The CRB Commodity Yearbook 2009

Commodity Research Bureau

WILEY

John Wiley & Sons, Inc.

Commodity Research Bureau
330 South Wells Street, Suite 612
Chicago, Illinois 60606-7110 USA
800.621.5271 or +1.312.554.8456
Fax: +1.312.939.4135
Website: www.crbtrader.com
Email: info@crbtrader.com

Table of Contents

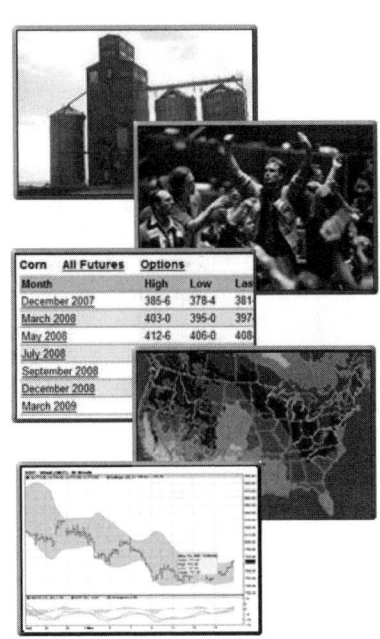

Acknowledgements

The editors wish to thank the following for source material:

Agricultural Marketing Service (AMS)

Agricultural Research Service (ARS)

American Bureau of Metal Statistics, Inc. (ABMS)

American Forest & Paper Association (AFPA)

The American Gas Association (AGA)

American Iron and Steel Institute (AISI)

American Metal Market (AMM)

Bureau of the Census

Bureau of Economic Analysis (BEA)

Bureau of Labor Statistics (BLS)

Chicago Board of Trade (CBT)

Chicago Mercantile Exchange (CME / IMM / IOM)

Coffee, Sugar & Cocoa Exchange (CSCE)

Commodity Credit Corporation (CCC)

Commodity Futures Trading Commision (CFTC)

The Conference Board

Economic Research Service (ERS)

Edison Electric Institute (EEI)

E D & F Man Cocoa Ltd

Farm Service Agency (FSA)

Federal Reserve Bank of St. Louis

Fiber Economics Bureau, Inc.

Florida Department of Citrus

Food and Agriculture Organization of the United Nations (FAO)

Foreign Agricultural Service (FAS)

Futures Industry Association (FIA)

International Cotton Advisory Committee (ICAC)

International Rubber Study Group (IRSG)

Johnson Matthey

Kansas City Board of Trade (KCBT)

Leather Industries of America

MidAmerica Commodity Exchange (MidAm)

Minneapolis Grain Exchange (MGE)

National Agricultural Statistics Service (NASS)

National Coffee Association of U.S.A., Inc. (NCA)

New York Cotton Exchange (NYCE / NYFE / FINEX)

New York Mercantile Exchange (NYMEX)

Commodity Exchange, Inc. (COMEX)

Oil World

The Organisation for Economic Co-Operation and Development (OECD)

Random Lengths

The Silver Institute

The Society of the Plastics Industry, Inc. (SPI)

United Nations (UN)

United States Department of Agriculture (USDA)

Wall Street Journal (WSJ)

Winnipeg Commodity Exchange (WCE)

The Commodity Price Trend

The Continuous Commodity Index (CCI) in 2008 peaked at a record high of 615.04 in July 2008, bringing the 2001-08 bull market to a post-war record of +236.4%. The CCI index was driven to that high by weakness in the dollar and speculative fever. However, the CCI index then plunged through the remainder of the year, falling by 48% from the record high posted in July 2008 to the 3-year low posted in December 2008. The CCI index ended 2008 down −23.7%, breaking the string of six consecutive annual increases (2002 +23.0%, 2003 +8.9%, 2004 +11.2%, 2005 +22.5%, 2006 +13.5%, 2007 +20.6%). The CCI index plunged in the latter half of 2008 as the global economy slowed and the global financial crisis emerged in September 2008. The global financial crisis caused a wash-out of speculative positions and the global recession meant a long period of weak demand for commodities.

All of the six CCI futures sub-sectors closed lower in 2008: Meats −2.7%, Softs −7.5%, Metals −19.0%, Grains −20.2%, Energy −46.1%. Reuters discontinued publishing the CCI sub-sector indexes in 2008. The sub-sector changes noted above are calculated by simply taking the average of the percentage changes of the constituents in each sub-sector.

Energy

The CCI Energy sub-sector, which is composed of Crude Oil, Heating Oil, and Natural Gas, accounts for 18% of the overall CCI Index. The constituents in the Energy sub-sector on average in 2008 closed down −46.1%, more than reversing the previous year's index gain of +39.5%. On a nearest-futures basis, crude oil in 2008 closed down −53.5%, gasoline closed down −59.3%, heating oil closed down −46.8%, and natural gas closed down −24.9%. Crude oil prices rallied sharply in the first half of 2008 due to the weak dollar and speculative fever. However, oil prices then plunged in the second half of 2008 as the U.S. economy due to the housing crisis and as the global financial crisis emerged in mid-September with the Lehman Brothers bankruptcy, which caused heavy long liquidation pressure and a sharp decline in global fuel demand.

Grains

The CCI Grains and Oilseeds sub-sector, which is composed of Corn, Soybeans, and Wheat, accounts for 18% of the overall CCI Index. The constituents in the Grains and Oilseeds sub-sector on average closed down −20.2% in 2008, reversing part of the +53.0% yr/yr index gain seen in 2007. On a nearest-futures basis, corn in 2008 fell −10.6%, soybeans fell −18.9%, and wheat closed −31.0%. Corn and soybean prices in the first half of 2008 extended the 2007 rally, which was sparked by the sharp increase in demand from ethanol producers for corn (which reduced soybean planting) and by the speculative bubble in commodity prices. However, corn, soybean and wheat plunged later in 2008 due to the global financial crisis.

Industrials

The CCI Industrials sub-sector, which is composed of Copper and Cotton, accounts for 12% of the overall Index. The constituents in the Industrials sub-sector on average showed a −40.9% decline in 2008, more than reversing the +13.4% gain in 2007. Copper closed sharply lower by −54.0% due to (1) heavy long liquidation pressure after the speculative run-up in commodity prices, and (2) the sharp drop in demand due to the global financial crisis and global recession. Cotton prices fell −27.9% in 2008, more than reversing the +21.0% gain in 2007. Cotton was undercut by falling demand for cotton.

Livestock

The CCI Livestock sub-sector, which is composed of Live Cattle and Lean Hogs, accounts for 12% of the CCI Index. The constituents in the Livestock sub-sector on average closed −2.7% lower in 2008 following the small increase of +0.1% seen in 2007. On a nearest-futures basis, cattle closed −10.5% while hogs closed +5.2%. Livestock prices were pressured in 2008 by weaker demand and by high feed and financing costs, which temporarily raised slaughter rates. On the bullish side, smaller herds were a supportive factor.

Precious Metals

The CCI Precious Metals sub-sector, which is composed of Gold, Platinum, and Silver, accounts for 17% of the overall Index. The constituents in the Precious Metals sub-sector on average closed −19.0% lower in 2008, reversing most of the +26.4% rally in 2007. Bearish factors for precious metals included the stronger dollar in the second half of 2008 and long liquidation pressure after the 2001-08 commodity bull market ended. Bullish factors included flight-to-safety during the global financial crisis and concerns that global central banks were debasing their currencies with extraordinary monetary rescue measures.

Softs

The CCI Softs sub-sector, which is composed of Cocoa, Coffee, Orange Juice, and Sugar #11, accounts for 23% of the CCI Index. The constituents in the Softs sub-sector on average in 2008 closed −7.5% lower. The big loser was orange juice with a −52.3% decline on weak demand and the lack of any hurricane damage during the season. Coffee prices closed −17.7%. Cocoa showed a sharp +31.0% gain while sugar rose +9.1% in 2008.

Continuous Commodity Index (CCI) (weekly close) as of January 02, 2009   Index Value

Continuous Commodity Index (CCI)   (High, Low and Close 1967 = 100)

Year		Jan.	Feb.	Mar.	Apr.	May	June	July	Aug.	Sept.	Oct.	Nov.	Dec.	Range
1999	High	198.96	191.45	193.28	192.89	193.99	193.43	192.91	199.59	209.41	209.91	207.54	206.20	209.91
	Low	187.18	182.76	183.38	187.14	185.05	185.07	182.67	190.14	199.03	199.66	202.23	200.74	182.67
	Settle	189.74	182.95	191.83	192.39	186.72	191.54	190.36	199.35	205.19	201.52	204.07	205.14	----
2000	High	213.70	215.29	217.88	214.15	226.12	227.29	225.69	228.02	232.20	234.38	231.46	233.37	234.38
	Low	201.43	206.74	209.61	207.61	211.86	222.23	217.42	217.76	224.74	218.38	220.93	225.46	201.43
	Settle	210.46	208.78	214.37	211.03	222.27	223.93	218.61	227.41	226.57	219.28	229.79	227.83	----
2001	High	232.58	228.34	225.75	216.39	219.29	212.39	209.27	202.90	202.34	191.09	192.74	193.94	232.58
	Low	223.02	219.68	210.24	208.87	208.43	203.86	201.84	197.02	188.24	182.83	181.83	187.73	181.83
	Settle	224.12	221.78	210.26	214.50	209.00	205.56	202.70	199.63	190.49	185.66	192.66	190.61	----
2002	High	195.97	193.53	205.45	208.39	205.33	209.33	215.10	219.24	229.62	231.67	231.83	238.39	238.39
	Low	186.38	187.19	192.26	195.21	197.42	199.56	207.24	208.46	217.60	223.82	223.29	230.17	186.38
	Settle	187.29	192.33	204.92	201.16	204.20	209.29	210.97	219.20	226.53	228.91	230.64	234.52	----
2003	High	248.92	251.59	247.23	236.62	242.16	238.25	237.20	243.74	246.07	250.67	257.54	263.60	263.60
	Low	234.58	245.39	228.10	228.77	231.26	231.39	230.36	233.96	236.79	241.68	244.79	249.60	228.10
	Settle	248.45	247.25	232.15	232.53	235.55	233.78	234.21	243.70	243.66	247.58	248.44	255.29	----
2004	High	271.08	275.02	285.28	284.42	277.94	282.03	275.38	278.10	285.37	289.29	292.49	291.02	292.49
	Low	257.49	258.94	270.52	268.53	266.80	264.34	265.50	265.20	269.12	280.53	280.20	276.15	257.49
	Settle	262.57	274.73	283.77	272.54	277.25	265.94	267.78	276.50	284.98	283.70	290.94	283.90	----
2005	High	288.38	305.00	323.33	313.23	304.25	315.79	316.46	321.60	333.58	338.19	332.58	349.20	349.20
	Low	277.07	280.19	304.22	297.47	292.06	300.76	302.71	309.21	317.05	326.36	326.09	332.62	277.07
	Settle	284.75	305.00	313.57	303.74	300.83	306.91	315.24	318.99	333.33	326.68	332.49	347.89	----
2006	High	363.70	364.28	365.66	382.46	399.66	387.52	396.16	399.90	393.51	389.24	408.91	409.65	409.65
	Low	348.57	345.49	346.56	360.85	376.35	363.63	375.73	380.15	359.07	361.19	385.23	391.77	345.49
	Settle	363.30	353.27	361.91	379.53	379.80	385.63	391.49	390.95	370.10	383.92	408.79	394.89	----
2007	High	396.93	414.62	411.26	411.97	408.05	418.59	426.79	424.78	450.36	454.40	461.06	477.48	477.48
	Low	377.59	390.76	395.75	401.53	401.16	402.80	409.78	395.03	412.70	436.88	446.46	450.94	377.59
	Settle	394.37	410.64	407.45	403.54	407.58	410.36	424.52	413.49	447.56	454.29	451.26	476.08	----
2008	High	503.45	567.84	577.64	556.09	556.84	599.36	615.04	553.81	517.81	457.69	388.82	364.82	615.04
	Low	475.91	501.42	509.00	507.82	523.37	539.42	538.86	498.36	449.70	350.53	341.55	322.53	322.53
	Settle	503.27	565.65	516.38	536.23	541.30	595.98	548.86	516.47	452.42	369.56	361.74	363.06	----

Source: Reuters

Continuous Commodity Index (CCI) vs. 30-year T-Bond Yield - 12-month (RoC)
(monthly close) through December 2008

Continuous Commodity Index (CCI) vs. CPI - 12-month Rate of Change
(monthly close) through December 2008

CCI Energy Sub-Index (1967=100) (monthly close) through June 2008

CRB Energy Sub-Index (1967=100) (weekly close) as of June 13, 2008

CCI Currencies Index (1977=100) (monthly close) through June 2008

CRB Currencies Index (1977=100) (weekly close) as of June 13, 2008

CRB Metals Sub-Index (1967=100) (monthly close) through December 2008

CRB Metals Sub-Index (1967=100) (weekly close) as of January 02, 2009

CRB Textiles Sub-Index (1967=100) (monthly close) through December 2008

CRB Textiles Sub-Index (1967=100) (weekly close) as of January 02, 2009

CRB Spot Index (monthly close) through December 2008

CRB Spot Index (weekly close) as of January 02, 2009

Reuters-CRB Index (CCI) and Goldman Sachs Commodity Index (GSCI$^{TM/SM}$) (weekly close) as of January 02, 2009

Reuters-CRB Index (CCI) and CRB Spot Index (weekly close) as of January 02, 2009

CRB INDICIES

Continuous Commodity Index (CCI)   (1967=100)

Year	Jan.	Feb.	Mar.	Apr.	May	June	July	Aug.	Sept.	Oct.	Nov.	Dec.	Average
1999	192.49	187.21	188.50	189.83	190.04	191.16	187.16	196.72	202.20	203.88	203.90	204.10	194.77
2000	207.65	211.28	213.87	211.29	220.42	224.73	220.51	220.84	228.23	226.36	226.56	228.98	220.06
2001	228.30	223.42	218.06	213.43	214.69	208.37	204.98	200.18	195.34	186.20	188.42	190.42	205.98
2002	191.44	190.91	201.86	200.74	201.69	203.92	211.42	214.01	226.00	227.52	228.54	234.62	211.06
2003	242.04	247.89	237.81	231.73	237.38	235.11	234.05	238.13	241.44	246.15	250.66	258.44	241.74
2004	266.65	264.93	278.19	276.48	272.78	270.78	270.41	271.18	276.47	285.36	286.02	283.28	275.21
2005	282.96	289.01	312.70	305.26	298.11	308.07	311.47	315.00	324.05	333.46	330.39	343.83	312.86
2006	354.56	354.30	353.74	371.33	385.81	374.50	386.50	389.11	372.98	376.70	395.21	397.28	376.00
2007	386.38	400.96	403.41	405.99	404.24	410.22	418.88	411.65	432.37	446.95	453.23	467.28	420.13
2008	490.38	531.00	547.16	538.62	544.56	572.19	573.12	517.71	475.59	392.21	360.19	346.15	490.74

Average.   *Source: Reuters*

Reuters/Jefferies-CRB Futures Index[1]   (1967=100)

Year	Jan.	Feb.	Mar.	Apr.	May	June	July	Aug.	Sept.	Oct.	Nov.	Dec.	Average
1999	192.49	187.21	188.50	189.83	190.04	191.16	187.16	196.72	202.20	203.88	203.90	204.10	194.77
2000	207.65	211.28	213.87	211.29	220.42	224.73	220.51	220.84	228.23	226.36	226.56	228.98	220.06
2001	228.30	223.42	218.06	213.43	214.69	208.37	204.98	200.18	195.34	186.20	188.42	190.42	205.98
2002	191.44	190.91	201.86	200.74	201.69	203.92	211.42	214.01	226.00	227.52	228.54	234.62	211.06
2003	242.04	247.89	237.81	231.73	237.38	235.11	234.05	238.13	241.44	246.15	250.66	258.44	241.74
2004	266.65	264.93	278.19	276.48	272.78	270.78	270.41	271.18	276.47	285.36	286.02	283.28	275.21
2005	282.96	289.01	312.70	305.26	298.11	306.97	308.04	318.76	326.19	326.44	315.27	327.58	309.77
2006	340.95	331.30	325.98	345.84	351.22	339.21	346.86	340.18	310.28	304.36	310.84	311.60	329.89
2007	292.18	305.63	309.03	314.35	310.77	314.32	320.89	308.89	323.89	336.20	349.82	349.36	319.61
2008	363.88	386.31	403.95	409.23	422.29	445.14	438.75	394.23	360.98	288.86	249.29	221.26	365.35

Average.   [1] New Calculation begins June 20, 2005.   *Source: Reuters*

Reuters/Jefferies-CRB Total Return Index[1]   (01/02/1982=100)

Year	Jan.	Feb.	Mar.	Apr.	May	June	July	Aug.	Sept.	Oct.	Nov.	Dec.	Average
1999	90.91	87.70	92.84	98.19	99.21	100.32	103.26	109.02	114.04	114.00	116.31	118.58	103.70
2000	122.59	128.50	132.60	128.43	139.10	144.80	143.12	147.23	155.89	155.00	157.45	158.74	142.79
2001	159.32	160.43	154.34	153.31	154.96	148.13	143.62	143.81	137.50	127.30	124.39	123.48	144.22
2002	123.82	124.53	135.70	138.03	138.93	138.66	143.23	145.91	153.53	153.91	151.63	161.51	142.45
2003	171.83	182.79	178.17	171.17	175.28	178.21	178.96	184.60	182.27	191.06	194.53	204.73	182.80
2004	213.15	215.30	226.72	227.21	234.19	230.03	232.57	236.76	238.75	254.24	248.91	241.10	233.24
2005	244.84	250.48	273.57	267.03	254.14	267.60	271.16	281.23	288.68	289.74	280.70	292.65	271.82
2006	305.70	298.05	294.39	313.52	319.76	310.00	318.32	313.52	287.18	282.84	290.08	291.98	302.11
2007	275.02	288.82	293.24	299.54	297.32	301.96	309.52	299.14	314.90	327.82	342.08	342.69	307.67
2008	357.92	380.80	398.78	404.43	417.85	441.16	435.51	391.90	359.36	287.82	248.68	220.56	362.06

Average.   [1] Theoretical data prior to June 20, 2005.   *Source: Reuters*

CCI Livestock Sub-Index   (1967=100)

Year	Jan.	Feb.	Mar.	Apr.	May	June	July	Aug.	Sept.	Oct.	Nov.	Dec.	Average
1999	206.47	220.47	218.75	222.97	226.14	219.14	198.18	206.89	209.31	221.68	227.97	239.13	218.09
2000	247.36	249.80	257.10	262.53	256.37	251.37	243.94	229.65	228.34	233.64	239.69	251.99	245.98
2001	254.81	254.62	262.97	259.27	252.40	257.32	257.15	248.31	240.83	230.82	227.86	237.26	248.64
2002	249.43	251.46	243.59	216.16	209.26	199.59	206.70	196.98	197.76	217.97	234.73	247.80	222.62
2003	252.70	242.32	240.06	237.27	251.07	248.86	245.33	244.63	261.29	264.33	264.96	255.07	250.66
2004	248.90	250.53	266.53	274.15	291.60	294.91	292.29	285.44	287.72	287.29	296.26	297.60	281.10
2005	305.39	294.73	302.88	295.95	293.97	269.99	266.35	269.80	280.26	288.27	292.59	297.62	288.15
2006	292.31	280.30	271.42	260.24	267.26	281.87	279.30	286.07	286.33	283.14	287.19	290.82	280.52
2007	297.80	310.65	314.13	312.66	308.79	303.77	307.72	311.64	304.89	293.76	287.43	297.95	304.27
2008	297.95	314.01	302.64	314.08	327.31	332.27							314.71

Average.   *Source: Reuters*

CCI Grains and Oilseeds Sub-Index   (1967=100)

Year	Jan.	Feb.	Mar.	Apr.	May	June	July	Aug.	Sept.	Oct.	Nov.	Dec.	Average
1999	174.76	165.92	170.54	166.69	163.22	163.11	152.45	166.33	170.88	161.96	158.72	155.35	164.16
2000	167.48	170.65	174.94	174.44	180.96	169.12	152.62	150.32	160.91	162.60	167.06	171.37	166.87
2001	171.45	163.23	164.33	158.41	155.93	156.71	170.42	168.74	167.95	161.37	163.22	162.14	163.66
2002	164.09	160.38	163.97	160.53	162.97	171.11	188.10	199.34	213.65	204.33	200.95	193.39	181.90
2003	187.57	189.29	183.12	185.98	194.62	193.35	181.84	192.82	201.68	209.28	222.27	226.46	197.36
2004	237.68	243.83	261.79	267.95	247.24	234.25	203.40	188.28	186.93	176.69	176.41	175.24	216.64
2005	173.61	175.50	198.55	189.30	190.57	203.73	209.28	193.48	187.59	186.48	181.90	186.72	189.73
2006	192.42	200.30	201.42	201.28	213.15	209.41	215.23	203.24	211.18	245.19	269.05	271.79	219.47
2007	276.60	289.85	286.56	274.99	283.75	309.16	306.13	317.68	362.96	364.93	375.95	419.17	322.31
2008	447.21	491.79	505.57	480.49	462.42	500.95							481.41

Average.   *Source: Reuters*

CCI Softs Sub-Index   (1967=100)

Year	Jan.	Feb.	Mar.	Apr.	May	June	July	Aug.	Sept.	Oct.	Nov.	Dec.	Average
1999	337.91	307.51	285.94	267.35	264.74	281.81	263.21	272.47	277.53	276.51	285.29	284.51	283.73
2000	268.52	254.77	259.39	260.26	267.91	280.26	285.20	273.72	270.43	270.05	257.94	255.68	267.01
2001	269.11	274.59	265.27	254.72	268.62	255.68	251.01	244.01	238.45	231.91	254.36	254.63	255.20
2002	256.23	246.71	259.73	256.73	254.63	252.54	270.15	278.25	307.15	311.84	311.53	311.73	276.44
2003	320.55	326.00	302.23	302.05	293.41	272.95	275.12	273.77	271.84	257.57	258.78	263.99	284.86
2004	265.93	259.29	265.98	259.39	256.91	266.95	285.81	289.61	304.70	309.01	318.42	339.23	285.10
2005	336.40	355.04	382.92	360.12	352.93	356.99	354.86	348.25	351.72	372.25	385.16	407.59	363.69
2006	443.78	452.96	448.44	458.99	460.75	447.03	460.34	451.85	433.83	433.57	461.09	476.10	452.39
2007	462.45	459.72	462.54	438.05	427.40	417.38	429.10	412.98	418.34	439.03	434.41	463.38	438.73
2008	479.96	518.98	507.19	483.25	475.12	476.96							490.24

Average.   *Source: Reuters*

CCI Precious Metals Sub-Index   (1967=100)

Year	Jan.	Feb.	Mar.	Apr.	May	June	July	Aug.	Sept.	Oct.	Nov.	Dec.	Average
1999	234.41	242.14	236.84	232.19	232.87	225.71	224.55	225.82	232.58	253.20	246.60	246.81	236.14
2000	247.16	266.43	256.51	253.53	255.44	268.03	267.08	266.97	269.50	263.47	261.97	266.96	261.92
2001	265.48	259.23	253.04	252.17	261.28	254.87	243.70	232.22	239.24	232.66	227.06	237.71	246.56
2002	241.90	245.33	254.47	261.61	266.59	276.27	268.03	264.27	269.19	267.88	272.29	281.24	264.09
2003	295.57	298.35	290.78	279.76	295.52	294.54	302.39	310.85	321.35	321.26	333.13	355.31	308.23
2004	377.11	375.30	400.41	390.82	351.29	354.67	366.98	380.85	377.08	394.42	408.67	402.12	381.64
2005	388.68	397.96	405.72	400.86	396.71	408.05	398.70	407.77	420.18	435.92	446.08	474.28	415.08
2006	505.52	514.07	530.47	595.40	651.48	572.29	599.67	619.15	587.59	567.40	618.12	613.96	581.26
2007	613.63	652.88	637.61	666.43	656.09	649.59	654.02	635.35	671.21	713.41	749.59	754.07	671.16
2008	823.60	927.66	973.02	918.83	910.40	902.48							909.33

Average.   *Source: Reuters*

CCI Industrials Sub-Index   (1967=100)

Year	Jan.	Feb.	Mar.	Apr.	May	June	July	Aug.	Sept.	Oct.	Nov.	Dec.	Average
1999	182.97	178.44	180.15	184.41	184.94	176.40	182.58	184.71	191.68	190.18	187.34	187.10	184.24
2000	201.37	202.67	204.59	194.18	207.18	200.83	207.37	217.64	224.10	217.16	217.11	219.27	209.46
2001	206.86	199.04	186.19	174.20	173.72	162.54	158.63	153.43	145.27	131.33	140.85	146.56	164.89
2002	150.49	151.21	156.49	152.31	152.59	167.27	172.54	164.08	161.79	162.28	176.79	178.53	162.20
2003	185.33	190.29	193.39	188.69	186.75	190.80	201.85	198.23	212.04	236.48	243.08	244.56	205.96
2004	262.68	269.43	273.02	256.62	249.14	234.34	224.38	226.27	233.50	227.52	223.80	223.54	242.02
2005	232.07	236.01	253.38	258.44	249.39	252.99	261.77	263.66	267.00	285.21	285.66	298.25	261.99
2006	314.02	326.07	322.13	358.06	398.97	383.23	401.59	408.38	394.84	380.43	372.50	373.90	369.51
2007	345.53	342.15	363.21	391.04	387.08	402.00	445.29	416.38	433.13	445.51	417.99	410.64	400.00
2008	437.26	469.27	499.57	492.00	480.95	459.82							473.15

Average.   *Source: Reuters*

CRB INDICIES

CCI Energy Sub-Index (1967=100)

Year	Jan.	Feb.	Mar.	Apr.	May	June	July	Aug.	Sept.	Oct.	Nov.	Dec.	Average
1999	134.58	129.41	146.56	169.80	174.02	180.31	196.88	219.08	228.80	225.66	225.76	223.94	187.90
2000	231.38	245.97	254.09	244.62	278.91	308.81	301.39	328.52	366.18	356.34	366.76	361.93	303.74
2001	345.00	328.00	312.27	319.96	308.23	292.65	267.20	269.05	253.17	232.68	214.70	206.92	279.15
2002	195.20	202.12	243.96	262.72	269.34	258.24	260.08	274.04	301.33	301.49	278.41	311.52	263.20
2003	337.33	375.64	346.99	313.78	328.18	342.51	332.71	343.58	317.98	338.95	331.81	361.52	339.25
2004	371.45	355.20	376.02	384.99	426.01	419.28	438.34	459.75	475.69	574.75	535.62	475.97	441.09
2005	478.71	491.25	563.52	567.69	526.48	595.62	628.00	716.27	803.00	797.33	716.36	733.16	634.78
2006	693.34	636.54	634.70	692.42	674.95	682.24	710.09	754.36	651.32	633.84	643.38	626.34	669.46
2007	564.23	618.69	627.96	666.41	671.37	688.51	693.20	680.59	724.00	770.61	827.14	794.45	693.93
2008	820.37	863.18	958.45	1,030.86	1,162.38	1,241.04							1,012.71

Average.   *Source: Reuters*

CCI Currencies Index (1977=100)

Year	Jan.	Feb.	Mar.	Apr.	May	June	July	Aug.	Sept.	Oct.	Nov.	Dec.	Average
1999	130.97	128.48	126.37	125.74	125.32	124.63	124.08	126.89	128.89	130.66	128.24	127.71	127.33
2000	127.65	124.37	124.01	123.43	119.42	122.54	121.59	119.04	117.11	115.99	114.89	117.55	120.63
2001	118.42	116.58	114.25	113.01	112.24	110.92	111.29	114.02	115.21	114.04	112.69	112.01	113.72
2002	110.20	109.38	110.40	111.33	114.54	117.39	121.30	119.68	119.54	119.02	120.77	121.97	116.29
2003	125.37	126.36	126.61	126.42	132.07	133.04	130.30	128.77	130.93	135.96	136.23	140.44	131.04
2004	143.44	143.23	140.68	139.36	137.62	140.48	141.81	140.92	141.25	144.04	149.66	152.54	142.92
2005	150.16	148.99	150.81	148.53	146.39	143.52	141.21	143.74	144.42	141.94	139.32	140.48	144.96
2006	142.95	140.86	141.45	143.36	149.49	147.98	147.20	148.24	147.65	146.19	147.72	149.64	146.06
2007	146.95	147.07	148.87	150.65	150.68	150.83	153.54	153.79	156.79	159.28	163.56	160.52	153.54
2008	162.09	162.68	168.94	168.21	166.42	165.36							165.62

Average.   *Source: Reuters*

CCI Interest Rates Index   (1977=100)

Year	Jan.	Feb.	Mar.	Apr.	May	June	July	Aug.	Sept.	Oct.	Nov.	Dec.	Average
1999	121.32	119.62	118.11	118.56	116.57	112.78	112.32	110.71	108.79	106.42	107.46	104.56	113.10
2000	100.05	101.51	102.61	103.99	101.80	103.65	104.12	105.21	105.10	105.57	105.94	108.44	104.00
2001	108.79	108.94	109.86	108.61	107.69	107.90	108.24	109.63	110.74	112.26	112.29	108.97	109.49
2002	109.51	110.34	107.65	108.31	109.04	110.08	111.45	114.14	116.24	115.54	115.44	115.27	111.92
2003	115.27	116.68	116.88	116.13	119.22	120.42	116.27	113.02	113.86	----	----	----	116.42
2004	----	----	123.94	118.47	115.30	114.52	117.46	119.91	121.02	121.71	121.25	120.64	119.42
2005	121.38	122.44	118.91	120.81	123.07	124.63	123.04	122.40	122.52	120.07	119.11	119.85	121.52
2006	120.69	119.33	117.83	115.44	114.45	114.57	115.02	116.87	118.33	118.28	119.64	119.86	117.53
2007	118.77	118.28	119.66	118.43	117.94	114.60	115.60	118.18	119.74	119.80	123.18	123.23	118.95
2008	126.72	126.13	127.26	126.04	124.37	121.95							125.41

Average.   *Source: Reuters*

CCI Energy Index   (1977=100)

Year	Jan.	Feb.	Mar.	Apr.	May	June	July	Aug.	Sept.	Oct.	Nov.	Dec.	Average
1999	121.00	116.39	136.44	152.20	153.53	157.52	176.40	185.48	196.52	192.71	202.36	207.81	166.53
2000	220.53	237.09	241.29	221.42	247.72	263.67	255.40	268.97	292.15	287.36	286.70	249.86	256.01
2001	251.05	256.70	246.06	258.47	264.15	248.51	231.56	238.47	231.53	201.64	180.55	180.49	232.43
2002	185.01	190.86	224.68	234.25	233.13	226.56	234.70	240.27	256.04	250.75	228.78	258.02	230.25
2003	279.06	307.09	282.73	243.10	243.92	256.78	264.31	275.82	248.55	265.44	271.25	284.02	268.51
2004	300.37	298.35	314.50	322.72	359.33	342.21	367.52	389.41	402.57	460.54	430.64	389.95	364.84
2005	415.65	428.72	493.69	497.67	461.97	515.29	537.91	593.73	624.18	584.79	538.28	548.87	520.06
2006	593.19	554.80	578.71	649.56	651.96	652.57	680.35	659.03	564.39	534.32	541.08	555.93	601.32
2007	516.96	549.35	581.59	624.67	630.15	645.30	668.27	635.37	684.53	727.59	811.45	803.94	656.60
2008	808.98	835.92	905.57	974.25	1,099.21	1,156.16							963.35

Average.   *Source: Reuters*

CRB Metals Sub-Index   (1967=100)

Year	Jan.	Feb.	Mar.	Apr.	May	June	July	Aug.	Sept.	Oct.	Nov.	Dec.	Average
1999	213.74	221.29	220.66	222.50	227.01	223.50	234.41	237.06	243.65	242.77	247.19	253.77	232.30
2000	261.71	248.29	240.26	237.57	241.56	239.24	232.04	226.20	228.82	225.15	216.25	215.36	234.37
2001	212.47	212.90	210.59	204.94	205.14	205.60	197.04	188.09	181.32	179.50	172.96	173.80	195.36
2002	174.76	176.41	181.22	186.31	189.12	189.38	192.66	184.51	184.03	185.61	183.21	186.27	184.46
2003	199.71	204.17	206.72	202.78	205.57	207.77	212.24	214.09	220.24	240.20	248.49	266.70	219.06
2004	287.40	306.07	320.96	321.90	314.73	308.28	312.29	318.21	333.97	350.45	359.77	361.92	324.66
2005	355.95	364.50	371.99	371.31	365.83	369.32	361.39	363.75	364.70	369.68	370.47	425.84	371.23
2006	458.64	485.21	504.91	571.37	623.28	616.35	621.31	617.86	623.05	660.11	681.87	693.51	596.46
2007	668.94	691.71	761.81	798.96	798.65	803.29	834.00	840.13	835.06	868.19	828.50	812.12	795.11
2008	800.80	839.03	908.64	934.68	921.35	828.98	803.21	754.15	699.10	562.36	477.58	419.81	745.81

Average.   *Source: Commodity Research Bureau*

CRB Textiles Sub-Index   (1967=100)

Year	Jan.	Feb.	Mar.	Apr.	May	June	July	Aug.	Sept.	Oct.	Nov.	Dec.	Average
1999	237.40	233.67	235.09	234.94	234.45	229.24	225.02	226.43	222.21	223.51	227.73	222.63	229.36
2000	226.56	227.69	234.87	234.25	242.70	243.76	241.28	243.73	244.33	244.90	248.17	248.57	240.07
2001	244.74	241.84	233.40	225.97	224.47	222.12	222.44	218.55	214.74	207.79	215.86	218.99	224.24
2002	218.08	216.84	218.40	214.72	211.21	220.16	222.95	221.74	219.02	220.10	225.85	227.76	219.74
2003	231.25	235.31	235.04	234.64	231.66	235.24	240.88	237.50	244.30	256.99	257.59	254.25	241.22
2004	257.58	253.15	252.37	247.97	249.74	242.65	233.48	233.58	237.31	235.03	235.88	236.39	242.93
2005	239.93	240.36	247.12	247.73	246.60	244.69	247.21	243.08	246.64	251.24	248.96	250.83	246.20
2006	255.02	255.52	251.74	248.26	244.26	244.16	242.03	243.89	245.78	244.89	246.37	251.15	247.76
2007	252.50	251.35	251.91	248.99	245.40	250.72	260.09	256.51	261.58	264.79	265.79	265.28	256.24
2008	267.18	269.60	271.76	267.02	264.71	262.29	263.92	261.98	255.47	241.15	231.28	235.84	257.68

Average.   *Source: Commodity Research Bureau*

CRB Raw Industrials Sub-Index   (1967=100)

Year	Jan.	Feb.	Mar.	Apr.	May	June	July	Aug.	Sept.	Oct.	Nov.	Dec.	Average
1999	262.81	259.65	255.03	251.75	250.07	248.91	253.43	255.96	262.56	266.37	270.39	267.30	258.69
2000	267.85	260.91	260.39	258.23	265.37	261.78	255.19	255.69	258.81	257.29	252.58	256.00	259.17
2001	254.54	248.53	246.35	244.03	244.29	245.92	244.22	238.10	228.30	220.52	218.94	221.57	237.94
2002	219.05	222.33	231.03	230.38	231.81	243.72	245.38	240.53	240.77	240.68	243.04	248.21	236.41
2003	255.85	258.59	260.97	258.79	257.65	260.47	263.77	263.99	273.24	291.18	295.88	302.30	270.22
2004	312.24	309.54	316.77	318.52	312.98	308.40	308.84	307.54	315.25	315.13	320.52	322.65	314.03
2005	320.94	324.57	333.31	336.68	331.99	331.88	325.29	324.52	329.36	332.79	332.83	349.53	331.14
2006	363.05	371.00	372.08	385.69	400.62	399.97	403.50	403.90	403.19	415.76	426.67	434.25	398.31
2007	430.87	434.54	452.81	465.37	468.44	475.75	485.36	478.47	483.09	492.43	486.68	475.95	469.15
2008	478.21	492.47	514.68	518.31	514.50	497.85	494.80	475.60	453.85	397.28	351.66	323.78	459.42

Average.   *Source: Commodity Research Bureau*

CRB Foodstuffs Sub-Index   (1967=100)

Year	Jan.	Feb.	Mar.	Apr.	May	June	July	Aug.	Sept.	Oct.	Nov.	Dec.	Average
1999	206.75	196.53	189.81	187.94	191.60	195.96	182.09	191.60	192.12	190.13	183.46	178.24	190.52
2000	180.37	175.68	183.76	189.88	194.32	190.42	176.52	171.63	175.02	183.53	186.75	186.58	182.87
2001	189.68	192.93	200.48	203.57	210.24	213.09	222.61	232.42	224.06	199.51	200.24	203.40	207.69
2002	203.33	202.39	204.04	197.88	195.85	207.11	218.25	222.32	226.98	230.63	230.76	237.99	214.79
2003	238.60	237.01	234.16	234.55	239.15	239.53	232.81	234.30	244.69	251.04	255.36	257.99	241.60
2004	263.90	275.85	287.49	287.41	285.33	278.05	273.83	270.42	272.10	257.76	268.47	261.77	273.53
2005	252.84	246.44	253.58	252.19	254.21	255.43	251.31	247.65	249.22	253.37	252.74	242.54	250.96
2006	243.31	241.95	239.60	243.17	250.70	253.86	261.17	267.04	269.14	267.52	271.19	273.16	256.82
2007	275.31	286.30	297.37	299.85	311.98	320.79	322.44	319.95	325.01	322.19	325.40	337.97	312.05
2008	346.56	383.11	390.10	391.07	405.44	421.87	427.47	405.89	385.15	334.27	303.48	284.65	373.26

Average.   *Source: Commodity Research Bureau*

CRB INDICIES

CRB Fats and Oils Sub-Index (1967=100)

Year	Jan.	Feb.	Mar.	Apr.	May	June	July	Aug.	Sept.	Oct.	Nov.	Dec.	Average
1999	230.99	194.96	172.59	174.97	176.78	187.84	178.61	191.19	209.68	209.53	194.38	177.98	191.63
2000	171.15	154.77	161.97	165.37	177.74	171.57	152.26	153.11	157.52	160.41	165.44	167.35	163.22
2001	170.49	158.27	165.77	177.63	177.95	196.02	232.89	259.60	237.33	177.05	174.66	184.78	192.70
2002	169.64	165.91	177.34	167.61	164.38	193.38	193.29	192.85	193.20	193.90	211.97	230.05	187.79
2003	222.39	209.89	215.72	216.91	219.56	229.01	225.83	223.36	251.40	285.47	288.08	292.22	239.99
2004	305.30	300.47	318.53	330.54	302.31	295.32	304.60	290.52	302.51	267.12	279.42	271.36	297.33
2005	248.45	238.13	252.70	263.98	262.93	266.01	245.81	243.51	259.50	268.43	269.77	231.17	254.20
2006	231.10	221.46	217.14	214.75	222.03	221.97	247.09	271.97	267.18	257.29	264.75	270.94	242.31
2007	274.74	274.35	300.01	313.08	339.65	366.31	376.09	357.79	365.74	365.51	381.69	364.06	339.92
2008	381.95	418.92	459.52	457.65	467.23	498.89	526.26	467.08	443.38	366.91	283.76	238.42	417.50

Average.   *Source: Commodity Research Bureau*

CRB Livestock Sub-Index (1967=100)

Year	Jan.	Feb.	Mar.	Apr.	May	June	July	Aug.	Sept.	Oct.	Nov.	Dec.	Average
1999	249.71	231.27	216.59	231.92	236.71	241.07	235.92	254.64	274.60	294.16	279.97	272.14	251.56
2000	261.83	245.67	252.65	258.44	268.41	260.53	241.72	238.62	245.35	252.78	240.45	259.65	252.18
2001	267.57	250.14	261.05	273.14	288.88	306.84	329.73	341.78	313.84	260.77	252.97	264.23	284.25
2002	251.61	260.32	274.95	257.32	256.33	289.40	288.22	279.03	274.13	276.94	288.86	313.14	275.85
2003	316.67	308.65	310.49	311.25	320.03	333.29	324.58	327.63	361.30	386.60	385.63	372.48	338.22
2004	372.16	353.19	362.41	369.65	369.31	374.28	395.48	392.33	395.40	365.68	373.69	370.63	374.52
2005	359.25	341.74	353.05	373.63	377.41	361.10	330.39	331.75	349.24	358.04	369.98	337.97	353.63
2006	331.93	328.72	320.09	314.72	327.28	340.29	359.18	388.13	384.78	366.35	364.05	372.08	349.80
2007	379.93	388.03	407.19	425.25	449.92	462.39	459.18	445.81	444.91	434.88	425.72	412.45	427.97
2008	417.36	451.42	468.41	483.09	510.01	522.82	556.10	526.98	492.24	426.75	342.41	288.42	457.17

Average.   *Source: Commodity Research Bureau*

CRB Spot Sub-Index (1967=100)

Year	Jan.	Feb.	Mar.	Apr.	May	June	July	Aug.	Sept.	Oct.	Nov.	Dec.	Average
1999	238.31	231.76	226.07	223.61	224.55	225.83	221.44	227.35	231.10	232.12	230.78	226.54	228.29
2000	227.91	222.00	225.85	227.78	233.68	229.89	219.54	217.28	220.60	224.15	223.29	224.99	224.75
2001	225.75	224.13	226.51	226.66	229.81	231.98	235.20	235.83	226.62	211.72	211.15	214.01	224.95
2002	212.55	214.02	219.65	216.54	216.43	228.09	233.96	232.98	235.10	236.59	238.01	244.06	227.33
2003	248.72	249.60	249.73	248.66	250.00	251.77	250.71	251.49	261.25	274.11	278.66	283.38	258.17
2004	291.55	295.38	304.54	305.49	301.44	295.70	294.10	291.86	296.90	290.35	298.19	296.26	296.81
2005	291.19	290.08	298.13	299.24	297.73	298.26	292.80	290.63	293.94	297.75	297.48	301.05	295.69
2006	308.31	311.58	310.86	319.47	330.81	332.19	337.82	341.11	341.85	347.18	354.58	359.35	332.93
2007	358.84	366.47	381.36	388.90	396.79	405.08	410.71	405.97	410.96	414.11	412.79	413.88	397.16
2008	419.30	444.52	459.65	462.04	466.86	465.36	466.20	445.87	424.50	370.28	331.17	307.24	421.92

Average.   *Source: Commodity Research Bureau*

Goldman Sachs Commodity Index (GSCI) (12/31/1969=100)

Year	Jan.	Feb.	Mar.	Apr.	May	June	July	Aug.	Sept.	Oct.	Nov.	Dec.	Average
1999	135.290	132.370	143.860	155.400	156.810	158.220	165.210	177.600	187.640	184.890	191.840	194.620	165.313
2000	200.140	211.150	214.190	200.420	219.110	230.070	222.130	230.880	247.730	243.670	251.820	244.790	226.342
2001	239.180	231.540	220.130	222.860	222.320	213.260	202.890	203.760	197.040	178.070	169.630	167.740	205.702
2002	168.970	172.750	193.580	199.870	200.650	197.070	203.120	208.760	223.690	222.700	212.180	230.030	202.781
2003	241.740	264.190	246.700	221.680	228.180	235.010	233.180	241.350	228.540	242.220	246.240	261.230	240.855
2004	269.180	266.230	280.100	284.060	303.190	292.630	298.970	308.010	315.290	356.700	341.120	314.250	302.478
2005	324.470	332.800	374.050	371.680	350.650	382.960	396.640	431.850	455.280	444.900	418.560	435.450	393.274
2006	442.120	422.490	427.470	469.730	477.930	471.650	490.320	485.650	434.560	431.130	442.050	444.620	453.310
2007	406.976	435.258	446.688	469.596	470.715	485.256	504.646	490.161	528.829	559.355	600.371	593.119	499.248
2008	606.714	638.875	689.259	717.944	778.146	832.309	818.904	716.837	644.004	496.045	405.956	338.266	640.272

Average.   *Source: Goldman Sachs*

Commodity Research Bureau Product Overview

Commodity Research Bureau

Commodity Research Bureau is the oldest and most respected information provider in the industry. CRB was founded in 1934 and is widely recognized in the industry for its accurate and professional products.

CRB's products are tailored for individual traders and brokerage firms. All of our products are available to brokerage firms on a bulk and private-label basis.

Product samples and pricing are located on our web site at www.crbtrader.com.

Please contact us for a free consultation about how our products can help your trading or your business.

Call +1.312.554.8456, or e-mail us at info@crbtrader.com

Commodity Research Bureau

330 South Wells Street, Suite 612
Chicago, Illinois 60606-7110
USA

Phone: +1.312.554.8456
or 800.621.5271
Fax: +1.312.939.4135
Email: info@crbtrader.com
Website: www.crbtrader.com

Price Data	
CRB DataCenter	End-of-day daily price files on futures, Commitments of Traders, options on futures, options volatility (implied/historic), equities and mutual funds. Available in various formats for direct upload to your chart/analysis software.
CRB InfoTech CD	The most comprehensive collection of commodity market information available anywhere, with decades of prices on over 600 cash, futures, foreign exchange, index markets, and option volatilities (implied/historic).
Custom Historical Data	Order a one-time package of price information according to your needs.

Charts	
CRB PriceCharts	Weekly 104-page magazine of charts on over 70 futures markets. Available in print and PDF formats.
PriceCharts.com	Over 400 pages of charts and technical studies covering the 77 major US, Europe, and Asia futures markets. Available in PDF format.
Wall Charts	Large poster-size charts on 35 futures markets with volume/open interest and Commitment of Traders data. Published annually each fall or on demand with your company logo.
Historical Desk Sets	Spiral-bound set of 86 charts on 48 markets with volume/open interest and Commitment of Traders data. Published each spring and fall.

Fundamental and Technical Research and Trading Systems	
Futures Market Service	Weekly 8-page newsletter on futures market fundamentals available in print or PDF formats.
Trends In Futures	Weekly 4-page newsletter on futures market technicals. Available in PDF format.
Electronic Futures Trend Analyzer	Computerized daily trading system started in 1963 with specific entry and exit points for over 60 Futures Markets.

Books	
CRB Commodity Yearbook	Annual publication of fundamental data, including supply/demand and production/consumption and price data, on over 100 commodity markets. Concise introductory articles that describe the salient features of each commodity. Available as a hardcover book with CD.
CRB Encyclopedia of Commodity and Financial Prices	Concise introductory articles on the fundamental market factors moving commodity and financial prices, providing a valuable complement to understanding price behavior on the long-term historical price charts. Available as a hardcover book with CD.

For more information and current specials, visit www.crbtrader.com or call +1.312.554.8456 or 800.621.5271

The Continuous Commodity Index (CCI) in the first half of 2008 extended its rally to post a new record high of 615.04 in July 2008. With that record high, the 2001-08 commodity bull market of +236.4% became the largest commodity bull market in post-war history, beating the previous record 1971-74 rally which totaled +146.7%. Moreover, the 2001-08 commodity rally became the longest-running rally at 81 months, far longer than 28 months for the second largest bull market of 1971-74.

The 1971-74 and 1977-80 commodity bull markets were separated by two years of consolidation in 1975-76. If those two rallies are counted as one large bull market, then that bull market would be the largest in post-war history at 250.2%. However, the 2001-08 bull market of 236.4% was still close behind that two-stage 1971-80 rally.

The Continuous Commodity Index (CCI) in 2007-08 performed similarly to the Reuters/Jefferies-CRB index, as illustrated by their parallel movement (see nearby chart). The RJ/CRB index was reformulated in June 2005 with a much heavier weighting on petroleum products of 33% versus the 12% weighting in the old CCI index. Strength in oil prices boosted the new RJ/CRB index in 2007, while strength in grain prices boosted the old CCI index.

The 2001-08 commodity bull market was driven by a progression of different factors, which helps explain the longevity of the rally. In the first three full years of the rally (2002-04), the commodity rally was driven mainly by the 33% plunge in the dollar, which resulted from the Fed's extraordinarily easy monetary policy during that time frame. The Fed during 2002-04 targeted the federal funds rate in the very low range of 1% to 2% to help the U.S. get through the tough times caused by the post2000 technology bust, the stock market bust, and the 9/11 terrorist attack in 2001. Commodities, as real assets, typically rise in price when the currency in which they are quoted depreciates in value.

The Fed finally started tightening its monetary policy in June 2004 due to the improved U.S. economic outlook and concerns that a bubble was emerging in the housing market from extremely low mortgage rates. The Fed's tighter monetary policy provided eventual support for the dollar and halted the dollar's decline, thus removing a linchpin of the commodity rally.

However, starting in 2004 strong commodity demand from China took over from the dollar as the major factor driving commodity prices higher. China's fast-growing demand for energy, industrial metals, and construction commodities was the key factor driving these sectors higher. In addition to strong demand, production supply

Commodity Bull Markets Ranked by Percentage Gain of Reuters-CRB Index (CCI) (1960-2009[1])						
	-------- Low --------		-------- High --------		Percent Rally	Rally Duration Months	Avg CPI (yr-yr%)
2001-08	Oct-01	182.83	Jul-08	615.04	236.4%	81	2.8%
1971-74	Oct-71	96.40	Feb-74	237.80	146.7%	28	4.9%
1977-80	Aug-77	184.70	Nov-80	337.60	82.8%	39	10.2%
1986-88	Jul-86	196.16	Jun-88	272.19	38.8%	23	3.2%
1992-96	Aug-92	198.17	Apr-96	263.79	33.1%	44	2.8%

[1] Data as of February 29, 2009. *Source: Commodity Research Bureau*

in those sectors could not keep up with the new demand because of years of underinvestment in new production, refining, and extraction facilities. That led to a squeeze in energy, industrial metals and construction commodity prices.

After the sharp rally in commodity prices during 2001-06, commodity prices then entered a sideways consolidation range from mid-2006 through mid-2007. That consolidation period was due to the relatively stable dollar and some concern about the U.S. economy following the Fed's tightening regime during 2004-06.

Commodity prices in mid-2007 then started a meteoric rise, sparked mainly by the Fed's aggressive easing in monetary policy after the U.S. banking crisis started in August 2007 with the insolvency of two Bear Stearns mortgage-related hedge funds. The Fed's easy monetary policy caused renewed weakness in the dollar, which in turn drove commodity prices higher. In addition, investors started pouring money into commodity funds because of concerns that the Fed's forced easing mode might cause an inflation outbreak. In addition, the stock market correction that emerged in the latter half of 2007 convinced some investors to withdraw money from stocks and invest it in commodities, which at least have a store of value during times of crisis.

The bull market in commodities abruptly ended in the latter half of 2008 when the U.S. housing and banking problems mushroomed into a financial crisis of global proportions. In the space of just five months, the CCI index plunged by 48% from the record high posted in July 2008 to the 3-year low posted in December 2008.

The plunge in commodity prices in late 2008 was due in part to extremely heavy long liquidation pressure by investors who had built up a huge long commodity position during the 2001-08 bull market. Investors during the crisis rushed to sell assets of all types in order to limit their losses and convert their portfolios into cash.

Commodity prices were also hurt by the sharp rally in the dollar that occurred during the crisis as global financial institutions rushed into dollars for safety. Commodity

prices were also pushed sharply lower in late 2008 a sit became clear that the financial crisis would spark a serious global recession, thus undercutting demand for commodities.

With 20-20 hindsight, it is now clear that many commodities traded at ridiculously high bubble levels. Oil prices reached $147 per barrel, natural gas prices rallied to $13.69 per MMBtu, copper rallied to $4.27 per pound, corn rallied to $7.62 per bushel, soybeans rallied to $16.60 per bushel, and wheat rallied to $13 per bushel. Speculative fever clearly pushed commodity prices to unsustainably high levels.

Looking ahead, commodity prices are likely to see continued downward pressure due to weak demand during the global recession and a possible further rally in the dollar. However, the outlook for commodity prices should turn bullish again once the global recession nears an end. Sharply lower commodity prices are forcing producers to shut down production and shelve expansion plans, meaning that commodities are likely to be in short supply when strong demand starts to emerge again. Moreover, the strong global development trend will eventually emerge again whereby countries such as China, India and Brazil will demand huge quantities of commodities to fuel their development.

The U.S. economy officially entered a recession in December 2007, according to the National Bureau of Economic Research (NBER), which is the official arbiter of recessions. The NBER did not make its determination on the beginning of the recession until a year later in December 2008.

As the U.S. recession began, GDP growth was actually positive in the first half of 2008 at +0.9% in Q1-2008 and +2.8% in Q2-2008. The NBER uses a more expansive definition of a recession than just negative GDP and includes other factors such as declines in real GDP, real income, employment, industrial production, and wholesale-retail sales. In fact, U.S. employment, as measured by non-farm payrolls, started falling in January 2008 and fell every month in 2008 by a total of 3.1 million persons in 2008.

U.S. GDP growth was mildly negative at -0.5% in Q32008 and then plunged by -6.2% in Q4-2008 after the crisis reached global proportions in September 2008 with the Lehman Brothers bankruptcy. The market consensus as of March 2009 was that U.S. GDP growth would show another sharp decline of about –6% in Q1-2009 and then improve a bit to –3% in Q2-2009. The market as of March 2009 was still hoping that the U.S. economy could bottom out sometime in the second half of 2009 and then show at least a small gain in 2010.

The 2008-09 recession could easily turn out to be the worst post-war recession. The largest post-war recession so far was the 1973-75 recession in which GDP fell by -4.7% on a peak-to-trough basis (i.e., measuring the overall decline

in GDP during the course of the recession). The peak-to-trough measurement is different than the quarterly GDP figures, which simply annualize the quarterly decline in GDP (e.g., the Q4-2008 GDP report of –6.2% was actually a decline of only about – 1.5% on a quarter-on-quarter basis). In the second half of 2008, the U.S. economy had shown a peak-to-trough decline of only –1.7%, which made it the 7th worst postwar recession. However, declines in GDP in the first two or three quarters of 2009 could push the economy down by an overall 5% from peak-to-trough, thus making the recession the worst in post-war history.

A "depression" is typically defined as an overall decline in real GDP of at least 10% or a decline in GDP lasting more than 3 years. By that definition, the last US depressions were during the Great Depression when GDP fell by 33% during 1929-33 and then by 18.2% in 1937

38. At present there appears to be little chance of a decline in GDP of more than 10% in the U.S. given the aggressive policy response of the U.S. Federal Reserve and Treasury and by overseas authorities as well.

The U.S. economy was muddling through the housing crisis, at least until the Lehman bankruptcy in 2008. The Lehman bankruptcy and the plunge in the global stock markets put the crisis front-and-center in the media and produced a panic situation among investors, consumers, and businesses. Consumers quickly stopped spending money except on essentials. The auto industry was stopped in its track, with auto sales plunging by roughly 40%.

Businesses rapidly started laying people off, thus causing further concern among consumers that they might lose their jobs. Payroll employment fell in the first half

S&P 500

10-year T-Note Yield

of 2008, but the monthly job losses accelerated to about 600,000 persons per month starting in November 2008. Some 2.6 million people lost their jobs in just the 4month period of November through February 2009. The U.S. unemployment rate rose to a 25-year high of 8.1% and Federal Reserve Chairman Ben Bernanke said he would not be surprised if the unemployment rate eventually rose as high as 10%. The record post-war high for the U.S. unemployment rate is 10.8% posted during the 1981-82 recession.

Looking ahead, there are three conditions that must be met for the U.S. economy to get back on its feet. First, the U.S. financial system needs to get stabilized so it can start getting credit back into the hands of consumers, home buyers, and businesses. Second, the U.S. housing market needs to bottom out and start back on a rising track. Third, the global economy needs to stabilize with adequate financing to get the developing world through the crisis.

The U.S. housing market, which was the original source of the problem, will take time to stabilize. Given the depths of the problems, there is little chance of a sustained recovery in the U.S. housing market until 2010 at the earliest. U.S. home sales in February 2009 were at record lows. There were few homes buyers in 2008 and early 2009 due to the ongoing decline in home prices, the severe recession and job losses, and the difficulty of obtaining mortgages. Mortgage rates were low, but it was difficult for potential homebuyers to meet the tight mortgage underwriting criteria. In addition, banks were requiring at least a 20% down payment in a big reversal from when it was easy to obtain 100% financing.

As of February 2009, home prices had fallen by 27%

from the peak. Of the homes that were being sold in late 2008 and early 2009, as many as 45% of the sales involved distressed sales at bargain prices involving a foreclosure or short sale. That indicated that there were buyers waiting in the wings, but only at rock bottom prices.

U.S. interest rates appear destined to remain low at least through the end of 2009. The Federal Reserve during the crisis in 2007-08 slashed its federal funds rate target from 5.25% to the range of zero to 0.25%. Moreover, the Fed promised to keep short-term rates low for an extended period of time. The 10-year T-note yield fell sharply during 2008 and hit a record low of 2.04% in January 2009. The Treasury was forced to sell huge quantities of Treasury securities to fund the ballooning U.S. budget deficit, which is expected to rise to $1.75 trillion in fiscal 2008-09, which would be 12% of GDP and the highest since World War II. However, global investors snapped up the Treasury securities, which were the safest place to be during the time of crisis. Moreover, the market viewed the low T-note yields as being reasonable given the possibility that deflation could emerge.

The S&P 500 index plunged in 2008 and hit new lows in March 2009, posting an overall decline of 58% from the record high in October 2007. Given the freefall in the U.S. economy in late 2008 and early 2009, the stock market had no real sense of how bad the earnings picture might get. In addition, there was concern about a spate of debt defaults and bankruptcies as corporations were hit with a plunge in revenue. The forward-looking price-to-earnings ratio was relatively cheap in early 2009, but it was only cheap if relatively optimistic earnings expectations panned out. Thus, U.S. stock investors remained very nervous as of March 2009.

US Dollar Index

Crude Oil (WTI, $/barrrel)

The global economy in 2009 will shrink for the first time in post-war history, according to a forecast released by the World Bank in March 2009. The World Bank also forecast that the world volume of trade would decline by the most in 80 years. The World Bank warned of a brewing financial crisis in the developing world, which had a financing short-fall of $270-700 billion to pay for imports and to service debts.

The global economy fell off a cliff when the U.S. banking problems mushroomed into a global crisis with the bankruptcy of Lehman Brothers in September 2008. In Q42008, GDP growth plunged by 6.2% (quarter-on-quarter annualized) in the U.S., 6.0% in the Euro-Zone, 6.0% in the U.K., and 12.1% in Japan. The market consensus was for sharp declines again in Q1-2009. For all of 2009, the market consensus was for GDP declines of at least 2% in the U.S., Euro-Zone, U.K., and Japan. Federal Reserve Chairman Ben Bernanke on February 25, 2009, said that "there is a reasonable prospect that the current recession will end in 2009 and that 2010 will be a year of recovery," but only if the various rescue measures by the Fed and the U.S. government restore "some measure of financial stability."

Governments around the world responded to the financial crisis with big fiscal stimulus programs. The U.S. Congress and the Obama Administration in February 2009 approved a $787 billion fiscal stimulus program. Europe announced a 200 billion euro program and China announced a $585 billion stimulus program.

Central banks around the world slashed interest rates to deal with the crisis. As of early March 2009, the following policy targets were in place: U.S. zero to 0.25%, European Central Bank 1.50%, Bank of England 0.50% (the lowest in the bank's 315 year history), Canada 0.50%, and Japan 0.10%. By March 2008, the central banks of the U.K., Japan, Switzerland and the U.S. had announced "quantitative easing" moves via the purchase of government bonds in the open market. The bond purchases directly increase the supply of money in the banking system and also seek to bring down long-term government bond yields, thus bringing down mortgage rates and corporate yields as well.

G7 bond yields fell sharply after the banking crisis emerged in September 2008 due to central bank rate cuts, falling inflation, and flight-to-quality purchases of government bonds. The average 10-year G7 bond yield fell by 84 bp from a 1-year high of 4.20% in June 2008 to 3.36% by February 2009. Global stock markets plunged in response to the financial crisis that emerged in September 2008. The MSCI Developed World Stock index plunged by a total of 59% from the record high of 1686.32 posted in October 2007 to the 13-1/2 year low of 684.07 posted in early March 2009.

The outlook for the global economy looked very negative as of early 2009. G7 governments had instituted a variety of monetary and fiscal support measures. However, the market consensus was that it will take an extended period of time for the global economy to stabilize given the depth of the problems.

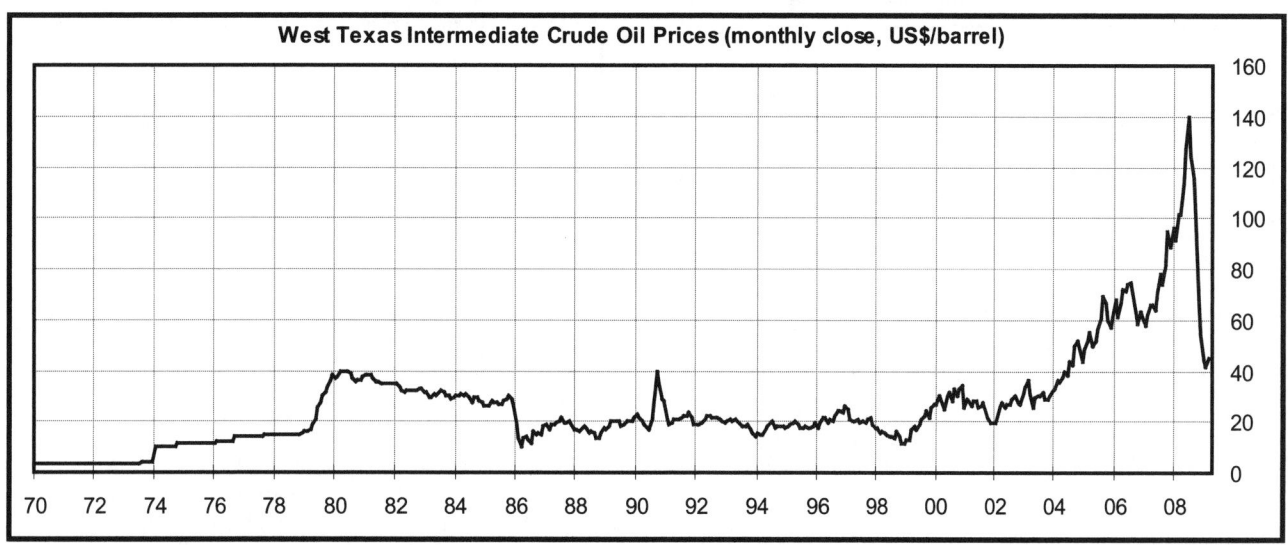

NYMEX West Texas Intermediate crude oil futures prices in 2007-08 nearly tripled in price from $50 per barrel in early-2007 to a record high of $147.27 per barrel in July 2008.

Oil prices started to rally in early 2007 after OPEC implemented production cuts to absorb excess inventories and prevent an extended period of $50 per barrel oil. Specifically, OPEC announced a 1.2 million barrel per day (bpd) production cut starting November 1, 2006, and then a further production cut of 500,000 bpd starting February 1, 2007. Oil prices were driven higher in early 2007 by those production cuts and also by a variety of U.S. refinery snafus during spring 2007, which caused a draw-down in gasoline inventories.

Oil prices were also boosted in 2007 by a steady increase in world demand. Specifically, world demand rose to a new record high of 87.2 million barrels per day in November 2007, up from 85.6 million bpd the previous November and 80 million bpd levels in 2004. China and other fast-growing countries such as India were the key consumers behind the steady increase in the demand for oil seen through 2007.

Crude oil prices in September 2007 then launched into a rally that culminated in the record high of $147.27 in July 2008. That rally was driven in large part by the

record low in the dollar, which was in turn caused by the Fed's interest rate cuts in response to the emerging U.S. housing and banking problems. Oil prices were also driven higher by heavy investment and speculative capi-tal flows into petroleum and other commodities from investors who were fleeing the weak stock market and who were trying to capitalize on the largest commodity bull market in post-war history.

As oil prices during 2007 progressively rallied toward $100 per barrel, OPEC started boosting its production to take advantage of high oil prices. More moderate OPEC

OPEC Oil Production (mln barrels/day)

Non-OPEC Crude Oil Production (mln bpd)

members such as Saudi Arabia were also boosting production to try to prevent a world recession in response to the surge in oil prices. OPEC production (excluding Iraq) rose sharply by 15% starting in mid-2007 from 26.415 barrels per day (bpd) to a peak of 30.315 million bpd in July 2008.

Finally in July 2008, the oil and commodity bubble burst and oil and commodity prices plunged through the end of 2008. The sell-off was initially due to emerging economic weakness and the rally in the dollar that started in July 2008. The oil and commodity sell-off was spurred on by heavy long liquidation pressure by speculators who were washed out of their long positions.

When the global financial crisis erupted in September 2008 with the bankruptcy of Lehman Brothers, oil prices plunged below $100 per barrel to a 5-year low of $32.40 by December 2008. The financial crisis pushed oil prices lower as more investors were forced out of their long positions and as crude oil demand plunged with the world economy going into a serious recession. World oil demand fell by 4.1% from the peak of 87.2 million bpd in November 2007 to the 2-1/2 year low of 83.6 million bpd posted in September 2008.

OPEC responded to the free-fall in oil prices by slashing production. From the peak of 30.315 million bpd in July 2008, OPEC (ex-Iraq) cut production by 16% to 25.390 million bpd by February 2009. That production cut, combined with a small increase in demand stemming from gasoline prices below $2 per gallon, was finally enough to allow crude oil prices to recover to the range of $40-50 per

barrel in early 2009.

Looking ahead, crude oil prices are likely to be in for an extended period of weakness due to the global recession and weak demand. OPEC showed enough cohesion with its production cuts to halt the price decline at $30-40 per barrel. However, it appears doubtful that OPEC members have the stomach for the further sharp production cuts that would be necessary to force oil prices closer to the $70 per barrel area that OPEC would like to target. The need for revenue by OPEC countries to support government spending programs should keep OPEC oil flowing even with oil prices at low levels.

The longer-term outlook for oil prices, however, is much more bullish once the global recession nears an end. The 2007-08 rally in oil prices to $147 per barrel showed that the world economy can absorb $100+ per barrel oil prices without an oil-induced recession (the global recession starting in 2008 was due to the financial crisis, not oil prices). Moreover, the current low level of oil prices is causing both OPEC and non-OPEC producers to shutter facilities and delay expansion plans. This cut in supply and capacity will eventually catch up with the market when demand emerges again.

The world is likely to eventually be back in the situation in 2007 when oil demand was rising sharply and oil producers are having trouble keeping up with demand. The boom-bust cycle of oil prices is only likely to make matters worse by discouraging producers from investing in the new capacity that will be needed in the future. The reality is that most of the cheap oil has already been found in the earth's crust. Major new sources of oil can usually be found only in very remote places or under miles of ocean, or need to be extracted from oil shale or tar sands, which is an expensive process. Oil producers will only invest the huge sums of capital that are necessary to find new oil supplies if they are relatively sure that oil prices will remain high.

The cost of developing new oil supplies is roughly in the neighborhood of $70 per barrel. That means that the longer oil prices remain below $70 per barrel, the longer oil producers will delay in finding new sources of oil and the more upside potential that oil prices will have down the road.

Crude Oil Inventories (mln bbls) vs 5-yr avg

The U.S. dollar index bottomed out a record low of 70.698 in March 2008. The dollar fell sharply from 2001 through early 2008 due to the relatively easy monetary policy by the Federal Reserve and the huge U.S. trade deficit.

The dollar index fell to new lows during 2007 and early2008 as the emerging U.S. housing crisis forced the Fed to start easing monetary policy before other major nations did. The Fed from September 2007 through February 2008 was forced to cut its federal funds rate target by a total of 225 bp from 5.25% in mid-2007 to 3.00% by February 2008, thus undercutting the dollar's interest rate differentials.

The dollar bottomed out in March 2008 when the U.S. banking problems started emerging on a larger scale with the near-failure of Bear Stearns. The dollar traded sideways from March 2008 through July 2008. The dollar then rallied sharply through the remainder of 2008 as the U.S. financial crisis hit full stride with the bankruptcy of Lehman Brothers in September 2008.

As the financial crisis emerged in late 2008, financial institutions around the world rushed into dollars and Treasury securities as a safe haven. The dollar was also pushed higher by U.S. investors, who engaged in a wholesale dumping of overseas investments during the crisis and brought their capital back home, thus forcing them to buy dollars to repatriate their capital.

The demand for dollars in Europe and Asia was so great that the Federal Reserve was forced to dramatically expand its currency swap lines with foreign central banks to meet the demand. Those swap lines reached $465 billion by January 2009. Through the swap lines, the Fed lends dollars to foreign central banks, which in turn lend those dollars to domestic financial institutions.

From a fundamental standpoint, the dollar during the financial crisis could have seen extreme weakness since the crisis originated in the U.S. housing market and since the Fed arguably was debasing its own currency with the $1 trillion injection of liquidity into the financial system (i.e., the amount by which the Fed's balance sheet rose during the crisis). However, the countervailing factor that pushed the dollar higher during the crisis was simply that financial institutions around the world rushed into dollars since the dollar is the de facto global reserve currency and is backed by the largest economy in the world. Thus, while the dollar's fundamentals were not strong during the crisis, the dollar was nevertheless the "least ugly" of the major currencies.

There was also a dramatic shift in investment capital flows during the crisis that worked in the dollar's favor. Global investors quickly pulled capital out of emerging markets, thus pushing the currencies of those countries down and pushing the dollar up. In Russia, for example, investors fled from Russian investments and the ruble because of political concerns (i.e., Russia's invasion of Georgia in August 2008), fears about a collapse in the

US Export & Import Growth (yoy%)

Export Growth — Import Growth

US Imports & Exports with China (US$ blns)

US Imports from China

US Exports to China

Russian banking system, and the plunge in oil prices which hurt the Russian energy industry. Many of those rubles ended up being converted into dollars.

The euro weakened during the financial crisis in late 2008 even though the European Central Bank was the most conservative central bank in addressing the crisis. The ECB did not start cutting interest rates until November 2008 and only cut rates to 1.50% by March 2009, which was much higher than Bank of England's 0.50% base rate, the Federal Reserve's federal funds target range of zero to 0.25%, and the Bank of Japan's policy target of 0.10%.

Regardless of strong European interest rate differentials, the euro was overshadowed by emergency demand for dollars during the crisis. In addition, there was concern during the crisis about the strains within the euro bloc that were caused by ballooning budget deficits and conflicting rescue measures. For example, early in the crisis Ireland moved to guarantee virtually all assets in the Irish banking system, thus drawing a quick flow of capital out of other euro bloc nations and creating serious political friction within the euro bloc.

The crisis made it clear that while the euro bloc has a common currency and a common central bank, it is still basically a free-for-all when it comes to supporting national banks, economies, and businesses during a crisis. Yet the euro in the end was a savior for Europe during the crisis. If Europe had not had the common currency and instead had all the old national currencies (deutschemark, franc, lira, etc.), then those currencies would have been under severe pressure during the crisis. A common currency backed by a decade of history and the steadfast European Central Bank was clearly a safety net for the euro bloc countries. Indeed, countries in eastern Europe that were not part of the euro block saw their currencies plunge as the crisis emerged, thus pushing up the cost of goods and services and the cost of servicing foreign debt.

The yen was buffeted by a variety of factors during the crisis. The yen initially saw strength as hedge funds and traders were forced to remove so-called "yen carry trades." In a yen carry trade, a hedge fund or trader borrows yen at very low interest rates, converts those yen into a foreign currency, and then enters an investment in that foreign currency with much higher return potential. During the crisis, however, stocks and bonds plunged the world over, thus forcing traders to exit those yen-carry-trade investments and buy back yen in order to repay their yen loans. The yen was also pushed higher by the repatriation of investment capital by Japanese investors who were dumping foreign investments.

On the bearish side, however, the yen saw downward pressure during the crisis from extremely low Japanese overnight interest rates (0.10%) and from the plunge in Japanese exports, which actually pushed the Japanese current account balance into a deficit in early 2009 for the first time in 13 years.

US - Europe 3-mo Rate Diff. vs. Dollar Index

Dollar Index (left scale)

US - Euro 3-mo rate (right scale)

US - Japan 3-mo Rate Diff. vs. Dollar Index

Dollar Index (left scale)

US - Japan 3-mo rate (right scale)

U.S. HOUSING PROBLEMS MUSHROOM INTO GLOBAL CRISIS

The problems that started to emerge in 2006 in the U.S. mortgage and housing market ultimately mushroomed into a crisis of global proportions when Lehman Brothers was forced into bankruptcy on September 15, 2008. The Lehman bankruptcy, plus the near-failure of Merrill Lynch and insurance-giant AIG during the same week, led to an all-out panic among investors and a plunge in global stocks. The crisis eventually led to a $50 trillion plunge in global financial assets, equivalent to a year's worth of global economic output, according to the Asian Development Bank in a report released in March 2009.

The U.S. had been struggling with the housing problems for more than a year before the crisis blew up into mammoth proportions with the Lehman bankruptcy. U.S. housing prices peaked in 2006 and home sales fell sharply during 2006 and 2007. By early 2007, a sharp rise in defaults on sub-prime mortgages led to a sharp sell-off in the value of mortgage securities backed by sub-prime loans. The first sign of real trouble in the mortgage securities market was the insolvency in June 2007 of two Bear Stearns hedge funds that held mortgage securities. Two months later in August 2007, French bank BNP Paribas was forced to freeze investor redemptions from three of its mortgage-backed hedge funds. That freeze sparked a run by institutional investors on other mortgage-related hedge funds.

The Fed starting cutting its federal funds rate target in October 2007. By February 2008, the Fed had cut its funds rate target from 5.25% to 3.00% and the Bush Administration had implemented a $168 billion stimulus package. However, the housing and mortgage markets continued to deteriorate, causing big losses among U.S. banks. In March 2008, Bear Stearns nearly failed due to losses on mortgage securities and a lack of market confidence in its ability to obtain funding and survive. The Federal Reserve and the Treasury engineered the sale of Bear Stearns to JPMorgan Chase with a $1.4 billion support package in order to prevent a Bear Stearns bankruptcy. Just six months later in September 2008, the U.S. government was forced to effectively nationalize Fannie Mae and Freddie Mac, which were having solvency and funding difficulties.

The U.S. stock market trended lower from the record high posted in November 2007 through the summer of 2008. But when the Lehman bankruptcy hit, an all-out global panic emerged and the S&P 500 index plunged by 43% from the August 2008 close to the 12-year low posted in December 2008. The U.S. stock market consolidated in January and February 2009, but then fell to a new 12-year low in March 2009. The plunge in the stock market, combined with the 15-20% decline in home prices, caused a plunge in U.S. household wealth by a record $5 trillion just in Q4-2008.

The global financial system nearly stopped functioned after the Lehman bankruptcy as liquidity froze up and panic emerged. There were widespread fears of more bank failures and investors rushed to sell any risky investments and get their cash into government-guaranteed securities or deposit accounts. The 3-month Libor rate, which is the rate at which banks lend money to each other, soared by 2 full percentage points from 2.80% to a peak of 4.82% in October 2008 as banks refused to lend money to each other due to uncertainty about which bank might be the next one to fail.

Starting in September 2008, the Federal Reserve and the U.S. Treasury swung into action with an unprecedented range of support programs. Fed Chairman Ben Bernanke had studied the Great Depression and was already aware of the drastic action that was necessary to arrest the panic. The Fed, aside from cutting its federal funds rate target from 5.25% to the range of zero to 0.25%, expanded its balance sheet by more than $1 trillion as it jammed liquidity into the financial system. The various support measures caused the U.S. federal budget deficit in fiscal 2008-09 to balloon to an estimated $1.75 trillion. Business-TV-network CNBC estimated the total tab of the various bailout programs at $7.4 trillion as of November 2008, which was double the cost of World War II in inflation-adjusted terms.

US Housing Starts (thous units)

US New & Existing Homes Median Price ($'000)

Existing Home Sale Prices — New Home Prices

The U.S. government implemented the following measures, among others, to address the financial crisis:

Term Auction Facility—The Federal Reserve created the Term Auction Facility (TAF) in December 2007 as a vehicle to provide funding to banking institutions for set periods of time. TAF is basically a supercharged version of the Fed's discount window, except with larger and longer funding periods and without the stigma of borrowing from the discount window.

Overseas currency swap lines—The Federal Reserve, starting in December 2007, expanded its currency swap lines with overseas central banks. Through those swap lines, the Fed lends dollars to foreign central banks, which in turn can lend those dollars to domestic financial institutions, thus satisfying the global demand for emergency dollar liquidity. As of January 2009, those currency swap lines totaled $465 billion.

Bush's $168 billion fiscal stimulus package—Congress and the Bush Administration in February 2008 passed the $168 billion Economic Stimulus Act of 2008. The main feature of the program was to send stimulus checks to millions of Americans, encouraging them to spend money to stimulate the economy. The program mildly boosted U.S. GDP in 2008 but had little lasting effect.

Primary Dealer Credit Facility—As a result of Bear Stearns' funding problems and near-failure in March 2008, the Federal Reserve started the Primary Dealer Credit Facility to make loans to government securities dealers such as Bear Stearns. Previously, the Fed was limited to making loans to commercial banks. The near-failure of Bear Stearns made it clear that the Fed needed to have a facility for quickly providing liquidity to investment banks and government securities dealers that were "too big to fail."

Term Security Lending Program—The Term Security Lending Program provided the Federal Reserve with a vehicle for lending securities to primary government securities dealers. The program was designed to alleviate shortages of Treasury securities that were needed by government securities dealers and their customers as collateral or for other transactions.

$540 billion money market rescue—The Federal Reserve in October 2008 announced a $540 billion lending program designed to provide funding for the money market industry, which saw a run on assets after the Lehman bankruptcy caused the Reserve Primary Fund to "break the buck" or fall below a net asset value of $1.00.

$700 billion TARP program—Congress and the Bush Administration in October 2008 approved the $700 billion Troubled Asset Relief Program (TARP) as part of the "Emergency Economic Stabilization Act of 2008." Treasury Secretary Henry Paulson initially intended to use the funds to buy toxic mortgage-backed securities from banks to clean up their balance sheets. However, the Treasury ended up using most of the funds to inject capital into banks to improve the solvency of the banking system.

FDIC bank debt guarantee program—The Temporary Liquidity Guarantee Program (TLGP) was created in October 2008. Under the program, the FDIC guaranteed the unsecured debt issued by banks and thrifts up to a total program size of $1 trillion. The program was designed to make it easier and less expensive for banks to get funding from investors, who might otherwise not be willing to fund banks in the crisis atmosphere.

Commercial paper program—The Treasury in October 2008 announced its Commercial Paper Funding Facility (CPFF), whereby the Fed bought commercial paper from highly rated corporations. The program was designed to get the commercial paper markets working again and to get short-term funding into the hands of large corporations that depend on the commercial paper market for their short-term cash needs. The Fed's facility held $258 billion in commercial paper as of late January 2009.

Fed's $1.45 trillion mortgage security purchase program—The Federal Reserve in November 2008 announced a $600 billion program to supply liquidity directly to the mortgage markets. The Fed earmarked $500 billion to buy mortgage-back securities and in March 2009 raised that amount to $1.25 trillion. The Fed initially said it would buy $100 billion worth of debt of mortgage-finance

US Existing Home Sales (mln units)

US New & Existing Homes Supply (months)

Existing Home Sale Prices — New Home Prices

companies Fannie Mae, Freddie Mac, and Ginnie Mae, and the Fed in March 2009 raised that amount to $200 billion. By March 2009, the Fed had so far purchased $237 billion of mortgage securities. The mortgage program was successful in bringing down mortgage rates, thus making home purchases more affordable and opening the door for a wave of mortgage refinancing, which reduced mortgage payments for many Americans.

TALF program—The Federal Reserve in November 2008 announced the $200 billion Term Asset-Backed Securities Loan Facility (TALF) program. The Fed later said the program would be expanded to $1 trillion. In the TALF program, the Fed provided funding for private investors to buy asset-backed securities backed by auto loans, student loans, credit card receivables, and small-business loans. The Fed in February 2009 said the program may be expanded to include commercial mortgage-backed securities (CMBS) and private-label residential mortgage-backed securities. The TALF program did not actually get started until late March 2009. The TALF program was designed to get the securitized lending channels working again, which were effectively shutdown after the various crisis events in 2007 and 2008. The securitized lending channels are critical for getting capital directly into the hands of consumer and small-business borrowers, thus bypassing the hobbled capital base of the U.S. commercial banks.

Obama $787 billion fiscal stimulus—Congress and the Obama Administration in February 2009 passed the $787 billion "American Recovery and Reinvestment Act of 2009." The bill included about $280 billion in tax cuts and $507 billion in spending programs.

Foreclosure prevention program—The Obama Administration in March 2009 proposed a $75 billion foreclosure-prevention program, which it said would help as many as 9 million homeowners obtain more affordable mortgage terms.

Quantitative easing—The Fed announced after its March 2009 FOMC meeting that it would buy $300 billion in Treasury notes over six months. Those purchases were designed to directly inject money into the banking system and bring down long-term Treasury yields.

Bank toxic asset plan—The Treasury in March 2009 announced its plan to partner with private investors to buy up to $1 trillion of mortgage-backed securities and other toxic assets from banks, thus clearing those impaired assets from bank balance sheets and boosting confidence in the financial strength of those banks.

There are many causes of the global financial crisis. The crisis began with a bubble in U.S. housing prices and reckless mortgage lending, which eventually caused huge losses for banks and hedge funds that held mortgage securities and a sharp decline in U.S. housing prices. However, the housing and mortgage problems exposed an even larger global problem, which was simply a bubble in debt and an over-reliance on leverage.

The rise in debt in the past decade in the U.S. was fostered by liberalized financial system regulation and a variety of new non-bank channels for creating debt such as securitization and finance companies, otherwise known as the "shadow banking system." U.S. consumers took on huge levels of debt as seen by the fact that the ratio of household debt to GDP in the U.S. rose from 66% in 1997 to 100% a decade later. The overall level of U.S. debt including government, households and business, reached nearly 350% of GDP, up from 160% in 1980. Banks and financial institutions operated on increasingly high levels of debt and leverage, thus leaving too little capital to absorb the massive losses that came in 2007 and 2008.

The world is slowly getting past the panic stage as government programs started to at least prevent new problems. However, the world is now going through a painful deleveraging process where debt is being wrung out of the system. Other problems include the fact that the U.S. banking system is not yet on a firm footing and that U.S. home prices have yet to hit bottom. Another major problem is the simultaneous shock to the entire global economy and the collapse in global trade, which means there are no obvious engines of growth to lead the world out of its recession. The world economy will eventually return to a healthy pace of growth, but it is likely to be a long and bumpy road.

Volume - U.S.

U.S. Futures Volume Highlights
2008 in Comparison with 2007

2008 Rank	Top 50 Contracts Traded in 2007	2008 Contracts	%	200876 Contracts	%	2008 Rank
1	E-Mini S&P 500 Index, CME	633,889,466	24.44%	415,348,228	16.01%	2
2	Eurodollars (3-month), CME	596,974,081	23.01%	621,470,328	23.96%	1
3	T-Notes (10-year), CBT	256,770,689	9.90%	349,229,371	13.46%	3
4	T-Notes (5-year), CBT	168,127,469	6.48%	166,207,391	6.41%	4
5	Crude Oil, NYMEX	134,674,264	5.19%	121,525,967	4.68%	5
6	E-Mini NASDAQ 100, CME	108,734,456	4.19%	95,309,053	3.67%	7
7	T-Bonds (30-year), CBT	89,464,546	3.45%	107,630,211	4.15%	6
8	T-Notes (2-year), CBT	79,311,002	3.06%	68,610,392	2.64%	8
9	Corn, CBT	59,957,118	2.31%	54,520,152	2.10%	10
10	Mini ($5) Dow Jones Industrial Index, CBT	55,348,312	2.13%	40,098,882	1.55%	12
11	Euro FX, CME	53,652,590	2.07%	43,063,060	1.66%	11
12	E-Mini Russell 2000 Index, CME	46,065,655	1.78%	60,731,902	2.34%	9
13	Natural Gas, NYMEX	38,730,519	1.49%	29,786,318	1.15%	15
14	Gold (100 oz.), COMEX Div. of NYMEX	38,377,367	1.48%	25,060,440	0.97%	16
15	Soybeans, CBT	36,373,096	1.40%	31,726,316	1.22%	13
16	Japanese Yen, CME	32,844,404	1.27%	30,820,442	1.19%	14
17	Henry Hub Swap, NYMEX	31,401,575	1.21%	16,207,044	0.62%	24
18	Sugar #11, NYBOT	27,019,704	1.04%	21,263,799	0.82%	17
19	Gasoline, RBOB, NYMEX	20,522,571	0.79%	19,791,439	0.76%	19
20	British Pound, CME	20,497,378	0.79%	20,799,827	0.80%	18
21	Heating Oil #2, NYMEX	19,583,052	0.75%	18,078,976	0.70%	21
22	Federal Funds (30-day), CBT	19,434,295	0.75%	16,597,188	0.64%	23
23	Wheat, CBT	19,011,928	0.73%	19,582,706	0.75%	20
24	Soybean Oil, CBT	16,928,361	0.65%	13,170,914	0.51%	27
25	S&P 500 Index, CME	16,763,071	0.65%	15,837,593	0.61%	25
26	E-Mini Russell 2000 Index, ICE	16,526,331	0.64%	57,540		
27	Swiss Franc, CME	14,814,153	0.57%	14,478,658	0.56%	26
28	Soybean Meal, CBT	13,354,174	0.51%	12,213,315	0.47%	29
29	Natural Gas Penultimate Swap, NYMEX	12,352,928	0.48%	10,117,889	0.39%	31
30	Rogers International TRAKRS, CME	11,621,869	0.45%	17,651,395	0.68%	22
31	Canadian Dollar, CME	11,378,024	0.44%	12,224,845	0.47%	28
32	Australian Dollar, CME	11,212,985	0.43%	10,785,897	0.42%	30
33	Live Cattle, CME	9,801,360	0.38%	8,587,973	0.33%	33
34	Silver (5,000 oz)	8,917,183	0.34%	6,817,137	0.26%	37
35	E-mini S&P MidCap 400 Index	8,580,467	0.33%	7,352,427	0.28%	35
36	Lean Hogs, CME	8,505,138	0.33%	7,264,832	0.28%	36
37	Cotton #2, NYBOT	6,162,963	0.24%	6,334,979	0.24%	38
38	E-Mini Crude Oil, NYMEX	5,641,145	0.22%	5,185,214	0.20%	39
39	Coffee "C", NYBOT	5,446,516	0.21%	5,128,623	0.20%	41
40	Mexican Peso, CME	5,302,297	0.20%	5,154,636	0.20%	40
41	Nikkei 225 Index (JPY), CME	4,769,567	0.18%	3,290,909	0.13%	46
42	High Grade Copper, NYMEX	4,618,074	0.18%	3,753,168	0.14%	43
43	Nikkei 225 Index (USD), CME	4,399,966	0.17%	3,421,085	0.13%	44
44	Wheat, KCBT	3,778,266	0.15%	4,318,007	0.17%	42
45	TRAKRS PIMCO, CME	3,668,906	0.14%	8,712,135	0.34%	32
46	Cocoa, NYBOT	3,592,268	0.14%	3,335,283	0.13%	45
47	Gold, CBT	3,466,009	0.13%	7,898,027	0.30%	34
48	Panhandle Basis Swap	2,017,371	0.08%	1,497,748		
49	US Dollar Index	1,825,326	0.07%	1,099,800		
50	NASDAQ 100 Index	1,407,413	0.05%	1,683,378	0.06%	50
	Top 50 Contracts	2,803,617,668	98.35%	2,590,832,839	97.97%	
	Contracts Below the Top 50	47,155,915	1.65%	53,731,835	2.03%	
	TOTAL	2,850,773,583	100.00%	2,644,564,674	100.00%	

* For 2007 Top 50 contracts totaled 2,594,078,567 including 3 contracts that are not among 2008's Top 50.

U.S. Futures Volume Highlights
2008 in Comparison with 2007

2008 Rank	EXCHANGE	2008 Contracts	%	2007 Contracts	%	2007 Rank
1	CME Group[2]	2,438,142,653	85.53%	2,310,944,764	87.38%	1
2	New York Mercantile Exchange (NYMEX)[1]	338,455,289	11.87%	277,408,465	10.49%	2
3	InterContinental Exchange (ICE)	63,433,647	2.23%	40,658,718	1.54%	3
4	OneChicago	4,012,281	0.14%	8,105,963	0.31%	4
5	Kansas City Board of Trade (KCBT)	3,778,266	0.13%	4,318,007	0.16%	5
6	Minneapolis Grain Exchange (MGE)	1,361,067	0.05%	1,792,453	0.07%	6
7	CBOE Futures Exchange (CFE)	1,161,397	0.04%	1,136,295	0.04%	7
8	Chicago Climate Exchange (CCFE)	370,505	0.01%	191,899	0.01%	8
9	Green Exchange	35,523	0.00%			
10	US Futures Exchange	22,955	0.00%	8,110	0.00%	9
	Total Futures	2,850,773,583	100.00%	2,644,564,674	100.00%	

[1] Includes Commodity Exchange, Inc. and GLOBEX. [2] In July 2007, the Chicago Mercantile Exchange and the Chicago Board of Trade merged and is now listed as one exchange.

CHICAGO CLIMATE FUTURES EXCHANGE (CCFE)

FUTURE	CONTRACT UNIT	2008	2007	2006		
Carbon Financial Instrument (CFI)		29,405	3,566			
European Carbon Financial Instrument		156	130			
Event Linked (IFEX)		10,373	2,321			
Event Linked (IFEX) FLW		2				
Certified Emissions Reduction (CER)		166	128			
Dow Jones Sustainability World Index		92				
ECO-Clean Energy Index (ECO)		792	1,054			
Nitrogen Financial Instrument - Annual		21,730	205			
Nitrogen Financial Instrument (NFI-OS)		1,348	3,465			
Regional Greenhouse Gas Initiatives		17,043				
Sulfur Financial Instrument (SFI)		289,398	181,030	28,924		
Total Futures		370,505	191,899	28,924		

CBOE FUTURES EXCHANGE (CFE)

FUTURE	CONTRACT UNIT	2008	2007	2006	2005	2004
CBOE Volatility Index (VIX)	100 USD x Index	1,088,105	1,046,475	434,478	128,927	89,622
CBOE S&P 500 12-Month Variance (VA)	50 USD per var pt	940	56	210		
DJIA Volatility Index (VXD)	100 USD x Index	40,706	43,555	38,892	9,546	
Nasdaq 100 Volatility Index (VXN)	1,000 USD x Index	2,581	3,163			
Russell 2000 Volatility Index (RVX)		26,956	30,011			
S&P 500 BuyWrite Index (BXM)	100 USD x Index	31	3,731	8		
S&P 500 3-Month Variance (VTI)	50 USD per point	2,078	9,302	3,787	5,033	1,129
Total Futures		1,161,397	1,136,295	478,424	177,632	91,332

CME Group (includes Chicago Mercantile Exchange and Chicago Board of Trade)

FUTURE	CONTRACT UNIT	2008	2007	2006	2005	2004
Wheat	5,000 bu	19,011,928	19,582,706	16,224,871	10,114,098	7,955,155
Mini Wheat	1,000 bu	70,971	79,282	67,637	32,295	31,044
Corn	5,000 bu	59,957,118	54,520,152	47,239,893	27,965,057	24,038,233
Mini Corn	1,000 bu	219,562	156,210	162,545	102,292	86,771
Oats	5,000 bu	441,588	432,741	427,315	351,539	416,448
Soybeans	5,000 bu	36,373,096	31,726,316	22,647,784	20,216,137	18,846,021
Mini Soybeans	1,000 bu	475,231	540,940	581,047	495,313	362,829
South American Soybeans	5,000 bu	2		226	12,088	
Soybean Oil	60,000 lbs	16,928,361	13,170,914	9,488,524	7,676,130	7,593,314
Soybean Meal	100 tons	13,354,174	12,213,315	9,350,043	8,324,616	8,569,243
Rough Rice	200,000 lbs	362,565	358,905	321,330	228,502	168,165
Live Cattle	40,000 lbs	9,801,360	8,587,973	8,209,698	5,833,556	4,510,128
Feeder Cattle	50,000 lbs	1,250,324	1,099,863	1,286,395	1,017,348	741,265
Lean Hogs	40,000 lbs	8,505,138	7,264,832	6,481,001	4,153,543	3,204,186
Pork Bellies, Frozen	40,000 lbs	56,705	68,409	107,564	124,418	151,949
Class III Milk	200,000 lbs	304,754	311,459	225,137	182,509	345,973
Class IV Milk	200,000 lbs	624	314	113	138	690
Nonfat Dry Milk	44,000 lbs	2,239	1,072	954	217	114
Butter	40,000 lbs	135	1,222	3,800	7,708	6,167
Cash Butter	20,000 lbs	17,495	20,067	18,673	2,337	
Dry Whey		4,141	6,378			
Wood Pulp		8,740	1,038			
Random Lumber	100,000 bd ft	437,613	334,689	271,024	236,241	242,873
Eurozone Harmonized CPI Index	10,000 EUR x Index	100	1,150	1,369	835	
Mini Silver	1,000 oz	490,434	462,406	547,182	163,395	204,255
Mini Gold	33.2 troy oz	1,403,986	1,452,314	1,994,920	389,737	420,604
Silver	5,000 oz	502,125	1,511,173	1,208,471	86,218	12,398
Gold	100 oz	3,466,009	7,898,027	8,452,484	626,901	89,539
T-Bonds (30-year)	100,000 USD	89,464,546	107,630,211	93,754,895	86,926,569	72,949,053
T-Notes (10-year)	100,000 USD	256,770,689	349,229,371	255,571,869	215,124,076	196,119,150
T-Notes (5-year)	100,000 USD	168,127,469	166,207,391	124,870,313	121,908,830	105,469,410
T-Notes (2-year)	200,000 USD	79,311,002	68,610,392	37,966,797	21,205,359	9,454,774
Interest Rate Swap (30-year)	100,000 USD	80,169	12,555			
Interest Rate Swap (10-year)	100,000 USD	1,004,309	848,372	520,090	655,711	856,968
Interest Rate Swap (7-year)	100,000 USD	320				
Interest Rate Swap (5-year)	100,000 USD	1,147,170	551,505	272,749	202,737	243,353
30-Day Federal Funds	5,000,000 USD	19,434,295	16,597,188	17,833,331	11,602,282	11,940,120
One Month LIBOR	3,000,000 USD	571,710	1,194,200	852,119	1,048,468	2,886,987
Eurodollar (3-month)	1,000,000 USD	596,974,081	621,470,328	502,077,391	410,355,384	297,284,038
E-Mini Eurodollar (5-year)		600	14,627	4,237		
Euroyen	1,000,000,000 JPY	122,917	561,220	662,653	200,958	224,821
2-Year SWAP		38,860	38,670	31,260	30,485	26,240
5-Year SWAP		29,990	74,950	56,320	35,315	56,438
10-Year SWAP		20,020	55,200	44,510	35,170	65,281
3M Overnight Index Swaps (OIS)		15,358				
Lehman Brothers Index	100 USD x Index	440	707			
Australian Dollar	100,000	11,212,985	10,785,897	6,567,650	4,749,093	2,672,733

CME Group (continued)

FUTURE	CONTRACT UNIT	2008	2007	2006	2005	2004
British Pound	62,500	20,497,378	20,799,827	16,099,540	8,769,751	4,676,512
Brazilian Real	100,000	67,168	127,879	94,514	23,144	2,911
Canadian Dollar	100,000	11,378,024	12,224,845	10,279,576	7,930,156	5,611,328
CME $ Index	1,000 USD x Index	5				306
Czech Koruna		787	496	461	118	31
Euro FX	125,000	53,652,590	43,063,060	40,790,379	34,530,730	20,456,672
E-Mini Euro FX	62,500	774,078	491,401	386,850	642,857	190,554
Hungarian Forint	30,000,000	901	148	620	77	10
Israeli Shekel	1,000,000	3,014	3,070	113		
Japanese Yen	12,500,000	32,844,404	30,820,442	19,677,365	12,471,672	7,395,322
E-Mini Japanese Yen	6,250,000	24,657	19,116	9,203	4,887	5,466
Korean Won	125,000,000	268	2,312	5,867		
Mexican Peso	500,000	5,302,297	5,154,636	3,795,538	3,674,886	3,247,222
New Zealand Dollar	100,000	808,296	928,816	529,782	187,437	162,370
Norwegian Krone	227,000	7,327	10,289	6,461	3,966	2,122
Polish Zloty	500,000	20,554	25,977	23,899	15,046	4,461
Russian Ruble	2500000	213,341	173,613	125,762	45,835	30,620
South African Rand	500,000	99,413	84,376	70,491	63,379	65,749
Swedish Krona	193,600	2,436	12,374	4,618	1,884	812
Swiss Franc	125,000	14,814,153	14,478,658	11,470,031	7,784,498	4,067,767
Australian Dollar / Canadian Dollar	200,000 AUD	2,762	1,749	6,708	1,797	676
Australian Dollar / Japanese Yen	200,000 AUD	1,088	44	19	836	1,066
Australian Dollar / New Zealand Dollar	200,000 AUD	1,346	903	39	1,990	639
British Pound / Japanese Yen	125,000 GBP	3,430	332	173	830	651
British Pound / Swiss Franc	125,000 GBP	702	3,031	6,151	3,209	689
Canadian Dollar / Japanese Yen	200,000 CAD	14	236	24	452	344
Chinese Renimibi / U.S. Dollar	1,000,000 CHR	16,790	8,179	5,407		
Swiss Franc / Japanese Yen	250,000 CHF	1,968	2,754	55	338	110
Euro / Australian Dollar	125,000 EUR	246	210	205	823	769
Euro / British Pound	125,000 EUR	73,554	80,232	42,053	39,069	43,635
Euro / Canadian Dollar	125,000 EUR	85	180	109	1,032	901
Euro / Czech Koruna	4,000,000 EUR	196	65		56	
Euro / Hungarian Forint	30,000,000 EUR	193	78	1,050	10	
Euro / Japanese Yen	125,000 EUR	320,060	365,895	272,182	123,805	118,614
Euro / Norwegian Krone	125,000 EUR	3,760	6,605	328	522	98
Euro / Polish Zloty	500,000	14,693	18,349	15,194	18,548	3,859
Euro / Swedish Krona	125,000 EUR	50	48	151	394	318
Euro / Swiss Franc	125,000 EUR	50,923	97,478	49,475	12,264	7,290
Ethanol	29,000 US Gallons	29,451	12,516	5,564	2,676	
OTC Ethanol Forward Swap	14,500 US Gallons	249,147	60,729	42		
Ethanol Gulf Coast Basis Swap	14,500 US Gallons	129				
Ethanol Los Angeles Basis Swap	14,500 US Gallons	126				
Dow Jones Industrial Index ($25)	25 USD x Index	12,392	14,301	18,686		
Dow Jones Industrial Index ($10)	10 USD x Index	1,147,657	1,483,817	1,919,847	1,787,405	2,577,138
Mini Dow Jones Industrial Index ($5)	5 USD x Index	55,348,312	40,098,882	26,792,373	24,892,328	20,695,848
Dow Jones US Real Estate	100 x Index	18	6,867			
S&P 500 Index	500 USD x Index	16,763,071	15,837,593	14,844,858	15,377,489	16,175,584
E-Mini S&P 500 Index	50 USD x Index	633,889,466	415,348,228	257,926,673	207,095,732	167,202,962
E-Mini S&P European		2,567				
E-mini S&P MidCap 400 Index	100 USD x Index	8,580,467	7,352,427	5,528,263	4,885,430	3,282,347
S&P MidCap 400 Index	500 USD x Index	97,224	118,140	153,268	205,058	260,764
S&P Citigroup Growth	250 USD x Index	8,163	25,132	5,473		
S&P Citigroup Value	250 USD x Index	6,450	6,418	7,289		
E-Mini Russell 2000 Index	100 USD x Index	46,065,655	60,731,902	41,748,538	28,902,033	17,121,233
Russell 2000 Index	500 USD x Index	459,695	696,006	619,286	571,055	614,040
E-Mini NASDAQ 100 Index	20 USD x Index	108,734,456	95,309,053	79,940,222	72,453,141	77,168,513
NASDAQ 100 Index	500 USD x Index	1,407,413	1,683,378	2,269,870	2,682,058	4,011,983
Nikkei 225 Index (USD)	5 USD x Index	4,399,966	3,421,085	2,809,839	1,886,270	1,239,010
Nikkei 225 Index (JPY)	5 USD x Index	4,769,567	3,290,909	2,126,654	952,618	260,128
S&P 500 Financial Sector	125 USD x Index	9,032	4,202		1,600	2,527
E-mini S&P SmallCap 600 Index	100 USD x Index	107,039	28,894			
S&P SmallCap 600 Index	200 USD x Index	341	1,028	130	1,882	2,354
E-Mini MSCI EAFE	50 USD x Index	450,138	172,371	17,461		
E-Mini FTSE/Xinhua China 25 Index	5 USD x Index	1	508			
E-mini MSCI Emerging Markets	50 USD x Index	171,064	26,793			
TRAKRS BXY	1 USD x Index	28,860	47,900	304,172		
TRAKRS PIMCO	1 USD x Index	3,668,906	8,712,135	24,471,474		
TRAKRS PIMCO SPTR	1 USD x Index	451,858	2,324,128	2,349,055		
Rogers International TRAKRS	1 USD x Index	11,621,869	17,651,395	26,486,999	36,081,429	
Dow Jones AIGER Index	100 x Index	73,445	51,651	5,990		
HDD Weather	20 USD x Index	119,533	135,702	115,763	75,266	16,404
HDD Seasonal Weather Strips	20 USD x Index	6,600	12,350	13,675	50	
CDD Weather	20 USD x Index	117,729	114,044	65,258	107,475	23,656
CDD Seasonal Weather Strips	20 USD x Index	3,610	7,300	8,450		

CME Group (continued)

FUTURE	CONTRACT UNIT	2008	2007	2006	2005	2004
Euro HDD Weather	20 GBP x Index	4,625	3,625	3,435	7,302	2,015
Euro CAT Weather	20 GBP x Index	350	750	950	3,332	535
Euro Seasonal HDD Weather	20 GBP x Index	2,850	1,750	1,225		
Weekly Average Temperature	1,000 USD x Index	100	5			
CSI Housing Index	250 USD x Index	1,178	2,995	3,632		
Goldman Sachs Commodity Index	250 USD x Index	526,036	644,761	615,260	498,424	450,036
GSCI Excess Return Index	100 USD x Index	27,206	15,136	13,141		
S&P 500 ETF	100 shares	1,109	1,165	2,009	4,522	
Russell 2000 ETF	200 shares	550	470	785	47	
Nasdaq 100 ETF	200 shares	833	1,470	1,849	3,817	
Total Futures		2,438,142,653	2,310,944,764	1,779,974,585	1,444,264,464	1,153,814,751

US FUTURES EXCHANGE (USFE) (formerly EUREX US)

FUTURE	CONTRACT UNIT	2008	2007	2006	2005	2004
USD SENSEX Index	100 USD x Index	9,923				
ISE Homebuild Index	100 USD x Index	40	35			
ISE Water Index	100 USD x Index	260	24			
ISE Natural Gas Index	100 USD x Index	20	12			
Mini Dolar Dax	10 USD x Index	3,309				
Morningstar Medium Cap Value Index	100 USD x Index	20	4			
FX Spot Equivalent Future on USD/CHF		367	195			
FX Spot Equivalent Future on GBP/USD	50,000	492	720			
FX Spot Equivalent Future on EUR/USD	50,000	5,717	4,363			
FX Spot Equivalent Future on USD/JPY	50,000	875	1,892			
FX Spot Equivalent Future on USD/CAD		430	272			
FX Spot Equivalent Future on USD/CAD		2				
FX Spot Equivalent Future on AUD/USD		1,500	423			
Total Futures		22,955	8,110	135,803	2,200,384	6,186,008

KANSAS CITY BOARD OF TRADE (KCBT)

FUTURE	CONTRACT UNIT	2008	2007	2006	2005	2004
Wheat	5,000 bu	3,778,266	4,318,007	4,763,168	3,682,919	2,833,370
Total Futures		3,778,266	4,318,007	4,771,711	3,690,025	2,834,799

MINNEAPOLIS GRAIN EXCHANGE (MGE)

FUTURE	CONTRACT UNIT	2008	2007	2006	2005	2004
Spring Wheat	5,000 bu	1,361,042	1,792,310	1,613,239	1,384,750	1,378,694
Hard Red Winter Wheat Index	5,000 bu	25	8	18	427	2,521
Total Futures		1,361,067	1,792,453	1,614,543	1,389,922	1,381,456

INTERCONTINENTINENAL EXCHANGE (ICE) (formerly NYBOT, NYFE, NYCE, FINEX and CSCE)

FUTURE	CONTRACT UNIT	2008	2007	2006	2005	2004
Coffee 'C'	37,500 lbs	5,446,516	5,128,623	4,407,512	3,987,778	4,193,303
Robusta Coffee	37,500 lbs	172	779			
Sugar #11	112,000 lbs	27,019,704	21,263,799	15,100,721	13,007,072	9,766,550
Sugar #14	112,000 lbs	92,365	108,603	120,685	136,676	114,619
Sugar #16	112,000 lbs	250				
Cocoa	10 metric tons	3,592,268	3,335,283	3,169,202	2,582,927	2,389,050
Cotton #2	50,000 lbs	6,162,963	6,334,979	4,490,407	3,848,990	3,156,018
Pulp	20 Airdry Metric Tons	39	2,281	20,627	20,500	
Orange Juice, Frozen Concentrate	15,000 lbs	710,512	845,792	923,696	902,019	970,437
US Dollar / Swedish Krona	200,000 USD	3,400	30,118	33,682	18,926	11,654
US Dollar / Swedish Krona (Half Size)	100,000 USD	50,858				
US Dollar / Norwegian Krone	200,000 USD	5,566	26,274	28,458	25,611	17,016
US Dollar / Norwegian Krone (Half Size)	100,000 USD	48,976				
US Dollar / Czech Koruna	200,000 USD	2,947	33,731	34,913	31,502	9,852
US Dollar / Czech Koruna (Half Size)	100,000 USD	12,711				
US Dollar / Hungarian Forint	200,000 USD	7,070	34,960	26,012	22,473	9,283
US Dollar / Hungarian Forint (Half Size)	100,000 USD	29,945				
US Dollar / South African Rand	100,000 USD	81,401	88,260	54,756	87,417	71,332
Canadian Dollar / Japanese Yen	200,000 CAD	13,078	20,463	13,215	9,238	16,604
Australian Dollar / US Dollar	100,000 AUD	4,920	17,666	29,069	39,578	13,141
Australian Dollar / Canadian Dollar	200,000 AUD	26,637	25,922	21,291	8,058	9,178
Australian Dolar / New Zealand Dollar	200,000 AUD	12,307	32,262	15,790	33,330	34,904
Australian Dollar / Japanese Yen	200,000 AUD	39,382	53,049	57,667	177,816	66,006
Colombian Peso / US Dollar	100,000,000 CP	1	7,664			
New Zealand Dollar / Japanese Yen	200,000 NZD	558	1,502	20		
New Zealand Dollar / US Dollar	200,000 NZD	45,134	61,657	53,413	70,364	37,899
Norwegian Krone / Swedish Koruna	500,000 NOK	38,021	20,866	15,172	11,797	10,192
British Pound / Swiss franc	125,000 GBP	43,558	66,586	84,210	49,597	31,151

VOLUME - U.S.

INTERCONTINENTINAL EXCHANGE (ICE) (continued)

FUTURE	CONTRACT UNIT	2008	2007	2006	2005	2004
British Pound / Japanese Yen	125,000 GBP	46,231	111,274	148,696	156,444	68,519
Swiss Franc / Japanese Yen	200,000 CHF	76,734	74,148	65,275	66,907	41,614
Euro / US Dollar, Small	100,000 EUR	112,675	24,382	116,029	110,186	12,409
Euro / Australian Dollar	100,000 EUR	62,986	73,821	58,144	59,644	44,000
Euro / Canadian Dollar	100,000 EUR	21,972	43,266	26,477	12,179	52,496
Euro / Czech Koruna	100,000 EUR	16,204	49,442	17,533	21,525	28,093
Euro / Hungarian Forint	100,000 EUR	18,525	31,105	11,615	12,905	17,640
Euro / Japanese Yen	100,000 EUR	346,417	418,725	586,129	448,372	363,069
Euro / Swedish Krona	100,000 EUR	55,039	64,617	54,571	129,028	64,334
Euro / British Pound	100,000 EUR	169,921	241,409	304,382	253,818	226,404
Euro / Norwegian	100,000 EUR	52,084	58,664	44,635	55,945	29,536
Euro / South African Rand	100,000 EUR	244	318	163		
Euro / Swiss Franc	100,000 EUR	159,849	215,173	183,446	261,897	143,274
Million Australian Dollar / US Dollar	1,000,000 AUD	3				
Million Euro / Japanese Yen	1,000,000 JPY	2				
Million Euro / US Dollar	1,000,000 EUR	4,804				
Million US Dollar / Swiss Franc	1,000,000 USD	49				
Million British Pound / US Dollar	1,000,000 GBP	327				
Million US Dollar / Japanese Yen	1,000,000 USD	1,783				
Million US Dollar / Canaddian Dollar	1,000,000 USD	1				
British Pound / Australian Dollar	125,000 GBP	8,104	5,994	10		
British Pound / Canadian Dollar	125,000 GBP	3,204	5,195	2		
British Pound / New Zealand Dollar	125,000 GBP	16				
British Pound / Swedish Krona	125,000 GBP	254				
Small British Pound / US Dollar	62,500 GBP	55,127	14,279	17,437	21,762	6,006
Small US Dollar / Canadian Dollar	100,000 USD	6,572	14,672	18,910	15,624	247
Small US Dollar / Japanese Yen	100,000 USD	26,973	28,251	142,751	39,715	5,664
Small US Dollar / Swiss Franc	100,000 USD	9,462	17,866	64,417	28,262	41
US Dollar Index	1,000 USD x Index	1,825,326	1,099,800	1,168,486	1,159,938	748,204
Revised NYSE Composite Index	50 USD x Index	698	4,605	3,213	14,047	14,678
Russell 1000 Mini Index	50 USD x Index	177,768	81,432			
Russell 1000 Index	500 USD x Index	46,309	61,205			
Russell 1000 Growth Index	500 USD x Index	1,725	2,112	2,730	2,905	2,442
Russell 1000 Value Index	500 USD x Index	1,476	1,474	2,031	2,391	2,392
Russell 2000 Index	500 USD x Index	87,884	1,913	1,038	298	424
Russell 2000 Mini Index	500 USD x Index	16,526,331	57,540			
Russell 2000 Value Index	500 USD x Index	10	135			2
Russell 3000 Index	500 USD x Index	70	10			20
Reuters-CRB Futures Index (CCI)	500 USD x Index	19,185	19,973	14,312	9,144	19,230
RJ/CRB Futures Index	200 USD x Index	44	3	150	7,424	
Total Futures		63,433,647	40,658,718	32,746,692	29,013,416	23,955,212

Green Exchange

FUTURE	CONTRACT UNIT	2008
EU Allowance		5,066
Certified Emission Reduction		25,083
Carbon RGGI Emissions		240
Seasonal Emission Allowance Current		20
Vintage 2009		45
Vintage 2010		35
Sulfur Dioxide (SO2) Emissions		5,034
Total Futures		35,523

NEW YORK MERCANTILE EXCHANGE (NYMEX)

COMEX DIVISION

FUTURE	CONTRACT UNIT	2008	2007	2006	2005	2004
Gold	100 oz	38,377,367	25,060,440	15,917,584	15,890,617	14,959,617
Silver	5,000 oz	8,917,183	6,817,137	5,433,063	5,536,351	5,006,125
High Grade Copper	25,000 lbs	4,618,074	3,753,168	3,281,312	3,950,842	3,190,625
Aluminum	44,000 lbs	9	723	9,149	28,491	72,169
Total Futures (COMEX)		51,912,633	35,631,468	24,641,108	25,406,301	23,228,536

NYMEX DIVISION

FUTURE	CONTRACT UNIT	2008	2007	2006	2005	2004
Palladium	100 oz	483,828	400,993	378,116	321,923	267,552
Platinum	50 oz	675,543	501,545	373,119	376,179	295,695
No. 2 Heating Oil, NY	42,000 gal	19,583,052	18,078,976	13,990,589	13,135,581	12,884,511
Crude Oil	1,000 bbl	134,674,264	121,525,967	71,053,203	59,650,468	52,883,200
NY Harbor RBOB Gasoline	42,000 gal	20,522,571	19,791,439	3,883,261	1,964	
Natural Gas	10,000 MMBTU	38,730,519	29,786,318	23,029,988	19,142,549	17,441,942
Natural Gas Penultimate Swap		12,352,928	10,117,889	7,973,290	2,751,455	294,011
Henry Hub Swap		31,401,575	16,207,044	24,157,726	10,406,462	5,353,792
AECO-C/NIT Basis Swap		533,158	860,885	1,317,291	1,247,570	488,699

NEW YORK MERCANTILE EXCHANGE (NYMEX) (continued)

NYMEX DIVISION (cont)

FUTURE	CONTRACT UNIT	2008	2007	2006	2005	2004
Algonquin City - gates Natural Gas Basis		214				
ANR - Louisiana Basis Swap		34,499	13,127	24,476	6,869	
ANR - Oklahoma Basis		124,501	99,106	47,516	57,584	52,967
Centerpoint Basis Swap		319,716	159,048	68,895		
Chicago Basis Swap		575,663	486,313	555,309	324,560	174,498
CIG Rockies		117,473	100,525	245,305	181,241	69,555
TCO Basis		236,679	394,285	333,867	316,053	244,049
Columbia Gulf Onshore Basis		211,645	80,422	68,181	27,332	24,272
Dominion Transmission - Appalachian		229,043	458,950	433,304	459,360	247,191
Permian Basis		432,177	521,914	520,763	306,329	128,814
Florida Gas Zone 3 Basis Swap		87,760	28,098	13,785	972	
Henry Hub Basis Swap		287,216	264,818	467,158	337,152	98,408
Houston Ship Channel Basis Swap		787,312	1,088,654	1,696,435	778,513	429,266
Kern River, Wyoming Basis Swap		151				
MichCon Basis Swap		283,962	289,738	484,925	158,667	94,137
NGPL Mid-Continent Swap		355,491	392,899	279,960	160,828	69,854
NGPL TEX/OK Basis Swap		524,326	675,365	1,119,784	401,241	60,266
NGPL STX Natural Gas Basis Swap		11,686				
Northern Natural Gas Demarcation Basis		334,235	278,478	162,381	73,501	17,651
Northwest Rockies Basis Swap		792,219	1,040,846	1,408,279	1,261,653	652,511
PG&E Citygate Basis Swap		387,422	328,283	356,769	642,845	209,906
Panhandle Basis Swap		2,017,371	1,497,748	1,404,498	870,855	224,329
PG&E Malin Basis		251,130	327,357	533,176	682,135	334,230
San Juan Basis Swap		169,655	246,858	181,765	160,530	62,048
Socal Basis Swap		1,082,052	1,784,378	2,311,008	1,580,162	569,540
Sonat Basis Swap		130,742	36,106	18,722	8,966	
Sumas Basis		63,684	83,641	205,978	429,597	320,144
Tennessee 500 Leg Basis Swap		79,271	29,621	19,071	8,600	
Tennessee Zone 0 Basis Swap		23,876	53,705	81,632	56,197	
Texas Eastern Zone M-3 Basis		412,686	765,236	642,301	716,299	278,235
Texas Gas Zone SL Basis Swap		71,598	46,454	49,163	10,640	
TETCO ELA Basis		43,217	5,382	11,811	8,196	24,755
TETCO STX Basis		37,702	51,664	69,669	36,481	19,790
Transco Zone 3 Basis Swap		157,593	126,442	58,349	92,944	56,993
Transco Zone 6 Basis Swap		165,105	545,492	313,674	529,577	480,197
Transco Zone 4 Basis Swap		107,097	11,004	13,652	1,394	
Trunkline, LA Basis Swap		31,481	17,364	7,001	3,972	
Northern Natural Gas Ventura Basis		361,503	353,186	306,787	207,843	21,771
WAHA Basis		624,817	727,707	611,795	338,241	184,909
ANR OK Natural Gas Index Swap		1,344				
Centerpoint East Index		4,644	1,671	1,378		
Chicago Index Swap		18,173	17,721	5,114	6,605	1,581
CIG Rockies Natural Gas Index Swap		1,041				
Demarc Natural Gas Index Swap		13,913	3,460	2,218		
Dominion Transmission - Appalachian		34,100	18,657	10,120	8,186	
El Paso, Permian Index Swap		46,469	34,194	16,710	11,740	2,250
Henry Hub Index Swap		187,463	207,234	332,129	271,791	65,860
Houston Ship Channel Index Swap		101,690	132,368	131,702	148,249	12,791
MichCon Natural Gas Index Swap		1,414				
NGPL Midcontinental Index		12,004	8,698	1,615		
NGPL TEXOK Index		43,322	14,304	3,537		
Panhandle Index Swap		37,250	31,609	9,444	6,171	1,798
PG&E Citygate Index		43,015	28,901	14,331	14,878	
Rockies Kern Opal - NW Index		26,500	19,440	29,994	8,562	
El Paso, San Juan Index Swap		2,766	3,425	3,702	924	
Socal Index		121,780	121,263	53,086	23,512	
Sumas Index		3,810	6,727	14,976	13,088	
TCO Natural Gas Index Swap		2,648				
TETCO M-3 Natural Gas Index Swap		121,290	54,619	44,685	19,601	
TETCO STX Natural Gas Index Swap		2,195				
Tennesse 500 Leg Natural Gas Index Swap		62				
Tennesse Zone 0 Natural Gas Index Swap		2,804				
Transco Zone 3 Natural Gas Index Swap		9,215				
Transco Zone 6 Natural Gas Index Swap		42,904	51,709	11,199	8,796	
Ventura Natural Gas Index Swap		17,671	12,748	2,508		
WAHA Index Swap		71,755	72,219	26,784	26,923	4,549
ANR OK Natural Gas Swing Swap		168				
Centerpoint Natural Gas Swing Swap		278	240	58		
Chicago Natural Gas Swing Swap		4,001	3,205	572	991	102
CIG Rockies Natural Gas Swing Swap		62				
Demarc Natural Gas Swing Swap		3,169	1,423	1,073		
Dominion Transmission - Appalachian		2,240	1,994	3,344	3,832	
El Paso Permian Swing		12,934	17,639	5,092	2,606	

VOLUME - U.S.

NEW YORK MERCANTILE EXCHANGE (NYMEX) (continued)

FUTURE	CONTRACT UNIT	2008	2007	2006	2005	2004
Henry Hub Swing		66,875	73,750	37,243	85,830	40,102
Houston Ship Channel Swing		41,940	19,333	10,247	6,384	1,078
Kern River Opal Plant Swing Swap		15,735	14,417	8,495	3,380	
Malin Natural Gas Swing Swap		2,402				
NGPL Midcontinental Swing Swap		2,481	856	202		
NGPL TEXOK Swing Swap		1,299	2,569	472		
Panhandle Swing		21,182	8,493	3,634	2,780	599
PG&E Citygate Swing Swap		12,387	9,100	2,960	4,147	
San Juan Swing Index		6,561	2,419	852	248	
Socal Swing Swap		62,728	50,013	19,888	11,528	
Sumas Swing Swap Future		606	165	2,546	1,434	
Texas Eastern Zone M-3 Swing		2,059	10,643	2,394	498	
Transco Zone 6 Swing Swap		798	3,214	1,515	914	
Ventura Natural Gas Swing Swap		3,131	610	434		
WAHA Swing		19,017	11,021	7,918	5,252	1,310
Brent Last Day Contract		465,056	506,075			
Brent (ICE) Calendar Swap		335,640	71,534	38,305		
Dated Brent Crude Oil Calendar Swap		34,610	7,815	1,425		
Dubai Crude Oil Calendar Swap		325,802	107,329	88,601		
Dubai Crude Oil BALMO Swap		2,276				
WTI Crude Oil Calendar Swap		847,658	489,274	377,086	41,931	152,680
Brent-Dubai Swap		60,009	19,400	15,455		
Dated-to-Frontline Brent Swap		183,262	90,783	21,394		
WTI-Brent (ICE) Bullet Swap		880	669	200		
WTI-Brent (ICE) Calendar Swap		240,916	60,008	35,343		
LLS (Argus) vs WTI Spread Calendar Swap		5,049				
LLS (Argus) vs WTI Spread Trade Month		902				
Mars (Argus) vs WTI Spread Trade Month		180				
WTS (Argus) vs WTI Spread Trade Month		3,082				
Gulf Coast Ultra Low Sulfur Diesel		448	2,753			
Gulf Coast Gasoline Calendar Swap		7,283	6,142	21,921	3,352	
Gulf Coast Heating Oil Calendar Swap		25	675	3,269	861	
Gulf Coast Jet Fuel Calendar Swap		960	1,725	3,052	615	
Gulf Coast No 6 Fuel Oil 3.0% Swap		180,907	53,150	27,673	21,515	200
Gulf Coast 3.0% Fuel Oil BALMO Swap		3,170				
Gulf Coast ULSD Calendar Swap		3,506	305			
Los Angeles CARB Gasoline Swap		25				
New York 0.3% Fuel Oil HiPr (Platts) Swap		775				
NY Harbor Heating Oil Calendar Swap		115,500	49,074	44,436	24,760	51,347
NY Harbor Residual Fuel 1.0% Sulfur Swap		93,845	67,130	38,366	15,163	625
NY Harbor Fuel Oil 1.0% Sulfur BALMO		1,161				
RBOB Calendar Swap		81,874	30,235	13,562		
RBOB Platts Calendar Swap Future		300	42			
EIA On-Highway Retail Diesel Swap		1,102				
New York 0.3% Fuel Oil Swap		325				
Europe 1% Fuel Oil Calendar Swap (NWE)		24,565	8,048	3,047	1,382	
European 1% Fuel Oil BALMO Swap		815	15			
Europe 1% Fuel Oil Rotterdam Calendar		18,743	2,872	681	707	
Europe 3.5% Fuel Oil MED Calendar Swap		244	15	105	20	
Europe 3.5% Fuel Oil Rotterdam Calendar		77,769	20,075	14,699	8,639	
European 3.5% Fuel Oil BALMO Swap		2,300	20			
European Gasoil 10PPM Rotterdam Barges		116				
European Gasoil (ICE) Calendar Swap		6,791	220	419		
European Gasoil (ICE) Bullet Swap		4,311	676			
European Jet Kero NWE CALS		250	71			
Europe Naptha Calendar Swap		5,430	1,143	811	140	
European Naptha BALMO Swap		139	9			
European Propane CIF ARA (Argus) Swap		389				
European ULSD PPM CIF MED Swap		105	21	6		
Euro ULSD 50ppm CIF NWE Swap		10	35	16		
Euro ULSD 50ppm FOB MED Swap		5				
Mediterranean Premium Unleaded		387	85	26		
NW Europe Gasoline Swap (Argus)		18,348	6,328	5,133	603	
Gasoil (ICE) Mini Calendar Swap		2,223				
Gasoil 0.1 Barges FOB Rotterdam Swap		965				
Gasoil 0.1 Cargoes FOB NWE Swap		30				
Gasoil 10ppm Cargoes CIF NWE Swap		42				
Gasoil 0.1 CIF MED vs ICE Gasoil Swap		124				
ULSD 10ppm CIF MED vs ICE Gasoil		125				
Jet Fuel Cargoes CIF NWE BALMO Swap		48				
ICE Gasoil BALMO Swap		114				
ULSD 10ppm Cargoes CIF NWE BALMO		30				
Gasoil 0.1 Barges FOB Rotterdam BALMO		3				
Diesel 10ppm Barges FOB Rotterdam		20				

NEW YORK MERCANTILE EXCHANGE (NYMEX) (continued)

NYMEX DIVISION (cont)

FUTURE	CONTRACT UNIT	2008	2007	2006	2005	2004
Argus Gasoline NWE BALMO Swap		352				
Singapore 380 Fuel Oil		650	150			
Japan C&F Naptha Swap		5,114	195			
Europe SINPO Fuel 180CST CALS		79,252	48,516	20,213	6,629	
Singapore 180 Fuel Oil BALMO		2,085	90			
Singapore 380CST Fuel Oil Swap		3,662	2,142	461	118	
Singapore 380 Fuel Oil BALMO		514	15			
Singapore Gasoil Swap		128,359	52,955	13,484	305	
Singapore Gasoil BALMO Swap		15,214	425			
Singapore Jet Kerosene Swap		36,688	20,045	4,898		
Singapore Jet Kerosene BALMO Swap		4,754	150			
Singapore Naptha Swap		25,374	9,955	2,750	150	
Singapore Naptha BALMO Swap		375				
Gasoline U-Down (Argus) Swap		125				
Gulf Coast Jet vs NYMEX HO Spread Swap		27,511	6,470	2,427	6,137	1,750
Gulf Coast No 6 Fuel Oil Crack Swap		30,872	1,400	360	1,875	
Gulf Coast ULSD Crack Spread Swap		825	325			
US Gulf Coast Unleaded 87 Crack Spread		10,724	8,517	19,933	5,876	45,775
Los Angeles Jet Fuel vs NYH #2 Heating		39	300	550		
Los Angeles CARBOB (OPIS) Spread Swap		1,542				
Los Angeles Jet (OPIS) Spread Swap		6,425	775			
Los Angeles CARB Diesel (OPIS) Spread		5,189	25			
NY Harbor No 2 Crack Spread Calendar		53,929	42,335	48,323	37,792	120,780
NY Harbor Residual Fuel Oil Crack Swap		5,255	11,464	4,877	4,700	
No 2 Up-Down Spread Calendar Swap		8,762	3,735	4,193	1,848	2,352
RBOB Crack Spread		83,269	57,793	13,254		
RBOB Up-Down Calendar Swap		53,431	22,724	6,169		
RBOB vs Heating Oil Swap		2,638	8,455	2,175		
NY Harbor Conv Gasoline vs RBOB		861	2,650	600		
NYMEX ULSD vs NYMEX Heating Oil		510	100			
Up Down GC LSD vs NYMEX Heating Oil		1,196	1,380			
Up Down GC ULSD vs NYMEX Heating		105,423	19,834			
New York 1% Fiel Oil vs Gulf Coast 3%		8,468				
New York Heating Oil (Platts) vs NYMEX		50				
1% Fuel Oil New Crack Spread Swap		5,322	1,385	95		
3.5% Fuel Oil FOB MED Crack Spread		918				
3.5% Fuel Oil Rotterdam Crack Swap		39,551	921	152		
3.5% Fuel Oil vs FOB MED Spread Swap		282	53	5		
Argus Gasoline Crack Spread SW		40,030	26,156	9,052		
European Gasoil 0.2 CIF NWE vs Gasoil		15	55	30		
European Gasoil 0.2 FOB MED vs Gasoil		244	1,186	75		
European Gasoil 0.2 Rotterdam Barges vs		110	418	15		
European Gasoil (10ppm) Rotterdam		2,850	436	27		
European Gasoil Crack Spread Swap		190,522	14,287	14,040		
European Jet CIF NWE vs Gasoil Swap		11,358	2,832	480		
European Jet Rotterdam Barges vs Gasoil		672				
European Naptha Crack Spread		34,053	13,268	2,332		
European ULSD 50ppm CIF MED vs Gasoil		205	170	70		
European ULSD (50ppm) CIF NWE vs		461	876	148		
European ULSD 50ppm FOB MED vs		5				
Heating Oil Arb Swap: NYMEX HO vs		16,561				
High-Low Sulfur Fuel Oil Spread Swap		14,528	2,860	1,701	592	
East-West Fuel Oil Spread Swap		11,622	2,532	2,069	668	
Singapore Gasoil vs Rotterdam Gasoil Swap		37,975	18,564	5,610		
Gasoil 0.1 Cargoes CIF NWE vs ICE Gasoil		773				
Gasoil 0.1 Barges FOB Rotterdam vs ICE		10,104				
Gasoil 10ppm Cargoes CIF NWE vs ICE		1,968				
Japan C&F Naptha Crack Spread (Platts)		15				
Singapore Fuel Oil Spread Swap		4,823	1,532	913	95	
Singapore Jet Kerosene vs Gasoil Spread		32,980	18,740	3,075		
NYMEX Ethanol		156				
Chicago Ethanol Swap		15,617	4,590			
New York Ethanol Swap		3,814	1,739			
Tanker Route TC2 Europe to US Atlantic		449	205	630	460	
Tanker Route TC4 Singapore to Japan		445	10		30	
Tanker Route TC5 Ras Tanura to Tokohama		560	50			
Tanker Route TD3 Middle Eastern Gulf to		460				
PJM AER-Dayton Hub Monthly Electricity		12,258	4,262	8,026	18,020	
PJM Northern Illinois Hub Monthly		23,978	19,359	38,220	21,038	
PJM Northern Illinois Hub Daily		180	548	1,080	700	
PJM Financially Settled Daily - Peak		1,626	26,610	3,530	217,349	190,591
PJM Financially Settled Monthly - Peak		77,287	84,154	171,655	652,077	234,207
Total Futures (NYMEX)		278,206,594	234,386,910	178,929,185	141,201,756	110,054,812

VOLUME - U.S.

NEW YORK MERCANTILE EXCHANGE (NYMEX) (continued)

GLOBEX Futured Traded on NYMEX

FUTURE	CONTRACT UNIT	2008	2007	2006		
Crude Oil miNY		5,641,145	5,185,214	9,323,467		
Heating Oil miNY		637	21,296	422,248		
RBOB Gasoline miNY		307	563	872		
Natural Gas miNY		1,058,665	1,403,525	2,035,824		
Brent Bullet Swap		114,701	42,053	20,432		
RBOB Financial		56,108	41,615	3,020		
WTI Financial		1,360,899	625,839	820,579		
Heating Oil Financial		70,561	46,828	19,231		
Gold miNY		20,034	10,988	313		
Silver miNY		8,115	5,120	40		
Copper miNY		4,890	4,927	77		
Total Futures (GLOBEX)		8,336,062	7,390,087	12,682,702		
Total Futures (COMEX, NYMEX, GLOBEX)		338,455,289	277,408,465	216,252,995	166,608,057	133,283,348

ONECHICAGO

FUTURE	CONTRACT UNIT	2007	2006	2005	2004	2003
Single Stock Futures		7,835,289	7,777,241	5,474,663	1,890,097	1,488,573
Exchange Traded Funds		51,034	9,124	14,162	29,585	127,424
Narrow-Based Equity Index		219,640	136,100	39,000		
Total Futures		8,105,963	7,922,465	5,528,046	1,922,726	1,619,194

Total Volume

	2008	2007	2006	2005	2004
Total Futures	2,850,773,583	2,644,564,674	2,043,926,142	1,652,871,946	1,323,726,632
Precent Change	7.80%	29.39%	23.66%	24.87%	26.92%

Options Traded on U.S. Securities Exchanges Volume Highlights
2008 in Comparison with 2007

2008 Rank	EXCHANGE	2008 Contracts	%	2007 Contracts	%	2007 Rank
1	Chicago Board of Options Exchange	1,193,355,070	33.60%	944,472,459	32.99%	1
2	International Securities Exchange	1,007,661,590	28.37%	804,347,677	28.10%	2
3	Philadelphia Stock Exchange	547,456,114	15.42%	407,972,525	14.25%	3
4	NYSE-ARCA[1]	416,938,764	11.74%	335,838,547	11.73%	4
5	American Stock Exchange	207,285,283	5.84%	240,383,466	8.40%	5
6	Boston Options Exchange	178,650,541	5.03%	129,797,339	4.53%	6
	Total Options	**3,551,347,362**	**100.00%**	**2,862,812,013**	**100.00%**	

[1] Formerly Pacific Stock Exchange.

Options Traded on U.S. Futures Exchanges Volume Highlights
2008 in Comparison with 2007

2008 Rank	EXCHANGE	2008 Contracts	%	2007 Contracts	%	2007 Rank
1	CME Group[2]	416,037,673	80.17%	494,053,527	95.21%	1
2	New York Mercantile Exchange (NYMEX)[1]	85,009,770	16.38%	75,976,972	14.64%	3
3	InterContinental Exchange (ICE)	17,521,134	3.38%	13,124,201	2.53%	4
4	Kansas City Board of Trade (KCBT)	187,658	0.04%	352,948	0.07%	5
5	Chicago Climate Futures Exchange (CCFE)	113,817	0.02%	91,859	0.02%	7
6	Minneapolis Grain Exchange (MGE)	47,935	0.01%	34,354	0.01%	6
7	US Futures Exchange (USFE)		0.00%	1	0.00%	8
	Total Options	**518,917,987**	**100.00%**	**583,633,862**	**100.00%**	

[1] Includes Commodity Exchange, Inc. and GLOBEX.   [2] In July 2007, the Chicago Mercantile Exchange and the Chicago Board of Trade merged and are now listed as one exchange.

CME Group (includes Chicago Mercantile Exchange and Chicago Board of Trade)

OPTION	CONTRACT UNIT	2008	2007	2006	2005	2004
Wheat	5,000 bu	4,060,865	3,893,354	2,597,975	1,870,541	1,465,760
Corn	5,000 bu	20,992,582	14,691,277	11,317,388	6,257,027	7,593,355
Oats	5,000 bu	23,843	16,381	25,738	22,320	36,498
Soybeans	5,000 bu	9,806,935	8,215,582	6,042,797	6,817,588	6,045,952
Soybean Crush	50,000 bu	2,452	3,267	6,828		
Soybean Oil	60,000 lbs	1,458,568	1,277,884	902,096	682,825	947,383
Soybean Meal	100 tons	884,721	713,821	746,185	685,830	971,335
Rough Rice	200,000 lbs	26,681	23,374	26,868	17,834	22,064
Live Cattle	40,000 lbs	1,226,704	726,003	930,169	502,021	500,927
Feeder Cattle	50,000 lbs	99,911	106,587	156,292	142,253	142,638
Lean Hogs	40,000 lbs	512,159	321,258	225,013	198,274	179,093
Pork Bellies, Frozen	40,000 lbs	211	575	1,198	3,228	4,010
Class III Milk	200,000 lbs	167,779	94,640	85,713	71,431	122,014
Nonfat Dry Milk	44,000 lbs	60		116		
Mini BFP Milk	100,000 lbs	367	967	549	796	1,654
Dry Whey	44,000 lbs	670				
Cash Butter	20,000 lbs	322	17			
Random Lumber	100,000 bd ft	17,485	18,127	20,909	25,171	20,056
Silver (5,000 oz)	5,000 oz	2,677	1,586	1,521		
Gold (100 oz)	100 oz	26,024	114,936	193,944		
Ethanol Forward Month Swap		42,477	6,048			
T-Bonds (30-year)	100,000 USD	18,209,855	17,391,744	20,731,673	15,661,021	13,788,908
T-Notes (10-year)	100,000 USD	56,753,688	61,528,219	61,888,144	55,648,782	56,878,013
T-Notes (5-year)	100,000 USD	12,752,318	15,392,035	11,585,131	17,691,564	17,215,903
T-Notes (2-year)	200,000 USD	2,333,092	1,056,738	804,975	23,251	10,206
30-Day Federal Funds	5,000,000 USD	7,478,025	8,020,547	9,424,628	6,534,587	4,707,103
Binary		8,144	92,211	47,237		
Flexible US T-Bonds		287,136	252,780	392,648	600,641	193,663
Flexible T-Notes (10-year)		12,575	910,609	311,295	259,295	96,192
Flexible T-Notes (5-year)		400	37,098	24,100	4,000	29,900
Eurodollar (3-month)	1,000,000 USD	228,224,397	313,032,284	268,957,052	188,001,048	130,598,377
Eurdollar Calendar Spreads		11,752				
Treasury Matched Eurodollar Mid-Curve		287,662				
Australian Dollar	100,000	206,649	74,874	36,562	109,970	60,593
British Pound	62,500	565,050	352,736	158,473	146,893	166,360
Canadian Dollar	100,000	380,894	530,023	375,257	231,329	190,976
Euro FX	125,000 EUR	2,696,811	1,801,681	1,849,119	2,100,595	1,492,887
Japanese Yen	12,500,000	850,340	929,733	544,716	419,232	465,261
Mexican Peso	500,000	768	51	371	1,284	3,664
Swiss Franc	125,000	198,694	78,675	47,984	50,107	55,596
Euro FX European	125,000 EUR	375,621	230,615	190,610	72,119	
British Pound European	62,500	89,910	98,323	18,191		
Canadian Dollar European	100,000	54,138	50,899	7,256		
Japanese Yen European	12,500,000 EUR	136,921	155,394	53,753	50,996	
Swiss Franc European	125,000	37,868	30,079	6,773		
Dow Jones Industrial Index	10 USD x Index	75,840	105,860	100,589	114,353	190,708
Mini ($5) Dow Jones Industrial Index	5 USD x Index	281,062	300,307	450,601	613,996	571,299
Nikkei 225	5 USD x Index	17,750	17,200	59,200	44,458	8,774
S&P 500 Index	500 USD x Index	16,378,218	19,458,815	15,785,802	9,810,489	5,834,225
E-Mini S&P 500 Index	50 USD x S&P Index	22,167,648	16,213,737	9,893,979	4,289,038	477,712
EOM S&P 500 Index	250 USD x Index	2,512,846	816,354	80,424		
EOM E-Mini S&P 500 Index	EOM x Index	1,028,368	950,829	147,471		
S&P MidCap 400 Index	500 USD x Index	441	400	435	670	375
E-Mini S&P MidCap 400 Index	100 USD x Index	5,507	235			
E-Mini SmallCap 600	100 USD x Index	34				
NASDAQ 100 Index	100 USD x Index	13,096	79,900	71,499	35,306	37,612
E-Mini NASDAQ 100 Index	20 USD x Index	542,497	742,395	317,765	110,093	10,015
Russell 2000 Index	500 USD x Index	6,701	7,667	5,812	4,779	6,205
E-Mini Russell 2000 Index	100 USD x Index	1,180,464	2,430,140	933,224	175,226	
CDD Weather	20 USD x Index	25,000	19,400	18,050	28,725	3,475
HDD Weather	20 USD x Index	50,850	63,835	75,277	16,400	11,527
CDD Seasonal Weather	20 USD x Index	100		27,100	225,550	5,650
HDD Seasonal Weather Strip	20 USD x Index	139,800	295,450	209,300	13,674	
CDD Seasonal Weather Strip	20 USD x Index	245,850	258,350	97,200		
Euro HDD Seasonal Weather	20 GBP x Index	4,200		2,000	33,625	13,950
Euro CAT Seasonal Strip Weather	20 GBP x Index	14,000	3,500			
Seasonal Max Hurricane	1,000 USD x Index	26,000				
Seasonal Accum Hurricane	1,000 USD x Index	2,000				
Binary Seasonal Hurricane	1,000 USD x Index	4,600				
Asian Seasonal Strip	250,000 JPY x Index	8,600				
Total Options		360,005,823	301,551,501	207,233,185	140,457,074	109,220,627

VOLUME - U.S.

CHICAGO CLIMATE FUTURES EXCHANGE (CCFE)

OPTION	CONTRACT UNIT	2008	2007			
Certified Emissions Reduction (CER)		1	1			
Carbon Financial Instrument (CFI)		11,753				
Nitrogen Financial Instrument - Annual		6,500				
Regional Greenhouse Gas Initiatives (RGGI)		10,373				
Sulfur Financial Instrument (SFI)		85,190	91,858			
Total Options		113,817	91,859			

KANSAS CITY BOARD OF TRADE (KCBT)

OPTION	CONTRACT UNIT	2008	2007	2006	2005	2004
Wheat	5,000 bu	187,658	352,948	515,479	263,511	254,304
Total Options		187,658	352,948	515,479	263,511	254,304

MINNEAPOLIS GRAIN EXCHANGE (MGE)

OPTION	CONTRACT UNIT	2008	2007	2006	2005	2004
American Spring Wheat	5,000 bu	47,935	34,354	40,468	27,245	34,260
Total Options		47,935	34,354	40,491	32,464	34,826

NEW YORK MERCANTILE EXCHANGE (NYMEX)

COMEX DIVISION

OPTION	CONTRACT UNIT	2008	2007	2006	2005	2004
Gold	100 oz	4,392,737	3,554,858	3,708,573	2,889,803	4,667,523
Silver	5,000 oz	1,700,882	1,257,505	1,646,959	1,131,812	1,022,348
High Grade Copper	25,000 lbs	22,559	24,467	75,403	143,609	216,350
Total Options (COMEX)		6,116,178	4,836,830	5,430,935	4,165,224	5,906,221

NYMEX DIVISION

OPTION	CONTRACT UNIT	2008	2007	2006	2005	2004
Heating Oil	42,000 gal	781,003	620,761	595,427	983,388	800,277
Heating Oil 1-month CSO		275		10,185	12,868	1,880
Crude Oil	1,000 bbl	35,255,326	28,398,793	21,016,562	14,726,263	11,512,918
Crude Oil 1-month CSO		1,016,327	1,851,827	1,209,952	440,234	357,156
Crude Oil 3-month CSO		500	500			
Crude Oil 6-month CSO		5,450	2,300	400		
Crude Oil 12-month CSO		70,137	83,126	24,750	12,267	9,600
Crude Oil One Day		132,590	134,537	21,416		
RBOB Gasoline		884,839	1,016,963	82,176		
RBOB Crack Spread		13,072	6,362	220		
Natural Gas	10,000 MMBTU	2,336,287	5,051,879	9,581,663	9,168,354	8,071,967
Natural Gas 1-month CSO		174,940	120,608	246,472	103,058	47,328
Natural Gas 2-month CSO		2,300	950	1,150	1,525	
Natural Gas 3-month CSO		26,605	14,233	24,556	3,175	500
Natural Gas 5-month CSO		250		5,500		
Natural Gas One Day		112,303	13,320	795		
Heating Oil-Crude Oil Spread	1,000 bbl	824	5,783	29,862	82,505	98,503
PJM Monthly Financially Settled Electricity		365,316	370,108	247,040	73,640	3,985
ISO New England Calendar-Month LMP		43,082	45,240			
Cinergy Calendar-Month LMP Swap		14,240	8,930			
Natural Gas European Style		31,158,326	29,921,068	19,515,968	6,968,569	2,012,703
PGE Citygate Pipe		3,600				
Alberta Pipe		1,800	200			
Northern Rockies Pipe		11,460	1,960			
San Juan Pipe		3,240				
SoCal Pipe		26,445				
Panhandle pipe		47,092				
Crude Oil European Style		3,580,861	1,879,999	379,250	119,218	17,080
Crude Oil APO		2,227,738	1,445,930	838,985	45,250	23,622
Brent Crude Oil American Style		8,904				
Brent Crude Oil European Style Look-Alike		31,181				
Brent Crude Oil Average Price		92,549				
RBOB Gasoline European style		84,382	44,382	995		
RBOB GasolineAverage Price		27,402	6,219	142		
Heating Oil European Style		112,488	32,438	1,525	24,339	8,023
Heating Oil APO		240,362	60,471	18,868	8,302	1,134
Average Price Gasoil		96				
Total Options		78,893,592	71,140,142	54,468,396	33,837,671	23,967,338
Total Options (COMEX, NYMEX)		85,009,770	75,976,972	59,899,331	38,002,895	29,873,559

INTERCONTINENTINENTAL EXCHANGE (ICE) (formerly NYBOT, NYFE, NYCE, FINEX and CSCE)

OPTION	CONTRACT UNIT	2008	2007	2006	2005	2004
Coffee 'C'	37,500 lbs	2,826,331	2,999,648	2,785,053	2,370,161	1,970,068
Sugar #11	112,000 lbs	9,179,779	5,548,668	6,250,162	3,631,939	2,854,683
Sugar #11 Options on Futures Spreads		145,368	204,100	54,880	14,861	
Cocoa	10 metric tons	376,444	370,429	377,905	512,259	429,769
Cotton #2	50,000 lbs	4,468,327	3,451,217	1,820,259	1,709,345	1,725,982
Orange Juice Frozen Concentrate	15,000 lbs	238,616	385,219	426,967	433,288	554,432
US Dollar Index	500 USD x Index	72,768	50,562	39,299	35,356	57,189
Russell 1000 Index	500 USD x Index	127,183	81,654	81,274	142,299	103,944
Russell 1000 Index Mini	100 USD x Index	877				
Russell 2000 Index	500 USD x Index	10,385	27,212	28,639	32,362	36,305
Russell 2000 Index Mini	100 USD x Index	73,634				
Russell 3000 Index	500 USD x Index	530	347	182	1,568	4,647
Reuters-CRB Futures Index (CCI)	500 USD x Index	892	435	6,320	1,539	
Total Options		17,521,134	13,124,201	11,920,477	8,932,169	7,774,379

Green Exchange

OPTION	CONTRACT UNIT	2008
EU Allowance		2,000
SO2		10
Carbon CER European		3,200
Total Options		5,210

Total Volume

	2008	2007	2006	2005	2004
Total Options	518,923,197	583,633,862	501,549,640	367,969,679	289,158,384
Percent Change	-11.09%	16.37%	36.30%	27.26%	30.43%

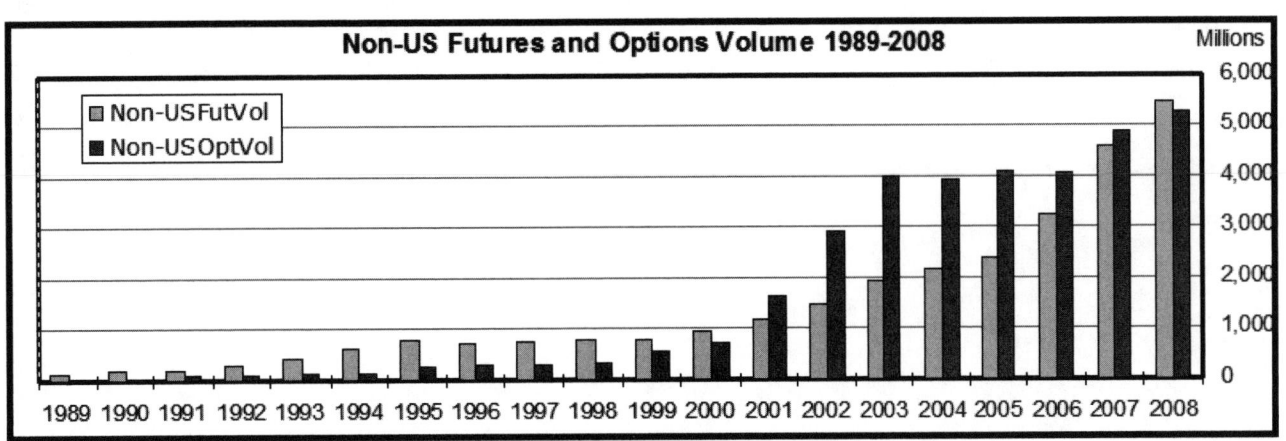

Volume - Worldwide

Australian Stock Exchange (ASX), Australia

	2008	2007	2006	2005	2004
S&P/ASX Index	309,499	238,823	110,769	106,237	66,256
All Futures on Individual Equities	971,261	706,656	693,683	490,238	460,501
Total Futures	**1,280,760**	**945,479**	**804,452**	**596,475**	**526,757**
S&P / ASX Index	2,819,582	1,797,754	1,170,793	1,163,213	794,121
All Options on Individual Equities	16,070,022	22,226,578	20,477,083	21,828,002	19,164,851
Total Options	**18,889,604**	**24,024,332**	**21,647,876**	**22,991,215**	**19,958,972**

BOVESPA, Brazil

	2008	2007	2006	2005	2004
Ibovespa Index	210,868	384,837	1,818,764	2,257,756	1,586,762
Exchange Traded Funds	17,063				
All Options on Individual Equities	350,046,567	367,305,446	285,699,806	266,362,631	233,759,713
Total Options	**350,274,498**	**367,690,283**	**287,518,570**	**268,620,460**	**235,349,514**

Bolsa de Mercadorias & Futuros (BM&F), Brazil

	2008	2007	2006	2005	2004
Arabica Coffee	760,761	724,319	528,462	485,902	620,997
Arabica Coffee Rollover	22,476				
Live Cattle	1,633,113	934,422	392,012	311,459	225,200
Feeder Cattle	10	159	296	3,031	1,024
Ethanol	16,608	17,234			
Sugar Crystal	7,039	45,112	69,351	63,385	47,347
Corn	403,258	207,724	135,188	97,795	52,600
Corn Basis Price	40				
Corn Cash Settled	7,767				
Soybean Futures	284,382	188,279	98,112	47,360	7,225
Gold Forward	520	283	308	668	15
Gold	1,280	2,100	3,180	2,640	2,742
Gold Spot	12,579	9,118	24,369	42,336	57,609
Bovespa Stock Index Futures	20,226,662	26,550,491	13,232,399	6,065,361	7,063,923
Bovespa Rollover	118,680				
Bovespa Mini Index	9,928,406	10,692,141	3,702,409	606,582	2,892,016
Interest Rate	166,983,583	221,627,417	161,654,736	121,249,186	100,290,263
Interest Rate Swap	547,146	91,503	192,356	260,404	1,005,212
Interest Rate x Stock Basket Swap	294	1,059			
Interest Rate x Exchange Rate Swap	449,784	483,342	398,757	382,326	1,189,805
Interest Rate x Reference Rate Swap	22,234	20,200	189,796	18,536	9,762
Interest Rate x Price Index Swap (formerly Inflation)	1,054,533	1,486,734	2,760,520	829,982	775,591
Interest Rate x Ibovespa Index Swap	596	2,292	1,813	1,760	1,175
Exchange Rate Swap	43,007	54,887	26,443	21,035	27,069
Price Index	7,200				
Interest Rate x IBrX-50	9,254	10,467	7,448	776	
ID x US Dollar Spread Futures	1,150,157	396,326	1,016,176	926,171	536,358
FRA on ID x US Dollar Spread	21,217,283	20,907,906	14,396,347	20,642,962	33,326,518
ID x US Dollar Spread Swap	336,560	44,049	145,943	232,609	126,525
ID x IPCA Spread	69,350	111,025	58,840		
CDS Brazil 5-Year	953				
Global 2019	8	91	273	760	
Global 2034	1,650	4,553	4,321		
Global 2037	1,813	6,385	270		
Global 2040	48,533	94,845	57,590	232,883	79,645
US T-Note	107,576	73,123	630		
US Dollar	87,442,346	84,774,568	52,350,517	33,466,104	23,943,757
US Dollar Rollover	7,179,600				
Mini US Dollar	147,424	3,460,153	5,053,580	827,427	608,772
US Dollar forward points	3,488,158	2,850,000	1,648,807	908,062	365,914
Euro	37,550	2,725	70		
Total Futures	**323,770,173**	**375,885,135**	**258,466,105**	**187,850,634**	**173,533,508**
Gold on Actuals	363,867	193,380	119,378	149,932	236,058
Gold Exercise	47,630	38,115	19,492	28,540	62,378
US $ Denominated Arabica Coffee	48,166	80,523	30,602	22,341	50,148
US $ Denominated Arabica Coffee Exercise	6,687	3,444	2,370	1,662	3,206
Corn	4,590	1,132	3,119		
Corn, Exercise	6	9	175		
Corn Cash Settled	51				
Soybeans	6,616	7,184	1,345		
Soybeans, Exercise	1,434	741			
Live Cattle	75,622	5,108	987	71	550
Live Cattle, Exercise	4,328	1,147	251		2
Bovespa Stock	1,229,734	727,015	26,625	6,344	21,730
Bovespa Stock Exercise	194,950	112,690	2,072	9,380	11,350
Bovespa Stock Volatility	85,270	40,230			
Interest Rate	7,317,364	1,886,247	945,250	268,819	1,253,545

Bolsa de Mercadorias & Futuros (BM&F), Brazil

	2008	2007	2006	2005	2004
Interest Rate (IDI) Exercise	1,511,261	273,500	18,080	147,840	154,100
Interest Rate (volatility)	3,724,645	2,436,765	933,445	539,825	879,575
Interest Rate (IDI)	13,915,878	12,316,359	9,279,101	2,058,806	2,224,832
IDI Index (exercise)	1,236,980	366,650	105,410	237,895	131,099
IDI Index (volatility)	1,823,370	3,068,460	1,848,810	351,575	143,180
Fexible Bovespa Stock Index	469,747	323,459	199,557	85,279	687,412
US Dollar on Actuals	30,588,575	24,682,702	9,766,867	6,251,235	2,708,961
US Dollar Exercise	1,805,319	1,332,280	552,837	391,221	147,645
US Dollar Volatility	2,887,345	2,241,390	1,042,235	793,665	255,150
Flexible Currency	495,007	339,827	206,128	207,585	866,474
Total Options	**67,844,442**	**50,478,357**	**25,104,136**	**11,595,830**	**9,894,430**

Budapest Stock Exchange (BSE), Hungary (BCE merged with BSE in 2005)

	2008	2007	2006	2005	2004
Feed Corn	6,879	7,452	5,050	6,431	9,617
Feed Wheat	1,213	528	840	755	1,351
Euro Wheat	2,819	3,447	126		
Feed Barley	621	260	238	41	366
Sunflower Seed	1,942	564	1,235	1,499	1,909
Rapeseed	1,426	428	471	148	270
Ammonium Nitrate	164	10	4	1	1
Budapest Stock Index (BUX)	3,082,870	3,950,947	1,879,034	529,512	376,679
CHF/HUF	159,947	91,977	100,200	31,208	71,800
CZK/HUF	1,370	4,730	48,180	61,120	26,410
EUR/HUF	2,481,943	2,669,580	2,688,100	682,116	583,060
GBP/HUF	22,050	42,750	82,415	54,850	28,000
JPY/HUF	14,350	62,877	29,267	18,000	41,350
PLN/HUF	40	880	33,600	21,550	42,092
TRY/HUF	138,400	131,950	66,500	41,500	
USD/HUF	1,446,993	1,152,754	814,635	494,057	227,235
AUD/JPY	3,300	2,700			
AUD/USD	150,650	32,940	46,400	950	
CAD/JPY	1,500	12,700	19,000	34,900	
CHF/JPY	2,750	5,050	19,050	46,000	
GBP/CHF	188,850	102,456	388,770	395,540	100,630
GBP/JPY	328,270	1,353,100	361,450	368,703	311,030
GBP/SEK	32,300	83,050	242,950	100,600	33,800
GBP/USD	146,068	354,640	631,500	1,137,635	197,560
EURO/CHF	18,700	86,650	86,350	67,850	38,700
EURO/CZK	10,400	3,200	35,600	58,620	2,200
EURO/GBP	210,150	100,700	227,500	106,800	17,500
EURO/HRK	6,200	7,600	13,000		
EURO/JPY	227,340	306,673	198,151	465,122	46,200
EURO/NOK	29,100	34,200	93,200	38,050	18,600
EURO/PLN	17,600	14,450	110,070	95,300	28,300
EURO/RON	20,300	3,500	16,400	29,100	
EURO/RSD	2,400				
EURO/RUB	8,350	7,700	19,600		
EURO/SEK	17,600	79,500	81,630	153,200	51,200
EURO/TRY	352,440	315,540	379,473	105,740	1,500
EURO/USD	999,736	1,555,406	1,117,803	1,112,158	501,448
NZD/JPY	5,000				
USD/BRL	600	900	6,700		
USD/CAD	78,332	251,316	345,405	17,750	
USD/CHF	73,900	183,200	258,422	249,547	117,700
USD/CZK	2,300	11,500	6,700	11,400	
USD/JPY	176,150	759,300	239,572	573,360	666,030
USD/MXN	900		3,400		
USD/NOK	1,000	25,900	2,200		
USD/PLN	4,600	52,600	8,600	57,500	5,400
USD/RUB	9,800	8,650	22,810		
USD/SEK	800	4,500	5,100		
USD/TRY	86,100	48,550	305,634	253,532	3,800
USD/UAH	5,400	5,000	10,000		
CHF/JPY	100				
EUR (1 week)	360,950	594,650	910,300	12,300	
GBP (1 week)	7,200	27,300	2,100		
USD (1 week)	111,920	71,500	24,000	12,500	
AUD/USD (1 week)	800	87,000	500		
EUR/GBP (1 week)	4,900	17,000			
EUR/JPY (1 week)	85,650	522,900	22,350		
EUR/PLN (1 week)	2,000	2,000	4,000		
EUR/USD (1 week)	189,250	330,900	100,690		

Budapest Stock Exchange (BSE), Hungary (continued)

	2008	2007	2006	2005	2004
GBP/CHF (1 week)	27,300	8,100	13,200		
GBP/JPY (1 week)	231,400	432,000	25,700		
GBP/USD (1 week)	57,200	232,400	34,350		
USD/CAD (1 week)	84,700	362,040	22,100		
USD/CHF (1 week)	26,200	22,400	4,900		
USD/JPY (1 week)	23,400	29,500	3,000		
All Futures on Individual Equities	1,163,252	1,529,194	919,426	737,069	707,875
Total Futures	**12,958,135**	**18,221,627**	**13,656,165**	**9,322,332**	**5,440,102**
Feed Corn	225	496	527	365	432
Euro Wheat	60				
Rapeseed	10				
Sunflower Seed	60	35	180	55	
US Dollar	31,450	21,240	2,000	11,000	
CHF	13,350	10,300			
EUR	130,559	126,766	205,000	92,200	113,970
JPY	1,300	3,379			
TRY	49,300	96,200			
EUR/CZK (HUF settlement)	1,200	1,900	2,200		
EUR/JPY (HUF settlement)	2,900	16,850	500		
EUR/PLN (HUF settlement)	800		1,200		
EUR/TRY (HUF settlement)	31,066	54,635			
EUR/USD (HUF settlement)	26,958	23,100	514,901		
GBP/CHF (HUF settlement)	15,850	9,100	500		
GBP/JPY (HUF settlement)	11,300	29,500	6,600		
GBP/USD (HUF settlement)	100	3,050	800		
USD/CAD (HUF settlement)	2,000	85,950			
USD/CHF (HUF settlement)	300		500		
USD/JPY (HUF settlement)	92,400	122,900	1,400		
USD/TRY	102	200			
Total Options	**411,290**	**606,601**	**1,026,764**	**160,617**	**115,219**

Dalian Commodity Exchange (DCE), China

	2008	2007	2006	2005	2004
Corn	59,436,742	64,976,076	21,859,732	5,828,045	
Corn	54,976,724	59,436,742	64,976,076	21,859,732	5,828,045
No 1 Soybeans	113,681,550	47,432,721	8,897,061	40,035,707	57,340,803
No 2 Soybeans	42,791	21,107	1,925,226	541,093	114,347
Palm Oil	6,302,478	339,175			
Soybean Oil	43,695,993	13,283,866	10,333,006		
Soybean Meal	81,265,439	64,719,466	31,549,669	36,738,182	24,750,958
Linear Low Density Polyethylene (LLDPE)	13,252,982	381,836			
Total Futures	**313,217,957**	**185,614,913**	**117,681,038**	**99,174,714**	**88,034,153**

Dubai Mercantile Exchange (DME)

	2008	2007
Oman Crude Oil	322,294	200,892
DME Brent	4,580	
Oman Crude Oil Financial	3,505	
Total Futures	**330,379**	**223,174**

EUREX, Frankfurt, Germany

	2008	2007	2006	2005	2004
DAX	49,237,082	50,413,122	40,425,513	32,722,572	29,229,847
RDXxt USD RDX Extended Index	1,217	26			
OMX-Helsinki 25	186,127	100,795	33,860	41,761	24,934
DivDAX	22,679				
MDAX	595,273	824,809	395,550	72,351	
MSCI Russia Index	94,697				
TecDAX	435,556	585,377	515,891	269,354	456,346
DJ Global Titans 50	646	10,358	6,481	2,038	333
Dow Jones Euro STOXX 50 Index Dividend	183,058				
DJ Euro STOXX 50	432,298,342	327,034,149	213,514,918	139,983,083	121,661,944
DJ Euro STOXX Automobiles	212,427	142,146	83,868	82,203	99,776
DJ Euro STOXX Banks	651,855	640,667	225,960	233,955	243,541
DJ Euro STOXX Basic Resources	39,168	22,501	21,200	31,221	18,018
DJ Euro STOXX Chemicals	39,868	18,750	12,464	9,464	5,254
DJ Euro STOXX Construction	34,171	36,663	7,492	2,343	573
DJ Euro STOXX Financial Services	34,470	27,007	15,804	5,111	1,050
DJ Euro STOXX Food and Beverage	36,888	11,226	9,161	22,700	16,382
DJ Euro STOXX Healthcare	50,893	40,201	12,982	9,694	4,288
DJ Euro STOXX Industry Goods and Services	26,200	29,283	17,537	11,220	844
DJ Euro STOXX Insurance	234,726	153,642	192,065	169,198	236,325
DJ Euro STOXX Media	39,198	39,462	30,860	26,035	8,863
DJ Euro STOXX Energy	182,422	107,664	101,586	118,601	118,457

EUREX, Frankfurt, Germany (continued)

	2008	2007	2006	2005	2004
DJ Euro STOXX Non-Cyclical Goods and Services	21,440	15,420	8,326	5,910	2,035
DJ Euro STOXX Real Estate	2,742				
DJ Euro STOXX Media	27,085	18,399	2,441	9,568	1,983
DJ Euro STOXX Technology	171,420	153,129	210,081	218,982	160,160
DJ Euro STOXX Telecom	257,493	274,843	246,288	177,863	182,949
DJ Euro STOXX Cyclical Goods and Services	36,451	24,433	17,618	12,963	5,358
DJ Euro STOXX Utilities	117,898	74,923	107,036	75,356	12,705
DJ Euro STOXX Select Dividend 30 Index	103,422	21,118			
DJ STOXX 50	1,607,048	1,387,401	1,064,167	807,761	798,106
DJ STOXX Mid 200 Index	471,758	279,128	36,901	3,554	
DJ STOXX Large 200 Index	140,741	9,866			
DJ STOXX Small 200 Index	279,477	21,848			
DJ STOXX 600	104,591	37,400	21,783	895	
DJ STOXX 600 Automobiles & Parts	377,947	184,908	43,692	30,368	
DJ STOXX 600 Banks	1,634,005	541,557	185,682	84,118	32,222
DJ STOXX 600 Basic Resources	441,871	214,640	90,361	30,441	647
DJ STOXX 600 Chemicals	89,156	72,184	18,340	3,861	
DJ STOXX 600 Construction & Materials	144,268	85,996	11,482	4,103	
DJ STOXX 600 Financial Services	69,389	96,472	14,349	9,695	166
DJ STOXX 600 Food & Beverage	175,795	85,753	91,537	24,807	347
DJ STOXX 600 Healthcare	379,849	305,236	171,262	117,720	70,931
DJ STOXX 600 Industrial G&S	285,522	174,806	81,265	21,844	1,527
DJ STOXX 600 Insurance	433,779	349,726	120,278	65,660	18,803
DJ STOXX 600 Media	273,233	74,664	25,242	14,955	305
DJ STOXX 600 Oil & Gas	534,071	387,825	146,585	35,459	3,261
DJ STOXX 600 Personal & Household Goods	60,153	15,092	21,262	7,187	
DJ STOXX 600 Real Estate	17,321				
DJ STOXX 600 Retail	221,545	105,297	32,829	6,161	
DJ STOXX 600 Technology	168,702	199,401	89,405	55,280	15,887
DJ STOXX 600 Telecom	386,335	268,292	164,519	112,686	19,596
DJ STOXX 600 Tracel & Leisure	113,510	86,329	25,622	9,706	
DJ STOXX 600 Utilities	266,804	153,117	59,958	63,814	29,622
Swiss Leader index (SLI)	122,721	36,577			
Swiss Market Index (SMI)	17,658,178	14,391,903	11,369,444	8,639,822	8,098,575
Swiss Market Index Mid-Cap (SMIM)	99,254	152,977	29,643	4,638	
DJ Euro STOXX 50 (VSTOXX)	13,133	6,590	1,406	109	
Swiss Government Bond (CONF)	407,583	360,355	334,314	372,385	308,206
Euro-BUND	257,827,619	338,319,416	319,889,369	299,287,916	239,787,517
Euro-BOBL	155,090,861	170,909,055	167,312,119	158,262,122	159,166,394
Euro-BUXL	1,155,127	1,582,859	1,265,079	470,831	
3-Month Euribor	703,273	792,635	767,458	688,831	585,142
Euro-SCHATZ	174,226,719	181,101,310	* 165,318,779	141,228,207	122,928,076
Euro Inflation	51				
EU Allowance	80,084				
Exchange Traded Funds	89	1,188	17,569	13,425	78,393
All Futures on Individual Equities	130,210,348	52,460,383	35,589,089	77,802	
Total Futures	**1,146,081,579**	**960,631,763**	**784,896,954**	**684,630,502**	**668,650,028**
DAX	104,939,881	91,850,835	61,411,659	53,633,130	42,184,611
DAX 1st Friday Weekly	136,941	192,587	148,881		
DAX 2nd Friday Weekly	99,993	149,972	100,406		
DAX 3rd Friday Weekly	118,099	209,868	122,774		
DAX 4th Friday Weekly	41,279	74,790	49,821		
DAX 5th Friday Weekly	187,159	91,140	10,543		
MSCI Russia Index	4,057				
HEX 25	20	1,307	1,075	1,201	1,050
TecDAX	52,968	37,848	33,025	23,923	27,370
DJ Euro STOXX Select Dividend 30 Index	1,415				
DJ Euro STOXX 50 Index	400,931,635	251,438,870	150,049,918	90,808,086	71,406,377
DJ Euro STOXX 50 Index - 1st Friday	36,992	149,414	90,475		
DJ Euro STOXX 50 Index - 2nd Friday	16,865	167,282	79,783		
DJ Euro STOXX 50 Index - 4th Friday	23,379	200,733	76,568		
DJ Euro STOXX 50 Index - 5th Friday	19,418	50,709	48,623		
DJ Euro STOXX Automobile	62,172	45,050	40,516	35,719	24,536
DJ Euro STOXX Banks	103,585	644,500	105,512	119,125	150,913
DJ Euro STOXX Basic Resources	50	415	50		
DJ Euro STOXX Chemicals	5,899	12,790	1,540	458	2
DJ Euro STOXX Construction & Materials	240	11,910	6,520		
DJ Euro STOXX Financial Services	1,575	5,381	2,000	250	160
DJ Euro STOXX Food and Beverage	104	3,486	2,000	17,910	300
DJ Euro STOXX Healthcare	502		2,460	5,250	600
DJ Euro STOXX Insurance	47,709	19,955	36,561	46,600	91,371
DJ Euro STOXX Media	5,408	16,559	7,300	22,492	799
DJ Euro STOXX Oil & Gas	14,544	17,870	108,053	90,726	46,243
DJ Euro STOXX Personal & Household Goods	165		906		
DJ Euro STOXX Technology	24,702	10,000	68,125	58,830	28,102

EUREX, Frankfurt, Germany (continued)

	2008	2007	2006	2005	2004
DJ Euro STOXX Telecom	51,047	40,018	49,856	113,758	39,396
DJ Euro STOXX Travel & Leisure	90	150	15,552	18,700	
DJ Euro STOXX Utilities	13,781	62,494	87,546	33,230	
DJ STOXX 50 Index	103,080	140,197	63,064	29,052	14,952
DJ STOXX 600 Index	37,529	30,593	4,208		
DJ STOXX 600 Automobiles & Parts	95,635	85,135	3,100		
DJ STOXX 600 Banks	535,531	377,343	30,701	10,887	1,865
DJ STOXX 600 Basic Resources	179,574	95,047	94,486	13,966	3,850
DJ STOXX 600 Chemicals	31,488	9,684	1,610		
DJ STOXX 600 Construction & Materials	60,216	50,582	305		
DJ STOXX 600 Financial Services	6,947	6,115	3,600		
DJ STOXX 600 Food & Beverage	29,802	623	568		
DJ STOXX 600 Healthcare	46,305	65,188	18,971	32,984	20,017
DJ STOXX 600 Industrial Goods & Services	111,988	142,189	41,602	1,360	
DJ STOXX 600 Insurance	525,853	195,790	11,604	8,399	
DJ STOXX 600 Media	15,632	10,744	5,206	310	
DJ STOXX 600 Oil & Gas	173,140	89,956	55,822	29,824	
DJ STOXX 600 Personal & Household Goods	4,587	7,063	320		
DJ STOXX 600 Retail	19,431				
DJ STOXX 600 Technology	11,612	11,539	4,081	600	1,000
DJ STOXX 600 Telecom	46,994	43,478	52,023	27,723	3,405
DJ STOXX 600 Travel & Leisure	922	9,653	18,761	486	
DJ STOXX 600 Utilities	84,162	106,487	23,308	13,679	1,000
DJ Stoxx Small 200 Index	31,998	7,607			
DJ STOXX Mid 200 Index	112,858	172,017	52,899	1,584	
Swiss Market Index (SMI)	5,588,591	5,773,269	3,948,593	4,134,470	3,645,596
Swiss Leader Index (SLI)	49,519	19,599			
Swiss Market Index Mid-Cap (SMIM)	49,610	44,920	14,616		
Euro-BUND	33,317,879	44,441,961	41,764,550	39,014,844	30,896,920
Euro-SCHATZ	20,438,378	19,085,515	17,344,245	11,546,405	9,782,863
Euro-BOBL	15,083,076	15,135,182	17,220,011	7,990,587	10,829,250
All Options on Individual SMI Component	75,864,298	68,122,792	57,323,550	58,463,793	47,714,268
All Options on Nordic Equities	18,414,654	17,291,936	16,396,662	16,109,249	17,836,215
All Options on Austrian Equities	113,901	19,025			
All Options on Belgian Equities	31,017				
All Options on Dutch Equities	7,243,976	11,811,227	10,420,237	12,834,633	8,364,977
All Options on Exchange Traded Funds	330,944	31,730	15,732	42,278	85,478
All Options on French Equities	9,429,765	7,795,177	6,667,994	4,867,961	2,743,950
All Options on German Equities	234,948,892	214,969,289	180,695,967	162,437,728	134,857,678
All Options on Italian Equities	1,784,585	1,146,488	1,006,419	785,918	187,948
All Options on Russian Equities	179,672	22,398			
All Options on Spanish Equities	1,319,054	860,700	22,988		
All Options on US Equities	1,590	8,221	9,235	419,511	15,207
Total Options	**933,396,359**	**753,780,347**	**566,120,139**	**463,851,198**	**381,008,508**

EURONEXT, Amsterdam (Formerly EOE, AFM and AEX, Netherlands)

	2008	2007	2006	2005	2004
AEX Stock Index (FTI)	12,477,916	12,850,137	11,165,258	7,397,665	5,651,747
Euro/US Dollar (FED)	5,124	5,087	7,474	5,640	2,026
US Dollar/Euro (FDE)	1,394	918	1,333	1,795	1,959
Total Futures	**12,484,434**	**12,856,367**	**11,190,181**	**7,447,671**	**5,701,122**
Euro / US Dollar (EDX)	394,315	439,811	651,810	290,839	139,758
US Dollar / Euro	55,414	52,499	81,229	113,118	99,322
AEX Stock Index (AEX)	27,534,800	26,292,719	23,694,580	19,753,393	17,093,573
All Options on Individual Equities	101,667,922	118,038,899	89,115,941	71,297,264	60,196,898
Total Options	**129,652,451**	**146,971,144**	**115,643,572**	**91,485,652**	**77,566,516**

EURONEXT, Brussels (Formerly BELFOX)

	2008	2007	2006	2005	2004
Bel 20 Index (BXF)	615,088	596,144	654,520	603,069	759,710
Total Futures	**615,088**	**596,144**	**654,520**	**603,069**	**759,710**
Bel 20 Index	15,404	133,467	127,000	117,795	271,717
All Options on Individual Equities	581,752	619,273	518,489	392,377	326,844
Total Options	**597,156**	**752,740**	**645,489**	**510,172**	**598,561**

EURONEXT, Lisbon

	2008	2007	2006	2005	2004
PSI-20 Index	75,904	110,485	88,557	64,252	114,955
All Futures on Individual Equities	413,987	894,753	584,957	413,315	520,966
Total Futures	**489,891**	**1,005,238**	**673,514**	**477,567**	**635,921**

EURONEXT, LIFFE, United Kingdom (LCE merged with LIFFE in 1996)

	2008	2007	2006	2005	2004
3-Month Short Sterling	104,572,875	119,675,947	83,003,622	68,029,052	51,324,125
3-Month Euroswiss	8,572,662	12,219,848	10,743,902	8,286,258	7,296,932
3-Month Euroyen Tibor	125,644	271,273	99,543	22	736
1-Month Eonia	1,553		5	2,640	35,152
3-Month Eonia	31,322				
3-Month Euribor	228,487,462	221,411,485	202,091,612	166,682,115	157,746,684
3-Month Eurodollar	26,692	15,926	69,760	5,662,806	4,666,508
Long Gilt	24,717,249	27,367,489	22,009,284	17,760,359	14,045,404
2-Year Swapnote EUR	703,608	512,872	274,459	322,212	458,492
5-Year Swapnote EUR	212,746	407,029	401,365	387,005	688,952
10-Year Swapnote EUR	104,460	273,961	405,011	434,759	653,046
Japanese Government Bond	105,584	173,810	140,487	101,127	80,569
FTSE 100 Index	42,314,080	33,535,934	25,120,880	21,522,583	20,772,878
FTSE Eurotop 100 Index	13,907	27,352	32,694	74,667	88,475
MSCI Euro Index	5,964	6,360	18,036	21,114	60,414
MSCI Pan-Euro Index	641,354	835,603	701,066	521,591	474,949
FTSE Mid 250 Index	163,652	181,735	62,304	39,238	32,896
Other Bclear	10,085	2,129	19,033		
Cocoa #7	3,577,010	3,319,396	3,095,346	2,690,105	2,643,199
Raw Sugar	6	7,196			
Robusta Coffee	3,959,277	4,435,793	3,550,938	3,263,253	3,054,386
Robusta Coffee - 10 Tonne	207,443				
Wheat	131,358	128,073	76,239	65,324	75,455
White Sugar	1,654,446	2,091,654	1,668,674	1,497,150	1,251,233
All Futures on Individual Equities	124,054,822	74,371,596	28,930,769	11,744,778	12,929,406
Total Futures	**544,395,261**	**501,332,214**	**383,367,780**	**309,779,562**	**279,474,981**
3-Month Short Sterling	59,079,440	50,747,710	34,231,229	25,096,889	16,139,006
3-Month Sterling Mid-curve	12,994,233	4,330,981	3,212,817	3,173,334	1,461,723
3-Month Euribor	106,730,522	74,276,297	48,176,163	44,138,922	52,245,463
3-Month Euribor Mid Curve	7,955,894	6,188,559	7,355,609	7,017,840	6,433,100
FTSE 100 Index (ESX)	29,261,814	23,700,667	15,717,186	14,473,441	17,866,310
FTSE 100 Index FLEX	1,434,196	1,021,680	1,979,620	1,189,652	1,178,067
Other Bclear	57,250	13,697	16,700		
Cocoa	251,614	177,788	102,819	95,814	170,079
Robusta Coffee	468,647	664,827	467,706	237,544	248,990
Robusta Coffee - 10 Tonne	48,987				
Wheat	523	5,284	2,320	3,070	2,387
White Sugar	224,977	254,307	81,647	81,598	94,705
All Options on Individual Equities	46,547,253	33,260,918	20,757,421	9,085,505	11,578,961
Total Options	**265,055,350**	**194,642,715**	**132,111,154**	**104,649,117**	**107,484,253**

EURONEXT, Paris (Formerly MATIF and MONEP, France)

	2008	2007	2006	2005	2004
Wheat #2	1,464,484	980,742	407,843	217,171	160,200
Corn	112,408	94,606	72,044	81,965	71,124
Rapeseed	680,765	438,849	238,594	211,281	191,644
CAC 40 Stock Index 10 Euro	49,242,000	44,668,975	33,405,804	25,011,372	24,058,528
FTSE EPRA Eurozone	12,265	3,742			
FTSE EPRA Europe	53,533	4,278			
FTSEurofirst 80	473,365	397,110	26,412		
FTSEurofirst 100	501	21,281	990		
Total Futures	**52,039,321**	**46,653,064**	**34,151,687**	**25,521,789**	**24,481,496**
Rapeseed	134,370	50,962	26,843	8,192	8,075
Wheat	325,464	129,365	41,398	9,810	7,109
Corn	3,738	4,656	1,818	1,622	
CAC 40 Index, 1 EUR	30	3,865	1,376	31,069,890	63,152,339
CAC 40 Index, 10 EUR	8,628,618	9,793,350	6,633,635	2,802,039	
All Options on Individual Equities*	35,308,480	34,233,628	45,160,159	183,560,708	230,863,609
Total Options	**44,400,700**	**44,215,826**	**51,865,229**	**217,452,261**	**294,031,132**

Italian Derivatives Market of the Italian Stock Exchange, Italy

	2008	2007	2006	2005	2004
MIB 30 Index	7,914,300	4,671,557	4,037,973	3,580,695	3,331,843
Mini FIB 30 Index	2,909,366	2,065,878	1,659,649	1,294,606	1,485,112
Electricity	634				
All Futures on Individual Equities	4,417,700	6,363,954	7,031,974	5,957,674	1,734,256
Total Futures	**15,242,000**	**13,101,389**	**12,729,596**	**10,832,975**	**6,551,211**
MIB 30 Index	3,630,359	3,658,686	2,819,916	2,597,830	2,220,807
All Options on Individual Equities	20,056,426	20,364,847	16,056,751	12,439,716	9,500,498
Total Options	**23,686,785**	**24,023,533**	**18,876,667**	**15,037,546**	**11,721,305**

VOLUME - WORLDWIDE

IntercontinentalExchange (ICE), United Kingdom (Formerly IPE, United Kingdom)

	2008	2007	2006	2005	2004
Crude Oil, Brent	68,368,145	59,728,941	44,345,927	30,412,027	25,458,259
Crude Oil, Brent - Quarters	3	12	150		
Crude Oil, Brent - Calendars	60				
Gas Oil	28,805,192	24,509,884	18,289,877	10,971,719	9,355,767
Natural Gas - Seasons	279,930	136,740	42,660	11,520	15,090
Natural Gas - Quarters	103,440	37,905	16,080	9,045	24,045
Natural Gas Monthly (NBP)	879,420	1,058,290	543,550	423,565	609,350
ECX European Emissions - Monthly	1,991,276	980,780	452,359	94,348	
WTI Crude - Monthly	51,091,712	51,388,362	28,672,639		
WTI Crude - Quarters	18	15			
WTI Crude - Calendars	12				
Middle-Eastern Sour Crude - Monthly	244	95,364			
Gasoline - Monthly	26,356	14,805	9,692		
Gasoline - Quarters	120				
Heating Oil - Monthly	116,911	205,072	199,187		
ECX CER - Monthly	507,779				
Rotterdam Coal - Monthly	5,895	465	45		
Rotterdam Coal - Quarters	24,720	3,870	630		
Rotterdam Coal - Seasons	630		30		
Rotterdam Coal - Calendar	70,860	4,500	120		
Richards Bay Coal - Monthly	1,900	240	60		
Richards Bay Coal - Quarters	8,880	525	15		
Richards Bay Coal - Calendar	34,020	480			
Richards Bay Coal - Seasons	30				
Electricity Baseload - Monthly	370	990	3,155	2,500	1,070
Electricity Baseload - Quarters	975	330	930	1,380	900
Electricity Baseload - Seasons	2,790	1,920	3,870	8,190	2,280
Electricity Peak - Monthly	40	205	490	420	
Electricity Peak - Quarters	540		345	30	
Total Futures	**152,322,268**	**138,169,680**	**92,582,921**	**41,936,609**	**35,466,941**
Crude Oil	121,024	74,056	33,249	44,421	28,688
ECX CFI	242,966	57,541	560		
ECX CER	69,565				
WTI Crude Oil	11,131	10,416			
Gasoil	183,179	159,263	104,320	74,055	45,154
Total Options	**627,865**	**301,276**	**138,129**	**118,476**	**73,842**

Korea Futures Exchange (KFE), Korea (* Transferred from KSE)

	2008	2007	2006	2005	2004
Korea Treasury Bonds	15,958,864	13,555,136	10,343,605	11,223,244	7,352,307
10-Year Treasury Bond	9,686				
*KOPSI 200	64,835,148	47,758,294	46,611,008	43,848,706	55,608,856
STAR Index	13,325	21,919	107,538	103,619	
Lean Hogs	16,258				
Gold	1,267	399			
US Dollar	6,672,438	5,752,134	3,104,641	2,667,005	2,090,291
Japanese Yen	104,012	271,043			
Euro	103,762	212,790			
All Futures on Individual Equities	11,293,134				
Total Futures	**99,007,894**	**67,571,815**	**60,169,114**	**57,883,098**	**65,261,326**
*KOPSI 200 Index	2,766,474,404	2,709,844,077	2,414,422,952	2,535,201,692	2,521,557,274
*All Options on Individual Equities	21	206	1,195	3,655	1
Total Options	**2,766,474,425**	**2,709,844,283**	**2,414,424,147**	**2,535,205,347**	**2,521,557,276**

Malaysia Derivatives Exchange, Malaysia

	2008	2007	2006	2005	2004
Crude Palm Oil (FCPO)	3,003,529	2,793,560	2,230,340	1,158,510	1,378,334
JSD Crude Palm Oil	72				
3-Month KLIBOR	195,203	239,314	272,502	162,592	141,969
5-Year Malaysian Gov't Securities (FMG5)	100	8,821	27,232	17,215	19,494
10-Year Malaysian Gov't Securities (FMG10)	400	2,950			
KLSE Composite Index (FKLI)	2,920,728	3,157,341	1,628,043	1,111,575	1,088,419
Total Futures	**6,120,032**	**6,202,686**	**4,161,024**	**2,459,745**	**2,632,543**

MEFF Renta Variable (RV), Spain

	2008	2007	2006	2005	2004
IBEX 35 Plus Index	7,275,299	8,435,258	6,408,961	4,591,196	4,354,868
Mini IBEX 35 Index	3,300,418	2,865,739	1,598,296	1,490,080	1,182,497
All Futures on Individual Equities	46,237,568	21,294,315	21,029,811	18,813,689	12,054,799
Total Futures	**56,813,285**	**32,595,312**	**29,037,068**	**24,894,965**	**17,592,164**
IBEX 35 Plus Index	8,286,224	5,670,773	5,510,621	4,407,465	2,947,529
All Options on Individual Equities	18,317,249	13,593,493	12,425,979	10,915,227	8,200,314
Total Options	**26,603,473**	**19,264,266**	**17,936,600**	**15,322,692**	**11,147,843**

London Metal Exchange (LME), United Kingdom

	2008	2007	2006	2005	2004
High Grade Primary Aluminium	48,307,389	40,229,693	36,418,131	30,426,465	29,232,921
Aluminium Alloy	582,398	492,868	444,738	501,960	429,459
North American Special Aluminium Alloy	1,519,811	1,236,484	1,031,411	1,001,412	1,192,100
Copper - Grade A	26,507,242	21,420,450	18,864,246	19,231,371	18,171,204
Standard Lead	6,188,753	4,697,862	4,568,140	4,061,819	3,786,375
Primary Nickel	5,202,609	3,792,788	4,177,557	3,482,593	3,177,206
Special High Grade Zinc	16,120,770	12,556,285	11,706,008	10,620,618	10,211,096
Far East Steel (MS)	2,760				
Mediterranean Steel (MS)	13,206				
Tin	1,410,450	1,293,722	1,283,897	1,095,031	971,612
LMEmini Copper Grade A	45	1,099	1,411		
LMEmini Primary Aluminium	200	729	1,987		
LMEmini Special High Grade Zinc	7	195	283		
Polypropylene	1,466	7,977	13,303	15,770	
PA Asia	33	102			
PE Europe	22	29			
PN North America	2,449	401			
LE Europe	80	16			
LL Global	24				
LA Asia	169				
LN North America	1,705	282			
Total Futures	**105,861,588**	**85,736,480**	**78,527,839**	**70,444,665**	**67,171,973**
High Grade Primary Aluminium	3,702,232	3,115,989	4,690,867	4,107,102	2,217,021
Aluminium Alloy	267,722	316,496	315	369,068	288
North American Special Aluminium Alloy	24,052	10,052	4,420	10,069	2,385
Copper - Grade A	1,987,291	2,027,181	1,850,993	2,091,198	1,721,914
Standard Lead	346,672	298,965	164,410	128,283	76,342
Primary Nickel	152,744	167,428	158,496	189,903	119,942
Special High Grade Zinc	715,970	1,111,080	1,335,184	1,011,429	471,097
Tin	67,716	18,407	17,315	14,012	3,227
Primary Aluminium TAPOS	37,748	43,621	93,540	129,657	55,539
Aluminium Alloy TAPOS	3,022	3,528	2,141		
Copper Grade A TAPOS	16,146	16,667	45,346	55,907	37,438
Lead TAPOS	9,411	3,210	3,335	8,116	10,653
Nickel TAPOS	11,347	35,220	14,502	12,610	4,014
Tin TAPOS	810	48	850	2,014	475
NASAA TAPOS	2,290	42	1,170	33,194	1,632
Special High Grade Zinc TAPOS	8,538	10,314	29,466	21,625	12,571
Total Options	**7,353,711**	**7,178,248**	**8,412,350**	**8,184,187**	**4,734,928**

MEFF Renta Fija (RF), Spain

	2008	2007	2006	2005	2004
10-Year Notional Bond	4	13	7	46	95
Total Futures	**4**	**13**	**7**	**46**	**95**

Mercado a Termino de Buenos Aires (MATBA), Argentina

	2008	2007	2006	2005	2004
Wheat	37,243	41,781	41,200	34,863	17,348
Corn	22,269	32,012	18,310	10,535	8,000
Sunflower	101	135	206	824	495
Soybean	82,164	80,016	59,279	68,598	42,701
Argentine Commodity Index (ICA)	96	84			
Total Futures	**141,873**	**154,069**	**118,995**	**114,820**	**68,544**
Wheat	1,449	5,243	7,934	7,074	3,302
Corn	1,538	4,068	5,021	569	811
Sunflower	64	1,221			
Soybean	10,831	12,963	15,195	13,146	12,233
Total Options	**13,882**	**23,495**	**28,150**	**20,915**	**17,049**

New Zealand Futures Exchange (NZFOE), New Zealand

	2008	2007	2006	2005	2004
10-Year Government Stock	691	664	594	891	788
90-Day Bank Bill	1,453,947	1,638,294	1,801,132	982,302	491,706
Total Futures	**1,454,638**	**1,638,988**	**1,801,726**	**983,223**	**492,666**
90-Day Bank Bill	1,850	4,450	24,190	2,850	4,515
All Options on Individual Equities	2,600	7,600	111		
Total Options	**4,450**	**12,050**	**24,301**	**2,850**	**4,515**

VOLUME - WORLDWIDE

Mercado a Termino de Rosario (ROFEX), Argentina

	2008	2007	2006	2005	2004
Wheat	106	405	1,039	41	36
Corn	208	294	538	8	
Soybeans	17,421	40,000	556	504	
Rosafe Soybean Index (ISR)	77,766	143,824	101,029	116,281	56,468
Rosafe Wheat Index (ITR)	5,631	10,661	5,061		
Rosafe Corn Index (IMR)	7,663	6,292	8,714	2,139	309
Government Bond (DICP)	12,784	4,657			
BODEN 2012 Government Bond (RG12)	55				
Badlar (BAR)	121				
US Dollar (EMT)	22,000				
US Dollar (DLR)	41,796,793	25,042,919	17,779,242	12,931,695	7,679,077
Euro (EC)	151,620	20	157,005	580	
Total Futures	**42,092,168**	**25,249,072**	**18,053,184**	**13,051,248**	**7,735,890**
Rosafe Soybean Index (ISR)	24,986	36,972	24,229	44,307	59,449
Rosafe Wheat Index (ITR)	410	6,460	3,836		
Rosafe Corn Index (IMR)	2,762	1,845	6,750	2,969	
Government Bond (DICP)	375				
US Dollar (DLR)	95,960	129,601	124,073	316,925	368,182
Total Options	**124,493**	**174,878**	**158,888**	**364,201**	**427,655**

Mexican Derivatives Exchange (MEXDER), Mexico

	2008	2007	2006	2005	2004
US Dollar	3,186,832	3,223,044	6,026,940	2,934,658	1,289,386
Euro FX	44,172	2,105	50,469	125	
IPC Stock Index	1,085,663	951,955	620,557	410,565	327,942
CETE 91	4,087,066	2,812,500	3,290,100	4,509,002	2,418,381
TIIE 28	57,881,101	220,608,024	264,160,131	99,830,916	206,027,203
M3 Bond	43,000	36,500	28,600		
M10 Bond	3,005,307	1,182,069	471,879	284,460	278,644
10-Year Interest Rate Swap	170,949	25,332			
All Futures on Individual Equities	2,000	2	3,000	19,400	13,455
Total Futures	**69,506,090**	**228,841,531**	**274,651,676**	**107,989,126**	**210,355,031**
MXN / USD	7	10	2,343		
IPC Stock Index	52,556	130,410	115,531	38,329	35,943
Exchange Traded Funds	7,585			730	
All Options on Individual Equities	577,452	78	448,120	149,091	4,290
Total Options	**637,600**	**130,498**	**565,994**	**188,150**	**40,233**

Montreal Exchange (ME), Canada

	2008	2007	2006	2005	2004
3-Month Bankers Acceptance (BAX)	9,958,833	15,237,958	16,702,302	11,157,298	7,765,060
10-Year Canadian Gov't Bond (CGB)	7,363,569	9,337,754	7,691,797	4,692,287	3,005,359
30-Day Overnight Repo Rate (ONX)	5				1,480
Canada Carbon Dioxide Equivalent Units (MCX)	1,179				
S&P Canada 60 Index (SXF)	4,575,352	3,885,872	3,064,695	2,234,406	1,906,038
Gold Index (SXA)	91,186	10,908	23,645	9,898	774
Banking Index (SXB)	24,129	9,014	140	266	186
Energy Index (SXY)	28,762	5,585	10,157	13,662	2,524
Total Futures	**22,043,015**	**28,493,454**	**27,578,059**	**18,240,633**	**12,900,821**
3-Month Bankers Acceptance (OBX)	282,190	748,991	605,806	377,370	265,937
30-yr Canadian Gov't Bond (LGB)	3,032	2,154			
10-yr Canadian Gov't Bond (OGB)	23,553	13,782	2,275		
US Dollar (USX)	23,795	34,889	31,262	7,264	
S&P Canada 60 Index (SXO)	38,666	26,484	57,974	27,897	38,892
Claymore Global Agriculture (COW)	64				
Horizons Beta Pro S&P/TSX 60 Bear Plus ETF (HXD)	3,896				
Horizons Beta Pro S&P/TSX 60 Bull Plus ETF (HXU)	7,651				
i60 Index (XIU)	661,286	364,924	317,637	176,498	120,502
CDN S&P/TSX Capped Gold Index Fund (XGD)	58,438	89,435	144,695	111,502	54,561
CDN S&P/TSX Capped Financials Index Fund (XFN)	195,820	101,499	130,730	99,079	73,006
CDN S&P/TSX Capped IT Index Fund (XIT)	3,248	14,989	10,018	7,942	11,800
CDN S&P/TSX Capped Materials Index Fund (XMA)	5,811	59,371	11,012		
CDN S&P/TSX Capped Energy Index Fund (XEG)	80,838	158,178	234,611	227,268	37,783
All Options on Individual Equities	14,633,599	12,634,060	11,416,758	9,409,938	8,311,818
Total Options	**16,021,887**	**14,248,756**	**12,962,778**	**10,444,758**	**8,914,307**

National Stock Exchange of India

	2008	2007	2006	2005	2004
S&P CNX Nifty Index	202,390,223	138,794,235	70,286,227	47,375,214	23,354,782
All Futures on Individual Equities	225,777,205	179,324,970	100,285,737	68,911,754	44,051,780
Total Futures	**428,167,428**	**318,119,205**	**170,571,964**	**116,286,968**	**67,406,562**
S&P CNX Nifty Index	150,916,778	52,707,150	18,702,248	10,140,239	2,812,109
All Options on Individual Equities	11,067,082	9,048,495	5,214,191	5,224,485	4,874,958
Total Options	**161,983,860**	**61,755,645**	**23,916,439**	**15,364,724**	**7,687,067**

OMX Exchanges, Sweden (formerly Copenhagen (FUTOP), FOME, Helsinki, Stockholm)

	2008	2007	2006	2005	2004
Interest Rate	25,226,793	22,522,968	12,205,955	8,223,372	6,546,035
OMX Index	39,307,915	31,609,782	24,374,765	20,259,029	16,460,920
All Futures on Individual Equities	15,841,312	9,013,489	8,459,165	5,659,824	4,257,168
Total Futures	**62,449,070**	**45,039,885**	**34,142,225**	**27,819,175**	**24,926,194**
Interest Rate	629,000	685,010			
OMX Index	19,654,145	19,715,476	13,613,210	12,229,146	8,946,939
All Options on Individual Equities	42,767,407	59,660,819	64,514,641	57,138,565	58,171,571
Total Options	**80,376,020**	**63,376,025**	**45,039,885**	**34,142,225**	**27,819,175**

Oslo Stock Exchange (OSE), Norway

	2008	2007	2006	2005	2004
Forwards	1,637,407	2,630,772	3,615,036	1,796,570	1,071,127
OBX	9,195,919	4,755,934	2,429,235	562,591	677,615
Total Futures	**10,833,326**	**7,386,706**	**6,044,271**	**2,359,161**	**1,748,742**
OBX	1,460,422	1,797,651	1,331,023	515,538	681,783
All Options on Individual Equities	3,754,682	4,783,490	5,781,666	3,325,368	2,921,209
Total Options	**5,215,104**	**6,581,141**	**7,112,689**	**3,840,906**	**3,602,992**

Shanghai Metal Exchange, China

	2008	2007	2006	2005	2004
Copper	20,773,258	16,328,011	5,393,419	12,352,026	21,248,370
Aluminum	14,788,920	4,823,552	13,931,476	2,125,020	6,829,499
Zinc	5,193,582	10,215,449			
Gold	22,235,782				
Rubber	46,461,103	42,191,727	26,047,061	9,503,158	9,680,649
Fuel Oil	30,810,540	12,005,094	12,734,045	9,809,550	2,818,855
Total Futures	**140,263,185**	**85,563,833**	**58,106,001**	**33,789,754**	**40,577,373**

Singapore Exchange (SGX), Singapore

	2008	2007	2006	2005	2004
Euroyen TIBOR	562,063	1,916,702	3,538,237	2,774,916	2,490,390
Mini Japanese Gov't Bond	831,196	1,457,309	1,427,458	1,241,616	931,110
Nikkei 225 Index	26,149,701	21,937,499	18,017,221	11,916,557	7,769,675
Nikkei 225 Index (USD)	3,154	10,913	871		
Mini Nikkei 225 Index	31,640	29,378			
Straits Times Index	2,734	22	4	546	1,830
FTSE/China A50 Index	34,232	12,349	8,932		
S&P CNX Nifty Index	12,435,118	750,361	134,445	9,910	38
MSCI Asia APEX 50 Index	6,658				
MSCI Singapore Index	4,635,517	4,012,860	2,214,521	1,707,865	1,658,600
MSCI Taiwan Index	16,913,325	13,611,314	10,824,249	8,100,202	6,998,626
Total Futures	**61,605,338**	**43,741,573**	**36,201,370**	**25,867,661**	**28,169,379**
EuroYen Tibor	2,000	51,539	8,700		
MSCI Taiwan Index	385	16,010	29,642	1,293	41,971
Nikkei 225 Index	233,545	397,704	358,031	156,449	205,417
Total Options	**235,930**	**465,253**	**396,373**	**158,467**	**249,378**

Taiwan Futures Exchange, Taiwan

	2008	2007	2006	2005	2004
TAIEX (TX)	19,819,775	11,813,150	9,914,999	6,917,375	8,861,278
Mini TAIEX (MTX)	9,058,436	2,964,042	1,760,583	1,088,523	1,943,269
Taiwan Stock Exchange Electronic Sector Index	1,356,290	1,004,603	1,459,821	1,179,643	1,568,391
Taiwan Stock Exchange Bank & Insurance Sector Index	1,285,074	909,383	786,477	909,621	2,255,478
Taiwan 50 Index	602	506	332	9,483	6,157
MSCI Taiwan Index (MSF)	1,425	1,132	9,894		
GreTai Securities Weighted Stock Index (GTF)	94,144	21,231			
Taiwan Stock Exch NonFin/NonElec SubIndex (XIF)	168,534	37,197			
10-Year Government Bond	471,508	151,247	40,675	2,887	67,705
30-Day Commercial Paper Interest Rate	114,558	36,243	1,022	217	209,561
Gold (GDF)	40,174	48,925	32,484		
NT Dollar Gold (TGF)	5,314,069				
Total Futures	**37,724,589**	**16,987,659**	**14,006,287**	**10,107,749**	**14,911,839**
TAIEX	92,757,254	92,585,637	96,929,940	80,096,506	43,824,511
TSE Electronic Sector Index	1,068,755	1,066,141	773,353	680,026	
TSE Financial Sector Index	927,888	1,203,084	937,044	756,570	
GreTai Securities Weighted Stock Index (GTO)	835,892	187,967			
Taiwan Stock Exch NonFin/NonElec SubIndex (XIO)	891,575	186,161			
MSCI Taiwan Index (MSO)	1,640,944	1,634,117	867,597		
All Options on Individual Equities	872,880	1,299,858	1,089,158	1,018,917	6,237,079
Total Options	**98,995,188**	**98,162,965**	**100,597,092**	**82,552,019**	**50,061,590**

VOLUME - WORLDWIDE

South African Futures Exchange (SAFEX), Africa

	2008	2007	2006	2005	2004
White Maize (WMAZ)	859,920	956,026	865,549	806,639	969,838
Yellow Maize (YMAZ)	337,429	268,780	164,601	198,625	228,709
WEAT	469,471	378,289	264,925	221,283	200,663
SUNS	165,088	64,402	68,882	78,093	56,285
SOYA	73,111	44,062	36,939	14,945	3,054
WOPT	80	14,500	18,913		
FTSE/JSE Top 40 Index (ALSI)	15,924,693	16,150,010	13,483,033	10,103,226	9,289,443
FTSE/JSE Top 40 Index - Mini (ALMI)	450				
FTSE/JSE 25 Index (INDI)	25,723	22,845	20,259	40,066	37,117
FTSE/JSE Gold Mining Index (GLDX)	1,651	7,893	11,517	336	9
FTSE/JSE FINI 15 Index (FINI)	43,660	16,309	6,421	6,439	15,931
FTSE/JSE FNDI 30 Index (FNDI)	217,863	125,960	319,247	33,663	4,892
FTSE/JSE Capped Top 40 Index (CTOP)	47,687	19,977	106,003		34,938
FTSE/JSE Shareholder Weighted Top 40 Index (DTOP)	3,037,960	2,359,997	1,321,011	460,071	37,596
FTSE/JSE SA Listed Property Index (SAPI)	370	684	12,245	6,184	
FTSE/JSE RESI 20 Index	14,528	5,390	8,254	1,419	2,004
Can Do (CDAA)	1,128,772	736,044	219,211		
Kruger Rand (KGRD)	519	9,922	6,654	16,381	15,798
Dividend Futures	20,097,204	11,891,790	420,266		
IDX Futures	28,362				
IDX Dividend Futures	1,364,561				
All Futures on Individual Equities	431,212,627	265,493,735	69,665,994	24,455,924	8,897,187
Total Futures	**475,051,729**	**298,567,616**	**87,036,273**	**36,456,767**	**19,811,664**
White Maize (WMAZ)	455,403	471,727	368,404	344,269	333,285
Yellow Maize (YMAZ)	69,339	55,695	20,746	23,694	33,385
WEAT	176,079	140,545	57,699	61,433	62,434
SUNS	21,073	5,983	9,179	21,115	5,089
SOYA	5,978	1,986	4,971	1,354	52
FTSE/JSE Top 40 Index (ALSI)	9,834,294	9,008,828	9,878,535	10,208,949	11,267,046
FTSE/JSE FINI 15 Index (FINI)	8				
FTSE/JSE FNDI 30 Index (FNDI)	50,987	70,110	219,444	124,638	1,717
FTSE/JSE Capped Top 40 Index (CTOP)	152	965	79,763	33,608	
FTSE/JSE Shareholder Weighted Top 40 Index (DTOP)	4,722,544	4,026,943	1,540,221	1,226,005	
CAN DO	3,604,877	2,978,981	73,454		
RESI	190				
All Options on Individual Equities	19,591,351	14,312,446	5,751,833	2,799,774	6,827,533
Total Options	**38,532,275**	**31,074,787**	**18,011,251**	**14,861,408**	**18,536,197**

Sydney Futures Exchange (SFE), Australia

	2008	2007	2006	2005	2004
SPI 200	10,174,823	8,407,052	6,516,247	5,597,066	4,622,139
30-Day Interbank Cash Rate	2,785,693	3,585,675	2,009,291	1,399,499	659,926
90-Day Bank Bills	20,192,284	22,682,851	19,501,781	16,119,237	14,213,188
3-Year Treasury Bonds	26,116,381	33,585,015	31,017,644	22,862,363	22,805,279
10-Year Treasury Bonds	13,188,549	19,169,641	15,051,399	11,021,452	8,557,437
d-cypha NSW Base Load Electricity	30,173	39,076	10,707	5,692	3,700
d-cypha VIC Base Load Electricity	23,870	34,788	13,581	2,341	2,693
d-cypha QLD Base Load Electricity	30,469	36,357	9,532	2,956	1,378
d-cypha SA Base Load Electricity	2,191	4,372	2,127	1,322	1,630
d-cypha NSW Peak Period Electricity	1,236	1,491	1,926	1,254	1,142
d-cypha VIC Peak Period Electricity	2,538	4,089	5,038	4,104	1,466
d-cypha QLD Peak Period Electricity	1,274	1,804	1,981	793	994
d-cypha SA Peak Period Electricity	251	338	110	161	358
d-cypha NSW Base $300 CAP	1,887	1,397	1,276	52	
d-cypha SA Base $300 CAP	101	260	62		
d-cypha QLD Base $300 CAP	1,625	902	986	595	
d-cypha VIC Base $300 CAP	3,621	2,422	1,590	308	10
Fine Wool	698	1,828	2,686	2,207	2,013
Broad Wool	69	119	53	409	826
Greasy Wool	21,612	19,629	16,869	15,767	9,520
MLA/SFE Cattle	651	1,140	1,860	1,167	1,354
All Futures on Individual Equities	100	11,242	10,843	38,156	29,986
Total Futures	**72,580,096**	**87,595,681**	**74,204,335**	**57,091,807**	**50,968,901**
SPI 200	436,869	564,156	636,033	673,899	518,511
90-Day Bank Bills	287,103	774,472	182,663	244,940	175,286
3-Year Treasury Bond	326,323	466,507	856,723	477,764	369,708
Overnight 3-Year Treasury Bond	680,333	1,121,860	1,522,000	1,212,700	1,262,942
3-Year Bonds Intra-Day	288,228	472,047	576,935	508,754	534,302
10-Year Treasury Bonds	5,034	38,217	52,623	40,041	60,619
10-Year Bonds Intra-Day	200	100	1,266	10,700	1,845
Overnight 10-Year Treasury Bond	1,200	19,115	76,909	57,700	71,140
d-cypha QLD Peak Period Electricity	30				
d-cypha SA Peak Period Electricity	20				
d-cypha VIC Peak Period Electricity	60	100	5		65
Total Options	**2,025,460**	**3,525,481**	**3,915,771**	**3,233,159**	**3,000,544**

Thailand Futures Exchange, Thailand

	2008	2007
SET 50	2,099,098	1,228,238
All Futures on Individual Equities	3,838	
Total Futures	**2,102,936**	**1,228,238**
TA-25 Index	2,428	45,684
Total Options	**2,428**	**45,684**

Tel-Aviv Stock Exchange (TASE), Israel

	2008	2007	2006	2005	2004
TA-25 Index	29,694	19,802	32,474	10,910	8,291
Shekel-Dollar Rate	80			140	44
Total Futures	**29,774**	**20,445**	**57,334**	**11,086**	**8,335**
TA-25 Index	81,483,701	94,520,236	75,486,658	63,096,635	36,921,511
TA-Banks Index	72,486	87,445	56,273	36,781	596
Shekel-Dollar Rate	10,596,199	9,508,185	7,344,622	6,640,621	5,847,295
Shekel-Euro Rate	391,882	235,452	103,095	303,822	598,206
Total Options	**92,544,268**	**104,351,318**	**82,990,648**	**70,077,859**	**43,367,608**

Turkish Derivatives Exchange (TurkDEX), Turkey

	2008	2007	2006	2005
Cotton	11	29	23	370
Wheat	5,503			45
Gold	21,641	81	1,618	
ISE-100 Index	2,961	1,561	39,809	26,700
ISE-30 Index	40,332,007	17,015,352	2,203,916	143,572
US Dollar	13,979,082	7,832,542	4,393,609	1,594,157
Euro	131,210	17,067	204,807	64,558
T-Benchmark	420	401	4,104	
Total Futures	**54,472,835**	**24,867,033**	**6,848,087**	**1,832,871**

Warsaw Stock Exchange, Poland

	2008	2007	2006	2005	2004
TECHWIG Index	1,141	8,204	13,419	7,617	7,961
WIG 20 Index	11,743,240	8,792,219	6,242,128	5,156,953	3,484,397
WIG 40 Index	25,349	15,819			
CHFPLN	5,669				
EURPLN	28,600	532	650	1,146	1,211
GBPPLN	71				
USDPLN	98,219	5,517	2,494	5,070	2,244
All Futures on Individual Equities	331,646	111,457	112,824	172,828	87,888
Total Futures	**12,233,935**	**8,936,225**	**6,386,377**	**5,378,517**	**3,609,125**
WIG20 Index	326,583	405,657	316,840	204,626	78,752
Total Options	**326,583**	**405,733**	**327,828**	**208,998**	**78,752**

Wiener Borse - Derivatives Market of Vienna, Austria (Formerly the AFOE)

	2008	2007	2006	2005	2004
ATF Index	32,408	35,043	46,517	35,973	25,607
ATX Index	156,376	108,020	108,004	68,704	50,743
IAX Index	5	5			
CeCe (5 Eastern European Indices)	59,692	89,335	65,953	63,722	40,108
All Futures on Individual Equities	6,981	11,199	12,371	23,748	7,862
Total Futures	**255,462**	**243,602**	**232,845**	**192,147**	**124,320**
ATX Index	22,894	28,067	23,462	34,631	36,738
ATF Index	3,236	8,117	1,938	2,496	4,097
CeCe (5 Eastern European Indices)	6	4			
All Options on Individual Equities	848,021	1,036,975	1,053,298	816,032	2,077,320
Total Options	**1,073,293**	**1,078,698**	**853,159**	**2,118,155**	**1,279,649**

ICE Futures Canada (ICE), Canada (Formerly the WCE)

	2008	2007	2006	2005	2004
Wheat	430	46,470	66,555	87,634	87,758
Canola (Rapeseed)	3,132,188	3,169,182	2,607,354	1,822,985	1,737,972
Western Barley	167,381	214,672	195,024	136,564	204,635
Total Futures	**3,299,999**	**3,430,324**	**2,868,933**	**2,047,183**	**2,030,455**
Western Barley	5	4,774	1,080	876	3,273
Canola	21,206	17,067	26,523	27,111	20,568
Total Options	**21,211**	**21,841**	**27,603**	**29,447**	**23,841**

Tokyo International Financial Futures Exchange (TIFFE), Japan

	2008	2007	2006	2005	2004
3-Month Euroyen TIBOR	22,372,133	38,952,553	31,495,084	10,977,591	7,259,779
US Dollar / Japanese Yen	13,177,698	7,629,879		600	200
Total Futures	**65,675,700**	**72,535,144**	**31,508,764**	**11,057,134**	**7,655,510**

VOLUME - WORLDWIDE

Hong Kong Futures Exchange (HKFE), Hong Kong

	2008	2007	2006	2005	2004
Hang Seng Index	21,716,508	17,160,964	12,718,380	9,910,565	8,601,559
Mini Hang Seng Index	7,961,028	4,325,977	2,140,242	1,501,342	1,457,681
H-Shares Index	14,440,965	10,846,277	4,880,470	1,978,673	1,743,700
Mini H-Shares Index	318,395				
Hang Seng China H-Financials Index	9	3,220			
FTSE/Xinhua China 25 Index	39	3,244	8,154	2,882	
1-Month HIBOR	881	574	155	246	733
3-Month HIBOR	23,818	31,678	13,888	24,935	58,307
3-Year Exchange Fund Note	10	150		1,250	2,225
Gold	3,075				
All Futures on Individual Equities	257,015	351,514	102,010	13,069	17,274
Total Futures	**44,721,743**	**32,723,598**	**19,863,299**	**13,433,386**	**11,884,152**
Hang Seng Index	3,820,797	7,480,183	4,095,679	3,071,822	2,029,068
Mini Hang Seng Index	156,957	69,512	53,456	30,595	26,882
FTSE/Xinhua China 25 Index	386	1,578	7,881	7,386	
H-Shares Index	1,613,988	1,727,847	758,247	257,425	77,758
All Options on Individual Equities	54,692,865	45,982,968	18,127,353	8,722,393	5,611,832
Total Options	**60,284,993**	**55,262,088**	**23,042,616**	**12,089,621**	**7,745,540**

Zhengzhou Commodity Exchange (ZCE), China

	2008	2007	2006	2005	2004
Cotton #1	5,400,835	2,955,235	2,084,541	10,870,825	2,994,046
Rapeseed Oil	6,429,404	659,612			
White Sugar	165,485,978	45,468,481	29,342,066		
Strong Gluten Wheat	27,509,312	38,982,788	14,676,238	16,620,096	11,587,269
Hard White Winter Wheat	164,309	25,719	28,052	981,649	9,655,959
PTA	17,567,296	4,960,879	167,220		
Total Futures	**222,557,134**	**93,052,714**	**46,298,117**	**28,472,570**	**24,237,274**

Kansai Commodities Exchange (KCE), Japan (Formerly KANEX, FFE, OGE, OSE, and KGE)

	2008	2007	2006	2005	2004
Red Beans	4,362	4,362	8,491	13,760	21,148
Imported Soybeans	12,638	19,712	1,497	10,264	31,310
Corn	133,592	101,401	121,135	765,921	2,406,808
Broiler	1,380	2,916	5,786	16,873	92,022
Raw Sugar	4,559	4,380	7,671	8,181	36,822
Raw Silk	358		1,446	6,346	6,665
Frozen Shrimp	5,853	6,248	66,651	511,944	1,385,143
Corn 75 Index	8,754	8,910	11,087	91,007	350,029
Coffee Index	8,903	11,248	59,627	269,269	726,741
Total Futures	**180,399**	**164,743**	**315,501**	**1,825,806**	**5,840,545**

Central Japan Commodity Exchange (CJCE), Japan (Formerly OME,KRE,OTE,CCE,NGSE,NTE, and TDCE)

	2008	2007	2006	2005	2004
Gasoline	1,745,785	3,635,329	4,953,168	11,972,407	15,869,951
Gas Oil	8,750	8,752	8,882	37,087	1,056,257
Kerosene	1,430,843	2,685,345	4,027,192	9,790,465	15,454,906
Hen Egg	6,362	7,077	12,275	65,142	798,308
Rubber (RSS3)	19,638	90,983	314,914	581,293	756,411
Rubber (TSR20)	8,776	11,620	34,031	212,805	826,045
Rubber Index	30,822	78,198	180,654	320,871	814,328
Ferrous Scrap	5,856	5,885	17,899	84,465	
Aluminum	9,534	15,016	75,659	459,244	1,101,198
Nickel	6,299	11,212	11,014	28,044	344,571
Total Futures	**3,272,665**	**6,549,417**	**9,635,688**	**23,551,823**	**37,035,812**

Osaka Securities Exchange (OSE), Japan

	2008	2007	2006	2005	2004
Nikkei 225 Index	35,546,016	30,084,781	25,151,924	17,909,404	14,415,884
Nikkei 225 Mini	95,446,729	49,107,059	6,348,382		
Nikkei 300 Index	35,509	81,907	153,439	141,534	167,399
Russell/Nomura Prime Index	80	17,317	7,586	19,414	
Total Futures	**131,028,334**	**79,291,064**	**31,661,331**	**18,070,352**	**14,583,283**
Nikkei 225 Index	32,126,060	29,181,438	28,230,767	24,894,389	16,560,874
All Options on Individual Equities	534,954	444,149	753,937	1,206,987	1,481,415
Total Options	**32,661,014**	**29,625,747**	**28,985,106**	**26,101,912**	**18,042,780**

Tokyo Commodity Exchange (TOCOM), Japan

	2008	2007	2006	2005	2004
Gold	15,163,975	18,203,194	22,228,198	17,958,240	17,385,766
Gold Mini	5,736,883	455,212			
Silver	301,216	536,583	858,153	817,624	1,473,370
Platinum	6,940,348	9,169,890	11,018,069	8,573,313	13,890,300
Platinum Mini	119,606				
Palladium	684,682	207,867	361,478	323,347	438,934
Aluminum	36,203	65,507	157,781	219,694	321,131
Gasoline	4,054,761	7,529,706	12,932,848	17,448,561	23,648,587
Kerosene	1,319,014	2,350,819	4,492,904	7,295,741	13,036,277
Crude Oil	755,520	1,489,018	1,961,190	1,981,389	2,284,572
Rubber	5,914,747	7,062,252	9,661,388	7,156,225	1,732,645
Total Futures	**41,026,955**	**47,070,048**	**63,672,011**	**61,780,446**	**74,447,426**

Tokyo Grain Exchange (TGE), Japan (Formerly YCE, TGE and TSE)

	2008	2007	2006	2005	2004
American Soybeans	910,992	1,247,786	1,259,515	2,050,803	2,125,458
Non-GMO Soybeans	2,899,301	12,280,932	9,885,557	10,964,812	9,971,499
Arabic Coffee	282,446	595,871	1,669,181	5,591,946	4,293,422
Azuki (Red Beans)	346,356	388,643	478,379	659,002	363,328
Corn	3,645,293	4,645,239	4,656,352	5,165,693	8,122,448
Raw Silk	2,923	3,096	14,170	113,938	239,446
Refined Sugar	2,862	2,862	2,896	2,860	2,854
Robusta Coffee	11,197	72,971	206,546	662,994	427,466
Raw Sugar	331,976	433,329	928,316	465,625	355,659
Total Futures	**8,433,346**	**19,674,560**	**19,116,748**	**25,957,307**	**26,870,498**

Tokyo Stock Exchange (TSE), Japan

	2008	2007	2006	2005	2004
10-Year Government Yen Bond	10,639,934	13,545,239	12,049,979	9,844,617	8,025,268
REIT Index	89,922				
TOPIX Stock Index	18,375,802	16,578,731	14,907,723	12,785,962	10,305,318
Mini TOPIX Stock Index	599,692				
TOPIX Core 30 Index	202,189				
Total Futures	**29,907,539**	**30,123,970**	**26,957,702**	**22,630,719**	**18,331,928**
TOPIX	62,045	19,555	18,354	20,004	17,643
10-Year Government Yen Bond	2,442,598	2,804,811	2,060,624	1,699,037	1,262,994
All Options on Individual Equities	88,256	145,449	190,876		
Total Options	**2,592,899**	**2,969,815**	**2,269,854**	**1,719,041**	**1,280,637**

Total Worldwide Volume

	2008	2007	2006	2005	2004
Total Futures	5,439,016,350	4,573,165,703	3,236,223,324	2,378,883,321	2,167,519,755
Percent Change	18.93%	41.31%	36.04%	9.75%	12.45%
Total Options	5,258,906,814	4,861,762,402	4,050,032,450	4,066,769,167	3,907,845,226
Percent Change	8.17%	20.04%	-0.41%	4.07%	-2.61%
Total Futures and Options	10,697,923,164	9,434,928,105	7,286,255,774	6,445,652,488	6,075,364,981
Percent Change	13.39%	29.49%	13.04%	6.09%	2.28%

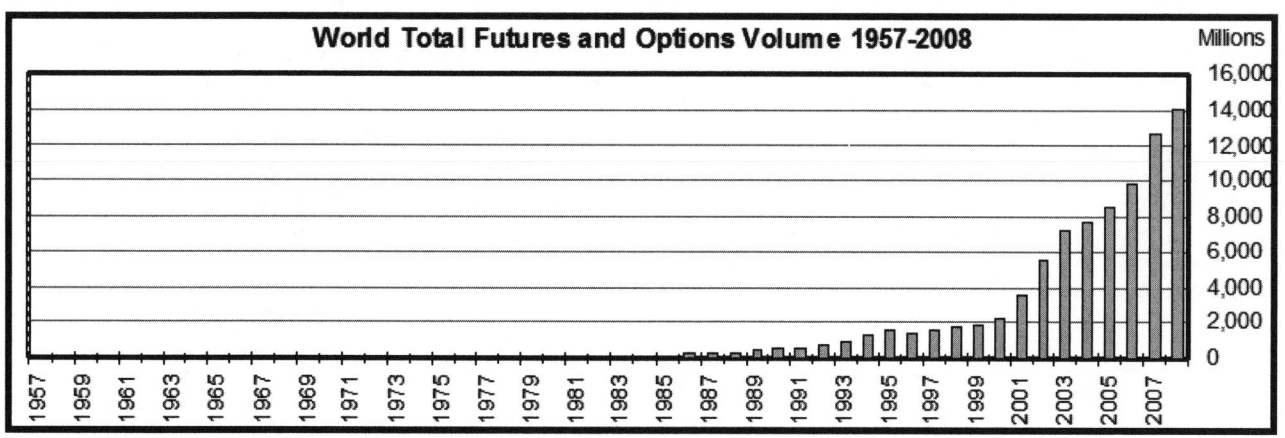

World Total Futures and Options Volume 1957-2008

Conversion Factors

Commonly Used Agricultural Weights and Measurements

Bushel Weights:
wheat and soybeans = 60 lbs.
corn, sorghum and rye = 56 lbs.
barley grain = 48 lbs.
barley malt = 34 lbs.
oats = 32 lbs.

Bushels to tonnes:
wheat and soybeans = bushels X 0.027216
barley grain = bushels X 0.021772
corn, sorghum and rye = bushels X 0.0254
oats = bushels X 0.014515

1 tonne (metric ton) equals:
2204.622 lbs.
1,000 kilograms
22.046 hundredweight
10 quintals

1 tonne (metric ton) equals:
36.7437 bushels of wheat or soybeans
39.3679 bushels of corn, sorghum or rye
45.9296 bushels of barley grain
68.8944 bushels of oats
4.5929 cotton bales (the statistical bale used by the USDA and ICAC contains a net weight of 480 pounds of lint)

Area Measurements:
1 acre = 43,560 square feet = 0.040694 hectare
1 hectare = 2.4710 acres = 10,000 square meters
640 acres = 1 square mile = 259 hectares

Yields:
wheat: bushels per acre X 0.6725 = quintals per hectare
rye, corn: bushels per acre X 0.6277 = quintals per hectare
barley grain: bushels per acre X 0.538 = quintals per hectare
oats: bushels per acre X 0.3587 = quintals per hectare

Commonly Used Weights

The troy, avoirdupois and apothecaries' grains are identical in U.S. and British weight systems, equal to 0.0648 gram in the metric system. One avoirdupois ounce equals 437.5 grains. The troy and apothecaries' ounces equal 480 grains, and their pounds contain 12 ounces.

Troy weights and conversions:
24 grains = 1 pennyweigh
20 pennyweights = 1 ounce
12 ounces = 1 pound
1 troy ounce = 31.103 grams
1 troy ounce = 0.0311033 kilogram
1 troy pound = 0.37224 kilogram
1 kilogram = 32.1507 troy ounces
1 tonne = 32,151 troy ounces

Avoirdupois weights and conversions:
27 11/32 grains = 1 dram
16 drams = 1 ounce
16 ounces = 1 lb.
1 lb. = 7,000 grains
14 lbs. = 1 stone (British)
100 lbs. = 1 hundredweight (U.S.)
112 lbs. = 8 stone = 1 hundredweight (British)
2,000 lbs. = 1 short ton (U.S. ton)
2,240 lbs. = 1 long ton (British ton)
160 stone = 1 long ton
20 hundredweight = 1 ton
1 lb. = 0.4536 kilogram
1 hundredweight (cwt.) = 45.359 kilograms
1 short ton = 907.18 kilograms
1 long ton = 1,016.05 kilograms

Metric weights and conversions:
1,000 grams = 1 kilogram
100 kilograms = 1 quintal
1 tonne = 1,000 kilograms = 10 quintals
1 kilogram = 2.204622 lbs.
1 quintal = 220.462 lbs.
1 tonne = 2204.6 lbs.
1 tonne = 1.102 short tons
1 tonne = 0.9842 long ton

U.S. dry volumes and conversions:
1 pint = 33.6 cubic inches = 0.5506 liter
2 pints = 1 quart = 1.1012 liters
8 quarts = 1 peck = 8.8098 liters
4 pecks = 1 bushel = 35.2391 liters
1 cubic foot = 28.3169 liters

U.S. liquid volumes and conversions:
1 ounce = 1.8047 cubic inches = 29.6 milliliters
1 cup = 8 ounces = 0.24 liter = 237 milliliters
1 pint = 16 ounces = 0.48 liter = 473 milliliters
1 quart = 2 pints = 0.946 liter = 946 milliliters
1 gallon = 4 quarts = 231 cubic inches = 3.785 liters
1 milliliter = 0.033815 fluid ounce
1 liter = 1.0567 quarts = 1,000 milliliters
1 liter = 33.815 fluid ounces
1 imperial gallon = 277.42 cubic inches = 1.2 U.S. gallons = 4.546 liters

Aluminum

Aluminum (symbol Al) is a silvery, lightweight metal that is the most abundant metallic element in the earth's crust. Aluminum was first isolated in 1825 by a Danish chemist, Hans Christian Oersted, using a chemical process involving a potassium amalgam. A German chemist, Friedrich Woehler, improved Oersted's process by using metallic potassium in 1827. He was the first to show aluminum's lightness. In France, Henri Sainte-Claire Deville isolated the metal by reducing aluminum chloride with sodium and established a large-scale experimental plant in 1854. He displayed pure aluminum at the Paris Exposition of 1855. In 1886, Charles Martin Hall in the U.S. and Paul L.T. Heroult in France simultaneously discovered the first practical method for producing aluminum through electrolytic reduction, which is still the primary method of aluminum production today.

By volume, aluminum weighs less than a third as much as steel. This high strength-to-weight ratio makes aluminum a good choice for construction of aircraft, railroad cars, and automobiles. Aluminum is used in cooking utensils and the pistons of internal-combustion engines because of its high heat conductivity. Aluminum foil, siding, and storm windows make excellent insulators. Because it absorbs relatively few neutrons, aluminum is used in low-temperature nuclear reactors. Aluminum is also useful in boat hulls and various marine devices due to its resistance to corrosion in salt water.

Aluminum futures and options are traded on the New York Mercantile Exchange (NYMEX) and the London Metal Exchange. Aluminum futures are traded on the Tokyo Commodity Exchange (TOCOM), the Osaka Mercantile Exchange (OME), and the Shanghai Futures Exchange (SHFE). The NYMEX aluminum futures contract calls for the delivery of 44,000 pounds of aluminum and the contract is priced in terms of cents per pound.

Prices – NYMEX aluminum futures prices showed sharp gains in the first half of 2008 but then collapsed in the second half of the year. Aluminum opened the year at about 120 cents per pound, rallied to 150 cents per pound in July, and then fell sharply to about 70 cents per pound by the end of the year. The decline continued into 2009 by moving lower to the 60 cent range.

Supply – World production of aluminum rose by +4.75% in 2008 to a record high of 39.700 million metric tons. The world's largest producers of aluminum are China with 34% of world production in 2008, Russia (11%), Canada (8%), U.S. (7%), and Australia (5%). U.S. production of primary aluminum in 2008 rose +3.915 yr/yr to 2.656 million metric tons. U.S. production of aluminum from secondary sources in 2007 (latest data available) rose +8.15% yr/yr to 3.850 million metric tons.

Demand – World consumption of aluminum in 2001, the latest reporting year for the series, fell 4.8% yr/yr to 23.613 million metric tons, which was moderately below the record high of 24.811 million metric tons consumed in 2000. U.S. consumption of aluminum in 2008 fell 42.28% yr/yr to 3.700 million metric tons which was a 33-year low.

Trade – U.S. exports in 2008 rose +33.8% yr/yr to a new record high of 3.800 million metric tons. U.S. imports of aluminum in 2008 fell 4.23% yr/yr to 4.300 million metric tons, down from the 2005 record high of 5.330 million metric tons. The U.S. was a net exporter in 2008 but in 2007 the U.S. relied on imports for 19% of its consumption.

World Production of Primary Aluminum   In Thousands of Metric Tons

Year	Australia	Brazil	Canada	China	France	Germany	Norway	Russia	Spain	United Kingdom	United States	Vene-zuela	World Total
1999	1,718	1,250	2,390	2,530	455	634	1,020	3,146	364	272	3,779	570	23,600
2000	1,769	1,277	2,373	2,800	441	644	1,026	3,245	366	305	3,668	571	24,300
2001	1,797	1,140	2,583	3,250	462	652	1,068	3,300	376	341	2,637	571	24,300
2002	1,836	1,318	2,709	4,300	463	653	1,096	3,347	380	344	2,707	605	26,100
2003	1,857	1,381	2,792	5,450	443	661	1,192	3,478	389	343	2,703	601	28,000
2004	1,894	1,457	2,592	6,670	451	668	1,322	3,592	398	360	2,516	624	29,900
2005	1,903	1,499	2,894	7,800	442	648	1,372	3,647	394	369	2,481	615	31,900
2006	1,932	1,604	3,051	9,360	442	516	1,331	3,718	394	360	2,284	610	33,900
2007[1]	1,960	1,610	3,083	12,600	428	551	1,304	3,955	350	365	2,554	610	37,900
2008[2]	1,960	1,660	3,100	13,500		590	1,100	4,200			2,640	550	39,700

[1] Preliminary.   [2] Estimate.   NA = Not available.   *Source: U.S. Geological Survey (USGS)*

Production of Primary Aluminum (Domestic and Foreign Ores) in the U.S.   In Thousands of Metric Tons

Year	Jan.	Feb.	Mar.	Apr.	May	June	July	Aug.	Sept.	Oct.	Nov.	Dec.	Total
1999	315	287	320	309	319	310	319	324	310	323	316	328	3,779
2000	329	308	327	316	327	299	296	296	291	300	289	291	3,668
2001	256	220	232	225	229	215	214	212	206	214	208	205	2,637
2002	210	197	220	216	228	225	238	237	227	235	232	241	2,707
2003	242	220	238	225	228	221	226	225	217	224	215	221	2,702
2004	216	202	217	209	217	204	209	210	203	211	207	211	2,516
2005	209	191	214	211	214	206	210	208	199	207	204	208	2,481
2006	197	179	198	190	197	189	192	185	183	190	188	197	2,285
2007	202	185	217	209	210	209	219	220	216	224	220	225	2,556
2008[1]	233	219	233	228	235	224	225	222	214	217	202	204	2,656

[1] Preliminary.   *Source: U.S. Geological Survey (USGS)*

1

ALUMINUM

Aluminum (monthly average) through December 2008 — Cents per pound

Salient Statistics of Aluminum in the United States   In Thousands of Metric Tons

	Net Import Reliance as a % of Apparent	-- Production ---		Primary Ship-	Recovery from Scrap		Apparent Con-	Plate, Sheet,	Rolled Structural	Ex- truded		Perma- nent				Total All Net Ship-
											Net Shipments[5] by Producers					
										Wrought Products		**Castings**				
Year	Consumption	Primary	Second-ary	ments	Old	New	sumption	Foil	Shapes[3]	Shapes[4]	All	Mold	Die	Sand	All	ments
1998	25	3,713	3,440	9,260	1,500	1,950	7,090	4,760	551	1,560	7,040	511	584	134	1,350	8,390
1999	30	3,779	3,700	9,840	1,570	2,120	7,770	5,000	549	1,640	7,360	484	1,020	158	1,790	9,150
2000	33	3,668	3,450	9,830	1,370	2,080	7,530	4,840	592	1,640	7,240	549	991	152	1,850	9,080
2001	35	2,637	2,970	9,310	1,210	1,760	6,230	4,370	512	1,550	6,580	484	873	251	1,760	8,340
2002	39	2,707	2,930	9,640	1,170	1,750	6,320	4,450	559	1,550	6,710	693	1,280	279	2,450	9,160
2003	38	2,703	2,820	9,760	1,070	1,750	7,120	4,370	531	1,670	6,580	719	1,210	285	2,400	8,970
2004	39	2,516	3,030	10,400	1,160	1,870	7,210	4,750	579	1,810	7,140	735	1,250	221	2,370	9,510
2005	41	2,481	3,030	10,461	1,080	1,950	7,270	5,330	1,080	2,090	8,500	785	1,110	289	2,290	10,790
2006	31	2,284	3,560	10,500	1,260	2,300	6,710	5,330	1,141	2,070	8,541	754	1,170	335	2,310	10,851
2007[1]	19	2,554	3,850	9,710	1,600	2,250	6,410	5,040	1,066	1,790	7,896	615	1,260	315	2,230	10,126

[1] Preliminary.   [2] To domestic industry.   [3] Also rod, bar & wire.   [4] Also rod, bar, tube, blooms & tubing.   [5] Consists of total shipments less shipments to other mills for further fabrication.   *Source: U.S. Geological Survey (USGS)*

Supply and Distribution of Aluminum in the United States   In Thousands of Metric Tons

	Apparent Con-	--- Production ---				Inventories - December 31 -			Apparent Con-	-- Production --				Inventories - December 31 -	
Year	sumption	Primary	From Old Scrap	Imports	Exports	Private	Govern-ment[2]	Year	sumption	Primary	From Old Scrap	Imports	Exports	Private	Govern-ment[2]
1997	6,720	3,603	1,530	3,080	1,570	1,860	[4]	2003	6,130	2,703	1,070	4,130	1,540	1,400	----
1998	7,090	3,713	1,500	3,550	1,590	1,930	----	2004	6,590	2,516	1,160	4,720	1,820	1,470	----
1999	7,770	3,779	1,570	4,000	1,650	1,870	----	2005	6,530	2,481	1,080	5,330	2,370	1,430	----
2000	7,530	3,668	1,370	3,910	1,760	1,550	----	2006	6,710	2,284	1,260	5,180	2,820	1,410	----
2001	6,230	2,637	1,210	3,740	1,590	1,300	----	2007[1]	6,410	2,554	1,600	4,490	2,840	1,400	----
2002	6,320	2,707	1,170	4,060	1,590	1,320	----	2008[2]	3,700	2,640	1,400	4,300	3,800	1,300	----

[1] Preliminary.   [2] Estimate.   [3] National Defense Stockpile.   [4] Less than 1/2 unit.   *Source: U.S. Geological Survey (USGS)*

Aluminum Products Distribution of End-Use Shipments in the United States In Thousands of Metric Tons

Year	Building & Construction	Consumer Durables	Containers and Packaging	Electrical	Exports	Machinery and Equipment	Trans-portation	Other	Total
1998	1,390	725	2,270	714	1,260	629	3,250	273	10,500
1999	1,470	760	2,320	739	1,330	661	3,600	293	11,200
2000	1,450	767	2,260	771	1,280	679	3,600	293	11,100
2001	1,500	681	2,250	686	902	641	3,190	367	10,200
2002	1,560	722	2,260	677	1,070	616	3,410	390	10,700
2003	1,560	689	2,240	653	905	659	3,540	415	10,700
2004	1,680	713	2,310	720	930	730	3,860	416	11,400
2005	1,671	708	2,320	746	1,125	741	3,939	336	11,586
2006	1,650	746	2,320	774	1,270	762	3,930	330	11,800
2007[1]	1,410	669	2,220	745	1,450	736	3,580	359	11,200

[1] Preliminary.   Source: U.S. Geological Survey (USGS)

World Consumption of Primary Aluminum   In Thousands of Metric Tons

Year	Brazil	Canada	China	France	Germany	India	Italy	Japan	Rep. of Korea	Russia	United Kingdom	United States	World Total
1992	377.1	420.4	1,253.8	730.5	1,457.1	414.3	660.0	2,271.6	397.0	1,242.0	550.0	4,616.9	18,529.5
1993	378.9	492.5	1,339.9	667.2	1,150.7	475.3	554.0	2,138.3	524.8	657.0	540.0	4,877.1	18,122.6
1994	414.1	559.0	1,500.1	736.3	1,370.3	475.0	660.0	2,344.8	603.9	470.0	570.0	5,407.1	19,670.8
1995	500.6	611.9	1,941.6	743.8	1,491.3	581.0	665.4	2,335.6	675.4	476.0	620.0	5,054.8	20,480.9
1996	497.0	619.9	2,135.3	671.7	1,355.4	584.8	585.1	2,392.6	674.3	443.8	571.0	5,348.0	20,596.4
1997	478.6	628.2	2,260.3	724.2	1,558.4	553.4	671.0	2,434.3	666.3	469.2	583.0	5,390.0	21,721.8
1998	521.4	720.6	2,425.4	733.8	1,519.0	566.5	675.4	2,082.0	505.7	489.2	579.0	5,813.6	21,797.2
1999	463.1	777.2	2,925.9	774.2	1,438.6	569.5	735.3	2,112.3	814.0	562.8	496.8	6,203.3	23,323.0
2000	513.8	798.7	3,499.1	780.4	1,490.3	602.4	780.3	2,224.9	822.6	748.4	575.5	6,079.5	24,811.4
2001[1]	550.8	759.6	3,545.4	772.9	1,590.9	558.0	770.4	2,014.0	849.6	786.2	433.3	5,117.0	23,612.8

[1] Preliminary.   Source: American Metal Market (AMM)

Salient Statistics of Recycling Aluminum in the United States

Year	Percent Recycled	New Scrap[1]	Old Scrap[2]	Recycled Metal[3]	Apparent Supply	New Scrap[1]	Old Scrap[2]	Recycled Metal[3]	Apparent Supply
		In Thousands of Metric Tons				Value in Millions of Dollars			
1997	41	2,020	1,530	3,550	8,740	3,430	2,590	6,020	14,800
1998	38	1,950	1,500	3,440	9,040	2,810	2,160	4,970	13,100
1999	37	2,120	1,570	3,700	9,890	3,070	2,280	5,350	14,300
2000	36	2,080	1,370	3,450	9,610	3,420	2,260	5,670	15,800
2001	37	1,760	1,210	2,970	7,990	2,670	1,830	4,500	12,100
2002	36	1,750	1,170	2,930	8,070	2,510	1,680	4,190	11,500
2003	36	1,750	1,070	2,820	7,880	2,620	1,610	4,230	11,800
2004	36	1,870	1,160	3,030	8,460	3,640	2,140	5,600	15,700
2005	36	1,950	1,080	3,030	8,480	3,910	2,170	6,080	17,000
2006	43	2,310	1,200	3,510	8,160	6,180	3,200	9,380	21,800

[1] Scrap that results from the manufacturing process.   [2] Scrap that results from consumer products.   [3] Metal recovered from new plus old scrap.
Source: U.S. Geological Survey (USGS)

Producer Prices for Aluminum Used Beverage Can Scrap   In Cents Per Pound

Year	Jan.	Feb.	Mar.	Apr.	May	June	July	Aug.	Sept.	Oct.	Nov.	Dec.	Average
1999	44.50	44.50	44.20	45.68	47.45	46.50	48.40	49.00	49.00	53.79	55.50	57.64	48.84
2000	58.58	62.90	61.50	56.85	54.50	54.50	56.50	57.00	57.00	56.20	53.50	53.50	56.88
2001	54.26	55.50	55.45	54.50	54.23	50.79	46.93	45.50	45.50	44.63	44.50	44.50	49.71
2002	44.50	44.66	47.21	49.41	48.68	48.50	46.89	45.06	46.36	47.07	49.76	50.29	47.37
2003	50.50	52.30	52.45	49.43	50.17	49.75	49.22	49.83	47.43	50.17	52.00	53.73	50.58
2004	57.44	61.64	61.65	63.00	57.85	60.00	62.23	60.57	59.48	62.07	61.45	63.81	60.93
2005	64.80	65.79	71.91	71.40	64.75	62.23	60.05	62.96	60.40	61.76	65.25	72.90	65.35
2006	81.03	85.76	85.13	91.08	99.41	83.50	83.40	82.74	80.70	79.66	83.90	85.00	85.11
2007	89.05	89.58	90.18	93.14	93.16	87.86	85.90	80.39	76.37	79.57	82.98	79.68	85.66
2008	82.81	90.35	100.19	100.09	97.52	98.88	98.75	88.83	79.38	63.43	55.67	46.33	83.52

Source: American Metal Market (AMM)

ALUMINUM

Average Price of Cast Aluminum Scrap (Crank Cases) in Chicago[1]   In Cents Per Pound

Year	Jan.	Feb.	Mar.	Apr.	May	June	July	Aug.	Sept.	Oct.	Nov.	Dec.	Average
1999	25.50	25.50	25.50	25.50	26.45	29.23	36.83	37.50	37.50	37.50	37.50	37.50	31.87
2000	37.50	37.50	37.50	35.55	31.09	30.32	30.30	32.00	32.00	31.09	31.00	31.00	33.04
2001	31.00	31.00	31.00	31.00	31.00	31.00	28.29	28.00	28.00	28.00	26.40	26.00	29.25
2002	26.00	27.47	28.95	30.00	30.00	30.00	30.00	29.64	28.00	28.00	28.00	28.00	28.67
2003	28.10	30.00	30.00	29.00	29.00	27.90	26.68	26.00	26.00	26.00	26.00	26.00	27.56
2004	30.00	31.26	36.00	36.00	33.00	29.00	29.00	29.00	29.00	29.00	29.00	29.00	30.77
2005	29.00	29.00	31.61	33.00	31.33	28.00	28.00	28.00	28.00	28.00	28.00	39.71	30.14
2006	42.50	42.50	43.80	47.50	47.50	55.91	46.48	45.46	44.50	46.45	51.15	51.10	47.07
2007	52.50	52.50	54.00	55.50	55.50	53.07	52.50	52.50	51.34	50.50	50.50	50.50	52.58
2008	50.50	52.00	58.50	62.09	60.12	57.50	60.00	60.60	53.69	35.76	26.94	18.45	49.68

[1] Dealer buying prices - prior to 1986 prices are for the New York area.   Source: American Metal Market (AMM)

Aluminum Exports of Crude Metal and Alloys from the United States   In Thousands of Metric Tons

Year	Jan.	Feb.	Mar.	Apr.	May	June	July	Aug.	Sept.	Oct.	Nov.	Dec.	Total
1999	18.6	26.7	23.9	22.7	25.2	27.7	23.7	27.5	26.1	31.4	30.3	34.8	318.6
2000	18.7	27.2	30.2	21.9	24.4	22.4	20.5	24.2	20.5	20.7	20.7	21.6	273.0
2001	19.6	16.1	18.9	14.7	16.8	15.6	12.4	14.5	12.6	18.9	16.7	15.1	191.9
2002	17.1	15.2	15.6	16.4	19.4	18.3	15.0	15.5	17.5	19.8	19.4	16.4	205.6
2003	14.3	14.8	14.5	16.9	17.0	17.8	16.5	20.4	18.7	22.9	20.4	19.7	213.9
2004	18.2	20.8	24.3	25.2	25.1	27.6	23.7	23.0	28.3	26.9	28.0	27.4	298.5
2005	26.5	23.4	24.3	27.0	28.9	29.6	25.9	33.1	27.2	29.5	29.6	23.9	328.9
2006	40.0	26.0	30.5	29.4	38.8	25.3	23.7	32.0	26.1	25.8	27.0	22.0	346.6
2007	32.1	27.1	27.0	28.6	33.8	31.1	26.4	30.3	28.5	29.9	29.6	24.5	348.9
2008[1]	30.8	26.8	26.4	30.4	28.4	27.6	25.9	26.4	27.4	25.3	17.3		319.3

[1] Preliminary.   Source: U.S. Geological Survey (USGS)

Aluminum General Imports of Crude Metal and Alloys into the United States   In Thousands of Metric Tons

Year	Jan.	Feb.	Mar.	Apr.	May	June	July	Aug.	Sept.	Oct.	Nov.	Dec.	Total
1999	191.0	200.0	240.0	311.0	281.0	258.0	213.0	219.0	178.0	202.0	178.0	180.0	2,651.0
2000	246.0	213.0	206.0	211.0	233.0	234.0	250.0	206.0	189.0	186.0	181.0	137.0	2,490.0
2001	193.0	200.0	237.0	197.0	209.0	179.0	201.0	198.0	252.0	220.0	248.0	227.0	2,561.0
2002	272.0	205.0	223.0	221.0	221.0	263.0	228.0	279.0	235.0	196.0	264.0	186.0	2,793.0
2003	215.0	246.0	350.0	202.0	265.0	261.0	233.0	194.0	215.0	210.0	233.0	243.0	2,867.0
2004	211.0	288.0	248.0	254.0	282.0	309.0	297.0	225.0	279.0	286.0	272.0	294.0	3,245.0
2005	334.0	289.0	262.0	372.0	372.0	324.0	324.0	264.0	282.0	298.0	240.0	299.0	3,660.0
2006	348.0	247.0	289.0	353.0	315.0	298.0	249.0	315.0	289.0	259.0	233.0	241.0	3,436.0
2007	251.0	258.0	238.0	259.0	220.0	254.0	236.0	266.0	268.0	244.0	238.0	215.0	2,947.0
2008[1]	240.0	208.0	247.0	238.0	237.0	263.0	227.0	204.0	229.0	249.0	219.0		2,793.8

[1] Preliminary.   Source: U.S. Geological Survey (USGS)

Average Open Interest of Aluminum Futures in New York   In Contracts

Year	Jan.	Feb.	Mar.	Apr.	May	June	July	Aug.	Sept.	Oct.	Nov.	Dec.
2002	3,277	2,744	2,738	2,250	2,397	2,902	3,903	4,618	4,643	5,139	8,057	10,479
2003	9,573	9,163	6,960	7,190	7,686	8,529	8,402	8,445	7,655	7,283	8,434	9,427
2004	8,815	7,384	9,666	10,575	10,363	10,370	9,626	10,287	10,292	10,035	9,706	8,879
2005	8,183	8,487	7,464	6,612	5,654	5,061	4,359	3,223	3,225	2,676	2,232	1,670
2006	1,066	708	482	1,110	948	816	1,068	1,125	1,116	865	994	950
2007	608	614	491	450	415	368	329	276	237	194	156	132
2008	0	0	0	0	0	0	0	0	0	0	0	0

Source: CME Group; New York Mercantile Exchange (NYMEX)

Volume of Trading of Aluminum Futures in New York   In Contracts

Year	Jan.	Feb.	Mar.	Apr.	May	June	July	Aug.	Sept.	Oct.	Nov.	Dec.	Total
2002	2,774	4,635	4,924	2,593	5,388	5,389	8,953	4,194	2,571	7,328	16,185	9,066	74,000
2003	12,565	9,625	8,163	5,440	10,567	8,463	11,797	9,451	5,119	6,222	8,536	11,542	107,490
2004	9,425	9,621	9,548	9,770	5,438	5,453	5,280	2,063	5,533	4,822	2,525	2,691	72,169
2005	5,294	2,829	3,244	2,627	2,613	1,832	1,247	902	1,625	623	3,135	2,520	28,491
2006	633	245	1,343	1,558	210	471	1,046	1,546	662	323	842	270	9,149
2007	94	332	82	28	2	56	84	19	25	0	1	0	723
2008	0	0	0	0	0	0	0	0	0	0	0	0	

Source: CME Group; New York Mercantile Exchange (NYMEX)

Antimony

Antimony (symbol Sb) is a lustrous, extremely brittle and hard crystalline semi-metal that is silvery white in its most common allotropic form. Antimony is a poor conductor of heat and electricity. In nature, antimony has a strong affinity for sulfur and for such metals as lead, silver, and copper. Antimony is primarily a byproduct of the mining, smelting and refining of lead, silver, and copper ores. There is no longer any mine production of antimony in the U.S.

The most common use of antimony is in antimony trioxide, a chemical that is used as a flame retardant in textiles, plastics, adhesives and building materials. Antimony trioxide is also used in battery components, ceramics, bearings, chemicals, glass, and ammunition.

Prices – Antimony prices in 2008 rose by +13.0% to a record high average of 287.00 cents per pound. Antimony prices in 2008 were more than four times the 33-year low price of 66.05 cents per pound posted as recently as 1999. Bullish factors included stronger U.S. and global economic growth in 2008, the weak dollar, and tight supplies.

Supply – World mine production of antimony in 2008 fell by 2.94% to 165,000 metric tons. China accounted for 91% of world antimony production in 2008. After China, the only significant producers were Bolivia (2% of world production) and South Africa (1.8%). U.S. secondary production of antimony in 2008 fell by -3.74%yr/yr to 3,350 metric tons from 3,480 metric tons in 2007.

Demand – U.S. industrial consumption of antimony in 2007 (latest data available) fell 7.79% to 9,590 metric tons from 10,400 metric tons in 2006. Of the consumption in the U.S. in 2007, 29% was used for flame-retardants, 26% was used for metal products, and 36% was used for non-metal products.

Trade –Total U.S. imports of antimony ore in 2007 (latest data available) fell by -5.78% from 2006. Gross weight rose by 53% to 313 metric tons and antimony content rose by 48% to 226 metric tons. U.S. exports of antimony oxide in 2007 fell by -2.28% to 1,640 metric tons from 1,680metric tons in 2006.

World Mine Production of Antimony (Content of Ore)   In Metric Tons

Year	Australia	Bolivia	Canada	China[2]	Guat-emala	Kyrgy-zstan	Mexico[3]	Peru[4]	Russia	South Africa	Thailand	Turkey	World Total
2004	120	2,633	105	125,000	2,686	20	----	356	3,000	4,967	52	900	142,000
2005	120	5,098	79	152,000	1,007	10	----	807	3,000	5,979	347	1,000	171,000
2006[1]	1,600	5,460	90	153,000	----	50	----	810	3,500	4,362	936	1,300	173,000
2007[2]	2,000	5,500	90	150,000	----	30	----	810	3,500	4,400	----	1,500	170,000

[1] Preliminary.   [2] Estimate.   [3] Includes antimony content of miscellaneous smelter products.   [4] Recoverable.
Source: U.S. Geological Survey (USGS)

Salient Statistics of Antimony in the United States   In Metric Tons

Year	Avg. Price Cents/lb. C.i.F. U.S. Ports	Primary[2] Mine	Primary[2] Smelter	Secondary (Alloys)[2]	Ore Gross Weight	Ore Antimony Content	Oxide (Gross Weight)	Exports (Oxide)	Metallic	Oxide	Sulfide	Other	Total
2004	130.3	----	W	3,650	1,820	1,750	28,300	3,240	483	2,330	W	16	2,830
2005	160.5	----	W	3,030	207	204	27,300	1,400	417	1,680	W	17	2,110
2006[1]	238.0	----	W	3,520	205	153	27,700	1,680	421	1,690	W	15	2,120
2007[2]	257.3	W	W	3,480	313	226	26,100	1,640	424	1,450	W	18	1,900

[1] Preliminary.   [2] Estimate.   [3] Antimony content.   [4] Including primary antimony residues & slag.   W = Withheld proprietary data.
Source: U.S. Geological Survey (USGS)

Industrial Consumption of Primary Antimony in the United States   In Metric Tons (Antimony Content)

Year	Ammu-nition	Anti-monial Lead[3]	Sheet Metal & Pipe[4]	Bearing Metal & Bearings	Solder	Products	Flame Retardants Plastics	Flame Retardants Total	Ceramics & Glass	Pigments	Plastics	Total	Grand Total
2004	W	1,200	W	51	85	3,020	4,680	5,910	535	536	W	2,480	11,400
2005	W	W	W	33	81	2,940	2,880	3,840	421	530	W	2,360	9,140
2006	W	W	W	20	61	3,000	2,810	3,810	258	215	W	3,600	10,400
2007[1]	W	W	W	21	71	2,520	2,820	2,710	231	329	W	3,500	9,590

[1] Preliminary.   [2] Estimated coverage based on 77% of the industry.   W = Withheld proprietary data.   *Source: U.S. Geological Survey (USGS)*

Average Price of Antimony[1] in the United States   In Cents Per Pound

Year	Jan.	Feb.	Mar.	Apr.	May	June	July	Aug.	Sept.	Oct.	Nov.	Dec.	Average
2005	138.35	138.35	146.63	147.42	147.42	148.66	156.49	157.48	168.96	174.63	174.63	170.72	155.81
2006	172.99	183.14	212.50	242.22	244.94	238.86	241.81	252.39	255.15	250.30	252.47	252.88	233.30
2007	252.88	252.88	252.26	251.75	251.75	250.42	249.74	258.55	254.24	255.39	258.24	258.55	253.89
2008	257.27	275.29	281.23	281.23	287.42	292.57	294.84	294.84	294.84	294.84	294.84	294.84	287.00

[1] Prices are for antimony metal (99.65%) merchants, minimum 18-ton containers, c.i.f. U.S. Ports.   *Source: American Metal Market (AMM)*

Apples

The apple tree is the common name of trees from the rose family, Rosaceae, and the fruit that comes from them. The apple tree is a deciduous plant and grows mainly in the temperate areas of the world. The apple tree is believed to have originated in the Caspian and Black Sea area. Apples were the favorite fruit of the ancient Greeks and Romans. The early settlers brought apple seeds with them and introduced them to America. John Champman, also known as Johnny Appleseed, was responsible for extensive planting of apple trees in the Midwestern United States.

Prices – The average monthly price of apples received by growers in the U.S. rose by +20.1% yr/yr to 39.4 cents per pound in 2008.

Supply – World apple production in the 2008-09 marketing year rose +7.9% yr/yr to 56.234 million metric tons. The world's largest apple producers in 2008-09 were China (with 51% of world production), the European Union (20%), the U.S. (7%), and Russia (3%). U.S. apple production in 2008-09 fell -0.3% to 4.102 million metric tons, but remained above the 2-decade low of 3.798 million metric tons posted in 2002-03.

Demand – The utilization breakdown of the 2007 apple crop showed that 67% of apples were for fresh consumption, 33% for canning, 14% for juice and cider, 2% for frozen apples, and 2% for dried apples. U.S. per capita apple consumption in 2007 was 16.4 pounds.

World Production of Apples[3], Fresh (Dessert & Cooking)   In Thousands of Metric Tons

Year	Argentina	Canada	Chile	China	European Union	Japan	Mexico	New Zealand	Russia	South Africa	Turkey	United States	World Total
2003-04	900	379	1,252	21,100	----	842	494	550	1,489	725	2,600	3,947	44,988
2004-05	1,200	381	1,120	23,675	----	755	573	504	1,500	659	2,300	4,699	46,097
2005-06	1,040	409	1,240	20,400	----	819	587	440	1,563	638	2,570	4,355	41,691
2006-07	1,100	403	1,250	26,059	11,134	860	505	453	1,250	712	2,002	4,433	53,832
2007-08[1]	940	406	1,350	24,800	9,724	860	530	441	1,800	720	2,458	4,113	52,101
2008-09[2]	970	360	1,390	28,500	11,239	860	540	470	1,800	725	1,300	4,102	56,234

[1] Preliminary.   [2] Estimate.   NA = Not available.   Source: Foreign Agricultural Service, U.S. Department of Agriculture (FAS-USDA)

Salient Statistics of Apples[2] in the United States

Year	Production Total	Production Utilized	Growers Prices Fresh Cents/lb.	Growers Prices Processing $/ton	Fresh	Canned	Dried	Frozen	Juice & Cider	Other[3]	Avg. Fram Price Cents/lb.	Farm Value Million $	Exports Fresh	Dried[5]	Imports Fresh & Dried[5]	Fresh Per Capita Consumption Lbs.
2002	8,524	8,374	25.8	130.0	5,366	3,008	208	192	1,479	51	18.9	1,572.2	519.3	26.3	187.1	16.0
2003	8,793	8,703	29.4	131.0	5,462	3,241	182	283	1,435	106	20.9	1,817.2	447.4	33.0	214.4	16.9
2004	10,441	10,361	18.1	107.0	6,638	3,723	201	256	1,876	79	13.5	1,403.0	607.4	32.4	119.2	18.8
2005	9,705	9,603	24.4	106.0	6,117	3,485	191	259	1,709	64	17.4	1,675.1	675.1		158.2	16.7
2006	9,872	9,776	31.7	132.0	6,342	3,434	253	200	1,561	61	22.9	2,236.1	638.0		194.0	17.8
2007[1]	9,114	9,070	37.7	189.0	6,091	2,979	204	178	1,264	63	28.4	2,579.7	652.5		206.6	16.4

Utilization of Quantities Sold — Processed[5] — Millions of Pounds. Foreign Trade[4] — Domestic. Metric Tons.

[1] Preliminary.   [2] Commercial crop.   [3] Mostly crushed for vinegar, jam, etc.   [4] Year beginning July.   [5] Fresh weight basis.
NA = Not available.   Source: Economic Research Service, U.S. Department of Agriculture (ERS-USDA)

Price of Apples Received by Growers (for Fresh Use) in the United States   In Cents Per Pound

Year	Jan.	Feb.	Mar.	Apr.	May	June	July	Aug.	Sept.	Oct.	Nov.	Dec.	Average
2003	25.8	24.6	22.6	23.4	21.8	22.4	20.8	34.6	27.1	27.9	29.7	27.9	25.7
2004	30.4	30.0	30.4	29.8	29.6	30.1	30.0	26.8	26.8	26.1	24.5	22.2	28.1
2005	21.6	20.3	18.4	17.3	17.4	16.2	15.7	21.1	30.9	28.8	29.4	25.8	21.9
2006	21.7	20.6	19.8	19.3	18.9	22.9	42.3	35.9	42.0	36.2	36.1	31.0	28.9
2007	29.9	29.7	29.2	28.1	26.9	29.6	30.6	34.4	40.2	37.9	40.3	35.0	32.7
2008[1]	35.5	34.7	34.4	33.5	33.9	40.9	44.6	53.4	53.6	44.2	34.2	29.6	39.4

[1] Preliminary.   Source: Economic Research Service, U.S. Department of Agriculture (ERS-USDA)

Apples (monthly average) through December 2008   Cents per pound

Arsenic

Arsenic (symbol As) is a silver-gray, extremely poisonous, semi-metallic element. Arsenic, which is odorless and flavorless, has been known since ancient times, but it wasn't until the Middle Ages that its poisonous characteristics first became known. Metallic arsenic was first produced in the 17th century by heating arsenic with potash and soap. Arsenic is rarely found in nature in its elemental form and is generally recovered as a by-product of ore processing. Recently, small doses of arsenic have been found to put some forms of cancer into remission. It can also help thin blood. Homoeopathists have successfully used undetectable amounts of arsenic to cure stomach cramps.

The U.S. does not produce any arsenic and instead imports all its consumption needs for arsenic metals and compounds. More than 95 percent of the arsenic consumed in the U.S. is in compound form, mostly as arsenic trioxide, which in turn is converted into arsenic acid. Production of chromated copper arsenate, a wood preservative, accounts for about 90% of the domestic consumption of arsenic trioxide. Three companies in the U.S. manufacture chromate copper arsenate. Another company used arsenic acid to produce an arsenical herbicide. Arsenic metal is used to produce nonferrous alloys, primarily for lead-acid batteries.

One area where there is increased consumption of arsenic is in the semiconductor industry. Very high-purity arsenic is used in the production of gallium arsenide. High speed and high frequency integrated circuits that use gallium arsenide have better signal reception and lower power consumption. An estimated 30 metric tons per year of high-purity arsenic is used in the production of semiconductor materials.

In the early 2000's, as much as 88% of U.S. arsenic production was used for wood preservative treatments, so the demand for arsenic was closely tied to new home construction, home renovation, and deck construction. However, the total demand for arsenic in 2004 dropped by 69% from 2003, and due to arsenic's toxicity and tighter environmental regulation; only 65% of that much smaller amount was used for wood preservative treatments. Since then the specific percentage used for wood preservative treatments is no longer available.

Supply –World production of white arsenic (arsenic trioxide) in 2008 fell by -4.29% to 53,500 metric tons from the 2007 level of 55,900 metric tons. The world's largest producer is China with about 47% of world production, followed by Chile with 22% of world production, Peru with 7%, Mexico with 3%, and Russia with 3%. China's production of arsenic was fairly constant at about 40,000 metric tons per year but that has dropped to about 25,000 to 30,000 in the last five years. The U.S. supply of arsenic in 2008 rose by 9.41% to 8,500 metric tons, up further from 2004's 30-year low of 7,022 metric tons.

Demand – U.S. demand for arsenic in 2008 rose by +36.4% to 7,200 metric tons. Use of arsenic since 2004 is not available but in 2004 about 65% was for wood preservatives, 10% was for non-ferrous alloys and electric usage, 10% was for glass, and 3% was for other uses.

Trade – U.S. imports of trioxide arsenic in 2007 (latest data available) fell by -25.6% to 9,220 metric tons from 12,400 metric tons in 2006. U.S. exports of trioxide arsenic in 2008 fell 47.8% to 1,300 metric tons, down further from the record high of 3,273 metric tons in 2005.

World Production of White Arsenic (Arsenic Trioxide) In Metric Tons

Year	Belgium	Bolivia	Canada[4]	Chile	China	France	Germany	Mexico	Namibia[3]	Peru	Philip-pines	Russia	World Total
2000	1,500	318	250	8,000	40,000	1,000	200	2,522	----	2,495	----	1,500	62,800
2001	1,000	846	250	11,500	39,500	1,000	200	2,381	----	2,800	----	1,500	63,000
2002	1,000	237	250	11,400	40,000	1,000	100	1,946	----	2,970	----	1,500	62,400
2003	1,000	276	250	11,600	40,000	----	----	1,729	----	4,640	----	1,500	69,700
2004	1,000	168	250	11,500	30,000	----	----	1,829	----	3,037	----	1,500	57,800
2005	1,000	120	250	11,700	30,000	----	----	1,664	----	3,150	----	1,500	60,000
2006[1]	1,000	240	250	11,700	30,000	----	----	1,595	----	4,399	----	1,500	61,200
2007[2]	1,000	200	250	11,400	25,000	----	----	1,600	----	4,320	----	1,500	55,900

[1] Preliminary. [2] Estimate. [3] Output of Tsumeb Corp. Ltd. only. [4] Includes low-grade dusts that were exported to the U.S. for further refining.
Source: U.S. Geological Survey (USGS)

Salient Statistics of Arsenic in the United States (In Metric Tons -- Arsenic Content)

	Supply				Distribution		Estimated Demand Pattern							Average Price			
	Imports		Industry			Industry	Agricul-tural			Non-Ferrous				Trioxide	Metal		
	Metal	Com-pounds	Stocks Jan. 1	Total	Apparent Demand	Stocks Dec. 31	Chem-icals	Glass	Wood Preserv-atives	Alloys & lectric	Other	Total		Mexican	Chinese	Imports Trioxide[3]	Exports
Year													-- Cents/Pound --				
2001	1,030	23,900	----	24,930	24,900	----	----	750	21,900	1,000	250	24,900	----	----	31,500	57
2002	879	18,800	----	19,679	19,600	----	----	700	17,300	650	200	19,600	----	----	24,700	100
2003	990	20,800	----	21,790	21,600	----	----	660	19,200	660	200	21,600	----	----	27,300	173
2004	872	6,150	----	7,022	6,800	----	----	650	4,450	650	200	6,800	----	----	8,090	220
2005	812	8,330	----	9,142	5,870	----	----	NA	NA	NA	NA	5,870	----	----	11,000	3,270
2006	1,070	9,430	----	10,500	7,450	----	----	NA	NA	NA	NA	7,450	----	----	12,400	3,060
2007[1]	759	7,010	----	7,769	5,280	----	----	NA	NA	NA	NA	5,280	----	----	9,220	2,490
2008[2]	500	8,000	----	8,500	7,200	----	----	NA	NA	NA	NA	7,200	----	----		1,300

[1] Preliminary. [2] Estimate. [3] For Consumption. *Source: U.S. Geological Survey (USGS)*

Barley

Barley is the common name for the genus of cereal grass and is native to Asia and Ethiopia. Barley is an ancient crop and was grown by the Egyptians, Greek, Romans and Chinese. Barley is now the world's fourth largest grain crop, after wheat, rice, and corn. Barley is planted in the spring in most of Europe, Canada and the United States. The U.S. barley crop year begins June 1. It is planted in the autumn in parts of California, Arizona and along the Mediterranean Sea. Barley is hardy and drought resistant and can be grown on marginal cropland. Salt-resistant strains are being developed for use in coastal regions. Barley grain, along with hay, straw, and several by-products are used for animal feed. Barley is used for malt beverages and in cooking. Barley, like other cereals, contains a large proportion of carbohydrate (67%) and protein (12.8%). Barley futures are traded on the Winnipeg Commodity Exchange (WCE), the London International Financial Futures and Options Exchange (LIFFE) and the Budapest Commodity Exchange.

Prices – The monthly average price for all barley received by U.S. farmers in the 2008-09 marketing year (through January 2009) rose by +27.7% yr/yr to $5.28 per bushel.

Supply – World barley production in the 2008-09 marketing year rose +15.0% yr/yr to a 14-year high of 154.637 million metric tons. The world's largest barley crop of 179.038 million metric tons occurred in 1990-91. The world's largest barley producers are the European Union with 42.3% of world production in 2008-09, Russia (14.9%), Ukraine (8.2%), Canada (7.6%), Australia (4.5%), Turkey (3.6%), and the U.S. (3.4%).

U.S. barley production in the 2008-09 marketing year rose by +13.1% yr/yr to 239.498 million bushels but that was still only about 40% of the record U.S. barley crop of 608.532 million bushels seen in 1986-87. U.S. farmers harvested 3.767 million acres of barley in 2008-09. That is up +7.4% from the 2006-07 level of 2.951 million acres which was the lowest acreage since 1885. Furthermore, the barley yield in 2008-09 rose 5.3% yr/yr to 63.6 bushels per acre, but still below the 2004-05 record high yield of 69.6 bushels per acre. Ending stocks for the 2008-09 marketing year fell -4.1% to 71.0 million bushels which is far below the 10-year high of 128.4 million bushels in 2004-05.

Demand – U.S. total barley disappearance in 2008-09 fell -3.1% yr/yr to 235.0 million bushels. About 66% of barley is used for food and alcoholic beverages, 31% for animal feed, and 3% for seed.

Trade – World exports of barley in 2008-09 rose by +3.14% yr/yr to a 12-year high of 18.990 million metric tons. The largest world exporters of barley in 2008-09 were the European Union with 21% of world exports, Australia with 18%, Canada with 11%, and the U.S. with only 2%. The single largest importer of barley is Saudi Arabia with 7.000 million metric tons of imports in 2008-09.

World Barley Supply and Demand   In Thousands of Metric Tons

| | ----- Exports ----- | | | | | | ----- Imports ----- | | | | ----- Utilization ----- | | ----- Ending Stocks ----- | | |
Year	Aus-tralia	Can-ada	European Union	Total Non-US	United States	Total	Saudi Arabia	Unac-counte	Total	Russia	United States	Total	Can-ada	United States	Total
1999-00	2,870	1,806	10,738	17,927	853	18,780	5,900	110	18,780	11,441	6,571	132,196	2,838	2,424	24,047
2000-01	3,924	1,956	6,049	15,162	1,068	16,230	5,100	537	15,774	12,700	6,407	133,973	2,516	2,314	22,214
2001-02	4,590	1,126	3,654	16,656	517	17,173	6,200	489	16,902	14,250	5,661	136,203	2,047	2,006	28,850
2002-03	2,159	304	6,102	15,754	552	16,306	7,650	225	16,161	15,500	5,179	137,538	1,475	1,510	26,678
2003-04	6,104	1,937	986	14,444	384	14,828	5,700	444	14,572	18,600	4,990	145,552	2,102	2,619	22,513
2004-05	4,481	1,476	4,240	16,194	771	16,965	6,500	530	16,536	16,500	5,672	143,271	3,435	2,796	32,786
2005-06	5,231	1,876	2,587	17,210	357	17,567	7,100	660	16,791	15,500	4,570	139,989	3,289	2,350	28,546
2006-07	1,927	1,337	4,389	13,994	528	14,522	6,000	350	14,233	16,400	4,596	144,365	1,492	1,500	21,048
2007-08[1]	3,377	2,947	3,888	17,511	901	18,412	7,800	455	18,121	15,050	4,376	135,797	1,573	1,485	20,186
2008-09[2]	3,500	2,100	4,000	18,540	450	18,990	7,000		18,560	17,900	5,225	145,967	1,953	1,692	28,794

[1] Preliminary.   [2] Estimate.   *Source: Foreign Agricultural Service, U.S. Department of Agriculture (FAS-USDA)*

World Production of Barley   In Thousands of Metric Tons

Year	Australia	Belarus	Canada	China	European Union	India	Iran	Kazakhstan	Russia	Turkey	Ukraine	United States	World Total
1999-00	5,032	1,181	13,196	2,970	59,253	1,470	1,600	2,250	10,600	6,600	6,425	5,922	127,490
2000-01	6,743	1,378	13,172	2,646	59,936	1,447	1,686	14,100	7,400	6,872	6,919	133,093
2001-02	8,280	1,700	10,846	2,893	58,767	1,432	2,423	2,200	19,500	6,900	10,186	5,407	143,347
2002-03	3,865	1,681	7,489	3,322	58,168	1,500	3,085	2,200	18,700	7,200	10,364	4,940	134,950
2003-04	10,387	1,800	12,164	2,717	55,818	1,410	2,908	2,100	18,000	6,900	6,850	6,059	142,539
2004-05	7,740	2,000	12,557	3,222	64,085	1,300	2,940	1,500	17,200	7,400	11,100	6,091	152,674
2005-06	9,483	1,800	11,678	3,400	54,752	1,200	2,857	1,500	15,800	7,600	9,000	4,613	136,756
2006-07	4,257	1,350	9,573	3,300	56,220	1,220	3,000	1,900	18,100	7,500	11,350	3,923	137,430
2007-08[1]	7,191	1,700	10,984	3,185	57,732	1,330	3,000	2,500	15,650	6,000	6,000	4,575	134,439
2008-09[2]	7,000	2,000	11,780	3,400	65,477	1,400	2,000	1,800	23,100	5,600	12,600	5,214	154,637

[1] Preliminary.   [2] Estimate.   *Source: Foreign Agricultural Service, U.S. Department of Agriculture (FAS-USDA)*

Barley Acreage and Prices in the United States

Crop Year Beginning June 1	Acreage ------- 1,000 Acres ------ Planted	Harvested for Gain	Yield Per Harvested Acre -- Bushels --	------- Received by Farmers[3] ------- All	Feed[4]	Malting[4]	Portland No. 2 Western	National Average Loan Rate	Target Price	Put Under Support (mil. Bu.)	Percent of Production
				--------- Seasonal Prices ---------			------ Government Price Support Operations ------				
						Dollars per Bushel					
2001-02	4,967	4,289	58.2	2.18	1.74	2.57	2.31	1.65	NA	10.6	4.2
2002-03	5,008	4,123	55.0	2.54	2.16	2.96	2.71	1.88	2.21	10.4	4.6
2003-04	5,348	4,727	58.9	2.90	2.27	3.07	2.74	1.88	2.21	17.9	6.4
2004-05	4,527	4,021	69.6	2.46	1.76	2.79	2.39	1.85	2.24	8.3	3.0
2005-06	3,875	3,269	64.8	2.54	1.89	2.80	2.44	1.85	2.24	12.0	5.7
2006-07	3,452	2,951	61.0	2.90	2.72	2.98	4.08	1.85	2.24	9.3	5.2
2007-08[1]	4,020	3,508	60.4	4.13	4.42	4.00	5.71	1.85	2.24		
2008-09[2]	4,234	3,767	63.6	5.31	3.94	5.47					

[1] Preliminary. [2] Estimate. [3] Excludes support payments. *Source: Economic Research Service, U.S. Department of Agriculture (ERS-USDA)*

Salient Statistics of Barley in the United States   In Millions of Bushels

Crop Year Beginning June 1	------------------- Supply ------------------- Beginning Stocks	Pro- duction	Imports	Total Supply	Food & Alcohol Beverage	Seed	Feed & Residual	Total	Exports	Total Disap- pearance	-------- Ending Stocks -------- Gov't Owned	Privately Owned	Total Stocks
					------------------------- Disappearance -------------------------								
					-------------- Domestic Use --------------								
2001-02	106.3	248.3	23.9	378.5	147.3	8.3	104.3	260.0	26.4	286.4	0	92.1	92.1
2002-03	92.1	226.9	18.5	337.5	145.7	8.7	83.6	237.9	30.3	268.2	0	69.3	69.3
2003-04	69.3	278.3	20.6	368.3	147.5	7.4	74.3	229.2	18.8	247.9	0	120.3	120.3
2004-05	120.3	279.7	12.1	412.2	151.3	6.4	103.3	260.5	23.3	283.8	0	128.4	128.4
2005-06	128.4	211.9	5.4	345.7	152.2	5.7	52.0	209.9	27.8	237.8	0	107.9	107.9
2006-07	107.9	180.2	12.1	300.2	149.0	6.6	55.5	211.1	20.3	231.3	0	68.9	68.9
2007-08[1]	68.9	211.8	31.6	310.6	133.2	7.0	60.0	201.1	41.4	242.5	0	68.2	68.2
2008-09[2]	68.2	239.5	30.0	337.7	138.0	7.0	65.0	210.0	20.0	260.0	0	71.0	71.0

[1] Preliminary. [2] Estimate. [3] Uncommitted inventory. [4] Includes quantity under loan & farmer-owned reserve. [5] Included in Food & Alcohol.
Source: Economic Research Service, U.S. Department of Agriculture (ERS-USDA)

Barley (monthly average) through December 2008 — Cents per pound

BARLEY

Average Price Received by Farmers for All Barley in the United States   In Dollars Per Bushel

Year	June	July	Aug.	Sept.	Oct.	Nov.	Dec.	Jan.	Feb.	Mar.	Apr.	May	Average
2001-02	2.63	2.54	2.77	2.43	2.29	2.45	2.49	2.41	2.31	2.49	2.26	2.46	2.18
2002-03	2.54	2.37	2.50	2.36	2.41	2.58	2.48	2.42	2.55	2.70	2.65	2.97	2.54
2003-04	2.77	2.71	2.70	2.53	2.76	2.92	2.93	3.03	3.09	3.11	3.07	3.12	2.90
2004-05	2.63	2.54	2.77	2.43	2.29	2.45	2.49	2.41	2.31	2.49	2.26	2.46	2.46
2005-06	2.54	2.37	2.50	2.36	2.41	2.58	2.48	2.42	2.55	2.70	2.65	2.97	2.54
2006-07	2.77	2.71	2.70	2.53	2.76	2.92	2.93	3.03	3.09	3.11	3.07	3.12	2.90
2007-08	3.30	3.46	3.55	4.05	4.53	4.31	4.44	4.35	4.39	4.17	4.54	4.52	4.13
2008-09[1]	4.75	5.11	5.11	5.74	5.61	5.41	5.37	5.29	5.37				5.31

[1] Preliminary.   *Source: National Agricultural Statistical Service, U.S. Department of Agriculture (NASS-USDA)*

Average Price Received by Farmers for Feed Barley in the United States   In Dollars Per Bushel

Year	June	July	Aug.	Sept.	Oct.	Nov.	Dec.	Jan.	Feb.	Mar.	Apr.	May	Average
2001-02	1.76	1.61	1.54	1.71	1.86	1.79	1.77	1.67	1.69	1.75	1.79	1.89	1.74
2002-03	1.83	1.88	2.05	2.23	2.26	2.32	2.14	2.17	2.20	2.30	2.20	2.33	2.16
2003-04	2.33	2.22	2.39	2.27	2.24	2.43	2.26	2.15	2.16	2.19	2.17	2.39	2.27
2004-05	2.20	2.21	1.83	1.64	1.58	1.78	1.66	1.65	1.60	1.67	1.56	1.71	1.76
2005-06	1.91	1.88	1.77	1.84	1.81	1.91	1.76	1.94	1.83	1.80	1.81	2.45	1.89
2006-07	2.08	2.04	2.06	2.31	2.68	2.84	2.79	3.11	3.15	3.19	3.20	3.20	2.72
2007-08	3.50	3.27	3.60	4.47	4.89	5.05	4.79	4.89	4.67	4.22	4.65	4.99	4.42
2008-09[1]	5.53	4.70	4.55	4.50	4.14	3.32	3.04	2.96	2.74				3.94

[1] Preliminary.   *Source: National Agricultural Statistical Service, U.S. Department of Agriculture (NASS-USDA)*

Average Open Interest of Western Feed Barley Futures in Winnipeg   In Contracts

2001	19,453	20,515	19,163	19,458	16,020	15,778	16,475	17,202	16,926	13,577	11,407	10,480
2002	9,771	10,653	11,255	11,113	11,141	11,068	11,271	13,046	13,845	12,172	9,000	8,027
2003	8,559	8,203	8,546	9,028	9,631	10,290	10,676	9,580	8,409	7,154	7,524	5,346
2004	6,731	6,881	6,262	9,779	10,497	9,930	9,992	9,743	11,140	11,956	12,786	10,916
2005	9,321	8,164	9,144	9,476	9,475	9,140	6,481	6,880	6,046	5,839	6,538	7,281
2006	8,179	10,505	10,719	12,131	12,543	12,762	12,948	13,680	14,938	16,026	13,803	14,620
2007	16,178	16,769	16,969	15,901	16,351	16,951	13,808	13,941	14,270	15,480	14,337	13,830
2008	14,224	15,626	15,758	14,304	14,394	13,462	12,975	12,052	10,528	9,502	8,462	8,486
2007	16,178	16,769	16,969	15,901	16,351	16,951	13,808	13,941	14,270	15,480	14,337	13,830

Source: ICE Futures Canada; formerly Winnipeg Commodity Exchange (WCE)

Volume of Trading of Western Feed Barley Futures in Winnipeg   In Contracts

Year	Jan.	Feb.	Mar.	Apr.	May	June	July	Aug.	Sept.	Oct.	Nov.	Dec.	Total
2001	26,836	18,732	16,962	24,993	26,361	20,465	20,849	20,137	19,735	21,276	14,926	6,302	237,574
2002	14,268	16,370	15,924	17,663	21,440	18,349	19,860	23,436	22,431	14,471	17,035	10,772	212,019
2003	10,555	18,933	13,069	18,879	13,900	15,153	13,293	29,799	19,438	18,937	17,768	10,977	200,701
2004	11,405	16,265	12,784	23,806	13,179	27,081	15,326	14,933	23,072	15,790	22,516	8,478	204,635
2005	15,452	12,171	19,849	9,325	16,469	14,741	4,100	11,815	7,573	12,665	8,452	3,952	136,564
2006	16,241	9,238	23,987	9,361	26,466	8,083	4,294	25,858	14,903	37,489	12,620	6,484	195,024
2007	24,784	10,380	21,229	12,525	21,161	23,044	11,151	20,457	27,030	27,072	11,926	3,913	214,672
2008	20,247	15,642	20,495	12,950	19,547	14,392	5,719	15,473	13,251	14,171	11,529	3,815	167,231

Source: ICE Futures Canada; formerly Winnipeg Commodity Exchange (WCE)

Bauxite

Bauxite is a naturally occurring, heterogeneous material comprised of one or more aluminum hydroxide minerals plus various mixtures of silica, iron oxide, titanium, alumina-silicates, and other impurities in trace amounts. Bauxite is an important ore of aluminum and forms by the rapid weathering of granite rocks in warm, humid climates. It is easily purified and can be converted directly into either alum or metallic aluminum. It is a soft mineral with hardness varying from 1 to 3, and specific gravity from 2 to 2.55. Bauxite is dull in appearance and may vary in color from white to brown. It usually occurs in aggregates in pea-sized lumps.

Bauxite is the only raw material used in the production of alumina on a commercial scale in the United States. Bauxite is classified according to the intended commercial application, such as abrasive, cement, chemical, metallurgical, and refractory. Of all the bauxite mined, about 95 percent is converted to alumina for the production of aluminum metal with some smaller amounts going to nonmetal uses as various forms of specialty alumina. Small amounts are used in non-metallurgical bauxite applications. Bauxite is also used to produce aluminum chemicals and is used in the steel industry.

Supply – World production of bauxite rose +1.5% yr/yr in 2008 to a new record high of 205 million metric tons.

The world's largest producer of bauxite is Australia with 31% of the world's production in 2007, the latest breakdown available, followed by China (15%), Brazil (12%), India (10%), Guinea (9%), and Jamaica (7%). Chinese production of bauxite has quadrupled in the past 10 years. India's bauxite production has also risen rapidly and is more than triple the amount seen 15 years ago.

Demand – U.S. consumption of bauxite in 2007 fell by −20.1% yr/yr to 9.780 million metric tons from 12.300 million metric tons in 2006. That was still well below the record high of 15.962 million metric tons seen in 1980. The alumina industry took 96% of bauxite production in 2007, or 9.430 million metric tons. According to 2004 data (the latest data available) the refractory industry usually takes about 1.4% of the U.S. bauxite supply, the abrasive industry takes about 0.2%, and the chemical industry takes the rest.

Trade – The U.S. relies on imports for almost 100% of its consumption needs. Domestic ore, which provides less than 1 percent of the U.S. requirement for bauxite, is mined by one company from surface mines in the states of Alabama and Georgia. U.S. imports of bauxite fell 25.0% yr/yr to 9.840 million metric tons in 2007, which was well below the record of 14.976 million metric tons seen in 1974. U.S. exports of bauxite in 2007 were negligible at 15,000 metric tons.

World Production of Bauxite   In Thousands of Metric Tons

Year	Australia	Brazil	China	Greece	Guinea	Guyana[3]	Hungary	India	Jamaica[3]	Russia[3]	Sierra Leone	Suriname	Total
1999	48,416	14,372	8,500	1,883	15,590	2,359	935	6,712	11,688	3,750	----	3,715	129,000
2000	53,802	13,866	9,000	1,991	15,700	2,471	1,047	7,562	11,127	4,200	----	3,610	136,000
2001	53,799	13,032	9,800	2,052	15,100	1,950	1,000	7,864	12,370	4,000	----	4,394	137,000
2002	54,135	13,260	12,000	2,492	15,300	1,690	720	9,647	13,120	4,500	----	4,002	144,000
2003	55,602	17,363	13,000	2,418	15,000	1,846	666	10,414	13,444	5,500	----	4,215	153,000
2004	56,593	20,950	17,000	2,444	15,254	1,506	647	11,285	13,296	6,000	----	4,052	164,000
2005	59,959	22,034	22,000	2,495	16,817	1,648	511	12,385	14,116	6,400	----	4,757	179,000
2006	61,780	22,055	27,000	2,163	16,956	1,558	538	13,940	14,865	6,600	1,072	4,924	190,000
2007[1]	62,400	24,800	30,000	2,220	18,000	1,600	546	19,200	14,600	6,400	1,168	4,900	202,000
2008[2]	63,000	25,000	32,000	2,200	18,000	1,600		20,000	15,000	6,400		4,500	205,000

[1] Preliminary.   [2] Estimate.   [3] Dry Bauxite equivalent of ore processed.   *Source: U.S. Geological Survey (USGS)*

Salient Statistics of Bauxite in the United States   In Thousands of Metric Tons

Year	Net Import Reliance as a % of Apparent Consumption	Average Price F.O.B. Mine $ per Ton	Consumption by Industry Total	Alumina	Abrasive	Chemical	Refractoty	Dry Equivalent Imports[4]	Exports[3]	Consumption	Stocks, December 31 Producers & Consumers	Gov't Owned	Total
1998	100	23	12,700	12,000	135	W	332	11,393	99	12,700	1,860	11,000	12,800
1999	100	22	11,700	11,100	113	W	251	10,189	149	11,700	1,440	6,800	8,250
2000	100	23	10,800	10,100	111	W	160	8,550	133	10,800	1,300	5,710	7,000
2001	100	23	9,770	9,010	61	W	175	8,300	67	9,770	1,740	2,070	3,810
2002	100	20	9,980	9,290	52	W	115	7,340	27	9,980	1,280	1,770	3,050
2003	100	19	11,300	10,600	53	W	150	8,390	55	11,300	3,830	66	3,830
2004	100	22	13,600	12,500	53	W	260	10,000	42	13,600	3,120	----	3,120
2005	100	26	12,400	11,900	W	W	W	11,800	34	12,400	W	----	W
2006[1]	100	28	12,300	11,800	W	W	W	11,600	20	12,300	W	----	W
2007[2]	100		9,780	9,430	W	W	W	9,840	15	9,780	W	----	W

[1] Preliminary.   [2] Estimate.   [3] Including concentrates.   [4] For consumption.   W = Withheld.   *Source: U.S. Geological Survey (USGS)*

Bismuth

Bismuth (symbol Bi) is a rare metallic element with a pinkish tinge. Bismuth has been known since ancient times, but it was confused with lead, tin, and zinc until the middle of the 18th century. Among the elements in the earth's crust, bismuth is ranked about 73rd in natural abundance. This makes bismuth about as rare as silver. Most industrial bismuth is obtained as a by-product of ore extraction.

Bismuth is useful for castings because of the unusual way that it expands after solidifying. Some of bismuth's alloys have unusually low melting points. Bismuth is one of the most difficult of all substances to magnetize. It tends to turn at right angles to a magnetic field. Because of this property, it is used in instruments for measuring the strength of magnetic fields.

Bismuth finds a wide variety of uses such as pharmaceutical compounds, ceramic glazes, crystal ware, and chemicals and pigments. Bismuth is found in household pharmaceuticals and is used to treat stomach ulcers. Bismuth is opaque to X-rays and can be used in fluoroscopy. Bismuth has also found new use as a nontoxic substitute for lead in various applications such as brass plumbing fixtures, crystal ware, lubricating greases, pigments, and solders. There has been environmental interest in the use of bismuth as a replacement for lead used in shot for waterfowl hunting and in fishing sinkers. Another use has been for galvanizing to improve drainage characteristics of galvanizing alloys. Zinc-bismuth alloys have the same drainage properties as zinc-lead without being as hazardous.

Prices – The average price of bismuth (99.99% pure) in the U.S. in 2008 fell by -9.3% to $12.08 per pound, down from $13.32 per pound in 2007. Up until 2007 the prices were in the $3.00 to $4.00 per pound range.

Supply – World mine production of bismuth in 2008 fell -7.9% to 5,800 metric tons, down from last year's record high of 6,300 metric tons. The world's largest producer in 2008 was China with 52% of world production, followed by Mexico with 21%, Peru with 17%, and Canada with 3%. Regarding production of the refined metal, China had 71% of production, Mexico had 10%, Belgium had 7%, and Peru had 5% in 2006, which is the latest data available. The U.S. does not have any significant domestic refinery production of bismuth.

Demand – U.S. consumption of bismuth in 2008 fell −31.2% to 1,080 metric tons, down from the record high of 2,420 metric tons in 2004. In 2006, the latest data available for consumption, 46% went for metallurgical additives, 29% for fusible alloys, 25% for chemicals, and 1% for other uses.

Trade – U.S. imports of bismuth in 2008 rose +13.4% to a record high of 3,480 metric tons. Of U.S. imports, 38% came from Belgium and 24% came from Mexico. U.S. exports of bismuth and alloys 2008 were at a record high of 566 metric tons, up 34.4% from the previous year.

World Production of Bismuth   In Metric Tons (Mine Output=Metal Content)

| | Mine Output, Metal Content | | | | | | Refined Metal | | | | | | |
Year	Canada	China	Japan	Mexico	Peru	Total	Belgium	China	Kazak-hastan[3]	Japan	Mexico	Peru	Total
2002	189	2,000	----	1,126	1,000	4,600	1,000	3,000	130	474	1,126	568	6,700
2003	145	2,500	----	1,064	1,000	5,100	1,000	5,000	130	513	1,064	600	8,700
2004	185	3,000	----	1,064	1,000	5,600	800	11,700	130	522	1,064	600	15,000
2005	185	3,000	----	970	952	5,400	800	8,500	120	463	970	600	12,000
2006	190	3,000	----	1,180	950	5,700	800	8,500	115	510	1,180	600	12,000
2007[1]	190	3,500	----	1,200	950	6,300							
2008[2]	190	3,000		1,200	960	5,800							

[1] Preliminary.   [2] Estimate.   *Source U.S. Geological Survey (USGS)*

Salient Statistics of Bismuth in the United States   In Metric Tons

| | | | Bismuth Consumed, By Uses | | | | | Imports from | | | | |
| | Metal-lurgical | Other Alloys | Fusible | Chem- | Total Con- | Consumer Stocks | Exports of Metal | Metallic Bismuth from | | | | Dealer Price $ Per |
Year	Additives	& Uses	Alloys	icals[3]	sumption	Dec. 31	& Alloys	Belgium	Mexico	Preu	Total	Pound
2001	369	45	981	805	2,200	95	541	728.0	605.0	----	2,220	3.74
2002	388	50	1,070	813	2,320	111	131	724.0	518.0	19.5	1,930	3.14
2003	833	25	646	616	2,120	279	108	778.0	532.0	0.1	2,320	2.87
2004	1,110	22	703	584	2,420	134	109	793.0	495.0	39.8	1,990	3.35
2005	1,150	14	685	498	2,340	136	142	1,050.0	480.0	----	2,530	3.91
2006[1]	923	24	591	510	1,980	158	311	876.0	552.0	17.6	2,300	5.04
2007[2]					1,570	156	421				3,070	14.07

[1] Preliminary.   [2] Estimate.   [3] Includes pharmaceuticals.   *Source: U.S. Geological Survey (USGS)*

Average Price of Bismuth (99.99%) in the United States   In Dollars Per Pound

Year	Jan.	Feb.	Mar.	Apr.	May	June	July	Aug.	Sept.	Oct.	Nov.	Dec.	Average
2005	2.98	2.98	2.98	2.98	2.98	2.98	3.20	4.10	4.17	4.30	4.54	4.63	3.57
2006	4.63	4.63	4.63	4.63	4.63	4.63	4.63	4.63	4.63	4.63	4.63	4.63	4.63
2007	4.63	4.63	8.36	13.00	17.02	18.36	17.64	17.08	15.92	14.89	14.63	13.63	13.32
2008	13.00	12.35	12.00	12.00	14.94	13.70	12.75	12.21	10.50	10.50	10.50	10.50	12.08

Source: American Metal Market (AMM)

Broilers

Broiler chickens are raised for meat rather than for eggs. The broiler industry was started in the late 1950's when chickens were selectively bred for meat production. Broiler chickens are housed in massive flocks mainly between 20,000 and 50,000 birds, with some flocks reaching over 100,000 birds. Broiler chicken farmers usually rear five or six batches of chickens per year.

After just six or seven weeks, broiler chickens are slaughtered (a chicken's natural lifespan is around seven years). Chickens marketed as pouissons, or spring chickens, are slaughtered after four weeks. A few are kept longer than seven weeks to be sold as the larger roasting chickens.

Prices – The average monthly price received by farmers for broilers (live weight) rose in 2008 by +4.5% yr/yr to a record high of 46.9 cents per pound. The average monthly price for wholesale broilers (ready-to-cook) in 2008 rose +4.3% to a record high of 79.67 cents per pound.

Supply – Total production of broilers in 2008 rose by +2.9% yr/yr to 36.975 billion pounds, which was a new record high. The number of broilers raised for commercial production in 2007 (latest data available) was up +0.3% yr/yr to a record high of 8.898 billion birds. The average live-weight per bird rose by +0.4% to 5.53 pounds, which was a new record high and was about 50% heavier than the average bird weight of 3.62 pounds seen in 1970, attesting to the increased efficiency of the industry.

Demand – U.S. per capita consumption of broilers in 2008 rose by +2.4% to 86.8 pounds (ready-to-cook) per person per year, down very slightly from the 2006 record high of 86.9. U.S. consumption of chicken has nearly doubled in the past two decades, up from 47.0 pounds in 1980, as consumers have increased their consumption of chicken because of the focus on low-carb diets and because chicken is a leaner and healthier meat than either beef or pork.

Broiler Supply and Prices in the United States

Years and Quarters	Number (Million)	Average Weight (Pounds)	Liveweight Pounds (Mil. Lbs.)	Certified RTC[3] Weight (Mil. Lbs.)	Total Production RTC[3] (Mil. Lbs.)	Per Capita Consumption RTC[3] Basis (Mil. Lnbs.)	Farm	Georgia Dock[4]
							Cents per Pound	
2003	8,522	5.19	44,247	32,700	32,749	81.6	35.33	64.80
2004	8,762	5.26	46,097	34,064	34,063	84.2	45.17	74.69
2005	8,842	5.37	47,475	35,238	35,365	85.6	43.33	72.83
2006	8,838	5.47	48,333	35,750	35,752	86.9	38.92	68.25
2007[1]	8,889	5.51	48,983	35,964	35,949	84.8	44.92	77.46
2008[2]	8,915	5.58	49,753	35,863	36,975	86.8	46.92	83.11
I	2,225	5.56	12,359	9,108	8,950	21.2	46.67	77.85
II	2,281	5.58	12,736	8,432	9,350	22.1	47.33	81.94
III	2,283	5.58	12,732	9,455	9,350	22.0	47.33	86.72
IV	2,127	5.61	11,926	8,869	9,325	21.6	46.33	85.92

[1] Preliminary.　[2] Estimate.　[3] Total production equals federal inspected slaughter plus other slaughter minus cut-up & further processing condemnation.
[4] Ready-to-cook basis.　*Source: Economic Research Service, U.S. Department of Agriculture (ERS-USDA)*

Salient Statistics of Broilers in the United States

	Commercial Production		Average				Total Chickens[3] Supply and Distribution						Broiler Consumption		
	Number (Mil. Lbs.)	Liveweight (Mil. Lbs.)	Liveweight Per Bird (Mil. Lbs.)	Average Price (cents Lb.)	Value of Production (Mil. $)	Production Federally Inspected	Other Chickens	Total	Storage Stocks January 1	Exports		Feed Ratio (pounds)	Total (Mil. Lbs.)	Per Capita[4] (Pounds)
Year						In Millions of Pounds								
2002	8,591	44,059	5.13	30.5	13,437	31,895	547	32,442	720	4,941		5.5	27,467	80.50
2003	8,493	43,958	5.18	34.6	15,215	32,399	502	32,901	768	4,920		5.4	32,749	81.60
2004	8,741	45,796	5.24	44.6	20,446	33,699	504	34,203	611	4,783		5.9	34,063	84.30
2005	8,872	47,856	5.39	43.6	20,878	34,986	515	35,331	716	5,203		7.0	35,293	85.60
2006	8,868	48,830	5.51	36.3	17,739	35,120	525	35,461	926	5,205		6.2	36,325	87.90
2007[1]	9,036	49,885	5.52	43.6	21,460	35,739			750	5,801		5.1	29,827	85.00
2008[2]	9,075	50,672	5.58			36,505			743	5,900		3.7	30,800	87.00

Preliminary.　[2] Estimate.　[3] Ready-to-cook.　[4] Retail weight basis.　Source: Economic Research Service, U.S. Department of Agriculture (ERS-USDA)

Average Wholesale Broiler[1] Prices RTC (Ready-to-Cook)　In Cents Per Pound

Year	Jan.	Feb.	Mar.	Apr.	May	June	July	Aug.	Sept.	Oct.	Nov.	Dec.	Average
2002	56.86	55.91	55.17	53.47	56.42	58.44	57.47	55.72	55.88	52.97	53.42	54.74	55.54
2003	60.46	60.49	60.02	57.78	59.44	61.56	62.80	63.20	64.08	63.59	64.45	65.71	61.97
2004	68.66	74.96	75.94	76.40	79.54	82.00	81.59	75.44	70.07	68.79	68.08	68.01	74.12
2005	71.40	71.43	72.81	73.21	72.54	72.19	72.47	71.45	72.51	69.02	66.95	63.98	70.83
2006	63.13	63.19	61.77	58.91	59.57	64.44	67.10	68.26	68.18	65.16	65.93	66.48	64.34
2007	70.43	75.89	78.66	78.63	81.00	81.34	80.68	78.82	78.19	70.60	71.74	71.06	76.42
2008[2]	75.91	78.79	79.51	77.84	81.58	82.48	84.60	79.34	77.98	77.65	78.51	81.90	79.67

[1] 12-city composite wholesale price.　[2] Preliminary.　*Source: Economic Research Service, U.S. Department of Agriculture (ERS-USDA)*

Butter

Butter is a dairy product produced by churning the fat from milk, usually cow's milk, until it solidifies. In some parts of the world, butter is also made from the milk of goats, sheep, and even horses. Butter has been in use since at least 2,000 BC. Today butter is used principally as a food item, but in ancient times it was used more as an ointment, medicine, or illuminating oil. Butter was first churned in skin pouches thrown back and forth over the backs of trotting horses.

It takes about 10 quarts of milk to produce 1 pound of butter. The manufacture of butter is the third largest use of milk in the U.S.. California is generally the largest producing state, followed closely by Wisconsin, with Washington as a distant third. Commercially finished butter is comprised of milk fat (80% to 85%), water (12% to 16%), and salt (about 2%). Although the price of butter is highly correlated with the price of milk, it also has its own supply and demand dynamics.

The consumption of butter has dropped in recent decades because pure butter has a high level of animal fat and cholesterol that have been linked to obesity and heart disease. The primary substitute for butter is margarine, which is produced from vegetable oil rather than milk fat. U.S. per capita consumption of margarine has risen from 2.6 pounds in 1930 to recent levels near 8.3 pounds, much higher than U.S. butter consumption.

Futures on butter are traded at the CME Group (CME). The CME's butter futures contract calls for the delivery of 40,000 pounds of Grade AA butter and is priced in cents per pound.

Prices – The average monthly price of butter at the CME Group in 2008 rose by +8.7% yr/yr to 148.70 cents/pound. That is still down from the 2004 record high of 181.66 cents per pound, but higher than the 12-year low of 110.59 cents per pound posted in 2002.

Supply – World production of butter in 2008 fell -18.1% yr/yr to 7.773 million metric tons, down from the record high of 9.492 million metric tons in 2007. The world's largest producers of butter are India with 48% of the world production in 2008, the European Union with 27%, the United States with 10%, New Zealand with 5%, and Russia with 4%. Production of creamery butter by U.S. factories in 2008 rose +7.7% yr/yr to 1.651 billion pounds. That was the highest level since 1943.

Demand – Total commercial use of creamery butter in the U.S rose by +13.0% yr/yr to a record high of 1.716 billion pounds. That is about one-third higher that the commercial use of butter back in the 1950's. Cold storage stocks of creamery butter in the U.S. on December 1, 2008 fell -16.3% yr/yr to 119.946 million pounds.

Trade – World imports of butter in 2008 fell -29.8% yr/yr to 357 thousand metric tons. U.S. imports of butter in 2008 fell -72.2% yr/yr to 5 thousand metric tons. World exports of butter in 2008 fell -35.6% yr/yr to 683 thousand metric tons. U.S exports in 2008 rose +156% yr/yr to a 15-year high of 105 million pounds.

Supply and Distribution of Butter in the United States — In Millions of Pounds

	Supply				Distribution						93 Score	
		Cold			-- Domestic Disappearance --			-- Department of Agriculture --			AA Wholesale Price	
		Storage				Per				Removed		
	Pro-	Stocks[3]		Total		Capita		Stocks[4]	Stocks[4]	by USDA	Total	
Year	duction	Jan. 1	Imports	Supply	Total	(Pounds)	Exports	Jan. 1	Dec 31	Programs	Use	----- $ per Pound -----
1999	1,167	26	39.806	1,337	1,307	4.7	20	0	0	3.7	1,314	1.2396
2000	1,274	25	32.400	1,331	1,329	4.5	7	0	0	8.9	1,289	1.1768
2001	1,237	24	75.000	1,336	1,268	4.4	18	0	0		1,275	1.6630
2002	1,355	56	34.800	1,446	1,293	4.4	8	0	1		1,288	1.1059
2003	1,242	158	32.200	1,432	1,307	4.5	9	1	6	29.1	1,332	1.1450
2004	1,250	100	50.600	1,400	1,326	4.6	26	6	0	-6.6	1,356	1.8166
2005	1,347	45	31.418	1,424	1,335			0			1,370	1.5484
2006[1]	1,448	59									1,435	1.2360
2007[2]	1,533	109									1,516	1.3680

[1] Preliminary. [2] Estimates. [3] Includes butter-equivalent. [4] Includes butteroil. [5] Includes stocks held by USDA.
Source: Economic Research Service, U.S. Department of Agriculture (ERS-USDA)

Quarterly Commercial Disappearance of Creamery Butter in the United States — In Millions of Pounds

Year	First Quarter	Second Quarter	Third Quarter	Fourth Quarter	Total	Year	First Quarter	Second Quarter	Third Quarter	Fourth Quarter	Total
1997	302.7	250.7	265.8	287.6	1,109.0	2003	304.2	275.4	317.2	411.8	1,308.6
1998	289.0	276.3	255.3	308.6	1,137.0	2004	286.3	303.2	340.8	421.1	1,351.4
1999	299.3	316.4	318.3	374.8	1,308.8	2005	287.1	304.9	349.6	423.1	1,364.7
2000	300.8	286.9	332.3	380.6	1,300.6	2006	320.2	308.5	333.2	471.6	1,433.5
2001	290.9	278.4	316.1	397.0	1,282.4	2007	344.6	299.2	376.8	498.3	1,518.9
2002	313.5	263.5	317.4	393.4	1,287.8	2008[1]	399.3	381.4	424.7	510.9	1,716.3

[1] Preliminary. *Source: Economic Research Service, U.S. Department of Agriculture (ERS-USDA)*

14

World Production of Butter[3]   In Thousands of Metric Tons

Year	Australia	Brazil	Canada	Egypt	European Union	India	Japan	Mexico	New Zealand	Russia	Ukraine	United States	World Total
2002	164	70	77	12	2,233	2,400	83	70	380	280	131	615	8,798
2003	163	72	84	13	2,153	2,450	80	77	405	280	148	564	8,766
2004	132	75	84	12	2,164	2,600	80	88	418	270	138	568	8,792
2005	131	77	84	12	2,155	2,749	84	93	379	275	118	615	8,923
2006	129	79	75	10	2,035	3,050	80	109	390	290	105	659	9,078
2007	117	82	79	10	2,053	3,360	75	126	419	300	100	704	9,492
2008[1]	111	84	84		2,060	3,695	73	130	391	305	89	751	7,773
2009[2]	113	86	80		2,075	4,065	75	132	405	310	88	740	8,169

[1] Preliminary.   [2] Forecast.   [3] Factory (including creameries and dairies) & farm.   NA = Not available.
Source: Foreign Agricultural Service, U.S. Department of Agriculture (FAS-USDA)

Production of Creamery Butter in Factories in the United States   In Millions of Pounds

Year	Jan.	Feb.	Mar.	Apr.	May	June	July	Aug.	Sept.	Oct.	Nov.	Dec.	Total
2001	127.4	111.8	111.4	109.0	111.0	86.8	84.2	75.6	86.7	109.9	100.1	123.0	1,236.8
2002	140.1	124.2	127.7	131.6	125.5	95.8	94.4	88.9	92.8	102.6	103.9	127.6	1,355.1
2003	141.9	128.1	126.4	122.8	114.9	84.2	80.1	70.9	73.3	96.8	88.4	114.6	1,242.4
2004	129.3	108.6	100.4	100.3	110.1	99.2	92.6	90.3	94.2	104.4	101.4	118.8	1,249.7
2005	128.0	116.9	122.4	117.1	120.7	106.6	95.9	93.2	100.6	108.9	110.9	126.0	1,347.2
2006	149.8	136.8	141.7	127.7	128.6	101.1	94.7	88.9	104.3	119.1	118.1	137.6	1,448.5
2007	150.6	134.0	138.4	133.0	124.0	110.0	116.5	110.9	112.9	130.4	130.8	141.5	1,532.9
2008[1]	168.8	146.8	151.9	150.1	142.6	119.8	114.2	115.7	121.0	130.0	133.7	156.3	1,651.1

[1] Preliminary.   *Source: Economic Research Service, U.S. Department of Agriculture (ERS-USDA)*

Cold Storage Holdings of Creamery Butter in the United States, on First of Month   In Millions of Pounds

Year	Jan.	Feb.	Mar.	Apr.	May	June	July	Aug.	Sept.	Oct.	Nov.	Dec.
2001	24.1	68.4	86.1	96.2	112.3	138.0	153.5	151.1	118.0	110.9	100.8	57.9
2002	55.9	99.2	130.1	145.2	196.6	226.8	243.0	245.3	229.5	209.1	164.6	135.6
2003	157.8	204.8	239.9	249.0	263.7	298.0	301.4	283.9	253.9	207.2	170.2	122.5
2004	99.6	152.4	159.1	158.1	155.7	178.7	189.2	193.5	161.0	133.0	107.2	57.2
2005	45.0	77.2	110.9	132.4	164.5	178.0	179.6	176.7	148.9	124.1	98.1	60.4
2006	58.6	125.3	169.1	195.3	227.7	261.5	263.0	259.8	215.2	190.6	157.6	108.1
2007	108.6	148.7	185.4	193.1	245.9	270.2	273.0	271.5	260.9	240.3	196.6	143.2
2008[1]	155.2	188.1	210.4	224.8	251.5	269.5	258.4	246.1	213.7	186.9	149.4	119.9

[1] Preliminary.   *Source: Agricultural Statistics Board, U.S. Department of Agriculture (ASB-USDA)*

Average Price of Butter at Chicago Mercantile Exchange[1]   In Cents Per Pound

Year	Jan.	Feb.	Mar.	Apr.	May	June	July	Aug.	Sept.	Oct.	Nov.	Dec.	Average
2001	122.3	138.1	154.9	174.7	190.4	197.4	192.4	204.5	219.7	151.9	135.2	130.2	167.6
2002	134.5	124.3	124.7	117.1	105.9	104.3	103.0	97.5	96.4	103.2	104.3	112.0	110.6
2003	108.2	104.1	109.2	109.1	109.2	111.4	119.9	117.1	117.3	118.5	120.6	129.7	114.5
2004	143.2	171.3	213.5	222.0	203.6	193.0	174.6	154.1	176.6	164.8	192.4	170.8	181.7
2005	157.8	161.5	155.3	149.3	140.4	153.1	162.1	168.6	169.9	162.0	142.6	135.5	154.8
2006	133.7	119.3	116.6	116.3	117.6	116.4	116.5	130.4	131.7	132.1	129.2	124.1	123.6
2007	122.5	121.9	132.2	137.3	148.3	150.2	149.1	144.6	137.8	130.2	135.9	131.9	136.8
2008	122.5	120.9	134.5	139.1	147.5	150.0	153.9	162.8	169.7	173.2	161.7	120.1	146.3

[1] Data through December 2001 are for Wholesale Price of 92 Score Creamery (Grade A) Butter, Central States.
Source: Economic Research Service, U.S. Department of Agriculture (ERS-USDA)

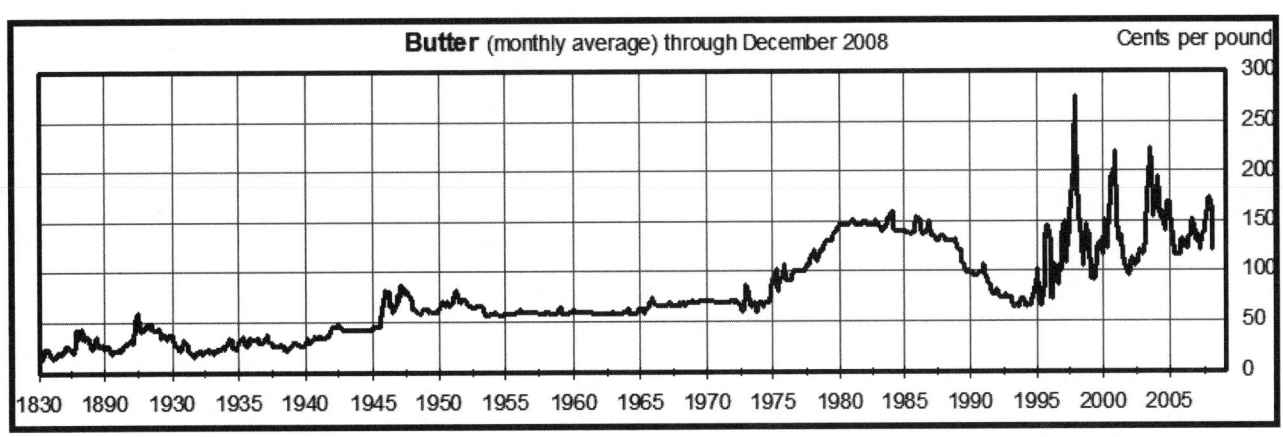

15

Cadmium

Cadmium (symbol Cd) is a soft, bluish-white, metallic element that can easily be shaped and cut with a knife. Cadmium melts at 321 degrees Celsius and boils at 765 degrees Celsius. Cadmium burns brightly in air when heated, forming the oxide CdO. In 1871, the German chemist Friedrich Stromeyer discovered cadmium in incrustations in zinc furnaces.

Rare greenockite is the only mineral bearing cadmium. Cadmium occurs most often in small quantities associated with zinc ores, such as sphalerite. Electrolysis or fractional distillation is used to separate the cadmium and zinc. About 80% of world cadmium output is a by-product from zinc refining. The remaining 20% comes from secondary sources and recycling of cadmium products. Cadmium recycling is practical only from nickel-cadmium batteries and from some alloys and dust from electric-arc furnaces.

Cadmium is used primarily for metal plating and coating operations in transportation equipment, machinery, baking enamels, photography, and television phosphors. It is also used in pigments and lasers, and in nickel-cadmium and solar batteries.

Prices – Cadmium prices for the 8 years up to 2005 were at severely depressed levels, reflecting the decreased demand for the substance. In 2005, however, cadmium prices rose very sharply by +172.7% to $1.50 cents per pound. In 2007 the price rose further to a 19-year high of $3.45 per pound then in 2008 the price fell by -9.9% to $3.11 per pound. The record high of $7.89 per pound was posted in 1988.

Supply – World cadmium production in 2008 rose +2.0% yr/yr to 20,800 metric tons, well above the 23-year low of 17,800 metric tons in 2002. The largest producer was China with 20% of total world production followed by Japan with 10%. The U.S. in 2008 produced 745 metric tons which accounted for 3.6% of world cadmium production, which was up 1.36% from the 2007 level. In 2006 the U.S produced a record low of only 723 metric tons.

Demand – Consumption of cadmium has been declining fairly steeply in the last few years due to environmental concerns. U.S. cadmium consumption fell by 3.6% yr/yr in 2008 to 564 metric tons, which was a new 10-decade low. Of the total apparent consumption, about 75% is used for batteries, 12% for pigments, 8% for coatings and plating, 4% for nonferrous alloys, and 1% for other uses.

Trade – The U.S. in 2004 relied on imports for 20% of its cadmium usage, down from 38% as recently as 1998. U.S. imports of cadmium plunged over the past 13 years but recovered to post a 6-year high in 2005 at 288 metric tons. That, however, was still far below the 1,110 metric tons seen as recently as 1994. In 2008 the U.S. imported 221 metric tons which was down -30% from 2007. U.S. exports of cadmium in 2008 rose by +3.8% yr/yr to 440 metric tons.

World Refinery Production of Cadmium   In Metric Tons

Year	Australia	Belgium	Canada	China	Finland	Germany	Italy	Japan	Kazakhstan	Mexico	United Kingdom	United States[3]	World Total
2001	378	1,236	1,493	2,510	604	539	312	2,460	1,250	1,421	485	1,450	20,000
2002	370	117	1,706	2,440	4	422	391	2,444	1,300	1,382	422	1,280	17,800
2003	560	----	1,759	2,710	----	640	22	2,497	1,351	1,590	529	1,450	18,400
2004	347	----	1,880	2,800	----	640	10	2,233	1,900	1,615	532	1,480	18,700
2005	358	----	1,727	4,080	----	640	10	2,297	2,000	1,653	481	1,470	20,200
2006	329	----	2,094	3,790	----	640	10	2,287	2,000	1,401	416	723	19,900
2007[1]	350	----	2,100	4,000	----	640	10	1,930	2,100	1,620	420	735	20,400
2008[2]	350	----	2,100	4,100	----	640		2,000	2,100	1,620		745	20,800

[1] Preliminary.   [2] Estimate.   [3] Primary and secondary metal.   *Source: U.S. Geological Survey (USGS)*

Salient Statistics of Cadmium in the United States   In Metric Tons of Contained Cadmium

Year	Net import Reliance As a % of Apparent Consumption	Production (Metal)	Producer Shipments	Cadmium Sulfide Production	Production Other Compounds	Imports of Cadmium Metal[3]	Exports[4]	Apparent Consumption	Industry Stocks Dec. 31[5]	New York Dealer Price $ Per Lb.
2001	3	1,450	1,040	31	----	107	216	1,000	1,090	.23
2002	E	1,280	1,470	33	----	81	264	1,700	1,360	.29
2003	E	1,450	1,200	----	----	112	615	1,020	1,430	.59
2004	20	1,480	1,410	----	----	263	154	1,840	1,170	.55
2005	E	1,470	1,680	----	----	288	686	699	1,540	1.50
2006	E	723	833	----	----	180	483	568	1,400	1.35
2007[1]	E	735	692	----	----	316	424	585	1,440	3.45
2008[2]	E	745		----	----	221	440	564	1,400	3.11

[1] Preliminary.   [2] Estimate.   [3] For consumption.   [4] Cadmium metal, alloys, dross, flue dust.   [5] Metallic, Compounds, Distributors.   [6] Sticks & Balls in 1 to 5 short ton lots of metal (99.95%).   E = Net exporter.   *Source: U.S. Geological Survey (USGS)*

Average Price of Cadmium (99.95%) in the United States   In Dollars Per Pound

Year	Jan.	Feb.	Mar.	Apr.	May	June	July	Aug.	Sept.	Oct.	Nov.	Dec.	Average
2006	162.75	140.00	140.00	140.00	144.55	171.36	175.00	169.78	155.00	136.36	145.00	167.75	153.96
2007	185.00	195.53	204.09	242.86	368.75	604.17	524.40	396.74	362.50	347.28	290.00	290.00	334.28
2008	301.90	315.00	315.00	315.00	315.00	315.00	315.00	306.67	280.00	280.00	280.00	280.00	301.55

Source: American Metal Market (AMM)

Canola (Rapeseed)

Canola is a genetic variation of rapeseed that was developed by Canadian plant breeders specifically for its nutritional qualities and its low level of saturated fat. The term Canola is a contraction of "Canadian oil." The history of canola oil begins with the rapeseed plant, a member of the mustard family. The rape plant is grown both as feed for livestock and birdfeed. For 4,000 years, the oil from the rapeseed was used in China and India for cooking and as lamp oil. During World War II, rapeseed oil was used as a marine and industrial lubricant. After the war, the market for rapeseed oil plummeted. Rapeseed growers needed other uses for their crop, and that stimulated the research that led to the development of canola. In 1974, Canadian plant breeders from the University of Manitoba produced canola by genetically altering rapeseed. Each canola plant produces yellow flowers, which then produce pods. The tiny round seeds within each pod are crushed to produce canola oil. Each canola seed contains approximately 40% oil. Canola oil is the world's third largest source of vegetable oil accounting for 13% of world vegetable oils, following soybean oil at 32%, and palm oil at 28%. The rest of the seed is processed into canola meal, which is used as high protein livestock feed.

The climate in Canada is especially suitable for canola plant growth. Today, over 13 million acres of Canadian soil are dedicated to canola production. Canola oil is Canada's leading vegetable oil. Due to strong demand from the U.S. for canola oil, approximately 70% of Canada's canola oil is exported to the U.S. Canola oil is used as a salad oil, cooking oil, and for margarine as well as in the manufacture of inks, biodegradable greases, pharmaceuticals, fuel, soap, and cosmetics.

Canola futures and options are traded at the Winnipeg Exchange. The futures contract calls for the delivery of 20 metric tons of canola and 5 contracts are together called a "1 board lot." The futures contract is priced in Canadian dollars per metric ton.

Prices – Canola prices on the Winnipeg nearest-futures chart started 2008 at about CD$580 per metric ton and rose to hit a high of $745 per metric ton in March. Except for a brief recovery in June, canola prices moved lower to end the year at about $400 per metric ton. That was down 31.0% from the start of the year and down 46.3% from the March high of $745.

The average monthly wholesale price of canola oil in the Midwest in 2007 rose +36.3% yr/yr to 45.45 cents per pound, to post a 10-year high. The average monthly wholesale price of canola meal (delivery Pacific Northwest) in the 2008-09 crop year (through Dec 2008) fell by -15.2% to $213.05 per short ton.

Supply – World canola production in the 2008-09 marketing year rose by +17.4% yr/yr to a new record high of 56.840 million metric tons. The world's largest canola producers were the European Union with 34% of world production in 2008-09, Canada (22%), China (20%), and India (12%). U.S. production of canola and canola oil in 2008-09 rose +0.9% yr/yr to 656,000 metric tons. Regarding canola products, world production of canola oil in 2008-09 rose +10.4% to 20.210 million metric tons, which was a new record high. U.S. production of canola oil in 2008-09 rose +14.6% to 502,000 metric tons which is a new record high. World production of canola meal in 2008-09 rose +10.4% to a record high of 30.591 million metric tons.

Demand – World crush demand for canola in 2008-09 rose +10.5% yr/yr to 51.479 million metric tons, which was a new record high. World consumption of canola oil in 2008-09 rose +8.6% yr/yr to a new record high of 19.936 million metric tons. World consumption of canola meal in 2008-09 rose +10.5% to a record high of 30.414 million metric tons.

Trade – World canola exports in 2008-09 rose +31.1% to a record high of 10.748 million metric tons, world canola oil exports rose +15.1% to a record high of 2.188 million metric tons, and world canola meal exports rose +0.3% yr/yr to a record high of 3.739 million metric tons. World canola imports in 2008-09 rose +38.0% to a record high of 10.344 million metric tons, world canola oil imports rose +3.6% to 2.015 million metric tons, and world canola meal imports rose 2.4% to a record high of 3.608 million metric tons. Regarding U.S. canola trade, U.S. canola imports in 2008-09 rose +3.0% to a record high of 900,000 metric tons and U.S. exports rose +16.3% to a record high 1.207 million metric tons.

World Production of Canola (Rapeseed) In Thousands of Metric Tons

Year	Australia	Canada	China	Bangla-desh	Belarus	European Union	India	Pakistan	Romania	Russia	Ukraine	United States	World Total
1999-00	2,460	8,798	10,132	254	57	14,361	5,110	290		135	148	621	42,481
2000-01	1,775	7,205	11,381	249	73	11,364	3,725	231		148	132	909	37,325
2001-02	1,756	5,017	11,331	238	95	11,585	4,500	221		140	135	908	36,010
2002-03	871	4,521	10,552	233	60	11,752	4,050	235		115	61	697	33,256
2003-04	1,703	6,771	11,420	218	55	11,185	6,800	238		192	51	686	39,428
2004-05	1,542	7,674	13,182	211	143	15,432	6,500	215		276	149	613	46,085
2005-06	1,419	9,483	13,052	191	150	15,523	7,000	181		303	285	718	48,504
2006-07[1]	573	9,000	10,966	235	115	16,092	5,800	318		523	600	633	45,163
2007-08[2]	1,065	9,528	10,573	210	250	18,412	5,450	190		632	1,100	650	48,426
2008-09[3]	1,400	12,600	11,500	220	550	19,085	6,580	225		700	2,900	656	56,830

[1] Preliminary.   [2] Estimate.   [3] Forecast.   Source: Economic Research Service, U.S. Department of Agriculture (ERS-USDA); The Oil World

CANOLA

Volume of Trading of Canola Futures in Winnipeg   In 20 Metric Ton Units

Year	Jan.	Feb.	Mar.	Apr.	May	June	July	Aug.	Sept.	Oct.	Nov.	Dec.	Total
1999	129,758	59,772	132,732	143,282	102,838	134,179	94,256	113,913	130,505	184,973	157,428	179,798	1,563,434
2000	137,528	182,744	163,038	169,807	168,164	152,358	79,071	91,762	146,890	208,639	154,727	204,045	1,858,773
2001	196,137	292,226	286,463	247,744	205,798	188,175	163,901	155,531	143,220	205,016	174,910	165,852	2,424,973
2002	164,945	179,753	166,889	159,981	133,202	139,256	132,524	174,527	131,034	170,873	105,661	169,477	1,828,122
2003	129,903	152,738	108,991	153,528	120,178	152,979	90,909	66,768	109,760	217,310	90,950	153,269	1,547,283
2004	145,339	204,567	178,516	192,429	120,218	128,843	73,417	97,483	113,368	175,776	110,922	196,094	1,736,972
2005	116,678	207,198	141,717	124,636	102,424	178,001	87,724	121,749	138,701	200,004	145,231	258,922	1,822,985
2006	195,189	240,070	237,537	229,470	211,688	238,967	129,433	145,133	212,164	284,033	191,676	291,994	2,607,354
2007	204,893	309,278	198,589	273,755	281,240	321,022	160,846	181,145	212,288	396,852	268,743	360,531	3,169,182
2008	333,852	388,180	307,536	296,455	209,631	290,152	172,089	170,596	220,479	293,978	126,273	265,670	3,074,891

Source: Winnipeg Commodity Exchange (WCE)

Average Open Interest of Canola Futures in Winnipeg   In 20 Metric Ton Units

Year	Jan.	Feb.	Mar.	Apr.	May	June	July	Aug.	Sept.	Oct.	Nov.	Dec.
1999	57,958	64,014	57,851	57,351	51,808	53,039	49,273	41,819	53,425	67,244	63,780	64,286
2000	59,057	65,545	65,296	66,253	65,855	59,673	46,813	51,367	59,342	72,618	64,862	65,170
2001	57,537	73,539	88,111	78,143	77,425	84,315	72,430	70,137	67,275	71,651	65,580	66,884
2002	57,821	56,443	53,321	56,830	50,924	38,901	48,329	54,286	53,630	50,379	56,896	57,983
2003	52,818	54,749	55,369	53,480	50,549	49,930	47,479	45,314	44,510	49,008	45,423	48,655
2004	54,524	57,944	71,624	77,357	69,783	59,012	50,669	51,009	49,659	53,855	65,215	68,719
2005	64,147	75,090	65,205	63,514	54,341	53,390	57,706	56,305	65,700	68,186	66,117	87,246
2006	82,651	88,576	84,828	88,970	84,710	81,561	81,243	77,356	81,597	80,800	90,694	102,651
2007	103,317	103,250	94,001	102,050	114,244	124,321	117,967	111,470	121,589	122,965	146,879	156,698
2008	164,326	172,229	165,282	135,226	111,687	102,353	91,891	82,272	90,075	90,062	91,459	88,373

Source: Winnipeg Commodity Exchange (WCE)

World Supply and Distribution of Canola and Products   In Thousands of Metric Tons

| | Canola | | | | | Canola Meal | | | | | Canola oil | | | | |
Year	Pro-duction	Exports	Imports	Crush	Ending Stocks	Pro-duction	Exports	Imports	Con-sumption	Ending Stocks	Pro-duction	Exports	Imports	Con-sumption	Ending Stocks
2001-02	36,010	4,895	4,947	33,482	2,778	19,950	1,512	1,535	19,959	303	13,059	1,031	1,124	13,255	670
2002-03	33,256	4,129	4,034	31,588	2,171	18,810	1,615	1,726	18,945	279	12,251	911	892	12,343	559
2003-04	39,428	5,481	5,145	36,422	2,099	21,877	2,456	2,490	21,542	648	14,095	1,327	1,358	14,289	396
2004-05	46,085	4,872	5,015	40,603	4,747	24,249	2,512	2,291	24,189	487	15,724	1,304	1,195	15,520	491
2005-06	48,504	6,991	6,684	44,610	5,506	26,575	2,781	2,558	26,267	572	17,244	1,742	1,463	16,865	591
2006-07[1]	45,163	6,635	7,019	43,678	4,659	26,007	2,903	3,039	26,365	350	17,029	1,943	2,201	17,450	428
2007-08[2]	48,426	8,196	7,494	46,584	3,388	27,700	3,727	3,523	27,534	312	18,310	1,901	1,945	18,352	430
2008-09[3]	56,830	10,748	10,344	51,479	5,454	30,591	3,739	3,608	30,414	358	20,210	2,188	2,015	19,936	531

[1] Preliminary.   [2] Estimate.   [3] Forecast.   *Source: Economic Research Service, U.S. Department of Agriculture (ERS-USDA); The Oil World*

Salient Statistics of Canola and Canola Oil in the United States   In Thousands of Metric Tons

| | Canola | | | | | | | Canola Oil | | | | | | |
| | Supply | | | Disappearance | | | | Supply | | | Disappearance | | |
Year	Stocks June 1	Pro-duction	Imports	Total Supply	Crush	Exports	Total[3]	Stocks Oct. 1	Pro-duction	Imports	Total Supply	Domestic	Exports	Total
2001-02	38	908	125	1,071	217	766	983	51	269	503	823	683	116	799
2002-03	68	697	197	962	287	586	873	24	230	445	699	591	73	664
2003-04	72	686	244	1,002	305	640	945	35	276	555	866	698	126	824
2004-05	40	613	467	1,120	140	901	1,041	42	363	514	919	739	122	861
2005-06	60	718	518	1,296	157	1,030	1,187	58	381	726	1,165	831	214	1,045
2006-07	87	633	647	1,367	246	963	1,209	120	376	712	1,208	854	286	1,140
2007-08[1]	135	650	874	1,659	435	1,038	1,473	68	438	1,017	1,523	1,305	158	1,463
2008-09[2]	158	656	900	1,714	230	1,207	1,437	60	502	1,163	1,725	1,540	130	1,670

[1] Preliminary.   [2] Forecast.   [3] Includes planting seed and residual.   *Source: Economic Research Service, U.S. Department of Agriculture (ERS-USDA)*

Wholesale Price of Canola Oil in Midwest   In Cents Per Pound

Year	Jan.	Feb.	Mar.	Apr.	May	June	July	Aug.	Sept.	Oct.	Nov.	Dec.	Average
2001	14.81	15.19	16.69	16.69	18.00	19.25	22.50	21.80	19.94	19.00	20.56	21.88	18.86
2002	20.81	21.31	27.44	21.94	21.95	23.19	25.06	28.45	29.81	30.75	34.19	41.19	27.17
2003	24.30	28.88	27.63	27.44	28.13	27.13	26.56	26.30	28.44	31.88	32.67	33.92	28.61
2004	33.44	37.19	38.19	36.81	35.60	32.88	31.63	29.50	31.38	28.35	31.75	31.75	33.21
2005	29.80	28.88	31.38	31.00	31.25	33.00	31.95	29.75	30.50	31.50	30.88	28.81	30.73
2006	38.63	29.06	30.19	29.70	31.56	31.69	33.95	33.06	32.94	34.50	37.63	37.42	33.36
2007	38.56	40.06	38.95	38.44	40.44	42.56	45.00	44.25	48.00	50.38	57.30	61.50	45.45
2008[1]	64.94	71.80	70.56	71.38	73.05	76.69	74.13	61.05	54.88	42.85	39.81	37.19	61.53

[1] Preliminary.   *Source: Economic Research Service, U.S. Department of Agriculture (ERS-USDA)*

Average Price of Canola in Vancouver   In Canadian Dollars Per Metric Ton

Year	Jan.	Feb.	Mar.	Apr.	May	June	July	Aug.	Sept.	Oct.	Nov.	Dec.	Average
2001	279.07	285.05	302.04	299.59	310.00	320.79	356.98	368.33	351.01	332.16	328.99	334.53	322.38
2002	329.23	328.38	329.39	316.74	318.67	330.21	369.42	401.78	408.43	413.64	436.25	418.74	366.74
2003	396.78	380.81	351.97	362.89	344.59	333.48	322.64	319.37	324.07	338.93	343.65	338.57	346.48
2004	345.51	370.53	402.02	395.92	384.09	378.62	360.93	349.57	341.29	288.64	275.37	265.15	346.47
2005	261.56	250.02	270.29	273.13	275.58	286.78	279.45	259.58	240.30	235.00	233.21	226.39	257.61
2006	230.48	231.43	241.57	248.63	267.11	263.66	277.90	265.70	265.20	295.90	335.39	348.60	272.63
2007	354.09	357.65	350.26	348.36	357.87	368.11	372.55	380.70	401.35	402.61	417.23	453.82	380.38
2008	519.88	608.92	618.85	594.74	578.47	616.27	601.79	517.00	457.86	391.62	399.41	371.48	523.02

Source: Winnipeg Commodity Exchange (WCE)

Average Wholesale Price of Canola Meal, 36% Pacific Northwest   In Dollars Per Short Ton

Year	June	July	Aug.	Sept.	Oct.	Nov.	Dec.	Jan.	Feb.	Mar.	Apr.	May	Average
2001-02	142.85	142.44	129.48	135.34	137.33	150.15	146.60	141.90	142.10	153.40	149.10	149.30	143.33
2002-03	131.50	134.70	142.17	154.10	155.80	147.55	145.60	148.50	146.95	137.10	135.50	149.20	144.06
2003-04	169.65	187.19	181.35	201.07	205.50	228.65	214.40	200.03	189.00	192.09	146.99	145.55	188.46
2004-05	133.39	138.81	135.13	129.21	139.55	146.08	140.85	139.25	153.98	150.48	138.12	132.10	139.75
2005-06	130.13	139.55	158.06	150.05	143.94	134.74	136.04	136.59	139.63	137.83	143.28	136.38	140.52
2006-07	149.77	166.80	163.17	173.30	198.37	195.37	169.01	168.19	189.11	171.14	159.33	176.98	173.38
2007-08	167.24	192.25	226.30	276.78	285.83	276.85	268.14	258.75	293.20	310.19	239.88	220.42	251.32
2008-09[1]	192.55	217.99	228.62	279.23	243.30								232.34

[1] Preliminary.   *Source: Economic Research Service, U.S. Department of Agriculture (ERS-USDA)*

Cassava

Cassava is a perennial woody shrub with an edible root. Cassava, which is also called manioc, mandioca, or yucca, grows in tropical and subtropical areas of the world. Cassava has been known since the 1500s and originates in Latin America. The cassava's starchy roots are a major source of dietary energy for more than 500 million people. Cassava is the highest producer of carbohydrates among staple crops, and it ranks fourth in food crops in developing countries. The leaves of the cassava plant are also edible and are relatively rich in protein and vitamins A and B.

Cassava is drought-tolerant and needs less soil preparation and weeding than other crops. Because cassava can be stored in the ground for up to 3 years, it also serves as a reserve food when other crops fail. The cassava is propagated by cuttings of the woody stem, thereby resulting in a low multiplication rate compared to crops propagated by true seeds.

One problem with cassava is the poisonous cyanides, which need to be destroyed before consumption. The cyanide content differs with each variety of cassava, but higher cyanide is usually correlated to high yields. The cyanide content can be destroyed through heat and various processing methods such as grating, sun drying, and fermenting.

Cassava is the primary source of tapioca. Cassava is also eaten raw or boiled, and is processed into livestock feed, starch and glucose, flour, and pharmaceuticals. One species of cassava has been successfully grown for its rubber.

Prices – The average price of tapioca (hard pellets, FOB Rotterdam) rose by +15.9% (over the 2005 price of $144) in the first four months of 2007 to a 12-year high of $167 per metric ton. The 2007 price was more than double the record low of $82 in 2001.

Supply – World production of cassava in 2006 (latest data available) rose by +7.1% to a record high of 226.337 million metric tons. The world's largest producers of cassava in 2006 were Nigeria (with 20% of world production), Brazil (12%), Thailand (10%), and Indonesia (9.0%).

Trade – World exports of tapioca in 2007 (latest available) rose +11.7% to a 14-year high of 6.358 million metric tons. Thailand accounted for 76% of world exports in 20076, followed by Vietnam with 20%, and Indonesia with 3%. The world's two main importers of tapioca in 2007 were China with 72% of world imports, the European Union with 21%, and the Republic of Korea with 5%.

World Cassava Production   In Thousands of Metric Tons

Year	Brazil	China	Ghana	India	Indonesia	Mozam-bique	Nigeria	Paraguay	Tanzania	Thailand	Uganda	Congo[2]	World Total
2000	23,336	3,822	8,107	6,014	16,089	5,362	32,010	2,719	7,120	19,064	4,966	15,959	178,471
2001	22,577	3,873	8,966	7,124	17,055	5,975	32,068	3,568	6,884	18,396	5,265	15,436	185,226
2002	23,066	3,925	9,731	6,834	16,913	5,925	34,120	4,430	6,888	16,868	5,373	14,930	186,953
2003	21,961	4,015	10,239	5,426	18,524	6,150	36,304	4,669	5,284	19,718	5,450	14,945	192,836
2004	23,927	3,816	9,739	5,945	19,425	6,413	38,845	5,500	6,152	21,440	5,500	14,951	205,079
2005	25,872	4,017	9,567	5,855	19,321	6,500	41,565	4,785	7,000	16,938	5,576	14,974	207,437
2006	26,639	4,318	9,638	7,620	19,928	7,500	45,721	4,800	6,500	22,584	4,926	14,989	222,559
2007[1]	27,313	4,370	9,650	7,600	19,610	7,350	45,750	5,100	6,600	26,411	4,456	15,000	228,138

[1] Estimate.   [2] Formerly Zaire.   *Source: Food and Agriculture Organization of the United Nations (FAO-UN)*

World Trade in Tapioca   In Thousands of Metric Tons

| | --------- Exports --------- | | | | --------- Imports --------- | | | | | | |
Year	Costa Rica	Indonesia	Thailand	Vietnam	World Total	China	European Union	Japan	Korea	Philippines	Singapore	World Total
2000	7	151	3,915	215	4,334	170	3,765	19	292	12	20	4,543
2001	9	177	4,494	409	5,140	1,950	2,915	20	445	17	19	5,475
2002	12	130	3,067	308	3,556	1,760	1,560	14	157	10	19	3,580
2003	14	42	3,994	681	4,785	2,368	1,869	21	247	6	19	4,624
2004	17	234	4,579	730	5,626	3,442	2,075	30	460	12	19	6,134
2005	18	230	3,028	545	3,889	3,335	362	23	265	----	21	4,062
2006	22	132	4,361	1,106	5,690	4,950	263	20	268	3	22	5,570
2007[1]	25	210	4,798	1,251	6,358	4,625	1,325	27	302	----	21	6,440

[1] Estimate.   [2] Intra-EU trade is excluded.   *Source: The Oil World*

Prices of Tapioca, Hard Pellets, F.O.B. Rotterdam   U.S. Dollars Per Tonne

Year	Jan.	Feb.	Mar.	Apr.	May	June	July	Aug.	Sept.	Oct.	Nov.	Dec.	Average
2000	94	90	88	92	85	88	88	81	78	74	76	79	84
2001	83	80	77	78	80	82	84	84	87	83	84	84	82
2002	86	82	82	84	87	91	96	97	95	93	93	89	90
2003	91	92	95	96	101	101	103	108	114	134	138	143	110
2004	138	132	121	118	117	118	120	122	128	134	139	148	128
2005	147	149	153	145	142	130	----	----	----	----	----	----	144
2006	----	----	----	----	----	----	----	----	----	----	----	----	----
2007	165	169	164	171									167

Source: The Oil World

Castor beans

Castor bean plants are native to the Ethiopian region of tropical east Africa. The seeds of the castor bean are used to produce castor oil. The average castor bean seed contains 35% to 55% oil. The oil is removed from the bean seeds by either pressing or solvent extraction. Castor oil is used in many products. In the U.S., the paint and varnish industry is the single largest market for castor oil. Castor oil is also used for coating fabrics, insulation, cosmetics, skin emollients, hair oils, inks, nylon plastics, greases, and hydraulic fluids.

Ricin is found in all parts of the castor bean plant, but the most concentrated amounts are found in the cake by-product after oil extraction. Ricin is one of the most deadly, naturally occurring poisons known. Ricin received attention when it was used in a subway attack in Japan in 1995 and again when it was sent to a Congressional office in an envelope in February 2004. One non-deadly use for ricin is for medical research where it is being studied for use as a potential treatment for cancer.

Supply – World production of castor-seed beans in the 2007-08 marketing year (the latest data available) rose by +8.8% to 1.314 million metric tons. The world's largest producer of castor-seed beans by far is India with 68% of world production in 2007-08 at 900,000 metric tons. The second and third largest producers are China with 16% of world production (210,000 metric tons) and Brazil with 8% of world production (94,000 metric tons).

Demand – U.S. consumption of castor oil in 2007-08 rose sharply by +124.6% to a record high of 97.769 million pounds.

World Production of Castorseed Beans   In Thousands of Metric Tons

Year	Brazil	China	Ecuador	India	Mexico	Paraguay	Pakistan	Philip-pines	Sudan	Tanzania	Thailand	Former U.S.S.R.	Total
2000-01	116	300	4	867	1	11	1	4	1	3	9	2	1,353
2001-02	100	260	4	610	1	13	3	4	1	3	9	2	1,044
2002-03	72	265	4	650	1	7	1	4	1	3	10	2	1,055
2003-04	78	258	4	720	1	10	10	4	1	3	10	2	1,154
2004-05	129	250	2	870	1	11	5	4	1	3	10	2	1,350
2005-06[1]	162	220	2	920	1	12	8	4	1	3	10	2	1,407
2006-07[2]	92	200	3	810	1	9	8	4	1	3	10	2	1,208
2007-08[3]	94	210	3	900	1	12	8	4	1	3	10	2	1,314

[1] Preliminary.   [2] Estimate.   [3] Forecast.   *Sources: Foreign Agricultural Service, U.S.Department of Agriculture (FAS-USDA); The Oil World*

Castor Oil Consumption[2] in the United States   In Thousands of Pounds

Year	Oct.	Nov.	Dec.	Jan.	Feb.	Mar.	Apr.	May	June	July	Aug.	Sept.	Total
2002-03	3,281	1,887	1,528	1,641	1,642	1,629	1,123	1,315	1,518	1,839	1,449	2,119	20,971
2003-04	2,072	1,836	1,779	1,526	1,251	2,241	2,396	2,250	1,905	1,542	2,382	2,366	23,546
2004-05	2,155	1,391	1,581	1,365	1,915	1,992	2,175	2,211	1,827	1,689	2,021	1,162	21,484
2005-06	1,389	1,761	1,654	1,602	1,610	1,426	1,457	1,766	1,899	1,516	1,768	1,379	19,227
2006-07	1,583	2,026	1,642	2,021	4,011	6,577	5,105	4,107	5,360	5,123	2,161	3,813	43,529
2007-08	2,616	4,583	W	7,664	7,890	7,942	9,327	9,190	9,101	10,361	11,406	9,542	97,769
2008-09[1]	10,137	7,106											103,458

[1] Preliminary.   [2] In inedible products (Resins, Plastics, etc.).   W = Withheld.   *Source: Bureau of the Census, U.S. Department of Commerce*

Castor Oil Stocks in the United States, on First of Month   In Thousands of Pounds

Year	Oct.	Nov.	Dec.	Jan.	Feb.	Mar.	Apr.	May	June	July	Aug.	Sept.
2002-03	41,322	37,282	33,195	32,983	25,926	20,551	22,460	15,337	23,212	24,138	32,110	27,827
2003-04	26,463	17,753	16,630	18,582	14,097	13,985	7,507	22,751	W	25,593	18,381	14,922
2004-05	34,525	31,608	24,287	19,476	32,641	25,318	27,876	19,098	31,493	22,919	15,963	35,604
2005-06	38,357	45,720	37,111	29,428	21,047	25,076	15,756	25,543	25,070	22,165	21,329	14,389
2006-07	39,635	24,055	18,780	43,896	30,734	46,850	58,989	50,455	49,276	46,715	37,668	26,019
2007-08	16,945	34,444	23,661	36,046	30,034	20,303	22,240	14,167	39,649	27,285	14,907	W
2008-09[1]	W	W	46,722									

[1] Preliminary.   W = Withheld proprietary data.   *Source: Bureau of the Census, U.S. Department of Commerce*

Average Wholesale Price of Castor Oil No. 1, Brazilian Tanks in New York   In Cents Per Pound

2001	48.00	48.00	48.00	48.00	48.00	48.00	48.00	48.00	48.00	48.00	47.50	47.50	47.92
2002	47.50	47.50	47.50	47.50	47.50	47.50	47.00	47.00	47.00	47.00	47.00	47.00	47.25
2003	47.00	47.00	47.00	47.00	47.00	47.00	47.00	47.00	47.00	47.00	47.00	47.00	47.00
2004	47.00	47.00	47.00	47.00	47.00	47.00	47.00	47.00	47.00	47.00	47.00	48.00	47.08
2005	50.00	50.00	50.00	50.00	50.00	50.00	50.00	49.00	49.00	47.00	45.50	45.00	48.79
2006	45.00	45.00	44.00	43.00	43.00	43.00	43.00	43.00	44.00	44.00	44.00	43.50	43.71
2007	46.60	49.75	52.00	54.60	58.00	57.50	56.00	NA	60.00	60.00	60.00	60.29	55.89
2006	45.00	45.00	44.00	43.00	43.00	43.00	43.00	43.00	44.00	44.00	44.00	43.50	43.71

Source: Foreign Agricultural Service, U.S.Department of Agriculture (FAS-USDA)

Cattle and Calves

The beef cycle begins with the cow-calf operation, which breeds the new calves. Most ranchers breed their herds of cows in summer, thus producing the new crop of calves in spring (the gestation period is about nine months). This allows the calves to be born during the milder weather of spring and provides the calves with ample forage through the summer and early autumn. The calves are weaned from the mother after 6-8 months and most are then moved into the "stocker" operation. The calves usually spend 6-10 months in the stocker operation, growing to near full-sized by foraging for summer grass or winter wheat. When the cattle reach 600-800 pounds, they are typically sent to a feedlot and become "feeder cattle." In the feedlot, the cattle are fed a special food mix to encourage rapid weight gain. The mix includes grain (corn, milo, or wheat), a protein supplement (soybean, cottonseed, or linseed meal), and roughage (alfalfa, silage, prairie hay, or an agricultural by-product such as sugar beet pulp). The animal is considered "finished" when it reaches full weight and is ready for slaughter, typically at around 1,200 pounds, which produces a dressed carcass of around 745 pounds. After reaching full weight, the cattle are sold for slaughter to a meat packing plant. Futures and options on live cattle and feeder cattle are traded at the Chicago Mercantile Exchange. Both the live and feeder cattle futures contracts trade in terms of cents per pound.

Prices – Live cattle futures prices rallied in the first half of 2008 and posted a record high of 104.7 cents per pound in July 2008. Live cattle prices then fell sharply by a total of 23.0% in the latter half of 2008 to a 2-1/2 year low of 80.65 cents in December 2008. Live cattle prices closed 2008 at 84.475 cents, down −11.775 cents (-12.2%) from the 2007 close of 96.25 cents. Cattle prices in early 2008 were pulled higher by the weak dollar and the feverish rally in commodity prices. However, cattle prices then fell sharply in the latter half of 2008 as the global economy slowed and the financial crisis emerged. Cattle producers during the financial crisis ran into problems financing their herds and therefore sent cattle to slaughter in relatively high numbers, increasing the supply of beef on the market and pushing prices lower. In 2008 as a whole, the number of cattle on feed fell by -4.7% to 22.31 million head. The smaller herds, however, should set the cattle market up for an upward rebound in prices once demand emerges.

Supply – The world cattle and buffalo figures showed a small +0.5% increase in 2008 (as of Jan 1, 2007) to 978.829 million head, which is still somewhat above the 3-decade low of 935 million head seen in 1995. As of January 1, 2008 there were 96.669 million cattle and calves on U.S. farms, down -0.3% yr/yr but still above the 94.888 million in 2004, which was the lowest level since 1959. World production of beef and veal in 2008 rose +0.4% to 59.250 million metric tons (carcass weight equivalent) but the USDA is forecasting a drop of -0.4% to 57.974 million metric tons in 2009. U.S. commercial production of beef in 2008 rose +0.6% to 26.589 billion pounds and the USDA is forecasting about the same for 2009.

Demand – World consumption of beef and veal in 2008 was virtually unchanged from 2007 at 58.299 million metric tons and the USDA is forecasting a drop of 0.6% in 2009 to 57.974 million metric tons. U.S. consumption of beef and veal in 2008 fell 2.4% to 12.520 million metric tons and the USDA is forecasting a further drop of 0.3% in 2009 to 12.483 million metric tons.

Trade – U.S. imports of live cattle in 2008 (annualized through the 3rd quarter) fell by -16.2% to 2.092 million head, but remained well above the low levels seen when mad cow disease caused the U.S. to close the Canadian border to live cattle in 2003. U.S. exports of live cattle in 2008 rose by +66.4% yr/yr to 110,455 head, up sharply from the multi-decade low of 21,155 in 2005 caused by to cattle trading bans by key U.S. trading partners.

By weight, U.S. imports of beef in 2008 fell -19.7% to 2.452 billion pounds but the USDA is forecasting an increase of +5.8% to 2.595 billion pounds in 2008. U.S. exports of beef in 2008 rose by +30.0% to 1.860 billion pounds and the USDA is forecasting a further rise of +3.2% to 1.920 billion pounds in 2008. That, however, remains far below the levels of about 2.5 billion pounds seen before mad cow disease hit in December 2003 and largely shut down U.S. beef exports.

World Cattle and Buffalo Numbers as of January 1   In Thousands of Head

Year	Argentina	Australia	Brazil	Canada	China	European Union	India	Mexico	Russia	South Africa	Ukraine	United States	World Total (Mil. Head)
2000	50,332	27,588	146,272	13,201	126,983	96,704	285,220	28,313	27,000	13,580	10,627	98,199	1,029.3
2001	51,167	27,720	150,382	13,608	123,532	94,289	284,822	28,449	25,500	13,460	9,424	97,298	1,018.1
2002	52,369	27,870	156,314	13,752	118,092	93,234	285,124	28,481	24,510	13,505	9,433	96,723	1,020.3
2003	53,069	27,870	161,463	13,466	115,678	91,597	286,079	29,224	23,500	13,635	9,108	96,100	1,001.6
2004	53,968	26,640	165,492	14,555	114,344	90,375	283,103	28,437	22,285	13,540	7,712	94,888	996.0
2005	53,767	27,270	169,567	14,925	112,354	89,319	282,500	27,572	21,100	13,510	6,992	95,438	995.6
2006	54,266	27,782	172,111	14,655	109,908	89,672	282,300	26,949	19,850	13,790	6,514	96,702	996.3
2007	55,664	28,400	173,830	14,155	104,651	88,463	282,000	26,644	19,000	13,934	6,175	97,003	991.7
2008[1]	55,662	28,100	175,437	13,895	105,948	88,300	281,700	26,725	18,370	14,082	5,491	96,669	987.2
2009[2]	55,162	28,300	177,492	13,350	107,095	88,000	281,400	27,094	17,800	14,195	4,971	96,200	978.8

[1] Preliminary.   [2] Forecast.   *Source: Foreign Agricultural Service, U.S. Department of Agriculture (FAS-USDA)*

Cattle Supply and Distribution in the United States   In Thousands of Head

	Cattle & Calves on Farms Jan. 1	Imports	Calves Born	Total Supply	Livestock Slaughter - Cattle and Calves — Federally Inspected	Commercial — Other[3]	All Commercial	Farm	Total Slaughter	Deaths on Farms	Exports	Total Disappearance
Year												
1999	99,115	1,945	38,796	139,856	36,738	695	37,432	210	37,642	4,114	329	42,085
2000	98,198	2,187	38,631	139,016	36,720	658	37,378	210	37,588	4,097	481	42,166
2001	97,277	2,437	38,280	137,994	35,751	625	36,377	200	36,577	4,209	678	41,464
2002	96,704	2,503	38,224	137,431	36,139	641	36,780	190	36,970	4,076	243	41,289
2003	96,100	1,752	37,903	135,754	35,883	611	36,494	192	36,686	4,030	100	40,816
2004	94,888	1,374	37,505	133,767	32,979	592	33,571	189	33,760	4,003	30	37,792
2005	95,438	1,815	37,575	134,828	32,549	573	33,122	189	33,311	4,052	21	37,385
2006	96,702	2,289	37,519	136,509	33,844	566	34,410	187	34,597	4,167	50	38,813
2007[1]	97,003	2,495	36,759	136,257	34,465	557	35,022	187	35,209	4,251	66	39,526
2008[2]	96,669	2,092	36,113	134,873	34,747	580	35,327				110	

[1] Preliminary.   [2] Estimate.   [3] Wholesale and retail.   *Source: Economic Research Service, U.S. Department of Agriculture (ERS-USDA)*

Beef Supply and Utilization in the United States

Years and Quarters	Beginning Stocks	Production — Commercial	Total	Imports	Total Supply	Exports	Ending Stocks	Total Disappearance	Per Capita Disappearance — Carcass Weight	Retail Weight Total
2005	----	24,683	24,683	3,599	28,282	698	----	----	----	65.4
I	----	5,725	5,725	831	6,556	130	----	----	----	15.6
II	----	6,189	6,189	1,065	7,254	189	----	----	----	16.8
III	----	6,560	6,560	906	7,466	150	----	----	----	17.0
IV	----	6,209	6,209	797	7,006	220	----	----	----	16.0
2006	----	26,153	26,153	3,085	29,238	1,145	----	----	----	65.7
I	----	6,082	6,082	843	6,925	215	----	----	----	15.8
II	----	6,724	6,724	789	7,513	315	----	----	----	16.8
III	----	6,834	6,834	731	7,565	307	----	----	----	16.8
IV	----	6,513	6,513	722	7,235	308	----	----	----	16.2
2007	----	26,421	26,421	3,052	29,473	1,431	----	----	----	65.2
I	----	6,237	6,237	770	7,007	269	----	----	----	15.9
II	----	6,649	6,649	884	7,533	363	----	----	----	16.6
III	----	6,802	6,802	774	7,576	424	----	----	----	16.4
IV	----	6,733	6,733	624	7,357	375	----	----	----	16.2
2008[1]	----	26,564	26,564	2,497	29,061	1,880	----	----	----	62.7
I	----	6,371	6,371	637	7,008	360	----	----	----	15.6
II	----	6,897	6,897	661	7,558	471	----	----	----	16.3
III	----	6,911	6,911	584	7,495	609	----	----	----	15.8
IV	----	6,385	6,385	615	7,000	440	----	----	----	15.0
2009[2]	----	26,110	26,110	2,680	28,790	1,880	----	----	----	61.6
I	----	6,225	6,225	625	6,850	415	----	----	----	15.0
II	----	6,630	6,630	710	7,340	495	----	----	----	15.7
III	----	6,830	6,830	690	7,520	490	----	----	----	15.9
IV	----	6,425	6,425	655	7,080	480	----	----	----	15.0

[1] Preliminary.   [2] Forecast.   *Source: Economic Research Service, U.S. Department of Agriculture (ERS-USDA)*

United States Cattle on Feed in 13 States   In Thousands of Head

Year	Number on Feed[3]	Placed on Feed	Marketings	Other Disappearance	Year	Number on Feed[3]	Placed on Feed	Marketings	Other Disappearance
2005	11,299	23,556	22,172	879	2007[1]	11,974	23,400	22,461	821
I	11,299	5,161	5,369	218	I	11,974	5,309	5,395	244
II	10,873	5,652	5,881	250	II	11,644	5,384	6,041	250
III	10,394	6,026	5,767	171	III	10,737	6,156	5,761	165
IV	10,482	6,717	5,155	240	IV	10,967	6,551	5,264	162
2006	11,804	23,595	22,477	948	2008[2]	12,092	22,309	22,414	753
I	11,804	5,624	5,370	246	I	12,092	5,246	5,471	183
II	11,812	5,468	6,143	265	II	11,684	4,954	6,128	215
III	10,872	6,475	5,777	185	III	10,295	6,008	5,743	145
IV	11,385	6,028	5,187	252	IV	10,415	6,101	5,072	210

[1] Preliminary.   [2] Estimate.   [3] Beginning of period.   *Source: Economic Research Service, U.S. Department of Agriculture (ERS-USDA)*

CATTLE AND CALVES

Live Cattle (monthly average) through December 2008 — Cents per pound

United States Cattle on Feed, 1000+ Capacity Feedlots[2], on First of Month   In Thousands of Head

Year	Jan.	Feb.	Mar.	Apr.	May	June	July	Aug.	Sept.	Oct.	Nov.	Dec.
1999	9,021	8,917	8,878	8,899	8,583	8,547	8,183	7,889	8,185	8,793	9,789	10,020
2000	9,752	9,885	9,695	9,593	9,391	9,411	8,959	8,812	8,972	9,502	10,192	10,213
2001	11,798	11,941	11,695	11,523	11,170	11,245	11,011	10,891	10,855	11,125	11,863	11,891
2002	11,565	11,572	11,518	11,587	10,971	10,990	10,507	10,109	10,159	10,452	10,785	10,946
2003	10,658	10,700	10,546	10,713	10,535	10,539	9,923	9,590	9,839	10,218	11,043	11,335
2004	11,253	11,138	10,987	10,763	10,375	10,640	10,132	9,868	9,988	10,502	11,334	11,334
2005	11,299	11,342	11,154	10,873	10,641	10,771	10,394	10,093	10,000	10,482	11,473	11,726
2006	11,804	12,110	12,023	11,812	11,559	11,187	10,872	10,822	10,986	11,385	11,969	11,973
2007	11,974	11,726	11,599	11,644	11,297	11,272	10,737	10,299	10,302	10,967	11,769	12,099
2008[1]	12,092	11,966	11,853	11,684	11,135	10,815	10,295	9,869	9,997	10,415	10,972	11,346

[1] Preliminary.   [2] 7 States through 2000.   *Source: Economic Research Service, U.S. Department of Agriculture (ERS-USDA)*

United States Cattle Placed on Feed, 1000+ Capacity Feedlots[2]   In Thousands of Head

Year	Jan.	Feb.	Mar.	Apr.	May	June	July	Aug.	Sept.	Oct.	Nov.	Dec.	Total
1999	1,681	1,563	1,741	1,443	1,733	1,515	1,565	2,085	2,345	2,629	1,823	1,408	21,531
2000	1,931	1,606	1,736	1,470	1,998	1,413	1,674	2,091	2,286	2,387	1,678	1,440	21,710
2001	2,263	1,580	1,842	1,551	2,372	1,965	1,986	2,204	2,141	2,702	1,908	1,578	24,092
2002	2,179	1,810	1,963	1,463	2,267	1,644	1,840	2,228	2,194	2,396	1,982	1,610	23,576
2003	2,089	1,650	2,032	1,870	2,307	1,672	1,997	2,384	2,474	2,781	1,926	1,748	24,930
2004	1,754	1,612	1,810	1,600	2,370	1,647	1,719	2,102	2,375	2,701	1,743	1,834	23,267
2005	1,888	1,523	1,750	1,660	2,223	1,769	1,678	1,993	2,355	2,788	2,045	1,884	23,556
2006	2,199	1,588	1,837	1,619	1,903	1,946	1,958	2,290	2,227	2,430	1,884	1,714	23,595
2007	1,690	1,659	1,960	1,568	2,159	1,657	1,622	2,119	2,415	2,725	2,125	1,701	23,400
2008[1]	1,787	1,723	1,736	1,536	1,900	1,518	1,666	2,061	2,281	2,438	2,016	1,647	22,309

[1] Preliminary.   [2] 7 States through 2000.   *Source: Economic Research Service, U.S. Department of Agriculture (ERS-USDA)*

Live Cattle Futures - CME Group
(weekly close) as of January 02, 2009

Cents per pound

United States Cattle Marketings, 1000+ Capacity Feedlots[2]   In Thousands of Head

Year	Jan.	Feb.	Mar.	Apr.	May	June	July	Aug.	Sept.	Oct.	Nov.	Dec.	Total
1999	1,738	1,560	1,668	1,681	1,696	1,835	1,816	1,747	1,682	1,570	1,530	1,601	20,124
2000	1,747	1,749	1,764	1,601	1,863	1,828	1,784	1,895	1,708	1,647	1,568	1,500	20,654
2001	2,042	1,745	1,916	1,815	2,196	2,122	2,047	2,186	1,825	1,896	1,800	1,811	23,401
2002	2,083	1,801	1,825	1,996	2,171	2,076	2,193	2,135	1,848	1,979	1,731	1,799	23,637
2003	1,972	1,733	1,803	1,985	2,238	2,227	2,270	2,075	2,032	1,855	1,537	1,740	23,467
2004	1,775	1,694	1,967	1,891	2,026	2,085	1,925	1,926	1,800	1,803	1,635	1,777	22,304
2005	1,772	1,634	1,963	1,801	1,997	2,083	1,918	2,033	1,816	1,739	1,701	1,715	22,172
2006	1,810	1,602	1,958	1,785	2,160	2,198	1,950	2,067	1,760	1,765	1,797	1,625	22,477
2007	1,841	1,711	1,843	1,816	2,085	2,140	1,999	2,066	1,696	1,876	1,738	1,650	22,461
2008[1]	1,853	1,776	1,842	2,010	2,140	1,978	2,047	1,884	1,812	1,814	1,575	1,683	22,414

[1] Preliminary.   [2] 7 States through 2000.   *Source: Economic Research Service, U.S. Department of Agriculture (ERS-USDA)*

Quarterly Trade of Live Cattle in the United States   In Head

	Imports					Exports				
Year	First Quarter	Second Quarter	Third Quarter	Fourth Quarter	Total	First Quarter	Second Quarter	Third Quarter	Fourth Quarter	Total
1999	549,847	424,182	313,211	657,836	1,945,076	51,830	59,195	47,049	171,245	329,319
2000	580,174	537,009	346,087	724,016	2,187,286	117,889	67,895	72,028	223,430	481,242
2001	700,239	612,645	444,637	679,194	2,436,715	111,549	75,152	297,069	194,683	678,453
2002	785,559	398,072	474,128	845,214	2,502,973	73,401	62,140	49,930	57,472	242,943
2003	630,303	408,833	142,780	569,669	1,751,585	38,246	34,145	10,953	16,926	100,270
2004	309,712	315,800	281,020	467,236	1,373,768	2,727	20,955	2,216	3,652	29,550
2005	335,687	348,897	341,834	788,270	1,814,688	5,128	6,446	5,977	3,604	21,155
2006	708,680	470,176	418,117	691,870	2,288,843	8,721	12,473	10,249	18,235	49,678
2007	629,157	518,173	462,359	885,276	2,494,965	13,723	15,112	10,441	27,107	66,383
2008[1]	682,174	562,566	405,199	634,054	2,283,993	38,319	30,575	15,181	23,417	107,492

[1] Preliminary.   *Source: Economic Research Service, U.S. Department of Agriculture (ERS-USDA)*

Feeder Cattle (monthly average) through December 2008   Cents per pound

Average Slaughter Steer Price, Choice 2-4, Nebraska Direct (1100-1300 Lb.)[1]   In Dollars Per 100 Pounds

Year	Jan.	Feb.	Mar.	Apr.	May	June	July	Aug.	Sept.	Oct.	Nov.	Dec.	Average
2002	67.25	70.72	72.59	67.79	65.32	63.64	62.49	62.96	64.43	64.93	70.12	72.24	67.04
2003	77.18	78.77	77.52	79.24	79.50	76.73	76.89	81.74	90.59	105.50	101.88	90.75	84.69
2004	80.36	79.15	86.96	87.04	88.22	89.19	84.27	84.15	82.33	84.03	84.64	86.60	84.75
2005	87.77	87.73	91.78	91.98	88.83	83.06	79.37	80.80	85.19	87.40	90.32	93.08	87.28
2006	92.90	89.09	85.73	81.30	79.02	80.85	81.14	85.87	89.18	87.43	86.56	85.83	85.41
2007	86.75	88.68	96.39	98.04	95.50	86.81	89.09	91.49	93.49	91.69	93.37	90.50	91.82
2008	88.63	90.85	89.28	89.04	93.86	95.55	98.83	99.14	97.37	90.61	90.40	83.66	92.27

Source: Economic Research Service, U.S. Department of Agriculture (ERS-USDA)

Average Price of Feeder Steers in Oklahoma City   In Dollars Per 100 Pounds

Year	Jan.	Feb.	Mar.	Apr.	May	June	July	Aug.	Sept.	Oct.	Nov.	Dec.	Average
2002	92.43	93.66	94.06	91.76	90.78	85.68	83.29	85.19	84.71	84.23	85.69	89.43	88.41
2003	87.76	88.84	91.31	92.94	93.58	96.04	99.28	99.15	102.68	102.63	106.87	98.09	96.60
2004	79.35	80.18	107.35	109.99	115.40	121.10	124.63	124.65	116.97	116.96	117.13	113.01	110.56
2005	112.40	116.87	120.48	126.77	127.13	126.91	122.73	119.96	119.61	120.29	122.84	122.75	121.56
2006	125.49	123.56	121.41	122.29	119.35	122.29	124.55	120.35	123.90	114.85	100.78	99.80	118.22
2007	96.54	97.50	103.38	107.97	107.74	107.65	112.29	116.30	117.20	112.79	108.80	105.13	107.77
2008	98.62	102.81	100.17	100.45	107.08	108.90	111.07	112.53	109.69	98.84	95.76	90.76	103.06

Source: Economic Research Service, U.S. Department of Agriculture (ERS-USDA)

Federally Inspected Slaughter of Cattle in the United States   In Thousands of Head

Year	Jan.	Feb.	Mar.	Apr.	May	June	July	Aug.	Sept.	Oct.	Nov.	Dec.	Total
2002	2,999	2,564	2,688	2,899	3,098	3,017	3,141	3,163	2,816	3,205	2,812	2,719	35,120
2003	2,950	2,519	2,725	2,918	3,201	3,208	3,245	3,094	3,082	2,953	2,387	2,626	34,907
2004	2,527	2,381	2,818	2,654	2,792	2,949	2,745	2,775	2,689	2,693	2,492	2,642	32,156
2005	2,477	2,297	2,675	2,517	2,751	2,894	2,677	2,948	2,729	2,625	2,623	2,619	31,831
2006	2,591	2,302	2,806	2,566	2,993	3,116	2,795	3,089	2,721	2,803	2,797	2,566	33,145
2007	2,748	2,518	2,747	2,660	3,008	3,035	2,860	3,088	2,621	3,046	2,787	2,603	33,721
2008[1]	2,847	2,598	2,684	2,914	3,095	2,912	3,017	2,866	2,842	2,933	2,475	2,623	33,805

[1] Preliminary.   *Source: National Agricultural Statistics Service, U.S. Department of Agriculture (NASS-USDA)*

Feeder Cattle Futures - CME Group
(weekly close) as of January 02, 2009

Cents per Pound

Average Open Interest of Live Cattle Futures in Chicago   In Contracts

Year	Jan.	Feb.	Mar.	Apr.	May	June	July	Aug.	Sept.	Oct.	Nov.	Dec.
1999	115,254	115,283	115,410	104,482	103,290	101,078	96,843	101,858	121,305	123,466	126,040	120,204
2000	128,918	123,980	123,925	122,596	117,834	106,196	116,266	120,526	123,945	123,517	131,773	132,239
2001	132,298	132,866	131,312	123,075	112,180	114,970	116,162	105,252	114,214	109,677	108,574	95,182
2002	93,589	91,566	98,176	98,343	98,846	91,129	93,541	92,966	109,651	111,338	121,671	116,588
2003	111,874	105,882	98,943	96,875	107,193	111,397	113,324	115,417	130,836	124,525	113,224	106,522
2004	98,752	99,491	112,449	124,930	128,727	126,481	114,656	109,588	104,928	109,832	112,709	123,483
2005	142,333	140,869	146,062	141,610	145,235	133,768	135,971	134,329	148,094	167,175	174,496	197,090
2006	225,313	220,947	220,042	240,567	261,496	235,783	231,914	213,918	214,583	205,776	211,814	224,501
2007	257,373	273,121	296,235	281,239	261,866	240,526	235,110	212,154	234,754	234,584	240,710	241,614
2008	252,555	273,397	276,043	285,956	298,370	298,937	300,862	278,808	265,436	227,860	215,054	211,836

Source: Chicago Mercantile Exchange (CME)

Volume of Trading of Live Cattle Futures Chicago   In Thousands of Contracts

Year	Jan.	Feb.	Mar.	Apr.	May	June	July	Aug.	Sept.	Oct.	Nov.	Dec.	Total
1999	298,814	342,572	338,076	320,457	296,512	342,854	287,557	266,544	371,735	345,269	375,960	253,198	3,839,548
2000	347,290	323,524	356,258	236,494	302,001	244,755	248,377	293,450	277,913	293,972	397,879	359,599	3,681,512
2001	511,050	357,474	385,581	302,829	348,294	289,093	318,564	324,614	340,969	403,101	403,009	294,695	4,279,273
2002	331,026	275,699	387,115	448,508	304,900	247,940	286,248	288,525	314,927	352,487	315,658	298,703	3,851,736
2003	378,862	343,931	334,007	306,713	391,477	311,239	449,966	319,677	473,218	469,405	324,732	332,862	4,436,089
2004	362,295	265,370	442,636	353,886	419,888	345,611	381,151	340,973	382,536	344,517	511,516	359,749	4,510,128
2005	519,794	395,847	598,171	377,494	503,753	405,687	506,253	406,010	569,040	438,631	627,585	485,291	5,833,556
2006	783,018	498,779	849,546	570,015	817,491	709,706	718,772	670,410	698,285	631,911	757,795	503,970	8,209,698
2007	907,155	663,121	1,046,653	575,800	814,423	513,667	849,053	634,475	724,467	638,942	761,870	458,347	8,587,973
2008	982,593	596,374	954,198	724,449	936,181	731,340	1,006,398	738,206	998,230	801,087	773,949	558,355	9,801,360

Source: Chicago Mercantile Exchange (CME)

CATTLE AND CALVES

Beef Steer-Corn Price Ratio[1] in the United States

Year	Jan.	Feb.	Mar.	Apr.	May	June	July	Aug.	Sept.	Oct.	Nov.	Dec.	Average
2001	40.1	40.2	41.1	42.1	42.5	43.6	40.1	38.7	37.7	38.1	36.6	34.6	39.6
2002	36.1	38.1	38.2	37.0	35.3	34.0	31.2	28.3	27.4	29.3	31.5	32.3	33.2
2003	33.4	33.4	32.9	33.7	33.4	33.6	36.4	38.6	40.6	46.1	45.4	41.4	37.4
2004	35.7	31.5	32.0	30.8	32.3	33.6	36.4	38.9	40.7	42.6	44.0	45.0	37.0
2005	44.5	47.7	47.1	49.1	48.5	45.3	41.8	45.0	48.5	52.8	54.9	51.9	48.1
2006	51.0	48.3	45.0	42.3	39.8	41.2	42.1	43.8	43.3	36.7	31.3	29.6	41.2
2007	29.4	26.6	28.5	29.4	28.1	26.4	28.0	29.4	30.0	29.4	27.9	25.3	28.2
2008[2]	23.5	20.8	19.7	17.8	18.2	17.6	19.0	19.0	19.8	21.3	21.4	20.9	19.9

[1] Bushels of corn equal in value to 100 pounds of steers and heifers.   [2] Preliminary.   *Source: Economic Research Service, U.S. Department of Agriculture*

Farm Value, Income and Wholesale Prices of Cattle and Calves in the United States

Year	----- January 1 ----- Per Head Dollars	Total Million $	Gross Income From C & C[2] Million $	At Omaha Steers Choice	Steers Select	Heifers[4] Select	Heifers[4] Choice	Feeder Heifers at Oklahoma City[5]	Cows, Boning Utility Sioux Falls[6]	Cows, Commercial Sioux Falls	Wholesale Prices, Central U.S. Choice 700-850 lb.	Select 700-850 lb.	Cow[6], Canner, Cutter
							Dollars per 100 Pounds						
2002	747	72,284	38,429	66.39	----	----	67.39	76.70	40.47	39.63	113.59	107.66	NA
2003	728	69,949	45,477	82.37	----	----	82.06	85.88	49.74	46.62	143.20	130.07	NA
2004	818	77,595	47,935	84.78	----	----	84.40	100.09	55.20	52.35	141.33	132.65	NA
2005	916	87,386	49,668	86.54	----	----	87.35	106.87	55.52	54.36	145.78	136.36	NA
2006	1,009	97,579	49,423	85.55	----	----	86.58	102.00	50.50	47.56	146.82	132.56	NA
2007	922	89,447	50,162					102.06	54.77	52.12	149.80	140.09	NA
2008[1]	987	95,401						96.85	57.75	54.92	153.17	147.68	NA

[1] Preliminary.   [2] Excludes interfarm sales & Gov't. payments. Cash receipts from farm marketings + value of farm home consumption.
[3] 1,000 to 1,100 lb.   [4] 1,000 to 1,200 lb.   [5] 700 to 750 lb.   [6] All weights.
Source: Economic Research Service, U.S. Department of Agriculture (NASS-USDA)

Average Price Received by Farmers for Beef Cattle in the United States   In Dollars Per 100 Pounds

Year	Jan.	Feb.	Mar.	Apr.	May	June	July	Aug.	Sept.	Oct.	Nov.	Dec.	Average
2001	74.80	74.70	76.00	75.40	73.60	73.60	71.80	70.60	69.00	66.50	64.00	64.80	71.23
2002	67.10	70.00	70.60	67.30	65.10	64.00	63.70	64.40	64.50	64.60	67.30	70.40	66.58
2003	73.20	73.90	72.60	74.50	75.50	74.90	75.80	79.30	84.90	91.50	93.40	90.40	79.99
2004	80.90	78.50	83.70	85.00	88.50	89.80	88.10	87.70	85.90	86.50	85.40	86.80	85.57
2005	89.40	88.80	91.00	93.70	92.10	88.00	85.00	84.40	88.00	90.40	90.80	93.30	89.58
2006	95.10	92.40	87.90	84.80	82.20	84.00	85.80	87.20	90.00	88.20	84.40	83.10	87.09
2007	84.30	86.10	91.60	93.70	92.80	88.80	89.00	91.40	93.10	90.90	89.90	89.20	90.07
2008[1]	87.30	89.00	87.70	86.60	91.10	92.00	95.10	96.10	94.40	87.90	84.90	79.80	89.33

[1] Preliminary.   *Source: National Agricultural Statistics Service, U.S. Department of Agriculture (NASS-USDA)*

Average Price Received by Farmers for Calves in the United States   In Dollars Per 100 Pounds

Year	Jan.	Feb.	Mar.	Apr.	May	June	July	Aug.	Sept.	Oct.	Nov.	Dec.	Average
2001	108.00	109.00	112.00	112.00	111.00	110.00	108.00	106.00	107.00	99.70	96.70	101.00	106.70
2002	102.00	105.00	105.00	101.00	99.50	96.50	92.40	94.90	92.40	92.00	91.90	95.30	97.33
2003	96.80	97.20	96.70	98.90	100.00	101.00	102.00	106.00	109.00	112.00	111.00	112.00	103.55
2004	110.00	111.00	115.00	117.00	121.00	125.00	130.00	131.00	128.00	126.00	123.00	122.00	121.58
2005	125.00	129.00	136.00	141.00	143.00	140.00	133.00	133.00	135.00	135.00	137.00	137.00	135.33
2006	141.00	143.00	139.00	137.00	134.00	135.00	137.00	136.00	136.00	128.00	119.00	116.00	133.42
2007	115.00	114.00	122.00	125.00	124.00	124.00	126.00	127.00	126.00	123.00	122.00	120.00	122.33
2008[1]	117.00	120.00	119.00	116.00	119.00	118.00	115.00	116.00	113.00	107.00	106.00	100.00	113.83

[1] Preliminary.   *Source: National Agricultural Statistics Board, U.S. Department of Agriculture (NASS-USDA)*

Federally Inspected Slaughter of Calves and Vealers in the United States   In Thousands of Head

Year	Jan.	Feb.	Mar.	Apr.	May	June	July	Aug.	Sept.	Oct.	Nov.	Dec.	Total
2001	89	77	82	72	77	75	81	92	77	91	85	82	981
2002	86	71	76	80	76	74	94	94	87	98	88	96	1,019
2003	92	81	83	77	74	72	83	78	80	85	76	95	976
2004	77	70	75	69	63	65	67	71	66	61	66	73	823
2005	66	61	67	60	57	58	57	64	60	54	55	59	718
2006	54	52	58	47	56	58	57	66	57	62	66	67	699
2007	73	66	70	56	58	60	62	65	55	64	58	60	745
2008[1]	70	68	70	72	70	74	87	78	86	94	80	93	942

[1] Preliminary.   *Source: Crop Reporting Board, U.S. Department of Agriculture (CRB-USDA)*

Cement

Cement is made in a wide variety of compositions and is used in many different ways. The best-known cement is Portland cement, which is bound with sand and gravel to create concrete. Concrete is used to unite the surfaces of various materials and to coat surfaces to protect them from various chemicals. Portland cement is almost universally used for structural concrete. It is manufactured from lime-bearing materials, usually limestone, together with clays, blast-furnace slag containing alumina and silica or shale. The combination is usually approximately 60 percent lime, 19 percent silica, 8 percent alumina, 5 percent iron, 5 percent magnesia, and 3 percent sulfur trioxide. To slow the hardening process, gypsum is often added. In 1924, the name "Portland cement" was coined by Joseph Aspdin, a British cement maker, because of the resemblance between concrete made from his cement and Portland stone. The United States did not start producing Portland cement in any great quantity until the 20th century. Hydraulic cements are those that set and harden in water. Clinker cement is an intermediate product in cement manufacture. The production and consumption of cement is directly related to the level of activity in the construction industry.

Prices – The average value (F.O.B. mill) of Portland cement in 2008 rose +1.9% yr/yr to $107.00 per ton, which was a new record high.

Supply – World production of hydraulic cement in 2008 rose +4.7% yr/yr to a new record high of 2.900 billion metric tons. The world's largest hydraulic cement producers were China with 50% of world production in 2008, India (6%), U.S. (3%), and Japan (2%).

U.S. production of Portland cement in 2006 (latest data available) fell -1.2% yr/yr to 92.768, down from last the 2005 record high of 93.904 million tons. U.S. shipments of finished Portland cement from mills in the U.S. in 2008 fell 8.5% to 84.413 million metric tons, falling farther below the 2005 record high of 95.588 million metric tons.

Demand – U.S. consumption of cement in 2008 fell 15.5% to 98.600 million metric tons, falling farther below the 2005 record high of 128.250 million metric tons.

Trade – The U.S. relied on imports for 12% of its cement consumption in 2008. The two main suppliers of cement to the U.S. were Canada and Mexico. U.S. exports of cement in 2008 rose +7.3% yr/yr to a record high of 950.000 million metric tons.

World Production of Hydraulic Cement   In Thousands of Short Tons

Year	Brazil	China	France	Germany	India	Italy	Japan	Rep. of Korea	Russia	Spain	Turkey	United States	World Total
2001	38,927	661,040	19,839	32,118	105,000	39,804	76,550	52,046	35,300	40,512	30,125	90,450	1,740,000
2002	38,027	725,000	19,437	31,009	115,000	41,722	71,828	55,514	37,700	42,417	32,577	91,266	1,850,000
2003	34,010	862,080	19,655	32,749	123,000	43,580	68,766	59,194	41,000	44,747	35,077	94,329	2,030,000
2004	34,413	970,000	20,962	31,854	130,000	45,343	67,376	54,330	45,700	46,593	38,796	99,015	2,190,000
2005	36,673	1,068,850	21,277	30,629	145,000	40,284	69,629	51,391	48,500	50,347	42,787	100,903	2,350,000
2006	39,540	1,204,110	22,270	33,516	160,000	47,814	69,942	54,971	54,700	54,033	47,499	99,712	2,560,000
2007[1]	46,400	1,350,000	22,300	33,400	170,000	47,500	67,700	57,000	59,900	54,500	49,500	96,500	2,770,000
2008[2]	48,000	1,450,000	22,000	33,000	175,000	47,000	67,000	56,000	61,000	55,000	48,000	89,100	2,900,000

[1] Preliminary.   [2] Estimate.   *Source: U.S. Geological Survey (USGS)*

Salient Statistics of Cement in the United States

Year	Net Import Reliance as a % of Apparent Consumption	Production Portland 1,000 Metric tons	Production Other[3]	Production Total	Capacity Used at Portland Mills %	Shipments From Mills Total (Mil. MT)	Shipments From Mills Value[4] (Mil. $)	Average Value (F.O.B. Mill) $ per MT	Stocks at Mills Dec. 31	Exports	Apparent Consumption	Imports for Consumption[5] by Country Canada	Japan	Mexico	Spain	Total
2001	21	84,450	4,450	88,900	79.1	112,510	8,600	76.50	6,600	746	112,810	5,110	----	1,645	651	25,861
2002	20	85,283	4,449	89,732	78.7	108,500	8,250	76.00	7,680	834	110,020	5,181	----	1,228	327	24,169
2003	20	88,106	4,737	92,843	78.5	111,000	8,340	75.00	6,610	837	114,090	6,319	----	891	355	23,959
2004	21	92,434	5,000	97,434	81.6	120,731	9,520	79.50	6,970	749	121,950	5,753	2	1,429	408	27,026
2005	23	93,904	5,415	99,319	82.3	129,791	11,700	91.00	7,450	766	128,250	5,404	4	2,173	236	33,261
2006	23	92,768	5,399	98,167	80.6	129,240	12,900	101.50	9,380	723	127,660	5,059	3	2,264	69	35,566
2007[1]	17			95,464		115,426		105.00	8,760	885	116,700					22,468
2008[2]	12			87,700		99,000		107.00	7,900	950	98,600					11,610

[1] Preliminary.   [2] Estimate.   [3] Masonry, natural & pozzolan (slag-line).   [4] Value received F.O.B. mill, excluding cost of containers.   [5] Hydraulic & clinker cement for consumption.   [6] Less than 1/2 unit.   *Source: U.S. Geological Survey (USGS)*

Shipments of Finished Portland Cement from Mills in the United States   In Thousands of Metric Tons

Year	Jan.	Feb.	Mar.	Apr.	May	June	July	Aug.	Sept.	Oct.	Nov.	Dec.	Total
2002	5,554	5,369	6,134	7,860	8,291	8,136	8,467	8,676	7,910	8,326	6,956	5,293	86,973
2003	5,486	4,560	6,483	8,009	8,288	8,492	9,064	8,829	8,755	9,781	6,987	6,348	91,082
2004	5,241	5,146	8,059	8,837	8,624	9,103	9,134	9,326	8,883	8,609	7,417	6,528	94,908
2005	5,337	5,732	7,498	8,316	9,102	9,595	8,305	9,604	8,847	8,870	8,065	6,317	95,588
2006	6,542	6,088	7,704	7,763	8,871	9,230	7,917	9,144	8,011	8,539	7,549	6,097	93,456
2007	5,574	5,207	7,241	7,697	9,082	8,869	8,693	9,426	8,218	9,182	7,890	5,189	92,268
2008[1]	5,441	5,317	6,355	7,769	8,058	8,181	8,652	7,954	7,830	8,277	6,025	4,553	84,413

[1] Preliminary.   *Source: U.S. Geological Survey (USGS)*

Cheese

Since prehistoric times, humans have been making and eating cheese. Dating back as far as 6,000 BC, archaeologists have discovered that cheese had been made from cow and goat milk and stored in tall jars. The Romans turned cheese making into a culinary art, mixing sheep and goat milk and adding herbs and spices for flavoring. By 300 AD, cheese was being exported regularly to countries along the Mediterranean coast.

Cheese is made from the milk of cows and other mammals such as sheep, goats, buffalo, reindeer, camels, yaks, and mares. More than 400 varieties of cheese exist. There are three basic steps common to all cheese making. First, proteins in milk are transformed into curds, or solid lumps. Second, the curds are separated from the milky liquid (or whey) and shaped or pressed into molds. Finally, the shaped curds are ripened according to a variety of aging and curing techniques. Cheeses are usually grouped according to their moisture content into fresh, soft, semi-soft, hard, and very hard. Many classifications overlap due to texture changes with aging.

Cheese is a multi-billion-dollar a year industry in the U.S. Cheddar cheese is the most common natural cheese produced in the U.S., accounting for 35% of U.S. production. Cheeses originating in America include Colby, cream cheese, and Monterey Jack. Varieties other than American cheeses, mostly Italian, now have had a combined level of production that easily exceeds American cheeses.

Prices – Average monthly cheese prices at the Chicago Mercantile Exchange in 2008 rose by +7.3% yr/yr to a new record high of 188.69 cents per pound.

Supply – World production of cheese in 2008 fell -32.6% yr/yr to 14.366 million metric tons, down from last year's record high of 21.326 million metric tons. The European Union is the world's largest producer of cheese with 48% of the total world production in 2008. The U.S. production was the next largest with 31% of the total. U.S. production of cheese in 2008 rose +1.4% to 9.840 billion pounds, which was a new record high.

Demand – U.S. consumption of cheese in 2007 (latest data available) rose +2.5% to 10.112 billion pounds. U.S. per capita cheese consumption in 2002 (latest data available) rose +2.0% to 30.60 pounds per person per year which is a new record high.

Trade – U.S. imports of cheese in 2005 (latest data available) fell -2.5% to 460 million pounds. U.S. exports of cheese in 2005 fell 4.9% to 128 million pounds, down from 2004's record high of 134 million pounds.

World Production of Cheese   In Thousands of Metric Tons

Year	Argentina	Australia	Brazil	Canada	Egypt	European Union	Japan	Mexico	New Zealand	Russia	Ukraine	United States	World Total
2000	445	373	445	328	380	5,976	34	134	297	220	67	3,746	18,475
2001	440	374	460	329	395	5,965	34	140	281	260	105	3,747	18,567
2002	370	413	470	350	410	6,106	36	145	312	340	129	3,877	19,125
2003	325	368	460	342	450	6,205	35	126	301	335	169	3,882	19,219
2004	370	389	470	345	455	6,481	35	134	305	350	224	4,025	20,019
2005	400	375	495	352	480	6,625	39	143	297	375	274	4,150	20,582
2006	480	362	528	291	408	6,801	40	145	292	405	210	4,320	20,965
2007	520	360	580	308	420	6,760	43	147	308	435	244	4,400	21,326
2008[1]	540	344	630	306	----	6,840	55	150	314	425	256	4,465	14,366
2009[2]	550	350	660	305	----	6,870	60	152	345	435	260	4,595	14,624

[1] Preliminary.   [2] Forecast.   NA = Not available.   Source: Foreign Agricultural Service, U.S. Department of Agriculture (FAS-USDA)

Supply and Distribution of All Cheese in the United States   In Millions of Pounds

	Supply					Cheese 40-lb. Blocks Wisconsin Assembly Points (Cents/Lb.)	Distribution				Domestic Disappearance		
	Production		Commercial					Gov't -	American Cheese				
Year	Whole Milk[2]	All Cheese[3]	Stocks Jan. 1	Imports[4]	Total Supply		Exports & Shipments[5]	Stocks Dec. 31	Removed by USDA Programs	Total Disappearance	American Cheese Donated	Total	Per Capita
1998	3,315	7,492	481	371	8,344	158.10	81	.6	8.2	7,797	----	7,664	27.70
1999	3,533	7,894	518	436	8,847	142.28	85	1.0	4.6	8,219	----	8,086	29.00
2000	3,642	8,258	621	416	9,295	116.14	105	2.3	28.0	8,555	----	8,406	29.80
2001	3,544	8,261	706	445	9,412	144.93	115	4.0	3.9	8,741	----	8,586	30.00
2002	3,691	8,547	659	475	9,681	118.22	119	2.7	15.8	8,933	----	8,819	30.60
2003	3,622	8,557	730	476	9,763	131.24	115	27.4	41.3	9,007			
2004	3,739	8,873	715	472	10,060	164.92	134	9.0	5.9	9,342			
2005	3,808	9,149	701	460	10,310	145.53	128			9,519			
2006	3,913	9,525	758			123.85				9,869			
2007[1]		817				175.78				10,112			

[1] Preliminary.   [2] Whole milk American cheddar.   [3] All types of cheese except cottage, pot and baker's cheese.   [4] Imports for consumption.
[5] Commercial.   Source: Economic Research Service, U.S. Department of Agriculture (ERS-USDA)

Production of Cheese in the United States   In Millions of Pounds

Year	American Whole Milk	American Part Skim	American Total	Swiss, Including Block	Munster	Brick	Lim- burger	Crean & Neufchatel Cheese	Italian Varieties	Blue Mond	All Other Varieties	Total of All Cheese[2]	Cottage Cheese Lowfat	Curd[3]	Creamed[4]
1998	3,315	NA	3,315	206.4	94.6	7.6	.9	621.3	3,004.7	[5]	166.0	7,492	361.2	465.8	366.8
1999	3,533	NA	3,533	221.0	80.3	8.1	.7	639.3	3,144.7	[5]	181.0	7,894	359.3	464.8	360.6
2000	3,642	NA	3,642	229.3	85.5	8.6	.6	687.4	3,288.9	[5]	219.7	8,258	363.7	461.0	371.5
2001	3,544	NA	3,544	245.5	82.2	8.7	.7	645.1	3,425.9	[5]	199.6	8,261	370.2	453.2	371.6
2002	3,691	NA	3,691	254.1	81.1	10.0	.7	686.2	3,470.0	[5]	229.8	8,547	374.3	436.6	374.2
2003	3,622	NA	3,622	264.7	79.4	9.8	.7	676.7	3,524.0	[5]	246.7	8,557	384.4	448.0	385.2
2004	3,739	NA	3,739	281.3	72.8	8.1	.9	699.1	3,661.6	[5]	268.1	8,873	396.4	464.0	382.4
2005	3,808	NA	3,808	300.1	77.9	8.9	.8	714.8	3,803.0	[5]	268.3	9,149	407.9	468.6	376.7
2006	3,913	NA	3,913	314.5	95.5	8.6	.8	756.2	3,972.9	[5]	281.5	9,525	409.2	459.0	368.8
2007[1]	3,878	NA	3,878	313.7	103.5	7.4	.7	772.8	4,134.2	[5]	299.8	9,700	420.8	460.6	360.7

[1] Preliminary.   [2] Excludes full-skim cheddar and cottage cheese.   [3] Includes cottage, pot, and baker's cheese with a butterfat content of less than 4%.
[4] Includes cheese with a butterfat content of 4 to 19 %.   [5] Included in All Other Varieties.   NA = Not available.
Source: Economic Research Service, U.S. Department of Agriculture ERS-USDA)

Average Price of Cheese, 40-lb. Blocks, Chicago Mercantile Exchange[2]   In Cents Per Pound

Year	Jan.	Feb.	Mar.	Apr.	May	June	July	Aug.	Sept.	Oct.	Nov.	Dec.	Average
1999	162.4	131.5	134.0	133.6	124.8	138.1	159.7	189.0	167.3	134.0	117.3	115.7	142.3
2000	114.6	111.6	112.2	110.7	110.6	120.0	125.2	125.5	133.4	109.4	107.5	113.0	116.1
2001	110.3	120.0	131.9	140.5	160.3	166.8	168.5	171.8	173.9	139.7	126.4	129.1	144.9
2002	132.4	120.8	121.3	124.5	120.1	113.0	108.9	115.8	120.4	119.5	108.9	113.1	118.2
2003	109.3	109.2	108.2	112.3	114.2	118.6	151.2	160.0	160.0	158.8	139.3	133.8	131.2
2004	130.6	139.6	182.0	216.9	199.3	171.1	144.9	157.3	157.0	151.7	169.6	159.2	164.9
2005	162.7	149.3	153.2	154.1	147.7	150.7	105.4	142.5	156.4	144.7	137.6	142.2	145.5
2006	133.4	119.9	116.4	116.5	118.6	119.2	116.3	123.5	129.3	123.5	137.5	132.2	123.8
2007	131.8	134.1	138.2	146.3	172.1	201.0	191.4	195.5	199.3	189.6	209.3	200.8	175.8
2008[1]	182.6	200.2	182.3	188.3	209.8	203.5	196.7	174.0	187.6	179.6	171.0	151.3	185.6

[1] Preliminary.   [2] Data through December 2001 are for Wholesale Price of Cheese, 40-lb. Blocks, Wisconsin Assembly Points.
Source: Economic Research Service, U.S. Department of Agriculture (ERS-USDA)

Production[2] of Cheese in the United States   In Millions of Pounds

Year	Jan.	Feb.	Mar.	Apr.	May	June	July	Aug.	Sept.	Oct.	Nov.	Dec.	Total
1999	631.6	591.7	698.2	663.8	668.9	664.4	641.3	642.6	637.6	666.5	683.4	704.2	7,894
2000	692.9	649.5	714.8	694.0	730.4	695.7	687.6	683.8	653.8	688.5	675.0	688.4	8,255
2001	680.3	625.3	713.7	670.2	706.8	678.5	676.0	660.0	641.8	682.1	691.2	703.1	8,129
2002	717.5	667.9	742.8	719.2	748.3	708.3	692.2	714.3	683.9	732.2	725.4	747.2	8,599
2003	714.8	648.6	730.3	718.8	737.0	712.3	718.3	700.1	708.7	740.0	710.0	758.9	8,598
2004	738.0	705.5	785.6	761.0	752.1	715.3	708.7	719.5	714.4	748.0	754.3	773.9	8,876
2005	754.0	704.6	797.5	754.8	783.9	764.5	739.5	757.4	745.5	760.4	766.1	798.9	9,127
2006	782.7	720.5	820.8	793.6	820.0	796.1	775.4	795.1	788.6	812.3	798.1	831.1	9,534
2007	822.9	754.1	840.5	803.8	824.6	792.6	799.5	797.0	777.2	825.8	815.2	847.3	9,700
2008[1]	812.7	784.6	834.7	810.2	831.8	809.4	813.2	820.7	796.5	843.5	824.0	859.0	9,840

[1] Preliminary.   [2] Excludes cottage cheese.   *Source: National Agricultural Statistics Service, U.S. Department of Agriculture (NASS-USDA)*

Cold Storage Holdings of All Varieties of Cheese in the United States, on First of Month   In Millions of Pounds

Year	Jan.	Feb.	Mar.	Apr.	May	June	July	Aug.	Sept.	Oct.	Nov.	Dec.
1999	517.2	622.4	635.9	645.1	688.7	741.3	728.4	748.7	694.7	651.3	622.0	591.7
2000	621.3	728.1	757.2	765.1	794.0	811.4	828.1	870.3	839.9	780.9	732.0	696.0
2001	707.8	709.9	723.9	711.6	711.8	712.1	739.2	752.6	721.2	708.7	672.2	631.3
2002	660.0	693.6	720.3	731.7	765.6	789.0	797.6	833.6	801.5	753.9	720.4	697.1
2003	730.1	761.2	770.0	771.3	781.1	791.0	800.1	809.0	794.2	762.2	722.4	695.5
2004	724.4	756.9	766.1	759.5	767.6	804.5	842.0	870.0	811.5	790.7	756.1	704.3
2005	705.8	713.8	723.7	749.2	780.8	815.6	823.4	837.2	812.9	769.0	755.9	720.8
2006	758.2	765.0	782.8	810.7	832.8	863.3	876.0	898.9	862.3	843.1	810.2	784.8
2007	817.4	850.0	875.7	892.9	894.3	898.9	891.2	886.0	846.2	820.4	810.6	805.9
2008[1]	798.3	781.4	801.0	824.3	855.9	881.3	902.5	902.8	880.3	834.2	829.0	818.6

Quantities are given in "net weight."   [1] Preliminary.   *Source: National Agricultural Statistics Service, U.S. Department of Agriculture (NASS-USDA)*

Chromium

Chromium (symbol Cr) is a steel-gray, hard, and brittle, metallic element that can take on a high polish. Chromium and its compounds are toxic. Discovered in 1797 by Louis Vauquelin, chromium is named after the Greek word for color, khroma. Vauquelin also discovered that an emerald's green color is due to the presence of chromium. Many precious stones owe their color to the presence of chromium compounds.

Chromium is primarily found in chromite ore. The primary use of chromium is to form alloys with iron, nickel, or cobalt. Chromium improves hardness and resistance to corrosion and oxidation in iron, steel, and nonferrous alloys. It is a critical alloying ingredient in the production of stainless steel, making up 10% or more of the final composition. More than half of the chromium consumed is used in metallic products, and about one-third is used in refractories. Chromium is also used as a lustrous decorative plating agent, in pigments, leather processing, plating of metals, and catalysts.

Supply – World production of chromium in 2008 was unchanged yr/yr at the record high of 21.500 million metric tons, which remained up sharply from the 12-year low of 12.100 million metric tons in 2001. The world's largest producers of chromium in 2006 (latest data available) were South Africa with 38% of world production, Kazakhstan with 18%, India with 18%, and with Turkey and Zimbabwe far behind with 5% and 3% respectively. India has emerged as a major producer of chromium in the past two decades. India's 2008 production level of 3.300 million metric tons was almost ten times the level of 360,000 metric tons seen 20 years earlier. South Africa's production in 2008 at 9.600 million metric tons was down less than 1.00% yr/yr from the 2007 record high of 9.650 million metric tons, but that is still more than double the levels seen as recently as the early-1990s. Kazakhstan's production in 2008 of 3.700 million was an 18-year high. Zimbabwe's chromium production in 2006 (latest data) was 600,000 metric tons. U.S. Government stocks of chromium as of Dec 31, 2006 (latest data available) fell 98.4% yr/yr to a record low of 1.160 metric tons.

Demand – Based on the most recently available data from 2004, the metallurgical and chemical industry accounts for 94% of chromium usage in the U.S., with the remaining 6% used by the refractory industry.

Trade – The U.S. relied on imports for a record low of 54% of its chromium consumption in 2008. That is well below the record high of 91% posted back in the 1970s. U.S. chromium imports in 2006 fell -3.3% yr/yr to 341,800 metric tons. U.S. exports of chromium in 2006 fell -1.6% yr/yr to 56.4 metric tons.

World Mine Production of Chromite   In Thousands of Metric Tons (Gross Weight)

Year	Albania	Brazil	Cuba	Finland	India	Iran	Kazak-hstan	Mada-gascar	philip-pines	South Africa	Turkey	Zim-babwe	Total[1]
1998	102	537	46	498	1,311	212	1,603	104	54	6,480	1,404	605	13,700
1999	71	458	52	597	1,473	255	2,406	----	20	6,817	770	653	14,200
2000	120	550	56	628	1,947	153	2,607	131	26	6,622	546	668	14,700
2001	130	409	50	575	1,678	145	2,046	24	27	5,502	390	780	12,200
2002	73	284	20	566	2,699	513	2,369	11	22	6,436	314	749	14,600
2003	98	377	33	549	2,210	97	2,928	45	34	7,405	229	637	15,500
2004	54	593	40	580	2,949	139	3,267	77	42	7,645	506	668	17,600
2005	66	616	34	572	3,255	224	3,579	141	38	7,493	859	618	19,000
2006[1]	65	616	34	549	3,600	225	3,600	132	47	7,418	1,060	600	19,700
2007[2]					3,320		3,690			9,650			21,500

[1] Preliminary.   [2] Estimate.   Source: U.S. Geological Survey (USGS)

Salient Statistics of Chromite in the United States   In Thousands of Metric Tons (Gross Weight)

Year	Net Import Reliance as a % of Appearent Consumption	Production of Ferro-chromium	Exports	Imports for Con-sumption	Reexports	Consumption by -- Primary Consumer Group -- Total	Metal-lurgical & Chemical	Refractory	Government[5] Stocks, Dec. 31 - Metal-lurgical & Chemical	Refractory	Total Stocks	$/Metric Ton South Africa[3]	Turkish[4]
1997	75	61	27	349	----	W	W	W	167	8	175	75	150
1998	80	W	55	383	----	W	W	W	W	W	159	68	145
1999	80	W	53	475	----	W	W	W	W	W	130	63	145
2000	77	W	86	453	----	W	W	W	396	241	637	60-65	140-150
2001	63	W	43	239	----	W	W	W	396	241	637	NA	NA
2002	69	W	29	263	----	W	W	W	78	126	204	NA	NA
2003	57	W	46	317	----	W	W	W	79	156	235	NA	NA
2004	64	W	35	326	----	W	W	W	46	88	135	NA	NA
2005[1]	59	W	57	353	----	W	W	W	4	70	73	NA	NA
2006[2]	64	W			----	W	W	W				NA	NA

[1] Preliminary.   [2] Estimate.   [3] Cr_2O_3, 44% (Transvaal).   [4] 48% Cr_2O_3.   [5] Data through 1999 are for Consumer.   W = Withheld.
Source: U.S. Geological Survey (USGS)

Coal

Coal is a sedimentary rock composed primarily of carbon, hydrogen, and oxygen. Coal is a fossil fuel formed from ancient plants buried deep in the Earth's crust over 300 million years ago. Historians believe coal was first used commercially in China for smelting copper and for casting coins around 1,000 BC. Almost 92% of all coal consumed in the U.S. is burned by electric power plants, and coal accounts for about 55% of total electricity output. Coal is also used in the manufacture of steel. The steel industry first converts coal into coke, then combines the coke with iron ore and limestone, and finally heats the mixture to produce iron. Other industries use coal to make fertilizers, solvents, medicine, pesticides, and synthetic fuels.

There are four types of mined coal: anthracite (used in high-grade steel production), bituminous (used for electricity generation and for making coke), sub-bituminous, and lignite (both used primarily for electricity generation).

Coal futures trade at the New York Mercantile Exchange (NYMEX). The contract trades in units of 1,550 tons and is priced in terms of dollars and cents per short ton.

Supply – U.S. production of bituminous coal in 2008 (annualized through Dec) rose +2.4% yr/yr to a new record high of 1.172 tons.

Demand – U.S. consumption of coal in 2007 (latest data available) rose by +1.5% to a new record high of 1.129 billion tons.

Trade – U.S. exports of coal in 2007 (latest data available) rose +19.2% yr/yr to a 9-year high of 59.163 million tons, and imports rose +0.3% yr/yr to a record high of 36.346 million tons. The major exporting destinations for the U.S. are Canada and Europe.

World Production[3] of Coal (Monthly Average)   In Thousands of Metric Tons

Year	Australia	Canada	China	Czech-Republic	Germany	India	Indonesia	Kazakhstan	Poland	Russia	Ukraine	United Kingdom	United States
1999	18,643	3,043	80,200	1,193	3,657	25,004	5,892	4,644	9,301	13,799	6,804	3,090	66,796
2000	19,958	2,817	70,782	1,238	3,111	25,802	6,402	5,960	8,598	14,292	6,749	2,600	65,220
2001	22,018	2,845	80,040	1,261	2,406	26,563	7,554	4,429	8,658	15,507	6,908	2,677	68,666
2002	23,123	5,573	92,339	1,206	2,197	27,938	8,588	6,493	8,676	15,198	5,163	2,499	66,565
2003	30,000	5,177	109,602	1,137	2,396	29,036	9,551	7,073	8,529	16,329	5,354	2,353	81,023
2004	31,250	5,499	130,434	1,109	2,429	31,438	11,021	7,240	8,414	17,495	4,947	2,089	92,953
2005	32,917	5,445	150,891	1,104	2,335	33,129	11,755	7,218	8,154	18,472	5,029	1,667	94,439
2006	33,084	5,244	171,288	1,111	1,980	35,088	12,571	6,428	7,940	19,468	5,135	1,506	96,782
2007[1]	33,667	5,780	191,562	1,074	1,794	37,121	14,569	6,636	7,316	20,178	4,895	1,419	95,390
2008[2]	33,334	5,771	213,275	1,049	1,579	38,999	12,516	9,076	7,111	20,449	4,991	1,426	97,415

[1] Preliminary.   [2] Estimate.   [3] All grades of anthracite and bituminous coal, but excludes recovered slurries, lignite and brown coal.
Source: United Nations

Production of Bituminous & Lignite Coal in the United States   In Thousands of Short Tons

Year	Alabama	Colorado	Illinois	Indiana	Kentucky	Montana	Ohio	Pennsylvania	Texas	West Virginia	Virginia	Wyoming	Total
1998	23,224	30,825	38,182	36,297	145,609	42,092	28,600	76,519	53,578	34,059	175,794	313,983	1,109,768
1999	19,504	29,989	40,417	34,004	139,626	41,102	22,480	76,368	53,071	32,181	157,919	337,119	1,095,474
2000	19,324	29,137	33,444	27,965	130,688	38,352	22,269	74,619	49,498	32,834	158,257	338,900	1,073,612
2001	19,513	33,372	33,783	36,738	134,298	39,143	25,400	74,784	45,042	33,060	162,631	368,749	1,125,749
2002	19,062	35,103	33,358	35,513	124,388	37,386	21,157	67,104	45,247	30,126	150,222	373,161	1,092,916
2003	20,207	35,831	31,760	35,512	113,126	36,994	22,009	63,792	47,517	31,771	139,755	376,270	1,071,753
2004	22,329	39,870	31,912	35,206	114,743	39,989	23,222	66,023	45,863	31,647	148,017	396,493	1,110,393
2005	21,453	38,510	32,014	34,457	120,029	40,354	24,718	65,852	45,939	27,964	153,655	404,319	1,129,794
2006[1]	18,830	36,322	32,729	35,119	120,848	41,823	22,722	64,500	45,548	29,740	152,374	446,742	1,162,750
2007[2]	19,321	36,384	32,445	35,003	114,970	43,390	22,558	63,498	41,948	25,268	153,223	453,568	1,145,567

[1] Preliminary.   [2] Estimate.   *Source: Energy Information Administration, U.S. Department of Energy (EIA-DOE)*

Production[2] of Bituminous Coal in the United States   In Thousands of Short Tons

Year	Jan.	Feb.	Mar.	Apr.	May	June	July	Aug.	Sept.	Oct.	Nov.	Dec.	Total
1999	90,928	92,015	98,672	88,630	84,436	89,734	87,759	92,600	92,248	89,146	90,885	92,450	1,089,503
2000	87,222	86,846	99,045	81,793	88,715	90,583	84,442	96,361	88,848	92,542	94,035	87,272	1,077,704
2001	96,721	86,802	99,176	89,954	94,840	92,657	89,037	99,048	88,985	99,529	93,736	88,234	1,118,719
2002	101,939	90,208	90,108	90,039	91,673	85,555	86,190	92,054	92,212	94,033	87,836	91,058	1,092,905
2003	92,649	82,130	88,976	89,202	90,435	88,348	88,301	89,355	90,344	93,928	84,155	94,154	1,071,977
2004	93,182	86,306	94,876	91,739	87,210	94,835	92,260	95,209	93,525	92,618	92,268	95,478	1,109,506
2005	92,804	89,039	102,178	93,296	90,168	95,374	91,930	97,907	95,493	93,532	94,842	92,774	1,129,337
2006	98,385	88,826	101,339	95,288	99,706	97,023	94,861	100,504	94,029	98,674	96,400	95,939	1,160,974
2007	99,221	88,084	97,490	92,923	96,867	95,432	92,884	100,493	92,288	98,691	96,769	93,010	1,144,152
2008[1]	98,488	93,428	98,870	97,832	97,375	90,798	98,476	99,763	98,679	103,786	94,907	99,179	1,171,581

[1] Preliminary.   [2] Includes small amount of lignite.   *Source: Energy Information Administration, U.S. Department of Energy (EIA-DOE)*

COAL

Production[2] of Pennsylvania Anthracite Coal In Thousands of Short Tons

Year	Jan.	Feb.	Mar.	Apr.	May	June	July	Aug.	Sept.	Oct.	Nov.	Dec.	Total
1999	355	369	389	354	459	402	343	436	479	414	407	406	4,808
2000	271	283	382	342	375	383	366	430	412	417	402	366	4,432
2001	302	275	323	283	300	297	328	358	318	375	349	173	3,681
2002	131	117	116	121	122	240	116	126	119	130	120	126	1,584
2003	108	98	98	115	114	107	97	95	101	130	111	116	1,290
2004	197	183	147	111	101	214	141	145	150	145	151	127	1,812
2005	133	129	149	137	135	157	125	140	135	156	179	127	1,704
2006	138	121	147	117	128	125	124	140	115	134	126	123	1,538
2007	141	125	139	125	133	134	120	135	116	134	141	128	1,568
2008[1]	131	126	127	158	160	102	149	147	149	168	140	154	1,712

[1] Preliminary. [2] Represents production in Pennsylvania only. *Source: Energy Information Administration, U.S. Department of Energy (EIA-DOE)*

Salient Statistics of Coal in the United States In Thousands of Short Tons

Year	Production	Imports	Consumption	Exports Brazil	Exports Canada	Exports Europe	Exports Asia	Exports Total	Total Ending Stocks[2]	Losses & Unaccounted For[3]
1998	1,117,535	8,724	1,037,103	6,475	19,901	33,773	12,311	77,295	164,602	-13,118
1999	1,100,431	9,089	1,038,648	4,442	19,826	22,508	9,157	58,476	188,590	-11,592
2000	1,073,612	12,513	1,084,094	4,536	18,769	24,969	6,702	58,489	140,282	938
2001	1,127,689	19,787	1,060,146	4,574	17,633	20,821	3,246	48,666	181,912	7,120
2002	1,094,283	16,875	1,066,355	3,538	16,686	15,574	1,735	39,601	192,127	4,039
2003	1,071,753	25,044	1,094,861	3,514	20,760	15,148	266	43,014	165,468	-4,403
2004	1,112,099	27,280	1,107,255	4,361	17,760	15,211	7,475	47,998	154,006	6,887
2005	1,131,498	30,460	1,125,978	4,199	19,466	18,825	5,082	49,942	144,304	9,092
2006	1,162,750	36,246	1,112,292	4,534	19,889	20,805	2,008	49,647	186,946	8,824
2007[1]	1,145,567	36,347	1,128,836	6,512	18,389	27,119	1,202	59,163	189,443	5,505

[1] Preliminary. [2] Producer & distributor and consumer stocks, excludes stocks held by retail dealers for consumption by the residential and commercial sector. [3] Equals production plus imports minus the change in producer & distributor and consumer stocks minus consumption minus exports.
Source: Energy Information Administraion, U.S. Department of Energy (EIA-DOE)

Consumption and Stocks of Coal in the United States In Thousands of Short Tons

Year	Consumption Electric Utilities Anthracite	Bituminous	Lignite	Total	Industrial Coke Plants	Other Industrial[2]	Residential and Commercial	Total	Stocks, Dec. 31 Consumer Electric Utilities	Coke Plants	Other Industrials	Producers and Distributors[3]
1998	867	832,094	77,906	936,619	28,189	67,439	4,856	1,037,103	120,501	2,026	5,545	36,530
1999	686	815,909	77,525	940,922	28,108	64,738	4,878	1,038,647	141,604	1,943	5,569	39,475
2000	NA	781,821	75,794	985,821	28,939	65,208	4,127	1,084,095	102,296	1,494	4,587	31,905
2001	NA	NA	NA	964,433	26,075	65,268	4,369	1,060,146	138,496	1,510	6,006	35,900
2002	NA	NA	NA	977,507	23,656	60,747	4,445	1,066,355	141,714	1,364	5,792	43,257
2003	NA	NA	NA	1,005,116	24,248	61,261	4,236	1,094,861	121,567	905	4,718	38,277
2004	NA	NA	NA	1,016,268	23,670	62,195	5,122	1,107,255	106,669	1,344	4,842	41,151
2005	NA	NA	NA	1,037,485	23,434	60,340	4,719	1,125,978	101,237	2,615	5,582	34,971
2006	NA	NA	NA	1,026,636	22,957	59,472	3,227	1,112,292	140,964	2,928	6,506	36,548
2007[1]	NA	NA	NA	1,046,424	22,715	56,470	3,227	1,128,836	151,127	1,936	5,624	30,757

[1] Preliminary. [2] Including transportation. [3] Excludes stocks held at retail dealers for consumption by the residential and commercial sector.
Source: Energy Information Administration, U.S. Department of Energy (EIA-DOE)

Average Prices of Coal in the United States In Dollars Per Short Ton

Year	End-Use Sector Electric Utilities	Coke Plants	Other Industrial[2]	Imports[3]	Exports Steam	Metal-lurgical	Total Average[3]	Year	End-Use Sector Electric Utilities	Coke Plants	Other Industrial[2]	Imports[3]	Exports Steam	Metal-lurgical	Total Average[3]
1998	25.64	46.06	32.30	32.18	30.27	44.53	38.89	2003	25.29	50.63	34.70	31.45	26.94	44.55	35.98
1999	24.72	45.85	31.59	30.77	29.91	41.91	36.50	2004	27.30	61.50	39.30	37.52	42.03	63.63	54.11
2000	24.28	44.38	31.46	30.10	29.67	38.99	34.89	2005	31.22	83.79	47.63	46.71	47.64	81.56	67.10
2001	24.68	46.42	32.26	34.00	31.88	41.63	36.97	2006	34.26	92.87	51.67	49.10	46.25	90.81	70.93
2002	24.74	50.67	35.49	35.51	34.51	45.41	40.44	2007[1]	NA	94.97	54.42	47.64	47.90	88.99	70.25

[1] Preliminary. [2] Manufacturing plants only. [3] Based on the free alongside ship (F.A.S.) value.
Source: Energy Information Administration, U.S. Department of Energy (EIA-DOE)

Trends in Bituminous Coal, Lignite and Pennsylvania Anthracite in the United States In Thousands of Short Tons

	Bituminous Coal and Lignite								Pennsylvania Anthracite				All Mines
	Production				Labor Productivity								
	Under-			Miners[1]	Under-Ground	Surface	Average	Under-			Miners[1]	Labor Productivity Short Tons	All Mines Labor Productivity Short Tons
Year	Ground	Surface	Total	Employed	Short Tons Per Miner Per Hour -			Ground	Surface	Total	Employed	Miner/Hr.	Miner/Hr.
1998	417,728	699,807	1,117,535	85,418	3.90	9.58	6.20	408	4,823	5,231	1,281	2.04	6.20
1999	391,790	708,642	1,100,431	78,723	3.99	10.39	6.61	377	4,376	4,753	1,326	1.76	6.61
2000	373,659	699,953	1,073,612	72,748	4.15	11.01	6.99	301	4,271	4,572	1,272	1.89	6.99
2001	380,627	745,308	1,127,689	77,088	4.02	10.60	6.82	341	1,143	1,484	955	.81	6.82
2002	357,385	735,910	1,094,283	75,466	3.98	10.38	6.80	305	998	1,303	872	.78	6.80
2003	352,785	717,870	1,071,753	71,023	4.04	10.76	6.95	282	961	1,243	814	.82	6.95
2004	367,557	743,552	1,112,099	73,912	3.96	10.57	6.80	271	1,408	1,679	890	.97	6.80
2005	368,612	762,190	1,131,498	79,283	3.62	10.04	6.36	264	1,296	1,560	891	.95	6.36
2006	359,022	802,976	1,161,998	82,959	3.37	10.19	6.26	239	1,132	1,371	869	.95	6.26
2007	351,790	793,690	1,145,480	81,278	3.34	10.25	6.27	196	1,199	1,395	910	.89	6.27

[1] Excludes miners employed at mines producing less than 10,000 tons.
Source: Energy Information Administration, U.S. Department of Energy (EIA-DOE)

Average Mine Prices of Coal in the United States In Dollars Per Short Ton

	Average Mine Prices by Method			Average Mine Prices by Rank				Bituminous & Lignite	Anthracite	All Coal CIF[3]
Year	Under-ground	Surface	Total	Lignite	Sub-bituminous	Bituminous	Anthracite[1]	FOB Mines[2]	FOB Mines[2]	Electric Utility Plants
1998	25.64	12.92	17.67	10.80	6.96	24.87	42.91	24.87	42.91	25.64
1999	24.33	12.37	16.63	11.04	6.87	23.92	35.13	23.92	35.13	24.72
2000	23.84	12.26	16.44	11.41	7.12	24.15	40.90	24.15	40.90	24.28
2001	25.37	13.18	17.38	11.52	6.67	25.36	47.67	25.36	47.67	24.68
2002	26.68	13.65	17.98	11.07	7.34	26.57	47.78	26.57	47.78	24.74
2003	26.71	13.42	17.85	11.20	7.73	26.73	49.55	26.73	49.55	25.29
2004	30.36	14.75	19.93	12.27	8.12	30.56	39.77	30.56	39.77	27.30
2005	36.42	17.37	23.59	13.49	8.68	36.80	41.00	36.80	41.00	31.22
2006	38.28	18.88	25.16	14.00	9.95	39.32	43.61	39.32	43.61	34.26
2007	40.29	19.41	26.20	14.89	10.69	40.80	52.24	40.80	52.24	36.06

[1] Produced in Pennsylvania.   [2] FOB = free on board.   [3] CIF = cost, insurance and freight.   W = Withheld data.
Source: Energy Information Adminstration, U.S. Department of Energy (EIA-DOE)

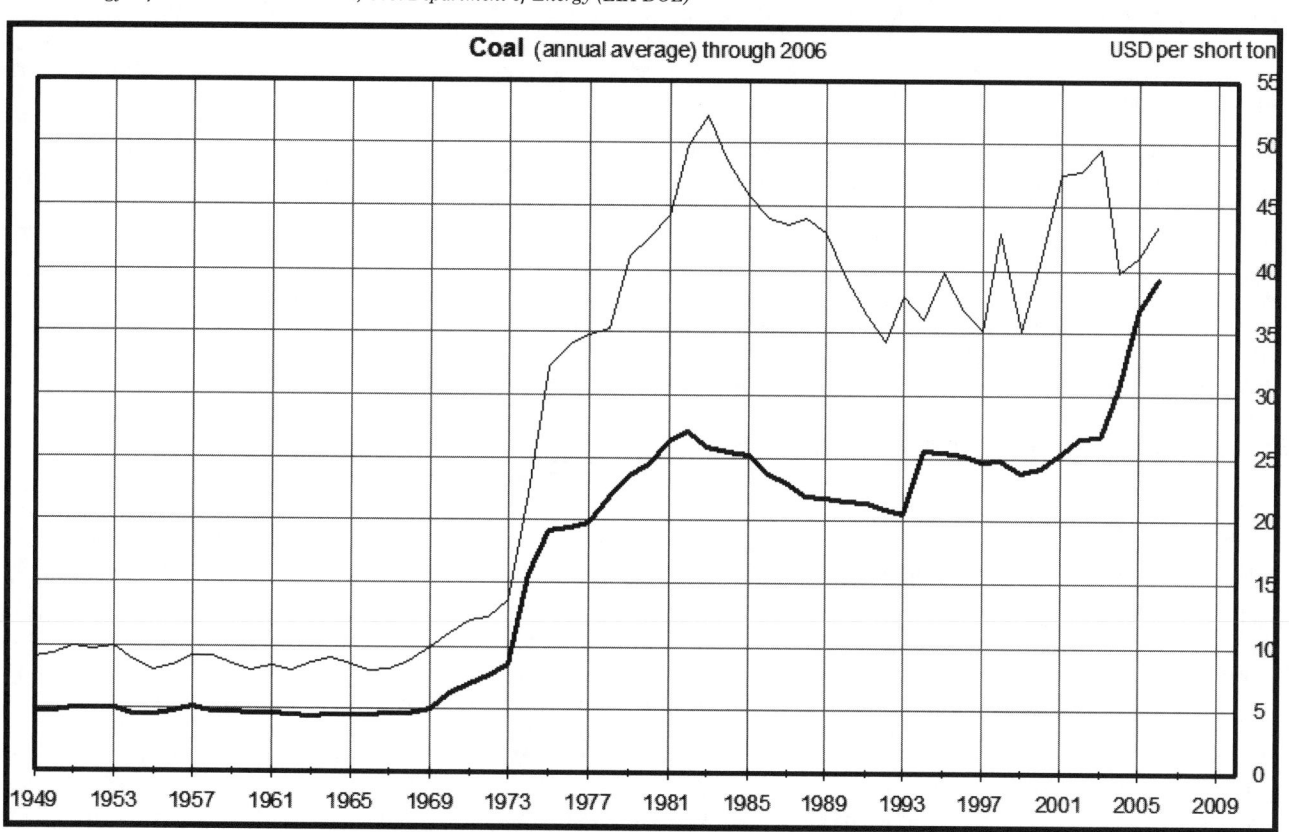

Coal (annual average) through 2006   USD per short ton

Cobalt

Cobalt (symbol Co) is a lustrous, silvery-white, magnetic, metallic element used chiefly for making alloys. Cobalt was known in ancient times and used by the Persians in 2250 BC to color glass. The name cobalt comes from the German word kobalt or kobold, meaning evil spirit. Miners gave cobalt its name because it was poisonous and troublesome since it polluted and degraded other mined elements, like nickel. In the 1730s, George Brandt first isolated metallic cobalt and was able to show that cobalt was the source of the blue color in glasses. In 1780, it was recognized as an element. Cobalt is generally not found in nature as a free metal and is instead found in ores. Cobalt is generally produced as a by-product of nickel and copper mining.

Cobalt is used in a variety of applications: high temperature steel alloys; fasteners in gas turbine engines; magnets and magnetic recording media; drying agents for paints and pigments; and steel-belted radial tires. Cobalt-60, an important radioactive tracer and cancer-treatment agent, is an artificially produced radioactive isotope of cobalt.

Prices – The price of cobalt rose sharply by +32.2% in 2008 to a new record high of $40.40 per pound. That is more than five times the 20-year low of $6.91 per pound in 2002, just six years ago.

Supply – World production of cobalt in 2008 rose by +9.6% to a new record high of 71,800 metric tons. The world's largest cobalt mine producers are the Congo with 45% of world production in 2008, Canada (12%), Canada (12%), Zambia (11%), and Australia (9%).

The U.S. does not specifically mine or refine cobalt although some cobalt is produced as a by-product of other mining operations. Imports, stock releases, and secondary materials comprise the U.S. cobalt supply. Secondary production includes extraction from super-alloy scrap, cemented carbide scrap, and spent catalysts. In the U.S. there are two domestic producers of extra-fine cobalt powder. One company produces the powder from imported primary metal and the other from recycled materials. There are only about seven companies that produce cobalt compounds. U.S. secondary production of cobalt in 2008 fell 1.6% yr/yr to 1,900 metric tons and remains well below the record high of 3,080 metric tons seen in 1998.

Demand – U.S. consumption of cobalt in 2008 rose by +6.3% yr/yr to 10,200 metric tons, but still below the 2005 record high of 11,800 metric tons. The largest use of cobalt by far was for super-alloys 38% of consumption in 2006 consumption. Other smaller-scaled applications for cobalt include cutting and wear-resistant materials (7.2%), magnetic alloys (3.5%), and welding materials (2.0%). Demand for some other uses is withheld as proprietary information.

Trade – U.S. imports of cobalt in 2008 rose +6.8% to 11,000 metric tons, but that is still below the 2006 record high of 11,600 metric tons. In 2008 the U.S. relied on imports for 81% of its cobalt consumption, which is down from the 99% level seen in the early 1970s.

World Mine Production of Cobalt   In Metric Tons (Cobalt Content)

Year	Australia	Botswana	Canada	Cuba	Finland (Refinery)	France (Refinery)	Japan (Refinery)	New Caledonia	Norway (Refinery)	Russia	Congo[3]	Zambia	World Total
1998	3,300	335	5,861	2,665	10,600	300	480	1,000	4,500	3,600	5,000	11,900	35,300
1999	4,100	331	5,323	2,537	10,000	300	480	1,100	4,500	3,900	7,000	5,640	32,700
2000	5,600	308	5,298	2,852	7,700	204	311	1,200	3,433	4,000	11,000	4,600	37,900
2001	6,300	325	5,326	3,425	8,100	199	350	1,400	3,314	4,600	12,000	8,000	44,800
2002	6,800	269	5,148	3,442	8,240	176	354	2,780	3,994	4,600	14,600	10,000	52,200
2003	7,300	294	4,327	3,274	7,989	181	379	2,602	4,556	4,800	14,800	11,300	52,700
2004	7,000	223	5,060	3,554	7,893	199	429	2,726	4,670	4,700	20,200	10,000	58,400
2005	7,200	326	5,767	3,768	8,171	280	471	1,769	5,021	5,000	24,500	9,300	63,500
2006[1]	7,400	303	6,976	3,800	8,582	256	920	1,900	4,927	5,100	28,000	8,000	67,500
2007[2]	5,900		8,300	3,800				1,600		6,300	25,300	7,600	65,500

[1] Preliminary.   [2] Estimate.   [3] Formerly Zaire.   *Source: U.S. Geological Survey (USGS)*

Salient Statistics of Cobalt in the United States   In Metric Tons (Cobalt Content)

Year	Net Import Reliance As a % of Apparent Consumption	Cobalt Secondary Production	Processor and Consumer Stocks Dec. 31	Imports for Consumption	Ground Coat Frit	Stainless & Heat Resisting	Catalysts	Super-alloys	Tool Steel	Magnetic Alloys	Pigments	Drier in Paints etc.	Cutting & Wear-Resistant Material	Welding Materials	Total Apparent Uses	Price $ Per Pound[4]
1998	73	3,080	750	7,670	W	38	W	4,060	96	771	W	W	844	421	11,500	21.43
1999	73	2,720	738	8,150	W	W	W	3,830	W	794	W	W	755	291	10,700	17.02
2000	78	2,550	820	8,770	W	W	W	4,070	W	625	W	W	760	867	11,600	15.16
2001	76	2,780	852	9,410	W	W	W	4,850	W	472	W	W	720	661	11,800	10.55
2002	72	2,800	917	8,450	W	W	W	3,700	W	416	W	W	618	634	9,830	6.91
2003	79	2,130	649	8,080	W	W	W	3,400	W	282	W	W	662	632	10,000	10.60
2004	77	2,300	719	8,720	W	W	W	3,650	W	396	W	W	765	627	9,950	23.93
2005	83	2,030	705	11,100	W	W	W	4,140	W	343	W	W	762	227	11,800	15.96
2006[1]	82	2,010	711	11,600	W	W	W	4,180	W	386	W	W	796	224	11,000	17.22
2007[2]	80	1,930		10,300											9,600	30.55

[1] Preliminary.   [2] Estimate.   [3] Or related usage.   [4] Annual spot for cathodes.   W = Withheld.   *Source: U.S. Geological Survey (USGS)*

Cocoa

Cocoa is the common name for a powder derived from the fruit seeds of the cacao tree. The Spanish called cocoa "the food of the gods" when they found it in South America 500 years ago. Today, it remains a valued commodity. Dating back to the time of the Aztecs, cocoa was mainly used as a beverage. The processing of the cacao seeds, also known as cocoa beans, begins when the harvested fruit is fermented or cured into a pulpy state for three to nine days. The cocoa beans are then dried in the sun and cleaned in special machines before they are roasted to bring out the chocolate flavor. After roasting, they are put into a crushing machine and ground into cocoa powder. Cocoa has a high food value because it contains as much as 20 percent protein, 40 percent carbohydrate, and 40 percent fat. It is also mildly stimulating because of the presence of theobromine, an alkaloid that is closely related to caffeine. Roughly two-thirds of cocoa bean production is used to make chocolate and one-third to make cocoa powder.

Four major West African cocoa producers, the Ivory Coast, Ghana, Nigeria and Cameroon, together account for about two-thirds of world cocoa production. Outside of West Africa, the major producers of cocoa are Indonesia, Brazil, Malaysia, Ecuador, and the Dominican Republic. Cocoa producers like Ghana and Indonesia have been making efforts to increase cocoa production while producers like Malaysia have been switching to other crops. Ghana has had an ongoing problem with black pod disease and with smuggling of the crop into neighboring Ivory Coast. Brazil was once one of the largest producers of cocoa but has had problems with witches' broom disease. In West Africa, the main crop harvest starts in the September-October period and can be extended into the January-March period. Cocoa trees reach maturity in 5-6 years but can live to be 50 years old or more. During the course of a growing season, the cocoa tree will produce thousands of flowers but only a few will develop into cocoa pods.

Cocoa futures and options are traded at the CSCE Division of the New York Board of Trade (NYBOT) and on the London International Financial Futures and Options Exchange (LIFFE). The futures contracts call for the delivery of 10 metric tons of cocoa and the contract is priced in US dollars per metric ton.

Prices – Cocoa prices in 2007 on the nearest-futures chart moved higher early in the year and then traded sideways until the fourth quarter when they moved up to 4-3/4 year highs, just below the more-than-two decade high of $2,420 posted in early 2003. Cocoa futures closed 2007 at $2,035 per metric ton, up +24.5% from the close of $1635 in 2006. Bullish factors for cocoa in 2007 included (1) a higher global cocoa deficit as demand in 2007 exceeded supply by 299,000 metric tons, (2) weather concerns as drought in early 2007 slowed cocoa bean growth and too much rain near the end of the growing season caused an outbreak of black pod disease (a fungal disease due to excessive moisture), (3) labor unrest in the Ivory Coast where ongoing strikes slowed cocoa exports, and (4) a surge in commodity fund buying due to the weak dollar as funds bought commodities as an inflation hedge. The Ivory Coast is the world's largest cocoa producer with 40% of world production.

Supply – The world net cocoa crop in 2005-06 (latest data available) fell −2.8% yr/yr to 3.190 million metric tons, down farther from the record high of 3.492 million metric tons seen in 2003-04. The drop in production caused closing stocks in 2005-06 to fall −15.3% yr/yr to 1.227 million metric tons, and the stocks/consumption ratio to fall to a low level of 36%. World grindings in 2005-06 rose by +2.7% yr/yr to 3.411 million metric tons, which was a new record high. The world's largest cocoa producer by far is the Ivory Coast where production in 2005-06 fell 6.1% yr/yr to 1.195 million metric tons from the record high of 1.386 million metric tons in 2003-04. The Ivory Coast accounted for 37% of world cocoa production in 2005-06. Other major cocoa producers included Ghana with 20% of world production, Indonesia with 14%, Cameroon with 5%, Brazil with 5%, and Nigeria with 5.0%.

Demand – World consumption of cocoa in 2004-05 (latest data available) rose +2.8% yr/yr to a new record high of 3.321 million metric tons. The world's largest cocoa consumers are the European Union with 40% of world consumption in 2004-05, followed by the U.S. with 12% of world consumption. U.S. consumption of cocoa in 2004-05 rose by +2.0% to 409,000 metric tons. There were large consumption increases in 2004-05 in Malaysia (+14%), in Russia (+8%), and in the European Union (+6%). There were large consumption decreases in Turkey (-18%), in Canada (-10%) and in Japan (7%).

Trade – U.S. imports of cocoa and cocoa products in 2007(annualized through October) fell by 9.6% yr/yr to 1.337 million metric tons, down from the record high of 1.317 million metric tons in 2005.

World Supply and Demand Cocoa   In Thousands of Metric Tons

Crop Year Beginning Oct. 1	Stocks Oct. 1	Net World Production[4]	Total Availability	Seasona Grindings	Closing Stocks	Stock Change	Stock/Consumption Ratio %
1996-97	1,602	2,690	4,292	2,730	1,562	-40	57.2
1997-98	1,562	2,605	4,167	2,773	1,394	-168	50.3
1998-99	1,394	2,786	4,180	2,757	1,423	29	51.6
1999-00	1,423	3,030	4,453	2,975	1,478	55	49.7
2000-01	1,478	2,766	4,244	3,072	1,172	-306	38.2
2001-02	1,172	2,793	3,965	2,843	1,123	-49	39.5
2002-03	1,123	3,115	4,238	3,014	1,224	101	40.6
2003-04[1]	1,224	3,492	4,716	3,230	1,486	262	46.0
2004-05[2]	1,486	3,283	4,769	3,321	1,448	-38	43.6
2005-06[3]	1,448	3,190	4,638	3,411	1,227	-221	36.0

[1] Preliminary.   [2] Estimate.   [3] Forecast.   [4] Obtained by adjusting the gross world crop for a one percent loss in weight.
Source: ED&F Man Cocoa Limited

COCOA

World Production of Cocoa Beans   In Thousands of Metric Tons

Crop Year Beginning Oct. 1	Brazil	Came-roon	Colom-bia	Dominican Republic	Ecuador	Ghana	Indo-nesia	Ivory Coast	Malaysia	Mexico	Nigeria	Papau New Guinea	World Total
1998-99	138	123	39	22	72	398	396	1,175	79	25	200	35	2,808
1999-00	124	115	37	28	92	435	428	1,404	37	31	180	46	3,054
2000-01	197	123	45	37	100	437	421	1,401	70	28	338	47	3,380
2001-02	186	122	44	45	76	390	428	1,212	58	47	340	39	3,112
2002-03	175	125	48	45	88	341	571	1,265	48	46	362	42	3,284
2003-04	170	155	42	47	88	497	573	1,352	36	50	385	43	3,581
2004-05	196	167	36	48	124	737	642	1,407	33	44	412	39	4,044
2005-06[1]	209	179	37	31	106	740	643	1,286	28	36	441	48	3,992
2006-07[2]	212	165	37	32	88	734	580	1,255	32	38	485	51	3,939
2007-08[3]	222	179	37	32	88	690	620	1,300	30	39	500	50	4,012

[1] Preliminary.   [2] Estimate.   [3] Forecast.   *Source: Food and Agricultural Organization of the United Nations (FAO-UN)*

World Consumption of Cocoa[4]   In Thousands of Metric Tons

Crop Year Beginning Oct. 1	Canada	Brazil	European Union	Ghana	Indonesia	Ivory Coast	Japan	Malaysia	Singa-pore	Turkey	United States	Russia	World Total
1995-96	39	183	1,225	60	60	130	49	96	63	16	345	75	2,655
1996-97	35	180	1,203	68	72	145	53	103	61	16	394	74	2,730
1997-98	53	188	1,228	67	74	195	43	94	68	22	399	50	2,773
1998-99	42	191	1,186	65	83	210	47	109	63	22	406	48	2,757
1999-00	56	202	1,235	75	88	230	48	117	60	25	439	62	2,975
2000-01	58	195	1,263	80	91	285	49	121	59	39	445	67	3,072
2001-02	56	173	1,159	80	108	265	50	93	62	39	393	69	2,843
2002-03[1]	57	196	1,190	69	115	290	64	129	71	50	400	60	3,014
2003-04[2]	72	207	1,256	78	122	321	57	200	59	71	401	63	3,230
2004-05[3]	65	209	1,328	76	111	320	53	228	57	58	409	68	3,321

[1] Preliminary.   [2] Estimate.   [3] Forecast.   [4] Figures represent the "grindings" of cocoa beans in each country.   NA = Not available.
Source: ED&F Man Cocoa Limited

Imports of Cocoa Butter in Selected Countries   In Metric Tons

Year	Australia	Austria	Belgium	Canada	France	Germany	Italy	Japan	Nether-lands	Sweden	Switzer-land	United Kingdom	United States
1997	16,000	6,917	34,222	16,781	46,514	71,094	9,698	16,609	30,549	7,431	19,057	34,749	87,689
1998	18,000	5,954	25,722	17,000	43,721	76,059	8,950	15,371	25,624	7,403	19,856	33,355	65,307
1999	22,473	5,356	42,278	17,323	56,923	70,455	8,277	17,824	36,799	6,948	21,278	38,023	80,475
2000	20,590	4,325	51,826	22,009	54,197	72,014	12,071	21,695	37,261	6,010	19,922	38,770	94,648
2001	20,633	3,945	51,577	23,307	51,145	80,839	11,765	21,665	36,687	6,349	20,604	41,827	80,806
2002	20,800	3,777	48,992	24,397	63,814	82,313	12,099	20,212	47,562	6,401	21,545	46,912	84,788
2003	22,310	3,823	54,621	26,309	58,759	77,880	13,337	22,579	55,523	6,564	21,555	39,092	78,035
2004	23,514	4,536	56,328	27,646	70,386	79,155	13,891	22,166	63,657	6,668	22,960	50,593	94,890
2005	21,527	4,281	61,200	28,382	72,561	82,050	16,114	24,633	70,255	6,276	24,264	70,777	96,876
2006[1]	19,172	4,729	68,173	23,803	75,572	82,726	16,285	25,603	82,864	5,774	25,725	48,447	96,455

[1] Preliminary.   NA = Not available.   *Sources: Food and Agricultural Organization of the United Nations (FAO)*

Imports of Cocoa Liquor and Cocoa Powder in Selected Countries   In Metric Tons

	Cocoa Liquor						Cocoa Powder						
Year	France	Germany	Japan	Nether-lands	United Kingdom	United States	Denmark	France	Germany	Italy	Japan	Nether-lands	United States
1997	61,148	10,299	1,393	8,401	5,860	17,850	4,317	26,016	42,370	15,909	9,159	27,904	106,811
1998	70,883	9,121	1,144	12,534	3,813	21,894	3,816	25,091	38,742	17,164	9,151	17,237	128,771
1999	74,721	13,833	1,421	25,639	4,396	12,823	4,410	27,229	38,681	16,885	10,227	17,469	113,746
2000	67,812	14,295	1,618	33,815	8,529	10,902	3,661	37,165	39,498	18,249	11,765	29,044	130,610
2001	67,500	17,548	1,553	41,913	10,289	17,940	3,792	25,631	32,621	19,224	12,004	29,866	113,592
2002	64,820	28,100	1,193	46,369	14,038	22,215	2,895	35,128	39,871	19,642	10,859	54,422	126,443
2003	71,337	31,391	1,764	35,089	20,154	20,018	3,142	43,915	37,065	18,757	12,895	38,713	136,813
2004	72,057	42,975	2,773	40,847	17,753	20,758	3,447	44,213	35,460	19,538	14,973	38,692	147,392
2005							3,996	43,626	33,202	23,085	13,705	45,859	141,044
2006[1]							3,053	39,833	41,050	22,485	15,831	34,770	145,820

[1] Preliminary.   NA = Not available.   *Source: Food and Agricultural Organization of the United Nations (FAO)*

Imports of Cocoa and Products in the United States   In Thousands of Metric Tons

Year	Jan.	Feb.	Mar.	Apr.	May	June	July	Aug.	Sept.	Oct.	Nov.	Dec.	Total
1999	100	79	81	93	51	60	77	62	68	67	82	102	922
2000	111	128	101	91	70	67	70	70	86	76	59	69	999
2001	108	97	77	47	68	61	80	78	76	86	92	118	989
2002	87	74	73	61	76	72	87	98	61	66	90	72	916
2003	115	74	92	71	68	74	95	82	79	95	85	116	1,046
2004	110	82	130	100	101	103	94	94	100	90	80	89	1,171
2005	129	109	156	108	104	93	91	104	84	97	113	129	1,317
2006	114	104	109	94	92	89	108	140	103	91	90	124	1,258
2007	111	121	110	102	82	76	83	83	84	95	76	106	1,130
2008[1]	108	115	109	87	80	65	88	82	79	90	83	129	1,114

[1] Preliminary.   *Source: Foreign Agricultural Service, U.S. Department of Agriculture (FAS-USDA)*

Visible Stocks of Cocoa in Port of Hampton Road Warehouses[1], at End of Month   In Thousands of Bags

Year	Jan.	Feb.	Mar.	Apr.	May	June	July	Aug.	Sept.	Oct.	Nov.	Dec.
1999	661.6	693.2	642.5	579.7	536.9	500.7	489.0	472.7	473.4	451.8	438.9	421.2
2000	469.7	448.4	571.7	583.4	711.1	672.4	720.3	925.2	921.4	839.7	762.9	816.0
2001	741.9	657.4	632.0	607.7	577.3	518.8	498.2	487.5	475.2	506.8	509.0	511.4
2002	504.7	462.8	436.7	424.0	383.8	353.4	327.4	273.3	255.4	194.8	181.5	169.9
2003	149.9	121.7	103.1	102.3	80.5	71.9	69.2	67.7	56.9	53.0	49.6	49.3
2004	48.6	47.8	47.5	47.5	44.3	43.9	41.2	40.4	40.1	38.0	38.0	36.8
2005	31.1	30.9	28.6	28.0	28.0	27.4	27.4	27.4	27.4	27.4	27.4	27.4
2006	18.3	17.9	17.6	17.3	17.3	17.3	17.3	17.3	17.1	17.1	17.1	17.1
2007	16.8	16.8	16.8	16.8	16.8	16.8	15.9	15.6	15.6	15.6	15.6	15.6
2008	15.6	15.6	15.6	15.6	15.8	15.8	15.8	15.8	15.8	15.6	15.6	15.6

[1] Licensed warehouses approved by ICE.   *Source: IntercontinentalEchange (ICE) formerly New York Board of Trade (NYBOT)*

Visible Stocks of Cocoa in Philadelphia (Del. River) Warehouses[1], at End of Month   In Thousands of Bags

Year	Jan.	Feb.	Mar.	Apr.	May	June	July	Aug.	Sept.	Oct.	Nov.	Dec.
1999	1,763.0	1,832.8	1,982.7	2,217.8	2,019.4	1,999.6	2,084.6	2,133.4	2,144.1	2,015.5	1,774.4	1,608.5
2000	1,619.0	1,801.7	2,466.4	2,582.0	2,581.6	2,363.7	2,168.3	2,101.6	2,105.1	2,039.1	1,697.4	1,589.4
2001	1,844.0	2,082.3	2,173.3	1,960.0	1,785.9	1,610.4	1,391.6	1,543.0	1,391.3	1,131.4	1,303.2	1,682.1
2002	1,701.5	1,876.7	1,849.3	1,708.0	1,746.4	1,689.5	1,793.1	1,832.7	1,750.9	1,334.5	1,162.7	1,250.6
2003	1,347.2	1,422.0	1,327.9	1,326.5	1,217.2	1,202.3	1,229.2	1,123.7	930.6	798.9	723.7	806.0
2004	1,294.9	1,061.5	1,259.1	1,187.1	1,238.8	1,342.0	1,432.6	1,529.3	1,366.4	1,569.4	1,312.8	1,335.7
2005	1,588.9	1,809.8	2,066.3	2,264.5	2,439.3	2,258.3	2,465.0	2,481.0	2,470.5	2,373.5	2,635.5	2,712.8
2006	2,888.5	2,828.9	3,018.9	3,208.9	3,095.0	2,913.8	3,005.2	3,404.0	3,382.1	3,307.2	3,135.3	3,293.0
2007	3,488.8	4,169.2	4,410.9	4,299.6	4,198.0	3,860.3	3,424.2	3,106.8	2,883.0	2,660.0	2,327.4	2,334.5
2008	2,435.5	2,679.8	2,920.4	2,787.6	2,733.9	2,486.3	2,223.6	2,110.8	1,717.5	1,571.2	1,390.4	1,533.4

[1] Licensed warehouses approved by ICE.   *Source: IntercontinentalEchange (ICE) formerly New York Board of Trade (NYBOT)*

Visible Stocks of Cocoa in New York Warehouses[1], at End of Month   In Thousands of Bags

Year	Jan.	Feb.	Mar.	Apr.	May	June	July	Aug.	Sept.	Oct.	Nov.	Dec.
1999	1,085.0	1,089.3	1,083.1	1,134.1	1,139.4	1,114.3	1,093.5	974.5	941.9	821.7	847.5	1,573.1
2000	1,633.7	1,689.5	1,926.9	2,049.8	1,926.7	1,789.6	1,632.2	1,383.7	1,323.7	1,234.8	1,100.0	1,019.4
2001	1,005.6	1,173.8	1,119.6	1,024.9	967.5	906.6	776.2	758.5	657.6	687.4	750.8	1,196.2
2002	1,088.9	870.8	892.0	816.1	739.1	736.0	640.9	553.6	670.1	525.7	473.1	554.8
2003	614.6	625.4	593.7	612.9	515.1	476.1	423.6	388.2	483.4	301.9	391.3	342.9
2004	229.9	415.2	616.1	579.9	712.7	680.1	676.3	596.1	486.3	334.5	272.0	209.6
2005	201.2	446.3	495.9	677.7	806.6	916.5	805.2	625.2	457.2	430.3	388.3	599.2
2006	758.4	971.5	894.9	818.3	759.3	691.8	618.7	685.8	654.2	649.1	528.0	502.8
2007	532.2	457.4	635.5	666.5	612.3	605.4	576.2	530.5	496.8	442.2	394.8	343.2
2008	422.4	411.1	574.4	618.7	614.0	554.4	527.9	434.6	396.1	375.6	323.1	242.5

[1] Licensed warehouses approved by ICE.   *Source: IntercontinentalEchange (ICE) formerly New York Board of Trade (NYBOT)*

COCOA

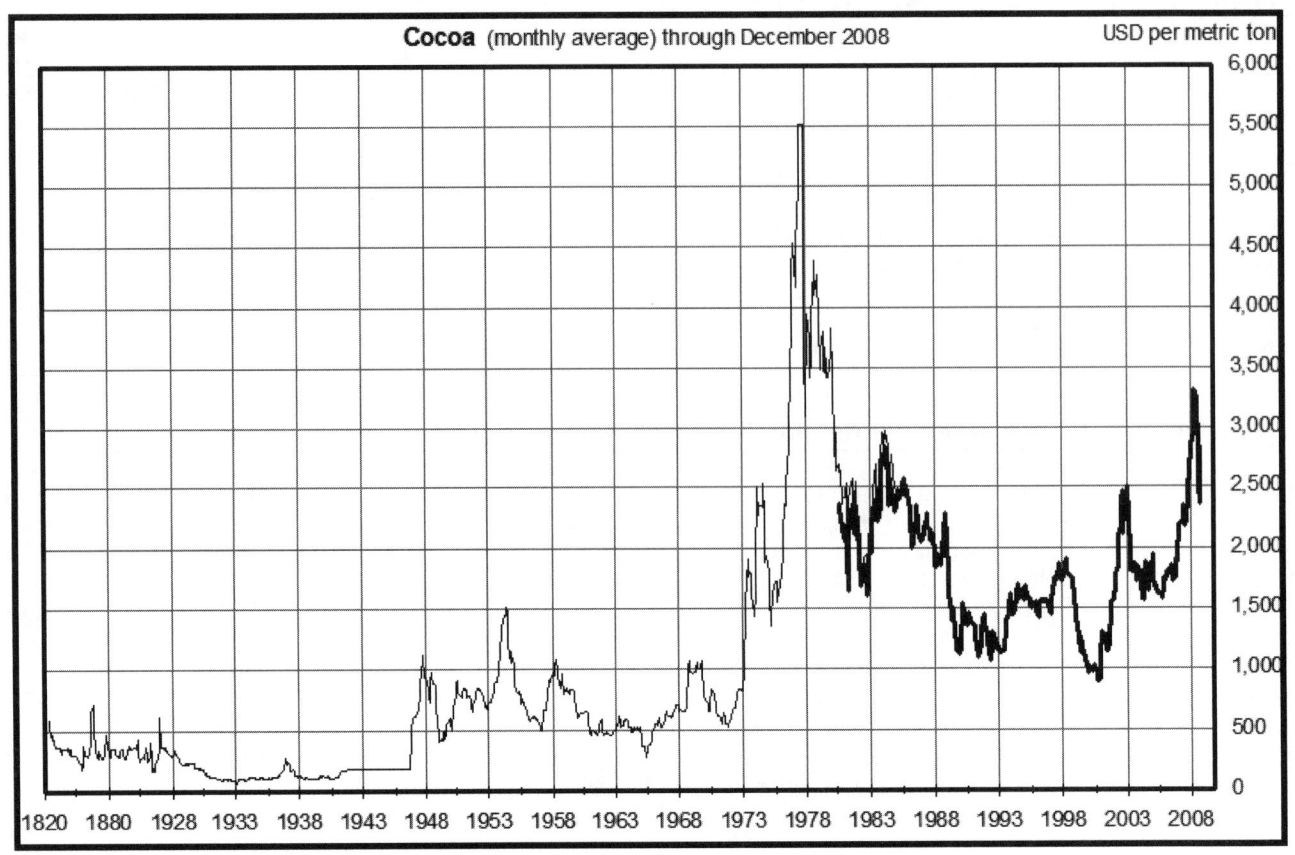

Cocoa (monthly average) through December 2008 — USD per metric ton

Average Cash Price of Cocoa, Ivory Coast in New York — In Dollars Per Metric Ton

Year	Jan.	Feb.	Mar.	Apr.	May	June	July	Aug.	Sept.	Oct.	Nov.	Dec.	Average
1999	1,565	1,498	1,415	1,276	1,144	1,263	1,209	1,154	1,156	1,133	1,037	1,027	1,240
2000	1,027	962	1,025	993	998	1,033	1,034	980	988	991	905	911	987
2001	1,093	1,299	1,290	1,244	1,281	1,146	1,152	1,200	1,183	1,288	1,439	1,543	1,263
2002	1,586	1,674	1,794	1,800	1,814	1,836	2,081	2,191	2,391	2,471	2,123	2,322	2,007
2003	2,483	2,506	2,258	2,232	1,996	1,818	1,803	1,843	1,877	1,713	1,737	1,832	2,008
2004	1,840	1,763	1,695	1,610	1,588	1,571	1,733	1,889	1,698	1,654	1,867	1,848	1,730
2005	1,740	1,827	1,950	1,744	1,656	1,687	1,625	1,626	1,640	1,598	1,585	1,670	1,696
2006	1,752	1,729	1,739	1,749	1,806	1,794	1,862	1,795	1,764	1,725	1,773	1,897	1,782
2007	1,883	1,996	2,120	2,169	2,214	2,225	2,361	2,185	2,242	2,198	2,251	2,396	2,187
2008	2,486	2,806	2,922	2,867	2,971	3,307	3,248	3,078	2,972	2,533	2,371	2,837	2,867

Source: Economic Research Service, U.S. Department of Agriculture (ERS-USDA)

Cocoa Futures - New York Board of Trade
(weekly close) as of January 02, 2009

USD per metric ton

Average Open Interest of Cocoa Futures in New York   In Contracts

Year	Jan.	Feb.	Mar.	Apr.	May	June	July	Aug.	Sept.	Oct.	Nov.	Dec.
1999	77,067	72,324	69,221	65,856	71,990	75,195	70,787	69,939	74,572	79,770	89,035	92,609
2000	100,540	110,316	106,056	102,382	113,239	111,948	112,864	117,260	123,463	138,523	139,141	138,266
2001	132,711	119,459	114,036	102,275	107,008	111,224	104,473	99,280	92,235	96,204	93,088	92,326
2002	97,563	98,169	96,336	98,851	103,746	100,701	107,080	102,441	107,294	107,880	82,236	82,844
2003	96,375	91,944	83,625	83,230	95,307	96,813	89,846	78,197	76,468	86,392	99,038	94,010
2004	88,879	84,078	99,918	100,429	108,150	99,476	103,350	111,318	101,998	119,033	117,876	118,769
2005	117,091	115,007	144,055	124,417	124,925	128,203	126,388	129,562	118,468	132,629	131,733	123,302
2006	131,527	127,471	129,426	129,814	131,035	138,004	154,163	134,942	139,544	153,485	136,329	140,099
2007	145,503	152,358	172,846	157,373	154,649	148,608	167,565	134,823	123,171	133,362	137,208	165,522
2008	188,039	182,389	166,939	136,591	146,759	160,366	151,896	134,715	127,674	122,381	113,422	113,240

Source: IntercontinentalEchange (ICE) formerly New York Board of Trade (NYBOT)

Volume of Trading of Cocoa Futures in New York   In Contracts

Year	Jan.	Feb.	Mar.	Apr.	May	June	July	Aug.	Sept.	Oct.	Nov.	Dec.	Total
1999	136,109	155,090	141,090	180,837	130,019	230,925	125,360	144,290	147,124	143,335	209,608	124,249	1,868,036
2000	156,812	231,562	232,803	186,837	147,072	267,470	124,906	191,849	111,740	174,216	186,515	98,266	2,110,048
2001	311,900	168,587	164,131	136,021	154,397	201,299	108,189	207,569	118,428	124,884	202,847	107,565	2,005,817
2002	155,699	187,550	129,833	217,590	160,364	220,289	176,450	209,249	138,394	207,310	162,982	114,270	2,079,980
2003	172,845	215,240	136,564	179,956	176,969	207,255	143,888	206,428	146,113	197,316	209,775	135,857	2,128,206
2004	174,684	180,693	181,667	244,946	174,452	238,201	219,018	260,025	146,090	150,443	290,227	128,604	2,389,050
2005	185,624	239,511	231,917	249,209	134,330	288,809	151,339	252,868	222,122	182,337	283,663	161,198	2,582,927
2006	235,410	264,557	201,604	295,814	244,032	333,275	331,108	313,591	174,246	264,490	308,782	202,293	3,169,202
2007	239,568	338,998	273,605	333,551	212,318	328,646	242,710	378,897	213,143	265,018	273,419	235,410	3,335,283
2008	322,864	434,965	316,509	328,551	293,874	353,593	280,275	345,973	197,765	313,220	228,699	175,550	3,591,838

Source: IntercontinentalEchange (ICE) formerly New York Board of Trade (NYBOT)

Coconut Oil and Copra

Coconut oil and copra come from the fruit of the coconut palm tree, which originated in Southeast Asia. Coconut oil has been used for thousands of years as cooking oil, and is still a staple in the diets of many people living in tropical areas. Until shortages of imported oil developed during WWII, Americans also used coconut oil for cooking.

Copra is the meaty inner lining of the coconut. It is an oil-rich pulp with a light, slightly sweet, nutty flavor. Copra is used mainly as a source of coconut oil and is also used shredded for baking. High-quality copra contains about 65% to 72% oil, and oil made from the copra is called crude coconut oil. Crude coconut oil is processed from copra by expeller press and solvent extraction. It is not considered fit for human consumption until it has been refined, which consists of neutralizing, bleaching and deodorizing it at high heat with a vacuum. The remaining oil cake obtained as a by-product is used for livestock feed.

Premium grade coconut oil, also called virgin coconut oil, is oil made from the first pressing without the addition of any chemicals. Premium grade coconut oil is more expensive than refined or crude oil because the producers use only selected raw materials and there is a lower production yield due to only one pressing.

Coconut oil accounts for approximately 20% of all vegetable oils used worldwide. Coconut oil is used in margarines, vegetable shortening, salad oils, confections, and in sports drinks to boost energy and enhance athletic performance. It is also used in the manufacture of soaps, detergents, shampoos, cosmetics, candles, glycerin and synthetic rubber. Coconut oil is very healthy, unless it is hydrogenated, and is easily digested.

Prices – The average monthly price of coconut oil (crude) in 2007 rose +42.2% yr/yr to 41.68 cents per pound. The record high of 60.21 cents per pound was posted in 1984.

Supply – World production of copra in 2007 fell by 6.9% yr/yr to 4.652 million metric tons, and remains far below the record high of 5.662 million metric tons posted in 2001. The world's largest producers of copra are the Philippines with 37% of world production, Indonesia with 29%, India with 13%, and Mexico with 4%. World production of coconut oil in the 2007-08 marketing year rose by +7.0% yr/yr to 3.282 million metric tons.

Demand – Virtually all of world production of copra in 2007-08 went for crushing into coconut meal and oil (over 99%). World consumption of coconut oil in 2007-08 rose by +3.8% yr/yr to 3.280 million metric tons, but still below the record high of 3.349 million metric tons in 2000-01.

Trade – Copra is generally crushed in the country of origin, meaning that less than 4% of copra itself is exported; the rest is exported in the form of coconut oil. World exports of coconut oil in 2007-08 rose by +10.5% yr/yr to 2.108 million metric tons, but still below the 2005-06 record high of 2.178 million metric tons.

World Production of Copra   In Thousands of Metric Tons

Year	India	Indonesia	Ivory Coast	Malaysia	Mexico	Mozam-bique	Papua New Guinea	Philip-pines	Sri Lanka	Thailand	Vanuatu	Vietnam	World Total
1999	718	860	36	48	199	73	146	1,250	68	65	30	72	3,874
2000	700	1,330	45	49	202	75	152	2,140	98	69	27	45	5,248
2001	690	1,185	45	47	198	75	95	2,790	113	60	30	41	5,662
2002	713	1,290	45	50	203	50	71	2,010	59	61	25	46	4,920
2003	690	1,260	45	51	185	55	85	2,406	50	68	25	49	5,267
2004	700	1,300	45	51	182	50	90	1,980	60	71	35	49	4,911
2005	660	1,460	45	48	184	50	112	2,100	67	72	30	50	5,186
2006[1]	650	1,370	45	51	174	48	94	2,100	65	65	30	51	5,058
2007[2]	620	1,570	45	49	204	46	97	1,810	69	68	30	52	4,974
2008[3]	650	1,560	46	52	190	48	100	2,120	73	68	32	53	5,311

[1] Preliminary.   [2] Estimate.   [3] Forecast.   *Source: The Oil World*

World Supply and Distribution of Coconut Oil   In Thousands of Metric Tons

Year		Prod	uction						Cons	umptio	n			Ending Stocks		
	India	Indo-nesia	Malay-sia	Philip-pines	Total	Exports	Imports	European Union	India	Indo-nesia	Philip-pines	United States	Total	Philip-pines	United States	Total
1998-99	431	458	51	783	2,370	1,040	1,142	578	446	110	295	461	2,750	58	69	319
1999-00	421	787	54	1,198	3,084	1,788	1,718	770	435	110	299	420	2,921	112	62	411
2000-01	419	700	48	1,731	3,496	2,159	2,173	751	439	277	348	437	3,349	60	118	572
2001-02	421	773	45	1,403	3,183	1,846	1,872	712	448	278	332	506	3,274	62	103	507
2002-03	418	758	41	1,425	3,180	1,958	1,991	786	454	273	352	384	3,301	53	98	418
2003-04	419	731	41	1,379	3,106	1,860	1,833	713	428	246	311	399	3,127	58	60	370
2004-05	402	881	42	1,263	3,153	2,106	2,079	814	421	175	253	361	3,093	73	110	401
2005-06[1]	392	789	45	1,450	3,218	2,178	2,194	768	420	180	253	494	3,233	66	101	402
2006-07[2]	377	960	47	1,133	3,067	1,908	1,954	727	392	186	306	441	3,159	63	58	356
2007-08[3]	386	916	49	1,373	3,282	2,108	2,100	780	397	186	340	450	3,280	66	60	350

[1] Preliminary.   [2] Estimate.   [3] Forecast.   *Source: The Oil World*

Supply and Distribution of Coconut Oil in the United States In Millions of Pounds

Year	Rotterdam Copra Tonne $ U.S.	Rotterdam Coconut Oil, CIF $ U.S.	Imports For Consumption	Stocks Oct. 1	Total Supply	Exports	Disapearance Total Domestic	Edible Products	Inedible Products	Total	Oct.-Dec.	Jan.-Mar.	April-June	July-Sept.
1998-99	468	748	791	392	1,183	11	1,021	144	380	363.2	89.6	82.9	99.3	91.4
1999-00	357	539	926	152	1,078	14	927	221	371	442.3	69.1	117.0	129.6	126.7
2000-01	208	323	1,100	136	1,236	8	968	237	297	534.9	135.7	128.3	146.9	124.0
2001-02	245	388	1,150	260	1,410	11	1,100	294	302	501.8	139.5	126.1	115.4	120.8
2002-03	286	450	866	226	1,092	28	1,205	305	310	546.7	128.8	137.0	155.6	125.2
2003-04	424	630	812	216	1,028	17	1,312	330	274	594.9	160.7	132.8	162.8	138.6
2004-05	431	636	936	131	1,067	29	1,374	341	280	623.3	153.7	157.5	160.8	151.3
2005-06	387	583	1,127	242	1,369	58	1,323	366	270	599.9	141.9	156.2	160.5	141.4
2006-07[1]	537	812	905	222	1,127	27	1,443	339	309	654.6	162.6	152.2	165.4	174.4
2007-08[2]	839	1,268	1,025	129	1,154	29	1,383	373	447	627.4	139.9	165.9	161.1	160.5

[1] Preliminary. [2] Forecast. *Source: Bureau of Census, U.S. Department of Commerce*

Consumption of Coconut Oil in End Products (Edible and Inedible) in the United States In Millions of Pounds

Year	Jan.	Feb.	Mar.	Apr.	May	June	July	Aug.	Sept.	Oct.	Nov.	Dec.	Total
1999	39.9	44.7	50.8	43.0	41.4	45.4	36.9	33.3	46.2	41.5	43.6	38.8	505.5
2000	49.4	44.0	52.7	54.6	51.4	56.5	49.1	56.2	54.7	44.1	44.3	43.0	600.0
2001	49.3	40.6	45.5	42.5	48.3	43.3	46.5	45.6	48.4	50.3	44.4	45.5	550.2
2002	55.4	41.3	50.8	59.3	53.9	46.4	50.7	51.8	45.9	54.3	56.1	49.4	615.4
2003	51.2	49.3	56.8	50.6	52.3	46.7	48.9	49.6	50.3	47.8	41.8	38.5	583.7
2004	50.0	51.7	58.5	54.6	48.5	55.6	52.9	55.1	48.9	48.2	64.3	51.7	640.0
2005	46.7	52.0	47.9	48.8	51.4	55.5	47.2	58.1	49.2	52.8	53.4	58.1	621.1
2006	70.4	62.7	50.4	47.5	50.7	51.6	43.1	51.6	43.8	49.6	44.4	40.8	606.4
2007	49.8	48.5	47.0	51.2	53.7	60.3	60.3	74.2	67.5	71.8	71.3	62.7	718.3
2008[1]	69.8	72.1	64.8	74.4	69.7	70.4	65.8	67.6	65.8	63.0	63.6	53.6	800.7

[1] Preliminary. *Source: Bureau of Census, U.S. Department of Commerce*

Stocks of Coconut Oil (Crude and Refined) in the United States, on First of Month In Millions of Pounds

Year	Jan.	Feb.	Mar.	Apr.	May	June	July	Aug.	Sept.	Oct.	Nov.	Dec.
1999	401.7	446.5	387.5	366.3	309.8	240.5	134.7	197.5	191.8	152.0	106.4	142.2
2000	93.6	123.6	100.1	99.6	102.3	104.0	137.7	163.6	161.4	136.4	178.1	161.6
2001	245.4	280.3	357.8	276.5	286.9	194.3	254.4	260.9	246.4	259.7	234.1	231.3
2002	245.9	238.8	249.6	251.3	233.5	231.6	303.3	301.6	245.8	226.5	273.8	264.1
2003	195.2	194.0	214.3	224.9	223.7	187.8	162.2	202.9	195.6	218.9	184.6	186.1
2004	167.2	160.3	192.6	181.7	131.4	108.7	90.6	132.8	149.2	131.3	147.7	182.5
2005	225.9	163.7	188.4	191.0	170.6	187.7	263.5	250.4	253.7	242.1	252.3	273.3
2006	268.3	236.9	224.5	227.3	260.2	229.1	213.8	214.4	204.7	224.5	179.2	180.2
2007	214.4	228.5	261.5	223.1	191.8	157.9	171.2	154.4	127.7	128.4	142.5	212.6
2008[1]	205.6	192.9	180.9	191.9	223.9	203.9	187.8	181.5	180.4	182.2	163.3	174.6

[1] Preliminary. *Source: Bureau of Census, U.S. Department of Commerce*

Average Price of Coconut Oil (Crude) Tank Cars in New York In Cents Per Pound

Year	Jan.	Feb.	Mar.	Apr.	May	June	July	Aug.	Sept.	Oct.	Nov.	Dec.	Average
1999	35.38	35.00	34.00	34.06	38.25	42.13	39.83	36.08	46.00	46.00	46.00	46.00	39.89
2000	40.88	32.94	28.81	26.63	24.25	21.90	19.63	18.58	16.40	16.81	17.50	15.70	23.34
2001	26.00	24.00	22.75	22.50	21.00	21.00	24.00	26.50	26.50	26.50	24.50	24.50	24.15
2002	16.38	17.38	17.25	18.75	20.05	21.13	21.06	21.35	28.50	28.25	27.13	26.00	21.94
2003	26.00	26.00	24.60	24.50	24.50	25.00	25.00	25.00	25.00	25.00	28.75	31.00	25.86
2004	32.00	33.38	34.56	39.20	45.00	46.00	46.00	46.00	39.25	32.65	31.25	31.25	38.05
2005	31.05	31.00	32.67	35.00	34.67	34.00	33.00	33.00	33.00	35.00	29.13	27.75	32.44
2006	27.75	27.75	27.75	27.75	27.75	27.75	27.75	27.75	29.25	30.75	32.25	34.95	29.10
2007	35.75	36.00	36.00	37.50	40.13	45.75	48.00	NA	42.50	45.16	45.38	46.32	41.68
2008[1]	58.02	62.33	70.98	67.38	67.38	71.73	70.33	59.62	55.82	47.73	37.46	35.51	58.69

[1] Preliminary. *Source: Economic Research Service, U.S. Department of Agriculture (ERS-USDA)*

Coffee

Coffee is one of the world's most important cash commodities. Coffee is the common name for any type of tree in the genus madder family. It is actually a tropical evergreen shrub that has the potential to grow 100 feet tall. The coffee tree grows in tropical regions between the Tropics of Cancer and Capricorn in areas with abundant rainfall, year-round warm temperatures averaging about 70 degrees Fahrenheit, and no frost. In the U.S., the only areas that produce any significant amount of coffee are Puerto Rico and Hawaii. The coffee plant will produce its first full crop of beans at about 5 years old and then be productive for about 15 years. The average coffee tree produces enough beans to make about 1 to 1 ½ pounds of roasted coffee per year. It takes approximately 4,000 handpicked green coffee beans to make a pound of coffee. Wine was actually the first drink made from the coffee tree using the coffee cherries, honey, and water. In the 17th century, the first coffee house, also known as a "penny university" because of the price per cup, opened in London. The London Stock Exchange grew from one of these first coffee houses.

Coffee is generally classified into two types of beans: arabica and robusta. The most widely produced coffee is arabica, which makes up about 70 percent of total production. It grows mostly at high altitudes of 600 to 2,000 meters, with Brazil and Colombia being the largest producers. Arabic coffee is traded on the New York Board of Trade. The stronger of the two types is robusta. It is grown at lower altitudes with the largest producers being Indonesia, West Africa, Brazil, and Vietnam. Robusta coffee is traded on the LIFFE exchange.

Ninety percent of the world coffee trade is in green (unroasted) coffee beans. Seasonal factors have a significant influence on the price of coffee. There is no extreme peak in world production at any one time of the year, although coffee consumption declines by 12 percent or more below the year's average in the warm summer months. Therefore, coffee imports and roasts both tend to decline in spring and summer and pick up again in fall and winter.

The very low prices for coffee in 2000-03 created serious problems for coffee producers. When prices fall below the costs of production, there is little or no economic incentive to produce coffee. The result is that coffee trees are neglected or completely abandoned. When prices are low, producers cannot afford to hire the labor needed to maintain the trees and pick the crop at harvest. The result is that trees yield less due to reduced use of fertilizer and fewer employed coffee workers. One effect is a decline in the quality of the coffee that is produced. Higher quality Arabica coffee is often produced at higher altitudes, which entails higher costs. It is this coffee that is often abandoned. Although the pressure on producers can be severe, the market eventually comes back into balance as supply declines in response to low prices.

Coffee prices are subject to upward spikes in June, July and August due to possible freeze scares in Brazil during the winter months in the Southern Hemisphere. The Brazilian coffee crop is harvested starting in May and extending for several weeks into what are the winter months in Brazil. A major freeze in Brazil occurs roughly every five years on average.

Coffee futures are traded on the Bolsa de Mercadorias & Futuros (BM&F), the Tokyo Grain Exchange (TGE), the London International Financial Futures and Options Exchange (LIFFE), and the IntercontinentalExcange (ICE). Options are traded on the BM&F, the LIFFE and the CSCE.

Prices – Nybot Arabica coffee futures prices in early 2008 extended the rally seen in the second half of 2007 and posted a 10-year high of 166.75 cents per pound in February 2008. That rally was driven by commodity fund buying, the decline in Brazilian inventories to a 50-year low, and the -8.6% decline in the 2007-08 coffee crop. However, coffee prices in March 2008 then fell sharply on a washout of commodity fund long positions. Coffee prices recovered through August 2008 but then fell sharply in September when the global financial crisis emerged, causing heavy long liquidation pressure in the commodity markets and reduced global demand for coffee. Coffee prices closed 2008 at 112.05 cents per pound, which was down -24.15 cents or -17.7% from the 2007 close of 136.20 cents. Coffee production in 2008-09 production year is forecasted to rise 14.5% to 138.4 million bags, which kept a damper on coffee prices in late 2008 and early 2009. However, global coffee inventories in 2008-09 are expected to remain relatively low, thus keeping the supply situation in check and providing some underlying support for coffee prices.

Supply – World coffee production in the 2008-09 marketing year (July-June) rose 14.5% yr/yr to a new record high of 138.414 million bags (1 bag equals 60 kilograms or 132.3 pounds). The increase in production caused the 2008-09 ending stocks to rise +14.7% to 39.597 million bags.

Brazil is the world's largest coffee producer by far with 51.1 million bags of production in 2008-09, accounting for 37% of total world production. Other key producers include Vietnam with 14% of the world's production and Columbia with 90%. Brazil's coffee production in 2008-09, rose +35.9% y/y from 2007-08's 37.6 million bags. Vietnam in recent years has become a major coffee producer, boosting its production to 19.500 million bags in 2008-09, up from less than a million bags in 1990.

Demand – U.S. coffee consumption was virtually unchanged in 2008 (latest data available) at 23.217 million bags in 2007, not far below the record high of 25.377 million bags seen in 1968.

Trade – World coffee exports in 2008-09 rose 5.8% yr/yr to a new record high of 102.710 million bags. The world's largest exporters of coffee were Brazil with 28% of world exports in 2008-09, Vietnam with 18%, and Columbia with 11%. U.S. coffee imports in 2008 was virtually unchanged at 23.217 million bags. The all-time high of 24.549 million bags was posted in 1962. The key countries from which the U.S. imported coffee in 2008 were Brazil (which accounted for 21% of U.S. imports), Columbia (18%), Guatemala (8%), and Mexico (6%).

World Supply and Distribution of Coffee for Producing Countries   In Thousands of 60 Kilogram Bags

Year	Beginning Stocks	Production	Imports	Total Supply	Total Exports	Bean Exports	Rst/Grn Exports	Soluble Exports	Domestic Use	Ending Stocks
1999-00	24,400	113,553	1,303	139,256	92,733	87,572	288	4,873	25,648	20,875
2000-01	20,875	117,521	1,478	139,874	90,937	84,853	289	5,795	26,319	22,618
2001-02	22,618	111,518	1,647	135,783	88,292	81,739	337	6,216	27,774	19,717
2002-03	19,717	127,762	3,498	150,977	95,231	88,499	293	6,439	27,252	28,494
2003-04	28,494	110,311	43,335	182,140	91,172	83,758	317	7,097	49,086	41,882
2004-05	41,882	120,766	84,491	247,139	91,142	83,778	294	7,070	110,391	45,606
2005-06	45,606	111,523	85,148	242,277	87,036	80,187	350	6,499	116,639	38,602
2006-07[1]	38,602	132,364	89,535	260,501	101,925	94,285	344	7,296	116,808	41,768
2007-08[2]	41,768	120,915	89,162	251,845	97,054	89,066	444	7,544	120,273	34,518
2008-09[3]	34,518	138,414	90,914	263,846	102,710	94,514	460	7,736	121,539	39,597

[1] Preliminary.   [2] Estimate.   [3] Forecast.   132.276 Lbs. Per Bag   *Source: Foreign Agricultural Service, U.S. Department of Agriculture (FAS-USDA)*

World Production of Green Coffee   In Thousands of 60 Kilogram Bags

Crop Year	Brazil	Colombia	Costa Rica	El Salvador	Ethiopia	Guate-mala	India	Indo-nesia	Ivory Coast	Mexico	Uganda	Vietnam	World Total
1999-00	30,800	9,512	2,688	2,612	3,505	4,364	4,870	6,660	5,700	6,193	3,097	11,010	113,553
2000-01	34,100	10,500	2,502	1,624	2,768	4,564	5,020	6,495	5,100	4,800	3,401	15,333	117,521
2001-02	35,100	11,950	2,338	1,610	3,756	3,530	5,010	6,160	3,568	4,200	3,158	12,833	111,518
2002-03	53,600	11,712	2,207	1,351	3,693	3,802	4,588	6,140	3,145	4,350	2,890	11,167	127,762
2003-04	33,200	11,053	2,106	1,343	3,875	3,671	4,508	6,000	2,689	4,428	2,599	15,000	110,311
2004-05	43,600	11,532	1,907	1,329	4,575	3,817	4,672	6,600	2,301	3,900	2,593	14,500	120,766
2005-06	36,100	11,953	1,751	1,387	4,000	3,605	4,617	6,750	1,962	4,000	2,159	13,666	111,523
2006-07[1]	46,700	12,164	1,782	1,300	4,650	4,050	4,800	6,665	2,847	4,200	2,700	19,500	132,364
2007-08[2]	37,600	12,392	1,882	1,480	5,000	3,960	4,367	6,650	1,600	4,500	3,200	18,333	120,915
2008-09[3]	51,100	12,250	1,880	1,400	5,000	3,910	4,667	6,600	2,500	4,500	3,400	19,500	138,414

[1] Preliminary.   [2] Estimate.   [3] Forecast.   132.276 Lbs. Per Bag   *Source: Foreign Agricultural Service, U.S. Department of Agriculture (FAS-USDA)*

World Exportable[4] Production of Green Coffee   In Thousands of 60 Kilogram Bags

Crop Year	Brazil	Colombia	Ethiopia	Guate-mala	Honduras	India	Indo-nesia	Ivory Coast	Mexico	Peru	Uganda	Vietnam	World Total
1999-00	20,164	9,060	2,005	4,234	2,825	4,250	5,657	5,797	5,138	2,380	2,917	11,433	92,733
2000-01	19,676	9,460	1,418	4,414	2,470	3,702	5,536	4,045	3,822	2,664	3,075	14,667	90,937
2001-02	24,795	10,665	1,939	3,330	2,617	3,442	4,729	3,058	3,200	2,360	3,153	12,000	88,292
2002-03	29,396	10,478	2,277	3,500	2,438	3,567	4,801	5,166	3,400	2,575	2,810	11,176	95,231
2003-04	24,920	10,154	2,375	3,314	2,794	3,826	4,408	2,622	3,550	2,685	2,523	14,500	91,172
2004-05	27,920	11,032	2,625	3,451	2,450	2,790	4,600	1,984	2,107	3,306	2,489	13,992	91,142
2005-06	24,543	10,752	2,550	3,325	2,978	3,580	5,070	1,645	2,600	2,225	2,002	12,958	87,036
2006-07[1]	29,260	11,237	2,775	3,700	3,248	3,664	4,710	2,691	2,720	4,430	2,700	18,600	101,925
2007-08[2]	27,290	11,774	2,850	3,800	3,430	3,850	4,640	1,800	2,730	2,700	3,200	16,140	97,054
2008-09[3]	28,000	11,500	3,800	3,600	3,677	3,750	4,585	2,200	2,730	4,180	3,100	18,670	102,710

[1] Preliminary.   [2] Estimate.   [3] Forecast.   [4] Marketing year begins in October in some countries and April or July in others. Exportable production represents total harvested production minus estimated domestic consumption.   132.276 Lbs. Per Bag
Source: Foreign Agricultural Service, U.S. Department of Agriculture (FAS-USDA)

Coffee[2] Imports in the United States   In Thousands of 60 Kilogram Bags

Year	Brazil	Colombia	Costa Rica	Republic	Ecuador	El Salvador	Ethiopia	Guate-mala	Indo-nesia	Mexico	Peru	Vene-zuela	World Total
1999	4,847	3,418	783	80	461	550	77	2,149	724	3,276	766	372	21,787
2000	2,747	3,191	780	73	177	1,209	91	2,380	693	3,725	868	32	22,840
2001	3,007	3,272	915	50	230	507	80	2,040	887	2,057	692	4	20,490
2002	5,060	3,596	987	51	145	470	74	1,626	759	2,034	842	170	20,631
2003	5,321	3,883	914	80	133	569	101	2,023	966	1,510	807	180	21,694
2004	4,475	3,714	957	2	157	524	121	1,624	1,636	1,477	788	103	22,046
2005	4,464	4,090	920	2	74	406	177	1,752	1,599	1,285	587	0	21,791
2006	4,794	3,904	751	60	147	435	250	1,654	1,677	1,528	850	2	22,657
2007	4,968	4,064	823	35	123	565	234	1,815	1,122	1,495	919	25	23,215
2008[1]	4,971	4,245	952	35	40	657	349	1,901	1,351	1,427	963	93	23,217

[1] Preliminary.   132.276 Lbs. Per Bag   *Source: Bureau of Census, U.S. Department of Commerce*

COFFEE

Coffee (monthly average) through December 2008 — Cents per pound

Monthly Coffee[2] Imports in the United States — In Thousands of 60 Kilogram Bags (132.276 Lbs. Per Bag)

Year	Jan.	Feb.	Mar.	Apr.	May	June	July	Aug.	Sept.	Oct.	Nov.	Dec.	Total
1999	1,742	1,866	2,243	1,787	1,602	1,691	1,488	1,639	1,491	1,470	1,639	1,903	20,561
2000	2,189	2,092	2,416	2,003	2,199	1,960	1,912	1,815	1,598	1,583	1,546	1,527	22,840
2001	1,747	1,690	1,906	1,825	1,823	1,685	1,863	1,605	1,430	1,502	1,581	1,833	20,490
2002	1,652	1,364	1,613	1,697	1,672	1,547	1,802	1,794	1,850	1,877	1,807	1,958	20,631
2003	1,994	1,755	2,007	1,916	1,715	1,710	2,015	1,732	1,712	1,750	1,525	1,863	21,694
2004	1,813	1,635	1,967	1,862	2,049	2,034	1,784	1,766	1,708	1,684	1,798	1,947	22,047
2005	1,939	1,942	2,072	1,965	1,893	1,891	1,781	1,606	1,481	1,718	1,699	1,803	21,791
2006	1,852	1,647	2,042	1,672	2,007	1,916	1,780	2,091	2,089	1,894	1,834	1,833	22,657
2007	2,167	1,760	1,992	2,015	1,887	1,743	2,005	2,249	2,037	2,038	1,712	1,608	23,215
2008[1]	1,987	1,867	2,117	2,073	2,002	1,945	1,980	1,851	1,977	1,863	1,542	2,012	23,217

[1] Preliminary.   [2] Data through 1999 are for Green Coffee.   *Source: Bureau of the Census, U.S. Department of Commerce*

Average Price of Brazilian[1] Coffee in New York — In Cents Per Pound

Year	Jan.	Feb.	Mar.	Apr.	May	June	July	Aug.	Sept.	Oct.	Nov.	Dec.	Average
1999	99.43	91.72	88.90	86.14	96.29	91.69	78.13	76.67	70.43	78.74	98.41	109.47	88.84
2000	97.68	91.51	89.93	86.46	87.23	78.32	79.89	70.57	71.14	72.28	68.95	64.39	79.86
2001	62.38	62.50	60.35	55.11	57.19	51.86	46.43	46.49	42.42	38.63	42.28	41.60	50.60
2002	42.56	42.79	48.79	49.90	45.19	42.96	43.58	40.55	44.46	45.28	48.37	46.70	45.09
2003	49.14	48.54	43.77	48.71	51.06	47.11	49.64	52.88	55.19	53.51	54.15	56.92	50.89
2004	64.32	66.08	65.79	62.89	64.31	67.62	59.39	60.25	69.46	68.63	80.20	89.17	68.18
2005	94.00	108.05	117.03	112.82	111.89	105.08	94.66	95.66	87.02	94.54	99.35	96.23	101.36
2006	115.89	109.51	103.52	105.89	99.00	91.26	91.01	98.90	97.36	97.39	109.34	115.60	102.89
2007	111.99	109.78	102.34	100.84	99.66	105.89	105.25	112.47	116.43	120.95	118.99	124.06	110.72
2008	126.26	142.25	130.45	123.15	125.18	130.52	131.10	131.85	126.82	104.57	102.74		124.99

[1] And other Arabicas.   *Source: Foreign Agricultural Service, U.S. Department of Agriculture (FAS-USDA)*

Average Monthly Retail[1] Price of Coffee in the United States   In Cents Per Pound

Year	Jan.	Feb.	Mar.	Apr.	May	June	July	Aug.	Sept.	Oct.	Nov.	Dec.	Average
2001	322.4	321.7	320.5	312.8	309.7	315.6	309.7	304.6	302.5	301.5	298.8	291.3	309.3
2002	293.6	294.6	285.9	297.6	301.1	293.8	297.7	292.9	292.1	287.2	288.2	283.8	292.4
2003	299.9	292.4	293.3	300.8	293.7	293.1	294.4	292.1	291.9	282.5	277.9	287.5	291.6
2004	289.2	285.6	293.2	290.8	283.1	275.0	287.8	287.8	287.4	284.0	277.8	277.6	284.9
2005	304.9	294.0	300.9	324.0	332.9	341.6	333.4	342.8	337.6	344.7	329.3	323.5	325.8
2006	323.2	317.4	330.1	329.2	334.9	315.8	315.4	319.6	317.3	313.8	315.8	311.3	320.3
2007	328.8	345.6	347.5	343.7	330.8	340.7	352.9	349.7	NA	NA	360.7	368.5	346.9
2008	NA	NA	NA	NA	NA	NA	NA	NA	NA	NA	NA	NA	NA

[1] Roasted in 13.1 to 20 ounce cans.   *Source: Foreign Agricultural Service, U.S. Department of Agriculture (FAS-USDA)*

Average Price of Colombian Mild Arabicas[1] in the United States   In Cents Per Pound

Year	Jan.	Feb.	Mar.	Apr.	May	June	July	Aug.	Sept.	Oct.	Nov.	Dec.	Average
2001	75.33	76.70	76.94	78.25	80.92	74.38	69.70	73.50	68.80	62.88	65.72	62.57	72.14
2002	63.46	65.64	71.16	70.17	63.44	60.86	59.60	58.98	62.49	66.54	72.83	67.92	65.26
2003	69.68	69.60	61.82	66.12	67.56	65.01	67.84	68.65	68.37	66.59	67.04	69.38	67.31
2004	76.61	79.34	80.12	77.08	80.61	85.62	78.27	78.85	85.71	85.52	95.63	106.48	84.15
2005	110.03	124.34	137.10	129.80	128.36	122.47	112.48	111.21	101.31	108.77	111.66	106.54	117.01
2006	129.64	123.17	117.00	119.87	113.03	106.84	109.45	116.22	112.26	113.73	126.23	132.85	118.36
2007	127.54	125.54	119.92	117.51	116.14	122.35	122.32	126.68	131.51	137.71	133.81	139.87	126.74
2008	143.37	161.30	151.48	142.41	143.51	150.60	151.56	154.23	150.20	133.37	133.40		146.86

[1] ICO monthly and composite indicator prices on the New York Market, 1979 ICA Agreement basis.   *Source: Foreign Agricultural Service, U.S. Department of Agriculture (FAS-USDA)*

Average Price of Other Mild Arabicas[1] in the United States   In Cents Per Pound

Year	Jan.	Feb.	Mar.	Apr.	May	June	July	Aug.	Sept.	Oct.	Nov.	Dec.	Average
2001	64.98	67.00	65.88	65.68	68.94	63.79	58.47	59.68	57.71	56.23	58.96	55.63	61.91
2002	57.34	60.51	66.38	65.78	58.45	55.12	53.07	52.02	57.58	64.05	70.15	64.75	60.43
2003	65.22	67.60	61.66	65.35	66.47	61.34	62.32	63.60	65.50	62.58	62.36	65.01	64.08
2004	74.25	77.51	77.29	74.24	76.40	82.24	73.64	72.99	81.22	79.90	89.88	102.19	80.15
2005	107.07	122.20	134.81	128.80	126.21	119.87	108.45	108.43	98.17	106.09	108.81	102.68	114.30
2006	124.26	118.46	112.20	114.65	107.96	101.21	102.77	112.13	109.36	110.91	123.57	129.93	113.95
2007	124.40	122.34	116.44	114.59	112.35	118.76	116.80	123.53	128.04	134.43	130.28	136.47	123.20
2008	139.10	158.03	148.07	138.06	139.32	144.90	145.13	146.03	141.50	122.04	120.76		140.27

[1] ICO monthly and composite indicator prices on the New York Market, 1979 ICA Agreement basis.   *Source: Foreign Agricultural Service, U.S. Department of Agriculture (FAS-USDA)*

Average Price of Robustas 1976[1] in the United States   In Cents Per Pound

Year	Jan.	Feb.	Mar.	Apr.	May	June	July	Aug.	Sept.	Oct.	Nov.	Dec.	Average
2001	31.00	31.96	30.96	28.59	29.71	29.33	27.59	25.86	23.79	21.26	22.03	23.57	27.14
2002	22.88	24.46	29.77	30.35	29.43	29.26	29.31	28.74	33.31	34.44	39.38	38.68	30.83
2003	42.75	42.35	38.26	38.68	38.90	35.33	36.71	37.92	38.76	37.32	36.05	37.59	38.39
2004	41.32	39.10	38.61	38.02	38.04	41.09	36.44	34.81	35.10	31.77	34.07	38.98	37.28
2005	39.63	44.61	50.70	53.32	58.66	62.96	60.57	55.60	50.07	50.84	54.72	58.79	53.37
2006	66.46	65.50	62.92	64.45	63.97	64.14	68.66	75.73	77.88	76.26	79.67	77.71	70.28
2007	80.55	80.97	78.95	81.64	86.06	94.76	93.47	88.51	93.61	97.34	92.28	91.37	88.29
2008	100.68	117.10	122.44	112.06	109.58	112.16	115.09	113.48	106.67	89.69	92.81		108.34

[1] ICO monthly and composite indicator prices on the New York Market, 1979 ICA Agreement basis.   *Source: Foreign Agricultural Service, U.S. Department of Agriculture (FAS-USDA)*

Average Price of Composite 1979[1] in the United States   In Cents Per Pound

Year	Jan.	Feb.	Mar.	Apr.	May	June	July	Aug.	Sept.	Oct.	Nov.	Dec.	Average
2001	49.19	49.39	48.52	47.31	49.38	46.54	43.07	42.77	41.17	42.21	44.24	43.36	45.60
2002	43.46	44.30	49.49	50.19	47.30	45.56	44.70	42.79	47.96	50.79	54.69	51.68	47.74
2003	54.04	54.07	49.61	51.87	53.19	48.90	50.89	52.22	54.10	51.72	49.81	52.44	51.91
2004	58.69	59.87	60.80	58.80	59.91	64.28	58.46	56.98	61.47	61.10	67.74	77.72	62.15
2005	79.35	89.40	101.44	98.20	99.78	96.29	88.48	85.31	78.79	82.55	85.93	86.85	89.36
2006	101.20	97.39	92.76	94.20	90.00	86.04	101.20	95.78	95.98	95.53	103.48	108.01	96.80
2007	105.81	104.18	100.09	99.30	100.09	107.03	106.20	107.98	113.20	115.71	114.43	118.16	107.68
2008	122.33	138.82	136.17	126.55	126.76	130.51	132.78	131.14	126.69	108.31	107.88		126.18

[1] ICO monthly and composite indicator prices on the New York Market, 1979 ICA Agreement basis.   *Source: Foreign Agricultural Service, U.S. Department of Agriculture (FAS-USDA)*

COFFEE

Coffee 'C' Futures - ICE Futures U.S.
(weekly close) as of January 02, 2009

Cents per pound

Average Open Interest of Coffee "C" Futures in New York   In Contracts

Year	Jan.	Feb.	Mar.	Apr.	May	June	July	Aug.	Sept.	Oct.	Nov.	Dec.
1999	36,194	36,693	41,294	43,846	45,947	45,675	45,411	46,725	46,255	47,956	46,271	46,764
2000	47,829	50,620	50,565	53,662	49,692	50,293	45,513	40,177	40,133	42,906	43,187	45,086
2001	48,914	53,050	58,111	57,722	53,481	58,311	57,888	57,243	55,674	58,345	55,317	53,953
2002	57,897	66,825	66,798	66,207	66,289	68,994	69,197	69,635	70,079	73,753	73,431	69,343
2003	69,508	71,682	76,934	77,954	72,716	72,155	72,110	68,259	73,809	79,038	81,253	76,670
2004	92,388	103,966	102,281	98,430	96,738	102,276	89,446	88,021	83,001	78,047	83,360	107,832
2005	102,163	107,715	117,419	105,245	96,063	94,139	93,303	89,662	85,518	86,489	81,525	81,234
2006	102,195	102,614	99,982	102,882	104,230	120,907	120,007	107,928	105,175	111,392	117,469	123,259
2007	128,158	132,849	141,033	146,723	159,011	157,086	168,019	163,288	162,445	173,426	158,146	160,331
2008	176,128	193,555	179,957	160,544	150,017	146,166	147,056	133,178	126,573	132,112	116,643	118,223

Source: IntercontinentalEchange (ICE) formerly New York Board of Trade (NYBOT)

Volume of Trading of Coffee "C" Futures in New York   In Contracts

Year	Jan.	Feb.	Mar.	Apr.	May	June	July	Aug.	Sept.	Oct.	Nov.	Dec.	Total
1999	216,810	201,670	252,841	243,630	237,968	243,164	187,019	232,817	151,724	270,013	244,258	177,309	2,659,223
2000	158,962	232,174	166,970	224,266	177,753	218,467	198,975	175,868	119,304	163,399	187,230	111,593	2,134,961
2001	189,977	221,775	167,466	236,757	182,621	220,708	134,809	250,151	100,443	153,739	229,495	111,430	2,199,371
2002	201,327	279,966	229,764	295,701	159,670	225,177	174,567	254,563	232,255	250,483	236,307	178,728	2,718,508
2003	205,420	283,317	169,611	334,188	255,935	270,424	237,210	278,746	332,473	309,930	314,182	219,595	3,211,031
2004	389,864	397,656	301,270	395,552	324,849	467,887	247,439	366,171	305,196	280,733	424,146	292,540	4,193,303
2005	280,912	469,605	356,855	459,018	240,989	428,227	224,531	404,307	259,177	266,697	376,844	220,616	3,987,778
2006	357,994	416,964	326,256	429,249	322,932	476,542	289,027	481,870	238,953	313,459	492,904	261,362	4,407,512
2007	334,593	468,712	383,506	474,542	373,291	600,122	361,467	596,622	373,925	484,038	468,987	208,818	5,128,623
2008	419,096	729,397	515,528	556,002	354,887	642,074	317,917	512,002	381,241	384,451	383,346	250,575	5,446,516

Source: IntercontinentalEchange (ICE) formerly New York Board of Trade (NYBOT)

Coke

Coke is the hard and porous residue left after certain types of bituminous coals are heated to high temperatures (up to 2,000 degrees Fahrenheit) for about 17 hours. It is blackish-gray and has a metallic luster. The residue is mostly carbon. Coke is used as a reducing agent in the smelting of pig iron and the production of steel. Petroleum coke is made from the heavy tar-like residue of the petroleum refining process. It is used primarily to generate electricity.

Supply – Production of petroleum coke in the U.S. in 2008 fell by 0.6% yr/yr to 298.706 million barrels. That was down from the 2006 three-decade high of 309.980 and far below the U.S. production record of 369.305 million barrels posted back in 1957. U.S. stocks of coke at coke plants (Dec 31) in 2007 fell by -7.7% yr/yr to 632,000 short tons.

Trade – U.S. coke exports in 2007 fell by 10.7% to 1.444 million tons, and almost one-half of those exports were to Canada. U.S. coke imports in 2007 fell by -39.5% yr/yr to 2.460 million short tons. About 32% of the imports were from Japan.

Salient Statistics of Coke in the United States — In Thousands of Short Tons

Year	Coke and Breeze Production at Coke Plants — By Census Division — Middle Atlantic	East North Central	East South Central	Other	Total	Coke Total	Breeze Total	Con- sumption[2]	Producer and Distributor Stocks Dec. 31	Exports Canada	Total	Imports Japan	Total
2002	W	8,287	1,925	7,712	17,924	16,778	1,146	19,603	606	610	792	1,554	3,242
2003	W	8,642	2,068	7,738	18,448	17,173	1,275	19,436	380	436	722	1,395	2,759
2004	W	8,614	2,104	7,356	18,074	16,909	1,165	22,492	351	596	1,319	943	6,873
2005	W	8,448	W	9,456	17,904	16,719	1,184	18,239	614	764	1,747	699	3,529
2006	W	8,439	W	9,112	17,551	16,404	1,147	18,784	685	840	1,616	838	4,068
2007[1]	W	8,009	W	9,409	17,418	16,201	1,217	17,270	632	589	1,444	791	2,460

[1] Preliminary. [2] Equal to production plus imports minus the change in producer and distributor stocks minus exports.
W = Withheld. *Source: Energy Information Administration, U.S. Department of Energy (EIA-DOE)*

Production of Petroleum Coke in the United States — In Thousands of Barrels

Year	Jan.	Feb.	Mar.	Apr.	May	June	July	Aug.	Sept.	Oct.	Nov.	Dec.	Total
2002	24,543	22,849	23,529	23,850	24,713	23,305	24,556	23,939	23,465	22,527	23,497	24,913	285,686
2003	23,420	20,030	23,810	23,768	24,831	24,054	26,080	25,746	24,072	24,588	24,208	26,560	291,167
2004	25,640	22,380	24,025	25,086	26,789	25,874	26,263	26,151	24,259	25,899	25,897	27,599	305,862
2005	25,093	23,806	26,896	25,648	27,209	26,950	26,612	26,410	22,209	22,039	24,372	26,575	303,819
2006	26,180	23,706	25,722	24,987	26,690	26,128	26,372	26,395	26,300	25,957	25,048	26,495	309,980
2007	25,883	22,117	25,369	24,592	26,071	24,904	26,345	26,316	24,613	24,143	24,220	26,050	300,623
2008[1]	25,862	22,994	24,616	24,100	25,432	25,801	26,691	25,993	21,350	24,796	25,196	25,875	298,706

[1] Preliminary. *Source: Energy Information Administration, U.S. Department of Energy (EIA-DOE)*

Coal Receipts and Average Prices at Coke Plants in the United States

Year	Coal Receipts at Coke Plants — By Census Division, in Thousands of Short Tons — Middle Atlantic	East North Central	East South Central	Other	Total	Average Price of Coal Receipts at Coke Plants — By Census Division, In Dollars per Short Ton — Middle Atlantic	East North Central	East South Central	Other	Total
2002	W	11,184	2,335	10,136	23,655	W	52.80	50.03	W	50.67
2003	W	11,252	2,452	10,019	23,723	W	52.94	48.20	W	50.63
2004	W	11,591	2,710	9,795	24,096	W	63.30	59.16	W	61.50
2005	W	11,523	W	12,778	24,301	W	89.97	W	W	83.79
2006	W	11,488	W	11,865	23,353	W	99.48	W	W	92.87
2007[1]	W	9,907	W	11,725	21,632	W	99.20	W	W	94.97

[1] Preliminary. W = Withheld. *Source: Energy Information Administration, U.S. Department of Energy (EIA-DOE)*

Coal Carbonized and Coke and Breeze Stocks at Coke Plants in the United States — In Thousands of Short Tons

Year	Coal Carbonized at Coke Plants — By Census Division — Middle Atlantic	East North Central	East South Central	Other	Total	Stocks at Coke Plants, Dec. 31 — By Census Division — Middle Atlantic	East North Central	East South Central	Other	Total	Coke Total	Breeze Total
2002	W	11,154	2,319	10,183	23,656	W	424	155	169	748	606	141
2003	W	11,410	2,541	10,297	24,248	W	233	135	144	512	380	132
2004	W	11,322	2,644	9,704	23,670	W	166	154	144	464	351	113
2005	W	11,064	W	12,370	23,434	W	363	W	383	746	614	132
2006	W	11,100	W	11,857	22,957	W	487	W	284	771	685	87
2007[1]	W	10,486	W	12,229	22,715	W	414	W	296	710	632	78

[1] Preliminary. W = Withheld. *Source: Energy Information Administration, U.S. Department of Energy (EIA-DOE)*

Copper

The word *copper* comes from name of the Mediterranean island Cyprus that was a primary source of the metal. Dating back more than 10,000 years, copper is the oldest metal used by humans. From the Pyramid of Cheops in Egypt, archeologists recovered a portion of a water plumbing system whose copper tubing was found in serviceable condition after more than 5,000 years.

Copper is one of the most widely used industrial metals because it is an excellent conductor of electricity, has strong corrosion-resistance properties, and is very ductile. It is also used to produce the alloys of brass (a copper-zinc alloy) and bronze (a copper-tin alloy), both of which are far harder and stronger than pure copper. Electrical uses of copper account for about 75% of total copper usage, and building construction is the single largest market (the average U.S. home contains 400 pounds of copper). Copper is biostatic, meaning that bacteria will not grow on its surface, and it is therefore used in air-conditioning systems, food processing surfaces, and doorknobs to prevent the spread of disease.

Copper futures and options are traded on the London Metal Exchange (LME) and the NYMEX Division of the CME Group. Copper futures are traded on the Shanghai Futures Exchange. The Nymex copper futures contract calls for the delivery of 25,000 pounds of Grade 1 electrolyte copper and is priced in terms of cents per pound.

Prices – NYMEX copper futures prices rallied in early 2008 to post a record high of $4.27 per pound in May 2008 on support from precious metals and the overall rally in commodity prices. Copper also continued to see strong demand through early 2008. However, copper prices then fell sharply during the remainder of 2008 as the global financial crisis emerged and the global economy headed toward its first post-war recession, thus severely undercutting copper demand. Copper prices in December 2008 fell to a 4-year low of $1.2475 per pound, down 70.8% from the record high. Copper prices closed 2008 at $1.395, down $1.6355 per pound or -54.0%.

Supply – World production of copper in 2008 rose by +2.0% yr/yr to 15.700 million metric tons, which was a new record high. The largest producer of copper was Chili with 36% of the world's production, followed by the U.S. with 8%, Peru with 8%, and China with 7%. U.S. production of refined copper in 2007 (annualized through December) rose +4.9% yr/yr to 1.311 million short tons, which was far below the record U.S. production level of 2.490 million short tons seen in 1998.

Demand – U.S. consumption of copper in 2006 (latest available data) fell 7.1% yr/yr to 2.110 million metric tons. The primary users of copper in the U.S. in 2006 by class of consumer were wire rod mills with 74% of usage, brass mills with 23% of usage, and nominal use of 1% or less by each of foundries, ingot makers, and chemical plants.

Trade – U.S. exports of refined copper in 2007 (annualized through November) fell sharply by 51.2% to a 5-year low of 51.807 metric tons. U.S. imports of copper in 2007 (annualized through November) fell by 23.5% yr/yr to 841 thousand metric tons.

World Mine Production of Copper (Content of Ore)   In Thousands of Metric Tons

Year	Australia	Canada[3]	Chile	China	Indonesia	Mexico	Peru	Poland	Russia	South Africa	United States[3]	Zambia	World Total[2]
1999	739.9	620.1	4,391.2	533	766.0	381.2	536.4	463.2	530	144.3	1,600	280.0	12,800
2000	829.0	633.9	4,602.4	613	1,012.1	364.6	553.9	454.1	570	137.1	1,440	249.1	13,300
2001	871.0	633.5	4,739.0	605	1,081.0	371.1	722.3	474.0	600	141.9	1,340	312.0	13,700
2002	867.8	603.5	4,581.0	593	1,171.7	329.9	844.6	502.8	695	129.6	1,140	330.0	13,600
2003	839.6	557.1	4,904.2	620	1,005.8	355.7	862.6	495.0	675	120.8	1,120	349.0	13,800
2004	854.1	562.8	5,412.5	752	840.3	405.5	1,035.6	531.0	675	102.6	1,160	426.9	14,700
2005	916.3	595.4	5,320.5	777	1,065.0	429.1	1,009.9	523.0	700	97.0	1,140	423.0	15,000
2006	858.8	607.0	5,360.8	889	816.0	338.0	1,048.9	512.0	725	97.0	1,200	476.0	15,100
2007[1]	870.0	589.0	5,560.0	946	797.0	347.0	1,190.0	452.0	740		1,170	520.0	15,400
2008[2]	850.0	590.0	5,600.0	1000	650.0	270.0	1,220.0	430.0	750		1,310	560.0	15,700

[1] Preliminary.   [2] Estimate.   [3] Recoverable.   *Source: U.S. Geological Survey (USGS)*

Commodity Exchange Inc. Warehouse Stocks of Copper, on First of Month   In Thousands of Short Tons

Year	Jan.	Feb.	Mar.	Apr.	May	June	July	Aug.	Sept.	Oct.	Nov.	Dec.
1999	93.9	101.8	112.3	123.1	132.6	131.7	133.7	120.2	108.8	97.5	90.9	90.9
2000	91.6	95.6	95.6	95.9	865.2	75.0	73.6	73.2	62.8	62.3	63.4	64.9
2001	64.7	79.3	90.0	105.1	126.5	150.9	165.1	176.1	186.8	199.6	211.0	236.5
2002	269.2	284.8	304.0	314.1	326.0	337.4	355.7	374.6	375.9	380.3	381.6	382.8
2003	399.3	395.2	373.7	362.7	351.2	336.7	320.5	310.6	303.9	299.0	294.4	288.1
2004	280.9	262.7	241.9	213.3	171.7	130.7	95.1	79.0	62.3	49.2	45.5	42.4
2005	48.2	45.8	46.8	43.3	30.1	22.0	15.3	11.0	9.3	7.2	3.7	3.7
2006	6.8	11.7	30.4	20.7	16.7	9.5	7.9	6.8	12.4	22.3	23.2	31.3
2007	34.0	36.2	37.0	36.4	33.7	27.2	22.1	21.8	20.7	20.1	19.0	18.0
2008	14.1	14.0	13.1	11.9	10.8	11.1	11.0	5.4	5.4	9.9	9.9	24.5

Source: New York Mercantile Exchange (NYMEX), COMEX division

Salient Statistics of Copper in the United States   In Thousands of Metric Tons

Year	Mines	Smelters	Refineries	From Foreign Ores	Total New	Secondary Recovery	Unmanufactured	Refined	Ore, Concentrate6	Refined7	COMEX	Primary Producers (Refined)	Blister & Material in Solution	Refined Copper (Reported)	Primary & Old Copper8
1998	1,860	1,490	1,290	238	2,140	466	1,190	683	37	86	85	532	160	2,890	3,030
1999	1,600	1,090	1,110	196	1,890	381	1,280	837	63	25	83	566	138	2,980	3,130
2000	1,450	1,000	865	163	1,580	358	1,350	1,060	107	94	59	345	122	3,020	3,090
2001	1,340	919	808	192	1,630	317	1,400	991	45	23	244	952	98	2,620	2,500
2002	1,140	683	725	116	1,440	190	1,230	927	23	27	362	1,030	44	2,370	2,610
2003	1,120	539	532	130	1,250	207	1,140	882	10	93	255	656	57	2,290	2,430
2004	1,160	542	531	140	1,260	191	1,060	807	24	118	44	134	51	2,410	2,550
2005	1,140	523	524	130	1,210	183	1,230	1,000	137	40	6	66	44	2,270	2,400
2006[1]	1,200	501	531	144	1,210	150	1,320	1,070	108	106	31	196	19	2,110	2,190
2007[2]	1,170				1,280	150	1,100	829	90	51		130		2,140	2,280

[1] Preliminary.   [2] Estimate.   [3] Also from matte, etc., refinery reports.   [4] From old scrap only.   [5] For consumption.   [6] Blister (copper content).   [7] Ingots, bars, etc.   [8] Old scrap only.   W = Withheld.   *Source: U.S. Geological Survey (USGS)*

Consumption of Refined Copper³ in the United States   In Thousands of Metric Tons

Year	Cathodes	Wire Bars	Ingots and Ingot Bars	Cakes & Slabs	Billets	Other4	Wire Rod Mills	Brass Mills	Chemical Plants	Ingot Makers	Foundries	Miscellaneous5	Total Consumption
1997	2,490.0	W	29.4	81.1	W	194.0	2,140.0	597.0	1.0	4.2	16.6	29.9	2,790.0
1998	2,600.0	W	30.7	76.2	W	184.0	2,170.0	659.0	1.1	5.4	19.2	31.8	2,890.0
1999	2,710.0	W	24.4	79.3	W	166.0	2,230.0	691.0	1.2	4.5	21.2	29.8	2,980.0
2000	2,730.0	W	23.8	101.0	W	175.0	2,240.0	723.0	1.2	4.6	24.3	32.5	3,030.0
2001	2,360.0	W	24.0	95.9	W	140.0	1,940.0	623.0	1.2	4.6	21.6	28.6	2,620.0
2002	2,140.0	W	22.8	72.6	W	126.0	1,710.0	593.0	1.0	4.6	19.8	35.7	2,370.0
2003	2,070.0	W	22.3	41.8	W	153.0	1,640.0	587.0	1.0	4.6	21.9	36.7	2,290.0
2004	2,160.0	W	21.4	57.0	W	173.0	1,780.0	573.0	1.2	4.6	21.0	35.2	2,410.0
2005[1]	2,040.0	W	28.8	35.3	W	167.0	1,680.0	528.0	1.2	4.5	20.2	39.3	2,270.0
2006[2]	1,910.0	W	43.7	37.1	W	135.0	1,570.0	490.0	1.0	4.5	21.4	21.4	2,110.0

[1] Preliminary.   [2] Estimate.   [3] Primary & secondary.   [4] Includes Wirebars and Billets.   [5] Includes iron and steel plants, primary smelters producing alloys other than copper, consumers of copper powder and copper shot, and other manufacturers.   W = Withheld.
Source: U.S. Geological Survey (USGS)

London Metals Exchange Warehouse Stocks of Copper, at End of Month   In Thousands of Metric Tons

Year	Jan.	Feb.	Mar.	Apr.	May	June	July	Aug.	Sept.	Oct.	Nov.	Dec.
1999	646.9	695.9	722.2	748.2	776.6	754.8	769.6	789.0	774.0	793.8	779.7	790.5
2000	807.3	824.1	755.4	697.8	605.7	553.4	487.8	449.2	401.5	380.9	349.4	357.4
2001	349.9	327.9	400.5	445.2	431.3	464.7	651.9	661.2	729.0	737.2	780.4	799.5
2002	855.5	910.9	950.9	973.8	958.3	892.1	893.6	896.6	870.6	863.2	862.8	855.9
2003	833.8	825.9	813.2	768.2	740.8	665.8	612.6	620.3	580.4	516.5	467.0	430.7
2004	358.2	281.6	187.5	151.3	132.3	101.5	87.7	111.3	91.8	77.9	59.8	48.9
2005	46.4	52.5	45.3	61.0	44.4	28.9	31.6	68.0	79.9	65.1	72.6	92.3
2006	96.0	115.3	120.7	117.6	111.2	93.6	100.6	125.4	116.9	135.2	156.8	190.7
2007	216.2	205.4	181.1	156.6	127.5	112.6	103.5	139.1	130.7	167.1	189.6	199.0
2008[1]	177.9	141.4	111.3	110.1	124.0	122.4	144.6	173.8	199.1	238.0	291.3	

[1] Preliminary.   *Source: American Bureau of Metal Statistics (ABMS)*

Copper Refined from Scrap in the United States   In Thousands of Metric Tons

Year	Jan.	Feb.	Mar.	Apr.	May	June	July	Aug.	Sept.	Oct.	Nov.	Dec.	Total
1998	25.9	28.6	23.7	31.0	17.8	21.4	24.2	23.9	23.8	31.8	23.2	26.3	336.0
1999	20.1	21.8	23.7	17.6	16.2	17.5	21.2	18.2	21.3	21.0	17.7	20.0	230.0
2000	19.4	18.6	25.8	22.5	22.1	15.4	11.7	19.7	14.1	14.3	19.7	15.6	208.0
2001	15.4	14.2	15.2	13.4	12.8	13.2	13.9	13.5	12.3	10.2	6.4	5.7	154.0
2002	7.1	6.2	7.2	7.6	8.2	7.8	7.0	7.6	7.1	4.5	5.1	3.9	81.1
2003	5.8	3.9	5.7	3.9	4.1	4.9	4.9	3.9	4.2	4.5	4.2	4.0	53.8
2004	4.2	3.9	4.3	4.4	4.2	4.5	4.1	3.9	4.7	4.5	4.2	3.9	50.8
2005	4.4	4.4	4.2	4.2	3.8	3.6	3.9	3.6	3.6	3.8	3.8	3.9	47.1
2006	3.8	3.7	3.8	3.7	3.7	3.7	3.7	3.7	3.8	3.7	3.7	3.8	44.8
2007[1]	3.9	3.9	3.4	3.5	3.4	3.4	3.4	3.4	3.5	3.4	3.6	3.5	42.1

[1] Preliminary.   *Source: U.S. Geological Survey (USGS)*

COPPER

Copper (monthly average) through December 2008   Cents per pound

Average Open Interest of Copper Futures in New York   In Contracts

Year	Jan.	Feb.	Mar.	Apr.	May	June	July	Aug.	Sept.	Oct.	Nov.	Dec.
1999	76,861	73,109	75,318	70,534	76,341	70,842	75,640	70,084	80,188	72,240	69,179	69,819
2000	82,289	73,778	68,026	75,520	69,531	63,786	71,389	79,565	83,546	73,609	74,161	70,349
2001	77,952	76,721	78,034	83,647	72,970	85,495	83,690	88,782	87,004	88,166	85,809	68,981
2002	72,823	79,806	79,156	75,229	74,350	80,981	82,661	102,056	99,225	99,470	89,213	79,218
2003	81,820	81,499	72,484	85,485	77,704	81,509	82,868	94,517	92,768	106,924	103,218	90,208
2004	91,726	88,136	77,158	71,705	65,531	64,879	65,310	71,096	81,162	85,421	81,928	88,822
2005	85,363	96,537	116,004	120,138	98,240	106,218	109,156	109,481	102,652	106,829	110,972	104,062
2006	102,227	93,813	93,069	97,283	83,758	75,841	74,471	72,158	69,004	72,023	72,517	68,402
2007	69,972	70,373	69,324	78,919	80,834	79,257	88,691	78,113	72,469	86,909	78,385	71,626
2008	81,778	94,021	101,503	105,050	98,787	103,055	109,591	96,254	76,523	80,961	76,869	71,809

Source: New York Mercantile Exchange (NYMEX), COMEX division

Volume of Trading of Copper Futures in New York   In Contracts

Year	Jan.	Feb.	Mar.	Apr.	May	June	July	Aug.	Sept.	Oct.	Nov.	Dec.	Total
1999	159,147	288,394	230,716	296,162	224,221	319,157	244,567	267,325	220,958	193,628	231,399	177,288	2,852,962
2000	220,488	276,374	195,668	261,971	232,971	241,854	187,453	283,328	171,080	243,342	266,051	197,544	2,778,124
2001	240,588	246,052	247,722	279,348	260,697	317,001	159,394	298,639	129,622	190,469	337,589	149,520	2,856,641
2002	217,598	233,704	164,747	254,259	218,091	267,201	263,395	303,642	195,637	232,731	276,492	179,789	2,807,286
2003	232,921	269,806	249,306	274,079	221,364	301,709	252,713	324,175	196,481	230,413	363,865	172,438	3,089,270
2004	213,536	385,848	265,312	340,236	203,906	280,882	208,415	310,299	212,082	245,011	317,220	207,878	3,190,625
2005	199,938	391,949	298,181	469,849	288,399	475,756	227,917	435,848	252,733	265,234	458,258	186,780	3,950,842
2006	234,295	401,404	284,478	406,984	260,422	321,626	182,175	310,023	189,405	216,369	320,780	153,351	3,281,312
2007	241,333	333,967	264,511	402,764	292,359	367,217	272,429	451,599	225,624	289,319	412,949	199,097	3,753,168
2008	345,506	459,539	298,485	466,514	344,500	462,033	382,095	463,234	349,541	403,803	414,380	228,444	4,618,074

Source: New York Mercantile Exchange (NYMEX), COMEX division

Producers' Price of Electrolytic (Wirebar) Copper, Delivered to U.S. Destinations   In Cents Per Pound

Year	Jan.	Feb.	Mar.	Apr.	May	June	July	Aug.	Sept.	Oct.	Nov.	Dec.	Average
1999	77.07	75.96	74.50	78.79	81.07	77.23	88.02	87.88	92.89	91.26	91.10	93.35	84.09
2000	96.83	94.41	91.63	89.32	94.80	92.74	95.81	98.67	103.49	99.63	95.25	98.92	95.96
2001	95.70	94.01	92.07	88.27	88.85	84.58	81.44	79.34	77.41	75.21	78.13	79.83	84.57
2002	81.79	84.23	86.60	85.11	85.22	88.23	84.44	79.82	79.71	80.16	84.57	75.56	82.62
2003	78.62	80.21	78.87	75.60	78.56	80.44	81.55	83.51	85.34	91.50	96.47	103.72	84.53
2004	113.93	129.91	139.96	135.82	129.44	129.11	134.34	135.50	138.74	142.01	147.99	151.88	135.72
2005	151.25	152.89	154.68	155.42	154.19	168.31	169.62	178.39	182.00	197.61	208.60	224.25	174.77
2006	225.07	230.74	238.31	302.74	382.65	346.65	368.49	359.91	353.01	345.83	322.45	307.00	315.24
2007	263.89	265.67	298.65	356.76	355.24	346.59	370.42	343.65	351.87	364.48	318.93	306.74	328.57
2008	325.53	364.78	385.98	399.96	383.39	375.08	382.31	349.89	320.54	224.32	174.59	145.09	319.29

Source: American Metal Market (AMM)

Dealers' Buying Price of No. 2 Heavy Copper Scrap in Chicago   In Cents Per Pound

Year	Jan.	Feb.	Mar.	Apr.	May	June	July	Aug.	Sept.	Oct.	Nov.	Dec.	Average
1999	36.32	36.00	36.00	36.00	39.60	41.77	41.00	45.09	46.19	48.00	48.00	48.67	41.90
2000	50.00	50.00	50.00	49.15	49.00	49.00	49.30	52.65	54.60	55.00	52.65	51.00	51.04
2001	51.62	49.16	49.00	49.81	50.00	50.00	49.14	44.00	44.00	43.48	41.45	41.47	46.93
2002	41.00	41.00	41.00	41.00	41.00	41.00	41.00	41.00	41.00	41.00	41.00	41.00	41.00
2003	41.00	41.00	41.00	41.00	41.00	41.00	41.00	41.00	41.00	48.17	56.00	56.00	43.99
2004	56.65	69.00	69.00	69.32	76.00	76.00	76.64	90.00	90.00	90.00	90.00	90.00	78.55
2005	90.00	90.00	90.00	90.00	90.00	94.09	100.00	100.00	100.00	100.00	100.00	129.52	97.80
2006	137.50	137.50	139.46	145.00	145.00	171.36	175.25	185.89	184.10	192.09	192.85	183.30	165.78
2007	155.83	153.92	164.32	197.83	210.09	203.60	216.83	219.89	213.97	224.72	210.20	191.87	196.92
2008	198.21	210.00	238.21	246.82	247.02	237.50	240.00	233.93	226.07	141.85	97.50	87.02	200.34

Source: American Metal Market (AMM)

COPPER

Imports of Refined Copper into the United States   In Thousands of Metric Tons

Year	Jan.	Feb.	Mar.	Apr.	May	June	July	Aug.	Sept.	Oct.	Nov.	Dec.	Total
1998	62.8	49.6	59.9	64.7	57.6	52.8	45.0	51.7	71.1	52.7	62.0	63.4	683.0
1999	64.7	53.2	68.1	59.9	62.3	63.8	73.0	84.5	90.3	81.0	59.0	77.5	837.0
2000	84.9	67.8	85.5	92.1	83.6	84.5	89.4	83.0	98.6	112.0	100.0	73.7	1,060.0
2001	105.0	91.6	90.1	94.4	70.3	72.7	61.7	66.3	83.5	71.0	110.0	74.4	991.0
2002	82.5	87.8	53.0	92.6	59.9	76.2	80.3	90.5	69.9	79.0	82.0	73.0	927.0
2003	60.7	87.8	69.9	78.5	72.7	62.3	74.0	78.1	81.7	82.0	73.2	61.1	882.0
2004	55.4	48.8	70.7	59.3	70.8	51.3	83.9	78.7	91.7	68.4	77.0	51.1	807.1
2005	85.2	66.5	75.8	63.7	107.0	64.7	75.8	79.4	79.4	99.4	101.0	106.0	1,003.9
2006	138.0	108.0	80.1	69.1	100.0	94.1	91.4	101.0	106.0	96.4	58.3	56.5	1,098.9
2007[1]	87.3	76.4	68.4	65.8	80.1	58.9	66.6	77.7	68.5	66.9	54.5		841.2

[1] Preliminary.   *Source: U.S. Geological Survey (USGS)*

Exports of Refined Copper from the United States   In Thousands of Metric Tons

Year	Jan.	Feb.	Mar.	Apr.	May	June	July	Aug.	Sept.	Oct.	Nov.	Dec.	Total
1998	6.2	12.1	12.2	7.5	7.8	6.4	7.5	6.4	5.8	5.0	3.6	6.2	86.2
1999	2.4	1.1	1.8	1.3	1.6	4.2	1.6	1.5	1.2	1.4	3.7	3.3	25.2
2000	1.6	5.3	22.0	12.2	18.1	12.8	6.7	4.4	2.9	4.3	1.2	2.1	93.6
2001	1.2	.9	.8	1.9	1.0	.8	1.7	2.6	1.2	4.6	5.3	.6	22.5
2002	.4	.7	3.2	.7	.8	6.8	7.7	2.6	1.3	.6	.5	1.5	26.6
2003	2.5	.8	1.5	.6	15.9	23.0	5.1	4.1	4.3	4.6	8.5	22.3	93.2
2004	11.0	18.5	23.9	28.4	3.7	2.7	5.5	9.4	.6	3.9	2.5	8.4	118.4
2005	4.5	3.2	2.8	1.9	7.2	4.3	3.0	2.7	1.8	3.3	3.3	3.0	40.9
2006	5.6	7.3	6.8	9.6	6.3	13.1	6.0	9.6	9.3	13.7	6.2	12.6	106.1
2007[1]	3.1	2.7	5.1	3.6	3.9	6.6	3.6	3.4	5.4	7.1	3.0		51.8

[1] Preliminary.   *Source: U.S. Geological Survey (USGS)*

Stocks of Refined Copper in the United States, on First of Month   In Thousands of Short Tons

Year	Jan.	Feb.	Mar.	Apr.	May	June	July	Aug.	Sept.	Oct.	Nov.	Dec.
1999	562.6	593.1	614.6	653.5	676.6	687.8	668.4	657.2	639.7	611.2	626.5	608.2
2000	619.2	620.8	619.5	582.9	537.0	508.8	467.8	418.0	397.7	394.3	379.1	344.2
2001	383.8	408.4	416.2	481.9	552.6	585.7	626.7	733.1	767.4	895.6	916.6	985.7
2002	1,045.1	1,096.2	1,132.4	1,155.3	1,175.0	1,158.8	1,126.7	1,132.2	1,123.0	1,123.7	1,110.5	1,109.0
2003	1,119.8	109.7	1,038.8	1,042.1	998.3	959.8	891.8	848.9	855.6	825.5	761.2	768.0
2004	733.8	646.3	566.7	463.9	367.0	311.8	247.8	218.3	194.5	169.2	158.9	147.4
2005	145.8	151.0	143.4	134.4	129.3	116.2	105.3	98.5	83.0	68.2	56.8	59.4
2006	66.8	76.9	103.3	109.0	88.2	84.5	68.3	76.4	80.1	88.4	103.4	152.3
2007	194.9	222.1	216.8	197.7	165.8	130.7	114.3	118.8	114.0	110.3	115.0	123.8
2008[1]	147.2	122.5	106.3	105.9	74.4	81.3	72.8	83.8	107.0	124.3	135.3	

Recoverable Copper Content.   [1] Preliminary.   *Source: American Bureau of Metal Statistics (ABMS)*

Stocks of Refined Copper Outside the United States, on First of Month   In Thousands of Short Tons

Year	Jan.	Feb.	Mar.	Apr.	May	June	July	Aug.	Sept.	Oct.	Nov.	Dec.
1999	922.6	944.3	960.3	963.0	990.5	1,008.3	993.3	990.0	1,017.0	996.9	1,001.5	992.0
2000	983.8	1,034.9	1,040.7	1,011.4	988.6	880.9	866.0	857.3	837.0	826.7	784.1	764.8
2001	795.0	999.5	986.4	971.2	995.7	969.4	1,000.8	1,091.0	1,108.7	1,083.3	1,021.0	1,104.5
2002	1,241.3	1,273.5	1,291.5	1,370.4	1,391.1	1,399.4	1,289.0	1,342.6	1,369.1	1,321.1	1,219.7	1,224.5
2003	1,238.8	2,147.6	1,188.0	1,216.3	1,147.4	1,109.8	1,129.2	1,139.9	1,150.9	1,140.2	1,170.8	1,157.1
2004	1,191.5	1,149.9	1,139.5	995.5	968.4	826.0	807.1	812.4	830.2	825.2	778.0	816.8
2005	833.8	802.2	929.8	848.0	758.2	771.3	822.6	786.4	846.9	774.3	803.4	805.0
2006	871.2	956.8	923.2	797.7	816.4	819.2	789.1	812.9	872.4	830.1	877.6	905.9
2007	1,016.2	969.5	966.6	994.3	973.0	873.8	893.9	845.9	880.9	894.4	884.8	860.7
2008	947.7	920.0	833.9	1,257.0	1,253.4	1,311.1	1,309.1	1,315.5	1,317.3	1,362.4	1,361.8	

Recoverable Copper Content.   *Source: American Bureau of Metal Statistics (ABMS)*

Production of Refined Copper in the United States   In Thousands of Short Tons

Year	Jan.	Feb.	Mar.	Apr.	May	June	July	Aug.	Sept.	Oct.	Nov.	Dec.	Total
1998	214.0	204.0	216.0	209.0	197.0	188.0	197.0	203.0	201.0	217.0	207.0	217.0	2,490
1999	185.0	178.0	220.0	198.0	186.0	175.0	163.0	161.0	172.0	172.0	157.0	162.0	2,130
2000	157.0	149.0	173.0	144.0	161.0	146.0	134.0	149.0	141.0	140.0	147.0	154.0	1,800
2001	155.0	144.0	156.0	145.0	155.0	157.0	146.0	143.0	148.0	149.0	152.0	150.0	1,800
2002	134.0	117.0	124.0	129.0	134.0	128.0	130.0	124.0	120.0	129.0	120.0	119.0	1,508
2003	124.0	110.0	118.0	98.7	98.8	106.0	110.0	110.0	112.0	108.0	101.0	111.0	1,308
2004	104.0	98.9	105.0	111.0	109.0	113.0	104.0	107.0	112.0	111.0	109.0	123.0	1,307
2005	102.0	102.0	104.0	105.0	109.0	101.0	100.0	102.0	103.0	104.0	108.0	115.0	1,255
2006	99.9	101.0	117.0	109.0	113.0	114.0	100.0	101.0	102.0	89.8	94.4	108.0	1,249
2007[1]	101.0	97.1	116.0	113.0	116.0	112.0	116.0	117.0	108.0	120.0	91.5	103.0	1,311

Recoverable Copper Content.   [1] Preliminary.   *Source: U.S. Geological Survey (USGS)*

Production of Refined Copper Outside North America   In Thousands of Short Tons

Year	Jan.	Feb.	Mar.	Apr.	May	June	July	Aug.	Sept.	Oct.	Nov.	Dec.	Total
1999	1,192.3	1,252.1	1,240.7	1,303.4	1,364.9	1,413.8	1,404.9	1,393.2	1,377.8	1,334.3	1,363.2	1,331.7	15,972
2000	1,179.5	1,121.6	1,205.2	1,178.1	1,227.4	1,188.6	1,198.2	1,204.8	1,230.0	1,253.8	1,238.2	1,251.8	14,477
2001	1,279.1	1,188.0	1,316.5	1,243.6	1,295.9	1,241.7	1,269.8	1,296.1	1,247.1	1,308.5	1,299.8	1,318.5	15,305
2002	1,310.4	1,190.9	1,307.8	1,268.2	1,294.3	1,257.6	1,254.9	1,272.7	1,242.9	1,293.6	1,263.1	1,282.0	15,238
2003	1,274.4	1,188.2	1,283.9	1,244.3	1,292.2	1,253.9	1,289.6	1,272.9	1,268.6	1,320.6	1,302.4	1,349.4	15,340
2004	1,286.7	1,256.0	1,344.1	1,290.0	1,277.3	1,291.9	1,358.8	1,366.5	1,370.6	1,390.0	1,402.4	1,406.5	16,041
2005	1,407.9	1,252.0	1,388.1	1,343.0	1,390.5	1,389.3	1,402.3	1,409.2	1,407.9	1,429.0	1,444.8	1,493.6	16,758
2006	1,423.7	1,346.1	1,466.0	1,435.9	1,459.1	1,457.0	1,476.2	1,459.2	1,460.0	1,521.8	1,494.8	1,566.7	17,567
2007	1,568.4	1,443.8	1,541.9	1,502.0	1,520.9	1,483.0	1,491.6	1,501.0	1,531.9	1,549.1	1,570.6	1,601.4	18,306
2008[1]	1,663.2	1,582.5	1,720.2	1,679.6	1,676.2	1,712.8	1,741.0	1,747.4	1,713.5	1,738.2	1,685.4		20,356

Recoverable Copper Content.   [1] Preliminary.   *Source: American Bureau of Metal Statistics (ABMS)*

Deliveries of Refined Copper to Fabricators in the United States   In Thousands of Short Tons

Year	Jan.	Feb.	Mar.	Apr.	May	June	July	Aug.	Sept.	Oct.	Nov.	Dec.	Total
1999	199.6	202.8	235.0	221.4	206.3	201.9	188.0	186.8	193.7	182.3	182.4	175.2	2,375
2000	166.8	161.3	176.3	157.0	173.7	161.3	145.2	149.7	150.6	154.8	149.8	162.7	1,909
2001	166.1	150.8	167.4	148.4	167.6	165.2	162.7	154.0	151.6	160.7	154.7	147.5	1,897
2002	152.1	126.0	140.7	149.3	148.6	136.2	147.9	141.1	129.5	141.6	124.5	129.7	1,667
2003	136.4	123.4	124.6	106.6	107.7	117.0	127.1	120.6	125.8	127.9	114.4	133.8	1,465
2004	126.4	131.1	137.6	137.7	130.9	143.5	133.3	132.9	136.8	129.3	128.8	137.5	1,606
2005	120.1	120.0	131.2	125.4	125.7	119.2	106.9	112.8	108.0	110.9	112.6	115.9	1,409
2006	124.8	110.3	131.5	121.9	121.8	132.7	117.5	119.9	112.7	95.5	95.6	100.5	1,385
2007	115.9	118.9	131.9	127.4	128.1	126.2	131.3	132.3	112.2	134.9	113.3	100.9	1,473
2008[1]	134.1	118.8	123.2	114.7	111.6	120.8	105.4	118.3	121.4	130.0	109.7		1,427

Recoverable Copper Content.   [1] Preliminary.   *Source: American Bureau of Metal Statistics (ABMS)*

Deliveries of Refined Copper to Fabricators Outside the United States   In Thousands of Short Tons

Year	Jan.	Feb.	Mar.	Apr.	May	June	July	Aug.	Sept.	Oct.	Nov.	Dec.	Total
1990	419.9	466.3	436.7	392.9	408.3	466.7	303.7	373.5	370.8	448.9	469.1	420.7	4,972
1991	405.0	404.4	391.5	361.2	406.3	433.5	368.5	323.4	420.7	499.1	391.4	483.4	4,807
1992	453.7	408.9	441.8	416.4	413.4	432.4	410.4	364.7	432.6	403.5	406.1	461.3	5,045
1993	427.9	392.9	452.3	361.7	422.2	442.6	384.4	347.9	387.5	414.8	463.4	458.5	4,956
1994	399.8	429.5	481.2	466.5	468.9	428.1	387.9	369.2	423.5	448.9	457.1	436.0	5,197
1995[2]	758.5	810.1	892.8	882.2	853.0	867.3	863.7	814.1	803.4	835.1	796.6	726.2	9,903
1996	875.2	859.4	934.3	907.2	816.7	950.7	908.3	817.4	911.5	1,056.0	922.7	918.3	10,878
1997	862.2	889.7	977.9	1,007.1	991.1	982.7	897.8	873.9	886.2	1,009.0	980.4	966.6	11,349
1998	1,091.7	973.8	1,062.0	1,055.5	995.7	1,014.8	986.8	924.8	913.3	987.9	982.1	1,023.0	12,011
1999[1]	314.5	745.5	NA	NA	NA	NA	NA	NA	NA	NA	NA	NA	6,360

Recoverable Copper Content.   [1] Preliminary.   [2] New reporting method beginning January 1995, includes crude copper deliveries.
Source: American Bureau of Metal Statistics (ABMS)

Corn

Corn is a member of the grass family of plants and is a native grain of the American continents. Fossils of corn pollen that are over 80,000 years old have been found in lake sediment under Mexico City. Archaeological discoveries show that cultivated corn existed in the southwestern U.S. for at least 3,000 years, indicating that the indigenous people of the region cultivated corn as a food crop long before the Europeans reached the New World. Corn is a hardy plant that grows in many different areas of the world. It can grow at altitudes as low as sea level and as high as 12,000 feet in the South American Andes Mountains. Corn can also grow in tropical climates that receive up to 400 inches of rainfall per year, or in areas that receive only 12 inches of rainfall per year. Corn is used primarily as livestock feed in the United States and the rest of the world. Other uses for corn are alcohol additives for gasoline, adhesives, corn oil for cooking and margarine, sweeteners, and as food for humans. Corn is the largest crop in the U.S., both in terms of the value of the crop and of the acres planted.

The largest futures market for corn is at the Chicago Board of Trade. Corn futures also trade at the Bolsa de Mercadorias & Futuros (BM&F) in Brazil, the Budapest Commodity Exchange, the Marche a Terme International de France (MATIF), the Mercado a Termino de Buenos Aires in Argentina, the Kanmon Commodity Exchange (KCE) in Korea, and the Tokyo Grain Exchange (TGE). The CBOT futures contract calls for the delivery of 5000 bushels of No. 2 yellow corn at par contract price, No. 1 yellow at 1-1/2 cents per bushel over the contract price, or No. 3 yellow at 1-1/2 cents per bushel below the contract price.

Prices – Corn futures prices in early 2008 extended the rally that began in late 2007 and reached a record high of $7.625 per bushel in June 2008. Corn prices then fell sharply in the latter half of 2008, particularly after the global financial crisis emerged in September 2008. Corn prices in December 2008 hit a 2-year low of $2.90, selling off by a total of 62% from the record high. Corn prices closed 2008 at $4.07, down -48.5 cents or -10.6%. Corn prices rallied sharply in 2006-07 as ethanol producers quickly ramped up production and took increasing amounts of corn to produce ethanol. Corn usage for ethanol was at 11% of the overall U.S. corn crop in 2002-04 but then ramped up to 20% in 2006-07, 23% in 2007-08 and 30% in 2008/09. In the 2007-08 marketing year, U.S. farmers sharply boosted corn planting by 19.4% to 93.527 million acres in response to the sharp rally in corn prices. However, soybean prices rallied sharply as well during that time and in 2008/09, U.S. farmers cut back corn planting by 8% to 85.982 million acres. Corn prices in early 2008 extended the 2006-07 rally due to the weak dollar and the feverish commodity bull market. However, corn prices peaked in mid-2008 as the U.S. economy started to slow and the dollar started to rally. Corn prices then plunged during the financial crisis as investors were washed out of their long positions and as global demand for corn receded from livestock and ethanol producers. In addition, the weather was generally favorable during the 2008 growing season, leading to a 12.101 billion bushel crop, the second highest ever. The U.S. corn carry-over in 2008/09 rose about 10% to 1.79 billion bushels and was higher than in the two previous years.

Supply – World production of corn in the 2008-09 marketing year fell by -0.6% to 786.473 million metric tons, down from last year's record high of 791.422 million metric tons. The world's largest corn producers are the U.S. with 39% of world production, China (21%), and Brazil (6%). Corn production in both China and Brazil has nearly doubled since 1980. Production in the U.S. over that same time frame has risen by about 50%. The world area harvested with corn in 2007-08 (latest data available) rose +3.5% yr/yr to 314.7 million hectares, which was an 11-year high. World ending stocks of corn and coarse grains in 2007-08 fell –7.7% to 126.0 million metric tons, which is a 3-decade low.

U.S. corn production in the 2008-09 marketing year (Sep-Aug) fell by -7.4% yr/yr to 12.101 billion bushels, down from last year's record high. U.S. farmers harvested 78.640 million acres of corn for grain usage in 2008-09, which was down -9.1% yr/yr, down from last year's record high. U.S. corn yield in 2008-09 rose +1.9% to 153.9 bushels per acre but that is still below the record high of 160.4 bushels per acre seen in 2004-05. U.S. carry-over stocks on June 1, 2008 rose +14.0% to 4.028 million bushels from 3.533 billion bushels in 2007. The largest corn producing states in the U.S. in 2008 were Iowa with 17.8% of U.S. production, Illinois (17.3%), Nebraska (11.4%), Minnesota (10.1%), and Indiana (7.2%). The value of the U.S. corn crop in 2007-08 was $52.090 billion.

Demand – World consumption of corn and rough grains in 2007-08 (latest data) rose by +5.2% yr/yr to 1,062.5 million metric tons, which was a new record high. The U.S. distribution tables for corn show that in 2008-09 the largest category of usage, aside from animal feed, is for ethanol production (alcohol fuel) with 4.000 billion bushels. That was up +33% from 2007-08 and is 75.0% of total non-feed usage. Corn usage for ethanol is more than five times the usage in 2000 and that usage category is likely to grow if there is a return of the high prices of crude oil and gasoline. After ethanol, the largest non-feed usage categories are for high fructose corn syrup (HFCS) with 9% of U.S. usage, corn starch (5%), glucose and dextrose sugars (5%), cereal and other corn products (4%), and alcoholic beverages (3%).

Trade – U.S. exports of corn in 2007-08 (latest data available) rose +12.1% yr/yr to 60.685 million metric tons, which is getting close to the record high of 61.417 million metric tons posted in 1979-80. The largest destination countries for U.S. corn exports are Japan, which accounted for 25% of U.S. corn exports in 2007-08, Mexico (16%), South Korea (14%), Taiwan (6%), Egypt (5%), and Canada (5%).

World Production of Corn or Maize In Thousands of Metric Tons

Crop Year Beginning Oct. 1	Argentina	Brazil	Canada	China	European Union	Egypt	India	Mexico	Romania	South Africa	United States	Ukraine	World Total
1999-00	17,200	31,641	9,161	128,086	57,329	5,678	11,470	19,240	10,500	11,455	239,549	1,737	607,630
2000-01	15,400	41,536	6,827	106,000	50,089	5,636	12,068	17,917	4,800	8,040	251,854	3,848	590,831
2001-02	14,700	35,501	8,389	114,088	58,022	6,160	13,510	20,400	7,000	10,050	241,377	3,641	600,339
2002-03	15,500	44,500	8,999	121,300	57,660	6,000	11,100	19,280	7,300	9,675	227,767	4,180	603,561
2003-04	15,000	42,000	9,587	115,830	47,905	5,740	14,980	21,800	7,020	9,700	256,229	6,850	627,545
2004-05	20,500	35,000	8,837	130,290	66,471	5,840	14,180	22,050	12,000	11,716	299,876	8,800	715,732
2005-06	15,800	41,700	9,332	139,365	60,668	5,932	14,710	19,500	10,300	6,935	282,263	7,150	699,127
2006-07[1]	22,500	51,000	8,990	151,600	53,829	6,149	15,100	22,350	8,500	7,300	267,503	6,400	712,277
2007-08[2]	20,850	58,600	11,649	152,300	47,666	6,174	19,310	22,650		13,164	331,177	7,400	791,422
2008-09[3]	13,500	49,500	10,600	165,500	61,357	6,175	17,500	25,000		10,500	307,386	11,400	786,473

[1] Preliminary. [2] Estimate. [3] Forecast. *Source: Foreign Agricultural Service, U.S. Department of Agriculture (FAS-USDA)*

World Supply and Demand of Course Grains In Millions of Metric Tons/Hectares

Crop Year Beginning Oct. 1	Area Harvested	Yield	Production	World Trade	Total Consumption	Ending Stocks	Stocks as % of Consumption[3]
1999-00	299.0	2.90	878.0	102.4	882.8	232.5	26.3
2000-01	296.1	2.90	863.0	102.7	884.5	210.9	23.8
2001-02	301.0	3.00	895.1	100.5	907.4	198.6	21.9
2002-03	293.0	3.00	875.8	102.7	903.9	170.5	18.9
2003-04	307.0	3.00	916.6	102.6	945.5	141.6	15.0
2004-05	300.3	3.40	1,016.4	101.2	979.4	178.6	18.2
2005-06	302.0	3.20	980.4	108.5	993.7	165.3	16.6
2006-07	306.1	3.20	988.0	114.3	1,014.8	138.4	13.6
2007-08[1]	319.6	3.40	1,080.6	128.8	1,059.3	159.8	15.1
2008-09[2]	313.8	3.50	1,100.1	102.1	1,072.6	187.2	17.5

[1] Preliminary. [2] Estimate. [3] Represents the ratio of marketing year ending stocks to total consumption. *Source: Foreign Agricultural Service, U.S. Department of Agriculture (FAS-USDA)*

Acreage and Supply of Corn in the United States In Millions of Bushels

Crop Year Beginning Sept. 1	Planted	Harvested For Grain	Harvested For Silage	Yield Per Harvested Acre Bushels	Carry-over, Sept. 1 On Farms	Carry-over, Sept. 1 Off Farms	Supply Beginning Stocks	Supply Production	Supply Imports	Total Supply
		In Thousands of Acres		Bushels						
1999-00	77,386	70,487	6,037	133.8	797.0	990.0	1,787	9,431	15	11,239
2000-01	79,551	72,440	6,082	136.9	793.0	924.5	1,718	9,915	7	11,693
2001-02	75,752	68,808	6,148	138.2	753.2	1,146.0	1,899	9,507	10	11,412
2002-03	78,894	69,330	7,122	129.3	586.8	1,009.6	1,596	8,967	14	10,578
2003-04	78,603	70,944	6,583	142.2	484.9	601.8	1,087	10,089	14	11,190
2004-05	80,930	73,632	6,103	160.4	438.0	520.1	958	11,807	11	12,776
2005-06	81,759	75,107	5,920	147.9	820.5	1,293.5	2,114	11,112	9	13,237
2006-07	78,327	70,648	6,477	149.1	749.5	1,217.7	1,967	10,535	12	12,514
2007-08[1]	93,600	86,542	6,071	151.1	460.1	843.5	1,304	13,074	15	14,393
2008-09[2]	85,982	78,640	5,965	153.9	500.0	1,124.2	1,433	12,101	15	13,183

[1] Preliminary. [2] Estimate. *Source: Economic Research Service, U.S. Department of Agriculture (ERS-USDA)*

Production of Corn (For Grain) in the United States, by State In Million of Bushels

Year	Illinois	Indiana	Iowa	Kansas	Michigan	Minnesota	Missouri	Nebraska	Ohio	South Dakota	Texas	Wisconsin	Total
1999	1,491.0	748.4	1,758.2	420.2	253.5	990.0	247.4	1,153.7	403.2	367.3	228.3	407.6	9,430.6
2000	1,668.6	810.3	1,728.0	412.1	241.8	964.3	396.1	1,014.3	485.1	425.6	235.6	363.0	9,915.1
2001	1,649.2	884.5	1,664.4	387.4	199.5	806.0	345.8	1,139.3	437.5	370.6	167.6	330.2	9,506.8
2002	1,471.5	631.6	1,931.6	301.6	234.0	1,051.9	283.5	940.8	264.3	308.8	202.3	391.5	8,966.8
2003	1,812.2	786.9	1,868.3	300.0	259.8	970.9	302.4	1,124.2	478.9	427.4	194.7	367.7	10,089.2
2004	2,088.0	929.0	2,244.4	432.0	257.3	1,121.0	466.6	1,319.7	491.4	539.5	233.5	353.6	11,807.2
2005	1,708.9	888.6	2,162.5	465.8	288.9	1,191.9	329.7	1,270.5	464.8	470.1	210.9	429.2	11,112.1
2006	1,817.5	844.7	2,050.1	345.0	288.1	1,102.9	362.9	1,178.0	470.6	312.3	175.5	400.4	10,534.9
2007	2,283.8	987.4	2,368.4	518.0	291.4	1,138.8	461.5	1,472.0	541.5	544.5	296.0	442.8	13,073.9
2008[1]	2,094.3	872.0	2,150.0	493.2	283.6	1,218.0	364.0	1,376.6	427.0	554.7	270.9	411.0	12,101.2

[1] Preliminary. *Source: National Agricultural Statistics Service, U.S. Department of Agriculture (NASS-USDA)*

CORN

Quarterly Supply and Disappearance of Corn in the United States   In Millions of Bushels

Crop Year Beginning Sept. 1	Beginning Stocks	Pro-duction	Imports[3]	Total Supply	Food & Alcohol	Seed	Feed & Residual	Total	Exports[3]	Total Disap-pearance	Gov't Owned[4]	Privately Owned[5]	Total Stocks
						Domestic Use					**Ending Stocks**		
2004-05	958	11,807	11.0	12,776	2,686	0	6,158	8,844	1,818	10,662			2,114
Sept.-Nov.	958	11,807	2.0	12,767	643	0	2,175	2,818	499	3,316			9,451
Dec.-Feb.	9,451	----	2.0	9,452	637	0	1,620	2,257	439	2,696			6,756
Mar.-May	6,756	----	4.0	6,760	700	0	1,611	2,311	428	2,440			4,321
June-Aug.	4,321	----	3.0	42,324	706	0	1,053	1,759	452	2,210			2,114
2005-06	2,114	11,114	9.0	13,237	2,981	0	6,141	9,122	2,147	11,270			1,967
Sept.-Nov.	2,114	11,114	1.0	13,230	697	0	2,241	2,938	477	3,415			9,815
Dec.-Feb.	9,815	----	4.0	9,816	708	0	1,636	2,344	485	2,829			6,987
Mar.-May	6,987	----	1.0	6,991	774	0	1,291	2,065	565	2,630			4,362
June-Aug.	4,362	----	9.0	4,363	802	0	974	1,776	620	2,396			1,967
2006-07	1,967	10,535	12.0	12,514	3,488	0	5,598	9,086	2,125	11,207			1,304
Sept.-Nov.	1,967	10,535	1.0	12,503	799	0	2,176	2,975	596	3,567			8,933
Dec.-Feb.	8,933	----	2.0	8,934	821	0	1,533	2,354	513	2,866			6,068
Mar.-May	6,068	----	5.0	6,074	918	0	1,144	2,062	478	2,540			3,533
June-Aug.	3,533	----	4.0	3,537	950	0	745	1,695	538	2,233			1,304
2007-08[1]	1,304	13,038	20.0	14,362	4,363	0	5,938	10,301	2,436	12,737			1,624
Sept.-Nov.	1,304	13,038	2.0	14,344	971	0	2,402	3,373	693	4,066			10,278
Dec.-Feb.	10,278	----	3.0	10,281	1,021	0	1,759	2,780	643	3,422			6,859
Mar.-May	6,859	----	10.0	6,868	1,165	0	1,096	2,261	580	2,840			4,028
June-Aug.	4,028	----	5.0	4,033	1,207	0	681	1,888	520	2,409			1,624
2008-09[2]	1,624	12,101	15.0	13,740	4,900	0	5,300	10,200	1,750	11,950			1,790
Sept.-Nov.	1,624	12,101	3.0	13,728	1,204	0	1,984	3,188	456	3,644			10,084

[1] Preliminary.   [2] Estimate.   [3] Uncommitted inventory.   [4] Includes quantity under loan and farmer-owned reserve.   *Source: Economic Research Service, U.S. Department of Agriculture (ERS-USDA)*

Corn Production Estimates and Cash Price in the United States

Year	Aug. 1	Sept. 1	Oct. 1	Nov. 1	Final	St. Louis No. 2 Yellow	Omaha No. 2 Yellow	Gulf Ports No. 2 Yellow	Kansas City No. 2 White	Chicago No. 2 Yellow	Average Farm Price[2]	Value of Pro-duction (Mil. $)
	Corn for Grain Production Estimates											
	In Thousands of Bushels					**Dollars Per Bushel**						
1999-00	9,560,919	9,380,947	9,466,977	9,537,137	9,430,612	2.02	1.80	2.23	1.98	1.97	1.82	17,104
2000-01	10,369,369	10,362,374	10,191,817	10,053,942	9,915,051	2.01	1.82	2.26	2.06	1.99	1.85	18,499
2001-02	9,266,397	9,238,356	9,429,543	9,545,513	9,506,840	2.15	1.95	2.35	2.20	2.13	1.98	18,888
2002-03	8,886,009	8,848,529	8,969,836	9,003,364	8,966,787	2.49	2.29	2.71	2.94	2.46	2.32	20,882
2003-04	10,064,452	9,944,418	10,207,141	10,277,932	10,089,222	2.49	2.29	2.94	2.66	2.66	2.50	24,477
2004-05	10,923,099	10,960,710	11,613,226	11,740,920	11,807,217	2.73	2.50	2.48	2.01	2.08	2.05	24,381
2005-06	10,349,841	10,638,661	10,857,440	11,032,105	11,112,072	2.13	1.82	2.69	2.11	2.10	2.01	22,198
2006-07	10,975,740	11,113,766	10,905,194	10,744,806	10,534,868	2.19	1.88	3.95	4.18	3.46	3.13	32,083
2007-08	13,053,617	13,307,999	13,318,102	13,167,741	13,073,893	3.60	3.33	5.54	5.19	4.98	4.45	54,667
2008-09[1]	12,287,875	12,072,365	12,199,908	12,019,894	12,101,238	5.05	4.84	4.63	4.41	4.01	4.38	47,378

[1] Preliminary.   [2] Season-average price based on monthly prices weigthed by monthly marketings.
Source: Economic Research Service, U.S. Department of Agriculture (ERS-USDA)

Distribution of Corn in the United States   In Millions of Bushels

Crop Year Beginning Sept. 1	HFCS	Glucose & Dextrose	Starch	Fuel	Bev-rage[3]	Seed	Cereal & Other Products	Total	Livestock Feed[4]	Exports (Including Grain Equiv. of Products)	Domestic Disap-pearance	Total Utilization
	Food, Seed and Industrial Use											
				Alcohol								
1999-00	540	222	251	566	130	20.3	185	1,893	5,665	1,936.6	7,578	9,515
2000-01	530	218	247	628	130	19.3	185	1,938	5,842	1,941.3	7,799	9,740
2001-02	541	217	246	706	131	20.1	186	2,046	5,864	1,904.8	7,911	9,815
2002-03	532	219	256	996	131	20.0	187	2,340	5,563	1,587.9	7,903	9,491
2003-04	530	228	271	1,168	132	20.6	187	2,537	5,793	1,899.8	8,330	10,230
2004-05	521	222	277	1,323	133	20.8	189	2,666	6,155	1,818.1	8,842	10,661
2005-06	529	229	275	1,603	135	19.9	190	2,961	6,152	2,133.8	9,134	11,268
2006-07	510	239	272	2,117	136	23.8	190	3,464	5,591	2,125.4	9,081	11,207
2007-08[1]	500	240	270	3,000	135	22.2	193	4,338	5,938	2,435.8	10,302	12,737
2008-09[2]	500	240	270	4,000	134	23.3	193	5,337	5,300	1,750.0	10,200	11,950

[1] Preliminary.   [2] Estimate.   [3] Also includes nonfuel industrial alcohol.   [4] Feed and waste (residual, mostly feed).
Source: Economic Research Service, U.S. Department of Agriculture (ERS-USDA)

Corn (monthly average) through December 2008 — Cents per bushel

Average Cash Price of Corn, No. 2 Yellow in Central Illinois   In Dollars Per Bushel

Year	Sept.	Oct.	Nov.	Dec.	Jan.	Feb.	Mar.	Apr.	May	June	July	Aug.	Average
1999-00	1.81	1.72	1.82	1.84	1.95	2.03	2.08	2.09	2.15	1.83	1.53	1.49	1.86
2000-01	1.58	1.81	1.96	2.01	1.99	1.95	1.92	1.87	1.78	1.76	1.92	2.00	1.88
2001-02	1.94	1.84	1.90	1.97	1.95	1.92	1.92	1.89	1.96	2.04	2.22	2.50	2.00
2002-03	2.57	2.41	2.36	2.32	2.29	2.33	2.31	2.36	2.40	2.37	2.13	2.26	2.34
2003-04	2.25	2.11	2.26	2.38	2.52	2.73	2.89	3.03	2.90	2.76	2.26	2.17	2.52
2004-05	1.98	1.77	1.79	1.87	1.86	1.86	1.97	1.94	1.93	2.02	2.20	1.98	1.93
2005-06	1.75	1.67	1.75	1.89	1.98	2.07	2.04	2.18	2.22	2.15	2.22	2.07	2.00
2006-07	2.21	2.82	3.43	3.53	3.66	3.90	3.76	3.36	3.52	3.68	3.03	3.08	3.33
2007-08	3.15	3.28	3.66	4.03	4.55	4.91	5.15	5.59	5.58	6.55	5.97	5.04	4.79
2008-09[1]	5.00	3.90	3.61	3.52	3.81								3.97

[1] Preliminary.   *Source: Economic Research Service, U.S. Department of Agriculture (ERS-USDA)*

Average Cash Price of Corn, No. 2 Yellow at Gulf Ports[2]   In Dollars Per Bushel

Year	Sept.	Oct.	Nov.	Dec.	Jan.	Feb.	Mar.	Apr.	May	June	July	Aug.	Average
1999-00	2.21	2.17	2.17	2.21	2.36	2.42	2.42	2.43	2.43	2.13	1.91	1.91	2.23
2000-01	2.03	2.15	2.26	2.45	2.40	2.35	2.32	2.22	2.14	2.11	2.30	2.36	2.26
2001-02	2.27	2.19	2.28	2.35	2.34	2.30	2.28	2.21	2.29	2.37	2.53	2.79	2.35
2002-03	2.89	2.79	2.77	2.71	2.69	2.69	2.67	2.68	2.74	2.72	2.48	2.56	2.70
2003-04	2.63	2.65	2.75	2.85	2.95	3.12	3.27	3.39	3.29	3.13	2.66	2.64	2.94
2004-05	2.49	2.37	2.39	2.43	2.44	2.40	2.54	2.45	2.42	2.49	2.69	2.59	2.48
2005-06	2.47	2.58	2.44	2.61	2.61	2.72	2.67	2.74	2.81	2.78	2.90	2.92	2.69
2006-07	3.05	3.82	4.17	4.08	4.19	4.50	3.81	3.88	4.07	4.20	3.73	3.84	3.95
2007-08	4.05	4.17	4.35	4.58	5.25	5.59	5.99	6.26	6.18	7.29	6.74	5.97	5.54
2008-09[1]	5.94	4.65	4.16	4.02	4.39								4.63

[1] Preliminary.   [2] Barge delivered to Louisiana Gulf.   *Source: Economic Research Service, U.S. Department of Agriculture (ERS-USDA)*

CORN

Weekly Outstanding Export Sales and Cumulative Exports of U.S. Corn   In Thousands of Metric Tons

Marketing Year 2006/0007 Week Ending	Out- standing Sales	Cumu- lative Exports	Marketing Year 2007/0008 Week Ending	Out- standing Sales	Cumu- lative Exports	Marketing Year 2008/0009 Week Ending	Out- standing Sales	Cumu- lative Exports
Sep 07, 2006	11,500.7	1,103.2	Sep 06, 2007	15,761.7	904.2	Sep 04, 2008	11,883.8	199.3
Sep 14, 2006	11,138.2	2,478.4	Sep 13, 2007	16,919.9	1,778.3	Sep 11, 2008	11,346.4	1,062.1
Sep 21, 2006	10,731.6	3,714.7	Sep 20, 2007	17,414.7	2,981.4	Sep 18, 2008	10,900.0	2,056.3
Sep 28, 2006	10,706.6	4,897.9	Sep 27, 2007	17,340.6	4,206.1	Sep 25, 2008	10,302.6	3,220.2
Oct 05, 2006	10,893.3	5,998.0	Oct 04, 2007	18,468.1	5,398.3	Oct 02, 2008	10,435.2	4,045.5
Oct 12, 2006	10,625.6	7,086.0	Oct 11, 2007	19,158.2	6,503.3	Oct 09, 2008	10,486.9	4,918.6
Oct 19, 2006	10,871.5	7,886.0	Oct 18, 2007	19,421.3	7,760.5	Oct 16, 2008	10,522.9	5,672.2
Oct 26, 2006	10,796.9	8,987.8	Oct 25, 2007	18,806.4	9,010.7	Oct 23, 2008	10,332.9	6,275.3
Nov 02, 2006	11,552.1	10,161.8	Nov 01, 2007	18,788.3	10,533.9	Oct 30, 2008	10,185.9	6,893.6
Nov 09, 2006	11,943.8	11,165.7	Nov 08, 2007	18,642.4	12,043.6	Nov 06, 2008	9,732.8	7,702.2
Nov 16, 2006	11,765.1	12,386.6	Nov 15, 2007	19,111.3	13,420.3	Nov 13, 2008	9,410.7	8,458.1
Nov 23, 2006	11,889.0	13,283.9	Nov 22, 2007	19,513.3	14,859.8	Nov 20, 2008	9,110.1	9,224.0
Nov 30, 2006	11,329.3	14,656.3	Nov 29, 2007	19,044.3	16,387.9	Nov 27, 2008	8,523.5	10,154.5
Dec 07, 2006	11,493.0	15,892.9	Dec 06, 2007	19,144.2	17,432.0	Dec 04, 2008	8,763.6	10,843.1
Dec 14, 2006	11,854.8	16,792.6	Dec 13, 2007	19,082.5	18,662.1	Dec 11, 2008	8,665.9	11,553.3
Dec 21, 2006	11,890.1	17,911.0	Dec 20, 2007	19,243.4	19,924.6	Dec 18, 2008	8,386.0	12,384.6
Dec 28, 2006	11,503.1	18,871.5	Dec 27, 2007	18,803.5	21,065.3	Dec 25, 2008	8,053.8	12,986.7
Jan 04, 2007	11,827.1	19,724.4	Jan 03, 2008	18,496.3	21,979.3	Jan 01, 2009	7,702.9	13,598.2
Jan 11, 2007	12,245.8	20,729.5	Jan 10, 2008	19,363.1	23,481.8	Jan 08, 2009	7,307.4	14,209.9
Jan 18, 2007	12,204.2	21,755.3	Jan 17, 2008	19,623.4	24,816.6	Jan 15, 2009	7,709.4	14,893.9
Jan 25, 2007	11,799.6	22,957.2	Jan 24, 2008	20,019.7	26,308.0	Jan 22, 2009	8,078.4	15,632.6
Feb 01, 2007	11,687.2	23,987.0	Jan 31, 2008	19,799.4	27,549.9	Jan 29, 2009	8,497.0	16,378.2
Feb 08, 2007	12,076.9	24,983.6	Feb 07, 2008	19,586.3	28,695.4	Feb 05, 2009	9,473.4	16,945.6
Feb 15, 2007	11,657.4	26,214.1	Feb 14, 2008	19,316.2	30,106.9	Feb 12, 2009	9,894.4	17,856.9
Feb 22, 2007	11,083.8	27,105.8	Feb 21, 2008	18,669.7	31,354.7	Feb 19, 2009	9,571.6	18,628.6
Mar 01, 2007	10,730.9	28,531.5	Feb 28, 2008	17,985.6	32,686.8	Feb 26, 2009	9,455.4	19,536.7
Mar 08, 2007	10,329.7	29,682.2	Mar 06, 2008	17,692.1	33,749.1	Mar 05, 2009		
Mar 15, 2007	10,065.6	30,587.2	Mar 13, 2008	16,968.9	35,221.9	Mar 12, 2009		
Mar 22, 2007	10,042.6	31,733.7	Mar 20, 2008	16,312.3	36,511.0	Mar 19, 2009		
Mar 29, 2007	9,655.9	32,670.0	Mar 27, 2008	15,871.1	37,651.1	Mar 26, 2009		
Apr 05, 2007	10,246.5	33,405.0	Apr 03, 2008	15,090.3	38,905.8	Apr 02, 2009		
Apr 12, 2007	10,152.3	34,302.4	Apr 10, 2008	14,847.0	40,018.0	Apr 09, 2009		
Apr 19, 2007	10,350.4	35,209.9	Apr 17, 2008	14,512.4	41,127.9	Apr 16, 2009		
Apr 26, 2007	9,879.7	36,296.4	Apr 24, 2008	14,059.9	42,131.6	Apr 23, 2009		
May 03, 2007	9,467.7	37,161.7	May 01, 2008	13,459.6	43,069.1	Apr 30, 2009		
May 10, 2007	9,834.8	38,308.5	May 08, 2008	13,011.9	44,064.0	May 07, 2009		
May 17, 2007	9,682.1	39,119.4	May 15, 2008	12,775.0	44,808.1	May 14, 2009		
May 24, 2007	9,268.2	40,209.4	May 22, 2008	12,180.0	45,880.6	May 21, 2009		
May 31, 2007	8,642.3	41,211.1	May 29, 2008	11,725.0	46,865.7	May 28, 2009		
Jun 07, 2007	8,343.1	42,037.0	Jun 05, 2008	11,084.7	48,030.7	Jun 04, 2009		
Jun 14, 2007	8,273.7	42,933.2	Jun 12, 2008	10,340.6	49,117.7	Jun 11, 2009		
Jun 21, 2007	8,170.7	43,788.9	Jun 19, 2008	9,588.0	50,096.6	Jun 18, 2009		
Jun 28, 2007	8,377.6	44,649.8	Jun 26, 2008	8,724.4	51,286.1	Jun 25, 2009		
Jul 05, 2007	8,572.8	45,462.4	Jul 03, 2008	8,132.2	52,216.7	Jul 02, 2009		
Jul 12, 2007	8,041.4	46,663.4	Jul 10, 2008	7,811.3	52,905.7	Jul 09, 2009		
Jul 19, 2007	7,540.4	47,576.9	Jul 17, 2008	7,387.6	53,652.9	Jul 16, 2009		
Jul 26, 2007	7,270.4	48,652.9	Jul 24, 2008	6,215.7	54,887.9	Jul 23, 2009		
Aug 02, 2007	6,844.0	49,366.3	Jul 31, 2008	5,677.2	55,764.3	Jul 30, 2009		
Aug 09, 2007	5,488.5	50,509.7	Aug 07, 2008	5,124.0	56,703.4	Aug 06, 2009		
Aug 16, 2007	4,677.3	51,459.5	Aug 14, 2008	4,230.2	57,793.9	Aug 13, 2009		
Aug 23, 2007	3,583.6	52,726.2	Aug 21, 2008	3,711.7	58,615.4	Aug 20, 2009		
Aug 30, 2007	2,770.7	53,799.3	Aug 28, 2008	2,861.0	59,666.4	Aug 27, 2009		

Source: Foreign Agricultural Service, U.S. Department of Agriculture (FAS-USDA)

<<TOC3>> Average Price Received by Farmers for Corn in the United States   In Dollars Per Bushel

Year	Sept.	Oct.	Nov.	Dec.	Jan.	Feb.	Mar.	Apr.	May	June	July	Aug.	Average
1999-00	1.75	1.69	1.70	1.82	1.91	1.98	2.03	2.03	2.11	1.91	1.64	1.52	1.84
2000-01	1.61	1.74	1.86	1.97	1.98	1.96	1.96	1.89	1.82	1.76	1.87	1.90	1.86
2001-02	1.91	1.84	1.85	1.98	1.97	1.93	1.94	1.91	1.93	1.97	2.13	2.38	1.98
2002-03	2.47	2.34	2.28	2.32	2.33	2.34	2.33	2.34	2.38	2.34	2.17	2.15	2.32
2003-04	2.20	2.12	2.20	2.31	2.39	2.61	2.75	2.89	2.87	2.79	2.51	2.34	2.50
2004-05	2.20	2.14	2.05	2.04	2.12	1.95	2.02	2.00	1.98	2.03	2.11	1.95	2.05
2005-06	1.90	1.82	1.77	1.92	2.00	2.02	2.06	2.11	2.17	2.14	2.14	2.09	2.01
2006-07	2.20	2.55	2.88	3.01	3.05	3.44	3.43	3.39	3.49	3.53	3.32	3.26	3.13
2007-08	3.28	3.29	3.44	3.77	3.98	4.53	4.70	5.15	5.28	5.48	5.24	5.26	4.45
2008-09[1]	5.02	4.37	4.26	4.10	4.15								4.38

[1] Preliminary.   *Source: Economic Research Service, U.S. Department of Agriculture (ERS-USDA)*

Corn Price Support Data in the United States

Crop Year Beginning Sept. 1	National Average Loan Rate[3] --- Dollars Per Bushel -----	Target Price	Placed Under Loan	% of Production	Acquired by CCC	Owned by CCC Aug. 31	CCC Inventory ----- As of Dec. 31 ----- CCC Owned	Under CCC Loan	Quantity Pledged (Thousands of Bushels)	Face Amount (Thousands of Dollars)
					--------------------------- Millions of Bushels -----------------------------					
1997-98	1.89	NA	1,141	12.4	2	4	2	81	1,129,915	2,062,308
1998-99	1.89	NA	1,775	18.2	24	12	15	----	1,129,915	2,062,308
1999-00	1.89	NA	1,421	15.1	32	14	26	----	1,420,878	2,590,443
2000-01	1.89	NA	1,394	14.1	27	8	36	----	1,393,947	2,562,172
2001-02	1.89	NA	1,395	14.7	0	6	24	----	1,394,561	2,557,874
2002-03	1.98	2.60	1,367	15.2	0	4	18	----	1,366,513	2,622,823
2003-04	1.98	2.60	1,327	13.2	1	0	16	----	1,326,884	2,555,183
2004-05	1.95	2.63	1,366	11.6	25	0	----	----	40,814	87,053
2005-06[1]	1.95	2.63	1,064	9.6	2	2	----	----	47,595	99,406
2006-07[2]	1.95	2.63							31,873	65,968

[1] Preliminary.   [2] Estimate.   [3] Findley or announced loan rate.   NA = Not available.
Source: National Agricultural Statistics Service, U.S. Department of Agriculture (NASS-USDA)

U.S. Exports[1] of Corn (Including Seed), By Country of Destination   In Thousands of Metric Tons

Crop Year Beginning Oct. 1	Algeria	Canada	Egypt	Israel	Japan	Mexico	Rep. of Korea	Russia	Saudi Arabia	Spain	Taiwan	Vene-zuela	Total
1998-99	947	898	2,954	395	15,375	5,576	6,659	405	1,175	92	4,538	1,329	51,949
1999-00	1,099	1,080	3,542	748	14,939	4,910	2,822	491	1,197	16	4,989	1,146	49,378
2000-01	1,180	2,797	4,116	621	14,091	5,928	3,109	26	1,003	0	4,894	1,152	48,192
2001-02	1,343	3,979	4,283	847	14,817	4,025	1,085	86	670	5	4,599	502	47,058
2002-03	1,009	3,811	2,904	313	14,384	5,220	272	0	222	0	4,139	651	40,780
2003-04	1,158	2,014	3,120	1,154	14,968	5,730	3,942	70	402	5	4,757	669	48,724
2004-05	1,036	2,210	3,738	393	15,036	5,935	2,210	13	126	14	4,446	90	45,262
2005-06	1,255	1,901	4,156	725	16,361	6,755	5,866	15	619	8	4,519	133	56,038
2006-07	940	2,142	3,522	844	14,840	8,886	3,873	9	540	3	4,213	514	54,159
2007-08[2]	898	3,069	2,971	1,207	15,102	9,526	8,421	7	985	10	3,792	1,085	60,685

[1] Excludes exports of corn by-products.   [2] Preliminary.   *Source: Foreign Agricultural Service, U.S. Department of Agriculture (FAS-USDA)*

Stocks of Corn (Shelled and Ear) in the United States   In Millions of Bushels

Year	On Farms Mar. 1	June 1	Sept. 1	Dec. 1	Off Farms Mar. 1	June 1	Sept. 1	Dec. 1	Total Stocks Mar. 1	June 1	Sept. 1	Dec. 1
1999	3,570.0	2,257.0	797.0	5,195.0	2,128.4	1,359.2	990.0	2,844.4	5,698.4	3,616.2	1,787.0	8,039.4
2000	3,300.0	2,029.8	793.0	5,550.0	2,301.9	1,556.1	924.5	2,972.2	5,601.9	3,585.9	1,717.5	8,522.2
2001	3,600.0	2,230.8	753.2	5,275.0	2,443.0	1,693.2	1,146.0	2,989.7	6,043.0	3,924.0	1,899.1	8,264.7
2002	3,355.0	2,020.6	586.8	4,800.0	2,440.3	1,576.3	1,009.6	2,838.0	5,795.3	3,596.9	1,596.4	7,638.0
2003	2,940.0	1,620.2	484.9	5,286.0	2,191.9	1,364.7	601.8	2,667.8	5,131.9	2,984.9	1,086.7	7,953.8
2004	3,030.0	1,540.0	438.0	6,144.0	2,241.5	1,430.1	520.1	3,308.5	5,271.5	2,970.1	958.1	9,452.5
2005	4,137.0	2,462.3	820.5	6,325.0	2,619.3	1,858.5	1,293.5	3,490.0	6,756.3	4,320.8	2,114.0	9,815.0
2006	4,055.0	2,350.5	749.5	5,627.0	2,932.3	2,011.2	1,217.7	3,305.7	6,987.3	4,361.7	1,967.2	8,932.7
2007	3,330.0	1,826.6	460.1	6,530.0	2,738.3	1,706.8	843.5	3,748.1	6,068.3	3,533.4	1,303.6	10,278.1
2008[1]	3,780.0	1,970.9	500.0	6,482.0	3,078.7	2,057.1	1,124.2	3,602.5	6,858.7	4,028.0	1,624.2	10,084.5

[1] Preliminary.   *Source: National Agricultural Statistics Service, U.S. Department of Agriculture (NASS-USDA)*

CORN

Corn Futures - Chicago Board of Trade
(weekly close) as of January 02, 2009

Cents per bushel

Volume of Trading of Corn Futures in Chicago   In Thousands of Contracts

Year	Jan.	Feb.	Mar.	Apr.	May	June	July	Aug.	Sept.	Oct.	Nov.	Dec.	Total
1999	955.1	1,374.2	1,440.1	1,420.6	975.1	1,597.4	1,708.0	1,669.8	1,131.9	1,096.2	1,500.9	855.6	15,724.8
2000	1,502.2	1,580.9	1,713.1	1,386.3	1,789.7	1,830.7	1,178.3	1,291.8	1,057.4	1,256.1	1,612.8	986.1	17,185.4
2001	1,397.2	1,197.4	1,329.5	1,518.7	1,173.2	1,612.1	2,023.5	1,549.0	1,072.3	1,223.3	1,741.2	891.4	16,728.7
2002	996.3	1,449.6	944.7	1,498.0	1,434.5	1,851.5	1,958.4	2,158.7	1,635.4	1,523.3	1,801.4	880.5	18,132.4
2003	1,204.0	1,559.1	1,156.9	1,633.1	1,657.0	1,951.2	1,499.3	1,830.6	1,389.7	2,057.7	1,815.9	1,364.3	19,118.7
2004	2,025.7	2,367.0	2,190.9	2,870.9	1,855.3	2,538.6	1,740.5	1,883.0	1,446.9	1,476.4	2,473.3	1,169.6	24,038.2
2005	1,467.8	2,680.8	2,278.1	2,519.1	2,188.3	3,446.1	2,626.0	2,993.6	1,618.5	1,504.2	2,892.2	1,750.3	27,965.1
2006	2,494.6	3,599.1	3,041.0	3,507.5	3,773.1	4,693.4	3,743.6	4,226.9	3,760.5	5,300.2	6,279.4	2,820.6	47,239.9
2007	5,166.5	5,111.6	4,959.0	6,095.4	4,519.9	6,090.9	4,035.7	4,344.1	3,128.9	3,306.5	4,615.6	3,145.9	54,520.2
2008	4,213.2	5,808.2	4,350.8	6,501.1	4,876.9	7,593.8	5,402.2	4,989.1	3,934.7	4,572.5	4,448.6	3,266.2	59,957.1

Source: CME Group; Chicago Board of Trade (CBT)

Average Open Interest of Corn Futures in Chicago   In Thousands of Contracts

Year	Jan.	Feb.	Mar.	Apr.	May	June	July	Aug.	Sept.	Oct.	Nov.	Dec.
1999	357.7	363.2	357.1	343.6	338.5	323.7	329.5	315.9	316.2	411.0	461.0	389.2
2000	446.0	478.9	482.1	487.8	476.9	445.0	392.0	387.3	356.6	398.0	454.9	414.9
2001	454.3	469.0	440.5	455.7	424.4	423.8	389.9	387.7	370.3	419.4	462.9	416.6
2002	459.3	464.4	431.9	430.7	411.3	430.9	458.1	509.1	501.5	485.9	497.0	450.0
2003	456.0	469.6	445.3	412.0	407.0	385.8	384.6	383.6	356.2	420.7	470.2	447.5
2004	544.0	641.4	678.0	704.9	637.4	621.9	566.5	562.2	548.8	606.3	639.5	588.9
2005	629.3	654.1	659.7	673.8	677.3	702.4	713.1	733.6	714.2	794.4	852.5	774.2
2006	875.3	1,048.8	1,066.0	1,176.0	1,288.2	1,327.8	1,360.2	1,347.2	1,302.1	1,312.6	1,405.7	1,381.5
2007	1,448.2	1,498.8	1,427.3	1,345.9	1,257.6	1,244.1	1,213.4	1,132.8	1,108.5	1,161.7	1,202.6	1,211.5
2008	1,383.2	1,463.1	1,421.8	1,445.3	1,409.2	1,396.1	1,279.9	1,170.4	1,050.9	995.5	967.6	820.5

Source: CME Group; Chicago Board of Trade (CBT)

Corn Oil

Corn oil is a bland, odorless oil produced by refining the crude corn oil that is mechanically extracted from the germ of the plant seed. High-oil corn, the most common type of corn used to make corn oil, typically has an oil content of 7% or higher compared to about 4% for normal corn. Corn oil is widely used as cooking oil, for making margarine and mayonnaise, and for making inedible products such as soap, paints, inks, varnishes, and cosmetics. For humans, studies have shown that no vegetable oil is more effective than corn oil in lowering blood cholesterol levels.

Prices –The average monthly price of corn oil (wet mill price in Chicago) in the 2007-08 marketing year (Oct-Sep) rose +118.1% yr/yr to a record high of 69.37 cents per pound. Seasonally, prices tend to be highest around March/April and lowest late in the calendar year.

Supply – U.S. corn oil production in the 2007-08 marketing year fell by -1.2% yr/yr to 2.560 billion pounds, down from last year's record high of 2.590 billion pounds. Seasonally, production tends to peak around December and March and reaches a low in July. U.S. stocks in the 2007-08 marketing year (Oct 1) fell -9.5% yr/yr to 181 million pounds.

Demand – U.S. usage (domestic disappearance) in 2007-08 fell -0.2% to 1.856 billion pounds.

Exports – U.S. corn oil exports in 2007-08 fell -6.7% to 740 million pounds. U.S. corn oil imports in 2007-08 rose 4.7% to 45 million pounds.

Supply and Disappearance of Corn Oil in the United States In Millions of Pounds

| | Supply | | | | Disappearance | | | | | | |
Year	Stocks Oct. 1	Pro- duction	Imports	Total Supply	Baking and Frying Fats	Salad and Cooking Oil	Marg- arine	Total Edible Products	Domestic Disap- pearance	Exports	Total Disap- pearance
2001-02	117	2,461	61.0	2,639	W	W	W	950	1,363	1,172	2,535
2002-03	104	2,453	66.0	2,623	W	W	W	W	1,615	888	2,503
2003-04	119	2,396	66.0	2,582	W	W	W	1,724	1,662	767	2,429
2004-05	153	2,396	49.0	2,598	W	1,466	W	1,690	1,653	789	2,442
2005-06	156	2,483	45.0	2,683	W	1,407	W	1,607	1,685	799	2,483
2006-07[1]	200	2,590	43.0	2,833	W	1,335	W	1,735	1,859	793	2,652
2007-08[2]	181	2,560	45.0	2,786	W	1,740	W	1,606	1,856	740	2,596

[1] Preliminary. [2] Estimate. W = Withheld. *Source: Economic Research Service, U.S. Department of Agriculture (ERS-USDA)*

Production[2] of Crude Corn Oil in the United States In Millions of Pounds

Year	Oct.	Nov.	Dec.	Jan.	Feb.	Mar.	Apr.	May	June	July	Aug.	Sept.	Total
2002-03	218.6	195.0	212.3	206.8	181.7	206.0	199.7	203.6	207.1	216.5	202.5	203.2	2,453
2003-04	209.1	196.5	193.2	201.0	182.9	195.8	200.0	197.7	210.7	204.3	205.2	200.1	2,397
2004-05	208.8	187.1	191.0	205.2	182.5	206.6	217.2	188.2	211.5	206.7	198.5	189.0	2,392
2005-06	207.5	199.9	200.3	209.2	184.8	217.6	191.7	218.7	206.7	215.3	222.0	209.0	2,483
2006-07	228.7	216.0	226.1	224.7	187.9	216.4	194.1	214.4	212.7	219.8	209.5	209.4	2,560
2007-08	213.5	213.0	214.0	205.8	193.7	222.5	190.7	220.9	193.7	214.9	217.3	207.3	2,507
2008-09[1]	206.3	210.6	198.7	198.4									2,442

[1] Preliminary. [2] Not seasonally adjusted. *Source: Bureau of the Census, U.S. Department of Commerce*

Consumption Corn Oil, in Refining, in the United States In Millions of Pounds

Year	Oct.	Nov.	Dec.	Jan.	Feb.	Mar.	Apr.	May	June	July	Aug.	Sept.	Total
2002-03	W	W	W	W	W	W	W	W	W	W	W	W	W
2003-04	W	W	W	W	W	W	134.6	W	152.8	W	W	W	1,724
2004-05	W	165.4	131.6	140.3	W	147.3	132.2	124.8	149.0	142.9	142.4	132.1	1,690
2005-06	148.4	140.4	140.3	148.4	123.4	128.0	110.8	145.2	138.9	121.6	131.6	130.0	1,607
2006-07	143.6	146.7	153.3	155.3	131.1	137.2	W	W	147.7	142.2	146.0	143.0	1,735
2007-08	155.2	W	133.8	119.5	119.2	143.8	124.2	142.9	109.7	131.8	150.3	141.8	1,606
2008-09[1]	137.8	132.1	130.8	131.6									1,597

[1] Preliminary. W = Withheld proprietary data. *Source: Bureau of Census, U.S. Department of Commerce*

Average Corn Oil Price, Wet Mill in Chicago In Cents Per Pound

Year	Oct.	Nov.	Dec.	Jan.	Feb.	Mar.	Apr.	May	June	July	Aug.	Sept.	Average
2002-03	22.45	26.90	28.25	29.30	28.90	27.20	27.55	29.10	30.15	29.90	30.68	27.71	28.17
2003-04	26.99	27.56	28.73	29.26	30.16	30.56	30.36	30.34	28.36	27.33	25.61	25.07	28.36
2004-05	23.10	24.24	26.67	27.41	27.58	28.08	29.29	30.65	30.73	30.01	28.83	27.75	27.86
2005-06	27.50	27.08	26.08	25.22	23.65	22.61	23.19	25.25	25.70	25.75	25.42	24.71	25.18
2006-07	24.70	26.47	28.05	28.05	28.66	29.08	29.93	31.56	34.71	37.25	39.61	43.61	31.81
2007-08	52.50	56.32	59.47	63.67	74.89	83.55	87.09	87.29	82.33	76.64	60.00	48.71	69.37
2008-09[1]	34.76	31.06	26.88	25.19	29.05								29.39

[1] Preliminary. *Source: Economic Research Service, U.S. Department of Agriculture (ERS-USDA)*

Cotton

Cotton is a natural vegetable fiber that comes from small trees and shrubs of a genus belonging to the mallow family, one of which is the common American Upland cotton plant. Cotton has been used in India for at least the last 5,000 years and probably much longer, and was also used by the ancient Chinese, Egyptians, and North and South Americans. Cotton was one of the earliest crops grown by European settlers in the U.S.

Cotton requires a long growing season, plenty of sunshine and water during the growing season, and then dry weather for harvesting. In the United States, the Cotton Belt stretches from northern Florida to North Carolina and westward to California. In the U.S., planting time varies from the beginning of February in Southern Texas to the beginning of June in the northern sections of the Cotton Belt. The flower bud of the plant blossoms and develops into an oval boll that splits open at maturity. At maturity, cotton is most vulnerable to damage from wind and rain. Approximately 95% of the cotton in the U.S. is now harvested mechanically with spindle-type pickers or strippers and then sent off to cotton gins for processing. There it is dried, cleaned, separated, and packed into bales.

Cotton is used in a wide range of products from clothing to home furnishings to medical products. The value of cotton is determined according to the staple, grade, and character of each bale. Staple refers to short, medium, long, or extra-long fiber length, with medium staple accounting for about 70% of all U.S. cotton. Grade refers to the color, brightness, and amount of foreign matter and is established by the U.S. Department of Agriculture. Character refers to the fiber's diameter, strength, body, maturity (ratio of mature to immature fibers), uniformity, and smoothness. Cotton is the fifth leading cash crop in the U.S. and is one of the nation's principal agricultural exports. The weight of cotton is typically measured in terms of a "bale," which is deemed to equal 480 pounds.

Cotton futures and options are traded on the New York Cotton Exchange, a division of the New York Board of Trade. Cotton futures are also traded on the Bolsa de Mercadorias & Futuros (BM&F). Cotton yarn futures are traded on the Central Japan Commodity Exchange (CCOM) and the Osaka Mercantile Exchange (OME). The New York Cotton Exchange's futures contract calls for the delivery of 50,000 pounds net weight (approximately 100 bales) of No. 2 cotton with a quality rating of Strict Low Middling and a staple length of 1-and-2/32 inch. Delivery points include Texas (Galveston and Houston), New Orleans, Memphis, and Greenville/Spartanburg in South Carolina.

Prices – Cotton prices on the New York Board of Trade nearest-futures chart in early 2008 extended the rally that began in mid-2007 and posted a record high of 91.38 cents per pound in March 2008. Cotton prices then fell back through summer and plunged to a 6-1/2 year low of 36.70 cents in November 2008. Cotton prices closed 2008 at 49.02 cents per pound, down -18.99 cents (or −27.9%) from the 2007 close of 68.01 cents. Cotton prices in early 2008 were pulled higher by the overall commodity rally and by strength in corn and soybean prices. However, cotton prices then plunged through the remainder of

the 2008 as the financial crisis emerged and the global economy headed toward a recession. World cotton demand fell sharply in 2008 due to the weak economy and due to reduced use of cotton for clothing. U.S. farmers planted only 9.47 million acres with cotton in 2008-09, which was the lowest level since 1967. The size of the U.S. cotton crop plunged by −26.3% y/y to 7.73 million bales, which was the smallest U.S. crop in 25 years. However, the sharp drop in demand roughly matched the decline in supply and the U.S. 2008-09 carry-over of 7.7 million bales was the third highest in the past 25 years. The 2008-09 global carry-over of 61.7 million bales was also comfortable, thus keeping downward pressure on cotton prices.

Supply – World cotton production in 2008-09 fell -9.2% yr/yr to 109.510 million bales (480 pounds per bale) farther below from the record high of 121.990 million bales seen in 2006-07. The world's largest cotton producers were China with 33% of world production in 2008-09, India with 21%, the U.S. with 12%, and Pakistan with 8%. World beginning stocks in 2008-09 rose +0.9% yr/yr to a record high of 62.796 million bales.

The U.S. cotton crop in 2008-09 fell by −32.1% yr/yr to 13.036 million bales, well down from the 2005-06 record high of 23.890 million bales. U.S. farmers harvested 7.728 million acres of cotton in 2008-09, down 26.3% yr/yr. The U.S. cotton yield in 2008-09 fell -7.9% to 810 pounds per acre, down from last year's record high. The leading U.S. producing states of Upland cotton are Texas with 40% of U.S. production in 2008 (latest data available), Georgia (13%), Arkansas (10%), North Carolina (6%), California (6%), Mississippi (5), and Missouri (5%). U.S. production of cotton cloth has fallen sharply by almost half in the past decade due to the movement of the textile industry out of the U.S. to low-wage foreign countries. Specifically, U.S. production of cotton cloth in 2008 fell −8.0% yr/yr to a record low of 1.811 billion square yards, less than one-fourth of the production level seen in 1950.

Demand – World consumption of cotton in 2008-09 fell by -8.7% yr/yr to 110.145 million bales, which was down further from the 2006-07 record high. Consumption of cotton continues to move toward countries with low wages, where the raw cotton is utilized to produce textiles and other cotton products. The largest consumers of cotton in 2008-09 were China (40%), India (16%), and Pakistan (10%). U.S. consumption of cotton by mills in 2008-09 fell −4.5% yr/yr to 4.400 million bales, and accounted for 25% of U.S. production. The remaining 75% of U.S. cotton production went for exports.

Trade – World exports of cotton in 2008-09 fell by -23.7% yr/yr to 29.333 million bales, down from the 2005-06 record high of 44.584 million bales. The U.S. is the world's largest cotton exporter by far and accounts for 39% of world cotton exports. Key world cotton importers include Turkey with 7% of total world imports in 2008-09, Indonesia with 7%, Mexico with 4%, and Russia with 3%. U.S. cotton exports in 2007-08 (latest data) rose by +14.4% yr/yr to a new record high of 13.982 million bales. The main destinations for U.S. exports in 2007-08 were China (32%), Mexico (10%), Indonesia (9%), Taiwan (6%), and Thailand (3%).

Supply and Distribution of All Cotton in the United States   In Thousands of 480-Pound Bales

Crop Year Beginning Aug. 1	Acre Planted (1,000 Acres)	Harvested (1,000 Acres)	Yield Lbs./Acre	Beginning Stocks[3]	Pro- duction[4]	Imports	Total	Mill Use	Exports	Total	Unac- counted	Ending Stocks	Farm Price[5]	"A" Index Price[6]	Value of Pro- duction Million USD
1999-00	14,874	13,425	607	3,939	16,968	97	21,004	10,240	6,750	16,944	-145	3,915	46.8	52.85	3,809.6
2000-01	15,517	13,053	632	3,915	17,188	16	21,119	8,862	6,740	15,602	483	6,000	51.6	57.25	4,260.4
2001-02	15,769	13,828	705	6,000	20,303	21	26,324	7,696	11,000	18,696	-180	7,448	32.0	41.88	3,121.8
2002-03	13,958	12,417	665	7,448	17,209	67	24,724	7,273	11,900	19,173	-166	5,385	45.7	55.81	3,777.1
2003-04	13,480	12,003	730	5,385	18,255	45	23,685	6,266	13,758	20,024	-211	3,450	63.0	69.24	5,516.8
2004-05	13,659	13,057	855	3,450	23,251	29	26,730	6,691	14,436	21,127	-108	5,495	43.5	53.53	4,993.6
2005-06	14,245	13,803	831	5,495	23,890	28	29,413	5,871	17,549	23,420	76	6,069	49.7	57.10	5,695.2
2006-07	15,274	12,732	814	6,069	21,588	19	27,676	4,935	13,010	17,945	-252	9,479	48.4	60.77	5,013.2
2007-08[1]	10,827	10,489	879	9,479	19,207	12	28,698	4,609	13,653	18,262	-392	10,044	61.1		5,196.7
2008-09[2]	9,470	7,728	810	10,044	13,036	15	23,587	4,400	13,000	17,400	13	6,200	47-57		

[1] Preliminary.   [2] Estimate.   [3] Excludes preseason ginnings (adjusted to 480-lb. bale net weight basis).   [4] Includes preseason ginnings.   [5] Marketing year average price.   [6] Average of 5 cheapest types of SLM 1 3/32" staple length cotton offered on the European market.
Source: Economic Research Service, U.S. Department of Agriculture (ERS-USDA)

World Production of All Cotton   In Thousands of 480-Pound Bales

Crop Year Beginning Aug. 1	Argentina	Australia	Brazil	Burkina	China	Egypt	Greece	India	Pakistan	Turkey	United States	Uzbek- istan	Total
1999-00	615	3,458	3,216	505	17,600	1,068	2,021	12,180	8,776	3,634	16,968	5,180	87,932
2000-01	758	3,700	4,312	525	20,300	965	2,035	10,931	8,379	3,600	17,188	4,400	89,099
2001-02	300	3,340	3,519	725	24,400	1,454	2,093	12,300	8,286	3,975	20,303	4,900	98,702
2002-03	290	1,680	3,890	750	25,200	1,331	1,715	10,600	7,972	4,179	17,209	4,600	90,977
2003-04	515	1,700	6,015	965	23,800	920	1,530	14,000	7,845	4,100	18,255	4,100	96,758
2004-05	675	3,000	5,900	1,180	30,300	1,356	1,800	19,000	11,138	4,150	23,251	5,200	121,437
2005-06	625	2,800	4,700	1,367	28,400	938	1,975	19,050	10,165	3,550	23,890	5,550	116,579
2006-07	800	1,350	7,000	1,300	35,500	975	1,400	21,800	9,900	3,800	21,588	5,350	121,990
2007-08[1]	703	620	7,360	675	37,000	1,000	1,325	24,600	8,900	3,100	19,207	5,500	120,536
2008-09[2]	650	1,350	5,800	850	36,500	475	1,100	23,000	9,200	2,300	13,036	5,000	109,510

[1] Preliminary.   [2] Estimate.   *Source: Foreign Agricultural Service, U.S. Department of Agriculture (FAS-USDA)*

World Stocks and Trade of Cotton   In Thousands of 480-Pound Bales

Crop Year Beginning Aug. 1	Beginning Stocks United States	Uzbek- istan	China	World Total	Imports Indo- nesia	Mexico	Russia	Turkey	World Total	Exports United States	Uzbek- istan	China	World Total
1999-00	3,939	603	26,928	52,822	2,076	1,813	1,600	2,411	27,976	6,750	4,200	1,692	27,195
2000-01	3,915	738	22,378	51,079	2,650	1,865	1,650	1,758	26,227	6,740	3,450	442	26,200
2001-02	6,000	668	19,741	49,411	2,356	2,065	1,800	2,977	29,304	11,000	3,500	342	29,149
2002-03	7,448	918	18,848	54,532	2,228	2,330	1,650	2,265	30,187	11,900	3,400	751	30,457
2003-04	5,385	1,018	17,474	47,628	2,150	1,858	1,475	2,370	34,012	13,758	3,100	173	33,198
2004-05	3,450	923	18,983	48,061	2,200	1,810	1,450	3,414	33,449	14,436	3,950	30	35,014
2005-06	5,495	1,298	18,388	60,444	2,200	1,744	1,425	3,501	44,484	17,549	4,800	36	44,584
2006-07	6,069	1,248	22,536	62,212	2,200	1,353	1,400	4,029	37,407	13,010	4,500	88	37,096
2007-08[1]	9,479	1,198	20,536	62,796	2,300	1,530	1,200	3,268	38,032	13,653	4,400	62	38,420
2008-09[2]	10,044	1,298	20,004	62,346	2,000	1,300	950	2,150	29,335	11,500	3,250	100	29,333

[1] Preliminary.   [2] Estimate.   *Source: Foreign Agricultural Service, U.S. Department of Agriculture (FAS-USDA)*

World Consumption of All Cottons in Specified Countries   In Thousands of 480-Pound Bales

Crop Year Beginning Aug. 1	Bangla- desh	Brazil	China	Egypt	India	Indonesia	Mexico	Pakistan	Russia	Thailand	Turkey	United States	Total
1999-00	801	4,111	20,575	823	13,547	2,050	2,425	7,675	1,550	1,606	5,600	10,339	90,456
2000-01	1,001	4,025	22,725	773	13,544	2,500	2,125	8,125	1,600	1,685	5,167	8,379	90,819
2001-02	1,201	3,689	25,400	798	13,275	2,350	2,225	8,525	1,800	1,825	6,150	7,876	93,736
2002-03	1,552	3,585	28,950	913	13,300	2,300	2,125	9,425	1,650	1,975	6,300	7,439	97,611
2003-04	1,727	3,865	30,950	913	13,500	2,200	2,025	9,625	1,500	1,875	6,000	6,477	97,139
2004-05	1,880	4,160	37,250	963	14,800	2,200	2,125	10,525	1,425	2,125	7,100	6,799	107,489
2005-06	2,205	4,302	43,500	1,013	16,700	2,225	2,125	11,525	1,425	2,075	6,900	5,795	114,711
2006-07	2,490	4,423	48,000	1,013	18,100	2,225	2,125	12,525	1,400	1,975	7,300	5,187	121,717
2007-08[1]	2,760	4,450	49,000	963	18,300	2,275	2,025	12,425	1,225	1,975	6,000	5,001	120,598
2008-09[2]	2,860	4,250	44,500	813	17,200	2,050	1,875	11,525	975	1,950	4,700	3,890	110,145

[1] Preliminary.   [2] Estimate.   *Source: Foreign Agricultural Service, U.S. Department of Agriculture (FAS-USDA)*

COTTON

Cotton (monthly average) through December 2008 — Cents per pound

Average Spot Cotton Prices[2], C.I.F. Northern Europe   In U.S. Cents Per Pound

Crop Year Beginning Aug. 1	Argentina "C"[3] 1 1/16"	Australia M 1 3/32"	Cotlook Index A	Cotlook Index B	Egypt Giza[4] 81 M 1 3/32"	Greece M 1 3/32"	Mexico[5] M 1 3/32"	Pakistan Sind/ Punjab[6]	Tanzania AR[7] Type 3	Turkey Izmir[8] 1 3/32"	U.S. Calif. ACALA SJV[9]	U.S. Memphis Terr.[10] M 1 3/32"	U.S. Orleans/ Texas[11] M 1 1/32"
1990-1	77.06	85.58	82.90	77.80	177.43	84.24	84.46	77.19	89.62	81.32	92.84	88.13	80.35
1991-2	55.08	65.97	63.05	58.50	128.10	65.90	68.19	58.14	68.90	74.66	74.47	66.35	63.41
1992-3	64.31	64.01	57.70	53.70	99.24	56.92	----	52.66	62.24	----	68.37	63.08	58.89
1993-4	80.20	72.81	70.60	67.30	88.35	58.81	----	54.42	69.83	59.80	77.55	72.80	69.78
1994-5	101.88	81.05	92.75	92.40	93.70	88.64	82.65	73.75	----	----	106.40	98.67	95.70
1995-6	82.98	93.75	85.61	81.06	----	84.95	94.94	81.86	96.20	90.38	103.49	94.71	90.37
1996-7	79.71	83.24	78.59	74.80	----	75.85	79.60	73.37	79.22	----	89.55	82.81	79.77
1997-8	69.96	77.49	72.19	70.69	----	72.03	81.70	72.93	84.04	----	85.11	78.12	74.74
1998-9	57.19	66.48	58.94	54.26	----	58.66	65.78	----	72.70	----	78.57	74.20	70.95
1999-00[1]	----	61.97	52.85	49.55	----	51.71	56.43	----	55.67	----	68.76	66.29	55.67

[1] Preliminary.   [2] Generally for prompt shipment.   [3] 1-1/32" prior to January 20, 1984; 1-1/16" since.   [4] Dendera until 1969/70; Giza 67 1969/70 until December 1983; Giza 69/75/81 until November 1990; Giza 81 since.   [5] S. Brazil Type 5, 1-1/32" prior to 1968-69; 1-1/16" until 1987/88; Brazilian Type 5/6, 1-1/16" since.   [6] Punjab until 1979/80; Sind SG until June 1984; Sind/Punjab SG until January 1985; Afzal 1" until January 1986; Afzal 1-1/32" since.   [7] No. 1 until 1978/79; No. 1/2 until February 1986; AR' Mwanza No. 3 until January 1992; AR' Type 3 since.   [8] Izmir ST 1 White 1-1/16" RG prior to 1981/82; 1-3/32" from 1981/82 until January 1987; Izmir/Antalya ST 1 White 1-3/32" RG since.   [9] SM 1-3/32" prior to 1975/76; SM 1-1/8" since.   [10] SM 1-1/16" prior to 1981/82; Middling 1-3/32" since.   [11] Middling 1" prior to 1988/89; Middling 1-1/32" since.
Source: International Cotton Advisory Committee (ICAC)

Average Producer Price Index of Gray Cotton Broadwovens   Index 1982 = 100

Year	Jan.	Feb.	Mar.	Apr.	May	June	July	Aug.	Sept.	Oct.	Nov.	Dec.	Average
1999	117.1	117.3	118.8	116.5	116.4	116.1	116.5	112.9	112.9	113.1	112.6	108.6	114.9
2000	112.1	111.1	106.9	108.2	108.6	107.7	108.3	108.8	110.1	110.2	112.3	112.3	109.7
2001	112.8	113.1	113.1	112.7	112.8	112.9	113.2	112.9	112.9	112.0	111.2	111.1	112.6
2002	110.7	109.9	110.1	108.1	107.3	108.0	106.9	107.0	106.9	105.9	105.7	106.2	107.7
2003	105.7	105.2	105.0	105.9	106.0	106.7	107.2	109.1	110.1	111.0	110.6	108.9	107.6
2004	109.9	111.2	110.6	111.5	112.3	112.6	113.7	113.2	113.5	113.6	113.3	112.5	112.3
2005	112.6	112.0	111.9	111.8	111.2	111.2	111.1	111.2	111.2	111.3	110.9	111.1	111.5
2006	111.1	110.5	109.9	109.9	110.1	110.1	110.1	110.1	110.1	110.0	110.0	109.9	110.2
2007	110.0	109.9	109.9	110.1	109.8	109.9	109.9	109.9	109.9	110.0	109.9	109.9	109.9
2008[1]	110.1	110.1	110.1	110.1	110.0	109.9	110.2	111.7	111.7	111.7	111.5	110.2	110.6

[1] Preliminary.   *Source: Bureau of Labor Statistics (0337-01), U.S. Department of Commerce*

Average Price of SLM 1-1/16", Cotton/5 at Designated U.S. Markets   In Cents Per Pound (Net Weight)

Year	Aug.	Sept.	Oct.	Nov.	Dec.	Jan.	Feb.	Mar.	Apr.	May	June	July	Average
1999-00	49.72	48.39	49.46	48.12	46.65	51.92	54.29	57.67	53.76	58.31	54.97	55.13	52.36
2000-01	59.33	60.62	60.54	62.16	61.04	56.66	54.10	47.22	42.19	40.02	37.38	37.48	51.56
2001-02	36.05	33.22	28.42	31.23	32.21	32.13	31.60	33.23	31.86	31.14	36.36	39.78	33.10
2002-03	39.20	37.91	39.62	44.98	46.38	48.60	51.35	53.82	53.38	48.94	50.92	54.45	47.46
2003-04	51.94	58.02	69.38	68.88	65.09	68.21	63.35	61.78	57.50	60.22	52.35	45.05	60.15
2004-05	44.92	47.48	44.55	42.62	41.68	43.21	42.90	48.19	49.58	48.57	45.92	47.78	45.62
2005-06	45.38	47.43	51.02	48.80	49.53	51.91	52.39	50.04	49.00	47.00	47.90	47.15	48.96
2006-07	48.65	46.80	45.15	46.32	49.85	49.90	48.77	49.21	46.97	44.62	50.35	57.50	48.67
2007-08	53.46	57.08	59.06	59.59	59.44	63.34	65.92	69.27	63.91	60.67	63.34	62.85	61.49
2008-09[1]	60.93	56.72	46.90	39.83	42.07	44.87							48.55

[1] Preliminary.   [2] Grade 41, leaf 4, staple 34, mike 35-36 and 43-49 , strength 23.5-26.4.   *Source: Agricultural Marketing Service, U.S. Department of Agriculture (AMS-USDA)*

Average Spot Cotton, 1-3/32", Price (SLM) at Designated U.S. Markets[2]   In Cents Per Pound (Net Weight)

Year	Aug.	Sept.	Oct.	Nov.	Dec.	Jan.	Feb.	Mar.	Apr.	May	June	July	Average
1999-00	52.90	51.27	52.43	51.51	49.73	55.02	57.38	61.02	57.52	63.09	59.28	58.80	55.83
2000-01	62.60	63.62	63.13	65.08	64.73	60.18	57.18	50.08	44.94	42.54	39.88	39.96	54.49
2001-02	38.88	36.11	31.55	34.03	34.82	34.55	34.08	36.04	34.84	34.03	39.31	42.86	35.93
2002-03	42.31	41.07	43.08	48.78	50.70	52.87	55.34	57.88	57.54	52.96	55.09	58.46	51.34
2003-04	55.87	61.76	73.27	72.63	68.90	71.96	67.34	66.42	63.11	65.97	57.99	51.11	64.69
2004-05	50.45	52.55	49.45	47.23	46.41	48.16	48.17	53.37	54.67	53.76	51.26	52.97	50.70
2005-06	50.59	52.81	56.01	53.78	54.47	56.69	57.16	55.03	54.07	52.02	52.97	52.35	54.00
2006-07	53.80	51.95	50.20	51.13	54.71	54.75	53.66	54.05	51.59	49.12	54.71	61.59	53.44
2007-08	57.53	61.15	63.08	63.71	63.50	67.22	69.73	72.68	67.25	63.99	66.67	66.17	65.22
2008-09[1]	64.25	60.01	50.52	43.76	45.95	48.76							52.21

[1] Preliminary.   *Source: Agricultural Marketing Service, U.S. Department of Agriculture (AMS-USDA)*

Average Spot Prices of U.S. Cotton,[2] Base Quality (SLM) at Designated Markets   In Cents Per Pound

Crop Year Beginning Aug. 1	Dallas (EastTex.-Okl.)	Fresno (San Joaquin Valley)	Greenville (Southeast)	Greenwood (South Delta)	Lubbock (West Texas)	Memphis (North Delta)	Phoenix Desert (Southwest)	Average
1998-99	57.66	63.78	62.06	61.82	57.76	61.82	55.92	60.12
1999-00	50.49	56.67	53.81	53.34	50.12	53.34	48.79	52.36
2000-01	51.03	52.45	52.63	52.32	50.71	52.32	49.47	51.56
2001-02	32.59	34.64	33.02	33.24	32.39	33.24	32.60	33.10
2002-03	46.76	47.52	48.28	48.46	46.51	48.47	46.27	47.46
2003-04	59.95	59.71	60.80	60.85	59.71	60.78	59.23	60.15
2004-05	44.22	47.38	45.91	46.02	44.08	46.02	45.66	45.61
2005-06	47.69	50.06	49.65	49.63	47.78	49.67	48.26	48.96
2006-07	48.17	48.58	49.90	49.46	48.06	49.46	47.08	48.67
2007-08[1]	60.89	60.57	63.95	62.67	60.64	62.67	59.07	61.50

[1] Preliminary   [2] Prices are for mixed lots, net weight, uncompressed in warehouse.
Source: Agricultural Marketing Service, U.S. Department of Agriculture (AMS-USDA)

Average Price[1] Received by Farmers for Upland Cotton in the United States   In Cents Per Pound

Year	Aug.	Sept.	Oct.	Nov.	Dec.	Jan.	Feb.	Mar.	Apr.	May	June	July	Average
1999-00	52.7	45.3	46.3	44.3	42.8	43.1	46.8	47.7	45.4	47.6	45.1	48.8	45.0
2000-01	51.4	50.6	55.5	58.0	57.8	52.1	48.5	41.1	42.6	40.9	39.2	38.9	49.8
2001-02	37.3	36.5	30.7	27.8	30.8	27.3	28.0	28.4	27.2	26.7	33.7	35.3	29.8
2002-03	33.0	35.2	39.4	43.0	44.3	45.5	46.5	48.6	45.4	45.9	45.5	46.3	43.2
2003-04	46.3	55.7	67.8	63.0	63.3	62.2	61.9	61.6	60.3	59.7	59.9	53.8	59.6
2004-05	53.7	49.3	50.6	43.2	39.3	38.5	38.3	40.3	41.4	39.6	41.9	41.1	43.1
2005-06	42.1	44.3	48.5	48.5	48.0	48.6	48.9	50.0	48.5	46.4	47.4	46.8	47.3
2006-07	45.8	47.3	45.9	47.4	49.0	49.4	47.4	46.4	46.3	44.0	45.4	45.2	46.6
2007-08	44.9	52.0	55.5	57.4	59.6	61.5	61.9	60.5	62.1	60.5	60.4	59.3	58.0
2008-09[2]	58.5	61.1	55.5	63.1	51.9	47.4							56.3

[1] Weighted average by sales.   [2] Preliminary.   *Source: Agricultural Marketing Service, U.S. Department of Agriculture (AMS-USDA)*

COTTON

Purchases Reported by Exchanges in Designated U.S. Spot Markets[1]   In Running Bales

Crop Year Beginning Aug. 1	Aug.	Sept.	Oct.	Nov.	Dec.	Jan.	Feb.	Mar.	Apr.	May	June	July	Market Total
1999-00	83,564	95,241	195,370	320,434	517,579	744,400	294,843	189,460	89,473	129,879	49,012	33,942	2,743,197
2000-01	63,607	69,083	143,938	323,891	288,242	217,755	215,318	191,667	274,185	193,774	152,905	167,647	2,302,012
2001-02	118,000	94,697	214,785	644,860	225,869	289,778	180,362	278,853	84,259	155,391	143,422	93,489	2,523,765
2002-03	43,047	49,671	194,020	204,564	369,838	481,730	432,055	169,064	170,951	213,679	149,780	86,830	2,565,229
2003-04	125,240	245,295	273,028	167,285	321,083	417,090	267,237	167,357	62,031	70,979	79,061	58,400	2,254,086
2004-05	135,568	46,749	91,390	263,999	369,597	402,504	445,448	424,472	210,285	93,471	95,154	20,398	2,599,035
2005-06	67,318	63,884	138,910	220,961	363,287	434,818	183,744	183,273	62,703	73,726	117,934	60,708	1,971,266
2006-07	87,527	58,849	111,619	112,634	214,384	174,852	140,273	125,562	207,478	310,748	168,730	137,204	1,849,860
2007-08	85,183	133,709	126,008	149,748	197,651	359,180	303,523	95,053	104,513	64,281	119,022	46,555	1,784,426
2008-09	79,487	75,191	89,246	92,960	113,117	149,362							1,198,726

[1] Seven markets.   *Source: Agricultural Marketing Service, U.S. Department of Agriculture (AMS-USDA)*

Production of Cotton (Upland and American-Pima) in the United States   In Thousands of 480-Pound Bales

Year	Alabama	Arizona	Arkansas	California	Georgia	Louisiana	sippi	Missouri	Carolina	Carolina	nessee	Texas	Total American-Pima
1999	625	716	1,428	1,580	1,567	901	1,731	472	816	281	595	5,050	674.3
2000	543	791	1,425	2,210	1,663	911	1,711	540	1,429	379	710	3,940	389.1
2001	920	690	1,833	1,770	2,220	1,034	2,396	695	1,673	423	978	4,260	700.4
2002	570	613	1,669	1,460	1,578	739	1,935	610	806	131	818	5,040	678.3
2003	820	550	1,804	1,495	2,110	1,027	2,120	700	1,037	326	890	4,330	432.3
2004	814	723	2,089	1,790	1,797	885	2,346	830	1,360	390	984	7,740	745.6
2005	848	622	2,202	1,623	2,140	1,098	2,147	864	1,437	410	1,122	8,484	630.5
2006	675	556	2,525	779	2,334	1,241	2,107	985	1,285	433	1,368	5,800	765.4
2007[1]	416	519	1,896	1,443	1,660	699	1,318	764	783	160	600	8,296	851.8
2008[2]	500	402	1,320	770	1,650	280	710	670	770	260	535	5,137	444.0

[1] Preliminary.   [2] Forecast.   *Source: Agricultural Statistics Board, U.S. Department of Agriculture (ASB-USDA)*

Cotton Production and Yield Estimates

Year	Forecasts of Production (1,000 Bales of 480 Lbs.[1]) Aug.1	Sept.1	Oct. 1	Nov. 1	Dec. 1	Jan. 1	Actual Crop	Forecasts of Yield (Lbs. Per Harvested Acre) Aug.1	Sept.1	Oct. 1	Nov. 1	Dec. 1	Jan. 1	Actual Yield
1999	18,304	17,535	16,430	16,531	16,875	----	16,968	649	621	588	592	604	----	607
2000	19,159	18,315	17,485	17,510	17,399	----	17,188	648	622	620	622	619	----	632
2001	20,003	19,992	20,072	20,175	20,064	----	20,303	670	679	681	685	691	----	705
2002	18,439	18,134	18,070	17,815	17,375	----	17,209	675	675	674	665	648	----	665
2003	17,104	16,939	17,559	18,215	18,215	----	18,255	667	667	696	722	722	----	730
2004	20,183	20,895	21,545	22,545	22,815	----	23,251	727	758	782	818	828	----	855
2005	21,291	22,282	22,717	23,161	23,703	----	23,890	748	782	797	813	832	----	831
2006	20,431	20,345	20,659	21,299	21,297	----	21,588	765	762	774	798	798	----	814
2007	17,346	17,812	18,154	18,862	18,987	----	19,207	783	811	826	859	864	----	879
2008	13,767	13,846	13,711	13,528	13,613	----	13,036	842	849	849	837	843	----	810

[1] Net weight bales.   *Source: Agricultural Statistics Board, U.S. Department of Agriculture (ASB-USDA)*

Supply and Distribution of Upland Cotton in the United States   In Thousands of 480-Pound Bales

Crop Year Beginning Aug. 1	Area Planted (1,000 Acres)	Harvested (1,000 Acres)	Yield Lbs./Acre	Beginning Stocks[3]	Supply Production	Imports	Total Supply	Mill Use	Exports	Total	Ending Stocks	Farm Price[5] Cents/ Lb.
1999-00	14,584	13,138	595	3,836	16,294	53	20,183	10,055	6,303	16,358	3,665	45.0
2000-01	15,347	12,884	626	3,665	16,799	8	20,472	8,738	6,303	15,041	5,879	49.8
2001-02	15,499	13,560	694	5,879	19,603	6	25,488	7,592	10,603	18,195	7,120	29.8
2002-03	13,714	12,174	652	7,120	16,530	10	23,661	7,170	11,266	18,436	5,140	43.2
2003-04	13,301	11,826	723	5,140	17,823	4	22,967	6,204	13,220	19,424	3,384	59.6
2004-05	13,409	12,809	843	3,384	22,505	8	25,897	6,629	13,645	20,274	5,482	43.1
2005-06	13,975	13,534	825	5,482	23,260	9	28,751	5,820	17,029	22,849	5,991	47.3
2006-07	14,948	12,408	806	5,991	20,822	10	26,824	4,896	12,338	17,234	9,338	46.6
2007-08[1]	10,535	10,201	864	9,338	18,355	6	27,699	4,573	12,820	17,393	9,905	58.0
2008-09[2]	9,296	7,559	799	9,905	12,589	5	22,979	4,365	12,500	16,865	6,137	56.3

[1] Preliminary.   [2] Estimate.   [3] Excludes preseason ginnings (adjusted to 480-lb. bale net weight basis).   [4] Includes preseason ginnings.
[5] Marketing year average price.   *Source: Economic Research Service, U.S. Department of Agriculture (ERS-USDA)*

Cotton Futures - ICE Futures U.S.
(weekly close) as of January 2, 2009

Cents per pound

Average Open Interest of Cotton #2 Futures in New York   In Contracts

Year	Jan.	Feb.	Mar.	Apr.	May	June	July	Aug.	Sept.	Oct.	Nov.	Dec.
1999	79,598	75,794	62,857	60,384	61,470	66,789	68,975	65,690	63,976	60,369	63,746	61,474
2000	63,987	67,720	69,788	56,038	54,058	48,024	53,621	63,069	73,735	67,767	65,017	62,931
2001	71,849	73,383	71,389	70,407	66,680	64,032	61,183	65,257	65,496	59,777	56,896	58,156
2002	64,096	64,572	63,451	63,827	67,601	65,848	74,892	72,612	69,554	71,526	82,802	74,685
2003	83,775	89,852	91,336	78,658	73,146	69,137	62,565	62,781	80,348	108,981	97,809	79,627
2004	93,191	81,871	84,600	89,082	81,988	79,310	77,029	75,449	69,514	76,556	86,280	84,409
2005	92,651	94,047	118,183	120,416	103,446	93,818	92,284	99,959	105,874	117,889	103,466	100,660
2006	118,234	129,108	129,728	141,156	165,386	170,190	161,719	166,806	178,539	184,002	170,275	164,797
2007	177,495	199,342	214,628	225,473	223,839	212,296	214,893	206,042	215,820	239,217	229,629	219,185
2008	264,235	279,240	286,505	259,800	258,309	239,935	219,979	216,387	211,933	177,277	146,431	127,380

Source: ICE Futures U.S.; formerly New York Board of Trade (NYBOT)

Volume of Trading of Cotton #2 Futures in New York   In Contracts

Year	Jan.	Feb.	Mar.	Apr.	May	June	July	Aug.	Sept.	Oct.	Nov.	Dec.	Total
1999	179,049	244,300	209,127	250,622	157,552	260,649	187,631	178,236	175,282	193,552	298,531	120,120	2,454,651
2000	270,792	279,566	248,017	220,222	232,947	272,023	147,878	175,707	154,735	172,875	242,013	180,982	2,597,757
2001	267,930	270,876	237,356	215,903	175,808	214,513	132,065	118,685	98,947	152,702	258,847	116,033	2,259,665
2002	156,834	248,299	162,781	237,861	188,340	234,442	170,893	128,185	145,946	199,779	296,859	157,741	2,327,960
2003	202,615	267,234	217,791	325,627	249,314	271,822	164,027	127,080	283,988	422,132	356,052	148,310	3,035,992
2004	272,948	359,105	300,820	376,669	184,869	357,548	159,924	195,886	196,739	224,431	341,709	185,370	3,156,018
2005	356,817	407,277	317,486	465,210	306,971	456,584	171,139	189,584	271,268	290,650	408,580	207,424	3,848,990
2006	311,926	495,729	375,624	515,709	330,785	601,971	184,482	259,259	268,847	308,584	587,710	249,781	4,490,407
2007	366,579	713,894	375,964	765,244	439,838	745,901	428,059	445,099	435,529	520,221	759,829	338,822	6,334,979
2008	684,489	971,319	730,160	651,281	427,731	690,183	281,522	306,004	418,279	401,064	426,785	174,146	6,162,963

Source: ICE Futures U.S.; formerly New York Board of Trade (NYBOT)

COTTON

Daily Rate of Upland Cotton Mill Consumption[2] on Cotton-System Spinning Spindles in the United States
In Thousands of Running Bales

Crop Year Beginning Aug. 1	Aug.	Sept.	Oct.	Nov.	Dec.	Jan.	Feb.	Mar.	Apr.	May	June	July	Average
1998-99	39.3	38.7	39.9	37.4	37.5	38.6	38.2	37.9	37.8	37.5	37.7	36.8	38.1
1999-00	36.1	36.4	37.3	37.2	37.6	36.8	37.5	37.6	37.5	37.0	38.1	36.5	37.1
2000-01	36.4	35.6	34.5	33.0	34.4	33.5	31.9	31.8	30.6	29.7	27.6	28.6	32.3
2001-02	28.8	28.1	27.5	26.3	27.1	27.1	27.5	27.9	27.4	28.4	29.3	30.6	28.0
2002-03	28.0	28.3	27.9	27.4	27.2	26.5	26.8	26.4	26.0	25.0	24.3	24.7	26.5
2003-04	23.0	22.7	22.6	23.0	22.7	22.4	23.1	23.1	22.8	23.1	23.2	24.2	23.0
2004-05	25.1	25.1	24.9	24.4	25.2	24.8	23.7	23.7	24.0	23.6	25.2	24.4	24.5
2005-06	23.2	22.0	22.6	21.2	20.5	22.9	23.1	22.4	20.7	20.2	19.9	19.5	21.5
2006-07	18.9	18.8	18.5	W	W	W	W	W	W	W	W	W	18.7
2007-[8]	W	W	W	W	W	W	W	W	W	W	W	W	W

[1] Preliminary. [2] Not seasonally adjusted. W = Withheld. *Source: Bureau of the Census: U.S. Department of Commerce*

Consumption of American and Foreign Cotton in the United States   In Thousands of Running Bales

Year	Aug.	Sept.	Oct.	Nov.	Dec.	Jan.	Feb.	Mar.	Apr.	May	June	July	Total
1998-99	835	1,013	834	758	796	979	795	983	777	793	970	678	10,210
1999-00	762	949	793	757	801	736	769	966	772	771	990	670	9,735
2000-01	766	929	741	663	749	661	657	837	641	628	727	510	8,510
2001-02	616	751	600	521	563	541	580	759	575	594	754	571	7,425
2002-03	574	733	585	545	598	671	556	708	541	523	616	456	7,106
2003-04	476	599	482	468	504	478	475	609	461	473	582	446	6,053
2004-05	484	604	483	460	500	470	472	601	469	463	581	449	6,035
2005-06	454	574	472	415	438	452	476	593	430	422	531	381	5,637
2006-07	385	492	389	357	370	361	363	461	371	371	476	348	4,744
2007-08[1]	358	467	366	343	362	423	341	402	346	333	430	329	4,499

[1] Preliminary. *Source: Bureau of the Census, U.S. Department of Commerce*

Exports of All Cotton[2] from the United States   In Thousands of Running Bales

Year	Aug.	Sept.	Oct.	Nov.	Dec.	Jan.	Feb.	Mar.	Apr.	May	June	July	Total
1998-99	402	280	265	795	1,027	156	182	221	169	256	260	330	4,344
1999-00	254	146	167	455	654	658	736	978	708	659	508	479	6,402
2000-01	430	336	382	435	541	564	614	720	568	692	784	648	6,715
2001-02	612	824	678	649	927	964	1,042	1,225	999	842	1,067	679	10,505
2002-03	472	653	373	626	935	1,206	873	1,597	1,174	1,150	1,273	1,231	11,561
2003-04	810	555	446	758	1,116	1,194	1,238	1,869	1,453	1,117	1,576	1,021	13,154
2004-05	760	374	422	632	1,087	1,179	1,214	1,839	1,461	1,094	1,411	1,828	13,301
2005-06	1,407	742	533	763	1,236	946	1,541	2,195	1,758	1,725	1,906	1,903	16,655
2006-07	688	412	487	599	812	683	824	1,266	1,269	1,385	2,174	1,745	12,342
2007-08[1]	1,116	1,337	883	977	781	981	945	955	1,096	1,360	1,292	1,427	13,150

[1] Preliminary. *Source: Foreign Agricultural Service, U.S. Department of Agriculture (FAS-USDA)*

U.S. Exports of American Cotton to Countries of Destination   In Thousands of 480-Pound Bales

Crop Year Beginning Aug. 1	Canada	China	Hong Kong	Indonesia	Italy	Japan	Rep. of Korea	Mexico	Philippines	Taiwan	Thailand	United Kingdom	Total
1998-99	281	71	245	229	29	406	381	1,359	59	82	249	6	4,298
1999-00	245	147	316	573	61	424	307	1,500	71	257	476	4	6,401
2000-01	322	124	287	558	52	355	489	1,760	42	237	367	1	6,740
2001-02	235	306	407	947	58	385	577	1,516	126	693	693	0	10,397
2002-03	303	1,840	364	869	81	380	480	1,777	104	592	556	4	11,607
2003-04	303	4,919	169	889	63	284	469	1,620	100	527	396	20	13,758
2004-05	305	4,085	274	1,138	75	301	643	1,589	110	846	711	60	14,436
2005-06	178	9,095	280	933	33	265	431	1,511	46	530	660	23	18,039
2006-07[1]	101	3,641	238	928	36	265	307	1,200	39	456	429	0	12,219
2007-08[2]	40	4,516	177	1,259	62	376	361	1,434	26	838	390	0	13,982

[1] Preliminary. [2] Estimate. *Source: Foreign Agricultural Service, U.S. Department of Agriculture (FAS-USDA)*

Cotton[1] Government Loan Program in the United States

Crop Year Beginning Aug. 1	Support Price --- Cents Per Lb. ---	Target Price --- Cents Per Lb. ---	Put Under Support Ths Bales	% of Production	Acquired ----- Ths. Bales -----	Owned July 31 ----- Ths. Bales -----	Crop Year Beginning Aug. 1	Support Price --- Cents Per Lb. ---	Target Price --- Cents Per Lb. ---	Put Under Support Ths Bales	% of Production	Acquired ----- Ths. Bales -----	Owned July 31 ----- Ths. Bales -----
1997-98	51.92	NA	4,281	23.5	1	0	2002-03	52.00	72.4	12,740	77.1	0	106
1998-99	51.92	NA	4,724	36.8	31	3	2003-04	52.00	72.4	10,466	58.7	16	0
1999-00	51.92	NA	8,721	54.9	0	1	2004-05	52.00	72.4	17,095	76.0	8	0
2000-01	51.92	NA	8,837	52.6	69	5	2005-06	52.00	72.4	17,779	76.4	60	11
2001-02	51.92	NA	13,655	69.7	31	2	2006-07[2]	52.00	72.4				

[1] Upland. [2] Preliminary. NA = Not applicable. Source: Economic Research Service, U.S. Department of Agriculture (ERS-USDA)

Production of Cotton Cloth[1] in the United States   In Millions of Square Yards

Year	First Quarter	Second Quarter	Third Quarter	Fourth Quarter	Total	Year	First Quarter	Second Quarter	Third Quarter	Fourth Quarter	Total
1999	1,170	1,164	1,078	1,039	4,451	2004	648	644	640	614	2,547
2000	1,075	1,129	1,111	1,079	4,395	2005	672	640	653	664	2,629
2001	1,047	976	873	811	3,706	2006	583	609	551	487	2,230
2002	893	912	894	825	3,524	2007	521	507	488	453	1,969
2003	836	780	662	620	2,898	2008[2]	447	460	451		1,811

[1] Cotton broadwoven goods over 12 inches in width.   [2] Preliminary.   Source: Bureau of Census, U.S. Department of Commerce

Cotton Ginnings[1] in the United States To: In Thousands of Running Bales

Crop Year	Aug. 1	Sept. 1	Sept. 15	Oct. 1	Oct. 15	Nov. 1	Nov. 15	Dec. 1	Dec. 15	Jan. 1	Jan. 15	Feb. 1	Total Crop
1999-00	81	561	1,018	2,690	4,885	8,263	11,006	13,379	14,992	15,965	16,322	16,468	16,528
2000-01	245	842	1,454	3,264	5,930	9,221	11,546	13,657	15,364	16,097	16,518	16,648	16,742
2001-02	99	609	802	2,072	4,616	8,806	12,558	15,564	17,606	18,759	19,268	19,532	19,771
2002-03	56	538	898	1,656	3,520	6,697	9,265	12,368	14,392	15,654	16,285	16,576	16,710
2003-04	29	567	958	2,001	3,819	7,393	10,507	13,466	15,678	16,883	17,409	17,601	17,709
2004-05	48	563	1,157	2,227	4,788	8,758	12,019	14,754	17,072	18,925	20,155	21,249	22,556
2005-06	69	592	976	2,314	4,556	8,691	12,569	15,991	18,401	20,108	21,282	22,255	23,253
2006-07	23	406	996	2,572	5,039	8,604	11,833	15,139	17,657	19,212	20,062	20,559	20,998
2007-08	W	182	375	1,561	3,793	7,072	10,099	12,594	14,341	15,700	16,690	17,585	18,909
2008-09[2]	13	338	476	817	2,073	4,365	6,834	8,946	10,479	11,612	12,139	12,375	

[1] Excluding linters.   [2] Preliminary.   W = Withheld.   Source: National Agricultural Statistics Service, U.S. Department of Agriculture (NASS-USDA)

Fiber Prices in the United States   In Cents Per Pound

Year	Cotton[1] Actual	Cotton[1] Raw[5] Equivalent	Rayon[2] Actual	Rayon[2] Raw[5] Equivalent	Polyester[3] Actual	Polyester[3] Raw[5] Equivalent	Price Ratios[4] In Percent Cotton/ Rayon	Price Ratios[4] In Percent Cotton/ Polyester
2000	64.06	71.17	97.58	101.65	57.08	59.46	70.0	119.1
2001	47.08	52.32	98.50	102.61	60.42	62.93	52.0	83.0
2002	45.56	50.63	97.83	101.91	61.17	63.72	50.0	79.0
2003	62.54	69.49	90.25	94.01	60.67	63.20	74.1	111.0
2004	60.42	67.13	99.08	103.21	62.67	65.28	66.5	103.5
2005	54.75	60.00	114.58	119.36	67.75	70.57	51.0	86.2
2006	56.70	63.00	113.00	117.71	69.00	71.86	53.5	88.0
2007	61.97	68.86	113.00	117.71	74.00	77.08	58.5	89.3
2008[6]	73.79	82.01	113.00	117.71	74.00	77.08	69.7	121.1
Jan.	73.32	81.47	113.00	117.71	74.00	77.08	69.2	120.3
Feb.	74.25	82.54	113.00	117.71	74.00	77.08	70.1	121.8
Mar.	NA	NA	NA	NA	NA	NA	NA	NA
Apr.	NA	NA	NA	NA	NA	NA	NA	NA
May	NA	NA	NA	NA	NA	NA	NA	NA
June	NA	NA	NA	NA	NA	NA	NA	NA
July	NA	NA	NA	NA	NA	NA	NA	NA
Aug.	NA	NA	NA	NA	NA	NA	NA	NA
Sept.	NA	NA	NA	NA	NA	NA	NA	NA
Oct.	NA	NA	NA	NA	NA	NA	NA	NA
Nov.	NA	NA	NA	NA	NA	NA	NA	NA
Dec.								

[1] SLM-1 1/16" at group B Mill points, net weight.   [2] 1.5 and 3.0 denier, regular rayon staples.   [3] Reported average market price for 1.5 denier polyester staple for cotton blending.   [4] Raw fiber equivalent.   [5] Actual prices converted to estimated raw fiber equivalent as follows: cotton, divided by 0.90, rayon and polyester, divided by 0.96.   [6] Preliminary.
Source: Economic Research Service, U.S. Department of Agriculture (ERS-USDA)

Cottonseed and Products

Cottonseed is crushed to produce both oil and meal. Cottonseed oil is typically used for cooking oil and cottonseed meal is fed to livestock. Before the cottonseed is crushed for oil and meal, it is de-linted of its linters. Linters are used for padding in furniture, absorbent cotton swabs, and for the manufacture of many cellulose products. The sediment left by cottonseed oil refining, called foots, provides fatty acids for industrial products. The value of cottonseeds represents a substantial 18% of a cotton producer's income.

Prices – The average monthly price of cottonseed oil in 2008 rose by +56.43% yr/yr to 68.09 cents per pound. The average monthly price of cottonseed meal in 2008 rose by +63.7% yr/yr to a record high of $265.22 per short ton.

Supply – World production of cottonseed in the 2007-08 marketing year fell –1.1% yr/yr to 43.981 million metric tons, down from the record high of 45.230 million metric tons posted in 2004-05. The world's largest cottonseed producers are China with 28% of world production, India with 24%, the U.S. with 14%, and Pakistan with 9%. U.S. production of cottonseed in the 2007-08 marketing year fell by –9.91% yr/yr to 6.620 million tons. U.S. production of cottonseed oil in 2008-09 fell by –11.8% yr/yr to 755 million pounds, down from the 10-year high of 957 million pounds posted in 2004-05. U.S. annualized production of cottonseed cake and meal for the first five months of the 2008-09 marketing year (Aug-Jul) fell by 15.7% yr/yr to 1.059 million short tons.

Demand – U.S. cottonseed crushed (consumed) in the U.S. annualized for the first five months of the 2008-09 marketing year fell by –14.6% to 2.307 million tons, far below the levels of over 4 million tons seen in the 1970s.

Trade – U.S. exports of cottonseed in 2008-09 fell -41.6% to 350,000 short tons, while imports were very low at only 50,000 short tons.

World Production of Cottonseed   In Thousands of Metric Ton

Crop Year Beginning Oct. 1	Argentina	Australia	Brazil	China	Egypt	Greece	India	Mexico	Pakistan	Turkey	United States	Former USSR	World Total
1999-00	223	1,047	1,310	6,817	385	740	5,300	237	3,824	1,159	5,764	2,832	33,398
2000-01	257	1,062	1,720	7,868	371	726	4,760	128	3,651	1,289	5,838	2,531	33,914
2001-02	102	1,054	1,407	9,476	527	743	5,372	152	3,610	1,354	6,761	2,749	37,365
2002-03	90	470	1,451	8,750	475	718	4,624	68	3,472	1,457	5,610	2,584	33,641
2003-04	159	494	2,390	8,651	338	611	6,018	115	3,416	1,337	6,046	2,442	36,044
2004-05	200	912	2,309	11,257	487	645	8,250	212	4,853	1,390	7,437	2,885	45,230
2005-06	187	770	1,816	10,240	335	677	8,200	221	4,428	1,230	7,414	3,102	42,790
2006-07[1]	245	320	2,347	12,200	350	520	9,300	249	4,422	1,340	6,666	3,045	44,482
2007-08[2]	198	150	2,340	12,200	390	520	10,500	209	3,900	1,160	5,977	3,054	43,981

[1] Preliminary.   [2] Estimate.   *Source: The Oil World*

Salient Statistics of Cottonseed in the United States   In Thousands of Short Tons

Crop Year Beginning Aug. 1	Stocks	Supply — Production	Total Supply	Disappearance — Crush	Exports	Other	Total	Farm Price USD/Ton	Value of Production Mil. USD	Products Produced	Total
			In Thousands of Short Tons								
2000-01	274	6,436	7,084	2,753	235	3,669	6,657	105	675.7	847	1,338
2001-02	427	7,452	8,206	2,791	274	4,742	7,807	91	667.3	876	1,294
2002-03	400	6,184	6,687	2,495	370	3,477	6,341	101	616.4	725	1,115
2003-04	347	6,665	7,013	2,643	354	3,595	6,592	117	779.0	874	1,244
2004-05	421	8,242	8,664	2,923	379	4,770	8,072	107	872.8	957	1,362
2005-06	592	8,172	8,764	3,010	523	4,630	8,163	96	779.5	951	1,372
2006-07	602	7,348	7,950	2,680	616	4,165	7,461	111	814.2	849	1,241
2007-08[1]	489	6,589	7,080	2,706	599	3,132	6,437	160	1,060.8	856	1,262
2008-09[2]	643	4,429	5,122	2,400	350	2,042	4,792	160-220		755	1,105

[1] Preliminary.   [2] Estimate.   *Source: Economic Research Service, U.S. Department of Agriculture (ERS-USDA)*

Average Wholesale Price of Cottonseed Meal (41% Solvent)[2] in Memphis   In Dollars Per Short Ton

Year	Jan.	Feb.	Mar.	Apr.	May	June	July	Aug.	Sept.	Oct.	Nov.	Dec.	Average
2000	126.88	130.50	129.38	125.00	123.25	130.63	131.88	130.50	153.12	150.00	141.88	160.83	136.15
2001	184.00	148.75	138.13	140.00	137.50	126.88	129.69	130.63	131.25	131.25	128.13	134.17	138.37
2002	133.13	125.00	131.88	124.30	120.88	137.50	151.50	159.75	156.38	150.10	150.00	156.00	141.37
2003	157.38	143.60	142.40	142.40	131.75	131.50	143.00	151.70	153.20	163.50	182.50	185.00	152.33
2004	188.00	193.00	205.10	219.67	203.00	185.40	177.50	156.20	142.75	126.75	119.00	117.00	169.45
2005	112.50	111.25	110.80	108.00	110.40	138.75	151.00	143.00	140.00	133.13	132.50	175.00	130.53
2006	172.50	152.50	148.75	144.38	131.50	135.00	132.50	134.50	139.00	132.40	131.88	152.50	142.28
2007	161.00	174.75	185.50	148.25	137.00	131.25	137.50	144.75	167.50	183.40	176.25	196.67	161.99
2008[1]	273.60	292.00	245.00	230.00	240.50	293.25	333.00	290.00	292.00	238.75	225.00	229.50	265.22

[1] Preliminary.   *Source: Economic Research Service, U.S. Department of Agriculture (ERS-USDA)*

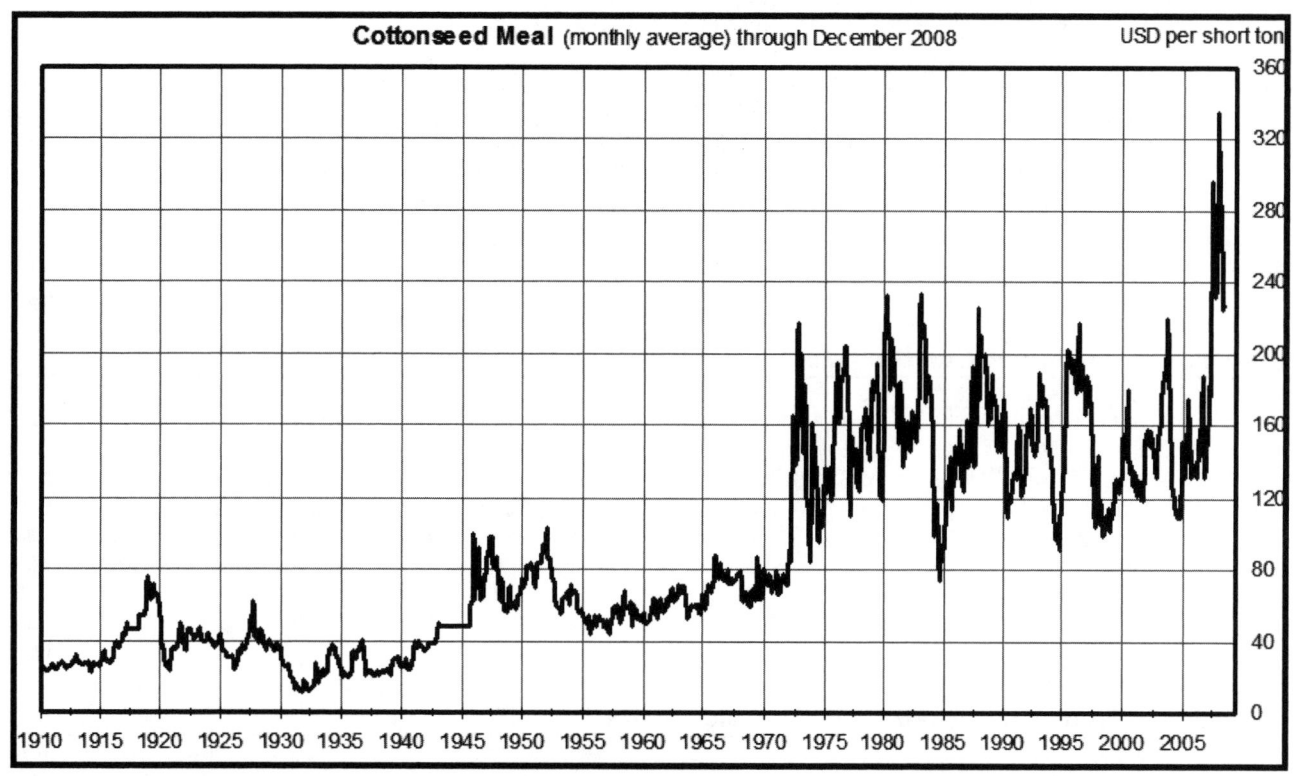

Cottonseed Meal (monthly average) through December 2008   USD per short ton

Supply and Distribution of Cottonseed Oil in the United States   In Millions of Pounds

Crop Year Beginning Oct. 1	Supply				Disappearance			Per Capita Consumption of Salad & Cooking Oils --- In Lbs. ---	Utilization Food Uses			Prices	
	Stocks	Pro-duction	Imports	Total Supply	Domestic	Exports	Total		Short-ening	Salad & Cooking Oils	Total	U.S.[3] (Crude) --- $/Metric Ton ---	Rott[4] (Cif)
2002-03	39	725	21.0	786	640	110	750	40	195	302	427	832	920
2003-04	36	874	0	910	690	111	801	40	167	295		688	752
2004-05	109	957	2.0	1,068	935	57	991	40	166	304		617	649
2005-06	76	951	1.0	1,028	860	67	927	43	213	389		649	669
2006-07	101	849	1.0	951	714	138	852	44	162	547		787	726
2007-08[1]	99	856	0	956	623	186	809	51	172	571		1,622	
2008-09[2]	147	755	0	902	686	131	817					818	

[1] Preliminary.   [2] Estimate.   [3] Valley Points FOB; Tank Cars.   [4] Rotterdam; US, PBSY, fob gulf.   W = Withheld.
Source: Economic Research Service, U.S. Department of Agriculture (ERS-USDA)

Consumption of Crude Cottonseed Oil, in Refining[2], in the United States   In Millions of Pound

Year	Oct.	Nov.	Dec.	Jan.	Feb.	Mar.	Apr.	May	June	July	Aug.	Sept.	Total
2002-03	48.5	59.5	56.0	66.8	55.8	57.1	59.2	49.7	42.4	31.9	38.7	34.9	600.5
2003-04	60.1	63.5	61.6	64.5	58.6	68.5	55.1	55.2	52.5	43.8	53.6	52.2	689.1
2004-05	60.0	66.4	67.0	73.7	69.2	66.8	72.6	52.9	64.7	57.0	71.8	55.2	777.1
2005-06	72.7	79.0	75.1	70.9	64.0	71.1	58.2	71.6	61.2	52.6	61.4	52.4	790.2
2006-07	65.7	55.7	61.4	63.9	55.3	63.7	60.1	63.6	54.1	56.3	56.5	55.6	711.9
2007-08	59.6	60.9	61.7	74.0	70.2	68.0	70.9	62.2	52.3	55.3	57.1	52.8	744.8
2008-09[1]	47.2	56.4	63.5	58.3									676.0

[1] Preliminary.   *Source: U.S. Bureau of Census, U.S. Department of Commerce*

Exports of Cottonseed Oil (Crude and Refined) from the United States   In Thousands of Pounds

Year	Jan.	Feb.	Mar.	Apr.	May	June	July	Aug.	Sept.	Oct.	Nov.	Dec.	Total
2002	12,905	17,550	12,137	8,319	21,013	9,444	7,863	8,727	6,831	12,698	11,105	10,761	139,352
2003	7,017	8,483	10,054	8,234	9,706	8,161	6,593	8,663	8,764	8,640	9,349	8,176	101,839
2004	14,203	8,982	8,321	10,399	9,632	10,720	7,931	9,891	4,617	5,669	7,619	7,507	105,492
2005	3,490	3,161	5,191	3,461	5,873	3,029	3,147	3,763	4,823	3,847	2,926	4,676	47,387
2006	5,084	5,724	5,410	7,738	5,519	6,640	7,539	6,608	5,755	8,827	9,377	14,365	88,586
2007	7,461	17,932	9,732	14,573	10,676	10,647	11,768	10,404	12,055	12,697	17,137	11,420	146,503
2008[1]	11,089	21,546	25,577	11,565	12,436	17,019	17,441	11,300	17,263	22,083	20,819		205,240

[1] Preliminary.   *Source: Economic Research Service, U.S. Department of Agriculture (ERS-USDA)*

COTTONSEED AND PRODUCTS

Cottonseed Crushed (Consumption) in the United States   In Thousands of Short Tons

Year	Aug.	Sept.	Oct.	Nov.	Dec.	Jan.	Feb.	Mar.	Apr.	May	June	July	Total
2000-01	170.8	141.1	265.9	252.3	241.5	295.2	268.7	261.9	186.0	228.3	241.9	199.2	2,753
2001-02	186.8	147.6	267.5	287.0	273.1	281.3	253.2	251.8	243.0	233.3	200.3	166.3	2,791
2002-03	195.1	131.4	207.8	242.5	236.6	274.5	224.5	230.4	241.5	203.6	179.4	127.4	2,495
2003-04	138.7	98.9	251.6	254.8	252.0	265.2	242.3	278.0	217.1	240.2	217.7	182.4	2,639
2004-05	193.8	141.0	247.9	260.3	263.5	283.1	266.3	270.2	287.7	221.0	266.6	221.6	2,923
2005-06	240.7	170.3	272.2	289.4	296.9	291.3	245.0	276.7	235.0	280.3	227.2	203.4	3,028
2006-07	204.8	158.2	252.4	223.3	236.7	251.2	222.5	249.1	230.8	243.2	204.6	203.3	2,680
2007-08	173.4	163.8	242.5	241.2	252.1	267.5	264.1	236.3	245.2	233.4	190.3	193.1	2,703
2008-09[1]	202.3	147.4	175.2	206.5	230.0	234.3							2,391

[1] Preliminary.   *Source: Economic Research Service, U.S. Department of Agriculture (ERS-USDA)*

Production of Cottonseed Cake and Meal in the United States   In Thousands of Short Tons

Year	Aug.	Sept.	Oct.	Nov.	Dec.	Jan.	Feb.	Mar.	Apr.	May	June	July	Total
2000-01	74.1	79.3	134.1	121.4	117.1	136.0	118.9	120.3	83.4	101.0	114.3	89.7	1,290
2001-02	83.9	70.8	118.5	126.5	118.2	129.0	112.5	115.0	109.2	107.9	96.3	73.7	1,261
2002-03	92.4	79.3	95.5	112.6	108.0	123.0	100.3	96.7	108.9	89.8	81.4	63.0	1,151
2003-04	74.9	59.5	112.3	111.0	112.5	113.9	105.1	123.4	94.2	104.7	97.7	91.0	1,200
2004-05	95.3	82.5	105.4	110.4	118.7	125.7	119.3	120.4	124.4	103.6	121.0	106.2	1,333
2005-06	116.4	91.1	109.6	134.6	129.3	128.8	108.2	119.4	104.5	129.3	107.2	99.0	1,377
2006-07	102.0	83.0	118.8	101.8	102.4	115.3	101.8	114.6	105.9	112.6	97.4	102.3	1,258
2007-08	81.3	87.3	112.5	111.0	111.9	125.6	119.9	116.3	110.4	103.2	86.8	90.7	1,257
2008-09[1]	96.5	76.9	74.8	89.7	103.5	102.7							1,088

[1] Preliminary.   *Source: Bureau of Census, U.S. Department of Commerce*

Production of Crude Cottonseed Oil[2] in the United States   In Millions of Pounds

Year	Aug.	Sept.	Oct.	Nov.	Dec.	Jan.	Feb.	Mar.	Apr.	May	June	July	Total
2000-01	55.1	52.1	84.3	76.8	73.5	85.9	78.4	76.4	53.9	66.8	66.6	55.7	826
2001-02	57.5	42.2	79.4	86.2	81.7	87.5	78.3	78.2	74.6	74.5	61.8	50.6	853
2002-03	60.2	53.7	62.8	72.1	67.9	80.8	65.6	66.7	71.0	59.9	52.8	39.9	753
2003-04	45.0	40.7	77.5	78.2	79.0	82.4	75.7	87.2	67.0	73.8	66.7	59.7	833
2004-05	68.6	58.1	77.1	82.2	81.4	88.7	83.4	84.3	90.7	71.3	81.6	69.5	937
2005-06	84.3	62.0	86.9	95.7	90.9	92.8	77.2	87.8	70.9	90.4	70.4	68.1	977
2006-07	68.4	59.2	77.1	71.7	73.9	78.6	67.1	78.1	72.5	77.2	65.2	66.7	856
2007-08	58.2	62.5	77.5	73.8	76.8	83.5	82.1	77.1	77.1	70.3	58.5	60.3	858
2008-09[1]	64.4	55.0	49.4	64.4	71.2	70.4							750

[1] Preliminary.   [2] Not seasonally adjusted.   *Source: Bureau of Census, U.S. Department of Commerce*

Production of Refined Cottonseed Oil in the United States   In Millions of Pounds

Year	Aug.	Sept.	Oct.	Nov.	Dec.	Jan.	Feb.	Mar.	Apr.	May	June	July	Total
2000-01	44.4	36.2	55.1	52.2	54.9	65.7	59.8	57.8	36.9	44.8	50.0	41.5	599
2001-02	49.4	29.6	48.2	63.6	61.3	64.9	58.0	58.5	56.2	56.7	45.2	36.8	628
2002-03	52.7	47.1	48.3	59.2	55.7	66.5	55.6	56.8	58.9	49.4	42.4	31.7	624
2003-04	38.5	34.6	59.8	63.5	61.4	64.3	58.4	68.3	55.1	55.1	52.4	43.8	655
2004-05	53.4	52.0	59.7	66.1	66.9	73.4	68.8	66.6	72.3	52.7	64.6	56.6	753
2005-06	71.2	54.7	72.8	78.5	74.7	70.3	63.8	70.8	57.8	71.2	60.8	52.3	799
2006-07	61.0	52.0	65.2	55.3	61.1	63.5	55.3	62.9	58.9	63.5	54.0	56.1	709
2007-08	56.4	55.5	59.6	60.9	61.6	73.8	70.0	67.8	70.5	62.1	52.3	55.2	746
2008-09[1]	56.9	52.6	46.9	56.3	63.2	57.9							668

[1] Preliminary.   *Source: Bureau of the Census, U.S. Department of Commerce*

Stocks of Cottonseed Oil (Crude and Refined) in the U.S., at End of Month   In Millions of Pounds

Year	Aug.	Sept.	Oct.	Nov.	Dec.	Jan.	Feb.	Mar.	Apr.	May	June	July
2000-01	59.9	49.0	66.5	75.2	95.0	109.5	134.4	139.9	133.5	123.5	126.8	114.0
2001-02	97.7	91.8	113.8	112.9	109.8	124.9	120.3	106.9	110.3	97.3	82.7	61.8
2002-03	46.1	39.7	32.8	40.2	38.0	46.1	58.8	72.2	83.3	84.2	91.4	64.0
2003-04	50.5	36.0	51.9	56.1	68.7	85.9	100.6	117.6	116.8	125.7	121.0	123.0
2004-05	123.3	109.0	106.6	110.6	111.3	116.6	122.0	112.9	121.2	111.5	90.0	86.2
2005-06	90.6	76.4	69.0	76.1	74.0	84.0	99.0	108.5	103.3	110.8	105.8	95.6
2006-07	98.9	101.1	93.2	92.3	106.8	119.2	117.0	112.2	124.5	126.1	119.5	160.2
2007-08	132.9	105.8	92.8	91.6	94.9	114.3	138.4	143.5	156.1	161.4	158.7	143.1
2008-09[1]	153.8	146.6	139.7	124.7	120.0	126.7						

[1] Preliminary.   *Source: Bureau of the Census, U.S. Department of Commerce*

Cottonseed Oil (monthly average) through December 2008   Cents per pound

Average Price of Crude Cottonseed Oil, PBSY, Greenwood, MS.[1] in Tank Cars   In Cents Per Pound

Year	Jan.	Feb.	Mar.	Apr.	May	June	July	Aug.	Sept.	Oct.	Nov.	Dec.	Average
1999	31.72	28.21	26.27	24.39	24.25	25.19	24.70	21.39	20.22	20.15	19.69	21.25	23.95
2000	21.98	22.65	23.70	24.57	22.97	21.54	21.03	20.17	18.52	18.16	17.83	17.25	20.86
2001	16.24	15.20	15.53	14.03	14.53	13.27	16.78	17.18	15.78	14.44	15.91	16.07	15.41
2002	16.38	15.89	16.77	16.98	17.95	19.48	21.30	22.32	22.32	26.84	36.90	46.89	23.34
2003	49.82	49.90	47.52	44.57	42.33	28.69	24.38	25.51	29.64	32.93	32.24	33.26	36.73
2004	32.76	34.21	34.91	34.47	32.57	30.72	27.83	25.29	23.29	22.74	23.88	23.81	28.87
2005	23.70	24.38	28.19	29.80	30.63	33.13	34.15	30.44	31.25	34.44	34.09	30.50	30.39
2006	29.63	29.50	29.75	27.05	28.06	27.25	29.20	26.69	27.13	27.44	30.25	30.75	28.56
2007	31.00	32.69	33.00	34.38	37.75	40.00	42.44	42.15	46.56	52.20	63.60	66.63	43.53
2008	71.69	78.60	78.94	79.75	82.75	87.56	86.06	72.55	62.44	46.45	37.38	32.88	68.09

Source: Economic Research Service, U.S. Department of Agriculture (ERS-USDA)

Exports of Cottonseed Oil to Important Countries from the United States   In Thousands of Metric Tons

Year	Canada	Dominican Republic	Egypt	Guate-mala	Japan	Mexico	Nether-lands	El Salvador	Rep. of Korea	Turkey	Venez-uela	Total
1999	37.5	0	0	0	4.2	5.4	.5	.8	.0	0	0	57.0
2000	40.2	.0	0	0	7.6	7.9	.4	0	.1	0	0	58.5
2001	26.0	.0	0	.5	6.5	8.6	3.1	4.8	2.5	0	0	64.6
2002	36.4	0	3.0	0	5.4	6.9	0	1.8	4.7	.3	0	63.2
2003	33.6	0	0	0	3.5	7.2	0	.0	.7	0	0	46.2
2004	26.5	0	0	0	11.6	8.6	0	0	.0	0	0	47.9
2005	12.7	0	0	0	1.0	6.5	0	0	.1	0	0	21.5
2006	10.0	.0	0	.0	1.3	11.2	0	0	14.1	0	.1	40.2
2007	24.0	.1	0	0	7.1	11.6	0	0	17.3	0	.0	66.5
2008[1]	37.5	.1	0	0	8.4	20.4	0	0	14.0	0	0	85.3

[1] Preliminary.   *Source: Foreign Agricultural Service, U.S. Department of Agriculture (FAS-USDA)*

Continuous Commodity Index (CCI)

The Continuous Commodity Index (CCI) was first calculated by Commodity Research Bureau, Inc. in 1957 and made its inaugural appearance in the 1958 CRB Commodity Year Book.

The Index originally consisted of two cash markets and 26 futures markets which were traded on exchanges in the U.S. and Canada. It included barley and flaxseed from the Winnipeg exchange; cocoa, coffee "B", copper, cotton, cottonseed oil, grease wool, hides, lead, potatoes, rubber, sugar #4, sugar #6, wool tops and zinc from New York exchanges; and corn, oats, wheat, rye, soybeans, soybean oil, soybean meal, lard, onions, and eggs from Chicago exchanges. In addition to those 26, the Index also included the spot New Orleans cotton and Minneapolis wheat markets.

Like the Bureau of Labor Statistics spot index, the CCI is calculated to produce an unweighted geometric mean of the individual commodity price relatives. In other words, a ratio of the current price to the base year average price. Currently, 1967 is the base year the Index is calculated against (1967=100).

The formula considers all future delivery contracts that expire on or before the end of the sixth calendar month from the current date, using up to a maximum of five contracts per commodity. However, a minimum of two contracts must be used to calculate the current price, even if the second contract is outside the six-month window. Contracts are excluded when in their delivery period.

The 2008 closing value of 363.06 was 23.74 percent lower than the 2007 close of 476.08. 13 of the 17 component commodities finished lower for the year.

Futures and options on the CCI are traded on the ICE Futures U.S. exchange.

Continuous Commodity Index (CCI) Component Commodities by Group

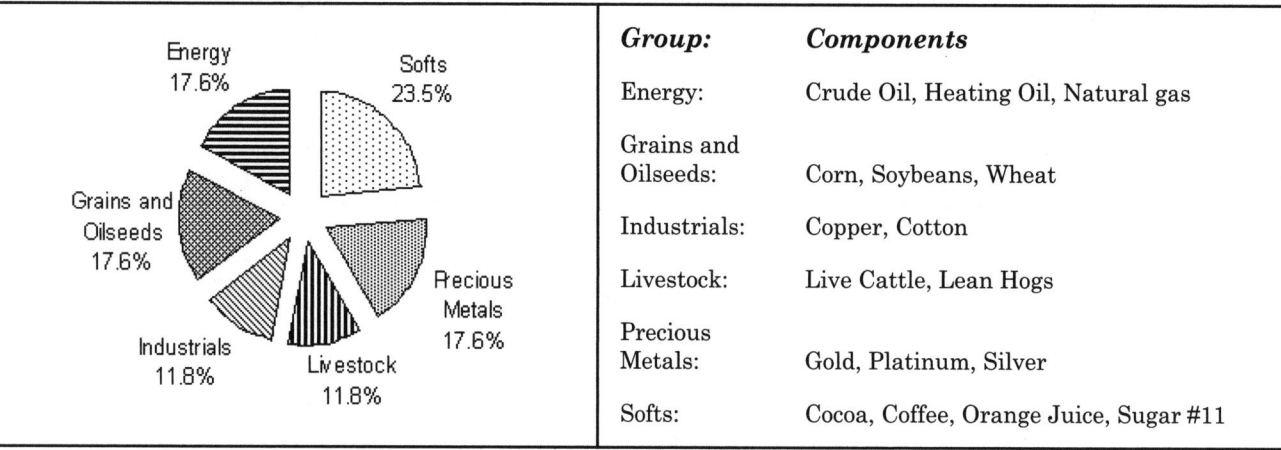

Group:	Components
Energy:	Crude Oil, Heating Oil, Natural gas
Grains and Oilseeds:	Corn, Soybeans, Wheat
Industrials:	Copper, Cotton
Livestock:	Live Cattle, Lean Hogs
Precious Metals:	Gold, Platinum, Silver
Softs:	Cocoa, Coffee, Orange Juice, Sugar #11

The Continuous Commodity Index (CCI) is computed using a three-step process:

1) Each of the Index's 17 component commodities is arithmetically averaged using the prices for all of the designated contract months which expire on or before the end of the sixth calendar month from the current date, except that: a) no contract shall be included in the calculation while in delivery; b) there shall be a minimum of two contract months for each component commodity (adding contracts beyond the six month window if necessary); c) there shall be a maximum of five contract months for each commodity (dropping the most deferred contracts to remain at five, if necessary). The result is that the Index extends six to seven months into the future depending on where one is in the current month. For example, live cattle's average price on October 30, 1995 would be computed as follows:

$$\text{Cattle Average} = \frac{\text{Dec. '96} + \text{Feb. '97}}{2}$$

2) These 17 component averages are then geometrically averaged by multiplying all of the numbers together and taking the 17th root.

$$\text{Geometric Average} = \sqrt[17]{\text{Crude Avg.} * \text{Heating Oil Avg.} * \text{Sugar Avg.}\ldots}$$

3) The resulting average is divided by 30.7766, the 1967 base-year average for these 17 commodities. That result is then multiplied by an adjustment factor of .8486. This adjustment factor is necessitated by the nine revisions to the Index since its inception in 1957. Finally, that result is multiplied by 100 in order to convert the Index into percentage terms:

$$\text{CCI} = \frac{\text{Current Geometric Average}}{\text{1967 Geometric Avg. (30.7766)} * .8486 * 100}$$

Continuous Commodity Index (CCI) - ICE Futures U.S.
(weekly close) as of January 02, 2009

Average Open Interest of Reuters-CRB Index (CCI) in New York   In Contracts

Year	Jan.	Feb.	Mar.	Apr.	May	June	July	Aug.	Sept.	Oct.	Nov.	Dec.
1999	2,863	3,027	3,153	3,041	3,785	3,388	3,300	3,443	4,231	4,851	4,579	4,087
2000	3,487	3,525	3,271	3,117	3,155	2,737	2,104	1,640	1,551	1,632	1,544	1,438
2001	1,280	1,063	1,032	1,036	969	1,006	1,058	1,048	993	559	354	404
2002	422	514	458	384	400	412	489	399	583	646	684	710
2003	748	877	835	849	939	905	858	917	1,078	1,029	1,013	760
2004	838	870	942	704	357	305	413	412	539	600	581	604
2005	540	561	710	663	644	683	861	1,023	1,016	1,024	1,016	1,035
2006	1,045	1,025	998	1,061	1,045	964	939	919	935	948	955	959
2007	927	914	995	1,251	1,526	1,500	1,409	1,560	1,416	1,603	1,864	1,484
2008	1,349	1,355	1,241	1,159	1,168	1,226	1,329	1,302	1,435	1,677	1,541	1,392

Source: ICE Futures U.S.; formerly New York Board of Trade (NYBOT)

Volume of Trading of Reuters-CRB Index (CCI) in New York   In Contracts

Year	Jan.	Feb.	Mar.	Apr.	May	June	July	Aug.	Sept.	Oct.	Nov.	Dec.	Total
1999	7,606	7,766	7,556	7,808	4,986	8,404	4,378	12,053	6,660	8,063	9,497	3,932	88,709
2000	14,975	6,760	3,941	7,582	7,402	8,924	2,023	3,973	1,333	2,122	3,254	1,205	63,494
2001	2,428	1,823	1,310	2,062	930	1,965	880	2,021	625	1,263	843	728	16,878
2002	1,251	1,231	896	1,472	785	1,191	1,217	915	1,100	1,654	1,430	1,141	14,283
2003	2,289	2,154	1,826	1,634	1,514	2,106	1,632	1,350	1,712	2,123	2,502	2,314	23,156
2004	2,477	1,695	3,169	2,672	1,209	1,618	792	1,341	759	813	1,630	979	19,154
2005	1,154	861	2,023	1,891	1,027	2,105	1,623	1,931	605	707	1,258	882	16,067
2006	2,231	1,114	1,017	1,836	1,563	1,323	927	1,020	892	461	1,220	708	14,312
2007	1,156	249	1,698	1,648	885	3,164	1,716	927	802	1,837	5,615	276	19,973
2008	1,888	1,454	2,139	2,186	745	1,758	2,162	1,311	1,408	499	2,692	943	19,185

Source: ICE Futures U.S.; formerly New York Board of Trade (NYBOT)

Currencies

A currency rate involves the price of the base currency (e.g., the dollar) quoted in terms of another currency (e.g., the yen), or in terms of a basket of currencies (e.g., the dollar index). The world's major currencies have traded in a floating-rate exchange rate regime ever since the Bretton-Woods international payments system broke down in 1971 when President Nixon broke the dollar's peg to gold. The two key factors affecting a currency's value are central bank monetary policy and the trade balance. An easy monetary policy (low interest rates) is bearish for a currency because the central bank is aggressively pumping new currency reserves into the marketplace and because foreign investors are not attracted to the low interest rate returns available in the country. By contrast, a tight monetary policy (high interest rates) is bullish for a currency because of the tight supply of new currency reserves and attractive interest rate returns for foreign investors.

The other key factor driving currency values is the nation's current account balance. A current account surplus is bullish for a currency due to the net inflow of the currency, while a current account deficit is bearish for a currency due to the net outflow of the currency. Currency values are also affected by economic growth and investment opportunities in the country. A country with a strong economy and lucrative investment opportunities will typically have a strong currency because global companies and investors want to buy into that country's investment opportunities. Futures on major currencies and on cross-currency rates are primarily traded at the Chicago Mercantile Exchange.

Dollar – The U.S. dollar index in early 2008 extended the downmove seen since 2001 and hit a record low of 73.560 in March 2008. The dollar during 2006 and 2007 sold off steadily as the U.S. housing crisis emerged and eventually forced the Federal Reserve into easing monetary policy, thus undercutting the dollar's interest rate differentials. The Fed started cutting interest rates in September 2007 and in the span of just 16 months the Fed slashed the federal funds target rate from 5.25% to the range of zero to 0.25% by December 2008.

However, the downtrend in the dollar halted in March 2008 when Bear Stearns nearly failed and was quickly merged into JPMorgan Chase. The dollar traded sideways through the summer of 2008 and then rallied sharply when Lehman Brothers went bankrupt in September and the global financial crisis erupted in full force. The dollar rallied as global financial institutions rushed for safe-haven into the world's reserve currency. The dollar was also boosted during the crisis as U.S. investors sold their overseas investments and repatriated that cash back into dollars.

The dollar also received a boost in the latter half of 2008 when the U.S. trade deficit narrowed sharply, mainly because of the plunge in crude oil prices, which reduced the dollar value of U.S. oil imports. The U.S. trade deficit moved sideways in the range of $55-62 billion during 2007 and early 2008, but then narrowed sharply to $36 billion in January 2009, the narrowest U.S. trade deficit since 2002. The U.S. trade deficit ex-petroleum actually started narrowing sharply in early 2007 due to an improvement in demand for U.S. exports due to the weak dollar and strong economic growth overseas.

Euro – The euro through 2007 and early 2008 rallied to a record high of $1.6038 per euro in July 2008 due the emerging U.S. housing and banking crisis, which undercut the dollar. However, the euro then fell sharply in late 2008 when the global financial crisis emerged as investors dumped euros and rushed into dollars for safety. The European Central Bank lagged the other major central banks on cutting interest rates during the crisis, thus providing some underlying support for the euro via strong interest rate differentials. However, the market was also worried about the euro because of political conflicts within the euro bloc during the crisis and because of downward pressure on the euro from banking crises in Russia and eastern Europe.

Yen – The yen was generally strong against the dollar during 2007 and 2008. That yen strength was due to the downtrend in the dollar seen in 2007 and early 2008 as the U.S. housing crisis emerged. The yen then rallied sharply when the global financial crisis emerged in full force in September 2008 as traders were forced out of their yen carry trades. As global markets plunged during the global crisis, traders were forced to sell their positions and then repatriate back into yen in order to repay the cheap yen loans that financed the positions in the first place. The yen was also boosted as Japanese financial institutions sold overseas investments and repatriated their remaining portfolio cash into yen. The yen showed strength against the dollar in late 2007 and during 2008 despite the Bank of Japan's extremely easy monetary policy. The Bank of Japan was already targeting its overnight target rate at a very low 0.50% during 2008 and then cut the rate to 0.10% by the end of 2008 in response to the global financial crisis.

U.S. Dollars per British Pound

Year	Jan.	Feb.	Mar.	Apr.	May	June	July	Aug.	Sept.	Oct.	Nov.	Dec.	Average
1999	1.6495	1.6269	1.6213	1.6085	1.6147	1.5957	1.5754	1.6051	1.6237	1.6570	1.6206	1.6131	1.6176
2000	1.6395	1.6007	1.5810	1.5807	1.5084	1.5102	1.5082	1.4885	1.4341	1.4509	1.4252	1.4657	1.5161
2001	1.4767	1.4522	1.4438	1.4350	1.4268	1.4025	1.4149	1.4376	1.4646	1.4520	1.4358	1.4422	1.4403
2002	1.4314	1.4233	1.4233	1.4434	1.4601	1.4849	1.5566	1.5375	1.5562	1.5576	1.5718	1.5882	1.5029
2003	1.6184	1.6077	1.5832	1.5751	1.6230	1.6606	1.6242	1.5942	1.6141	1.6778	1.6899	1.7536	1.6352
2004	1.8223	1.8675	1.8273	1.8050	1.7888	1.8292	1.8433	1.8195	1.7932	1.8069	1.8608	1.9298	1.8328
2005	1.8783	1.8883	1.9034	1.8961	1.8538	1.8179	1.7518	1.7947	1.8078	1.7649	1.7355	1.7454	1.8198
2006	1.7665	1.7478	1.7446	1.7690	1.8693	1.8435	1.8451	1.8934	1.8858	1.8766	1.9124	1.9634	1.8431
2007	1.9585	1.9586	1.9479	1.9874	1.9834	1.9870	2.0344	2.0112	2.0202	2.0453	2.0709	2.0168	2.0018
2008	1.9692	1.9640	2.0012	1.9815	1.9662	1.9675	1.9897	1.8870	1.7997	1.6899	1.5290	1.4869	1.8526

Average.   *Source: FOREX*

Volume of Trading of British Pound Futures in Chicago   In Thousands of Contracts

Year	Jan.	Feb.	Mar.	Apr.	May	June	July	Aug.	Sept.	Oct.	Nov.	Dec.	Total
1999	182.4	151.8	350.2	205.3	285.0	332.1	250.3	178.2	275.9	177.9	163.2	181.5	2,734.0
2000	199.6	179.8	270.9	138.9	133.3	225.8	136.2	155.9	245.1	100.7	100.7	152.5	2,039.3
2001	125.6	126.2	198.7	127.0	166.3	248.9	164.2	183.6	197.1	178.9	161.4	187.4	2,065.4
2002	182.0	168.2	230.4	168.2	174.1	239.8	133.3	138.3	185.3	177.5	160.9	198.0	2,155.9
2003	158.3	161.8	217.4	158.1	164.7	288.6	214.9	163.5	284.5	212.6	206.2	364.5	2,595.2
2004	310.3	291.6	470.3	293.1	282.5	427.8	373.4	367.1	471.4	405.4	348.4	635.2	4,676.5
2005	376.7	410.5	628.7	453.3	555.5	763.5	640.2	735.3	1,034.5	887.8	1,080.6	1,203.1	8,769.8
2006	1,013.7	1,012.0	1,479.2	1,207.6	1,465.1	1,262.1	963.1	1,262.2	1,486.2	1,387.1	1,563.9	1,997.4	16,099.5
2007	1,639.3	1,485.2	2,151.4	1,330.1	1,705.8	2,066.0	1,946.6	1,964.1	1,668.3	1,729.8	1,793.9	1,319.3	20,799.8
2008	1,541.0	1,442.5	1,886.1	1,979.0	1,633.7	2,058.8	1,896.4	1,805.7	2,151.8	1,584.1	1,240.3	1,278.1	20,497.4

Source: International Monetary Market (IMM), division of the Chicago Mercantile Exchange (CME)

Average Open Interest of British Pound Futures in Chicago   In Contracts

Year	Jan.	Feb.	Mar.	Apr.	May	June	July	Aug.	Sept.	Oct.	Nov.	Dec.
1999	51,519	59,705	66,913	64,937	58,744	60,414	65,206	54,373	50,949	65,038	49,468	34,191
2000	37,192	45,329	51,645	41,488	51,965	43,009	30,766	36,320	42,781	30,978	34,627	32,913
2001	28,776	30,555	36,532	34,713	39,836	48,310	33,273	40,935	50,083	38,579	40,461	35,424
2002	26,450	31,023	30,474	39,952	46,178	47,355	38,138	31,320	31,513	29,599	40,901	36,671
2003	36,892	33,066	27,042	25,274	36,171	50,118	41,702	46,979	40,183	55,884	66,660	70,197
2004	61,694	68,173	51,968	43,830	45,843	53,615	68,262	71,503	60,274	66,565	87,487	86,572
2005	67,140	70,872	81,799	80,850	88,397	79,278	75,387	73,199	81,479	79,854	84,884	91,497
2006	83,051	97,226	83,641	83,275	106,555	98,417	91,563	129,334	120,737	106,288	145,026	157,837
2007	147,183	152,892	135,618	130,611	130,861	145,405	157,336	124,948	110,905	118,737	128,761	96,974
2008	87,465	94,154	98,154	109,464	158,836	126,688	100,775	105,857	112,717	110,761	113,147	93,313

Source: International Monetary Market (IMM), division of the Chicago Mercantile Exchange (CME)

CURRENCIES

Canadian Dollars per U.S. Dollar

Year	Jan.	Feb.	Mar.	Apr.	May	June	July	Aug.	Sept.	Oct.	Nov.	Dec.	Average
1999	1.5189	1.4971	1.5174	1.4868	1.4614	1.4691	1.4877	1.4921	1.4772	1.4767	1.4671	1.4713	1.4852
2000	1.4480	1.4499	1.4600	1.4681	1.4944	1.4762	1.4778	1.4819	1.4841	1.5119	1.5425	1.5219	1.4847
2001	1.5021	1.5227	1.5579	1.5581	1.5403	1.5238	1.5294	1.5384	1.5665	1.5708	1.5934	1.5793	1.5486
2002	1.5996	1.5961	1.5872	1.5814	1.5491	1.5312	1.5447	1.5685	1.5747	1.5783	1.5715	1.5588	1.5701
2003	1.5395	1.5119	1.4752	1.4567	1.3819	1.3520	1.3801	1.3948	1.3638	1.3226	1.3128	1.3121	1.4003
2004	1.2967	1.3292	1.3282	1.3410	1.3774	1.3582	1.3225	1.3127	1.2880	1.2476	1.1958	1.2177	1.3013
2005	1.2248	1.2386	1.2157	1.2368	1.2553	1.2402	1.2239	1.2048	1.1781	1.1777	1.1813	1.1619	1.2116
2006	1.1573	1.1488	1.1571	1.1440	1.1094	1.1139	1.1287	1.1191	1.1161	1.1281	1.1365	1.1531	1.1343
2007	1.1757	1.1708	1.1687	1.1351	1.0948	1.0655	1.0512	1.0585	1.0260	0.9752	0.9680	1.0021	1.0743
2008	1.0114	1.0001	1.0031	1.0130	0.9999	1.0170	1.0133	1.0539	1.0582	1.1797	1.2204	1.2337	1.0670

Average.　　*Source: FOREX*

Volume of Trading of Canadian Dollar Futures in Chicago　In Thousands of Contracts

Year	Jan.	Feb.	Mar.	Apr.	May	June	July	Aug.	Sept.	Oct.	Nov.	Dec.	Total
1999	171.0	173.0	279.9	203.4	164.4	309.7	216.1	186.0	263.4	167.7	165.6	277.2	2,577.5
2000	184.2	182.5	280.9	155.0	162.8	295.5	166.0	188.5	241.2	161.6	150.3	265.8	2,434.1
2001	194.7	201.1	317.9	188.2	228.4	351.0	221.6	235.9	265.1	214.1	218.1	287.3	2,923.3
2002	222.9	191.5	338.3	249.6	222.2	358.7	278.8	204.2	279.1	245.3	207.4	324.4	3,122.3
2003	270.8	256.7	475.5	289.2	353.1	494.2	331.3	266.2	393.3	285.7	294.4	509.3	4,219.6
2004	380.7	328.0	516.3	380.3	337.1	504.0	366.5	419.4	640.8	512.0	499.5	726.8	5,611.3
2005	548.6	483.0	678.0	592.9	555.2	761.5	562.2	566.3	914.2	671.3	736.0	861.0	7,930.2
2006	695.1	648.6	1,040.9	654.9	816.6	1,043.4	658.3	811.0	1,073.7	805.8	960.8	1,070.4	10,279.6
2007	795.9	724.5	1,089.4	749.9	949.9	1,348.4	1,101.2	1,015.5	1,226.6	1,054.0	1,238.3	931.2	12,224.8
2008	960.2	957.8	1,202.2	948.1	958.2	1,151.9	932.0	966.4	1,240.9	812.9	601.8	645.8	11,378.0

Source: International Monetary Market (IMM), division of the Chicago Mercantile Exchange (CME)

Average Open Interest of Canadian Dollar Futures in Chicago　In Contracts

Year	Jan.	Feb.	Mar.	Apr.	May	June	July	Aug.	Sept.	Oct.	Nov.	Dec.
1999	50,061	71,819	63,782	73,773	84,885	71,923	65,877	71,458	61,994	58,749	59,941	51,967
2000	66,374	64,528	58,621	60,389	76,444	69,033	67,198	65,370	65,779	81,995	77,746	65,452
2001	54,369	58,660	72,051	64,550	65,407	62,489	54,742	54,580	73,647	71,610	82,083	67,578
2002	68,927	72,132	70,484	68,120	81,574	86,250	74,347	63,116	63,605	57,031	60,648	71,852
2003	82,870	105,051	107,507	97,515	96,689	85,665	68,741	63,518	70,261	79,754	82,366	74,271
2004	74,577	64,032	61,981	72,750	84,356	68,458	73,164	83,483	97,486	112,648	110,035	81,976
2005	74,703	84,753	93,986	77,680	95,229	79,464	86,451	101,128	120,542	108,095	106,773	122,584
2006	103,427	118,978	103,066	92,541	114,587	107,605	89,443	91,591	112,788	99,209	121,729	146,474
2007	151,511	144,025	140,775	119,430	163,570	180,961	147,966	132,910	136,952	145,923	120,912	99,261
2008	86,448	99,650	109,567	103,486	115,665	103,145	95,618	120,175	116,163	103,135	94,297	66,313

Source: International Monetary Market (IMM), division of the Chicago Mercantile Exchange (CME)

Euro FX Futures - International Monetary Market
(weekly close) as of January 02, 2009

USD per EUR

Euro[1] per U.S. Dollar

Year	Jan.	Feb.	Mar.	Apr.	May	June	July	Aug.	Sept.	Oct.	Nov.	Dec.	Average
1999	1.1584	1.1202	1.0882	1.0700	1.0622	1.0385	1.0366	1.0603	1.0501	1.0705	1.0327	1.0117	1.0666
2000	1.0135	.9842	.9644	.9450	.9080	.9496	.9394	.9042	.8706	.8533	.8554	.9004	.9240
2001	.9380	.9208	.9085	.8931	.8747	.8536	.8616	.9023	.9123	.9062	.8882	.8913	.8959
2002	.8828	.8706	.8767	.8866	.9179	.9567	.9924	.9781	.9810	.9818	1.0020	1.0210	.9456
2003	1.0636	1.0778	1.0795	1.0875	1.1580	1.1670	1.1374	1.1154	1.1260	1.1701	1.1714	1.2314	1.1321
2004	1.2604	1.2633	1.2263	1.1999	1.2013	1.2147	1.2265	1.2192	1.2226	1.2504	1.3001	1.3415	1.2439
2005	1.3110	1.3020	1.3178	1.2940	1.2685	1.2156	1.2049	1.2299	1.2246	1.2030	1.1796	1.1861	1.2448
2006	1.2121	1.1940	1.2033	1.2282	1.2773	1.2665	1.2693	1.2811	1.2734	1.2623	1.2893	1.3200	1.2564
2007	1.2989	1.3087	1.3249	1.3512	1.3511	1.3422	1.3720	1.3620	1.3918	1.4234	1.4681	1.4561	1.3709
2008	1.4722	1.4759	1.5527	1.5760	1.5560	1.5569	1.5765	1.4954	1.4367	1.3286	1.2723	1.3518	1.4709

Average.   [1] Data through December 1998 are theoretical based on DEM * 1.95583.   Source: FOREX

Volume of Trading of Euro FX Futures in Chicago   In Thousands of Contracts

Year	Jan.	Feb.	Mar.	Apr.	May	June	July	Aug.	Sept.	Oct.	Nov.	Dec.	Total
1999	69.0	96.6	288.4	157.6	183.7	276.4	259.7	258.1	422.8	302.5	303.1	383.0	3,000.8
2000	404.9	335.0	452.4	289.4	318.3	382.2	234.9	303.3	486.3	287.7	297.0	466.7	4,258.2
2001	453.5	373.2	556.4	368.3	407.7	585.3	425.1	494.7	533.9	533.6	545.0	781.1	6,057.8
2002	567.8	582.3	783.3	650.2	611.4	917.7	821.6	525.5	675.3	525.2	426.7	625.4	7,712.3
2003	610.6	749.2	977.9	785.5	902.7	1,103.8	866.2	824.5	1,112.4	1,069.6	958.9	1,232.6	11,193.9
2004	1,487.3	1,469.2	1,837.7	1,326.7	1,328.9	1,682.2	1,491.2	1,518.5	1,798.7	1,786.0	2,138.5	2,591.9	20,456.7
2005	2,646.0	2,266.4	2,772.9	2,992.0	2,771.6	3,656.1	2,732.6	2,765.1	3,206.6	2,613.6	3,164.2	2,943.6	34,530.7
2006	2,956.0	2,563.9	3,411.2	2,984.4	4,496.3	3,765.7	2,789.0	3,229.5	3,364.0	3,123.5	3,790.4	4,316.6	40,790.4
2007	3,701.9	3,032.1	4,427.3	2,979.1	3,337.4	3,877.6	3,560.5	4,074.2	3,286.6	3,831.5	3,793.1	3,161.6	43,063.1
2008	3,669.9	3,327.5	4,709.2	4,596.3	4,537.8	5,312.0	4,661.3	5,009.7	6,216.8	4,556.3	3,607.9	3,447.8	53,652.6

Source: International Monetary Market (IMM), division of the Chicago Mercantile Exchange (CME)

Average Open Interest of Euro FX Futures in Chicago   In Contracts

Year	Jan.	Feb.	Mar.	Apr.	May	June	July	Aug.	Sept.	Oct.	Nov.	Dec.
1999	8,261	30,546	37,837	37,881	46,446	50,615	46,777	55,858	49,352	57,380	58,846	65,346
2000	63,124	68,413	61,180	59,110	67,644	63,361	57,723	69,561	77,617	73,314	79,577	92,730
2001	89,049	91,130	90,127	78,762	89,390	94,160	84,637	104,437	112,797	108,445	108,999	104,323
2002	100,258	108,955	113,075	112,413	136,660	135,364	112,462	101,992	99,365	85,462	103,156	108,602
2003	105,762	106,905	100,759	85,604	108,619	111,651	96,338	98,671	95,553	102,568	113,601	131,560
2004	125,879	133,690	115,712	112,361	138,193	120,281	140,430	160,315	121,180	136,959	202,074	175,374
2005	135,748	152,110	140,879	130,131	154,751	163,584	142,826	148,309	149,184	142,879	171,035	160,065
2006	133,092	150,085	152,674	166,920	196,057	177,700	155,865	173,151	155,567	152,410	182,079	214,241
2007	173,989	196,963	205,366	217,899	222,019	204,945	218,401	221,095	221,268	207,644	221,736	204,536
2008	179,767	206,661	200,084	178,993	211,068	193,878	170,675	153,423	163,948	180,955	169,315	144,926

Source: International Monetary Market (IMM), division of the Chicago Mercantile Exchange (CME)

CURRENCIES

Japanese Yen Futures - International Monetary Market
(weekly close) as of January 02, 2009
USD per JPY

Japanese Yen per U.S. Dollar

Year	Jan.	Feb.	Mar.	Apr.	May	June	July	Aug.	Sept.	Oct.	Nov.	Dec.	Average
1999	113.23	116.62	119.49	119.73	121.88	120.69	119.38	113.16	107.00	105.94	104.62	102.64	113.70
2000	105.29	109.49	106.34	105.65	108.19	106.15	108.03	108.06	106.79	108.39	108.94	112.18	107.79
2001	116.83	116.17	121.44	123.64	121.66	122.38	124.45	121.29	118.64	121.35	122.39	127.72	121.50
2002	132.77	133.50	131.11	130.75	126.29	123.25	118.02	119.04	120.88	123.92	121.50	121.83	125.24
2003	118.76	119.39	118.76	119.81	117.37	118.31	118.64	118.61	114.94	109.51	109.17	107.70	115.91
2004	106.38	106.70	108.51	107.61	112.05	109.44	109.46	110.24	110.10	108.81	104.71	103.79	108.15
2005	103.29	104.98	105.35	107.19	106.71	108.75	111.92	110.62	111.19	114.84	118.42	118.39	110.14
2006	115.53	117.92	117.31	116.97	111.77	114.65	115.69	115.95	117.14	118.61	117.28	117.43	116.35
2007	120.45	120.40	117.33	118.96	120.82	122.65	121.47	116.78	115.08	115.92	110.92	112.37	117.76
2008	107.71	107.11	100.80	102.69	104.33	106.88	106.87	109.41	106.62	100.15	96.80	91.13	103.37

Average.   *Source: FOREX*

Volume of Trading of Japanese Yen Futures in Chicago   In Thousands of Contracts

Year	Jan.	Feb.	Mar.	Apr.	May	June	July	Aug.	Sept.	Oct.	Nov.	Dec.	Total
1999	418.1	524.6	672.7	400.4	473.4	687.1	476.9	422.3	679.1	310.5	390.5	469.1	5,924.8
2000	433.9	299.1	569.7	250.5	265.8	427.4	248.8	285.9	367.1	213.9	222.7	405.2	3,990.0
2001	258.6	223.7	598.4	295.4	351.2	459.4	307.4	369.4	518.6	286.2	350.1	595.9	4,614.1
2002	415.7	417.5	630.8	391.7	318.5	461.7	301.2	234.2	499.2	349.5	255.4	535.8	4,811.1
2003	423.9	388.3	634.4	453.4	495.6	621.0	518.8	427.0	731.0	396.6	353.4	641.8	6,085.2
2004	410.1	484.9	741.8	516.4	415.5	685.8	487.5	490.7	807.6	629.6	650.5	1,074.9	7,395.3
2005	789.9	718.8	1,045.2	915.4	876.2	1,263.0	946.9	1,012.4	1,285.4	963.7	1,001.0	1,653.9	12,471.7
2006	1,221.1	1,128.7	1,950.5	1,385.9	1,890.9	1,905.3	1,317.9	1,395.9	1,965.8	1,525.1	1,852.8	2,137.5	19,677.4
2007	1,602.2	2,006.6	3,286.7	1,771.1	1,802.4	2,777.8	3,083.8	3,954.2	2,860.7	2,493.1	3,125.2	2,056.6	30,820.4
2008	3,013.2	2,558.7	3,384.5	2,632.6	2,502.9	3,193.9	2,898.0	2,428.9	3,446.2	3,117.8	1,937.5	1,730.2	32,844.4

Source: International Monetary Market (IMM), division of the Chicago Mercantile Exchange (CME)

Average Open Interest of Japanese Yen Futures in Chicago   In Contracts

Year	Jan.	Feb.	Mar.	Apr.	May	June	July	Aug.	Sept.	Oct.	Nov.	Dec.
1999	78,767	81,859	96,271	87,829	118,819	120,681	118,329	136,826	115,884	82,657	87,869	87,595
2000	93,785	125,318	95,034	75,631	80,840	68,359	60,966	79,195	64,845	64,648	68,719	100,713
2001	89,680	90,652	109,536	96,244	89,377	82,838	93,430	107,588	102,710	75,096	97,368	137,756
2002	129,917	123,735	95,535	72,358	88,905	88,324	77,168	71,683	79,980	80,104	74,584	99,643
2003	116,574	107,929	101,809	81,168	107,090	102,507	107,450	125,884	149,978	152,368	138,799	147,255
2004	156,929	156,416	120,848	117,483	108,078	105,505	106,280	110,234	93,780	127,644	181,093	172,526
2005	164,708	155,593	132,268	134,802	172,574	164,580	161,763	170,290	159,227	186,631	202,939	191,591
2006	168,309	198,855	203,450	201,459	210,578	197,160	191,480	218,893	239,426	258,509	242,216	265,490
2007	312,252	338,933	246,715	234,352	303,537	347,031	302,278	272,937	227,242	225,047	202,361	195,324
2008	197,886	233,558	224,932	176,577	171,298	171,516	185,657	207,309	168,119	142,938	128,891	130,118

Source: International Monetary Market (IMM), division of the Chicago Mercantile Exchange (CME)

Swiss Franc Futures - International Monetary Market
(weekly close) as of January 02, 2009
USD per CHF

Swiss Francs per U.S. Dollar

Year	Jan.	Feb.	Mar.	Apr.	May	June	July	Aug.	Sept.	Oct.	Nov.	Dec.	Average
1999	1.3856	1.4273	1.4656	1.4972	1.5078	1.5359	1.5472	1.5092	1.5251	1.4891	1.5541	1.5827	1.5022
2000	1.5888	1.6326	1.6624	1.6638	1.7151	1.6422	1.6503	1.7146	1.7564	1.7727	1.7772	1.6778	1.6878
2001	1.6296	1.6681	1.6903	1.7115	1.7525	1.7842	1.7564	1.6791	1.6338	1.6337	1.6501	1.6569	1.6872
2002	1.6710	1.6972	1.6741	1.6527	1.5868	1.5389	1.4731	1.4968	1.4929	1.4922	1.4647	1.4360	1.5564
2003	1.3748	1.3609	1.3617	1.3770	1.3091	1.3196	1.3597	1.3813	1.3741	1.3234	1.3314	1.2627	1.3446
2004	1.2425	1.2458	1.2773	1.2954	1.2818	1.2501	1.2458	1.2625	1.2624	1.2338	1.1702	1.1455	1.2428
2005	1.1802	1.1906	1.1763	1.1955	1.2183	1.2663	1.2935	1.2626	1.2657	1.2872	1.3100	1.3056	1.2460
2006	1.2781	1.3056	1.3044	1.2822	1.2185	1.2319	1.2362	1.2319	1.2440	1.2597	1.2351	1.2102	1.2532
2007	1.2438	1.2385	1.2179	1.2128	1.2217	1.2329	1.2076	1.2034	1.1847	1.1743	1.1229	1.1397	1.2000
2008	1.1001	1.0894	1.0116	1.0141	1.0443	1.0363	1.0278	1.0843	1.1091	1.1429	1.1923	1.1393	1.0826

Average.   Source: FOREX

Volume of Trading of Swiss Franc Futures in Chicago   In Thousands of Contracts

Year	Jan.	Feb.	Mar.	Apr.	May	June	July	Aug.	Sept.	Oct.	Nov.	Dec.	Total
1999	294.6	262.1	417.0	284.0	323.3	384.7	351.1	311.8	482.4	407.6	287.2	304.5	4,110.3
2000	326.2	313.1	385.3	252.1	247.7	301.2	214.6	216.6	344.5	176.2	185.4	267.3	3,230.2
2001	193.5	203.0	280.3	168.7	191.6	326.0	257.6	229.4	261.8	227.5	238.2	297.3	2,874.8
2002	195.3	183.2	281.3	211.5	208.1	297.0	187.2	218.5	323.1	237.6	207.8	271.6	2,822.1
2003	236.1	289.9	412.7	256.9	277.8	384.9	315.0	252.1	349.9	237.2	283.8	300.5	3,596.7
2004	216.1	230.1	359.6	260.0	255.7	370.9	331.4	313.7	404.5	428.3	329.0	568.4	4,067.8
2005	444.3	389.1	575.5	605.0	521.4	753.4	546.4	596.4	888.8	765.9	797.1	901.2	7,784.5
2006	803.5	745.9	1,129.0	837.5	1,011.3	993.3	771.2	1,014.8	1,046.8	919.6	1,078.1	1,118.9	11,470.0
2007	994.4	998.5	1,418.5	959.4	1,100.0	1,507.0	1,660.0	1,588.2	1,113.7	1,129.8	1,067.3	941.8	14,478.7
2008	1,090.5	1,082.4	1,311.8	1,350.7	1,362.8	1,789.1	1,650.0	1,330.3	1,578.9	1,042.4	574.0	651.3	14,814.2

Source: International Monetary Market (IMM), division of the Chicago Mercantile Exchange (CME)

Average Open Interest of Swiss Franc Futures in Chicago   In Contracts

Year	Jan.	Feb.	Mar.	Apr.	May	June	July	Aug.	Sept.	Oct.	Nov.	Dec.
1999	39,434	58,279	66,250	66,530	73,322	75,322	66,603	71,060	60,214	65,020	67,936	64,507
2000	55,660	69,983	57,703	41,732	46,159	41,727	36,894	50,595	57,439	47,313	48,870	55,982
2001	50,121	44,405	46,470	41,641	53,265	60,943	53,687	60,986	61,689	48,962	53,445	46,771
2002	35,116	44,388	45,434	38,248	55,039	54,573	42,060	38,102	37,675	54,259	62,584	60,475
2003	56,268	57,099	50,008	37,451	53,642	49,688	41,489	50,677	52,641	54,259	62,584	60,475
2004	45,259	42,950	41,250	38,563	38,024	48,654	51,116	40,256	33,539	47,200	74,988	70,330
2005	51,858	56,240	50,827	41,322	55,995	78,794	72,596	67,489	66,009	75,088	91,072	98,443
2006	80,904	107,509	101,445	82,280	98,416	89,254	67,127	69,406	83,545	97,034	89,039	74,522
2007	83,176	103,073	70,627	66,246	89,737	121,557	108,394	118,597	100,948	73,433	81,366	73,025
2008	67,993	67,786	71,972	60,528	65,029	58,511	56,337	61,521	53,448	39,448	42,315	31,420

Source: International Monetary Market (IMM), division of the Chicago Mercantile Exchange (CME)

CURRENCIES

United States Merchandise Trade Balance[1]   In Millions of Dollars

Year	Jan.	Feb.	Mar.	Apr.	May	June	July	Aug.	Sept.	Oct.	Nov.	Dec.	Total
1999	-23,409	-25,233	-25,741	-25,851	-27,753	-30,381	-31,227	-30,518	-30,573	-31,576	-32,401	-32,255	-345,434
2000	-34,116	-34,708	-37,215	-36,934	-36,910	-37,827	-38,091	-36,839	-39,682	-40,205	-38,955	-39,360	-452,423
2001	-39,161	-34,648	-38,815	-37,270	-34,690	-35,760	-35,633	-34,458	-35,660	-35,034	-34,095	-31,534	-427,215
2002	-33,407	-31,405	-31,865	-39,875	-39,229	-37,590	-46,642	-44,082	-43,241	-45,583	-44,076	-45,303	-482,298
2003	-43,619	-38,301	-43,538	-46,145	-43,275	-43,882	-51,798	-45,166	-49,478	-51,812	-42,937	-47,345	-547,296
2004	-46,104	-42,621	-50,545	-52,314	-49,848	-60,221	-60,068	-60,752	-57,766	-62,556	-66,320	-56,294	-665,409
2005	-57,625	-54,860	-56,700	-60,386	-61,475	-64,686	-66,999	-70,417	-73,183	-77,869	-72,663	-65,876	-782,739
2006	-71,051	-58,418	-63,754	-65,314	-73,033	-71,405	-79,477	-80,243	-71,951	-65,492	-66,256	-68,590	-834,984
2007	-64,906	-65,782	-70,712	-68,754	-68,472	-68,661	-67,794	-66,672	-66,738	-67,713	-71,697	-69,509	-817,410
2008[2]	-70,664	-73,000	-68,920	-73,467	-72,628	-71,785	-74,633	-71,575	-70,054	-69,566	-53,292	-51,570	-821,154

[1] Not seasonally adjusted.   [2] Preliminary.   *Source: Bureau of Economic Analysis, U.S. Department of Commerce (BEA)*

Index of Real Trade-Weighted Dollar Exchange Rates for Total Agriculture[3]   (2000 = 100)

Year		Jan.	Feb.	Mar.	Apr.	May	June	July	Aug.	Sept.	Oct.	Nov.	Dec.
2002	U.S. Markets	111.5	112.0	111.6	111.3	110.2	109.6	108.7	109.7	110.5	111.4	110.1	109.4
	U.S. Competitors	125.1	127.6	127.2	126.5	124.5	122.3	120.5	122.4	122.5	123.2	120.5	118.5
2003	U.S. Markets	108.9	109.9	109.8	108.5	105.3	105.5	106.4	107.2	106.2	104.4	103.7	102.9
	U.S. Competitors	115.1	114.6	114.3	112.2	107.1	106.9	108.8	110.5	109.3	106.1	105.4	102.4
2004	U.S. Markets	101.3	102.0	102.9	103.5	105.9	104.9	103.8	103.5	103.6	102.3	99.7	98.4
	U.S. Competitors	100.2	100.5	102.7	103.9	105.3	104.8	103.4	103.6	103.0	101.2	98.2	95.7
2005	U.S. Markets	98.7	99.0	98.8	100.1	99.6	100.1	100.6	99.9	100.6	101.6	101.3	100.1
	U.S. Competitors	96.8	97.0	96.6	97.9	98.7	101.0	102.0	100.6	101.3	102.4	102.6	101.7
2006	U.S. Markets	99.2	99.3	99.9	100.0	98.7	100.1	100.1	99.2	98.9	98.6	97.7	97.0
	U.S. Competitors	100.7	101.1	101.1	100.1	97.8	99.2	99.1	98.0	97.8	97.6	95.8	93.9
2007	U.S. Markets	98.3	98.4	98.5	97.8	96.9	97.0	95.8	95.6	94.3	92.3	91.4	91.7
	U.S. Competitors	95.0	94.7	94.3	92.7	91.6	92.6	90.9	91.6	90.2	87.6	86.0	86.2
2008[1]	U.S. Markets	91.3	90.3	89.0	88.9	89.4	89.9	89.4	90.5	92.2	97.1	97.6	95.5
	U.S. Competitors	85.8	85.0	82.5	81.9	82.5	82.8	82.0	84.7	88.3	94.8	97.3	93.4
2009[2]	U.S. Markets	95.1	96.9	99.0	99.3	98.9	97.7	96.6	95.7	95.1	94.2	92.7	91.0
	U.S. Competitors	93.3	95.3	96.4	96.8	96.0	94.0	92.1	90.8	89.9	88.9	87.3	85.5

[1] Not seasonally adjusted.   [2] Preliminary.   *Source: Bureau of Economic Analysis, U.S. Department of Commerce (BEA)*

United States Balance on Current Account[1]   In Millions of Dollars

Year	First Quarter	Second Quarter	Third Quarter	Fourth Quarter	Annual
1999	-53,707	-72,549	-90,734	-84,640	-301,630
2000	-87,401	-100,735	-117,474	-111,816	-417,426
2001	-95,797	-98,218	-100,881	-89,803	-384,699
2002	-91,548	-116,530	-128,386	-124,811	-461,275
2003	-122,951	-131,513	-141,850	-127,086	-523,400
2004	-123,272	-156,955	-166,241	-178,525	-624,993
2005	-157,567	-180,310	-182,422	-208,694	-728,993
2006	-178,298	-201,502	-224,820	-183,497	-788,117
2007	-177,982	-193,372	-186,525	-173,336	-731,215
2008[2]	-155,302	-182,722	-200,782	-134,459	-673,265

[1] Not seasonally adjusted.   [2] Estimate.   *Source: Bureau of Economic Analysis, U.S. Department of Commerce (BEA)*

Merchandise Trade and Current Account Balances[1]   In Billions of Dollars

	Merchanise Trade Balance					Current Account Balance				
Year	Canada	Germany	Japan	Switzerland	United Kingdom	Canada	Germany	Japan	Switzerland	United Kingdom
2000	41.6	7.0	68.0	14.6	-27.2	19.7	-33.6	118.7	30.1	-38.9
2001	41.2	38.3	26.1	12.6	-34.6	16.3	.5	88.4	19.7	-30.4
2002	32.4	93.3	51.2	18.4	-42.2	12.6	41.2	112.3	23.6	-27.9
2003	32.5	97.9	69.3	21.4	-42.7	10.6	45.5	136.4	42.0	-30.0
2004	42.7	138.6	89.0	25.1	-60.0	22.9	125.8	170.9	46.9	-46.1
2005	42.4	148.3	63.3	24.2	-77.5	22.1	144.9	166.6	51.0	-58.9
2006	31.4	165.8	54.5	29.9	-79.8	17.8	178.2	172.0	56.4	-83.3
2007	27.2	235.8	73.3	39.3	-95.1	12.3	255.3	211.8	57.1	-105.0
2008[2]	21.6	225.3	43.4	53.2	-80.0	7.6	233.7	187.2	39.5	-53.5
2009[3]	-10.4	191.6	94.3	55.0	-62.3	-20.6	193.7	230.9	44.3	-34.9

[1] Not seasonally adjusted.   [2] Estimate.   [3] Projection.   *Source: Organization for Economic Cooperation and Development (OECD)*

Euro / Swiss Franc (weekly close) as of January 02, 2009   EUR per CHF

Euro / British Pound (weekly close) as of January 02, 2009   EUR per GBP

Japanese Yen / British Pound (weekly close) as of January 02, 2009   JPY per GBP

Euro / Japanese Yen (weekly close) as of January 02, 2009   JPY per EUR

Diamonds

The diamond, which is the mineral form of carbon, is the hardest, strongest natural material known on earth. The name *diamond* is derived from *adamas*, the ancient Greek term meaning "invincible." Diamonds form deep within the Earth's crust and are typically billions of years old. Diamonds have also have been found in and near meteorites and their craters. Diamonds are considered precious gemstones but lower grade diamonds are used for industrial applications such as drilling, cutting, grinding and polishing.

Supply – World production of natural gem diamonds in 2006 (latest data available) fell by -0.5% yr/yr to 91.300 million carats, down from the 2005 record high of 91.800

million carats (one carat equals 1/5 gram or 200 milligrams). The world's largest producers of natural gem diamonds are Botswana with 26.3% of world production in 2006, Russia a close second with 25.6%, Australia with 8%, South Africa with 7%, and the Congo with 6%. World production of natural industrial diamonds in 2007 was down -3.6% yr/yr to 77.000 million carats. World production of synthetic diamonds was up +0.5% yr/yr to 566.000 million carats. The main producer of synthetic diamonds was the U.S. with 46% of world production.

Trade – The U.S. in 2008 relied on net imports for 92% of its consumption of natural diamonds.

World Production of Natural Gem Diamonds   In Thousands of Carats

Year	Angola	Australia	Botswana	Brazil	Central African Republic	China	Dem Rep. of Congo[3]	Ghana	Namibia	Russia	Suerra Leone	South Africa	World Total
2001	4,643	14,397	19,812	700	340	100	3,638	936	1,487	17,500	102	4,465	72,900
2002	4,520	15,136	21,297	500	312	100	4,223	770	1,562	17,400	162	4,351	76,400
2003	5,130	13,981	22,800	400	250	100	5,381	724	1,481	20,000	233	5,144	87,800
2004	5,490	6,058	23,300	300	263	100	6,180	725	2,004	21,400	318	5,800	86,200
2005[1]	6,300	8,577	23,900	300	285	100	6,100	850	1,902	23,000	395	6,400	91,800
2006[2]	7,000	7,305	24,000	300	315	100	5,600	780	2,200	23,400	360	6,240	91,300

[1] Preliminary.   [2] Estimate.   [3] Formerly Zaire.   *Source: U.S. Geological Survey (USGS)*

World Production of Natural Industrial Diamonds[4]   In Thousands of Carats

Year	Angola	Australia	Botswana	Brazil	Central African Republic	China	Ghana	Russia	Leone	South Africa	Vene-zuela	Dem. Rep of Congo[3]	World Total
2001	516	11,779	6,604	600	113	950	14,560	234	11,700	120	6,698	28	54,300
2002	502	18,500	7,100	600	104	955	17,456	193	11,600	190	6,526	61	64,200
2003	570	17,087	7,600	600	83	955	21,600	180	13,000	274	7,540	24	69,900
2004	610	18,172	7,800	600	88	960	24,700	180	14,200	374	8,500	60	76,700
2005[1]	700	25,730	8,000	600	95	960	24,200	213	15,000	374	8,500	60	85,700
2006[2]	800	21,915	8,000	600	105	965	22,400	190	15,000	252	9,130	70	79,900

[1] Preliminary.   [2] Estimate.   [3] Formerly Zaire.   *Source: U.S. Geological Survey (USGS)*

World Production of Synthetic Diamonds   In Thousands of Carats

Year	Belarus	China	Czech Republic	France	Greece	Ireland	Japan	Russia	South Africa	Sweden	Ukraine	United States	World Total
2001	25,000	17,000	----	3,000	----	60,000	33,000	80,000	60,000	20,000	8,000	202,000	508,000
2002	25,000	17,000	5	3,000	----	60,000	34,000	80,000	60,000	20,000	8,000	222,000	529,000
2003	25,000	17,000	5	3,000	----	60,000	34,000	80,000	60,000	20,000	8,000	236,000	543,000
2004	25,000	17,000	5	3,000	----	60,000	34,000	80,000	60,000	20,000	8,000	252,000	559,000
2005[1]	25,000	17,000	5	3,000	----	60,000	34,000	80,000	60,000	20,000	8,000	256,000	563,000
2006[2]	25,000	18,000	5	3,000	----	60,000	34,000	80,000	60,000	20,000	8,000	258,000	566,000

[1] Preliminary.   [2] Estimate.   *Source: U.S. Geological Survey (USGS)*

Salient Statistics of Industrial Diamonds in the United States   In Millions of Carats

	Bort, Grit & Powder & Dust Natural and Synthetic								Stones (Natural)					Net
	--- Production ---													
Year	Manu-factured Diamond	Secon-dary	Imports for Con-sumption	Exports & Reexports	In Manu-factured Products	Gov't Sales	Apparent Con-sumption	Price Value of Imports $/Carat	Secondary Pro-duction	Imports for Con-sumption	Exports & Reexports	Gov't Sales	Apparent Con-sumption	Price Value of Imports $/Carat	Net Import Reliance Imports % of Con-sumption
2003	236.0	4.7	250.0	74.0	----	----	417.0	.26	[3]	1.8	[3]	.4	2.1	3.09	91
2004	252.0	4.6	240.0	86.0	----	----	411.0	.25	[3]	1.8	.5	.4	2.1	7.77	80
2005	256.0	4.6	284.0	92.0	----	----	453.0	.27	[3]	2.1	[3]	----	2.2	13.91	77
2006	258.0	34.2	371.0	90.0	----	----	573.0	.22	[3]	2.2	1.6	.1	2.8	12.61	80
2007[1]	260.0	34.4	411.0	107.0	----	----	598.0	.19	[3]	3.1	----	[3]	3.5	11.54	89
2008[2]	261.0	34.4	493.0	122.0	----	----	666.0	.12	----		----	----	4.6	10.41	92

[1] Preliminary.   [2] Estimate.   [3] Less than 1/2 unit.   *Source: U.S. Geological Survey (USGS)*

Eggs

Eggs are a low-priced protein source and are consumed worldwide. Each commercial chicken lays between 265-280 eggs per year. In the United States, the grade and size of eggs are regulated under the federal Egg Products Inspection Act (1970). The grades of eggs are AA, A, and B, and must have sound, whole shells and must be clean. The difference among the grades of eggs is internal and mostly reflects the freshness of the egg. Table eggs vary in color and can be determined by the color of the chicken's earlobe-
-white earlobes lay white eggs, reddish-brown earlobes lay brown eggs, etc. In the U.S., egg size is determined by the weight of a dozen eggs, not individual eggs, and range from Peewee to Jumbo. Store-bought eggs in the shell stay fresh for 3 to 5 weeks in a home refrigerator, according to the USDA.

Eggs are primarily used as a source of food, although eggs are also widely used for medical purposes. Fertile eggs, as a source of purified proteins, are used to produce many vaccines. Flu vaccines are produced by growing single strains of the flu virus in eggs, which are then extracted to make the vaccine. Eggs are also used in biotechnology to create new drugs. The hen's genetic make-up can be altered so the whites of the eggs are rich in tailored proteins that form the basis of medicines to fight cancer and other diseases. The U.S. biotech company Viragen and the Roslin Institute in Edinburgh have produced eggs with 100 mg or more of the easily-extracted proteins used in new drugs to treat various illnesses including ovarian and breast cancers.

Prices – The average monthly price of all eggs received by farmers in the U.S. in 2008 rose by +15.9% yr/yr to 108.2 cents per dozen, which was a record high.

Supply – World egg production in 2007, the latest reporting year, was 1,183.0 billion eggs. The world's largest egg producers at that time were China with 44% of world production, the U.S. with 8%, Japan with 4%, Mexico with 4%, Russia with 3%, and Brazil with 3%. U.S. egg production in 2008 fell -0.36% to 83.512 billion eggs, down from the 2006 record high of 90.895. The average number of hens and pullets on U.S. farms in 2008 fell by -2.0% yr/yr to 339.572 million, down from the 2006 record high of 347.880 million.

Demand – U.S. consumption of eggs in 2007 fell -2.0% yr/yr to 6.297 billion dozen eggs. That was down from the 2006 record high of 6.428 billion dozen, but still up about 20% from ten years earlier, reflecting sharply higher egg consumption due to the popularity of a low-carbohydrate diet since eggs are high in protein. U.S. per capita egg consumption in 2008 fell 0.7% yr/yr to 248.3 eggs per year per person. Per capita egg consumption was at a high of 277.2 eggs in 1970, then fell sharply in the 1990s to a low of 174.9 in 1995, and then began rebounding in 1997 to current levels of about 250 eggs per year.

Trade – U.S. imports of eggs in 2008 rose +13.2% yr/yr to a 19-year high of 15.4 million dozen eggs. U.S. exports of eggs in 2008 fell by -17.0% yr/yr to 207.8 million dozen eggs, well below the record export level of 253.1 million dozen eggs in 1996.

World Production of Eggs   In Millions of Eggs

Year	Brazil	China	France	Germany	Italy	Japan	Mexico	Russia	Spain	Ukraine	United Kingdom	United States	World Total
1999	29,340	370,201	17,550	14,204	12,909	42,324	32,696	32,971	10,170	8,578	10,102	82,944	937,377
2000	30,189	388,659	17,317	14,400	12,252	42,257	35,759	33,911	11,742	8,675	9,804	84,402	974,162
2001	30,783	404,594	16,940	14,167	12,830	41,985	37,843	35,002	11,928	9,553	10,332	85,884	1,005,729
2002	30,951	425,759	16,480	14,262	12,855	42,157	38,012	36,106	13,113	11,159	10,272	87,216	1,041,789
2003	31,423	450,244	16,598	12,588	12,838	42,173	37,451	36,296	13,722	11,380	10,116	87,473	1,068,867
2004	32,319	470,054	14,246	12,353	13,054	41,346	40,033	35,562	15,213	11,883	10,704	89,091	1,100,826
2005	33,499	478,994	14,045	12,028	12,896	41,377	40,494	36,691	14,785	12,955	10,608	90,027	1,124,415
2006[1]	35,207	506,650	13,745	12,137	12,500	41,611	45,801	37,651	13,500	14,122	10,236	90,877	1,172,864
2007[2]	33,560	517,000	12,750	12,150	12,000	42,083	46,000	37,528	14,025	13,500	9,900	89,968	1,183,009

[1] Preliminary.   [2] Forecast.   [3] Selected countries.   *Source: Food and Agricultural Organization of the United Nations (FAO)*

Salient Statistics of Eggs in the United States

	--- Hens & Pullets ---		Rate of Lay	----- Eggs -----						----- Consumption -----		
	On Farm Dec. 1[3]	Average Number During Year	Per Layer During Year[4]	Total Produced	Price in cents Per Dozen	Value of Production[5] Million USD	Total Egg Production	Imports[6]	Exports[6]	Used for Hatching	Total	Per Capita Eggs[6]
Year	----- Thousands -----		(Number)	----- Millions -----			------------------- Million Dozen -------------------					Number
2000	332,410	327,985	257	84,386	61.8	4,346	7,062	8.4	171.1	940.2	5,955	252.1
2001	338,628	335,012	256	85,745	62.2	4,446	7,187	8.9	190.0	964.2	6,043	252.7
2002	339,827	339,024	257	87,252	58.9	4,281	7,270	15.0	174.0	961.3	6,150	256.0
2003	340,979	338,393	259	87,473	73.2	5,333	7,296	13.3	146.0	959.4	6,201	255.7
2004	344,278	341,956	261	89,091	71.4	5,299	7,440	12.7	167.6	988.1	6,296	256.9
2005	347,917	343,792	262	90,027	54.0	4,049	7,511	8.5	203.3	996.7	6,318	255.3
2006	348,719	347,880	263	91,328	58.2	4,432	7,610	8.6	202.1	992.2	6,428	257.8
2007[1]	344,492	346,498	263	91,101	88.5	6,678	7,547	13.6	250.3	1,014.5	6,297	250.1
2008[2]	340,473	339,572	266	90,151			7,499	15.4	207.8	992.5	6,309	248.3

[1] Preliminary.   [2] Forecast.   [3] All layers of laying age.   [4] Number of eggs produced during the year divided by the average number of all layers of laying age on hand during the year.   [5] Value of sales plus value of eggs consumed in households of producers. 6/ Shell-egg equivalent of eggs and egg products.   *Source: National Agricultural Statistics Service, U.S. Department of Agriculture (NASS-USDA)*

EGGS

Eggs (monthly average) through December 2008 — Cents per dozen

Average Price Received by Farmers for All Eggs in the United States   In Cents Per Dozen

Year	Jan.	Feb.	Mar.	Apr.	May	June	July	Aug.	Sept.	Oct.	Nov.	Dec.	Average
1999	72.5	66.1	68.6	60.3	54.9	56.2	58.8	59.7	57.5	52.0	64.1	60.3	60.9
2000	57.8	67.8	56.9	64.7	52.0	61.8	56.5	66.4	59.2	66.8	72.0	80.7	63.6
2001	67.2	68.2	69.1	65.0	55.2	55.0	54.0	56.6	55.5	59.9	64.1	59.0	60.7
2002	62.3	55.9	68.5	52.2	50.5	62.1	60.8	66.4	57.1	56.0	70.7	62.8	60.4
2003	63.6	59.3	68.7	68.6	58.7	67.2	68.7	80.8	77.6	83.8	102.0	86.8	73.8
2004	92.6	87.5	110.0	76.7	62.6	77.3	64.0	52.6	53.8	49.4	60.4	65.4	71.0
2005	55.8	55.1	52.6	47.4	45.6	45.2	52.7	47.1	63.6	51.1	65.0	71.9	54.4
2006	61.0	49.5	67.0	51.2	42.7	54.7	43.5	55.0	53.4	54.1	81.2	80.7	57.8
2007	91.5	78.1	82.8	72.9	78.0	73.4	94.5	86.6	107.0	93.5	126.0	136.0	93.4
2008[1]	129.0	131.0	138.0	103.0	106.0	106.0	84.1	96.5	99.8	102.0	103.0	99.9	108.2

[1] Preliminary.   Source: Economic Research Service, U.S. Department of Agriculture (ERS-USDA)

Average Wholesale Price of Shell Eggs (Large) Delivered, Chicago   In Cents Per Dozen

Year	Jan.	Feb.	Mar.	Apr.	May	June	July	Aug.	Sept.	Oct.	Nov.	Dec.	Average
1999	72.34	62.13	67.85	52.74	51.35	47.86	58.40	59.30	52.86	48.38	59.26	56.38	57.40
2000	54.97	59.65	52.93	61.71	42.59	55.18	52.80	64.39	58.08	66.45	74.26	84.90	60.66
2001	68.52	64.45	69.00	66.12	50.61	49.81	52.83	55.46	50.21	57.41	62.50	58.05	58.75
2002	60.43	52.00	68.00	47.23	43.73	56.40	53.02	57.16	53.20	54.43	74.00	66.38	57.17
2003	69.57	65.39	71.05	68.83	59.10	68.76	72.39	88.26	86.21	92.07	113.16	101.09	79.66
2004	105.10	103.89	115.00	86.88	67.28	70.00	63.12	59.45	55.81	53.79	60.36	69.83	75.88
2005	54.78	60.26	48.32	42.00	41.57	40.72	51.38	42.78	61.19	48.38	62.41	70.21	52.00
2006	65.40	46.08	65.11	57.11	41.32	56.14	40.30	57.46	54.97	55.64	84.38	87.65	59.30
2007	91.75	92.71	89.23	80.00	83.55	69.60	99.95	97.37	117.50	101.89	128.93	147.70	100.02
2008[1]	144.55	142.70	150.15	115.23	90.64	107.33	95.43	100.07	108.98	103.85	110.50	109.50	114.91

[1] Preliminary.   Source: National Agricultural Statistics Service, U.S. Department of Agriculture (NASS-USDA)

Total Egg Production in the United States   In Millions of Eggs

Year	Jan.	Feb.	Mar.	Apr.	May	June	July	Aug.	Sept.	Oct.	Nov.	Dec.	Total
1999	6,979	6,281	7,052	6,784	6,941	6,742	6,903	6,971	6,860	7,131	7,016	7,279	82,939
2000	7,157	6,648	7,234	7,013	7,104	6,801	7,061	7,104	6,854	7,130	7,027	7,287	84,420
2001	7,226	6,524	7,336	7,099	7,240	6,992	7,195	7,221	7,044	7,347	7,191	7,420	85,835
2002	7,264	6,581	7,417	7,105	7,297	7,126	7,347	7,356	7,147	7,412	7,226	7,451	86,729
2003	7,390	6,665	7,424	7,187	7,327	7,105	7,403	7,367	7,112	7,439	7,326	7,554	87,299
2004	7,386	6,901	7,547	7,358	7,513	7,289	7,557	7,538	7,344	7,659	7,482	7,721	89,295
2005	7,626	6,928	7,738	7,407	7,572	7,346	7,563	7,528	7,348	7,665	7,514	7,793	90,028
2006	7,727	6,980	7,843	7,543	7,637	7,401	7,645	7,647	7,430	7,678	7,549	7,815	90,895
2007	7,675	6,951	7,806	7,472	7,622	7,380	7,599	7,594	7,393	7,726	7,542	7,808	90,568
2008[1]	7,647	7,114	7,675	773	7,564	7,367	7,599	7,551	7,339	7,625	7,490	7,768	83,512

[1] Preliminary.   *Source: National Agricultural Statistics Service, U.S. Department of Agriculture (NASS-USDA)*

Per Capita Disappearance of Eggs[4] in the United States   In Number of Eggs

Year	First Quarter	Second Quarter	Third Quarter	Fourth Quarter	Total	Total Consumption (Million Dozen)	Year	First Quarter	Second Quarter	Third Quarter	Fourth Quarter	Total	Total Consumption (Million Dozen)
1998	60.5	60.5	61.1	63.2	244.9	5,522	2004	63.7	63.9	64.1	65.5	257.3	6,296
1999	62.7	62.8	63.8	66.2	255.7	5,817	2005	63.4	63.0	63.5	65.0	255.8	6,318
2000	64.5	64.0	64.2	65.6	252.1	5,955	2006	64.1	63.7	63.9	64.7	257.8	6,428
2001	64.5	64.2	64.7	66.6	252.7	6,043	2007[1]	62.2	61.7	62.4	63.8	250.1	6,297
2002	62.4	62.6	64.0	64.6	256.0	6,150	2008[2]	61.9	61.4	62.0	63.9	249.1	6,309
2003	62.6	63.0	63.8	65.3	255.7	6,201	2009[3]	61.1	60.6	61.8	63.3	246.7	

[1] Preliminary.   [2] Estimate.   [3] Forecast.   *Source: Economic Research Service, U.S. Department of Agriculture (ERS-USDA)*

Egg-Feed Ratio[1] in the United States

Year	Jan.	Feb.	Mar.	Apr.	May	June	July	Aug.	Sept.	Oct.	Nov.	Dec.	Average
1999	11.7	10.6	11.3	9.2	7.8	8.2	9.9	10.1	9.3	8.0	11.9	10.1	9.8
2000	8.9	11.3	8.0	9.9	6.4	9.5	9.2	12.9	10.3	12.2	13.1	15.0	10.6
2001	10.9	11.4	11.6	11.3	8.6	8.5	7.9	8.4	8.5	10.3	11.5	9.3	9.9
2002	10.2	8.4	11.6	7.4	6.7	9.5	7.5	7.9	7.1	6.6	10.5	8.9	8.5
2003	9.0	8.0	9.5	9.3	6.9	8.8	9.8	12.7	11.6	12.6	15.7	12.2	10.5
2004	12.9	10.7	13.2	7.8	6.0	6.6	5.9	5.6	6.5	5.8	8.8	9.8	8.3
2005	7.2	7.4	6.3	5.2	4.6	4.4	5.9	5.1	9.3	6.6	10.3	11.3	7.0
2006	8.5	5.9	9.8	6.3	4.2	7.1	4.6	7.5	6.9	6.4	10.6	10.1	7.3
2007	11.7	8.4	9.1	7.6	8.1	6.4	10.7	9.5	12.3	10.2	13.9	13.9	10.2
2008[2]	12.7	11.1	11.7	7.4	5.8	7.2	5.3	6.6	7.7	8.9	9.3	9.2	8.6

[1] Pounds of laying feed equivalent in value to one dozen eggs.   [2] Preliminary.   *Source: Economic Research Service, U.S. Department of Agriculture (ERS-USDA)*

Hens and Pullets of Laying Age (Layers) in the United States, on First of Month   In Thousands

Year	Jan.	Feb.	Mar.	Apr.	May	June	July	Aug.	Sept.	Oct.	Nov.	Dec.
1999	322,137	322,382	323,161	322,162	320,783	320,211	320,672	318,944	321,349	323,365	327,135	329,320
2000	328,307	328,767	330,876	330,807	327,597	325,012	324,843	326,240	325,212	327,219	329,092	332,410
2001	332,107	335,449	336,131	337,472	336,755	333,522	332,274	332,148	333,417	336,573	337,549	338,625
2002	339,423	338,465	337,478	337,376	336,131	335,547	335,236	335,717	336,561	337,923	338,350	339,827
2003	340,752	341,019	340,080	339,645	336,678	335,611	333,925	334,381	334,248	334,103	336,528	339,989
2004	338,272	338,774	340,479	342,879	342,305	343,233	342,392	342,522	343,405	344,794	345,267	344,278
2005	347,273	348,412	349,117	344,759	342,346	341,247	338,424	338,674	339,984	341,803	343,789	347,917
2006	349,763	349,930	350,452	350,453	346,809	343,596	341,733	340,728	342,309	343,946	345,090	348,719
2007	349,192	348,563	349,081	347,280	343,835	341,057	339,373	340,648	340,604	341,322	343,909	344,492
2008/1	345,535	343,891	342,080	341,686	340,683	339,791	337,390	334,950	335,353	333,349	335,728	340,473

[1] Preliminary.   *Source: National Agricultural Statistics Service, U.S. Department of Agriculture (NASS-USDA)*

EGGS

Eggs Laid Per Hundred Layers in the United States   In Number of Eggs

Year	Jan.	Feb.	Mar.	Apr.	May	June	July	Aug.	Sept.	Oct.	Nov.	Dec.	Average
1999	2,165	1,946	2,185	2,110	2,166	2,104	2,158	2,177	2,128	2,192	2,138	2,214	2,140
2000	2,178	2,016	2,186	2,130	2,177	2,093	2,169	2,181	2,101	2,173	2,125	2,193	2,144
2001	2,165	1,943	2,178	2,106	2,160	2,100	2,166	2,170	2,103	2,180	2,130	2,188	2,132
2002	2,143	1,947	2,198	2,110	2,173	2,125	2,190	2,188	2,119	2,192	2,139	2,189	2,143
2003	2,168	1,957	2,184	2,125	2,180	2,122	2,215	2,203	2,128	2,218	2,166	2,223	2,157
2004	2,182	2,032	2,209	2,148	2,192	2,126	2,207	2,198	2,134	2,220	2,170	2,234	2,171
2005	2,192	1,986	2,230	2,156	2,215	2,162	2,234	2,218	2,155	2,236	2,172	2,234	2,183
2006	2,210	1,994	2,238	2,164	2,212	2,160	2,240	2,239	2,165	2,228	2,176	2,234	2,188
2007	2,200	1,993	2,242	2,162	2,226	2,169	2,235	2,229	2,168	2,255	2,191	2,255	2,194
2008[1]	2,218	2,073	2,244	2,163	2,225	2,177	2,260	2,252	2,194	2,276	2,216	2,283	2,215

[1] Preliminary.   Source: National Agricultural Statistics Service, U.S. Department of Agriculture (NASS-USDA)

Egg-Type Chicks Hatched by Commercial Hatcheries in the United States   In Thousands

Year	Jan.	Feb.	Mar.	Apr.	May	June	July	Aug.	Sept.	Oct.	Nov.	Dec.	Total
1999	35,242	36,367	41,172	42,285	40,726	41,439	34,275	35,518	39,287	39,044	32,802	33,564	451,721
2000	34,181	34,659	38,877	36,653	41,185	37,268	33,240	34,328	36,325	36,080	32,438	35,178	430,412
2001	36,728	37,836	41,015	42,789	42,655	40,822	38,651	34,987	37,140	35,825	32,355	31,870	452,673
2002	35,655	34,473	36,985	38,096	38,760	35,144	35,581	35,689	35,742	32,157	31,154	32,113	421,549
2003	33,521	30,474	36,775	37,820	37,630	36,602	35,578	33,199	35,763	34,812	30,241	33,588	416,003
2004	35,155	31,923	37,545	37,466	38,347	37,508	34,919	36,854	36,631	34,866	38,758	37,332	437,304
2005	38,291	34,427	41,701	38,049	38,792	35,034	34,897	38,700	33,623	35,461	32,285	35,917	437,177
2006	35,159	33,409	38,805	35,435	39,744	37,406	32,727	35,611	36,873	36,162	31,554	33,183	426,068
2007	36,195	36,739	38,561	39,254	38,080	40,641	35,952	36,930	35,327	36,332	36,232	35,866	446,109
2008[1]	40,167	37,549	39,547	41,051	42,724	42,538	37,929	36,301	36,428	39,998	36,607	36,393	467,232

[1] Preliminary.   Source: National Agricultural Statistics Service, U.S. Department of Agriculture (NASS-USDA)

Cold Storage Holdings of Frozen Eggs in the United States, on First of Month   In Millions of Pounds[2]

Year	Jan.	Feb.	Mar.	Apr.	May	June	July	Aug.	Sept.	Oct.	Nov.	Dec.
1999	11.0	11.0	10.8	9.2	9.4	9.7	11.3	11.1	8.8	9.5	9.0	8.5
2000	10.1	17.6	14.8	14.0	12.8	13.5	14.1	14.4	14.9	14.4	16.6	15.4
2001	15.0	16.9	15.5	14.6	15.9	15.8	14.4	16.7	17.8	17.7	15.5	13.9
2002	13.7	13.1	13.9	11.7	10.2	11.1	12.7	12.9	13.2	13.2	13.1	11.2
2003	13.5	15.3	17.1	17.0	15.7	17.7	18.0	18.6	18.0	16.6	16.9	14.9
2004	18.0	21.3	21.1	19.2	20.9	20.6	18.3	16.7	17.3	18.7	17.9	17.3
2005	19.1	18.6	17.9	18.5	18.9	17.7	19.7	19.6	19.9	18.8	17.6	17.6
2006	21.0	22.5	24.5	20.8	23.3	21.0	22.1	23.6	21.6	19.0	16.3	17.1
2007	16.5	17.2	15.7	14.6	14.3	15.2	17.4	17.5	18.5	17.7	17.6	15.2
2008[1]	14.7	12.0	16.7	16.3	16.0	12.4	16.1	21.1	20.8	21.9	22.4	21.3

[1] Preliminary.   [2] Converted on basis 39.5 pounds frozen eggs equals 1 case.   Source: National Agricultural Statistics Service, U.S. Department of Agriculture (NASS-USDA)

Electric Power

The modern electric utility industry began in the 1800s. In 1807, Humphry Davy constructed a practical battery and demonstrated both incandescent and arc light. In 1831, Michael Faraday built the first electric generator proving that rotary mechanical power could be converted into electric power. In 1879, Thomas Edison perfected a practical incandescent light bulb. The electric utility industry evolved from gas and electric carbon-arc commercial and street lighting systems. In 1882, in New York City, Thomas Edison's Pearl Street electricity generating station established the industry by displaying the four key elements of a modern electric utility system: reliable central generation, efficient distribution, successful end use, and a competitive price.

Electricity is measured in units called watts and watt-hours. Electricity must be used when it is generated and cannot be stored to any significant degree. That means the power utilities must match the level of electricity generation to the level of demand in order to avoid wasteful over-production. The power industry has been deregulated to some degree in the past decade and now major utility companies sell power back and forth across major national grids in order to meet supply and demand needs. The rapid changes in the supply-demand situation mean that the cost of electricity can be very volatile.

Electricity futures trade at the New York Mercantile Exchange (NYMEX). The futures contract is a financially settled contract, which is priced based on electricity prices in the PJM western hub at 111 delivery points, mainly on the utility transmission systems of Pennsylvania Electric Co. and the Potomac Electric Co. The contract is priced in dollars and cents per megawatt hours.

Supply – U.S. electricity production in 2008 (through November, annualized) fell -1.0% yr/yr to 2.479 trillion kilowatt-hours. That was well below the record high of 3.212 trillion kilowatt-hours in 1998 and indicated that recent electricity production has been reduced by more efficient production and distribution systems, and to some extent by conservation of electricity by both business and residential consumers.

U.S. electricity generation in 2006 (latest data available) required the use of 2.478 trillion cubic feet of natural gas (+16.1% yr/yr), 753 million tons of coal (1.0% yr/yr), and 54 million barrels of fuel oil (-45.5% yr/yr).

In terms of kilowatt-hours, coal is the most widely used source of electricity production in the U.S. accounting for 59% of electricity production in 2006, followed by nuclear (17%), hydro (11%), natural gas (11%), and fuel oil (2%). Alternative sources of fuel for electricity generation that are gaining favor include geothermal, biomass, solar, wind, etc. but so far account for only 0.3% of total electricity production in the U.S.

Demand – Residential use of electricity accounts for the largest single category of electricity demand with usage of 1.352 trillion kilowatt hours in 2006 accounting for 35% of overall usage. Business users in total use more electricity than residential users, but business users are broken into the categories of commercial with 34% of usage and industrial with 27% of usage.

World Electricity Production (Monthly Average)   In Millions of Kilowatt Hours

Year	Australia	Canada	China	Germany	India	Italy	Japan	Rep. of Korea	Russia	South Africa	Ukraine	United Kingdom	United States
1999	15,399	55,809	100,345	45,820	40,148	22,136	76,755	19,944	70,611	16,961	14,342	28,095	308,572
2000	15,712	58,337	109,426	46,417	41,725	22,986	78,391	22,200	73,117	17,557	14,287	28,484	316,845
2001	15,548	56,576	118,439	47,107	42,434	23,242	77,742	23,768	74,031	17,508	14,414	29,415	311,387
2002	15,646	57,873	133,513	47,211	44,141	23,638	77,139	25,500	74,078	18,142	14,477	29,220	321,538
2003	15,564	56,294	153,229	49,060	52,773	24,386	76,661	26,856	76,158	19,267	15,030	35,006	307,250
2004	16,095	56,844	176,169	44,439	48,968	24,975	71,574	28,472	77,562	20,648	15,180	34,924	316,000
2005	16,336	49,559	199,780	48,840	51,125	25,754	72,667	30,357	79,355	20,673	15,505	33,377	336,499
2006	19,077	48,756	229,119	45,030	54,309	26,037	81,401	31,773	82,619	21,396	16,017	33,272	337,747
2007[1]	18,958	50,318	265,047	43,565	57,839	26,070	82,974	33,594	84,656	21,861	16,269	29,943	346,386
2008[2]	19,455	50,200	288,869	43,537	60,098	26,698	84,119	35,191	84,573	21,831	16,620	28,783	350,695

[1] Preliminary.   [2] Estimate.   NA = Not avaliable.   *Source: United Nations*

Installed Capacity, Capability & Peak Load of the U.S. Electric Utility Industry   In Thousands of Megawatts (Nameplate)

		------- Type of Prime Mover -------			-------------- Type of Ownership --------------					Capability at Winter Peak Load	Non-Coincident Winter Peak Load	Capacity Margin Non-Coincident Peak Load (%)	Total Electric Utility Industry Generation (Mil. kWh)	Annual Peak Load Factor (%)
Year	Total Electric Utility Industry	Hydro & Steam	Gas Turbine Nuclear Power	Internal Combustion	Investor	Cooper-ative	Sub-total Gov't.	Munic-ipal Utilities	Federal	Power Districts, State Projects					
1990	735.1	87.2	531.1	108.0	8.7	568.8	26.3	139.9	40.1	65.4	34.4	696.8	484.8	20.4	2,901.3	60.4
1991	740.0	88.7	534.1	108.4	8.8	573.0	26.5	140.5	40.4	65.6	34.5	703.2	486.4	20.2	2,935.6	60.9
1992	741.7	89.7	534.5	107.9	9.6	572.9	26.0	142.7	41.6	66.1	35.0	707.8	493.6	21.1	2,934.4	61.1
1993	744.7	90.2	536.9	107.8	9.8	575.2	26.1	143.4	41.8	66.1	35.5	712.0	522.4	17.1	3,043.9	61.0
1994	764.0	90.3	537.9	107.9	9.9	574.8	26.4	144.7	42.0	66.3	36.4	715.1	518.9	16.7	3,088.7	61.2
1995	769.0	91.1	541.6	107.9	9.9	578.7	27.1	144.8	42.2	65.9	36.6	727.7	545.4	13.2	3,194.2	59.8
1996	463.0	91.0	546.6	109.0	9.9	582.2	27.2	147.1	43.0	67.2	36.9	740.5	554.1	27.7	3,284.1	61.0
1997	775.9	92.5	549.7	107.6	10.0	582.5	28.0	149.4	43.8	68.9	36.7	743.8	529.9	26.0	3,329.4	61.3
1998	778.6	91.2	522.1	104.8	10.2	531.3	32.5	164.5	50.5	68.7	45.3	835.3	567.6	25.7	3,457.4	62.0
1999[1]	775.9	89.8	476.3	102.3	9.6	483.7	34.6	159.6	50.2	68.7	40.7	848.9	570.9	26.7	3,530.0	61.2

[1] Preliminary.   *Source: Edison Electric Institute (EEI)*

ELECTRIC POWER

Available Electricity and Energy Sales in the United States   In Billions of Kilowatt Hours

	Net Generation — Electric Utility Industry								Sales to Ultimate Customer							
Year	Total[2]	Hydro	Natural Gas	Coal	Fuel Oil	Nuclear	Other Sources[3]	Total	Total Million $	Total	Residential	Interdepartmental	Commercial	Industrial	Street & highway Lighting	Other Public Auth.	Railways & Railroads
1997	3,123	341.3	283.6	1,788	77.8	628.6	7.5	3,492	215,334	3,302	1,076	2.6	928.6	1,037	19.7	75.6	5.3
1998	3,212	308.8	309.2	1,807	110.2	673.7	7.2	3,620	219,848	3,425	1,130	[4]	979.4	1,051	16.3	87.2	[4]
1999	3,174	299.9	296.4	1,768	86.9	725.0	3.7	3,695	219,896	3,484	1,145	[4]	1,002.0	1,058	15.9	107.0	[4]
2000	3,015	253.2	290.7	1,697	72.2	705.4	2.2	3,802	233,163	3,592	1,192	[4]	1,055.2	1,064	[4]	109.5	[4]
2001	2,630	197.8	264.4	1,560	78.9	534.2	2.2	3,737	247,343	3,557	1,202	[4]	1,083.1	997	[4]	108.4	[4]
2002	2,549	242.3	229.6	1,515	59.1	507.4	3.8	3,858	249,411	3,632	1,265	[4]	1,104.5	990	[4]	105.8	[4]
2003	2,462	249.6	187.0	1,500	69.9	458.8	4.2	3,883	259,767	3,662	1,276	[4]	1,198.7	1,012	[4]	NA	[4]
2004	2,505	245.5	199.7	1,514	73.7	475.7	4.5	3,971	270,119	3,716	1,292	[4]	1,230.4	1,018	[4]	NA	[4]
2005	2,475	245.6	238.2	1,485	69.7	436.3	5.6	4,055	298,003	3,811	1,359	[4]	1,275.1	1,019	[4]	NA	[4]
2006[1]	2,484	261.9	282.1	1,471	40.9	425.3	7.3	4,065	326,506	3,817	1,352	[4]	1,299.7	1,011	[4]	NA	[4]

[1] Preliminary.   [2] Includes internal combustion.   [3] Includes electricity produced from geothermal, wood, waste, wind, solar, etc.   [4] Included in Other.
NA = Not available.   *Source: Edison Electric Institute (EEI)*

Electric Power Production by Electric Utilities in the United States   In Millions of Kilowatt Hours

Year	Jan.	Feb.	Mar.	Apr.	May	June	July	Aug.	Sept.	Oct.	Nov.	Dec.	Total
1999	275,230	239,825	258,678	238,969	255,266	281,233	318,745	307,835	261,347	243,212	235,129	258,205	3,173,674
2000	265,991	237,324	241,397	227,031	253,890	268,128	279,421	286,682	245,137	228,389	226,765	255,229	3,015,383
2001	236,467	199,802	211,942	197,499	215,508	233,622	253,400	258,901	214,236	204,307	192,518	211,742	2,629,946
2002	215,684	187,929	200,833	194,038	208,436	227,940	248,962	241,449	215,408	201,705	194,205	212,868	2,549,457
2003	217,338	189,944	193,305	181,914	200,634	212,297	234,888	234,675	201,966	192,198	189,362	213,758	2,462,281
2004	221,782	198,675	193,763	182,744	207,224	219,767	235,266	227,785	209,507	197,320	191,813	219,585	2,505,231
2005	212,654	185,283	196,136	178,408	197,082	221,116	239,381	238,790	211,139	193,687	188,255	212,914	2,474,845
2006	204,976	192,304	197,249	184,803	204,107	223,950	243,526	242,624	200,655	193,321	189,435	206,705	2,483,655
2007	218,288	197,329	197,229	184,017	202,783	218,554	234,728	246,147	209,641	197,285	189,498	208,631	2,504,130
2008[1]	220,619	198,266	195,810	184,352	203,149	227,204	239,761	229,255	201,218	187,502	185,444		2,479,178

[1] Preliminary.   *Source: Energy Information Administration, U.S. Department of Energy (EIA-DOE)*

Use of Fuels for Electric Generation in the United States

Year	Coal (Thousand ShortTons)	Consumption of Fuel Fuel Oil (Thousand Barrels)	Gas (Million Cubic Feet)	Total Fuel in Coal Equivalent[3]	Net Generation by Fuels[4] (Million Kilowatt Hour)	Pounds of Coal Per Kilowatt Hour (Pounds)	Cost of Fossil-Fuel at Elec. Utilities (Cents/MMBTU)	Average Cost of Fuel Per Kilowatt Hour (In Cents)	Heat Rate BTU Per Kilowatt Hour	Cost Per Million BTU Consumed (In Cents)
1997	900,361	125,146	2,968,453	1,103,037	2,148,756	1.005	152.2	1.53	10,081	152.2
1998	910,867	178,614	3,258,054	1,147,317	2,226,860	.996	143.8	1.49	10,360	143.8
1999	894,120	143,830	3,113,419	1,113,614	2,150,989	1.012	144.1	1.48	10,301	144.1
2000	859,335	120,129	3,043,094				173.8			
2001	806,269	126,367	2,686,287				173.0			
2002	767,803	88,595	2,259,684				151.5			
2003	757,384	105,319	1,763,764							
2004	772,224	103,793	1,809,443							
2005	761,349	98,223	2,134,859							
2006[1]	753,390	53,529	2,478,396							

[1] Preliminary.   [2] 42-gallon barrels.   [3] Coal equivalents are calculated on the basis of Btu instead of generation data.   [4] Excludes wood & waste fuels.
Source: Edison Electric Institute (EEI)

Ethanol

World Production of Ethanol   In Millions of Gallons

Year	Brazil	China	France	Germany	India	Russia	Saudi Arabia	South Africa	Spain	Thailand	United Kingdom	United States	World Total
2004	3,989	964	219	71	462	198	79	110	79	74	106	3,535	10,770
2005	4,227	1,004	240	114	449	198	32	103	93	79	92	4,264	12,150
2006[1]	4,491	1,017	251	202	502	171	52	102	122	93	74	4,855	13,489
2007[2]	5,019	486			53					79		6,499	13,102

[1] Preliminary.   [2] Estimate.   *Source: Renewable Fuels Association*

Salient Statistics of Ethanol in the United States

Year	Ethanol Plants	Ethanol Production Capacity (mgy)	Plants Under Con-struction	Capacity Under Construction (mgy)	Farmer Owned Plants	Farmer Owned Capacity (mgy)	Percent of Total Capacity Farmer	Farmer Owned UC Plants	Farmers Owned UC Capacity	Percent of Total UC Capacity	States with Ethanol Plants
2001	56	1,921.9	5	64.7	21	473.0	25	3	60	71	18
2002	61	2,347.3	13	390.7	25	645.6	28	10	335	86	19
2003	68	2,706.8	11	483.0	28	796.6	29	8	318	66	20
2004	72	3,100.8	15	598.0	33	1,041.1	34	12	447	75	19
2005	81	3,643.7	16	754.0	40	1,388.6	38	10	450	60	18
2006	95	4,336.4	31	1,778.0	46	1,677.1	39	4	187	11	20
2007[1]	110	5,493.4	76	5,635.5	46	1,677.1	39	4	187	11	21
2008[2]	134	7,229.4	77	6,216.9	49	1,948.6	28	13	771	12	26

[1] Preliminary.   [2] Estimate.   *Source: Renewable Fuels Association*

Production of Fuel Ethanol in the United States   In Thousands of Barrels Per Day

Year	Jan.	Feb.	Mar.	Apr.	May	June	July	Aug.	Sept.	Oct.	Nov.	Dec.	Average
1999	102	99	102	99	93	83	77	93	97	106	100	100	96
2000	110	108	104	110	103	104	103	98	101	111	109	113	106
2001	115	116	113	108	108	110	112	113	116	121	126	124	115
2002	135	122	128	126	129	123	128	136	145	159	166	176	139
2003	177	169	175	179	175	181	178	180	190	188	194	207	183
2004	211	212	214	218	221	222	218	225	226	226	232	232	221
2005	241	245	243	238	237	249	258	260	261	269	275	280	255
2006	288	302	301	289	293	318	316	329	333	333	343	356	317
2007	375	386	384	391	406	418	421	434	441	452	479	489	423
2008[1]	510	518	561	562	598	585	614	647	640	647	668	656	601

[1] Preliminary.   *Source: Energy Information Administration, U.S. Department of Energy (EIA-DOE)*

Production of Fuel Ethanol in the United States   In Thousands of Barrels

Year	Jan.	Feb.	Mar.	Apr.	May	June	July	Aug.	Sept.	Oct.	Nov.	Dec.	Total
1999	3,170	2,551	2,928	3,169	2,877	2,372	2,362	2,831	2,958	3,195	2,995	3,473	34,881
2000	3,204	3,025	3,231	3,311	3,309	2,928	3,299	2,926	3,103	3,429	3,297	3,565	38,627
2001	3,574	3,249	3,500	3,226	3,339	3,310	3,472	3,515	3,470	3,743	3,794	3,836	42,028
2002	4,189	3,429	3,968	3,788	4,007	3,705	3,970	4,203	4,342	4,939	4,965	5,451	50,956
2003	5,497	4,734	5,430	5,384	5,426	5,440	5,529	5,589	5,685	5,829	5,806	6,423	66,772
2004	6,551	6,155	6,648	6,525	6,857	6,648	6,749	6,977	6,766	7,007	6,946	7,229	81,058
2005	7,461	6,847	7,530	7,135	7,357	7,463	8,007	8,050	7,841	8,335	8,259	8,676	92,961
2006	8,935	8,463	9,333	8,663	9,086	9,531	9,791	10,235	10,088	10,512	10,442	11,215	116,294
2007	11,621	10,795	11,892	11,716	12,573	12,553	13,051	13,458	13,222	14,018	14,356	15,161	154,416
2008[1]	15,818	15,025	17,387	16,868	18,543	17,544	19,042	20,059	19,197	20,048	20,054	20,342	219,927

[1] Preliminary.   *Source: Energy Information Administration, U.S. Department of Energy (EIA-DOE)*

Stocks of Fuel Ethanol in the United States   In Thousands of Barrels

Year	Jan.	Feb.	Mar.	Apr.	May	June	July	Aug.	Sept.	Oct.	Nov.	Dec.
1999	3,576	3,612	3,859	4,553	4,938	4,572	4,593	4,740	5,009	4,862	4,423	4,024
2000	3,923	4,208	4,082	4,487	4,466	4,869	5,071	4,582	4,542	4,200	3,760	3,400
2001	2,811	2,771	2,691	2,936	3,172	4,152	3,503	4,226	4,438	3,783	4,038	4,298
2002	4,828	4,757	5,691	5,853	5,994	6,188	6,070	6,212	6,485	6,530	6,009	6,200
2003	6,933	5,943	6,549	6,528	6,507	6,753	6,975	6,744	7,256	7,201	6,472	5,978
2004	5,830	5,469	5,578	5,433	5,796	5,345	5,971	6,367	6,641	6,664	6,414	6,002
2005	6,142	6,261	6,605	6,861	6,810	6,064	5,926	5,398	5,317	5,591	5,723	5,563
2006	6,099	7,268	8,626	8,990	7,767	6,675	7,706	9,133	9,725	9,723	9,232	8,760
2007	8,593	8,749	8,529	8,791	8,950	9,067	9,696	10,309	11,509	11,423	11,194	10,509
2008[1]	10,674	10,465	11,391	11,539	12,044	12,304	13,186	14,882	15,994	15,192	15,227	14,219

[1] Preliminary.   *Source: Energy Information Administration, U.S. Department of Energy (EIA-DOE)*

ETHANOL

Ethanol Futures - Chicago Board of Trade
(weekly close) as of January 02, 2009

Cents per pound

Average Price of Ethanol in the United States[1]   In Dollars Per Gallon

Year	Jan.	Feb.	Mar.	Apr.	May	June	July	Aug.	Sept.	Oct.	Nov.	Dec.	Average
1999	1.033	1.032	1.044	1.023	1.016	0.992	0.986	0.990	0.991	0.996	1.032	1.170	1.025
2000	1.285	1.275	1.331	1.329	1.314	1.471	1.402	1.405	1.533	1.558	1.687	1.696	1.441
2001	1.783	1.737	1.579	1.571	1.707	1.646	1.457	1.551	1.593	1.375	1.188	1.012	1.517
2002	0.979	0.973	1.125	1.070	0.982	1.046	1.156	1.330	1.335	1.238	1.263	1.210	1.142
2003	1.151	1.278	1.427	1.269	1.131	1.242	1.234	1.262	1.388	1.381	1.645	1.716	1.344
2004	1.423	1.398	1.666	1.791	1.753	1.862	1.762	1.624	1.585	1.878	1.995	1.812	1.712
2005	1.733	1.597	1.365	1.237	1.221	1.405	1.786	2.031	2.695	2.511	2.130	1.916	1.802
2006	1.967	2.428	2.450	2.475	2.903	3.597	3.208	2.668	2.148	1.815	2.045	2.234	2.495
2007	2.144	1.899	2.185	2.159	2.169	2.089	1.970	1.849	1.581	1.523	1.739	1.950	1.938
2008	2.188	2.129	2.316	2.455	2.485	2.535	2.642	2.224	2.150	1.846	1.648	1.493	2.176

[1] Northeast and Northwest Iowa.   *Source: Agricultural Marketing Service, U.S. Department of Agriculture (AMS-USDA)*

Volume of Trading of Ethanol Futures in Chicago   In Contracts

Year	Jan.	Feb.	Mar.	Apr.	May	June	July	Aug.	Sept.	Oct.	Nov.	Dec.	Total
2005	----	----	350	119	222	61	155	321	227	390	559	272	2,676
2006	443	508	329	421	330	686	1,141	365	779	348	97	117	5,564
2007	191	526	945	1,153	784	1,163	792	969	704	966	1,436	2,887	12,516
2008	1,889	11,459	1,634	2,594	1,956	2,843	2,156	3,556	2,969	2,857	2,327	3,625	39,865

Source: Chicago Board of Trade (CBT)

Month-End Open Interest of Ethanol Futures in Chicago   In Contracts

Year	Jan.	Feb.	Mar.	Apr.	May	June	July	Aug.	Sept.	Oct.	Nov.	Dec.
2005	----	----	246	215	88	39	61	208	301	461	759	778
2006	774	856	860	900	745	735	829	599	474	442	396	322
2007	402	478	593	623	842	1,227	1,100	1,378	1,326	1,642	1,853	2,141
2008	2,328	2,245	2,257	1,862	2,053	2,659	2,763	2,447	2,641	3,055	3,114	2,935

Source: Chicago Board of Trade (CBT)

Fertilizer

Fertilizer is a natural or synthetic chemical substance, or mixture, that enriches soil to promote plant growth. The three primary nutrients that fertilizers provide are nitrogen, potassium, and phosphorus. In ancient times, and still today, many commonly used fertilizers contain one or more of the three primary ingredients: manure (containing nitrogen), bones (containing small amounts of nitrogen and large quantities of phosphorus), and wood ash (containing potassium).

At least fourteen different nutrients have been found essential for crops. These include three organic nutrients (carbon, hydrogen, and oxygen, which are taken directly from air and water), three primary chemical nutrients (nitrogen, phosphorus, and potassium), and three secondary chemical nutrients (magnesium, calcium, and sulfur). The others are micronutrients or trace elements and include iron, manganese, copper, zinc, boron, and molybdenum.

Prices – The average price of ammonia, a key source of ingredients for fertilizers, rose by +2.3% yr/yr in 2007 (latest data available) to $309 per metric ton. The average price of phosphate rock in the U.S. in 2006 (latest data available) rose by 3.1% yr/yr to a record high of $30.52 per metric ton. The average price of potash in the U.S. in 2007 rose by +37.9% yr/yr to a record high of $400.00 per metric ton.

Supply – World production of nitrogen (as contained in ammonia) in 2007 rose by +4.0% yr/yr to a new record high of 131.000 million metric tons. The world's largest producers of nitrogen in 2007 were China with 32% of world production, India (8%), Russia (8%), and the U.S. (7%). U.S. nitrogen production in 2007 rose +7.9% to 8,840

million metric tons.

World production of phosphate rock, basic slag and guano in 2007 rose +3.3% yr/yr to 156.000 million metric tons. The world's largest producers of phosphate rock in 2007 were China (with 29% of world production), U.S. (19%), Morocco (17%), and Russia (7%). U.S. production in 2007 fell -1.3% y/y to 29.7 million metric tons.

World production of marketable potash in 2007 rose +18.9% yr/yr to a record high of 34.6 million metric tons. The world's largest producers of potash in 2007 were Canada with 32% of world production, Russia (19%), Belarus (15%), and Germany (10%). U.S. production of potash in 2007 was unchanged from 2006 at 1.100 million metric tons.

Demand – U.S. consumption of nitrogen in 2007 rose +9.1% yr/yr to a 7-year high of 12.000 million metric tons. U.S. consumption of phosphate rock in 2007 rose +3.7% to 33.8000 million metric tons, up from the 25-year low of 32.600 million metric tons in 2006. U.S. consumption of potash in 2007 rose +13.5% to 5.9 million metric tons, down from the 2004 10-year high of 6.000 million metric tons.

Trade – U.S. imports of nitrogen in 2007 rose +10.3% to 6.530 million metric tons and the U.S. relied on imports for 42% of consumption. U.S. imports of phosphate rock in 2007 rose +10.3% yr/yr to 2.670 million metric tons, just below the 2002 record high of 2.700 million metric tons. U.S. imports of potash in 2007 rose +11.2% to 4.970 million metric tons, and imports accounted for 81% of U.S. consumption.

World Production of Ammonia   In Thousands of Metric Tons of Contained Nitrogen

Year	Canada	China	France	Germany	India	Indonesia	Japan	Mexico	Nether-lands	Poland	Russia	United States	Total
2000	4,130	27,700	1,620	2,473	10,148	3,620	1,410	701	2,540	1,862	8,735	11,800	108,000
2001	3,439	28,200	1,380	2,522	10,081	3,655	1,318	548	1,989	1,735	8,690	9,120	105,000
2002	3,700	30,200	1,172	2,560	9,827	4,200	1,192	559	2,053	1,311	8,600	10,300	109,000
2003	3,662	31,500	1,153	2,803	10,048	4,250	1,061	439	1,750	1,906	9,100	8,450	110,000
2004	4,107	34,770	1,120	2,741	10,718	4,120	1,101	560	1,970	1,984	9,800	8,990	117,000
2005	4,100	37,850	1,206	2,789	10,800	4,400	1,083	423	1,700	2,080	10,000	8,340	123,000
2006	4,100	40,660	616	2,718	10,900	4,300	1,091	487	1,800	2,100	10,500	8,190	126,000
2007[1]	4,100	42,480	800	2,746	11,000	4,400	1,090	487	1,800	1,900	10,500	8,840	131,000
2008[2]	4,100	44,600		2,800	11,000	4,400	1,360		1,800	1,900	11,000	8,240	136,000

[1] Preliminary.   [2] Estimate.   *Source: U.S. Geological Survey (USGS)*

Salient Statistics of Nitrogen[3] (Ammonia) in the United States   In Thousands of Metric Tons

Year	Net Import Reliance As a % of Apparent Consumption	Production[3] (Fixed) Fertilizer	Production[3] (Fixed) Non-fertilizer	Production[3] (Fixed) Total	Imprts[4] (Fixed)	Exports	Nitrogen[5] Compounds Pro-duced	Nitrogen[5] Compounds Con-sumption	Stocks, Dec. 31 Am-monia	Stocks, Dec. 31 Fixed Nitrogen Com-pounds	Ammonia Con-sumption (Apparent)	Average Price ($/Metric Ton) Urea FOB Gulf[6] Coast	Average Price Urea FOB Corn Belt	Ammonium Nitrate: FOB Corn Belt	Ammonia FOB Gulf Coast
2000	21	10,300	1,510	11,800	3,880	662	10,272	12,500	1,120	1,400	14,900	158-161	175-180	140-150	169
2001	31	8,190	929	9,120	4,550	647	7,852	10,600	261	1,340	13,200	104-108	130-135	120-130	183
2002	29	9,300	1,030	10,300	4,670	437	9,937	11,000	286	1,140	14,500	128-132	150-160	120-130	137
2003	39	7,490	961	8,450	5,720	400	9,122	11,000	195	476	13,900	192-195	215-225	190-195	245
2004	38	8,470	524	8,990	5,900	381	9,258	11,900	298	590	14,400	225-230	255-270	195-210	274
2005	42	7,450	884	8,340	6,520	525	9,099	11,300	254	605	14,400	260-267	300-325	265-270	304
2006	41	7,270	921	8,190	5,920	194	9,083	11,000	170	485	14,000	265-280	295-305	250-260	302
2007[1]	42	7,890	949	8,840	6,530	145	9,387	12,000	155	467	15,200	435-445	465-490	380-385	309
2008[2]	48			8,240	7,720	166			188		15,800				500

[1] Preliminary.   [2] Estimate.   [3] Anhydrous ammonia, synthetic.   [4] For consumption.   [5] Major downstream nitrogen compounds.   [6] Granular.
Source: U.S. Geological Survey (USGS)

FERTILIZER

World Production of Phosphate Rock, Basic Slag & Guano — In Thousands of Metric Tons (Gross Weight)

Year	Brazil	China	Egypt	Israel	Jordan	Morocco	Russia	Senegal	Syria	Togo	Tunisia	United States	World Total
1999	4,344	20,000	1,018	4,128	6,014	22,163	11,400	1,814	2,084	1,600	8,006	40,600	134,000
2000	4,725	19,400	1,096	4,110	5,526	21,463	11,100	1,738	2,166	1,370	8,339	38,600	132,000
2001	4,805	21,000	972	3,511	5,843	21,983	10,500	1,708	2,043	1,067	8,144	31,900	126,000
2002	5,084	23,000	1,550	4,091	7,179	23,028	10,700	1,551	2,483	1,271	7,461	36,100	136,000
2003	5,584	25,200	2,183	3,708	6,650	23,338	11,000	1,765	2,414	1,471	7,890	35,000	138,000
2004	5,690	25,500	2,219	3,290	6,188	26,675	11,000	1,580	2,883	1,115	8,051	35,800	143,000
2005	5,450	30,400	2,144	3,236	6,375	28,788	11,000	1,455	3,500	1,350	8,220	36,100	150,000
2006	5,930	38,600	2,200	2,949	5,805	27,000	11,000	584	3,664	1,650	7,801	30,100	151,000
2007[1]	6,000	45,400	2,200	3,100	5,540	27,000	11,000	600	3,700	800	7,800	29,700	156,000
2008[2]	6,000	50,000	3,000	3,100	5,500	28,000	11,000	600	3,700	800	7,800	30,900	167,000

[1] Preliminary. [2] Estimate. *Source: U.S. Geological Survey (USGS)*

Salient Statistics of Phosphate Rock in the United States — In Thousands of Metric Tons

Year	Mine Production	Marketable Production	Value Million Dollars	Imports for Consumption	Exports	Apparent Consumption	Producer Stocks, Dec. 31	Avg. Price FOB Mine $/Metric Ton	Avg. Price of Florida & N. Carolina - $/Met. Ton - FOB Mine (-60% to +74%) - Domestic	Export	Average
1999	161,000	40,600	1,240	2,170	272	43,500	6,920	31.49	30.56	41.96	31.49
2000	163,000	38,600	932	1,930	299	39,000	8,170	24.29	24.14	40.38	24.29
2001	130,000	31,900	856	2,500	9	35,300	7,510	26.82	26.82	W	26.81
2002	154,000	36,100	993	2,700	62	37,400	8,860	27.47	27.69	W	27.69
2003	153,000	35,000	946	2,400	64	38,800	7,540	27.01	26.95	W	26.95
2004	146,000	35,800	995	2,500	----	39,000	7,220	27.79	27.76	NA	27.76
2005	151,000	36,100	1,070	2,630	----	37,800	6,970	29.61	29.67	NA	29.60
2006	111,000	30,100	919	2,420	----	32,600	7,070	30.49	W	NA	30.52
2007[1]	126,000	29,700	1,520	2,670	----	33,800	4,970	51.10			
2008[2]		30,900		3,000		34,000	4,900	113.00			

[1] Preliminary. [2] Estimate. *Source: U.S. Geological Survey (USGS)*

World Production of Marketable Potash — In Thousands of Metric Tons (K_2O Equivalent)

Year	Belarus	Brazil	Canada	China	France	Germany	Israel	Jordan	Russia	Spain	United Kingdom	United States	World Total
1999	4,553	348	8,475	260	345	3,543	1,700	1,080	4,200	656	495	1,200	27,300
2000	3,786	352	9,202	380	320	3,407	1,750	1,160	3,700	653	600	1,300	27,000
2001	3,700	319	8,237	385	244	3,549	1,770	1,180	4,300	471	532	1,200	26,400
2002	3,800	337	8,515	450	130	3,472	1,950	1,191	4,400	481	540	1,200	27,100
2003	4,230	416	9,104	500	----	3,564	1,990	1,190	4,740	506	620	1,100	28,600
2004	4,600	403	10,100	551	----	3,627	2,170	1,175	5,600	553	550	1,200	31,100
2005	4,844	405	10,596	600	----	3,664	2,260	1,115	6,270	494	480	1,200	32,500
2006	4,605	405	8,360	600	----	3,620	2,200	1,036	5,720	537	480	1,100	29,100
2007[1]	4,970	405	11,100	2,000	----	3,600	2,200	1,090	6,600	580	427	1,100	34,600
2008[2]	5,100	430	11,000	2,100	----	3,600	2,400	1,200	6,900	590	480	1,200	36,000

[1] Preliminary. [2] Estimate. *Source: U.S. Geological Survey (USGS)*

Salient Statistics of Potash in the United States — In Thousands of Metric Tons (K_2O Equivalent)

Year	Net Import Reliance As a % of Apparent Consumption	Production	Sales by Producers	Value Million Dollars	Imports for Consumption	Exports	Apparent Consumption	Producer Stocks Dec. 31	Avg Value of Product	Avg Value of K_2O Equiv	Avg. Price[3] (Metric Ton)
1999	80	1,200	1,200	280.0	4,470	459	5,100	300	110.00	230.00	150.00
2000	80	1,300	1,200	290.0	4,600	367	5,600	----	110.00	230.00	157.50
2001	80	1,200	1,100	260.0	4,540	366	5,300	----	110.00	230.00	165.00
2002	80	1,200	1,200	280.0	4,620	371	5,400	----	110.00	230.00	155.00
2003	80	1,100	1,200	280.0	4,720	329	5,600	----	110.00	230.00	170.00
2004	80	1,200	1,300	340.0	4,920	233	6,000	----	125.00	270.00	200.00
2005	80	1,200	1,200	410.0	4,920	200	5,900	----	165.00	350.00	280.00
2006	79	1,100	1,100	410.0	4,470	332	5,200	----	170.00	375.00	290.00
2007[1]	81	1,100			4,970	199	5,900	----			400.00
2008[2]	81	1,200			5,250	275	6,200	----			717.00

[1] Preliminary. [2] Estimate. [3] Unit of K_2O, standard 60% muriate F.O.B. mine. *Source: U.S. Geological Survey (USGS)*

Fish

Fish are the primary source of protein for a large portion of the world's population. The worldwide yearly harvest of all sea fish (including aquaculture) is between 85 and 130 million metric tons. There are approximately 20,000 species of fish, of which 9,000 are regularly caught. Only 22 fish species are harvested in large amounts. Ground-fish, which are fish that live near or on the ocean floor, account for about 10% of the world's fishery harvest, and include cod, haddock, pollock, flounder, halibut and sole. Large pelagic fish such as tuna, swordfish, marlin, and mahi-mahi, account for about 5% of world harvest. The fish eaten most often in the United States is canned tuna.

Rising global demand for fish has increased the pressure to harvest more fish to the point where all 17 of the world's major fishing areas have either reached or exceeded their limits. Atlantic stocks of cod, haddock and blue-fin tuna are all seriously depleted, while in the Pacific, anchovies, salmon and halibut are all over-fished. Aquaculture, or fish farming, reduces pressure on wild stocks and now accounts for nearly 20% of world harvest.

Supply – The U.S. grand total of fishery products rose +1.7% to a record high of 20.966 billion pounds in 2006 (latest data available). The U.S. total domestic catch in 2006 fell by -2.3% to 9.489 billion pounds, and that comprised 45% of total U.S. supply. Of the U.S. total domestic catch in 2006, 71% of the catch was finfish for human consumption, 18% of the catch was a variety of fish for industrial use, and 12% was shellfish for human consumption. The principal species of U.S. fishery landings in 2006 were Pollock (with 3.414 billion pounds landed), Menhaden (1.304 billion pounds), Pacific Salmon (663 million pounds), Flounder (446 million pounds), and Sea Herring (365 million pounds).

About 30% of the fish harvested in the world are processed directly into fishmeal and fish oil. Fishmeal is used primarily in animal feed. Fish oil is used in both animal feed and human food products. World fishmeal production in the 2007-08 marketing year rose by +2.4% to 5.537 million metric tons. World production of fish oil in 2007-08 rose +1.0% to 1,055.500 million metric tons. Peru and Chile are the world's largest producers of fishmeal and fish oil.

Trade – U.S. imports of fishery products in 2006 rose +5.3% yr/yr to a record high of 11.477 billion pounds, comprising 55% of total U.S. supply.

Year	Grand Total	For Human Food - Finfish	For Human Food - Shellfish[3]	For Industrial Use[4]	Domestic Catch - Total	Percent of Grand Total	For Human Food - Finfish	For Human Food - Shellfish[3]	For Industrial Use[4]	Imports - Total	Percent of Grand Total	For Human Food - Finfish	For Human Food - Shellfish[3]	For Industrial Use[4]
2000	17,339	11,006	3,734	2,599	9,068	52.3	5,637	1,275	2,157	8,271	47.7	5,369	2,459	442
2001	18,119	11,330	3,977	2,812	9,492	52.4	6,162	1,152	2,178	8,627	47.6	5,168	2,825	634
2002	19,028	11,770	4,237	3,022	9,397	49.4	6,013	1,192	2,193	9,631	50.6	5,757	3,045	829
2003	19,850	12,617	4,570	2,663	9,507	47.9	6,388	1,133	1,986	10,343	52.1	6,229	3,437	677
2004	20,413	12,959	4,689	2,765	9,683	47.4	6,641	1,153	1,889	10,730	52.6	6,318	3,536	876
2005	20,612	13,567	4,588	2,457	9,707	47.1	6,914	1,084	1,710	10,905	52.9	6,653	3,505	747
2006[1]	20,966	13,507	5,054	2,404	9,489	45.3	6,694	1,115	1,680	11,477	54.7	6,813	3,939	725

[1] Preliminary. [2] Live weight, except percent. [3] For univalue and bivalues mollusks (conchs, clams, oysters, scallops, etc.) the weight of meats, excluding the shell is reported. [4] Fish meal and sea herring. *Source: Fisheries Statistics Division, U.S. Department of Commerce*

Fisheries -- Landings of Principal Species in the United States   In Millions of Pounds

Year	Cod, Atlantic	Flounder	Halibut	Herring, Sea	Man-haden	Pollock	Salmon, Pacific	Tuna	Whiting	Clams (Meats)	Crabs	Lobsters American	Oysters (Meats)	Scallops (Meats)	Shrimp
2000	25	413	75	235	1,760	2,616	629	51	27	118	299	83	41	33	332
2001	33	352	78	300	1,741	3,188	723	52	28	123	272	74	33	47	324
2002	29	373	82	214	1,751	3,349	567	49	18	130	308	82	34	53	317
2003	24	365	80	287	1,599	3,372	674	62	19	128	332	74	37	56	315
2004	16	360	80	265	1,498	3,365	739	57	19	119	316	88	39	65	309
2005	14	419	76	303	1,244	3,426	899	44	17	106	299	88	34	57	261
2006[1]	13	446	72	365	1,304	3,414	663	49	13	108	322	93	27	59	292

[1] Preliminary. *Source: National Marine Fisheries Service, U.S. Department of Commerce*

U.S. Fisheries: Quantity & Value of Domestic Catch & Consumption & World Fish Oil Production

Year	Disposition - Fresh & Frozen	Canned	Cured	For Meal, Oil, etc.	Total	For Human Food	For Industrial Products	Ex-vessel Value[3]	Average Price	Fish Per Capita Consumption	World[2] Fish Oil Production
	Millions of Pounds							Million $	Cents /Lb.	Pounds	1,000 Tons
2000	6,657	530	119	1,763	9,069	6,912	2,157	3,550	39.1	NA	1,428
2001	7,085	536	123	1,748	9,492	7,314	2,178	3,228	34.0	NA	1,132
2002	6,826	652	117	1,802	9,397	7,205	2,192	3,092	32.9	NA	946
2003	7,266	498	119	1,624	9,507	7,521	1,986	3,347	35.2	NA	1,006
2004	7,488	552	137	1,506	9,683	7,794	1,889	3,756	38.8	NA	1,129
2005	7,776	563	160	1,208	9,707	7,997	1,710	3,942	40.6	NA	987
2006[1]	7,752	463	108	1,166	9,489	7,809	1,680	3,993	42.1	NA	1,021

[1] Preliminary. [2] Crop years on a marketing year basis. [3] At the Dock Prices. Source: Fisheries Statistics Division, U.S. Department of Commerce

FISH

Imports of Seafood Products into the United States   In Thousands of Pounds

Year	Atlantic Salmon	Pacific Salmon[2]	Shrimp	Fresh & Frozen Trout	Atlantic Salmon	Pacific Salmon[2]	Shrimp	Canned & Prepared Salmon[3]	Fresh & Prepared Shrimp[4]	Oysters[5]	Mussels[6]	Clams[7]	Tilapia[8]
2000	7,095	119,366	19,908	10,658	12,844	620,890	159,254	9,453	140,865	89,202	20,790	43,118	27,791
2001	7,294	132,601	17,592	8,387	10,515	714,340	217,270	11,513	169,225	124,312	18,438	39,973	31,485
2002	9,752	149,083	23,063	6,629	18,354	729,903	257,175	16,417	217,629	148,034	19,084	45,696	30,507
2003	9,044	132,801	22,462	8,776	27,309	879,924	272,802	25,312	234,834	198,955	22,283	43,275	34,416
2004	8,580	121,724	22,396	7,917	40,860	871,856	264,586	24,632	271,199	249,167	23,120	50,817	31,111
2005	7,171	142,244	22,514	5,052	42,270	870,595	275,501	25,672	301,534	297,639	22,912	51,662	32,912
2006	10,215	171,848	20,905	5,137	52,161	920,922	257,970	27,456	385,701	348,707	24,599	50,796	34,454
2007[1]	11,679	178,932	17,583	6,596	52,688	913,977	265,404	30,490	317,811	383,065	24,040	53,104	30,638

[1] Preliminary.   [2] Also contains salmon with no specific species noted.   [3] Includes smoked and cured salmon.   [4] Shrimp, canned, breaded, or prepared.   [5] Oysters fresh or prepared.   [6] Mussels fresh or prepared.   [7] Clams, fresh or prepared.   [8] Tilapia, frozen whole fish plus fresh and frozen fillets.
Source: Bureau of the Census, U.S. Department of Commerce

Exports of Seafood Products From the United States   In Thousands of Pounds

Year	Atlantic Salmon	Pacific Salmon[2]	Shrimp	Fresh & Frozen Trout	Atlantic Salmon	Pacific Salmon[2]	Shrimp	Canned & Prepared Salmon[3]	Fresh & Prepared Shrimp[4]	Oysters[5]	Mussels[6]	Clams[7]
2000	1,818	15,798	39,393	299	161,785	15,158	99,206	14,759	3,230	1,568	4,483	7,250
2001	1,080	18,431	25,198	84	167,558	13,956	128,154	14,320	3,932	1,424	4,232	9,273
2002	1,163	8,444	29,884	84	132,605	13,899	116,419	15,519	3,928	1,179	11,285	10,049
2003	2,600	11,388	39,846	99	155,256	16,395	121,038	16,172	5,905	1,340	10,071	13,443
2004	1,180	13,995	34,249	197	187,954	12,730	138,455	14,620	7,688	924	12,506	16,909
2005	972	11,760	18,965	379	261,124	9,105	146,064	13,026	7,852	1,026	10,523	25,591
2006	875	8,759	19,869	106	219,019	7,544	137,538	12,944	6,241	2,525	12,257	29,110
2007[1]	797	7,255	15,671	257	300,340	8,565	138,950	14,137	6,192	1,886	12,467	24,141

[1] Preliminary.   [2] Also contains salmon with no specific species noted.   [3] Includes smoked and cured salmon.   [4] Shrimp, canned, breaded, or prepared.   [5] Oysters fresh or prepared.   [6] Mussels fresh or prepared.   [7] Clams, fresh or prepared.   *Source: Bureau of the Census, U.S. Department of Commerce*

World Production of Fish Meal   In Thousands of Metric Tons

Year	Chile	Spain	Denmark	European Union	Former USSR	Iceland	Japan	Norway	Peru	South Africa	Thailand	United States	World Total
2000-01	731.0	116.6	311.9	577.7	102.8	283.0	350.0	238.8	2,144.2	97.8	385.9	337.1	6,763.8
2001-02	766.0	95.5	308.2	562.8	72.9	307.9	318.0	222.9	1,688.1	115.7	390.9	349.8	6,212.4
2002-03	858.9	98.0	238.9	495.8	71.8	268.5	326.0	199.2	1,344.6	115.3	398.8	322.4	5,770.4
2003-04	929.7	83.4	255.9	505.5	61.3	214.6	319.0	234.2	1,842.2	136.6	404.3	305.0	6,269.1
2004-05	886.1	79.1	231.2	484.6	59.6	202.1	318.0	155.6	1,949.2	121.3	407.9	308.1	6,134.4
2005-06[1]	857.2	82.3	213.7	473.9	64.0	137.7	315.0	162.4	1,493.3	72.7	430.0	305.1	5,584.9
2006-07[2]	816.7	82.0	164.8	429.3	67.3	149.6	308.0	173.1	1,341.7	88.6	467.0	299.1	5,406.2
2007-08[3]	820.0	81.0	182.0	448.1	70.3	122.0	315.0	158.0	1,450.0	86.1	452.0	305.0	5,536.7

[1] Preliminary.   [2] Estimate.   [3] Forecast.   *Source: The Oil World*

World Production of Fish Oil   In Thousands of Metric Tons

Year	Canada	Chile	China	Denmark	Iceland	Japan	Norway	Peru	Africa	Former USSR	United States	World Total	Fish Oil CIF[4] $ Per Tonne
2000-01	4.1	142.9	17.6	121.3	98.0	65.8	66.4	400.8	4.5	2.7	123.3	1,209.4	375
2001-02	4.3	140.2	22.5	104.1	84.6	64.7	61.2	162.2	5.3	2.9	103.9	935.0	593
2002-03	4.5	152.1	18.3	112.9	122.0	65.6	51.6	208.0	5.4	3.5	89.6	1,017.2	560
2003-04	4.8	176.5	14.0	107.4	74.2	68.1	40.5	263.5	7.1	3.6	81.9	1,038.3	648
2004-05	5.2	182.3	12.0	74.7	59.1	65.8	29.7	342.2	7.1	3.7	77.6	1,048.3	716
2005-06[1]	5.0	179.0	12.1	75.0	51.6	68.5	36.1	287.4	7.5	3.8	62.7	1,008.4	792
2006-07[2]	5.2	172.2	13.0	52.6	53.4	66.9	41.5	334.3	4.5	3.9	73.9	1,044.8	885
2007-08[3]	5.4	180.0	14.5	64.0	46.0	68.0	42.0	320.0	5.3	4.0	74.0	1,055.5	1,500

[1] Preliminary.   [2] Estimate.   [3] Forecast.   [4] Any origin, N.W. Europe.   *Source: The Oil World*

Monthly Production of Catfish--Round Weight Processed--in the United States   In Thousands of Pounds (Live Weight)

Year	Jan.	Feb.	Mar.	Apr.	May	June	July	Aug.	Sept.	Oct.	Nov.	Dec.	Total
2001	46,999	50,257	57,766	52,478	51,736	47,883	47,829	51,690	49,699	52,264	44,670	43,837	597,108
2002	52,551	52,856	58,340	50,694	52,902	49,450	52,363	54,383	53,366	56,576	50,072	48,048	631,601
2003	55,523	55,461	65,007	57,105	58,424	52,441	54,089	54,153	51,885	57,652	51,246	48,518	661,504
2004	53,849	54,173	60,272	53,896	52,324	50,155	51,055	53,295	51,329	52,396	49,536	48,170	630,450
2005	53,856	51,720	57,117	50,306	51,552	49,626	47,241	50,686	47,151	49,034	46,674	45,707	600,670
2006	50,703	49,145	56,315	43,126	42,865	41,214	45,528	51,736	47,296	50,788	45,680	41,735	566,131
2007	46,079	44,083	45,477	37,954	38,867	37,275	39,168	42,626	39,519	45,890	40,307	39,001	496,246
2008[1]	45,992	47,634	47,908	45,018	44,326	43,265	42,583	40,985	39,057	43,344	36,869	32,616	509,597

[1] Preliminary.   *Source: Economic Research Service, U.S. Department of Agriculture ERS-USDA)*

Average Price Paid to Producers for Farm-Raised Catfish in the United States   In Cents Per Pound (Live Weight)

Year	Jan.	Feb.	Mar.	Apr.	May	June	July	Aug.	Sept.	Oct.	Nov.	Dec.	Average
2001	69.3	69.6	69.7	69.4	68.7	66.9	65.6	62.4	61.0	59.6	56.6	55.4	64.5
2002	54.9	55.5	56.5	56.1	57.4	58.8	59.0	58.2	57.6	56.8	56.0	54.4	56.8
2003	52.9	54.4	58.5	63.0	61.8	58.6	56.4	55.2	56.0	56.7	61.0	62.9	58.1
2004	66.8	70.3	72.3	72.8	72.0	68.9	68.2	68.3	68.3	69.5	68.9	69.0	69.6
2005	72.5	73.1	73.3	72.5	72.2	72.1	72.3	72.4	72.4	72.4	72.4	72.6	72.5
2006	72.7	72.9	74.5	78.5	79.6	80.7	81.2	81.1	83.2	83.6	83.7	83.8	79.6
2007	83.7	83.8	83.8	84.1	84.0	81.7	76.2	73.1	69.7	68.2	66.6	65.0	76.7
2008[1]	65.8	68.8	74.3	75.7	77.6	79.4	81.8	82.7	82.7	82.5	82.3	82.1	78.0

[1] Preliminary.   *Source: Economic Research Service, U.S. Department of Agriculture (ERS-USDA)*

Sales of Fresh Catfish in the United States   In Thousands of Pounds

Year	Jan.	Feb.	Mar.	Apr.	May	June	July	Aug.	Sept.	Oct.	Nov.	Dec.	Total
Whole													
2001	3,516	3,242	4,260	3,644	3,271	3,166	3,233	3,204	3,174	3,294	2,865	2,803	39,672
2002	3,713	3,656	3,826	3,373	3,644	3,313	3,477	3,733	3,418	3,822	3,031	2,986	41,992
2003	3,833	3,785	4,339	3,643	3,692	3,266	3,553	3,510	3,233	3,231	2,798	2,693	41,576
2004	3,205	3,266	3,808	3,001	2,853	2,707	2,875	3,002	2,861	3,076	2,950	2,704	36,308
2005	3,111	3,177	3,402	2,938	2,679	2,765	2,686	2,673	2,687	2,546	2,615	2,784	34,063
2006[1]	3,195	3,331	4,024	2,940	2,795	2,464	2,716	2,711					36,264
Fillets[2]													
2001	4,884	6,112	6,751	5,709	5,587	5,122	5,191	5,313	5,264	5,273	4,463	4,489	64,158
2002	5,684	6,132	6,010	5,236	5,682	5,093	5,327	5,442	5,317	5,420	4,447	4,119	63,909
2003	5,362	5,158	6,715	5,700	6,364	5,737	5,984	6,013	5,308	6,082	5,187	4,710	68,320
2004	5,964	6,455	6,815	5,887	5,688	5,500	5,559	5,483	4,865	4,992	4,336	4,162	65,706
2005	5,274	5,615	5,795	4,979	5,274	4,987	4,714	4,998	4,848	5,072	4,291	4,209	60,056
2006[1]	5,160	5,109	6,090	5,077	4,653	4,446	4,279	4,447					58,892
Other[3]													
2001	1,443	1,292	2,156	1,309	1,282	1,298	1,375	1,436	1,449	1,430	1,223	1,252	16,945
2002	1,526	1,446	1,375	1,356	1,732	1,527	1,576	1,569	1,441	1,596	1,165	1,205	17,514
2003	1,668	1,532	1,599	1,458	1,472	1,319	1,425	1,366	1,473	1,361	1,138	1,134	16,945
2004	1,435	1,518	1,567	1,426	1,299	1,248	1,181	1,173	1,228	1,263	1,152	1,095	15,585
2005	1,300	1,295	1,370	1,271	1,204	1,130	1,097	1,128	1,084	1,121	965	900	13,865
2006[1]	1,126	1,024	1,214	987	915	807	863	879					11,723

[1] Preliminary.   [2] Includes regular, shank and strip fillets; excludes breaded products.   [3] Includes steaks, nuggets and all other products not reported.
Source: Economic Research Service, U.S. Department of Agriculture (ERS-USDA)

Prices of Fresh Catfish in the United States   In Dollars Per Pound

Year	Jan.	Feb.	Mar.	Apr.	May	June	July	Aug.	Sept.	Oct.	Nov.	Dec.	Average
Whole													
2001	1.59	1.68	1.63	1.65	1.65	1.62	1.59	1.55	1.53	1.49	1.42	1.37	1.56
2002	1.36	1.35	1.30	1.34	1.36	1.37	1.35	1.32	1.32	1.28	1.24	1.25	1.32
2003	1.28	1.30	1.35	1.37	1.36	1.39	1.33	1.33	1.34	1.36	1.40	1.43	1.35
2004	1.49	1.53	1.57	1.60	1.60	1.57	1.57	1.58	1.56	1.59	1.51	1.57	1.56
2005	1.64	1.64	1.61	1.61	1.61	1.58	1.58	1.57	1.58	1.63	1.55	1.50	1.59
2006[1]	1.53	1.49	1.54	1.65	1.70	1.74	1.72	1.76					1.64
Fillets[2]													
2001	2.80	2.79	2.80	2.80	2.80	2.78	2.77	2.75	2.69	2.63	2.60	2.55	2.73
2002	2.52	2.49	2.49	2.51	2.53	2.55	2.55	2.54	2.54	2.52	2.49	2.47	2.52
2003	2.44	2.45	2.44	2.49	2.51	2.50	2.48	2.48	2.49	2.49	2.50	2.54	2.48
2004	2.59	2.62	2.71	2.73	2.74	2.74	2.73	2.73	2.74	2.76	2.77	2.77	2.72
2005	2.81	2.75	2.85	2.87	2.86	2.85	2.84	2.83	2.83	2.84	2.84	2.84	2.83
2006[1]	2.86	2.87	2.89	2.98	3.08	3.14	3.18	3.20					3.03
Other[3]													
2001	1.64	1.68	1.57	1.64	1.69	1.64	1.61	1.57	1.52	1.59	1.59	1.53	1.61
2002	1.53	1.57	1.54	1.51	1.45	1.51	1.51	1.50	1.54	1.48	1.55	1.46	1.51
2003	1.40	1.41	1.51	1.53	1.47	1.54	1.52	1.58	1.50	1.58	1.60	1.64	1.52
2004	1.63	1.70	1.71	1.78	1.78	1.78	1.62	1.76	1.69	1.72	1.70	1.71	1.72
2005	1.67	1.67	1.74	1.71	1.77	1.78	1.72	1.68	1.64	1.65	1.60	1.65	1.69
2006[1]	1.64	1.63	1.65	1.75	1.73	1.86	1.86	1.85					1.75

[1] Preliminary.   [2] Includes regular, shank and strip fillets; excludes breaded products.   [3] Includes steaks, nuggets and all other products not reported.
Source: Economic Research Service, U.S. Department of Agriculture (ERS-USDA)

Flaxseed and Linseed Oil

Flaxseed, also called linseed, is an ancient crop that was cultivated by the Babylonians around 3,000 BC. Flaxseed is used for fiber in textiles and to produce oil. Flaxseeds contain approximately 35% oil, of which 60% is omega-3 fatty acid. Flaxseed or linseed oil is obtained through either the expeller extraction or solvent extraction method. Manufacturers filter the processed oil to remove some impurities and then sell it as unrefined. Unrefined oil retains its full flavor, aroma, color, and naturally occurring nutrients. Flaxseed oil is used for cooking and as a dietary supplement as well as for animal feed. Industrial linseed oil is not for internal consumption due to possible poisonous additives and is used for making putty, sealants, linoleum, wood preservation, varnishes, and oil paints.

Flaxseed futures and options trade at the Winnipeg Commodity Exchange. The futures contract calls for the delivery of 20 metric tons of flaxseed. The contract is now priced in U.S. dollars per metric ton.

Prices – The average monthly price received by U.S. farmers for flaxseed in the 2008-09 marketing year (through January 2009) rose by +2.7% yr/yr to a record high of $13.93 per bushel.

Supply – World production of flaxseed in the 2007-08 marketing year fell by -23.3% yr/yr to 1.997 million metric tons, down from the 16-year high of 2.898 million metric tons in 2005-06. The world's largest producer of flaxseed is Canada with 35% of world production in 2007-08, followed by the China (24%), India (10%), the former USSR (7%), and the U.S. (7%). U.S. production of flaxseed in 2007-08 fell sharply by -46.4% to 5.904 million bushels, down from the record high of 19.695 million bushels in 2005-06. North Dakota is by far the largest producing state of flaxseed and accounted for 94.0% of flaxseed production in 2007, followed by South Dakota with 1.5% of production and Minnesota with 1.5% of production

World production of linseed oil in 2007-08 rose sharply by +89.5% yr/yr to 1.533 million metric tons. The world's largest producers of linseed oil are China (with 23% of world production in 2007-08), the U.S. (18%), Belgium (18%), and India (9%). U.S. production of linseed oil in 2007-08 fell by −27.2% yr/yr to 212 million pounds.

Demand – U.S. distribution of flaxseed in 2007-08 fell by −19.4% yr/yr to 14.160 million bushels. The breakdown was 77% for crushing into meal and oil, 14% for exports, 4.7% for seed, and 4.6% for residual. U.S. consumption of linseed oil (inedible products) in the 2007-08 marketing year rose by +52.0% yr/yr to 86.430 million pounds.

Trade – U.S. exports of flaxseed in 2007-08 rose by +11.8% yr/yr to 2.000 million bushels. U.S. imports of flaxseed in 2007-08 rose by +34.2% yr/yr to a 10-year high of 7.312 million bushels.

World Production of Flaxseed   In Thousands of Metric Tons

Crop Year	Argen-tina	Australia	Bang-ladesh	Canada	China	Egypt	France	Hungary	India	Romania	United States	Former USSR	World Total
1998-99	85	10	50	1,210	523	24	29	1	265	3	170	55	2,828
1999-00	47	9	46	1,100	404	30	34	2	289	3	200	42	2,868
2000-01	22	9	48	775	520	30	38	1	240	1	273	74	2,361
2001-02	16	9	50	770	273	26	23	1	240	2	291	82	1,980
2002-03	11	9	50	750	409	15	17	1	200	2	301	60	1,974
2003-04	29	9	50	835	450	22	11	1	230	2	265	89	2,221
2004-05	36	10	50	592	460	31	13	2	200	3	263	106	1,990
2005-06[1]	54	10	26	1,150	475	28	25	3	210	1	480	111	2,898
2006-07[2]	38	7	26	1,060	480	27	43	3	200	1	280	148	2,603
2007-08[3]	13	9	27	690	480	27	33	2	190	1	150	152	1,997

[1] Preliminary.   [2] Estimate.   [3] Forecast.   *Source: The Oil World*

Supply and Distribution of Flaxseed in the United States   In Thousands of Bushels

Crop Year Beginning June 1	Planted	Harvested	Yield Per Acre (Bushels)	Beginning Stocks	Pro-duction	Imports	Total Supply	Seed	Crush	Exports	Residual	Total
	---- 1,000 Acres ----			------- Supply -------				------- Distribution -------				
1998-99	336	329	20.4	1,181	6,708	5,992	13,881	313	10,600	476	333	11,723
1999-00	387	381	20.6	2,158	7,864	6,629	16,651	434	11,500	201	2,735	14,884
2000-01	536	517	20.8	1,767	10,730	2,849	15,346	474	12,000	1,017	572	14,038
2001-02	585	578	19.8	1,308	11,455	1,904	14,667	635	10,000	2,386	753	13,774
2002-03	784	703	16.9	893	11,863	2,901	15,657	482	10,500	3,181	416	14,579
2003-04	595	588	17.9	1,078	10,516	4,580	16,174	424	11,260	2,516	686	14,886
2004-05	523	516	20.3	1,288	10,471	5,413	17,069	796	13,600	1,510	301	16,206
2005-06[1]	983	955	20.6	863	19,695	4,256	24,814	659	16,400	3,779	441	21,279
2006-07[2]	813	767	14.4	3,535	11,019	4,501	19,055	650	13,500	2,000	405	16,555
2007-08[3]	354	349	16.9		5,904							

[1] Preliminary.   [2] Estimate.   [3] Forecast.   NA = not avaliable.   *Source: Economic Research Service, U.S. Department of Agriculture (ERS-USDA)*

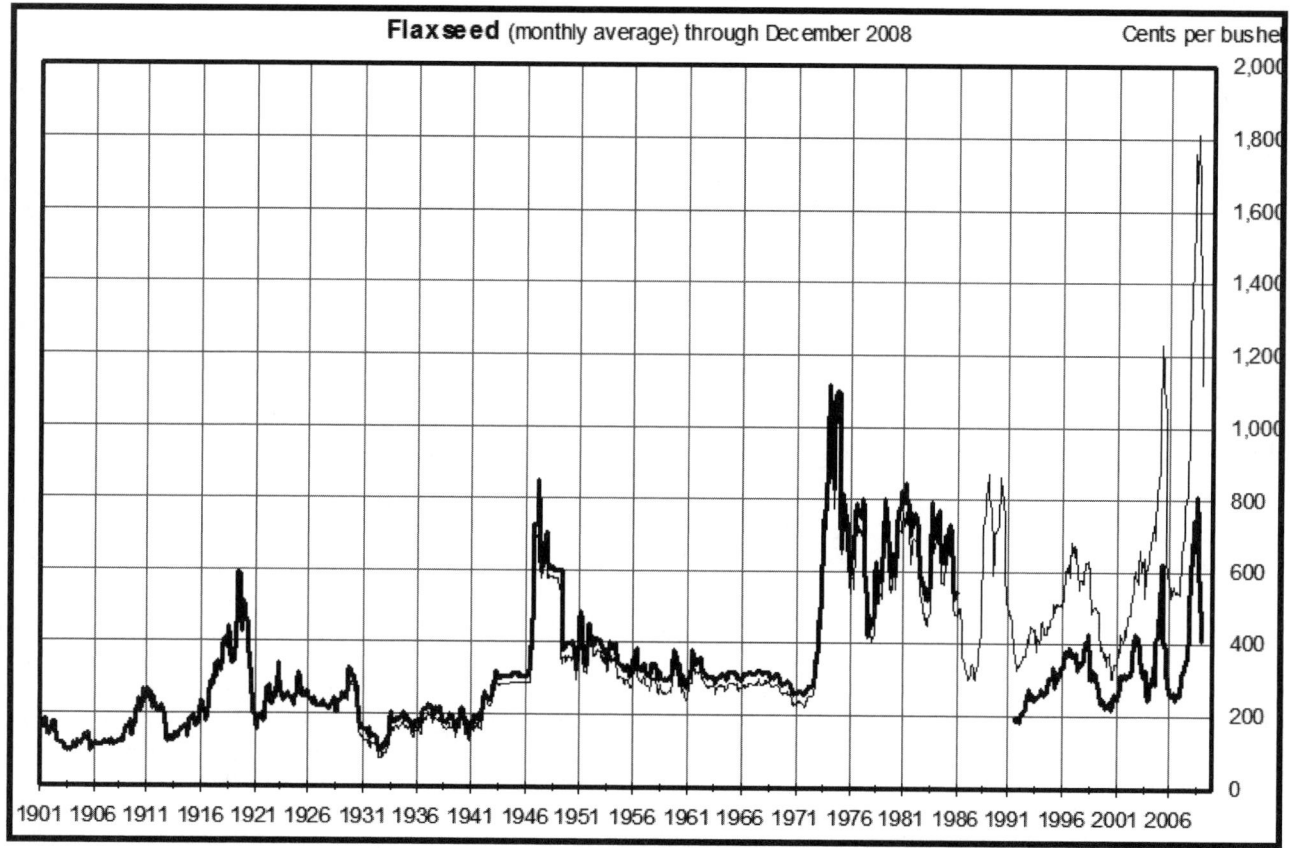

Flaxseed (monthly average) through December 2008 — Cents per bushel

Production of Flaxseed in the United States, by States In Thousands of Bushels

Year	Minnesota	North Dakota	South Dakota	Montana[2]	Total	Year	Minnesota	North Dakota	South Dakota	Montana[2]	Total
1999	198	6,867	357	340	7,864	2004	51	9,840	135	342	10,471
2000	198	9,975	361	196	10,730	2005	132	18,165	480	918	19,695
2001	52	10,900	323	180	11,455	2006	126	10,368	228	297	11,019
2002	64	11,560	44	195	11,863	2007	72	5,548	96	180	5,904
2003	161	9,990	144	221	10,516	2008[1]	69	5,491	84	72	5,716

[1] Preliminary.   [2] Data through 1999 are "Other".   *Source: National Agricultural Statistics Service, U.S. Department of Agriculture (NASS-USDA)*

Factory Shipments of Paints, Varnish and Lacquer in the United States In Millions of Dollars

Year	First Quarter	Second Quarter	Third Quarter	Fourth Quarter	Total	Year	First Quarter	Second Quarter	Third Quarter	Fourth Quarter	Total
1999	3,926.2	4,452.2	4,216.5	3,925.7	16,521	2004	4,306.1	5,000.1	4,843.2	4,104.7	18,254
2000	4,073.1	4,573.5	4,082.0	3,474.7	16,203	2005	4,061.1	5,268.4	4,953.6	4,254.9	18,538
2001	3,625.0	4,345.4	4,094.5	3,652.6	15,718	2006	4,626.5	5,408.8	5,050.5	4,305.7	19,392
2002	3,729.9	4,440.7	4,251.4	3,600.7	16,023	2007	4,311.4	5,483.2	5,245.9	4,277.0	19,318
2003	3,981.5	4,671.8	4,374.7	3,905.8	16,934	2008[1]	4,203.2	5,151.7	5,189.8	3,876.5	18,421

[1] Preliminary.   *Source: Bureau of the Census, U.S. Department of Commerce*

Consumption of Linseed Oil (Inedible Products) in the United States In Millions of Pounds

Year	July	Aug.	Sept.	Oct.	Nov.	Dec.	Jan.	Feb.	Mar.	Apr.	May	June	Average
2001-02	9.6	8.4	9.2	7.4	5.3	5.0	8.2	7.1	6.9	8.0	7.7	8.7	91.3
2002-03	11.7	9.6	10.0	7.0	5.7	7.3	6.8	6.4	8.7	8.5	6.6	6.7	94.9
2003-04	7.9	6.9	6.0	6.8	3.5	5.0	5.6	7.3	6.0	7.7	8.1	8.2	79.1
2004-05	7.3	7.3	6.7	5.6	4.8	5.1	3.7	4.8	4.9	4.0	5.7	4.7	64.6
2005-06	4.8	4.5	4.2	3.7	2.7	2.7	3.9	3.8	4.9	3.3	5.9	6.0	50.5
2006-07	4.4	5.8	5.7	3.5	3.7	2.8	3.6	4.3	4.2	5.0	6.8	7.2	56.8
2007-08	8.6	W	W	W	W	W	5.8	W	W	W	W	W	86.4
2008-09[1]	W	W	W	W	W	W	W						

[1] Preliminary.   W = Withheld.   *Source: Bureau of the Census, U.S. Department of Commerce*

FLAXSEED AND LINSEED OIL

Supply and Distribution of Linseed Oil in the United States   In Millions of Pounds

Crop Year Beginning June 1	Stocks June 1	Production	Total	Exports	Domestic	Total	Average Price at Minneapolis Cents/Lb.
		---- Supply ----		---- Disappearance ----			
1998-99	42	207	261	63	150	213	36.4
1999-00	48	224	285	74	162	236	35.8
2000-01	49	234	295	73	179	252	36.0
2001-02	43	195	249	50	167	218	38.1
2002-03	31	205	249	70	149	219	39.9
2003-04	30	220	265	76	169	245	42.0
2004-05	20	265	301	107	149	256	59.5
2005-06	45	320	375	98	232	330	54.0
2006-07[1]	45	291	344	76	217	293	44.4
2007-08[2]	52	212	276	75	171	246	67.5-71.5

[1] Preliminary.   [2] Forecast.   *Source: Economic Research Service, U.S. Department of Agriculture (ERS-USDA)*

World Production and Price of Linseed Oil   In Thousands of Metric Tons

Year	Argentina	Bangladesh	Belgium	China	Egypt	Germany	India	Japan	United Kingdom	United States	Former USSR	World Total	Rotterdam Ex-TankUSD $/Tonne
1998-99	24.5	13.6	59.2	150.0	15.2	74.1	80.1	26.5	34.3	107.6	10.7	731.1	575
1999-00	13.1	12.6	68.8	118.3	15.0	73.6	85.9	23.8	34.1	124.9	7.9	709.4	413
2000-01	6.2	12.9	75.2	133.0	23.0	63.4	74.7	21.1	17.0	114.7	16.4	669.0	378
2001-02	3.8	13.5	95.0	75.3	15.6	57.3	72.4	18.9	9.9	95.7	20.7	584.1	454
2002-03	2.1	7.5	92.1	111.4	15.1	64.4	63.3	8.6	5.9	105.5	15.1	582.4	679
2003-04	2.3	7.7	119.6	124.0	11.3	66.6	67.7	7.5	6.7	103.8	17.1	631.2	757
2004-05	6.9	7.5	97.9	127.0	12.0	37.9	62.7	6.8	3.5	135.5	16.3	628.9	1,191
2005-06	13.1	9.0	97.9	137.6	14.8	65.2	63.7	5.7	3.5	147.7	16.2	696.2	686
2006-07[1]	5.0	10.6	135.9	146.6	16.5	59.3	61.7	6.2	5.3	140.3	14.1	729.8	809
2007-08[2]	2.2	10.1	120.0	150.5	12.5	51.8	59.2	4.6	2.8	119.6	24.8	672.1	1,533

[1] Preliminary.   [2] Forecast.   *Source: The Oil World*

Average Price Received by Farmers for Flaxseed in the United States   In Dollars Per Bushel

Year	July	Aug.	Sept.	Oct.	Nov.	Dec.	Jan.	Feb.	Mar.	Apr.	May	June	Average
1999-00	4.40	3.86	4.00	3.76	3.66	3.61	3.75	3.43	3.70	3.66	3.77	3.64	3.77
2000-01	3.25	3.05	3.10	3.17	3.39	4.45	3.42	3.43	3.90	3.68	3.91	4.10	3.57
2001-02	4.28	4.09	4.10	4.21	4.33	4.55	4.22	4.75	4.75	4.80	5.02	5.29	4.53
2002-03	5.38	5.27	5.55	5.76	6.04	5.92	5.71	6.25	6.47	6.57	6.05	6.02	5.92
2003-04	6.38	5.30	5.43	5.77	6.02	6.15	6.08	6.39	6.53	7.01	7.10	7.23	6.28
2004-05	7.33	6.90	7.19	7.36	8.62	8.42	8.89	10.90	11.40	12.30	11.60	11.20	9.34
2005-06	10.40	6.28	6.10	6.05	5.94	5.81	5.64	5.59	5.31	5.56	5.59	5.40	6.14
2006-07	5.47	5.50	5.46	5.41	5.38	5.73	6.03	6.39	6.79	6.72	7.08	7.81	6.15
2007-08	8.14	8.64	9.55	11.60	12.90	13.10	13.50	15.70	17.60	17.30	16.80	18.00	13.57
2008-09[1]	18.10	16.50	15.60	12.60	13.00	11.20	10.50						13.93

[1] Preliminary.   *Source: National Agricultural Statistics Service, U.S. Department of Agriculture (NASS-USDA)*

Stocks of Linseed Oil (Crude and Refined) at Factories and Warehouses in the U.S.   In Millions of Pounds

Year	July 1	Aug. 1	Sept. 1	Oct. 1	Nov. 1	Dec. 1	Jan. 1	Feb. 1	Mar. 1	Apr. 1	May 1	June 1
1999-00	68.7	65.5	68.9	74.0	92.4	69.6	72.0	69.5	65.7	53.9	49.1	44.2
2000-01	39.5	42.5	41.3	54.3	58.7	87.0	61.6	50.1	50.5	51.2	39.2	44.8
2001-02	29.1	30.2	22.6	38.4	32.4	29.9	33.4	36.6	26.8	33.4	32.3	31.1
2002-03	27.8	17.7	12.8	21.8	30.5	29.0	31.9	35.9	34.6	36.2	33.7	33.7
2003-04	30.2	27.2	22.3	78.5	42.0	35.0	40.0	43.4	37.6	32.9	24.5	19.9
2004-05	15.1	15.8	8.0	13.0	17.1	26.9	31.3	35.4	35.4	41.0	43.9	47.2
2005-06	38.1	24.8	14.1	33.9	31.1	21.0	29.4	38.4	42.2	32.2	25.5	29.8
2006-07	22.2	27.9	21.6	23.6	28.4	33.5	38.5	41.5	44.9	44.3	49.6	51.6
2007-08	41.5	44.4	49.5	39.4	50.3	49.9	34.3	22.8	37.1	28.0	35.6	26.5
2008-09[1]	22.4	26.1	31.8	28.5	30.3	37.7	37.6	47.5				

[1] Preliminary.   *Source: Bureau of the Census, U.S. Department of Commerce*

Wholesale Price of Raw Linseed Oil at Minneapolis in Tank Cars   In Cents Per Pound

Year	Jan.	Feb.	Mar.	Apr.	May	June	July	Aug.	Sept.	Oct.	Nov.	Dec.	Average
1998-99	37.00	37.00	37.00	37.00	37.00	37.00	36.00	36.00	36.00	36.00	36.00	36.00	36.50
1999-00	36.00	36.00	36.00	36.00	36.00	36.00	36.00	36.00	36.00	36.00	36.00	36.00	36.00
2000-01	36.00	36.00	36.00	36.00	36.00	36.00	36.00	36.00	36.00	36.00	36.00	32.00	35.67
2001-02	35.50	38.00	39.00	39.00	39.00	39.00	39.00	39.00	39.00	39.00	39.65	40.35	38.79
2002-03	40.00	38.00	41.00	31.75	41.00	41.00	41.00	41.00	41.00	41.00	41.19	41.75	39.97
2003-04	41.75	41.75	42.00	42.75	43.13	43.25	42.60	40.00	40.00	40.00	45.00	45.50	42.31
2004-05	48.50	50.00	55.00	57.20	60.00	58.17	60.80	64.00	66.00	73.75	75.00	75.00	61.95
2005-06	75.00	75.00	75.00	48.75	42.75	43.50	42.40	42.00	42.38	42.94	43.10	42.35	51.26
2006-07	43.30	43.25	43.44	43.83	44.00	44.38	44.60	44.67	46.00	46.10	46.50	47.75	44.82
2007-08[1]	49.00	NA	65.67	70.00	72.64	75.00							66.46

[1] Preliminary.   *Source: Economic Research Service, U.S. Department of Agriculture (ERS-USDA)*

Average Price of Linseed Meal (34% protein) at Minneapolis   In Dollars Per Ton

Year	Jan.	Feb.	Mar.	Apr.	May	June	July	Aug.	Sept.	Oct.	Nov.	Dec.	Average
1999-00	75.00	71.30	80.00	89.40	119.50	105.00	91.80	92.60	108.80	111.00	101.00	106.30	95.98
2000-01	115.10	106.50	95.70	110.00	113.80	121.30	140.00	130.00	121.90	116.30	116.80	110.00	116.45
2001-02	135.00	135.60	111.30	114.00	122.50	124.40	123.70	119.20	114.50	112.80	112.50	113.50	119.92
2002-03	127.50	143.80	127.10	114.00	113.10	112.50	118.40	120.10	133.00	126.70	125.00	127.30	124.04
2003-04	129.10	130.60	125.20	139.90	178.80	162.30	166.30	174.40	193.60	197.80	181.80	151.80	160.97
2004-05	139.80	112.40	112.40	99.50	114.60	109.10	111.60	109.90	109.80	104.00	96.00	116.00	111.26
2005-06	159.40	157.80	99.00	100.40	113.60	118.00	127.30	130.20	129.00	126.60	119.10	116.90	124.78
2006-07	111.50	101.10	92.80	100.80	118.10	123.30	134.20	156.40	156.30	149.00	135.10	132.00	125.88
2007-08	135.80	123.90	131.40	170.20	184.60	186.80	242.70	250.00	247.10	253.70	240.30	265.40	202.66
2008-09[1]	273.70	231.30	200.00	160.80	164.00	189.60							203.23

[1] Preliminary.   *Source: Economic Research Service, U.S. Department of Agriculture (ERS-USDA)*

Volume of Trading of Flaxseed Futures in Winnipeg   In Contracts

Year	Jan.	Feb.	Mar.	Apr.	May	June	July	Aug.	Sept.	Oct.	Nov.	Dec.	Total
1996	9,617	8,301	4,110	13,531	10,855	7,997	6,517	4,153	5,430	11,126	7,532	10,720	99,889
1997	7,640	6,486	7,123	10,912	6,256	7,851	7,662	7,081	20,967	23,418	20,049	15,311	140,756
1998	15,713	19,906	8,275	9,060	5,231	7,642	4,468	4,062	7,328	13,085	13,824	6,958	115,552
1999	4,855	8,922	4,383	8,460	5,241	5,891	4,863	2,833	5,852	12,078	7,710	7,345	78,433
2000	9,022	9,340	9,292	12,604	7,372	7,393	2,676	2,525	9,822	11,915	14,436	7,819	100,040
2001	8,232	6,428	6,928	7,117	6,514	6,745	4,344	2,620	5,242	7,291	4,689	6,326	72,476
2002	2,990	2,838	2,519	3,832	3,320	3,018	1,153	810	777	3,030	955	344	25,586
2003	333	724	412	368	452	738	343	96	491	273	183	25	4,438
2004	35	10	15	0	0	0	0	0	15	0	0	15	90
2005	0	0	0	0	0	0	0	0	0	0	0	0	

Source: Winnipeg Commodity Exchange (WCE)

Flaxseed Futures - Winnipeg Commodity Exchange
(weekly close) as of October 31, 2005
CAD per metric ton

Fruits

A fruit is any seed-bearing structure produced from a flowering plant. A widely used classification system divides fruit into fleshy or dry types. Fleshy fruits are juicy and include peaches, mangos, apples, and blueberries. Dry fruits include tree nuts such as almonds, walnuts, and pecans. Some foods that are commonly called vegetables, such as tomatoes, squash, peppers and eggplant, are technically fruits because they develop from the ovary of a flower.

Worldwide, over 430 million tons of fruit are produced each year and are grown everywhere except the Arctic and the Antarctic. The tropics, because of their abundant moisture and warm temperatures, produce the most diverse and abundant fruits. Mexico and Chile produce more than half of all the fresh and frozen fruit imported into the U.S. In the U.S., the top three fruits produced are oranges, grapes, and apples. Virtually all U.S. production of almonds, pistachios, and walnuts occurs in California, which leads the U.S. in tree nut production.

Prices – Overall fruit prices were fairly strong in 2007 with the fresh fruit Consumer Price Index (CPI) rising +4.5% to 329.5 and the processed fruit CPI index rising +2.1% to 125.2. Individual fruit prices, however, were mixed in 2007: Red Delicious Apples (+4.6% to $1.115 per pound), bananas (+2.0% to 51.0 cents per pound), Anjou pears (+12.3% to $1.273 per pound), Thompson seedless grapes (-6.9% to $2.092 per pound), lemons (+21.5% to $1.857 per pound), grapefruit (-13.4% to $0.964 per pound), navel oranges (+18.2% to $1.284 cents per pound), and Valencia oranges (+7.3% to $1.074 per pound).

Supply – U.S. commercial production of selected fruits in 2007 fell –4.5% to 27.152 million short tons. By weight, oranges accounted for 28% of that U.S. fruit production figure, followed by grapes at 26%, and apples at 17%. The value of U.S. fruit production in 2007 rose +9.0% yr/yr to $18.525 billion.

Demand – U.S. per capita fresh fruit consumption in 2007 fell -3.6% to 97.46 pounds per year, but remained below the 2004 record high of 102.3. The highest per capita consumption categories for non-citrus fruits in 2007 were bananas (25.93 pounds) and apples (16.43 pounds). Per capital consumption of citrus fruits were oranges (7.44 pounds), grapefruit (2.83 pounds, lemons (2.80 pounds), and Tangerines & Tangelos (2.55 pounds). The utilization breakdown for 2007 shows that total U.S. non-citrus fruit was used for fresh fruit (41%), wine (23%), dried fruit (12%), canned fruit (8%), juice (7%), and frozen fruit (4%). The value of utilized non-citrus fruit production in 2007 rose +7.8% yr/yr to $11.406 billion.

Commercial Production for Selected Fruits in the United States   In Thousands of Short Tons

Year	Apples	Cherries[2]	Cran-berries	Grapes	Grape-fruit	Lemons	Nect-arines	Oranges	Peaches	Pears	Pine-apple[3]	Prunes & Plums	Straw-berries	Tang-elos	Tang-erines	Total All Fruits
2001	4,712	415	267	6,569	2,462	996	275	12,221	1,204	1,027	323	651	826	95	373	32,916
2002	4,262	213	285	7,339	2,424	801	300	12,374	1,268	890	320	736	942	97	420	33,173
2003	4,397	359	310	6,644	2,063	1,026	273	11,545	1,260	934	300	803	1,078	105	382	31,992
2004	5,220	390	309	6,240	2,165	798	269	12,872	1,307	878	220	325	1,107	45	417	33,027
2005	4,853	386	312	7,814	1,018	870	251	9,252	1,185	823	212	476	1,161	70	335	29,572
2006	4,936	425	345	6,377	1,232	980	232	9,021	1,010	842	185	813	1,202	63	417	28,417
2007[1]	4,557	437	328	7,018	1,627	798	283	7,625	1,129	873		405	1,250	56	361	27,152

[1] Preliminary.   [2] Sweet and tart.   [3] Utilized production.   *Source: Economic Research Service, U.S. Department of Agriculture (ERS-USDA)*

Utilized Production for Selected Fruits in the United States   In Thousands of Short Tons

	---------------------- Utilized Production ----------------------				-------------------------- Value of Production --------------------------			
	Citrus[2]	Noncitrus	Tree nuts[3]	Total	Citrus[2]	Noncitrus	Tree nuts[3]	Total
Year	---------------------- In Thousands of Short Tons ----------------------				-------------------------- In Thousands of Dollars --------------------------			
2001	16,216	16,740	1,304	34,260	2,319,917	7,918,636	1,513,063	11,751,616
2002	16,194	17,122	1,448	34,764	2,610,559	8,137,640	2,078,670	12,826,869
2003	15,180	16,853	1,458	33,491	2,259,976	8,617,592	2,472,480	13,350,048
2004	16,360	16,837	1,524	34,720	2,485,052	8,549,887	3,527,904	14,562,843
2005	11,574	18,294	1,467	31,335	2,303,425	9,830,977	4,175,893	16,310,295
2006	11,745	16,852	1,598	30,195	2,738,361	10,581,944	3,680,383	17,000,688
2007[1]	10,467	17,065	1,992	29,524	3,147,755	11,406,349	3,971,000	18,525,104

[1] Preliminary.   [2] Year harvest was completed.   [3] Tree nuts on an in-shell equivalent.
Source: Economic Research Service, U.S. Department of Agriculture (ERS-USDA)

Annual Average Retail Prices for Selected Fruits in the United States   In Dollars Per Pound

Year	Red Delicious Apples	Bananas	Anjou Pears	Thompson Seedless Grapes	Lemons	Grapefruit	------------ Oranges ------------	
							Navel	Valencias
2001	.868	.507	.966	1.850	1.265	.651	.722	.524
2002	.948	.508	.997	1.887	1.391	.648	.836	.565
2003	.980	.509	NA	1.899	1.317	.723	.838	.575
2004	1.043	.495	NA	2.059	1.235	.819	.859	.691
2005	.949	.492	1.114	2.078	1.411	.998	.996	.897
2006	1.067	.500	1.133	2.246	1.529	1.114	1.087	1.001
2007[1]	1.115	.510	1.273	2.092	1.857	.964	1.284	1.074

[1] Estimate.   *Source: Economic Research Service, U.S. Department of Agriculture (ERS-USDA)*

Utilization of Noncitrus Fruit Production, and Value in the United States   1,000 Short Tons (Fresh Equivalent)

Year	Utilized Production	Fresh	Canned	Dried	Juice	Frozen	Wine	Other Processed	Value of Utilized Production $1,000
1998	16,552	6,514	1,845	1,911	1,786	711	3,315	198	7,251,032
1999	17,347	6,691	1,986	2,154	1,887	717	3,351	244	8,077,404
2000	18,854	7,015	1,812	3,023	1,712	691	4,130	191	7,883,036
2001	16,740	6,488	1,859	2,290	1,462	665	3,568	169	7,918,636
2002	17,122	6,549	1,727	2,582	1,251	591	3,999	138	8,137,640
2003	16,853	6,676	1,762	2,293	1,295	716	3,582	219	8,617,592
2004	16,837	7,177	1,711	1,425	1,421	685	3,819	290	8,549,887
2005	18,294	7,202	1,575	2,101	1,562	713	4,551	277	9,830,977
2006	16,852	6,959	1,401	2,219	1,262	675	3,725	271	10,581,944
2007[1]	17,065	7,063	1,435	2,012	1,260	709	3,920	338	11,406,349

[1] Preliminary.   *Source: Economic Research Service, U.S. Department of Agriculture (ERS-USDA)*

Average Price Indexes for Fruits in the United States

Year	Index of all Fruit & Nut Prices Received by Growers (1990-92=100)	Fresh Fruit	Dried Fruit	Canned Fruits and Juices	Frozen Fruits and Juices	Fresh Fruit	Processed Fruit
1998	111	90.5	121.8	134.3	101.5	246.5	101.9
1999	115	103.6	122.9	137.0	106.1	266.3	105.4
2000	98	91.4	122.4	139.5	108.9	258.3	106.9
2001	109	97.7	120.3	143.3	111.9	265.1	109.0
2002	105	91.5	120.7	141.7	111.2	270.2	111.6
2003	106	84.1	122.1	142.3	115.7	279.1	113.7
2004	124	104.9	NA	143.1	113.3	286.8	114.0
2005	131	102.8	NA	148.1	112.4	297.4	118.4
2006	154	111.0	NA	153.0	113.2	315.2	121.5
2007[1]	157	123.4	NA	156.9	117.9	329.5	125.2

Columns: Index of all Fruit & Nut Prices (1990-92=100); Producer Price Index (Fresh Fruit, Dried Fruit, Canned Fruits and Juices, Frozen Fruits and Juices) 1982 = 100; Consumer Price Index (Fresh Fruit, Processed Fruit) 1982-84 = 100.

[1] Estimate.   NA = Not availavle.   *Source: Economic Research Service, U.S. Department of Agriculture (ERS-USDA)*

Fresh Fruit: Per Capita Consumption[1] in the United States   In Pounds

Year	Oranges	Tangerines & Tangelos	Lemons	Grapefruit	Total	Apples	Apricots	Avocados	Bananas	Cherries	Cranberries
1998	14.61	2.17	2.46	5.94	26.58	18.98	.12	1.52	28.01	.52	.08
1999	8.38	2.30	2.61	5.75	20.37	18.50	.12	1.92	30.70	.63	.11
2000	11.74	2.86	2.44	5.09	23.51	17.45	.15	2.21	28.44	.60	.14
2001	11.87	2.72	2.96	4.84	23.90	15.59	.08	2.50	26.62	.77	.13
2002	11.73	2.55	3.33	4.62	23.33	15.98	.09	2.33	26.75	.70	.11
2003	11.88	2.71	3.32	4.09	23.92	16.90	.13	2.74	26.13	.92	.10
2004	10.78	2.76	3.12	4.13	22.67	18.82	.12	3.06	25.73	.99	.11
2005	11.39	2.49	2.94	2.64	21.60	16.72	.13	3.47	25.17	.81	.09
2006	10.19	2.68	4.14	2.30	21.49	17.83	.08	3.59	25.09	1.09	.09
2007[2]	7.44	2.55	2.80	2.83	18.00	16.43	.16	3.40	25.93	1.25	.10

Columns: Cutrus Fruit (Oranges, Tangerines & Tangelos, Lemons, Grapefruit, Total); Noncitrus Fruit (Apples, Apricots, Avocados, Bananas, Cherries, Cranberries).

[1] All data on calendar-year basis except for citrus fruits; apples, August; grapes and pears, July; grapefruit, September; lemons, August of prior year; all other citrus, November.   [2] Preliminary.   *Source: Economic Research Service, U.S. Department of Agriculture (ERS-USDA)*

Fresh Fruit: Per Capita Consumption[1] in the United States   In Pounds

Noncitrus Fruit Continued

Year	Grapes	Kiwifruit	Mangos	& Peaches	Pears	Pineapples	Papaya	Prunes	Strawberries	Total Noncitrus	Total Fruit
1998	7.17	.53	1.49	4.69	3.43	2.75	.47	1.18	3.92	75.19	101.77
1999	7.97	.52	1.62	5.29	3.53	3.03	.62	1.28	4.57	80.72	101.09
2000	7.44	.56	1.75	5.30	3.39	3.22	.68	1.19	4.86	77.66	101.17
2001	7.37	.44	1.79	5.16	3.25	3.16	.78	1.33	4.21	73.53	97.43
2002	8.40	.38	1.97	5.22	3.06	3.81	.79	1.25	4.65	75.88	99.21
2003	7.64	.38	2.06	5.16	3.07	4.39	.87	1.24	5.28	77.40	101.32
2004	7.78	.41	2.01	5.13	2.95	4.42	1.03	1.12	5.47	79.67	102.34
2005	8.59	.45	1.88	4.82	2.91	4.90	.94	1.11	5.82	78.25	99.85
2006	7.59	.47	2.10	4.58	3.19	5.20	1.04	1.02	6.13	79.64	101.12
2007[2]	8.01	.41	2.10	4.47	3.09	5.02	1.08	1.01	6.44	79.46	97.46

[1] All data on calendar-year basis except for citrus fruits; apples, August; grapes and pears, July; grapefruit, September; lemons, August of prior year; all other citrus, November.   [2] Preliminary.   *Source: Economic Research Service, U.S. Department of Agriculture (ERS-USDA)*

Gas

Natural gas is a fossil fuel that is colorless, shapeless, and odorless in its pure form. It is a mixture of hydrocarbon gases formed primarily of methane, but it can also include ethane, propane, butane, and pentane. Natural gas is combustible, clean burning, and gives off a great deal of energy. Around 500 BC, the Chinese discovered that the energy in natural gas could be harnessed. They passed it through crude bamboo-shoot pipes and then burned it to boil sea water to create potable fresh water. Around 1785, Britain became the first country to commercially use natural gas produced from coal for streetlights and indoor lights. In 1821, William Hart dug the first well specifically intended to obtain natural gas and he is generally regarded as the "father of natural gas" in America. There is a vast amount of natural gas estimated to still be in the ground in the U.S. Natural gas as a source of energy is significantly less expensive than electricity per Btu.

Natural gas futures and options are traded on the New York Mercantile Exchange (NYMEX). The NYMEX natural gas futures contract calls for the delivery of natural gas representing 10,000 million British thermal units (mmBtu) at the Henry Hub in Louisiana, which is the nexus of 16 intra-state and inter-state pipelines. The contract is priced in terms of dollars per mmBtu. NYMEX also has basic swap futures contracts available for 30 different natural gas pricing locations versus the benchmark Henry Hub location. Natural gas futures are also listed in London on the International Petroleum Exchange (IPE).

Prices – NYMEX natural gas futures on the nearest-futures chart in 2008 started the year at about $7.84 per mmBtu. The price was already in an uptrend and continued to move higher to reach a high of $13.69 per mmBtu in July. From there the price moved sharply lower and ended the year at about $5.87 per mmBtu.

Supply –U.S. recovery of natural gas in 2007 (latest data available) rose +4.5% to a record high of 24,591 billion cubic feet. The top U.S. producing states for natural gas were Texas with 29% of U.S. production in 2006, (latest data) Oklahoma with 9%, Wyoming with 9%, New Mexico with 8%, and Louisiana with 7%. In 2008 the world's largest natural gas producers were Russia with 1,922,240 terajoules of production and the U.S. with 1,870,393 terajoules.

Demand – U.S.- delivered consumption of natural gas in 2007 (latest data available) rose +6.28% yr/yr to 23,047 billion cubic feet, of which about 30% was delivered to electrical utility plants, 29% to industrial establishments, 21% to residences, and 13% to commercial establishments.

Trade – U.S. imports of natural gas (consumed) in 2006 (latest data available) fell -3.6% yr/yr to 4,186 billion cubic feet, down from last year's record high of 4,341 billion cubic feet. U.S. exports of natural gas in 2006 fell –0.6% yr/yr to 724 billion cubic feet, down further from the 2004 record high of 854 billion cubic feet.

World Production of Natural Gas (Monthly Average Marketed Production[3])   In Terajoule[4]

Year	Australia	Canada	China	Germany	Indonesia	India	Italy	Mexico	Nether-lands	Romania	Russia	United Kingdom	United States
1999	92,440	569,819	79,523	62,651	282,485	91,468	56,616	182,610	186,672	38,952	1,807,313	345,040	1,790,617
2000	92,746	588,447	90,287	59,164	267,707	94,783	54,289	178,861	178,989	38,254	1,898,046	377,565	1,812,716
2001	96,523	550,463	98,431	60,463	258,122	91,063	48,008	171,940	192,180	40,422	1,887,953	370,237	1,848,810
2002	96,841	553,183	106,720	61,147	280,939	92,568	46,190	168,675	186,206	38,004	1,934,011	361,414	1,792,367
2003	99,771	534,434	111,352	61,441	289,371	89,570	42,812	174,733	178,853	38,831	2,016,895	358,798	1,726,221
2004	104,731	537,643	132,281	55,108	282,364	83,996	39,760	177,650	232,485	41,725	2,055,061	333,492	1,564,674
2005	108,249	547,204	163,802	55,089	267,057	92,451	38,167	187,151	218,699	40,959	2,065,477	307,775	1,636,149
2006	115,535	551,397	193,124	55,557	279,573	101,003	34,670	208,018	191,741	33,977	2,134,095	277,025	1,682,950
2007[1]	118,726	539,861	223,107	55,914	276,893	101,146	30,839	234,278	189,494	34,001	2,117,364	251,428	1,745,050
2008[2]	110,356	513,966	262,827	57,664	267,073	102,887	29,253	266,328	200,641	32,204	1,922,240	238,928	1,870,393

[1] Preliminary.   [2] Estimate.   [3] Compares all gas collected & utilized as fuel or as a chemical industry raw material, including gas used in oilfields and/or gasfields as a fuel by producers.   [4] Terajoule = 10 to the 12th power Joule = approximately 10 to the 9th power BTU.   *Source: United Nations*

Marketed Production of Natural Gas in the United States, by States   In Million Cubic Feet

Year	Alaska	California	Colorado	Kansas	Louisiana[2]	Michigan	Mississippi	Mexico	Oklahoma	Texas[2]	Wyoming	Total
1999	462,967	382,715	722,738	553,419	1,566,916	277,364	111,021	1,511,671	1,594,002	5,054,486	971,230	19,804,848
2000	458,995	376,580	752,985	525,729	1,455,014	296,556	88,558	1,695,295	1,612,890	5,282,104	1,088,328	20,197,511
2001	471,440	377,824	817,206	480,145	1,502,086	275,036	107,541	1,689,125	1,615,384	5,282,723	1,363,879	20,570,295
2002	463,301	360,205	937,245	454,901	1,361,751	274,476	112,980	1,632,080	1,581,606	5,141,075	1,453,957	19,884,780
2003	489,757	337,216	1,011,285	418,893	1,350,399	236,987	133,901	1,604,015	1,558,155	5,243,567	1,539,318	19,974,360
2004	471,899	319,919	1,079,235	397,121	1,353,249	259,681	63,353	1,632,539	1,655,769	5,067,315	1,592,203	19,517,491
2005	487,282	317,637	1,133,086	377,229	1,296,048	261,112	52,923	1,645,166	1,670,137	5,276,401	1,639,317	18,927,095
2006	444,724	315,209	1,202,821	371,044	1,361,119	365,294	60,531	1,609,223	1,688,985	5,548,022	1,816,201	19,409,674
2007	433,485				1,363,538			1,544,830	1,744,393	6,091,724	1,923,224	20,019,321
2008[1]	404,410				1,354,075			1,468,180	1,880,334	6,981,519	2,266,412	21,452,377

[1] Preliminary.   *Source: Energy Information Administration, U.S. Department of Energy (EIA-DOE)*

World Production of Natural Gas Plant Liquids   Thousand Barrels per Day

Year	Algeria	Canada	Mexico	Saudi Arabia	Russia	United States	Persian Gulf[2]	OAPEC[3]	OPEC-12[4]	OPEC-11[4]	World
2000	230	699	438	1,008	232	1,911	1,556	1,837	2,101	2,101	6,466
2001	250	709	433	1,051	237	1,868	1,721	2,029	2,304	2,304	6,766
2002	270	698	408	1,095	246	1,880	1,797	2,137	2,403	2,403	6,877
2003	280	724	418	1,220	390	1,719	1,972	2,312	2,551	2,548	7,152
2004	292	658	442	1,310	456	1,809	2,100	2,437	2,707	2,702	7,393
2005	295	645	426	1,460	457	1,717	2,282	2,654	2,943	2,930	7,654
2006	310	685	427	1,427	417	1,739	2,289	2,688	3,024	2,999	7,795
2007	342	728	396	1,440	426	1,783	2,313	2,769	3,096	3,083	7,956
2008[1]	357	682	365	1,434	422	1,781	2,339	2,808	3,152		7,943

Average. [1] Preliminary. [2] Bahrain, Iran, Iraq, Kuwait, Qatar, Saudi Arabia, and the United Arab Emirates. [3] Organization of Arab Petroleum Exporting Countriess: Algeria, Iraq, Kuwait, Libya, Qatar, Saudi Arabia, and the United Arab Emirates. [4] OPEC-12: Organization of the Petroleum Exporting Countries: Algeria, Angola, Indonesia, Iran, Iraq, Kuwait, Libya, Nigeria, Qatar, Saudi Arabia, the United Arab Emirates, and Venezuela. OPEC-11 does not include Angola. *Source: Energy Information Administration, U.S. Department of Energy (EIA-DOE)*

Recoverable Reserves and Deliveries of Natural Gas in the United States   In Billions of Cubic Feet

Year	Gross With-drawals	Recoverable Reserves of Natural Gas Dec. 31[2]	Residential	Commercial	Electric Utility Plants[3]	Industrial	Total	Lease & Plant Fuel	Used as Pipline Fuel	Heating Value BTU per Cubic Foot
1999	23,823	167,406	4,726	3,045	4,820	8,079	20,681	1,079	645	1,027
2000	24,174	177,427	4,996	3,182	5,206	8,142	21,540	1,151	642	1,025
2001	24,501	183,460	4,771	3,023	5,342	7,344	22,239	1,119	625	1,028
2002	23,941	186,946	4,889	3,144	5,672	7,507	23,007	1,113	667	1,027
2003	24,119	189,044	5,079	3,179	5,135	7,150	22,277	1,122	591	1,031
2004	23,970	192,513	4,869	3,129	5,464	7,243	22,389	1,098	566	1,027
2005	23,457	204,385	4,827	2,999	5,869	6,597	22,011	1,112	584	1,029
2006	23,535	211,085	4,368	2,832	6,222	6,512	21,685	1,142	584	1,028
2007[1]	24,591	237,726	4,717	3,017	6,841	6,625	23,047	1,199	623	1,029

[1] Preliminary. [2] Estimated proved recoverable reserves of dry natural gas. [3] Figures include gas other than natural (impossible to segregate); therefore, shown separately from other consumption. *Source: Energy Information Administration, U.S. Department of Energy (EIA-DOE)*

Gas Utility Sales in the United States by Types and Class of Service   In Trillions of BTUs

Year	Total Utility Sales	Number of Customers (Millions)	Resi-dential	Commer-cial	Industrial	Electric Generation	Other	Total	Resi-dental	Commer-cial	Industrial	Electric Generation	Other
1998	8,781	61.5	4,534	2,063	1,370	810	5	47,084	30,130	11,020	4,189	1,726	20
1999	8,975	60.8	4,622	2,067	1,553	729	5	47,202	30,095	10,731	4,715	1,641	21
2000	9,232	61.3	4,741	2,077	1,698	709	6	59,243	35,828	13,338	7,432	2,612	33
2001	8,667	61.4	4,525	2,053	1,461	620	8	69,150	42,454	16,848	7,513	2,286	49
2002	8,864	62.0	4,589	2,055	1,748	459	13	57,112	35,062	13,512	6,840	1,639	59
2003	8,927	62.6	4,722	2,125	1,672	397	11	72,606	43,664	17,349	9,478	2,048	68
2004	8,766	63.3	4,566	2,075	1,763	351	12	79,929	47,275	18,689	11,230	2,653	83
2005[1]	8,848	64.4	4,516	2,056	1,654	610	12	96,909	55,680	22,653	13,751	4,718	107
2006[2]	8,222	65.0	4,117	1,861	1,576	606	62	91,928	53,961	21,557	12,006	3,921	484

Class of Service — Revenue - Million $ From Sales to Customers

[1] Preliminary. [2] Estimate. *Source: American Gas Association (AGA)*

Salient Statistics of Natural Gas in the United States

Supply — Disposition — Average Price Delivered to Customers

Year	Mar-keted Pro-duction	Extrac-tion Loss	Dry Pro-duction	Storage With-drawals	Imports (Con-sumed)	Total Supply	Con-sump-tion	Exports	Added to Storage	Total Dis-position	Well-head Price	Imports	Exports	Resi-dential	Com-mercial	Indus-trial	Electric Utilities
1999	23,823	973	18,832	2,808	3,586	25,699	22,405	163	2,636	25,699	2.19	2.24	2.61	6.69	5.33	3.12	2.62
2000	24,174	1,016	19,182	3,550	3,782	26,815	23,333	244	2,721	26,815	3.68	3.95	4.10	7.76	6.59	4.45	4.38
2001	24,501	954	19,616	2,344	3,977	26,697	22,239	373	3,510	26,697	4.00	4.43	4.19	9.63	8.43	5.24	4.61
2002	23,941	957	18,928	3,180	4,015	26,767	23,007	516	2,713	26,767	2.95	3.14	3.41	7.89	6.63	4.02	3.68
2003	24,119	876	19,099	3,161	3,944	26,963	22,277	680	3,358	26,963	4.88	5.17	5.54	9.63	8.40	5.89	5.57
2004	24,055	927	18,591	3,088	4,259	26,985	22,389	854	3,202	26,985	5.46	5.81	6.09	10.75	9.43	6.53	6.11
2005	23,457	876	18,051	3,057	4,341		22,011	729	3,002		7.33	8.12	7.59	12.70	11.34	8.56	8.47
2006[1]	23,507	906	18,476	2,493	4,186		21,653	724	2,924		6.40	6.88	6.83	13.75	11.99	7.86	7.11
2007[2]	24,528	874	19,078	2,688			23,005		3,080		6.39			13.01	11.31	7.60	

In Billions of Cubic Feet — Dollars Per Thousand Cubic Feet

[1] Preliminary. [2] Estimate. *Source: Energy Information Administration, U.S. Department of Energy (EIA-DOE)*

Natural Gas Futures - CME Group (NYMEX)
(weekly close) as of January 02, 2009
USD per MMBtu

Average Price of Natural Gas at Henry Hub   In Dollars Per MMBtu

Year	Jan.	Feb.	Mar.	Apr.	May	June	July	Aug.	Sept.	Oct.	Nov.	Dec.	Average
1999	1.85	1.77	1.79	2.15	2.25	2.30	2.31	2.79	2.54	2.72	2.35	2.36	2.27
2000	2.42	2.65	2.79	3.03	3.58	4.28	3.96	4.41	5.11	5.02	5.54	8.95	4.31
2001	8.18	5.62	5.16	5.16	4.21	3.71	3.11	2.95	2.15	2.45	2.35	2.43	3.96
2002	2.25	2.31	3.03	3.42	3.49	3.22	2.98	3.09	3.55	4.12	4.04	4.75	3.35
2003	5.49	7.41	6.08	5.27	5.81	5.83	5.03	4.97	4.61	4.66	4.47	6.13	5.48
2004	6.17	5.39	5.38	5.71	6.30	6.29	5.93	5.44	5.11	6.39	6.15	6.64	5.91
2005	6.13	6.13	6.91	7.22	6.48	7.15	7.63	9.46	11.87	13.42	10.28	13.05	8.81
2006	8.65	7.54	6.90	7.16	6.23	6.19	6.22	7.14	4.90	5.84	7.36	6.73	6.74
2007	6.60	7.92	7.10	7.59	7.63	7.35	6.21	6.23	6.08	6.78	7.15	7.13	6.98
2008	7.98	8.54	9.44	10.13	11.28	12.68	11.06	8.25	7.67	6.73	6.67	5.81	8.85

Source: Energy Information Administration, U.S. Department of Energy (EIA-DOE)

Volume of Trading of Natural Gas Futures in New York   In Thousands of Contracts

Year	Jan.	Feb.	Mar.	Apr.	May	June	July	Aug.	Sept.	Oct.	Nov.	Dec.	Total
1999	1,296.7	1,158.6	1,788.5	1,655.8	1,465.3	1,474.2	1,865.8	1,892.1	1,978.6	1,676.5	1,552.3	1,360.7	19,165.1
2000	1,388.8	1,470.9	1,505.0	1,179.3	1,822.2	1,853.7	1,331.4	1,483.9	1,510.2	1,594.9	1,759.5	975.1	17,875.0
2001	1,044.4	1,044.6	1,131.7	1,144.8	1,632.5	1,536.9	1,350.3	1,510.9	901.1	1,639.7	1,891.7	1,639.6	16,468.1
2002	1,942.5	1,668.6	2,381.1	2,421.7	2,281.4	1,911.7	2,266.1	2,115.6	1,990.0	2,103.4	1,569.2	1,706.4	24,357.8
2003	2,134.4	1,909.1	1,362.4	1,321.3	1,521.7	1,584.8	1,543.7	1,315.3	1,503.7	1,948.9	1,376.6	1,515.2	19,037.1
2004	1,162.1	1,125.1	1,420.3	1,443.1	1,587.5	1,588.5	1,508.8	1,724.1	1,885.6	1,458.3	1,320.0	1,218.6	17,441.9
2005	1,442.2	1,490.4	1,653.3	1,586.0	1,504.1	1,931.9	1,528.4	2,044.4	1,587.6	1,433.1	1,449.5	1,491.7	19,142.5
2006	1,609.9	1,833.9	1,682.2	1,911.6	2,272.5	1,920.6	1,786.2	2,428.7	2,017.7	1,935.1	1,799.6	1,832.0	23,030.0
2007	2,597.6	2,417.5	1,922.6	2,163.2	2,266.2	2,683.7	2,346.7	3,049.9	2,468.5	3,044.3	2,452.0	2,374.2	29,786.3
2008	2,921.9	3,330.7	2,983.6	3,382.9	3,168.0	3,379.1	4,274.0	3,756.1	3,295.8	3,151.7	2,539.9	2,384.3	38,567.9

Source: New York Mercantile Exchange (NYMEX)

Average Open Interest of Natural Gas Futures in New York   In Contracts

Year	Jan.	Feb.	Mar.	Apr.	May	June	July	Aug.	Sept.	Oct.	Nov.	Dec.
1999	244,472	268,649	284,312	315,336	332,398	330,725	316,034	353,767	336,622	316,157	309,130	292,161
2000	262,845	266,826	295,176	313,739	342,455	347,353	330,604	339,025	373,654	369,448	389,363	377,470
2001	364,532	346,343	360,032	380,632	421,145	456,512	473,675	497,972	494,475	488,187	455,766	415,882
2002	458,924	491,215	527,765	559,413	556,277	526,016	494,133	437,285	419,532	413,312	393,953	391,424
2003	415,642	420,329	367,673	354,154	365,838	366,610	357,299	343,622	354,568	352,685	356,622	340,756
2004	322,762	312,475	322,366	338,786	382,160	366,135	373,853	378,787	393,477	392,626	383,712	387,605
2005	401,829	405,692	458,013	479,880	480,318	472,631	498,440	524,235	544,165	551,121	545,270	551,444
2006	545,165	582,231	634,072	700,588	795,375	851,655	883,492	938,024	940,339	931,949	903,355	889,759
2007	905,449	839,142	761,701	747,721	752,596	787,099	823,127	776,747	778,512	749,480	789,360	843,361
2008	881,812	942,089	906,497	875,484	885,165	946,673	963,953	922,474	915,638	859,278	744,821	702,918

Source: New York Mercantile Exchange (NYMEX)

Gasoline

Gasoline is a complex mixture of hundreds of lighter liquid hydrocarbons and is used chiefly as a fuel for internal-combustion engines. Petroleum crude, or crude oil, is still the most economical source of gasoline with refineries turning more than half of every barrel of crude oil into gasoline. The three basic steps to all refining operations are the separation process (separating crude oil into various chemical components), conversion process (breaking the chemicals down into molecules called hydrocarbons), and treatment process (transforming and combining hydrocarbon molecules and other additives). Another process, called hydro treating, removes a significant amount of sulfur from finished gasoline as is currently required by the state of California.

Octane is a measure of a gasoline's ability to resist pinging or knocking noise from an engine. Most gasoline stations offer three octane grades of unleaded fuel—regular at 87 (R+M)/2, mid-grade at 89 (R+M)/2, and premium at 93 (R+M)/2. Additional refining steps are needed to increase the octane, which increases the retail price. This does not make the gasoline any cleaner or better, but yields a different blend of hydrocarbons that burn more slowly.

In an attempt to improve air quality and reduce harmful emissions from internal combustion engines, Congress in 1990 amended the Clean Air Act to mandate the addition of ethanol to gasoline. Some 2 billion gallons of ethanol are now added to gasoline each year in the U.S. The most common blend is E10, which contains 10% ethanol and 90% gasoline. Auto manufacturers have approved that mixture for use in all U.S. vehicles. Ethanol is an alcohol-based fuel produced by fermenting and distilling crops such as corn, barley, wheat and sugar.

Unleaded gasoline futures and options trade at the New York Mercantile Exchange (NYMEX). The NYMEX gasoline futures contract calls for the delivery of 1,000 barrels (42,000 gallons) of unleaded gasoline in the New York harbor and is priced in terms of dollars and cents per gallon.

Prices – NYMEX gasoline futures prices fluctuated widely in 2008. They started the year at about $2.32 per gallon, and rallied to a high of $3.57 in early July. From there the price moved sharply lower to about $0.84 per gallon at the end of the year. The average monthly retail price of regular unleaded gasoline in 2008 (through December) rose +16.7% yr/yr to $3.27 per gallon, which was a new record high. The average monthly retail price of unleaded premium motor gasoline in the U.S. in 2008 (through December) rose by +16.0% to $3.52 per gallon, which was a new record high. The average monthly refiner price of finished aviation gasoline to end users in 2008 (through November) rose by +21.5% yr/yr to a new record high of $3.42 per gallon.

Supply – U.S. production of gasoline in 2007 (through December, annualized) rose +0.2% yr/yr to 8.369 million barrels per day. Gasoline stocks in December of 2008 were 98.2 million barrels, down from 110.0 million barrels in December of 2007.

Demand – U.S. consumption of finished motor gasoline in 2008 (through December, annualized) fell 3.4% yr/yr to 8.972 million barrels per day, down from last year's record high of 9.284 million barrels per day.

Production of Finished Motor Gasoline in the United States   In Thousand Barrels per Day

Year	Jan.	Feb.	Mar.	Apr.	May	June	July	Aug.	Sept.	Oct.	Nov.	Dec.	Average
1999	7,886	7,607	7,531	8,138	8,207	8,402	8,280	8,183	8,187	8,266	8,142	8,471	8,111
2000	7,798	7,658	8,032	8,130	8,398	8,550	8,320	8,251	8,358	8,031	8,394	8,298	8,186
2001	7,888	7,822	8,011	8,450	8,651	8,637	8,481	8,277	8,381	8,446	8,366	8,301	8,312
2002	8,160	8,117	8,072	8,626	8,729	8,661	8,665	8,666	8,320	8,190	8,738	8,734	8,475
2003	7,870	7,800	7,724	8,161	8,311	8,293	8,320	8,355	8,228	8,253	8,450	8,540	8,194
2004	7,956	7,979	8,102	8,233	8,447	8,336	8,370	8,357	7,993	8,384	8,346	8,659	8,264
2005	8,157	8,194	8,119	8,549	8,475	8,589	8,352	8,326	8,129	7,953	8,468	8,503	8,318
2006	8,189	7,969	7,765	8,032	8,613	8,957	8,624	8,610	8,465	8,210	8,335	8,567	8,361
2007	8,348	8,012	8,101	8,122	8,491	8,686	8,504	8,547	8,320	8,276	8,353	8,501	8,355
2008[1]	8,427	8,364	8,230	8,471	8,492	8,375	8,405	8,301	7,631	8,739	8,449	8,540	8,369

[1] Preliminary.   Source: Energy Information Administration, U.S. Department of Energy (EIA-DOE)

Disposition of Finished Motor Gasoline, Total Product Supplied in the United States   In Thousand Barrels per Day

Year	Jan.	Feb.	Mar.	Apr.	May	June	July	Aug.	Sept.	Oct.	Nov.	Dec.	Average
1999	7,701	8,031	8,128	8,506	8,420	8,886	8,942	8,579	8,305	8,542	8,240	8,859	8,431
2000	7,653	8,291	8,305	8,375	8,661	8,824	8,642	8,921	8,518	8,417	8,384	8,670	8,472
2001	8,099	8,234	8,532	8,575	8,706	8,690	9,023	8,953	8,557	8,655	8,677	8,585	8,610
2002	8,227	8,607	8,655	8,766	9,078	9,140	9,143	9,313	8,687	8,814	8,829	8,893	8,848
2003	8,414	8,525	8,602	8,838	9,042	9,170	9,192	9,411	8,926	9,108	8,946	9,011	8,935
2004	8,705	8,838	9,024	9,126	9,179	9,322	9,357	9,327	9,015	9,097	9,055	9,206	9,104
2005	8,813	8,861	8,994	9,128	9,278	9,373	9,534	9,537	8,915	9,036	9,115	9,296	9,157
2006	8,839	8,911	9,054	9,154	9,308	9,478	9,607	9,564	9,236	9,267	9,244	9,338	9,250
2007	8,886	9,006	9,178	9,215	9,434	9,491	9,640	9,582	9,254	9,236	9,229	9,251	9,284
2008[1]	8,814	8,842	9,069	9,117	9,216	9,071	9,072	9,090	8,469	8,986	8,889	9,033	8,972

[1] Preliminary.   Source: Energy Information Administration, U.S. Department of Energy (EIA-DOE)

GASOLINE

Average Spot Price of Unleaded Gasoline in New York   In Cents Per Gallon

Year	Jan.	Feb.	Mar.	Apr.	May	June	July	Aug.	Sept.	Oct.	Nov.	Dec.	Average
1999	34.24	31.81	42.33	50.11	48.86	48.65	58.35	63.89	69.37	62.63	69.57	70.55	54.20
2000	70.43	81.30	89.11	73.15	89.06	96.18	86.76	86.97	96.04	94.71	93.94	73.66	85.94
2001	83.32	82.56	78.18	94.95	92.37	71.85	68.31	77.18	75.00	59.79	51.34	51.85	73.89
2002	54.30	55.41	69.64	74.66	70.32	71.65	76.62	76.75	78.36	82.34	76.08	80.56	72.22
2003	87.56	99.62	95.51	80.08	76.16	80.65	87.17	100.42	90.41	87.12	87.33	88.37	88.37
2004	99.66	104.63	109.12	112.02	133.98	115.70	122.65	120.89	126.17	137.75	126.96	106.90	118.04
2005	123.85	122.42	143.90	147.06	137.06	151.02	158.89	191.13	214.78	170.87	147.73	159.88	155.72
2006	173.39	149.98	175.87	214.62	204.68	206.50	223.99	203.23	158.42	152.00	158.71	166.70	182.34
2007	141.63	164.55	193.58	210.05	224.09	218.30	213.51	199.83	209.72	216.93	242.33	232.69	205.60
2008	233.09	238.37	249.09	277.45	309.23	329.79	315.86	290.20	280.69	190.84	129.29	97.18	245.09

Source: Energy Information Administration, U.S. Department of Energy (EIA-DOE)

Volume of Trading of Gasoline, RBOB[1] Futures in New York   In Contracts

Year	Jan.	Feb.	Mar.	Apr.	May	June	July	Aug.	Sept.	Oct.	Nov.	Dec.	Total
1999	561.5	619.7	876.4	741.5	721.1	737.7	822.0	800.4	751.3	705.1	748.8	615.7	8,701.2
2000	693.6	721.9	921.6	730.0	927.5	838.5	650.6	677.2	641.2	635.7	612.1	595.1	8,645.2
2001	825.2	701.2	809.2	981.0	1,056.5	895.0	737.3	790.8	581.9	664.9	613.3	567.2	9,223.4
2002	795.0	744.7	942.7	1,019.3	985.2	834.5	967.8	893.6	867.6	1,105.0	865.9	958.4	10,979.7
2003	1,054.1	968.7	1,010.9	909.0	933.7	944.0	987.5	1,021.5	943.0	877.1	760.8	761.6	11,172.1
2004	956.1	998.7	1,169.2	1,169.0	1,203.8	1,194.5	1,027.0	1,177.7	1,052.9	983.7	849.0	995.9	12,777.5
2005	974.6	1,000.9	1,193.5	1,252.5	1,060.2	1,104.7	1,103.2	1,341.3	1,221.3	999.2	928.1	989.0	13,168.4
2006	1,149.6	1,233.0	1,259.1	1,079.6	1,122.7	1,039.8	939.8	1,145.5	891.4	839.6	838.1	966.0	12,504.2
2007	1,172.9	1,272.2	1,722.5	1,826.7	2,134.5	1,811.8	1,770.2	1,872.8	1,627.3	1,706.1	1,531.3	1,343.2	19,791.4
2008	1,660.6	1,887.5	2,111.9	1,986.3	1,917.6	1,854.4	1,621.6	1,667.7	1,774.1	1,452.9	1,193.4	1,306.4	20,434.6

[1] Data thru September 2005 are Unleaded, October 2005 thru December 2006 are Unleaded and RBOB.   *Source: New York Mercantile Exchange*

Average Open Interest of Gasoline, RBOB[1] Futures in New York   In Contracts

Year	Jan.	Feb.	Mar.	Apr.	May	June	July	Aug.	Sept.	Oct.	Nov.	Dec.
1999	105,532	113,683	111,449	110,531	107,644	102,927	113,619	120,468	120,328	111,758	109,428	96,652
2000	89,049	103,586	105,448	105,133	103,831	96,772	80,886	66,598	74,735	80,446	88,509	92,041
2001	117,540	126,762	124,631	124,162	111,576	103,058	101,249	92,156	87,841	102,414	115,699	126,634
2002	136,795	139,191	133,649	129,274	120,224	114,663	106,463	94,648	95,754	100,427	105,175	109,737
2003	117,558	124,288	113,380	98,627	96,405	93,285	95,433	99,394	85,457	90,007	95,002	105,919
2004	125,207	141,837	150,573	146,375	148,782	138,248	140,691	146,532	147,088	150,643	138,280	153,907
2005	162,432	161,603	172,012	166,620	145,587	148,482	156,730	156,282	140,270	134,833	138,659	144,396
2006	157,562	173,978	168,067	165,233	150,913	138,578	146,173	135,367	131,771	124,963	128,906	135,085
2007	161,557	161,335	166,936	170,675	172,870	183,443	189,084	184,342	188,954	196,730	206,392	208,238
2008	230,032	253,303	241,781	250,852	264,988	256,220	238,170	219,229	198,263	162,480	172,267	194,234

[1] Data thru September 2005 are Unleaded, October 2005 thru December 2006 are Unleaded and RBOB.   *Source: New York Mercantile Exchange*

RBOB Gasoline (monthly Average) through December 2008 — USD per gallon

Stocks of Finished Gasoline² on Hand in the United States, at End of Month   In Millions of Barrels

Year	Jan.	Feb.	Mar.	Apr.	May	June	July	Aug.	Sept.	Oct.	Nov.	Dec.
1999	185.2	178.4	167.8	168.9	176.5	172.3	163.6	158.6	159.2	158.8	160.5	151.6
2000	165.3	156.4	157.1	160.6	162.2	164.5	164.6	151.0	154.2	147.4	156.7	153.0
2001	158.7	154.6	144.7	150.3	160.1	169.4	162.3	150.6	158.0	160.2	161.2	161.5
2002	169.7	165.5	159.8	167.0	168.3	167.6	164.8	157.3	157.4	148.2	158.0	161.9
2003	157.2	151.1	144.7	151.4	155.2	153.0	150.1	145.2	146.1	140.4	146.3	146.9
2004	138.7	133.5	132.1	133.1	137.2	140.2	140.5	137.9	135.7	138.4	141.5	143.2
2005	144.8	148.4	137.8	141.6	141.0	141.9	135.1	125.0	128.1	130.0	132.9	135.0
2006	142.2	137.9	124.2	115.4	121.5	119.1	117.9	116.6	120.5	112.8	113.8	116.1
2007	125.0	115.7	108.8	108.5	114.7	116.7	114.4	110.7	112.3	107.7	108.8	110.0
2008[1]	117.3	118.9	110.0	105.2	105.6	107.0	102.3	97.3	92.3	95.9	97.0	98.2

[1] Preliminary.   [2] Includes oxygenated and other finished.   *Source: Energy Information Administration, U.S. Department of Energy (EIA-DOE)*

Average Refiner Price of Finished Motor Gasoline to End Users¹ in the United States   In Cents Per Gallon

Year	Jan.	Feb.	Mar.	Apr.	May	June	July	Aug.	Sept.	Oct.	Nov.	Dec.	Average
1999	59.2	56.8	65.1	79.0	78.2	75.6	80.6	86.5	88.8	87.1	88.4	90.3	78.1
2000	91.7	98.7	113.1	108.7	110.3	121.3	117.3	110.3	117.5	115.5	113.5	106.3	110.6
2001	106.8	106.7	103.9	117.7	130.1	120.7	103.2	102.5	1,009.2	89.9	76.9	68.5	103.2
2002	70.6	71.8	87.2	100.4	99.9	99.1	100.3	100.1	100.1	104.0	101.2	98.1	94.7
2003	106.0	122.1	130.0	120.1	110.0	109.3	110.6	123.1	126.5	115.0	109.5	106.5	115.7
2004	117.3	125.6	133.8	139.6	156.9	154.4	148.3	145.1	145.0	158.6	155.1	141.3	143.4
2005	139.5	146.8	163.7	180.3	171.4	172.1	185.0	208.0	241.7	226.2	182.4	173.9	182.6
2006	187.2	183.3	198.3	233.1	245.8	243.6	252.8	248.6	207.6	178.9	178.8	186.8	212.1
2007	179.1	184.2	213.8	240.5	266.9	256.9	248.8	232.0	233.7	235.0	261.4	255.2	234.0
2008[2]	257.3	256.9	278.4	298.4	331.6	357.9	356.7	327.8	320.7	253.4	161.5		291.0

[1] Excludes aviation and taxes.   [2] Preliminary.   *Source: Energy Information Administration, U.S. Department of Energy (EIA-DOE)*

GASOLINE

Average Retail Price of Unleaded Premium Motor Gasoline[2] in the United States   In Cents per Gallon

Year	Jan.	Feb.	Mar.	Apr.	May	June	July	Aug.	Sept.	Oct.	Nov.	Dec.	Average
1999	117.1	115.5	118.6	136.7	137.0	133.9	137.8	144.1	146.8	146.4	145.4	148.6	135.7
2000	148.6	155.1	172.3	169.8	168.2	178.6	177.3	168.9	176.4	174.4	173.8	167.9	169.3
2001	165.7	167.1	163.8	174.8	193.4	188.1	169.5	163.6	172.6	156.0	142.7	131.2	165.7
2002	132.3	133.0	145.0	162.2	162.5	160.8	160.7	162.0	161.9	164.3	164.3	158.9	157.8
2003	166.6	182.8	192.4	184.6	172.9	170.0	171.0	180.8	191.1	178.9	172.4	168.6	177.7
2004	177.9	185.8	194.9	201.2	218.6	222.5	213.0	209.1	208.2	221.5	220.3	208.0	206.8
2005	201.7	210.5	225.1	246.8	240.3	236.5	250.2	270.1	313.0	300.1	256.0	239.3	249.1
2006	252.1	251.9	260.3	296.7	316.9	313.9	321.9	320.7	281.9	249.3	245.9	255.0	280.5
2007	250.1	250.9	281.8	309.3	334.8	328.1	320.0	301.8	302.1	303.7	330.7	326.4	303.3
2008[1]	329.1	327.2	350.2	369.0	400.3	431.9	435.0	404.5	394.0	343.2	243.3	195.1	351.9

[1] Preliminary.   [2] Including taxes.   *Source: Energy Information Administration, U.S. Department of Energy (EIA-DOE)*

Average Retail Price of Unleaded Regular Motor Gasoline[2] in the United States   In Cents per Gallon

Year	Jan.	Feb.	Mar.	Apr.	May	June	July	Aug.	Sept.	Oct.	Nov.	Dec.	Average
1999	97.2	95.5	99.1	117.7	117.8	114.8	118.9	125.5	128.0	127.4	126.4	129.8	116.5
2000	130.1	136.9	154.1	150.6	149.8	161.7	159.3	151.0	158.2	155.9	155.5	148.9	151.0
2001	147.2	148.4	144.7	156.4	172.9	164.0	148.2	142.7	153.1	136.2	126.3	113.1	146.1
2002	113.9	113.0	124.1	140.7	142.1	140.4	141.2	142.3	142.2	144.9	144.8	139.4	135.8
2003	147.3	164.1	174.8	165.9	154.2	151.4	152.4	162.8	172.8	160.3	153.5	149.4	159.1
2004	159.2	167.2	176.6	183.3	200.9	204.1	193.9	189.8	189.1	202.9	201.0	188.2	188.0
2005	182.3	191.8	206.5	228.3	221.6	217.6	231.6	250.3	292.7	278.5	234.3	218.6	229.5
2006	231.5	231.0	240.1	275.7	294.7	291.7	299.9	298.5	258.9	227.2	224.1	233.4	258.9
2007	227.4	228.5	259.2	286.0	313.0	305.2	296.1	278.2	278.9	279.3	306.9	302.0	280.1
2008[1]	304.7	303.3	325.8	344.1	376.4	406.5	409.0	378.6	369.8	317.3	215.1	168.9	326.6

[1] Preliminary.   [2] Including taxes.   *Source: Energy Information Administration, U.S. Department of Energy (EIA-DOE)*

Average Retail Price of All-Types[2] Motor Gasoline[3] in the United States   In Cents per Gallon

Year	Jan.	Feb.	Mar.	Apr.	May	June	July	Aug.	Sept.	Oct.	Nov.	Dec.	Average
1999	103.1	101.4	104.8	123.2	123.3	120.4	124.4	130.9	133.4	132.9	131.9	135.3	122.1
2000	135.6	142.2	159.4	156.1	155.2	166.6	164.2	155.9	163.5	161.3	160.8	154.4	156.3
2001	152.5	153.8	150.3	161.7	181.2	173.1	156.5	150.9	160.9	144.2	132.4	120.0	153.1
2002	120.9	121.0	132.4	149.3	150.8	148.9	149.6	150.8	150.7	153.5	153.4	147.7	144.1
2003	155.7	168.6	179.1	170.4	158.7	155.8	156.7	167.1	177.1	164.6	157.8	153.8	163.8
2004	163.5	171.5	180.9	187.5	205.0	208.3	198.2	194.1	193.4	207.2	205.3	192.6	192.3
2005	186.6	196.0	210.7	232.5	225.7	221.8	235.7	254.8	296.9	283.0	238.7	223.0	233.8
2006	235.9	235.4	244.4	280.1	299.3	296.3	304.6	303.3	263.7	231.9	228.7	238.0	263.5
2007	232.1	233.3	263.9	290.9	317.6	310.0	301.3	283.3	283.9	284.3	311.8	306.9	284.9
2008[1]	309.6	308.3	330.7	349.1	381.3	411.5	414.2	383.8	374.9	322.5	220.8	174.2	331.7

[1] Preliminary.   [2] Also includes types of motor oil not shown separately.   [3] Including taxes.   *Source: Energy Information Administration, U.S. Department of Energy (EIA-DOE)*

Average Refiner Price of Finished Aviation Gasoline to End Users[2] in the United States   In Cents per Gallon

Year	Jan.	Feb.	Mar.	Apr.	May	June	July	Aug.	Sept.	Oct.	Nov.	Dec.	Average
1999	87.1	85.1	90.1	101.4	104.2	104.1	107.9	113.2	115.4	117.6	116.4	119.6	105.9
2000	118.7	119.5	129.1	124.3	126.8	139.8	142.6	NA	138.2	134.9	134.9	126.1	130.6
2001	128.5	129.2	124.5	134.9	150.9	145.1	134.6	136.3	142.4	125.3	119.4	115.8	132.3
2002	111.8	110.6	122.6	129.8	128.9	127.3	139.2	136.9	139.1	143.0	141.8	139.8	128.8
2003	139.7	W	W	W	139.8	145.1	151.9	162.2	158.9	150.8	W	146.6	149.4
2004	W	W	W	177.4	194.4	192.3	185.4	184.9	187.8	195.5	187.0	176.7	186.8
2005	173.8	186.7	201.5	221.7	212.1	211.6	223.0	238.6	280.8	270.8	218.6	219.3	221.5
2006	239.1	232.4	247.3	286.9	301.3	305.7	310.3	305.8	253.2	238.5	235.3	234.9	265.9
2007	217.9	228.5	262.7	296.9	309.6	297.8	305.3	282.3	290.0	285.5	306.7	297.5	281.7
2008[1]	304.5	307.0	337.0	359.7	382.7	396.5	395.5	379.2	383.6	297.5	223.0		342.4

[1] Preliminary.   [2] Excluding taxes.   NA = Not available.   W = Withheld proprietary data.   *Source: Energy Information Administration, U.S. Department Energy (EIA-DOE)*

Gold

Gold is a dense, bright yellow metallic element with a high luster. Gold is an inactive substance and is unaffected by air, heat, moisture, and most solvents. Gold has been coveted for centuries for its unique blend of rarity, beauty, and near indestructibility. The Egyptians mined gold before 2,000 BC. The first known, pure gold coin was made on the orders of King Croesus of Lydia in the sixth century BC.

Gold is found in nature in quartz veins and secondary alluvial deposits as a free metal. Gold is produced from mines on every continent with the exception of Antarctica, where mining is forbidden. Because it is virtually indestructible, much of the gold that has ever been mined still exists above ground in one form or another. The largest producer of gold in the U.S. by far is the state of Nevada, with Alaska and California running a distant second and third.

Gold is a vital industrial commodity. Pure gold is one of the most malleable and ductile of all the metals. It is a good conductor of heat and electricity. The prime industrial use of gold is in electronics. Another important sector is dental gold where it has been used for almost 3,000 years. Other applications for gold include decorative gold leaf, reflective glass, and jewelry.

In 1792, the United States first assigned a formal monetary role for gold when Congress put the nation's currency on a bimetallic standard, backing it with gold and silver. Under the gold standard, the U.S. government was willing to exchange its paper currency for a set amount of gold, meaning the paper currency was backed by a physical asset with real value. However, President Nixon in 1971 severed the convertibility between the U.S. dollar and gold, which led to the breakdown of the Bretton Woods international payments system. Since then, the prices of gold and of paper currencies have floated freely. U.S. and other central banks now hold physical gold reserves primarily as a store of wealth.

Gold futures and options are traded at the New York Mercantile Exchange. Gold futures are traded on the Bolsa de Mercadorias and Futuros (BM&F) and on the Tokyo Commodity Exchange (TOCOM), the Chicago Board of Trade (CBOT) and the Korea Futures Exchange (KOFEX). The Nymex gold futures contract calls for the delivery of 100 troy ounces of gold (0.995 fineness), and the contract trades in terms of dollars and cents per troy ounce.

Prices – Nymex gold futures prices in early 2008 extended the sharp rally seen in 2007, reaching a record high of $1,033.90 per ounce in March 2008. That rally was driven by the weak dollar and strong investment and speculative demand for gold. Gold prices consolidated through the summer and then fell sharply when the global financial crisis emerged in September 2008 as traders were forced to liquidate long positions, as the dollar rallied, and as concern grew about deflation. Gold prices bottomed out fairly quickly at $681 per ounce in October 2008 and then began a new rally back up to the $1,000 per ounce mark by February 2009. Gold prices rallied because the U.S., European and Japanese governments, with their extraordinary monetary and fiscal stimulus measures, fueled market concerns about currency debasement and a potential outbreak of inflation down the road.

Supply – World mine production of gold fell -2.1% yr/yr to 2.470 million kilograms in 2008, and was still below the record high of 2.570 million kilograms seen in 1999 and 2000 (1 kilogram = 32.1507 troy ounces). The world's largest producers of gold in 2008 were China with 12.7% of world production, followed by South Africa (10.7%), the U.S (9.9%), Australia (9.7%), and Russia (7.1%).

Gold mine production has been moving lower in most major gold-producing countries such as South Africa, Australia, and the U.S. For example, South Africa's production of 250,000 kilograms in 2008 was down -0.9% yr/yr and that was less than half the production levels of more than 600,000 kilograms seen in the 1980s and early 1990s. On the other hand, China's gold production in 2008 rose +7.3% to a record 295,000 kilograms. U.S. gold mine production in 2008 fell 3.4% yr/yr to 230,000 kilograms, which was the lowest production level since 1988. U.S. refinery production of gold from domestic and foreign ore sources in 2008 fell 3.4% yr/yr to 170,000 kilograms. U.S. refinery production of gold from secondary scrap sources in 2008 fell by 11.1% yr/yr to 120,000 kilograms.

Demand – U.S. consumption of gold in 2008 was unchanged from last year at 180,000 kilograms. The most recent data available from the early 1990s showed that 71% of gold demand came from jewelry and the arts, 22% from industrial uses, and 7% from dental uses.

Trade – U.S. exports of gold (excluding coinage) in 2008 rose by +214.6% yr/yr to 595,000 kilograms, up from the 18-year low of 257,000 kilograms seen in 2004. U.S. imports of gold for consumption in 2008 rose +35.3% yr/yr to 230,000 kilograms, down from the 2005 level of 341,000 kilograms, which was a 22-year high.

World Mine Production of Gold   In Kilograms (1 Kilogram = 32.1507 Troy Ounces)

Year	Australia	Brazil	Canada	Chile	China	Ghana	Indonesia	Papua New Guinea	Russia	South Africa	United States	Uzebistan	World Total
2000	296,410	50,393	156,207	54,143	180,000	72,100	124,596	74,540	143,000	430,800	353,000	85,000	2,570,000
2001	280,100	42,884	158,875	42,673	185,000	68,341	166,091	67,043	152,500	394,800	335,000	87,000	2,560,000
2002	266,100	41,662	151,904	38,688	192,000	69,271	142,238	61,379	168,411	398,523	298,000	90,000	2,530,000
2003	282,000	40,416	140,861	38,954	205,000	70,749	141,019	67,832	170,068	373,300	277,000	90,000	2,560,000
2004	259,000	47,596	129,478	39,986	215,000	63,139	91,710	73,670	163,148	337,223	258,000	93,000	2,440,000
2005	262,000	38,292	119,549	40,447	225,000	66,852	130,620	68,483	164,186	294,671	256,000	90,000	2,470,000
2006	244,000	41,154	103,890	42,100	245,000	66,205	164,400	50,000	159,340	272,128	252,000	85,000	2,460,000
2007[1]	246,000	40,000	101,000	42,000	275,000	84,000	118,000	65,000	157,000	252,000	238,000	85,000	2,380,000
2008[2]	225,000	40,000	100,000	42,000	295,000	84,000	90,000	65,000	165,000	250,000	230,000	85,000	2,330,000

[1] Preliminary.   [2] Estimate.   *Source: U.S. Geological Survey (USGS)*

GOLD

Gold (monthly average) through December 2008 — USD per troy ounce

Salient Statistics of Gold in the United States   In Kilograms (1 Kilogram = 32.1507 Troy Ounces)

Year	Mine Pro-duction	Value Million $	Domestic & Foreign Ores	Secondary (Old Scrap)	Exports, Excluding Coinage	Imports for Con-sumption	Treasury Depart-ment[3]	Futures Exchange	Industry	Official World Reserves[4]	Dental	Indus-trial[5]	Jewelry & Arts	Total
1998	366,000	3,480.0	277,000	163,000	522,000	278,000	8,130,000	25,200	16,600	33,600	----	----	----	219,000
1999	341,000	3,070.0	265,000	143,000	523,000	221,000	8,170,000	37,900	14,700	33,500	----	----	----	245,000
2000	353,000	3,180.0	197,000	81,600	547,000	223,000	8,140,000	52,900	9,300	33,000	----	----	----	183,000
2001	335,000	2,940.0	191,000	82,700	489,000	194,000	8,120,000	38,000	3,670	33,000	----	----	----	179,000
2002	298,000	2,980.0	196,000	78,100	257,000	217,000	8,140,000	63,900	3,490	32,200	----	----	----	163,000
2003	277,000	3,250.0	194,000	89,100	352,000	249,000	8,140,000	97,100	3,590	31,800	----	----	----	183,000
2004	258,000	3,400.0	222,000	91,700	257,000	283,000	8,140,000	180,000	1,080	31,400	----	----	----	185,000
2005	256,000	3,670.0	195,000	81,300	324,000	341,000	8,140,000	211,000	2,040	30,800	----	----	----	183,000
2006[1]	252,000	4,910.0	181,000	89,100	389,000	263,000	8,140,000	234,000	2,000	30,400	----	----	----	185,000
2007[1]	238,000		176,000	135,000	519,000	170,000	8,140,000				----	----	----	180,000

[1] Preliminary.   [2] Estimate.   [3] Includes gold in Exchange Stabilization Fund.   [4] Held by market economy country central banks and governments and international monetary orgainzations.   [5] Including space and defense.   NA = Not available.   *Source: U.S. Geological Survey (USGS)*

Monthly Average Gold Price (Handy & Harman) in New York   Dollars Per Troy Ounce

Year	Jan.	Feb.	Mar.	Apr.	May	June	July	Aug.	Sept.	Oct.	Nov.	Dec.	Average
1999	287.05	287.22	285.96	282.45	276.94	261.31	255.81	256.56	265.23	310.72	292.74	283.69	278.81
2000	284.26	299.60	286.39	279.75	275.10	285.73	281.01	274.44	273.53	270.00	266.05	271.68	278.96
2001	265.58	261.99	263.03	260.56	272.07	270.23	267.53	272.40	283.78	283.06	276.49	275.98	271.06
2002	281.47	295.40	294.06	302.68	314.08	321.81	313.51	310.18	319.49	316.56	319.14	333.21	310.13
2003	356.91	359.60	340.55	328.25	355.03	356.35	351.01	359.91	379.07	378.92	389.13	407.44	363.51
2004	414.09	404.52	405.99	403.96	383.94	392.73	398.08	400.86	405.45	420.46	438.21	442.20	409.21
2005	424.39	423.15	433.91	429.23	422.53	430.66	424.33	438.03	456.52	469.90	474.87	510.01	444.79
2006	549.27	555.02	557.09	610.41	673.97	596.15	634.89	632.10	596.76	585.78	627.12	629.38	604.00
2007	630.97	664.43	655.30	679.20	667.86	655.40	665.83	665.21	714.79	749.73	806.68	803.20	696.55
2008[1]	890.47	923.25	966.30	909.70	886.29	889.49	940.16	838.30	830.30	806.62			888.09

[1] Preliminary.   *Source: U.S. Geological Survey (USGS)*

Gold Futures - CME Group (NYMEX)
(weekly close) as of January 02, 2009

USD per troy ounce

Volume of Trading of Gold Futures in New York (COMEX)   In Thousands of Contracts

Year	Jan.	Feb.	Mar.	Apr.	May	June	July	Aug.	Sept.	Oct.	Nov.	Dec.	Total
1999	860.8	517.4	1,147.6	561.1	1,069.6	573.6	964.3	709.6	1,067.3	993.8	674.7	436.1	9,575.8
2000	616.4	833.5	767.7	362.2	701.5	625.5	532.5	374.4	403.2	424.9	625.7	349.0	6,616.5
2001	755.2	483.3	766.6	438.1	971.6	481.4	578.3	547.4	341.0	481.4	573.6	367.4	6,785.3
2002	733.6	613.2	717.7	559.8	1,089.6	775.5	998.9	585.8	621.8	669.0	844.8	808.5	9,018.2
2003	1,260.1	1,007.5	987.6	667.8	1,160.3	824.3	1,191.7	837.5	1,034.0	1,091.3	1,397.3	776.3	12,235.5
2004	1,581.3	962.6	1,649.5	1,202.9	1,344.8	960.6	1,405.0	953.0	944.9	1,067.2	1,864.7	1,053.2	14,989.6
2005	1,502.3	944.4	1,599.0	858.1	1,451.7	1,240.0	1,432.4	1,234.4	1,380.2	1,174.0	1,852.7	1,221.5	15,890.6
2006	2,018.8	1,162.7	2,052.7	1,302.9	2,071.0	1,148.6	1,487.2	804.5	884.7	857.1	1,284.7	842.7	15,917.6
2007	1,929.8	1,455.9	2,195.9	1,405.2	2,336.6	1,610.8	2,292.2	1,710.7	2,024.6	2,584.4	3,837.1	1,677.2	25,060.4
2008	4,041.7	2,617.6	3,901.8	2,765.5	3,328.0	2,624.0	4,269.9	3,066.1	4,109.4	3,045.1	2,687.1	1,921.1	38,377.4

Source: New York Mercantile Exchange (NYMEX), COMEX division

Average Open Interest of Gold in New York (COMEX)   In Thousands of Contracts

Year	Jan.	Feb.	Mar.	Apr.	May	June	July	Aug.	Sept.	Oct.	Nov.	Dec.
1999	179,726	185,345	178,456	198,202	193,978	207,122	205,687	193,023	206,186	216,034	189,433	156,754
2000	149,606	158,026	160,325	155,188	162,516	144,099	133,087	126,893	132,731	132,546	134,630	113,830
2001	134,401	142,673	126,558	120,111	118,426	116,788	114,098	116,687	125,907	125,639	114,238	111,622
2002	124,222	142,763	142,638	159,892	190,845	174,123	166,042	146,596	167,620	162,456	164,581	191,594
2003	221,495	210,247	186,656	176,033	191,459	198,808	199,741	224,694	284,906	258,238	275,346	277,183
2004	283,813	238,816	256,873	274,898	250,963	225,001	239,579	237,940	259,181	306,522	344,665	329,669
2005	277,112	263,191	301,758	283,546	277,469	275,508	268,068	304,000	339,269	356,526	334,562	331,527
2006	348,949	338,851	331,223	350,380	336,735	288,309	316,969	309,186	320,850	330,152	346,141	335,204
2007	350,958	387,321	372,781	377,094	405,645	401,337	379,066	339,923	394,400	479,735	530,775	500,409
2008	556,302	487,373	471,320	418,693	435,847	401,914	460,178	382,302	378,216	321,545	290,706	280,402

Source: New York Mercantile Exchange (NYMEX), COMEX division

GOLD

Commodity Exchange, Inc. (COMEX) Depository Warehouse Stocks of Gold   In Thousands of Troy Ounces

Year	Jan. 1	Feb. 1	Mar. 1	Apr. 1	May 1	June 1	July 1	Aug. 1	Sept. 1	Oct. 1	Nov. 1	Dec. 1
1999	809.5	809.1	859.7	1,034.0	895.9	879.3	818.3	936.1	1,198.2	928.0	874.4	1,137.4
2000	1,219.4	1,392.9	1,373.9	1,968.1	1,966.7	1,900.6	1,890.1	2,012.6	1,961.1	1,918.1	1,865.5	1,863.6
2001	1,701.2	1,775.3	1,653.7	1,302.4	858.3	864.2	891.3	901.1	793.6	824.3	1,164.6	1,425.7
2002	1,220.3	1,186.7	1,285.7	1,322.3	1,372.3	1,764.1	1,850.7	1,835.6	1,915.0	1,892.4	1,994.9	2,046.5
2003	2,056.5	2,159.8	2,262.4	2,383.9	2,460.7	2,474.9	2,675.1	2,743.8	2,729.4	2,822.6	2,912.1	3,058.9
2004	3,122.2	3,324.0	3,476.9	3,677.1	4,142.0	4,391.8	4,399.6	4,657.0	4,880.1	5,122.4	5,334.7	5,374.3
2005	5,795.6	5,962.6	5,913.9	5,960.7	6,156.7	6,036.6	5,751.0	5,713.8	6,008.5	6,737.1	6,351.5	6,614.3
2006	6,657.7	7,320.9	7,518.9	7,426.6	7,334.4	7,796.0	8,031.2	8,199.0	7,980.8	7,695.2	7,565.8	7,491.1
2007	7,534.5	7,459.2	7,487.2	7,302.5	7,624.8	7,633.1	7,276.1	7,130.5	7,077.1	7,211.9	7,346.7	7,366.1
2008	7,492.5	7,588.0	7,371.3	7,623.1	7,760.4	7,588.9	7,611.6	8,266.0	8,442.8	8,594.9	8,171.8	8,540.3

Source: New York Mercantile Exchange (NYMEX), COMEX Division

Central Gold Bank Reserves   In Millions of Troy Ounces

																Bank	
												Deve-	Deve-		for Int'l	
		Can-		Ger-			Nether-	Switzer-	United	United	Industrial	loping	loping		Settle-	World
Year	Belgium	ada	France	many	Italy	Japan	lands	land	Kingdom	States	Total	Oil	Non-Oil	IMF[2]	ments	Total
1992	25.0	9.9	81.9	95.2	66.7	24.2	43.9	83.3	18.6	261.8	877.4	42.0	100.3	103.4	6.8	1,129.9
1993	25.0	6.1	81.9	95.2	66.7	24.2	35.1	83.3	18.5	261.8	860.4	42.4	108.1	103.4	8.6	1,123.0
1994	25.0	3.9	81.9	95.2	66.7	24.2	34.8	83.3	18.4	261.7	856.9	42.4	106.6	103.4	7.0	1,116.2
1995	20.5	3.4	81.9	95.2	66.7	24.2	34.8	83.3	18.4	261.7	848.7	41.9	111.9	103.4	7.3	1,113.2
1996	15.3	3.1	81.9	95.2	66.7	24.2	34.8	83.3	18.4	261.7	840.1	42.5	115.5	103.4	6.6	1,108.2
1997	15.3	3.1	81.9	95.2	66.7	24.2	27.1	83.3	18.4	261.6	821.9	42.3	115.8	103.4	6.2	1,089.7
1998	9.5	2.5	102.4	119.0	83.4	24.2	33.8	83.3	23.0	261.6	809.0	41.6	115.7	103.4	6.4	1,076.1
1999	8.3	1.8	97.2	111.5	78.8	24.2	31.6	83.3	20.6	261.7	810.4	41.2	112.9	103.4	6.5	1,074.5
2000	8.3	1.2	97.3	111.5	78.8	24.6	29.3	78.8	16.5	261.6	796.5	41.6	112.0	103.4	6.5	1,060.1
2001[1]	8.0	1.2	97.0	112.0	79.0	24.6	29.0	74.6	13.4	261.6	791.3	42.3	111.3	103.4	6.5	1,054.7

[1] Preliminary.   [2] International Monetary Fund.   *Source: American Metal Market (AMM)*

Mine Production of Recoverable Gold in the United States   In Kilograms

Year	Arizona	California	Idaho	Montana	Nevada	Alaska	Colorado	South Dakota	New Mexico	Utah	Other States	Total
1998	1,840	18,700	W	8,200	273,000	18,300	W	12,100	W	W	33,860	366,000
1999	786	17,500	W	7,540	9,310	16,200	W	10,300	W	W	279,364	341,000
2000	442	17,200	W	9,310	268,000	15,600	W	8,230	W	W	34,218	353,000
2001	W	13,800	W	W	253,000	16,700	W	W	W	W	51,500	335,000
2002	W	9,180	W	W	240,000	W	W	W	W	W	48,820	298,000
2003	W	4,270	W	W	227,000	W	W	W	W	W	45,730	277,000
2004	W	3,260	W	W	216,000	W	W	W	W	W	38,740	258,000
2005	W	W	W	W	212,000	W	W	W	W	W	44,200	256,000
2006	W	W	W	W	206,000	W	W	W	W	W	45,800	252,000
2007[1]	W	W	W	W	186,000	W	W	W	W	W	52,400	238,000

[1] Preliminary.   W = Withheld proprietary data, included in "Other States."   *Source: U.S. Geological Survey (USGS)*

Consumption of Gold, By End-Use in the United States   In Kilograms

| | Jewelry and the Arts | | | | Industrial | | | | | |
Year	Gold-Filled & Other	Electro-plating	Karat Gold	Total	Dental	Gold-Filled & Other	Electro-plating	Karat Gold	Total	Grand Total
1989	7,364	1,283	60,877	69,524	7,927	15,723	20,684	1,215	37,621	115,078
1990	8,132	429	69,952	78,514	8,700	12,725	17,251	1,020	30,996	118,216
1991	3,848	373	79,875	84,096	8,485	8,102	12,624	1,068	21,793	114,375
1992	3,546	581	79,381	83,508	6,543	8,802	10,476	1,082	20,360	110,410
1993	3,530	373	61,700	65,600	6,170	9,470	9,090	1,100	19,700	91,400
1994	3,650	369	49,700	53,700	5,430	7,450	9,470	96	17,000	76,100
1995	NA	NA	NA	NA	NA	NA	NA	NA	NA	NA
1996	NA	NA	NA	NA	NA	NA	NA	NA	NA	NA
1997	NA	NA	NA	NA	NA	NA	NA	NA	NA	NA
1998	NA	NA	NA	NA	NA	NA	NA	NA	NA	NA

[1] Preliminary.   NA = Not available.   *Source: U.S. Geological Survey (USGS)*

Grain Sorghum

Grain sorghums include milo, kafir, durra, feterita, and kaoliang. Grain sorghums are tolerant of drought by going into dormancy during dry and hot conditions and then resuming growth as conditions improve. Grain sorghums are a staple food in China, India, and Africa but in the U.S. they are mainly used as livestock feed. The two key U.S. producing states are Texas and Kansas, each with about one-third of total U.S. production. U.S. sorghum production has become more popular with the breeding of dwarf grain sorghum hybrids which are only about 3 feet tall (versus up to 10 feet tall for wild sorghum) and are easier to harvest with a combine. The U.S. sorghum crop year begins September 1.

Prices – The monthly average price for sorghum grain received by U.S. farmers in the 2007-08 (Sep 07-Aug 08) rose by +35.7% yr/yr to $8.04 per hundred pounds. The value of U.S. grain sorghum production in the 2007-08 marketing year is estimated to rise +118.0% to $1.925 billion.

Supply – World production of sorghum in the 2007-08 (latest data available) marketing year is estimated to rise +12.2% to an eleven-year high of 63.533 million metric tons, remaining well above the 52.889 million metric ton crop in 2002-03 that was the smallest crop since 1968-69. U.S. grain sorghum production in 2007-08 is estimated to rise +81.9% yr/yr to 504.993 million bushels. Sorghum acreage harvested in 2007-08 is estimated to rise +37.8% to 6.805 million acres, up sharply from last year which was the smallest sorghum acreage to be harvested since the late 1930s. Yield will be above average in 2007-08 and is estimated to be 74.2 bushels per acre, which would be a record high.

Demand – World utilization (consumption) of grain sorghum in the 2007-08 (latest data available) marketing year is estimated to rise +11.9% to 63.055 million metric tons, which would be an eleven-year high.

Trade – World exports of sorghum in the 2007-08 (latest data available) marketing year is estimated to rise +73.7% to 9.457 million metric tons, which would be a 19-year high. U.S. exports in 2007-08 is estimated to rise +81.9% yr/yr to 7.052 million metric tons, and accounted for 74% of total world exports. Argentina is the world's other major exporter with 1.100 million metric tons of exports in 2007-08, accounting for 12% of total world exports. Major world importers are Mexico and Japan.

World Supply and Demand of Grain Sorghum   In Thousands of Metric Tons

Crop Year	Exports Argentina	Exports Non-U.S.	Exports U.S.	Exports Total	Imports Japan	Imports Mexico	Imports Unaccounted	Total Total	Pro-duction	Utilization China	Utilization Mexico	Utilization U.S.	Utilization Total	Ending Stocks Non-U.S.	Ending Stocks U.S.	Ending Stocks Total
2003-04	192	1,490	5,049	6,539	1,434	3,002	49	6,519	58,407	3,000	9,800	5,637	57,604	3,809	852	4,661
2004-05	351	728	4,675	5,403	1,374	2,931	147	5,304	57,529	2,400	9,300	6,254	57,794	2,851	1,446	4,297
2005-06	197	443	4,936	5,379	1,393	3,029	176	5,245	58,365	2,500	8,600	4,818	58,004	2,856	1,668	4,524
2006-07[1]	1,083	1,585	3,876	5,461	1,276	1,954	406	4,753	56,628	1,950	8,100	4,012	56,327	3,303	814	4,117
2007-08[2]	1,100	2,435	7,052	9,487	1,084	1,156	525	9,310	63,533	1,700	7,100	5,059	63,055	3,078	1,340	4,418
2008-09[3]	800	1,900	3,302	5,202	1,350	2,300		4,978	64,192	1,800	8,400	8,383	63,393	3,337	1,656	4,993

[1] Preliminary.   [2] Estimate.   [3] Forecast.   Source: Foreign Agricultural Service, U.S. Department of Agriculture (FAS-USDA)

Salient Statistics of Grain Sorghum in the United States

Crop Year Beginning Sept. 1	Acreage Planted[4] for All Purposes	Acreage Harvested	For Grain Production (1,000 Bushels)	For Grain Yield Per Acre Harvested (Bushels)	For Grain Price in Cents Per Bushel	For Grain Value of Production (Million $)	For Silage Acreage Harvested (1,000 Acres)	For Silage Production (1,000 Tons)	For Silage Yield Per Acre Harvested (Tons)	Sorghum Grain Stocks Dec. 1 On Farms	Sorghum Grain Stocks Dec. 1 Off Farms	Sorghum Grain Stocks June 1 On Farms	Sorghum Grain Stocks June 1 Off Farms
2003-04	9,420	7,798	411,237	52.7	239	965.0	343	3,552	10.4	45,200	190,736	7,650	72,944
2004-05	7,486	6,517	453,650	69.8	179	843.5	352	4,763	13.5	78,700	203,505	16,000	97,170
2005-06	6,454	5,736	392,933	68.7	186	737.0	311	4,218	13.6	55,000	235,376	12,650	102,213
2006-07[1]	6,522	4,937	277,538	56.2	329	885.4	347	4,642	13.4	38,100	174,094	5,380	69,490
2007-08[2]	7,718	6,805	504,993	74.2	408	1,950.9	399	6,206	15.6	51,400	239,850	7,000	94,019
2008-09[3]	7,271	7,236	464,186	64.1	305-335					54,400	257,351		

[1] Preliminary.   [2] Estimate.   [3] Forecast.   Source: Foreign Agricultural Service, U.S. Department of Agriculture (FAS-USDA)

Production of All Sorghum for Grain in the United States, by States   In Thousands of Bushels

Year	Arkansas	Colorado	Illinois	Kansas	Louisiana	Mississippi	Missouri	Nebraska	New Mexico	Oklahoma	South Dakota	Texas	Total
2003	17,220	4,320	8,610	130,500	14,025	6,132	16,170	31,000	1,674	9,250	6,750	153,900	411,237
2004	4,704	5,400	8,938	220,400	5,200	1,422	15,660	33,615	4,232	14,400	6,300	127,100	453,650
2005	4,960	3,410	7,636	195,000	8,712	----	9,880	21,750	4,365	11,520	4,420	111,000	392,933
2006	5,100	3,380	6,408	145,000	8,352	----	8,075	19,200	2,100	6,800	2,880	62,400	277,538
2007	20,210	5,550	6,237	212,000	23,765	----	10,080	23,520	3,000	12,760	8,060	161,700	504,993
2008[1]	10,800	4,860	6,545	209,000	10,695	----	8,075	19,580	3,280	15,040	7,150	153,400	464,186

[1] Preliminary.   Source: National Agricultural Statistics Service, U.S. Department of Agriculture (NASS-USDA)

Quarterly Supply and Disappearance of Grain Sorghum in the United States In Millions of Bushels

Crop Year Beginning Sept. 1	Supply Beginning Stocks	Pro-duction	Imports[3]	Total Supply	Food & Alcohol	Seed	Feed & Residual	Total	Exports[3]	Total Disap-pearance	Gov't Owned[4]	Privately Owned[5]	Total Stocks
2005-06	56.9	392.9	0	449.9	50.0		139.5	384.2	194.7	578.9			65.7
Sept.-Nov.	56.9	392.9	0	449.9	12.3		107.2	159.5	40.0	199.5			290.4
Dec.-Feb.	290.4	----	0	290.4	15.5		24.0	97.2	57.7	154.9			193.1
Mar.-May	193.1	----	0	193.1	11.8		3.7	78.3	62.8	141.1			114.9
June-Aug.	114.9	----	0	114.9	10.4		4.6	49.2	34.2	83.4			65.7
2006-07	65.7	276.8	.1	342.6	45.0		112.9	310.5	152.6	463.1			32.1
Sept.-Nov.	65.7	276.8	0	342.5	13.2		80.7	130.3	36.4	166.7			212.2
Dec.-Feb.	212.2	----	.0	212.2	13.2		13.9	70.0	42.9	112.9			142.2
Mar.-May	142.2	----	0	142.2	13.8		18.3	67.4	35.2	102.6			74.9
June-Aug.	74.9	----	.0	74.9	4.7		.1	42.9	38.1	80.9			32.1
2007-08[1]	32.1	497.5	.0	529.5	35.2		164.0	476.8	277.6	754.4			52.8
Sept.-Nov.	32.1	497.5	.0	529.5	8.5		136.1	238.3	93.7	332.0			291.3
Dec.-Feb.	291.3	----	0	291.3	8.5		5.0	105.3	91.9	197.2			185.9
Mar.-May	185.9	----	0	185.9	9.3		17.9	84.9	57.7	142.6			101.0
June-Aug.	101.0	----	0	101.0	8.9		5.1	48.3	34.3	82.6			52.8
2008-09[2]	52.8	472.3	.1	525.2	110.0		220.0	460.0	130.0	590.0			65.2
Sept.-Nov.	52.8	472.3	.1	525.2	27.3		142.0	213.5	44.2	257.6			311.8

[1] Preliminary. [2] Estimate. [3] Uncommitted inventory. [4] Includes quantity under loan and farmer-owned reserve. *Source: Economic Research Service, U.S. Department of Agriculture (ERS-USDA)*

Average Price of Sorghum Grain, No. 2, Yellow in Kansas City In Dollars Per Hundred Pounds (Cwt.)

Year	Sept.	Oct.	Nov.	Dec.	Jan.	Feb.	Mar.	Apr.	May	June	July	Aug.	Average
2001-02	3.55	3.38	3.44	3.59	3.61	3.55	3.58	3.47	3.44	3.57	3.97	4.60	3.65
2002-03	4.86	4.70	4.72	4.62	4.52	4.43	4.07	4.24	4.12	4.06	3.71	4.00	4.34
2003-04	4.15	4.18	4.50	4.61	4.71	4.88	5.18	5.37	4.94	4.67	3.92	3.75	4.57
2004-05	3.45	3.21	3.17	3.21	3.13	3.23	3.44	3.30	3.36	3.56	3.90	3.53	3.37
2005-06	3.22	3.08	2.93	3.30	3.46	3.58	3.65	3.79	4.03	3.90	4.15	3.79	3.57
2006-07	3.82	5.07	5.97	6.03	6.36	6.72	6.38	5.69	5.97	6.09	5.33	5.50	5.74
2007-08	5.68	5.60	6.13	7.34	8.36	8.86	9.13	9.70	9.65	11.63	10.10	8.37	8.38
2008-09[1]	8.43	5.92	3.68	5.19	5.67								5.78

[1] Preliminary. *Source: Economic Research Service, U.S. Department of Agriculture (ERS-USDA)*

Exports of Grain Sorghum, by Country of Destination from the United States In Metric Tons

Year	Canada	Ecuador	Ethiopia	Israel	Japan	Jordan	Mexico	South Africa	Spain	Sudan	Turkey	World Total
2001-02	4,912	0	0	25,082	1,233,799	0	4,695,814	37,272	8,193	0	0	6,014,304
2002-03	5,921	91	48,000	65,725	1,035,634	0	3,150,014	43,918	266,892	5,880	0	4,690,875
2003-04	8,025	210	54,320	105,170	889,054	0	2,814,386	156	267,691	11,430	0	4,626,171
2004-05	5,270	0	53,540	26,654	1,088,171	0	2,883,335	2,000	167,896	116,577	0	4,474,017
2005-06	4,227	0	31,500	16,177	1,193	0	3,004,518	30,398	131,995	211,021	0	4,929,700
2006-07[1]	3,999	0	4,100	54,533	674,824	0	1,914,111	0	1,018,325	299,650	0	4,333,212
2007-08[2]	5,801	0	27,600	137,284	505,919	125	1,150,231	45,498	1,929,955	303,818	0	6,676,002

[1] Preliminary. [2] Estimate. *Source: Economic Research Service, U.S. Department of Agriculture (ERS-USDA)*

Grain Sorghum Price Support Program and Market Prices in the United States

Year	Price Support Quantity	% of Pro-duction	Aquired by CCC	Owned by CCC at Year End	Basic Loan Rate	Target Price	Findley Loan Rate	Effective Base[3] (Million Acres)	Partici-pation Rate[4] % of Base	No. 2 Yellow Kansas City	Texas High Plains	Los Angeles	Gulf Ports
	Million Cwt.				Dollars Per Bushel								
2000-01	8.6	3.3	.2	0	3.05	NA	1.71	13.6	----	3.41	3.94	----	4.22
2001-02	9.6	3.3	0	.1	3.05	NA	1.71	13.6	----	3.65	4.05	----	4.34
2002-03	3.7	1.8	0	0	3.54	2.54	1.98	12.1	----	4.34	4.69	----	5.01
2003-04	3.5	1.5	0	0	3.54	2.54	1.98	12.1	----	4.57	5.01	----	5.45
2004-05	5.5	2.1	.2	0	3.48	2.57	1.95			3.37	3.95	----	4.42
2005-06[1]	5.4	2.4	0	0	3.48	4.59				3.57	3.84	----	5.04
2006-07[2]	1.9	1.2	0	0	3.48	4.59				5.74	6.09	----	7.39

[1] Preliminary. [2] Estimate. [3] National effective crop acreage base as determined by ASCS. [4] Percentage of effective base acres enrolled in acreage reduction programs. 5/ Beginning with the 1996-7 marketing year, target prices are no longer applicable. *Source: Economic Research Service, U.S. Department of Agriculture (ERS-USDA)*

Hay

Hay is a catchall term for forage plants, typically grasses such as timothy and Sudan-grass, and legumes such as alfalfa and clover. Alfalfa and alfalfa mixtures account for nearly half of all hay production. Hay is generally used to make cured feed for livestock. Curing, which is the proper drying of hay, is necessary to prevent spoilage. Hay, when properly cured, contains about 20% moisture. If hay is dried excessively, however, there is a loss of protein, which makes it less effective as livestock feed. Hay is harvested in virtually all of the lower 48 states.

Prices – The average monthly price of hay received by U.S. farmers in the first nine months of the 2008-09 marketing year (May 2008 through April 2009) as of January 2009 rose by +17.6% yr/yr to a record high of $155.33 per ton The farm production value of hay produced in 2007-08 (latest data available) was $16.961 million.

Supply – U.S. hay production in 2007-08 rose +6.1% yr/yr to 150.3 million tons. U.S. farmers harvested 61.625 million acres of hay in 2007-08, up +1.4% yr/yr. The yield in 2007-08 was 2.44 tons per acre, down from the 2004-05 record high of 2.55. U.S. carryover (May 1) in 2007-08 fell 29.7% to 15.0 million tons.

The largest hay producing states in the U.S. for 2007 are Texas (with 10.2% of U.S. hay production), California (6.3%), Missouri (5.0%), South Dakota (5.0), Oklahoma (4.7%), Nebraska (4.2%), Idaho (3.6%), and Minnesota (3.1%).

Salient Statistics of All Hay in the United States

Crop Year Beginning May 1	Acres Harvested (1,000 Acres)	Yield Per Acre (Tons)	Pro-duction	Carry-over May 1	Disap-pearance	Supply Per Animal Unit	Disap-pearance Per Animal Unit	Animal Units Fed[3] (Millions)	Farm Price ($ Per Ton)	Farm Pro-duction Value Million $	Alfalfa (Certified)	Timothy	Red Clover	Sudan-grass
			Millions of Tons			**In Tons**					**Dollars Per Cwt.**			
2003-04	63,371	2.48	157.4	22.0	153.7	2.54	2.17	70.7	85.7	12,007	286.00	107.00	144.00	55.30
2004-05	61,944	2.55	158.1	25.9	156.4	2.58	2.19	71.3	92.1	12,212	291.00	110.00	145.00	55.60
2005-06	61,637	2.44	150.5	27.8	NA	2.49	2.19	72.4	98.4	12,585	281.00	105.00	174.00	57.40
2006-07	60,632	2.32	140.8	21.3	NA	2.24	2.04	73.1	111.1	13,791	286.00	106.00	177.00	50.20
2007-08[1]	61,006	2.41	146.9	15.0		2.24	1.94		132.1	16,961	292.00	112.00	202.00	56.70
2008-09[2]	60,062	2.43	145.7	21.6		2.31			155.3					

[1] Preliminary.   [2] Estimate.   [3] Roughage-consuming animal units fed annually.   NA = Not available.
Source: Economic Research Service, U.S. Department of Agriculture (ERS-USDA)

Production of All Hay in the United States, by States   In Thousands of Tons

Year	California	Idaho	Iowa	Minne-sota	Missouri	New York	North Dakota	Ohio	Okla-homa	South Dakota	Texas	Wisconsin	Total
2003	9,485	4,950	5,515	5,245	8,122	7,600	4,598	3,974	5,304	7,210	12,388	4,380	157,390
2004	9,220	5,350	6,240	5,895	9,420	6,423	3,666	3,232	5,958	6,870	12,295	4,880	158,122
2005	9,206	5,382	5,860	6,055	6,718	6,945	5,646	3,630	5,084	7,560	9,140	4,470	150,461
2006	9,568	5,505	5,189	5,679	6,944	5,588	3,137	3,421	3,556	4,180	8,675	5,264	140,783
2007	9,042	6,530	4,944	4,240	7,528	6,185	5,063	2,804	6,858	7,275	14,740	4,392	146,901
2008[1]	8,816	6,765	5,330	5,265	8,820	6,232	4,118	2,802	5,536	7,840	9,211	4,810	145,672

[1] Preliminary.   *Source: Agricultural Statistics Board, U.S. Department of Agriculture (ASB-USDA)*

Hay Production and Farm Stocks in the United States   In Thousands of Short Tons

Year	Alfalfa & Mixtures	All Others	All Hay	Corn for Silage[1]	Sorghum Silage[1]	May 1	Dec. 1
		Production				Farm Stocks	
2003	76,098	81,292	157,390	107,378	3,552	22,013	111,011
2004	75,375	82,747	158,122	107,293	4,776	25,947	114,489
2005	75,610	74,851	150,461	106,486	4,218	27,758	105,181
2006	70,548	70,235	140,783	105,294	4,612	21,345	96,400
2007	69,880	77,021	146,901	106,229	5,246	14,990	104,089
2008[2]	69,620	76,052	145,672	111,619	5,646	21,585	103,658

[1] Not included in all tame hay.   [2] Preliminary.   *Source: Agricultural Statistics Board, U.S. Department of Agriculture (ASB-USDA)*

Mid-Month Price Received by Farmers for All Hay (Baled) in the United States   In Dollars Per Ton

Year	May	June	July	Aug.	Sept.	Oct.	Nov.	Dec.	Jan.	Feb.	Mar.	Apr.	Average
2003-04	98.0	94.6	89.0	85.0	84.4	83.7	81.5	80.6	80.1	81.2	81.8	88.9	85.7
2004-05	101.0	95.2	90.4	92.2	91.4	92.8	88.7	86.0	87.8	88.2	92.6	99.4	92.1
2005-06	107.0	102.0	99.7	99.7	99.0	97.7	91.7	92.0	93.1	95.8	97.5	105.0	98.4
2006-07	113.0	109.0	107.0	106.0	108.0	109.0	106.0	110.0	109.0	113.0	119.0	124.0	111.1
2007-08	138.0	131.0	131.0	124.0	127.0	128.0	129.0	127.0	126.0	133.0	139.0	152.0	132.1
2008-09[1]	166.0	161.0	164.0	165.0	161.0	157.0	147.0	141.0	136.0				155.3

[1] Preliminary.   [2] Marketing year average.   *Source: Economic Research Service, U.S. Department of Agriculture (ERS-USDA)*

Heating Oil

Heating oil is a heavy fuel oil that is derived from crude oil. Heating oil is also known as No. 2 fuel oil and accounts for about 25% of the yield from a barrel of crude oil. That is the second largest "cut" after gasoline. The price to consumers of home heating oil is generally comprised of 42% for crude oil, 12% for refining costs, and 46% for marketing and distribution costs (Source: EIA's Petroleum Marketing Monthly, 2001). Generally, a $1 increase in the price of crude oil translates into a 2.5-cent per gallon rise in heating oil. Because of this, heating oil prices are highly correlated with crude oil prices, although heating oil prices are also subject to swift supply and demand shifts due to weather changes or refinery shutdowns.

The primary use for heating oil is for residential heating. In the U.S., approximately 8.1 million households use heating oil as their main heating fuel. Most of the demand for heating oil occurs from October through March. The Northeast region, which includes the New England and the Central Atlantic States, is most reliant on heating oil. This region consumes approximately 70% of U.S. heating oil. However, demand for heating oil has been dropping as households switch to a more convenient heating source like natural gas. In fact, demand for heating oil is down by about 10 billion gallons/year from its peak use in 1976 (Source: American Petroleum Institute).

Refineries produce approximately 85% of U.S. heating oil as part of the "distillate fuel oil" product family, which includes heating oil and diesel fuel. The remainder of U.S. heating oil is imported from Canada, the Virgin Islands, and Venezuela.

Recently, a team of Purdue University researchers developed a way to make home heating oil from a mixture of soybean oil and conventional fuel oil. The oil blend is made by replacing 20% of the fuel oil with soybean oil, potentially saving 1.3 billion gallons of fuel oil per year. This soybean heating oil can be used in conventional furnaces without altering existing equipment. The soybean heating oil is relatively easy to produce and creates no sulfur emissions.

The "crack-spread" is the processing margin earned when refiners buy crude oil and refine it into heating oil and gasoline. The crack-spread ratio commonly used in the industry is the 3-2-1, which involves buying 1 heating oil contract and 2 gasoline futures contracts, and then selling 3 crude oil contracts. As long as the crack spread is positive, it is profitable for refiners to buy crude oil and refine it into products. The NYMEX has a crack-spread calculator on their web site at www.NYMEX.com.

Heating oil futures and options trade at the New York Mercantile Exchange (NYMEX). The heating oil futures contract calls for the delivery of 1,000 barrels of fungible No. 2 heating oil in the New York harbor. In London, gas/oil futures and options are traded on the International Petroleum Exchange (IPE).

Prices – NYMEX heating oil futures prices on the nearest-futures chart started the year 2008 at around $2.68 per gallon and rallied to a record high of $4.08 per gallon in early July. From there the priced moved lower to end the year at about $1.48 per gallon. The downmove continued into early 2009.

Supply – U.S. production of distillate fuel oil in 2008 (through December, annualized) rose by +3.8% yr/yr to a new record high of 4.289 million barrels per day. Stocks of distillate fuel oil in December 20087 were 135.8 million barrels. U.S. production of residual fuel in 2008 (through December, annualized) fell by -8.2% yr/yr to an average of 617,000 barrels per day, which less than half the production levels of well over 1 million barrels per day produced in the 1970s. U.S. stocks of residual fuel oil as of January 1, 2009 rose +0.3% to 38.7 million barrels from 38.6 million barrels a year earlier.

Demand – U.S. usage of distillate fuel oil in 2008 (through November, annualized) fell 6.0% yr/yr to 3.946 million barrels per day, down from last year's record high 4.198 million barrels per day.

Trade – U.S. imports of distillate fuel oil in 2008 (through December, annualized) fell 31.6% to an average of 206,000 barrels per day, down from the 2006 record high of 365,000 barrels per day. U.S. exports of distillate fuel oil in 2007 (through November, annualized) rose by +2.7% yr/yr to a 13-year high average of 221 barrels per day. U.S. imports of residual fuel oil in 2007 rose +5.1% yr/yr to 368,000 barrels per day, which was less than a third of the levels of over 1 million barrels per day seen back in the 1970s. U.S. exports of residual fuel oil in 2007 rose +9.2% to 309,000 barrels per day, which was a new record high.

Average Price of Heating Oil #2   In Cents Per Gallon

Year	Jan.	Feb.	Mar.	Apr.	May	June	July	Aug.	Sept.	Oct.	Nov.	Dec.	Average
1999	33.41	30.48	38.74	43.07	41.68	43.36	50.02	54.81	60.27	58.34	64.89	67.36	48.87
2000	91.32	94.37	77.29	75.32	75.88	78.32	78.14	89.13	98.87	97.46	102.70	94.08	87.74
2001	84.30	78.55	74.17	78.02	77.11	75.74	69.88	73.41	71.65	62.63	54.37	52.60	71.04
2002	53.52	54.03	63.52	66.60	66.54	64.50	67.79	69.81	77.25	76.55	72.14	81.70	67.83
2003	90.09	112.84	99.70	79.75	74.31	75.95	79.03	81.61	73.54	81.97	83.35	89.04	85.10
2004	97.91	91.19	90.88	91.87	101.65	99.41	109.42	116.86	125.73	148.55	138.16	127.32	111.58
2005	132.01	134.26	155.44	152.35	140.89	161.20	163.71	180.75	196.50	188.75	168.67	170.32	162.07
2006	174.99	163.68	177.70	198.27	197.17	191.76	192.30	198.25	169.17	154.53	165.00	167.85	179.22
2007	151.99	169.48	174.05	186.30	188.47	200.31	206.99	198.36	218.06	228.32	258.79	257.54	203.22
2008	255.64	264.17	306.80	322.96	361.64	379.99	375.67	317.16	290.76	222.44	185.15	138.93	285.11

Source: Energy Information Administration, U.S. Department of Energy (EIA-DOE)

HEATING OIL

Heating Oil Futures - CME Group (NYMEX)
(weekly close) as of January 02, 2009

USD per gallon

Average Open Interest of Heating Oil #2 Futures in New York   In Contracts

Year	Jan.	Feb.	Mar.	Apr.	May	June	July	Aug.	Sept.	Oct.	Nov.	Dec.
1999	167,686	160,388	166,472	172,127	170,842	168,307	182,383	188,726	192,883	179,040	165,334	146,997
2000	135,431	132,407	108,646	100,389	117,055	129,872	153,914	169,092	177,997	168,388	155,475	142,145
2001	138,980	127,219	120,899	127,395	130,328	141,436	149,577	145,605	145,692	155,540	162,392	153,850
2002	166,824	173,110	160,205	144,936	139,979	136,201	131,742	141,084	147,692	153,739	161,137	156,268
2003	178,932	174,224	134,616	111,706	118,822	124,675	127,273	146,821	150,893	156,142	145,857	145,555
2004	153,794	145,924	161,945	174,618	176,784	167,331	193,291	206,099	197,783	188,843	176,298	163,629
2005	155,528	152,479	174,437	179,923	176,770	185,831	182,710	185,185	174,229	172,772	178,199	178,008
2006	170,094	165,627	168,415	170,955	171,732	169,123	179,773	185,648	208,848	221,942	228,152	216,033
2007	219,690	219,715	209,805	208,829	210,128	224,289	239,109	218,913	235,403	232,165	224,475	209,578
2008	202,976	220,716	230,646	227,140	224,480	218,004	223,645	221,733	212,561	212,981	224,465	224,359

Source: New York Mercantile Exchange (NYMEX)

Volume of Trading of Heating Oil #2 Futures in New York   In Thousands of Contracts

Year	Jan.	Feb.	Mar.	Apr.	May	June	July	Aug.	Sept.	Oct.	Nov.	Dec.	Total
1999	738.9	662.3	973.3	706.3	768.1	802.7	770.4	707.9	720.1	819.6	818.6	712.7	9,200.7
2000	914.0	770.3	645.2	556.1	673.3	705.9	663.0	1,004.4	954.9	878.1	939.0	927.3	9,631.4
2001	914.4	650.7	758.0	728.6	722.8	849.9	712.9	745.8	694.0	853.8	835.5	798.1	9,264.5
2002	998.5	810.8	885.5	844.1	789.8	720.1	798.8	866.0	794.4	1,017.9	1,039.5	1,129.9	10,695.2
2003	1,340.1	1,158.9	965.9	757.7	811.6	802.9	849.9	891.3	1,118.5	1,095.5	817.3	971.8	11,581.7
2004	1,153.8	1,059.7	1,139.9	1,007.8	910.0	1,100.5	920.7	1,105.7	1,060.8	1,148.6	1,112.7	1,164.4	12,884.5
2005	1,090.6	1,046.1	1,204.2	1,062.5	999.7	1,193.5	1,058.5	1,150.4	1,165.1	1,019.5	1,009.5	1,136.0	13,135.6
2006	1,157.5	1,131.2	1,121.7	974.8	1,185.1	1,114.0	1,027.1	1,166.1	1,235.9	1,291.1	1,228.6	1,357.5	13,990.6
2007	1,655.6	1,507.5	1,370.3	1,326.0	1,462.2	1,605.8	1,478.9	1,579.8	1,394.7	1,687.2	1,544.1	1,467.0	18,079.0
2008	1,611.7	1,726.3	1,763.3	1,639.2	1,825.3	1,651.9	1,571.3	1,641.9	1,510.9	1,646.4	1,297.3	1,630.4	19,516.0

Source: New York Mercantile Exchange (NYMEX)

Heating Oil (monthly average) through December 2008 — USD per gallon

Stocks of Distillate and Residual Fuel in the United States, on First of Month   In Millions of Barrels

Year	Jan.	Feb.	Mar.	Apr.	May	June	July	Aug.	Sept.	Oct.	Nov.	Dec.	Residual Fuel --- Oil Stocks --- Jan. 1	July 1
1999	156.2	147.9	142.3	125.7	125.3	134.8	133.2	138.1	142.0	145.2	137.6	140.6	44.9	42.5
2000	124.1	106.7	105.2	96.0	100.1	105.4	106.4	112.9	111.0	115.3	116.5	121.1	35.8	37.0
2001	118.0	118.2	117.0	105.0	104.9	107.1	113.9	125.2	122.0	127.0	128.9	138.9	36.2	41.7
2002	144.5	137.8	130.0	123.0	122.6	127.4	130.9	133.4	130.6	126.9	121.4	124.4	41.0	32.7
2003	134.1	112.6	97.7	98.6	97.2	106.7	112.2	118.0	126.5	131.3	132.1	136.1	31.3	35.3
2004	136.5	122.8	112.2	104.4	101.5	107.5	114.3	121.9	130.8	123.1	118.3	123.2	37.8	37.5
2005	126.3	121.4	116.4	104.5	104.5	111.0	118.8	132.0	139.4	127.7	124.8	133.8	42.4	37.4
2006	136.0	139.4	135.6	120.5	116.5	124.0	129.9	137.5	145.1	149.3	142.8	140.6	37.4	43.2
2007	143.7	139.5	123.2	119.7	120.9	124.8	123.4	130.6	133.5	133.6	133.9	134.4	42.4	36.1
2008[1]	133.5	129.6	117.0	107.2	106.1	112.8	121.1	130.4	132.5	127.2	127.4	135.8	38.6	41.6

[1] Preliminary.   Source: Energy Information Administration; U.S. Department of Energy (EIA-DOE)

Production of Distillate Fuel Oil in the United States   In Thousand Barrels per Day

Year	Jan.	Feb.	Mar.	Apr.	May	June	July	Aug.	Sept.	Oct.	Nov.	Dec.	Average
1999	3,176	3,253	3,183	3,407	3,458	3,374	3,521	3,419	3,482	3,506	3,608	3,401	3,399
2000	3,123	3,348	3,342	3,533	3,650	3,481	3,520	3,678	3,844	3,774	3,785	3,872	3,580
2001	3,609	3,612	3,483	3,650	3,652	3,702	3,837	3,654	3,625	3,796	3,968	3,744	3,695
2002	3,508	3,498	3,360	3,647	3,709	3,679	3,561	3,538	3,536	3,380	3,768	3,922	3,592
2003	3,403	3,459	3,732	3,796	3,833	3,728	3,673	3,730	3,721	3,750	3,800	3,845	3,707
2004	3,592	3,446	3,550	3,874	3,857	3,956	3,902	3,981	3,625	3,808	4,004	4,159	3,813
2005	3,777	3,797	3,874	4,028	4,179	4,274	4,236	4,108	3,570	3,585	3,966	4,044	3,953
2006	3,840	3,941	3,736	3,833	4,105	4,107	4,065	4,234	4,300	4,090	4,070	4,159	4,040
2007	4,027	3,883	4,009	4,102	4,142	4,050	4,145	4,244	4,158	4,208	4,278	4,326	4,131
2008[1]	4,110	3,973	3,940	4,287	4,459	4,572	4,509	4,466	3,681	4,437	4,490	4,544	4,289

[1] Preliminary.   Source: Energy Information Administration; U.S. Department of Energy (EIA-DOE)

HEATING OIL

Imports of Distillate Fuel Oil in the United States   In Thousand of Barrels per Day

Year	Jan.	Feb.	Mar.	Apr.	May	June	July	Aug.	Sept.	Oct.	Nov.	Dec.	Average
2001	789	635	348	288	310	302	209	212	317	253	244	241	344
2002	298	248	234	219	193	204	188	205	196	350	373	496	267
2003	325	503	460	246	287	337	299	375	352	281	241	305	333
2004	370	507	449	267	275	324	283	313	272	243	319	292	326
2005	353	344	257	264	281	236	243	263	275	507	486	435	329
2006	552	388	292	297	437	297	361	363	438	307	288	355	365
2007	352	334	360	322	272	273	318	346	261	288	245	241	301
2008[1]	307	248	241	255	188	179	181	109	195	166	203	200	206

[1] Preliminary.   Source: Energy Information Administration, U.S. Department of Energy (EIA-DOE)

Exports of Distillate Fuel Oil from the United States   In Thousand of Barrels per Day

Year	Jan.	Feb.	Mar.	Apr.	May	June	July	Aug.	Sept.	Oct.	Nov.	Dec.	Average
2000	132	112	211	178	127	149	132	253	194	255	191	135	173
2001	67	77	75	107	146	120	113	140	152	99	132	202	119
2002	109	279	67	68	74	93	44	119	127	96	114	171	112
2003	119	132	161	139	162	101	103	80	43	62	81	100	107
2004	72	86	99	92	100	163	113	120	88	101	102	176	109
2005	49	102	165	192	199	227	189	163	108	109	92	65	138
2006	123	156	120	200	229	187	231	191	456	291	252	149	215
2007[1]	253	202	155	167	227	240	243	311	274	173	188	NA	221

[1] Preliminary.   Source: Energy Information Administration, U.S. Department of Energy (EIA-DOE)

Disposition of Distillate Fuel Oil, Total Product Supplied in the United States   In Thousand of Barrels per Day

Year	Jan.	Feb.	Mar.	Apr.	May	June	July	Aug.	Sept.	Oct.	Nov.	Dec.	Average
2001	4,325	4,212	4,143	3,834	3,746	3,659	3,569	3,829	3,624	3,888	3,746	3,604	3,847
2002	3,940	3,714	3,750	3,821	3,679	3,587	3,683	3,728	3,730	3,808	3,929	3,934	3,776
2003	4,301	4,362	4,001	3,951	3,651	3,781	3,680	3,752	3,871	3,945	3,824	4,037	3,927
2004	4,334	4,232	4,152	4,145	3,840	3,888	3,827	3,887	4,065	4,104	4,058	4,176	4,059
2005	4,223	4,202	4,349	4,101	4,037	4,038	3,854	4,020	4,116	4,079	4,061	4,339	4,118
2006	4,159	4,308	4,395	4,065	4,072	4,019	3,950	4,162	4,141	4,315	4,180	4,268	4,170
2007	4,256	4,582	4,334	4,214	4,068	4,114	4,026	4,146	4,161	4,213	4,074	4,193	4,198
2008[1]	4,209	4,251	4,140	4,108	3,936	3,728	3,672	3,657	3,740	4,004	3,960		3,946

[1] Preliminary.   Source: Energy Information Administration, U.S. Department of Energy (EIA-DOE)

Production of Residual Fuel Oil in the United States   In Thousands of Barrels per Day

Year	Jan.	Feb.	Mar.	Apr.	May	June	July	Aug.	Sept.	Oct.	Nov.	Dec.	Average
2001	809	743	750	817	786	783	639	622	653	710	685	655	721
2002	625	613	617	601	582	540	566	583	607	593	648	641	601
2003	658	683	652	632	729	666	632	663	662	640	616	686	660
2004	656	659	635	701	668	648	618	631	617	610	703	723	656
2005	701	691	619	598	645	673	614	594	555	530	642	674	628
2006	670	635	644	643	580	645	658	652	619	597	624	656	635
2007	667	650	656	658	647	628	708	698	698	689	694	676	672
2008[1]	591	645	664	710	734	695	584	579	485	575	588	555	617

[1] Preliminary.   Source: Energy Information Administration, U.S. Department of Energy (EIA-DOE)

Supply and Disposition of Residual Fuel Oil in the United States

Year	Supply — Total Production	Imports	Disposition — Stock Change	Exports	Product Supplied	Ending Stocks (Million Barrels)	Average Sales to End Users[3] (Cents per Gallon)
2000	696	352	1	139	909	36	60.2
2001	721	295	13	191	811	41	53.1
2002	601	249	-27	177	700	31	56.9
2003	660	327	18	197	772	38	69.8
2004	655	426	12	205	865	42	73.9
2005	628	530	-14	251	920	37	104.8
2006	635	350	14	283	689	42	121.8
2007[1]	669	368	-13	309	742	38	

In Tousands of Barrels Per Day

[1] Preliminary.   [2] Less than +500 barrels per day and greater than -500 barrels per day.   [3] Refiner price excluding taxes.
Source: Energy Information Administration, U.S. Department of Energy (EIA-DOE)

Hides and Leather

Hides and leather have been used since ancient times for boots, clothing, shields, armor, tents, bottles, buckets, and cups. Leather is produced through the tanning of hides, pelts, and skins of animals. The remains of leather have been found in the Middle East dating back at least 7,000 years.

Today, most leather is made of cowhide but it is also made from the hides of lamb, deer, ostrich, snakes, crocodiles, and even stingray. Cattle hides are the most valuable byproduct of the meat packing industry. U.S. exports of cowhides bring more than $1 billion in foreign trade, and U.S. finished leather production is worth about $4 billion.

Prices – The average monthly price of wholesale cattle hides (packer heavy native steers FOB Chicago) in 2008 fell -10.8% yr/yr to 80.75 cents per pound, down from last year's record high of 90.53 cents per pound.

Supply – World production of cattle and buffalo hides in 2005 (latest data available) rose by +2.9% yr/yr to a record high of 8.769 million metric tons. The world's largest producers of cattle and buffalo hides in 2005 were the U.S. with 11% of world production, Brazil with 10%, and Argentina with 5%. U.S. new supply of cattle hides from domestic slaughter in 2004 (latest data available) fell 7.8% yr/yr to 32,728 million hides, which is far below the record high of 43.582 million hides posted in 1976.

U.S. production of leather footwear has been dropping off sharply in recent years due to the movement of production offshore to lower cost producers. U.S. production of leather footwear in 2003 (latest data available) fell -46% yr/yr to 22.3 million pairs and was a mere 4% of the 562.3 million pairs produced in 1970.

Demand – World consumption of cowhides and skins in 2000, the last reporting year for the series, rose +1.4% to 4,774 metric tons, which was a record high for the data series, which goes back to 1984. The world's largest consumers of cowhides and skins in 2000 were the U.S. with 13.0% of world consumption, Italy (10.6%), Brazil (8.9%), Mexico, (6.0%), Argentina (6.0%), and South Korea (5.9%).

Trade – U.S. net exports of cattle hides in 2004 (latest data available) fell –4.3% yr/yr to 17.388 million hides from the 15-year high of 21.750 million hides posted in 2001. The total value of U.S. leather exports in 2004 rose +16.8% yr/yr to $1.344 billion. The largest destinations for U.S. exports in 2008 were South Korea (which took 15% of U.S. exports), Mexico (7%), Taiwan (5%), Thailand (3%), and Italy (2%). World imports of cowhides and skins in 2000 (latest data available) rose +2.8% yr/yr to a record high of 2,058 metric tons. The world's largest importers of cowhides and skins in 2000 were South Korea (with 13% of world imports in 2000), Italy (11%) and Taiwan (7%).

World Production of Cattle and Buffalo Hides   In Thousands of Metric Tons

Year	Argentina	Australia	Brazil	Canada	Colombia	France	Germany	Italy	Mexico	Russia	United Kingdom	United States	World Total
1996	388	206	605	88	84	164	176	150	160	325	67	1,065	6,927
1997	384	219	622	91	81	163	176	148	161	294	64	1,063	7,195
1998	338	233	637	94	81	154	161	142	170	275	65	1,070	7,214
1999	364	241	667	98	86	151	162	145	170	229	64	1,099	7,304
2000	372	238	670	96	82	150	152	143	175	232	68	1,116	7,416
2001	348	254	725	95	76	150	153	130	176	220	61	1,031	7,266
2002	345	243	750	96	72	160	151	132	176	224	65	1,054	7,444
2003	375	248	770	88	72	157	141	130	176	229	63	1,046	7,642
2004[1]	432	243	792	111	80	150	141	132	176	223	66	1,046	7,894
2005[2]	432	255	792	115	80	150	141	132	176	220	66	1,046	8,033

[1] Preliminary.   [2] Forecast.   *Source: Food and Agricultural Organization of the United Nations (FAO-UN)*

Salient Statistics of Hides and Leather in the United States   In Thousands of Equivalent Hides

	New Supply of Cattle hides — Domestic Slaughter				Wholesale Prices - Cents Per Pound		Production		Value of Leather Exports ($1,000)	Wholesale Leather Indicies (1982 = 100)		Footwear	
Year	Federally Inspected	Unin- spected[4]	Total Production	Net Exports	Heavy Native Cows[2]	Heavy Native[3] Steers	All U.S. Tanning In 1,000 Equiv. Hides	Cattle- hide		Men	Women	Pro- duction[5] Million Pairs	Exports
1996	36,583	177	36,760	18,626	92.15	86.4	18,769	18,135	950,510	152.4	132.1	127,315	23,726
1997	35,567	751	36,492	17,562	90.99	86.1	19,592	18,930	1,145,664	156.4	132.2	124,444	21,958
1998	34,787	677	35,637	15,937	75.45	69.5	20,297	19,706	1,289,547	158.0	132.4	108,536	19,009
1999	36,150	664	36,320	15,700	73.80	73.1	21,342	20,620	1,137,534	157.0	133.0	78,581	18,176
2000	36,246	615	36,416	19,670	83.41	81.2	17,332	16,746	1,125,957	157.2	133.6	58,870	20,157
2001	34,771	599	35,370	21,750	85.52	89.8	14,212	13,779	1,221,131	158.4	133.8	55,600	19,472
2002	35,120	614	35,734	19,484	85.73	82.3		16,403	1,161,944	158.8	133.5	41,100	21,582
2003	34,907	590	35,493	18,177	88.34	83.8		17,470	1,150,212	161.4	132.1	22,300	21,319
2004[1]	32,156		32,728	17,388		82.2		15,492	1,344,017	161.7	129.2		21,464
2005[1]										163.5	132.1		

[1] Preliminary.   [2] Central U.S., heifers.   [3] F.O.B. Chicago.   [4] Includes farm slaughter; diseased & condemned animals & hides taken off fallen animals.
[5] Other than rubber.   *Sources: Leather Industries of America (LIA); Bureau of Labor Statistics, U.S. Department of Commerce (BLS)*

HIDES AND LEATHER

Production of All Footwear (Shoes, Sandals, Slippers, Athletic, Etc.) in the United States   In Millions of Pairs

Year	First Quarter	Second Quarter	Third Quarter	Fourth Quarter	Total	Year	First Quarter	Second Quarter	Third Quarter	Fourth Quarter	Total
1994	42.5	40.8	40.1	39.5	163.0	1999	26.7	26.1	24.5	21.7	78.5
1995	37.2	38.3	34.8	36.7	147.0	2000	----	----	----	----	58.8
1996	33.2	31.8	29.7	33.2	128.0	2001	----	----	----	----	55.6
1997	31.4	33.1	28.6	30.6	124.4	2002	----	----	----	----	41.1
1998	32.8	31.8	29.3	28.6	108.5	2003[1]	----	----	----	----	22.3

[1] Preliminary.   *Source: Bureau of the Census, U.S. Department of Commerce*

Average Factory Price[2] of Footwear in the United States   In Dollars Per Pair

Year	First Quarter	Second Quarter	Third Quarter	Fourth Quarter	Total	Year	First Quarter	Second Quarter	Third Quarter	Fourth Quarter	Total
1994	25.77	23.60	21.49	22.44	23.22	1999	23.33	22.70	19.90	19.50	21.19
1995	19.61	21.46	25.37	21.26	21.79	2000	----	----	----	----	24.14
1996	23.65	22.78	22.14	20.38	22.07	2001	----	----	----	----	25.66
1997	22.42	21.56	22.21	22.24	22.11	2002	----	----	----	----	24.12
1998	24.39	24.21	20.27	19.78	21.84	2003[1]	----	----	----	----	45.95

[1] Preliminary.   [2] Average value of factory shipments per pair.   *Source: Bureau of the Census, U.S. Department of Commerce*

Imports and Exports of All Cattle Hides in the United States   In Thousands of Hides

| | ----- Imports ----- | | ---- U.S. Exports - by Country of Destination ---- | | | | | | | | | | |
Year	Total	From Canada	Total	Canada	Italy	Japan	Rep of Korea	Mexico	Portugal	Romania	Spain	Taiwan	Thailand
1999	1,906	1,742	17,621	829	738	1,252	6,038	2,723	46	0	262	2,863	343
2000	1,972	1,876	21,658	875	1,163	1,529	7,673	2,196	37	0	189	2,844	562
2001	1,721	1,615	23,471	716	920	1,343	7,602	1,647	54	0	159	2,751	888
2002	1,298	1,227	20,784	837	1,099	584	5,812	1,470	14	0	189	2,145	914
2003	2,934	1,888	19,139	530	779	483	4,784	1,257	6	0	63	1,982	788
2004	7,342	6,165	18,795	346	417	468	4,218	1,419	4	0	16	1,842	684
2005	3,698	2,888	19,231	141	568	334	4,048	1,288	2	0	8	1,730	652
2006	2,175	1,602	20,059	57	523	277	3,455	1,225	5	0	41	1,902	441
2007	1,924	1,182	17,687	91	191	234	2,867	1,243	3	0	44	1,260	724
2008[1]	1,722	1,100	15,157	111	246	150	2,240	1,045	0	0	99	749	428

[1] Preliminary.   *Source: Leather Industries of America*

Imports of Bovine Hides and Skins by Selected Countries   In Metric Tons

Year	Brazil	Canada	Hong Kong	Italy	Japan	Mexico	Portugal	Rep. of Korea	Spain	Taiwan	Turkey	United States	World Total
1992	11	17	80	131	188	71	32	385	26	91	28	65	1,266
1993	21	26	81	141	188	71	39	372	35	94	37	57	1,426
1994	16	28	95	243	139	60	56	356	29	112	17	49	1,556
1995	33	35	100	250	152	30	43	342	42	112	43	57	1,715
1996	20	34	79	263	123	71	42	341	33	124	50	60	1,692
1997	13	39	64	254	114	96	37	323	44	140	68	60	1,985
1998	10	42	71	249	96	110	39	229	44	142	45	59	1,876
1999[1]	8	34	91	215	95	115	42	254	29	142	55	57	2,002
2000[2]	8	36	93	220	95	115	43	260	30	142	60	57	2,058

[1] Preliminary.   [2] Forecast.   *Source: Foreign Agricultural Service, U.S. Department of Agriculture (FAS-USDA)*

Exports of Bovine Hides and Skins by Selected Countries   In Metric Tons

Year	Australia	Brazil	Canada	Germany	Hong Kong	Italy	Netherlands	New Zealand	Poland	Russia	United Kingdom	United States	World Total
1992	144	71	74	38	75	9	66	31	17	28	19	610	1,261
1993	142	76	87	40	76	7	35	21	5	150	25	581	1,374
1994	96	84	79	24	93	10	37	22	2	216	22	455	1,271
1995	85	148	90	34	100	10	47	22	2	195	22	510	1,351
1996	93	174	97	33	72	20	47	28	3	212	24	506	1,423
1997	115	216	97	35	60	16	48	27	3	210	25	473	1,475
1998	111	220	86	31	69	24	32	28	6	202	17	443	1,400
1999[1]	115	230	83	28	90	7	30	30	7	190	15	436	1,389
2000[2]	108	250	85	31	92	8	25	30	7	170	15	427	1,399

[1] Preliminary.   [2] Forecast.   *Source: Foreign Agricultural Service, U.S. Department of Agriculture (FAS-USDA)*

Hides (monthly average) through December 2008 — Cents per pound

Utilization of Bovine Hides and Skins by Selected Countries   In Metric Tons

Year	Argentina	Brazil	Colombia	Germany	Italy	Japan	Mexico	Rep. of Korea	Spain	Taiwan	Turkey	United States	World Total
1992	298	382	97	129	435	229	231	400	98	91	90	528	3,977
1993	302	510	94	100	435	226	232	385	98	94	95	554	4,322
1994	304	505	96	83	550	200	226	374	94	112	85	536	4,282
1995	300	493	89	79	570	191	200	355	98	112	100	523	4,365
1996	308	461	91	80	615	165	230	353	95	124	110	548	4,332
1997	332	387	89	101	570	150	251	347	106	140	120	572	4,609
1998	285	412	91	100	540	135	275	265	108	142	100	603	4,584
1999[1]	300	415	89	102	500	130	280	280	104	142	110	623	4,707
2000[2]	285	425	89	103	505	130	285	283	108	142	120	623	4,774

[1] Preliminary.   [2] Forecast.   *Source: Foreign Agricultural Service, U.S. Department of Agriculture (FAS-USDA)*

Wholesale Price of Hides (Packer Heavy Native Steers) F.O.B. Chicago   In Cents Per Pound

Year	Jan.	Feb.	Mar.	Apr.	May	June	July	Aug.	Sept.	Oct.	Nov.	Dec.	Average
1999	69.42	69.97	70.84	67.36	65.96	66.89	68.17	72.41	77.52	80.43	79.67	78.00	72.22
2000	75.92	76.29	77.86	78.83	79.24	75.18	77.25	81.64	85.60	84.89	84.41	85.31	80.20
2001	85.33	84.12	93.02	102.64	106.19	97.31	87.59	77.28	73.51	70.58	73.30	69.16	85.00
2002	68.23	72.39	80.41	83.21	84.32	86.72	84.43	85.77	85.84	85.75	83.35	85.18	82.13
2003	83.77	85.81	86.04	85.81	79.42	77.64	80.53	84.09	86.78	86.13	85.89	86.05	84.00
2004	85.17	81.79	82.89	79.15	80.16	82.43	85.11	84.54	85.05	82.23	81.42	78.02	82.33
2005	78.14	80.90	79.04	80.45	79.49	83.07	82.70	81.78	80.58	80.44	80.07	79.03	80.47
2006	79.28	81.01	83.86	84.95	87.76	88.07	87.93	87.15	88.29	88.08	88.81	90.50	86.31
2007	93.75	95.85	95.66	98.13	97.68	93.19	87.36	86.95	86.14	83.08	84.72	83.83	90.53
2008	79.55	79.43	82.79	85.58	85.82	87.01	87.55	87.49	85.10	85.31	78.38	44.98	80.75

Source: National Agricultural Statistics Service, U.S. Department of Agriculture (NASS-USDA)

Hogs

Hogs are generally bred twice a year in a continuous cycle designed to provide a steady flow of production. The gestation period for hogs is 3-1/2 months and the average litter size is 9 pigs. The pigs are weaned at 3-4 weeks of age. The pigs are then fed so as to maximize weight gain. The feed consists primarily of grains such as corn, barley, milo, oats, and wheat. Protein is added from oilseed meals. Hogs typically gain 3.1 pounds per pound of feed. The time from birth to slaughter is typically 6 months. Hogs are ready for slaughter at about 254 pounds, producing a dressed carcass weight of around 190 pounds and an average 88.6 pounds of lean meat. The lean meat consists of 21% ham, 20% loin, 14% belly, 3% spareribs, 7% Boston butt roast and blade steaks, and 10% picnic, with the remaining 25% going into jowl, lean trim, fat, miscellaneous cuts, and trimmings. Futures on lean hogs are traded at the Chicago Mercantile Exchange. The futures contract is settled in cash based on the CME Lean Hog Index price, meaning that no physical delivery of hogs occurs. The CME Lean Hog Index is based on the 2-day average net price of slaughtered hogs at the average lean percentage level.

Prices – Lean hog futures prices on the nearest futures chart fell sharply in late 2007 and posted a 5-year low of 50.65 cents per pound in November 2007. Lean hog prices then recovered sharply in the first half of 2008 and posted a 12-year high of 90.00 cents in August 2008. Lean hog prices then plunged by 40% to a 1-year low of 53.90 cents in November 2008. Lean hog prices closed 2008 at 60.875 cents, up 3 cents (+5.2%) from the 2007 close of 57.875 cents. Lean hog prices came in to 2008 on a weak note after soaring grain and feed prices in 2007 caused producers to liquidate herds and caused a big supply of pork. However, lean hog prices then rallied in the first half of 2008 on the weak dollar and the overall rally in commodity prices. Hog prices then tumbled during the latter half of 2008 as the financial crisis encouraged producers to trim their herds and bring more hogs to slaughter. The number of hogs slaughtered rose by 4.2% in 2007 to 109.17 million head and rose by another 6.7% in 2008 to 116.46 million head.

Supply – World pork production in 2008 fell 2.8% yr/yr to 92.992 million metric tons. The USDA, however, is forecasting an increase of +4.4% in 2009 to 97.130 million metric tons. The world's largest pork producers are China with 52% of world production 2008, the European Union with 24%, and the U.S. with11%.

U.S. pork production in 2008 rose +1.5% to 10.108 million metric tons, and is forecasted by the USDA to rise another +5.7% to 10.684 million metric tons in 2009. The number of hogs and pigs on U.S. farms in 2008 (Dec 1) fell by -2.2% to 66.708 million, down from the more than 6-decade high of 68.117 in 2007. The federally-inspected hog slaughter in the U.S. in 2008 rose +6.7% to a record high of 115.420 million head.

Demand – World consumption of pork in 2008 fell by 3.5% yr/yr to 92.169 million metric tons. The USDA, however, is forecasting an increase of +5.2% in 2009 to 96.924 million metric tons. U.S. consumption of pork in 2008 rose +1.8% to 9.129 million metric tons, and the USDA is forecasting a further rise of +2.8% in 2009 to 9.384 million metric tons. The U.S. accounted for 9.9% of world consumption in 2008.

Trade – World pork exports in 2008 were virtually unchanged from 2007 at 5.516 million metric tons, but the USDA is an increase of +6.3% for 2009. The world's largest pork exporters are the U.S. with 28% of world exports in 2008, the European Union with 22%, Canada with 20%, and Brazil with 15%. U.S. pork exports in 2008 rose +1.2% yr/yr to 1.442 million metric tons and the USDA is forecasting a further rise of +1.7% in 2009 to 1.694 million metric tons.

World pork imports in 2008 fell -14 .8% to 4.30 million metric tons, but the USDA is forecasting a rise of +1.2% to 4.5.183 million metric tons in 2009. The world's largest pork importers are Japan, which accounted for 28% of world imports in 2008, Russia (20%), the U.S. (11%), South Korea (11%), and Mexico (9%).

Salient Statistics of Pigs and Hogs in the United States

	Pig Crop						Value of Hogs on Farms, Dec. 1-		Hog Mar-ketings	Quantity Pro-duced	Value of Pro-duction	Hogs Slaughtered, Thousand Head				
	Spring[3]			Fall[4]								Commercial				
	Sows Farrowed	Pig Crop	Pigs Per Litter	Sows Farrowed	Pig Crop	Pigs Per Litter	$ Per Head	Total Million $	(1,000 Head)	(Live Wt.) (Mil. Lbs.)	(Million $)	Federally Inspected	Other	Total	Farm	Total
Year	--- 1,000 Head ---			--- 1,000 Head ---												
1999	5,877	51,519	8.77	5,764	50,835	8.82	72.0	4,254	121,137	25,791	7,766	99,739	1,806	101,544	150	101,694
2000	5,683	50,087	8.81	5,727	50,660	8.85	77.0	4,542	118,418	25,717	10,791	96,436	1,540	97,976	130	98,106
2001	5,619	49,472	8.81	5,767	51,031	8.85	77.0	4,590	119,262	25,884	11,430	96,528	1,434	97,962	120	98,082
2002	5,776	50,858	8.81	5,716	50,820	8.89	71.0	4,231	124,013	26,274	8,691	98,915	1,348	100,263	115	100,378
2003	5,655	50,029	8.85	5,773	51,462	8.91	67.0	4,025	124,383	26,260	9,663	99,685	1,233	100,931	116	101,047
2004	5,706	50,737	8.89	5,793	52,043	8.98	103.0	6,303	127,563	26,689	13,072	102,361	1,103	103,463	114	103,577
2005	5,716	51,330	8.98	5,818	52,635	9.05	92.0	5,672	129,056	27,416	13,607	102,519	1,063	103,582	109	103,690
2006	5,768	52,242	9.06	5,862	53,376	9.11	89.0	5,586	132,262	28,149	12,702	103,689	1,048	104,737	105	104,842
2007[1]	5,935	54,266	9.14	6,312	58,608	9.28	73.0	4,917	137,759	29,567	13,468	108,138	1,034	109,172	106	109,278
2008[2]	6,126	57,044	9.31	6,065	57,660	9.51						115,420	1,038	116,458		

[1] Preliminary. [2] Estimate. [3] December-May. [4] June-November. *Source: Economic Research Service, U.S. Department of Agriculture (ERS-USDA)*

World Hog Numbers in Specified Countries as of January 1   In Thousands of Head

Year	Brazil	Canada	China	European Union	Japan	Rep. of Korea	Mexico	Philip-pines	Russia	Taiwan	Ukraine	United States	World Total
2000	31,860	12,904	431,442	163,746	9,805	7,000	10,781	10,764	16,100	7,243	10,073	59,335	778,366
2001	32,440	13,576	416,336	158,765	9,788	7,350	10,649	11,715	15,780	7,495	7,652	59,110	775,166
2002	32,710	14,375	419,505	158,250	9,612	7,856	10,569	11,816	16,570	7,165	8,317	59,722	782,964
2003	32,655	14,745	417,762	160,486	9,725	8,110	10,549	12,218	17,000	6,794	9,204	59,554	787,214
2004	32,081	14,725	413,818	158,970	9,724	8,367	10,668	12,518	17,200	6,779	7,321	60,444	782,324
2005	32,323	14,810	421,234	156,973	9,600	8,044	10,303	12,139	16,500	6,819	6,466	60,975	787,174
2006	32,938	15,110	433,191	159,115	9,620	8,098	10,125	13,041	16,550	7,172	7,052	61,449	805,751
2007	33,147	14,907	418,504	161,526	9,759	8,518	10,250	13,693	17,180	7,092	8,055	62,490	798,329
2008[1]	32,797	13,810	439,895	160,006	9,745	8,743	10,134		18,187		7,020	68,173	773,513
2009[2]	32,870	12,435	446,662	158,000	9,745	8,263	9,365		19,520		5,943	67,200	772,553

[1] Preliminary.   [2] Forecast.   *Source: Foreign Agricultural Service, U.S. Department of Agriculture (FAS-USDA)*

Hogs and Pigs on Farms in the United States on December 1   In Thousands of Head

Year	Georgia	Illinois	Indiana	Iowa	Kansas	Minne-sota	Missouri	Nebraska	North Carolina	Ohio	South Dakota	Wisconsin	Total
1999	480	4,050	3,250	15,400	1,460	5,500	3,150	3,000	9,500	1,480	1,260	570	59,342
2000	380	4,150	3,350	15,100	1,520	5,800	2,900	3,050	9,300	1,490	1,320	610	59,138
2001	315	4,250	3,200	15,400	1,570	5,800	3,000	2,900	9,800	1,430	1,290	540	59,804
2002	345	4,150	3,250	15,500	1,530	6,100	2,950	3,000	9,700	1,440	1,330	520	59,554
2003	295	4,000	3,100	15,900	1,650	6,500	2,950	2,900	10,000	1,520	1,280	480	60,444
2004	275	4,100	3,200	16,300	1,710	6,500	2,900	2,850	9,900	1,450	1,340	430	60,975
2005	270	4,000	3,250	16,600	1,790	6,600	2,700	2,850	9,800	1,560	1,490	430	61,449
2006	245	4,200	3,350	17,300	1,840	6,900	2,800	3,050	9,500	1,690	1,270	450	62,490
2007	265	4,350	3,700	19,400	1,880	7,700	3,150	3,350	10,200	1,830	1,460	440	68,177
2008[1]	230	4,350	3,500	19,800	1,730	7,400	3,100	3,350	9,600	1,930	1,320	360	66,708

[1] Preliminary.   *Source: National Agricultural Statistics Service, U.S. Department of Agriculture (NASS-USDA)*

Hog-Corn Price Ratio[2] in the United States

Year	Jan.	Feb.	Mar.	Apr.	May	June	July	Aug.	Sept.	Oct.	Nov.	Dec.	Average
1999	12.8	13.5	13.6	14.8	18.4	17.3	18.2	20.7	19.4	20.2	19.6	19.6	17.3
2000	19.3	20.2	20.5	23.3	22.9	25.6	29.5	28.8	25.8	23.8	19.8	20.2	23.3
2001	18.8	20.0	23.5	25.3	27.7	29.7	27.6	26.6	23.7	21.8	18.9	16.8	23.4
2002	19.1	19.9	18.6	16.6	17.2	18.2	18.4	13.4	10.7	13.2	12.2	13.1	15.9
2003	14.2	14.7	14.9	14.9	17.4	19.2	19.7	18.4	18.0	17.3	15.8	14.8	16.6
2004	15.4	16.3	17.2	16.4	19.7	20.3	22.7	23.6	24.9	24.4	27.1	25.7	21.1
2005	25.1	26.0	25.3	25.6	27.7	24.4	23.6	26.2	26.0	25.8	24.6	23.1	25.3
2006	20.4	21.1	20.8	19.6	22.2	25.1	23.5	24.7	22.2	18.2	15.6	14.5	20.7
2007	14.0	13.8	13.1	14.0	15.2	15.4	15.7	15.7	14.3	12.9	11.0	10.5	13.8
2008[1]	9.3	9.3	8.6	8.6	10.5	9.7	10.3	11.5	10.5	11.1	9.6	10.2	9.9

[1] Preliminary.   [2] Bushels of corn equal in value to 100 pounds of hog, live weight.   *Source: Economic Research Service, U.S. Department of Agriculture (ERS-USDA)*

Cold Storage Holdings of Frozen Pork[2] in the United States, on First of Month   In Millions of Pounds

Year	Jan.	Feb.	Mar.	Apr.	May	June	July	Aug.	Sept.	Oct.	Nov.	Dec.
1999	503.5	510.3	540.9	552.8	596.9	572.7	528.6	494.6	432.6	430.6	438.1	422.5
2000	415.4	481.4	523.5	534.7	532.1	537.9	495.5	478.5	455.6	439.5	438.6	445.6
2001	411.5	471.4	468.3	432.3	432.6	421.5	374.1	339.5	332.6	366.9	430.6	432.7
2002	465.0	503.9	510.9	531.5	567.7	548.0	497.8	472.2	464.4	480.2	489.8	463.9
2003	468.5	512.7	519.7	530.5	520.0	499.7	460.0	440.7	430.2	435.2	446.8	438.9
2004	470.7	504.1	477.1	447.3	448.6	412.8	373.0	366.8	382.1	413.8	423.1	436.3
2005	482.9	496.8	538.2	540.2	562.8	511.2	488.6	442.9	408.5	425.6	440.7	431.3
2006	421.3	527.7	528.0	505.0	520.0	477.0	412.6	417.8	415.6	458.4	488.4	468.5
2007	442.5	484.3	483.2	494.8	528.5	492.0	467.9	455.9	458.3	484.9	494.8	474.6
2008[1]	458.7	570.3	605.7	652.7	652.6	567.3	517.2	491.4	486.6	507.7	510.8	512.8

[1] Preliminary.   [2] Excludes lard.   *Source: Economic Research Service, U.S. Department of Agriculture (ERS-USDA)*

HOGS

Hogs (monthly average) through December 2008   Cents per pound

Average Price of Hogs, National Base 51-52% lean   In Dollars Per Hundred Pounds (Cwt.)

Year	Jan.	Feb.	Mar.	Apr.	May	June	July	Aug.	Sept.	Oct.	Nov.	Dec.	Average
1999	28.58	29.65	28.25	31.69	38.45	35.39	32.84	38.56	35.71	35.84	35.34	37.70	34.00
2000	38.32	41.58	43.52	49.59	50.21	51.48	50.45	45.35	43.49	43.09	37.84	41.40	44.69
2001	38.61	41.47	48.41	49.28	52.34	54.53	53.75	52.47	46.93	41.27	35.49	35.14	45.81
2002	40.16	40.65	37.47	32.97	34.64	37.32	40.53	34.00	26.98	31.69	29.99	32.35	34.90
2003	34.39	35.64	36.11	36.42	43.62	47.88	44.98	41.90	41.82	38.63	36.02	36.02	39.45
2004	39.02	45.21	48.30	48.34	58.45	57.95	58.21	56.19	55.34	53.68	56.23	53.15	52.51
2005	53.36	51.11	51.30	51.00	55.40	49.86	49.96	51.60	49.98	47.49	37.70	44.81	49.46
2006	41.37	43.17	43.34	41.45	49.00	54.90	51.89	53.32	50.28	47.57	45.97	44.84	47.26
2007	44.04	48.60	45.47	48.43	54.40	54.82	52.39	52.01	46.61	41.96	36.95	39.40	47.09
2008[1]	36.77	42.74	39.40	45.06	57.75	54.71	56.48	62.56	52.76	47.06	38.90	39.80	47.83

[1] Preliminary.   *Source: Economic Research Service, U.S. Department of Agriculture (ERS-USDA)*

Average Price Received by Farmers for Hogs in the United States   In Cents Per Pound

Year	Jan.	Feb.	Mar.	Apr.	May	June	July	Aug.	Sept.	Oct.	Nov.	Dec.	Average
1999	26.5	27.7	28.0	30.1	36.6	34.1	31.6	36.2	33.9	34.2	33.4	35.6	32.3
2000	36.8	39.9	41.7	47.4	48.3	48.9	48.3	43.8	41.6	41.4	36.8	39.8	42.9
2001	37.2	39.2	45.9	47.8	50.4	52.2	51.7	50.8	45.2	40.2	35.0	33.3	44.1
2002	37.7	38.5	36.0	31.7	33.2	35.8	39.2	31.9	26.5	30.8	27.8	30.3	33.3
2003	33.0	34.3	34.7	34.8	41.3	45.0	42.7	39.6	39.7	36.7	34.7	34.2	37.6
2004	36.8	42.6	47.2	47.4	56.6	56.7	57.1	55.3	54.8	52.2	55.6	52.4	51.2
2005	53.2	50.7	51.2	51.1	54.9	49.5	49.8	51.0	49.4	47.0	43.5	44.3	49.6
2006	40.7	42.6	42.8	41.3	48.2	53.8	50.2	51.6	48.9	46.5	44.9	43.5	46.3
2007	42.7	47.5	44.9	47.3	53.1	54.3	52.2	51.3	46.8	42.4	37.9	39.6	46.7
2008[1]	37.2	42.2	40.2	44.1	55.3	53.3	54.2	60.6	52.7	48.6	40.8	41.9	47.6

[1] Preliminary.   *Source: Economic Research Service, U.S. Department of Agriculture (ERS-USDA)*

Quarterly Hogs and Pigs Report in the United States, 10 States   In Thousands of Head

Year[2]	Inventory[3]	Breeding[3]	Market[3]	Farrowings	Pig Crop	Year[2]	Inventory[3]	Breeding[3]	Market[3]	Farrowings	Pig Crop
1999	62,206	6,682	55,523	11,641	102,354	2004	60,444	6,009	54,434	11,499	102,781
I	62,206	6,682	55,523	2,891	25,247	I	60,444	6,009	54,434	2,836	25,105
II	60,191	6,527	53,663	2,986	26,272	II	59,520	5,961	53,558	2,870	25,633
III	60,896	6,515	54,380	2,920	25,862	III	60,698	5,937	54,760	2,905	26,162
IV	60,776	6,301	54,474	2,844	24,973	IV	61,519	5,962	55,556	2,888	25,881
2000	59,342	6,234	53,109	11,410	100,747	2005	60,975	5,969	55,005	11,535	103,965
I	59,342	6,234	53,109	2,798	24,522	I	60,975	5,969	55,005	2,835	25,343
II	57,782	6,190	51,593	2,885	25,565	II	59,699	5,941	53,757	2,882	25,986
III	59,117	6,234	52,884	2,889	25,548	III	60,732	5,977	54,754	2,918	26,449
IV	59,495	6,246	53,250	2,838	25,112	IV	61,846	5,972	55,873	2,900	26,187
2001	59,138	6,270	52,868	11,385	100,503	2006	61,449	6,011	55,438	11,629	105,618
I	59,138	6,270	52,868	2,748	23,963	I	61,449	6,011	55,438	2,841	25,662
II	57,524	6,232	51,292	2,870	25,509	II	60,326	6,025	54,301	2,927	26,580
III	58,603	6,186	52,417	2,878	25,539	III	61,687	6,060	55,627	2,912	26,519
IV	59,777	6,158	53,619	2,889	25,492	IV	62,914	6,079	56,835	2,949	26,857
2002	59,804	6,209	53,594	11,492	101,677	2007	62,490	6,087	56,402	12,248	112,873
I	59,804	6,209	53,594	2,835	24,857	I	62,490	6,087	56,402	2,905	26,395
II	59,256	6,230	53,026	2,941	26,001	II	61,896	6,149	55,746	3,030	27,870
III	60,391	6,208	54,183	2,883	25,725	III	63,947	6,169	57,777	3,133	29,095
IV	60,753	6,051	54,702	2,833	25,094	IV	67,275	6,208	66,708	3,180	29,513
2003	59,554	6,058	53,496	11,429	101,491	2008[1]	68,177	6,233	61,944	12,191	114,704
I	59,554	6,058	53,496	2,769	24,400	I	68,177	6,233	61,944	3,071	28,387
II	58,183	6,027	52,156	2,886	25,629	II	67,218	6,200	61,018	3,055	28,657
III	59,602	6,026	53,576	2,918	25,974	III	67,400	6,131	61,269	3,075	29,250
IV	61,009	5,938	55,071	2,856	25,488	IV	68,196	6,061	62,135	2,990	28,410

[1] Preliminary.   [2] Quarters are Dec. preceding year-Feb.(I), Mar.-May(II), June-Aug.(III) and Sept.-Nov.(IV).
[3] Beginning of period.   *Source: National Agricultural Statistics Service, U.S. Department of Agriculture (NASS-USDA)*

Federally Inspected Hog Slaughter in the United States   In Thousands of Head

Year	Jan.	Feb.	Mar.	Apr.	May	June	July	Aug.	Sept.	Oct.	Nov.	Dec.	Total
1999	8,373	7,746	8,945	8,386	7,303	8,176	7,778	8,256	8,501	8,806	8,750	8,719	99,739
2000	8,010	7,955	8,695	7,108	7,816	7,823	7,235	8,481	7,992	8,746	8,633	7,943	96,436
2001	8,521	7,491	8,207	7,722	7,836	7,368	7,333	8,247	7,687	9,210	8,610	8,298	96,528
2002	8,552	7,400	7,879	8,321	8,215	7,425	7,957	8,425	8,384	9,276	8,548	8,534	98,915
2003	8,680	7,587	8,069	8,238	7,715	7,665	8,008	7,951	8,466	9,547	8,506	9,254	99,685
2004	8,704	7,805	8,942	8,567	7,494	8,415	8,008	8,616	8,897	8,883	8,881	9,150	102,361
2005	8,402	8,031	8,858	8,369	7,939	8,470	7,582	8,888	8,778	9,027	9,038	9,138	102,519
2006	8,834	7,978	9,148	7,884	8,450	8,256	7,805	8,991	8,738	9,541	9,276	8,788	103,689
2007	9,281	8,040	9,119	8,389	8,680	8,218	8,312	9,296	8,683	10,555	9,964	9,601	108,138
2008[1]	10,474	9,297	9,579	9,911	8,980	8,801	9,373	9,170	9,878	10,654	9,250	10,053	115,420

[1] Preliminary. *Source: National Agricultural Statistics Service, U.S. Department of Agriculture (NASS-USDA)*

Average Live Weight of all Hogs Slaughtered Under Federal Inspection   In Pounds Per Head

Year	Jan.	Feb.	Mar.	Apr.	May	June	July	Aug.	Sept.	Oct.	Nov.	Dec.	Average
1999	259	259	259	260	260	260	257	254	256	259	262	262	259
2000	262	262	263	263	264	263	260	258	260	263	266	265	262
2001	265	264	264	265	264	264	261	258	262	267	269	268	264
2002	268	267	267	268	267	266	261	259	261	264	268	268	265
2003	268	267	268	268	268	266	263	261	263	268	270	269	267
2004	269	268	268	268	266	265	263	263	266	267	270	270	267
2005	270	270	271	271	270	269	265	263	265	269	272	272	269
2006	273	272	272	272	271	267	264	262	267	269	272	271	269
2007	271	270	271	270	269	267	265	264	267	270	273	272	269
2008[1]	273	271	271	270	268	266	263	261	266	270	271	271	268

[1] Preliminary. *Source: National Agricultural Statistics Service, U.S. Department of Agriculture (NASS-USDA)*

HOGS

Average Open Interest of Lean Hog Futures in Chicago — In Contracts

Year	Jan.	Feb.	Mar.	Apr.	May	June	July	Aug.	Sept.	Oct.	Nov.	Dec.
1999	46,003	44,211	43,803	48,277	55,951	52,398	54,723	49,915	53,055	54,089	54,432	50,691
2000	49,209	54,094	57,472	68,535	64,938	54,208	45,730	38,233	38,802	38,254	40,075	45,141
2001	41,425	41,892	48,381	45,296	41,910	45,715	51,661	47,760	42,072	36,983	32,821	27,687
2002	28,720	31,662	33,056	33,472	33,161	28,719	29,338	32,030	36,136	35,245	42,852	43,974
2003	40,660	39,862	40,446	37,883	43,672	47,338	39,706	37,700	49,469	46,295	43,552	43,352
2004	46,380	55,058	63,889	77,756	80,271	81,370	79,860	84,840	86,092	86,423	94,336	98,328
2005	102,580	97,550	95,841	94,008	96,662	91,871	97,160	95,841	107,617	113,754	116,005	124,492
2006	133,258	144,506	145,020	144,250	157,259	158,276	157,899	165,781	176,336	174,971	188,965	179,057
2007	174,424	182,146	178,296	174,233	176,897	177,274	174,144	176,425	175,093	179,402	204,475	206,458
2008	212,644	227,377	219,938	232,309	252,497	242,588	238,162	231,283	206,602	171,506	168,129	159,600

Source: Chicago Mercantile Exchange (CME)

Volume of Trading of Lean Hog Futures in Chicago — In Contracts

Year	Jan.	Feb.	Mar.	Apr.	May	June	July	Aug.	Sept.	Oct.	Nov.	Dec.	Total
1999	218,608	171,108	196,825	189,773	214,852	237,240	239,096	167,787	190,238	187,794	205,505	139,270	2,358,096
2000	175,399	186,352	231,532	158,765	218,222	235,036	172,725	145,849	146,240	142,240	153,043	146,404	2,111,807
2001	183,493	159,020	197,004	142,892	165,220	184,421	198,503	164,712	152,178	177,601	163,798	129,497	2,018,339
2002	145,266	120,994	168,929	196,956	163,816	158,074	166,064	140,154	174,797	167,065	165,039	164,106	1,931,260
2003	186,436	137,479	186,511	156,370	209,740	210,901	199,782	124,677	232,705	207,247	164,190	148,117	2,164,155
2004	212,420	170,270	249,205	211,501	295,271	304,279	315,197	215,233	356,295	242,204	376,823	255,488	3,204,186
2005	347,467	237,079	380,658	287,828	412,655	398,201	354,819	315,949	391,121	295,817	421,714	310,235	4,153,543
2006	561,152	319,827	597,852	356,950	658,973	826,312	578,656	478,837	577,375	533,532	649,293	342,242	6,481,001
2007	687,585	449,649	721,014	423,223	620,985	744,799	865,371	559,139	591,564	485,066	730,036	386,401	7,264,832
2008	800,566	527,093	809,724	736,404	796,703	938,662	968,358	617,855	781,563	506,765	576,326	445,119	8,505,138

Source: Chicago Mercantile Exchange (CME)

Honey

Honey is the thick, supersaturated sugar solution produced by bees to feed their larvae. It is composed of fructose, glucose and water in varying proportions and also contains several enzymes and oils. The color of honey varies due to the source of nectar and age of the honey. Light colored honeys are usually of higher quality than darker honeys. The average honeybee colony can produce more than 700 pounds of honey per year but only 10 percent is usually harvested by the beekeeper. The rest of the honey is consumed by the colony during the year. American per capita honey consumption is 1 pound per person per year. Honey is said to be humanity's oldest sweet, and beeswax the first plastic.

Honey is used in many ways, including direct human consumption, baking, and medicine. Honey has several healing properties. Its high sugar content nourishes injured tissues, thus enhancing faster healing time. Honey's phytochemicals create a form of hydrogen peroxide that cleans out the wound, and the thick consistency protects the wound from contact with air Honey has also proven superior to antibiotic ointments for reducing rates of infection in people with burns.

Prices – U.S. average domestic honey prices in 2008 rose by +30.9% to a record high of 141.0 cents per pound. The value of U.S. honey production in 2008 rose +42.0% to $226.814 million, but stayed well below the 2003 record high of $253.106 million.

Supply – World production of honey in 2007 (latest data available) fell -25.4% to an 11-year low of 1.073 million metric tons, down from the 2006 record high of 1.438 million metric tons. Usually the world's largest producer of honey is China (at around 23% of total world production) but in 2007 China only produced 6,000 metric tons (vs. 301,978 in 2006). Major producers in 2007 were Argentina with 81,000 metric tons, the U.S. with 70,500 metric tons, and Mexico and Russia with each at 56,000 metric tons.

U.S. production of honey in 2008 rose +8.4% to 160.861 million pounds, remaining well below the 14-year high of 220.339 million pounds posted in 2000. Stocks fell by 4.2% to 50.445 million pounds in 2008 (Jan 1), but stayed well above the 25-year low of 39.4 million pounds posted in 2002. Yield per colony in 2008 rose +15.2% to 69.9 pounds per colony. The number of colonies in 2008 fell by -5.8% to a record low of 2.301 million.

Trade – U.S. imports of honey in 2008 fell by -0.7% to 231.4 million pounds, down from the 2006 record high of 277.7 million pounds. U.S. exports of honey are generally small and in 2008 they totaled only 10.1 million pounds, which was only 6.3% of U.S. production.

World Production of Honey   In Metric Tons

Year	Argentina	Australia	Brazil	Canada	China	Germany	Japan	Mexico	Russia	United States	Total
2001	80,000	19,000	22,220	35,388	254,358	25,951	3,300	59,069	52,659	84,335	1,264,604
2002	83,000	18,000	23,995	37,072	267,830	14,620	3,300	58,890	49,400	77,890	1,283,709
2003	75,000	16,000	30,022	34,602	298,197	23,691	3,300	57,045	48,048	82,431	1,334,229
2004	80,000	16,000	32,290	34,241	297,987	25,575	3,300	56,917	52,666	83,272	1,367,809
2005	110,000	16,000	33,750	36,109	299,327	21,232	3,300	50,631	52,123	72,927	1,410,455
2006	80,000	17,500	33,800	48,353	301,978	20,000	3,300	55,970	55,316	70,238	1,438,261
2007[1]	81,000	18,000	34,000	27,842	NA	NA	NA	56,000	56,000	70,500	1,073,017

[1] Preliminary.   NA = Not available.   *Source: Food and Agricultural Organization of the United Nations (FAO)*

Salient Statistics of Honey in the United States   In Millions of Pounds

Year	Number of Colonies (1,000)	Yield Per Colony (Pounds)	Stocks Jan. 1	Total U.S. Production	Imports for Consumption	Domestic Disappearance	Exports	Total Supply	Placed Under Loan	CCC Take Over	Net Gov't. Expenditure[3] (Million $)	Domestic Avg. Price All Honey - Cents Per Pound -	National Avg. Price Support	Per Capita Consumption (Pounds)
2003	2,599	70.0	40.8	181.7	200.4	----	6.9	422.9	----	----	----	138.7	----	----
2004	2,556	71.8	61.2	183.6	178.6	----	7.8	423.4	----	----	----	106.9	----	----
2005	2,413	72.4	62.5	174.8	233.0	----	7.6	470.3	----	----	----	91.8	----	----
2006	2,393	64.7	60.5	154.9	277.7	----	7.0	493.1	----	----	----	103.6	----	----
2007[1]	2,443	60.7	52.6	148.3	233.0	----	8.3	434.0	----	----	----	107.7	----	----
2008[2]	2,301	69.9	50.4	160.9	231.4	----	10.1	442.7	----	----	----	141.0	----	----

[1] Preliminary.   [2] Forecast.   [3] Fiscal year.   *Source: Economic Research Service, U.S. Department of Agriculture (ERS-USDA)*

Production and Yield of Honey in the United States

Year	Production in Thousands of Pounds						Value of Production ($1,000)	Yield Per Colony in Pounds					
	California	Florida	Minnesota	North Dakota	South Dakota	Total		California	Florida	Minnesota	North Dakota	South Dakota	Average
2003	32,160	14,910	9,960	29,580	15,050	181,727	253,106	67	71	83	87	70	70.0
2004	17,550	20,090	10,125	30,420	22,575	183,582	196,259	45	98	75	78	105	71.8
2005	30,000	13,760	8,880	33,670	17,380	174,818	160,428	75	86	74	91	79	72.4
2006	19,760	13,770	10,000	25,900	10,575	154,907	160,484	52	81	80	74	47	64.7
2007	13,600	11,360	8,840	31,080	13,260	148,341	159,763	40	71	68	74	52	60.8
2008[1]	18,360	11,850	9,516	35,100	21,375	160,861	226,814	51	79	78	90	95	69.9

[1] Preliminary.   *Source: National Agricultural Statistics Service, U.S. Department of Agriculture (NASS-USDA)*

Interest Rates - U.S.

US interest rates can be characterized in two main ways, by credit quality and maturity. Credit quality refers to the level of risk associated with a particular borrower. U.S. Treasury securities, for example, carry the lowest risk. Maturity refers to the time at which the security matures and must be repaid. Treasury securities carry the full spectrum of maturities, from short-term cash management bills, to T-bills (4-weeks, 3-months, and 6-months), T-notes (2-year, 3-year, 5-year and 10-year), and 30-year T-bonds. The most active futures markets are the Treasury note and bond futures traded at the Chicago Board of Trade (CBOT) and the Eurodollar futures traded at the Chicago Mercantile Exchange (CME).

Prices – T-note prices in 2008 extended the rally that began in mid-2007 when the U.S. mortgage and banking crisis started to emerge with the insolvency of two Bear Stearns hedge funds in June 2007 and the halt on investor redemptions in three BNP Paribas mortgage security hedge funds in August 2007. The Fed was forced to respond with liquidity injections and with a cut in the federal funds rate target. T-note prices rallied to a new high in March 2008 when Bear Stearns nearly went bankrupt and was acquired by JPMorgan Chase. T-note prices from mid-2007 through early 2008 rallied very sharply by 16 full points.

T-note prices settled back in the spring and summer of 2008 as it appeared that the U.S. economy and banking system might be able to muddle through the housing crisis. The U.S. economy received a boost during spring and summer 2008 from the Bush administration's $168 billion stimulus plan approved in February, which involved sending stimulus checks to millions of American taxpayers. T-note prices were also undercut in the first half of 2008 by the continued sharp rally in energy and commodity prices, which pushed the inflation figures to new highs.

However, the U.S. housing and banking crisis continued to fester during 2008 and finally blew wide open in September 2008. Fannie Mae and Freddie Mac were effectively nationalized in early September due to insolvency and funding problems. Then on September 15, 2008, Lehman Brothers was forced to declare bankruptcy due to mortgage losses and the inability to maintain funding. During the same week, Merrill Lynch and insurance-giant AIG nearly went bankrupt. Bank of America was acquired Merrill Lynch and AIG received a giant bailout package from the U.S. Treasury.

The global equity markets plunged as investors tried to preserve their capital and fled to the safety of government securities and government-insured bank deposits. T-note prices soared on safe-haven buying and the Federal Reserve's massive liquidity assault, which boosted the Fed's balance sheet by more than $1 trillion. The Fed cut its federal funds rate target to the range of zero to 0.25% by December 2008 and promised to keep rates low for an extended period of time.

T-note prices settled back in January and February 2009 as the Fed started to get a grip on the crisis and safe-haven demand for Treasury securities eased a bit. However, T-note prices then soared again in March 2009 when the Fed announced that it would buy up to $300 billion in longer-term Treasury securities in a "quantitative easing" move. The Fed's purchase of T-notes was designed to boost the supply of money and bring down long-term Treasury yields, which in theory should drive down mortgage rates, corporate bond rates, and other private longer-term rates that are tied to T-note yields.

U.S. Producer Price Index[2] for All Commodities   1982 = 100

Year	Jan.	Feb.	Mar.	Apr.	May	June	July	Aug.	Sept.	Oct.	Nov.	Dec.	Average
1999	122.9	122.3	122.6	123.6	124.7	125.2	125.7	126.9	128.0	127.7	128.3	127.8	125.5
2000	128.3	129.8	130.8	130.7	131.6	133.8	133.7	132.9	134.7	135.4	135.0	136.2	132.7
2001	140.0	137.4	135.9	136.4	136.8	135.5	133.4	133.4	133.3	130.3	129.8	128.1	134.2
2002	128.5	128.4	129.8	130.8	130.8	130.9	131.2	131.5	132.3	133.2	133.1	132.9	131.1
2003	135.3	137.6	141.2	136.8	136.7	138.0	137.7	138.0	138.5	139.3	138.9	139.5	138.1
2004	141.4	142.1	143.1	144.8	146.8	147.2	147.4	148.0	147.7	150.0	151.4	150.2	146.7
2005	150.9	151.6	153.7	155.0	154.3	154.3	156.3	157.6	162.2	166.2	163.7	163.0	157.4
2006	164.3	161.8	162.2	164.3	165.8	166.1	166.8	167.9	165.4	162.2	164.6	165.6	164.8
2007	164.0	166.8	169.3	171.4	173.3	173.8	175.1	172.4	173.5	174.7	179.0	178.6	172.7
2008[1]	181.0	182.7	187.9	190.9	196.6	200.5	205.5	199.0	196.9	186.4	177.5	171.3	189.7

[1] Preliminary.   [2] Not seasonally adjusted.   *Source: Bureau of Labor Statistics, U.S. Department of Commerce (BLS)*

U.S. Consumer Price Index[2] for All Urban Consumers   1982-84 = 100

Year	Jan.	Feb.	Mar.	Apr.	May	June	July	Aug.	Sept.	Oct.	Nov.	Dec.	Average
1999	164.3	164.5	165.0	166.2	166.2	166.2	166.7	167.1	167.9	168.2	168.3	168.3	166.6
2000	168.8	169.8	171.2	171.3	171.5	172.4	172.8	172.8	173.7	174.0	174.1	174.0	172.2
2001	175.1	175.8	176.2	176.9	177.7	178.0	177.5	177.5	178.3	177.7	177.4	176.7	177.1
2002	177.1	177.8	178.8	179.8	179.8	179.9	180.1	180.7	181.0	181.3	181.3	180.9	179.9
2003	181.7	183.1	184.2	183.8	183.5	183.7	183.9	184.6	185.2	185.0	184.5	184.3	184.0
2004	185.2	186.2	187.4	188.0	189.1	189.7	189.4	189.5	189.9	190.9	191.0	190.3	188.9
2005	190.7	191.8	193.3	194.6	194.4	194.5	195.4	196.4	198.8	199.2	197.6	196.8	195.3
2006	198.3	198.7	199.8	201.5	202.5	202.9	203.5	203.9	202.9	201.8	201.5	201.8	201.6
2007	202.4	203.5	205.4	206.7	207.9	208.4	208.3	207.9	208.5	208.9	210.2	210.0	207.3
2008[1]	211.1	211.7	213.5	214.8	216.6	218.8	220.0	219.1	218.8	216.6	212.4	210.2	215.3

[1] Preliminary.   [2] Not seasonally adjusted.   *Source: Bureau of Labor Statistics, U.S. Department of Commerce (BLS)*

3-Month Eurodollar Futures - CME Group
(weekly close) as of January 02, 2009

Points of 100%

Volume of Trading of 3-month Eurodollar Futures in Chicago   In Thousands of Contracts

Year	Jan.	Feb.	Mar.	Apr.	May	June	July	Aug.	Sept.	Oct.	Nov.	Dec.	Total
1999	7,470.9	7,674.5	8,718.6	7,346.5	8,957.0	9,649.8	7,746.3	8,898.0	7,629.1	7,500.6	6,223.2	5,604.0	93,418
2000	8,379.6	9,723.0	10,197.8	10,171.8	10,261.3	9,791.3	7,384.8	7,009.6	8,204.6	9,276.4	7,561.4	10,152.3	108,115
2001	17,515.1	12,908.4	15,478.5	15,191.7	15,691.1	14,309.9	12,673.1	14,947.9	16,776.2	14,139.1	21,150.1	13,234.4	184,015
2002	19,487.1	14,491.2	17,986.7	17,946.9	18,717.5	17,931.8	20,366.9	17,757.9	15,309.9	18,495.9	13,348.6	10,240.5	202,081
2003	13,534.2	12,314.9	18,275.3	15,392.9	19,403.0	21,162.6	18,732.5	18,724.3	18,817.0	20,004.3	15,431.9	16,978.2	208,771
2004	20,808.8	16,042.4	22,583.6	26,673.6	25,548.9	28,067.1	25,114.4	24,859.3	32,283.0	25,737.3	27,945.3	21,920.2	297,584
2005	27,793.8	28,549.2	34,472.4	42,437.2	36,599.9	37,997.0	26,794.7	32,920.8	45,483.5	35,148.8	34,775.7	27,382.0	410,355
2006	35,602.4	34,218.0	47,463.8	37,752.2	44,154.6	45,443.4	36,794.1	45,126.7	45,180.3	46,453.5	42,700.7	41,187.7	502,077
2007	43,204.2	46,365.8	63,154.7	39,567.7	50,305.2	58,372.0	53,290.3	77,539.0	49,528.8	45,862.8	53,795.1	40,484.5	621,470
2008	70,787.1	59,378.2	60,956.1	56,371.5	48,683.4	60,086.5	54,178.8	36,521.6	58,497.7	40,508.5	24,515.5	26,489.2	596,974

Source: International Monetary Market (IOM), division of the Chicago Mercantile Exchange (CME)

Average Open Interest of 3-month Eurodollar Futures in Chicago   In Thousands of Contracts

Year	Jan.	Feb.	Mar.	Apr.	May	June	July	Aug.	Sept.	Oct.	Nov.	Dec.
1999	2,917.9	3,039.5	2,973.5	2,894.7	3,183.2	3,208.8	3,064.4	3,115.6	2,904.0	2,918.2	2,879.7	2,859.4
2000	2,971.3	3,261.4	3,138.7	3,156.6	3,331.7	3,272.1	3,160.3	3,225.7	3,181.8	3,067.2	3,201.1	3,349.7
2001	3,576.4	3,878.6	4,117.4	4,109.3	4,316.3	4,471.7	4,452.4	4,753.5	4,567.8	4,524.0	4,950.8	4,559.1
2002	4,592.0	4,937.0	4,727.9	4,411.6	4,421.0	4,295.5	4,123.7	4,482.4	4,243.4	4,237.9	4,553.7	4,072.5
2003	4,007.1	4,500.1	4,517.3	4,448.6	5,098.7	5,514.2	5,218.4	5,277.9	5,034.1	4,935.4	5,024.2	4,936.1
2004	5,128.0	5,624.1	5,640.5	5,602.2	6,060.0	6,117.3	6,026.7	6,236.3	5,992.8	5,968.9	6,527.8	6,706.7
2005	7,163.3	7,858.5	8,124.1	8,244.1	8,604.5	8,045.7	7,416.0	8,044.7	8,054.2	8,471.9	9,264.8	9,145.1
2006	8,833.5	9,574.0	9,586.0	9,679.6	10,126.2	9,995.4	9,572.4	10,153.9	9,949.4	9,809.8	10,345.5	10,201.1
2007	9,682.3	10,400.5	10,847.9	10,827.1	11,895.5	11,285.2	11,166.9	11,416.3	10,782.6	10,019.4	10,631.2	10,515.5
2008	11,033.0	11,206.7	10,356.6	9,225.3	9,282.5	9,266.0	9,589.0	9,882.1	8,953.0	8,141.7	8,286.9	7,389.1

Source: International Monetary Market (IOM), division of the Chicago Mercantile Exchange (CME)

2-Year Treasury Note Futures - CME Group (CBT)
(weekly close) as of January 02, 2009

Nominal Value

Volume of Trading of 2-Year U.S. Treasury Note Futures in Chicago   In Thousands of Contracts

Year	Jan.	Feb.	Mar.	Apr.	May	June	July	Aug.	Sept.	Oct.	Nov.	Dec.	Total
1999	64.5	132.7	67.0	62.9	132.3	93.6	46.5	139.2	71.3	44.0	124.1	72.3	1,050
2000	51.5	159.3	97.9	76.9	160.2	105.2	43.0	181.0	107.4	97.4	287.6	126.5	1,494
2001	174.6	299.2	160.9	194.8	274.0	163.3	93.4	316.4	198.1	122.9	303.8	160.6	2,462
2002	195.0	332.9	290.4	159.2	377.0	242.9	177.0	377.0	253.0	174.8	387.2	232.3	3,199
2003	146.8	392.9	292.5	153.3	513.9	339.2	274.1	514.0	522.8	281.1	496.7	488.5	4,416
2004	310.4	829.8	630.0	462.4	872.2	788.8	406.7	1,009.9	1,014.5	678.0	1,393.3	1,058.5	9,455
2005	953.7	1,997.5	1,706.1	1,548.3	2,306.3	1,811.4	1,153.0	2,144.2	2,118.0	1,344.1	2,451.5	1,671.3	21,205
2006	2,053.3	3,223.3	3,206.5	2,090.0	4,690.9	2,837.1	2,525.1	4,461.0	2,768.3	2,422.9	4,826.4	2,862.0	37,967
2007	2,892.6	5,666.6	5,321.4	3,128.3	7,197.4	5,495.7	4,793.7	10,567.2	4,788.1	4,771.2	8,849.7	5,138.5	68,610
2008	7,526.1	10,092.8	7,515.4	5,102.6	8,195.6	7,207.2	6,366.1	7,529.6	8,126.5	5,355.3	4,067.9	2,225.8	79,311

Source: Chicago Board of Trade (CBT)

Average Open Interest of 2-Year U.S. Treasury Note Futures in Chicago   In Thousands of Contracts

Year	Jan.	Feb.	Mar.	Apr.	May	June	July	Aug.	Sept.	Oct.	Nov.	Dec.
1999	40.0	40.7	40.3	40.1	34.7	36.0	35.3	37.6	38.7	38.2	38.7	34.1
2000	34.3	43.0	44.5	43.8	49.0	51.2	55.8	53.4	47.9	53.3	60.9	77.9
2001	82.2	79.4	81.7	72.5	66.2	63.6	56.6	73.0	74.4	65.4	72.7	71.3
2002	86.5	103.3	103.6	87.9	102.0	105.9	99.4	108.0	110.4	108.1	115.5	113.6
2003	107.1	114.2	123.9	109.0	120.3	118.8	112.1	149.1	151.9	144.6	149.0	156.5
2004	161.9	195.2	186.8	172.4	198.9	210.7	191.7	207.1	216.4	205.5	221.6	248.5
2005	287.3	345.7	329.6	307.0	341.5	372.9	362.3	371.1	364.4	351.3	357.3	363.2
2006	437.8	489.3	469.0	489.5	607.6	541.1	595.1	701.4	683.6	680.7	698.4	716.0
2007	764.5	826.7	896.3	1,003.3	1,125.5	965.1	1,016.8	985.4	902.3	993.1	1,043.6	997.3
2008	1,101.2	1,313.0	1,187.3	1,110.0	1,166.8	972.5	895.4	922.6	783.7	735.0	648.0	503.4

Source: Chicago Board of Trade (CBT)

Volume of Trading of 5-Year U.S. Treasury Note Futures in Chicago   In Thousands of Contracts

Year	Jan.	Feb.	Mar.	Apr.	May	June	July	Aug.	Sept.	Oct.	Nov.	Dec.	Total
1999	1,119.7	1,553.6	1,336.6	1,115.0	1,906.4	1,543.9	1,166.4	2,163.6	1,034.1	1,245.2	1,606.6	1,192.8	16,984
2000	1,800.5	2,873.8	2,010.0	1,707.8	2,548.4	1,757.3	1,188.9	2,253.3	1,515.5	1,774.2	2,259.7	1,642.6	23,332
2001	2,422.8	2,591.5	2,281.2	2,062.8	3,221.5	2,264.0	1,702.0	2,697.4	2,617.3	2,525.7	4,052.5	2,683.6	31,122
2002	2,867.9	3,826.0	3,848.2	3,092.4	4,637.6	4,095.7	4,437.4	5,354.4	4,859.3	5,026.7	5,013.2	3,453.2	50,512
2003	4,435.6	5,178.5	5,533.7	4,623.6	7,267.6	6,165.7	6,462.6	7,090.2	7,453.9	6,364.3	6,885.3	6,285.6	73,746
2004	5,856.9	7,388.8	7,775.6	7,793.1	10,979.4	9,458.2	7,109.8	10,656.0	10,311.6	7,686.2	11,036.9	9,416.8	105,469
2005	7,797.7	11,168.4	11,848.9	10,720.3	12,320.4	9,164.3	7,698.0	12,662.9	10,999.9	8,510.5	11,996.4	7,021.1	121,909
2006	9,388.4	12,141.7	11,865.2	7,869.8	12,971.9	9,368.7	8,102.0	13,347.5	9,369.3	8,730.9	13,423.5	8,291.5	124,870
2007	9,208.6	14,410.2	14,156.0	8,372.3	15,673.4	13,243.1	13,001.7	22,354.8	11,376.0	12,495.6	21,271.6	10,644.1	166,207
2008	15,479.7	20,790.4	17,424.0	12,474.7	17,616.2	14,904.3	14,514.1	15,085.6	16,979.1	10,079.8	8,057.9	4,721.7	168,127

Source: Chicago Board of Trade (CBT)

Average Open Interest of 5-Year U.S. Treasury Note Futures in Chicago   In Thousands of Contracts

Year	Jan.	Feb.	Mar.	Apr.	May	June	July	Aug.	Sept.	Oct.	Nov.	Dec.
1999	290.4	268.6	247.5	246.9	311.1	348.6	325.3	341.5	298.9	328.6	272.6	288.5
2000	387.0	475.5	420.8	417.9	428.2	379.6	402.7	405.1	372.8	373.7	381.4	380.2
2001	377.7	392.0	374.5	376.9	436.3	422.0	461.0	483.3	451.4	463.2	554.6	491.1
2002	507.2	576.2	585.6	632.2	656.4	594.9	554.9	652.8	655.0	662.5	720.7	692.8
2003	685.1	743.2	777.8	835.5	856.3	827.5	781.7	840.4	737.0	819.4	925.6	880.1
2004	874.2	1,008.1	987.2	1,043.0	1,145.4	1,118.5	1,217.3	1,322.5	1,168.1	1,099.4	1,290.7	1,318.7
2005	1,160.2	1,237.0	1,325.0	1,383.0	1,320.9	1,127.9	1,247.7	1,450.3	1,190.2	1,342.0	1,397.6	1,126.8
2006	1,105.1	1,404.8	1,238.0	1,257.2	1,326.0	1,264.7	1,258.3	1,409.8	1,341.3	1,413.8	1,484.4	1,423.8
2007	1,468.1	1,499.6	1,481.0	1,614.9	1,763.5	1,601.5	1,586.9	1,648.0	1,564.9	1,666.1	1,932.4	1,841.2
2008	1,940.6	2,101.2	1,923.8	1,850.9	1,851.0	1,669.6	1,574.5	1,600.7	1,483.4	1,378.1	1,267.1	1,057.8

Source: Chicago Board of Trade (CBT)

INTEREST RATES - U.S.

10-Year Treasury Note Futures - CME Group (CBT)
(weekly close) as of January 02, 2009

Nominal Value

Volume of Trading of 10-year U.S. Treasury Note Futures in Chicago   In Thousands of Contracts

Year	Jan.	Feb.	Mar.	Apr.	May	June	July	Aug.	Sept.	Oct.	Nov.	Dec.	Total
1999	2,269.1	3,562.1	2,993.8	2,145.3	3,519.3	3,153.0	2,438.5	3,735.6	2,508.7	2,470.9	3,201.5	2,048.0	34,046
2000	3,557.0	4,974.7	3,750.4	3,529.7	4,711.6	3,706.0	2,580.9	4,459.8	3,779.5	3,824.3	4,513.6	3,313.1	46,701
2001	4,632.8	4,915.3	4,500.5	4,299.4	5,483.3	4,083.8	3,493.1	5,683.1	4,389.7	4,144.8	7,270.1	4,689.8	57,586
2002	5,539.7	6,407.2	6,520.6	5,463.3	8,309.1	7,547.7	8,980.8	10,590.5	8,529.1	11,198.8	9,679.2	7,020.2	95,786
2003	9,120.6	10,746.5	11,320.5	9,377.2	13,817.0	12,149.5	15,285.0	14,248.7	13,706.7	13,586.9	12,474.5	10,912.2	146,745
2004	13,608.5	14,569.4	16,984.0	16,478.4	17,785.8	15,184.2	12,954.3	17,419.5	18,467.8	16,622.0	21,006.4	15,038.9	196,119
2005	13,901.3	19,565.4	21,132.8	19,487.3	22,688.8	16,778.7	13,894.5	20,120.1	18,348.2	15,357.3	20,705.4	13,144.2	215,124
2006	17,188.6	21,262.7	22,739.9	17,241.5	26,174.6	20,311.2	16,645.2	24,796.6	22,125.2	20,602.6	28,413.8	18,070.1	255,572
2007	21,492.5	30,367.2	30,210.2	18,529.8	34,343.9	37,171.0	32,361.3	38,785.6	24,375.6	25,280.4	36,890.7	19,421.3	349,229
2008	28,924.8	33,426.2	23,331.5	19,043.9	27,414.0	22,591.8	22,903.0	21,069.7	23,265.1	15,101.1	11,826.6	7,873.1	256,771

Source: Chicago Board of Trade (CBT)

Average Open Interest of 10-year U.S. Treasury Note Futures in Chicago   In Thousands of Contracts

Year	Jan.	Feb.	Mar.	Apr.	May	June	July	Aug.	Sept.	Oct.	Nov.	Dec.
1999	528.5	549.5	515.4	510.1	541.1	574.5	588.3	623.8	607.3	653.1	582.0	487.9
2000	595.2	653.8	571.9	615.6	621.4	583.9	608.4	602.1	547.6	564.6	555.2	508.9
2001	550.3	541.6	560.0	595.1	628.7	512.1	550.2	627.3	610.4	590.3	662.0	559.9
2002	572.9	643.9	679.6	699.1	806.5	793.0	877.6	958.3	888.7	970.2	938.0	751.6
2003	772.9	896.9	914.9	897.1	968.1	993.6	1,009.5	1,032.5	856.2	985.7	1,140.7	965.0
2004	1,145.9	1,320.6	1,312.9	1,347.7	1,392.4	1,300.3	1,348.2	1,456.6	1,503.6	1,626.9	1,767.4	1,642.0
2005	1,671.3	1,888.6	1,980.2	2,003.5	2,140.8	1,869.0	1,859.3	1,992.8	1,749.4	1,677.7	1,778.6	1,635.6
2006	1,700.0	1,990.4	2,048.7	2,259.7	2,321.0	2,054.2	2,087.1	2,265.3	2,271.5	2,408.2	2,398.2	2,236.0
2007	2,343.6	2,367.3	2,294.0	2,586.9	2,878.3	2,853.9	2,871.5	2,820.5	2,269.5	2,497.2	2,661.6	2,313.2
2008	2,431.2	2,517.6	2,179.8	2,073.7	2,144.6	1,978.8	1,802.6	1,835.2	1,658.2	1,385.2	1,226.4	1,074.2

Source: Chicago Board of Trade (CBT)

30-Year Treasury Bond Futures - CME Group (CBT)
(weekly close) as of January 02, 2009

Nominal Value

Volume of Trading of 30-year U.S. Treasury Bond Futures in Chicago   In Thousands of Contracts

Year	Jan.	Feb.	Mar.	Apr.	May	June	July	Aug.	Sept.	Oct.	Nov.	Dec.	Total
1999	8,075.2	10,031.5	8,667.5	7,196.9	9,555.8	8,072.1	6,415.1	7,995.2	6,559.6	6,301.1	6,909.0	4,263.5	90,042
2000	7,966.4	8,157.4	5,378.6	5,282.3	5,972.9	4,458.6	3,080.0	4,709.9	4,529.2	4,460.4	5,072.8	3,682.3	62,751
2001	5,123.0	5,545.9	5,196.3	4,584.0	6,022.2	4,233.2	3,347.0	4,965.6	4,331.0	4,598.6	6,746.4	3,886.0	58,579
2002	4,132.7	4,721.1	4,504.8	3,932.8	5,191.4	4,722.2	5,157.9	5,666.5	4,534.5	5,190.1	4,722.8	3,605.6	56,082
2003	3,625.3	4,840.9	5,106.9	3,795.0	7,188.4	5,896.2	6,352.1	6,198.0	5,738.4	5,121.8	4,823.4	4,835.2	63,522
2004	5,025.4	5,762.8	6,687.9	5,983.2	6,463.8	5,556.9	4,540.1	6,343.5	7,638.7	5,658.6	7,374.2	5,914.0	72,949
2005	6,134.8	8,973.5	8,573.7	7,293.5	8,558.9	7,407.2	5,367.0	7,771.3	7,193.6	6,450.4	7,928.8	5,274.0	86,927
2006	7,044.8	8,511.6	8,980.6	6,969.2	10,354.4	7,564.5	5,854.2	8,736.7	7,553.9	6,375.1	9,461.6	6,348.2	93,755
2007	7,108.8	10,060.2	10,338.3	6,108.4	10,578.5	11,338.4	9,452.1	11,439.3	6,864.4	7,232.1	11,146.2	5,963.6	107,630
2008	9,667.3	11,646.2	8,739.1	5,835.3	9,173.4	7,176.8	7,429.4	7,521.6	7,830.0	5,559.1	5,267.6	3,618.7	89,465

Source: Chicago Board of Trade (CBT)

Average Open Interest of 30-year U.S. Treasury Bond Futures in Chicago   In Contracts

Year	Jan.	Feb.	Mar.	Apr.	May	June	July	Aug.	Sept.	Oct.	Nov.	Dec.
1999	657,180	801,115	664,131	618,453	717,453	674,225	672,983	748,974	647,816	621,816	637,656	561,919
2000	637,023	612,298	530,957	503,412	434,771	390,928	394,075	440,437	402,156	399,880	443,282	445,386
2001	413,244	479,165	519,987	509,558	503,194	455,799	458,613	531,098	525,972	567,177	602,647	478,418
2002	468,455	520,573	479,939	463,100	472,778	458,020	427,896	465,971	496,815	467,440	459,877	440,225
2003	420,797	506,910	487,277	449,286	566,887	596,186	554,632	521,928	423,995	443,177	489,185	471,848
2004	488,484	571,445	557,595	488,921	553,721	512,566	517,893	594,905	584,416	594,353	640,026	634,008
2005	674,170	792,247	749,403	710,061	735,910	665,235	579,724	600,565	595,736	586,653	618,647	574,121
2006	601,094	662,314	622,927	739,601	858,812	760,240	760,749	813,905	763,092	737,070	810,426	803,020
2007	816,747	903,121	852,305	875,810	949,173	980,004	988,995	991,513	915,693	948,940	1,022,623	947,588
2008	1,033,106	1,041,505	979,695	893,308	941,317	879,149	891,111	880,157	877,623	756,790	731,186	754,687

Source: Chicago Board of Trade (CBT)

U.S. Federal Funds Rate   In Percent

Year	Jan.	Feb.	Mar.	Apr.	May	June	July	Aug.	Sept.	Oct.	Nov.	Dec.	Average
1999	4.63	4.76	4.81	4.74	4.74	4.76	4.99	5.07	5.22	5.20	5.42	5.30	4.97
2000	5.46	5.73	5.85	6.02	6.27	6.53	6.54	6.50	6.52	6.51	6.51	6.40	6.24
2001	5.98	5.49	5.31	4.80	4.21	3.97	3.77	3.65	3.07	2.49	2.09	1.82	3.89
2002	1.73	1.74	1.73	1.75	1.75	1.75	1.73	1.74	1.75	1.75	1.34	1.24	1.67
2003	1.24	1.26	1.25	1.26	1.26	1.22	1.01	1.03	1.01	1.01	1.00	0.98	1.13
2004	1.00	1.01	1.00	1.00	1.00	1.03	1.26	1.43	1.61	1.76	1.93	2.16	1.35
2005	2.28	2.50	2.63	2.79	3.00	3.04	3.26	3.50	3.62	3.78	4.00	4.16	3.21
2006	4.29	4.49	4.59	4.79	4.94	4.99	5.24	5.25	5.25	5.25	5.25	5.24	4.96
2007	5.25	5.26	5.26	5.25	5.25	5.25	5.26	5.02	4.94	4.76	4.49	4.24	5.02
2008	3.94	2.98	2.61	2.28	1.98	2.00	2.01	2.00	1.81	0.97	0.39	0.16	1.93

Source: Bureau of Economic Analysis, U.S. Department of Commerce (BEA)

U.S. Municipal Bond Yield[1]   In Percent

Year	Jan.	Feb.	Mar.	Apr.	May	June	July	Aug.	Sept.	Oct.	Nov.	Dec.	Average
1999	5.02	5.03	5.10	5.08	5.18	5.37	5.36	5.58	5.69	5.92	5.86	5.95	5.43
2000	6.08	6.00	5.83	5.75	6.00	5.80	5.63	5.51	5.56	5.59	5.54	5.22	5.71
2001	5.10	5.18	5.13	5.27	5.29	5.20	5.20	5.03	5.09	5.05	5.04	5.25	5.15
2002	5.16	5.11	5.29	5.22	5.19	5.09	5.02	4.95	4.74	4.88	4.95	4.85	5.04
2003	4.90	4.81	4.76	4.74	4.41	4.33	4.74	5.10	4.92	4.89	4.73	4.65	4.75
2004	4.61	4.55	4.41	4.82	5.07	5.05	4.87	4.70	4.56	4.49	4.52	4.48	4.68
2005	4.41	4.35	4.57	4.46	4.31	4.23	4.31	4.32	4.29	4.48	4.57	4.46	4.40
2006	4.37	4.41	4.44	4.58	4.59	4.60	4.61	4.39	4.27	4.30	4.14	4.11	4.40
2007	4.23	4.22	4.15	4.26	4.31	4.60	4.56	4.64	4.51	4.39	4.46	4.42	4.40
2008	4.27	4.64	4.93	4.70	4.58	4.69	4.68	4.69	4.86	5.50	5.23		4.80

[1] 20-bond average.   *Source: Bureau of Economic Analysis, U.S. Department of Commerce (BEA)*

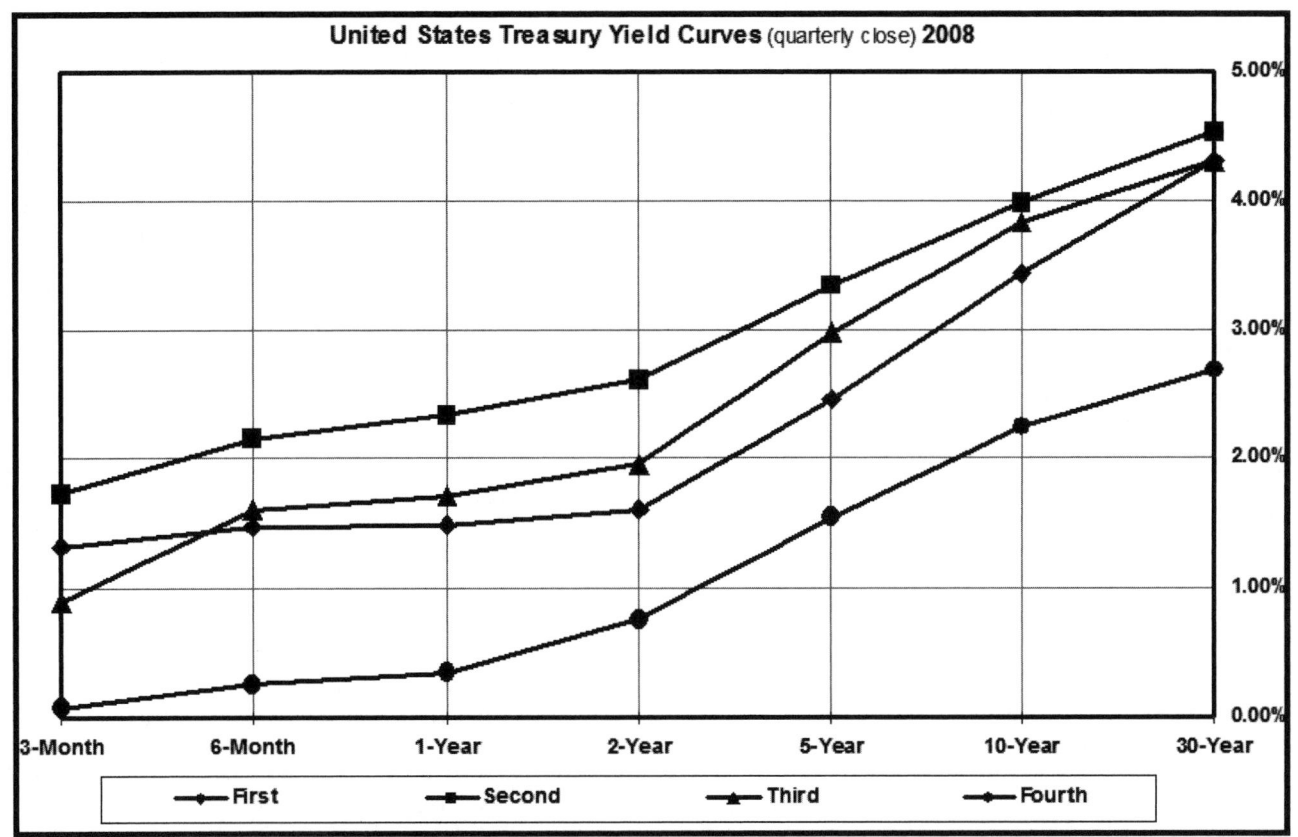

U.S. Industrial Production Index[1]   1997 = 100

Year	Jan.	Feb.	Mar.	Apr.	May	June	July	Aug.	Sept.	Oct.	Nov.	Dec.	Average
1999	134.1	134.5	135.1	135.5	136.2	136.6	137.4	137.7	138.1	139.1	141.9	142.8	139.2
2000	143.6	144.3	145.2	146.3	147.2	147.9	147.6	148.7	148.8	146.3	145.8	145.1	145.7
2001	143.9	143.5	142.9	142.0	141.6	140.3	140.4	140.0	138.5	137.7	108.8	108.3	111.5
2002	109.0	109.2	109.6	110.1	110.4	110.8	111.6	111.3	111.2	111.0	111.2	110.6	111.0
2003	111.2	111.6	110.8	110.1	110.0	110.0	110.8	110.9	111.5	111.8	112.7	112.9	110.9
2004	113.2	114.4	114.1	114.7	115.5	115.1	115.9	116.0	105.1	105.8	106.0	106.7	103.6
2005	106.9	107.4	107.3	107.2	107.4	108.3	108.3	108.6	107.2	107.1	108.2	109.2	106.9
2006	109.1	109.4	110.0	110.9	110.9	111.9	112.3	112.5	112.2	112.0	111.5	112.2	111.2
2007	111.7	112.5	110.4	111.0	111.0	111.4	112.0	112.0	112.3	111.8	112.3	112.4	111.7
2008[2]	112.6	112.3	112.0	111.4	111.2	111.3	111.3	109.8	105.2	106.8	106.1		110.0

[1] Total Index of the Federal Reserve Index of Quantity Output, seasonally adjusted.   [2] Preliminary.   *Source: Bureau of Economic Analysis, U.S. Department of Commerce (BEA)*

U.S. Gross National Product, National Income, and Personal Income   In Billions of Constant Dollars[1]

	---------- Gross Domestic Product ----------				--------------- National Income ---------------				--------------- Personal Income ---------------				
Year	First Quarter	Second Quarter	Third Quarter	Fourth Quarter	Total	First Quarter	Second Quarter	Third Quarter	Fourth Quarter	Total	First Quarter	Second Quarter	Third Quarter	Fourth Quarter	Total
1999	9,067	9,174	9,314	9,520	9,268	8,074	8,161	8,255	8,456	8,237	7,658	7,729	7,824	7,999	7,802
2000	9,629	9,823	9,862	9,954	9,817	8,681	8,750	8,858	8,892	8,795	8,266	8,372	8,514	8,566	8,430
2001	10,022	10,129	10,135	10,226	10,128	8,988	9,002	8,890	9,040	8,980	8,689	8,720	8,733	8,755	8,724
2002	10,333	10,427	10,527	10,591	10,470	9,131	9,212	9,248	9,327	9,229	8,815	8,892	8,895	8,926	8,882
2003	10,706	10,832	11,086	11,220	10,961	9,407	9,538	9,699	9,885	9,632	8,998	9,111	9,204	9,341	9,164
2004	11,406	11,610	11,779	11,949	11,686	10,090	10,248	10,318	10,571	10,307	9,483	9,630	9,771	10,026	9,727
2005	12,154	12,317	12,559	12,706	12,434	10,769	10,903	10,715	11,165	10,888	10,074	10,234	10,329	10,567	10,301
2006	12,960	13,134	13,250	13,370	13,178	11,611	11,739	11,849	11,985	11,796	10,782	10,913	11,056	11,225	10,994
2007	13,511	13,738	13,951	14,031	13,808	12,087	12,234	12,339	12,424	12,271	11,473	11,578	11,730	11,872	11,663
2008[2]	14,151	14,295	14,413	14,200	14,265	12,448	12,469	12,491		12,469	11,961	12,152	12,170	12,144	12,107

[1] Seasonally adjusted at annual rates.   [2] Preliminary.   *Source: Bureau of Economic Analysis, U.S. Department of Commerce (BEA)*

INTEREST RATES - U.S.

U.S. Money Supply M1[2]   In Billions of Dollars

Year	Jan.	Feb.	Mar.	Apr.	May	June	July	Aug.	Sept.	Oct.	Nov.	Dec.	Average
1999	1,097.8	1,097.0	1,097.8	1,101.9	1,102.6	1,099.7	1,098.7	1,099.0	1,096.3	1,102.3	1,111.7	1,122.6	1,102.3
2000	1,121.9	1,109.4	1,108.2	1,113.4	1,105.8	1,103.3	1,103.0	1,100.3	1,099.0	1,098.6	1,092.3	1,087.6	1,103.6
2001	1,097.6	1,101.5	1,109.8	1,114.9	1,119.5	1,126.4	1,139.6	1,149.6	1,203.9	1,165.9	1,171.5	1,182.3	1,140.2
2002	1,190.9	1,190.7	1,192.8	1,185.9	1,189.0	1,192.2	1,199.5	1,185.9	1,194.6	1,204.0	1,209.3	1,220.4	1,196.3
2003	1,226.8	1,238.6	1,238.9	1,248.4	1,268.0	1,280.2	1,287.9	1,293.9	1,297.0	1,297.3	1,298.0	1,306.8	1,273.5
2004	1,306.1	1,321.7	1,330.0	1,332.1	1,331.6	1,342.8	1,340.5	1,353.2	1,361.4	1,361.0	1,376.0	1,376.4	1,344.4
2005	1,366.6	1,372.5	1,372.6	1,357.8	1,365.5	1,379.2	1,366.6	1,376.2	1,377.8	1,375.0	1,376.9	1,374.2	1,371.7
2006	1,380.6	1,379.8	1,383.9	1,380.5	1,386.8	1,374.4	1,369.2	1,369.2	1,361.6	1,369.4	1,371.3	1,365.6	1,374.4
2007	1,373.6	1,366.0	1,368.1	1,378.8	1,379.7	1,364.5	1,366.6	1,368.4	1,366.2	1,371.7	1,366.7	1,364.5	1,369.6
2008[1]	1,368.4	1,371.1	1,372.9	1,373.7	1,373.7	1,383.6	1,400.1	1,392.2	1,452.1	1,475.2	1,524.0	1,595.9	1,423.6

[1] Preliminary.   [2] *M1* -- The sum of currency held outside the vaults of depository institutions, Federal Reserve Banks, and the U.S. Treasury; travelers checks; and demand and other checkable deposits issued by financial institutions (except demand deposits due to the Treasury and depository institutions), minus cash items in process of collection and Federal Reserve float. Seasonally adjusted.   *Source: Board of Governors of the Federal Reserve System*

U.S. Money Supply M2[2]   In Billions of Dollars

Year	Jan.	Feb.	Mar.	Apr.	May	June	July	Aug.	Sept.	Oct.	Nov.	Dec.	Average
1999	4,399.4	4,424.7	4,435.9	4,462.8	4,481.9	4,504.8	4,528.3	4,549.1	4,562.4	4,582.4	4,608.0	4,631.7	4,514.3
2000	4,658.0	4,675.3	4,702.2	4,753.2	4,747.6	4,761.4	4,774.8	4,808.3	4,839.8	4,858.3	4,866.8	4,910.7	4,779.7
2001	4,965.7	5,001.5	5,058.8	5,120.3	5,124.2	5,163.6	5,196.9	5,226.8	5,335.8	5,327.2	5,368.3	5,417.8	5,192.2
2002	5,448.2	5,474.4	5,483.0	5,489.2	5,510.8	5,533.0	5,583.0	5,620.2	5,644.7	5,696.1	5,739.1	5,764.6	5,582.2
2003	5,790.7	5,827.1	5,840.8	5,887.4	5,941.1	5,980.0	6,034.3	6,080.8	6,062.3	6,047.7	6,047.9	6,055.2	5,966.3
2004	6,059.4	6,097.4	6,135.4	6,177.4	6,244.9	6,258.9	6,264.4	6,288.4	6,322.6	6,347.6	6,384.7	6,399.8	6,248.4
2005	6,404.2	6,417.3	6,432.6	6,440.3	6,456.6	6,488.8	6,515.9	6,545.8	6,581.8	6,610.1	6,636.8	6,661.5	6,516.0
2006	6,712.2	6,731.7	6,749.0	6,772.1	6,785.3	6,816.9	6,844.6	6,865.3	6,890.8	6,945.3	6,978.3	7,021.5	6,842.8
2007	7,069.5	7,076.1	7,111.7	7,160.7	7,189.1	7,212.3	7,239.4	7,287.7	7,322.6	7,352.8	7,384.4	7,417.3	7,235.3
2008[1]	7,463.6	7,539.0	7,600.5	7,620.0	7,637.8	7,648.5	7,698.9	7,687.3	7,796.2	7,916.0	7,972.5	8,154.2	7,727.9

[1] Preliminary.   [2] *M2* -- M1 plus savings deposits (including money market deposit accounts) and small-denomination (less than $100,000) time deposits issued by financial institutions; and shares in retail money market mutual funds (funds with initial investments of less than $50,000), net of retirement accounts. Seasonally adjusted.   *Source: Board of Governors of the Federal Reserve System*

U.S. Money Supply M3[2]   In Billions of Dollars

Year	Jan.	Feb.	Mar.	Apr.	May	June	July	Aug.	Sept.	Oct.	Nov.	Dec.	Average
1997	5,013.2	5,041.7	5,080.2	5,119.8	5,147.1	5,177.4	5,235.8	5,291.4	5,332.3	5,376.3	5,417.1	5,460.5	5,224.4
1998	5,508.8	5,541.3	5,611.5	5,647.3	5,686.9	5,728.4	5,750.0	5,815.0	5,882.0	5,953.7	6,010.1	6,051.9	5,765.6
1999	6,080.7	6,129.5	6,133.6	6,172.3	6,201.0	6,237.7	6,269.0	6,299.1	6,323.0	6,378.4	6,464.1	6,551.8	6,270.0
2000	6,605.5	6,642.2	6,704.0	6,767.3	6,776.9	6,823.6	6,875.2	6,945.0	7,003.5	7,027.0	7,038.3	7,117.6	6,860.5
2001	7,237.2	7,308.5	7,372.0	7,507.8	7,564.1	7,644.7	7,691.9	7,696.3	7,853.2	7,897.8	7,973.0	8,035.4	7,648.5
2002	8,063.9	8,109.3	8,117.3	8,142.6	8,175.1	8,190.8	8,244.2	8,298.1	8,331.5	8,368.9	8,498.8	8,568.0	8,259.0
2003	8,588.1	8,628.7	8,648.8	8,686.0	8,741.9	8,791.6	8,888.7	8,918.2	8,906.5	8,896.8	8,880.3	8,872.3	8,787.3
2004	8,930.2	9,000.3	9,080.7	9,149.6	9,243.8	9,275.7	9,282.7	9,314.4	9,351.8	9,359.4	9,395.1	9,433.0	9,234.7
2005	9,487.2	9,531.6	9,565.3	9,620.9	9,665.0	9,725.3	9,762.4	9,864.6	9,950.8	10,032.0	10,078.5	10,154.0	9,786.5
2006[1]	10,242.8	10,298.7	Discontinued										10,270.8

[1] Preliminary.   [2] *M3* -- M2 plus large-denomination ($100,000 or more) time deposits; repurchase agreements issued by depository institutions; Eurodollar deposits, specifically, dollar-denominated deposits due to nonbank U.S. addresses held at foreign offices of U.S. banks worldwide and all banking offices in Canada and the United Kingdom; and institutional money market mutual funds (funds with initial investments of $50,000 or more). Seasonally adjusted. *Source: Board of Governors of the Federal Reserve System*

U.S. Money Supply MZM[2]   In Billions of Dollars

Year	Jan.	Feb.	Mar.	Apr.	May	June	July	Aug.	Sept.	Oct.	Nov.	Dec.	Average
1999	4,011.8	4,055.5	4,069.8	4,112.4	4,141.0	4,172.4	4,195.7	4,224.0	4,237.1	4,264.0	4,300.9	4,335.8	4,176.7
2000	4,369.7	4,380.6	4,415.5	4,463.5	4,460.5	4,474.2	4,505.2	4,548.4	4,593.2	4,615.3	4,625.9	4,679.7	4,511.0
2001	4,770.0	4,866.1	4,951.5	5,050.3	5,104.7	5,183.1	5,239.3	5,261.7	5,425.5	5,502.8	5,582.0	5,661.9	5,216.6
2002	5,701.1	5,745.6	5,763.2	5,786.0	5,815.6	5,836.9	5,888.3	5,917.2	5,930.2	5,967.5	6,087.0	6,138.9	5,881.5
2003	6,151.8	6,184.2	6,187.1	6,218.0	6,259.1	6,305.8	6,411.0	6,432.3	6,417.1	6,397.7	6,386.2	6,368.3	6,309.9
2004	6,378.7	6,416.5	6,463.6	6,510.4	6,585.6	6,594.5	6,588.0	6,599.8	6,617.8	6,622.9	6,652.4	6,653.1	6,556.9
2005	6,641.3	6,637.5	6,633.7	6,633.0	6,631.5	6,659.1	6,685.8	6,709.7	6,746.5	6,775.6	6,793.2	6,818.7	6,697.1
2006	6,869.8	6,876.0	6,883.0	6,903.5	6,916.6	6,952.8	6,979.0	6,999.8	7,027.2	7,090.2	7,134.1	7,205.5	6,986.5
2007	7,250.7	7,265.7	7,322.3	7,397.7	7,462.3	7,515.7	7,584.9	7,708.7	7,835.2	7,945.7	8,038.6	8,104.5	7,619.3
2008[1]	8,182.8	8,381.1	8,520.6	8,590.1	8,646.6	8,689.5	8,745.4	8,730.9	8,788.5	8,834.0	8,950.7	9,173.4	8,686.1

[1] Preliminary.   [2] *MZM* (money, zero maturity): M2 minus small-denomination time deposits, plus institutional money market mutual funds (that is, those included in M3 but excluded from M2). The label MZM was coined by William Poole (1991); the aggregate itself was proposed earlier by Motley (1988). Seasonally adjusted.   *Source: Board of Governors of the Federal Reserve System*

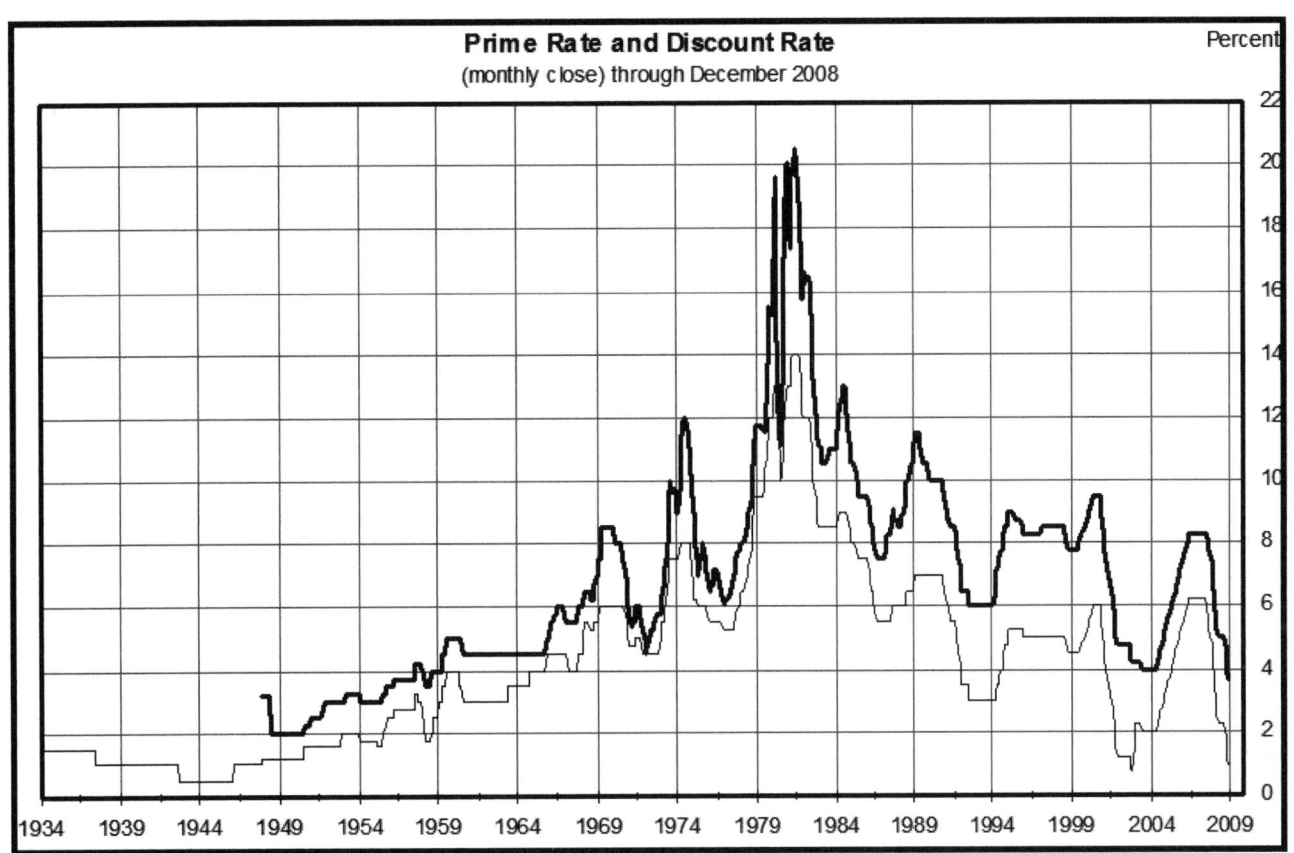

Prime Rate and Discount Rate
(monthly close) through December 2008

Percent

Municipal Bonds and Corporate AAA Bond Yields
(monthly average) through December 2008

Percent

Key Interest Rates
(weekly close) as of January 02, 2009

Percent

| Jan-99 | Jan-00 | Jan-01 | Jan-02 | Jan-03 | Jan-04 | Dec-04 | Dec-05 | Dec-06 | Dec-07 | Dec-08 | Dec-09 |

5-Year Treasury Note Yield
(monthly average) through December 2008

Percent

| 1953 | 1957 | 1961 | 1965 | 1969 | 1973 | 1977 | 1981 | 1985 | 1989 | 1993 | 1997 | 2001 | 2005 | 2009 |

Interest Rates - Worldwide

Interest rate futures contracts are widely traded throughout the world. The most popular futures contracts are generally 10-year government bonds and the 3-month interest rate contracts. In Europe, futures on German interest rates are traded at the all-electronic Eurex Exchange in Frankfurt. Futures on UK interest rates are traded at the Liffe Exchange in London. Futures on Canadian interest rates are traded at the Montreal Exchange. Futures on Japanese interest rates are traded at the Singapore Exchange (Simex) and at the Tokyo Stock Exchange. A variety of other interest rate futures contracts are traded throughout the rest of the world (please see the front of this Yearbook for a complete list).

Euro-Zone – The Eurex 10-year Euro Bund futures contract fell in the first half of 2008 by about 8 full points but then rallied by about 15 points in the second half of the year to close the year up +11.73 points at 124.84. The German 10-year government bund yield in the first half of 2008 rose to a 1-1/2 year high of 4.692% in July 2008 but then fell sharply in the second half of the year to close 2008 at 2.951%, down 136 bp on the year. The 3-month Euribor interbank lending rate rose to a 13-year high of 5.27% as the global financial crisis emerged in September 2008, but then fell sharply to close 2008 at 2.89%, down 178 bp from the 2007 close of 4.67%.

European interest rates rose in the first half of 2008 as the European Central Bank (ECB) stuck to its tight monetary policy and implemented its last 25 bp rate hike to 4.25% in July 2008. Euro-Zone GDP growth had averaged a relatively strong +2.5% in 2007 and showed a strong report of +2.8% (quarter-on-quarter annualized) in Q1-2008. However, the European economy started to slip in Q2 and showed negative growth in the last three quarters of 2008 (Q2 –1.2%, Q3 –0.8%, Q4 –6.0%).

When the global financial crisis emerged in September 2008, the ECB initially was slow to react. The ECB finally started cutting its key 2-week refinancing rate in November with a 50 bp rate cut to 3.75%. As the scope of the damage to the European economy became clearer, the ECB continued cutting rates to 1.50% by March 2009. The ECB also promised to provide as much liquidity to the banking system as it needed through at least the end of 2009. As of March 2009, however, the ECB had still not joined the central banks of the U.S., U.K., Switzerland and Japan in engaging in the quantitative easing move of buying longer-term government bonds.

The Euro-Zone economy in Q1-2009 was essentially in a free-fall along with the rest of the global economy. The market consensus was that Euro-Zone GDP would show a decline of at least 3% in 2009. Euro-Zone core inflation showed only a small decline to +1.6% by early 2009, but the market was expecting inflation to move lower as the economic crisis undercut demand and prices. The market generally expected European interest rates to remain low at least through the end of 2009 in response to the severe economic recession and falling inflation.

UK – The Liffe 10-year Gilt futures contract in 2008 displayed a similar pattern to that of T-note prices and Euro Bund prices, selling off early in the year and then rallying sharply in the second half of the year as the global financial crisis emerged. The Liffe 10-year Gilt futures closed 2008 +13.24 points higher at 123.47. The 3-month UK Libor rate traded in the range of 5.50% to 6.00% in the first half of 2008, spiked higher to 6.30% during the financial crisis, and then plunged to 2.77% by the end of 2008. The Bank of England started cutting its base rate in December 2007 as the U.K. housing market and economy started to show weakness about the same time as the U.S. housing market and economy. The Bank of England slashed its base rate by a total of 525 bp from 5.75% in November 2007 to 0.50% by March 2009. The BOE's base rate of 0.50% in March 2009 was the lowest rate in the BOE's 315-year history, attesting to the seriousness of the financial crisis. The BOE in March 2009 also announced a quantitative easing move of buying up to $75 billion of long-term government bonds, thus directly injecting liquidity into the banking system.

Canada – The Montreal Exchange's Canadian 10-year government note futures contract traded basically sideways in the first half of 2008 and then rallied sharply as the global crisis emerged in late 2008, finally closing the year up +11.84 points at 126.76. The Canadian 10-year government yield traded sideways in the range of 3.40% to 3.90% in the first half of 2008 and then fell sharply late in the year to close 2008 at 2.68%, down 131 bp on the year. The 3-month Canadian interbank lending rate declined all during 2008 as the Bank of Canada eased monetary policy and fell to 1.06% by March 2009. The well-regulated Canadian banking system was spared the debacle seen in the U.S., U.K., and European banking systems. Nevertheless, the Canadian economy was hit hard along with the rest of the world in response to the global financial crisis. The Bank of Canada slashed its overnight lending rate from 4.50% in November 2007 to 0.50% by March 2009. Canadian real GDP growth, which is reported on a monthly basis, did not turn negative until November with a report of –0.8% y/y. However, the market consensus was that Canada's GDP would show a decline of -1.6% in 2009.

Japan – The SGX 10-year JGB futures contract in early 2008 extended the rally that began in mid-2007 and rallied to a 5-year high of 141.96 in March 2008. JGBs fell to 132 by June 2008 but then started to rebound sharply as the global financial crisis and recession emerged later in 2008. JGBs closed 2008 at 139.75, up +2.99 points on the year. The 10-year JGB yield moved lower in the latter half of 2008 and closed the year down 31 bp at 1.17%. Japanese GDP growth fell in the last three quarters of 2008 by –4.5% in Q2, –1.4% in Q3, and –12.1% in Q4 (quarter-on-quarter annualized). Japan's economy was hit hard by the plunge in exports seen during the global financial crisis. The Bank of Japan started cutting its overnight benchmark rate from 0.50% in September 2008 to 0.10% by December. The Bank of Japan also reinstated its quantitative easing policy of buying government bonds to inject reserves into the banking system.

Long Gilt Futures - Euronext-LIFFE
(weekly close) as of January 02, 2009

Nominal Value

3-Month Sterling Futures - Euronext-LIFFE
(weekly close) as of January 02, 2009

Points of 100%

10-Year Japanese Government Bond Futures - Tokyo Stock Exch.
(weekly close) as January 02, 2009

Nominal Value

3-Month Euroyen Futures - TIFFE
(weekly close) as of January 02, 2009

Points of 100%

10-Year Canadian Government Bond Futures - Montreal Exch.
(weekly close) as of January 02, 2009

Nominal Value

3-Month Canadian Bankers' Acceptance Futures - Montreal Exch.
(weekly close) as of January 02, 2009

Points of 100%

Australia -- Economic Statistics   Percentage Change from Previous Period

Year	Real GDP	Nominal GDP	Real Private Consumption	Real Public Consumption	Grossed Fixed Investment	Real Total Domestic Demand	Real Exports of Goods & Services	Real Imports of Goods & Services	Consumer Prices[1]	Unemployment Rate
2001	2.1	6.1	2.9	1.7	-4.8	.6	2.2	-4.2	4.4	6.7
2002	4.0	7.1	3.8	3.0	17.0	6.3	.2	10.9	3.0	6.3
2003	3.4	6.3	3.6	3.7	9.4	6.1	-1.6	10.7	2.8	5.9
2004	3.2	7.5	5.9	3.9	6.9	5.3	4.6	15.3	2.3	5.4
2005	3.2	7.5	3.0	3.0	8.9	4.6	2.4	8.5	2.7	5.0
2006	2.5	7.5	3.1	3.2	4.7	2.7	3.3	7.3	3.5	4.8
2007	4.4	8.1	4.5	2.4	9.4	6.2	3.1	11.2	2.3	4.4
2008[1]	2.5	8.4	2.4	3.7	7.2	3.8	5.0	11.2	4.6	4.3
2009[3]	1.7	3.8	1.7	2.4	2.0	1.8	3.7	3.9	3.3	5.3

[1] National accounts implicit private consumption deflator.   [2] Estimate.   [3] Projection.   *Source: Organization for Economic Co-operation and Development (OECD)*

Canada -- Economic Statistics   Percentage Change from Previous Period

Year	Real GDP	Nominal GDP	Real Private Consumption	Real Public Consumption	Grossed Fixed Investment	Real Total Domestic Demand	Real Exports of Goods & Services	Real Imports of Goods & Services	Consumer Prices[1]	Unemployment Rate
2001	1.8	2.9	2.3	3.9	4.0	1.3	-3.0	-5.1	2.5	7.2
2002	2.9	4.0	3.6	2.5	1.6	3.2	1.2	1.7	2.3	7.6
2003	1.9	5.2	3.0	3.1	6.2	4.5	-2.3	4.1	2.8	7.6
2004	3.1	6.4	3.3	2.0	7.8	4.1	5.0	8.0	1.9	7.2
2005	2.9	6.3	3.7	1.5	9.2	4.8	1.8	7.1	2.2	6.8
2006	3.1	5.7	4.3	3.8	7.1	4.6	.6	4.6	2.0	6.3
2007	2.7	5.9	4.5	3.7	3.9	4.3	1.0	5.5	2.1	6.0
2008[1]	.5	3.8	3.4	4.3	1.0	2.7	-4.3	1.9	2.6	6.1
2009[3]	-.5	-1.5	-.6	2.4	-2.8	-.4	-2.9	-2.6	1.2	7.0

[1] National accounts implicit private consumption deflator.   [2] Estimate.   [3] Projection.   *Source: Organization for Economic Co-operation and Development (OECD)*

France -- Economic Statistics   Percentage Change from Previous Period

Year	Real GDP	Nominal GDP	Real Private Consumption	Real Public Consumption	Grossed Fixed Investment	Real Total Domestic Demand	Real Exports of Goods & Services	Real Imports of Goods & Services	Consumer Prices[1]	Unemployment Rate
2001	1.8	3.8	2.6	1.1	2.3	1.7	2.5	2.3	1.8	7.8
2002	1.1	3.5	2.3	1.9	-1.6	1.2	1.3	1.6	1.9	7.9
2003	1.1	3.0	2.0	2.0	2.2	1.7	-.7	1.5	2.2	8.5
2004	2.2	3.8	2.4	2.2	3.3	3.1	3.0	6.4	2.3	8.8
2005	1.9	4.0	2.5	1.3	4.5	2.6	3.5	6.0	1.9	8.8
2006	2.4	4.9	2.5	1.4	5.0	2.6	5.6	6.5	1.9	8.8
2007	2.1	4.6	2.4	1.4	4.9	2.9	3.2	5.9	1.6	8.0
2008[1]	.9	3.2	.9	1.4	.3	.9	2.2	1.9	3.3	7.3
2009[3]	-.4	1.3	.3	.8	-3.6	-.4	-.2	-.4	1.0	8.2

[1] National accounts implicit private consumption deflator.   [2] Estimate.   [3] Projection.   *Source: Organization for Economic Co-operation and Development (OECD)*

Germany -- Economic Statistics   Percentage Change from Previous Period

Year	Real GDP	Nominal GDP	Real Private Consumption	Real Public Consumption	Grossed Fixed Investment	Real Total Domestic Demand	Real Exports of Goods & Services	Real Imports of Goods & Services	Consumer Prices[1]	Unemployment Rate
2001	1.4	2.6	1.9	.5	-3.4	-.4	6.8	1.5	1.9	7.5
2002	.0	1.4	-.8	1.5	-6.2	-2.0	4.3	-1.4	1.4	8.3
2003	-.2	.9	.1	.4	-.3	.6	2.4	5.3	1.0	9.2
2004	.7	1.7	-.2	-.7	-1.3	-.6	9.4	6.5	1.8	9.7
2005	.9	1.6	.2	.4	1.3	.2	7.9	6.7	1.9	10.5
2006	3.2	3.7	1.2	.6	8.5	2.3	13.1	12.2	1.8	9.8
2007	2.6	4.5	-.3	2.2	4.5	1.2	7.7	5.2	2.3	8.3
2008[1]	1.4	3.0	-.6	1.9	3.6	1.7	4.2	5.4	2.9	7.4
2009[3]	-.8	1.0	.2	1.0	-2.8	.1	.7	2.8	1.1	8.1

[1] National accounts implicit private consumption deflator.   [2] Estimate.   [3] Projection.   *Source: Organization for Economic Co-operation and Development (OECD)*

INTEREST RATES - WORLDWIDE

Italy -- Economic Statistics   Percentage Change from Previous Period

Year	Real GDP	Nominal GDP	Real Private Consumption	Real Public Consumption	Grossed Fixed Investment	Real Total Domestic Demand	Real Exports of Goods & Services	Real Imports of Goods & Services	Consumer Prices[1]	Unemployment Rate
2001	1.7	4.8	.7	3.9	2.4	1.5	2.2	1.4	2.3	9.2
2002	.5	3.7	.2	2.4	3.7	1.3	-2.8	.2	2.6	8.8
2003	.0	3.2	1.0	1.9	-.9	.8	-1.6	1.5	2.8	8.6
2004	1.4	4.0	.8	2.2	1.6	1.2	3.8	3.3	2.3	8.1
2005	.7	2.8	.9	1.9	1.2	.9	1.8	2.7	2.2	7.8
2006	1.9	3.7	1.1	.8	2.7	1.8	6.5	6.1	2.2	6.8
2007	1.4	3.7	1.5	1.2	.8	1.3	4.5	4.0	2.0	6.2
2008[1]	-.4	3.5	-.5	1.2	-1.4	-.8	.4	-1.3	3.5	6.9
2009[3]	-1.0	1.5	-.3	.2	-4.6	-1.1	-.6	-.7	1.5	7.8

[1] National accounts implicit private consumption deflator.   [2] Estimate.   [3] Projection.   *Source: Organization for Economic Co-operation and Development (OECD)*

Japan -- Economic Statistics   Percentage Change from Previous Period

Year	Real GDP	Nominal GDP	Real Private Consumption	Real Public Consumption	Grossed Fixed Investment	Real Total Domestic Demand	Real Exports of Goods & Services	Real Imports of Goods & Services	Consumer Prices[1]	Unemployment Rate
2001	.2	-1.0	1.6	3.0	-.9	1.0	-6.9	.6	-.8	5.0
2002	.3	-1.3	1.1	2.4	-4.9	-.4	7.5	.9	-.9	5.4
2003	1.4	-.2	.4	2.3	-.5	.8	9.2	3.9	-.2	5.3
2004	2.7	1.6	1.6	1.9	1.4	1.9	13.9	8.1	.0	4.7
2005	1.9	.7	1.3	1.6	3.1	1.7	7.0	5.8	-.6	4.4
2006	2.4	1.4	2.0	-.4	1.3	1.6	9.7	4.2	.2	4.1
2007	2.1	1.3	1.5	.7	-.6	1.0	8.6	1.7	.1	3.9
2008[1]	.5	-.5	.7	.3	-2.4	-.3	5.3	.9	1.4	4.1
2009[3]	-.1	1.1	.6	1.4	-.1	.6	-2.9	1.2	.3	4.4

[1] National accounts implicit private consumption deflator.   [2] Estimate.   [3] Projection.   *Source: Organization for Economic Co-operation and Development (OECD)*

Switzerland -- Economic Statistics   Percentage Change from Previous Period

Year	Real GDP	Nominal GDP	Real Private Consumption	Real Public Consumption	Grossed Fixed Investment	Real Total Domestic Demand	Real Exports of Goods & Services	Real Imports of Goods & Services	Consumer Prices[1]	Unemployment Rate
2001	1.2	2.0	2.3	4.5	-3.5	2.0	.5	2.3	1.0	2.6
2002	.4	.9	.1	1.2	-.5	.1	-.1	-1.1	.6	3.2
2003	-.2	.8	.9	1.9	-1.2	.5	-.5	1.3	.6	4.3
2004	2.5	3.1	1.6	.8	4.5	1.9	7.9	7.3	.8	4.4
2005	2.5	2.6	1.8	1.0	3.8	1.9	7.3	6.6	1.2	4.4
2006	3.4	5.2	1.6	-.9	4.7	1.4	9.9	6.5	1.1	4.0
2007	3.3	5.2	2.1	-1.1	5.4	1.1	9.4	5.9	.7	3.6
2008[1]	1.9	4.7	2.0	-.8	-.7	.3	5.2	2.6	2.5	3.5
2009[3]	-.2	1.8	1.2	.9	-3.2	.1	2.1	3.0	1.0	3.9

[1] National accounts implicit private consumption deflator.   [2] Estimate.   [3] Projection.   *Source: Organization for Economic Co-operation and Development (OECD)*

United Kingdom -- Economic Statistics   Percentage Change from Previous Period

Year	Real GDP	Nominal GDP	Real Private Consumption	Real Public Consumption	Grossed Fixed Investment	Real Total Domestic Demand	Real Exports of Goods & Services	Real Imports of Goods & Services	Consumer Prices[1]	Unemployment Rate
2001	2.5	4.6	3.1	2.4	2.6	3.0	3.0	4.8	1.2	5.1
2002	2.1	5.3	3.5	3.4	3.6	3.2	1.0	4.9	1.3	5.2
2003	2.8	6.0	3.0	3.5	1.1	2.9	1.8	2.2	1.4	5.0
2004	2.8	5.3	2.9	3.4	4.9	3.4	4.8	6.8	1.3	4.8
2005	2.1	4.3	1.9	1.7	2.2	1.9	8.1	7.0	2.0	4.8
2006	2.8	5.5	2.1	1.6	6.0	2.6	11.0	9.6	2.3	5.4
2007	3.0	6.0	3.0	1.8	7.1	3.6	-4.5	-1.9	2.3	5.4
2008[1]	.8	4.1	1.8	2.3	-5.3	.5	1.2	.2	3.7	5.5
2009[3]	-1.1	1.3	-1.0	2.3	-9.0	-1.6	-1.8	-3.4	2.7	6.8

[1] National accounts implicit private consumption deflator.   [2] Estimate.   [3] Projection.   *Source: Organization for Economic Co-operation and Development (OECD)*

Iron and Steel

Iron (symbol Fe) is a soft, malleable, and ductile metallic element. Next to aluminum, iron is the most abundant of all metals. Pure iron melts at about 1535 degrees Celsius and boils at 2750 degrees Celsius. Archaeologists in Egypt discovered the earliest iron implements dating back to about 3000 BC, and iron ornaments were used even earlier.

Steel is an alloy of iron and carbon, often with an admixture of other elements. The physical properties of various types of steel and steel alloys depend primarily on the amount of carbon present and how it is distributed in the iron. Steel is marketed in a variety of sizes and shapes, such as rods, pipes, railroad rails, tees, channels, and I-beams. Steel mills roll and form heated ingots into the required shapes. The working of steel improves the quality of the steel by refining its crystalline structure and making the metal tougher. There are five classifications of steel: carbon steels, alloy steels, high-strength low-alloy steels, stainless steel, and tool steels.

Prices – In 2008 the average wholesale price (through June) for No. 1 heavy-melting steel scrap in Chicago rose by +59.8% to $419.87 per metric ton. That was a new record high.

Supply – World production of iron ore in 2006 (latest data available) rose by +16.9% to 1.800 billion metric tons, which was a new record high. The world's largest producers of iron ore are China (with 33% of world production in 2006), Brazil (with 18%), and Australia (with 15%). The U.S. accounted for only 3.0% of world iron ore production in 2006. World production of raw steel (ingots and castings) in 2006 rose +7.9 % yr/yr to 1,230 million metric tons, with the largest producers being China (with 34% of world production), Japan (with 9%), and the U.S. (with 8%). U.S. production of steel ingots in 2006 rose by +5.7% to an 8-year high of 108.621 million short tons. U.S. production of pig iron (excluding ferro-alloys) in 2008 was virtually unchanged at 36.060 million short tons in 2005.

Demand – U.S. consumption of ferrous scrap and pig iron fell −0.2% yr/yr in 2006 to 103.200 million metric tons, but still above the 102.900 million metric tons in 2003, which was the lowest level since 1986. The largest consumers of ferrous scrap and pig iron were the manufacturers of pig iron and steel ingots and castings with 88% of consumption at 91.200 million metric tons in 2006. Iron foundries and miscellaneous users accounted for 10% of consumption, and manufacturers of steel castings (scrap) accounted for 2% of consumption.

Trade – The U.S. imported 9.4 million metric tons of iron ore in 2007, down 18.4% yr/yr from 11.5 million metric tons in 2006. The bulk of U.S. iron ore imports came from Canada (59% with 5.520 million metric tons) and Brazil (34% with 3.210 million metric tons).

World Production of Raw Steel (Ingots and Castings)   In Thousands of Metric Tons

Year	Brazil	Canada	China	France	Germany	Italy	Japan	Rep. of Korea	Russia	Ukraine	United Kindom	United States	World Total
1997	26,153	15,554	108,911	19,767	45,007	25,842	104,545	42,554	48,502	25,629	18,489	98,486	798,892
1998	25,800	15,930	115,590	20,126	44,046	25,798	93,548	39,896	43,822	23,461	17,066	98,600	770,000
1999	24,600	16,300	124,260	20,211	42,056	24,964	94,192	41,042	51,524	27,390	16,634	97,400	790,000
2000	27,865	15,900	128,500	21,002	46,376	26,544	106,444	43,107	59,098	31,780	15,022	102,000	850,000
2001	26,718	16,300	151,630	19,431	44,775	26,483	102,866	43,852	59,030	33,110	13,610	90,100	853,000
2002	29,605	16,300	182,370	20,524	44,999	25,930	107,745	45,390	59,777	34,538	11,718	91,600	907,000
2003	31,150	17,000	222,340	19,578	44,809	26,832	110,511	46,310	62,710	36,900	13,128	93,700	974,000
2004	32,918	17,000	272,450	20,770	46,374	28,317	112,718	47,521	65,646	38,740	13,766	99,700	1,060,000
2005[1]	31,631	17,000	353,240	19,481	44,524	29,061	112,471	47,820	66,186	38,636	13,210	94,900	1,140,000
2006[2]	31,800	17,000	418,780	19,867	47,223	31,550	116,219	48,437	70,766	40,899	13,952	98,200	1,230,000

[1] Preliminary.   [2] Estimate.   *Source: U.S. Geological Survey (USGS)*

Average Wholesale Prices of Iron and Steel in the United States

	No. 1 Heavy Melting Steel Scrap		Sheet Bars			Pittsburg Prices				Rail Road	Used
Year	Pittsburg	Chicago	Hot Rolled	Hot Rolled	Cold Finished	Hot Rolled Strip	Carbon Steel Plates	Cold Rolled Strip	Galvan-ized Sheets	Steel Scrap[2]	Steel Cans[3]
	----- $ Per Gross Ton -----		-------------------------------- Cents Per Pound --------------------------------							---- $ Per Gross Ton ----	
1999	97.86	102.49	14.74	----	23.50	----	14.00	----	21.20	150.00	68.94
2000	103.73	96.07	15.67	----	23.08	----	15.69	----	21.38	150.00	82.23
2001	79.34	74.17	11.71	----	22.76	----	12.94	----	16.41	NA	68.52
2002	101.06	89.92	16.46	----	23.26	----	----	----	22.00	NA	66.71
2003	128.32	113.82	14.80	----	25.15	----	----	----	20.08	----	116.21
2004	221.05	220.13	30.84	----	38.67	----	----	----	36.69	----	192.80
2005	199.10	196.75	27.83	----	44.96	----	----	----	33.77	----	172.00
2006	222.39	225.21	29.78	----	44.02	----	----	----	38.09	----	212.63
2007	250.98	262.80	26.89	----	45.26	----	----	----	38.25	----	244.65
2008[1]	365.62	357.88	44.56	----	61.67	----	----	----	54.91	----	314.63

[1] Preliminary.   [2] Specialties scrap.   [3] Consumer buying prices.   NA = Not available.   *Source: American Metal Market (AMM)*

IRON AND STEEL

Salient Statistics of Steel in the United States   In Thousands of Short Tons

Year	Pig Iron Production	Producer Price Index for Steel Mill Products (1982=100)	Raw Steel Production By Type of Furnace — Basic Oxygen	Open Hearth	Electric[2]	Stainless	Carbon	Alloy	Total	Net Shipments Steel Mill Products	Total Steel Products — Exports	Imports
1997	54,679	116.4	61,053	----	47,508	2,382	95,933	10,246	108,561	105,858	7,369	34,389
1998	53,164	113.8	59,686	----	49,067	2,214	97,054	9,484	108,752	102,420	5,520	41,520
1999	51,002	105.3	57,722	----	49,673	2,086	98,694	5,421	107,395	106,201	5,426	35,731
2000	52,787	108.4	59,485	----	52,756	2,104	102,141	5,379	111,903	109,050	6,529	37,957
2001	46,424	101.3	52,204	----	47,118	1,836	92,946	4,666	99,322	99,448	6,144	30,080
2002	44,341	104.8	50,114	----	51,564	1,894	92,518	4,779	101,679	99,191	6,009	32,686
2003	43,122	109.5	50,942	----	48,751	1,952	98,772	4,901	99,693	105,625	8,220	23,125
2004	44,731	147.2	50,613	----	58,456	2,073	105,161	4,851	109,069	112,085	7,933	35,808
2005	40,036	159.7	45,231	----	57,599	1,903	96,636	4,935	102,830	103,474	9,393	32,108
2006[1]	41,781	174.1	46,802	----	61,838	2,081	101,572	4,956	108,640	108,609	9,728	45,272

[1] Preliminary.   [2] Includes crucible steels.   *Sources: American Iron & Steel Institute (AISI); U.S. Geological Survey (USGS)*

Production of Steel Ingots, Rate of Capability Utilization[1] in the United States   In Percent

Year	Jan.	Feb.	Mar.	Apr.	May	June	July	Aug.	Sept.	Oct.	Nov.	Dec.	Average
1998	90.0	95.2	93.1	92.5	89.1	86.1	83.0	86.4	83.0	81.0	74.4	74.8	85.7
1999	77.2	79.5	81.7	81.8	81.7	79.7	79.4	82.8	82.3	88.2	89.1	88.5	82.7
2000	89.7	89.4	91.2	92.0	91.3	89.6	85.3	83.5	82.7	81.0	75.1	72.0	85.2
2001	77.6	82.3	81.8	82.9	81.5	81.6	79.8	80.4	80.5	77.5	73.5	65.9	78.8
2002	84.5	88.4	86.7	90.3	89.4	92.5	86.8	91.0	94.0	90.8	86.8	83.9	88.8
2003	83.1	87.3	85.0	87.8	81.1	86.2	78.9	78.3	80.7	82.8	82.8	81.9	83.0
2004	88.0	90.9	93.8	93.3	92.9	94.4	93.5	95.0	97.3	97.5	94.8	91.5	93.6
2005	90.9	92.9	88.4	89.2	84.2	79.8	77.1	81.3	86.4	89.3	88.1	85.0	86.1
2006	85.6	89.5	92.8	91.4	92.5	92.1	88.7	88.7	91.2	86.2	81.5	75.0	87.9
2007[2]	78.2	87.8	86.3	85.0	88.4	88.6	87.0	87.7	86.5	88.5	88.5	88.1	86.7

[1] Based on tonnage capability to produce raw steel for a full order book.   [2] Preliminary.   *Sources: American Iron and Steel Institute (AISI); U.S. Geological Survey (USGS)*

Production of Steel Ingots in the United States   In Thousands of Short Tons

Year	Jan.	Feb.	Mar.	Apr.	May	June	July	Aug.	Sept.	Oct.	Nov.	Dec.	Total
1997	8,735	8,266	9,175	8,882	9,048	8,662	8,692	8,818	9,006	9,128	9,116	9,071	107,488
1998	9,510	9,087	9,839	9,524	9,483	8,863	8,832	9,194	8,548	8,681	7,710	8,013	107,643
1999	8,422	7,837	8,854	8,643	8,914	8,413	8,619	8,993	8,650	9,574	9,357	9,604	105,882
2000	9,838	9,170	10,009	9,843	10,097	9,592	9,411	9,213	8,830	8,978	8,054	7,982	111,015
2001	8,475	8,122	8,932	8,685	8,832	8,550	8,459	8,525	8,263	8,125	7,226	6,695	98,889
2002	8,050	7,609	8,261	8,214	8,401	8,414	8,510	8,918	8,916	9,015	8,340	8,329	100,976
2003	8,617	8,175	8,817	8,692	8,047	8,534	8,163	8,096	8,026	8,514	8,347	8,414	100,442
2004	8,656	8,400	9,268	8,901	9,163	9,006	9,164	9,314	9,234	9,551	8,989	8,660	108,305
2005	9,123	8,419	9,028	8,757	8,543	7,837	7,896	8,330	8,562	9,032	8,629	8,599	102,754
2006[1]	8,918	8,506	9,770	9,382	9,811	9,458	9,324	9,320	9,282	8,922	8,169	7,760	108,621

[1] Preliminary.   *Source: American Iron and Steel Institute (AISI)*

Shipments of Steel Products[1] by Market Classifications in the United States   In Thousands of Short Tons

Year	Appliances Utensils & Cutlery	Automotive	Containers, Packaging & Shipping Materials	Construction Including Maint.	Contactors Products	Electrical Equipment	Export	Machinery, Industrial Equip. & Tools	Oil and Gas	Rail Transportation	Steel for Converting & Processing[2]	Steel Service Center & Distributors	All Other[3]	Total Shipments
1997	1,635	15,251	4,163	15,885	[5]	2,434	2,610	2,355	3,811	1,410	11,263	27,800	17,241	105,858
1998	1,729	15,842	3,829	15,289	[5]	2,255	2,556	2,147	2,649	1,657	9,975	27,751	16,741	102,420
1999	1,712	15,639	3,768	14,685	[5]	2,260	2,292	1,547	1,544	876	7,599	21,439	32,840	106,201
2000	1,530	14,697	3,684	14,763	[5]	2,039	2,752	1,513	2,268	994	7,753	22,537	35,093	109,624
2001	1,675	12,767	3,193	16,339	[5]	1,694	2,281	1,210	2,134	720	7,462	23,887	26,086	99,448
2002	1,734	12,562	3,251	15,729	[5]	1,336	1,844	1,137	1,658	751	7,201	22,828	29,160	99,191
2003	1,891	11,937	2,949	14,403	[5]	1,200	2,572	1,108	1,800	799	6,798	24,266	35,905	105,628
2004	1,919	12,527	2,978	15,114	[5]	1,139	2,426	1,332	2,043	957	7,295	25,385	38,969	112,085
2005	1,895	13,031	2,504	15,858	[5]	1,088	2,592	1,300	2,056	1,019	7,559	23,213	31,359	103,474
2006[4]	1,781	14,003	2,535	17,544	[5]	1,228	3,068	1,360	2,459	1,242	8,531	23,706	31,153	108,609

[1] All grades including carbon, alloy and stainless steel.   [2] Net total after deducting shipments to reporting companies for conversion or resale.
[3] Includes agricultural; bolts, nuts rivets & screws; forgings (other than automotive); shipbuilding & marine equipment; aircraft; mining, quarrying & lumbering; other domestic & commercial equipment machinery; ordnance & other direct military; and shipments of non-reporting companies.
[4] Preliminary.   [5] Included in Construction.   *Source: American Iron and Steel Institute (AISI)*

Net Shipments of Steel Products[2] in the United States   In Thousands of Short Tons

Year	Cold Finished Bars	Rails & Accessories	Wire Drawn	Tin Mill Products	Plates Cut & Coils	Sheet & Strip[3] Galv, Hot Dipped	Hot Rolled Bars	Pipe & Tubing	Structural Shapes & Steel Piling	Reinforcing Bars	Hot Rolled Sheets	Cold Rolled Sheets	Carbon	Alloy	Stainless
1997	1,809	875	619	4,057	8,855	12,439	8,153	6,548	6,029	6,188	18,221	13,322	97,509	6,282	2,067
1998	1,780	938	725	3,714	8,864	13,481	8,189	5,409	5,595	5,909	15,715	13,185	94,536	5,847	2,037
1999	1,775	646	611	3,771	8,200	14,870	8,078	4,772	5,995	6,183	17,740	13,874	98,694	5,421	2,086
2000	1,756	783	579	3,742	8,898	14,917	7,901	5,385	7,402	6,893	19,236	14,802	102,141	5,379	2,104
2001	1,369	630	481	3,202	8,349	14,310	7,032	5,377	6,789	6,976	18,866	12,352	92,314	4,789	1,837
2002	1,404	789	733	3,419	8,769	14,944	6,581	4,809	6,729	6,359	19,243	12,673	92,518	4,779	1,894
2003	1,426	739	684	3,513	9,230	15,221	6,486	4,597	7,437	7,970	22,218	13,485	98,772	4,901	1,952
2004	1,520	843	428	3,247	10,740	16,306	7,181	5,328	7,812	8,274	23,106	14,762	105,161	4,851	2,073
2005	1,495	920	560	2,874	10,274	15,249	6,674	5,096	8,070	7,464	20,569	12,793	97,884	5,183	1,903
2006[1]	1,487	1,016	603	2,880	10,827	16,358	7,595	5,426	8,652	7,419	20,862	13,281	101,572	4,956	2,081

[1] Preliminary.   [2] All grades, including carbon, alloy and stainless steel.   *Source: American Iron and Steel Institute (AISI)*

World Production of Pig Iron (Excludes Ferro-Alloys)   In Thousands of Metric Tons

Year	Belgium	Brazil	China	France	Germany	India	Italy	Japan	Russia	Ukraine	United Kingdom	United States	World Total
1999	8,472	25,060	125,390	13,854	27,931	20,139	10,509	74,520	40,854	21,937	12,399	46,300	578,000
2000	8,472	27,952	131,010	13,621	30,846	21,321	11,223	81,071	44,618	25,700	10,891	47,900	616,000
2001	7,732	27,623	155,540	12,004	29,184	21,900	10,650	78,836	44,980	26,400	9,861	42,125	624,086
2002	8,053	29,667	170,850	13,217	29,427	24,315	9,736	80,979	46,060	27,560	8,561	40,200	653,000
2003	8,000	32,036	213,660	12,756	29,481	24,000	10,148	82,092	48,368	29,570	10,228	40,600	715,000
2004	8,000	34,579	251,850	13,198	30,018	25,000	10,604	82,974	50,427	31,000	10,180	42,300	764,000
2005	8,000	34,382	343,750	12,705	28,854	25,500	11,423	83,058	49,175	30,747	10,189	37,200	851,000
2006	8,000	34,500	404,170	13,013	30,360	26,000	11,535	84,270	51,683	32,926	10,736	37,900	925,000
2007[1]		36,000	469,000	12,000	31,000		11,000	87,000	52,000	36,000	11,000	36,000	947,000
2008[2]		37,000	478,000	12,000	30,000		11,000	88,000	52,000	34,000	11,000	36,000	958,000

[1] Preliminary.   [2] Estimate.   *Source: U.S. Geological Survey (USGS)*

Production of Pig Iron (Excludes Ferro-Alloys) in the United States   In Thousands of Short Tons

Year	Jan.	Feb.	Mar.	Apr.	May	June	July	Aug.	Sept.	Oct.	Nov.	Dec.	Total
1999	4,140	3,802	4,257	4,157	4,352	4,045	4,204	4,280	4,167	4,572	4,447	4,722	51,145
2000	4,571	4,325	4,793	4,741	4,887	4,577	4,454	4,387	4,262	4,138	3,675	3,781	52,591
2001	3,808	3,691	4,255	4,183	4,278	4,143	4,048	4,121	3,920	3,837	3,202	2,965	46,451
2002	3,493	3,308	3,616	3,480	3,584	3,612	3,854	3,983	4,006	4,018	3,710	3,677	44,341
2003	3,832	3,631	3,906	3,810	3,381	3,569	3,395	3,253	3,289	3,527	3,530	3,733	42,856
2004	3,682	3,524	4,018	3,749	3,670	3,633	3,590	3,839	3,818	3,940	3,668	3,389	44,520
2005	3,773	3,592	4,030	3,397	3,395	2,962	2,895	3,183	3,127	3,237	3,310	3,135	40,036
2006	3,519	3,421	3,765	3,612	3,816	3,667	3,540	3,525	3,544	3,403	3,059	2,909	41,780
2007	2,850	2,610	3,040	3,010	3,130	3,120	3,080	3,010	3,010	3,200	2,940	3,160	36,160
2008[1]	2,900	3,110											36,060

[1] Preliminary.   *Source: American Iron and Steel Institute*

Salient Statistics of Ferrous Scrap and Pig Iron in the United States   In Thousands of Metric Tons

	Consumption: Ferrous Scrap & Pig Iron Charged To											Stocks, Dec. 31		
	Mfg. of Pig Iron & Steel Ingots & Castings			Iron Foundries & Misc. Users			Mfg. of Steel Castings (Scrap)	All Uses			Imports of Scrap[2]	Exports of Scrap[3]	Ferrous Scrap & Pig Iron at Consumers	
Year	Scrap	Pig Iron	Total	Scrap	Pig Iron	Total		Ferrous Scrap	Pig Iron	Grand Total				Total
1997	58,000	51,000	109,000	13,000	1,200	14,200	1,800	73,000	52,000	125,000	2,870	8,930	5,500	510	6,010
1998	58,000	49,000	107,000	13,000	1,200	14,200	2,000	73,000	50,000	123,000	3,060	5,570	5,300	570	5,870
1999	56,000	48,000	104,000	13,000	1,100	14,100	1,900	71,000	49,000	120,000	3,360	5,000	5,450	724	6,174
2000	59,000	49,000	108,000	13,000	1,200	14,200	2,200	74,000	50,000	124,000	3,040	5,230	5,320	930	6,250
2001	56,700	46,900	103,600	12,000	1,100	13,100	2,200	71,000	48,000	119,000	2,630	7,440	4,880	787	5,667
2002	56,400	42,500	98,900	11,000	1,500	12,500	1,800	69,000	44,000	113,000	3,130	8,950	4,930	754	5,684
2003	55,200	39,700	94,900	4,460	655	5,115	2,680	61,900	41,000	102,900	3,480	10,800	4,410	381	4,791
2004	57,100	38,000	95,100	8,490	1,020	9,510	1,330	66,500	39,100	105,600	4,660	11,800	5,420	722	6,142
2005	54,600	36,900	91,500	9,010	1,090	10,100	1,810	65,400	38,000	103,400	3,840	13,000	5,100	665	5,765
2006[1]	54,500	36,700	91,200	9,370	857	10,227	1,640	65,600	37,600	103,200	4,820	14,900	4,740	701	5,441

[1] Preliminary.   [2] Includes tinplate and terneplate.   [3] Excludes used rails for rerolling and other uses and ships, boats, and other vessels for scrapping.
Source: U.S. Geological Survey (USGS)

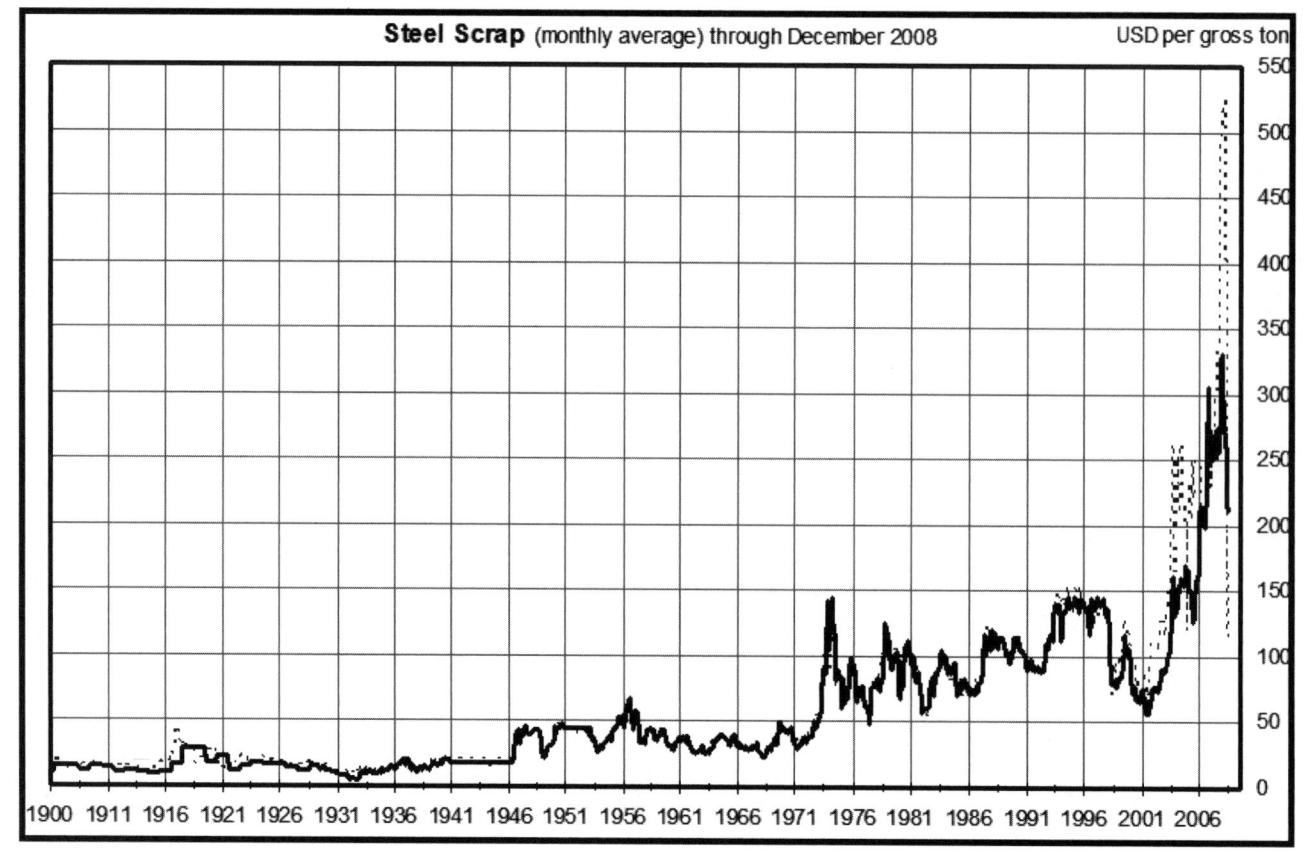

Steel Scrap (monthly average) through December 2008 — USD per gross ton

Consumption of Pig Iron in the United States, by Type of Furance or Equipment In Thousands of Metric Tons

Year	Open Hearth	Electric	Cupola	Basic Oxygen Process	Air & Other Furnace	Direct Casting	Total
1997	----	2,400	400	50,000	W	41	52,000
1998	----	4,000	590	46,000	W	36	50,000
1999	----	3,100	520	45,000	W	36	49,000
2000	----	2,900	530	47,000	W	35	50,000
2001	----	2,700	500	45,000	W	36	48,000
2002	----	3,200	520	40,000	W	36	44,000
2003	----	2,310	792	37,900	W	36	41,000
2004	----	3,030	354	35,700	W	36	39,100
2005[1]	----	3,040	528	34,400	W	36	38,000
2006[2]	----	3,380	435	33,800	W	36	37,600

[1] Preliminary.   [2] Estimate.   W = Withheld.   *Source: U.S. Geological Survey (USGS)*

Wholesale Price of No. 1 Heavy Melting Steel Scrap in Chicago In Dollars Per Metric Ton

Year	Jan.	Feb.	Mar.	Apr.	May	June	July	Aug.	Sept.	Oct.	Nov.	Dec.	Average
1999	89.66	101.50	90.89	90.50	100.00	104.32	100.98	105.95	106.50	106.50	113.40	120.17	102.49
2000	120.50	111.10	110.50	108.15	101.50	94.59	92.50	92.50	92.50	82.59	72.80	74.20	96.07
2001	83.55	74.50	74.50	74.50	73.23	72.50	75.93	76.50	76.50	72.54	67.50	67.50	74.17
2002	70.21	75.03	75.50	85.05	93.09	97.10	97.50	97.50	100.50	98.85	93.50	93.50	89.78
2003	96.93	101.97	105.07	105.50	101.69	96.88	101.05	116.79	122.02	122.50	138.22	159.74	114.03
2004	187.75	219.92	250.85	224.55	181.90	180.00	222.50	249.32	217.38	237.62	248.00	223.57	220.28
2005	203.00	190.00	190.00	217.14	180.95	124.32	135.50	189.78	241.19	204.29	246.25	242.43	197.07
2006	222.70	237.76	237.07	245.00	249.23	249.23	245.25	204.41	207.25	202.55	197.90	203.55	225.16
2007	225.24	252.37	305.00	291.90	255.36	254.71	250.71	257.04	268.74	265.65	252.10	273.42	262.69
2008	334.00	338.70	352.57	482.73	513.10	498.10	510.45	466.43	313.62	188.00	91.67	169.29	354.89

Source: American Metal Market (AMM)

World Production of Iron Ore[3]   In Thousands of Metric Tons (Gross Weight)

Year	Australia	Brazil	Canada	China	India	Maur-itania	Russia	South Africa	Sweden	Ukraine	United States	Venezula	World Total
1997	157,766	184,970	37,277	268,000	69,453	11,700	70,900	33,225	21,893	53,000	62,971	18,503	1,070,000
1998	155,731	197,500	37,808	247,000	72,532	11,400	72,343	32,948	20,930	50,758	62,931	16,553	1,050,000
1999	154,268	194,000	33,900	237,000	70,220	10,400	81,311	29,508	18,558	47,769	57,749	14,051	1,016,289
2000	167,935	212,576	35,427	223,000	75,950	11,345	86,630	33,707	20,557	55,883	63,089	17,353	1,078,746
2001	181,553	201,430	27,119	220,000	79,200	10,302	82,500	34,757	19,486	54,650	46,192	16,902	1,046,430
2002	187,198	214,560	30,902	231,000	86,400	9,553	84,236	36,484	20,300	58,900	51,600	16,684	1,100,000
2003	212,981	230,707	33,322	261,000	99,100	10,377	91,760	38,086	21,500	62,498	48,600	17,954	1,210,000
2004	233,994	261,675	28,596	320,000	120,600	10,674	96,980	39,322	22,300	65,550	54,700	19,196	1,360,000
2005[1]	261,855	281,430	30,387	420,000	140,000	10,752	96,764	39,542	23,300	68,570	54,300	20,000	1,540,000
2006[2]	275,042	318,000	33,551	588,000	160,000	11,155	102,000	41,326	23,300	74,000	52,700	23,000	1,800,000

[1] Preliminary.   [2] Estimate.   [3] Iron ore, iron ore concentrates and iron ore agglomerates.   Source: U.S. Geological Survey (USGS)

Salient Statistics of Iron Ore[3] in the United States   In Thousands of Metric Tons

Year	Net Import Reliance As a % of Apparent Consumption	Total	Production Lake Superior	Production Other Regions	Ship-ments	Value Million $ (at Mine)	Average Value $ at Mine Per Ton	Stock, Dec. 31 Mines	Stock, Dec. 31 Con-suming Plants	Stock, Dec. 31 Lake Erie Docks	Imports	Exports	Con-sumption	Total
1999	17	57,700	57,410	NA	58,500	1,550.0	26.47	5,710	17,900	2,770	14,300	6,120	75,100	399.0
2000	19	63,100	62,983	NA	61,000	1,560.0	25.57	9,150	16,800	2,860	15,700	6,150	76,500	420.0
2001	15	46,200	46,100	NA	50,600	1,210.0	23.87	3,800	12,300	1,960	10,700	5,610	65,700	293.0
2002	11	51,600	51,500	NA	51,500	1,340.0	26.04	4,090	12,400	1,820	12,500	6,750	59,700	313.0
2003	11	48,600	NA	NA	46,100	1,490.0	32.30	4,910	10,900	1,630	12,600	6,770	61,600	328.0
2004	6	54,700	NA	NA	54,900	2,080.0	37.92	3,930	NA	NA	11,800	8,400	64,500	371.0
2005	4	54,300	NA	NA	53,200	2,370.0	44.50	2,040	NA	NA	13,000	11,800	60,100	532.0
2006	8	52,700	NA	NA	52,700	2,840.0	53.88	1,380	NA	NA	11,500	8,270	58,200	611.0
2007[1]	E	52,500	NA	NA	50,900		59.64				9,400	9,300	54,800	
2008[2]	E	54,000	NA	NA	56,000		66.00				9,000	11,000	55,000	

[1] Preliminary.   [2] Estimate.   [3] Usable iron ore exclusive of ore containing 5% or more manganese and includes byproduct ore.
NA = Not available.   Source: U.S. Geological Survey (USGS)

U.S. Imports (for Consumption) of Iron Ore[2]   In Thousands of Metric Tons

Year	Australia	Brazil	Canada	Chile	Mauritania	Peru	Sweden	Venezuela	Total
1998	807	5,980	8,520	48	----	126	373	970	16,900
1999	694	5,540	6,860	69	----	63	421	327	14,300
2000	755	6,090	7,990	135	----	40	250	349	15,700
2001	576	4,260	4,530	711	----	71	70	87	10,700
2002	567	5,750	5,540	319	----	86	44	49	12,500
2003	128	4,980	6,970	296	----	77	88	21	12,600
2004	(/3)	5,020	5,830	244	----	56	111	262	11,800
2005	[1]	4,180	7,510	270	----	33	133	148	13,000
2006	8	4,530	6,240	283	----	52	(/3)	23	11,500
2007[1]	----	3,210	5,520	279	----	140	[141]	58	9,400

[1] Preliminary.   [2] Including agglomerates.   [3] Less than 1/2 unit.   Source: U.S. Geological Survey (USGS)

Iron Ore Stocks[2] in the United States, at End of Month   In Thousands of Metric Tons

Year	Jan.	Feb.	Mar.	Apr.	May	June	July	Aug.	Sept.	Oct.	Nov.	Dec.
1999	8,730	12,418	14,944	13,522	12,870	11,982	11,307	9,607	7,710	6,847	6,456	5,714
2000	6,847	11,027	13,209	12,227	11,508	11,258	10,358	10,143	10,022	9,519	9,127	9,146
2001	10,712	13,176	14,681	13,839	11,558	9,364	7,433	6,367	6,345	5,659	4,789	3,803
2002	4,980	6,810	8,270	7,740	7,270	6,330	5,020	4,080	3,420	3,290	3,540	3,210
2003	4,640	7,790	10,100	9,500	8,180	7,080	6,550	6,160	5,820	5,640	5,240	3,860
2004	4,220	7,260	8,780	8,360	7,660	7,080	5,670	4,500	3,470	3,850	3,700	2,990
2005	4,060	6,770	8,410	7,690	7,730	7,370	7,420	7,240	6,550	5,840	6,250	5,750
2006	6,750	9,620	11,900	11,100	10,800	10,100	9,353	8,760	8,090	8,120	7,590	5,880
2007	7,330	10,100	11,800	11,000	10,300	9,870	9,340	8,700	7,950	7,660	7,110	6,490
2008[1]	6,930	9,820	12,400	11,300	9,950	NA	8,170	6,910				

[1] Preliminary.   [2] Through August 1997 includes mines, plants and loading docks plus furnace yards and receiving/transfer docks; Beginning September 1997 includes mines, plants and loading docks.   Source: U.S. Geological Survey (USGS)

Lard

Lard is the layer of fat found along the back and underneath the skin of a hog. The hog's fat is purified by washing it with water, melting it under constant heat, and straining it several times. Lard is an important byproduct of the meatpacking industry. It is valued highly as cooking oil because there is very little smoke when it is heated. However, demand for lard in cooking is declining because of the trend toward healthier eating. Lard is also used for medicinal purposes such as ointments, plasters, liniments, and occasionally as a laxative for children. Lard production is directly proportional to commercial hog production, meaning the largest producers of hogs are the largest producers of lard.

Prices – The average monthly wholesale price of lard in 2008 (through December) rose by +25.6% to a record high of 39.34 cents per pound.

Supply – World production of lard in the 2007-08 marketing year rose by +2.3% yr/yr to 7.849 million metric tons, which was a new record high. The world's largest lard producers were China (with 42% of world production), the U.S (8%), Germany (6%), Brazil (5%), the former USSR (5%), Spain (4%), and Poland (3%). U.S. production of lard in 2007-08 rose 9.0% yr/yr to 1.338 billion pounds.

Demand – U.S. consumption of lard in 2008 (annualized through December) rose +73.5% to 490.602 million pounds, which was a new record high. The current level of consumption is still only about 30% of the consumption of 1.574 billion pounds in 1971.

Exports – U.S. exports of lard in 2007-08 rose by +1.4% to 73.0 million pounds, and accounted for only 6% of U.S. production.

World Production of Lard   In Thousands of Metric Tons

Year	Brazil	Canada	China	France	Germany	Italy	Japan	Poland	Romania	Spain	United States	Ex-USSR	World Total
1999-00	325.7	107.5	2,771.4	164.7	423.5	200.9	65.1	254.7	81.1	262.0	491.6	328.4	6,750.9
2000-01	336.8	112.6	2,832.1	155.7	415.2	195.9	62.3	239.5	72.7	264.9	488.6	314.8	6,748.6
2001-02	361.4	112.1	2,920.9	157.4	422.3	199.3	61.8	252.0	76.9	263.9	508.1	324.6	6,963.7
2002-03	350.2	124.2	3,040.4	156.2	433.7	204.8	59.3	272.5	60.1	280.9	510.0	346.0	7,166.8
2003-04	337.2	127.0	3,154.3	155.5	439.5	208.3	59.3	257.7	69.4	273.4	531.7	334.1	7,310.3
2004-05	344.2	127.4	3,317.8	153.4	456.9	199.2	59.4	243.8	58.9	278.1	532.4	315.1	7,478.0
2005-06[1]	368.9	126.5	3,414.7	151.3	471.3	200.9	55.9	266.4	66.7	282.1	541.3	340.8	7,705.6
2006-07[2]	382.5	126.8	3,204.8	152.2	501.2	207.7	54.2	270.9	76.2	300.5	552.7	382.4	7,670.1
2007-08[3]	393.9	126.5	3,257.3	153.0	509.0	211.9	56.0	269.2	76.8	306.3	599.6	405.1	7,848.8

[1] Preliminary.   [2] Estimate.   [3] Forecast.   *Source: The Oil World*

Supply and Distribution of Lard in the United States   In Millions of Pounds

	Supply			Disappearance						
Year	Production	Stocks Oct. 1	Total Supply	Domestic	Baking or Frying Fats	Margarine[3]	Exports	Total Disappearance	Direct Use	Per Capita (Lbs.)
1999-00	1,091.0	20.8	1,097.8	591.0	234.0	14.0	155.0	739.0	186.0	0.7
2000-01	1,058.0	27.0	1,087.0	558.0	W	12.0	174.0	731.0	221.0	0.8
2001-02	1,058.0	16.0	1,077.0	627.0	W	6.0	103.0	730.0	325.0	1.1
2002-03	1,083.0	14.0	1,105.0	671.0	W	7.0	84.0	755.0	370.0	1.3
2003-04	1,090.0	11.0	1,108.0	640.0	W	16.0	117.0	757.0	369.0	1.3
2004-05	1,117.0	13.0	1,136.0	488.0	W	6.0	289.0	777.0	220.0	0.7
2005-06	1,193.3	14.0	1,207.3	695.0	W	3.0	94.0	789.0	460.0	1.5
2006-07[1]	1,218.5	9.0	1,227.5	716.0	W	W	72.0	788.0	499.0	1.7
2007-08[2]	1,321.9	16.0	1,337.9	773.0	W	W	73.0	846.0	474.0	1.6

[1] Preliminary.   [2] Forecast.   [3] Includes edible tallow.   W = Withheld.
Source: Economic Research Service, U.S. Department of Agriculture (ERS-USDA)

Consumption of Lard (Edible and Inedible) in the United States   In Millions of Pounds

Year	Jan.	Feb.	Mar.	Apr.	May	June	July	Aug.	Sept.	Oct.	Nov.	Dec.	Total
1999	34.6	30.2	28.8	31.1	30.5	32.9	28.9	33.0	29.2	31.2	31.3	30.3	372.1
2000	27.3	25.7	29.1	23.3	30.3	27.6	24.4	31.3	31.1	32.6	29.6	31.7	343.9
2001	27.8	22.2	28.3	24.5	22.5	23.3	21.8	27.1	23.2	27.9	26.7	24.4	299.8
2002	26.4	26.1	21.8	26.7	24.8	21.2	22.9	26.4	23.6	26.4	28.1	28.7	303.2
2003	22.6	22.3	23.4	21.4	23.3	24.0	23.0	21.4	22.5	24.3	20.2	21.0	269.5
2004	22.9	25.8	25.9	23.9	23.5	22.0	19.1	19.7	21.3	22.4	21.9	19.9	268.1
2005	19.0	15.4	21.4	18.7	19.9	20.4	18.9	19.5	20.1	19.7	22.2	17.9	233.1
2006	15.7	16.4	20.6	21.4	20.2	16.7	14.9	17.7	17.8	18.9	22.3	20.9	223.4
2007	21.6	16.2	22.2	19.7	20.5	20.8	22.8	23.9	22.8	31.1	29.7	31.4	282.8
2008[1]	34.8	32.2	44.6	50.7	50.8	44.4	47.8	39.7	44.0	37.5	31.7	32.2	490.6

[1] Preliminary.   *Source: Bureau of the Census, U.S. Department of Commerce*

Lard (monthly average) through December 2008 — Cents per pound

Average Wholesale Price of Lard--Loose, Tank Cars, in Chicago   In Cents Per Pound

Year	Jan.	Feb.	Mar.	Apr.	May	June	July	Aug.	Sept.	Oct.	Nov.	Dec.	Average
1999	16.89	13.91	11.98	13.12	13.43	12.98	11.87	13.89	17.44	20.55	17.74	16.12	14.99
2000	15.66	12.38	11.99	11.96	12.68	12.64	10.32	10.35	11.14	13.04	12.06	12.14	12.20
2001	13.57	11.92	11.07	12.09	11.84	13.38	18.05	24.11	22.00	13.04	13.18	14.92	14.93
2002	12.69	12.50	13.07	12.42	11.38	14.64	14.60	15.00	15.21	14.39	16.28	18.42	14.22
2003	18.61	17.11	16.85	16.72	17.29	18.90	18.93	20.08	23.98	27.50	26.40	25.18	20.63
2004	26.50	25.83	23.77	22.58	21.31	22.50	27.53	32.06	32.38	27.95	27.26	26.50	26.35
2005	22.10	18.30	17.71	20.72	22.95	21.30	18.08	17.75	20.97	27.38	27.76	18.60	21.14
2006	17.16	16.44	16.82	18.00	17.13	17.63	22.21	29.91	31.86	23.55	20.78	22.58	21.17
2007	23.00	23.82	30.75	27.71	28.60	32.64	36.00	35.77	36.00	35.09	33.78	32.66	31.32
2008	33.01	38.33	46.00	43.04	42.27	44.93	52.82	46.50	41.73	37.07	26.40	20.00	39.34

Source: Economic Research Service, U.S. Department of Agriculture (ERS-USDA)

Cold Storage Holdings of all Lard[1] in the United States, on First of Month   In Millions of Pounds

Year	Jan.	Feb.	Mar.	Apr.	May	June	July	Aug.	Sept.	Oct.	Nov.	Dec.
1999	28.4	30.4	30.6	34.0	27.1	39.9	30.7	25.5	29.4	20.8	19.1	22.8
2000	26.7	27.8	29.2	30.1	20.2	22.5	18.9	19.3	17.3	17.4	16.3	16.8
2001	16.0	14.9	14.9	17.9	13.7	13.1	10.3	12.4	11.8	13.6	13.0	11.7
2002	13.2	18.0	16.4	16.5	20.3	22.4	18.9	18.3	12.0	10.5	14.6	11.3
2003	10.5	14.0	19.6	18.7	16.5	13.5	11.9	9.7	8.4	9.3	10.1	12.4
2004	13.3	19.8	18.6	20.3	20.5	15.0	12.9	10.8	10.3	11.8	11.4	13.2
2005	13.7	14.6	20.6	19.0	17.8	12.3	12.0	12.3	12.5	13.0	12.2	14.7
2006	9.6	11.5	13.7	13.6	9.3	9.9	13.0	12.4	13.0	11.5	16.1	16.0
2007	16.4	14.9	13.3	18.5	10.9	14.6	11.3	12.8	11.0	9.2	14.6	18.8
2008[2]	14.0	22.4	20.4	22.9	23.0	19.5	22.7	13.6	18.0	17.8	16.1	20.4

[1] Stocks in factories and warehouses (except that in hands of retailers).   [2] Preliminary.   *Source: Bureau of the Census, U.S. Department of Commerce*

Lead

Lead (symbol Pb) is a dense, toxic, bluish-gray metallic element, and is the heaviest stable element. Lead was one of the first known metals. The ancients used lead in face powders, rouges, mascaras, paints, condiments, wine preservatives, and water supply plumbing. The Romans were slowly poisoned from lead because of its diverse daily usage.

Lead is usually found in ore with zinc, silver, and most often copper. The most common lead ore is galena, containing 86.6% lead. Cerussite and angleside are other common varieties of lead. More than half of the lead currently used comes from recycling.

Lead is used in building construction, bullets and shot, tank and pipe lining, storage batteries, and electric cable sheathing. Lead is used extensively as a protective shielding for radioactive material (e.g., X-ray apparatus) because of its high density and nuclear properties. Lead is also part of solder, pewter, and fusible alloys.

Lead futures and options trade at the London Metal Exchange (LME). The LME lead futures contract calls for the delivery of 25 metric tons of at least 99.970% purity lead ingots (pigs). The contract is priced in U.S. dollars per metric ton. Lead first started trading on the LME in 1903.

Prices – The price of lead rose to its peak of about $3,400 per metric ton in late February of 2008 and except for a brief rally in June/July 2008 declined steadily from there. By the end of 2008, the price had dropped to about $900 per metric ton. The price started to rally early in 2009 but leveled off in the range of about $1,000 to $1,100 per metric ton by February.

Supply – World smelter production of lead (both primary and secondary) in 2007 (the latest data available) rose +4.9% yr/yr to 8.280 million metric tons to post a new record high production level. The world's largest smelter producers of lead (both primary and secondary) are China with 36% of world production in 2006, followed by the U.S. with 16%, Germany with 4%, and the UK with 4%.

U.S. mine production of recoverable lead rose +3.6% yr/yr to 434,000 metric tons in 2007, up from its 12-year low of 419,000 in 2006. Missouri was responsible for 92% of U.S. production, with the remainder produced mainly by Idaho and Montana. Lead recovered from scrap in the U.S. (secondary production) rose +0.5% yr/yr in 2008 (through October, annualized) to 1.196 million metric tons, to post a new record high. The amount of lead recovered from scrap is more than twice the amount of lead produced in the U.S. from mines (primary production). The value of U.S. secondary lead production in 2007 rose sharply by +62.6% to $3.220 billion, which was another new record high.

Demand – U.S. lead consumption in 2007 (through October, annualized) rose + 2.4% to 1.615 million metric tons, continuing to recover from the 10-year low of 1.417 million metric tons seen in 2004. The record level of U.S. lead consumption was 1.680 million metric tons posted in 1999.

Trade – The U.S. relied on imports for 8% of its lead consumption in 2001 but has been a net exporter ever since. U.S. imports of lead pigs and bars in 2007 fell -20.5% yr/yr to 263,000 metric tons. U.S. lead exports in 2007 were comprised of ore concentrate (300,000 metric tons), scrap (128,800 metric tons), unwrought lead (51,700 metric tons), and wrought lead (4,600 metric tons).

World Smelter (Primary and Secondary) Production of Lead   In Thousands of Metric Tons

Year	Australia[3]	Belgium[4]	Canada[3]	China[2]	France	Germany	Italy	Japan	Mexico[3]	Spain	United Kingdom[3]	United States	World Total
1999	272.8	103.2	266.4	918.0	279.0	373.6	215.3	293.4	221.1	96.0	348.1	1,460	6,280
2000	251.8	118.0	284.8	1,100.0	258.0	414.5	235.0	311.7	253.2	120.0	337.2	1,470	6,650
2001	303.0	96.0	230.9	1,200.0	238.0	373.4	203.0	302.4	253.5	98.0	366.0	1,390	6,600
2002	304.0	88.0	251.6	1,330.0	204.0	379.9	205.0	285.8	237.2	116.0	374.6	1,360	6,800
2003	295.0	65.0	223.4	1,580.0	96.7	356.9	246.0	295.3	247.5	102.0	364.6	1,380	6,990
2004	268.0	63.0	241.2	1,940.0	105.6	359.2	202.0	282.9	217.4	105.0	245.9	1,280	7,070
2005	263.0	83.4	229.4	2,390.0	104.4	348.1	211.5	274.6	226.5	110.0	304.4	1,300	7,640
2006[1]	233.0	54.0	235.0	2,720.0	104.2	320.5	190.5	279.4	212.5	131.0	307.7	1,310	7,890
2007[2]	227.0	117.0	230.0	3,000.0	104.2	320.0	210.0	276.3	212.0	130.0	300.0	1,300	8,280

[1] Preliminary.   [2] Estimate.   [3] Refineded & bullion.   [4] Includes scrap.   *Source: U.S. Geological Survey (USGS)*

Consumption of Lead in the United States, by Products   In Metric Tons

Year	Ammunition	Bearing Metals	Pipes, Traps & Bends[2]	Cable Covering	Calking Lead	Casting Metals	Other Metal Products[3]	Total Other Oxides[4]	Sheet Lead	Solder	Storage Battery -- Grids, Post, etc.	Oxides	Brass and Bronze	Total Consumption
1999	58,300	1,570	2,020	2,410	971	34,300	7,130	58,200	15,400	13,100	765,000	707,000	3,940	1,680,000
2000	63,700	1,490	2,010	W	1,140	35,100	25,800	52,400	23,800	11,500	796,000	690,000	3,670	1,720,000
2001	53,600	837	2,370	W	927	31,800	17,100	43,900	22,400	6,120	655,000	694,000	2,590	1,550,000
2002	57,600	406	2,250	W	1,060	34,800	24,200	51,900	25,600	6,450	554,000	641,000	2,730	1,440,000
2003	48,800	13,500	1,550	W	822	31,700	9,730	35,600	24,400	6,310	523,000	642,000	2,810	1,390,000
2004	61,500	1,300	W	W	W	17,900	W	25,700	31,600	7,440	657,000	630,000	2,390	1,480,000
2005	61,300	1,180	1,220	W	W	30,400	22,200	14,100	29,100	8,370	579,000	705,000	2,100	1,490,000
2006	65,700	1,240	1,440	W	W	29,900	23,400	16,000	28,400	7,280	586,000	710,000	3,130	1,490,000
2007[1]	69,400	1,410	1,320	W	W	31,500	23,500	15,800	28,600	7,220	640,000	738,000	2,870	1,570,000

[1] Preliminary.   [2] Including building.   [3] Including terne metal, type metal, and lead consumed in foil, collapsible tubes, annealing, plating, galvanizing and fishing weights.   [4] Includes paints, glass and ceramic products, and other pigments and chemicals.   W = Withheld.
Source: U.S. Geological Survey (USGS)

Salient Statistics of Lead in the United States   In Thousands of Metric Tons

Year	Net Import Reliance as a % of Apparent Consumption	Production of Refined Lead From Domestic Ores[3]	Foreign Ores[3]	Total Primary	Total Value of Refined Million $	As Soft Lead	In Anti-monial Lead	In Other Alloys	Total	Total Value of Secondary Million USD	Stocks, Dec. 31 Primary	Con-sumer[4]	New York	London
1998	21	337.0	W	337.0	336.0	667.0	417.0	16.1	1,120.0	1,110.0	10.9	77.9	45.27	23.96
1999	20	350.0	W	350.0	337.0	635.0	444.0	18.1	1,110.0	1,070.0	12.3	78.7	43.72	22.78
2000	13	341.0	W	341.0	328.0	651.0	428.0	36.8	1,130.0	1,090.0	18.6	106.0	43.57	20.57
2001	8	290.0	W	290.0	279.0	734.0	291.0	75.9	1,100.0	1,060.0	W	100.0	43.64	21.58
2002	E	262.0	W	262.0	252.0	754.0	289.0	72.8	1,120.0	1,070.0	W	111.0	43.56	20.52
2003	E	245.0	W	245.0	236.0	829.0	303.0	4.2	1,140.0	1,110.0	W	84.6	43.76	23.34
2004	E	148.0	W	148.0	143.0	841.0	283.0	3.0	1,130.0	1,370.0	W	59.0	55.14	40.19
2005	E	143.0	W	143.0		869.0	271.0	4.5	1,150.0	1,550.0	W	46.8	61.03	44.23
2006[1]	E	153.0	W	153.0		948.0	200.0	12.4	1,160.0	1,980.0	W	54.8	77.40	58.00
2007[2]	E	123.0	W	123.0		1,020.0	160.0	2.4	1,180.0	3,220.0	W	49.4	123.84	117.00

[1] Preliminary.   [2] Estimate.   [3] And base bullion.   [4] Also at secondary smelters.   W = Withheld.   E = Net exporter.
Source: U.S. Geological Survey (USGS)

U.S. Foreign Trade of Lead   In Thousands of Metric Tons

Year	Exports Ore Con-centrate	Un-wrought Lead[3]	Wrought Lead[4]	Scrap	Ash & Re-sidues[5]	Imports for Consumption Ores, Flue Dust or Fume & Mattes	Base Bullion	Pigs & Bars	Re-claimed Scrap, Etc.	Value Million $	Ore, Flue, Dust & Matte Aus-tralia	Can-ada	Peru	Pigs & Bars Can-ada	Mexico	Peru
1998	72.4	24.1	15.4	99.2	9.0	32.7	0.5	267.0	6	191.9	2.4	6.5	18.5	181.0	63.6	11.4
1999	93.5	23.4	13.9	117.0	1.4	12.3	0.1	311.0	----	196.5	0.1	1.2	8.8	198.0	27.2	6.9
2000	117.0	21.4	27.2	71.6	11.3	31.2	0.1	356.0	0.0	217.1	----	6	10.8	216.0	18.4	1.8
2001	181.0	17.0	17.7	108.0	14.2	2.2	----	271.0	10.2	166.8	----	----	----	167.0	12.4	2.3
2002	241.0	31.4	11.7	106.0	----	0.0	----	210.0	2.6	124.9	----	----	----	172.0	7.5	----
2003	253.0	92.1	30.5	92.8	----	----	----	175.0	4.2	111.9	----	----	----	167.0	8.3	----
2004	292.0	58.6	23.8	56.3	----	----	----	197.0	4.8	235.3	----	----	----	166.0	8.8	7.3
2005	390.2	45.5	19.0	67.3	----	----	----	298.0	3.3	334.8	----	----	----	190.0	15.2	23.9
2006[1]	297.6	52.7	15.8	120.9	----	----	0.5	331.0	1.6	235.3	----	----	----	222.0	15.8	34.6
2007[2]	300.0	51.8	4.6	128.8	----	----	2.0	263.0	2.4	334.8	----	----	----	208.0	35.6	16.5

[1] Preliminary.   [2] Estimate.   [3] And lead alloys.   [4] Blocks, pigs, etc.   [5] Less than 1/2 unit.   *Source: U.S. Geological Survey (USGS)*

Annual Mine Production of Recoverable Lead in the United States   In Metric Tons

Year	Total	Idaho	Missouri	Montana	Other States	Missouri's % of Total
1998	481,000	W	439,000	7,310	35,100	91%
1999	503,000	W	464,000	7,950	31,200	92%
2000	449,000	W	410,000	W	38,700	91%
2001	454,000	W	423,000	W	30,900	93%
2002	440,000	W	428,000	W	12,300	97%
2003	449,000	W	432,000	W	17,200	96%
2004	430,000	W	407,000	W	23,400	95%
2005	426,000	W	397,000	W	29,500	93%
2006[1]	419,000	W	393,000	W	26,100	94%
2007[2]	434,000	W	400,000	W	34,200	92%

[1] Preliminary.   [2] Estimate.   W = Withheld, included in Other States.   *Source: U.S. Geological Survey (USGS)*

Mine Production of Recoverable Lead in the United States   In Thousands of Metric Tons

Year	Jan.	Feb.	Mar.	Apr.	May	June	July	Aug.	Sept.	Oct.	Nov.	Dec.	Total
1999	41.2	42.1	44.4	43.1	41.7	42.6	47.2	43.6	41.5	41.2	37.8	38.1	505.0
2000	35.1	36.7	43.0	37.5	37.4	37.8	33.0	36.8	36.8	32.4	38.8	36.9	447.0
2001	42.9	37.8	39.4	33.7	35.0	32.2	38.2	39.6	32.4	39.5	32.1	35.4	450.0
2002	39.5	35.5	41.2	36.1	39.3	36.1	35.0	39.6	33.2	34.8	34.1	34.2	438.6
2003	33.7	34.9	38.5	36.2	38.8	39.2	41.3	38.0	38.3	37.2	34.0	33.9	444.0
2004	33.4	32.8	33.5	35.1	31.2	33.1	33.8	36.9	36.9	36.2	35.0	31.8	409.7
2005	31.1	31.1	34.6	35.2	33.4	41.4	39.5	37.4	38.2	37.9	34.6	37.9	432.3
2006	36.7	33.3	38.1	33.6	33.4	33.9	36.6	36.3	37.0	38.0	35.0	29.6	421.5
2007	38.1	33.9	36.7	31.6	36.9	34.5	38.7	41.3	34.6	39.4	31.5	37.1	434.3
2008[1]	38.0	36.9	36.1	33.0	31.0	34.4	37.8	34.2	33.8	34.0			419.0

[1] Preliminary.   *Source: U.S. Geological Survey (USGS)*

LEAD

Lead (monthly average) through December 2008 — Cents per pound

Average Price of Pig Lead, U.S. Primary Producers (Common Corroding)[1] In Cents Per Pound

Year	Jan.	Feb.	Mar.	Apr.	May	June	July	Aug.	Sept.	Oct.	Nov.	Dec.	Average
1999	45.00	45.00	45.00	45.00	45.00	45.00	45.00	45.00	45.00	45.00	45.00	45.00	45.00
2000	45.00	45.00	45.00	45.00	45.00	45.00	45.00	45.00	45.00	45.00	45.00	45.00	45.00
2001	45.00	45.00	45.00	45.00	45.00	45.00	45.00	45.00	45.00	45.00	45.00	45.00	45.00
2002	45.00	45.00	45.00	45.00	45.00	45.00	45.00	45.00	45.00	45.00	45.00	45.00	45.00
2003	23.14	24.65	23.81	23.13	24.56	24.77	26.93	26.05	27.23	30.16	32.09	35.46	26.83
2004	38.48	44.79	45.30	39.93	42.44	45.16	48.20	47.46	48.08	48.01	49.54	49.75	45.60
2005	50.46	52.20	54.00	53.25	53.41	53.26	47.22	47.53	49.76	54.01	54.68	59.63	52.45
2006	66.16	67.16	63.28	61.58	61.16	51.92	56.07	61.48	69.24	77.64	82.09	86.22	67.00
2007	83.62	88.42	94.72	98.73	103.14	117.95	148.17	148.47	153.50	175.59	159.80	124.81	124.74
2008	125.37	146.72	141.77	134.92	106.42	88.93	93.68	92.49	90.49	73.02	65.52	49.58	100.74

[1] New York Delivery. *Source: American Metal Market*

Refiners Production[1] of Lead in the United States In Metric Tons

Year	Jan.	Feb.	Mar.	Apr.	May	June	July	Aug.	Sept.	Oct.	Nov.	Dec.	Total
1999	NA	NA	NA	NA	NA	NA	NA	NA	NA	NA	NA	NA	350,000
2000	NA	NA	NA	NA	NA	NA	NA	NA	NA	NA	NA	NA	341,000
2001	NA	NA	NA	NA	NA	NA	NA	NA	NA	NA	NA	NA	290,000
2002	NA	NA	NA	NA	NA	NA	NA	NA	NA	NA	NA	NA	262,000
2003	NA	NA	NA	NA	NA	NA	NA	NA	NA	NA	NA	NA	245,000
2004	NA	NA	NA	NA	NA	NA	NA	NA	NA	NA	NA	NA	NA
2005	NA	NA	NA	NA	NA	NA	NA	NA	NA	NA	NA	NA	143,000
2006	NA	NA	NA	NA	NA	NA	NA	NA	NA	NA	NA	NA	143,000
2007	NA	NA	NA	NA	NA	NA	NA	NA	NA	NA	NA	NA	
2008[2]	NA	NA	NA	NA	NA	NA	NA	NA	NA	NA			

[1] Represents refined lead produced from domestic ores by primary smelters plus small amounts of secondary material passing through these smelters. Includes GSA metal purchased for remelt. [2] Preliminary. NA = Not available. *Source: U.S. Geological Survey (USGS)*

Total Stocks of Lead[1] in the United States at Refiners, at End of Month   In Metric Tons

Year	Jan.	Feb.	Mar.	Apr.	May	June	July	Aug.	Sept.	Oct.	Nov.	Dec.
1999	NA	NA	NA	NA	NA	NA	NA	NA	NA	NA	NA	12,300
2000	NA	NA	NA	NA	NA	NA	NA	NA	NA	NA	NA	18,600
2001	NA	NA	NA	NA	NA	NA	NA	NA	NA	NA	NA	NA
2002	NA	NA	NA	NA	NA	NA	NA	NA	NA	NA	NA	NA
2003	NA	NA	NA	NA	NA	NA	NA	NA	NA	NA	NA	NA
2004	NA	NA	NA	NA	NA	NA	NA	NA	NA	NA	NA	NA
2005	NA	NA	NA	NA	NA	NA	NA	NA	NA	NA	NA	NA
2006	NA	NA	NA	NA	NA	NA	NA	NA	NA	NA	NA	NA
2007	NA	NA	NA	NA	NA	NA	NA	NA	NA	NA	NA	NA
2008[2]	NA	NA	NA	NA	NA	NA	NA	NA	NA	NA		

[1] Primary refineries.   [2] Preliminary.   NA = Not available.   *Source: U.S. Geological Survey (USGS)*

Total[1] Lead Consumption in the United States   In Thousands of Metric Tons

Year	Jan.	Feb.	Mar.	Apr.	May	June	July	Aug.	Sept.	Oct.	Nov.	Dec.	Total
1999	128.0	129.0	130.0	127.0	128.0	130.0	137.0	136.0	141.0	136.0	140.0	133.0	1,680
2000	139.0	139.0	139.0	139.0	140.0	140.0	135.0	141.0	139.0	139.0	136.0	132.0	1,660
2001	145.0	135.0	133.0	130.0	138.0	136.0	135.0	136.0	142.0	146.0	138.0	138.0	1,652
2002	132.0	131.0	133.0	142.0	142.0	144.0	143.0	145.0	141.0	145.0	142.0	133.0	1,673
2003	134.0	129.0	126.0	120.0	121.0	121.0	121.0	122.0	123.0	127.0	122.0	125.0	1,491
2004	119.0	118.0	119.0	119.0	117.0	119.0	118.0	118.0	117.0	117.0	117.0	119.0	1,417
2005	125.0	117.0	109.0	108.0	134.0	130.0	124.0	129.0	126.0	126.0	126.0	126.0	1,480
2006	124.0	130.0	129.0	128.0	128.0	128.0	125.0	126.0	127.0	128.0	126.0	126.0	1,525
2007	130.0	128.0	129.0	128.0	131.0	139.0	131.0	134.0	132.0	137.0	132.0	127.0	1,578
2008[2]	140.0	136.0	130.0	135.0	135.0	141.0	134.0	129.0	134.0	132.0			1,615

[1] Represents total consumption of primary & secondary lead as metal, in chemicals, or in alloys.   [2] Preliminary.   *Source: U.S. Geological Survey (USGS)*

Lead Recovered from Scrap in the United States   In Thousands of Metric Tons (Lead Content)

Year	Jan.	Feb.	Mar.	Apr.	May	June	July	Aug.	Sept.	Oct.	Nov.	Dec.	Total
1999	89.5	89.1	88.9	91.0	90.2	91.1	81.3	91.9	91.6	93.5	91.4	93.1	1,110.0
2000	91.0	88.0	91.1	91.4	90.5	91.3	88.6	95.1	94.0	96.0	95.4	93.7	1,110.0
2001	90.3	90.4	86.7	92.6	93.7	93.6	90.4	95.1	93.9	96.7	94.6	94.6	1,112.6
2002	89.3	82.3	88.2	93.1	93.9	93.6	88.0	96.1	93.3	97.5	95.0	95.7	1,106.0
2003	95.7	83.6	86.2	85.1	94.0	94.8	95.7	93.9	93.3	102.0	93.7	95.2	1,113.2
2004	94.0	94.2	96.3	97.9	94.4	96.6	97.4	96.3	94.8	96.8	94.9	95.4	1,149.0
2005	94.4	95.1	86.8	86.8	87.1	94.6	94.7	94.8	93.0	95.9	96.4	92.4	1,112.0
2006	90.2	96.7	97.4	98.2	99.5	95.7	94.9	97.0	95.6	98.4	98.4	95.9	1,157.9
2007	99.0	96.5	98.6	93.5	94.5	100.0	103.0	103.0	101.0	104.0	104.0	94.6	1,191.7
2008[1]	104.0	98.2	102.0	100.0	105.0	102.0	92.0	102.0	91.7	100.0			1,196.3

[1] Preliminary.   *Source: U.S. Geological Survey (USGS)*

Domestic Shipments[1] of Lead in the United States, by Refiners   In Thousands of Short Tons

Year	Jan.	Feb.	Mar.	Apr.	May	June	July	Aug.	Sept.	Oct.	Nov.	Dec.	Total
1989	29.3	28.5	32.2	35.7	45.1	36.4	32.8	41.5	40.0	44.2	40.2	31.1	437.1
1990	39.3	33.9	39.1	33.5	38.4	32.9	32.6	38.9	36.6	38.9	37.9	31.7	433.7
1991	35.4	33.8	34.3	39.8	33.9	26.0	31.8	37.9	35.1	35.7	28.7	26.7	399.2
1992	31.3	23.9	30.4	26.3	25.6	27.2	27.3	28.7	26.3	28.5	26.3	21.7	323.5
1993	24.6	23.6	32.5	30.0	31.3	35.1	28.9	34.0	35.5	35.5	31.7	33.5	376.2
1994	35.9	32.8	35.2	32.7	34.7	36.7	31.6	33.4	34.8	34.3	34.0	33.3	409.3
1995	36.5	30.3	35.1	31.1	33.7	31.9	28.6	40.3	34.9	40.9	33.2	29.8	406.4
1996	37.2	32.4	29.5	30.2	29.4	26.7	27.7	33.5	30.1	33.5	28.1	27.6	366.0
1997[2]	31.5	27.8	24.7	35.2	39.2	36.1	33.4	29.4	26.4	31.5	30.4	28.1	377.8
1998[2]	Data no longer available.												

[1] Includes GSA metal.   [2] Preliminary.   *Source: American Metal Market (AMM)*

Lumber and Plywood

Humans have utilized lumber for construction for thousands of years, but due to the heaviness of timber and the manual methods of harvesting, large-scale lumbering didn't occur until the mechanical advances of the Industrial Revolution. Lumber is produced from both hardwood and softwood. Hardwood lumber comes from deciduous trees that have broad leaves. Most hardwood lumber is used for miscellaneous industrial applications, primarily wood pallets, and includes oak, gum, maple, and ash. Hardwood species with beautiful colors and patterns are used for such high-grade products as furniture, flooring, paneling, and cabinets and include black walnut, black cherry, and red oak. Wood from cone-bearing trees is called softwood, regardless of its actual hardness. Most lumber from the U.S. is softwood. Softwoods, such as southern yellow pine, Douglas fir, ponderosa pine, and true firs, are primarily used as structural lumber such as 2x4s and 2x6s, poles, paper and cardboard.

Plywood consists of several thin layers of veneer bonded together with adhesives. The veneer sheets are layered so that the grain of one sheet is perpendicular to that of the next, which makes plywood exceptionally strong for its weight. Most plywood has from three to nine layers of wood. Plywood manufacturers use both hard and soft woods, although hardwoods serve primarily for appearance and are not as strong as those made from softwoods. Plywood is primarily used in construction, particularly for floors, roofs, walls, and doors. Homebuilding and remodeling account for two-thirds of U.S. lumber consumption. The price of lumber and plywood is highly correlated with the strength of the U.S. home-building market.

The forest and wood products industry is dominated by Weyerhaeuser Company (ticker symbol WY), which has about $20 billion in annual sales. Weyerhaeuser is a forest products conglomerate that engages not only in growing and harvesting timber, but also in the production and distribution of forest products, real estate development, and construction of single-family homes. Forest products include wood products, pulp and paper, and containerboard. The timberland segment of the business manages 7.2 million acres of company-owned land and 800,000 acres of leased commercial forestlands in North America. The company's Canadian division has renewable, long-term licenses on about 35 million acres of forestland in five Canadian provinces. In order to maximize its long-term yield from its acreage, Weyerhaeuser engages in a number of forest management activities such as extensive planting, suppression of non-merchantable species, thinning, fertilization, and operational pruning.

Lumber futures and options are traded on the Chicago Mercantile Exchange (CME). The CME's lumber futures contract calls for the delivery of 111,000 board feet (one 73 foot rail car) of random length 8 to 12 foot 2 x 4s, the type used in construction. The contract is priced in terms of dollars per thousand board feet.

Prices – CME lumber futures prices fluctuated widely around $220 between January and May of 2008, hitting a low of $188 in March and a high of $229 in April. Starting in early May the price began a rally that went to a high of $266 in August. From there the price fell steadily through December to end the year at about $170. The downmove continued into early 2009.

Supply – The U.S. led the world in the production of industrial round wood but in 2007 (latest data available) production fell -4.6% yr/yr to 393.313 million cubic meters, followed by Canada with 192.995 million cubic meters (+4.2% yr/yr), and Russia with 162.500 million cubic meters (+12.0% yr/yr). The U.S. also led the world in the production of plywood with 12.437 million cubic meters of production in 2007 (-8.9% yr/yr), followed by Russia with 2.763 million cubic meters (+5.7% yr/yr), and then Canada with 2.065 million cubic meters (8.3% yr/yr). U.S. softwood lumber production in latest data from the series of 2006 (through November, annualized) fell 4.4% yr/yr to 38.503 billion board feet.

Demand – U.S. consumption of softwood lumber in 2006, the last full reporting year, fell by 1.9% yr/yr to 63.080 billion board feet.

Trade – U.S. total lumber imports in 2006, the last full reporting year, fell 1.8% to 25.285 billion board feet, down from last year's record high. U.S. imports of hardwood in 2006 fell by 3.1% to 1,042 million board feet. U.S. imports of softwood in 2006 fell by 1.7% to 24.214 billion board feet. The leading softwood import was spruce with 1.730 billion board feet of imports in 20065, followed by cedar at 721 million board feet.

Total U.S. exports of lumber in 2006 rose +3.6% yr/yr to 2.779 billion board feet, which is a 6-year high. The record high was 4.528 billion board feet in 1988. U.S. exports of hardwood in 2006 rose by +21.7% yr/yr to 1.797 billion board feet. U.S. exports of softwood in 2006 rose by 9.5% yr/yr to 982 million board feet. The largest types of U.S. softwood exports in 2006 were southern pine with 232 million board feet of exports, Ponderosa white pine (114 million board feet), and Douglas Fir (76 million board feet). The world's largest exporter of plywood in 2007 was Russia with 1.503 million cubic meters of exports, followed by Finland with 1.229 million cubic meters, and Canada with 964,000 thousand cubic meters.

World Production of Industrial Roundwood by Selected Countries   In Thousands of Cubic Meters

Year	Austria	Canada	Czech Republic	Finland	France	Germany	Poland	Romania	Russia	Spain	Sweden	Turkey	United States
1998	10,858	173,901	13,171	49,541	32,718	36,441	21,793	8,629	77,400	13,164	54,700	9,979	422,034
1999	10,988	190,988	13,363	49,593	33,237	35,063	22,842	9,484	94,600	13,160	52,800	10,065	423,298
2000	10,416	198,918	13,501	50,147	43,440	51,088	24,489	10,116	105,800	12,721	57,400	10,429	420,619
2001	10,562	182,945	13,364	47,727	37,471	36,502	23,375	9,806	117,800	13,276	57,300	9,976	403,212
2002	11,810	195,211	13,534	48,529	32,736	37,755	24,995	12,092	118,600	13,850	60,700	11,191	404,958
2003	13,719	176,799	13,960	49,246	30,540	45,415	27,204	12,537	126,600	14,075	61,200	10,729	405,613
2004	12,943	205,273	14,411	49,281	31,289	48,657	29,337	12,794	130,600	14,235	61,400	11,225	418,131
2005	12,786	200,247	14,285	47,116	28,253	50,905	28,531	11,542	138,000	13,351	92,300	11,202	423,456
2006[1]	14,430	185,196	16,333	45,521	28,592	54,000	28,767	9,454	144,600	14,109	58,700	12,253	412,134
2007[2]	16,521	192,995	16,738	51,662	29,330	68,029	32,461	11,572	162,000	12,546	71,300	13,019	393,313

[1] Preliminary.   [2] Estimate.   NA = Not available.   *Source: Food and Agriculture Organization of the United Nations (FAO-UN)*

LUMBER AND PLYWOOD

Lumber Production and Consumption in the United States   In Millions of Board Feet

Year	California Redwood	Inland Region	Southern Pine	West Coast	Other Softwood	Total Softwood	Inland Region	California Redwood	Southern Pine	West Coast	Other Softwood	Softwood Imports	Total Softwood
	Production						Domestic Consumption						
1998	1,391	7,298	16,151	7,797	2,040	34,677	7,256	1,409	15,788	7,502	1,567	18,686	52,209
1999	1,325	7,580	16,922	8,625	2,153	36,605	7,445	1,358	16,525	8,115	1,641	19,178	54,262
2000	1,320	7,078	16,672	8,782	2,115	35,967	6,926	1,257	16,374	8,300	1,629	19,449	53,934
2001	1,121	6,563	16,094	8,764	2,035	34,577	6,490	1,132	15,937	8,471	1,724	20,075	53,828
2002	1,035	6,759	16,686	9,244	2,106	35,830	6,641	1,056	16,571	8,966	1,832	20,986	56,050
2003	977	6,716	16,841	9,904	2,151	36,591	6,709	976	16,759	9,585	1,751	21,188	56,969
2004	1,049	6,742	18,050	10,934	2,300	39,075	6,600	1,021	17,935	10,705	1,971	23,584	61,819
2005	1,048	21,386	18,986	11,599	2,139	40,458	6,635	1,060	18,829	11,346	1,781	24,626	64,279
I	280	1,789	4,725	2,914	542	10,250	1,712	246	4,615	2,708	455	5,632	15,368
II	265	16,394	4,939	2,928	548	10,374	1,690	283	4,934	2,948	472	6,685	17,014
III	271	1,692	4,731	-2,877	535	10,106	1,709	291	4,720	2,844	446	6,297	16,308
IV	232	1,511	4,591	2,880	514	9,728	1,524	240	4,560	2,846	408	6,012	15,589
2006¹	972	6,404	19,560	11,700	2,156	40,792	6,320	760	18,772	11,332	1,680	24,212	63,080
I	243	1,601	4,890	2,925	539	10,198	1,580	190	4,693	2,833	420	6,053	15,770
II													
III													

¹ Preliminary.   Source: American Forest & Paper Association (AFPA)

U.S. Housing Starts: Seasonally Adjusted Annual Rate   In Thousands

Year	Jan.	Feb.	Mar.	Apr.	May	June	July	Aug.	Sept.	Oct.	Nov.	Dec.	Average
1999	1,748	1,670	1,710	1,553	1,611	1,559	1,669	1,648	1,635	1,608	1,648	1,708	1,647
2000	1,636	1,737	1,604	1,626	1,575	1,559	1,463	1,541	1,507	1,549	1,551	1,532	1,573
2001	1,600	1,625	1,590	1,649	1,605	1,636	1,670	1,567	1,562	1,540	1,602	1,568	1,601
2002	1,698	1,829	1,642	1,592	1,764	1,717	1,655	1,633	1,804	1,648	1,753	1,788	1,710
2003	1,853	1,629	1,726	1,643	1,751	1,867	1,897	1,833	1,939	1,967	2,083	2,057	1,854
2004	1,911	1,846	1,998	2,003	1,981	1,828	2,002	2,024	1,905	2,072	1,782	2,042	1,950
2005	2,144	2,207	1,864	2,061	2,025	2,068	2,054	2,095	2,151	2,065	2,147	1,994	2,073
2006	2,273	2,119	1,969	1,821	1,942	1,802	1,737	1,650	1,720	1,491	1,570	1,649	1,812
2007	1,382	1,486	1,492	1,487	1,436	1,458	1,371	1,337	1,185	1,275	1,179	1,000	1,341
2008¹	1,064	1,107	988	1,004	982	1,089	949	854	824	767	655	560	904

¹ Preliminary.   Total Privately owned.   Source: Bureau of the Census, U.S. Department of Commerce

Stocks (Gross) of Softwood Lumber in the United States, on First of Month   In Millions of Board Feet

Year	Jan.	Feb.	Mar.	Apr.	May	June	July	Aug.	Sept.	Oct.	Nov.	Dec.
1997	3,973	4,019	4,113	4,067	3,963	4,017	3,915	3,871	3,875	3,927	3,925	3,865
1998	3,884	3,970	4,048	4,062	4,158	4,084	NA	NA	NA	NA	NA	NA
1999	3,519	3,595	3,688	3,726	3,698	3,581	3,512	3,485	3,533	3,491	3,562	3,536
2000	3,639	3,704	3,811	3,887	3,960	2,738	3,902	3,936	3,878	3,848	3,957	3,875
2001	3,919	3,864	4,013	3,951	4,095	3,955	NA	3,961	3,938	4,076	4,100	4,248
2002	4,784	3,735	3,826	3,756	3,273	3,316	3,242	3,230	3,136	3,098	3,173	3,127
2003	3,175	3,177	3,202	3,249	3,308	3,211	3,075	3,085	3,081	3,158	3,076	3,055
2004	2,904	2,904	2,904	2,873	2,966	2,966	2,966	2,966	3,030	3,030	3,031	2,450
2005	2,912	2,994	3,076	3,056	2,866	2,687	2,554	2,641	2,497	2,986	3,059	2,913
2006¹	3,004	3,100	3,111	2,978	2,952	2,925	2,918	2,917	2,956	2,960	2,954	

¹ Preliminary.   NA = Not available.   Source: American Forest & Paper Association (AFPA)

Lumber (Softwood) Production in the United States   In Millions of Board Feet

Year	Jan.	Feb.	Mar.	Apr.	May	June	July	Aug.	Sept.	Oct.	Nov.	Dec.	Total
1997	3,012	2,791	2,866	3,149	2,890	3,027	3,097	2,889	2,905	3,094	2,536	2,487	34,743
1998	2,767	2,760	2,928	3,084	2,647	3,051	3,079	2,930	2,953	3,167	2,667	2,754	34,787
1999	2,783	2,921	3,190	3,227	3,071	3,318	3,115	3,054	2,992	3,096	2,954	2,795	36,516
2000	3,020	3,128	3,474	3,058	3,276	3,249	2,730	2,971	2,839	3,041	2,761	2,342	35,889
2001	2,832	2,457	2,918	2,928	NA	3,032	2,812	3,240	2,743	3,188	2,740	2,372	34,104
2002	3,019	2,761	3,074	3,284	3,126	3,200	3,104	3,128	2,862	3,386	2,599	2,482	36,025
2003	2,971	2,801	2,937	2,994	2,931	3,109	3,088	2,981	3,052	3,335	2,793	2,740	35,732
2004	3,037	2,978	3,380	3,434	3,021	3,329	3,227	3,271	3,147	3,321	3,082	2,931	38,158
2005	3,233	3,169	3,596	3,486	3,339	3,535	3,248	3,490	3,385	3,574	3,180	3,052	40,287
2006¹	3,511	3,216	3,550	3,294	3,360	3,420	3,195	3,349	2,877	3,154	2,368		38,503

¹ Preliminary.   Source: American Forest & Paper Association (AFPA)

LUMBER AND PLYWOOD

Lumber and Plywood (monthly average) through December 2008 — USD per 1,000 board feet

Lumber (Softwood) Shipments in the United States — In Millions of Board Feet

Year	Jan.	Feb.	Mar.	Apr.	May	June	July	Aug.	Sept.	Oct.	Nov.	Dec.	Total
1997	2,966	2,697	2,890	3,253	2,834	3,126	3,139	2,885	2,852	3,096	2,598	2,461	34,797
1998	2,685	2,685	2,863	3,019	2,684	3,175	3,132	2,963	2,948	3,205	2,703	2,865	34,927
1999	2,689	2,829	3,177	3,227	3,071	3,383	3,141	3,004	3,037	3,021	2,944	2,691	36,214
2000	2,953	3,039	3,394	2,974	3,292	3,309	2,686	3,027	2,871	2,931	2,752	2,444	35,672
2001	2,859	2,372	2,981	2,974	NA	2,961	2,936	3,279	2,644	3,166	2,732	2,396	34,145
2002	3,032	2,815	3,049	3,212	3,064	3,260	3,234	3,111	2,858	3,299	2,675	2,501	36,110
2003	3,018	2,742	2,843	3,134	2,969	3,173	3,209	3,137	3,030	3,413	2,787	2,722	36,177
2004	3,067	2,840	3,262	3,582	3,061	3,385	3,485	3,372	3,086	3,345	3,135	2,964	38,584
2005	3,264	3,087	3,506	3,506	3,542	3,696	3,389	3,512	3,413	3,542	3,145	3,196	40,798
2006[1]	3,423	3,122	3,536	3,280	3,386	3,447	3,202	3,349	2,838	3,151	2,374		38,300

[1] Preliminary. *Source: American Forest & Paper Association (AFPA)*

Imports and Exports of Lumber in the United States, by Type — In Millions of Board Feet

| | ---------- Imports[2] ---------- | | | | | | | | ---------- Exports[2] ---------- | | | | | | |
| | ---- Softwood ---- | | | | | | | | ---- Softwood ---- | | | | | | |
Year	Cedar	Douglas Fir	Hem-lock	Pine	Spruce	Total	Total Hard-wood	Total Lumber	Douglas Fir	Hem-lock	Pond-erosa/ White Pine	South-ern Pine	Total	Total Hard-wood	Total Lumber
1997	586	264	250	314	1,040	18,014	465	18,506	436	105	122	299	1,820	1,281	3,189
1998	514	417	268	363	849	18,686	589	19,306	252	39	113	279	1,265	1,119	2,601
1999	591	426	259	449	803	19,178	708	19,903	249	54	140	326	1,431	1,242	2,867
2000	694	455	184	450	812	19,449	795	20,268	232	46	116	298	1,355	1,319	2,822
2001	667	471	199	365	838	20,075	645	20,737	168	26	86	232	968	1,222	2,351
2002	648	385	69	445	1,046	20,986	739	21,774	111	19	83	205	848	1,219	2,313
2003	536	356	53	472	854	21,188	794	22,023	96	18	100	132	948	1,236	2,368
2004	630	570	67	580	1,183	23,483	995	24,499	88	19	93	156	821	1,496	2,533
2005	637	494	76	439	1,769	24,626	1,075	25,738	93	19	112	235	897	1,477	2,682
2006[1] I	180	88	31	100	432	6,054	261	6,321	19	3	29	58	246	449	695
II															
III															

Average Open Interest of Random Lumber Futures in Chicago   In Contracts

Year	Jan.	Feb.	Mar.	Apr.	May	June	July	Aug.	Sept.	Oct.	Nov.	Dec.
1999	4,864	5,497	4,698	4,456	4,927	6,405	6,263	4,882	3,457	3,704	2,963	2,868
2000	3,004	3,131	2,728	3,175	3,171	3,218	3,064	3,638	3,845	4,277	4,208	4,405
2001	4,605	4,494	3,654	3,644	3,867	3,733	2,612	2,949	2,148	2,102	2,173	2,416
2002	2,106	2,382	2,441	2,011	1,502	2,136	1,879	2,265	2,654	2,974	3,315	3,249
2003	3,238	3,222	2,521	2,804	2,937	3,188	2,370	2,827	3,492	3,033	1,824	1,887
2004	2,884	3,996	3,790	5,414	5,436	5,042	5,123	6,216	4,667	3,826	3,489	3,540
2005	3,759	5,169	5,040	4,705	3,463	3,576	3,401	4,227	3,913	3,883	4,713	5,202
2006	5,893	5,144	4,084	4,959	4,586	5,449	5,317	6,429	5,912	6,351	6,121	7,018
2007	6,466	7,807	7,684	8,680	7,726	8,206	7,130	7,666	6,493	9,356	8,960	9,731
2008	9,827	13,134	13,385	14,637	14,801	14,275	14,417	14,016	12,110	9,466	7,744	8,084

Source: CME Group; Chicago Mercantile Exchange (CME)

Volume of Trading of Random Lumber Futures in Chicago   In Contracts

Year	Jan.	Feb.	Mar.	Apr.	May	June	July	Aug.	Sept.	Oct.	Nov.	Dec.	Total
1999	25,962	22,184	28,151	22,618	23,835	30,410	30,791	25,683	24,177	18,125	20,802	15,118	287,856
2000	19,871	19,486	18,936	16,136	21,003	18,057	16,636	16,563	19,037	17,155	20,706	17,582	221,168
2001	21,567	15,076	24,561	22,458	23,681	18,878	15,210	16,440	12,882	11,608	11,989	12,490	206,840
2002	15,328	13,239	16,401	13,910	12,427	11,950	12,046	10,154	13,518	13,442	15,828	16,180	164,423
2003	24,241	17,533	17,027	11,573	20,132	21,840	21,097	22,418	22,891	19,387	12,480	13,272	223,891
2004	17,921	17,713	22,544	25,743	19,951	17,190	22,672	20,902	24,238	17,111	17,271	19,617	242,873
2005	20,838	20,257	24,595	20,360	17,338	17,115	16,244	19,590	22,895	15,896	23,404	17,709	236,241
2006	26,803	19,152	18,504	21,358	21,619	23,959	21,568	23,800	22,618	24,804	22,385	24,454	271,024
2007	26,214	28,328	24,741	26,433	31,540	28,545	23,462	28,610	24,841	33,876	29,738	28,361	334,689
2008	31,401	43,338	37,899	50,586	37,909	38,362	41,612	40,693	32,155	36,226	20,277	27,155	437,613

Source: CME Group; Chicago Mercantile Exchange (CME)

LUMBER AND PLYWOOD

Production of Plywood by Selected Countries   In Thousands of Cubic Meters

Year	Austria	Canada	Finland	France	Germany	Italy	Japan	Poland	Romania	Russia	Spain	Sweden	United States
2000	155	2,244	1,170	558	357	450	3,218	261	72	1,484	380	110	17,271
2001	186	2,026	1,140	509	321	488	2,771	242	79	1,590	380	106	15,417
2002	186	2,176	1,240	459	285	520	2,735	261	90	1,821	360	87	15,307
2003	186	2,206	1,300	415	245	511	3,024	289	94	1,978	370	75	14,870
2004	186	2,344	1,350	435	283	485	3,149	342	117	2,246	375	71	14,833
2005	195	2,322	1,305	415	236	390	3,212	361	126	2,556	557	92	14,449
2006[1]	178	2,252	1,415	431	235	334	3,314	385	188	2,614	468	92	13,651
2007[2]	258	2,065	1,410	378	229	420	3,073	440	107	2,763	450	92	12,437

[1] Preliminary.   [2] Estimate.   NA = Not available.   *Source: Food and Agricultural Organization of the United Nations (FAO-UN)*

Imports of Plywood by Selected Countries   In Thousands of Cubic Meters

Year	Austria	Belgium	Canada	Denmark	France	Germany	Italy	Japan	Netherlands	Sweden	Switzerland	United Kingdom	United States
2000	151	534	230	247	272	965	422	5,033	594	178	153	1,207	2,385
2001	138	526	520	250	358	954	425	5,021	600	157	143	1,300	3,009
2002	156	505	489	254	349	905	558	5,119	541	152	128	1,297	3,890
2003	180	572	509	394	363	1,103	558	4,221	527	161	130	1,253	4,249
2004	144	624	350	413	383	1,214	581	5,122	542	164	140	1,474	5,900
2005	140	521	690	371	411	1,142	532	4,732	526	189	145	1,456	6,181
2006[1]	140	610	685	402	445	1,314	575	5,046	603	197	143	1,497	6,393
2007[2]	267	660	1,048	389	461	1,433	588	4,064	608	240	126	1,624	5,633

[1] Preliminary.   [2] Estimate.   NA = Not available.   *Source: Food and Agricultural Organization of the United Nations (FAO-UN)*

Exports of Plywood by Selected Countries   In Thousands of Cubic Meters

Year	Austria	Baltic States	Belgium	Canada	Finland	France	Germany	Italy	Netherlands	Poland	Russia	Spain	United States
2000	246	194	380	941	1,006	231	210	146	55	109	974	104	673
2001	286	232	378	1,030	1,009	200	232	125	57	128	1,032	88	530
2002	240	238	371	1,056	1,117	190	167	204	43	138	1,157	82	523
2003	262	245	436	1,017	1,172	187	200	208	32	149	1,438	88	512
2004	265	255	474	1,027	1,234	192	265	201	46	171	1,527	114	525
2005	287	253	423	1,118	1,173	196	287	146	40	177	1,527	117	503
2006[1]	311	282	470	950	1,250	225	321	238	60	137	1,577	124	492
2007[2]	525	318	480	964	1,229	229	341	295	55	148	1,503	162	602

[1] Preliminary.   [2] Estimate.   NA = Not available.   *Source: Food and Agricultural Organization of the United Nations (FAO-UN)*

Imports of Industrial Roundwood by Selected Countries   In Thousands of Cubic Meters

Year	Austria	Belgium	Canada	Finland	France	Germany	Italy	Norway	Poland	Portugal	Spain	Sweden	United States
2000	8,451	3,992	6,507	9,875	2,012	3,549	5,805	3,315	732	1,340	3,771	11,721	2,453
2001	7,493	4,505	7,557	11,869	1,994	3,493	5,211	2,772	882	1,109	4,128	9,505	2,430
2002	7,289	2,653	6,941	12,586	1,993	2,623	4,703	2,561	726	901	3,374	9,705	2,687
2003	7,498	2,667	6,615	12,869	2,250	2,519	4,323	2,722	663	468	3,191	9,021	2,551
2004	8,812	2,879	5,961	12,961	2,175	2,227	4,614	2,866	943	364	2,973	9,398	2,437
2005	8,629	3,187	6,274	16,031	2,344	3,005	4,755	3,145	2,009	362	3,640	8,686	3,569
2006[1]	9,102	3,284	5,787	14,655	2,601	3,669	4,486	2,346	1,814	335	3,841	6,664	2,922
2007[2]	8,722	3,577	5,154	12,942	2,897	4,486	4,299	2,547	2,088	746	3,965	7,364	2,242

[1] Preliminary.   [2] Estimate.   NA = Not available.   *Source: Food and Agricultural Organization of the United Nations (FAO-UN)*

Exports of Industrial Roundwood by Selected Countries   In Thousands of Cubic Meters

Year	Canada	Czech Republic	Estonia	France	Germany	Hungary	Latvia	Lithuania	Russia	Slovakia	Sweden	Switzerland	United States
2000	2,903	1,857	4,257	5,522	5,558	1,282	4,190	1,200	30,835	1,550	1,431	3,754	11,952
2001	3,835	2,276	3,482	5,116	4,906	1,227	3,990	1,314	31,693	1,550	1,303	3,149	11,412
2002	4,471	2,302	3,132	4,244	4,907	1,210	4,225	1,420	36,800	1,187	1,755	1,970	11,067
2003	5,004	2,955	3,029	4,111	4,592	1,366	3,922	1,378	37,518	1,034	1,520	1,748	10,288
2004	3,899	2,858	2,297	3,851	5,589	1,137	4,136	1,178	41,553	1,142	1,522	1,741	10,402
2005	5,592	2,942	1,806	3,862	6,819	871	3,919	1,131	48,020	1,691	3,095	1,416	9,815
2006[1]	4,640	2,679	1,606	3,695	7,557	1,095	3,419	1,061	50,900	1,218	3,004	1,727	9,638
2007[2]	3,571	3,014	1,502	3,612	6,661	1,054	3,690	1,671	49,100	1,457	3,808	2,005	9,949

[1] Preliminary.   [2] Estimate.   NA = Not available.   *Source: Food and Agricultural Organization of the United Nations (FAO-UN)*

Magnesium

Magnesium (symbol Mg) is a silvery-white, light, and fairly tough, metallic element and is relatively stable. Magnesium is one of the alkaline earth metals. Magnesium is the eighth most abundant element in the earth's crust and the third most plentiful element found in seawater. Magnesium is ductile and malleable when heated, and with the exception of beryllium, is the lightest metal that remains stable under ordinary conditions. First isolated by the British chemist Sir Humphrey Davy in 1808, magnesium today is obtained mainly by electrolysis of fused magnesium chloride.

Magnesium compounds, primarily magnesium oxide, are used in the refractory material that line the furnaces used to produce iron and steel, nonferrous metals, glass, and cement. Magnesium oxide and other compounds are also used in the chemical, agricultural, and construction industries. Magnesium's principal use is as an alloying addition for aluminum. These aluminum-magnesium alloys are used primarily in beverage cans. Due to their lightness and considerable tensile strength, the alloys are also used in structural components in airplanes and automobiles.

Prices – The average price of magnesium in 2008 rose +48.9% to a new record high of $3.38 per pound, up from $1.73 in 2007 .

Supply – World primary production of magnesium in 2008 rose +7.9% yr/yr to a new record high of 808,000 metric tons. The current level of magnesium production has more than tripled since the mid-1970s (production was 249,367 metric tons in 1976). The world's largest primary producers of magnesium in 2008 were China with 700,000 metric tons, Russia with 35,000 metric tons, and Brazil with 18,000 metric tons. The U.S. production amount is not available because it is considered proprietary data but is probably less than about 50,000 metric tons. China's production has increased almost ten-fold over the past 10 years from 70,500 metric tons in 1998 to 700,000 metric tons in 2008. By 2006 Canada's production had grown by more than seven-fold from the mid-1980s, but that fell sharply in 2007 by -75% to 16,300 metric tons. Russia's production is less than half of what it was in the mid 1980s.

Demand – Total U.S. consumption of primary magnesium in 2007 fell 6.8% to 72,249 metric tons. U.S. consumption of magnesium for structural products in 2007 rose +1.0% yr/yr to 28,649. metric tons. Of the structural product consumption category, 91% was for castings and the remaining 9% was for wrought products. U.S. consumption of magnesium for aluminum alloys fell -11.6% yr/yr in 2007 to 29,800 metric tons. The consumption of magnesium for other uses fell by −10.4% yr/yr in 2007 to 13,800 metric tons.

Trade – U.S. exports of magnesium in 2008 fell −12.2% yr/yr to 13,000 metric tons, up from the 2005 record low of 9,650 metric tons. U.S. imports of magnesium in 2008 rose +14.2% yr/yr to 82,000 metric tons.

World Production of Magnesium (Primary and Secondary)   In Metric Tons

	---------------------------------- Primary Production ----------------------------------								---------------- Secondary Production -----------------				
Year	Brazil	Canada	China	France	Norway	Russia	United States	Total	Japan	United Kingdom	United States	Former USSR	Total
2003	6,000	78,000	340,000	----	----	43,000	W	509,000	----	----	----	----	----
2004	6,000	54,000	442,000	----	----	45,000	W	595,000	----	----	----	----	----
2005	6,000	50,000	470,000	----	----	45,000	W	622,000	----	----	----	----	----
2006	6,000	65,000	520,000	----	----	35,000	W	675,000	----	----	----	----	----
2007[1]	18,000	16,300	627,000	----	----	37,000	W	749,000	----	----	----	----	----
2008[2]	18,000	----	700,000	----	----	35,000	W	808,000	----	----	----	----	----

[1] Preliminary.   [2] Estimate.   W = Withheld.   *Source: U.S. Geological Survey (USGS)*

Salient Statistics of Magnesium in the United States   In Metric Tons

	--------------- Production ---------------								------- Domestic Consumption of Primary Magnesium -------					
	Primary	---- Secondary ----			Total	Imports for Con-	Stocks	Price $ Per	Castings	Wrought	Total	Aluminum	Other	Total
Year	(Ingot)	New Scrap	Old Scrap	Total	Exports[3]	sumption	Dec. 31[4]	Pound[5]	----- Structural Products -----			Alloys	Uses	
2003	W	44,700	25,400	70,100	20,400	83,400	W	1.14	49,565	3,190	52,755	33,800	16,200	50,000
2004	W	W	20,500	72,000	11,800	98,600	W	1.58	48,629	2,240	50,869	33,900	16,400	50,300
2005	W	W	19,400	72,900	9,650	84,700	W	1.23	34,024	2,890	36,914	30,300	14,800	45,100
2006	W	W	21,700	75,800	12,300	75,300	W	1.40	26,007	2,410	28,417	33,700	15,400	49,100
2007[1]	W	W	23,800	75,000	14,800	71,800	W	2.25	25,929	2,720	28,649	29,800	13,800	43,600
2008[2]	W	W		85,000	13,000	82,000	W	3.50						

[1] Preliminary.   [2] Estimate.   [3] Metal & alloys in crude form & scrap.   [4] Estimate of Industry Stocks, metal.   [5] Magnesium ingots (99.8%),
f.o.b. Valasco, Texas.   [6] Distributive or sacrificial purposes.   W = Withheld proprietary data.   *Source: U.S. Geological Survey (USGS)*

Average Price of Magnesium   In Dollars Per Pound

Year	Jan.	Feb.	Mar.	Apr.	May	June	July	Aug.	Sept.	Oct.	Nov.	Dec.	Average
2004	1.08	1.11	1.23	1.30	1.42	1.55	1.55	1.55	1.55	1.55	1.60	1.60	1.42
2005	1.60	1.57	1.57	1.57	1.54	1.48	1.40	1.40	1.33	1.32	1.29	1.25	1.44
2006	1.25	1.18	1.18	1.16	1.16	1.16	1.16	1.16	1.20	1.21	1.29	1.33	1.20
2007	1.42	1.56	1.58	1.62	1.65	1.65	1.65	1.65	1.65	1.98	2.09	2.20	1.73
2008	2.89	3.08	3.27	3.39	3.55	3.55	3.55	3.55	3.55	3.50	3.43	3.22	3.38

Source: American Metal Market (AMM)

Manganese

Manganese (symbol Mn) is a silvery-white, very brittle, metallic element used primarily in making alloys. Manganese was first distinguished as an element and isolated in 1774 by Johan Gottlieb Gahn. Manganese dissolves in acid and corrodes in moist air.

Manganese is found in the earth's crust in the form of ores such as rhodochrosite, franklinite, psilomelane, and manganite. Pyrolusite is the principal ore of manganese. Pure manganese is produced by igniting pyrolusite with aluminum powder or by electrolyzing manganese sulfate.

Manganese is used primarily in the steel industry for creating alloys, the most important ones being ferromanganese and spiegeleisen. In steel, manganese improves forging and rolling qualities, strength, toughness, stiffness, wear resistance, and hardness. Manganese is also used in plant fertilizers, animal feed, pigments, and dry cell batteries.

Prices – The average monthly price of ferromanganese (high carbon, FOB plant) rose sharply by +114.7% yr/yr in 2008 to $2,953.84 per gross ton, which was a new record high. The 2008 price was more than five times the 21-year low price of $447.44 per gross ton posted as recently as 2001.

Supply – World production of manganese ore in 2006 (latest data available) rose by +7.4% to 33.4 million metric tons, which was a record high. That was well above the record low of 17.8 million metric tons posted in 1999. The world's largest producers of manganese ore are China with 24% of world production in 2006, South Africa with 16%, Australia with 14%, Brazil with 9%, and the Ukraine with 7%. China's production in 2006 was up +6.7% yr/yr at 8.000 million metric tons.

Demand – U.S. consumption of manganese ore in 2008 fell –0.7% to a record low of 298,000 metric tons. U.S. consumption of ferromanganese in 2008 rose +7.4% yr/yr to 292,000 metric tons, but remains below the 11-year high of 315,000 metric tons posted in 2004. The 2008 figure is about one-third of the U.S. consumption in the early 1970s.

Trade – The U.S. still relies on imports for 100% of its manganese consumption, as it has since 1985. U.S. imports of manganese ore for consumption in 2008 fell –6.3% yr/yr to 564,000 metric tons. U.S. imports of ferromanganese for consumption in 2008 rose 52.75 yr/yr to a 20-year high of 481,000 metric tons. U.S. imports of silico-manganese in 2008 fell 10.9% yr/yr to 369,000 metric tons. The primary sources of U.S. imports of manganese ore in 2006 were Gabon with 44% imports, South Africa with 34%, and Australia with 5%.

World Production of Manganese Ore   In Thousands of Metric Tons (Gross Weight)

Year	Australia[2] 37-53[4]	Brazil 37[4]	China 20-30[4]	Gabon 45-53[4]	Georgia[5] 29-30[4]	Ghana 32-34[4]	India 10-54[4]	Kazakhstan[5] 29-30[4]	Mexico 27-50[4]	South Africa 30-48+[4]	Ukraine[5] 30-35[4]	Other	World Total
1997	2,136	2,124	6,000	1,904	----	437	1,596	400	534	3,121	3,040	608	21,900
1998	1,500	1,940	5,300	2,092	----	537	1,557	634	510	3,044	2,226	522	19,900
1999	1,892	1,656	3,190	1,908	----	639	1,500	980	459	3,122	1,985	458	17,800
2000	1,614	1,925	3,500	1,743	----	896	1,550	1,136	435	3,635	2,741	433	19,600
2001	2,069	1,970	4,300	1,791	----	1,077	1,600	1,387	277	3,266	2,700	490	20,900
2002	2,189	2,529	4,500	1,856	----	1,136	1,553	1,792	245	3,322	2,470	526	22,100
2003	2,564	2,544	4,600	2,000	----	1,509	1,650	2,361	320	3,501	2,591	529	24,200
2004	3,431	3,143	5,500	2,460	----	1,597	1,776	2,318	377	4,282	2,362	696	27,900
2005	3,136	3,200	7,500	2,859	----	1,715	2,386	2,208	369	4,612	2,260	829	31,100
2006[1]	4,556	3,128	8,000	3,000	----	1,700	2,003	2,250	370	5,213	2,400	750	33,400

[1] Preliminary.   [2] Metallurgical Ore.   [3] Concentrate.   [4] Ranges of percentage of manganese.   *Source: U.S. Geological Survey (USGS)*

Salient Statistics of Manganese in the United States   In Thousands of Metric Tons (Gross Weight)

Year	Net Import Reliance As a % of Apparent Consumption	Manganese Ore (35% or More Manganese) Imports for Consumption	Exports	Consumption	Stocks Dec. 31[3]	Ferromanganese Imports for Consumption	Exports	Consumption	Avg Price Mn. Metallurgical Ore $/Lg. Ton Unit[4]	Silicomanganese Exports	Imports
1999	100	460	4	479	172	312	12	281	2.26	3.7	301.0
2000	100	447	10	486	226	312	8	300	2.39	1.9	378.0
2001	100	358	9	425	138	251	9	266	2.44	3.6	269.0
2002	100	427	15	360	151	275	9	253	2.30	0.5	247.0
2003	100	347	18	398	156	238	11	248	2.41	0.6	267.0
2004	100	451	123	441	159	429	9	315	2.89	0.5	422.0
2005	100	656	13	368	337	255	14	286	4.39	0.9	327.0
2006	100	572	2	365	159	358	22	297	3.51	0.9	400.0
2007[1]	100	602	29	300	100	315	29	272	3.48		414.0
2008[2]	100	564	42	298	100	481	25	292	12.97		369.0

[1] Preliminary.   [2] Estimate.   [3] Including bonded warehouses; excludes Gov't stocks; also excludes small tonnages of dealers' stocks.
[4] 46-48% Mn, C.I.F. U.S. Ports.   *Source: U.S. Geological Survey (USGS)*

Ferromanganese (monthly average) through December 2008 — USD per gross ton

Imports[3] of Manganese Ore (20% or More Mn) in the United States — In Metric Tons (Mn Content)

Year	Australia	Brazil	Gabon	Mexico	Morocco	South Africa	Total	Customs Value ($1,000)
1997	16,400	9,100	99,400	30,100	37	----	156,000	30,800
1998	18,700	12,100	94,900	14,600	----	13,800	160,000	27,800
1999	23,500	1	142,000	9,130	----	39,100	224,000	37,200
2000	18,100	3,250	188,000	3,250	----	----	219,000	32,100
2001	18,000	3,480	158,000	1,720	----	17,400	199,000	28,000
2002	18,400	12,900	140,000	1,100	----	41,800	214,000	29,200
2003	12,900	7	123,000	1,520	----	36,900	175,000	27,000
2004	27,700	23	188,000	1,640	----	13,200	234,000	37,700
2005[1]	21,300	----	252,000	4,320	----	33,100	334,000	58,200
2006[2]	12,800	1,790	230,000	2,950	38	98,300	371,000	42,100

[1] Preliminary.   [2] Estimate.   [3] Imports for consumption.   *Source: U.S. Geological Survey (USGS)*

Average Price of Ferromanganese[1] — In Dollars Per Gross Ton -- Carloads

Year	Jan.	Feb.	Mar.	Apr.	May	June	July	Aug.	Sept.	Oct.	Nov.	Dec.	Average
1999	510.00	510.00	510.00	510.00	510.00	498.75	482.50	482.50	482.50	482.50	482.50	482.50	495.21
2000	482.50	482.50	482.50	482.50	482.50	482.50	501.63	505.00	509.00	510.00	510.00	477.50	492.40
2001	473.93	467.89	460.00	454.29	450.00	450.00	446.90	444.57	430.79	430.00	430.00	430.00	447.44
2002	430.00	430.00	437.14	447.73	449.55	456.75	481.82	556.14	597.00	589.67	552.89	518.93	495.64
2003	509.52	510.00	502.38	497.61	492.50	481.79	477.27	470.00	478.57	497.83	516.67	559.76	499.49
2004	610.00	790.00	1,382.61	1,700.00	1,700.00	1,674.43	1,490.34	1,488.64	1,500.00	1,371.43	1,207.50	1,019.52	1,327.87
2005	904.50	818.68	739.46	651.67	586.19	547.39	528.13	512.07	522.14	550.24	597.75	694.05	637.69
2006	707.25	712.50	737.50	759.00	764.55	870.23	987.50	1,025.00	1,021.25	946.25	836.25	790.00	846.44
2007	834.29	930.00	949.55	1,000.00	1,074.43	1,633.33	1,705.00	1,620.00	1,620.00	1,656.96	1,700.00	1,785.53	1,375.76
2008	1,978.57	2,262.75	2,734.29	3,145.45	3,200.00	3,200.00	3,175.00	3,150.00	3,150.00	3,150.00	3,150.00	3,150.00	2,953.84

[1] Domestic standard, high carbon, FOB plant, carloads.   *Source: American Metal Market (AMM)*

Meats

U.S. commercial red meat includes beef, veal, lamb, and pork. Red meat is a good source of iron, vitamin B12, and protein, and eliminating it from the diet can lead to iron and zinc deficiencies. Today, red meat is far leaner than it was 30 years ago due to newer breeds of livestock that carry less fat. The leanest cuts of beef include tenderloin, sirloin, and flank. The leanest cuts of pork include pork tenderloin, loin chops, and rib chops.

The USDA (United States Department of Agriculture) grades various cuts of meat. "Prime" is the highest USDA grade for beef, veal, and lamb. "Choice" is the grade designation below Prime for beef, veal, and lamb. "Commercial" and "Cutter" grades are two of the lower designations for beef, usually sold as ground meat, sausage, and canned meat. "Canner" is the lowest USDA grade designation for beef and is used primarily in canned meats not sold at retail.

Supply – World meat production in 2008 rose +1.5% to a new record high of 155.960 million metric tons. China was the world's largest meat producer in 2008 with 50.853 million metric tons of production (up +3.8% yr/yr), accounting for 33% of world production.

U.S. production of meat in 2008 rose by +3.6% yr/yr to 50.567 billion pounds, which was a new record high. U.S. production of beef in 2008 rose 0.6% yr/yr to 26.682 billion

pounds, which will be just moderately below the record of 27.192 billion pounds in 2002. Beef accounted for 53.0% of all U.S. meat production. U.S. production of pork in 2008 rose +7.3% yr/yr to a new record high of 23.554 billion pounds. Pork accounts for 47.0% of U.S. meat production. Veal accounts for only 0.3% of U.S. meat production, and lamb and mutton account for only 0.4% of U.S. meat production.

Demand – U.S. per capita meat consumption in 2008 rose by 0.9% to 119.0 pounds per person per year, but that is only slightly above the 2006/7 record low of 117 pounds per person reflecting the trend towards eating more chicken and fish and the availability of meat substitutes. Per capita beef consumption in 2008 was unchanged at 65.0 pounds per person per year, which was about half the record high of 127.5 pounds seen in 1976. Per capita pork consumption in 2008 rose by +4.0% to 53.0 pounds per person per year from he record low of 49.0 pounds posted in 2006. Per capita consumption of veal is negligible at .5 pounds per person and lamb/mutton consumption is also negligible at 1.0 pound per person.

Trade – World red meat exports in 2008 rose 8.0% to a new record high of 13.909 million metric tons. The world's largest red meat exporters will be the U.S. with 23% of world exports in 2008, Brazil with 19%, the European Union with 12%, and Australia and Canada each with 11%.

World Total Meat Production[4]   In Thousands of Metric Tons

Year	Argentina	Australia	Brazil	Canada	China[4]	European Union	India	Mexico	New Zealand	Russia	South Africa	United States	World Total
2000	3,094	2,353	8,530	2,886	44,791	29,793	----	2,935	628	3,340	734	20,894	138,790
2001	2,838	2,428	9,125	2,993	45,603	29,300	----	2,990	624	3,320	776	20,674	139,361
2002	2,865	2,496	9,805	3,152	46,450	29,928	----	3,015	635	3,370	770	21,356	143,317
2003	2,950	2,492	9,945	3,066	47,811	30,016	----	3,050	729	3,380	756	21,095	144,959
2004	3,308	2,475	10,575	3,432	49,014	29,998	----	3,249	749	3,315	801	20,573	147,649
2005	3,388	2,487	11,302	3,443	51,234	29,766	----	3,320	711	3,260	829	20,710	151,221
2006	3,310	2,572	11,855	3,289	52,272	29,941	----	3,283	699	3,235	876	21,539	154,310
2007	3,515	2,558	12,293	3,173	49,012	31,061	----	3,352	658	3,280	828	22,058	153,719
2008[1]	3,420	2,467	12,260	3,115	50,853	30,520	----	3,395	670	3,370	826	22,908	155,960
2009[2]	3,385	2,431	12,555	3,030	52,360	30,270	----	3,463	652	3,480	832	22,710	156,817

[1] Preliminary.   [2] Forecast.   [3] Data through 2000, includes beef, veal, pork, sheep and goat meat. Beginning 2001, excludes sheep and goat.
[4] Predominately pork production.   *Source: Foreign Agricultural Service, U.S. Department of Agriculture (FAS-USDA)*

Production and Consumption of Red Meats in The United States

	Beef			Veal			Lamb & Mutton			Pork (Excluding Lard)			All Meats		
	Commercial Production	Consumption		Commercial Production	Consumption		Commercial Production	Consumption		Commercial Production	Consumption		Commercial Production	Consumption	
		Total	Per Capita		Total	Per Capita		Total	Per Capita		Total	Per Capita		Total	Per Capita
Year	- Million Pounds -		Lbs.	- Million Pounds -		Lbs.	- Million Pounds -		Lbs.	- Million Pounds -		Lbs.	- Million Pounds -		Lbs.
1999	26,493	26,936	68.0	235	235	1.0	248	358	1.0	19,308	18,954	53.0	46,284	46,483	122.0
2000	26,888	27,338	68.0	225	225	1.0	234	354	1.0	18,952	18,643	51.0	46,299	46,560	121.0
2001	26,212	27,026	66.0	205	204	1.0	227	368	1.0	19,160	18,492	50.0	45,804	46,089	118.0
2002	27,192	27,877	68.0	205	204	1.0	223	381	1.0	19,685	19,146	52.0	47,305	47,608	121.0
2003	26,339	27,000	65.0	202	204	0.6	203	367	1.0	19,966	19,436	52.0	46,710	47,006	118.0
2004	24,650	27,750	66.0	176	177	0.6	200	373	1.0	20,529	19,437	51.0	45,555	47,737	119.0
2005	24,787	27,754	66.0	165	164	0.6	191	355	1.0	20,705	19,112	50.0	45,848	47,385	117.0
2006	26,256	28,137	66.0	156	155	0.5	190	356	1.0	21,074	19,048	49.0	47,675	47,696	117.0
2007[1]	26,523	28,144	65.0	145	144	0.5	188	384	1.0	21,962	19,763	51.0	48,817	48,435	118.0
2008[2]	26,682	28,127	65.0	150	153	0.5	181	367	1.0	23,554	20,686	53.0	50,567	48,333	119.0

[1] Preliminary.   [2] Estimate.   [3] Forecast.   *Source: Economic Research Service, U.S. Department of Agriculture (ERS-USDA)*

Total Red Meat Imports[3] (Carcass Weight Equivalent) of Principal Countries   In Thousands of Metric Tons

Year	Brazil	Canada	European Union	Egypt	Hong Kong	Japan	Rep of Korea	Mexico	Philippines	Russia	Taiwan	United States	World Total
2000	71	358	448	228	285	1,992	517	709	150	695	130	1,813	8,737
2001	44	421	449	147	296	2,004	385	732	136	1,130	93	1,866	9,000
2002	77	431	563	178	312	1,805	606	828	155	1,507	116	1,945	10,063
2003	62	395	593	127	343	1,924	620	752	149	1,416	144	1,901	10,418
2004	52	228	694	173	367	1,903	457	754	185	1,333	134	2,168	10,677
2005	48	290	810	221	353	2,000	595	755	160	1,730	129	2,096	11,532
2006	28	325	842	292	368	1,832	708	829	160	1,774	128	1,848	11,705
2007	30	413	675	293	397	1,896	755	854	179	1,924	120	1,823	12,192
2008[1]	33	475	450	225	467	1,923	780	980	230	1,950	122	1,508	12,554
2009[2]	30	495	475	240	490	1,932	780	965	210	1,990	117	1,585	12,612

[1] Preliminary.   [2] Forecast.   [3] Data through 2000, includes beef, veal, pork, sheep and goat meat. Beginning 2001, excludes sheep and goat.
Source: Foreign Agricultural Service, U.S. Department of Agriculture (FAS-USDA)

Total Red Meat Exports[3] (Carcass Weight Equivalent) of Principal Countries   In Thousands of Metric Tons

Year	Argentina	Australia	Brazil	Canada	China	Denmark	France	India	Ireland	Netherlands	New Zealand	United States	World Total
2000	354	1,368	650	1,223	191	1,997	344	474	7	167	1,704	236	9,003
2001	168	1,446	1,078	1,347	276	1,580	365	483	7	100	1,736	145	9,067
2002	345	1,424	1,462	1,521	344	1,573	411	475	7	187	1,841	225	10,168
2003	382	1,318	1,765	1,388	433	1,578	432	548	10	227	1,921	282	10,661
2004	616	1,431	2,231	1,575	589	1,665	492	594	10	127	1,198	354	11,363
2005	755	1,444	2,606	1,680	578	1,396	617	577	12	91	1,525	418	12,311
2006	553	1,490	2,723	1,558	643	1,502	681	530	9	24	1,878	461	12,748
2007	535	1,454	2,919	1,490	431	1,425	765	496	9	52	2,075	386	12,884
2008[1]	401	1,434	2,600	1,540	259	1,625	810	515	13	25	3,263	401	13,909
2009[2]	480	1,402	2,720	1,550	218	1,575	815	497	13	13	3,247	420	13,919

[1] Preliminary.   [2] Forecast.   [3] Data through 2000, includes beef, veal, pork, sheep and goat meat. Beginning 2001, excludes sheep and goat.
Source: Foreign Agricultural Service, U.S. Department of Agriculture (FAS-USDA)

United States Meat Imports by Type of Product   In Metric Tons

Year	Beef and Veal — Fresh	Beef and Veal — Frozen	Beef and Veal — Other Prepared or Preserved	Lamb, Mutton and Goat, Except Canned	Pork — Fresh and Chilled	Pork — Frozen	Pork — Other Prepared or Preserved	Variety Meats, Fresh or Frozen	Other Livestock Meats NSE	Total
1996	227,874	412,805	66,719	33,009	125,220	58,336	72,650	32,579	13,744	1,042,934
1997	262,985	469,949	63,181	37,848	126,061	65,000	72,903	44,317	14,215	1,156,457
1998	295,820	527,063	68,884	51,630	146,965	70,227	76,230	47,031	13,058	1,296,907
1999	337,899	542,524	82,669	50,209	188,556	77,638	84,207	51,640	13,625	1,428,966
2000	336,117	608,737	73,750	59,968	229,395	91,446	92,672	57,388	14,281	1,563,753
2001	368,529	618,897	73,713	66,785	240,275	84,687	83,724	62,541	16,723	1,615,873
2002	400,484	586,500	84,640	73,863	276,639	90,423	91,379	55,384	19,401	1,678,713
2003	285,772	612,569	85,439	77,546	293,169	107,749	107,964	47,688	21,367	1,639,263
2004	387,758	717,942	92,123	82,930	266,583	109,915	96,840	33,776	55,737	1,843,604
2005[1]	406,431	669,935	96,181	83,957	266,544	93,063	78,594	41,067	25,426	1,761,198

[1] Preliminary.   NSE = Not specified elsewhere.   *Source: Foreign Agricultural Service, U.S. Department of Agriculture (FAS-USDA)*

United States Meat Exports by Type of Product   In Metric Tons

Year	Beef and Veal — Fresh	Beef and Veal — Frozen	Beef and Veal — Other Prepared or Preserved	Lamb and Mutton, Fresh or Frozen	Pork — Fresh and Chilled	Pork — Frozen	Pork — Other Prepared or Preserved	Variety Meats, Fresh, Chilled or Frozen	Other Meats	Total
1996	273,276	324,329	14,577	2,478	101,975	166,057	32,190	495,343	434,759	1,844,984
1997	316,534	359,460	15,227	2,545	134,706	151,121	31,215	469,789	435,258	1,915,854
1998	346,403	352,050	17,966	2,528	147,006	209,135	37,907	495,643	423,980	2,032,618
1999	370,184	414,458	19,323	2,219	160,910	225,492	40,463	524,325	455,561	2,212,935
2000	395,588	417,538	21,791	2,184	208,055	185,240	36,915	604,738	503,942	2,372,990
2001	393,105	362,972	23,932	2,770	227,807	247,461	44,494	685,063	513,969	2,501,573
2002	407,599	393,836	27,232	3,042	235,547	231,274	69,030	592,185	619,491	2,579,236
2003	430,071	390,543	37,572	2,909	237,129	257,360	69,693	598,726	567,565	2,591,568
2004	114,966	20,458	9,068	3,671	352,173	298,786	74,963	456,480	189,127	1,519,691
2005[1]	173,337	31,714	19,027	4,885	404,601	401,115	75,096	497,346	274,990	1,882,111

[1] Preliminary.   *Source: Foreign Agricultural Service, U.S. Department of Agriculture (FAS-USDA)*

Exports and Imports of Meats in the United States (Carcass Weight Equivalent)[3]

	-------- Exports --------				-------- Imports --------			
Year	Beef and Veal	Lamb and Mutton	Pork[3]	All Meat	Beef and Veal	Lamb and Mutton	Pork[3]	All Meat
1997	2,136	5	1,044	3,185	2,343	83	634	3,061
1998	2,171	6	1,230	3,407	2,643	112	705	3,461
1999	2,412	5	1,277	3,694	2,873	112	827	3,813
2000	2,468	5	1,287	3,760	3,032	130	965	4,127
2001	2,269	7	1,559	3,835	3,163	146	951	4,260
2002	2,448	7	1,612	4,067	3,218	160	1,071	4,448
2003	2,518	7	1,717	4,242	3,006	168	1,185	4,359
2004	460	9	2,181	2,650	3,679	180	1,099	4,959
2005[1]	644	9	2,683	3,336	3,587	179	1,002	4,768
2006[2]	680	8	2,785	3,473	3,560	175	960	4,695

[1] Preliminary. [2] Estimate. [3] Includes meat content of minor meats and of mixed products.
Source: Economic Research Service, U.S. Department of Agriculture (FAS-USDA)

Average Wholesale Prices of Meats in the United States   In Cent Per Pound

	Composite ----- Retail Price -----		Wholesale --------- Value[4] -------		Net Farm Value[5]	Cow Beef Canner & Cutter, Central US	Boxed Beef Cut-out, Choice1-3, Central US	Pork Carcass Cut-out, U.S.,	Lamb Carcass, Choice-Prime, E. Coast,	Pork[6] Loins, Central US	Skinned Ham, Central US	Pork Bellies, Central US
Year	of Beef, Choice, Grade 3	of Pork[3]	Beef	Pork	of Pork	Central US	550-700 Lb.	No. 2	55-65 lbs.	14-18 lbs.	17-20 lbs.	12-14 lbs.
1999	287.76	241.44	171.55	99.00	60.40	66.51	111.06	53.45	170.29	100.38	51.35	57.12
2000	306.42	258.20	182.27	114.50	79.40	72.57	117.51	64.07	177.78	117.13	60.85	77.46
2001	337.73	269.39	192.12	117.80	81.30	79.50	122.61	66.83	148.96	116.97	64.86	78.61
2002	331.53	265.75	180.02	100.70	61.90	NA	114.42	53.49	151.28	97.98	47.52	69.91
2003	374.62	265.82	222.90	107.40	69.60	NA	143.58	58.87	185.21	100.96	45.48	86.42
2004	406.53	279.16	218.90	127.40	92.10	NA	142.15	73.53	189.08	117.14	64.98	99.35
2005	409.22	282.69	226.10	124.90	88.00	NA	145.78	69.84	209.88	113.22	64.07	81.46
2006	397.02	280.72	228.17	121.38	83.27	NA	146.82	67.62	199.10	104.46	64.04	82.81
2007[1]	415.85	287.03	231.08	121.44	81.98	NA	149.80	67.54	215.96	104.17	57.96	88.97
2008[2]	432.45	293.65	235.04	124.73	82.48	NA	153.17	69.24	226.63	106.63	63.52	69.86

[1] Preliminary. [2] Estimate. [3] Sold as retail cuts (ham, bacon, loin, etc.). [4] Quantity equivalent to 1 pound of retail cuts.
[5] Portion of gross farm value minus farm by-product allowance.   *Source: Economic Research Service, U.S. Department of Agriculture (ERS-USDA)*

Average Wholesale Price of Boxed Beef Cut-Out[1], Choice 1-3, at Central US   In Cents Per Pound

Year	Jan.	Feb.	Mar.	Apr.	May	June	July	Aug.	Sept.	Oct.	Nov.	Dec.	Average
1999	101.37	99.37	103.62	107.55	110.89	115.39	111.14	114.00	115.13	119.21	117.38	117.71	111.06
2000	114.74	112.59	118.42	123.45	124.88	123.30	115.85	111.20	108.68	112.58	118.05	126.41	117.51
2001	129.78	128.87	129.58	128.93	129.03	126.82	118.93	120.20	119.30	115.93	110.95	113.04	122.61
2002	111.99	111.53	120.54	116.61	115.14	114.06	109.88	110.93	111.83	111.64	116.41	122.45	114.42
2003	128.59	128.77	126.35	133.03	141.44	141.16	130.13	139.91	156.64	176.06	167.15	153.71	143.58
2004	138.60	129.29	141.34	157.53	155.70	148.54	140.27	139.33	137.82	138.45	135.64	143.31	142.15
2005	148.93	143.02	150.66	157.34	156.82	140.02	131.19	132.85	137.97	144.30	148.81	157.49	145.78
2006	155.60	149.71	144.94	141.83	147.45	153.09	147.01	146.22	144.69	144.79	143.64	142.92	146.82
2007	149.15	149.54	159.23	163.23	160.20	145.59	141.47	144.51	146.99	144.09	145.39	148.25	149.80
2008[2]	146.41	149.63	144.42	147.47	156.07	159.10	167.33	162.31	159.56	148.03	153.29	144.42	153.17

[1] Data through 2004: 550-750 pounds; beginning 2005: 600-900 pounds.   [2] Preliminary.   *Source: Economic Research Service, U.S. Department of Agriculture (ERS-USDA)*

Production (Commercial) of All Red Meats in the United States   In Millions of Pounds (Carcass Weight)

Year	Jan.	Feb.	Mar.	Apr.	May	June	July	Aug.	Sept.	Oct.	Nov.	Dec.	Total
1999	3,833	3,535	4,016	3,824	3,604	3,940	3,781	3,913	3,933	4,002	3,895	3,862	46,138
2000	3,784	3,767	4,044	3,460	3,878	3,941	3,644	4,113	3,861	4,096	3,919	3,619	46,126
2001	3,935	3,761	3,761	3,506	3,881	3,758	3,643	4,060	3,664	4,264	3,970	3,813	46,016
2002	4,081	3,501	3,677	3,902	4,018	3,813	4,016	4,141	3,873	4,382	3,908	3,859	47,171
2003	4,075	3,496	3,705	3,845	3,944	3,948	4,046	3,913	4,007	4,155	3,524	3,876	46,534
2004	3,713	3,404	3,944	3,713	3,597	3,928	3,708	3,878	3,905	3,921	3,770	3,931	45,412
2005	3,648	3,423	3,879	3,622	3,714	3,963	3,616	4,100	3,933	3,926	3,942	3,954	45,719
2006	3,890	3,485	4,111	3,614	4,048	4,120	3,782	4,245	3,933	4,182	4,136	3,862	47,408
2007	4,091	3,615	4,013	3,753	4,075	4,028	3,940	4,026	3,864	4,614	4,300	4,059	48,378
2008[1]	4,416	3,968	4,090	4,297	4,223	4,050	4,252	4,097	4,273	4,530	3,872	4,162	50,230

[1] Preliminary.   *Source: Economic Research Service, U.S. Department of Agriculture (ERS-USDA)*

Cold Storage Holdings of All[2] Meats in the United States, on First of Month   In Millions of Pounds

Year	Jan.	Feb.	Mar.	Apr.	May	June	July	Aug.	Sept.	Oct.	Nov.	Dec.
1999	821.0	833.0	863.1	883.5	936.4	901.2	843.9	810.4	834.9	746.3	780.3	750.5
2000	748.3	853.1	913.9	934.3	951.3	963.5	926.7	896.2	881.0	871.1	868.0	883.0
2001	836.2	907.8	852.6	787.9	771.4	772.5	742.2	717.4	732.6	775.3	849.0	880.9
2002	946.8	982.6	970.7	961.9	996.6	973.0	918.0	912.6	950.7	997.8	1,038.9	997.7
2003	1,011.5	1,015.2	978.2	951.9	926.8	901.5	847.5	825.0	817.3	832.1	836.9	828.1
2004	879.0	953.7	926.9	879.4	883.6	829.3	797.9	807.7	841.9	886.1	889.2	912.6
2005	979.0	965.0	953.2	928.0	908.5	847.0	847.8	850.8	842.9	884.9	900.1	882.1
2006	877.2	1,012.4	987.3	959.8	979.1	940.8	880.9	915.5	918.2	969.4	994.0	1,009.9
2007	946.6	977.3	963.4	943.5	970.3	925.7	919.7	943.5	958.7	991.8	1,003.2	968.4
2008[1]	961.6	1,037.2	1,054.1	1,098.8	1,106.6	1,005.9	963.9	939.8	947.7	984.5	1,004.6	1,017.3

[1] Preliminary.   [2] Includes beef and veal, mutton and lamb, pork and products, rendered pork fat, and miscellaneous meats. Excludes lard.
Source: Economic Research Service, U.S. Department of Agriculture (ERS-USDA)

Cold Storage Holdings of Frozen Beef in the United States, on First of Month   In Millions of Pounds

Year	Jan.	Feb.	Mar.	Apr.	May	June	July	Aug.	Sept.	Oct.	Nov.	Dec.
1999	296.4	301.1	300.1	309.2	316.8	306.7	293.1	292.7	377.9	294.4	322.5	308.9
2000	314.2	350.9	369.0	378.2	396.1	401.1	405.1	391.5	398.8	405.7	404.4	411.8
2001	401.7	410.9	360.2	332.6	315.3	325.1	340.8	351.4	373.2	382.8	395.1	427.6
2002	460.7	455.5	439.0	410.5	405.7	401.8	396.9	416.5	461.8	494.9	525.2	512.6
2003	524.6	482.4	441.9	403.1	389.7	385.1	371.5	368.2	371.0	379.8	375.2	373.8
2004	395.1	434.4	435.0	416.8	421.2	402.8	411.8	427.0	446.0	457.2	452.6	463.3
2005	484.3	453.3	400.2	372.3	329.4	318.2	342.1	385.2	410.6	438.8	439.2	429.9
2006	434.4	465.9	440.6	436.2	441.3	446.3	449.1	479.2	484.5	491.9	485.7	520.3
2007	482.1	470.6	458.9	427.2	417.3	411.5	430.3	467.7	480.9	486.7	488.0	475.3
2008[1]	482.5	445.1	424.1	423.2	430.0	413.9	421.2	423.9	434.0	448.1	465.1	474.9

[1] Preliminary.   *Source: Economic Research Service, U.S. Department of Agriculture (ERS-USDA)*

Mercury

Mercury (symbol Hg) was known to the ancient Hindus and Chinese, and was also found in Egyptian tombs dating back to 1500 BC. The ancient Greeks used mercury in ointments, and the Romans used it in cosmetics. Alchemists thought mercury turned into gold when it hardened.

Mercury, also called quicksilver, is a heavy, silvery, toxic, transitional metal. Mercury is the only common metal that is liquid at room temperatures. When subjected to a pressure of 7,640 atmospheres (7.7 million millibars), mercury becomes a solid. Mercury dissolves in nitric or concentrated sulfuric acid, but is resistant to alkalis. It is a poor conductor of heat. Mercury has superconductivity when cooled to sufficiently low temperatures. It has a freezing point of about –39 degrees Celsius and a boiling point of about 357 degrees Celsius.

Mercury is found in its pure form or combined in small amounts with silvers, but is found most often in the ore cinnabar, a mineral consisting of mercuric sulfide. By heating the cinnabar ore in air until the mercuric sulfide breaks down, pure mercury metal is produced. Mercury forms alloys called amalgams with all common metals except iron and platinum. Most mercury is used for the manufacture of industrial chemicals and for electrical and electronic applications. Other uses for mercury include its use in gold recovery from ores, barometers, diffusion pumps, laboratory instruments, mercury-vapor lamps, pesticides, batteries, and catalysts. A decline in mercury production and usage since the 1970s reflects a trend for using mercury substitutes due to its toxicity.

Prices – The average monthly price of mercury in 2008 rose by +6.0% yr/yr to $573.83 per flask (34.5 kilograms). That is still below the 2005 record high price of $774.04.

Supply – World mine production of mercury in 2008 fell by -18.8% yr/yr to a record low of 950 metric tons. The record high of 10,364 metric tons was posted in 1971. The world's largest miners of mercury are China with 63% of world production and Kyrgyzstan with 26%. China's production in 2008 was 600 metric tons. China's production was as high as 1,140 metric tons as recently as 2004. China's record high production of 1,200 metric tons was posted in 1989 and its record low of 190 metric tons was posted in 2001. Spain is also a large producer but their data has not been available since 2004.

Demand – The breakdown of domestic consumption of mercury by particular categories is no longer available. However, as of 1997 records showed that chlorine and caustic soda accounted for 46% of U.S. mercury consumption, followed by wiring devices and switches (17%), dental equipment (12%), electrical lighting (8%), and measuring control instruments (7%). Substitutes for mercury include lithium and composite ceramic materials.

Trade – U.S. foreign trade in mercury has been relatively small but U.S. imports of mercury in 2008 rose by +123.9% yr/yr to 150 metric tons from last year's 5-year low of 67 metric tons. U.S. imports were mostly from Chile and Peru. U.S. exports of mercury in 2008 rose sharply by +971.4% to a record high of 900 metric tons from last year's 9-year low of 84 metric tons in 2007.

World Mine Production of Mercury   In Metric Tons (1 tonne = 29.008216 flasks)

Year	Algeria	China	Finland	Kyrgyzstan	Mexico	Spain	Tajikistan	Russia	Ukraine	United States	World Total
1999	240	200	40	300	15	433	35	50	NA	NA	1,320
2000	216	200	76	257	15	500	40	50	NA	NA	1,360
2001	321	190	71	300	15	500	40	50	----	NA	1,500
2002	307	495	51	300	15	727	20	50	NA	NA	1,980
2003	176	610	25	300	15	500	30	50	----	NA	1,730
2004	73	1,140	24	300	15	250	30	50	----	NA	1,900
2005	4	1,100	20	200	6	----	30	50	----	NA	1,520
2006	----	760	20	250	8	----	30	50	----	NA	1,150
2007[1]	----	800	20	250	8	----	30	50	----	NA	1,170
2008[2]	----	600	----	250	----	----	----	----	----	NA	950

[1] Preliminary.   [2] Estimate.   [4] Less than 1/2 unit.   NA = Not available   W = Withheld.   *Source: U.S. Geological Survey (USGS)*

Salient Statistics of Mercury in the United States   In Metric Tons

Year	Producing Mines	Secondary Production Industrial	Secondary Production Government[3]	NDS[4] Shipments	Consumer & Dealer Stocks, Dec. 31	Industrial Demand	Exports	Imports
2000	NA	NA	----	----	NA	NA	182	103
2001	NA	NA	----	----	NA	NA	108	100
2002	NA	NA	----	----	40	NA	201	209
2003	NA	NA	----	----	94	72	287	46
2004	NA	NA	----	----	62	91	278	92
2005	NA	NA	----	----	38	40	319	212
2006	NA	NA	----	----	19	38	390	94
2007[1]	NA	NA	----	----	18	31	84	67
2008[2]	NA	NA	----	----			900	150

[1] Preliminary.   [2] Estimate.   [3] Secondary mercury shipped from the Department of Energy.   [4] National Defense Stockpile.   NA = Not available.
E = Net exporter.   *Source: U.S. Geological Survey (USGS)*

Mercury (monthly average) through December 2008   Cents per pound

Average Price of Mercury in New York   In Dollars Per Flask of 76 Pounds (34.5 Kilograms)

Year	Jan.	Feb.	Mar.	Apr.	May	June	July	Aug.	Sept.	Oct.	Nov.	Dec.	Average
1999	175.00	152.63	150.00	150.00	150.00	150.00	150.00	150.00	150.00	150.00	150.00	150.00	152.09
2000	150.00	157.88	167.50	167.50	167.50	158.23	142.00	142.00	142.00	142.00	142.00	142.00	151.90
2001	142.00	142.00	142.00	142.00	142.00	143.71	154.00	154.00	154.00	154.00	154.00	154.00	148.12
2002	154.00	154.00	154.00	154.00	154.00	154.00	154.00	154.00	154.00	154.00	154.00	154.00	154.00
2003	165.43	175.00	175.00	175.00	185.23	187.50	187.50	187.50	187.50	187.50	195.63	200.00	184.07
2004	200.00	256.25	297.61	305.00	305.00	305.00	305.00	305.00	417.05	485.12	649.24	650.00	373.36
2005	678.57	747.50	867.39	873.81	850.00	817.05	759.52	750.00	813.64	730.95	700.00	700.00	774.04
2006	700.00	700.00	691.30	552.50	574.02	582.50	582.50	582.50	582.50	576.59	513.64	500.00	594.84
2007	500.00	500.00	500.00	500.00	500.00	573.81	600.00	600.00	572.50	550.00	550.00	550.00	541.36
2008	550.00	550.00	550.00	550.00	550.00	550.00	550.00	550.00	590.91	600.00	645.00	650.00	573.83

Source: American Metal Market (AMM)

Mercury Consumed in the United States   In Metric Tons

Year	Batteries[3]	Chlorine & Caustic Soda	Catalysts, Misc.	Dental Equip.	Electrical Lighting[3]	General Lab Use	Measuring Control Instrument	Paints	Wiring Devices & Switches[3]	Other Uses	Grand Total
1989	250	379	40	39	31	18	87	192	141	32	1,212
1990	106	247	29	44	33	32	108	14	70	38	720
1991	18	184	26	41	39	30	90	6	71	49	554
1992	13	209	20	42	55	28	80	----	82	92	621
1993	10	180	18	35	38	26	65	----	83	103	558
1994	6	135	25	24	27	24	53	----	79	110	483
1995	----	154	----	32	30	----	43	----	84	93	436
1996[1]	----	136	----	31	29	----	41	----	49	86	372
1997[2]	----	160	----	40	29	----	24	----	57	36	346
	Data No Longer Available										

[1] Preliminary.   [2] Estimate.   W = Withheld proprietary data.   *Source: U.S. Geological Survey (USGS)*

Milk

Evidence of man's use of animal milk as food was discovered in a temple in the Euphrates Valley near Babylon, dating back to 3,000 BC. Humans drink the milk produced from a variety of domesticated mammals, including cows, goats, sheep, camels, reindeer, buffaloes, and llama. In India, half of all milk consumed is from water buffalo. Camels' milk spoils slower than other types of milk in the hot desert, but the vast majority of milk used for commercial production and consumption comes from cows.

Milk directly from a cow in its natural form is called raw milk. Raw milk is processed by spinning it in a centrifuge, homogenizing it to create a consistent texture (i.e., by forcing hot milk under high pressure through small nozzles), and then sterilizing it through pasteurization (i.e., heating to a high temperature for a specified length of time to destroy pathogenic bacteria). Condensed, powdered, and evaporated milk are produced by evaporating some or all of the water content. Whole milk contains 3.5% milk fat. Lower-fat milks include 2% low-fat milk, 1% low- fat milk, and skim milk, which has only 1/2 gram of milk fat per serving.

The CME Group has three different milk futures contracts: Milk Class III which is milk used in the manufacturing of cheese, Milk Class IV which is milk used in the production of butter and all dried milk products, and Nonfat Dry Milk which is used in commercial or consumer cooking or to reconstitute nonfat milk by the consumer. The Milk Class III contract has the largest volume and open interest.

Prices – The average monthly price received by farmers for all milk sold to plants in 2008 fell by -4.3% yr/yr to $18.32 per hundred pounds, down from last year's record high. The average monthly price received by farmers for fluid grade milk in 2008 fell by -4.3% yr/yr to $18.31. The average monthly price received by farmers for manufacturing grade milk in 2008 fell by 0.8% to $18.03.

Supply – World milk production in 2008 fell -23.0% to 437.640 million metric tons. The biggest producers were the European Union with 31% of world production, the U.S. with 20%, and India with10%. U.S. 2008 milk production in pounds rose +2.4% yr/yr to 189.992 billion pounds, which was a new record high. The number of dairy cows on U.S. farms has fallen sharply in the past 3 decades from the 12 million seen in 1970. In 2008, there were 9.315 million dairy cows on U.S. farms. Dairy farmers have been able to increase milk production even with fewer cows because of a dramatic increase in milk yield per cow. In 2008, the average cow produced a record 20,724 pounds of milk per year, more than double the 9,751 pounds seen in 1970.

Demand – Per capita consumption of milk in the U.S. fell to a new record low of 206 pounds per year in 2002 (the latest data available), down sharply by 26% from 277 pounds in 1977. The utilization breakdown for 2002 shows the largest manufacturing usage categories are cheese (64.504 billion pounds of milk) and creamery butter (30.250 billion pounds).

Trade – U.S. imports of milk in 2008 fell by -26.7% yr/yr to 3.400 billion pounds, far below the record high of 5.716 billion pounds posted in 2001.

World Fluid Milk Production (Cow's Milk)   In Thousands of Metric Tons

Year	Argentina	Australia	Brazil	China	European Union	India	Japan	Mexico	New Zealand	Russia	Ukraine	United States	World Total
2002	8,500	11,608	22,635	12,998	134,086	36,200	8,385	9,560	13,925	33,500	13,860	77,140	536,352
2003	7,950	10,636	22,860	17,463	135,069	36,500	8,400	9,784	14,346	33,000	13,400	77,289	541,446
2004	9,250	10,377	23,317	22,606	133,969	37,500	8,329	9,874	15,000	32,000	13,787	77,534	546,305
2005	9,500	10,429	24,250	27,534	134,672	37,520	8,285	9,855	14,500	32,000	13,423	80,254	553,049
2006	10,200	10,395	25,230	31,934	132,206	41,000	8,137	10,051	15,200	31,100	12,890	82,462	558,120
2007	9,550	9,870	26,750	35,252	132,604	42,890	8,007	10,657	15,640	32,200	11,997	84,188	568,260
2008[1]	10,100	9,500	28,890	36,700	134,000	44,100	7,990	10,814	15,141	32,500	11,070	86,026	437,640
2009[2]	10,400	9,675	30,335	38,630	134,400	45,140	8,010	11,030	16,350	32,830	10,350	86,817	444,799

[1] Preliminary.   [2] Forecast.   *Source: Foreign Agricultural Service, U.S. Department of Agriculture (FAS-USDA)*

Salient Statistics of Milk in the United States   In Millions of Pounds

Year	Number of Milk Cows on Farms[3] (Thousands)	Production Per Cow[4] (Pounds)	Production Total[4]	Beginning Stocks[5]	Imports	Total Supply	Exports[5]	Domestic Fed to Calves	Domestic Humans	Total Use	All Milk, Wholesale	Milk, Eligible for Fluid Market	Milk, Manufacturing Grade	Per Capita Consumption[6] (Fluid Milk in Lbs)
2001	9,114	18,158	165,497	7,010	5,716	178,223	----	1,036	164,123	165,159	14.98	14.99	14.78	208
2002	9,139	18,608	170,063	7,259	5,103	182,425	----	959	168,944	169,903	12.10	12.10	10.92	206
2003	9,083	18,761	170,394	9,891	5,040	185,325	----	964	169,276	170,240	12.52	12.53	11.77	
2004	9,010	18,958	170,805	8,333	5,278	184,416	----	956	169,699	170,655	16.04	16.04	15.41	
2005	9,040	19,577	176,989	7,154	5,071	189,214	3,300	987	175,788	180,075	15.14	15.14	14.45	
2006	9,112	19,951	181,798	8,007	4,981	194,786	3,400	1,001	180,640	185,041	12.91	12.92	12.28	
2007[1]	9,158	20,266	185,602	9,500	4,638	199,740	5,700	1,014	184,435	191,149	19.13	19.13	18.18	
2008[2]	9,315	20,396	189,992	10,355	3,400	203,747	8,700				18.32	18.31	18.03	

[1] Preliminary.   [2] Estimate.   [3] Average number on farms during year including dry cows, excluding heifers not yet fresh.   [4] Excludes milk sucked by calves.   [5] Government and commercial.   [6] Product pounds of commercial sales and on farm consumption.
Source: Economic Research Service, U.S. Department of Agriculture (ERS-USDA)

Utilization of Milk in the United States   In Millions of Pounds (Milk Equivalent)

Year	Butter from Whey Cream	Creamery Butter[2]	Cheese[3]	Cottage Cheese (Creamed)	Canned Milk[4]	Bulk Condensed Whole Milk Unsweet-ened	Sweet-ened	Dry Whole Milk Products	Ice Cream[5]	Other Frozen Dairy Products	Other Manu-factured Pro-ducts[6]	Used on Farms Farm-Churned Butter	Total
1999	5,392	28,657	60,154	NA	1,037	216	171	868	2,305	14,370	682	219	1,328
2000	5,538	28,059	62,257	NA	965	180	163	815	2,218	14,447	700	196	1,303
2001	5,612	27,557	61,804	NA	991	170	163	303	2,220	14,395	701	170	1,181
2002	5,791	30,250	64,504	374	593	77	56	47	2,320	14,373	706	160	1,119
2003	NA	NA	NA	385	595	128	76	39	NA	NA	NA	149	1,105
2004	NA	NA	NA	382	549	117	76	42	NA	NA	NA	147	1,103
2005	NA	NA	NA	377	548	124	67	32	NA	NA	NA	153	1,140
2006[1]	NA	NA	NA	367	517	115	68	31	NA	NA	NA	150	1,143

[1] Preliminary.   [2] Excludes whey butter.   [3] American and other.   [4] Includes evaporated and sweetened condensed.   [5] Milk equivalent of butter and condensed milk used in ice cream.   [6] Whole milk equivalent of dry cream, malted milk powder, part-skim milk, dry or concentrated ice cream mix, dehydrated butterfat and other miscellaneous products using milkfat.
Source: National Agricultural Statistics Service, U.S. Department of Agriculture (NASS-USDA)

Milk-Feed Price Ratio[1] in the United States   In Pounds

Year	Jan.	Feb.	Mar.	Apr.	May	June	July	Aug.	Sept.	Oct.	Nov.	Dec.	Average
2001	3.08	3.03	3.24	3.29	3.41	3.74	3.60	3.62	3.75	3.55	3.29	2.99	3.38
2002	3.03	3.00	2.89	2.81	2.64	2.54	2.34	2.27	2.30	2.46	2.44	2.44	2.60
2003	2.40	2.35	2.27	2.25	2.19	2.21	2.60	2.89	3.16	3.23	3.05	2.89	2.62
2004	2.70	2.60	2.80	3.11	3.15	3.12	2.96	2.93	3.22	3.27	3.57	3.67	3.09
2005	3.45	3.50	3.35	3.18	2.93	2.87	2.93	3.08	3.27	3.42	3.45	3.28	3.23
2006	3.17	2.93	2.70	2.48	2.32	2.35	2.33	2.48	2.61	2.53	2.44	2.43	2.56
2007	2.45	2.33	2.39	2.51	2.54	2.88	3.16	3.19	3.19	3.10	3.05	2.85	2.80
2008[2]	2.65	2.24	2.07	1.89	1.83	1.88	1.91	1.81	1.89	2.00	2.02	1.92	2.01

[1] Pounds of 16% protein mixed dairy feed equal in value to one pound of whole milk.   [2] Preliminary.   *Source: Economic Research Service, U.S. Department of Agriculture (ERS-USDA)*

Milk Production[1] in the United States   In Millions of Pounds

Year	Jan.	Feb.	Mar.	Apr.	May	June	July	Aug.	Sept.	Oct.	Nov.	Dec.	Total
2002	14,304	13,229	14,864	14,580	15,118	14,317	14,196	14,128	13,467	13,866	13,478	14,211	170,063
2003	14,584	13,441	15,044	14,634	15,003	14,328	14,263	14,015	13,468	13,898	13,470	14,164	170,394
2004	14,402	13,595	14,762	14,519	15,012	14,293	14,405	14,215	13,619	14,070	13,610	14,303	170,805
2005	14,614	13,530	15,206	15,047	15,697	15,087	14,978	14,896	14,260	14,611	14,209	14,854	176,989
2006	15,343	14,238	15,966	15,538	16,068	15,324	15,168	15,061	14,481	14,857	14,523	15,231	181,798
2007	15,605	14,321	16,132	15,763	16,180	15,476	15,714	15,525	14,871	15,370	15,013	15,632	185,602
2008[1]	15,976	15,176	16,458	16,125	16,707	15,942	15,995	15,757	15,129	15,615	15,212	15,900	189,992

[1] Preliminary.   [2] Excludes milk sucked by calves.   *Source: Economic Research Service, U.S. Department of Agriculture (ERS-USDA)*

Average Price Received by Farmers for All Milk (Sold to Plants)   In Dollars Per Hundred Pounds (Cwt.)

Year	Jan.	Feb.	Mar.	Apr.	May	June	July	Aug.	Sept.	Oct.	Nov.	Dec.	Average
2002	13.40	13.10	12.70	12.50	12.10	11.50	11.10	11.30	11.60	12.10	11.90	11.90	12.10
2003	11.70	11.40	11.00	11.00	11.00	11.00	12.10	13.30	14.50	15.00	14.40	13.80	12.52
2004	13.20	13.60	15.40	18.10	19.30	18.20	16.10	14.90	15.50	15.60	16.20	16.40	16.04
2005	15.90	15.50	15.60	15.20	14.70	14.40	14.80	14.80	15.30	15.60	15.10	14.80	15.14
2006	14.50	13.50	12.60	12.10	11.90	11.90	11.70	12.00	13.00	13.60	13.90	14.20	12.91
2007	14.50	14.90	15.60	16.60	18.00	20.20	21.60	21.60	21.80	21.40	21.90	21.50	19.13
2008[1]	20.50	19.10	18.10	18.00	18.40	19.30	19.40	18.40	18.20	17.70	17.10	15.60	18.32

[1] Preliminary.   *Source: Economic Research Service, U.S. Department of Agriculture (ERS-USDA)*

Average Price Received by Farmers for Fluid Grade Milk   In Dollars Per Hundred Pounds (Cwt.)

Year	Jan.	Feb.	Mar.	Apr.	May	June	July	Aug.	Sept.	Oct.	Nov.	Dec.	Average
2002	13.40	13.10	12.70	12.50	12.10	11.50	11.10	11.30	11.60	12.10	11.90	11.90	12.10
2003	11.80	11.40	11.00	11.00	11.00	11.00	12.10	13.30	14.50	15.00	14.40	13.80	12.53
2004	13.20	13.60	15.40	18.10	19.30	18.20	16.10	14.90	15.50	15.60	16.20	16.40	16.04
2005	15.90	15.50	15.60	15.20	14.70	14.40	14.80	14.80	15.30	15.60	15.10	14.80	15.14
2006	14.50	13.50	12.60	12.10	11.90	11.90	11.70	12.10	13.00	13.60	13.90	14.20	12.92
2007	14.50	14.90	15.60	16.60	18.00	20.20	21.60	21.60	21.80	21.40	21.90	21.50	19.13
2008[1]	20.50	19.10	18.00	18.00	18.40	19.30	19.40	18.40	18.20	17.70	17.10	15.60	18.31

[1] Preliminary.   *Source: Economic Research Service, U.S. Department of Agriculture (ERS-USDA)*

Molybdenum

Molybdenum (symbol Mo) is a silvery-white, hard, malleable, metallic element. Molybdenum melts at about 2610 degrees Celsius and boils at about 4640 degrees Celsius. Swedish chemist Carl Wilhelm Scheele discovered molybdenum in 1778.

Molybdenum occurs in nature in the form of molybdenite and wulfenite. Contributing to the growth of plants, it is an important trace element in soils. Approximately 70% of the world supply of molybdenum is obtained as a by-product of copper mining. Molybdenum is chiefly used as an alloy to strengthen steel and resist corrosion. It is used for structural work, aircraft parts, and forged automobile parts because it withstands high temperatures and pressures and adds strength. Other uses include lubricants, a refractory metal in chemical applications, electron tubing, and as a catalyst.

Prices – The average monthly U.S. merchant price of molybdic oxide in 2008 rose by +0.6% yr/yr to $29.74 per pound. That was below the 2005 record high of $32.70 per pound but still almost 11 times higher than the decade low of $2.37 seen in 2001.

Supply – World production of molybdenum in 2008 rose by +3.4% yr/yr to a record high of 212,000 metric tons, continuing the recovery from the 14-year low of 122,000 metric tons seen in 2002. The world's largest producers of molybdenum are the U.S. with 29% of world production in 2008, China with 28%, and Chili with 21%

U.S. production of molybdenum concentrate in 2008 rose +7.7% yr/yr to 61,400 metric tons, continuing the recovery from the 25-year low of 32,300 metric tons posted in 2002. U.S. production of molybdenum primary products in 2006 rose +2.7% to 30,600 metric tons, with 29,000 metric tons of that production in molybdic oxide and 1,600 metric tons in molybdenum metal powder.

Demand – U.S. consumption of molybdenum concentrate in 2006 (latest data available) fell by 4.7% yr/yr to 44,400 metric tons, but remained well above the 12-year low of 21,200 metric tons posted in 2002. U.S. consumption of molybdenum concentrate has more than doubled over the last 10 years. U.S. consumption of molybdenum primary products rose by +11.7% yr/yr in 2008 to 22,900 metric tons.

Trade – U.S. imports of molybdenum concentrate for consumption in 2006 fell -8.4% yr/yr to 10,900 metric tons, but still well above the 12-year low of 4,710 metric tons posted in 2002.

World Mine Production of Molybdenum In Metric Tons (Contained Molybdenum)

Year	Armenia	Canada[3]	Chile	China	Iran	Kazak-hstan	Mexico	Mongolia	Peru	Russia	United States	Uzbek-isten	World Total
2002	2,884	8,043	29,466	29,300	2,300	230	3,428	1,590	8,613	2,900	32,300	500	122,000
2003	2,763	9,090	33,374	31,000	2,200	230	3,524	1,793	9,561	2,900	33,500	500	131,000
2004	2,950	9,520	41,883	38,500	1,800	230	3,730	1,141	14,246	2,900	41,500	500	159,000
2005	3,000	7,935	48,041	40,000	2,000	230	4,246	1,188	17,325	3,000	58,000	575	186,000
2006	3,000	7,840	43,278	43,900	2,000	250	2,500	1,200	17,209	3,100	59,800	600	185,000
2007[1]	4,080	12,000	44,912	59,800	2,600	400	2,500	1,300	16,737	3,300	57,000	600	205,000
2008[2]	4,100	12,000	45,000	59,800	2,600	400	4,000	1,300	17,000	3,500	61,400	600	212,000

[1] Preliminary. [2] Estimate. [3] Shipments. *Source: U.S. Geological Survey (USGS)*

Salient Statistics of Molybdenum in the United States In Metric Tons (Contained Molybdenum)

| | Concentrate | | | | | | | | Primary Products[4] | | | | | |
| | | Shipments | | | | | | | Net Production | | | Shipments | | |
Year	Production	Total (Including Exports)	Value Million $	For Exports	Con-sumption	Imports For Con-sumption	Stocks Dec. 31[3]	Grand Total	Molybdic Oxide[5]	Molyb-denum Metal Powder	Avg Price Value $ / Kg.[6]	To Oxide for Domestic Dest-inations	Exports, Gross Weight	Con-sumption	Producer Stocks, Dec. 31
2002	32,300	32,300	232.0	----	21,200	4,710	3,870	10,500	10,000	513	8.27	27,500	1,670	15,300	4,300
2003	33,500	33,600	324.0	----	27,500	5,190	2,520	11,800	11,000	760	11.75	30,100	2,580	16,400	2,760
2004	41,500	42,000	1,420.0	----	38,700	8,780	2,610	24,300	23,400	868	36.73	39,300	5,280	17,400	2,840
2005	58,000	57,900	NA	----	46,600	11,900	3,620	29,800	28,700	1,050	70.11	46,700	14,600	18,900	3,770
2006	59,800	59,900	NA	----	44,400	10,900	2,120	30,600	29,000	1,620	54.62	51,000	11,600	19,000	3,210
2007[1]	57,000										66.79			20,500	
2008[2]	61,400										73.30			22,900	

[1] Preliminary. [2] Estimate. [3] At mines & at plants making molybdenum products. [4] Comprises ferromolybdenum, molybdic oxide, & molybdenum salts & metal. [5] Includes molybdic oxide briquets, molybdic acid, molybdenum trioxide, all other. [6] U.S. producer price per kilogram of molybdenum oxide contained in technical-grade molybdic oxide. W = Withheld proprietary data. E = Net exporter. *Source: U.S. Geological Survey (USGS)*

US Merchant Price of Molybdic Oxide In Dollars Per Pound

Year	Jan.	Feb.	Mar.	Apr.	May	June	July	Aug.	Sept.	Oct.	Nov.	Dec.	Average
2002	2.33	2.33	2.33	2.75	2.99	6.93	5.32	4.75	4.73	4.70	3.82	3.48	3.87
2003	3.63	3.74	4.62	5.20	5.20	5.77	5.86	5.60	5.84	6.25	6.25	6.25	5.35
2004	7.63	8.15	8.93	13.11	14.00	15.03	15.75	16.70	18.27	19.50	22.66	27.50	15.60
2005	33.00	30.15	33.59	34.79	36.41	38.32	32.79	30.00	31.93	32.33	30.33	28.72	32.70
2006	23.70	24.54	23.12	22.93	24.82	26.31	26.01	25.60	26.96	26.02	25.41	25.50	25.08
2007	25.22	25.53	27.77	28.52	30.05	33.71	32.23	31.39	23.00	32.00	32.80	32.63	29.57
2008	32.74	32.88	32.88	32.88	32.88	32.88	32.88	33.17	33.75	33.75	15.58	10.62	29.74

Source: American Metal Market (AMM)

Nickel

Nickel (symbol Ni) is a hard, malleable, ductile metal that has a silvery tinge that can take on a high polish. Nickel is somewhat ferromagnetic and is a fair conductor of heat and electricity. Nickel is primarily used in the production of stainless steel and other corrosion-resistant alloys. Nickel is used in coins to replace silver, in rechargeable batteries, and in electronic circuitry. Nickel plating techniques, like electro-less coating or single-slurry coating, are employed in such applications as turbine blades, helicopter rotors, extrusion dies, and rolled steel strip.

Nickel futures and options trade at the London Metal Exchange (LME). The nickel futures contract calls for the delivery of 6 metric tons of primary nickel with at least 99.80% purity in the form of full plate, cut cathodes, pellets or briquettes. The contract is priced in terms of U.S. dollars per metric ton.

Prices – Nickel prices varied widely during 2008. Nickel started the year at about $28,000 per metric ton in the midst of a sharp downturn from the record high of $54,200 per metric ton in June 2007. Except for a brief rally in March to about $32,700, the price continued to move lower during the rest of 2008 to end the year at about $13,000 per metric ton.

Supply – World mine production of nickel in 2008 fell -3.0% yr/yr to 1.610 million metric tons, down slightly from the 2007 record high production of 1.660 million metric tons. That is more than double the production seen in 1970. The world's largest mine producers of nickel in 2008 were Russia (with 17% of world production), Canada (16%), Indonesia (13%), Australia (11%), and New Caledonia (6%). In 2006 (latest data available) U.S. secondary nickel production rose +6.6% to a record high of 108,210 metric tons. That was well up from the 5-year low of 81,200 metric tons in 2001.

Demand – U.S. consumption of nickel in 2006 (latest data available) rose +8.7% to a record high of 213,000 metric tons. The primary U.S. nickel consumption use is for stainless and heat-resisting steels, which accounted for 62% of U.S. consumption in 2005. Other consumption uses were nickel alloys (9%), super alloys (8%), electro-plating anodes (5%), copper base alloys (3%), alloy steels (2%), and chemicals (1%).

Trade – The U.S. relied on imports for 33% of its nickel consumption in 2008, down from 64% in 1998. U.S. imports of primary and secondary nickel in 2008 rose +15.6% to 163,200 metric tons, up from 2002's 16-year low of 130,110 metric tons. U.S. exports of primary and secondary nickel in 2008 rose +6.8% to 124,000 metric tons, which was a new record high.

World Mine Production of Nickel   In Metric Tons (Contained Nickel)

Year	Australia[3]	Botswana	Brazil	Canada	China	Republic	Greece	Indonesia	New Caledonia	Philippines	Russia	South Africa	Total
2002	188,000	28,600	45,456	189,297	53,700	38,859	22,670	143,000	99,841	24,148	310,000	38,546	1,350,000
2003	191,000	38,230	44,928	163,244	61,000	45,253	21,410	144,000	112,013	19,537	300,000	40,842	1,370,000
2004	187,000	35,163	51,886	186,694	75,600	46,000	21,700	136,000	119,199	16,973	315,000	39,851	1,420,000
2005	189,000	39,305	74,198	199,932	72,700	53,124	23,210	135,000	111,939	22,555	315,000	42,392	1,500,000
2006	185,000	38,000	82,492	233,461	82,100	46,526	21,670	140,000	102,986	50,637	320,000	41,599	1,580,000
2007[1]	161,000	38,000	75,300	255,000	85,000	47,100	21,200	229,000	125,000	79,500	280,000	37,900	1,660,000
2008[2]	180,000	36,000	75,600	250,000	85,000	47,000	20,100	211,000	92,600	88,400	276,000	38,000	1,610,000

[1] Preliminary.   [2] Estimate.   [3] Content of nickel sulfate and concentrates.   *Source: U.S. Geological Survey (USGS)*

Salient Statistics of Nickel in the United States   In Metric Tons (Contained Nickel)

Year	Net Import Reliance As a % of Apparent Consumption	Production - Plant[4]	Secondary[5]	Alloy Sheets	Cast Iron	Copper Base Alloys	Electro-plating Anodes	Nickel Alloys	Stainless & Heat Resisting Steels	Super Alloys	Chemicals	Apparent Consumption	Stocks, Dec. 31 At Consumer Plants	Stocks, Dec. 31 At Producer Plants	Primary & Secondary Exports	Primary & Secondary Imports	Avg. Price LME $/Lb.
2002	46	----	99,250	3,920	427	5,280	12,300	14,200	135,000	12,600	1,280	197,000	11,540	6,150	45,920	130,110	3.07
2003	45	----	100,900	3,730	591	5,200	11,400	14,600	114,000	13,400	2,400	165,000	11,680	8,040	53,630	136,500	4.37
2004	49	----	103,210	3,770	306	5,990	11,900	15,400	115,000	15,700	6,270	183,000	11,880	6,580	56,300	154,800	6.27
2005	48	----	101,520	4,020	179	6,090	11,300	18,800	131,000	18,000	2,030	196,000	13,470	5,940	63,230	158,500	6.69
2006	49	----	108,210	4,070	180	7,010	10,700	19,600	151,000	20,500	1,930	213,000	14,100	6,450	67,350	173,300	11.00
2007[2]	21		5,350										14,100	6,600	116,100	141,200	16.88
2008[3]	33												14,300	6,700	124,000	163,200	9.69

[1] Exclusive of scrap.   [2] Preliminary.   3/ Estimate.   [4] Smelter & refinery.   [5] From purchased scrap (ferrous & nonferrous).
W = Withheld proprietary data.   NA = Not available.   *Source: U.S. Geological Survey (USGS)*

Average Price of Nickel[1] in the United States   In Cents Per Pound

Year	Jan.	Feb.	Mar.	Apr.	May	June	July	Aug.	Sept.	Oct.	Nov.	Dec.	Average
2004	734.25	725.15	659.93	625.29	542.52	648.94	715.77	656.11	640.61	689.95	673.15	656.37	664.00
2005	696.18	733.52	773.94	772.25	813.21	788.04	707.58	720.47	692.83	610.92	594.54	657.44	713.41
2006	705.36	718.05	716.83	854.01	994.34	996.93	1,273.06	1,461.61	1,424.67	1,545.18	1,511.97	1,629.01	1,152.59
2007	1,734.23	1,930.47	2,172.62	2,378.64	2,476.96	2,002.41	1,618.56	1,342.03	1,425.77	1,489.95	1,477.33	1,254.00	1,775.25
2008	1,328.12	1,341.80	1,475.21	1,376.29	1,243.11	1,094.23	986.01	929.79	870.45	612.68	551.36	501.41	1,025.87

[1] Plating material, briquettes.   *Source: American Metal Market (AMM)*

Oats

Oats are seeds or grains of a genus of plants that thrive in cool, moist climates. There are about 25 species of oats that grow worldwide in the cooler temperate regions. The oldest known cultivated oats were found inside caves in Switzerland and are believed to be from the Bronze Age. Oats are usually sown in early spring and harvested in mid to late summer, but in southern regions of the northern hemisphere, they may be sown in the fall. Oats are used in many processed foods such as flour, livestock feed, and furfural, a chemical used as a solvent in various refining industries. The oat crop year begins in June and ends in May. Oat futures and options are traded on the Chicago Board of Trade (CBOT) and the Winnipeg Commodity Exchange (WCE).

Prices – Oat prices on the CBOT weekly nearest futures chart started the year 2008 at about $3.30 per bushel, and moved higher to close at $3.91 per bushel in March. Oats then moved lower to $3.34 before rallying to the year's high at $4.55 per bushel at the end of June. From there the price moved steadily lower to end the year at about $2.30 per bushel. The down move continued into early 2009 with the price reaching about $1.75 per bushel in March 2009.

Regarding cash prices, the average monthly price received by farmers for oats in the U.S. in the first eight months of the 2008-09 marketing year (i.e., June 2008 to May 2009) rose +10.5% yr/yr to $3.13 per bushel.

Supply – World oat production in 2008-09 rose +4.6% yr/yr at 26.741 million metric tons, up from the record low of 23.163 in 2006-07. World annual oat production in the past three decades has dropped very sharply from levels above 50 million metric tons in the early 1970s. The world's largest oat producers are the European Union with 33% of world production in 2008-09, Russia with 22%, Canada with 16%, the U.S. with 5%, and Australia with 4%.

U.S. oat production in the 2008-09 marketing year fell by –3.2% yr/yr to 88.635 million bushels, which was a new record low. U.S. oat production has fallen sharply from levels mostly above 1 billion bushels seen from the early 1900s into the early 1960s. U.S. farmers harvested only 1.395 million acres of oats in 2008-09, which was down –7.3% from the previous year and posted a new record low. That is down from the almost 40 million acres harvested back in the 1950s. The oat yield in 2008-09 rose +4.3% to 63.5 bushels per acre. Oat stocks in the U.S. as of December 2008 were up +21.7% yr/yr to a 5-year high for December. The largest U.S. oat-producing states in 2006 were the states of Wisconsin (with 13% of U.S. production), Minnesota (13%), South Dakota (10%), Texas (6%), Iowa (6%), and Pennsylvania (5%).

Demand – U.S. usage of oats in 2008-09 fell -0.4% yr/yr to a record low of 198.0 million bushels. Regarding U.S. usage of oats in 2008-09, 60.6% was for feed and residual, 33.4% for food, alcohol and industrial, 4.5% for seed, and 1.5% for exports.

Trade – U.S. exports of oats rose +3.1% to a mere 3.0 million bushels in 2008-09. U.S. imports of oats in 2008-09 fell -10.8% yr/yr to 110.0 million bushels, down from last year's record high of 123.29 million bushels.

World Production of Oats   In Thousands of Metric Tons

Crop Year	Argentina	Australia	Belarus	Brazil	Canada	China	European Union	Norway	Turkey	Ukraine	United States	Russia	World Total
1999-00	555	1,118	368	250	3,641	600	8,542	356	290	760	2,114	4,400	24,110
2000-01	645	1,050	495	330	3,389	600	8,783	397	314	881	2,165	6,000	25,977
2001-02	645	1,434	530	277	2,691	600	8,491	330	265	1,116	1,707	7,700	27,033
2002-03	500	957	575	390	2,911	600	9,680	279	290	943	1,684	5,700	25,599
2003-04	348	2,018	500	413	3,377	600	9,019	333	285	925	2,096	5,200	26,259
2004-05	508	1,283	770	433	3,467	600	9,146	359	290	1,000	1,679	4,950	25,667
2005-06	350	1,690	600	517	3,283	600	7,968	360	290	800	1,667	4,550	23,861
2006-07[1]	400	748	550	475	3,852	600	7,768	360	290	700	1,357	4,900	23,163
2007-08[2]	470	843	600	475	4,696	600	8,823	360	290	550	1,313	5,400	25,577
2008-09[3]	500	1,200	900	475	4,270	600	8,952	360	290	950	1,287	5,800	26,741

[1] Preliminary.   [2] Estimate.   [3] Forecast.   Source: Foreign Agricultural Service, U.S. Department of Agriculture (FAS-USDA)

Official Oats Crop Production Reports in the United States   In Thousands of Bushels

Year	July 1	Aug. 1	Sept. 1	Oct. 1	Dec. 1	Final	Year	July 1	Aug. 1	Sept. 1	Oct. 1	Dec. 1	Final
1997	182,672	187,127	----	----	----	167,246	2003	147,895	151,345	----	----	----	144,383
1998	183,201	177,211	----	----	----	165,768	2004	121,860	127,950	----	----	----	115,695
1999	----	162,096	----	----	----	145,628	2005	131,314	127,819	----	----	----	114,878
2000	151,380	152,745	----	----	----	149,165	2006	110,322	107,423	----	----	----	93,638
2001	132,150	135,445	----	----	----	117,024	2007	100,921	98,341	----	----	----	91,599
2002	147,584	142,580	----	----	----	116,002	2008[1]	92,872	89,897	----	----	----	88,635

[1] Preliminary.   Source: National Agricultural Statistics Service, U.S. Department of Agriculture (NASS-USDA)

Oat Stocks in the United States   In Thousands of Bushels

	On Farms				Off Farms				Total Stocks			
Year	Mar. 1	June 1	Sept. 1	Dec. 1	Mar. 1	June 1	Sept. 1	Dec. 1	Mar. 1	June 1	Sept. 1	Dec. 1
1999	61,700	40,700	97,300	79,800	50,850	40,678	51,151	53,872	112,550	81,378	148,451	133,672
2000	53,300	36,000	101,200	86,900	48,500	40,031	49,177	57,237	101,800	76,031	150,377	144,137
2001	55,800	32,050	74,800	58,100	54,128	40,677	41,592	56,117	109,928	72,727	116,392	114,217
2002	40,200	28,650	70,500	52,500	53,158	34,552	41,212	51,284	93,358	63,202	111,712	103,784
2003	35,000	20,600	82,100	64,400	47,879	29,233	49,637	54,900	82,879	49,833	131,737	119,300
2004	45,600	27,500	74,300	60,400	49,414	37,348	41,458	44,513	95,014	64,848	115,758	104,913
2005	43,500	25,350	71,700	60,100	38,946	32,592	41,803	35,617	82,446	57,942	113,503	95,717
2006	42,200	25,190	60,800	53,000	32,673	27,376	39,284	45,889	74,873	52,566	100,084	98,889
2007	33,900	18,400	53,650	43,100	37,158	32,198	34,710	51,331	71,058	50,598	88,360	94,431
2008[1]	31,000	16,100	52,800	42,600	47,988	50,674	66,296	72,278	78,988	66,774	119,096	114,878

[1] Preliminary.   Source: National Agricultural Statistics Service, U.S. Department of Agriculture (NASS-USDA)

Supply and Utilization of Oats in the United States   In Millions of Bushels

Crop Year Beginning June 1	Acreage Planted	Acreage Harvested	Yield Per Acre (Bushels)	Pro-duction	Imports	Total Supply	Feed & Residual	Food, Alcohol & Industrial	Seed	Exports	Total Use	Ending Stocks	Farm Price	Findley Loan Rate	Target Price
	--- 1,000 Acres ---			In Millions of Bushels									Dollars Per Bushel		
1999-00	4,668	2,445	59.6	145.6	99.0	326.0	180.0	56.8	11.2	1.8	250.0	76.0	1.12	1.13	NA
2000-01	4,473	2,325	64.2	149.2	106.0	332.0	189.0	57.0	11.0	1.7	259.0	73.0	1.10	1.16	NA
2001-02	4,403	1,905	61.4	117.0	96.0	286.3	148.3	59.2	12.8	2.8	223.1	63.2	1.59	1.21	NA
2002-03	4,995	2,058	56.4	116.0	95.1	274.3	149.9	60.2	11.8	2.6	224.5	49.8	1.81	1.35	1.40
2003-04	4,597	2,220	65.0	144.4	89.7	284.0	143.7	62.4	10.5	2.5	219.1	64.9	1.48	1.35	1.40
2004-05	4,085	1,787	64.7	115.7	90.3	270.9	136.3	63.0	11.0	2.7	212.9	57.9	1.48	1.33	1.44
2005-06	4,246	1,823	63.0	114.9	91.2	264.0	135.7	62.9	10.8	2.1	211.4	52.6	1.63		
2006-07	4,168	1,566	59.8	93.6	106.2	252.4	125.1	64.5	9.7	2.6	201.8	50.6	1.87		
2007-08[1]	3,760	1,505	60.9	91.6	123.3	265.5	120.8	66.0	9.0	2.9	198.7	66.8	2.60		
2008-09[2]	3,217	1,395	63.5	88.6	110.0	265.4	120.0	66.1	8.9	3.0	198.0	67.4	3.70-4.70		

[1] Preliminary.   [2] Forecast.   [3] Less than 500,000 bushels.   NA = Not available.
Source: Economic Research Service, U.S. Department of Agiculture (ERS-USDA)

Production of Oats in the United States, by States   In Thousands of Bushels

Year	Illinois	Iowa	Michigan	Minne-sota	Nebraska	New York	North Dakota	Ohio	Penn-slyvania	South Dakota	Texas	Wisconsin	Total
1999	4,260	11,375	4,875	17,700	4,650	4,760	16,830	7,000	7,975	12,800	4,840	18,600	145,628
2000	4,015	12,060	4,800	22,320	1,890	3,900	19,845	6,840	8,265	13,420	4,300	19,040	149,165
2001	3,200	9,100	3,520	12,600	3,660	5,520	14,880	6,205	7,475	7,800	7,200	12,480	117,024
2002	3,285	13,300	4,160	14,840	2,365	4,160	12,600	3,355	7,015	5,400	6,160	15,000	116,002
2003	4,450	10,790	5,250	18,815	6,570	4,410	21,240	3,960	6,490	15,640	6,300	15,410	144,383
2004	2,450	10,080	4,420	13,300	3,400	3,250	14,080	3,150	6,050	13,940	6,400	13,650	115,695
2005	3,160	9,875	4,575	12,710	4,380	4,050	14,160	3,600	6,050	12,960	4,730	13,760	114,878
2006	3,080	8,360	4,030	11,200	2,025	4,958	4,920	4,125	7,040	5,415	3,700	14,490	93,638
2007	1,632	4,757	3,190	10,800	2,380	3,420	15,340	3,410	4,480	9,250	4,000	10,720	91,599
2008[1]	2,100	4,875	3,960	11,900	2,450	4,224	6,630	3,500	4,640	8,760	5,000	11,780	88,635

[1] Preliminary.   Source: National Agricultural Statistics Service, U.S. Department of Agriculture (NASS-USDA)

Average Cash Price of No. 2 Heavy White Oats in Toledo   In Dollars Per Bushel

Year	Jan.	Feb.	Mar.	Apr.	May	June	July	Aug.	Sept.	Oct.	Nov.	Dec.	Average
1996-97	NQ	2.45	2.34	2.19	2.02	1.96	1.96	1.99	2.16	2.26	2.12	2.08	2.14
1997-98	2.12	1.79	1.84	1.80	1.77	NQ	NQ	NQ	NQ	NQ	NQ	NQ	1.86
1998-99	NQ	NQ	NQ	NQ	NQ	NQ	NQ	NQ	NQ	NQ	NQ	NQ	NQ
1999-00	NQ	NQ	NQ	NQ	NQ	NQ	NQ	NQ	NQ	NQ	NQ	NQ	NQ
2000-01	NQ	NQ	NQ	NQ	NQ	NQ	NQ	NQ	NQ	NQ	NQ	NQ	NQ
2001-02	NQ	NQ	NQ	NQ	NQ	NQ	NQ	NQ	NQ	NQ	NQ	NQ	NQ
2002-03	NQ	NQ	NQ	NQ	NQ	NQ	NQ	NQ	NQ	NQ	NQ	NQ	NQ
2003-04	NQ	NQ	NQ	NQ	NQ	NQ	NQ	NQ	NQ	NQ	NQ	NQ	NQ
2004-05	NQ	NQ	NQ	NQ	NQ	NQ	NQ	NQ	NQ	NQ	NQ	NQ	NQ
2005-06[1]	NQ	NQ	NQ										

[1] Preliminary.   NQ = No quotes.   Source: Economic Research Service, U.S. Department of Agriculture (ERS-USDA)

OATS

Oat Futures - CME Group (CBT)
(weekly close) as of January 02, 2009
Cents per bushel

Volume of Trading in Oats Futures in Chicago   In Contracts

Year	Jan.	Feb.	Mar.	Apr.	May	June	July	Aug.	Sept.	Oct.	Nov.	Dec.	Total
1999	23,747	35,706	43,671	44,974	22,399	40,722	35,812	27,928	17,893	16,155	42,029	20,370	371,406
2000	27,073	43,332	29,707	31,653	38,647	50,461	30,885	42,814	21,846	21,476	48,890	15,406	402,190
2001	26,377	38,040	24,903	41,482	20,516	41,926	50,440	22,883	31,252	50,580	53,578	38,877	440,854
2002	41,516	46,435	30,662	51,889	32,386	39,229	35,217	29,647	23,968	32,847	35,412	15,932	415,140
2003	26,149	31,892	27,766	26,022	20,442	24,113	23,230	21,562	26,658	33,621	30,273	27,170	318,898
2004	33,743	34,605	55,216	49,746	38,951	35,356	25,451	31,023	32,322	25,443	33,942	20,650	416,448
2005	26,439	35,921	36,808	35,199	24,696	33,748	28,353	26,134	17,708	27,080	32,687	26,766	351,539
2006	25,667	40,534	30,437	35,799	39,362	42,812	35,751	30,790	25,700	43,724	51,304	25,435	427,315
2007	42,231	41,327	41,259	46,054	31,288	43,157	32,977	30,240	24,565	29,484	48,488	21,671	432,741
2008	44,184	61,469	44,478	47,918	37,813	52,116	27,923	32,074	19,009	31,829	23,978	18,797	441,588

Source: Chicago Board of Trade (CBT)

Average Open Interest of Oats in Chicago   In Contracts

Year	Jan.	Feb.	Mar.	Apr.	May	June	July	Aug.	Sept.	Oct.	Nov.	Dec.
1999	17,126	17,019	16,677	15,398	13,491	12,705	11,927	11,670	9,802	10,638	12,754	12,360
2000	15,343	17,521	17,719	18,183	176,686	16,178	15,550	15,225	13,176	13,985	14,377	14,119
2001	14,093	15,060	14,873	14,962	14,875	13,695	11,861	11,707	10,059	12,111	14,453	12,142
2002	12,640	13,137	11,833	10,976	9,047	10,381	10,230	10,970	9,881	9,550	9,134	6,008
2003	6,929	6,715	5,945	6,135	5,833	5,640	5,811	5,958	6,261	6,194	6,268	5,122
2004	6,284	6,314	10,018	12,988	11,903	11,339	10,293	9,153	6,669	7,010	7,753	6,724
2005	7,691	8,482	7,346	8,110	7,746	7,686	7,779	6,721	5,847	6,914	7,565	9,385
2006	10,200	11,697	10,960	10,961	13,529	14,128	13,965	11,620	11,178	13,483	14,714	13,818
2007	16,176	18,406	19,178	19,255	18,061	17,909	14,824	13,387	14,158	14,251	13,223	10,914
2008	13,696	14,812	14,764	15,097	15,957	16,802	16,667	15,027	14,740	15,495	15,108	16,848

Source: Chicago Board of Trade (CBT)

Oats (monthly average) through December 2008 — Cents per bushel

Average Cash Price of No. 2 Heavy White Oats in Minneapolis   In Dollars Per Bushel

Year	Jan.	Feb.	Mar.	Apr.	May	June	July	Aug.	Sept.	Oct.	Nov.	Dec.	Average
1999-00	1.34	1.25	1.20	1.17	1.20	1.20	1.28	1.21	1.19	1.34	1.45	NQ	1.26
2000-01	.73	.72	.69	.68	.70	.72	.70	.70	.75	.77	.80	.82	.73
2001-02	.83	.95	1.08	1.04	1.29	1.41	1.48	1.41	1.47	1.51	1.31	1.29	1.26
2002-03	1.40	1.24	1.23	1.36	1.36	1.33	1.36	1.44	1.28	1.28	1.22	1.08	1.30
2003-04	1.05	NQ	.98	1.01	1.00	.99	1.04	.99	1.14	1.08	1.22	1.08	1.05
2004-05	1.04	.96	.99	1.11	1.01	1.04	1.13	1.18	1.15	1.16	1.13	.99	1.07
2005-06	.99	1.20	1.12	1.09	1.16	1.16	1.37	1.33	1.29	1.23	1.25	1.33	1.21
2006-07	1.38	1.41	1.29	1.36	1.52	1.69	1.76	1.74	1.66	1.78	1.76	1.73	1.59
2007-08	1.81	1.68	1.63	1.67	NQ	1.74	2.43	2.02	2.28	3.18	2.35	2.47	2.12
2008-09[1]	2.54	2.60	NQ	NQ	NQ	1.33	1.33	1.36					1.83

[1] Preliminary.   NQ = No qoute.   *Source: Economic Research Service, U.S. Department of Agriculture (ERS-USDA)*

Average Price Received by Farmers for Oats in the United States   In Dollars Per Bushel

Year	Jan.	Feb.	Mar.	Apr.	May	June	July	Aug.	Sept.	Oct.	Nov.	Dec.	Average
1999-00	1.22	1.09	.97	1.08	1.06	1.12	1.18	1.20	1.27	1.28	1.35	1.31	1.18
2000-01	1.24	1.08	.93	.95	1.08	1.22	1.14	1.21	1.28	1.24	1.28	1.28	1.16
2001-02	1.38	1.32	1.25	1.39	1.64	1.79	1.92	1.93	1.91	1.99	1.99	1.99	1.71
2002-03	1.95	1.69	1.67	1.80	1.80	1.91	1.95	2.04	2.11	2.08	1.98	1.95	1.91
2003-04	1.83	1.46	1.39	1.39	1.44	1.29	1.58	1.48	1.58	1.60	1.63	1.70	1.53
2004-05	1.61	1.36	1.32	1.42	1.45	1.51	1.60	1.64	1.67	1.73	1.65	1.64	1.55
2005-06	1.75	1.59	1.49	1.54	1.59	1.64	1.73	1.73	1.82	1.82	1.75	1.85	1.69
2006-07	1.90	1.78	1.67	1.70	1.77	2.05	2.01	2.20	2.35	2.40	2.46	2.49	2.07
2007-08	2.54	2.32	2.24	2.47	2.45	2.63	2.69	2.88	3.20	3.44	3.48	3.63	2.83
2008-09[1]	3.49	3.46	3.15	3.29	3.25	2.99	3.10	2.30					3.13

[1] Preliminary.   *Source: National Agricultural Statistics Service, U.S. Department of Agriculture (NASS-USDA)*

Olive Oil

Olive oil is derived from the fruit of the olive tree and originated in the Mediterranean area. Olives designated for oil are picked before ripening in the fall. Olive picking is usually done by hand. The olives are then weighed and washed in cold water. The olives, along with their oil-rich pits, are then crushed and kneaded until a homogeneous paste is formed. The paste is spread by hand onto metal plates, which are then stacked and pressed hydraulically to yield a liquid. The liquid is then centrifuged to separate the oil. It takes 1,300 to 2,000 olives to produce 1 quart of olive oil. The best olive oil is still produced from the first pressing, which is usually performed within 24 to 72 hours after harvest and is called extra virgin olive oil.

Supply – World production of olive oil (pressed oil) in the marketing year 2007-08 rose +4.4% to 3.110 million metric tons, which was a new record high. The world's largest producers of olive oil in 2007-08 were Spain (with 44% of world production), Italy (18%), Greece (13%),

Tunisia (7%), Turkey (5%), and Syria (4%). Production levels in the various countries vary considerable from year-to-year depending on various weather and crop conditions.

Demand – World consumption of olive oil in the 2007-08 marketing year rose +1.3% yr/yr to a new record high of 3.038 million metric tons. The U.S. is the world's largest consumer of olive oil with 8.4% of world consumption in 2007-08. The U.S. consumption of olive oil set a new record high of 254,000 metric tons.

Trade – World olive oil imports in 2007-08 fell -1.6% to 777,000 metric tons. The U.S. was the world's largest importer in 2007-08 with 265,000 metric tons, representing 34% of world imports. World olive oil exports in 2007-09 fell -4.2% to 766,000 metric tons. The world's largest exporters were Italy (with 27% of world exports), Tunisia (24%), Spain (22%), and Turkey (7%).

World Production of Olive Oil (Pressed Oil)   In Thousands of Metric Tons

Crop Year	Algeria	Argentina	Greece	Italy	Jordan	Libya	Morocco	Portugal	Spain	Syria	Tunisia	Turkey	World Total
1999-00	33.5	11.5	454.0	670.0	7.0	7.0	45.0	58.3	694.1	88.0	225.0	61.0	2,412.4
2000-01	26.5	3.0	467.0	508.0	29.5	4.0	39.5	28.5	1,040.0	183.0	141.0	197.5	2,742.7
2001-02	25.5	10.0	388.3	500.0	16.0	7.0	66.0	36.7	1,468.0	104.0	40.0	71.0	2,791.1
2002-03	15.0	11.0	449.0	620.0	30.0	6.5	48.5	31.9	949.4	184.5	76.0	187.0	2,698.0
2003-04	69.5	13.5	332.0	470.0	21.0	6.5	110.0	38.2	1,566.0	121.5	296.0	80.0	3,178.1
2004-05	33.5	18.0	470.0	785.0	49.0	12.5	54.0	46.7	1,034.0	195.0	139.5	157.0	3,077.6
2005-06[1]	32.0	23.0	455.5	635.0	23.0	9.0	81.0	35.5	887.0	110.0	236.5	119.0	2,710.6
2006-07[2]	21.5	16.5	398.0	610.0	39.0	11.0	81.0	51.8	1,139.0	171.5	182.5	174.5	2,977.8
2007-08[3]	34.0	20.0	388.0	550.0	25.0	11.0	91.7	39.0	1,360.0	120.0	220.0	168.0	3,110.0

[1] Preliminary.   [2] Estimate.   [3] Forecast.   *Source: The Oil World*

World Imports and Exports of Olive Oil (Pressed Oil)   In Thousands of Metric Tons

Crop Year	Imports							Exports					
	Australia	Brazil	Italy	Japan	Spain	United States	World Total	Greece	Italy	Spain	Tunisia	Turkey	World Total
1999-00	24.2	25.6	105.1	27.2	23.4	189.3	507.1	8.8	176.8	95.6	122.4	25.8	496.9
2000-01	29.5	24.7	110.5	29.6	13.3	212.5	549.1	6.3	194.1	97.9	101.0	77.5	543.8
2001-02	26.4	24.0	50.8	31.2	6.6	218.0	491.6	9.4	199.0	116.8	33.0	37.3	470.0
2002-03	32.0	21.1	70.1	31.4	16.6	220.1	536.5	10.4	197.3	118.4	42.9	60.8	532.9
2003-04	30.5	23.2	178.2	33.1	49.1	244.8	721.6	9.3	199.9	123.0	197.0	55.9	725.9
2004-05	28.9	25.7	154.6	32.8	40.7	248.7	716.1	8.9	217.0	125.1	119.9	88.4	725.7
2005-06[1]	32.7	26.0	136.6	30.2	51.1	242.3	695.4	9.8	203.6	114.6	109.7	56.0	685.5
2006-07[2]	42.1	36.6	154.1	32.0	71.3	262.5	789.3	17.8	208.6	148.5	211.0	47.2	799.2
2007-08[3]	41.8	37.0	155.0	33.0	54.0	265.0	777.0	12.0	205.0	165.0	180.0	50.0	766.0

[1] Preliminary.   [2] Estimate.   [3] Forecast.   *Source: The Oil World*

World Consumption and Ending Stocks of Olive Oil (Pressed Oil)   In Thousands of Metric Tons

Crop Year	Consumption							Ending Stocks					
	Brazil	Morocco	Syria	Tunisia	Turkey	United States	World Total	European Union	Morocco	Syria	Tunisia	Turkey	World Total
1999-00	25.6	55.7	99.0	63.3	76.3	180.1	2,614.0	668.9	21.0	36.6	55.0	9.9	836.4
2000-01	24.7	49.6	121.6	61.3	79.9	205.5	2,751.0	568.6	16.0	97.2	34.0	50.0	833.3
2001-02	24.0	61.1	111.6	38.4	73.7	211.5	2,750.6	709.0	25.3	86.5	3.0	12.0	895.4
2002-03	21.1	64.2	117.7	31.7	91.6	218.7	2,797.3	535.0	19.0	130.9	4.6	47.0	799.6
2003-04	23.2	69.8	133.4	59.2	61.8	225.3	2,924.9	791.0	35.0	95.0	45.0	10.0	1,048.6
2004-05	25.7	62.4	142.8	55.8	65.7	235.9	2,931.3	964.7	11.0	105.0	9.0	13.0	1,185.3
2005-06[1]	26.0	60.4	135.8	57.8	66.1	233.0	2,872.6	863.7	3.0	37.0	79.0	10.0	1,033.1
2006-07[2]	36.6	65.4	136.5	43.9	97.4	244.2	2,998.7	861.7	16.0	27.0	9.0	40.0	1,002.3
2007-08[3]	37.0	69.0	125.0	42.0	120.1	254.0	3,038.0	963.0	15.0	10.0	10.0	38.0	1,085.3

[1] Preliminary.   [2] Estimate.   [3] Forecast.   *Source: The Oil World*

Onions

Onions are the bulbs of plants in the lily family. Onions can be eaten raw, cooked, pickled, used as a flavoring or seasoning, or dehydrated. Onions rank in the top 10 vegetables produced in the U.S. in terms of dollar value. Since 1629, onions have been cultivated in the U.S., but are believed to be indigenous to Asia.

The two main types of onions produced in the U.S. are yellow and white onions. Yellow varieties comprise approximately 75% of all onions grown for bulb production in the U.S. Onions that are planted as a winter crop in warm areas are milder in taste and odor than onions planted during the summer in cooler regions.

Prices – Onion prices in 2008 averaged $12.33 per hundred pounds, up +7.2% from $11.50 in 2007. Monthly onion prices were very weak in early 2008 at a low of $2.71 per hundred pounds in March, moved up to a high of $23.30 in May, but then faded to end the year at $13.40 per hundred pounds.

Supply – U.S. production in 2007 rose +7.8% to 7.888 billion pounds, but still below the 2004 record high of 8.307 billion pounds. The farm value of the U.S. production crop in 2007 fell 20.5% to 840.002 million, down from the 2006 record high of $1.057 billion. U.S. farmers harvested 159,480 acres in 2007, down –3.3% yr/yr. The yield per acre in 2007 was 495 pounds per acre.

Demand – U.S. per capita consumption of onions in 2007 rose +7.4% to a record high of 23.2 pounds.

Trade – U.S. exports of fresh onions in 2006 totaled 659 million pounds, and imports were not far behind at 643 million pounds.

Salient Statistics of Onions in the United States

Crop Year	Harvested Acres	Yield Per Acre	Pro- duction 1,000 Cwt.	Price Per Cwt.	Farm Value $1,000	Jan. 1 Pack Frozen	Anual Pack Frozen	Imports Canned	Exports (Fresh)	Imports (Fresh)	Per Capita[3] Utilization -- Lbs., Farm Weight -- All	Fresh
2002	162,720	429	69,844	12.10	764,994	29.9	387.1	7.1	637.1	595.8	20.4	19.3
2003	160,090	442	73,636	13.70	929,274	39.5	207.2	10.3	679.0	646.1	21.3	19.5
2004	169,150	491	83,065	9.06	671,626	38.6	218.2	10.5	620.1	689.3	23.1	21.6
2005	165,220	445	73,504	12.40	848,798	39.9		22.9	667.2	659.2	22.2	21.0
2006	163,780	444	73,066	16.10	1,084,099	48.1			658.5	643.2	21.6	19.8
2007[1]	160,080	495	79,638	11.10	816,061	44.9					23.2	21.7
2008[2]	153,490	492	73,837	12.70	865,442	39.4						

[1] Preliminary. [2] Forecast. [3] Includes fresh and processing. *Source: Economic Research Service, U.S. Department of Agiculture (ERS-USDA)*

Production of Onions in the United States   In Thousands of Hundredweight (Cwt.)

Crop Year	Arizona	Cali- fornia (Spring)	Texas	Total (All)	Cali- fornia (Summer)	Colo- rado	Idaho	Mich- igan	Minne- sota	Mexico	New York	Oregon, Malheur	Texas	Total (All)	Grand Total
2002	690	2,708	4,725	9,561	11,562	4,400	6,272	897	78	----	2,829	7,800	----	60,283	69,844
2003	750	3,675	3,520	10,133	14,700	3,696	5,880	1,152	65	----	3,808	7,198	----	63,230	73,363
2004	800	3,586	3,875	12,031	13,200	5,500	8,008	986	----	----	5,200	8,658	----	71,034	83,065
2005	920	3,800	4,650	11,575	12,240	4,180	6,080	754	----	----	3,808	7,360	----	61,929	73,504
2006	490	3,279	4,104	11,128	13,515	3,800	5,076	650	----	----	4,224	6,084	----	62,049	73,177
2007	540	3,330	3,120	10,230	12,975	3,157	6,825	650	----	----	4,428	9,360	----	68,652	78,882
2008[1]	780	2,925	3,800	10,955	12,900	3,024	5,865	650	----	----	3,780	7,526	----	61,883	72,883

[1] Preliminary. *Source: Agricultural Statistics Board, U.S. Department of Agiculture (ASB-USDA)*

Cold Storage Stocks of Frozen[2] Onions in the United States, on First of Month   In Thousands of Pounds

Year	Jan.	Feb.	Mar.	Apr.	May	June	July	Aug.	Sept.	Oct.	Nov.	Dec.
2003	39,480	39,764	43,624	37,569	35,625	35,617	36,529	35,590	35,907	33,844	38,693	39,467
2004	38,632	32,515	34,080	36,724	39,364	41,525	37,408	34,845	34,888	35,826	38,098	39,789
2005	39,865	40,428	44,191	48,695	50,579	47,418	45,605	47,231	44,834	40,718	43,751	45,690
2006	48,106	52,207	55,141	54,638	54,276	53,331	45,724	43,707	47,176	47,636	50,175	48,731
2007	44,919	42,027	45,810	46,244	40,350	32,240	34,663	30,966	36,734	39,096	37,653	37,929
2008[1]	39,438	40,120	43,487	44,181	39,503	42,726	45,115	41,249	42,324	42,786	41,006	40,102

[1] Preliminary. *Source: National Agricultural Statistics Service, U.S. Department of Agiculture (NASS-USDA)*

Average Price Received by Growers for Onions in the United States   In Dollars Per Hundred Pounds (Cwt.)

Year	Jan.	Feb.	Mar.	Apr.	May	June	July	Aug.	Sept.	Oct.	Nov.	Dec.	Season Average
2003	12.30	14.90	21.80	39.30	32.00	22.10	16.70	13.80	12.20	12.60	13.90	12.70	13.70
2004	18.20	21.30	12.80	20.80	18.10	16.50	16.40	13.40	11.30	9.22	9.01	8.58	9.06
2005	6.29	5.61	6.13	18.20	19.70	17.80	14.00	11.10	13.10	12.90	14.00	12.30	12.40
2006	11.70	8.04	7.45	15.10	15.60	17.00	16.80	13.70	12.30	10.90	11.10	16.60	16.10
2007	22.10	26.20	35.00	55.20	24.20	24.60	15.40	10.80	5.57	4.47	4.70	4.39	11.10
2008[1]	4.13	3.55	2.71	17.40	23.30	17.60	15.10	12.00	13.30	14.00	10.60	13.40	

[1] Preliminary. *Source: Economic Research Service, U.S. Department of Agiculture (ERS-USDA)*

Oranges and Orange Juice

The orange tree is a semi-tropical, non-deciduous tree, and the fruit is technically a hesperidium, a kind of berry. The three major varieties of oranges include the sweet orange, the sour orange, and the mandarin orange (or tangerine). In the U.S., only sweet oranges are grown commercially. Those include Hamlin, Jaffa, navel, Pineapple, blood orange, and Valencia. Sour oranges are mainly used in marmalade and in liqueurs such as triple sec and curacao.

Frozen Concentrated Orange Juice (FCOJ) was developed in 1945, which led to oranges becoming the main fruit crop in the U.S.. The world's largest producer of orange juice is Brazil, followed by Florida. Two to four medium-sized oranges will produce about 1 cup of juice, and modern mechanical extractors can remove the juice from 400 to 700 oranges per minute. Before juice extraction, orange oil is recovered from the peel. Approximately 50% of the orange weight is juice, the remainder is peel, pulp, and seeds, which are dried to produce nutritious cattle feed.

The U.S. marketing year for oranges begins December 1 of the first year shown (e.g., the 2005-06 marketing year extends from December 1, 2005 to November 30, 2006). Orange juice futures prices are subject to upward spikes during the U.S. hurricane season (officially June 1 to November 30), and the Florida freeze season (late-November through March).

Frozen concentrated orange juice future and options are traded on the Intercontinental Exchange (ICE). The ICE orange juice futures contract calls for the delivery of 15,000 pounds of orange solids and is priced in terms of cents per pound.

Prices – ICE orange juice futures prices posted a 31-year high of 209.50 cents per pound in February 2007 (which was just 10.5 cents shy of the record high of 220 cents per pound posted in November 1977) but then spent most of the remainder of 2007 and all of 2008 in a steep slump. OJ prices hit a 4-1/2 year low of 64.60 cents per pound in February 2009, which was down by 69.2% from the 31-year high posted in February 2007. Bearish factors for OJ included (1) the lack of any hurricane damage to Florida orange trees in 2007 or 2008, (2) a rebound in Florida orange production in the 2007/08 and 2008/09 marketing years after the poor crops seen in the previous 3 years due to hurricane damage, and (3) a long-term slump in orange juice demand due to the plethora of new drinks available and perceptions that carbohydrate-heavy orange juice is not healthful.

Supply – World production of oranges in the 2008-09 marketing year rose +0.6% y/y to 50.905 million metric tons, to post a new record high. The world's largest producers of oranges in 2008-09 were Brazil with 33% of world production, followed by the U.S. (16%), and Mexico (8%).

U.S. production of oranges in 2007-08 (latest data available) rose +33.6% y/y to 236.814 million boxes, but still well below the record high of 315.525 million boxes in 1997-98. (1 box equals 90 lbs.) Florida's production in 2007-08 rose +31.9% y/y to 170.200 million boxes but still well below the record high of 244.000 million boxes in 1997-98.

World Production of Oranges   In Thousands of Metric Tons

Year	Argentina	Australia	Brazil	Egypt	Greece	Italy	Mexico	Morocco	South Africa	Spain	Turkey	United States	World Total
1999-00	789	624	17,136	1,637	1,040	1,750	3,385	845	1,119	2,828	1,100	11,875	48,286
2000-01	913	437	14,729	1,610	976	1,800	3,885	693	1,119	2,688	1,070	11,139	44,588
2001-02	780	633	18,360	1,696	1,076	1,724	4,020	720	1,263	2,822	1,250	11,290	49,828
2002-03	700	407	15,382	1,734	1,145	1,723	3,734	800	1,148	2,950	1,250	10,527	45,829
2003-04	750	453	19,054	1,740	550	1,835	3,901	705	1,113	3,052	1,250	11,734	50,805
2004-05	770	547	16,565	1,775	764	2,105	4,000	813	1,038	2,691	1,300	8,419	45,493
2005-06	840	470	17,993	1,800	1,017	2,261	4,157	784	1,167	2,376	1,445	8,212	47,453
2006-07[1]	990	419	18,482	1,830			4,248	721	1,412		1,536	6,917	49,462
2007-08[2]	800	440	16,320	2,759			4,300	732	1,550		1,427	9,223	50,588
2008-09[3]	1,000	480	16,730	3,500			3,900	790	1,470		1,450	8,270	50,905

[1] Preliminary.   [2] Estimate.   [3] Forecast.   NA = Not available.   *Source: Foreign Agricultural Service, U.S. Department of Agriculture (FAS-USDA)*

Salient Statistics of Oranges & Orange Juice in the United States

	--------- Production[4] ---------				--------- Florida Crop Processed ---------					Frozen Concentrated --------- Orange Juice - Florida ---------			
Year	California	Florida	Total U.S.	Farm Price $ Per Box	Farm Value Million $	Frozen Concen-trates	Chilled Products	Total Pro-cessed	Yield Per Box Gallons[5]	Carry-in	Pack	Total Supply	Total Season Movement
	-------- Million Boxes ---------				------------- Million Boxes -------------				---- In Millions of Gallons (42 Deg. Brix) ----			
1998-99	36.0	186.0	224.6	7.41	1,687.9	97.2	80.1	175.1	1.6	104.7	216.9	321.6	209.1
1999-00	64.0	233.0	299.8	5.56	1,666.1	134.2	90.1	226.7	1.5	105.2	254.0	359.2	239.7
2000-01	54.5	223.3	280.9	5.88	1,682.8	124.1	89.6	215.9	1.6	112.6	245.2	357.8	226.0
2001-02	51.5	230.0	283.8	6.37	1,846.2	136.0	85.9	223.2	1.6	128.3	253.2	381.5	249.9
2002-03	62.0	203.0	267.0	5.80	1,564.7	102.1	92.5	196.0	1.5	120.2	203.3	323.5	200.1
2003-04	50.5	242.0	294.6	5.88	1,774.5	139.7	93.4	233.6	1.6	124.0	249.7	373.7	213.8
2004-05	64.5	149.8	216.5	6.68	1,475.4	54.3	88.5	143.9	1.6	151.8	86.3	238.1	175.2
2005-06[1]	61.0	147.7	210.8	8.60	1,829.9	51.9	88.7	141.7	1.6	107.8	85.2	193.0	160.8
2006-07[2]	46.0	129.0	177.3	12.56	2,216.5	48.0	74.5	123.4	1.6	67.2	79.6	146.8	149.2
2007-08[3]	64.5	170.2	236.8	8.99	2,135.5	80.8	84.7	165.5	1.7				

[1] Preliminary.   [2] Estimate.   [3] Forecast.   4/ Fruit ripened on trees, but destroyed prior to picking not included.   [5] 42 deg. Brix equivalent.
Source: Economic Research Service, U.S. Department of Agriculture (ERS-USDA); Florida Department of Citrus

Average Open Interest of Frozen Concentrated Orange Juice Futures in New York   In Contracts

Year	Jan.	Feb.	Mar.	Apr.	May	June	July	Aug.	Sept.	Oct.	Nov.	Dec.
1999	25,917	28,965	28,707	31,199	26,669	28,362	28,087	30,021	28,922	27,498	26,893	25,887
2000	23,727	24,647	19,684	22,475	23,456	27,087	27,386	30,272	30,090	32,328	30,192	30,757
2001	28,852	28,011	28,073	27,794	24,199	24,428	22,591	22,073	17,789	18,026	21,506	19,275
2002	15,716	16,593	18,515	22,328	23,498	26,581	28,137	33,206	27,323	23,758	22,651	23,461
2003	25,080	26,588	22,707	21,466	20,634	23,794	25,467	26,518	27,788	30,767	31,575	36,336
2004	36,079	35,325	32,806	36,112	34,704	42,299	39,970	38,259	39,877	38,990	33,342	36,072
2005	33,821	33,619	30,008	32,523	26,171	28,730	32,221	29,034	23,603	28,602	34,966	35,795
2006	30,485	35,479	36,603	36,617	34,418	29,180	27,169	29,872	29,515	30,852	29,873	28,342
2007	29,484	28,370	32,312	29,430	28,830	31,917	30,457	29,540	28,335	29,599	26,608	27,412
2008	24,919	26,603	29,806	32,831	32,102	33,136	28,353	31,133	29,112	31,060	28,254	28,802

Source: IntercontinentalEchange (ICE) (formerly New York Board of Trade (NYBOT))

Volume of Trading of Frozen Concentrated Orange Juice Futures in New York   In Contracts

Year	Jan.	Feb.	Mar.	Apr.	May	June	July	Aug.	Sept.	Oct.	Nov.	Dec.	Total
1999	64,149	92,868	40,027	92,522	49,180	78,627	48,177	99,531	49,323	71,914	42,532	68,734	797,584
2000	45,680	78,532	33,617	71,024	50,475	80,372	46,548	67,312	38,485	64,831	45,966	89,362	712,204
2001	46,655	66,561	27,994	63,012	38,447	66,773	40,870	64,860	22,246	68,364	23,376	48,338	577,496
2002	31,709	50,898	30,316	58,644	37,283	52,238	45,316	78,111	36,053	71,635	24,111	61,443	577,757
2003	45,945	63,224	23,926	70,846	35,791	64,209	27,056	73,792	40,782	87,055	42,084	78,005	652,715
2004	52,908	86,600	41,941	99,532	45,741	123,815	105,220	118,021	65,655	89,064	56,502	85,438	970,437
2005	54,140	85,349	57,557	87,595	40,785	94,913	61,610	92,195	46,868	117,355	50,098	113,574	902,039
2006	65,978	98,034	82,293	92,312	73,517	87,429	63,429	84,160	50,871	95,955	54,975	74,743	923,696
2007	70,773	84,076	63,417	87,759	59,937	84,150	50,721	78,502	48,392	103,218	45,539	69,308	845,792
2008	57,421	78,860	52,166	80,331	43,942	70,780	51,859	67,402	41,353	78,327	29,013	59,058	710,512

Source: IntercontinentalEchange (ICE) (formerly New York Board of Trade (NYBOT))

ORANGES AND ORANGE JUICE

Cold Storage Stocks of Orange Juice Concentrate[2] in the U.S., on First of Month   In Millions of Pounds

Year	Jan.	Feb.	Mar.	Apr.	May	June	July	Aug.	Sept.	Oct.	Nov.	Dec.
1999	1,791.9	1,999.4	2,204.2	2,191.3	2,485.7	2,115.6	1,969.7	1,823.0	1,618.5	1,443.4	1,182.0	1,102.7
2000	1,330.7	1,540.6	1,632.7	1,857.9	1,812.5	1,965.6	2,037.9	1,843.7	1,457.7	1,346.6	1,169.4	1,202.0
2001	1,382.0	1,610.8	1,825.1	1,735.5	1,872.2	2,061.8	2,035.6	1,913.2	1,691.1	1,537.7	1,398.9	1,406.7
2002	1,571.7	1,721.3	1,770.9	1,794.4	1,886.0	1,982.8	1,934.0	1,870.9	1,680.9	1,543.6	1,409.6	1,471.2
2003	1,673.6	1,851.9	1,833.4	1,856.6	1,936.8	2,102.6	2,021.2	1,848.9	1,672.2	1,529.9	1,335.6	1,428.5
2004	1,585.8	1,613.0	1,646.1	1,790.5	1,987.6	2,128.7	2,075.7	1,953.4	1,823.3	1,644.2	1,516.8	1,458.0
2005	1,468.8	1,553.8	1,578.9	1,578.2	1,652.4	1,668.1	1,548.8	1,501.6	1,397.3	1,243.3	1,139.9	1,027.5
2006	1,044.7	1,065.9	1,076.8	1,005.7	1,087.5	1,157.7	1,104.1	1,002.6	888.8	776.0	714.3	650.3
2007	678.2	726.0	751.1	825.1	901.5	960.7	909.7	849.1	761.2	620.4	582.2	563.7
2008[1]	682.5	837.8	942.4	1,031.9	1,210.6	1,442.7	1,514.9	1,424.9	1,319.4	1,199.7	1,086.0	1,034.6

[1] Preliminary.   [2] Adjusted to 42.0 degrees Brix equivalent (9.896 pounds per gallon).   Source: Agricultural Statistics Board, U.S. Department of Agriculture (ASB-USDA)

Producer Price Index of Frozen Orange Juice Concentrate   1982 = 100

Year	Jan.	Feb.	Mar.	Apr.	May	June	July	Aug.	Sept.	Oct.	Nov.	Dec.	Average
1999	119.7	118.6	118.0	115.5	113.3	113.2	112.5	111.3	112.4	112.5	113.1	112.4	114.4
2000	110.0	108.9	108.0	107.1	106.9	106.6	105.4	104.8	101.5	100.4	99.8	99.1	104.9
2001	98.9	99.2	98.3	96.8	96.8	97.4	97.3	97.2	97.3	97.3	99.6	102.5	98.2
2002	103.0	102.9	103.1	102.9	102.8	103.2	103.2	103.5	107.4	107.4	109.7	110.2	104.9
2003	110.2	110.2	110.7	110.4	108.5	109.4	109.1	108.9	107.1	106.6	105.1	103.0	108.3
2004	103.4	103.2	102.7	101.6	101.6	101.6	98.9	98.9	98.9	98.9	103.3	103.3	101.4
2005	103.3	103.3	105.0	109.0	109.0	109.0	109.3	109.3	108.1	107.9	108.4	126.4	109.0
2006	138.3	142.1	150.1	160.9	161.0	164.1	172.3	174.8	185.4	197.6	208.9	208.7	172.0
2007	198.1	191.7	198.5	179.6	187.7	184.1	173.6	171.5	152.9	159.3	162.6	168.2	177.3
2008[1]	168.0	166.6	160.0	159.2	159.3	159.6	126.0	121.8	121.4	117.4	115.2	112.8	140.6

[1] Preliminary.   NA = Not avaliable.   Source: Bureau of Labor Statistics, U.S. Department of Labor (BLS)

Average Price Received by Farmers for Oranges (Equivalent On-Tree) in the U.S.   In Dollars Per Box

Year	Jan.	Feb.	Mar.	Apr.	May	June	July	Aug.	Sept.	Oct.	Nov.	Dec.	Average
1999	4.52	4.99	5.90	5.96	6.48	8.04	8.58	6.66	9.96	9.50	4.70	3.42	6.56
2000	3.35	3.18	3.24	4.20	4.39	4.34	2.45	0.35	0.29	1.43	3.20	2.95	2.78
2001	2.85	3.20	4.93	4.84	4.64	4.47	4.63	5.01	6.20	4.99	2.90	3.20	4.32
2002	3.75	4.05	4.64	4.65	4.47	4.00	4.06	6.61	5.33	5.18	3.11	3.23	4.42
2003	3.00	3.14	4.17	4.43	4.43	4.41	3.91	4.27	2.80	2.78	2.32	2.55	3.52
2004	2.45	3.02	3.68	3.68	3.60	4.13	8.85	8.49	15.85	20.87	5.34	3.27	6.94
2005	3.39	3.69	4.84	4.80	5.11	5.43	6.55	4.90	4.29	4.04	5.90	4.46	4.78
2006	5.16	5.27	5.78	6.44	7.13	7.05	6.56	12.03	17.96	13.89	6.95	7.28	8.46
2007	8.25	8.11	10.58	10.62	11.12	11.07	8.95	8.81	7.84	9.60	8.14	5.80	9.07
2008[1]	5.77	5.74	6.07	6.21	6.95	6.91	5.59	4.78	5.71	4.22	5.26	4.75	5.66

[1] Preliminary.   [2] Data thru 1984 are for wholesale oranges (Calif.) F.O.B. packed fresh.   Source: Economic Research Service, U.S. Department of Agriculture (ERS-USDA)

188

Palm Oil

Palm oil is an edible vegetable oil produced from the flesh of the fruit of the oil palm tree. The oil palm tree is a tropical palm tree that is a native of the west coast of Africa and is different from the coconut palm tree. The fruit of the oil palm tree is reddish, about the size of a large plum, and grows in large bunches. A single seed, the palm kernel, is contained in each fruit. Oil is extracted from both the pulp of the fruit (becoming palm oil) and the kernel (palm kernel oil). About 1 metric ton of palm kernel oil is obtained for every 10 metric tons of palm oil.

Palm oil is commercially used in soap, ointments, cosmetics, detergents, and machinery lubricants. It is also used worldwide as cooking oil, shortening, and margarine. Palm kernel oil is a lighter oil and is used exclusively for food use. Crude palm oil and crude palm kernel oil are traded on the Kuala Lumpur Commodity Exchange.

Prices – The monthly average wholesale price of palm oil (CIF, bulk, U.S. ports) in 2007 rose by +41.1% yr/yr to 41.93 cents per pound, which was a new record high.

Supply – World production of palm oil in the 2007-08 marketing year rose by +11.6% to 41.727 million metric tons. World palm oil production has grown by about twenty times the production level of 1.922 million metric tons seen back in 1970. Indonesia and Malaysia are the world's two major global producers of palm oil. Indonesian production rose +10.9% to a record high of 18.360 million metric tons in 2007-08 and Indonesian production accounted for 44% of world production. Malaysian production in 2007-08 rose +13.9% to a record high of 17.424 million metric tons and Malaysian production accounted for 42% of world production. Other smaller global producers include Thailand with 2.7% of world production, Nigeria with 2.0%, and Columbia with (2.0%).

Demand – U.S. total disappearance of palm oil in 2007-08 rose +24.0% yr/yr to 800.0 metric tons which was a new record high.

Trade – World palm oil exports in 2007-08 rose by +10.5% to 32.842 million metric tons, which was a new record high. The world's largest exporters are Malaysia with a 46% share of world exports, followed by Indonesia with a 43% share. World palm oil imports in 2007-08 rose +11.1% to 32.752 million metric tons. The world's largest importers are China with an 19% share of world imports, followed by India with 14%.

World Production of Palm Oil   In Thousands of Metric Tons

Crop Year	Brazil	Came-roon	Colombia	Costa Rica	Ecuador	Ghana	Indonesia	Ivory Coast	Malaysia	Nigeria	Papua New Guinea	Thailand	World Total
1998-99	91	133	466	117	247	110	6,011	265	9,759	713	257	540	19,501
1999-00	105	136	513	136	228	109	6,855	283	10,492	735	300	533	21,266
2000-01	109	138	561	147	199	108	7,775	211	11,940	763	334	601	23,773
2001-02	115	143	517	131	231	109	9,060	260	11,856	774	338	606	25,041
2002-03	128	142	537	148	265	111	10,370	245	13,180	782	310	669	27,811
2003-04	138	145	614	179	272	110	11,970	264	13,418	789	344	724	29,952
2004-05	155	152	653	183	316	116	13,560	311	15,195	798	330	709	33,508
2005-06[1]	171	159	699	193	320	120	15,520	320	15,486	815	315	795	36,024
2006-07[2]	179	169	738	203	409	123	16,550	320	15,294	830	417	989	37,400
2007-08[3]	215	182	832	228	406	127	18,360	328	17,424	850	400	1,123	41,727

[1] Preliminary.   [2] Estimate.   [3] Forecast.   *Source: The Oil World*

World Trade of Palm Oil   In Thousands of Metric Tons

	Imports							Exports					
Crop Year	China	Germany	India	Nether-lands	Pakistan	United Kingdom	Total	Hong Kong	Indonesia	Malaysia	Guinea	Sing-apore	Total
1998-99	1,433	406	2,762	738	1,053	528	12,977	113	3,219	8,482	248	289	13,246
1999-00	1,474	431	3,482	780	1,086	558	14,759	130	3,898	9,051	292	251	14,628
2000-01	2,147	497	3,856	907	1,191	607	17,356	180	4,617	10,707	334	228	17,340
2001-02	2,600	592	3,233	1,101	1,333	721	18,590	302	6,094	10,758	332	217	18,917
2002-03	3,167	562	4,110	1,132	1,442	776	21,467	209	7,167	12,133	329	253	21,531
2003-04	3,570	646	3,574	1,174	1,405	819	23,418	154	8,706	12,186	336	227	23,469
2004-05	4,319	766	3,342	1,438	1,683	869	26,184	59	9,862	13,585	322	223	26,157
2005-06[1]	5,182	662	2,820	1,589	1,728	885	28,111	14	11,590	13,718	317	206	28,121
2006-07[2]	5,543	711	3,664	1,710	1,743	854	29,469	27	12,465	13,768	406	185	29,735
2007-08[3]	6,200	710	4,560	1,850	1,720	850	32,752	37	14,150	15,200	385	200	32,842

[1] Preliminary.   [2] Estimate.   [3] Forecast.   *Source: The Oil World*

PALM OIL

Palm Oil (monthly average) through December 2008 — Cents per pound

Supply and Distribution of Palm Oil in the United States — In Thousands of Metric Tons

Crop Year Beginning Oct. 1	Stocks Oct. 1	Imports	Total Supply	Edible Products	Inedible Products	Total End Products	Total Disap-pearance	Exports	U.S. Import Value[4]	Malaysia, F.O.B., RBD	Palm Kernel Oil, Malaysia, C.I.F Rotterdam
				-------- In Millions of Pounds --------					--------- U.S. $ Per Metric Ton ---------		
1998-99	16.1	128.8	144.9	W	72.4	W	118.6	5.2	----	514	708
1999-00	21.1	156.6	177.7	W	55.0	W	148.5	3.4	----	338	533
2000-01	25.7	175.5	201.2	W	36.0	W	167.7	6.0	----	272	313
2001-02	27.5	217.2	244.7	W	22.6	75.1	214.4	6.2	----	359	379
2002-03	24.1	174.4	198.5	W	W	76.7	168.5	8.1	----	428	439
2003-04	22.1	281.5	303.6	51.9	37.5	67.9	226.4	13.1	----	489	619
2004-05	64.0	349.0	413.0	62.3	W	62.3	319.4	17.2	----	420	638
2005-06[1]	76.4	603.8	680.2	436.4	W	436.4	555.6	30.6	----	452	583
2006-07[2]	94.0	696.3	790.3	568.5	W	568.5	645.0	58.4	----	685	768
2007-08[3]	86.9	865.0	951.9	789.3	W	789.3	800.0	61.9	----	1061	1258

[1] Preliminary. [2] Estimate. [3] Forecast. [4] Market value in the foreign country, excluding import duties, ocean freight and marine insurance.
W = Withheld. *Sources: The Oil World; Economic Research Service, U.S. Department of Agriculture (ERS-USDA)*

Average Wholesale Palm Oil Prices, CIF, Bulk, U.S. Ports — In Cents Per Pound

Year	Jan.	Feb.	Mar.	Apr.	May	June	July	Aug.	Sept.	Oct.	Nov.	Dec.	Average
1999	31.06	28.58	25.52	25.52	24.50	21.30	18.15	18.70	21.00	20.00	20.00	20.00	22.86
2000	18.65	17.66	17.73	18.21	18.12	16.52	16.85	16.23	15.90	13.19	13.56	12.75	16.28
2001	18.05	18.05	13.50	13.50	12.50	13.00	15.50	18.00	16.75	15.60	16.85	17.45	15.73
2002	17.75	17.06	17.30	17.75	18.85	21.44	20.50	21.85	32.00	31.75	31.75	31.75	23.31
2003	31.75	31.75	31.35	31.25	31.25	31.75	32.25	32.25	32.25	32.25	32.44	33.75	32.02
2004	34.00	35.38	35.25	36.40	36.50	36.50	36.50	36.50	34.00	30.00	29.00	29.00	34.09
2005	28.20	28.00	28.67	30.00	30.00	30.00	30.00	30.00	30.00	30.00	29.25	29.00	29.43
2006	29.00	29.00	29.00	29.00	29.00	29.00	29.00	29.00	29.00	29.00	31.00	35.75	29.73
2007	38.00	34.50	34.50	36.00	42.38	48.63	50.00	NA	41.67	43.19	46.20	46.20	41.93
2008	51.48	54.66	64.63	61.96	61.90	59.70	55.41	44.43	38.52	30.11	27.41	26.91	48.09

Source: Economic Research Service, U.S. Department of Agriculture (ERS-USDA)

Paper

The earliest known paper that is still in existence was made from cotton rags around 150 AD. Around 800 AD, paper made its appearance in Egypt but was not manufactured there until 900 AD. The Moors introduced the use of paper to Europe, and around 1150, the first papermaking mill was established in Spain, followed by England in 1495, and the U.S. in 1690.

During the 17th and 18th centuries, the increased usage of paper created a shortage of cotton rags, which were the only source for papermaking. The solution to this problem lead to the introduction of the ground-wood process of pulp-making in 1840 and the first chemical pulp process 10 years later.

Today, the paper and paperboard industries, including newsprint, are sensitive to the economic cycle. As the economy strengthens, paper use increases, and vice versa.

Prices – The average monthly index price (1982 = 100) for paperboard in 2008 rose +8.0% yr/yr to 217.80, continuing to recover from the 9-year low of 162.7 posted in 2003. The average monthly producer price index of standard newsprint paper in 2008 rose by +12.3% to 147.8, down from the 12-year high of 151.8 posted in 2006.

Supply – U.S. production of paper and paperboard in 2007 fell -0.6% yr/yr to 83.826 million metric tons. The U.S. is the world's largest producer of paper and paperboard by far, followed by Germany with 23.172 million metric tons and Canada with 18.113 million metric tons.

U.S. production of newsprint fell by –2.4% yr/yr to a record low of 414.6 metric tons per month in 2005 which is the latest data available. U.S. production of newsprint is second in the world, after Canada, which had production of 657.200 metric tons per month in 2005.

Production of Paper and Paperboard by Selected Countries   In Thousands of Metric Tons

Year	Austria	Canada	Finland	France	Germany	Italy	Nether-lands	Norway	Russia/3	Spain	Sweden	United Kingdom	United States
2002	4,419	20,073	12,789	9,809	18,526	9,317	3,346	2,114	5,978	5,365	10,724	6,452	81,879
2003	4,565	19,964	13,058	9,939	19,310	9,491	3,339	2,186	6,377	5,437	11,062	6,455	80,712
2004	4,852	20,462	14,036	10,255	20,391	9,667	3,459	2,294	6,830	5,526	11,589	6,442	82,084
2005	4,950	19,498	12,391	10,332	21,679	9,999	3,471	2,223	7,126	5,697	11,775	6,241	83,697
2006	5,213	18,189	14,140	10,006	22,656	10,011	3,367	2,109	7,434	6,898	12,066	5,454	84,317
2007[1]	5,199	18,113	14,334	9,871	23,172	10,112	3,224	2,010	7,559	6,714	11,902	5,284	83,826

[1] Preliminary.   Source: Food and Agriculture Organization of the United Nations (FAO-UN)

Production of Newsprint by Selected Countires (Monthly Average)   In Thousands of Metric Tons

Year	Australia	Brazil	Canada	China	Finland	France	Germany	India	Japan	Rep. of Korea	Russia/3	Sweden	United States
2003	34.0	13.6	673.3	170.9	78.9	60.0	178.1	58.2	292.9	133.3	151.2	210.7	429.2
2004	35.2	11.1	648.0	248.4	60.2	93.8	185.9	58.1	307.6	145.4	164.8	220.8	424.7
2005	NA	11.0	657.2	283.2	47.9	95.7	226.0	71.9	311.2	135.8	152.8	213.0	414.6
2006	NA	11.0	NA	328.2	NA	NA	225.9	84.8	312.6	137.9	153.8	211.4	NA
2007[1]	NA	11.9	NA	382.4	NA	86.9	218.6	85.8	324.2	138.8	165.2	214.1	NA
2008[2]	NA	11.5	NA	363.7	NA	91.6	221.5	89.4	306.3	135.7	164.6	206.5	NA

[1] Preliminary.   [2] Estimate.   NA = Not available.   Source: United Nations

Index Price of Paperboard   (1982 = 100)

Year	Jan.	Feb.	Mar.	Apr.	May	June	July	Aug.	Sept.	Oct.	Nov.	Dec.	Average
2002	165.0	164.0	162.6	162.8	161.1	161.1	161.8	165.8	166.7	167.1	167.3	166.6	164.3
2003	166.8	166.5	164.4	163.5	163.6	163.4	162.5	162.5	160.5	159.9	159.6	159.7	162.7
2004	157.8	157.4	157.5	162.2	165.5	170.0	175.2	178.5	179.2	179.4	180.1	179.3	170.2
2005	179.7	180.0	180.1	180.7	180.9	176.6	174.6	168.5	168.5	168.6	174.1	173.9	175.5
2006	175.3	184.0	184.3	184.3	193.7	196.7	196.8	197.2	197.5	197.7	198.4	197.5	192.0
2007	198.0	198.1	198.2	199.0	198.8	198.7	199.0	199.1	203.1	209.5	209.2	209.4	201.7
2008[1]	209.7	209.8	209.7	209.7	209.7	210.3	211.5	226.0	229.5	230.0	229.3	228.8	217.8

[1] Preliminary.   Source: Bureau of Labor Statistics, U.S. Department of Commerce (BLS) (0914)

Producer Price Index of Standard Newsprint   (1982 = 100)

Year	Jan.	Feb.	Mar.	Apr.	May	June	July	Aug.	Sept.	Oct.	Nov.	Dec.	Average
2002	113.6	106.2	106.5	105.7	98.9	100.5	101.0	101.8	104.7	112.2	109.6	107.9	105.7
2003	106.1	107.4	106.3	110.2	112.6	112.5	111.0	114.3	116.8	118.1	114.6	115.0	112.1
2004	116.5	116.7	118.8	122.4	125.0	126.0	125.6	125.7	125.8	129.5	129.8	132.4	124.5
2005	130.3	131.9	131.6	132.8	133.2	135.9	138.8	141.4	152.2	143.5	144.9	145.6	138.5
2006	148.8	148.0	150.5	149.8	152.0	153.7	154.3	153.3	153.9	153.7	151.9	151.3	151.8
2007	150.3	146.1	145.0	143.1	127.9	127.5	125.8	124.1	122.5	121.8	121.1	124.4	131.6
2008[1]	125.8	129.6	133.4	136.2	142.7	146.5	151.0	156.1	158.6	161.5	166.3	165.4	147.8

[1] Preliminary.   Source: Bureau of Labor Statistics, U.S. Department of Commerce (BLS) (0913-02)

Peanuts and Peanut Oil

Peanuts are the edible seeds of a plant from the pea family. Although called a nut, the peanut is actually a legume. Ancient South American Inca Indians were the first to grind peanuts to make peanut butter. Peanuts originated in Brazil and were later brought to the U.S. via Africa. The first major use of peanuts was as feed for pigs. It wasn't until the Civil War that peanuts were used as human food when both Northern and Southern troops used the peanut as a food source during hard times. In 1903, Dr. George Washington Carver, a talented botanist who is considered the "father of commercial peanuts," introduced peanuts as a rotation crop in cotton-growing areas. Carver discovered over 300 uses for the peanut including shaving cream, leather dye, coffee, ink, cheese, and shampoo.

Peanuts come in many varieties, but there are four basic types grown in the U.S.: Runner, Spanish, Valencia, and Virginia. Over half of Runner peanuts are used to make peanut butter. Spanish peanuts are primarily used to make candies and peanut oil. Valencia peanuts are the sweetest of the four types. Virginia peanuts are mainly roasted and sold in and out of the shell.

Peanut oil is extracted from shelled and crushed peanuts through hydraulic pressing, expelled pressing, or solvent extraction. Crude peanut oil is used as a flavoring agent, salad oil, and cooking oil. Refined, bleached and deodorized peanut oil is used for cooking and in margarines and shortenings. The by-product called press cake is used for cattle feed along with the tops of the plants after the pods are removed. The dry shells can be burned as fuel.

Prices – The average monthly price received by farmers for peanuts (in the shell) in the first six months of the 2008-09 marketing year (i.e., Aug 2008-Jul 2009) rose +2.2% to 21.0 cents per pound. The record high is 34.7 cents posted in 1990-91. The average monthly price of peanut oil in the 2008-09 marketing year (through December 2008) fell -10.1% yr/yr to 90.75 cents per pound, down from last year's record 100.92 per pound. The average monthly price of peanut meal (50% Southeast Mills) fell by –8.0% yr/yr in 2006-07 (through February 2007, which is the latest data available) to a record low of $98.40 per short ton.

Supply – World peanut production in 2008-09 rose by +7.1% to a new record high of 34.250 million metric tons. The world's largest peanut producers are China with 39% of world production, India with 21%, U.S. with 7%, and Nigeria with 5%. U.S. peanut production in the 2008-09 marketing year rose by +37.6% to a new record high of 5.148 billion pounds.

U.S. farmers harvested 1.507 million acres of peanuts in 2008-09, up +26.1% yr/yr. That was down from the 15-year high harvest of 1.629 million acres in 2005-06. U.S. peanut yield in 2008-09 rose +9.1% yr/yr to 3,416 pounds per acre, which was a new record high. The largest peanut producing states in the U.S. are Georgia (with 44% of U.S. production in 2008), Texas (16%), Alabama (12%), Florida (9%), and North Carolina (7%). U.S. peanut oil production in 2008 fell -9.1% to 159.328 million pounds, which was only about half of the record high level of 358,195 million pounds posted in 1996.

Demand – U.S. disposition of peanuts in 2007-08 fell by -3.3% yr/yr to 4.033 billion pounds. Of that disposition, 62% of the peanuts went for food, 15% for exports, 13% for crushing into peanut oil, and 10% for seed, loss and residual. The most popular type of peanut grown in the U.S. is the Runner peanut with 85% of U.S. production in 2007-08. This was followed by the Virginia peanut with 13% of production and the Spanish peanut far behind with only 2% of production. Peanut butter is a primary use for Runner and Virginia peanuts. It accounts for 58% of Runner peanut usage and 56% of Virginia peanut usage. In a poor third place, only 5% of Spanish peanuts are used for peanut butter. Snack peanuts is also a key usage category and accounts for 31% of Spanish peanut usage, 31% of Virginia peanut usage, and 23% of Runner peanut usage. Candy accounts for 41% of Spanish peanut usage, 19% of Runner peanut usage, and 12% of Virginia peanut usage.

Trade – U.S. exports of peanuts in 2007-08 fell by -2.2% yr/yr to 590 million pounds. U.S. imports of peanuts fell by –5.2% yr/yr in 2007-08 to 55 million pounds.

World Production of Peanuts (in the Shell)   In Thousands of Metric Tons

Crop Year	Argen- tina	Burma	China	India	Indo- nesia	Nigeria	Senegal	South Africa	Sudan	Thailand	United States	Zaire	World Total
1999-00	600	562	12,639	5,500	1,020	1,450	764	165	370	137	1,737	396	29,417
2000-01	564	634	14,437	5,700	1,040	1,470	1,003	186	370	132	1,481	382	31,423
2001-02	517	731	14,415	7,600	1,033	1,490	903	120	370	107	1,940	368	33,816
2002-03	316	756	14,818	5,400	1,086	1,510	260	60	370	112	1,506	355	30,859
2003-04	420	878	13,420	7,700	1,130	1,510	445	115	370	113	1,880	360	32,834
2004-05	585	916	14,340	7,000	1,150	1,520	573	85	370	114	1,945	364	33,606
2005-06	510	770	14,340	6,300	1,170	1,520	703	93	370	114	2,209	365	33,075
2006-07	575	880	12,887	5,385	1,200	1,520	460	77	850	117	1,571	370	30,671
2007-08[1]	625	880	13,027	6,600	1,150	1,550	331	118	850	115	1,666	370	31,980
2008-09[2]	650	880	13,400	7,124	1,250	1,550	710	115	850	115	2,335	370	34,250

[1] Preliminary.   [2] Estimate.   *Source: Foreign Agricultural Service, U.S. Department of Agriculture (FAS-USDA)*

Salient Statistics of Peanuts in the United States

Crop Year Beginning Aug. 1	Acreage Planted	Acreage Harvested for Nuts	Average Yield Per Acre In Lbs.	Pro- duction (1,000 Lbs)	Season Farm Price (Cents Lb.)	Farm Value (Million Dollars)	In Thousands of Pounds Exports Unshelled	In Thousands of Pounds Exports Shelled	In Thousands of Pounds Imports Unshelled	In Thousands of Pounds Imports Shelled
	------ 1,000 Acres ------									
1999-00	1,534.5	1,436.0	2,667	3,829,490	25.4	971.6	727,000	----	178,000	----
2000-01	1,536.8	1,336.0	2,444	3,265,505	27.4	896.1	527,000	----	216,000	----
2001-02	1,541.2	1,411.9	3,029	4,276,704	23.4	1,000.5	700,000	----	203,000	----
2002-03	1,353.0	1,291.7	2,571	3,321,040	18.2	599.7	490,000	----	75,000	----
2003-04	1,344.0	1,312.0	3,159	4,144,150	19.3	799.4	516,000	----	39,000	----
2004-05	1,430.0	1,394.0	3,076	4,288,200	18.9	813.6	491,000	----	37,000	----
2005-06	1,657.0	1,629.0	2,989	4,869,860	17.3	843.4	491,000	----	32,000	----
2006-07	1,243.0	1,210.0	2,863	3,464,250	17.7	612.8	603,000	----	58,000	----
2007-08[1]	1,230.0	1,195.0	3,130	3,740,650	20.5	758.6	590,000	----	55,000	----
2008-09[2]	1,534.0	1,507.0	3,416	5,147,900	20.5	1,051.7				

[1] Preliminary.   [2] Estimate.   Source: Economic Research Service, U.S. Department of Agriculture (ERS-USDA)

Supply and Disposition of Peanuts (Farmer's Stock Basis) & Support Program in the United States

Crop Year Beginning Aug. 1	Supply Pro- duction	Supply Imports	Supply Stocks Aug. 1	Supply Total	Disposition Exports	Disposition Crushed for Oil	Disposition Seed, Loss & Residual	Disposition Food	Disposition Total Disap- pearance	Government Support Program Support Price	Government Support Program Addi- tional	Amount Put Under Support Quantity	Amount Put Under Support % of Pro- duction
	---------------------- In Millions of Pounds ----------------------									--- Cents Per Lb. ---		(Mil. Lbs.)	
1999-00	3,829	178	1,392	5,399	727	713	479	2,233	4,168	30.50	8.8	----	----
2000-01	3,266	216	1,233	4,715	527	548	360	2,184	3,618	30.50	6.6	----	----
2001-02	4,277	203	1,097	5,576	700	693	482	2,225	4,100	30.50	6.6	----	----
2002-03	3,321	75	1,476	4,873	490	857	410	2,241	3,998	NA	NA	----	----
2003-04	4,144	39	875	5,058	516	536	429	2,456	3,937	NA	NA	----	----
2004-05	4,288	37	1,121	5,446	491	393	547	2,600	4,031	NA	NA	----	----
2005-06	4,870	32	1,415	6,316	491	542	500	2,616	4,150	NA	NA	----	----
2006-07[1]	3,464	58	2,167	5,689	603	513	468	2,585	4,169	NA	NA	----	----
2007-08[2]	3,741	55	1,520	5,316	590	530	393	2,520	4,033	NA	NA	----	----

[1] Preliminary.   [2] Estimate.   Source: Economic Research Service, U.S. Department of Agriculture (ERS-USDA)

Production of Peanuts (Harvested for Nuts) in the United States, by States   In Thousands of Pounds

Crop Year	Alabama	Florida	Georgia	New Mexico	North Carolina	Oklahoma	South Carolina	Texas	Virgina	Total
1999	448,050	260,380	1,400,800	61,600	298,840	189,600	25,300	926,800	218,120	3,829,490
2000	271,180	213,710	1,328,400	54,990	338,250	120,600	29,500	698,500	210,375	3,265,505
2001	532,325	250,100	1,711,620	67,044	356,475	197,890	30,600	895,900	234,750	4,276,704
2002	379,800	197,800	1,313,000	54,000	210,000	159,600	19,140	868,000	119,700	3,321,040
2003	508,750	345,000	1,863,000	45,900	320,000	98,000	57,800	810,000	95,700	4,144,150
2004	557,200	364,000	1,817,800	59,500	367,500	102,300	112,200	803,700	104,000	4,288,200
2005	613,250	410,400	2,130,000	66,500	288,000	107,910	168,000	975,000	66,000	4,869,860
2006	407,500	300,000	1,598,500	43,200	268,800	62,700	168,000	514,750	54,400	3,464,250
2007	400,350	321,300	1,622,400	32,000	261,000	57,800	173,600	691,900	52,500	3,740,650
2008[1]	636,900	448,000	2,329,000	25,600	358,900	63,000	265,200	860,200	79,200	5,147,900

[1] Preliminary.   Source: Agricultural Statistics Board, U.S. Department of Agriculture (ASB-USDA)

Supply and Reported Uses of Shelled Peanuts and Products in the United States   In Thousands of Pounds

Crop Year Beginning Aug. 1	Shelled Peanuts Stocks, Aug. 1 Edible	Shelled Peanuts Stocks, Aug. 1 Oil Stock[2]	Shelled Peanuts Production Edible	Shelled Peanuts Production Oil Stock[2]	Reported Used — Edible Grades Used In Candy[3]	Reported Used Snack[4]	Reported Used Sandwich Spread	Reported Used Butter[5]	Reported Used Other Products	Reported Used Total	Shelled Peanuts Crushed[6]	Crude Oil Pro- duction	Cake & Meal Production
1999-00	855,572	16,587	2,157,828	448,875	354,953	394,121	----	772,104	20,227	1,541,405	536,164	228,839	291,491
2000-01	707,672	14,463	1,939,736	337,324	355,610	361,516	----	753,239	19,998	1,490,363	411,558	178,523	230,099
2001-02	680,850	16,648	2,090,776	485,092	349,729	360,916	----	818,927	17,284	1,546,856	521,173	230,791	296,874
2002-03	504,186	24,231	1,983,016	611,627	354,232	344,913	----	828,529	24,379	1,552,053	644,194	285,685	356,888
2003-04	603,529	17,686	2,439,231	390,893	365,983	414,588	----	901,637	15,930	1,698,138	402,958	172,977	226,995
2004-05	621,190	17,686	2,357,314	246,663	389,696	450,781	----	938,514	22,547	1,801,538	295,769	126,249	172,668
2005-06	501,868	15,305	2,411,471	357,600	376,777	454,324	----	974,223	12,092	1,817,416	407,817	181,085	232,868
2006-07	510,097	21,499	2,415,495	347,243	373,684	415,131	----	993,445	9,397	1,791,657	385,375	166,450	223,537
2007-08[1]	528,918	33,401	2,291,603	319,186	320,467	425,166	----	1,012,263	10,676	1,768,572	372,980	158,144	211,733

[1] Preliminary.   [2] Includes straight run oil stock peanuts.   [3] Includes peanut butter made by manufacturers for own use in candy.   [4] Formerly titled "Salted Peanuts."   [5] Includes peanut butter made by manufacturers for own use in cookies and sandwiches, but excludes peanut butter used in candy.   [6] All crushings regardless of grade.   Source: National Agricultural Statistics Service, U.S. Department of Agriculture (NASS-USDA)

PEANUTS AND PEANUT OIL

Shelled Peanuts (Raw Basis) Used in Primary Products, by Type   In Thousands of Pounds

Crop Year Beginning Aug. 1	Virginia Candy[2]	Virginia Peanuts	Virginia Butter[3]	Virginia Total	Runner Candy[2]	Runner Peanuts	Runner Butter[3]	Runner Total	Spanish Candy[2]	Spanish Peanuts	Spanish Butter[3]	Spanish Total
1998-99	36,178	99,401	57,864	196,935	321,838	234,486	670,705	1,244,748	22,161	15,919	16,137	55,137
1999-00	23,173	100,384	73,926	200,804	315,467	278,440	690,564	1,300,393	16,313	15,297	7,614	40,208
2000-01	19,101	100,650	102,050	225,072	320,304	247,739	643,229	1,227,156	16,205	13,127	7,960	38,135
2001-02	26,640	97,046	106,573	233,356	303,668	250,079	702,454	1,269,776	19,421	13,791	9,900	43,724
2002-03	26,930	75,100	77,018	183,226	312,192	257,259	734,844	1,323,846	15,110	12,555	16,667	44,981
2003-04	23,580	68,257	88,053	181,559	328,560	333,198	805,852	1,481,457	13,843	13,133	7,732	35,122
2004-05	25,466	70,216	112,027	209,411	349,437	367,671	824,876	1,562,692	14,793	12,894	1,611	29,435
2005-06	25,738	81,617	123,402	231,893	335,748	361,176	849,176	1,557,025	15,291	11,531	W	28,498
2006-07	29,542	75,858	113,689	220,196	329,806	328,167	869,014	1,535,250	14,335	11,104	W	36,211
2007-08[1]	27,909	71,059	125,497	225,445	279,564	344,551	878,026	1,511,807	12,994	9,556	W	31,321

[1] Preliminary.   [2] Includes peanut butter made by manufacturers for own use in candy.   [3] Includes peanut butter made by manufacturers for own use in cookies and sandwiches, but excludes peanut butter used in candy.
Source: National Agricultural Statistics Service, U.S. Department of Agriculture (NASS-USDA)

Production, Consumption, Stocks and Foreign Trade of Peanut Oil in the United States   In Millions of Pounds

Crop Year Beginning Aug. 1	Production Crude	Production Refined	Consumption In Refining	Consumption In End Products	Stocks, Dec. 31 Crude	Stocks, Dec. 31 Refined	Imports for Consumption	Exports
1999-00	262.9	195.9	238.9	260.4	19.7	1.7	9.6	5.8
2000-01	222.1	206.3	258.9	277.3	23.1	1.9	19.5	5.5
2001-02	278.5	179.1	291.9	282.5	8.2	1.7	----	----
2002-03	267.7	166.3	W	277.6	52.9	3.5	----	----
2003-04	180.7	115.8	W	203.8	23.0	1.8	----	----
2004-05	135.7	91.0	W	181.9	40.3	2.4	----	----
2005-06	188.0	119.9	W	152.1	15.4	3.7	----	----
2006-07	173.8	115.1	W	W	35.5	5.6	----	----
2007-08[1]	168.7	111.2	W	W	14.1	1.8	----	----
2008-09[2]	168.4	110.3	W	W	17.6	3.0	----	----

[1] Preliminary.   [2] Forecast.   W = Withheld.   *Source: Bureau of the Census, U.S. Department of Commerce*

Production of Crude Peanut Oil in the United States   In Millions of Pounds

Year	Jan.	Feb.	Mar.	Apr.	May	June	July	Aug.	Sept.	Oct.	Nov.	Dec.	Total
1999	16.2	18.2	15.8	18.2	16.4	20.7	20.8	17.8	16.3	13.5	22.6	22.7	219.2
2000	35.2	32.1	27.4	31.9	30.4	28.0	24.1	28.8	21.5	25.4	16.4	15.2	316.3
2001	17.3	15.7	20.1	15.3	12.4	19.1	16.3	16.7	12.9	17.1	13.8	25.6	202.4
2002	24.8	25.5	32.8	28.5	33.8	24.3	22.6	27.7	27.2	26.5	24.9	20.2	319.0
2003	21.7	16.6	19.4	20.5	20.0	23.2	19.8	17.3	18.3	24.1	15.6	13.2	229.6
2004	12.6	15.7	13.0	14.7	11.8	13.7	10.7	9.8	5.8	10.0	11.9	12.6	142.4
2005	14.4	13.1	9.9	11.3	13.3	14.6	8.9	14.5	11.3	15.3	16.4	17.7	160.8
2006	W	16.5	W	15.6	18.1	15.6	15.7	19.7	16.2	18.0	14.4	10.1	191.8
2007	14.3	12.8	14.3	14.9	9.7	15.2	14.1	17.7	19.0	17.3	12.0	14.0	175.3
2008[1]	14.9	6.0	14.3	14.2	13.8	12.6	13.0	11.8	14.6	17.8	12.4	13.9	159.2

[1] Preliminary.   W = Withheld.   *Source: Bureau of the Census, U.S. Department of Commerce*

Average Price of Peanut Meal 50% Southeast Mills   In Dollars Per Short Ton

Year	Jan.	Feb.	Mar.	Apr.	May	June	July	Aug.	Sept.	Oct.	Nov.	Dec.	Average
1999-00	98.00	103.00	103.00	104.00	104.75	110.00	115.00	115.00	119.60	118.00	118.00	118.00	108.15
2000-01	118.00	118.00	118.00	142.50	120.00	118.00	110.75	112.50	NA	123.50	130.50	126.25	121.64
2001-02	115.00	111.25	100.00	102.50	100.00	105.00	110.00	105.00	NA	130.00	135.00	136.88	113.69
2002-03	NA	130.00	122.50	118.50	114.25	124.00	125.00	135.00	135.00	135.75	130.00	130.00	127.27
2003-04	147.10	161.00	163.25	163.35	168.75	200.40	226.00	237.50	204.00	199.33	143.33	133.00	178.92
2004-05	100.38	99.25	93.50	93.25	99.25	112.00	122.75	137.25	145.25	140.83	132.50	109.00	115.43
2005-06	105.50	102.50	100.88	NA	114.50	113.50	113.17	113.33	107.13	107.50	100.00	98.75	106.98
2006-07	98.50	98.50	98.00	98.50	98.50	NA	NA	NA	NA	NA	NA	NA	98.40
2007-08	NA	NA	NA	NA	NA	NA	NA	NA	NA	NA	NA	NA	NA
2008-09[1]	NA	NA	NA	NA	NA								

[1] Preliminary.   NA = Not available.   *Source: Agricultural Marketing Service, U.S. Department of Agriculture (AMS-USDA)*

Peanuts (monthly average) through December 2008 — Cents per pound

Average Price Received by Farmers for Peanuts (in the Shell) in the United States — In Cents Per Pound

Year	Jan.	Feb.	Mar.	Apr.	May	June	July	Aug.	Sept.	Oct.	Nov.	Dec.	Average[1]
1999-00	25.7	27.0	25.4	24.1	21.8	14.9	NQ	NQ	NQ	NQ	NQ	NQ	23.2
2000-01	NQ	27.7	26.5	26.1	27.3	31.4	NQ	NQ	NQ	NQ	NQ	NQ	27.8
2001-02	24.1	24.9	22.8	21.0	19.5	13.5	10.7	NQ	NQ	NQ	NQ	NQ	19.5
2002-03	NQ	17.9	17.9	18.0	17.5	19.1	19.6	22.6	18.4	19.6	17.7	NQ	18.8
2003-04	NQ	18.3	18.5	18.4	19.6	20.6	18.9	18.6	19.8	20.6	20.3	17.4	19.2
2004-05	19.0	19.2	20.1	20.3	18.3	18.9	18.6	18.5	18.0	17.8	17.6	16.0	18.5
2005-06	17.0	17.0	17.4	17.5	17.4	17.3	18.6	16.9	17.4	17.3	17.0	17.0	17.3
2006-07	17.0	17.3	17.2	17.2	17.6	17.8	17.8	17.8	18.3	17.9	18.1	18.7	17.7
2007-08	18.0	18.6	21.4	21.7	21.3	21.6	21.0	20.7	20.0	20.4	20.1	21.1	20.5
2008-09[2]	18.9	21.1	20.6	20.1	21.7	23.3							21.0

[1] Weighted average by sales.   [2] Preliminarly.   NQ = No quote.   *Source: National Agricultural Statistics Service, U.S. Department of Agriculture (NASS-USDA)*

Average Price of Domestic Crude Peanut Oil (in Tanks) F.O.B. Southeast Mills — In Cents Per Pound

Year	Jan.	Feb.	Mar.	Apr.	May	June	July	Aug.	Sept.	Oct.	Nov.	Dec.	Average
1999-00	40.40	41.00	35.40	33.00	32.50	31.60	33.00	36.25	36.00	35.63	35.00	34.90	35.39
2000-01	34.63	35.50	36.40	37.25	37.00	35.90	34.00	33.00	33.00	33.00	34.00	34.00	34.81
2001-02	36.25	37.00	37.00	35.00	28.00	27.50	27.00	27.00	30.00	34.00	35.20	36.25	32.52
2002-03	NA	42.00	43.67	45.75	46.00	47.00	50.25	52.75	56.60	58.25	60.00	60.67	51.18
2003-04	61.60	63.25	64.50	65.00	61.67	60.00	60.00	56.50	NA	56.00	53.75	55.00	59.75
2004-05	55.00	55.00	55.67	56.00	55.00	50.00	50.00	53.25	52.50	52.38	52.25	50.06	53.09
2005-06	45.50	45.50	45.00	42.50	42.50	42.50	42.50	42.50	43.75	45.00	47.30	49.25	44.48
2006-07	52.67	52.50	50.00	49.25	46.25	48.20	52.63	55.63	62.56	69.63	70.00	73.00	56.86
2007-08	76.75	93.20	98.50	97.33	99.00	100.00	104.38	104.80	107.00	110.00	110.00	110.00	100.91
2008-09[1]	97.00	90.00	85.25	79.10	75.00								85.27

[1] Preliminary.   NA = Not available.   *Source: Agricultural Marketing Service, U.S. Department of Agriculture (AMS-USDA)*

Pepper

The pepper plant is a perennial climbing shrub that originated in India and Sri Lanka. Pepper is considered the world's most important spice and has been used to flavor foods for over 3,000 years. Pepper was once considered so valuable that it was used to ransom Rome from Attila the Hun. Black pepper alone accounts for nearly 35% of the world's spice trade. Unlike many other popular herbs and spices, pepper can only be cultivated in tropical climates. The pepper plant produces a berry called a peppercorn. Both black and white pepper are obtained from the same plant. The colors of pepper are determined by the maturity of the berry at harvest and by different processing methods.

Black pepper is picked when the berries are still green and immature. The peppercorns are then dried in the sun until they turn black. White pepper is picked when the berries are fully ripe and bright red. The red peppercorns are then soaked, washed to remove the skin of the berry, and dried to produce a white to yellowish-white peppercorn. Black pepper has a slightly hotter flavor and stronger aroma than white pepper. Piperine, an alkaloid of pyridine, is the active ingredient in pepper that makes it hot.

Black pepper oil is obtained from crushed berries using solvent extraction. Black pepper oil is used in the treatment of pain, chills, flu, muscular aches, and in some perfumes. It is also helpful in promoting digestion in the colon.

The world's key pepper varieties are known by their place of origin. Popular types of pepper include Lampong Black and Muntok White from Indonesia, Brazilian Black, and Malabar Black and Tellicherry from India.

Prices – The average monthly price for black pepper in 2007 (through June) rose sharply by +55.8% to 161.8 cents per pound, way up from the 14-year low of 75.6 cents per pound in 2004. The average monthly price for white pepper in 2007 rose sharply by +40.9% to 216.4 cents per pound, but that was still only 61% of the record high of 356.5 cents seen in 1998.

Trade – The world's largest exporters of pepper in 2006 (latest data available) were Vietnam (with 115,000 metric tons of exports), Brazil (42,200), Indonesia (36,953), India (35,499), and Malaysia (16,610). U.S. imports of black pepper in 2008 fell -2.6% yr/yr to 49,626 metric tons. The primary source of U.S. imports of black pepper in 2008 was Indonesia which accounted for 41% of U.S. imports, followed by India with 20%, and Brazil with 17%. Imports from Malaysia have dropped by over 95% since 2003. U.S. imports of white pepper in 2008 rose by +25.1% yr/yr to 6,960 metric tons. The primary source of U.S. imports of white pepper was Indonesia, which accounted for 69% of U.S. imports, followed by Malaysia with 5%, Brazil with 1%, and China with 1%.

World Exports of Pepper (Black and White) and Prices in the United States   In Metric Tons

| | Exports (In Metric Tons) | | | | | | | | New York Spot Prices (Cents Per Pound) | | | | |
| | | | | | | | | | Indonesian | | Indian | | |
Year	Brazil	India	Indonesia	Madagascar	Malaysia	Mexico	Sri Lanka	Vietnam	Lampong Black	Muntok White	Brazilian Black	Malabar Black	Telli-cherry[2]
1998	17,249	32,859	38,723	339	18,717	3,365	5,493	15,100	239.5	356.5	239.5	239.5	286.6
1999	19,617	35,635	36,293	619	21,804	4,026	3,754	34,800	254.5	334.9	254.5	254.5	296.3
2000	20,469	19,125	47,502	587	23,684	4,533	4,855	36,400	228.1	227.1	228.1	228.1	282.6
2001	36,975	19,641	53,432	811	25,537	4,658	2,161	57,000	116.2	132.6	116.2	116.2	179.3
2002	38,230	21,066	63,214	880	22,840	4,344	7,915	78,400	92.9	120.6	92.9	92.9	127.8
2003	38,972	15,319	51,546	863	18,346	3,861	7,740	73,900	85.8	139.3	85.8	85.8	128.8
2004	43,003	15,429	32,364	1,243	19,788	5,785	4,852	111,000	75.6	120.9	75.6	75.6	118.8
2005	38,424	21,470	34,531	1,229	18,097	15,415	8,131	109,000	76.0	116.0	76.0	76.0	109.9
2006[1]	42,200	35,499	36,953	1,776	16,610	6,593	7,596	115,000	103.9	153.5	103.9	103.9	136.4
2007[1]									161.8	216.4	161.8	161.8	

[1] Preliminary.   [2] Extra bold.   NA = not avaliable.   *Source: Foreign Agricultural Service, U.S. Department of Agriculture (FAS-USDA)*

United States Imports of Unground Pepper from Specified Countries   In Metric Tons

| | Black Pepper | | | | | | | White Pepper | | | | | |
Year	Brazil	India	Indonesia	Malaysia	Singapore	Sri Lanka	Total	Brazil	China	Indonesia	Malaysia	Singapore	Total
1999	7,093	24,931	8,429	2,392	525	441	47,591	32	451	5,202	420	342	6,789
2000	7,853	10,981	15,713	4,148	306	516	43,539	15	210	6,345	185	215	7,311
2001	11,699	7,998	19,606	2,957	508	279	48,749	48	7	5,807	120	161	6,365
2002	11,300	7,407	13,638	3,213	110	564	50,155	18	73	6,559	103	219	7,207
2003	13,792	4,950	16,370	1,416	163	504	51,124	198	180	4,567	224	904	6,758
2004	15,606	2,039	13,210	97	25	187	52,152	472	98	4,034	192	422	7,290
2005	13,935	3,828	13,502	144	50	269	52,152	460	73	4,134	192	300	7,248
2006	15,622	7,272	12,941	249	90	342	55,523	615	106	3,809	419	344	7,805
2007	14,148	14,763	14,201	162	75	281	50,934	122	121	3,991	520	140	5,564
2008[1]	8,224	9,699	20,180	35	126	665	49,626	88	82	4,783	381	36	6,960

[1] Preliminary.   *Source: Foreign Agricultural Service, U.S. Department of Agriculture (FAS-USDA)*

Pepper (monthly average) through June 2007 — Cents per pound

Average Black Pepper in New York (Brazilian)   In Cents Per Pound

Year	Jan.	Feb.	Mar.	Apr.	May	June	July	Aug.	Sept.	Oct.	Nov.	Dec.	Average
1998	199.4	205.5	243.8	262.8	262.8	247.5	253.0	253.8	246.3	243.0	231.3	225.0	239.5
1999	222.5	225.8	252.5	248.0	252.5	250.0	229.0	249.3	263.8	282.0	297.5	281.0	254.5
2000	260.0	256.3	246.0	260.0	265.0	265.0	263.8	252.5	205.0	167.5	147.5	149.0	228.1
2001	157.5	146.3	144.0	150.0	143.8	123.0	97.3	87.0	90.0	89.3	81.6	85.3	116.2
2002	85.0	80.0	81.4	100.5	101.0	92.0	84.8	86.8	93.5	103.5	106.0	100.8	92.9
2003	93.8	89.0	88.5	85.5	83.8	89.0	90.0	86.6	83.5	81.6	80.0	78.0	85.8
2004	78.0	75.5	75.5	75.4	77.3	78.0	76.8	75.0	75.0	74.2	73.3	73.0	75.6
2005	73.0	73.0	73.8	75.2	75.5	77.0	77.0	77.0	77.6	78.0	77.0	77.4	76.0
2006	78.0	78.0	77.8	78.5	80.0	80.4	89.0	112.7	146.0	152.0	139.5	134.3	103.9
2007	132.5	136.0	137.2	177.5	194.5	193.0							161.8

NA = Not available.   *Source: Foreign Agricultural Service, U.S. Department of Agriculture (FAS-USDA)*

Average White Pepper in New York (Indonesian)[1]   In Cents Per Pound

Year	Jan.	Feb.	Mar.	Apr.	May	June	July	Aug.	Sept.	Oct.	Nov.	Dec.	Average
1998	348.0	346.3	362.5	390.0	393.0	358.8	354.0	356.3	348.8	340.0	340.0	340.0	356.5
1999	361.3	355.0	365.0	355.0	352.5	335.0	310.0	313.8	325.0	327.0	316.3	303.0	334.9
2000	295.0	293.8	264.0	253.8	246.3	242.0	226.3	227.5	205.0	171.3	150.0	150.0	227.1
2001	159.0	151.3	144.0	133.8	130.0	127.0	122.5	129.6	128.0	125.5	120.0	120.0	132.6
2002	111.3	100.3	95.6	108.8	108.0	105.0	104.5	118.8	130.0	154.0	157.5	153.0	120.6
2003	152.4	148.8	150.0	150.0	142.6	133.0	133.0	138.2	137.5	133.6	127.5	125.0	139.3
2004	118.0	118.0	125.8	130.0	130.0	125.0	127.0	120.5	119.0	113.8	109.5	114.6	120.9
2005	119.0	118.0	118.0	116.4	115.0	115.0	115.0	115.0	115.2	115.0	115.0	115.0	116.0
2006	115.0	117.5	125.0	125.0	125.0	126.2	145.0	160.0	210.0	212.5	192.5	188.8	153.5
2007	191.3	195.0	197.0	225.0	245.0	245.0							216.4

[1] Muntok White.   *Source: Foreign Agricultural Service, U.S. Department of Agriculture (FAS-USDA)*

Petroleum

Crude oil is petroleum that is acquired directly from the ground. Crude oil was formed millions of years ago from the remains of tiny aquatic plants and animals that lived in ancient seas. Ancient societies such as the Persians, 10th century Sumatrans, and pre-Columbian Indians believed that crude oil had medicinal benefits. Around 4,000 BC in Mesopotamia, bitumen, a tarry crude, was used as caulking for ships, as a setting for jewels and mosaics, and as an adhesive to secure weapon handles. The walls of Babylon and the famed pyramids were held together with bitumen, and Egyptians used it for embalming. During the 19th century in America, an oil find was often met with dismay. Pioneers who dug wells to find water or brine, were disappointed when they struck oil. It wasn't until 1854, with the invention of the kerosene lamp, that the first large-scale demand for petroleum emerged. Crude oil is a relatively abundant commodity. The world has produced approximately 650 billion barrels of oil, but another trillion barrels of proved reserves have yet to be extracted. Crude oil was the world's first trillion-dollar industry and accounts for the single largest product in world trade.

Futures and options on crude oil trade at the New York Mercantile Exchange (Nymex) and at the International Petroleum Exchange in London (IPE). The Nymex trades two main types of crude oil: light sweet crude oil and Brent crude oil. The light sweet futures contract calls for the delivery of 1,000 barrels of crude oil in Cushing, Oklahoma. Light sweet crude is preferred by refiners because of its low sulfur content and relatively high yield of high-value products such as gasoline, diesel fuel, heating oil, and jet fuel. The Brent blend crude is based on a light, sweet North Sea crude oil. Brent blend crude production is approximately 500,000 barrels per day, and is shipped from Sullom Voe in the Shetland Islands.

Prices – NYMEX crude oil prices in the first half of 2008 extended the extraordinary rally that began in 2001 with oil prices at $16.70 per barrel. Oil prices, which closed 2007 at $95.98, pierced the $100 per barrel mark in January 2008 and rallied to a record high of $147.27 in July 2008. That rally was driven by the weak dollar, strong demand, lagging supply, and a heavy flow of investment capital into the commodity and petroleum markets. OPEC responded to the sharp rally in oil prices by boosting production by 15% to a record high of 30.315 million barrels per day (bpd) in July 2008. The commodity and oil price bubble finally burst in July 2008 as the weight of the U.S. banking and housing crises started to push the global economy lower. When the global financial crisis hit full stride in September 2008 with the bankruptcy of Lehman Brothers, oil prices accelerated downward to hit a 5-year low of $32.40 in December 2008. The global financial crisis not only forced capitulation by investors with long petroleum positions but also raised the specter of a long period of weak fuel demand during a global recession. In fact, the International Energy Agency was forced to repeatedly cut its petroleum demand forecasts for 2009 as the global economy entered its first recession in post-war history. The rally in the dollar during the global financial crisis was an additional bearish factor for crude oil prices. Oil prices finally bottomed out and started moving higher in early 2008 after OPEC slashed its production by 16% from July 2008 through February 2009. In addition, fuel demand stabilized after gasoline prices in the U.S. moved below $2 per gallon.

Supply – World crude oil production in 2008 rose +1.2% yr/yr to 73.885 million barrels per day, which was a new record high. The world's largest oil producers are Russia (with 12.7% of world production in 2006), Saudi Arabia (12.6%), the United States (6.7%), Iran (5.5%), China (5.1%), and Mexico (3.8%). U.S. crude oil production in 2007 fell 0.7% yr/yr to 5.064 million barrels per day, which was the lowest level in over 30 years. Alaskan production in 2007 fell –2.6% yr/yr to 722,000 barrels per day, the lowest level since 1977 and only 35% of the peak level of 2.107 million barrels per day seen in 1988.

Demand – U.S. demand for crude oil in 2007 (latest data available) fell -0.6% yr/yr to 15.156 million barrels per day, still below the 2004 record high of 15.475. Most of that demand went for U.S. refinery production of products such as gasoline fuel, diesel fuel, aviation fuel, heating oil, kerosene, asphalt, and lubricants.

Trade – The U.S. is highly dependent on imports of crude oil to meet its energy needs. U.S. imports in 2007 (latest data available) fell 0.9% yr/yr to 10.031 million barrels per day, down from the 2005 record high of 10.126. U.S. imports of petroleum products in 2007 fell –27.4% to 2.761 million barrels per day, imports of distillate fuel oil fell -20.1% yr/yr to 304,000 barrels per day, and imports of residual fuel oil rose +5.9% yr/yr to 372,000 barrels per day.

World Production of Crude Petroleum   In Thousands of Barrels Per Day

Year	Canada	China	Indo-nesia	Iran	Kuwait	Mexico	Nigeria	Russia/3	Saudi Arabia	United Kingdom	United States	Vene-zuela	World Total
1999	1,907	3,195	1,472	3,557	1,898	2,906	2,130	6,079	7,833	2,684	5,881	2,826	65,922
2000	1,977	3,249	1,428	3,696	2,079	3,012	2,165	6,479	8,404	2,275	5,822	3,155	68,495
2001	2,029	3,300	1,340	3,724	1,998	3,157	2,256	6,917	8,031	2,282	5,801	3,010	68,101
2002	2,171	3,390	1,249	3,444	1,894	3,177	2,275	8,132	8,775	2,093	5,681	2,335	69,434
2003	2,306	3,409	1,155	3,743	2,136	3,371	2,275	8,132	9,101	1,845	5,419	2,557	72,493
2004	2,398	3,485	1,096	4,001	2,376	3,383	2,329	8,805	9,101	1,845	5,419	2,557	72,493
2005	2,369	3,609	1,067	4,139	2,529	3,334	2,627	9,043	9,550	1,649	5,178	2,565	73,737
2006	2,525	3,673	1,019	4,028	2,535	3,256	2,440	9,247	9,152	1,490	5,102	2,511	73,461
2007[1]	2,616	3,729	964	3,912	2,464	3,082	2,350	9,437	8,722	1,498	5,064	2,433	73,012
2008[2]	2,586	3,799	972	4,037	2,594	2,806	2,173	9,359	9,330	1,380	4,940	2,399	73,885

Includes lease condensate.   [1] Preliminary.   [2] Estimate.   *Source: Energy Information Administration, U.S. Department of Energy (EIA-DOE)*

Refiner Sales Prices of Residual Fuel Oil　　In Cents Per Gallon

Year	Jan.	Feb.	Mar.	Apr.	May	June	July	Aug.	Sept.	Oct.	Nov.	Dec.	Average
2003	86.6	97.2	98.1	77.3	74.9	71.9	74.5	75.4	72.0	70.7	76.7	79.3	80.4
2004	84.3	80.6	76.3	75.7	80.7	80.5	78.2	81.8	90.3	91.5	96.6	87.2	83.6
2005	86.9	90.8	98.0	106.6	112.2	111.8	116.8	129.2	138.4	142.7	134.3	134.6	116.9
2006	134.6	137.8	136.0	139.7	143.5	148.1	145.1	145.1	132.4	120.1	117.6	119.9	135.0
2007	117.2	121.4	122.1	125.8	135.9	142.1	153.9	158.4	161.0	166.1	183.2	194.8	148.5
2008[1]	203.9	200.3	204.7	221.7	234.8	265.7	294.5	NA	266.6	216.6	161.2		227.0

Sulfur 1% or less, excluding taxes.　　[1] Preliminary.　　*Source: Energy Information Administration, U.S. Department of Energy (EIA-DOE)*

Refiner Sales Prices of No. 2 Fuel Oil　　In Cents Per Gallon

Year	Jan.	Feb.	Mar.	Apr.	May	June	July	Aug.	Sept.	Oct.	Nov.	Dec.	Average
2003	90.0	108.6	105.3	83.0	75.8	76.9	78.9	83.6	77.3	84.2	84.2	88.6	88.1
2004	97.0	93.0	93.6	95.4	103.0	101.9	109.5	118.8	127.0	147.9	139.4	129.9	113.0
2005	131.4	134.4	153.5	155.9	144.4	159.1	164.7	178.4	199.3	207.1	175.2	172.4	164.7
2006	175.6	171.1	179.1	197.2	201.3	198.4	200.6	206.1	179.7	172.2	169.9	175.3	185.5
2007	160.6	172.4	178.1	191.0	194.9	201.4	207.1	202.1	213.3	226.0	256.9	257.0	205.1
2008[1]	256.6	260.9	297.6	319.4	353.8	376.0	380.2	328.7	300.0	240.0	194.7		300.7

Excluding taxes.　　[1] Preliminary.　　*Source: Energy Information Administration, U.S. Department of Energy (EIA-DOE)*

Refiner Sales Prices of No. 2 Diesel Fuel　　In Cents Per Gallon

Year	Jan.	Feb.	Mar.	Apr.	May	June	July	Aug.	Sept.	Oct.	Nov.	Dec.	Average
2003	89.2	107.8	102.5	86.4	79.2	81.0	83.7	88.8	80.7	87.0	86.5	89.2	88.3
2004	96.2	96.8	101.0	107.6	112.1	107.1	115.4	124.4	133.0	153.0	142.2	127.2	118.0
2005	130.6	139.1	158.8	163.8	152.2	167.0	171.5	189.8	212.7	232.3	182.6	175.5	173.0
2006	181.0	180.6	190.1	212.2	218.7	218.7	225.0	234.3	191.3	182.7	186.8	188.6	200.8
2007	169.8	182.7	197.9	211.6	210.1	214.7	222.0	219.3	232.1	242.6	269.8	259.9	219.4
2008[1]	258.1	273.8	315.9	335.8	371.2	385.9	387.6	333.9	316.0	251.6	195.6		311.4

Excluding taxes.　　[1] Preliminary.　　*Source: Energy Information Administration, U.S. Department of Energy (EIA-DOE)*

Refiner Sales Prices of Kerosine-Type Jet Fuel　　In Cents Per Gallon

Year	Jan.	Feb.	Mar.	Apr.	May	June	July	Aug.	Sept.	Oct.	Nov.	Dec.	Average
2003	89.8	103.1	102.4	82.3	75.1	76.9	81.3	86.2	80.8	83.7	86.5	90.7	87.1
2004	99.7	100.0	101.4	103.3	114.9	108.5	115.6	126.9	132.6	155.1	145.2	132.8	119.7
2005	131.7	138.3	158.2	165.5	155.8	165.0	171.2	184.7	206.9	233.5	181.4	173.8	172.2
2006	182.4	182.5	186.2	203.2	213.2	213.3	217.4	221.4	194.7	181.5	177.8	190.6	197.0
2007	172.7	176.6	184.6	202.1	207.9	211.4	216.7	215.1	225.6	235.3	265.6	265.5	214.9
2008[1]	266.3	267.3	310.5	332.0	364.2	391.2	397.8	339.3	327.8	256.9	197.4		313.7

Excluding taxes.　　[1] Preliminary.　　*Source: Energy Information Administration, U.S. Department of Energy (EIA-DOE)*

Refiner Sales Prices of Propane[2]　　In Cents Per Gallon

Year	Jan.	Feb.	Mar.	Apr.	May	June	July	Aug.	Sept.	Oct.	Nov.	Dec.	Average
2003	60.5	72.7	69.2	53.8	54.3	57.1	55.9	58.6	56.7	59.7	58.7	64.8	60.7
2004	71.7	70.1	61.9	60.4	65.5	66.1	72.2	83.0	80.4	88.6	88.3	83.5	74.3
2005	NA	NA	NA	86.0	82.0	83.0	86.0	93.2	108.2	111.6	103.3	106.8	95.6
2006	104.4	97.5	96.7	102.3	102.9	106.7	110.8	111.3	103.2	100.3	101.3	103.3	103.4
2007	99.5	103.3	104.9	106.7	111.2	109.4	115.9	116.7	124.8	135.1	147.1	146.1	118.4
2008[1]	148.3	143.1	146.0	152.7	163.7	177.1	183.3	166.5	156.4	124.2	100.8		151.1

[1] Preliminary.　　[2] Consumer Grade, Excluding taxes.　　*Source: Energy Information Administration, U.S. Department of Energy (EIA-DOE)*

Supply and Disposition of Crude Oil in the United States　　In Thousands of Barrels Per Day

Year	Field Production Total Domestic	Alskan	Imports Total	Imports SPR[2]	Imports Other	Unaccounted for Crude Oil	Stock Withdrawal[3] SPR[2]	Stock Withdrawal[3] Other	Disposition Refinery Inputs	Disposition Exports	Ending Stocks Total	Ending Stocks SPR[2]	Ending Stocks Other Primary
	In Thousands of Barrels Per Day										*In Millions of Barrels*		
2000	5,822	970	9,071	8	9,062	155	-73	3	15,067	50	826	541	286
2001	5,801	963	9,328	11	9,318	117	26	73	15,128	20	862	550	312
2002	5,746	984	9,140	16	9,124	110	134	-94	14,947	9	877	599	278
2003	5,681	974	9,665	0	9,665	54	108	-24	15,304	12	907	638	269
2004	5,419	908	10,088	77	10,010	143	102	46	15,475	27	961	676	286
2005	5,178	864	10,126	52	10,074	76	25	104	15,220	32	1,008	685	324
2006	5,102	741	10,118	8	10,089	8	11	-37	15,242	25	1,001	689	312
2007[1]	5,064	722	10,031	7					15,156	27	983	697	286

[1] Preliminary.　　[2] Strategic Petroleum Reserve.　　[3] A negative number indicates a decrease in stocks and a positive number indicates an increase.
Source: Energy Information Administration, U.S. Department of Energy (EIA-DOE)

PETROLEUM

Crude Petroleum Refinery Operations Ratio[2] in the United States   In Percent of Capacity

Year	Jan.	Feb.	Mar.	Apr.	May	June	July	Aug.	Sept.	Oct.	Nov.	Dec.	Average
1999	90.4	90.0	90.9	94.6	93.9	93.5	94.9	95.5	94.1	91.1	92.0	90.4	92.7
2000	85.7	86.4	89.8	92.6	94.7	96.2	96.9	95.9	94.3	92.4	92.7	94.0	92.6
2001	90.2	90.5	89.4	94.9	96.4	95.6	93.9	93.3	92.2	92.0	92.2	90.2	92.6
2002	87.7	86.6	87.9	93.0	91.5	93.1	93.5	92.9	90.4	87.5	92.6	91.1	90.7
2003	87.2	87.4	90.5	94.1	95.8	94.7	94.0	95.0	93.1	92.4	93.6	93.0	92.6
2004	89.1	88.8	88.5	92.5	95.6	97.5	96.8	97.1	90.1	90.2	94.4	95.0	93.0
2005	91.3	90.6	90.2	92.6	94.1	96.7	94.0	92.1	83.9	81.6	89.0	89.0	90.4
2006	87.0	86.5	85.7	88.1	91.1	93.0	92.4	93.2	93.0	88.0	88.2	90.4	89.7
2007	88.1	84.7	87.0	88.2	89.7	88.5	91.2	90.8	88.9	87.4	88.9	88.7	88.5
2008[1]	85.8	85.0	83.2	86.2	88.8	89.5	88.8	87.1	74.6	85.3	85.8	83.9	85.3

[1] Preliminary.   [2] Based on the ration of the daily average crude runs to stills to the rated capacity of refineries per day.   *Source: Energy Information Administration, U.S. Department of Energy (EIA-DOE)*

Crude Oil Refinery Inputs in the United States   In Thousands of Barrels Per Day

Year	Jan.	Feb.	Mar.	Apr.	May	June	July	Aug.	Sept.	Oct.	Nov.	Dec.	Average
1999	14,442	14,309	14,498	15,094	14,973	14,959	15,237	15,299	15,107	14,589	14,704	14,410	14,804
2000	13,779	14,028	14,613	15,053	15,494	15,643	15,819	15,640	15,407	15,029	15,023	15,232	15,067
2001	14,789	14,813	14,649	15,536	15,763	15,650	15,369	15,259	15,005	15,002	15,001	14,688	15,128
2002	14,487	14,306	14,526	15,325	15,301	15,397	15,430	15,338	14,861	14,303	15,155	14,900	14,947
2003	14,338	14,381	14,933	15,575	15,910	15,620	15,546	15,693	15,446	15,342	15,455	15,345	15,304
2004	14,782	14,706	14,787	15,541	15,992	16,240	16,142	16,142	14,980	14,941	15,664	15,750	15,472
2005	15,254	15,142	15,214	15,494	15,905	16,401	15,850	15,664	13,986	13,646	15,032	15,046	15,220
2006	14,805	14,581	14,582	14,928	15,516	15,843	15,702	15,792	15,739	15,008	15,009	15,354	15,238
2007	14,992	14,435	14,840	15,045	15,380	15,248	15,671	15,685	15,226	14,933	15,151	15,202	15,151
2008[1]	14,799	14,625	14,361	14,799	15,291	15,384	15,236	14,947	12,759	14,551	14,605	14,509	14,656

[1] Preliminary.   *Source: Energy Information Administration, U.S. Department of Energy (EIA-DOE)*

Production of Major Refined Petroleum Products in Continental United States   In Millions of Barrels

Year	Asphalt	Aviation Gasoline	Fuel Oil Distillate	Fuel Oil Residual	Gasoline	Jet Fuel	Kero-sene	Natural Gas Plant Liquids	Lubri-cants	Liquified Gasses Total	at L.P.G.[2]	AT L.P.G.[3]
1999	184.3	7.5	1,240.8	254.8	2,896	571.3	24.4	675.1	66.8	811.0	564.5	246.5
2000	180.6	6.2	1,189.9	234.3	2,664	536.6	20.4	649.4	60.9	788.0	545.5	242.5
2001	177.3	6.5	1,348.4	262.8	2,913	558.2	26.7	680.3	64.1	810.1	569.1	241.0
2002	179.9	6.4	1,309.8	218.8	2,983	552.3	20.8	686.5	63.3	822.5	576.8	245.7
2003	181.0	5.8	1,355.5	241.8	2,992	543.1	20.4	626.7	60.6	766.1	526.4	239.6
2004	185.6	6.2	1,397.6	238.0	3,013	566.3	23.2	662.7	62.0	797.2	561.3	235.9
2005	186.0	6.1	1,441.4	227.9	3,014	561.5	23.6	623.9	60.8	736.9	527.2	209.8
2006	184.8	6.6	1,478.1	231.5	3,036	540.4	17.3	633.4	66.8	757.6	537.8	219.9
2007	166.1	6.0	1,507.7	244.4	3,045	528.6	12.7	648.3	65.1	789.0	552.8	236.2
2008[1]	150.9	5.5	1,569.5	227.1	3,072	539.5	12.0	651.9	63.2	786.1	556.2	229.9

[1] Preliminary.   [2] Gas processing plants.   [3] Refineries.   *Source: Energy Information Administration, U.S. Department of Energy (EIA-DOE)*

Stocks of Petroleum and Products in the United States on January 1   In Millions of Barrels

Year	Crude Petroleum	Strategic Reserve	Total	Asphalt	Aviation Gasoline	Fuel Oil Distillate	Fuel Oil Residual	Finished Gasoline	Jet Fuel	Kero-sene	Gases[2]	Lubri-cants	Motor Gasoline Total	Motor Gasoline Finished[3]
2000	851.7	567.2	407.1	16.9	1.6	125.5	35.8	154.1	40.5	4.9	89.3	11.8	196	154
2001	826.2	540.7	415.7	25.0	1.3	118.0	36.2	153.0	44.5	4.1	82.5	12.1	207	153
2002	862.2	550.2	445.6	20.6	1.5	144.5	41.0	161.5	42.0	5.4	120.9	13.8	214	161
2003	876.7	599.1	425.1	21.3	1.4	134.1	31.3	161.9	39.2	5.5	105.7	12.0	199	162
2004	906.3	638.4	413.1	19.3	1.2	136.8	37.8	146.8	38.7	5.6	94.4	10.0		147
2005	961.9	675.6	405.6	22.1	1.3	126.0	42.4	143.1	40.2	4.9	111.0	10.4		143
2006	1,007.8	684.5	403.6	21.0	1.2	136.0	37.3	134.8	41.8	5.1	117.6	9.7		135
2007	998.4	688.6	405.9	28.8	1.4	143.7	42.4	118.3	39.1	3.4	125.2	12.4		118
2008	982.8	696.9	374.3	22.2	1.2	133.5	38.6	110.0	39.5	2.8	105.5	10.6		110
2009[1]	1,026.1	701.8	367.8	20.3	1.2	145.9	36.2	98.2	38.2	2.2	126.9	10.7		98

[1] Preliminary.   [2] Includes ethane & ethylene at plants and refineries.   [3] Includes oxygenated.
Source: Energy Information Administration, U.S. Department of Energy (EIA-DOE)

Stocks of Crude Petroleum in the United States, on First of Month   In Millions of Barrels

Year	Jan.	Feb.	Mar.	Apr.	May	June	July	Aug.	Sept.	Oct.	Nov.	Dec.
1999	894.4	896.6	897.4	908.0	902.3	914.8	902.8	906.0	889.1	878.0	875.7	866.2
2000	851.6	852.4	855.2	866.5	873.2	864.1	859.5	852.6	858.7	848.2	842.4	833.9
2001	826.2	836.0	824.2	850.8	873.0	871.7	851.5	856.6	851.6	854.1	858.4	859.5
2002	862.2	874.9	887.4	895.0	891.3	898.3	894.1	882.8	878.5	857.8	881.1	884.0
2003	876.7	873.2	870.3	880.8	891.0	888.6	893.1	897.3	897.8	911.1	925.5	914.8
2004	907.3	912.8	931.2	949.4	961.5	965.8	967.2	960.1	947.6	943.3	957.0	961.0
2005	961.3	968.3	985.6	1,007.0	1,022.5	1,026.5	1,025.6	1,018.5	1,012.1	1,000.8	1,006.9	1,007.4
2006	1,007.7	1,006.8	1,027.4	1,028.8	1,035.6	1,029.2	1,024.5	1,019.3	1,020.7	1,020.5	1,027.9	1,023.1
2007	1,000.9	1,012.3	1,006.6	1,020.5	1,026.9	1,038.7	1,045.1	1,028.8	1,015.1	1,008.1	1,002.9	995.0
2008[1]	982.8	994.7	1,000.3	1,013.5	1,020.3	1,007.1	1,000.7	1,001.7	1,008.7	1,005.7	1,013.9	1,022.5

[1] Preliminary.   Source: Energy Information Administration; U.S. Department of Energy

Production of Crude Petroleum in the United States   In Thousands of Barrels Per Day

Year	Jan.	Feb.	Mar.	Apr.	May	June	July	Aug.	Sept.	Oct.	Nov.	Dec.	Average
1999	5,963	5,966	5,883	5,887	5,875	5,760	5,798	5,780	5,804	5,947	5,960	5,959	5,881
2000	5,784	5,852	5,918	5,854	5,847	5,823	5,739	5,789	5,758	5,809	5,833	5,855	5,822
2001	5,799	5,780	5,880	5,863	5,829	5,766	5,749	5,725	5,709	5,746	5,881	5,887	5,801
2002	5,848	5,871	5,883	5,859	5,924	5,915	5,770	5,811	5,411	5,363	5,597	5,699	5,746
2003	5,785	5,791	5,817	5,774	5,733	5,701	5,526	5,595	5,683	5,635	5,560	5,579	5,681
2004	5,570	5,556	5,607	5,527	5,548	5,398	5,458	5,333	5,062	5,156	5,396	5,413	5,419
2005	5,441	5,494	5,601	5,556	5,581	5,460	5,240	5,218	4,204	4,534	4,837	4,984	5,179
2006	5,106	5,045	5,045	5,128	5,161	5,160	5,102	5,059	5,037	5,106	5,105	5,166	5,102
2007	5,123	5,125	5,106	5,189	5,197	5,096	5,024	4,914	4,884	5,043	5,017	5,056	5,065
2008[1]	5,093	5,113	5,139	5,162	5,166	5,109	5,110	4,895	3,960	4,645	4,938	4,989	4,943

[1] Preliminary.   Source: Energy Information Administration, U.S. Department of Energy (EIA-DOE)

U.S. Foreign Trade of Petroleum and Products   In Thousands of Barrels Per Day

	----- Exports -----		-------------------- Imports --------------------						----- Exports -----		-------------------- Imports --------------------			
Year	Total[2]	Petroleum Products	Crude	Petroleum Products	Distillate Fuel Oil	Residual Fuel Oil	Net Imports[3]	Year	Total[2]	Petroleum Products	Crude	Petroleum Products	Distillate Fuel Oil	Residual Fuel Oil	Net Imports[3]
1989	859	717	5,843	2,217	306	629	7,202	1999	940	822	8,731	2,122	250	237	9,912
1990	857	748	5,894	2,123	278	504	7,161	2000	1,040	990	9,071	2,389	295	352	10,419
1991	1,001	885	5,782	1,844	205	453	6,626	2001	971	951	9,328	2,543	344	295	10,900
1992	950	861	6,083	1,805	216	375	6,938	2002	984	975	9,140	2,390	267	249	10,546
1993	1,003	904	6,787	1,833	184	373	7,618	2003	1,027	1,014	9,665	2,599	333	327	11,237
1994	942	843	7,063	1,933	203	314	8,054	2004	1,048	1,021	10,088	3,057	325	426	12,097
1995	949	855	7,230	1,605	193	187	7,886	2005	1,165	1,133	10,126	3,588	329	530	12,549
1996	981	871	7,508	1,971	230	248	8,498	2006	1,317	1,292	10,118	3,517	365	350	12,390
1997	1,003	896	8,225	1,936	228	194	9,158	2007	1,433	1,405	10,031	2,761	304	372	12,035
1998	945	835	8,706	2,002	210	275	9,764	2008[1]	1,792	1,764	9,776	2,561	206	349	11,100

[1] Preliminary.   [2] Includes crude oil.   [3] Equals imports minus exports.
Source: Energy Information Administration, U.S. Department of Energy (EIA-DOE)

Domestic First Purchase Price of Crude Petroleum at Wells[1]   In Dollars Per Barrel

Year	Jan.	Feb.	Mar.	Apr.	May	June	July	Aug.	Sept.	Oct.	Nov.	Dec.	Average
1999	8.57	8.60	10.76	12.82	13.92	14.39	16.12	17.58	20.03	19.71	21.35	22.55	15.56
2000	23.53	25.48	26.19	23.20	25.58	27.62	26.81	27.91	29.72	29.65	30.36	24.46	26.72
2001	24.58	25.27	23.02	23.41	24.06	23.43	22.94	23.08	22.37	18.73	16.49	15.54	21.84
2002	15.89	16.92	20.04	22.14	23.51	22.59	23.51	24.76	26.08	25.29	23.38	25.29	22.51
2003	28.35	31.85	30.09	25.46	24.96	26.83	27.53	27.94	25.23	26.52	27.21	28.54	27.54
2004	30.35	31.21	32.86	33.23	36.07	34.53	36.54	40.10	40.62	46.28	42.81	38.22	36.90
2005	40.18	42.19	47.56	47.26	44.03	49.83	53.35	58.90	59.64	56.99	53.20	53.24	50.53
2006	57.85	55.69	55.59	62.51	64.31	64.36	67.72	67.21	59.36	53.26	52.42	55.03	59.61
2007	49.32	52.94	54.95	58.20	58.90	62.35	69.23	67.78	73.16	79.32	87.16	85.29	66.55
2008[2]	87.06	89.41	98.44	106.64	118.55	127.47	128.08	112.83	98.50	73.22	53.70		99.45

[1] Buyers posted prices.   [2] Preliminary.   Source: Energy Information Administration, U.S. Department of Energy (EIA-DOE)

Light Crude Oil Futures - CME Group (NYMEX)
(weekly close) as of January 02, 2009
USD per barrel

Volume of Trading of Crude Oil Futures in New York In Thousands of Contracts

Year	Jan.	Feb.	Mar.	Apr.	May	June	July	Aug.	Sept.	Oct.	Nov.	Dec.	Total
1999	2,534	2,326	3,768	3,167	3,038	3,307	3,471	3,355	3,388	3,571	3,465	2,470	37,860
2000	3,139	3,077	3,380	2,579	3,002	3,232	2,750	3,149	3,712	3,418	2,824	2,620	36,883
2001	3,035	2,855	3,449	3,312	3,469	3,572	3,170	3,316	2,773	2,913	3,210	2,455	37,531
2002	3,481	3,150	3,790	4,315	4,317	3,429	3,466	3,883	3,939	4,397	3,478	4,034	45,679
2003	4,553	4,039	4,151	3,355	3,329	3,534	3,401	3,732	3,826	4,248	3,624	3,646	45,437
2004	4,118	3,887	4,495	4,326	4,250	4,633	4,063	4,987	4,711	4,794	4,510	4,108	52,883
2005	4,352	4,032	5,721	5,404	5,045	5,326	4,629	6,091	5,252	5,022	4,488	4,288	59,650
2006	5,482	5,594	5,937	5,285	5,861	5,134	4,500	5,409	6,067	7,492	7,555	6,739	71,053
2007	10,367	9,092	10,069	9,287	9,487	9,862	9,656	10,647	10,670	12,390	11,307	8,692	121,526
2008	10,815	10,100	12,577	11,066	13,497	12,453	11,321	10,589	11,554	11,638	8,662	9,910	134,183

Source: New York Mercantile Exchange (NYMEX)

Average Open Interest of Crude Oil Futures in New York In Thousands of Contracts

Year	Jan.	Feb.	Mar.	Apr.	May	June	July	Aug.	Sept.	Oct.	Nov.	Dec.
1999	501.7	524.7	581.1	611.7	594.0	582.1	601.2	585.0	622.3	595.7	564.5	531.6
2000	512.0	519.1	513.4	467.3	453.0	462.5	432.6	416.9	461.3	478.2	479.0	438.1
2001	432.9	437.2	432.6	419.9	443.0	462.3	451.0	461.9	435.0	430.8	435.2	436.3
2002	448.1	454.2	497.4	488.1	512.4	474.1	457.0	454.2	505.5	528.5	482.2	531.1
2003	608.3	641.0	568.5	495.5	478.9	494.1	517.5	542.6	507.2	532.0	550.4	580.6
2004	647.7	656.9	673.5	690.0	722.5	705.1	692.9	705.6	684.8	717.0	705.2	676.3
2005	707.9	745.2	829.2	833.8	799.0	785.4	820.1	901.6	870.6	848.7	832.3	841.3
2006	903.5	927.5	954.2	1,000.4	1,055.7	1,016.2	1,068.7	1,164.0	1,181.8	1,168.7	1,176.6	1,200.0
2007	1,284.9	1,281.7	1,314.3	1,328.0	1,390.4	1,431.6	1,523.6	1,477.4	1,483.3	1,447.1	1,451.8	1,362.3
2008	1,393.5	1,384.6	1,428.5	1,393.8	1,396.5	1,351.8	1,277.9	1,224.1	1,171.2	1,076.8	1,139.7	1,160.9

Source: New York Mercantile Exchange (NYMEX)

Plastics

Plastics are moldable, chemically fabricated materials produced mostly from fossil fuels, such as oil, coal, or natural gas. The word plastic is derived from the Greek *plastikos*, meaning "to mold," and the Latin **plasticus**, meaning "capable of molding." Leo Baekeland created the first commercially successful thermosetting synthetic resin in 1909. More than 50 families of plastics have since been produced.

All plastics can be divided into either thermoplastics or thermosetting plastics. The difference is the way in which they respond to heat. Thermoplastics can be repeatedly softened by heat and hardened by cooling. Thermosetting plastics harden permanently after being heated once.

Prices – Plastics prices in 2008 continued its 6-year strong showing after 2007's one weak year. Specifically, the average monthly producer price index (1982=100) of plastic resins and materials in the U.S. in 2008 rose +10.9% yr/yr to a new record high of 217.3. The average monthly producer price index of thermoplastic resins in the U.S. in 2008 rose +12.0% yr/yr to a record high of 218.6. The average monthly producer price index of styrene plastic materials (also a thermoplastic) in the U.S. in 2003 (latest available data) rose +21.2% to 115.7 from the 25-year low of 95.5 posted in 2002. The average monthly producer price index of thermosetting resins in the U.S. in 2008 rose +5.6% to a new record high of 233.3.

Supply – Total U.S. plastics production in 2007 (latest data available) rose by +1.5% yr/yr to a new record high of 115.793 billion pounds. U.S. plastics production has more than doubled in the past two decades. By sector, the thermoplastics sector is by far the largest, with 2007 production rising +1.8% yr/yr to 92.835 billion pounds and accounting for 80% of total U.S. plastic production. Production in the thermosetting plastic sector (polyester unsaturated, phenolic, and epoxy) rose +1.0% yr/yr in 2007 to 8.951 billion pounds and accounted for 8% of total U.S. plastics production. The category of "other plastics" rose by +0.3% to 14.007 billion pounds and accounted for 12% of total U.S. plastics production.

Demand – Total usage of plastic resins by important markets in 2007 (latest data available) in the U.S. fell by -1.9% to 83.354 billion pounds. The breakdown by market shows that the largest single consumption category is "Packaging" with 26.527 billion pounds of usage in 2007, accounting for 32% of total U.S. consumption. After packaging, the largest categories are "Consumer and Industrial" (21% of U.S. consumption), and "Building and Construction" (17% of U.S. consumption).

Trade – U.S. exports of plastics in 2007 (latest data available) rose +24.0% yr/yr to a new record high of 12.346 billion pounds. U.S. exports accounted for 15% of U.S. supply disappearance in 2005.

Plastics Production by Resin in the United States   In Millions of Pounds

| | ------------ Thermosets ------------ | | | | ------------------------------------ Thermoplastics ------------------------------ | | | | | | | | | | |
Year	Polyester Unsaturated	Phenolic	Epoxy	Total Thermosets	Thermoplastic Polyester	Polyvinyl Chloride	Polystyrene	Polypropylene	Nylon	Low Density Polyethylene[1]	High Density Polyethylene	Total Thermoplastics	Total Selected Plastics	Other Plastics	Total Plastics
1998	1,713	3,940	639	9,163	4,423	14,502	6,237	13,825	1,285	14,805	12,924	71,209	78,659	13,026	91,685
1999	2,985	4,388	657	8,030	6,735	14,912	7,075	15,493	1,349	15,807	13,864	78,457	86,487	13,467	99,954
2000	3,149	3,965	669	7,783	7,239	14,364	6,676	15,583	1,395	19,588	16,439	84,553	92,336	13,604	105,940
2001	3,021	3,894	597	7,512	6,972	14,626	6,223	16,135	1,159	18,389	15,195	81,726	89,238	12,720	101,958
2002	3,197	4,076	620	7,893	7,480	15,250	6,768	17,084	1,284	19,515	16,190	86,762	94,655	13,607	108,262
2003	3,152	4,015	587	7,754	7,950	14,938	6,478	17,497	1,306	18,915	15,906	86,071	93,825	13,641	106,466
2004	3,294	4,200	658	8,152	8,632	15,883	6,765	18,523	1,357	20,390	17,519	92,317	100,469	13,471	113,940
2005	3,359	4,689	609	8,657	7,749	15,259	6,293	17,965	1,252	19,736	16,155	87,524	96,181	13,595	109,776
2006	3,430	4,809	624	8,863	8,290	14,919	6,269	18,775	1,270	20,926	17,645	91,204	100,067	13,970	114,037
2007	3,471	4,838	642	8,951	8,745	14,606	6,015	19,445	1,295	21,511	18,222	92,835	101,786	14,007	115,793

[1] Includes LDPE and LLDPE.   *Source: American Plastics Council (APC)*

Total Resin Sales and Captive Use by Important Markets   In Millions of Pounds (Dry Weight Basis)

Year	Adhesive, Inks & Coatings	Building & Construction	Consumer & Industrial	Electrical & Electronics	Exports	Furniture & Furnishings	Industrial & Machinary	Packaging	Transportation	Other	Total
1998	1,758	12,077	11,031	2,816	8,208	3,293	710	19,396	3,588	9,211	71,994
1999	1,171	14,794	13,921	2,862	8,353	3,630	1,181	24,130	4,383	2,698	77,123
2000	1,167	14,439	16,487	2,787	9,771	3,572	1,084	20,941	4,389	3,003	77,640
2001	1,143	13,988	16,510	2,501	9,295	3,226	968	22,847	4,207	2,705	77,390
2002	1,165	14,729	17,649	3,037	10,048	3,507	998	24,170	4,738	2,283	82,324
2003	1,170	14,495	17,571	2,862	9,009	3,361	962	24,087	4,732	2,021	80,270
2004	1,196	15,676	18,714	3,096	9,900	3,458	1,042	25,952	4,899	2,168	86,101
2005	1,160	15,483	17,400	2,917	9,790	3,406	1,087	25,144	4,711	2,133	83,231
2006	1,113	15,429	17,735	2,661	9,957	3,332	1,004	26,161	4,558	2,019	83,970
2007	1,069	14,289	17,193	1,980	12,346	3,091	943	26,527	3,312	1,604	82,354

[1] Included in other.   *Source: American Plastics Council (APC)*

PLASTICS

Average Producer Price Index of Plastic Resins and Materials (066) in the United States (1982 = 100)

Year	Jan.	Feb.	Mar.	Apr.	May	June	July	Aug.	Sept.	Oct.	Nov.	Dec.	Average
1999	115.9	115.8	117.3	118.6	122.1	123.1	127.9	130.0	133.8	135.6	135.8	134.3	125.8
2000	133.2	135.7	139.4	143.7	147.4	147.8	146.4	146.3	142.4	140.7	138.8	137.3	141.6
2001	137.8	139.3	141.4	141.9	139.9	137.6	135.1	131.3	126.8	128.3	126.6	123.9	134.2
2002	122.0	121.3	123.1	125.4	128.0	130.1	135.3	136.4	136.7	138.2	137.0	135.3	130.7
2003	137.2	141.8	149.6	153.2	152.4	149.2	144.9	143.6	144.9	146.2	145.8	144.0	146.1
2004	146.2	150.4	151.4	154.8	156.5	159.6	161.1	164.9	170.6	175.6	181.4	185.2	163.1
2005	190.3	190.8	192.1	192.3	190.3	186.3	185.0	183.4	188.2	203.9	208.6	205.2	193.0
2006	203.9	200.0	198.9	194.3	195.9	198.5	199.2	202.3	202.4	200.0	196.2	189.1	198.4
2007	187.6	185.5	187.0	192.1	193.8	196.9	198.6	198.7	198.0	199.3	205.9	207.5	195.9
2008[1]	209.7	209.6	210.8	212.1	216.4	219.1	229.2	233.3	227.1	228.9	216.0	195.8	217.3

[1] Preliminary. *Source: Bureau of Labor Statistics, U.S. Department of Commerce (BLS)*

Average Producer Price Index of Thermoplastic Resins (0662) in the United States (1982 = 100)

Year	Jan.	Feb.	Mar.	Apr.	May	June	July	Aug.	Sept.	Oct.	Nov.	Dec.	Average
1999	112.3	112.5	114.4	116.1	120.4	121.6	127.5	129.9	134.5	136.7	137.0	135.2	124.9
2000	133.8	136.0	140.4	145.2	149.3	149.6	147.6	147.4	142.7	140.3	137.9	136.0	142.2
2001	136.3	138.0	140.2	140.8	138.4	135.7	133.1	128.6	123.4	125.7	123.9	120.8	132.1
2002	118.4	117.8	120.3	123.8	126.2	128.6	135.0	135.9	136.2	137.6	136.1	133.8	129.1
2003	136.3	142.2	151.4	155.8	153.6	149.5	144.3	142.8	144.7	146.3	146.2	143.9	146.4
2004	146.7	151.9	152.6	156.4	157.5	160.9	162.3	165.5	171.3	176.6	182.3	186.9	164.2
2005	193.2	193.8	195.3	194.9	192.0	187.0	185.4	183.7	189.3	208.4	213.7	209.4	195.5
2006	207.9	202.8	201.5	195.6	197.6	201.1	201.6	205.1	205.0	201.6	196.8	188.1	200.4
2007	186.0	183.4	185.3	190.7	193.0	196.2	198.2	198.4	197.6	199.3	206.6	208.2	195.2
2008[1]	209.9	209.9	211.5	213.2	218.4	221.2	232.4	236.5	229.0	231.1	216.5	193.8	218.6

[1] Preliminary. *Source: Bureau of Labor Statistics, U.S. Department of Commerce (BLS)*

Average Producer Price Index of Styrene Plastics Materials (0662-06) in the United States (1982 = 100)

Year	Jan.	Feb.	Mar.	Apr.	May	June	July	Aug.	Sept.	Oct.	Nov.	Dec.	Average
1995	129.0	127.0	132.5	134.7	135.9	137.5	135.1	133.2	132.1	130.1	127.9	126.1	131.8
1996	125.7	123.5	125.0	118.3	120.1	122.7	123.4	123.3	123.6	122.8	122.0	120.9	122.6
1997	120.6	123.1	123.0	121.6	121.6	121.6	122.7	117.7	118.0	116.5	113.5	113.7	119.5
1998	113.3	113.9	115.5	114.9	114.1	112.8	111.3	111.2	107.6	107.9	107.1	106.3	111.3
1999	103.5	102.4	103.5	104.7	103.0	102.3	103.1	101.5	101.4	99.8	99.4	100.5	102.1
2000	103.0	104.3	110.5	113.0	116.2	116.9	118.5	116.5	115.0	114.1	112.1	110.4	112.5
2001	110.5	109.2	107.9	108.0	101.8	99.9	97.6	95.7	87.3	89.4	90.0	85.4	98.6
2002	85.7	85.8	87.9	88.5	90.4	91.7	93.7	100.6	100.5	108.9	108.1	103.9	95.5
2003[1]	102.9	110.2	119.5	127.2	126.7	119.1	118.0	113.3	112.8	113.6	113.7	111.6	115.7
2004[1]	Data no longer available												

[1] Preliminary. *Source: Bureau of Labor Statistics, U.S. Department of Commerce (BLS)*

Average Producer Price Index of Thermosetting Resins (0663) in the United States (1982 = 100)

Year	Jan.	Feb.	Mar.	Apr.	May	June	July	Aug.	Sept.	Oct.	Nov.	Dec.	Average
1999	139.9	138.1	137.7	137.4	136.9	136.5	136.2	136.5	136.5	136.5	136.3	136.2	137.0
2000	136.8	141.1	141.3	142.8	144.9	146.0	147.6	147.8	147.5	149.5	150.3	151.0	145.6
2001	152.1	152.9	154.5	154.4	154.2	154.2	152.3	151.3	150.4	148.2	146.3	146.1	151.4
2002	146.2	144.6	143.8	141.2	144.1	145.5	145.8	147.6	148.4	150.3	150.3	150.6	146.5
2003	150.4	149.7	151.7	152.0	156.8	157.9	157.1	156.4	155.7	155.6	153.8	153.8	154.2
2004	154.0	154.2	155.9	158.3	162.2	164.3	166.4	173.2	179.0	183.0	189.3	189.8	169.1
2005	189.9	190.3	190.5	193.5	195.8	195.8	195.5	194.6	196.1	197.5	199.9	200.2	195.0
2006	200.0	200.8	200.8	201.7	201.6	200.5	202.1	203.6	204.2	206.3	206.6	206.3	202.9
2007	207.8	208.3	207.8	211.7	210.0	212.6	212.3	212.4	211.9	211.6	214.7	216.8	211.5
2008[1]	221.4	220.7	220.0	219.0	218.5	220.3	224.8	229.3	229.8	230.4	226.2	219.1	223.3

[1] Preliminary. *Source: Bureau of Labor Statistics, U.S. Department of Commerce (BLS)*

Platinum-Group Metals

Platinum is a relatively rare, chemically inert metallic element that is more valuable than gold. Platinum is a grayish-white metal that has a high fusing point, is malleable and ductile, and has a high electrical resistance. Chemically, platinum is relatively inert and resists attack by air, water, single acids, and ordinary reagents. Platinum is the most important of the six-metal group, which also includes ruthenium, rhodium, palladium, osmium, and iridium. The word "platinum" is derived from the Spanish word platina meaning silver.

Platinum is one of the world's rarest metals with new mine production totaling only about 5 million troy ounces a year. All the platinum mined to date would fit in the average-size living room. Platinum is mined all over the world with supplies concentrated in South Africa. South Africa accounts for nearly 80% of world supply, followed by Russia, and North America.

Because platinum will never tarnish, lose its rich white luster, or even wear down after many years, it is prized by the jewelry industry. The international jewelry industry is the largest consumer sector for platinum, accounting for 51% of total platinum demand. In Europe and the U.S., the normal purity of platinum is 95%. Ten tons of ore must be mined and a five-month process is needed to produce one ounce of pure platinum.

The second major consumer sector for platinum is for auto catalysts, with 21% of total platinum demand. Catalysts in autos are used to convert most of vehicle emissions into less harmful carbon dioxide, nitrogen, and water vapor. Platinum is also used in the production of hard disk drive coatings, fiber optic cables, infra-red detectors, fertilizers, explosives, petrol additives, platinum-tipped spark plugs, glassmaking equipment, biodegradable elements for household detergents, dental restorations, and in anti-cancer drugs.

Palladium is very similar to platinum and is part of the same general metals group. Palladium is mined with platinum, but it is somewhat more common because it is also a by-product of nickel mining. The primary use for palladium is in the use of automotive catalysts, with that sector accounting for about 63% of total palladium demand. Other uses for palladium include electronic equipment (21%), dental alloys (12%), and jewelry (4%).

Rhodium, another member of the platinum group, is also used in the automotive industry in pollution control devices. To some extent palladium has replaced rhodium. Iridium is used to process catalysts and it has also found use in some auto catalysts. Iridium and ruthenium are used in the production of polyvinyl chloride. As the prices of these metals change, there is some substitution. Therefore, strength of platinum prices relative to palladium should lead to the substitution of palladium for platinum in catalytic converters.

Platinum futures and options and palladium futures are traded on the NYMEX division of the CME Group. Platinum and palladium futures are traded on the Tokyo Commodity Exchange (TOCOM). The NYMEX platinum futures contract calls for the delivery of 50 troy ounces of platinum (0.9995 fineness) and the contract trades in terms of dollars and cents per troy ounce. The NYMEX palladium futures contract calls for the delivery of 50 troy ounces of palladium (0.9995 fineness) and the contract is priced in terms of dollars and cents per troy ounce.

Prices – NYMEX platinum futures prices started 2008 at about $1,539 per troy ounce, and moved higher to post a high of $21.64 in March. The prices then moved lower most of the year, except for a brief rally in May, to finally end the year at about $900 per troy ounce.

NYMEX palladium futures prices started 2008 at about $375 per troy ounce, rallied to a high of about $575 per troy ounce in March, but then moved lower to post a low of about $175 at the end of the year. There was a slight rally early in 2009 with the price rising to about $200 per troy ounce in February of 2009.

Supply – World mine production of platinum in 2008 fell by -6.1% yr/yr to 220,000 kilograms, down from the record high of 216,000 kilograms in 2006. South Africa is the world's largest producer of platinum by far with 77% of world production in 2006, followed by Russia (13%), Canada (4%) and the U.S. (2%). World mine production of palladium in 2008 fell -5.9% to 206,000 kilograms, which was a down from the record high production level of 222,000 in 2006. The world's largest palladium producers are Russia with 43% of world production in 2008, South Africa with 39%, Canada with 6%, and the U.S. with 6%. World production of platinum group metals other than platinum and palladium in 2007 (latest data available) rose by +2.9% yr/yr to a record high of 78,100 kilograms.

U.S. mine production of platinum in 2008 fell by -4.2% yr/yr to 3,700 kilograms, down from the record high of 4,390 kilograms posted in 2002. U.S. mine production of palladium in 2008 fell by -3.1% yr/yr to 12,400 kilograms, down from the record high of 14,800 kilograms posted in 2002. U.S. refinery production of scrap platinum and palladium in 2007, latest data available, rose +30.4% to 16,340 kilograms, up from the 2005 record low of 11,580 kilograms but still well below the 13-year high of 24,790 kilograms in 2001.

Demand – The total of platinum-group metals sold to consuming industries in the U.S. in 2004 (the latest data available) rose +7.1% to 91,434 kilograms. The two main U.S. industries that use platinum are the auto industry, which accounts for about 74% of U.S. platinum usage, and the jewelry industry, which accounts for about 26% of U.S. platinum usage.

Trade – U.S. imports of refined platinum and palladium in 2008 for consumption rose +4.2% yr/yr to 377,824 kilograms, which was well above the 13-year low of 222,356 kilograms seen in 2002. U.S. exports of refined platinum and palladium fell by -4.8% to 77,200 kilograms, down further from the record high of 103,590 kilograms in 2006. The U.S. relied on imports for 91% of its platinum and palladium consumption in 2008.

PLATINUM-GROUP METALS

World Mine Production of Platinum   In Kilograms

Year	Australia	Canada	Colombia[3]	Finland	Japan	Russia	Serbia/ Montenegro	Africa	United States	Zimbabwe	World Total
2000	171	6,302	339	441	782	34,000	5	114,459	3,110	505	160,000
2001	174	7,733	674	510	791	27,000	5	130,307	3,610	519	172,000
2002	200	9,202	661	508	762	27,000	5	132,897	4,390	2,306	178,000
2003	225	6,990	828	461	770	28,000	1	148,348	4,170	4,270	195,000
2004	200	7,000	1,209	705	750	28,000	1	153,239	4,040	4,438	200,000
2005	111	6,075	1,082	800	760	29,000	1	163,711	3,920	4,834	211,000
2006	112	6,120	1,438	800	760	29,000	1	168,125	4,290	4,998	216,000
2007[1]	130	6,200	1,400	800	770	27,000	1	166,000	3,860	5,300	213,000
2008[2]		7,200	1,700			25,000		153,000	3,700	5,600	200,000

[1] Preliminary.   [2] Estimate.   [3] Placer platinum.   W = Withheld.   *Source: U.S. Geological Survey (USGS)*

World Mine Production of Palladium and Other Group Metals   In Kilograms

	-- Palladium --										------ Other Group Metals ------		
Year	Australia	Canada	Finland	Japan	Russia	Serbia/ Montenegro	Africa	United States	Zim- babwe	Total	Russia	South Africa	World Total
2000	812	9,949	----	4,712	71,000	25	55,818	10,300	366	153,000	14,100	36,493	51,400
2001	828	8,972	----	4,805	96,000	25	62,601	12,100	371	187,000	14,500	37,005	52,300
2002	810	12,210	----	5,618	96,000	25	63,758	14,800	1,943	196,000	14,500	39,986	57,900
2003	820	12,808	----	5,500	97,000	8	70,946	14,000	3,449	207,000	15,000	46,856	64,400
2004	800	12,000	----	5,300	97,000	8	76,403	13,700	3,564	211,000	15,000	46,759	69,700
2005	550	10,415	----	5,400	97,400	8	82,961	13,300	3,879	216,000	15,500	56,309	77,700
2006	600	10,493	----	5,400	98,400	8	86,265	14,400	4,022	222,000	15,600	53,138	75,900
2007[1]	600	10,500	----	5,500	96,800	8	86,500	12,800	4,200	219,000	14,500	58,626	78,100
2008[2]		12,500	----		88,000		80,000	12,400	4,400	206,000			

[1] Preliminary.   [2] Estimate.   *Source: U.S. Geological Survey (USGS)*

Platinum Group Metals Sold to Consuming Industries in the United States   In Kilograms

	-- Automotive --		--- Chemical ---		---- Electrical ----		Dental & ---- Medical ----		Jewelry & -- Decorative --		--- Petroleum ---		----- All Platinum Group Metals -----			
Year	Platinum	Other[3]	Platinum	Other[3]	Platinum	Other[3]	Platinum	Other[3]	Platinum	Other[3]	Platinum	Other[3]	Platinum	Palladium	Other[3]	Total
1996	28,550	19,282	2,115	2,457	4,541	17,665	778	6,285	1,493	1,493	3,514	902	44,489	45,157	----	89,646
1997	28,923	20,402	2,239	2,426	4,945	19,997	840	6,376	2,115	1,617	3,390	871	46,184	50,227	----	96,411
1998	29,483	26,528	2,301	2,488	5,194	20,215	902	6,376	2,333	1,617	3,390	809	47,396	61,827	----	109,223
1999	31,100	29,390	2,364	2,519	5,443	21,148	933	6,065	3,110	1,679	3,514	778	50,310	65,248	----	115,558
2000	32,344	31,100	2,457	2,139	5,691	19,282	964	3,732	3,670	1,400	3,639	660	52,808	61,889	----	114,697
2001	33,411	34,832	2,644	715	5,909	17,354	995	3,670	4,043	1,431	4,199	715	55,399	62,293	----	117,692
2002	17,727	19,904	3,110	2,333	2,955	6,531	1,244	6,687	9,641		1,400		33,433	28,768	----	62,200
2003[1]	27,524	37,476	2,955	2,177	2,644	6,687	778	6,998	9,641		1,244		37,476	47,894	----	85,370
2004[2]	24,880	44,940	2,799	2,644	2,799	6,376	622	7,309	9,019		1,089		33,588	57,846	----	91,434

[1] Preliminary.   [2] Estimate.   [3] Includes Palladium, iridium, osmium, rhodium, and ruthenium.
Sources: U.S. Geological Survey (USGS); American Metal Market (AMM)

Salient Statistics of Platinum and Allied Metals[3] in the United States   In Kilograms

	Net Import Reliance as a % of Apparent	Mine ----- Production -----		Refinery Pro- duction (Secon-		Refiner, Importer & Dealer -------- Stocks as of Dec. 31 ---------				----- Imports -----		----- Exports -----		Apparent Con-
Year	Consumption	Platinum	Palladium	dary)	Total Refined	Platinum	Palladium	Other[4]	Total	Refined	Total	Refined	Total	sumptio
1999	----	2,920	9,800	23,300	23,300	7,060	28,200	784	36,044	337,973	----	64,165	----	----
2000	83	3,110	10,300	23,780	23,780	5,190	19,000	784	24,974	316,633	----	84,087	----	----
2001	66	3,610	12,100	24,790	24,790	3,680	16,300	784	20,764	267,957	----	67,334	----	----
2002	93	4,390	14,800	20,900	20,900	649	5,870	784	7,303	222,356	----	70,943	----	----
2003	91	4,170	14,000	24,250	24,250	649	1,170	562	2,381	223,653	----	45,124	----	----
2004	92	4,040	13,700	22,180	22,180	649	568	501	1,718	248,705	----	52,897	----	----
2005	93	3,920	13,300	11,580	11,580	261	----	189	450	284,849	----	49,395	----	----
2006	90	4,290	14,400	12,530	12,530	261	----	111	372	287,756	----	103,590	----	----
2007[1]	91	3,860	12,800	16,340	16,340	261	----	18	279	362,723	----	81,090	----	----
2008[2]	91	3,700	12,400							377,824	----	77,200	----	----

[1] Preliminary.   [2] Estimate.   [3] Includes platinum, palladium, iridium, osmium, rhodium, and ruthenium.   [4] Includes iridium, osmium, rhodium, and ruthenium.   W = Withheld.   *Source: U.S. Geological Survey (USGS)*

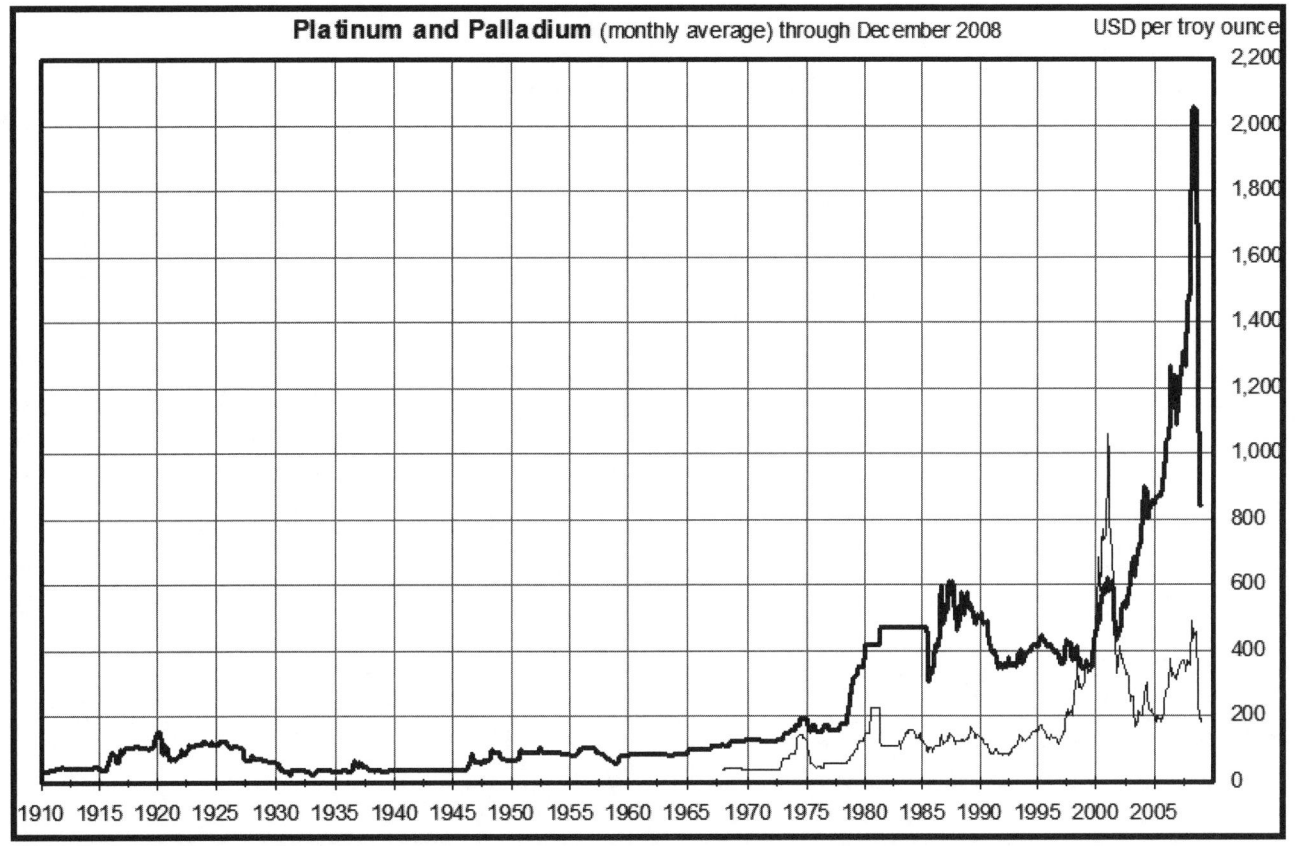

Average Merchant's Price of Platinum in the United States   In Dollars Per Troy Ounce

Year	Jan.	Feb.	Mar.	Apr.	May	June	July	Aug.	Sept.	Oct.	Nov.	Dec. Average
1999	353.53	361.55	370.80	357.30	354.75	357.75	350.30	352.24	365.62	421.52	436.48	438.00	376.44
2000	432.95	517.02	478.28	493.53	519.57	557.45	558.53	572.76	592.53	576.91	592.73	608.28	541.49
2001	623.43	453.56	566.67	589.63	611.07	588.91	643.88	457.37	453.50	437.43	427.25	450.24	531.93
2002	471.52	470.68	511.95	539.20	533.66	554.70	526.32	545.48	556.05	580.11	588.15	594.89	539.39
2003	633.09	684.47	677.05	627.19	651.43	664.19	684.68	695.12	707.90	734.91	762.78	810.48	691.78
2004	855.95	849.53	902.78	884.76	814.05	810.59	813.48	851.91	851.05	843.76	856.15	854.55	849.05
2005	861.80	867.40	870.23	867.71	869.00	883.23	876.60	901.04	918.10	933.76	964.00	9890.48	1641.95
2006	1032.48	1045.16	1044.39	1105.00	1264.05	1192.73	1233.03	1236.74	1183.30	1085.32	1183.73	1124.79	1144.23
2007	1151.90	1206.47	1222.77	1280.90	1306.50	1289.14	1307.38	1267.30	1313.00	1413.87	1449.45	1492.47	1308.43
2008	1585.09	2002.55	2043.65	1991.32	2053.57	2042.24	1904.68	1492.52	1221.71	917.13	841.22	842.40	1578.17

Source: American Metal Market (AMM)

Average Dealer Price[1] of Palladium in the United States   In Dollars Per Troy Ounce

Year	Jan.	Feb.	Mar.	Apr.	May	June	July	Aug.	Sept.	Oct.	Nov.	Dec. Average
1999	317.28	351.38	351.78	358.83	330.70	339.84	333.17	341.64	358.55	387.05	400.38	420.17	357.50
2000	447.45	607.33	687.72	580.00	574.89	640.80	686.63	759.63	731.15	734.91	778.73	887.33	676.55
2001	1054.10	984.37	792.68	699.15	663.41	619.67	525.90	459.83	444.47	340.52	333.14	405.95	610.27
2002	412.62	377.79	377.15	372.50	360.00	339.20	325.41	327.55	330.50	319.09	289.20	243.57	339.55
2003	258.41	255.68	226.38	164.76	169.00	181.76	175.27	185.76	214.29	203.74	200.17	200.86	203.01
2004	220.70	237.95	272.43	299.57	249.57	231.32	222.95	217.55	213.95	220.43	215.85	193.00	232.94
2005	188.45	184.15	200.09	200.76	191.38	188.50	186.95	188.13	191.19	209.71	246.35	266.24	203.49
2006	275.95	291.58	312.70	355.74	372.82	319.36	320.21	332.57	324.40	315.18	326.91	328.00	322.95
2007	339.81	344.26	352.27	370.35	369.50	370.76	368.67	344.61	337.63	368.70	366.75	355.42	357.39
2008	376.95	473.65	490.35	449.05	438.29	453.57	428.27	318.29	250.19	193.30	212.61	178.00	355.21

[1] Based on wholesale quantities, prompt delivery.   Source: American Metal Market (AMM)

Platinum Futures - CME Group (NYMEX)
(weekly close) as of January 02, 2009

USD Per Troy Ounce

Volume of Trading of Platinum Futures in New York   In Contracts

Year	Jan.	Feb.	Mar.	Apr.	May	June	July	Aug.	Sept.	Oct.	Nov.	Dec.	Total
1999	37,700	53,698	68,350	36,900	26,507	75,444	57,536	36,115	102,196	30,637	32,176	40,009	597,268
2000	33,226	31,352	35,013	28,057	22,741	47,197	16,527	14,739	36,643	12,122	12,662	30,645	320,924
2001	19,278	12,885	31,617	14,961	15,714	23,245	14,494	12,477	17,040	9,957	11,401	22,890	205,969
2002	12,848	13,807	24,434	11,066	12,294	27,176	14,198	18,583	29,762	11,834	9,878	33,891	219,771
2003	15,545	15,157	38,170	13,472	18,968	30,961	10,852	11,878	37,686	19,275	14,040	42,301	268,305
2004	16,337	15,574	42,249	29,228	13,125	28,495	15,598	18,180	34,076	24,393	18,606	39,834	295,695
2005	15,410	20,253	41,297	16,267	20,135	55,588	25,132	26,604	52,535	21,827	30,447	50,684	376,179
2006	20,604	27,572	42,804	17,215	34,684	45,985	16,220	21,428	44,000	21,182	46,754	34,671	373,119
2007	20,534	26,975	59,099	26,457	35,525	66,968	35,371	35,975	58,091	34,100	36,126	66,324	501,545
2008	54,479	71,978	84,901	41,283	54,476	66,398	43,127	47,539	70,624	38,107	30,011	39,079	642,002

Source: New York Mercantile Exchange (NYMEX)

Average Open Interest of Platinum Futures in New York   In Contracts

Year	Jan.	Feb.	Mar.	Apr.	May	June	July	Aug.	Sept.	Oct.	Nov.	Dec.
1999	12,311	14,481	16,493	11,471	12,256	12,436	14,703	13,777	15,014	14,892	13,402	12,017
2000	10,858	10,952	9,218	8,484	9,057	10,585	9,566	9,731	9,716	8,106	8,163	8,507
2001	8,449	7,311	6,855	6,715	7,436	5,751	6,210	5,996	5,646	5,395	6,102	6,033
2002	6,587	6,213	7,121	6,823	6,031	6,901	5,516	6,405	6,930	7,211	7,406	8,388
2003	8,694	8,132	8,034	6,322	6,599	6,847	7,450	8,556	8,794	8,489	9,421	9,373
2004	8,210	7,379	8,879	7,698	5,555	5,590	5,376	6,282	6,091	6,092	7,208	7,184
2005	6,800	7,486	8,047	8,132	8,496	10,109	8,497	11,729	12,478	13,024	12,377	11,327
2006	10,625	9,995	8,407	9,486	9,681	8,265	8,575	9,889	9,076	7,276	8,332	8,186
2007	8,810	10,752	11,154	13,413	15,173	15,033	16,641	12,347	12,341	15,199	14,427	15,404
2008	17,912	15,770	12,966	12,977	15,869	15,821	14,198	12,325	13,904	15,111	16,530	17,267

Source: New York Mercantile Exchange (NYMEX)

Palladium Futures - CME Group (NYMEX)
(weekly close) as of January 02, 2009
USD Per Troy Ounce

Volume of Trading of Palladium Futures in New York   In Contracts

Year	Jan.	Feb.	Mar.	Apr.	May	June	July	Aug.	Sept.	Oct.	Nov.	Dec.	Total
1999	3,092	11,614	4,082	7,097	8,890	3,411	5,053	6,868	5,826	3,722	10,670	5,069	75,394
2000	4,584	13,976	2,803	1,833	7,034	2,622	3,120	5,169	2,523	2,460	3,041	1,601	50,766
2001	2,171	6,090	1,397	1,121	3,325	1,013	1,173	3,221	523	1,255	3,261	1,375	25,925
2002	1,275	3,372	1,538	1,527	6,126	2,166	2,154	8,971	1,452	1,710	8,118	2,644	41,053
2003	4,200	7,266	3,256	3,971	8,420	3,430	4,221	15,645	8,152	7,587	18,323	11,142	95,613
2004	17,093	41,036	20,508	30,214	27,343	11,433	7,606	28,895	10,690	15,036	41,269	16,429	267,552
2005	7,728	43,268	16,979	13,316	46,112	13,594	17,185	49,268	17,747	21,680	50,643	24,403	321,923
2006	28,447	59,279	32,573	23,135	64,863	25,857	13,464	41,123	16,222	14,351	47,797	11,005	378,116
2007	23,636	62,815	14,987	25,166	69,089	16,322	15,072	65,106	16,975	26,385	52,411	13,029	400,993
2008	26,954	105,845	49,411	24,750	66,939	18,934	26,245	53,692	23,121	28,627	43,879	13,299	481,696

Source: New York Mercantile Exchange (NYMEX)

Average Open Interest of Palladium Futures in New York   In Contracts

Year	Jan.	Feb.	Mar.	Apr.	May	June	July	Aug.	Sept.	Oct.	Nov.	Dec.
1999	2,846	3,234	2,957	3,015	2,796	2,757	2,823	2,496	2,755	3,210	3,301	3,045
2000	3,129	3,101	2,367	2,359	2,628	2,015	2,118	1,974	1,757	1,905	1,859	1,837
2001	1,828	1,666	1,525	1,577	1,613	1,385	1,420	1,318	1,383	1,286	1,477	1,244
2002	1,217	1,208	1,042	1,199	1,554	1,806	2,103	2,298	1,878	1,976	1,977	2,025
2003	2,000	2,039	1,948	1,997	2,315	2,609	2,680	3,605	5,184	5,533	6,096	6,737
2004	9,119	11,878	11,465	11,039	8,828	7,861	8,055	8,688	8,933	9,965	11,192	12,188
2005	12,824	13,821	12,946	13,116	13,345	13,527	13,794	14,465	13,340	13,488	14,676	14,477
2006	14,353	16,632	15,426	17,783	18,002	14,251	14,087	13,166	11,247	11,836	12,511	11,210
2007	13,794	16,132	15,587	18,126	19,682	18,288	18,152	18,035	16,062	16,286	17,194	14,820
2008	18,184	20,999	20,227	19,571	19,197	17,106	15,223	13,821	14,294	14,656	13,435	12,688

Source: New York Mercantile Exchange (NYMEX)

Pork Bellies

Pork bellies are the cut of meat from a hog from which bacon is produced. A hog has two belly slabs, generally weighing 8-18 pounds each, depending on the hog's commercial slaughter weight. Total hog slaughter weights average around 255 pounds, equal to a dressed carcass weight of about 190 pounds. Bellies account for about 12% of a hog's live weight, but represent a larger 14% of the total cutout value of the realized pork products. Pork bellies can be frozen and stored for up to a year before processing. The pork belly futures contract at the Chicago Mercantile Exchange calls for the physical delivery of 40,000 pounds of frozen pork bellies, which have been slaughtered at USDA federally inspected slaughtering plants. Each deliverable belly typically weighs 12-14 pounds each.

There are definite seasonal patterns in pork belly prices. Bellies are storable and the movement into cold storage builds early in the calendar year, peaking about mid-year. Net withdrawals from storage then carry stocks to a low around October. The cycle then starts again. Retail bacon demand also follows a time worn trend, peaking in the summer and tapering off to a low during the winter months. While demand patterns would suggest the highest prices in the summer and the lowest in the winter, just the opposite is not unusual. Such contra-seasonal price moves can be partially attributed to supply logistics, notably the availability of frozen storage stocks deliverable against futures at CME exchange-approved warehouses. When stocks prove either too large or small, the underlying demand variables for bacon can be relegated to the backburner as a market-moving factor. The fact that no contract months are traded between August and the following February adds to the late fall futures price distortion.

Belly prices (cash and futures) are sensitive to the inventory in cold storage and to the weekly net movement in and out of storage, which affords some insight to demand, although a better measure is the weekly quantity of bellies being sliced into bacon. Higher retail prices tend to encourage placing more supply into storage because of lower retail bacon demand. Bacon is not a necessary foodstuff so demand can be buoyed by favorable consumer disposable income. However, dietary standards have changed dramatically in recent years and do not favor the consumption of high fat and salt content food, such as bacon. In addition, alternatives to pork bacon have emerged in recent years such as turkey bacon, which has lower fat and calorie content.

Prices – Pork belly futures prices fell sharply in the first half of 2008 and posted a 3-1/2 year low of 60.70 cents per pound in July 2008. Pork belly prices then rallied sharply in August and September 2008 to a 1-1/2 year high of 100.225 cents. Pork belly prices then faded in the latter half of 2008 as the U.S. economy slowed and the financial crisis emerged, finally closing 2008 at 87.375, up 1.4 cents (+1.6%) from the 2007 close of 85.975. Frozen pork bellies in cold storage were high in 2008 versus the previous 3 years, putting downward pressure on prices.

Supply – The average monthly level of frozen pork belly storage stocks in 2008 rose by +52.2% to a 9-year high of 60.988 million pounds. As of December 2007, there were 33.490 million pounds of pork bellies in storage.

Average Retail Price of Bacon, Sliced   In Dollars Per Pound

Year	Jan.	Feb.	Mar.	Apr.	May	June	July	Aug.	Sept.	Oct.	Nov.	Dec.	Average
1999	2.52	2.52	2.51	2.45	2.47	2.50	2.50	2.93	2.58	2.57	2.66	2.75	2.58
2000	2.75	2.87	2.93	2.95	3.01	3.13	3.17	3.20	3.21	3.07	3.05	3.03	3.03
2001	2.99	3.07	3.16	3.11	3.26	3.25	3.32	3.47	3.49	3.34	3.30	3.30	3.25
2002	3.27	3.32	3.27	3.26	3.18	3.19	3.23	3.29	3.16	3.24	3.21	3.24	3.24
2003	3.20	3.28	3.22	3.29	3.09	3.14	3.16	3.23	3.22	3.16	3.23	3.18	3.20
2004	3.16	3.19	3.13	3.20	3.33	3.42	3.47	3.62	3.59	3.61	3.44	3.37	3.38
2005	3.37	3.40	3.36	3.33	3.56	3.46	3.48	3.44	3.40	3.33	3.26	3.33	3.39
2006	3.36	3.39	3.36	3.34	3.31	3.40	3.51	3.56	3.55	3.61	3.44	3.46	3.44
2007	3.51	3.57	3.46	3.50	3.65	3.66	3.72	3.80	3.78	3.88	3.66	3.69	3.66
2008[1]	3.65	3.62	3.62	3.55	3.64	3.66	3.61	3.84	3.73	3.75	3.60	3.67	3.66

[1] Preliminary.   Source: Economic Research Service, U.S. Department of Agriculture (ERS-USDA)

Frozen Pork Belly Storage Stocks in the United States, on First of Month   In Thousands of Pounds

Year	Jan.	Feb.	Mar.	Apr.	May	June	July	Aug.	Sept.	Oct.	Nov.	Dec.
1999	72,657	82,605	93,323	106,194	109,521	108,257	93,383	69,675	34,814	19,273	22,489	26,170
2000	40,300	43,802	49,983	60,527	63,461	68,292	60,097	50,515	33,005	21,341	20,589	38,674
2001	47,099	50,145	47,154	45,440	43,878	46,029	39,552	24,996	12,754	8,960	28,216	36,297
2002	44,301	50,849	57,569	60,721	63,293	62,269	51,019	29,925	14,250	9,452	10,354	18,059
2003	28,254	35,354	38,278	42,971	48,542	45,870	43,504	32,075	17,900	10,180	21,135	33,073
2004	49,017	63,095	57,123	50,126	48,363	41,366	37,185	23,383	15,230	11,344	15,970	33,955
2005	56,026	61,528	72,324	77,718	88,367	80,033	66,775	45,254	16,175	8,094	9,421	22,490
2006	40,707	54,902	58,861	61,628	62,665	58,803	46,056	30,506	11,962	10,199	15,597	30,553
2007	41,917	46,227	46,643	55,160	61,796	57,294	47,214	31,619	21,410	17,050	20,356	34,328
2008[1]	54,746	70,647	79,282	98,896	100,189	87,428	74,372	57,964	31,878	21,270	21,696	33,490

[1] Preliminary.   Source: National Agricultural Statistics Service, U.S. Department of Agriculture (NASS-USDA)

Weekly Pork Belly Storage Movement

------------- Stocks[1] in Thousands of Pounds ---------------					------------- Stocks[1] in Thousands of Pounds ---------------				
Week Ending	In	Out	On Hand	Net Move-ment	Week Ending	In	Out	On Hand	Net Move-ment
Jan 06, 2007	2,123	0	28,403	2,123	Jan 05, 2008	2,548	-438	39,272	2,110
Jan 13, 2007	1,021	0	29,424	1,021	Jan 12, 2008	1,519	-492	40,299	1,027
Jan 20, 2007	1,364	-165	30,623	1,199	Jan 19, 2008	2,930	-322	42,907	2,608
Jan 27, 2007	1,002	-119	31,506	883	Jan 26, 2008	1,861	-239	44,381	1,622
Feb 03, 2007	405	0	31,911	405	Feb 02, 2008	2,487	-44	49,046	2,443
Feb 10, 2007	525	-486	31,950	39	Feb 09, 2008	2,529	-258	51,317	2,271
Feb 17, 2007	80	-763	31,267	-683	Feb 16, 2008	2,267	-80	53,504	2,187
Feb 24, 2007	742	-426	31,583	316	Feb 23, 2008	1,708	-80	55,132	1,628
Mar 03, 2007	412	-205	31,790	207	Mar 01, 2008	3,264	-108	58,288	3,156
Mar 10, 2007	539	-109	32,220	430	Mar 08, 2008	2,981	-234	61,035	2,747
Mar 17, 2007	1,421	-40	33,601	1,381	Mar 15, 2008	4,814	-121	65,727	4,693
Mar 24, 2007	3,567	0	37,168	3,567	Mar 22, 2008	1,678	0	67,405	1,678
Mar 31, 2007	3,016	-41	40,143	2,975	Mar 29, 2008	5,168	-80	72,493	5,088
Apr 07, 2007	2,211	0	42,354	2,211	Apr 05, 2008	1,446	0	73,939	1,446
Apr 14, 2007	2,087	0	44,441	2,087	Apr 12, 2008	845	-42	74,742	803
Apr 21, 2007	883	-10	45,314	873	Apr 19, 2008	275	-506	74,511	-231
Apr 28, 2007	736	-41	46,009	695	Apr 26, 2008	179	-767	73,923	-588
May 05, 2007	434	-722	45,721	-288	May 03, 2008	362	-727	73,558	-365
May 12, 2007	2	-908	57,745	-906	May 10, 2008	501	-2,143	71,916	-1,642
May 19, 2007	601	-1,463	43,912	-862	May 17, 2008	620	-2,234	70,302	-1,614
May 26, 2007	82	-1,322	42,672	-1,240	May 24, 2008	687	-5,120	65,869	-4,433
Jun 02, 2007	245	-1,246	41,671	-1,001	May 31, 2008	441	-3,028	63,282	-2,587
Jun 09, 2007	2	-1,601	40,072	-1,599	Jun 07, 2008	323	-1,943	61,662	-1,620
Jun 16, 2007	334	-811	39,595	-477	Jun 14, 2008	754	-1,554	60,862	-800
Jun 23, 2007	4	-1,688	37,911	-1,684	Jun 21, 2008	501	-1,328	60,035	-827
Jun 30, 2007	382	-2,580	33,677	-2,198	Jun 28, 2008	380	-1,802	58,613	-1,422
Jul 07, 2007	382	-2,580	33,677	-2,198	Jul 05, 2008	767	-1,740	57,640	-973
Jul 14, 2007	113	-3,528	30,262	-3,415	Jul 12, 2008	1,366	-3,134	55,872	-1,768
Jul 21, 2007	143	-4,324	26,081	-4,181	Jul 19, 2008	1,119	-3,471	53,520	-2,352
Jul 28, 2007	15	-3,202	30,990	-2,758	Jul 26, 2008	1,192	-4,449	50,263	-3,257
Aug 04, 2007	11	-2,504	21,054	-2,493	Aug 02, 2008	1,560	-3,789	48,034	-2,229
Aug 11, 2007	379	-2,212	19,221	-1,833	Aug 09, 2008	1,426	-4,267	45,193	-2,841
Aug 18, 2007	0	-2,478	16,743	-2,478	Aug 16, 2008	915	-4,044	42,064	-3,129
Aug 25, 2007	42	-2,701	14,082	-2,659	Aug 23, 2008	1,688	-4,327	39,425	-2,639
Sep 01, 2007	129	-2,799	11,412	-2,670	Aug 30, 2008	1,455	-3,434	21,364	-1,979
Sep 08, 2007	42	-2,243	9,211	-2,201	Sep 06, 2008	1,261	-3,176	19,449	-1,915
Sep 15, 2007	0	-1,362	7,891	-1,362	Sep 13, 2008	640	-3,111	16,976	-2,471
Sep 22, 2007	64	-1,576	6,379	-1,512	Sep 20, 2008	252	-2,580	14,648	-2,328
Sep 29, 2007	493	-1,152	5,720	-659	Sep 27, 2008	136	-1,610	13,174	-1,474
Oct 06, 2007	758	-112	6,366	646	Oct 04, 2008	182	-1,499	11,857	-1,317
Oct 13, 2007	889	-625	6,630	264	Oct 11, 2008	944	-1,319	11,482	-375
Oct 20, 2007	1,358	-734	7,254	624	Oct 18, 2008	1,094	-999	11,577	95
Oct 27, 2007	1,069	-619	7,704	450	Oct 25, 2008	1,411	-1,048	11,940	363
Nov 03, 2007	1,901	-426	9,179	1,475	Nov 01, 2008	2,168	-1,456	12,652	712
Nov 10, 2007	2,248	-164	11,263	2,084	Nov 08, 2008	2,555	-509	14,698	2,046
Nov 17, 2007	3,907	-80	15,090	3,827	Nov 15, 2008	1,939	-403	16,234	1,536
Nov 24, 2007	3,174	-351	17,914	2,823	Nov 22, 2008	2,904	-735	18,403	2,169
Dec 01, 2007	3,493	-135	21,272	3,358	Nov 29, 2008	3,001	-372	21,032	2,629
Dec 08, 2007	3,367	-128	24,511	3,239	Dec 06, 2008	3,426	-626	23,832	2,800
Dec 15, 2007	3,737	-85	28,163	3,652	Dec 13, 2008	5,292	-283	28,841	5,009
Dec 22, 2007	5,730	-141	33,752	5,589	Dec 20, 2008	4,897	-828	32,910	4,069
Dec 29, 2007	3,614	-204	37,162	3,410	Dec 27, 2008	3,618	-90	36,438	3,528

[1] 60 Chicago and Outside Combined Chicago Mercantile Exchange approved warehouses.   *Source: Chicago Mercantile Exchange (CME)*

PORK BELLIES

Pork Belly Futures - Chicago Mercantile Exchange
(weekly close) as of December 28, 2007
Cents Per Pound

Average Open Interest of Pork Belly Futures in Chicago   In Contracts

Year	Jan.	Feb.	Mar.	Apr.	May	June	July	Aug.	Sept.	Oct.	Nov.	Dec.
1999	7,217	6,192	4,623	5,113	6,030	6,639	5,003	2,415	2,320	3,206	4,011	4,868
2000	5,872	6,011	6,320	6,563	5,836	5,306	3,650	1,877	1,860	2,093	2,409	2,610
2001	2,719	2,908	2,935	3,138	2,808	2,354	2,526	2,579	2,695	2,321	2,441	2,451
2002	2,574	2,768	2,879	3,271	3,224	2,821	1,885	986	1,116	1,329	2,020	2,548
2003	2,842	2,805	2,915	3,082	3,383	3,410	2,858	1,632	1,899	1,885	2,075	2,484
2004	2,431	3,213	3,491	3,998	3,880	3,158	2,675	1,473	1,399	1,200	1,491	1,900
2005	2,013	3,010	2,858	2,891	3,743	3,725	2,507	1,599	1,143	1,451	1,323	1,868
2006	2,273	2,407	1,949	2,146	2,049	1,938	1,812	1,006	782	907	1,039	1,069
2007	1,257	1,520	1,391	1,259	1,256	1,369	1,146	851	941	1,532	1,911	1,850
2008	2,047	1,718	1,763	2,051	1,976	2,219	1,816	702	704	805	1,140	1,164

Source: Chicago Mercantile Exchange (CME)

Volume of Trading of Pork Belly Futures in Chicago   In Contracts

Year	Jan.	Feb.	Mar.	Apr.	May	June	July	Aug.	Sept.	Oct.	Nov.	Dec.	Total
1999	39,925	36,293	33,322	31,558	31,321	45,030	36,513	23,536	16,544	20,392	28,920	24,955	368,309
2000	37,650	38,943	39,061	31,464	40,311	31,229	25,051	17,875	10,711	11,854	11,737	13,690	309,576
2001	15,861	16,200	16,675	18,274	18,708	16,989	20,187	18,823	12,719	12,905	15,984	13,034	196,359
2002	16,495	16,650	14,279	17,758	13,648	15,764	16,773	7,490	6,857	8,107	8,659	9,574	152,054
2003	13,635	13,956	13,137	18,279	18,112	16,993	19,540	9,967	7,909	10,235	8,542	11,024	161,329
2004	11,519	14,738	17,699	18,412	17,366	15,136	16,012	10,518	9,410	5,713	7,643	7,783	151,949
2005	7,736	13,995	10,767	13,713	11,020	15,226	12,869	11,275	5,099	9,370	6,438	6,910	124,418
2006	10,806	12,890	11,682	13,183	10,342	12,616	9,842	9,634	4,885	4,375	4,568	2,741	107,564
2007	7,767	7,117	6,102	6,200	6,072	6,369	6,965	5,873	3,296	4,006	5,140	3,502	68,409
2008	6,159	5,741	5,396	6,289	4,695	5,608	7,993	4,163	2,377	2,463	2,060	3,761	56,705

Source: Chicago Mercantile Exchange (CME)

Pork Bellies (monthly average) through December 2007   Cents per pound

Average Price of Pork Bellies (12-14 lbs.), Central, U.S.   In Cents Per Pound

Year	Jan.	Feb.	Mar.	Apr.	May	June	July	Aug.	Sept.	Oct.	Nov.	Dec.	Average
1999	48.80	50.76	46.51	49.23	53.76	53.41	47.78	67.29	57.87	70.83	67.81	71.37	57.12
2000	80.45	82.40	85.00	93.70	97.85	91.99	90.38	75.64	63.94	57.83	51.97	58.36	77.46
2001	66.61	66.68	78.04	85.80	77.91	91.50	102.42	98.39	81.91	61.30	63.68	69.13	78.61
2002	70.87	70.75	72.55	63.48	58.65	65.90	81.06	67.98	57.05	76.24	75.50	78.92	69.91
2003	78.02	79.54	85.80	84.94	96.58	97.05	102.37	85.65	83.15	84.46	78.53	81.00	86.42
2004	79.78	90.76	103.67	109.15	117.53	113.00	118.22	99.92	92.00	88.90	91.50	87.81	99.35
2005	78.00	82.13	84.20	78.13	87.31	68.73	77.48	94.00	89.67	84.07	78.82	75.00	81.46
2006	75.00	71.83	78.67	78.83	87.00	101.25	94.29	90.67	82.56	75.44	78.64	79.50	82.81
2007	86.25	96.08	93.25	93.47	106.30	101.06	99.83	86.58	80.42	71.58	75.69	77.08	88.97
2008[1]	75.56	78.94	67.26	61.08	79.00	64.54	78.75	74.17	63.50	77.00	57.25	61.25	69.86

[1] Preliminary.   *Source: Economic Research Service, U.S. Department of Agriculture (ERS-USDA)*

Average Price of Pork Loins (12-14 lbs.)[2], Central, U.S.   In Cents Per Pound

Year	Jan.	Feb.	Mar.	Apr.	May	June	July	Aug.	Sept.	Oct.	Nov.	Dec.	Average
1999	105.82	92.35	83.47	99.35	107.44	97.62	105.72	111.55	104.99	98.98	94.64	102.57	100.38
2000	99.29	110.66	110.06	127.48	115.38	132.53	131.73	120.45	119.22	119.90	104.19	114.68	117.13
2001	110.80	114.32	128.53	117.98	130.72	132.33	126.41	121.22	116.21	108.69	97.87	98.50	116.97
2002	106.95	105.73	100.08	94.13	101.71	104.80	108.64	97.85	87.17	93.04	82.60	93.03	97.98
2003	91.83	95.75	92.43	96.90	108.93	126.51	102.50	104.85	111.38	97.71	89.06	93.72	100.96
2004	111.98	117.30	110.00	115.48	140.65	130.30	121.36	116.93	119.22	110.00	102.92	109.50	117.14
2005	116.08	114.83	115.88	115.03	133.45	115.62	115.03	119.82	111.31	103.78	96.72	101.12	113.22
2006	95.00	96.21	101.31	107.25	112.77	124.61	114.95	109.35	99.58	99.27	92.02	101.15	104.46
2007	100.96	112.08	101.04	108.99	121.61	113.58	111.78	111.66	100.18	93.41	88.25	86.46	104.17
2008[1]	87.70	90.22	90.33	108.10	130.43	115.19	117.11	128.86	114.54	111.10	92.88	93.10	106.63

[1] Preliminary.   *Source: Economic Research Service, U.S. Department of Agriculture (ERS-USDA)*

Potatoes

The potato is a member of the nightshade family. The leaves of the potato plant are poisonous and a potato will begin to turn green if left too long in the light. This green skin contains solanine, a substance that can cause the potato to taste bitter and even cause illness in humans. In Peru, the Inca Indians were the first to cultivate potatoes around 200 BC. The Indians developed potato crops because their staple diet of corn would not grow above an altitude of 3,350 meters. In 1536, after conquering the Incas, the Spanish Conquistadors brought potatoes back to Europe. At first, Europeans did not accept the potato because it was not mentioned in the Bible and was therefore considered an "evil" food. But after Marie Antoinette wore a crown of potato flowers, it finally became a popular food. In 1897, during the Alaskan Klondike gold rush, potatoes were so valued for their vitamin C content that miners traded gold for potatoes. The potato became the first vegetable to be grown in outer space in October 1995.

The potato is a highly nutritious, fat-free, cholesterol-free and sodium-free food, and is an important dietary staple in over 130 countries. A medium-sized potato contains only 100 calories. Potatoes are an excellent source of vitamin C and provide B vitamins as well as potassium, copper, magnesium, and iron. According to the U.S. Department of Agriculture, "a diet of whole milk and potatoes would supply almost all of the food elements necessary for the maintenance of the human body."

Potatoes are one of the largest vegetable crops grown in the U.S., and are grown in all fifty states. The U.S. ranks about 4th in world potato production. The top three types of potatoes grown extensively in the U.S. are white, red, and Russets (Russets account for about two-thirds the U.S. crop). Potatoes in the U.S. are harvested in all four seasons, but the vast majority of the crop is harvested in fall. Potatoes harvested in the winter, spring and summer are used mainly to supplement fresh supplies of fall-harvested potatoes and are also important to the processing industries. The four principal categories for U.S. potato exports are frozen, potato chips, fresh, and dehydrated. Fries account for approximately 95% of U.S. frozen potato exports.

Prices – The average monthly price received for potatoes by U.S. farmers in 2008 rose +28.8% to $9.17 per hundred pounds, which is a new record high.

Supply –The total potato crop in 2008 fell by -0.1% to 41.055 billion pounds, well below the record high of 50.936 billion pounds posted in 2000. The fall crop in 2008 also fell by -0.1% to 37.350 billion pounds and it accounted for 91% of the total crop. Stocks of the fall crop (as of Dec 1, 2007) were 27.010 billion pounds. In 2008, the spring crop rose +1.6% to 2.013 billion pounds, the summer crop fell 14.1% to 1.463 billion pounds, and the fall crop fell 8.00% to 37.639 billion pounds.

The largest producing states for the fall 2008 crop were Idaho (with 31% of the crop), Washington (25%), Wisconsin (7%), North Dakota (6%), and Colorado (5%). For the spring crop, the largest producing states were Florida with 40% of the crop and California with 34% of the crop. Farmers harvested 1.045 million acres in 2008, down -7.5% from 2007 which was a record low. The yield per harvested acre in 2008 fell by -0.5% to 39,500 pounds per acre.

Demand – Total utilization of potatoes in 2007 (latest data available) rose +1.2% yr/yr to 44.681 billion pounds. The breakdown shows that the largest consumption category for potatoes is frozen French fries with 32% of total consumption, followed closely by table stock (25%), chips and shoestrings (12%), and dehydration (11%). U.S. per capita consumption of potatoes in 2008 fell -0.6% to 125.3 pounds, well below the record high of 145.0 pounds per capita seen in 1996.

Trade – U.S. exports of potatoes in 2007 (latest data available) rose by +3.4% to 621.200 million pounds. U.S. exports hit a record high of 693.196 million pounds in 2002. U.S. imports rose sharply by +51.2% to 923.500 million pounds, which was a new record high.

Salient Statistics of Potatoes in the United States

Crop Year	Acreage Planted --- 1,000 Acres ---	Acreage Harvested	Yield Per Harvested Acre Cwt.	Total Production	Used Where Grown Seed & Feed	Used Where Grown Shrinkage & Loss	Sold[2]	Farm Price ($ Cwt.)	Value of Production[3] ---- Million $ ----	Value of sales	Stocks Jan. 1 (1,000 Cwt)	Exports (Fresh)	Imports -- Millions of Lbs. --	Consumption[4] Per Capita Fresh	Consumption[4] Per Capita Total
1998	1,417	1,388	343	475,771	5,766	35,454	434,551	5.56	2,635	2,416	246,230	650,918	737,223	46.9	137.7
1999	1,377	1,332	359	478,216	5,569	35,531	437,116	5.77	2,746	2,522	239,910	599,066	610,538	47.7	136.2
2000	1,384	1,348	381	513,621	5,288	43,688	464,645	5.08	2,591	2,360	275,270	676,577	502,706	47.1	137.9
2001	1,247	1,221	358	437,673	5,387	31,208	401,293	6.99	3,058	2,805	224,680	636,176	487,889	46.6	138.8
2002	1,300	1,266	362	458,171	5,622	30,905	421,644	6.67	3,045	2,812	231,490	693,196	621,475	44.3	132.1
2003	1,273	1,249	367	457,814	5,543	35,294	416,977	5.89	2,686	2,458	233,590	589,756	634,971	46.8	138.2
2004	1,193	1,167	391	456,041	4,796	37,408	413,837	5.66	2,575	2,344	236,700	433,700	575,400	45.8	134.7
2005	1,109	1,087	390	423,926	4,791	28,519	390,616	7.06	2,991	2,758	220,500	586,200	631,300	42.4	125.5
2006	1,140	1,122	393	441,348	4,738	29,852	406,758	7.33	3,226	2,981	226,100	600,700	611,200	42.0	123.7
2007[1]	1,149	1,129	398	449,156				7.12	3,198	3,031	237,500	621,200	923,500	43.6	126.0

[1] Preliminary.   [2] For all purposes, including food, seed processing & livestock feed.   [3] Farm weight basis, excluding canned and frozen potatoes.
[4] Calendar year.   *Source: Economic Research Service, U.S. Department of Agriculture (ERS-USDA)*

Cold Storage Stocks of All Frozen Potatoes in the United States, on First of Month   In Millions of Pounds

Year	Jan.	Feb.	Mar.	Apr.	May	June	July	Aug.	Sept.	Oct.	Nov.	Dec.
1998	1,163.5	1,147.2	1,235.7	1,278.3	1,225.1	1,282.8	1,316.5	1,234.7	1,204.5	1,266.8	1,341.0	1,290.5
1999	1,151.3	1,219.7	1,272.9	1,278.8	1,236.2	1,255.5	1,234.1	1,142.3	1,169.8	1,235.5	1,307.8	1,254.5
2000	1,165.4	1,140.9	1,270.1	1,283.4	1,239.4	1,250.4	1,186.3	1,180.3	1,185.7	1,291.5	1,351.5	1,285.9
2001	1,189.7	1,228.6	1,254.7	1,220.9	1,280.4	1,270.3	1,355.0	1,282.6	1,197.5	1,323.8	1,338.5	1,297.4
2002	1,239.8	1,274.2	1,271.5	1,271.4	1,222.7	1,182.3	1,223.5	1,106.6	1,040.6	1,141.4	1,252.2	1,214.4
2003	1,131.2	1,173.1	1,211.0	1,217.4	1,150.5	1,106.6	1,181.8	1,130.4	1,070.4	1,151.7	1,248.0	1,232.8
2004	1,120.4	1,167.3	1,207.4	1,192.5	1,158.7	1,185.9	1,128.7	1,117.1	1,127.0	1,178.6	1,274.9	1,219.3
2005	1,074.8	1,168.8	1,152.8	1,093.7	1,174.3	1,178.1	1,190.5	1,154.9	1,121.3	1,180.4	1,200.0	1,122.5
2006	1,051.1	1,076.2	1,147.0	1,158.9	1,176.6	1,104.9	1,108.1	996.4	964.1	1,009.6	1,066.6	1,052.1
2007[1]	954.8	1,041.3	1,063.6	1,114.6	1,102.2	1,070.7	1,078.2	990.3	999.0	1,080.0	1,133.4	1,077.2

[1] Preliminary.   *Source: Agricultural Statistics Board, U.S. Department of Agriculture (ASB-USDA)*

Potato Crop Production Estimates, Stocks and Disappearance in the United States   In Millions of Cwt.

	Crop Production Estimates			Total Storage Stocks[2]			Following Year					Fall Crop Production 1,000 Cwt.	Fall Crop Disappearance (Sold)	Fall Crop Stocks Dec. 1	Average Price ($/Cwt.)	Value of Sales ($1,000)
	Total Crop			Fall Crop												
Year	Oct. 1	Nov. 1	Dec. 1	Oct. 1	Nov. 1	Dec. 1	Jan. 1	Feb. 1	Mar. 1	Apr. 1	May 1					
1998	----	471.0	----	----	429.0	280.9	246.2	209.6	173.7	131.2	87.9	423,170	392,922	280,910	5.07	1,994,030
1999	----	481.5	----	----	435.6	275.1	239.9	207.2	169.6	128.4	86.9	420,567	390,210	275,100	5.29	2,064,564
2000	----	509.4	----	----	463.4	310.3	275.3	234.3	197.7	153.5	109.2	458,827	420,279	310,300	4.55	1,910,952
2001	----	441.8	----	----	400.7	258.8	224.7	192.1	158.6	120.0	81.2	387,033	358,812	258,750	6.54	2,348,006
2002	----	459.7	----	----	415.0	264.5	231.5	199.0	165.2	125.8	83.0	407,085	378,796	264,485	5.89	2,232,627
2003	----	459.2	----	----	413.5	267.9	233.6	200.2	166.3	126.1	85.0	403,181	371,755	267,900	5.23	1,943,986
2004	----	450.2	----	----	407.8	271.1	236.7	203.5	168.0	128.9	88.6	403,587	369,781	271,100	5.08	1,877,912
2005	----	421.3	----	----	382.2	253.8	220.5	189.1	155.5	115.7	75.9	382,743	351,083	253,800	6.53	2,290,850
2006	----	434.8	----	----	390.9	259.3	226.1	192.6	159.7	121.0	79.1	398,921	365,863	259,300	6.68	2,445,026
2007[1]	----	448.0	----	----	408.3	270.1	270.1	206.2				400,085		270,100	6.61	2,725,800

[1] Preliminary.   [2] Held by growers and local dealers in the fall producing areas.
Source: Agricultural Statistics Board, U.S. Department of Agriculture (ASB-USDA)

Production of Potatoes by Seasonal Groups in the United States   In Thousands of Cwt.

	Winter	Spring			Summer			Fall								
Year	Total	California	Florida	Total	Mexico	Virgina	Total	Colorado	Idaho	Maine	Minnesota	North Dakota	Oregan	Washington	Wisconsin	Total
1998	2,980	6,198	7,358	21,121	962	1,380	18,933	25,360	138,000	18,060	21,170	28,670	26,229	93,225	30,895	423,170
1999	4,070	7,600	8,820	25,327	1,247	1,050	18,972	25,762	133,330	17,813	18,020	26,400	28,020	95,200	34,000	420,567
2000	4,960	7,426	6,343	21,921	1,050	1,292	19,236	27,972	152,320	17,920	21,240	26,950	30,683	105,000	33,800	458,827
2001	4,115	6,045	7,970	21,814	770	1,386	18,209	21,357	120,200	16,430	18,425	26,400	20,730	94,400	31,955	387,033
2002	4,206	7,695	7,883	22,452	736	1,386	17,932	27,885	133,385	16,960	18,810	23,460	24,936	92,340	30,750	407,085
2003	4,027	8,360	8,008	24,433	532	1,550	18,766	23,652	123,180	17,030	22,330	27,440	20,991	93,150	32,800	403,181
2004	4,818	8,313	7,678	22,663	340	1,200	18,307	23,791	131,970	19,065	18,920	26,765	19,775	93,810	30,450	403,587
2005	4,892	6,116	6,527	18,724	----	1,029	17,567	22,910	118,288	15,455	17,630	20,500	22,023	95,480	27,880	382,743
2006	4,495	6,044	6,441	19,766	----	1,512	18,166	22,686	128,915	17,980	20,400	25,480	18,533	89,900	29,370	398,921
2007[1]	2,473	6,123	7,807	20,694	----	1,134	16,907	20,981	131,650	16,530	20,680	23,660	20,238	102,300	28,160	400,085

[1] Preliminary.   *Source: Agricultural Statistics Board, U.S. Department of Agriculture (ASB-USDA)*

Utilization of Potatoes in the United States   In Thousands of Cwt.

	Sales											Non-Sales			
				For Processing						Other Sales		Used on			
Crop Year	Table Stock	Chips, Shoe-strings	Dehyd-ration	Frozen French Fries	Other Frozen Products	Canned Potatoes	Other Canned Products[2]	Starch & Flour	Live-stock Feed	Seed	Total Sales	Farms Where Grown	Shrink-age & Loss	Total Non-Sales	Total
1997	131,670	48,130	48,389	131,628	33,397	2,822	2,675	1,311	3,603	25,808	429,433	4,167	32,183	37,658	467,091
1998	125,413	51,471	55,522	142,932	24,964	2,730	1,964	1,585	3,111	24,859	434,551	4,358	35,454	41,220	475,771
1999	134,130	52,916	50,831	140,196	23,593	3,311	2,394	1,310	3,141	25,294	437,116	4,415	35,531	41,100	478,216
2000	139,590	52,405	54,332	146,869	26,723	2,368	2,709	1,966	14,265	23,345	464,572	3,792	43,685	48,972	513,544
2001	122,552	54,080	40,759	126,711	23,598	2,590	1,722	1,015	3,496	24,537	401,060	4,088	31,227	36,613	437,673
2002	131,889	51,640	51,357	124,875	28,951	2,744	2,089	1,050	3,044	24,005	421,644	4,144	30,905	36,527	458,171
2003	133,143	52,790	48,418	126,515	23,870	3,086	1,168	1,379	2,005	24,603	416,977	4,000	35,294	40,837	457,814
2004	130,418	50,068	48,541	131,592	23,003	2,843	984	1,531	1,942	22,915	413,837	3,601	37,408	42,204	456,041
2005	120,372	50,998	42,312	123,298	24,747	2,120	934	1,582	1,999	22,254	390,616	3,595	28,519	33,310	423,926
2006[1]	101,383	67,034	54,590	129,469	24,859	2,200	795	1,097	1,660	23,671	406,758	3,503	29,852	34,590	441,348

[1] Preliminary.   [2] Hash, stews and soups.   *Source: Agricultural Statistics Board, U.S. Department of Agriculture (ASB-USDA)*

POTATOES

Potatoes (monthly average) through December 2008 — USD per 100 pounds

Per Capita Utilization of Potatoes in the United States   In Pounds (Farm Weight)

Year	Total	Fresh	Freezing	Chips & Shoe-string	Dehy-drating	Canning	Total Processing
2000	137.9	47.1	57.5	15.9	15.7	1.7	90.8
2001	138.8	46.6	58.2	17.6	14.8	1.6	92.2
2002	132.1	44.3	55.2	16.5	14.7	1.4	87.8
2003	138.4	46.9	57.3	17.3	15.5	1.4	91.5
2004	134.9	45.9	57.4	16.6	13.8	1.2	89.0
2005	125.8	41.4	54.5	16.2	12.8	0.9	84.4
2006	123.5	38.6	53.0	18.8	12.3	0.8	84.9
2007	125.4	39.1	53.6	18.7	13.1	0.9	86.3
2008[1]	120.4	36.9	53.6	16.4	12.6	0.9	83.5
2009[2]	121.0	37.4	53.6	16.6	12.5	0.9	83.6

[1] Preliminary.   [2] Forecast.   Source: Agricultural Statistics Board, U.S. Department of Agriculture (ASB-USDA)

Average Price Received by Farmers for Potatoes in the U.S.   In Dollars Per Hundred Pounds (Cwt.)

Year	Jan.	Feb.	Mar.	Apr.	May	June	July	Aug.	Sept.	Oct.	Nov.	Dec.	Season Average
1999	5.50	5.75	6.12	6.50	6.13	6.54	7.35	6.02	5.09	4.86	5.52	5.44	5.77
2000	5.68	5.92	6.26	6.46	6.31	6.14	6.93	5.56	4.49	4.27	4.31	4.48	5.08
2001	4.56	5.26	5.12	5.47	5.24	5.75	6.46	7.61	6.04	5.15	5.96	6.66	6.99
2002	6.90	7.34	8.26	8.00	8.62	9.39	10.40	8.00	6.14	5.44	6.38	6.67	6.67
2003	6.67	6.33	6.87	6.94	6.96	6.68	6.30	5.75	5.24	5.03	5.46	5.77	5.88
2004	5.75	5.87	6.09	6.62	6.47	6.16	6.46	5.77	5.32	4.70	5.02	5.36	5.65
2005	5.59	5.79	6.44	6.20	6.23	6.29	7.63	7.02	5.69	5.37	6.26	6.83	7.04
2006	7.07	6.76	8.50	8.35	7.83	8.41	10.46	8.23	6.12	5.76	6.59	6.79	7.31
2007	7.06	7.42	7.93	8.71	7.95	7.75	8.48	6.85	5.81	5.68	6.47	7.02	7.51
2008[1]	7.33	7.51	8.37	8.45	9.16	10.78	12.33	11.33	8.79	7.38	8.91	9.62	9.46

[1] Preliminary.   Source: Agricultural Statistics Board, U.S. Department of Agriculture (ASB-USDA)

Potatoes Processed[1] in the United States, Eight States   In Thousands of Cwt.

States	Storage Season	to Dec. 1	to Jan. 1	to Feb. 1	to Mar. 1	to Apr. 1	to May 1	to June 1	Entire Season
Idaho and Oregon-Malheur Co.	2000-01	29,290	35,720	43,470	50,580	58,910	66,760	75,270	93,460
	2001-02	20,940	27,330	33,620	40,860	47,710	54,150	61,200	73,390
	2002-03	28,380	34,860	41,200	48,600	56,240	63,840	71,280	85,390
	2003-04	24,310	30,730	36,260	43,640	49,570	56,380	63,770	77,530
	2004-05	24,360	30,840	36,820	44,610	51,000	58,090	65,800	84,600
	2005-06	22,840	29,300	35,970	43,300	50,820	57,830	65,030	77,360
	2006-07	27,090	34,070	41,350	49,840	56,650	63,680	71,220	85,630
	2007-08	26,230	33,250	40,310	48,660	55,460	63,000	70,700	88,030
	2008-09	22,360	28,980	35,430	42,150				
Maine[2]	2000-01	1,845	2,475	3,105	3,695	4,225	4,760	5,340	7,015
	2001-02	1,975	2,440	3,110	3,700	4,285	4,775	5,515	7,195
	2002-03	2,230	2,715	3,345	3,905	4,505	5,225	5,905	7,835
	2003-04	1,590	2,085	2,720	3,420	4,095	4,740	5,400	7,270
	2004-05	1,540	1,970	2,600	3,135	3,700	4,340	4,910	6,590
	2005-06	1,365	1,880	2,485	3,090	3,800	4,450	5,130	6,825
	2006-07	1,755	2,360	2,910	3,465	4,185	4,810	5,470	7,560
	2007-08	1,700	2,170	2,815	3,440	3,990	4,670	5,240	7,550
	2008-09	1,635	2,240	2,890	3,505				
Washington & Oregon-Other	2000-01	34,770	40,970	47,720	55,250	62,860	69,850	78,010	91,130
	2001-02	29,320	35,310	40,540	47,910	54,970	61,360	69,400	77,180
	2002-03	33,680	39,490	44,190	51,920	58,710	64,300	71,480	79,110
	2003-04	32,670	38,520	43,610	51,210	58,500	64,160	72,350	79,800
	2004-05	32,305	38,130	43,570	50,730	57,140	63,855	71,355	78,680
	2005-06	30,310	35,895	40,545	48,290	55,320	61,855	69,360	78,550
	2006-07	30,980	37,060	41,290	49,930	56,690	63,170	70,410	77,355
	2007-08	30,595	36,940	42,350	50,165	57,160	67,690	72,380	82,770
	2008-09	32,570	37,750	42,490	49,795				
Other States[3]	2000-01	12,665	16,215	18,975	22,095	25,410	28,695	31,765	39,020
	2001-02	13,170	14,925	19,000	22,115	24,655	27,815	30,460	37,740
	2002-03	12,675	15,530	18,735	21,780	24,810	27,405	30,655	38,700
	2003-04	13,835	16,505	19,590	22,685	25,920	29,480	32,845	42,160
	2004-05	12,490	15,000	17,965	20,910	24,150	27,480	30,945	41,175
	2005-06	11,055	14,070	17,005	19,895	22,520	25,270	27,740	35,535
	2006-07	14,355	17,800	21,415	24,690	28,205	31,560	35,040	43,565
	2007-08	15,040	17,535	20,755	23,900	26,650	29,710	32,600	39,430
	2008-09	12,535	15,190	18,250	21,150				
Total	2000-01	78,570	95,380	113,270	131,620	151,405	170,065	190,385	230,625
	2001-02	65,405	80,005	96,270	114,585	131,620	148,100	166,575	195,505
	2002-03	76,965	92,595	107,470	126,205	144,265	160,770	179,320	211,035
	2003-04	72,405	87,840	102,180	120,955	138,085	154,760	174,365	206,760
	2004-05	70,695	85,940	100,955	119,385	135,990	153,765	173,010	211,045
	2005-06	65,570	81,145	96,005	114,575	132,460	149,405	167,260	198,270
	2006-07	74,210	91,320	107,895	127,050	145,760	163,250	182,170	214,225
	2007-08	73,565	89,895	106,230	126,165	143,260	165,070	180,920	217,780
	2008-09	69,100	84,160	99,060	11,660				
Dehydrated[4]	2001-02	----	----	----	----	----	----	----	38,581
	2002-03	15,675	19,660	23,710	27,950	31,915	36,105	40,455	48,940
	2003-04	14,250	18,440	22,050	26,090	30,290	34,630	39,070	47,750
	2004-05	14,525	18,540	21,875	25,970	30,020	33,685	38,505	47,805
	2005-06	11,920	15,655	19,225	22,765	26,605	30,065	34,130	41,625
	2006-07	14,590	19,250	23,635	27,885	32,210	36,480	40,915	49,375
	2007-08	12,815	16,785	21,040	25,350	29,500	33,650	37,975	46,660
	2008-09	10,745	14,570	18,405	21,535				

[1] Total quantity received and used for processing regardless of the State in which the potatoes were produced. Amount excludes quantities used for potato chips in Maine, Michigan and Wisconsin.   [2] Includes Maine grown potatoes only.   [3] Colorado, Minnesota, , Nevada, North Dakota and Wisconsin.
[4] Dehydrated products except starch and flour. Included in above totals. Includes CO, ID, NV, ND, OR, WA, and WI.
Source: National Agricultural Statistics Service, U.S. Department of Agriculture (NASS-USDA)

Rayon and Other Synthetic Fibers

World Cellulosic Fiber Production In Thousands of Metric Tons

Year	Brazil	Bulgaria	China	CIS	Czech Republic	India	Indo-nesia	Japan	Mexico	Taiwan	Thailand	United States	World Total
1999	34.6	13.5	472.1	88.0	17.6	248.5	195.6	135.5	13.5	143.7	55.3	134.7	2,074
2000	36.2	15.0	552.3	83.7	7.1	297.5	207.0	126.2	14.8	141.5	65.0	158.8	2,215
2001	28.7	12.2	608.6	64.4	7.6	251.9	205.0	107.1	22.6	127.4	65.0	103.0	2,083
2002	34.2	5.6	682.1	72.9	7.3	285.7	214.0	68.1	16.8	114.2	71.1	80.7	2,125
2003	47.2	5.2	800.2	78.8	9.1	283.0	223.0	68.3	8.4	121.5	73.8	75.3	2,249
2004	46.8	5.0	966.1	77.2	9.2	311.5	234.0	67.1	8.4	134.9	79.4	66.8	2,465
2005	40.1	5.0	1,056.0	46.6	9.5	295.4	245.0	66.6	3.8	114.5	78.2	49.1	2,475
2006	34.3	5.0	1,175.0	22.7	9.7	309.5	278.0	65.8	----	132.3	79.2	24.3	2,616
2007[1]	46.6	6.0	1,520.0	57.3	9.7	362.9	310.0	96.3	----	149.6	110.0	25.0	3,212
2008[2]	46.6	6.0	1,800.0	57.3	9.7	426.7	347.0	96.3	----	149.6	142.0	25.0	3,624

[1] Preliminary. [2] Producing capacity. *Source: Fiber Economics Bureau, Inc. (FEB)*

World Noncellulosic Fiber Production (Except Olefin) In Thousands of Metric Tons

Year	Brazil	China	India	Indonesia	Japan	Rep. of Korea	Mexico	Pakistan	Taiwan	Thailand	Turkey	United States	World Total
1999	292.6	5,235.1	1,493.3	1,037.8	1,299.7	2,592.8	571.2	478.0	2,927.7	694.2	613.5	3,169.5	24,885
2000	311.1	6,158.4	1,568.4	1,142.7	1,307.9	2,659.0	586.8	503.9	3,122.9	769.5	744.5	3,149.2	26,219
2001	288.8	7,322.9	1,570.2	1,190.6	1,239.5	2,471.9	536.4	528.4	2,977.5	784.5	669.2	2,687.6	26,243
2002	293.1	8,849.4	1,695.3	1,132.8	1,129.1	2,455.7	509.6	581.5	3,091.3	852.6	728.1	2,805.0	28,052
2003	314.2	10,456.0	1,792.0	1,144.2	1,030.3	2,418.0	474.9	646.8	3,060.9	872.5	766.9	2,719.5	29,450
2004	330.9	12,474.1	1,904.2	1,064.5	989.2	2,194.3	474.9	659.3	2,965.0	905.9	849.5	2,858.2	31,429
2005	303.9	16,084.3	1,849.2	1,064.0	955.4	1,697.4	399.6	565.2	2,587.8	920.7	792.0	2,680.1	33,509
2006	263.0	18,012.5	2,159.4	1,097.7	928.9	1,487.5	280.8	550.7	2,399.0	851.4	787.7	2,486.2	34,803
2007[1]	369.0	26,739.0	3,434.0	1,406.0	1,189.8	1,617.6	363.0	781.0	3,033.1	1,093.0	1,004.2	2,879.9	48,324
2008[2]	369.0	28,094.0	3,949.0	1,431.0	1,182.8	1,427.6	388.0	851.0	2,693.1	1,022.0	1,009.2	2,847.7	49,810

[1] Preliminary. [2] Producing capacity. *Source: Fiber Economics Bureau, Inc. (FEB)*

World Production of Synthetic Fibers In Thousands of Metric Tons

| | Noncellulosic Fiber Production (Except Olefin) | | | | | | | | Glass Fiber Production | | | | | | | |
| | By Fibers | | | | World Total | | | | | | | | | | | |
Year	Acrylic & Mod-acrylic	Nylon & Aramid	Polyester	Other	Yarn & Monofil-aments	Staple & Tow & Fiberfill	Total	Europe	Japan	Other Americas	United States	Total	China	USSR	Cigarette Tow Pro-duction
1999	2,513	3,800	17,879	294	13,660	10,825	24,485	674	300	96	1,126	60	30	2,538	544
2000	2,634	4,117	19,155	313	14,771	11,448	26,219	728	280	96	1,143	60	28	2,580	570
2001	2,562	3,784	19,563	335	14,968	11,276	26,243	701	273	93	1,016	67	32	2,431	590
2002	2,713	3,941	21,048	350	15,993	12,059	28,052	718	251	96	1,222	90	34	2,661	612
2003	2,707	3,951	22,365	427	16,853	12,597	29,450	724	250	100	1,307	120	37	2,790	633
2004	2,824	3,976	24,136	492	17,957	13,472	31,429	740	250	104	1,363	150	40	2,903	651
2005	2,697	3,851	26,451	510	19,286	14,222	33,509								665
2006	2,534	3,883	27,808	578	20,592	14,211	34,803								680
2007[1]	3,147	5,101	39,322	755	28,388	19,937	48,324								
2008[2]	3,249	5,150	40,645	767	29,221	20,590	49,810								

[1] Preliminary. [2] Producing capacity. [3] Alginate, azion, spandex, saran, etc. *Source: Fiber Economics Bureau, Inc. (FEB)*

Artificial (Cellulosic) Fiber Distribution in the United States In Millions of Pounds

| | Yarn & Monofilament | | | | | Staple & Tow | | | | | Glass Fiber Ship-ments |
| | Producers' Shipments | | | | Domestic Con-sumption | Producers' Shipments | | | | Domestic Con-sumption | |
Year	Domestic	Exports	Total	Imports		Domestic	Exports	Total	Imports		
1999	84.2	30.4	114.6	28.2	112.4	168.8	29.9	198.7	47.5	216.3	----
2000	76.7	37.8	114.5	23.2	99.9	162.3	69.3	231.5	37.5	199.7	----
2001	54.3	33.7	88.0	14.5	68.8	117.2	35.5	152.7	33.9	151.2	----
2002	41.2	33.2	74.4	12.7	53.9	91.1	12.6	103.7	56.2	147.4	----
2003	32.5	35.5	68.0	11.7	44.2	86.7	13.1	99.8	44.5	131.2	----
2004	26.7	38.7	65.4	12.2	38.9	77.4	9.9	87.2	63.9	141.3	----
2005	22.6	41.4	64.0	9.3	31.9	40.2	8.1	48.2	91.0	131.2	----
2006	22.4	37.6	60.0	7.7	30.1		8.9	8.9	141.4	141.4	----
2007	18.7	41.3	60.0	17.0	35.7		5.4	5.4	200.7	200.7	----
2008[1]	15.4	44.6	60.0	11.8	27.2		6.8	6.8	179.8	179.8	----

[1] Preliminary. *Source: Fiber Economice Bureau, Inc.*

Man-Made Fiber Production in the United States   In Millions of Pounds

Year	Artificial (Cellulosic) Fibers - Rayon & Acetate - Filament Yarn & Monofilament	Staple & Tow	Total Cellulostic	Synthetic (Noncellulosic) Fibers Yarn & Monofilament Nylon	Polyester	Olefin	Total Yarn	Staple & Tow Nylon	Polyester	Acrylic & Modacrylic	Olefin	Total Staple	Total Noncellulosic Fibers	Total Manufactured Fibers	Total Glass Fiber
2000	114	232	345	1,947	1,509	2,406	5,860	733	2,405	339	816	4,293	10,153	10,236	2,738
2001	----	153	153	1,642	1,188	2,181	5,011	606	2,040	310	721	3,676	8,687		2,638
2002	----	104	104	1,772	1,218	2,331	5,321	681	2,050	340	749	3,820	9,141		2,759
2003	----	100	100	1,762	1,145	2,349	5,255	697	1,886	270	680	3,533	8,788		2,789
2004	----	----	----	1,837	1,242	2,383	5,462	680	2,064	240	676	3,660	9,123		
2005	----	----	----	1,788	1,111	2,395	5,294	598	2,019	140	699	3,455	8,749		
2006	----	----	----	1,739	1,919	2,223	5,034	515	1,864		622	3,001	8,036		
2007[1]	----	----	----	1,636	1,779	2,266	4,916	429	1,719		588	2,736	7,652		
2008[2]	----	----	----	1,359		1,957	4,230	275	1,423		488	2,186	6,416		

[1] Preliminary.   [2] Estimate.   *Source: Fiber Economics Bureau, Inc. (FEB)*

Domestic Distribution of Synthetic (Noncellulosic) Fibers in the United States   In Millions of Pounds

Year	Yarn & Monofilament Producers' Shipments Domestic Nylon	Polyester	Olefin	Total	Exports	Total	Imports	Domestic Consumption	Staple & Tow Producers' Shipments Domestic Nylon	Polyester	Acrylic & Modacrylic	Olefin	Total	Exports	Total	Imports	Domestic Consumption
2000	1,795	1,375	2,371	5,541	250	5,791	790	6,331	674	2,174	244	757	3,849	327	4,176	727	4,576
2001	1,606	1,215	2,144	4,964	155	5,119	697	5,661	607	1,881	228	673	3,389	308	3,698	757	4,146
2002	1,668	1,150	2,289	5,107	189	5,296	765	5,871	637	1,823	255	723	3,438	353	3,791	875	4,312
2003	1,666	1,109	2,318	5,093	179	5,272	766	5,859	673	1,688	211	635	3,206	246	3,452	829	4,035
2004	1,722	1,137	2,347	5,205	249	5,455	785	5,990	658	1,788	200	641	3,287	296	3,583	766	4,053
2005	1,688	1,052	2,369	5,109	197	5,306	849	5,958	582	1,765	122	650	3,120	292	3,411	914	4,034
2006	1,589	975	2,198	4,762	211	4,974	819	5,581	492	1,624	7	596	2,720	268	2,988	1,007	3,726
2007	1,526	928	2,219	4,672	199	4,871	739	5,411	407	1,506	8	549	2,469	256	2,725	1,029	3,498
2008[1]	1,334	1,072	1,921	4,327	141	4,468	692	5,019	264	1,279	8	448	1,999	184	2,183	1,038	3,037

[1] Preliminary.   *Source: Fiber Economics Bureau, Inc. (FEB)*

Mill Consumption of Fiber & Products and Per Capita Consumption in the United States   In Millions of Pounds

Year	Cellulosic Fibers Yarn & Monofilament	Staple & Tow	Net Waste	Total Cellulosic	Noncellulosic Fibers Noncellulosic	Net Waste	Total Noncellulosic	Total Manufactured Fibers[2]	Cotton	Wool	Other Fibers[3]	Grand Total	Per Capita[4] Mill Consumption (Lbs.) Manmade Finers	Cotton	Wool	Other Fibers[3]	Total
1999	112	216	1.6	330	10,575	177	10,752	11,082	4,996	99	213.3	16,391	46.9	34.5	1.2	2.5	85.1
2000	100	200	1.9	302	10,895	190	11,085	11,387	4,754	101	177.9	16,420	48.4	34.9	1.3	2.6	87.3
2001	69	151	2.4	222	9,939	193	10,133	10,355	3,983	87	168.1	14,593	44.8	33.1	1.4	2.1	81.4
2002	54	147	1.8	203	10,141	190	10,331	10,534	3,576	56	110.3	14,276	47.6	34.3	1.3	2.2	85.4
2003	44	131	1.3	177	10,369	177	10,546	10,722	3,210	43	106.3	14,082	50.2	34.8	1.4	2.7	89.2
2004	39	141	1.5	182	10,499	144	10,643	10,825	3,126	44	123.4	14,118	50.4	35.1	1.4	3.4	90.3
2005	32	131	2.0	165	10,568	166	10,734	10,899	3,005	36	141.3	14,081	52.0	37.7	1.4	3.1	94.2
2006	30	141	2.9	174	10,157	73	10,230	10,404	2,729	33	106.7	13,273	51.5	38.3	1.4	2.9	94.2
2007[1]	36	201	2.8	239	9,557	77	9,634	9,873	2,112	10		12,097	50.0	36.9	1.3	2.6	90.7

[1] Preliminary.   [2] Excludes Glass Fiber.   [3] Includes silk, linen, jute and sisal & others.   [4] Mill consumption plus inports less exports of semimanufactured and unmanufactured products.   *Source: Fiber Economics Bureau, Inc. (FEB)*

Producer Price Index of Grey Synthetic Broadwovens   (1982 = 100)

Year	Jan.	Feb.	Mar.	Apr.	May	June	July	Aug.	Sept.	Oct.	Nov.	Dec.	Average
1999	113.6	112.0	113.3	111.5	110.4	108.1	106.7	106.0	106.0	108.3	106.9	107.6	109.2
2000	108.1	109.3	110.6	110.6	109.0	107.7	109.6	110.6	109.4	109.3	110.6	110.9	109.6
2001	110.1	111.3	111.8	111.9	109.2	110.1	107.8	108.8	109.2	107.7	107.7	107.5	109.4
2002	106.7	106.4	108.0	108.5	107.7	108.2	107.3	108.1	108.0	107.2	107.3	108.4	107.7
2003	108.2	108.2	107.6	107.7	110.1	106.0	105.7	107.1	106.7	106.0	106.6	107.7	107.3
2004	107.3	106.9	106.2	107.4	108.9	109.0	107.5	106.2	106.3	106.3	106.2	106.2	107.0
2005	108.5	108.8	109.1	110.5	110.2	110.0	110.7	110.9	110.8	112.4	113.3	116.2	111.0
2006	118.2	119.5	119.8	119.2	119.4	119.4	119.5	120.4	119.1	119.5	119.0	118.1	119.3
2007	117.8	118.8	118.9	119.1	119.6	119.8	120.3	121.5	122.9	122.7	123.0	122.9	120.6
2008[1]	122.9	123.0	122.8	123.0	123.3	123.3	123.6	121.8	122.0	121.1	121.1	118.7	122.2

[1] Preliminary.   *Source: Bureau of Labor Statistics, U.S. Department of Commerce (BLS) (0337-03)*

Rice

Rice is a grain that is cultivated on every continent except Antarctica and is the primary food for half the people in the world. Rice cultivation probably originated as early as 10,000 BC in Asia. Rice is grown at varying altitudes (sea level to about 3,000 meters), in varying climates (tropical to temperate), and on dry to flooded land. The growth duration of rice plants is 3-6 months, depending on variety and growing conditions. Rice is harvested by hand in developing countries or by combines in industrialized countries. Asian countries produce about 90% of rice grown worldwide. Rough rice futures and options are traded on the Chicago Board of Trade (CBOT).

Prices – Rough rice prices on the CBOT nearest futures chart at the beginning of 2008 were about $14.00 per hundred pounds. Prices moved steadily higher to a high of about $24.50 per hundred pounds in April. From there the price dropped steadily, except for a brief rally in August, to end the year at about $15.00 per hundred pounds. The downmove continued into 2009 with the price reaching about $12.00 per hundred pounds in March 2009. Regarding cash prices, the average monthly price of rice received by farmers in the U.S. in the first six months of the 2008-09 marketing year (i.e., August 2008 through July 2009) rose by +32.6% yr/yr to $17.37 per hundred pounds (cwt.).

Supply – World rice production in the 2008-09 marketing year rose +1.8% to 655.489 million metric tons, down from the record high of 627.323 million metric tons in 2006-07. The world's largest rice producers were China with 29% of world production in 2008-09, India with 22% of world production, Indonesia with 9%, Bangladesh with 7%, Vietnam with 5%, and Thailand with 4%. U.S. production of rice in 2008-09 rose +3.0% yr/yr to 203.5 million cwt (hundred pounds), but still well below the 2004-05 record high of 232.4 million cwt.

Demand – World utilization of rice in 2008-09 rose +1.6% to a record high of 431.971 million metric tons. U.S. rice consumption in 2008-09 rose +2.2% yr/yr to 126.0 million cwt (hundred pounds), down from the 2006-07 record high of 127.2 million cwt (hundred pounds).

Trade – World exports of rice in 2008-09 fell -6.4% yr/yr to 28.969 million metric tons, down from last year's record high of 30.941 metric tons. The world's largest rice exporters are Thailand with 31% of world exports, Vietnam with 18%, Pakistan with 14%, the U.S. with 11%, and India with 7%. U.S. rice imports in 2008-090 fell by -5.9% yr/yr to 22.5 million cwt (hundred pounds), down from last year's record high of 23.9 million cwt. U.S. rice exports in 2008-09 fell by -1.8% yr/yr to 106.0 million cwt.

World Rice Supply and Distribution   In Thousands of Metric Tons

| | | | | | | | ----------------- Imports ----------------- | | | ---------- Utilization ----------- | | | --------- Ending Stocks ---------- | | |
Crop Year	Brazil	Indo-nesia	European Union	Iran	Nigeria	Saudi Arabia	Total	China	India	Total	China	India	Total
2003-04	881	650	1,125	950	1,448	1,150	24,963	132,100	85,630	411,886	43,915	10,800	81,145
2004-05	510	500	1,090	983	1,369	1,500	25,907	130,300	80,861	406,828	38,931	8,500	73,152
2005-06	750	539	1,126	1,251	1,777	1,357	26,582	128,000	85,088	412,171	36,783	10,520	75,676
2006-07[1]	732	2,000	1,338	1,144	1,600	1,448	28,846	127,200	86,940	418,441	35,915	11,430	75,389
2007-08[2]	400	500	1,566	1,100	1,550	958	27,696	127,450	90,360	425,029	37,994	13,000	78,981
2008-09[3]	500	800	1,050	1,400	1,600	1,015	26,822	130,500	93,000	431,971	41,624	15,500	84,601

[1] Preliminary.   [2] Estimate.   [3] Forecast.   Source: Foreign Agricultural Service, U.S. Department of Agriculture (FAS-USDA)

World Production of Rough Rice   In Thousands of Metric Tons

Year	Bang-ladesh	Brazil	Burma	China	India	Indo-nesia	Japan	Korea	Pakistan	Philip-pines	Thailand	Vietnam	World Total
2003-04	39,232	12,807	18,500	160,660	132,808	54,301	9,740	6,151	7,273	14,154	27,289	33,458	584,978
2004-05	38,404	13,229	16,500	179,090	124,707	54,000	10,912	6,737	7,538	14,500	26,303	34,418	597,333
2005-06	43,141	11,579	18,000	180,591	137,699	54,200	11,342	6,435	8,321	15,109	27,576	34,503	623,392
2006-07[1]	43,504	11,316	18,276	181,714	140,039	54,729	10,695	6,306	8,176	15,516	27,652	34,730	627,323
2007-08[2]	43,204	12,057	18,500	186,034	144,659	55,504	10,893	5,962	8,551	16,633	29,242	36,932	644,206
2008-09[3]	44,404	12,200	16,897	193,000	146,265	56,202	10,989	6,545	9,451	16,905	29,394	35,606	655,489

[1] Preliminary.   [2] Estimate.   [3] Forecast.   Source: Foreign Agricultural Service, U.S. Department of Agriculture (FAS-USDA)

World Exports of Rice (Milled Basis)   In Thousands of Metric Tons

Year	Argentina	Australia	Burma	China	European Union	Guyana	India	Pakistan	Thailand	Uruguay	Vietnam	United States	World Total
2003-04	294	175	130	880	225	200	3,100	1,868	10,137	725	4,295	3,310	27,418
2004-05	325	80	190	656	175	243	4,569	2,801	7,274	775	5,174	3,496	28,507
2005-06	484	326	47	1,216	161	182	4,688	3,664	7,376	834	4,705	3,661	30,374
2006-07[1]	450	200	31	1,340	148	250	5,500	2,839	9,557	734	4,522	2,923	31,343
2007-08[2]	520	92	541	945	152	210	4,500	3,000	10,016	775	4,649	3,452	30,941
2008-09[3]	550	20	500	1,300	150	210	2,000	4,000	9,000	800	5,200	3,134	28,969

[1] Preliminary.   [2] Estimate.   [3] Forecast.   Source: Foreign Agricultural Service, U.S. Department of Agriculture (FAS-USDA)

Rice (monthly average) through December 2008   USD per 100 pounds

Average Wholesale Price of Rice No. 2 (Medium)[1] Southwest Louisiana   In Dollars Per Cwt. Bagged

Year	Jan.	Feb.	Mar.	Apr.	May	June	July	Aug.	Sept.	Oct.	Nov.	Dec.	Average
1999-00	18.60	17.50	14.88	14.70	14.67	14.35	14.00	13.83	13.75	13.40	12.50	12.63	14.57
2000-01	13.00	12.34	12.48	12.41	12.38	12.38	12.25	12.00	11.82	11.53	11.25	11.25	12.09
2001-02	11.06	11.50	11.50	11.50	11.08	11.50	11.50	11.43	10.94	11.13	11.13	11.13	11.28
2002-03	11.13	11.50	12.25	12.25	12.25	12.63	13.50	14.05	14.25	14.44	14.50	14.88	13.13
2003-04	16.75	17.70	19.00	19.95	21.25	21.38	22.30	22.46	22.50	23.00	21.50	21.50	20.77
2004-05	18.60	15.69	15.23	15.13	15.13	16.31	14.88	14.88	14.88	14.88	14.88	14.94	15.45
2005-06	17.00	17.50	18.45	20.13	21.38	22.50	22.50	22.50	22.50	22.50	22.50	22.35	20.98
2006-07	21.94	22.00	22.00	23.50	23.50	23.50	23.50	23.50	23.50	23.50	23.50	23.50	23.12
2007-08	23.50	23.50	23.30	23.25	23.25	23.25	24.31	27.45	34.00	39.00	40.00	40.00	28.73
2008-09[2]	40.63	43.10	43.25	43.06	42.88								42.58

[1] U.S. No. 2 -- broken not to exceed 4%.   [2] Preliminary.   *Source: Economic Research Service, U.S. Department of Agriculture (ERS-USDA)*

Average Price Received by Farmers for Rice (Rough) in the United States   In Dollars Per Hundred Pounds (Cwt.)

Year	Jan.	Feb.	Mar.	Apr.	May	June	July	Aug.	Sept.	Oct.	Nov.	Dec.	Average[2]
1999-00	6.91	6.17	5.91	5.96	6.01	5.98	5.82	5.64	5.75	5.62	5.69	5.59	5.93
2000-01	5.72	5.53	5.57	5.72	5.69	5.86	5.72	5.66	5.68	5.40	5.14	5.32	5.61
2001-02	5.10	4.78	4.36	4.08	4.07	4.30	4.16	3.99	3.94	3.98	3.92	3.81	4.21
2002-03	3.71	3.94	3.69	3.70	4.13	4.66	4.24	4.31	4.61	4.84	5.43	5.31	4.38
2003-04	5.47	6.18	6.44	6.99	7.57	8.57	8.23	8.45	8.65	9.30	9.37	8.79	7.83
2004-05	8.96	8.47	7.60	7.36	7.37	7.39	6.90	6.97	6.98	6.98	6.96	6.82	7.40
2005-06	6.58	6.76	6.99	7.46	7.49	7.80	8.02	8.05	8.16	8.03	8.41	8.18	7.66
2006-07	8.81	9.03	9.65	10.10	9.91	10.40	10.10	10.00	10.20	10.00	10.00	10.10	9.86
2007-08	10.10	10.30	10.70	11.40	11.50	12.40	12.50	13.60	14.60	16.10	16.80	17.20	13.10
2008-09[1]	18.00	17.10	16.90	17.70	17.50	17.00							17.37

[1] Preliminary.   [2] Weighted average by sales.   *Source: Economic Research Service, U.S. Department of Agriculture (ERS-USDA)*

RICE

Salient Statistics of Rice, Rough & Milled (Rough Equivalent) in the United States   In Millions of Cwt.

Crop Year Beginning Aug. 1	Stocks Aug. 1	Pro- duction	Imports	Total Supply	Food	Brewers	Seed	Total	Resi- dual	Exports	Total Disap- pearance	CCC Stocks July 31	Put Under Price Support	Long	Med- ium	All Classes	Milled Long
2003-04	26.8	199.9	15.0	241.7	110.8	[4]	4.1	114.9	[4]	103.1	218.0	0	----	6.64	6.09	6.50	10.65
2004-05	23.7	232.4	13.2	269.3	118.5	[4]	4.2	122.7	[4]	108.8	231.5	0	----	6.66	6.04	6.50	10.61
2005-06	37.7	222.8	17.1	277.7	116.7	[4]	3.5	119.9	[4]	114.8	234.7	0	----	6.66	6.04	6.50	10.54
2006-07	43.0	194.6	20.6	258.2	123.8	[4]	3.4	128.1	[4]	90.8	218.8	0	----	6.64	6.07	6.50	10.52
2007-08[1]	39.3	198.4	23.9	261.6	119.7	[4]	3.6	124.2	[4]	107.9	232.1	0	----	6.59	6.20	6.50	10.12
2008-09[2]	29.4	203.7	18.0	251.2		[4]		127.0	[4]	94.0	221.0						

[1] Preliminary.   [2] Forecast.   [3] Loan rate for each class of rice is the sum of the whole kernels' loan rate weighted by its milling yield (average 56%) and the broken kernels' loan rate weighted by its milling yield (average 12%).   [4] Included in Food.
Source: Economic Research Service, U.S. Department of Agriculture (ERS-USDA)

Acreage, Yield, Production and Prices of Rice in the United States

Crop Year Beginning Aug. 1	Southern States	Cali- fornia	United States	Cali- fornia	United States	Southern States	Cali- fornia	United States	Value of Pro- duction ($1,000)	Arkan- sas[2]	Hous- ton[2]	U.S. No. 2[4]	Thai "A"[5]	Thai "B"[5]
2003-04	2,490	507	2,997	7,700	6,670	160,861	39,036	199,897	1,628,948	21.18	17.60	358	----	NA
2004-05	2,735	590	3,325	8,600	6,942	180,059	50,759	230,818	1,701,822	14.46	17.45	316	----	NA
2005-06	2,838	526	3,364	7,380	6,636	184,399	38,836	223,235	1,741,721	20.52	17.53	293	----	NA
2006-07	2,298	523	2,821	7,660	6,868	153,696	40,040	193,736	1,990,783	22.18	21.10			
2007-08	2,215	533	2,748	8,220	7,185	153,634	43,822	197,456	2,600,871	23.18	21.80			
2008-09[1]	2,478	517	2,995	8,100	6,848	161,856	41,877	203,733	3,390,666					

[1] Preliminary.   [2] F.O.B. mills, Arkansas, medium.   [3] Houston, Texas (long grain).   [4] Milled, 4%, container, FAS.
[5] SWR, 100%, bulk.   NA = Not available.   *Source: Economic Research Service, U.S. Department of Agriculture (ERS-USDA)*

U.S. Exports of Milled Rice, by Country of Destination   In Thousands of Metric Tons

Trade Year Beginning October	Canada	Haiti	Iran	Ivory Coast	Jamaica	Mexico	Nether- lands	Peru	Saudi Arabia	South Africa	Switzer- land	United Kingdom	Total
2002-03	168.6	324.8	10.3	65.8	60.7	740.6	71.7	23.8	97.6	73.1	26.2	126.4	4,469
2003-04	208.4	242.2	0	32.7	44.5	738.0	30.4	3.5	87.7	.0	10.6	100.2	3,690
2004-05	230.8	299.1	0	32.6	48.2	725.8	44.8	45.7	101.4	.6	18.0	130.9	4,248
2005-06	236.9	340.3	0	25.0	53.5	822.3	38.2	1.7	93.4	.0	12.4	118.0	4,014
2006-07	243.9	279.3	0	0	42.6	810.2	4.0	.1	96.8	.7	.2	37.6	3,306
2007-08[1]	255.5	314.1	0	15.0	60.0	896.0	6.2	2.9	150.4	20.2	1.0	63.5	4,036

[1] Preliminary.   *Source: Economic Research Service, U.S. Department of Agriculture (ERS-USDA)*

U.S. Rice Exports by Export Program   In Thousands of Metric Tons

Year	PL 480	Section 416	CCC Credit Pro- grams[2]	CCC African Relief Exports	EEP[3]	Export Pro- grams[4]	Exports Outside Specified Export Programs	Total U.S. Rice Exports	% Export Programs as a Share of Total Exports
2003	263	0	----	0	0	310	4,169	4,478	7
2004	129	0	----	0	0	214	3,484	3,699	6
2005	126	0	----	0	0	150	4,108	4,258	4
2006	53	0	----	0	0	96	3,928	4,024	2
2007	97	0	----	0	0	136	3,180	3,316	4
2008[1]	78	0	----	0	0	108	3,938	4,046	3

[1] Preliminary.   [2] May not completely reflect exports made under these programs.   [3] Sales not shipments.   [4] Adjusted for estimated overlap between CCC export credit and EEP shipments.   *Source: Economice Research Service, U.S. Department of Agriculture (ERS-USDA)*

Production of Rice (Rough) in the United States, by Type and Variety   In Thousands of Cwt.

Year	Long Grain	Medium Grain	Short Grain	Total	Year	Long Grain	Medium Grain	Short Grain	Total
1999	151,863	50,540	3,624	206,027	2004	170,445	58,689	3,228	230,818
2000	128,756	59,514	2,602	190,872	2005	177,527	42,408	3,300	223,235
2001	167,555	46,105	1,610	215,270	2006	146,214	43,802	3,720	193,736
2002	157,243	52,201	1,516	210,960	2007	142,182	51,184	4,090	197,456
2003	149,011	48,180	2,706	199,897	2008[1]	154,733	45,516	3,227	203,733

[1] Preliminary.   *Source: National Agricultural Statistics Service, U.S. Department of Agriculture (NASS-USDA)*

Rubber

Rubber is a natural or synthetic substance characterized by elasticity, water repellence, and electrical resistance. Pre-Columbian Native South Americans discovered many uses for rubber such as containers, balls, shoes, and waterproofing for fabrics such as coats and capes. The Spaniards tried to duplicate these products for many years but were unsuccessful. The first commercial application of rubber began in 1791 when Samuel Peal patented a method of waterproofing cloth by treating it with a solution of rubber and turpentine. In 1839, Charles Goodyear revolutionized the rubber industry with his discovery of a process called vulcanization, which involves combining rubber and sulfur and heating the mixture.

Natural rubber is obtained from latex, a milky white fluid, from the Hevea Brasiliensis tree. The latex is gathered by cutting a chevron shape through the bark of the rubber tree. The latex is collected in a small cup, with approximately 1 fluid ounce per cutting. The cuttings are usually done every other day until the cuttings reach the ground. The tree is then allowed to renew itself before a new tapping is started. The collected latex is strained, diluted with water, and treated with acid to bind the rubber particles together. The rubber is then pressed between rollers to consolidate the rubber into slabs or thin sheets and is air-dried or smoke-dried for shipment.

During World War II, natural rubber supplies from the Far East were cut off, and the rubber shortage accelerated the development of synthetic rubber in the U.S. Synthetic rubber is produced by chemical reactions, condensation or polymerization, of certain unsaturated hydrocarbons. Synthetic rubber is made of raw material derived from petroleum, coal, oil, natural gas, and acetylene and is almost identical to natural rubber in chemical and physical properties.

Natural rubber and Rubber Index futures are traded on the Osaka Mercantile Exchange (OME). The OME's natural rubber contract is based on the RSS3 ribbed smoked sheet No. 3. The OME's Rubber Index Futures Contract is based on a composite of 8 component grades from 6 rubber markets in the world. Rubber futures are also traded on the Shanghai Futures Exchange (SHFE) and the Tokyo Commodity Exchange (TOCOM).

Prices – The average monthly price for spot crude rubber (No.1 smoked sheets, ribbed, plantation rubber), basis in New York, in 2007 rose +7.0% to a record high of 112.24 cents per pound. A 3-decade low of 33.88 cents per pound was seen as recently as 2001 during that recessionary year.

Supply – World production of natural rubber in 2007 rose +2.1% to a record high of 9.893 million metric tons. The world's largest producers of natural rubber in 2007 were Thailand with 31% of world production, Indonesia (28%), Malaysia (12%), India (8%), Vietnam (6%), and China (6%).

In 2007 world production of synthetic rubber rose by +6.8% to a record high of 13.596 million metric tons. The world's largest producers of synthetic rubber in 2007 were the U.S. with 20% of world production, Japan (12%), Russia (9%), and Germany (7%). U.S. production of synthetic rubber in 2007 rose +4.0% to 2.708 million metric tons from the 14-year low of 2.064 million metric tons posted in 2001. U.S. production of car and truck tires in 2007 fell 6.8% to 186.000 million tires.

Demand – World consumption of natural rubber in 2007 rose by +5.6% to a record high of 9.735 million metric tons. The largest consumers of natural rubber in 2007 were the U.S. with 11% of consumption, Japan with 9%, Brazil with 3%, and France, Germany, and the UK with a combined 6.1%. The world's consumption of natural rubber has tripled since 1970. World consumption of synthetic rubber in 2007 rose by +6.7% to a record high of 13.197 million metric tons. The largest consumers of synthetic rubber in 2007 were the U.S. with 15% of consumption, Japan with 9%, and France, Germany, and the UK with a combined 9.1%. The world's consumption of synthetic rubber has more than doubled since 1970.

U.S. consumption of natural rubber in 2007 rose by +1.5% to 1.018 million metric tons. U.S. consumption of natural rubber has more than doubled since 1970. U.S. consumption of synthetic rubber in 2007 fell 3.0% to 1.941 million metric tons. The U.S. consumption of synthetic rubber is about the same as it was in the 1970s.

Trade – World exports of natural rubber in 2007 rose by +0.5% to a record 6.985 million metric tons. The world's largest exporters of natural rubber in 2007 were Thailand with 39% of world exports and Indonesia with 34% of world exports.

U.S. imports of natural rubber in 2007 rose +1.5% to a record high of 1.018 million metric tons. U.S. exports of synthetic rubber in 2007 rose +5.3% to a record high of 1.317 million metric tons.

U.S. Imports of Natural Rubber (Includes Latex & Guayule)   In Thousands of Metric Tons

Year	Jan.	Feb.	Mar.	Apr.	May	June	July	Aug.	Sept.	Oct.	Nov.	Dec.	Total
1999	91.8	90.7	93.4	101.6	84.8	80.0	76.6	112.2	88.7	127.5	83.1	85.9	1,116.3
2000	127.4	88.2	114.1	107.9	114.9	120.1	65.9	96.2	79.2	96.2	92.2	89.3	1,191.6
2001	85.2	69.1	93.9	80.0	74.9	63.8	101.1	109.2	69.9	92.4	69.2	63.4	972.1
2002	104.8	71.2	79.2	90.8	106.1	92.2	108.6	109.7	81.1	94.7	83.0	88.9	1,110.3
2003	104.1	86.2	106.8	99.8	91.4	97.6	94.5	67.4	100.1	70.6	72.3	86.2	1,077.0
2004	116.2	76.6	101.7	96.5	112.6	92.0	87.6	81.7	85.5	120.4	71.0	101.8	1,143.6
2005	99.8	101.9	97.1	115.5	80.9	95.7	84.5	91.7	113.5	92.2	82.7	103.7	1,159.2
2006	113.3	71.8	98.9	80.5	115.6	72.5	72.4	97.3	58.7	83.0	82.0	57.2	1,003.2
2007[1]	86.1	67.7	102.1	90.7	63.4	113.3	74.3	83.8	90.6	81.8	80.3	84.3	1,018.4

[1] Preliminary.   *Source: International Rubber Study Group (IRSG)*

RUBBER

World Production[1] of Rubber   In Thousands of Metric Tons

				Natural								Synthetic		
Year	China	India	Indonesia	Malaysia	Sri Lanka	Thailand	Vietnam	World Total	Germany	Japan	United States	Russia	World Total
1998	450.0	591.1	1,714.0	885.7	95.7	2,075.9	220.0	6,820	619.0	1,520.1	2,600.0	621.0	9,840
1999	460.0	620.1	1,599.2	768.9	96.6	2,154.6	262.0	6,872	720.1	1,576.7	2,354.0	737.0	10,336
2000	445.0	629.0	1,501.1	927.6	87.6	2,346.4	290.8	6,762	849.2	1,591.7	2,396.8	837.1	10,818
2001	478.0	631.5	1,607.3	882.1	86.2	2,319.5	312.6	7,332	828.4	1,465.5	2,062.1	919.2	10,483
2002	527.0	640.8	1,630.0	889.8	90.5	2,615.1	331.4	7,337	869.2	1,522.0	2,164.4	919.0	10,882
2003	565.0	707.1	1,792.2	985.6	92.0	2,876.0	363.5	8,033	888.0	1,577.4	2,270.1	1,070.0	11,390
2004	573.0	742.6	2,066.2	1,168.7	94.7	2,984.3	419.0	8,756	905.0	1,616.1	2,325.1	1,116.1	12,019
2005	510.0	771.5	2,271.0	1,126.0	104.4	2,937.2	468.6	8,892	855.0	1,626.9	2,365.8	1,146.0	12,151
2006[1]	533.0	853.3	2,637.0	1,283.6	109.2	3,137.0	553.5	9,686	865.0	1,607.0	2,606.3	1,219.0	12,733
2007[2]	600.0	811.0	2,797.0	1,201.0	120.0	3,063.0	602.0	9,893	901.0	1,654.6	2,708.0	1,209.0	13,596

[1] Including rubber in the form of latex.   [2] Preliminary.   *Source: International Rubber Study Group (IRSG)*

World Consumption of Natural and Synthetic Rubber   In Thousands of Metric Tons

			Natural							Synthetic			
Year	Brazil	France	Germany	Japan	United Kingdom	United States	Total	France	Germany	Japan	United Kingdom	United States	Total
1998	185.3	223.0	247.0	707.3	139.0	1,157.4	6,580	451.4	582.0	1,115.7	177.0	2,354.4	9,830
1999	184.1	240.0	226.0	734.2	127.0	1,116.3	6,646	434.3	565.0	1,132.9	189.0	2,217.5	10,196
2000	226.6	270.0	250.0	751.8	122.5	1,194.8	7,381	481.5	632.0	1,137.5	188.0	2,189.5	10,764
2001	215.9	282.0	246.0	729.2	98.0	974.1	7,333	464.5	613.0	1,085.1	167.0	1,839.5	10,253
2002	233.4	230.7	247.0	749.0	76.0	1,110.8	7,628	469.3	612.0	1,096.0	210.0	1,895.0	10,692
2003	255.5	300.2	260.3	784.2	90.9	1,078.5	8,033	493.2	615.0	1,110.7	203.9	1,926.4	11,371
2004	284.9	230.1	242.3	814.8	86.3	1,143.6	8,715	420.1	624.5	1,146.3	213.5	1,906.8	11,839
2005	301.8	230.0	263.0	857.4	82.3	1,159.2	9,082	354.9	635.0	1,156.0	222.3	2,002.1	11,895
2006	286.4	219.6	269.2	873.7	67.7	1,003.1	9,216	310.8	635.0	1,170.8	200.6	2,000.8	12,371
2007[1]	327.2	220.0	286.3	888.0	87.9	1,018.4	9,735	316.0	710.0	1,162.0	168.7	1,940.4	13,197

[1] Preliminary.   *Source: International Rubber Study Group (IRSG)*

World Stocks[1] of Natural & Synthetic Rubber (by Countries) on January 1   In Thousands of Metric Tons

			In Producing Countries							In Consuming Countries (Reported Stocks)			
Year	Total Synthetic	Africa	Indonesia	Malaysia	Sri Lanka	Thailand	Vietnam	Total Natural	Brazil	India	Japan	United States	Total
1998	185.3	223.0	247.0	707.3	139.0	1,157.4	6,580	451.4	582.0	1,115.7	177.0	2,354.4	9,830
1999	184.1	240.0	226.0	734.2	127.0	1,116.3	6,646	434.3	565.0	1,132.9	189.0	2,217.5	10,196
2000	226.6	270.0	250.0	751.8	122.5	1,194.8	7,381	481.5	632.0	1,137.5	188.0	2,189.5	10,764
2001	215.9	282.0	246.0	729.2	98.0	974.1	7,333	464.5	613.0	1,085.1	167.0	1,839.5	10,253
2002	233.4	230.7	247.0	749.0	76.0	1,110.8	7,628	469.3	612.0	1,096.0	210.0	1,895.0	10,692
2003	255.5	300.2	260.3	784.2	90.9	1,078.5	8,033	493.2	615.0	1,110.7	203.9	1,926.4	11,371
2004	284.9	230.1	242.3	814.8	86.3	1,143.6	8,715	420.1	624.5	1,146.3	213.5	1,906.8	11,839
2005	301.8	230.0	263.0	857.4	82.3	1,159.2	9,082	354.9	635.0	1,156.0	222.3	2,002.1	11,895
2006	286.4	219.6	269.2	873.7	67.7	1,003.1	9,216	310.8	635.0	1,170.8	200.6	2,000.8	12,371
2007[1]	327.2	220.0	286.3	888.0	87.9	1,018.4	9,735	316.0	710.0	1,162.0	168.7	1,940.4	13,197

[1] Preliminary.   *Source: International Rubber Study Group (IRSG)*

Net Exports of Natural Rubber from Producing Areas   In Thousands of Metric Tons

Year	Cambodia	Guatemala[4]	Indonesia	Liberia	Malaysia	Nigeria	Sri Lanka	Thailand	Vietnam	Other Africa[2]	Other Asia[3]	Total
1998	29.0	24.6	1,641.2	75.0	424.9	46.5	41.4	1,839.4	181.0	181.7	62.8	4,650
1999	42.0	27.7	1,494.6	75.0	435.5	38.0	42.7	1,886.3	218.0	200.4	60.5	4,648
2000	39.0	31.8	1,379.6	73.5	429.8	36.0	32.6	2,166.2	254.0	207.4	61.8	5,000
2001	38.0	33.0	1,496.9	71.7	345.2	30.0	32.0	2,042.1	270.0	212.4	85.5	5,193
2002	40.0	40.1	1,502.2	73.0	430.1	24.0	36.1	2,354.4	278.0	199.8	90.5	5,155
2003	41.0	41.0	1,660.5	69.6	509.9	22.0	35.2	2,573.4	302.5	211.8	101.2	5,639
2004	40.5	52.9	1,875.1	74.4	679.9	29.0	40.3	2,637.1	340.0	222.0	94.3	6,174
2005	41.0	54.6	2,025.0	72.2	666.0	25.0	31.6	2,632.4	445.0	248.6	96.6	6,416
2006	60.0	55.4	2,287.0	60.3	619.0	28.0	45.8	2,771.6	474.0	270.6	91.8	6,947
2007[1]	63.0	68.7	2,379.0	68.4	600.1	29.0	48.5	2,710.0	525.0	284.4	102.8	6,985

[1] Preliminary.   [2] Includes Cameroon, Cote d'Ivoire, Gabon, Ghana and Zaire.   [3] Includes Myanmar, Papua New Guinea and the Philippines.
Source: International Rubber Study Group (IRSG)

Rubber (monthly average) through December 2007

Average Spot Crude Rubber Prices (Smoked Sheets[1]) in New York   In Cents Per Pound

Year	Jan.	Feb.	Mar.	Apr.	May	June	July	Aug.	Sept.	Oct.	Nov.	Dec.	Average
2000	38.16	40.36	38.17	37.80	37.76	37.07	36.65	37.90	37.35	37.61	37.02	36.90	37.73
2001	35.98	35.66	34.78	34.50	34.80	35.00	34.80	34.48	33.07	31.98	31.14	30.35	33.88
2002	32.21	34.45	36.50	36.38	36.93	43.53	44.32	45.20	47.90	45.70	44.97	45.39	41.12
2003	47.95	49.25	54.96	52.04	49.32	51.76	51.99	53.71	57.61	65.88	67.63	65.20	55.61
2004	65.63	67.28	68.09	68.84	70.40	69.90	68.10	66.50	66.39	67.30	66.80	63.90	67.43
2005	64.20	66.18	66.80	66.70	68.07	73.75	80.50	82.34	85.51	87.90	83.75	81.99	75.64
2006	93.04	104.01	104.48	105.20	115.03	131.74	124.01	114.94	95.17	94.77	87.95	88.53	104.91
2007	104.90	113.90	109.86	112.81	114.76	111.72	105.30	106.90	106.49	113.29	123.08	123.85	112.24

[1] No. 1, ribbed, plantation rubber.   *Source: International Rubber Study Group (IRSG)*

Natural Rubber Prices in London

Year	Jan.	Feb.	Mar.	Apr.	May	June	July	Aug.	Sept.	Oct.	Nov.	Dec.	Average
Buyers' Price RSS 1 (CIF)			In British Pounds per Metric Ton										
2003	1,058.7	1,133.6	1,211.6	1,147.2	1,087.4	1,141.2	1,146.1	1,184.2	1,270.0	1,452.5	1,491.0	1,437.5	1,230.1
2004	1,446.8	1,483.2	1,501.2	1,517.6	1,552.1	1,541.0	1,501.3	1,466.1	1,463.6	1,483.7	1,472.7	1,408.8	1,486.5
2005	1,415.4	1,459.1	1,472.7	1,470.5	1,500.7	1,626.0	1,774.7	1,815.2	1,885.2	1,937.8	1,846.4	1,807.5	1,667.6
2006	2,051.1	2,293.1	2,303.3	2,319.2	2,536.0	2,904.3	2,734.0	2,533.9	2,098.2	2,089.4	1,938.9	1,951.7	2,312.8
2007	2,312.7	2,511.1	2,421.9	2,487.0	2,530.1	2,463.0	2,321.5	2,356.8	2,347.6	2,497.5	2,713.5	2,730.4	2,474.4
Buyers' Prices RSS 3 (CIF)			In Euro per Metric Ton										
2003	930.6	987.3	1,046.6	968.7	905.6	949.7	956.9	1,021.4	1,086.1	1,197.3	1,182.0	1,091.5	1,027.0
2004	1,063.3	1,084.9	1,172.4	1,219.8	1,206.4	1,204.9	1,123.4	1,101.9	1,051.4	1,045.6	1,026.6	973.2	1,106.2
2005	957.2	992.6	1,066.7	1,094.0	1,142.5	1,292.6	1,492.2	1,405.8	1,484.3	1,525.3	1,454.3	1,528.5	1,286.3
2006	1,657.1	1,840.3	1,846.7	1,864.2	2,016.0	2,267.5	2,112.0	1,839.5	1,487.3	1,511.1	1,327.8	1,356.6	1,760.5
2007	1,652.3	1,800.8	1,741.9	1,766.8	1,765.0	1,721.8	1,558.0	1,607.0	1,621.5	1,707.2	1,761.8	1,776.2	1,706.7
Sellers' Prices SMR 20 (CIF)			In Euro per Metric Ton										
2003	915.0	937.7	942.2	888.2	795.4	800.0	834.4	911.0	1,040.7	1,174.7	1,166.0	1,087.6	957.7
2004	1,030.2	1,072.0	1,104.7	1,118.2	1,094.0	1,042.5	996.8	1,006.9	1,008.1	1,037.3	1,000.2	959.5	1,039.2
2005	950.5	985.8	991.1	1,012.1	1,018.7	1,138.6	1,292.6	1,254.0	1,385.5	1,410.0	1,442.3	1,485.8	1,197.3
2006	1,564.6	1,727.5	1,704.7	1,694.2	1,788.7	1,952.6	1,949.4	1,797.4	1,490.4	1,475.6	1,313.3	1,294.3	1,646.1
2007	1,547.5	1,688.5	1,599.0	1,541.6	1,678.7	1,622.3	1,532.3	1,565.7	1,679.5	1,654.6	1,691.0	1,723.6	1,627.0

Source: International Rubber Study Group (IRSG)

RUBBER

Consumption of Natural Rubber in the United States   In Thousands of Metric Tons

Year	Jan.	Feb.	Mar.	Apr.	May	June	July	Aug.	Sept.	Oct.	Nov.	Dec.	Total
1998	104.4	76.6	102.7	81.0	98.0	92.9	96.4	91.7	119.1	104.8	78.4	111.4	1,157.4
1999	92.0	92.0	93.0	88.0	88.0	88.0	92.0	92.0	92.0	100.0	100.0	100.0	1,116.3
2000	110.0	110.0	110.0	114.0	114.0	114.0	80.0	80.0	80.0	93.0	93.0	93.0	1,194.8
2001	85.5	69.4	94.1	80.2	75.1	64.1	101.2	109.3	70.0	92.4	69.4	63.4	974.1
2002	104.9	71.3	79.2	90.4	106.3	92.3	108.7	109.7	81.2	94.7	83.1	89.0	1,110.8
2003	104.2	86.3	106.9	100.1	91.2	97.7	94.6	67.5	101.3	69.9	72.5	86.3	1,078.5
2004	116.0	76.5	101.5	96.5	112.5	92.5	87.5	82.0	86.0	120.0	71.0	101.8	1,143.8
2005	99.8	101.9	97.1	115.5	80.9	95.7	84.5	91.7	113.5	92.2	82.7	103.7	1,159.2
2006	113.3	71.8	98.9	80.5	115.6	72.5	72.4	97.3	58.7	83.0	82.0	57.2	1,003.2
2007[1]	86.1	67.7	102.1	90.7	63.4	113.3	74.3	83.8	90.6	81.8	80.3	84.3	1,018.4

[1] Preliminary.   Source: International Rubber Study Group (IRSG)

Stocks of Natural Rubber in the United States, on First of Month   In Thousands of Metric Tons

Year	Jan.	Feb.	Mar.	Apr.	May	June	July	Aug.	Sept.	Oct.	Nov.	Dec.
1998	57.2	61.2	65.5	63.5	60.9	66.7	53.6	57.9	54.7	58.3	58.9	66.5
1999	70.4	68.0	66.0	64.0	62.0	60.0	58.0	56.0	54.0	52.0	50.0	48.0
2000	46.0	63.4	41.6	45.7	39.6	40.5	46.6	32.5	48.7	47.9	51.1	50.3
2001	46.6	44.3	44.0	43.8	43.6	43.4	43.1	43.0	42.9	42.8	42.8	42.6
2002	42.6	42.5	42.4	42.4	42.8	42.6	42.5	42.4	42.4	42.3	42.3	42.2
2003	42.1	42.0	41.9	41.8	41.5	41.7	41.6	41.5	41.4	40.2	40.9	40.7
2004	40.6	40.8	40.9	40.9	40.9	40.9	40.9	40.9	40.9	40.9	40.9	40.9
2005	40.6	40.6	40.6	40.6	40.6	40.6	40.6	40.6	40.6	40.6	40.6	40.6
2006	40.6	40.6	40.6	40.6	40.6	40.6	40.6	40.6	40.6	40.6	40.6	40.6
2007[1]	40.6	40.6	40.6	40.6	40.6	40.6	40.6	40.6	40.6	40.6	40.6	40.6

[1] Preliminary.   Source: International Rubber Study Group (IRSG)

Stocks of Synthetic Rubber in the United States, on First of Month   In Thousands of Metric Tons

Year	Jan.	Feb.	Mar.	Apr.	May	June	July	Aug.	Sept.	Oct.	Nov.	Dec.
1998	377.7	382.2	375.7	379.5	387.5	402.8	394.6	406.8	394.2	398.7	395.7	396.5
1999	409.3	404.0	404.0	406.0	399.0	420.0	410.0	419.0	413.0	390.0	391.0	389.0
2000	406.0	416.0	413.0	402.0	405.0	416.0	409.0	418.0	400.0	412.0	407.0	419.0
2001	433.0	451.0	467.0	4,559.0	448.0	433.0	426.0	420.0	394.0	400.0	394.0	379.0
2002	392.0	377.0	379.0	393.0	398.0	384.0	385.0	381.0	364.0	375.0	364.0	358.0
2003	390.0	325.0	330.0	325.0	336.0	336.0	332.0	332.0	331.0	328.0	317.0	338.0
2004	343.0	347.0	335.0	315.0	310.0	300.0	300.0	290.0	280.0	280.0	280.0	270.0
2005	260.0	255.0	240.0	240.0	235.0	235.0	240.0	245.0	245.0	245.0	245.0	245.0
2006	248.0	240.0	225.0	215.0	210.0	210.0	210.0	210.0	210.0	210.0	210.0	210.0
2007[1]	210.0	210.0	210.0	210.0	210.0	210.0	210.0	210.0	210.0	210.0	210.0	210.0

[1] Preliminary.   Source: International Rubber Study Group (IRSG)

Production of Synthetic Rubber in the United States   In Thousands of Metric Tons

Year	Jan.	Feb.	Mar.	Apr.	May	June	July	Aug.	Sept.	Oct.	Nov.	Dec.	Total
1998	230.0	200.0	230.0	220.0	240.0	210.0	220.0	210.0	230.0	210.0	200.0	210.0	2,610
1999	200.0	181.0	209.0	195.0	205.0	190.0	199.0	192.0	180.0	204.0	197.0	202.0	2,354
2000	202.0	202.0	214.0	193.0	216.0	202.0	198.0	187.0	193.0	197.0	194.0	184.0	2,382
2001	203.0	188.6	184.3	172.1	175.5	162.3	166.7	164.7	174.3	178.6	155.1	139.2	2,064
2002	176.1	171.9	192.3	190.6	187.0	184.6	183.5	177.3	175.1	175.0	160.4	176.4	2,150
2003	185.6	180.9	193.6	179.8	182.9	166.3	174.2	172.9	188.4	189.7	192.0	185.6	2,192
2004	208.3	199.0	203.5	193.5	187.1	183.5	183.5	184.1	193.5	198.5	202.1	188.5	2,325
2005	206.9	204.8	209.4	202.7	196.9	188.9	187.3	193.7	182.7	185.8	206.9	199.8	2,366
2006	212.9	213.7	212.9	210.2	227.5	217.8	218.1	218.2	218.5	218.3	220.4	214.9	2,603
2007[1]	224.3	223.1	222.6	222.6	227.4	227.8	227.9	227.5	228.4	227.5	224.0	225.0	2,708

[1] Preliminary.   Source: International Rubber Study Group (IRSG)

Consumption of Synthetic Rubber in the United States   In Thousands of Metric Tons

Year	Jan.	Feb.	Mar.	Apr.	May	June	July	Aug.	Sept.	Oct.	Nov.	Dec.	Total
1998	196.5	192.5	214.8	194.4	199.8	201.4	192.0	204.5	202.2	200.3	181.2	174.8	2,354
1999	164.0	166.0	195.0	178.0	170.0	186.0	177.0	176.0	191.0	171.0	178.0	161.0	2,218
2000	173.0	185.0	202.0	178.0	194.0	196.0	177.0	189.0	172.0	182.0	168.0	147.0	2,190
2001	170.8	149.6	166.8	153.3	159.8	148.6	156.4	173.0	145.7	162.7	140.8	112.0	1,840
2002	155.5	146.8	153.0	165.8	173.4	160.4	161.5	169.3	154.8	166.7	148.2	139.6	1,895
2003	166.1	156.4	167.7	157.8	162.0	163.0	163.3	152.3	159.0	175.6	147.3	155.9	1,926
2004	170.0	166.2	176.0	156.5	152.2	141.9	158.8	149.2	152.9	155.0	170.0	158.1	1,907
2005	174.7	184.0	180.6	171.5	156.8	147.9	145.2	148.9	153.7	161.2	166.8	163.3	1,955
2006	173.7	182.7	178.0	170.7	172.2	167.4	157.7	158.1	161.5	161.5	160.9	156.6	2,001
2007[1]	157.8	155.0	155.6	164.6	163.8	166.1	165.6	160.4	166.6	163.6	163.0	158.4	1,941

[1] Preliminary.   *Source: International Rubber Study Group (IRSG)*

U.S. Exports of Synthetic Rubber   In Thousands of Metric Tons

Year	Jan.	Feb.	Mar.	Apr.	May	June	July	Aug.	Sept.	Oct.	Nov.	Dec.	Total
1998	61.1	60.8	62.8	59.8	66.9	61.8	60.1	64.4	63.7	62.3	59.2	59.2	742.1
1999	57.6	63.3	65.0	70.5	64.7	66.0	61.5	68.2	65.1	79.0	70.2	65.7	796.8
2000	64.3	73.4	83.8	70.2	73.2	72.3	72.4	78.6	78.6	75.2	73.3	70.7	886.0
2001	74.6	67.3	76.4	78.2	75.1	69.6	70.6	71.6	68.1	70.7	62.4	59.4	844.4
2002	67.9	71.6	69.5	74.9	78.5	73.6	74.5	72.8	70.9	73.1	70.8	66.3	864.4
2003	73.1	70.1	80.1	85.2	78.4	75.3	74.4	72.4	73.9	83.7	74.5	79.3	920.4
2004	82.0	87.3	97.0	90.9	96.8	92.6	88.9	91.6	94.8	89.0	87.0	81.6	1,079.5
2005	86.3	89.6	91.8	98.4	98.3	96.9	91.5	100.4	76.4	87.0	101.3	87.5	1,105.4
2006	103.4	97.3	106.7	103.2	109.2	106.8	110.0	112.5	101.3	103.3	97.8	98.5	1,250.0
2007[1]	110.5	108.6	118.0	107.8	116.0	109.7	108.8	112.9	106.3	111.7	104.1	102.1	1,316.5

[1] Preliminary.   *Source: International Rubber Study Group (IRSG)*

Production of Tyres (Car and Truck) in the United States   In Thousands of Units

Year	First Quarter	Second Quarter	Third Quarter	Fourth Quarter	Total	Year	First Quarter	Second Quarter	Third Quarter	Fourth Quarter	Total
1988	54,677	52,986	51,195	52,493	211,351	1998	----	----	----	----	270,905
1989	56,716	56,626	50,086	49,444	212,870	1999	----	----	----	----	267,652
1990	55,915	53,856	51,163	49,729	210,663	2000	----	----	----	----	276,765
1991	51,296	52,796	49,183	51,115	202,391	2001	65,367	62,809	62,366	56,106	255,700
1992	57,890	57,319	57,554	57,487	230,250	2002	62,937	64,362	60,524	58,241	246,064
1993	61,809	60,752	57,702	57,184	237,447	2003	62,686	59,311	58,441	55,565	236,003
1994	63,586	63,331	57,018	59,442	243,696	2004	60,272	59,774	58,389	54,824	233,259
1995	63,800	63,800	63,800	63,754	255,521	2005	57,377	58,832	54,920	52,074	223,203
1996	64,000	64,000	64,000	63,700	255,723	2006[1]	56,787	53,452	49,612	39,636	199,487
1997	----	----	----	----	263,860	2007[2]	46,600	44,500	45,700	49,200	186,000

[1] Preliminary.   [2] Estimate.   *Source: International Rubber Study Group (IRSG)*

U.S. Foreign Trade of Tyres (Car and Truck)   In Thousands of Units

Year	Imports — First Quarter	Second Quarter	Third Quarter	Fourth Quarter	Total	Exports — First Quarter	Second Quarter	Third Quarter	Fourth Quarter	Total
1998	17,046	17,728	18,016	19,346	72,124	12,840	10,678	10,018	10,372	43,923
1999	19,471	22,295	22,194	23,784	87,768	9,874	9,580	10,480	10,537	40,945
2000	24,200	24,698	23,561	22,123	94,019	11,200	10,200	10,200	10,100	44,164
2001	19,563	22,251	22,072	20,956	84,842	10,087	10,362	11,004	10,691	42,144
2002	21,554	25,831	24,868	24,950	97,203	10,438	10,379	10,167	10,380	41,363
2003	26,310	28,557	28,472	27,536	110,875	9,293	2,648	10,263	10,794	32,998
2004	28,996	31,998	30,788	32,707	124,489	10,272	10,902	10,108	10,299	41,581
2005	32,704	36,924	34,391	33,584	137,603	9,808	10,071	10,659	10,570	41,108
2006[1]	34,562	36,863	34,638	36,136	142,199	9,021	9,328	9,388	9,236	36,973
2007[2]	35,984	39,428	38,778	38,273	152,463	8,922	9,360	9,539	9,417	37,238

[1] Preliminary.   [2] Estimate.   *Source: International Rubber Study Group (IRSG)*

Rye

Rye is a cereal grain and a member of the grass family. Hardy varieties of rye have been developed for winter planting. Rye is most widely grown in northern Europe and Asia. In the U.S., rye is used as an animal feed and as an ingredient in bread and some whiskeys. Bread using rye was developed in northern Europe in the Middle Ages where bakers developed dark, hearty bread consisting of rye, oat and barley flours. Those were crops that grew more readily in the wet and damp climate of northern Europe, as opposed to wheat which fares better in the warmer and drier climates in central Europe. Modern rye bread is made with a mixture of white and rye flours. Coarsely ground rye flour is also used in pumpernickel bread and helps provide the dark color and course texture, along with molasses. The major producing states are North and South Dakota, Oklahoma, and Georgia. The crop year runs from June to May.

Supply – World rye production in 2008-09 marketing year rose by +21.6% yr/yr to 17.326 million metric tons, up from the 2006-07 record low of 12.382 million metric tons. The world's largest producers of rye are the European Union with 53% of world production in 2008-09, followed by Russia with 26%, Belarus with 9%, and the Ukraine with 6%. U.S. production of rye accounted for only 1.2% of world production.

U.S. production of rye in 2007 (latest data) rose +10.0% to 7.914 million bushels but that was far below the production levels of over 20 million bushels seen from the late 1800s through the 1960s. U.S. production of rye fell off in the 1970s, and fell to a record low of 6.971 million bushels in 2002.

U.S. acreage harvested with rye in 2008-09 fell -8.0% to 266,000 acres, down from last year's level of 289,000 acres. U.S. farmers in the late 1800s through the 1960s typically harvested more than 1 million acres of rye, showing how domestic planting of rye has dropped off sharply in the past several decades.

Rye yield in 2007-08 rose +4.2% to 27.4 bushels per acre, but that is still well below the record high of 33.1 bushels per acre posted in 1984-85. Modern rye production yields are, however, more than double the levels in the teens seen prior to the 1960s when yields started to rise.

Demand – Total U.S. domestic usage of rye in 2007-08 fell 3.4% yr/yr to 12.800 million bushels. The breakdown of domestic usage shows that 26% of rye in 2007-08 was used for food, 23% by industry, 23% as seed, and 3% as feed and residual.

Trade – World exports of rye in the 2008-09 marketing year rose +0.8% yr/yr to 560.000 metric tons, up from the record low of 556,000 metric tons last year. The largest exporter was the European Union with exports of 250,000 metric tons. World imports of rye rose +18.2% to 513,000 metric tons. U.S. imports of rye in 2008-09 fell 29.1% yr/yr to 127,000 metric tons.

World Production of Rye   In Thousands of Metric Tons

Crop Year	Argentina	Australia	Belarus	Canada	European Union	Kazakhstan	Romania	Russia	Switzerland	Turkey	Ukraine	United States	World Total
1999-00	116	20	929	387	11,478	20		4,800	20	233	919	280	19,278
2000-01	125	20	1,360	260	10,268	50		5,450	20	260	966	213	19,064
2001-02	81	20	1,294	228	11,956	75		6,600	20	220	1,822	175	22,562
2002-03	80	20	1,600	134	9,255	50		7,150	20	255	1,511	165	20,308
2003-04	37	20	1,200	327	6,972	50		4,200	20	240	625	219	13,983
2004-05	89	20	1,400	398	10,031	50		2,850	20	240	1,600	210	17,002
2005-06	55	20	1,150	330	7,688	50		3,600	20	240	1,050	191	14,492
2006-07[1]	55	20	1,200	383	6,541	50		3,000	20	240	600	183	12,382
2007-08[2]	55	20	1,300	233	7,620	50		3,900	20	240	550	160	14,245
2008-09[3]	55	20	1,600	320	9,171	50		4,500	20	240	1,050	203	17,326

[1] Preliminary.   [2] Estimate.   [3] Forecast.   *Source: Foreign Agricultural Service, U.S. Department of Agriculture (FAS-USDA)*

World Imports and Exports of Rye   In Thousands of Metric Tons

	Imports							Exports					
Year	European Union	Japan	Rep. of Korea	Turkey	Russia	United States	World Total	Belarus	Canada	European Union	Russia	United States	World Total
1999-00	3	397	476	142	464	87	1,979	----	87	1,794	----	7	2,096
2000-01	2	337	57	----	193	82	765	50	91	814	----	10	966
2001-02	307	335	121	20	7	126	1,056	30	66	647	4	5	1,046
2002-03	436	414	31	14	----	156	1,356	110	53	669	291	3	1,414
2003-04	99	341	114	43	6	83	845	60	171	506	156	1	905
2004-05	----	261	8	59	172	143	782	50	122	574	----	4	854
2005-06	9	279	7	7	49	139	623	50	132	359	----	----	610
2006-07[1]	25	258	8	5	50	150	623	75	208	424	----	2	709
2007-08[2]	98	83	6	25	5	179	434	150	191	76	119	7	556
2008-09[3]	50	225	5	5	----	127	513	50	50	250	100	10	560

[1] Preliminary.   [2] Estimate.   [3] Forecast.   *Source: Foreign Agricultural Service, U.S. Department of Agriculture (FAS-USDA)*

Rye (monthly average) through 2007/08   Cents per bushel

Production of Rye in the United States   In Thousands of Bushels

Year	Georgia	Kansas	Mich-igan	Minne-sota	Neb-raska	Dakota	Okla-homa	Penn-ylvania	Carolina	Dakota	Texas	Wis-consin	Total
1999	1,050	300	756	775	405	1,517	1,045	600	500	1,012	450	384	11,038
2000	1,170	2	2	2	2	704	1,470	2	2	546	2	2	8,386
2001	875	2	2	2	2	340	1,150	2	2	350	2	2	6,971
2002	560	2	2	2	2	210	1,300	2	2	270	2	2	6,488
2003	800	2	2	2	2	750	1,540	2	2	672	2	2	8,634
2004	600	2	2	2	2	780	1,620	2	2	649	2	2	8,255
2005	810	2	2	2	2	2	1,400	2	2	2	2	2	7,537
2006	650	2	2	2	2	2	1,040	2	2	2	2	2	7,193
2007	800	2	2	2	2	2	1,080	2	2	2	2	2	6,311
2008[1]	1,200	2	2	2	2	2	1,045	2	2	2	2	2	7,979

[1] Preliminary.   [2] Estimates not published beginning in 2000.   *Source: Agricultural Statistics Board, U.S. Department of Agriculture (ASB-USDA)*

Salient Statistics of Rye in the United States   In Thousands of Bushels

Crop Year Beginning June 1	Supply — Stocks June 1	Supply — Pro-duction	Supply — Imports	Supply — Total Supply	Domestic Use — Food	Domestic Use — Industry	Domestic Use — Seed	Domestic Use — Feed & Residual	Domestic Use — Total	Exports	Total Disap-pearance	Acreage — Planted 1,000 Acres	Acreage — Harvested for Grain 1,000 Acres	Yield Per Harvested Acre (Bushels)
1999-00	2,449	11,038	3,424	16,911	3,300	3,000	3,000	5,736	15,036	286	15,322	1,582	383	28.8
2000-01	1,589	8,386	3,230	13,205	3,300	3,000	3,000	2,325	11,625	390	12,015	1,329	296	28.3
2001-02	1,190	6,971	4,945	13,106	3,300	3,000	3,000	2,970	12,270	193	12,463	1,328	255	27.3
2002-03	568	6,488	6,140	13,196	3,300	3,000	3,000	3,329	12,629	122	12,751	1,355	263	24.8
2003-04	445	8,634	3,286	12,365	3,300	3,000	3,000	2,425	11,725	60	11,785	1,348	319	27.1
2004-05	584	8,255	5,626	14,465	3,300	3,000	3,000	4,237	13,537	145	13,682	1,380	300	27.5
2005-06	790	7,537	5,480	13,807	3,300	3,000	3,000	3,790	13,090	10	13,110	1,433	279	27.0
2006-07[1]	710	7,193	5,900	13,803	3,300	3,000	3,000	3,950	13,250	70	13,320	1,396	274	26.3
2007-08[2]	480	6,311	5,000	11,791	3,300	3,000	3,000	350	12,800	100	12,900	1,334	252	25.0
2008-09[3]		7,979										1,260	269	29.7

[1] Preliminary.   [2] Estimate.   [3] Forecast   *Source: Economic Research Service, U.S. Department of Agriculture (ERS-USDA)*

Salt

Salt, also known as sodium chloride, is a chemical compound that is an essential element in the diet of humans, animals, and even many plants. Since prehistoric times, salt has been used to preserve foods and was commonly used in the religious rites of the Greeks, Romans, Hebrews, and Christians. Salt, in the form of salt cakes, served as money in ancient Ethiopia and Tibet. As long ago as 1450 BC, Egyptian art shows records of salt production.

The simplest method of obtaining salt is through the evaporation of salt water from areas near oceans or seas. In most regions, rock salt is obtained from underground mining or by wells sunk into deposits. Salt is soluble in water, is slightly soluble in alcohol, but is insoluble in concentrated hydrochloric acid. In its crystalline form, salt is transparent and colorless, shining with an ice-like luster.

Prices – Salt prices in 2008 (FOB mine, vacuum and open pan) rose +0.3% yr/yr to $155.00 per ton, which was a new record high.

Supply – World production of salt in 2008 rose +1.2% yr/yr to 260.000 million metric tons. The world's largest salt producers were China with 23% and the U.S. with 18% of world production in 2008. U.S. salt production in 2008 rose +3.4% yr/yr to 46.000 million metric tons.

Demand – U.S. consumption of salt in 2008 rose +3.8% to 55.200 million metric tons, but that is still down from the 2005 record high of 56.200 million metric tons.

Trade – The U.S. relied on imports for 18% of its salt consumption in 2008, down from 23% in 2004. U.S. imports of salt for consumption in 2008 rose +15.7% yr/yr to 10.000 million metric tons, but still below 2003's record high of 12.9 million metric tons. U.S. exports of salt in 2008 fell by -4.0% to 800,000 metric tons, with the bulk of those exports going to Canada.

World Production of All Salt   In Thousands of Metric Tons

Year	Australia	Canada	China	France	Germany	India	Italy	Mexico	Poland	Spain	United Kingdom	United States	World Total
2001	9,536	13,725	34,105	7,000	14,343	14,503	3,600	8,501	3,476	3,200	5,800	44,800	214,000
2002	9,961	12,736	36,024	6,400	15,736	14,500	3,343	7,802	3,558	3,894	5,700	40,300	214,000
2003	10,256	13,718	32,424	6,673	16,424	15,000	2,922	7,547	4,660	3,963	5,900	43,700	225,000
2004	11,088	14,096	37,101	6,910	18,838	15,000	2,876	8,566	5,142	3,993	5,800	46,500	236,000
2005	12,444	13,643	46,610	6,730	19,333	15,500	3,476	9,508	4,190	4,550	5,800	45,200	250,000
2006	11,363	14,389	56,630	8,718	19,846	15,500	3,438	8,371	4,955	4,550	5,800	44,400	262,000
2007[1]	11,400	11,800	59,800	6,100	19,800	16,000	2,200	8,400	4,400	4,600	5,800	44,500	257,000
2008[2]	12,000	12,000	60,000	6,000	19,000	15,800	2,200	8,400	4,400	4,600	5,800	46,000	260,000

[1] Preliminary.   [2] Estimate.   *Source: U.S. Geological Survey (USGS)*

Salient Statistics of the Salt Industry in the United States   In Thousands of Metric Tons

Year	Net Import Reliance As a % of Apparent Consumption	Average Value FOB Mine Vacuum & Open Pan ($ Per Ton)	Production Total	Production Open & Vacuum Pan	Production Solar	Production Rock	Production Brine	Sold or Used, Producers Open & Vacuum Pan	Sold or Used, Producers Rock	Sold or Used, Producers Brine	Total Salt	Value[3] Million $	Imports for Consumption	Exports Total	Exports To Canada	Apparent Consumption
2000	15	113.95	45,600	4,200	3,810	15,000	22,500	4,190	13,600	22,500	43,300	1,040.0	8,960	642	500	51,600
2001	17	120.02	44,800	4,120	3,310	17,000	20,400	4,090	14,600	20,400	42,200	1,110.0	12,900	1,120	984	54,000
2002	18	120.02	40,300	4,100	3,390	13,500	19,300	4,070	11,400	19,300	37,700	1,010.0	8,160	689	585	45,100
2003	17	124.24	43,700	4,070	3,330	16,300	20,000	4,010	14,100	20,000	41,100	1,130.0	12,900	718	585	53,200
2004	23	128.39	46,500	4,100	3,520	18,300	20,500	4,040	17,400	20,500	45,000	1,270.0	11,900	1,110	971	55,800
2005	20	130.75	45,100	4,170	3,430	17,700	19,900	3,970	18,100	19,800	45,000	1,310.0	12,100	879	686	56,200
2006[1]	17	145.90	44,400	4,450	3,640	16,500	19,800	4,300	13,500	19,800	40,600	1,310.0	9,490	973	775	49,100
2007[1]	15	154.95	44,500	4,420	3,570	16,800	19,700	4,310	18,400	19,600	45,400	1,520.0	8,640	833	588	53,200

[1] Preliminary.   [2] Estimate.   [3] Values are f.o.b. mine or refinery & do not include cost of cooperage or containers.   *Source: U.S. Geological Survey (USGS)*

Salt Sold or Used by Producers in the U.S. by Classes & Consumers or Uses   In Thousands of Metric Tons

Year	Chemical[2]	Tanning Leather	Textile & Dyeing	Meat Packers[3]	Canning	Baking	Agricultural Distribution	Feed Dealers	Feed Manufacturers	Rubber	Oil	Paper & Pulp	Metal Processing	Water Treatment	Grocery Stores	Water Conditioning Distrib.	Ice Control and/or Stabilization
2000	22,400	82	209	402	220	234	262	1,240	540	71	2,510	106	112	589	823	568	19,700
2001	20,100	87	172	411	213	242	280	1,170	533	61	2,260	100	124	512	824	560	16,800
2002	19,500	79	154	395	230	215	245	1,040	507	61	2,010	93	118	662	781	525	13,300
2003	20,100	71	151	374	231	210	215	1,090	460	67	2,210	88	126	777	802	537	18,500
2004	20,400	56	145	385	225	209	242	1,090	451	69	2,350	86	112	858	794	514	18,000
2005	19,700	55	149	398	211	204	227	1,140	477	65	2,210	81	107	1,140	803	511	21,000
2006	18,400	50	121	380	208	203	211	1,090	502	66	2,150	72	49	952	770	489	12,400
2007[1]	21,400	41	98	305	198	149	385	1,160	457	6	211	60	36	1,120	943	522	20,800

[1] Preliminary.   [2] Chloralkali producers and other chemical.   *Source: U.S. Geological Survey (USGS)*

Sheep and Lambs

Sheep and lambs are raised for both their wool and meat. In countries that have high wool production, there is also demand for sheep and lamb meat due to the easy availability. Production levels have declined in New Zealand and Australia, but that has been counteracted by a substantial increase in China.

Prices – The average monthly price received by farmers for lambs in the U.S. in 2008 rose by +2.3% to 99.42 cents per pound, but remained well below the record high o 110.67 cents per pound seen in 2005. The average monthly price received by U.S. farmers for sheep in 2008 fell by 11.4% to a 15-year low of 27.41 cents per pound. The average monthly wholesale price of slaughter lambs

(choice) at San Angelo, Texas in 2008 rose by +0.8% to 85.66 cents per pound, but remained below the 2005 record high of 97.76 cents per pound.

Supply – World sheep and goat numbers in 2007 (latest data available) rose by +0.4% to a new record high of 1.963 billion head. The world's largest producers of sheep and goats are China with 19% of world production in 2008, India (10%), Australia (5%), and New Zealand (2%). The number of sheep and lambs on U.S. farms in 2007 (Jan 1) fell –0.7% to 6.185 million head. The U.S. states with the most sheep and lambs were Texas (with 17% of the U.S. total), California (10%), Wyoming (7%), Colorado (7%), and South Dakota (6%).

World Sheep and Goat Numbers in Specified Countries on January 1   In Thousands of Head

Year	Argen-tina	Australia	China	India	Kazak-hstan	New Zealand	Romania	Russia	South Africa	Spain	Turkey	United Kingdom	World Total
1998	16,900	117,711	256,073	181,128	10,384	44,628	9,548	18,774	35,903	27,864	38,614	44,548	1,739,316
1999	17,106	115,676	269,309	182,051	9,527	45,866	8,994	15,556	35,137	26,969	37,492	44,736	1,760,535
2000	17,052	118,812	279,496	182,980	9,657	42,443	8,679	14,751	35,257	26,592	38,030	42,341	1,776,344
2001	16,887	111,195	290,522	183,918	9,981	40,173	8,195	14,773	35,350	27,276	35,693	36,792	1,770,094
2002	16,400	106,566	297,370	184,864	10,479	39,725	7,776	15,327	32,452	26,860	33,994	35,909	1,779,675
2003	16,650	99,672	316,714	185,827	11,273	39,707	7,945	16,051	32,178	26,650	31,954	35,939	1,816,742
2004	16,650	101,882	340,693	186,789	12,247	39,424	8,125	17,030	31,732	25,743	32,203	35,937	1,877,702
2005	16,650	101,586	366,641	187,760	13,409	40,035	8,086	17,771	31,690	25,654	31,811	35,345	1,935,980
2006[1]	16,600	100,555	372,924	188,739	14,335	40,253	8,298	18,213	31,383	25,408	31,822	34,818	1,955,407
2007[2]	16,700	100,452	369,230	189,725	15,350	40,160	8,405	19,675	31,400	24,694	31,900	33,677	1,962,741

[1] Preliminary.   [2] Forecast.   *Source: Food and Agricultural Organization of the United Nations (FAO-UN)*

Salient Statistics of Sheep & Lambs in the United States (Average Live Weight)   In Thousands of Head

| | - Inventory, Jan. 1 - | | | | --- Marketings[3] --- | | ---------- Slaughter ---------- | | | | | Pro-duction (Live Weight) | Farm Value ------ Jan. 1 ------- | |
Year	Without New Crop Lambs	With New Crop Lambs	Lamb Crop	Total Supply	Sheep	Lambs	Farm	Com-mercial	Total[4]	Net Exports	Total Disap-pearance	(Mil. Lbs.)		Total
1999	7,215	7,215	4,733	11,948	790	5,208	65	3,701	3,766	393	4,922	533.6	637.6	88.0
2000	7,032	7,032	4,622	11,654	788	4,827	67	3,460	3,527	329	4,554	508.9	668.8	95.0
2001	6,965	6,965	4,495	11,460	711	4,795	68	3,222	3,290	299	4,303	495.6	694.5	100.0
2002	6,685	6,685	4,357	11,042	855	4,794	66	3,286	3,352	266	4,380	485.1	618.1	94.0
2003	6,300	6,321	4,140	10,461	828	4,387	67	2,979	3,046	105	3,804	470.1	656.6	104.0
2004	6,105	6,105	4,096	10,201	695	4,184	65	2,839	2,904			464.0	723.8	119.0
2005	6,135	6,135	4,117	10,252	669	4,200	64	2,698	2,762			473.3	799.3	130.0
2006	6,230	6,230	4,065	10,295	692	4,196	69	2,699	2,768			463.1	875.4	141.0
2007[1]	6,165	6,165	3,895	10,060	748	4,095	79	2,692	2,771			473.1	823.8	134.0
2008[2]	6,055	6,055	3,710	9,765								460.8	836.1	1,383.0

[1] Preliminary.   [2] Estimate.   [3] Excludes interfarm sales.   [4] Includes all commercial and farm.
Source: Economic Research Service, U.S. Department of Agriculture (ERS-USDA)

Sheep and Lambs[3] on Farms in the United States on January 1   In Thousands of Head

Year	Cali-fornia	Colo-rado	Idaho	Iowa	Minne-sota	Mon-tana	Mexico	Ohio	Dakota	Texas	Utah	Wyo-ming	Total
2001	840	420	275	270	170	360	255	142	420	1,150	390	530	6,965
2002	800	370	260	250	160	335	230	140	400	1,130	365	480	6,685
2003	730	380	260	255	145	310	175	150	380	1,040	310	460	6,300
2004	680	360	260	250	140	300	160	140	370	1,100	265	430	6,105
2005	670	365	270	245	145	305	145	142	375	1,070	270	450	6,135
2006	650	390	260	235	155	295	155	141	385	1,090	280	450	6,230
2007	610	400	260	235	150	290	130	141	380	1,050	295	460	6,165
2008[1]	620	420	235	225	145	270	130	125	340	960	280	425	5,950
2009[2]	660	410	210	200	140	255	120	130	305	870	290	420	5,747

[1] Preliminary.   [2] Estimate.   [3] Includes sheep & lambs on feed for market and stock sheep & lambs.   *Source: Economic Research Service, U.S. Department of Agriculture (ERS-USDA)*

SHEEP AND LAMBS

Average Wholesale Price of Slaughter Lambs (Choice[2]) at San Angelo Texas   In Dollars Per Hundred Pounds (Cwt.)

Year	Jan.	Feb.	Mar.	Apr.	May	June	July	Aug.	Sept.	Oct.	Nov.	Dec.	Average
2000	73.71	76.83	78.17	78.25	89.65	78.30	84.17	82.20	82.00	77.50	76.70	75.33	79.40
2001	81.25	87.00	82.63	83.30	86.07	75.21	69.82	54.47	56.50	57.67	59.00	71.60	72.04
2002	65.85	70.00	64.00	65.15	64.06	68.75	75.83	74.35	73.69	76.20	83.00	86.88	72.31
2003	89.25	90.25	96.25	88.13	95.75	97.25	87.88	85.81	91.44	91.31	91.00	96.17	91.71
2004	99.44	99.94	102.50	92.31	97.50	101.37	97.50	91.12	92.25	91.75	95.58	99.12	96.70
2005	107.25	109.69	101.37	99.37	96.94	99.50	95.00	92.14	91.56	93.00	93.33	94.00	97.76
2006	86.75	76.87	67.47	60.60	68.16	70.94	74.00	84.00	85.30	85.18	85.40	83.00	77.31
2007	81.00	82.27	84.50	85.25	84.20	77.40	86.38	86.19	89.44	84.90	84.83	92.92	84.94
2008[1]	86.63	88.82	83.25	74.70	77.75	86.75	88.81	88.13	89.54	85.55	85.46	95.83	85.94

[1] Preliminary.   *Source: Economic Research Service, U.S. Department of Agriculture (ERS-USDA)*

Federally Inspected Slaughter of Sheep & Lambs in the United States   In Thousands of Head

Year	Jan.	Feb.	Mar.	Apr.	May	June	July	Aug.	Sept.	Oct.	Nov.	Dec.	Total
2000	271	284	334	330	248	247	229	269	257	266	286	287	3,308
2001	258	236	316	275	227	221	229	258	230	274	273	266	3,065
2002	244	244	311	263	267	216	241	246	259	284	255	262	3,092
2003	227	211	252	280	209	216	225	226	241	251	223	246	2,805
2004	207	199	295	238	175	220	207	219	231	228	228	229	2,676
2005	195	204	268	208	198	210	188	216	219	217	213	219	2,555
2006	210	193	240	234	215	200	191	213	205	223	212	212	2,547
2007	204	194	267	203	205	188	191	212	197	232	223	212	2,529
2008[1]	202	202	219	207	195	181	193	186	27	209	180	213	2,213

[1] Preliminary.   *Source: Economic Research Service, U.S. Department of Agriculture (ERS-USDA)*

Cold Storage Holdings of Lamb and Mutton in the United States, on First of Month   In Thousands of Pounds

Year	Jan.	Feb.	Mar.	Apr.	May	June	July	Aug.	Sept.	Oct.	Nov.	Dec.
2000	8,740	10,394	10,335	11,437	13,345	13,137	13,984	13,557	14,042	12,867	12,195	12,486
2001	13,455	13,833	13,141	13,729	13,551	14,586	15,443	15,744	15,266	13,979	13,238	11,336
2002	11,905	13,110	11,269	10,528	13,172	12,938	13,553	14,215	14,458	11,961	12,004	9,255
2003	7,124	6,232	4,063	3,900	5,016	5,838	5,427	5,929	5,855	6,210	4,485	4,883
2004	3,795	3,671	3,355	3,164	3,251	3,504	3,872	3,376	3,878	4,179	4,166	3,715
2005	3,497	7,549	7,585	7,650	8,739	9,719	9,362	11,756	11,790	10,942	10,137	9,332
2006	9,967	15,730	15,777	15,454	15,247	15,215	15,126	15,254	15,353	15,228	15,452	15,862
2007	15,769	15,640	15,570	15,996	18,206	16,644	15,410	13,811	15,692	14,734	13,944	13,096
2008[1]	12,918	15,177	18,157	17,118	17,783	18,411	19,598	19,723	21,147	20,796	21,331	21,659

[1] Preliminary.   *Source: Economic Research Service, U.S. Department of Agriculture (ERS-USDA)*

Average Price Received by Farmers for Sheep in the United States   In Dollars Per Hundred Pounds (Cwt.)

Year	Jan.	Feb.	Mar.	Apr.	May	June	July	Aug.	Sept.	Oct.	Nov.	Dec.	Average
2000	36.80	39.50	38.80	35.00	30.50	30.00	34.20	30.70	30.30	29.50	33.60	36.20	33.76
2001	43.30	47.50	46.60	36.90	36.30	31.70	34.10	32.20	29.90	27.20	27.10	34.00	35.57
2002	36.20	34.30	31.80	26.00	25.30	23.50	25.60	25.60	24.50	25.60	31.30	38.70	29.03
2003	41.30	44.00	40.90	31.10	31.30	29.40	28.60	29.20	32.50	35.00	40.50	45.10	35.74
2004	43.80	40.80	36.70	36.70	36.00	31.30	37.10	37.30	41.20	40.40	41.40	44.60	38.94
2005	53.50	52.40	49.00	45.10	43.70	41.20	41.00	43.00	43.70	43.60	46.20	49.30	45.98
2006	47.70	45.90	40.10	35.20	32.50	28.20	27.60	27.90	32.20	31.40	30.30	34.80	34.48
2007	37.10	37.30	36.60	34.20	30.80	28.20	29.20	28.30	26.70	25.50	27.10	30.20	30.93
2008[1]	31.90	29.90	28.30	28.80	27.70	24.80	26.90	26.30	23.80	21.80	27.00	31.70	27.41

[1] Preliminary.   *Source: Economic Research Service, U.S. Department of Agriculture (ERS-USDA)*

Average Price Received by Farmers for Lambs in the United States   In Dollars Per Hundred Pounds (Cwt.)

Year	68.20	67.20	67.40	67.40	82.80	81.30	77.00	80.30	75.30	72.60	76.30	77.60	74.45
2000	70.90	72.00	80.20	82.60	96.40	89.70	87.00	83.60	80.80	76.80	71.50	71.80	80.28
2001	74.10	80.10	84.00	84.30	80.00	71.60	64.30	54.80	52.50	51.40	52.80	61.40	67.61
2002	65.50	67.80	66.70	64.70	64.40	72.90	75.60	75.30	76.30	79.60	84.00	87.20	73.33
2003	92.00	92.40	97.10	93.70	97.60	89.30	89.40	88.60	95.10	96.80	99.70	97.70	94.12
2004	104.00	106.00	103.00	100.00	103.00	105.00	101.00	97.90	100.00	97.70	99.90	101.00	101.54
2005	114.00	114.00	114.00	114.00	114.00	114.00	110.00	109.00	110.00	108.00	107.00	100.00	110.67
2006	96.10	97.80	92.10	87.20	88.90	92.10	93.40	95.40	98.30	98.50	95.60	94.00	94.12
2007	96.50	94.80	95.50	97.10	97.10	96.80	98.70	97.90	99.00	97.00	97.10	98.40	97.16
2008[1]	97.50	96.80	98.00	99.40	100.00	102.00	103.00	99.60	99.60	97.50	99.60	100.00	99.42

[1] Preliminary.   *Source: Economic Research Service, U.S. Department of Agriculture (ERS-USDA)*

Silk

Silk is a fine, tough, elastic fiber produced by caterpillars, commonly called silkworms. Silk is one of the oldest known textile fibers. Chinese tradition credits Lady Hsi-Ling-Shih, wife of the Emperor Huang Ti, with the discovery of the silkworm and the invention of the first silk reel. Dating to around 3000 BC, a group of ribbons, threads, and woven fragments was found in China. Also found, along the lower Yangzi River, were 7,000 year-old spinning tools, silk thread, and fabric fragments.

Silk filament was first woven into cloth in Ancient China. The Chinese successfully guarded this secret until 300AD, when Japan, and later India, learned the secret. In 550 AD, two Nestorian monks were sent to China to steal mulberry seeds and silkworm eggs, which they hid in their walking staffs, and then brought them back to Rome. By the 17th century, France was the silk center of the West. Unfortunately, the silkworm did not flourish in the English climate, nor has it ever flourished in the U.S.

Sericulture is the term for the raising of silkworms. The blind, flightless moth, Bombyx mori, lays more than 500 tiny eggs. After hatching, the tiny worms eat chopped mulberry leaves continuously until they are ready to spin their cocoons. After gathering the complete cocoons, the first step in silk manufacturing is to kill the insects inside the cocoons with heat. The cocoons are then placed in boiling water to loosen the gummy substance, sericin,

holding the filament together. The filament is unwound, and then rewound in a process called reeling. Each cocoon's silk filament is between 600 and 900 meters long. Four different types of silk thread may be produced: organzine, crepe, tram, and thrown singles. During the last 30 years, in spite of the use of man-made fibers, world silk production has doubled.

Raw silk is traded on the Kansai Agricultural Commodities Exchange (KANEX) in Japan. Dried cocoons are traded on the Chuba Commodity Exchange (CCE). Raw silk and dried cocoons are traded on the Yokohama Commodity Exchange.

Supply – World production of silk in 2005, the latest reporting year, rose +6.6% to 155,549 metric tons, which was a record high and sharply above the 14-year low of 79,458 posted in 1997. China is the world's largest producer of silk by far with 72% of world production in 2005. Other key producers include India with 11% of world production, Vietnam (8%), and Turkmenistan (3%).

Trade – In 2006, the latest reporting year, the world's largest exporters of silk were China with 79% of world exports, Japan with 4.8%, and North Korea with 1.6%. In 2006, the world's largest importers of silk were India (with 48% of world imports), Italy (12%), Japan (10%), and South Korea (8%).

World Production of Raw Silk   In Metric Tons

Year	Brazil	China	India	Iran	Japan	North Korea	Rep. of Korea	Kyrgy-zstan	Thailand	Turkmen-istan	Uzbek-istan	Viet Nam	World Total
1996	2,270	51,451	13,909	680	2,579	360	149	800	1,144	4,600	2,500	1,500	82,618
1997	2,120	50,751	14,126	720	1,902	200	46	300	1,039	4,600	2,000	1,000	79,458
1998	1,821	67,701	15,236	760	1,108	150	40	150	900	4,700	1,500	862	95,600
1999	1,554	70,201	15,544	800	650	150	29	80	1,000	5,000	923	780	97,403
2000	1,389	78,201	15,214	840	650	150	15	67	955	4,700	1,100	7,153	111,158
2001	1,554	94,201	15,857	900	559	150	6	76	1,510	5,000	1,260	10,866	132,694
2002	1,560	100,101	17,347	900	391	200	4	96	1,550	4,500	1,200	12,124	140,677
2003	1,580	95,761	16,319	900	287	320	3	50	1,550	4,500	1,200	11,582	134,887
2004[1]	1,580	104,801	15,742	900	250	350	3	17	1,600	4,500	1,200	12,323	145,931
2005[2]	1,580	111,951	17,500	900	220	350	3	50	1,600	4,500	1,200	13,000	155,549

[1] Preliminary.   [2] Estimate.   NA = Not avaliable.   *Source: Food and Agricultural Organization of the United Nations (FAO-UN)*

World Trade of Silk by Selected Countries   In Metric Tons

Year	France	Hong Kong	India	Italy	Japan	Rep. of Korea	World Total	Brazil	China	Hong Kong	Japan	Rep. of Korea	World Total
1997	423	3,570	2,346	3,144	2,251	2,509	21,940	----	11,118	3,813	1	80	37,233
1998	454	1,495	2,743	2,436	1,795	1,261	14,963	----	9,171	1,667	----	180	29,611
1999	287	1,059	5,018	2,695	2,596	2,107	18,957	----	12,089	1,048	3	130	35,041
2000	323	561	4,713	3,177	2,581	1,769	17,267	3	12,531	676	9	120	15,183
2001	327	175	6,809	2,760	1,893	1,582	16,410	23	11,266	186	2	90	13,003
2002	262	38	9,054	2,363	2,025	1,845	18,548	4	14,702	102	2	170	16,117
2003	147	67	9,258	2,219	1,949	1,648	18,439	2	13,931	31	96	296	15,866
2004	181	3	7,948	1,983	1,581	1,338	16,607	7	11,288	20	688	227	14,324
2005	262	14	8,383	1,974	1,406	1,359	17,863	36	10,972	11	202	219	13,699
2006[1]	212	3	5,565	2,146	1,295	1,095	14,719	4	6,712	4	11	223	10,012

[1] Preliminary.   *Source: Food and Agricultural Organization of the United Nations (FAO-UN)*

Silver

Silver is a white, lustrous metallic element that conducts heat and electricity better than any other metal. In ancient times, many silver deposits were on or near the earth's surface. Before 2,500 BC, silver mines were worked in Asia Minor. Around 700 BC, ancient Greeks stamped a turtle on their first silver coins. Silver assumed a key role in the U.S. monetary system in 1792 when Congress based the currency on the silver dollar. However, the U.S. discontinued the use of silver in coinage in 1965. Today Mexico is the only country that uses silver in its circulating coinage.

Silver is the most malleable and ductile of all metals, with the exception of gold. Silver melts at about 962 degrees Celsius and boils at about 2212 degrees Celsius. Silver is not very chemically active, although tarnishing occurs when sulfur and sulfides attack silver, forming silver sulfide on the surface of the metal. Because silver is too soft in its pure form, a hardening agent, usually copper, is mixed into the silver. Copper is usually used as the hardening agent because it does not discolor the silver. The term "sterling silver" refers to silver that contains at least 925 parts of silver per thousand (92.5%) to 75 parts of copper (7.5%).

Silver is usually found combined with other elements in minerals and ores. In the U.S., silver is mined in conjunction with lead, copper, and zinc. In the U.S., Nevada, Idaho, Alaska, and Arizona are the leading silver-producing states. For industrial purposes, silver is used for photography, electrical appliances, glass, and as an antibacterial agent for the health industry.

Silver futures and options are traded on the Comex division of the New York Mercantile Exchange, the Chicago Board of Trade (CBOT), and the London Metal Exchange (LME). Silver futures are traded on the Tokyo Commodity Exchange (TOCOM). The Nymex silver futures contract calls for the delivery of 5,000 troy ounces of silver (0.999 fineness) and is priced in terms of dollars and cents per troy ounce.

Prices – Nymex silver futures prices in early 2008 extended the 2007 rally to post a 28-year high of $21.185 per troy ounce in March 2008. The highest month-end price ever posted for cash silver was about $38 per troy ounce back in January 1980. Silver prices consolidated through summer of 2008 and then plunged in September 2008 when the global financial crisis emerged. Silver hit a 3-year low of $8.40 in October 2008, posting an overall sell-off of 60.3% from the March high. Silver closed 2008 at $11.295, down $3.625 or -24.3%. Silver in early 2008 rallied to the 28-year high on the weak dollar, strong industrial demand, and strong investment and speculative demand. Silver during the crisis initially fell on a washout of long positions and fears about deflation, but then rallied along with gold in early 2009 as the market became concerned about the extraordinarily easy monetary policies from major central banks, which could debase paper currency values and cause inflation down the road.

Supply – World mine production of silver in 2008 rose +0.5% yr/yr to a new record high of 20,900 metric tons, continuing to show some improvement after flat production figures in 2000-03. The world's largest silver producers in 2007 were Peru with 17% of world production, Mexico (14%), China (12%), Chili (9%), Australia (9%), and the U.S. (6%). U.S. production of refined silver in 2007 (through December, annualized) fell by 6.4% to 4,671 metric tons (latest data available), but remained above the 10-year low of 4,442 metric tons seen in 2004.

Demand – U.S. consumption of silver in 2003, the latest reporting year, fell –1.0% yr/yr to 175.3 million troy ounces. The largest consumption of silver is for photographic materials with 35% of total usage, followed by electrical contacts and conductors (23%), jewelry (9%), coinage (7%), and brazing alloys and solders (5%). The world's largest consuming nation of silver for industrial purposes is the U.S. with 20% of world consumption in 2004, followed by Japan (16%), India (10%), and Italy (7%).

Trade – U.S. exports of refined silver in 2005 (latest available data) fell –21.4% yr/yr to 9.709 million troy ounces, which was less that one tenth of the record high of 99.022 million troy ounces seen in 1997. The major destinations for U.S. silver exports are Canada (38%), Switzerland (29%), and the UK (12%). U.S. imports of silver ore and concentrates in 2005 (latest available data) fell –80.5% yr/yr to 14,000 troy ounces. U.S. imports of refined silver bullion rose +11.2% yr/yr to 134.387 million troy ounces in 2005. The bulk of those imports came from Mexico (65.908 million troy ounces), Canada (41.474 million troy ounces), and Peru (20.319 million troy ounces).

World Mine Production of Silver — In Thousands of Kilograms (Metric Ton)

Year	Australia	Bolivia	Canada[3]	Chile	China	Kazakhstan	Mexico	Peru	Poland	Russia	Sweden	United States	World Total[2]
1999	1,720	422	1,174	1,381	1,320	905	2,467	2,231	1,100	375	284	1,950	17,100
2000	2,060	434	1,212	1,242	1,600	927	2,620	2,438	1,148	370	329	1,980	18,100
2001	1,970	411	1,320	1,349	1,910	982	2,760	2,571	1,194	380	306	1,740	18,700
2002	2,077	450	1,408	1,210	2,200	893	2,727	2,870	1,229	400	294	1,350	18,800
2003	1,868	465	1,310	1,313	2,400	827	2,569	2,921	1,237	700	307	1,240	18,800
2004	2,224	407	1,337	1,360	2,450	733	2,569	3,060	1,344	1,277	293	1,250	19,900
2005	2,417	419	1,124	1,400	2,500	832	2,894	3,193	1,263	1,350	310	1,230	20,600
2006	1,727	500	983	1,607	2,600	830	2,700	3,471	1,325	1,300	268	1,140	20,200
2007[1]	1,880		800	1,900	2,560		3,000	3,500	1,200			1,260	20,800
2008[2]	1,800		800	2,000	2,600		3,000	3,600	1,300			1,120	20,900

[1] Preliminary. [2] Estimate. [3] Shipments. *Source: U.S. Geological Survey (USGS)*

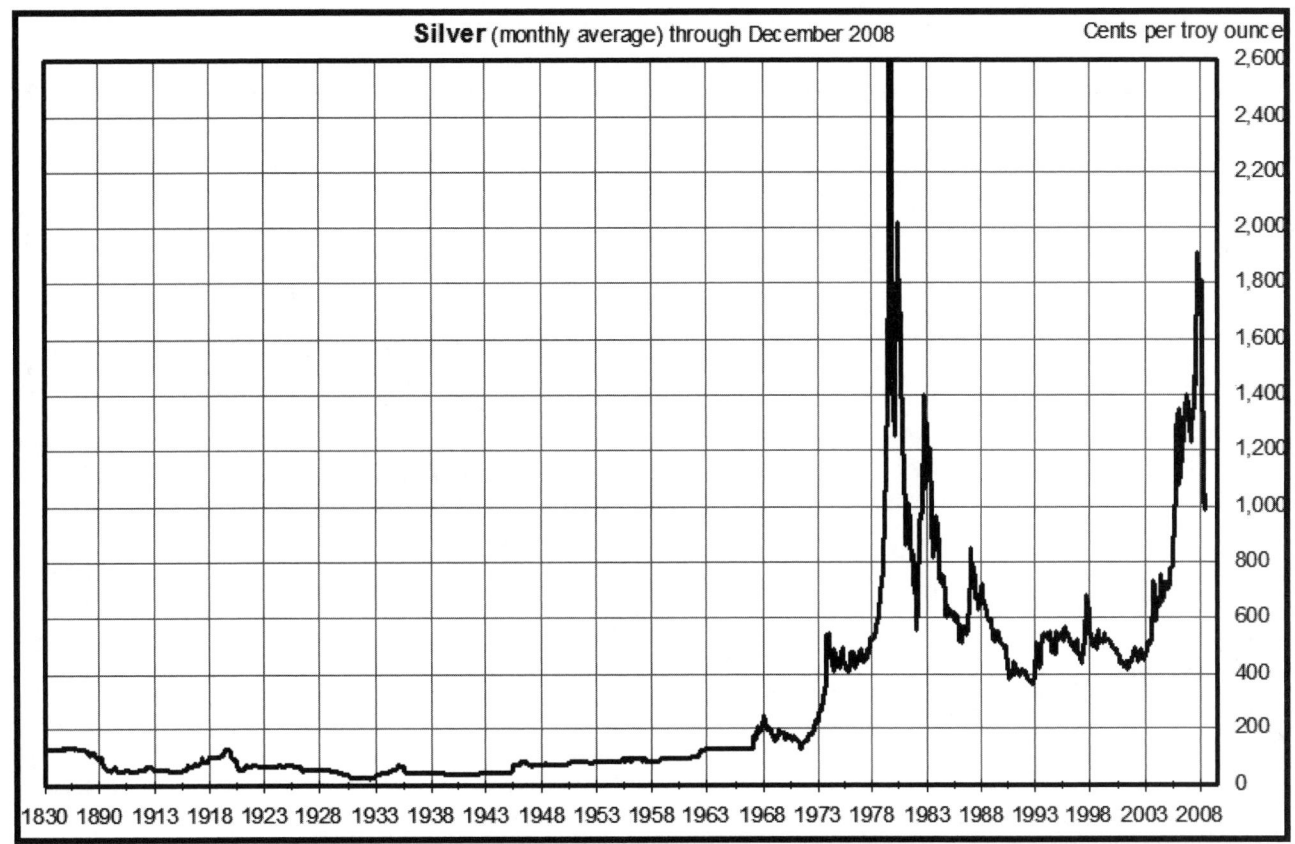

Silver (monthly average) through December 2008 — Cents per troy ounce

Average Price of Silver in New York (Handy & Harman)   In Cents Per Troy Ounce (.999 Fine)

Year	Jan.	Feb.	Mar.	Apr.	May	June	July	Aug.	Sept.	Oct.	Nov.	Dec.	Average
1999	511.61	554.55	519.85	509.21	529.83	507.73	522.81	529.36	527.86	541.67	519.20	521.95	524.75
2000	523.47	529.65	510.15	510.37	504.30	505.20	501.82	492.76	494.50	488.14	471.93	466.40	499.89
2001	470.19	457.34	439.93	439.25	443.59	436.79	425.45	420.72	441.09	441.87	412.35	437.98	438.88
2002	450.17	444.79	457.00	460.50	473.55	492.13	494.57	456.16	458.93	442.28	453.87	465.78	462.39
2003	485.62	468.11	454.74	453.40	475.29	455.62	486.48	502.90	520.62	503.91	520.64	565.33	491.06
2004	637.13	647.71	729.48	708.57	589.19	588.38	637.55	670.98	641.93	717.55	751.43	712.43	669.36
2005	665.45	709.18	728.50	715.74	705.29	733.64	704.40	702.72	719.33	769.90	786.35	865.88	733.87
2006	918.48	952.13	1,037.52	1,263.71	1,337.84	1,077.41	1,121.24	1,225.39	1,159.93	1,161.55	1,298.45	1,329.83	1,156.96
2007	1,286.63	1,394.58	1,316.27	1,373.23	1,319.27	1,315.48	1,295.21	1,233.22	1,292.92	1,372.17	1,467.15	1,431.24	1,341.45
2008	1,605.90	1,766.63	1,921.60	1,751.57	1,704.90	1,703.95	1,806.41	1,457.81	1,219.33	1,042.72	986.78	1,031.66	1,499.94

Source: American Metal Market (AMM)

Average Price of Silver in London (Spot Fix)   In Pence Per Troy Ounce (.999 Fine)

Year	Jan.	Feb.	Mar.	Apr.	May	June	July	Aug.	Sept.	Oct.	Nov.	Dec.	Average
1999	312.69	340.46	320.27	315.12	326.80	315.51	328.86	327.98	322.20	326.42	317.53	319.87	322.75
2000	316.08	327.90	320.87	319.61	330.53	331.24	329.35	327.80	340.75	332.24	327.71	317.47	326.94
2001	315.87	312.57	304.50	304.36	310.19	309.54	300.97	277.97	297.93	289.21	286.92	306.25	302.43
2002	315.08	310.55	318.27	316.61	322.58	329.32	316.07	295.93	292.38	282.49	286.93	291.52	306.48
2003	297.21	289.23	287.39	285.06	292.05	272.79	295.53	313.01	320.30	298.01	306.53	320.48	298.13
2004	347.36	339.49	395.67	391.14	327.03	320.36	342.32	368.78	356.35	392.94	402.52	368.43	362.70
2005	354.28	375.57	382.74	377.48	380.46	403.56	402.10	391.55	397.90	436.23	453.10	496.09	404.26
2006	519.94	544.76	594.70	714.36	715.69	584.44	607.69	647.19	615.09	618.97	678.96	677.31	626.59
2007	656.95	712.03	675.74	690.95	665.15	662.06	636.65	613.19	639.99	670.90	708.45	709.65	670.14
2008	815.50	899.50	960.24	883.98	867.12	866.05	907.89	772.57	677.51	617.03	645.37	693.86	800.55

Source: American Metal Market (AMM)

SILVER

Silver Futures - CME Group (NYMEX)
(weekly close) as of January 02, 2009

Cents per troy ounce

Average Open Interest of Silver Futures in New York (COMEX)   In Contracts

Year	Jan.	Feb.	Mar.	Apr.	May	June	July	Aug.	Sept.	Oct.	Nov.	Dec.
1999	77,946	97,593	82,435	82,824	78,745	78,943	78,151	86,601	77,490	86,577	80,564	70,275
2000	76,187	81,398	75,765	76,213	75,001	76,466	75,199	91,083	73,441	78,222	83,142	73,644
2001	69,408	72,798	74,337	71,589	67,328	67,429	75,019	75,830	65,533	66,530	74,228	66,903
2002	67,442	65,355	67,405	76,158	82,525	100,837	94,731	82,349	80,511	89,094	85,434	78,174
2003	98,561	94,472	84,485	87,445	85,232	80,001	91,544	108,118	110,423	92,216	101,303	103,007
2004	109,860	113,764	117,848	113,172	90,493	87,201	89,062	97,844	85,245	108,762	121,221	107,136
2005	97,744	98,644	101,200	103,562	104,680	124,317	124,521	121,133	117,121	135,335	146,409	136,502
2006	131,767	129,928	132,140	137,121	110,400	110,631	98,733	110,635	102,159	105,167	114,132	105,741
2007	105,692	122,515	113,749	118,275	109,070	120,179	117,817	118,292	110,958	123,781	144,897	146,891
2008	174,969	182,076	157,971	143,333	123,649	128,645	136,866	131,931	110,333	97,927	91,983	84,986

Source: New York Mercantile Exchange (NYMEX), COMEX Division

Volume of Trading of Silver Futures in New York (COMEX)   In Contracts

Year	Jan.	Feb.	Mar.	Apr.	May	June	July	Aug.	Sept.	Oct.	Nov.	Dec.	Total
1999	315,165	550,271	355,559	424,822	274,002	373,662	288,480	422,653	328,907	318,256	344,289	161,434	4,157,500
2000	258,053	425,910	231,336	318,752	216,938	407,455	175,235	370,739	146,007	149,252	303,673	113,667	3,117,017
2001	175,026	302,035	155,658	252,486	204,552	281,846	112,956	267,711	160,329	210,266	266,077	180,256	2,569,198
2002	265,773	271,293	163,898	325,889	243,475	389,798	281,214	296,579	164,537	209,249	292,861	230,998	3,135,564
2003	291,120	409,737	216,660	315,240	251,096	352,729	407,931	442,762	335,508	373,493	464,244	250,835	4,111,355
2004	385,058	544,939	408,447	671,204	278,703	425,501	316,264	427,973	281,737	364,158	541,366	360,775	5,006,125
2005	285,449	513,617	370,338	485,832	392,156	621,647	334,903	600,961	455,033	424,972	652,917	398,526	5,536,351
2006	495,649	624,491	562,330	807,269	513,822	508,746	255,777	452,551	268,393	244,152	424,771	275,112	5,433,063
2007	364,565	589,332	479,896	635,023	417,343	680,612	404,108	783,999	469,459	581,062	1,018,495	393,243	6,817,137
2008	719,308	989,601	188,396	912,952	580,959	859,976	706,778	953,123	792,072	594,307	578,009	332,437	8,207,918

Source: New York Mercantile Exchange (NYMEX), COMEX Division

Mine Production of Recoverable Silver in the United States   In Metric Tons

Year	Arizona	California	Colorado	Idaho	Missouri	Montana	Nevada	New Mexico	South Dakota	Washington	Other States	Total
1997	190	23	W	341	W	W	787	W	4	2	833	2,180
1998	211	11	W	447	W	W	670	W	2	1	723	2,060
1999	183	8	W	416	W	W	597	W	W	W	748	1,950
2000	W	8	3	W	W	W	734	W	W	2	1,240	1,980
2001	W	8	3	W	W	W	544	W	W	W	1,180	1,740
2002	W	3	W	W	W	W	424	W	W	W	927	1,350
2003	W	1	W	W	W	W	322	W	W	W	916	1,240
2004	W	1	W	W	W	W	302	W	W	W	943	1,250
2005	W	W	W	W	W	W	276	W	W	W	949	1,230
2006[1]	W	W	W	W	W	W	245	W	W	W	895	1,140

[1] Preliminary.   W = Withheld proprietary data; included in "Other States".   *Source: U.S. Geological Survey (USGS)*

Consumption of Silver in the United States, by End Use   In Millions of Troy Ounces

Year	Brazing Alloys & Solders	Catalysts	Batteries	Mirrors	Electrical Contacts & Conductors	Photographic Materials	Silverplate	Jewerly	Sterling Ware	Total Net Industrial Consumption	Coinage	Total Consumption
1994	7.7	4.2	3.6	1.5	31.6	57.6	3.1	3.7	4.2	130.2	9.5	139.7
1995	8.0	4.9	4.1	1.7	36.0	59.7	3.5	4.1	4.4	138.1	9.0	147.1
1996	8.2	5.5	4.5	2.1	36.3	59.9	3.9	4.4	4.8	140.5	7.1	147.6
1997	8.4	5.7	4.8	2.4	41.9	62.9	4.1	4.9	5.1	150.7	6.5	157.2
1998	8.6	5.9	4.9	2.6	44.1	69.4	4.5	5.5	5.7	163.0	7.0	170.0
1999	9.0	5.9	5.0	2.6	47.1	73.8	4.4	5.7	5.8	175.5	10.7	186.2
2000	8.7	6.3	5.2	2.6	50.6	73.9	4.5	6.1	5.6	181.9	13.4	195.3
2001	8.3	6.1	5.3	2.5	34.1	65.8	4.0	4.9	4.6	157.6	12.3	169.9
2002	8.4	NA	NA	NA	37.6	66.2	[3]	13.7	[3]	162.9	14.2	177.1
2003[1]	7.9	NA	NA	NA	39.5	61.6	[3]	15.1	[3]	162.8	12.5	175.3

[1] Preliminary.   [3] Included in Jewelry beginning 2002.   NA = Not available.   *Source: American Metal Market*

Commodity Exchange, Inc. (COMEX) Warehouse of Stocks of Silver   In Thousands of Troy Ounces

Year	Jan.	Feb.	Mar.	Apr.	May	June	July	Aug.	Sept.	Oct.	Nov.	Dec.
1999	75,807	75,108	78,135	79,605	78,819	77,512	73,514	77,592	79,606	79,391	79,155	78,416
2000	75,945	73,948	93,782	104,259	102,589	99,285	102,713	102,291	97,879	99,552	95,749	95,717
2001	93,983	93,195	98,659	96,694	95,745	96,090	98,700	100,494	102,770	101,538	103,982	105,235
2002	104,547	102,395	100,983	102,540	104,526	107,766	105,938	105,563	108,090	107,495	107,440	107,090
2003	107,394	107,610	109,153	108,521	108,168	105,092	107,222	105,406	104,862	106,283	118,238	124,498
2004	124,271	124,181	123,195	122,087	122,687	118,442	118,369	116,253	109,311	107,789	104,624	102,831
2005	103,590	102,390	101,494	103,627	103,995	104,257	104,719	109,467	115,588	116,687	116,257	117,608
2006	119,974	124,793	127,898	125,763	123,627	108,443	102,268	102,086	103,634	105,451	105,313	107,770
2007	111,071	113,970	117,637	126,433	131,343	130,497	139,935	132,106	133,057	133,474	133,891	134,533
2008	130,072	135,414	135,037	135,881	133,512	134,896	135,959	138,061	137,821	135,719	130,204	127,170

Source: New York Mercantile Exchange (NYMEX), COMEX Division

Production[2] of Refined Silver in the United States, from All Sources   In Metric Tons

Year	Jan.	Feb.	Mar.	Apr.	May	June	July	Aug.	Sept.	Oct.	Nov.	Dec.	Total
1999	424	420	441	356	368	394	404	316	354	371	364	396	4,608
2000	436	1,177	551	399	431	390	361	402	400	469	386	401	5,780
2001	405	343	405	360	360	331	395	380	338	403	442	383	4,545
2002	544	387	465	532	509	398	398	419	473	437	394	485	5,441
2003	483	426	320	412	357	431	430	373	361	809	363	471	5,235
2004	407	418	460	337	361	177	175	351	433	255	390	678	4,442
2005	402	505	515	568	450	558	556	440	356	376	485	439	5,650
2006	506	434	500	445	381	554	489	431	349	387	209	305	4,990
2007	401	405	445	436	476	452	335	438	290	388	267	339	4,671
2008[1]	322	357	391	459	482								4,825

[1] Preliminary.   [2] Includes U.S. mine production of recoverable silver plus imports of refined silver.   *Source: U.S. Geological Survey (USGS)*

SILVER

U.S. Exports of Refined Silver to Selected Countries   In Thousands of Troy Ounces

Year	Canada	France	Germany	Hong Kong	Japan	Sing- apore	Rep of Korea	Switzer- land	United Arab Emirates	United Kingdom	Uruguay	Other Countries	Total
1996	489	[2]	2	646	4,662	3,601	383	2,413	15,850	35,366	624	40	93,346
1997	1,861	[2]	2	797	6,044	[2]	547	5,369	16,750	62,693	402	4,557	99,022
1998	669	2,205	347	45	585	210	----	604	3,569	62,693	688	8,760	80,375
1999	2,180	2	1	----	585	37	31	624	4,244	7,716	180	4,205	19,804
2000	1,906	22	2	----	3,504	1	----	727	----	3,311	109	2,634	12,217
2001	1,598	----	----	11	1,202	2	----	354	----	20,029	105	7,659	30,960
2002	466	----	1	4	466	10	----	727	----	14,532	----	11,990	28,196
2003	524	3	----	3	17	2	16	630	----	3,086	----	2,534	6,816
2004	7,009	1	3	24	585	166	1	2,321	----	3	108	2,125	12,346
2005[1]	3,729	----	25	3	1	95	18	2,829	----	1,145	563	1,302	9,709

[1] Preliminary.   [2] Included in "Other Countries", if any.   NA = Not available.   *Source: American Bureau of Metal Statistics, Inc. (ABMS)*

U.S. Imports of Silver From Selected Countries   In Thousands of Troy Ounces

Year	Canada	Mexico	Other Countries	Total	Canada	Chile	Mexico	Peru	Uruguay	Other Countries	Total
1996	256	4,662	----	4,918	35,365	1,874	30,285	12,153	[2]	3,122	82,799
1997	7	4,437	90	4,533	29,385	608	28,774	8,873	----	518	68,158
1998	24	5,851	427	6,301	34,722	813	41,152	9,388	----	3,945	90,020
1999	11	334	2	347	43,403	1,048	33,115	5,433	----	2,521	85,519
2000	46	----	----	46	38,902	225	44,689	2,787	----	35,899	122,502
2001	243	----	----	243	44,046	2,054	41,152	5,498	----	1,771	94,521
2002	149	1,813	----	1,961	48,868	2,331	67,837	6,430	----	6,350	131,815
2003	82	----	----	82	41,795	1,987	62,050	18,261	----	12,223	136,316
2004	71	----	----	71	37,616	2,042	59,156	17,297	----	4,774	120,884
2005[1]	14	----	----	14	41,474	2,514	65,908	20,319	----	4,173	134,387

[1] Preliminary.   [2] Included in "Other Countries", if any.   NA = Not available.   Source: American Bureau of Metal Statistics, Inc. (ABMS)

World Silver Consumption   In Millions of Troy Ounces

Year	Can- ada	France	Ger- many	India	Italy	Japan	Mex- ico	United Kingdom	United States	World Total	Austria	Can- ada	France	Ger- many	Mex- ico	United States	Total Coinage	World Total
											----- Coinage -----								
1995	2.0	30.0	43.6	101.3	49.5	112.7	16.9	31.6	148.7	752.7	.5	.7	1.2	2.4	.6	9.0	24.7	777.4
1996	2.0	26.9	41.0	122.2	51.7	112.1	20.3	33.8	155.0	785.8	.5	.7	.3	4.6	.5	7.1	23.3	809.1
1997	2.2	28.3	42.3	122.9	56.1	119.9	23.3	34.9	166.3	828.2	.4	.6	.3	3.7	.4	6.5	28.5	856.7
1998	2.3	28.4	38.4	114.7	55.9	112.8	21.7	38.6	162.6	801.2	.3	1.1	.3	10.0	.2	7.0	27.8	829.0
1999	2.1	26.6	35.1	121.5	61.8	122.5	21.3	39.3	175.2	838.7	.3	1.4	.3	7.0	.4	10.7	29.2	867.8
2000	2.0	28.8	31.8	131.0	65.1	135.0	16.6	42.7	179.1	871.8	.3	1.0	.4	8.8	.6	13.4	32.1	904.0
2001	2.0	28.7	32.4	154.0	58.2	119.3	15.9	45.9	157.3	836.5	.3	.9	.4	8.1	1.1	12.3	30.5	867.0
2002	2.1	27.1	29.4	122.5	56.0	118.7	17.0	43.1	161.6	807.0	.4	1.0	.5	6.0	1.1	15.3	31.6	838.6
2003	2.2	25.6	29.4	122.5	55.0	115.9	18.7	44.1	160.8	817.5	.4	.3	.5	10.3	1.1	14.5	35.8	853.4
2004[2]	2.1	12.0	30.7	79.2	54.8	125.1	18.6	52.2	164.8	807.0	.5	1.3	.5	10.3	.9	15.5	41.1	836.6

[2] Preliminary.   NA = Not available.   *Source: The Silver Institute*

Soybean Meal

Soybean meal is produced through processing and separating soybeans into oil and meal components. By weight, soybean meal accounts for about 35% of the weight of raw soybeans (at 13% moisture). If the soybeans are of particularly good quality, then the processor can get more meal weight by including more hulls in the meal while still meeting the 48% protein minimum. Soybean meal can be further processed into soy flour and isolated soy protein, but the bulk of soybean meal is used as animal feed for poultry, hogs and cattle. Soybean meal accounts for about two-thirds of the world's high-protein animal feed, followed by cottonseed and rapeseed meal, which together account for less than 20%. Soybean meal consumption has been moving to record highs in recent years. The soybean meal marketing year begins in October and ends in September. Soybean meal futures and options are traded on the Chicago Board of Trade (CBOT). The CBOT soybean meal futures contract calls for the delivery of 100 tons of soybean meal produced by conditioning ground soybeans and reducing the oil content of the conditioned product and having a minimum of 48.0% protein, minimum of 0.5% fat, maximum of 3.5% fiber, and maximum of 12.0% moisture.

Soybean crush – The term soybean "crush" refers to both the physical processing of soybeans and also to the dollar-value premium received for processing soybeans into their component products of meal and oil. The conventional model says that processing 60 pounds (one bushel) of soybeans produces 11 pounds of soybean oil, 44 pounds of 48% protein soybean meal, 3 pounds of hulls, and 1 pound of waste. The Gross Processing Margin (GPM) or crush equals (0.22 times Soybean Meal Prices in dollars per ton) + (11 times Soybean Oil prices in cents/pound) – Soybean prices in $/bushel. A higher crush value will occur when the price of the meal and oil products are strong relative to soybeans, e.g., because of supply disruptions or because of an increase in demand for the products. When the crush value is high, companies will have a strong incentive to buy raw soybeans and boost the output of the products. That supply increase should eventually bring the crush value back into line with the long-term equilibrium.

Prices – Soybean meal futures prices at the Chicago Board of Trade in 2008 started the year at about $350 per ton. After a brief rally, the price traded generally sideways until June and then rallied sharply to a high of about $450 per ton in July. From there, meal prices moved steadily downward to a low of about $250 per ton in October and then rallied to end the year at about $300 per ton. The price faded into the beginning of 2009 to about $275 in March 2009. Regarding cash prices, the average price of soybean meal (48% solvent) in Decatur, Illinois in the 2008-09 marketing year (i.e., October 2008 to September 2009) through December of 2008, averaged $265.42 per short ton, down by -21.0% yr/yr.

Supply – World soybean meal production in 2008-09 fell -2.5% yr/yr to 154.378 million metric tons, down from last year's record high of 158.339 million metric tons. The world's largest soybean meal producers are the U.S. with 23% of world production in 2008-09, China with 21%, Brazil with 16%, and the European Union with 7%. U.S. production of soybean meal in 2008-09 fell 5.7% yr/yr 39.841 million short tons, which was down from last year's record high of 42.242 million metric tons. U.S. soybean meal stocks in 2008-09 (Oct 1) fell 15.0% yr/yr to 294,000 short tons, down from last year's 7-year high of 346,000 short tons.

Demand – World consumption of soybean meal in 2008-09 fell -1.9% yr/yr to 154.494 million metric tons, which was down from last year's record high of 157.509. The U.S. accounted for 18% of that consumption and the European Union accounted for 21%. U.S. consumption of soybean meal in 2008-09 fell -7.3% yr/yr to 27.896 million metric tons.

Trade – World exports of soybean meal in 2008-09 fell -2.4% to 54.359 million metric tons. Brazil accounted for 23% of world exports in 2004-05 and the U.S. accounted for 14%. World imports of soybean meal in 2008-09 fell 2.2% yr/yr to 53.538 million metric tons. U.S. exports of soybean meal in 2008-09 fell -9.5% yr/yr to 8.400 million short tons. U.S. imports of soybean meal in 2008-09 rose +17.0% yr/yr to 165,000 short tons, remaining well below the record high of 285,000 short tons seen in 2003-04.

World Supply and Distribution of Soybean Meal   In Thousands of Metric Tons

Crop Year Beginning Oct. 1	Production Brazil	China	European Union	United States	Total	Exports Brazil	United States	Total	Imports European Union	Total	Consumption European Union	United States	Total	Ending Stocks Brazil	United States	Total
1999-00	16,478	11,975	11,331	34,102	107,158	9,950	6,912	34,119	17,963	34,922	29,294	27,269	108,613	1,080	266	5,901
2000-01	17,725	15,050	13,175	35,730	116,151	10,673	7,335	36,245	17,712	35,926	30,711	28,359	116,038	1,253	348	5,695
2001-02	19,407	16,300	14,042	36,552	125,070	11,862	7,271	41,688	19,961	40,392	33,406	29,541	123,619	1,560	218	5,850
2002-03	21,449	21,000	12,950	34,649	130,647	13,657	5,728	42,781	20,545	42,467	33,335	29,096	130,157	1,647	200	6,026
2003-04	22,360	20,190	11,084	32,953	128,673	14,792	4,690	45,653	22,012	44,944	32,729	28,530	128,501	1,801	191	5,489
2004-05	22,740	24,026	11,300	36,936	138,999	14,256	6,659	47,213	21,910	45,925	32,680	30,446	136,756	1,577	156	6,444
2005-06	21,920	27,296	10,760	37,416	145,869	12,895	7,301	51,884	22,829	51,201	32,875	30,114	145,530	1,469	285	6,100
2006-07	24,110	28,465	11,550	39,058	154,159	12,715	7,987	54,274	22,213	52,491	33,228	31,184	152,195	1,913	314	6,281
2007-08[1]	24,670	31,280	11,715	38,322	158,339	12,138	8,419	55,689	24,072	54,760	35,169	30,078	157,509	2,588	267	6,182
2008-09[2]	24,180	32,534	10,277	35,372	154,378	12,400	7,620	54,359	22,500	53,538	32,842	27,896	154,494	2,163	272	5,245

[1] Preliminary.   [2] Forecast.   *Source: Foreign Agricultural Service, U.S. Department of Agriculture (FAS-USDA)*

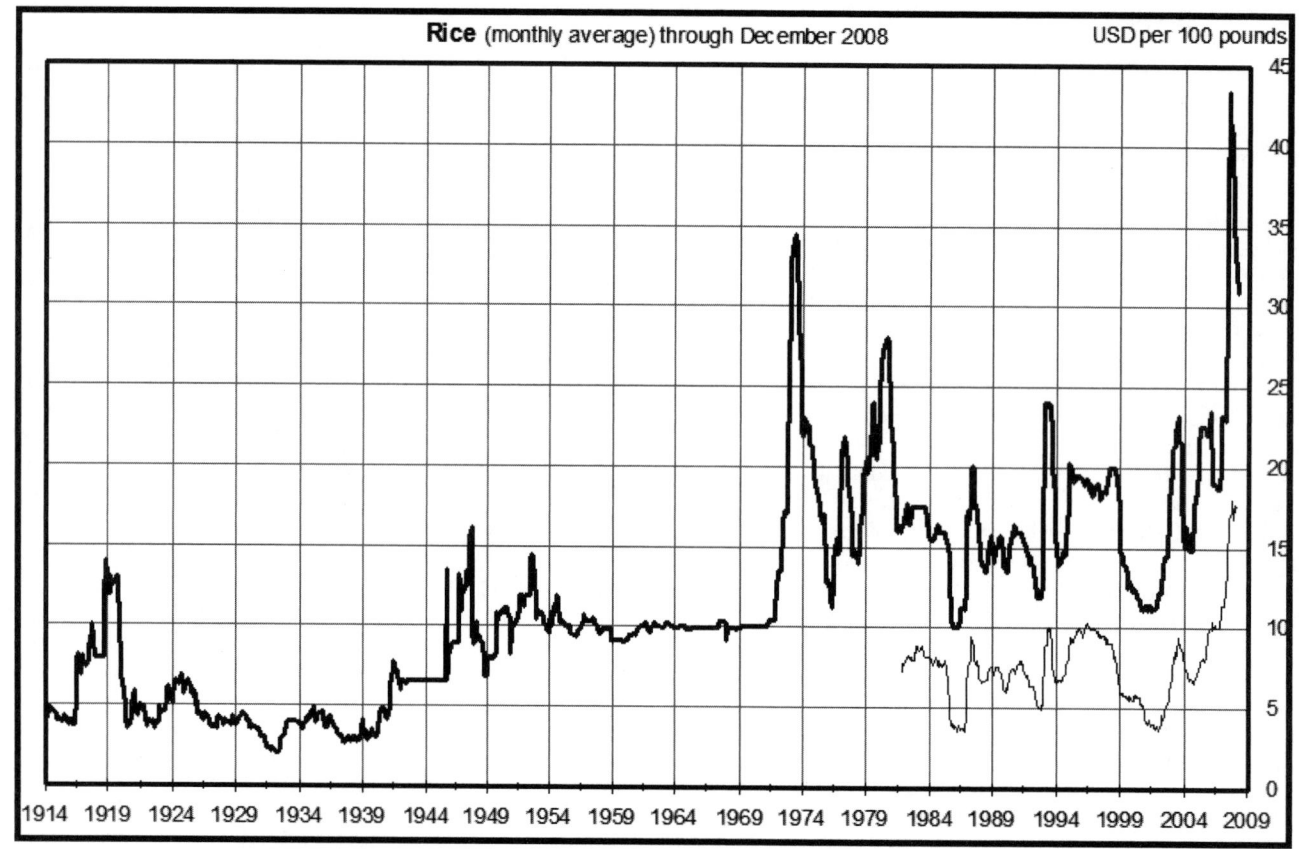

Rice (monthly average) through December 2008 — USD per 100 pounds

Volume of Trading of Soybean Meal Futures in Chicago   In Thousands of Contracts

Year	Jan.	Feb.	Mar.	Apr.	May	June	July	Aug.	Sept.	Oct.	Nov.	Dec.	Total
1999	420.2	509.3	476.1	477.1	390.5	646.8	710.1	597.0	568.9	511.5	572.2	447.1	6,326.9
2000	455.3	537.5	556.0	467.7	566.6	606.2	488.2	469.0	484.6	483.2	690.3	513.3	6,318.0
2001	530.2	431.8	470.6	485.1	584.4	625.1	710.0	630.9	491.4	652.9	659.3	472.1	6,743.8
2002	610.3	398.3	424.7	618.9	567.2	664.7	806.4	673.7	581.2	613.7	657.8	557.7	7,174.5
2003	639.6	551.4	527.7	676.7	599.6	749.8	772.1	692.8	677.2	896.4	700.7	674.3	8,158.4
2004	648.7	767.1	740.7	819.6	795.8	821.6	873.2	638.9	547.3	559.7	703.5	653.2	8,569.2
2005	658.7	857.6	713.4	661.8	571.3	1,025.0	632.8	693.4	602.9	497.9	694.0	715.8	8,324.6
2006	506.9	605.0	575.3	785.6	716.8	976.1	801.5	819.1	807.7	906.1	1,064.2	785.7	9,350.0
2007	768.9	1,018.8	822.1	985.7	798.9	1,217.3	1,107.9	1,025.1	1,028.6	1,016.4	1,218.8	1,204.7	12,213.3
2008	1,260.6	1,235.1	1,240.4	1,257.7	922.5	1,359.0	1,258.6	1,074.5	1,069.3	1,020.3	837.1	818.9	13,354.2

Source: CME Group; Chicago Board of Trade (CBT)

Average Open Interest of Soybean Meal Futures in Chicago   In Contracts

Year	Jan.	Feb.	Mar.	Apr.	May	June	July	Aug.	Sept.	Oct.	Nov.	Dec.
1999	123,041	130,473	121,435	112,155	104,176	108,134	116,464	121,202	120,462	112,426	117,523	104,246
2000	115,285	124,822	120,157	123,957	123,691	112,425	105,230	94,469	105,240	103,263	120,164	127,529
2001	111,880	108,047	107,253	116,888	119,644	135,046	134,982	129,536	123,644	121,845	145,996	147,576
2002	146,674	137,425	134,880	130,138	132,376	143,956	142,728	132,996	137,799	131,249	137,836	140,902
2003	154,821	168,036	157,670	163,532	163,096	154,985	152,121	146,582	153,505	169,709	170,707	176,191
2004	183,462	186,137	185,647	175,069	162,284	149,584	135,675	134,987	133,045	137,447	152,846	147,307
2005	154,984	165,403	146,326	133,578	129,372	149,882	122,088	109,976	121,833	135,970	140,102	140,959
2006	127,922	132,833	147,837	172,905	181,823	182,940	196,236	230,082	236,351	206,002	216,854	206,762
2007	201,214	227,905	213,708	216,258	212,398	217,576	210,612	201,339	219,046	225,683	248,277	251,133
2008	234,286	234,695	225,607	218,126	199,422	216,039	208,444	178,191	163,511	152,968	138,111	124,898

Source: CME Group; Chicago Board of Trade (CBT)

Supply and Distribution of Soybean Meal in the United States   In Thousands of Short Tons

Crop Year Beginning Oct. 1	For Stocks Oct. 1	Pro-duction	Total Supply	Domestic	Exports	Total	Decatur 48% Protein Solvent	Decatur 44% Protein Solvent	Brazil FOB 45-46% Protein	Rotter-dam CIF
1999-00	330	37,591	37,970	30,346	7,331	37,677	167.70	185	182	180
2000-01	293	39,385	39,729	31,643	7,703	39,346	173.60	191	187	188
2001-02	383	40,292	40,818	33,070	7,508	40,578	167.73	180	174	174
2002-03	240	38,194	38,600	32,361	6,019	38,380	181.57	200	163	197
2003-04	220	36,324	36,830	31,449	5,170	36,619	256.05	282	211	273
2004-05	211	40,715	41,073	33,559	7,343	40,902	182.90	202	172	231
2005-06	172	41,244	41,557	33,195	8,048	41,243	174.17	192	176	215
2006-07[1]	314	43,054	43,524	34,374	8,804	43,178	205.44	226	199	276
2007-08[2]	346	42,242	42,729	33,155	9,280	42,435	335.94			
2008-09[3]	294	38,841	39,300	30,600	8,400	39,000	260-320			

[1] Preliminary.   [2] Estimate.   [3] Forecast.   *Source: Economic Research Service, U.S. Department of Agriculture (ERS-USDA)*

U.S. Exports of Soybean Cake & Meal by Country of Destination   In Thousands of Metric Tons

Year	Algeria	Australia	Canada	Dominican Republic	Italy	Japan	Mexico	Nether-lands	Philip-pines	Russia	Spain	Vene-zuela	Total
1999	213.2	199.1	813.4	309.9	61.0	228.3	435.6	231.6	1,033.4	289.4	77.7	359.6	7,252
2000	205.6	200.3	845.1	357.4	19.1	256.5	274.3	96.0	943.9	90.7	96.5	248.1	6,760
2001	186.8	191.3	1,069.9	370.9	132.9	298.6	433.1	241.2	720.9	114.0	132.4	137.8	7,777
2002	266.5	294.2	1,156.9	358.8	34.4	157.7	514.4	107.5	756.9	121.3	79.7	60.3	7,141
2003	184.7	384.3	1,091.4	317.5	0.4	331.0	762.4	84.3	238.5	60.7	5.6	190.5	5,951
2004	176.2	209.4	1,212.9	156.9	1.1	220.9	944.1	127.6	299.0	18.2	48.4	193.5	5,526
2005	63.0	74.9	1,208.8	264.7	0.5	523.7	1,512.5	46.5	442.3	16.8	26.1	112.5	6,905
2006	18.4	54.5	1,415.1	424.7	1.4	481.4	1,892.2	76.4	520.5	36.6	4.8	27.9	7,943
2007	39.5	1.2	1,490.5	448.9	0.2	415.9	1,803.8	11.7	626.9	31.8	0.8	49.3	8,272
2008[1]	50.1	45.1	1,318.6	340.0	59.0	400.7	1,529.3	36.9	539.5	27.3	0.3	488.8	7,868

[1] Preliminary.   *Source: Foreign Agricultural Service, U.S. Department of Agriculture (FAS-USDA)*

Production of Soybean Cake & Meal[2] in the United States   In Thousands of Short Tons

Year	Jan.	Feb.	Mar.	Apr.	May	June	July	Aug.	Sept.	Oct.	Nov.	Dec.	Total	Yield in lbs.
1999-00	3,573.4	3,400.4	3,413.5	3,332.8	2,998.2	3,123.6	2,906.1	2,882.5	2,845.4	3,118.8	2,906.8	3,089.7	37,591	47.76
2000-01	3,573.9	3,432.8	3,399.4	3,521.6	3,083.0	3,412.5	3,152.3	3,181.0	3,091.6	3,256.6	3,203.6	3,076.8	39,385	48.06
2001-02	3,534.4	3,538.7	3,655.3	3,703.1	3,313.2	3,589.7	3,315.7	3,344.2	3,194.1	3,085.4	3,106.7	2,911.3	40,292	44.27
2002-03	3,499.3	3,424.7	3,526.8	3,358.4	3,048.4	3,360.1	2,994.7	3,072.4	2,873.4	3,064.4	2,966.6	3,023.5	38,213	43.90
2003-04	3,462.1	3,465.9	3,483.7	3,479.3	3,144.9	3,092.4	2,682.4	2,792.4	2,616.2	2,752.2	2,480.2	2,872.6	36,324	44.32
2004-05	3,685.2	3,584.2	3,567.9	3,553.6	3,293.3	3,547.6	3,328.0	3,396.8	3,160.9	3,320.4	3,122.1	3,157.0	40,717	44.26
2005-06	3,700.9	3,562.3	3,518.0	3,589.5	3,215.3	3,504.0	3,212.6	3,474.6	3,250.9	3,507.8	3,351.7	3,354.5	41,242	43.83
2006-07	3,823.2	3,671.9	3,733.0	3,697.5	3,257.2	3,721.5	3,444.5	3,627.3	3,532.6	3,572.4	3,474.6	3,498.2	43,054	43.85
2007-08	3,870.8	3,711.6	3,889.0	3,792.6	3,424.7	3,701.1	3,500.6	3,634.5	3,350.6	3,316.9	3,053.0	2,996.9	42,242	
2008-09[1]	3,520.1	3,412.8	3,345.6	3,439.5									41,154	

[1] Preliminary.   [2] At oil mills; including millfeed and lecithin.   *Sources: Economic Research Service, U.S. Department of Agriculture (ERS-USDA)*

Stocks (at Oil Mills)[2] of Soybean Cake & Meal in the United States, on First of Month   In Thousands of Short Tons

Year	Jan.	Feb.	Mar.	Apr.	May	June	July	Aug.	Sept.	Oct.	Nov.	Dec.
1999-00	330.2	467.6	460.2	436.5	489.8	482.5	350.2	441.2	325.0	260.2	305.8	225.9
2000-01	292.9	317.4	343.8	423.7	333.9	325.8	309.1	313.3	286.9	341.3	338.1	273.9
2001-02	383.3	305.5	302.9	393.7	289.7	272.0	336.5	253.8	212.7	343.3	202.4	256.5
2002-03	240.0	285.2	371.7	337.0	299.1	259.5	335.7	263.5	311.8	271.6	228.4	266.9
2003-04	219.9	317.8	432.4	280.7	328.9	415.8	375.0	338.6	465.5	314.9	344.6	196.3
2004-05	210.7	357.7	286.8	271.3	340.9	310.4	248.0	307.5	349.0	244.8	362.3	238.3
2005-06	171.8	316.1	304.9	338.0	326.6	301.6	286.5	415.4	303.5	266.2	372.6	225.8
2006-07	313.8	388.4	373.6	468.9	372.4	289.4	329.9	328.6	279.0	316.8	314.9	231.9
2007-08	346.0	313.3	294.8	422.0	288.5	335.8	395.4	339.9	433.2	424.3	299.3	415.3
2008-09[1]	293.9	372.1	599.8	413.9								

[1] Preliminary.   [2] Including millfeed and lecithin.   *Sources: Economic Research Service, U.S. Department of Agriculture (ERS-USDA)*

SOYBEAN MEAL

Soybean Meal (monthly average) through December 2008 — USD per ton

Average Price of Soybean Meal (48% Solvent) in Decatur Illinois   In Dollars Per Short Ton -- Bulk

Year	Jan.	Feb.	Mar.	Apr.	May	June	July	Aug.	Sept.	Oct.	Nov.	Dec.	Average
1999-00	153.57	154.70	154.00	163.41	170.85	175.50	177.53	189.34	177.45	163.38	157.48	174.60	167.65
2000-01	171.52	179.95	195.65	183.17	166.08	156.32	158.48	165.14	172.60	184.43	178.46	171.67	173.62
2001-02	165.45	166.10	154.18	158.01	153.11	160.49	161.57	164.28	170.33	187.45	186.25	185.45	167.72
2002-03	168.20	163.20	163.60	167.40	176.80	175.40	182.10	195.40	191.90	187.30	189.70	217.95	181.58
2003-04	225.20	242.00	231.54	252.15	257.39	301.14	311.83	300.69	285.81	284.05	205.34	175.51	256.05
2004-05	155.37	153.90	161.60	167.34	167.95	187.96	193.19	198.68	219.28	215.75	198.43	175.40	182.90
2005-06	166.22	170.32	193.17	183.64	176.73	175.07	174.64	175.77	176.83	168.97	159.76	168.87	174.17
2006-07	177.71	190.67	180.63	190.36	208.81	205.26	189.37	198.66	229.70	222.05	217.63	254.41	205.44
2007-08	260.55	280.76	314.78	331.28	345.87	331.57	329.94	325.48	390.72	412.25	355.35	352.70	335.94
2008-09	260.66	267.37	268.24	306.85	297.42								280.11

Source: Economic Research Service, U.S. Department of Agriculture (ERS-USDA)

Average Price of Soybean Meal (44% Solvent) in Decatur Illinois   In Dollars Per Short Ton -- Bulk

Year	Jan.	Feb.	Mar.	Apr.	May	June	July	Aug.	Sept.	Oct.	Nov.	Dec.	Average
1992-93	168.6	170.9	176.4	175.6	167.5	172.4	175.6	181.7	181.3	217.6	206.9	186.5	181.8
1993-94	180.6	195.7	192.5	185.9	184.4	182.0	176.4	191.1	183.0	168.1	165.6	162.5	180.7
1994-95	156.4	150.9	145.4	145.1	149.4	145.7	151.0	148.1	149.1	160.1	157.5	171.8	152.5
1995-96	183.4	194.1	213.6	220.5	216.7	215.7	237.9	232.3	227.9	242.3	251.1	265.5	225.1
1996-97	238.0	242.7	240.9	240.7	253.6	270.4	277.7	296.0	275.9	261.5	261.6	265.7	260.4
1997-98	216.0	231.6	214.9	193.1	182.1	165.3	152.8	150.3	157.8	173.3	135.7	126.9	175.0
1998-99	129.4	139.3	139.6	131.0	124.4	127.2	128.6	127.0	131.7	125.7	135.9	144.1	132.0
1999-00	147.2	148.1	145.4	155.0	163.6	166.6	168.1	180.1	170.2	156.8	151.4	166.9	160.0
2000-01	166.0	173.7	187.9	175.6	158.3	149.1	149.7	155.6	163.1	183.9	170.6	163.5	166.4
2001-02	157.7	157.2	146.6	Disc.	Disc.	Disc.	Disc.	Disc.	Disc.	Disc.	Disc.	Disc.	153.8

Source: Economic Research Service, U.S. Department of Agriculture (ERS-USDA)

Soybean Oil

Soybean oil is the natural oil extracted from whole soybeans. Typically, about 19% of a soybean's weight can be extracted as crude soybean oil. The oil content of U.S. soybeans correlates directly with the temperatures and amount of sunshine during the soybean pod-filling stages. Edible products produced with soybean oil include cooking and salad oils, shortening, and margarine. Soybean oil is the most widely used cooking oil in the U.S. It accounts for 80% of margarine production and for more than 75% of total U.S. consumer vegetable fat and oil consumption. Soy oil is cholesterol-free and high in polyunsaturated fat. Soy oil is also used to produce inedible products such as paints, varnish, resins, and plastics. Of the edible vegetable oils, soy oil is the world's largest at about 32%, followed by palm oil and rapeseed oil. Soybean oil futures and options are traded on the Chicago Board of Trade (CBOT).

Prices – Soybean oil futures prices at the Chicago Board of Trade in 2008 were at about 50.00 cents per pound in January. Prices moved sharply higher and reach a record high of about 70.00 cents per pound in early March. The price dropped sharply to about 55.00 cents per pound by the end of March, and then rebounded to about 67.00 cents per pound in July. From there, the prices moved steadily lower to end the year at about 33.5 cents per pound. There was a brief rally into the new year but then prices again turned lower to reach about 30.00 cents per pound in early March of 2009. Regarding cash prices, for the year 2007-08 (through September 2008), the average monthly price of crude domestic soybean oil (in tank cars) in Decatur (F.O.B.) rose +67.7% yr/yr to 52.03 cents per pound.

Supply – World production of soybean oil in 2008-09 fell -2.8% yr/yr to 36.463 million metric tons, down from last year's record high of 37.511 million metric tons. The U.S. accounts for 23% of world soybean oil production, while Brazil accounts for 16%, and the European Union accounts for 6%. U.S. production of soybean oil in 2008-09 fell -6.6% yr/yr to 19.210 billion pounds.

Demand – World consumption of soybean oil in 2008-09 fell -2.6% yr/yr to 36.517 million metric tons, down from last year's record high of 37.486. The U.S. accounted for 22% of world consumption, while Brazil accounted for 11%, the European Union for 8%, and India for 6%. U.S. consumption of soybean oil in 2008-09 fell -2.6% yr/yr to 17.850 billion pounds.

Trade – World exports of soybean oil in 2008-09 fell -14.2% yr/yr to 9.287 million metric tons. U.S. exports of soybean oil in 2008-09 fell sharply by -39.8% yr/yr to 1.750 billion pounds.

World Supply and Demand of Soybean Oil   In Thousands of Metric Tons

Crop Year Beginning Oct. 1	Brazil	European Union	United States	Total	Brazil	United States	Total	India	Total	Brazil	European Union	India	United States	Total	United States	Total
	Production				Exports			Imports		Consumption					End Stocks[3]	
1999-00	3,943	2,529	8,085	24,491	1,137	624	6,219	790	6,078	2,899	1,666	1,582	7,283	23,956	904	2,866
2000-01	4,333	2,984	8,355	26,736	1,533	636	7,049	1,400	6,948	2,952	2,137	2,024	7,401	26,367	1,255	3,134
2001-02	4,700	3,198	8,572	28,897	1,775	1,143	8,348	1,479	7,737	2,949	2,291	2,300	7,635	28,304	1,070	3,116
2002-03	5,205	2,950	8,360	30,583	2,394	1,027	9,032	1,197	8,272	2,920	2,304	1,900	7,748	30,166	676	2,773
2003-04	5,588	2,531	7,748	30,183	2,718	425	8,804	906	8,333	2,954	2,107	1,885	7,650	30,082	488	2,403
2004-05	5,630	2,575	8,782	32,604	2,414	600	9,116	2,026	8,907	3,130	2,210	2,627	7,911	31,697	771	3,101
2005-06	5,430	2,460	9,248	34,605	2,466	523	9,829	1,727	9,008	3,133	2,915	2,938	8,147	33,507	1,365	3,378
2006-07	5,970	2,640	9,294	36,387	2,462	851	10,570	1,403	9,821	3,510	3,368	2,598	8,426	35,785	1,399	3,231
2007-08[1]	6,110	2,667	9,329	37,511	2,388	1,319	10,825	733	10,392	3,802	3,377	2,269	8,313	37,486	1,126	2,823
2008-09[2]	5,984	2,348	8,532	36,463	2,140	680	9,287	600	8,932	3,976	2,863	2,130	7,984	36,517	1,017	2,414

[1] Preliminary.   [2] Forecast.   [3] End of season.   *Source: Foreign Agricultural Service, U.S. Department of Agriculture (FAS-USDA)*

Supply and Distribution of Soybean Oil in the United States   In Millions of Pounds

Crop Year Beginning Oct. 1	Production	Imports	Stocks Oct. 1	Exports	Total Domestic	Shortening	Margarine	Cooking & Salad Oils	Other Edible	Total Food	Paint & Varnish	Resins & Plastics	Total Non-Food	Total Disappearance
						Domestic Disappearance								
						Food					Non-Food			
1999-00	17,825	83	1,520	1,376	16,057	7,153	1,481	7,075	132	15,841	65	96	586	17,433
2000-01	18,420	73	1,995	1,401	16,210	7,908	1,465	7,361	125	16,859	60	86	535	17,611
2001-02	18,898	46	2,767	2,519	16,833	8,234	1,298	7,373	125	17,030	60	85	519	19,352
2002-03	18,430	46	2,359	2,261	17,085	8,566	1,212	7,886	119	17,783	64	88	520	19,346
2003-04	17,080	306	1,489	936	16,864	8,304	1,138	7,933	NA	17,375	71	100	623	17,800
2004-05	19,360	26	1,076	1,324	17,439	7,938	1,227	7,790	NA	16,955	81	81	747	18,763
2005-06	20,387	35	1,699	1,153	17,959	7,779	848	8,700	NA	17,327	117	85	1,866	19,112
2006-07	20,489	37	3,010	1,877	18,574	6,617	972	9,307	NA	16,896	63	98	3,445	20,451
2007-08[1]	20,568	65	3,085	2,907	18,328						33	108	3,466	21,235
2008-09[2]	18,645	50	2,483	1,500	16,900							110	2,837	18,400

[1] Preliminary.   [2] Forecast.   *Source: Economic Research Service, U.S. Department of Agriculture (ERS-USDA)*

SOYBEAN OIL

Stocks of Crude Soybean Oil in the United States, at End of Month

Year	Oct	Nov	Dec	Jan	Feb	Mar	Apr	May	June	July	Aug	Sept
2002-03	2,097.1	2,114.3	2,197.2	2,186.9	2,062.5	2,028.7	1,916.0	1,843.0	1,706.4	1,595.1	1,458.4	1,282.4
2003-04	1,236.8	1,329.7	1,390.1	1,737.3	1,797.5	1,675.7	1,452.3	1,410.3	1,296.4	1,198.0	1,001.8	887.7
2004-05	1,019.5	1,013.1	1,111.1	1,348.2	1,425.3	1,588.7	1,560.0	1,658.1	1,622.4	1,715.6	1,525.2	1,505.9
2005-06	1,641.0	1,706.5	2,029.6	2,247.4	2,392.2	2,433.1	2,454.7	2,576.8	2,605.3	2,762.9	2,740.2	2,703.5
2006-07	2,680.0	2,719.5	2,700.0	2,739.4	2,853.0	2,974.9	2,897.9	2,928.5	2,962.3	2,816.3	2,666.4	2,558.1
2007-08	2,701.1	2,736.4	2,713.9	2,860.0	2,713.1	2,714.6	2,573.4	2,633.8	2,554.7	2,482.8	2,265.2	2,200.4
2008-09[1]	2,084.0	2,197.8	2,346.7	2,619.2								

Crop year beginning October 1. [1] Preliminary. *Source: Bureau of the Census, U.S. Department of Commerce*

Stocks of Refined Soybean Oil in the United States, at End of Month   In Millions of Pounds

Year	Oct	Nov	Dec	Jan	Feb	Mar	Apr	May	June	July	Aug	Sept
2002-03	197.1	212.0	202.3	209.8	209.5	215.9	204.1	210.8	222.1	199.1	196.0	208.3
2003-04	175.0	200.8	189.9	208.3	190.5	180.2	191.9	241.2	217.7	214.0	178.8	187.8
2004-05	235.8	178.4	200.3	212.6	222.0	222.7	243.4	236.6	216.2	273.8	200.7	193.6
2005-06	254.1	178.9	199.4	251.3	281.2	285.0	300.8	308.2	313.9	343.2	320.9	315.3
2006-07	334.7	355.6	381.7	442.4	427.7	386.5	403.5	382.4	397.9	408.2	380.0	346.1
2007-08	352.1	319.3	364.8	374.5	362.5	360.7	344.1	344.7	338.8	300.8	286.3	282.3
2008-09[1]	307.3	337.6	298.5	313.5								

Crop year beginning October 1. [1] Preliminary. *Source: Bureau of the Census, U.S. Department of Commerce*

U.S. Exports of Soybean Oil[1], by Country of Destination   In Metric Tons

Crop Year Beginning Oct. 1	Canada	Ecuador	Ethiopia	Haiti	India	Mexico	Morocco	Pakistan	Panama	Peru	Turkey	Venezuela	Total
1998-99	11,316	4,858	2,933	44,957	71,685	99,112	43,346	0	1,369	62,085	8,497	1,464	1,075,699
1999-00	22,715	0	13,627	25,214	23,413	118,079	14,091	0	299	66,686	15,680	414	623,651
2000-01	54,909	9,849	5,224	5,793	54,062	72,456	0	62,999	4,558	60,606	0	577	635,493
2001-02	87,047	0	2,225	9,452	88,529	161,760	39,439	59,999	12,616	37,677	85,199	635	1,142,755
2002-03	124,667	0	11,997	1,997	42,727	188,993	26,517	38,215	2,241	20,349	26,500	311	1,026,638
2003-04	96,450	10	3,665	1,298	14,561	97,099	15,518	17	2,834	25,097	0	169	424,554
2004-05	68,162	0	1,529	4,375	29,385	162,913	6,579	15,506	7,247	15,459	21	6,063	600,399
2005-06	76,342	2	3,270	3,972	23,031	108,515	21,951	12,000	1,546	19,588	4,032	38	523,153
2006-07	80,068	3	550	1,962	14,301	151,641	60,347	2	3,409	5,940	16	26,806	851,221
2007-08[2]	90,917	3,009	2,141	14,138	11	268,986	107,323	0	6,817	183	73	82,035	1,318,834

[1] Crude & Refined oil combined as such. [2] Preliminary. *Source: Foreign Agricultural Service, U.S. Department of Agriculture (FAS-USDA)*

Production of Crude Soybean Oil in the United States   In Millions of Pounds

Year	Oct.	Nov.	Dec.	Jan.	Feb.	Mar.	Apr.	May	June	July	Aug.	Sept.	Total
2000-01	1,672.7	1,590.8	1,579.0	1,642.3	1,435.7	1,602.4	1,485.2	1,478.7	1,448.8	1,525.6	1,506.1	1,452.5	18,420
2001-02	1,680.1	1,629.0	1,696.4	1,706.7	1,543.7	1,661.9	1,550.6	1,574.0	1,506.1	1,461.2	1,474.8	1,413.8	18,898
2002-03	1,692.6	1,631.5	1,696.0	1,612.8	1,473.6	1,633.3	1,447.5	1,491.7	1,391.0	1,482.4	1,440.4	1,445.2	18,438
2003-04	1,630.8	1,610.6	1,604.6	1,618.3	1,462.4	1,461.4	1,260.3	1,314.6	1,236.0	1,304.0	1,185.9	1,391.7	17,081
2004-05	1,759.6	1,688.0	1,682.3	1,680.2	1,564.1	1,686.4	1,579.6	1,620.1	1,497.3	1,586.7	1,484.4	1,531.1	19,360
2005-06	1,828.6	1,756.7	1,717.3	1,765.2	1,594.8	1,746.5	1,586.3	1,709.3	1,608.7	1,737.6	1,657.7	1,684.1	20,393
2006-07	1,829.5	1,725.0	1,771.0	1,747.2	1,548.3	1,766.9	1,626.3	1,729.9	1,693.5	1,710.7	1,662.8	1,678.0	20,489
2007-08	1,868.6	1,805.4	1,879.4	1,855.2	1,663.2	1,827.8	1,707.0	1,756.9	1,633.3	1,616.9	1,508.0	1,445.9	20,568
2008-09[1]	1,716.4	1,623.3	1,597.4	1,618.7									19,667

Crop year beginning October 1. [1] Preliminary. *Source: Bureau of the Census, U.S. Department of Commerce*

Production of Refined Soybean Oil in the United States   In Millions of Pounds

Year	Oct.	Nov.	Dec.	Jan.	Feb.	Mar.	Apr.	May	June	July	Aug.	Sept.	Total
2000-01	1,260.3	1,159.7	1,093.4	1,107.5	1,166.8	1,211.3	1,170.0	1,234.1	1,204.6	1,222.8	1,317.4	1,201.2	14,349
2001-02	1,383.2	1,363.5	1,266.9	1,231.8	1,183.9	1,330.0	1,270.5	1,297.9	1,287.7	1,272.8	1,308.4	1,362.4	15,559
2002-03	1,451.2	1,367.2	1,262.2	1,224.5	1,181.0	1,308.2	1,238.6	1,378.8	1,316.1	1,293.8	1,290.5	1,334.8	15,647
2003-04	1,393.0	1,350.9	1,226.6	1,205.6	1,196.0	1,330.6	1,210.3	1,267.4	1,195.9	1,246.8	1,268.8	1,306.3	15,198
2004-05	1,377.6	1,331.1	1,243.2	1,243.4	1,188.1	1,321.6	1,324.5	1,287.4	1,253.6	1,295.9	1,324.1	1,324.7	15,515
2005-06	1,389.3	1,307.4	1,245.2	1,273.9	1,132.9	1,409.3	1,326.6	1,361.5	1,352.9	1,329.1	1,399.7	1,400.0	15,928
2006-07	1,477.9	1,309.3	1,303.9	1,269.3	1,165.2	1,361.0	1,361.8	1,409.8	1,340.8	1,457.5	1,404.0	1,421.0	16,281
2007-08	1,468.6	1,372.3	1,359.7	1,350.5	1,259.6	1,400.0	1,346.2	1,277.0	1,257.6	1,354.7	1,371.8	1,314.7	16,133
2008-09[1]	1,388.0	1,248.3	1,102.6	1,121.3									14,580

Crop year beginning October 1. [1] Preliminary. *Source: Bureau of the Census, U.S. Department of Commerce*

Coconut Oil and Corn Oil (monthly average) through December 2008   Cents per pound

Consumption of Soybean Oil in End Products in the United States   In Millions of Pounds

Year	Jan.	Feb.	Mar.	Apr.	May	June	July	Aug.	Sept.	Oct.	Nov.	Dec.	Total
1999	1,031.5	979.0	1,156.1	1,087.7	1,091.9	1,079.5	1,082.9	1,185.0	1,185.7	1,183.0	1,199.3	1,135.6	13,397
2000	1,096.6	1,050.5	1,217.9	1,158.9	1,183.6	1,102.9	1,121.1	1,226.4	1,163.6	1,306.1	1,139.7	1,079.6	13,847
2001	1,065.9	1,151.7	1,308.8	1,202.4	1,224.2	1,261.6	1,307.6	1,557.5	1,411.0	1,687.3	1,624.0	1,485.8	16,288
2002	1,461.5	1,395.3	1,568.0	1,505.1	1,549.7	1,492.4	1,490.5	1,545.5	1,543.7	1,710.2	1,587.2	1,458.8	18,308
2003	1,418.1	1,347.4	1,490.0	1,494.9	1,552.6	1,493.1	1,509.5	1,483.5	1,577.7	1,660.7	1,544.2	1,451.4	18,023
2004	1,388.1	1,417.6	1,555.2	1,468.0	1,506.7	1,421.1	1,429.2	1,473.6	1,483.2	1,558.3	1,533.7	1,368.9	17,604
2005	1,365.4	1,609.2	1,609.2	1,587.2	1,589.5	1,496.2	1,523.3	1,570.4	1,527.2	1,589.6	1,546.9	1,416.2	18,430
2006	1,505.2	1,368.8	1,661.4	1,561.1	1,634.9	1,653.2	1,575.5	1,746.2	1,727.9	1,775.6	1,638.6	1,571.5	19,420
2007	1,547.3	1,357.8	1,624.8	1,586.7	1,728.6	1,640.3	1,812.9	1,793.1	1,699.5	1,757.8	1,618.9	1,548.4	19,716
2008[1]	1,623.6	1,476.9	1,625.3	1,580.9	1,510.8	1,528.4	1,589.8	1,624.2	1,559.2	1,662.7	1,500.3	1,348.5	18,630

[1] Preliminary.   *Source: Bureau of the Census, U.S. Department of Commerce*

U.S. Exports of Soybean Oil (Crude and Refined)   In Millions of Pounds

Year	Jan.	Feb.	Mar.	Apr.	May	June	July	Aug.	Sept.	Oct.	Nov.	Dec.	Total
1999	246.1	231.1	130.8	230.8	91.3	135.0	111.7	91.2	196.2	209.1	114.9	157.6	1,946
2000	103.0	146.1	161.3	91.5	48.2	109.8	105.8	57.0	69.0	43.9	115.2	261.6	1,313
2001	130.4	184.5	142.4	105.8	51.2	109.9	89.1	96.3	70.6	233.9	138.6	164.8	1,518
2002	249.9	446.7	233.3	233.3	87.3	345.4	180.8	95.3	109.8	113.5	194.9	210.2	2,501
2003	277.5	319.1	273.9	211.6	109.5	96.6	234.5	116.0	105.9	152.5	111.3	133.2	2,142
2004	71.2	62.8	73.5	38.8	44.0	39.3	53.9	68.8	86.8	59.9	184.5	239.5	1,023
2005	77.0	217.2	74.6	74.8	71.9	68.5	52.4	137.3	65.9	76.3	154.1	107.8	1,178
2006	71.3	67.0	178.2	96.8	53.8	82.0	89.4	64.7	111.8	167.1	120.3	276.7	1,379
2007	176.4	125.2	81.2	102.7	121.3	123.5	202.1	201.9	190.8	132.9	198.0	391.3	2,047
2008[1]	157.6	507.7	384.5	426.0	163.6	172.3	125.5	183.8	64.1	138.1	102.4	119.9	2,546

[1] Preliminary.   *Source: Bureau of the Census, U.S. Department of Commerce*

Soybean Oil (monthly average) through December 2008 — Cents per pound

Stocks of Soybean Oil (Crude and Refined) at Factories and Warehouses in the U.S.   In Millions of Pounds

Year	Oct.	Nov.	Dec.	Jan.	Feb.	Mar.	Apr.	May	June	July	Aug.	Sept.
1999-00	1,519.6	1,616.4	1,663.6	1,791.1	2,013.7	2,099.8	2,092.7	2,099.2	1,991.9	2,028.3	2,120.4	2,018.1
2000-01	1,995.3	2,060.8	2,167.5	2,298.0	2,379.7	2,474.0	2,504.0	2,505.8	2,656.1	2,776.7	2,895.5	2,869.9
2001-02	2,877.2	2,724.9	2,787.4	2,868.1	3,038.5	2,896.4	2,952.7	2,856.8	2,943.2	2,735.9	2,529.7	2,521.7
2002-03	2,358.6	2,280.1	2,326.1	2,398.0	2,395.7	2,271.9	2,244.6	2,120.2	2,053.9	1,928.5	1,794.2	1,654.4
2003-04	1,490.6	1,411.8	1,530.4	1,579.9	1,945.6	1,988.0	1,855.9	1,644.1	1,651.6	1,514.0	1,412.0	1,180.6
2004-05	1,075.6	1,269.4	1,191.2	1,311.1	1,560.1	1,646.8	1,812.7	1,797.1	1,888.7	1,838.0	1,988.8	1,727.0
2005-06	1,699.0	1,883.5	1,851.8	2,190.5	2,498.7	2,673.4	2,718.1	2,755.4	2,885.0	2,919.2	3,106.1	3,061.2
2006-07	3,009.8	3,012.3	3,081.9	3,090.6	3,356.7	3,477.7	3,558.4	3,500.0	3,468.7	3,549.8	3,399.6	3,200.4
2007-08	3,085.2	3,224.9	3,235.2	3,277.0	3,234.2	3,075.6	3,075.3	2,917.4	2,979.2	2,893.5	2,783.6	2,551.5
2008-09[1]	2,482.7	2,391.2	2,535.4	2,645.2								

On First of Month.   [1] Preliminary.   *Source: Economic Research Service, U.S. Department of Agriculture (ERS-USDA)*

Average Price of Crude Domestic Soybean Oil (in Tank Cars) F.O.B. Decatur   In Cents Per Pound

Year	Oct.	Nov.	Dec.	Jan.	Feb.	Mar.	Apr.	May	June	July	Aug.	Sept.	Average
1999-00	16.08	15.63	15.30	15.63	15.09	16.21	17.52	16.75	15.65	14.70	14.34	14.24	15.60
2000-01	13.50	13.37	13.12	12.53	12.38	13.90	13.53	13.53	14.21	16.49	17.08	15.46	14.09
2001-02	14.38	15.23	15.10	14.82	14.15	14.75	15.31	15.98	17.69	19.12	20.61	20.32	16.46
2002-03	20.75	23.00	22.60	21.50	21.20	21.56	22.40	23.17	22.90	21.80	20.40	23.20	22.04
2003-04	27.40	27.76	29.54	30.34	33.05	34.66	34.19	32.68	30.07	28.05	25.98	25.87	29.97
2004-05	23.23	22.95	21.79	20.46	20.70	23.60	23.09	23.38	24.70	25.46	23.59	23.19	23.01
2005-06	24.26	22.52	21.00	21.63	22.21	23.21	22.98	24.76	24.20	25.86	24.80	23.54	23.41
2006-07	24.80	27.64	27.63	28.00	28.94	29.74	31.06	32.90	34.01	35.74	34.87	36.89	31.02
2007-08	38.10	42.68	45.16	49.77	56.68	57.27	56.58	58.27	62.43	60.54	50.78	46.09	52.03
2008-09[1]	35.50	31.55	29.30	32.16	28.93								31.49

[1] Preliminary.   *Source: Economic Research Service, U.S. Department of Agriculture (ERS-USDA)*

Soybean Oil Futures - CME Group (CBT)
(weekly close) as of January 02, 2009

Cents per pound

Volume of Trading of Soybean Oil Futures in Chicago   In Thousands of Contracts

Year	Jan.	Feb.	Mar.	Apr.	May	June	July	Aug.	Sept.	Oct.	Nov.	Dec.	Total
1999	367.3	555.1	520.6	463.2	350.9	489.2	516.2	552.2	523.4	395.2	497.1	433.5	5,663.9
2000	424.2	451.7	483.2	438.5	451.2	533.4	422.4	456.2	436.8	378.4	507.0	386.8	5,369.9
2001	327.6	458.4	416.7	443.5	403.1	541.2	751.3	612.3	447.4	551.0	579.5	502.3	6,034.3
2002	474.8	497.4	468.9	497.0	526.9	588.4	701.5	648.9	529.4	549.9	705.4	628.0	6,816.5
2003	522.9	540.6	473.7	618.5	520.0	740.5	761.5	594.7	636.5	733.4	656.5	618.5	7,417.3
2004	521.3	722.6	736.2	760.2	631.2	642.9	657.5	549.5	565.4	552.9	654.3	599.3	7,593.3
2005	475.1	799.9	579.6	636.3	565.5	852.3	548.3	637.1	594.8	607.1	672.8	707.4	7,676.1
2006	531.9	611.2	597.6	866.4	688.6	1,024.5	801.2	816.7	729.0	939.3	1,003.3	878.8	9,488.5
2007	784.1	1,091.9	765.0	1,218.3	805.3	1,476.9	1,113.7	1,092.0	947.7	1,213.6	1,324.4	1,337.9	13,170.9
2008	1,294.7	1,541.4	1,291.0	1,551.1	1,107.0	1,467.6	1,624.2	1,386.9	1,441.7	1,414.4	1,252.4	1,455.9	16,828.4

Source: CME Group; Chicago Board of Trade (CBT)

Average Open Interest of Soybean Oil Futures in Chicago   In Contracts

Year	Jan.	Feb.	Mar.	Apr.	May	June	July	Aug.	Sept.	Oct.	Nov.	Dec.
1999	115,407	131,875	136,967	133,404	131,993	147,749	157,999	147,280	146,239	155,768	163,439	144,798
2000	131,948	135,196	143,699	155,114	134,093	140,582	134,392	135,506	136,590	135,584	142,712	134,873
2001	134,677	133,497	123,770	128,360	142,877	151,713	162,395	166,318	159,467	164,521	167,803	154,589
2002	149,103	158,157	149,913	136,198	128,707	129,480	135,762	143,144	146,759	139,626	169,978	155,871
2003	143,607	140,272	131,323	142,123	147,584	143,218	147,610	157,066	141,596	161,556	183,747	191,176
2004	198,361	212,204	186,745	159,478	141,772	136,887	135,649	142,574	132,936	147,046	154,316	151,800
2005	159,229	174,091	161,971	145,808	135,515	155,962	147,542	132,351	139,489	165,634	175,229	186,760
2006	171,317	183,717	192,643	204,132	244,580	241,962	276,251	269,208	259,464	256,153	279,091	273,375
2007	256,800	283,761	285,436	312,454	301,566	309,109	294,005	285,255	277,219	276,874	306,390	298,906
2008	289,892	292,918	287,995	275,016	253,974	259,416	258,412	254,496	256,621	257,226	252,077	220,725

Source: CME Group; Chicago Board of Trade (CBT)

Soybeans

Soybean is the common name for the annual leguminous plant and its seed. The soybean is a member of the oilseed family and is not considered a grain. The soybean seeds are contained in pods and are nearly spherical in shape. The seeds are usually light yellow in color. The seeds contain 20% oil and 40% protein. Soybeans were an ancient food crop in China, Japan, and Korea and were only introduced to the U.S. in the early 1800s. Today, soybeans are the second largest crop produced in the U.S. behind corn. Soybean production in the U.S. is concentrated in the Midwest and the lower Mississippi Valley. Soybean crops in the U.S. are planted in May or June and are harvested in autumn. Soybean plants usually reach maturity 100-150 days after planting depending on growing conditions.

Soybeans are used to produce a wide variety of food products. The key value of soybeans lies in the relatively high protein content, which makes it an excellent source of protein without many of the negative factors of animal meat. Popular soy-based food products include whole soybeans (roasted for snacks or used in sauces, stews and soups), soy oil for cooking and baking, soy flour, protein concentrates, isolated soy protein (which contains up to 92% protein), soy milk and baby formula (as an alternative to dairy products), soy yogurt, soy cheese, soy nut butter, soy sprouts, tofu and tofu products (soybean curd), soy sauce (which is produced by a fermentation process), and meat alternatives (hamburgers, breakfast sausage, etc).

The primary market for soybean futures is at the Chicago Board of Trade. The CBOT's soybean contract calls for the delivery of 5,000 bushels of No. 2 yellow soybeans (at contract par), No. 1 yellow soybeans (at 6 cents per bushel above the contract price), or No. 3 yellow soybeans (at a 6 cents under the contract price). Soybean futures are also traded at exchanges in Brazil, Argentina, China, and Tokyo.

Prices – Soybean futures prices in early 2008 extended the rally that began in late 2006. Soybean prices hit a record high of $16.60 per bushel in July 2008. Soybean prices in the second half of 2008 then plunged by an overall 53% to post a 1-1/2 year low of $7.77 per bushel in December 2008. Soybean futures prices closed 2008 at $9.7225, down $2.2675 per bushel (or −18.9%) from the 2007 close of $11.99. Soybean prices from late 2006 through early 2008 more than doubled in price as ethanol producer demand for corn took planted acres away from soybeans and created a short supply. U.S. planted soybean acreage in 2007/08 plunged by -14.3% as U.S. farmers switched land to corn from soybeans. The lower soybean acreage produced a sharp -16% decline in the size of the U.S. soybean crop in 2007-08 to 2.68 billion bushels, pushing the U.S. soybean carry-over down by 64% to a 4-year low of 205 billion bushels. The tight soybean supply created a sharp rally in soybean prices and U.S. farmers in spring 2008 therefore boosted their planting of soybeans by 17% and the size of the U.S. soybean crop in 2008-09 recovered by 10.5% to 2.96 billion bushels. The sharp rally in petroleum and fertilizer prices in 2007 and 2008 also prompted some switching by U.S. farmers to soybean planting since corn requires more costly fertilization. Soybean prices plunged in the latter half of 2008 as commodity prices in general plunged and the global recession reduced demand for soybeans for food and for biodiesel production.

Supply – World soybean production during the 2008-09 marketing year (Sep-Aug) rose by +1.5% yr/yr to 224.147 million metric tons, but still down from the 2006-07 record high. World soybean production has more than doubled from the 81 million metric ton level seen in 1980. The world's largest soybean producers were the U.S. with 36% of world production in 2008-09, Brazil (25%), Argentina (20%), China (8%), and India (4%). China's soybean production has roughly doubled since 1980. Brazil's production has risen by almost 4 times since 1980.

U.S. soybean production in 2008-09 rose by +10.6% yr/yr to 2.959 billion bushels, but still down from the 2006-07 record high. U.S. farmers harvested a record high of 74.641 million acres of soybeans in 2008-09, which is up +18.8% yr/yr. The average yield of 39.6 bushels per acre in 2008-09 is down ¬-5.0% yr/yr, down from the 2005-06 record high of 43.0. U.S. ending stocks for the 2008-09 marketing year (September 1), fell sharply by -64.3% to 205 million bushels but still above the 3-decade low of 112 million bushels seen in 2003-04.

Demand – Total U.S. distribution in 2008-09 fell -3.5% to 2.948 billion bushels. The distribution tables for U.S. soybeans for the 2008-09 marketing year show that 57% of U.S. soybean usage went for crushing into soybean oil and meal, 37% for exports, and 6% for seed and residual. The quantity of soybeans that went for crushing fell -6.4% yr/yr in 2008-09 to 1.685 billion bushels. The world soybean crush fell -2.7% yr/yr in 2008-09 to 196.221 million metric tons, which was down from last year's record high but was more than double the level seen in 1980.

Trade – World exports of soybeans in 2008-09 fell -5.8% yr/yr to 74.849 million metric tons, down from last year's record high. The world's largest soybean exporters in 2008-09 were the U.S. with 40% of world exports, Brazil with 32% of world exports, and Argentina with 17% of world exports. U.S. soybean exports in 2008-09 fell -1.0% yr/yr to 31.298 million metric tons, down from last year's record high. Brazil's soybean exports have more than doubled in the past decade.

World imports in 2008-09 fell -6.2% yr/yr to 73.988 million metric tons, down from last year's record high. The world's largest importers of soybeans in 2008-09 were China with 49% of world imports, the European Union with 18%, Japan with 5%, and Mexico with 5%. China's imports in 2008-09 fell -4.8% yr/yr to 36.000 million metric tons, down from last year's record high but way up from negligible levels prior to 1994.

World Production of Soybeans   In Thousands of Metric Tons

Crop Year[4]	Argen-tina	Bolivia	Brazil	Canada	China	India	Indo-nesia	Mexico	Para-guay	Thailand	United States	Russia	World Total
1999-00	21,200	1,200	34,700	2,776	14,290	5,200	1,300	123	2,911	330	72,224	334	160,349
2000-01	27,800	1,150	39,500	2,703	15,400	5,250	1,020	103	3,502	312	75,055	342	175,759
2001-02	30,000	1,245	43,500	1,635	15,410	5,400	870	66	3,547	270	78,672	350	184,818
2002-03	35,500	1,650	52,000	2,336	16,510	4,000	780	89	4,500	250	75,010	423	196,864
2003-04	33,000	1,850	51,000	2,263	15,394	6,800	820	125	3,911	220	66,783	393	186,638
2004-05	39,000	2,027	53,000	3,042	17,400	5,850	825	132	4,040	217	85,019	555	215,774
2005-06	40,500	2,060	57,000	3,161	16,350	7,000	832	185	3,640	226	83,507	689	220,670
2006-07[1]	48,800	1,650	59,000	3,460	15,967	7,690	815	80	6,200	210	87,001	807	237,541
2007-08[2]	46,200	1,050	61,000	2,700	14,000	9,300	780	76	6,800	210	72,859	652	220,882
2008-09[3]	43,800	1,200	57,000	3,300	16,800	10,000	800	160	4,000	180	80,536	700	224,147

[1] Preliminary.   [2] Estimate.   [3] Forecast.   [4] Spilt year includes Northern Hemisphere crops harvested in the late months of the first year shown combined with Southern Hemisphere crops harvested in the early months of the following year.   Sources: Oil World; Foreign Agricultural Service, U.S. Department of Agriculture (FAS-USDA)

World Crushings and Ending Stocks of Soybeans   In Thousands of Metric Tons

Crop Year	Argen-tina	Brazil	China	European Union	India	Japan	Mexico	Taiwan	United States	World Total	Brazil	United States	World Total
	Crushings										Ending Stocks		
1999-00	17,074	21,084	15,070	14,139	4,400	3,750	4,100	2,098	42,927	135,084	9,418	7,897	30,176
2000-01	17,300	22,742	18,900	16,728	4,525	3,775	4,450	2,128	44,625	146,602	9,448	6,743	33,696
2001-02	20,859	24,693	20,250	17,819	4,629	3,885	4,610	2,187	46,259	158,018	12,593	5,663	35,526
2002-03	23,533	27,168	26,540	16,480	3,420	4,217	4,335	2,135	43,948	165,634	16,636	4,853	42,870
2003-04	25,040	29,323	25,439	14,084	5,534	3,536	3,889	2,046	41,632	163,767	15,507	3,059	37,848
2004-05	27,313	29,344	30,362	14,350	5,030	3,149	3,729	2,013	46,160	175,749	16,658	6,960	47,449
2005-06	31,888	28,285	34,500	13,670	5,990	2,820	3,823	2,190	47,324	185,222	16,641	12,229	53,090
2006-07[1]	33,586	31,109	35,970	14,670	6,615	2,925	3,900	2,161	49,198	195,898	18,190	15,617	62,688
2007-08[2]	34,607	31,838	39,518	14,870	7,998	2,890	3,700	1,927	49,024	201,681	19,178	5,580	53,207
2008-09[3]	33,720	31,200	41,104	13,050	8,640	2,840	3,515	2,075	44,906	196,221	17,122	5,710	49,873

[1] Preliminary.   [2] Estimate.   [3] Forecast.   Sources: Oil World; Foreign Agricultural Service, U.S. Department of Agriculture (FAS-USDA)

World Imports and Exports of Soybeans   In Thousands of Metric Tons

Crop Year	China	European Union	Japan	Rep. of Korea	Mexico	Taiwan	World Total	Argen-tina	Brazil	Canada	Para-guay	United States	World Total
	Imports							Exports					
1999-00	10,100	14,122	4,907	1,606	4,039	2,408	45,568	4,125	11,101	949	2,025	26,537	45,616
2000-01	13,245	17,602	4,767	1,389	4,381	2,330	53,052	7,304	15,469	747	2,509	27,103	53,756
2001-02	10,385	18,675	5,023	1,434	4,510	2,578	54,387	5,960	14,504	502	2,285	28,948	52,896
2002-03	21,417	16,943	5,087	1,516	4,230	2,351	62,923	8,624	19,629	726	2,806	28,423	60,982
2003-04	16,933	14,675	4,688	1,368	3,797	2,217	54,000	6,741	20,417	914	2,776	24,128	56,204
2004-05	25,802	14,539	4,295	1,240	3,640	2,256	63,484	9,568	20,137	1,124	2,888	29,860	64,787
2005-06	28,317	13,937	3,962	1,190	3,667	2,498	64,172	7,249	25,911	1,318	2,315	25,579	63,780
2006-07[1]	28,726	15,291	4,094	1,231	3,844	2,436	69,162	9,559	23,485	1,683	4,500	30,386	71,502
2007-08[2]	37,816	15,148	4,014	1,231	3,650	2,149	78,889	13,830	25,364	1,775	5,080	31,598	79,477
2008-09[3]	36,000	13,550	4,000	1,260	3,400	2,350	73,988	12,700	24,900	1,830	2,400	31,298	74,849

[1] Preliminary.   [2] Estimate.   [3] Forecast.   Sources: Oil World; Foreign Agricultural Service, U.S. Department of Agriculture (FAS-USDA)

Supply and Distribution of Soybeans in the United States   In Millions of Bushels

Crop Year Beginning Sept. 1	Farms	Mills, Elevators[3]	Total	Production	Total Supply	Crushings	Exports	Seed, Feed & Residual Use	Total Distri-bution
	Supply					Distribution			
	Stocks, Sept. 1								
1999-00	145.0	203.5	348.5	2,653.8	3,006.0	1,578.0	973.0	165.0	2,716.0
2000-01	112.5	177.7	290.2	2,757.8	3,052.0	1,640.0	996.0	168.0	2,804.0
2001-02	83.5	164.2	247.7	2,890.7	3,141.0	1,700.0	1,064.0	169.0	2,933.0
2002-03	62.7	145.3	208.0	2,756.1	2,969.0	1,615.0	1,044.0	131.0	2,791.0
2003-04	58.0	120.3	178.3	2,453.7	2,638.0	1,530.0	887.0	109.0	2,525.0
2004-05	29.4	83.0	112.4	3,123.7	3,242.0	1,696.0	1,097.0	193.0	2,986.0
2005-06	99.7	156.0	255.7	3,063.2	3,322.0	1,739.0	940.0	194.0	2,873.0
2006-07	176.3	273.0	449.3	3,188.2	3,655.0	1,808.0	1,116.0	157.0	3,081.0
2007-08[1]	143.0	430.8	573.8	2,675.8	3,261.0	1,801.0	1,161.0	93.0	3,056.0
2008-09[2]	47.0	158.0	205.0	2,959.2	3,173.0	1,640.0	1,185.0	163.0	2,988.0

[1] Preliminary.   [2] Estimate.   [3] Also warehouses.   Source: Economic Research Service, U.S. Department of Agriculture (ERS-USDA)

SOYBEANS

Salient Statistics & Official Crop Production Reports of Soybeans in the United States   In Millions of Bushels

Year	Planted ---- 1,000 Acres ----	Acreage Harvested	Yield Per Acre (Bu.)	Farm Price ($/Bu.)	Farm Value (Million Dollars)	Yield of Oil (Lbs. Per Bushel Crushed)	Yield of Meal (Lbs. Per Bushel Crushed)	Aug. 1	Sept. 1	Oct. 1	Nov. 1	Dec. 1	Final
1999-00	73,730	72,446	36.6	4.63	12,287	11.34	47.76	2,869,519	2,778,392	2,696,272	2,672,972	----	2,653,758
2000-01	74,266	72,408	38.1	4.54	12,548	11.24	48.06	2,988,669	2,899,571	2,822,821	2,777,036	----	2,757,810
2001-02	74,075	72,975	39.6	4.38	12,606	11.14	44.27	2,867,474	2,833,511	2,907,042	2,922,914	----	2,890,682
2002-03	73,963	72,497	38.0	5.64	15,253	11.39	43.90	2,628,387	2,655,819	2,653,798	2,689,691	----	2,756,147
2003-04	73,404	72,476	33.9	7.95	18,014	11.20	44.32	2,862,039	2,642,644	2,468,390	2,451,759	----	2,453,665
2004-05	75,208	73,958	42.2	5.90	17,895	11.33	44.26	2,876,627	2,835,989	3,106,861	3,150,441	----	3,123,686
2005-06	72,032	71,251	43.0	5.63	17,269	11.64	43.83	2,791,133	2,856,449	2,967,075	3,043,116	----	3,063,237
2006-07	75,522	74,602	42.9	6.67	20,468	11.34	43.85	2,927,634	3,092,970	3,188,576	3,203,908	----	3,188,247
2007-08[1]	63,631	62,820	41.7	11.04	26,974			2,625,274	2,618,796	2,598,046	2,594,275	----	2,675,822
2008-09[2]	75,718	74,641	39.6	9.84	27,399			2,972,577	2,933,888	2,983,023	2,920,589		2,959,174

Crop Production Reports ---------------------- In Thousands of Bushels ----------------------

[1] Preliminary.   [2] Forecast.   NA = Not available.   Source: National Agricultural Statistics Service, U.S. Department of Agriculture (NASS-USDA)

Stocks of Soybeans in the United States   In Thousands of Bushels

Year	Mar. 1	June 1	Sept. 1	Dec. 1	Mar. 1	June 1	Sept. 1	Dec. 1	Mar. 1	June 1	Sept. 1	Dec. 1
	On Farms				Off Farms				Total Stocks			
1999	815,000	458,000	145,000	1,150,000	642,338	390,573	203,482	1,032,666	1,457,338	848,573	348,482	2,182,666
2000	730,000	370,000	112,500	1,217,000	665,986	404,425	177,662	1,022,791	1,395,986	774,425	290,162	2,239,791
2001	780,000	365,000	83,500	1,240,000	623,908	343,180	164,247	1,035,713	1,403,908	708,180	247,747	2,275,713
2002	687,000	301,200	62,700	1,170,000	648,987	383,721	145,320	943,641	1,335,987	684,921	208,020	2,113,641
2003	636,500	272,500	58,000	820,000	565,528	329,862	120,329	868,653	1,201,028	602,362	178,329	1,688,653
2004	355,900	110,000	29,400	1,300,000	549,947	300,604	83,014	1,004,640	905,847	410,604	112,414	2,304,640
2005	795,000	356,100	99,700	1,345,000	586,364	343,174	156,038	1,157,098	1,381,364	699,274	255,738	2,502,098
2006	872,000	495,500	176,300	1,461,000	797,206	495,199	273,026	1,240,366	1,669,206	990,699	449,326	2,701,366
2007	910,000	500,000	143,000	1,100,000	876,887	592,185	430,810	1,231,860	1,786,887	1,092,185	573,810	2,331,860
2008[1]	593,000	226,600	47,000	1,189,000	840,982	449,543	158,034	1,086,593	1,433,982	676,143	205,034	2,275,593

[1] Preliminary.   Source: National Agricultural Statistics Service, U.S. Department of Agriculture (NASS-USDA)

Commercial Stocks of Soybeans in the United States, on First of Month   In Millions of Bushels

Year	Jan.	Feb.	Mar.	Apr.	May	June	July	Aug.	Sept.	Oct.	Nov.	Dec.
1999	39.1	31.5	29.0	28.7	25.0	18.9	16.1	17.3	14.1	19.5	46.9	42.3
2000	34.1	28.3	30.0	23.9	23.8	20.6	17.0	12.3	8.6	15.5	38.2	37.9
2001	34.5	28.8	25.2	22.5	16.3	15.0	12.9	13.4	11.9	9.6	34.7	38.2
2002	29.6	27.0	22.2	21.0	18.4	15.4	14.4	10.2	4.6	8.4	26.9	28.4
2003	25.9	13.2	13.9	12.8	9.7	9.4	11.7	7.6	4.5	7.0	33.0	36.7
2004	35.5	26.2	26.0	19.4	15.7	13.5	8.0	5.9	4.4	10.8	31.1	32.9
2005	26.5	21.5	19.5	16.0	14.8	12.1	11.5	8.8	5.4	17.0	36.7	36.1
2006	36.8	30.2	26.1	25.7	17.6	20.5	14.6	14.5	14.5	19.0	40.1	43.7
2007	42.0	36.5	37.3	34.3	29.7	27.4	26.6	24.6	25.5	32.0	54.0	61.3
2008	51.1	45.5	41.8	36.3	28.2	25.6	19.2	14.8	11.4	19.6	40.5	46.1

Source: Livestock Division, U.S. Department of Agriculture (LD-USDA)

Stocks of Soybeans at Mills in the United States, on First of Month   In Millions of Bushels

Year	Sept.	Oct.	Nov.	Dec.	Jan.	Feb.	Mar.	Apr.	May	June	July	Aug.
1997-98	28.3	37.0	126.4	124.3	110.3	98.7	93.4	72.0	56.9	41.0	42.5	44.1
1998-99	32.8	66.5	175.0	154.3	131.0	109.6	102.5	93.7	80.5	56.9	55.5	48.1
1999-00	41.7	70.8	162.9	144.7	144.2	140.3	137.8	129.6	98.7	78.7	78.4	52.1
2000-01	52.1	56.8	179.4	166.8	137.8	143.3	127.0	120.6	94.9	86.1	79.3	69.0
2001-02	69.0	41.3	152.8	137.1	121.4	129.6	128.2	112.9	104.2	88.2	67.9	65.4
2002-03	46.4	36.3	114.5	113.5	106.0	109.2	102.9	91.5	91.6	76.0	64.9	55.6
2003-04	35.3	31.9	129.9	121.0	121.7	125.6	124.5	134.3	114.8	91.2	76.0	61.4
2004-05	37.0	74.8	114.1	113.1	100.3	85.6	88.1	88.8	70.9	59.2	66.1	51.7
2005-06	43.7	66.2	158.3	129.7	114.1	117.4	108.0	90.0	69.5	64.0	63.1	51.5
2006-07[1]	52.7	48.7	124.7	132.4	127.0	132.9	121.7	123.5	113.6	101.9	103.4	99.0

[1] Preliminary.   Source: Economic Research Service, U.S. Department of Agriculture (ERS-USDA)

Production of Soybeans for Beans in the United States, by State   In Millions of Bushels

Year	Arkan-sas	Illinois	Indiana	Iowa	Ken-tucky	Mich-igan	Minn-esota	Miss-issippi	Missouri	Neb-raska	Ohio	Tenn-essee	Total
1999-00	92.4	443.1	216.5	478.4	24.4	77.6	289.8	44.7	147.1	180.6	162.0	22.8	2,653.8
2000-01	80.3	459.8	252.1	464.6	45.2	73.1	293.2	34.8	175.0	173.9	186.5	28.8	2,757.8
2001-02	91.2	477.9	273.9	480.5	48.8	63.9	266.4	37.0	186.2	223.0	187.8	35.4	2,890.7
2002-03	96.5	453.7	239.5	499.2	42.6	78.5	308.9	43.8	170.0	176.3	151.0	34.7	2,756.1
2003-04	111.3	379.6	204.1	342.9	53.9	54.7	238.4	55.8	146.0	182.3	164.8	47.0	2,453.7
2004-05	122.9	495.0	284.3	497.4	57.2	75.2	232.7	61.5	223.2	218.5	207.7	48.4	3,123.7
2005-06	102.0	439.4	263.6	525.0	53.3	76.6	306.0	58.0	181.7	235.3	201.6	41.8	3,063.2
2006-07	107.5	482.4	284.0	510.1	60.3	89.6	319.0	42.9	191.2	250.5	217.1	44.1	3,188.2
2007-08	101.5	360.2	220.3	448.8	30.3	70.7	267.3	58.3	175.1	196.4	199.3	19.2	2,675.8
2008-09[1]	130.0	416.3	237.6	441.6	47.3	69.9	269.1	75.2	191.9	223.1	161.3	45.3	2,959.2

[1] Preliminary.   Source: Agricultural Statistics Board, U.S. Department of Agriculture (ASB-USDA)

U. S. Exports of Soybeans   In Millions of Bushels

Year	Sept.	Oct.	Nov.	Dec.	Jan.	Feb.	Mar.	Apr.	May	June	July	Aug.	Total
1999-00	69.4	122.8	104.5	109.1	104.0	103.1	109.7	50.6	45.6	46.0	50.3	58.4	973.4
2000-01	51.4	141.4	123.0	106.6	103.3	126.5	135.2	52.8	39.8	39.5	33.1	43.4	995.9
2001-02	31.7	158.9	158.0	133.2	157.2	132.0	63.8	46.0	45.6	43.2	56.0	38.0	1,063.7
2002-03	30.9	136.7	152.8	114.7	159.3	151.5	92.1	66.4	35.9	31.9	37.9	34.3	1,044.4
2003-04	34.0	165.3	186.4	143.2	109.3	82.6	69.9	28.7	19.1	20.2	14.8	10.8	884.2
2004-05	47.2	177.7	181.0	155.0	121.9	123.2	96.4	65.2	49.6	35.2	20.0	30.3	1,102.7
2005-06	32.3	143.1	140.1	83.1	111.8	111.3	95.6	43.4	46.5	39.0	47.6	51.0	944.8
2006-07	64.9	182.6	126.4	122.7	147.2	126.5	96.9	71.1	41.9	48.9	37.9	49.6	1,116.6
2007-08	62.0	138.6	127.4	146.0	140.9	139.8	119.2	74.9	54.7	62.6	50.6	44.1	1,160.8
2008-09[1]	36.0	178.1	173.5	170.8									1,675.2

[1] Preliminary.   Source: Economic Research Service, U.S. Department of Agriculture (ERS-USDA)

Spread Between Value of Products and Soybean Price in the United States   In Cents Per Bushel

Year	Sept.	Oct.	Nov.	Dec.	Jan.	Feb.	Mar.	Apr.	May	June	July	Aug.	Average
1997-98	177	96	108	87	57	51	35	33	33	29	53	43	67
1998-99	53	53	38	40	33	30	35	37	34	36	47	45	40
1999-00	48	61	64	58	75	61	70	70	80	81	69	62	66
2000-01	81	76	77	89	85	59	65	72	67	81	96	92	78
2001-02	102	108	106	83	86	65	65	65	57	63	64	89	79
2002-03	77	73	52	60	53	52	61	53	62	59	72	74	62
2003-04	117	88	94	81	84	81	96	96	85	97	150	127	99
2004-05	132	95	70	66	75	76	67	78	69	75	73	82	79
2005-06	100	102	70	91	90	84	94	102	106	104	106	110	97
2006-07[1]	126	105	81	74	73	72	80	64	78	113	110	88	87

[1] Preliminary.   Source: Economic Research Service, U.S. Department of Agriculture (ERS-USDA)

Soybean Crushed (Factory Consumption) in the United States   In Millions of Bushels

Year	Jan.	Feb.	Mar.	Apr.	May	June	July	Aug.	Sept.	Oct.	Nov.	Dec.	Total
1999-00	133.8	150.2	142.8	143.0	139.2	125.4	130.4	121.5	121.0	117.9	130.2	122.2	1,578
2000-01	128.9	149.1	143.1	142.3	146.7	128.9	141.8	131.1	132.7	128.0	133.6	133.5	1,640
2001-02	128.2	150.2	149.1	153.4	155.1	139.0	149.8	139.2	140.6	134.6	129.8	130.6	1,700
2002-03	122.3	149.5	145.7	150.2	142.7	129.2	142.8	127.0	129.8	121.4	129.3	125.1	1,615
2003-04	127.6	146.2	145.6	145.8	146.0	131.4	129.6	112.5	117.5	109.4	115.3	103.0	1,530
2004-05	121.0	155.3	151.1	150.0	148.6	137.6	148.5	139.4	142.8	132.0	139.5	130.3	1,696
2005-06	133.2	157.7	151.5	148.4	152.4	136.3	149.5	135.5	146.2	137.4	148.5	142.1	1,739
2006-07	142.4	161.7	155.1	157.4	155.5	136.9	156.1	145.0	152.1	148.9	150.4	146.2	1,808
2007-08	147.3	163.7	156.3	164.1	160.5	144.4	156.0	147.5	152.6	141.0	139.3	128.7	1,801
2008-09[1]	125.7	150.1	144.7	141.3	145.2								1,697

[1] Preliminary.   Source: Economic Research Service, U.S. Department of Agriculture (ERS-USDA)

SOYBEANS

Soybean Futures - CME Group (CBT)
(weekly close) as of January 02, 2009
Cents per bushel

Volume of Trading of Soybean Futures in Chicago   In Thousands of Contracts

Year	Jan.	Feb.	Mar.	Apr.	May	June	July	Aug.	Sept.	Oct.	Nov.	Dec.	Total
1999	871.1	1,025.3	1,440.1	963.5	823.6	1,149.5	1,502.5	1,669.8	903.0	1,158.6	839.4	872.3	12,482
2000	1,071.9	1,099.3	1,191.6	1,079.1	1,321.6	1,302.0	883.4	801.4	860.9	1,188.8	932.5	895.3	12,628
2001	935.0	947.4	843.1	916.3	909.5	1,155.6	1,508.1	1,122.0	648.7	1,356.1	964.7	844.1	12,150
2002	1,078.8	899.9	1,065.7	1,238.6	1,048.3	1,311.8	1,762.2	1,346.4	1,002.9	1,486.1	1,070.9	1,163.5	14,475
2003	1,267.3	1,222.9	997.1	1,588.9	1,368.2	1,723.4	1,385.7	1,193.5	1,308.5	2,416.3	1,535.4	1,538.5	17,546
2004	1,509.7	1,879.6	1,957.2	2,036.2	1,593.2	1,601.7	1,551.3	1,107.6	1,052.8	1,635.3	1,395.3	1,526.1	18,846
2005	1,398.6	2,085.8	1,959.9	1,656.5	1,454.6	2,577.3	1,675.4	1,487.2	1,069.1	1,765.0	1,241.5	1,845.1	20,216
2006	1,503.4	1,889.1	1,501.2	1,916.6	1,682.6	2,443.2	1,798.2	1,638.5	1,420.2	2,884.7	2,017.4	1,952.6	22,648
2007	1,976.3	2,620.6	2,251.0	2,641.2	2,107.2	3,461.3	2,734.6	2,323.7	2,315.2	3,680.4	2,521.3	3,093.5	31,726
2008	3,528.7	3,746.2	2,895.0	3,786.1	2,272.2	3,731.2	3,134.9	2,454.4	2,615.1	3,719.0	1,910.5	2,579.7	36,373

Source: Chicago Board of Trade (CBT)

Average Open Interest of Soybean Futures in Chicago   In Contracts

Year	Jan.	Feb.	Mar.	Apr.	May	June	July	Aug.	Sept.	Oct.	Nov.	Dec.
1999	152,757	166,003	162,690	166,565	164,777	163,663	157,433	134,105	146,087	174,583	164,306	153,693
2000	149,468	172,494	174,465	195,189	193,500	167,678	140,894	126,952	149,074	183,734	168,023	177,324
2001	160,730	164,017	148,190	156,781	137,227	153,190	181,194	165,630	167,677	195,366	175,522	173,116
2002	156,898	169,242	169,882	164,388	156,548	188,692	220,758	201,494	201,808	210,033	208,099	213,868
2003	201,536	217,680	226,421	251,314	230,325	222,185	190,206	190,533	232,030	265,088	241,320	252,874
2004	258,708	267,482	263,737	262,919	222,310	199,108	172,194	171,791	190,006	242,654	228,700	241,972
2005	244,197	266,745	295,324	268,081	252,582	313,724	278,738	256,853	249,030	285,070	275,308	290,370
2006	315,640	359,379	354,211	374,507	375,124	371,155	336,000	348,321	361,643	384,069	394,259	414,374
2007	416,459	478,579	474,466	470,517	465,303	549,655	536,595	495,302	526,913	580,446	586,635	582,502
2008	563,927	598,278	543,451	506,423	458,047	489,069	446,006	388,939	364,679	348,438	312,905	304,252

Source: Chicago Board of Trade (CBT)

Soybeans (monthly average) through December 2008 — Cents per bushel

Average Cash Price of No. 1 Yellow Soybeans at Illinois Processor   In Cents Per Bushel

Year	Jan.	Feb.	Mar.	Apr.	May	June	July	Aug.	Sept.	Oct.	Nov.	Dec.	Average
1997-98	703	684	727	699	679	680	662	649	649	640	642	556	664
1998-99	533	536	572	558	532	490	475	480	468	462	425	465	500
1999-00	485	470	464	460	473	500	513	529	542	510	474	463	490
2000-01	484	468	483	506	477	457	451	441	457	474	517	510	477
2001-02	469	430	441	438	437	440	464	471	492	519	575	567	479
2002-03	579	541	575	566	570	590	580	611	640	635	601	589	590
2003-04	639	729	763	772	823	872	975	992	958	890	809	641	822
2004-05	562	519	534	545	539	544	628	622	644	701	703	639	598
2005-06	565	553	574	592	576	575	569	562	581	576	577	542	570
2006-07[1]	535	580	66	657	683	735	730	718	749	792	801	804	704

[1] Preliminary.   *Source: Economic Research Service, U.S. Department of Agriculture (ERS-USDA)*

Average Price Received by Farmers for Soybeans in the United States   In Dollars Per Bushel

Year	Jan.	Feb.	Mar.	Apr.	May	June	July	Aug.	Sept.	Oct.	Nov.	Dec.	Average
1999-00	4.57	4.48	4.45	4.43	4.62	4.79	4.91	5.00	5.19	4.93	4.53	4.45	4.63
2000-01	4.59	4.45	4.55	4.78	4.68	4.46	4.39	4.22	4.33	4.46	4.79	4.85	4.54
2001-02	4.53	4.09	4.16	4.20	4.22	4.22	4.38	4.47	4.64	4.88	5.35	5.53	4.38
2002-03	5.39	5.20	5.46	5.46	5.51	5.55	5.59	5.82	6.07	6.09	5.82	5.68	5.64
2003-04	6.06	6.60	7.05	7.17	7.35	8.28	9.28	9.62	9.56	9.08	8.46	6.83	7.95
2004-05	5.83	5.56	5.36	5.45	5.57	5.42	5.95	6.03	6.21	6.58	6.65	6.15	5.90
2005-06	5.77	5.67	5.62	5.78	5.87	5.67	5.57	5.52	5.68	5.62	5.61	5.23	5.63
2006-07	5.23	5.52	6.08	6.18	6.37	6.87	6.95	6.88	7.12	7.51	7.56	7.72	6.67
2007-08	8.15	8.36	9.42	10.00	9.95	11.70	11.50	12.00	12.10	13.20	13.30	12.80	11.04
2008-09[1]	10.70	9.94	9.38	9.24	9.92								9.84

[1] Preliminary.   *Source: Economic Research Service, U.S. Department of Agriculture (ERS-USDA)*

Stock Index Futures - U.S.

A stock index simply represents a basket of underlying stocks. Indices can be either price-weighted or capitalization-weighted. In a price-weighted index, such as the Dow Jones Industrials Average, the price of each of the stocks are simply added up and then divided by a divisor, meaning that stocks with higher prices have a higher weighting in the index value. In a capitalization-weighted index, such as the Standard and Poor's 500 index, the weighting of each stock corresponds to the size of the company as determined by its capitalization (i.e., the total dollar value of its stock). Stock indices cover a variety of different sectors. For example, the Dow Jones Industrials Average contains 30 blue-chip stocks that represent the industrial sector. The S&P 500 index includes 500 of the largest blue-chip U.S. companies. The NYSE index includes all the stocks that trade at the New York Stock Exchange. The Nasdaq 100 includes the largest 100 companies that trade on the Nasdaq Exchange. The most popular U.S. stock index futures contract is the S&P 500 at the Chicago Mercantile Exchange (CME).

Prices – The S&P 500 index peaked at a record high of 1576.09 in October 2007. The S&P 500 index then proceeded to plunge through 2008 and early 2009. The S&P 500 index in 2008 closed down –38.5%, breaking the string of five consecutive yearly gains (2007 +3.5%, 2006 +13.6%, 2005 +3.0%, 2004 +9.0%, 2003 +26.4%). In March 2009, the S&P 500 posted a new 12-year low of 666.79, posting an overall sell-off of 57.7% from the record high posted in October 2007.

The S&P 500 started lower in late 2007 after the U.S. housing situation worsened and losses started to grow on mortgage-backed securities. By the end of August 2008, the S&P 500 had fallen by 18.6% from the record high. The sell-off then kicked into high gear during the third week in September 2008 when Lehman Brothers went bankrupt and Merrill Lynch and insurance-giant AIG nearly went bankrupt as well. The global equity markets went into a free-fall after the U.S. government was either unwilling or unable to save Lehman Brothers and investors responded by selling everything in sight to try to preserve what little capital they had left. The global banking system nearly stopped functioning due to concerns about which major financial institution might be the next to fail. In addition, there was concern that the multi-trillion-dollar credit default swaps market might blow up, taking down a series of financial institutions as well.

The Federal Reserve and the U.S. Treasury responded to the crisis with an unprecedented array of liquidity and rescue programs, which eventually succeeded in slowing investor panic. However, stock prices were unable to recover as the market worried about a deep recession and a plunge in corporate earnings. Global trade collapsed due to weak demand and the difficulty of obtaining trade finance. Businesses responded to the crisis by laying off workers at a fast pace, thus causing even more panic among U.S. consumers. The S&P 500 index in early March 2009 fell to a new 12-year low as the market started to doubt whether an economic recovery might even occur in 2009. By March 2009, the S&P 500 was trading at a relatively cheap level using the price/earnings ratio as a benchmark. However, there was little confidence in earnings projections given the high degree of economic and financial uncertainty, making it difficult for stock prices to show a sustained recovery.

Average Value of Dow Jones Industrials Index (30 Stocks)

Year	Jan.	Feb.	Mar.	Apr.	May	June	July	Aug.	Sept.	Oct.	Nov.	Dec.	Average
1999	9,345.9	9,323.0	9,753.6	10,443.5	10,853.9	10,704.0	11,052.2	10,935.5	10,714.0	10,396.9	10,809.8	11,246.4	10,464.9
2000	11,281.3	10,541.9	10,483.4	10,944.4	10,580.3	10,582.9	10,663.0	11,014.5	10,967.9	10,441.0	10,666.1	10,652.4	10,734.9
2001	10,682.7	10,774.6	10,081.3	10,234.5	11,005.0	10,767.2	10,444.5	10,314.7	9,042.6	9,220.8	9,721.8	9,979.9	10,189.1
2002	9,923.8	9,891.1	10,501.0	10,165.2	10,080.5	9,492.4	8,616.5	8,685.5	8,160.2	8,048.1	8,625.7	8,526.7	9,226.4
2003	8,474.4	7,916.2	7,977.7	8,332.1	8,623.4	9,098.1	9,154.5	9,284.8	9,492.5	9,683.6	9,762.2	10,124.7	8,993.7
2004	10,540.1	10,601.5	10,323.7	10,419.9	10,083.8	10,364.9	10,152.1	10,032.8	10,204.6	10,001.6	10,411.8	10,673.4	10,317.5
2005	10,539.5	10,723.8	10,682.1	10,283.2	10,377.2	10,486.6	10,545.4	10,554.3	10,532.5	10,324.3	10,695.3	10,827.8	10,547.7
2006	10,872.5	10,971.2	11,144.5	11,234.7	11,333.9	10,998.0	11,032.5	11,257.4	11,533.6	11,963.1	12,185.2	12,377.6	11,408.7
2007	12,512.9	12,631.5	12,268.5	12,754.8	13,407.8	13,480.2	13,677.9	13,239.7	13,557.7	13,901.3	13,200.5	13,406.9	13,170.0
2008	12,537.4	12,419.6	12,193.9	12,656.6	12,812.5	12,056.7	11,322.4	11,530.8	11,114.1	9,176.7	8,614.6	8,595.6	11,252.6

Source: New York Stock Exchange (NYSE)

Average Value of Dow Jones Transportation Index (20 Stocks)

Year	Jan.	Feb.	Mar.	Apr.	May	June	July	Aug.	Sept.	Oct.	Nov.	Dec.	Average
1999	3,172.0	3,188.3	3,296.4	3,477.7	3,628.2	3,396.1	3,423.7	3,207.0	3,006.2	2,928.7	2,988.7	2,902.1	3,217.9
2000	2,812.2	2,483.4	2,534.5	2,823.9	2,813.2	2,717.2	2,822.3	2,835.6	2,641.5	2,491.0	2,792.3	2,822.9	2,715.8
2001	3,029.9	3,010.2	2,792.5	2,776.6	2,908.2	2,770.4	2,887.3	2,852.1	2,344.8	2,217.3	2,404.6	2,603.0	2,716.4
2002	2,735.3	2,719.1	2,942.9	2,776.0	2,734.8	2,702.2	2,432.1	2,318.5	2,216.0	2,216.6	2,321.6	2,331.7	2,537.2
2003	2,297.3	2,102.5	2,094.6	2,278.7	2,429.9	2,459.6	2,554.5	2,617.3	2,744.7	2,841.3	2,920.0	2,969.3	2,525.8
2004	3,021.0	2,889.4	2,838.3	2,941.1	2,877.1	3,069.0	3,099.8	3,065.8	3,205.1	3,372.6	3,589.4	3,750.0	3,143.2
2005	3,587.0	3,614.5	3,779.4	3,527.8	3,548.8	3,542.1	3,663.1	3,726.1	3,637.0	3,673.1	4,051.7	4,152.1	3,708.6
2006	4,224.5	4,362.5	4,519.5	4,679.6	4,761.4	4,663.1	4,636.1	4,291.1	4,363.3	4,654.7	4,761.6	4,660.0	4,548.1
2007	4,752.2	5,024.6	4,817.3	5,059.2	5,174.8	5,137.2	5,258.8	4,889.0	4,812.7	4,891.2	4,605.9	4,686.4	4,925.8
2008	4,348.7	4,720.0	4,641.9	4,996.9	5,304.5	5,166.7	4,899.2	5,057.0	4,889.3	3,815.4	3,518.5	3,369.2	4,560.6

Source: New York Stock Exchange (NYSE)

Dow Jones 30 Industrials - Logarithmic Scale
(monthly close) through December 2008

Average Value of Dow Jones Utilities Index (15 Stocks)

Year	Jan.	Feb.	Mar.	Apr.	May	June	July	Aug.	Sept.	Oct.	Nov.	Dec.	Average
1999	307.4	293.9	299.4	299.9	320.5	327.8	319.9	317.3	306.8	298.8	294.9	277.4	305.3
2000	300.6	302.3	285.4	307.0	325.2	322.2	325.0	355.6	384.2	386.9	392.5	394.9	340.2
2001	360.9	385.1	375.7	387.0	388.9	367.2	356.8	345.4	321.3	308.8	291.4	284.0	347.7
2002	290.7	279.6	298.4	305.1	297.3	276.1	235.5	241.0	221.7	189.2	200.4	208.5	253.6
2003	217.7	199.5	203.3	215.9	232.3	250.4	240.3	236.8	246.5	253.1	249.2	258.4	233.6
2004	268.8	272.2	278.2	275.6	268.4	275.4	278.8	285.3	293.3	303.3	324.9	327.8	287.7
2005	331.9	351.5	356.3	364.5	364.4	376.3	392.5	397.4	422.7	401.3	395.3	409.0	380.2
2006	416.7	408.2	401.7	392.1	401.0	409.2	424.1	436.9	430.1	439.8	449.1	458.5	422.3
2007	449.9	474.1	486.1	516.9	526.2	498.2	502.3	489.0	499.5	514.0	523.5	540.9	501.7
2008	518.8	499.0	480.3	506.2	516.7	519.1	500.8	472.4	446.3	370.1	368.1	362.7	463.4

Source: New York Stock Exchange (NYSE)

Average Value of Standard & Poor's 500 Index

Year	Jan.	Feb.	Mar.	Apr.	May	June	July	Aug.	Sept.	Oct.	Nov.	Dec.	Average
1999	1,248.7	1,246.6	1,281.7	1,334.8	1,332.1	1,322.6	1,381.0	1,327.5	1,318.2	1,300.0	1,391.0	1,428.7	1,326.1
2000	1,425.6	1,388.9	1,442.2	1,461.4	1,418.5	1,462.0	1,473.0	1,485.5	1,468.0	1,390.1	1,375.0	1,330.9	1,426.8
2001	1,335.6	1,305.8	1,185.9	1,189.8	1,270.4	1,238.8	1,204.5	1,178.5	1,047.6	1,076.6	1,129.7	1,144.9	1,192.3
2002	1,140.2	1,100.7	1,153.8	1,112.0	1,079.3	1,014.1	903.6	912.6	867.8	854.6	909.9	899.2	995.6
2003	895.8	837.6	846.6	890.0	936.0	988.0	992.5	989.5	1,019.4	1,038.7	1,049.9	1,080.6	963.7
2004	1,132.5	1,143.4	1,124.0	1,133.1	1,102.8	1,132.8	1,105.9	1,088.9	1,117.7	1,118.1	1,168.9	1,199.2	1,130.6
2005	1,181.4	1,199.6	1,194.9	1,164.4	1,178.3	1,202.3	1,222.2	1,224.3	1,225.9	1,192.0	1,237.3	1,262.1	1,207.1
2006	1,278.7	1,276.7	1,293.7	1,302.2	1,290.0	1,253.1	1,260.2	1,287.2	1,317.8	1,363.3	1,388.6	1,416.4	1,310.7
2007	1,424.2	1,444.8	1,407.0	1,463.7	1,511.1	1,514.5	1,520.7	1,454.6	1,497.1	1,539.7	1,463.4	1,479.2	1,476.7
2008	1,378.8	1,354.9	1,316.9	1,370.5	1,403.2	1,341.3	1,257.3	1,281.5	1,217.0	968.8	883.0	877.4	1,220.9

Source: Index and Option Market (IOM), division of the Chicago Mercantile Exchange (CME)

STOCK INDEX FUTURES - U.S.

Composite Index of Leading Indicators   (1992 = 100)

Year	Jan.	Feb.	Mar.	Apr.	May	June	July	Aug.	Sept.	Oct.	Nov.	Dec.	Average
1999	83.4	84.1	84.0	83.9	84.3	84.7	85.1	85.2	85.3	85.5	86.0	86.5	84.8
2000	86.8	86.3	86.7	87.2	86.6	86.7	86.5	86.3	86.3	85.9	85.6	85.0	86.3
2001	84.9	84.5	84.2	84.1	84.5	84.6	84.8	84.9	84.2	84.3	85.3	86.6	84.7
2002	87.1	87.7	88.0	88.1	89.0	89.0	89.1	89.3	89.3	89.4	90.2	90.5	88.9
2003	90.6	90.5	90.6	91.1	92.5	93.1	93.8	94.3	95.0	95.8	96.4	96.9	93.4
2004	97.5	97.8	99.1	99.3	100.0	100.2	100.6	100.6	100.8	100.7	101.4	102.0	100.0
2005	101.8	102.2	101.7	101.8	102.1	103.1	102.9	103.1	102.4	103.3	104.2	104.2	102.7
2006	104.7	104.4	104.6	104.4	103.7	103.9	103.7	103.3	103.7	103.9	103.8	104.4	104.0
2007	104.0	103.7	104.1	103.9	104.0	103.9	104.6	103.6	103.7	103.2	102.8	102.6	103.7
2008[1]	102.1	101.9	101.9	102.0	101.9	101.9	101.2	100.3	100.3	99.4	99.0		101.1

[1] Preliminary.   Source: The Conference Board

Consumer Confidence, The Conference Board   (2004 = 100)

Year	Jan.	Feb.	Mar.	Apr.	May	June	July	Aug.	Sept.	Oct.	Nov.	Dec.	Average
1999	128.9	133.1	134.0	135.5	137.7	139.0	136.2	136.0	134.2	130.5	137.0	141.7	135.3
2000	144.7	140.8	137.1	137.7	144.7	139.2	143.0	140.8	142.5	135.8	132.6	128.6	139.0
2001	115.7	109.3	116.9	109.9	116.1	118.9	116.3	114.0	97.0	85.3	84.9	94.6	106.6
2002	97.8	95.0	110.7	108.5	110.3	106.3	97.4	94.5	93.7	79.6	84.9	80.7	96.6
2003	78.8	64.8	61.4	81.0	83.6	83.5	77.0	81.7	77.0	81.7	92.5	94.8	79.8
2004	97.7	88.5	88.5	93.0	93.1	102.8	105.7	98.7	96.7	92.9	92.6	102.7	96.1
2005	105.1	104.4	103.0	97.5	103.1	106.2	103.6	105.5	87.5	85.2	98.3	103.8	100.3
2006	106.8	102.7	107.5	109.8	104.7	105.4	107.0	100.2	105.9	105.1	105.3	110.0	105.9
2007	110.2	111.2	108.2	106.3	108.5	105.3	111.9	105.6	99.5	95.2	87.8	90.6	103.4
2008[1]	87.3	76.4	65.9	62.8	58.1	51.0	51.9	58.5	61.4	38.8	44.7		59.7

[1] Preliminary.   Source: The Conference Board (TCB) Copyrighted.

Capacity Utilization Rates (Total Industry)   In Percent

Year	Jan.	Feb.	Mar.	Apr.	May	June	July	Aug.	Sept.	Oct.	Nov.	Dec.	Average
1999	82.0	82.0	81.8	81.7	82.0	81.6	81.8	81.9	81.3	82.0	82.2	82.6	81.9
2000	82.4	82.4	82.4	82.6	82.5	82.4	81.9	81.5	81.6	81.0	80.7	80.2	81.8
2001	79.4	78.7	78.2	77.8	77.1	76.4	75.9	75.4	74.9	74.3	73.8	73.6	76.3
2002	73.8	73.8	74.2	74.4	74.7	75.4	75.1	75.2	75.2	75.0	75.4	75.1	74.8
2003	75.6	75.9	75.9	75.3	75.4	75.6	75.9	75.9	76.3	76.4	77.0	77.0	76.0
2004	77.2	77.6	77.1	77.5	78.0	77.4	77.9	78.1	78.0	78.7	79.0	79.4	78.0
2005	79.8	80.2	80.1	80.0	80.2	80.5	80.4	80.5	79.0	79.8	80.6	80.9	80.2
2006	80.9	80.7	80.8	81.1	80.9	81.2	81.3	81.3	80.9	80.8	80.5	80.9	80.9
2007	80.5	80.9	80.7	81.0	80.9	81.0	81.4	81.2	81.3	80.9	81.1	81.0	81.0
2008[1]	81.0	80.7	80.4	79.9	79.6	79.6	79.4	78.3	75.0	76.2	75.2	73.3	78.2

[1] Preliminary.   Source: Bureau of Economic Analysis, U.S. Department of Commerce (BEA)

Manufacturers New Orders, Durable Goods   In Billions of Constant Dollars

Year	Jan.	Feb.	Mar.	Apr.	May	June	July	Aug.	Sept.	Oct.	Nov.	Dec.	Average
1999	211.18	203.31	209.39	204.68	206.78	207.27	216.02	218.02	214.83	212.77	215.34	229.47	209.76
2000	225.14	221.12	230.44	217.17	232.76	254.20	220.74	227.27	232.41	217.30	221.14	220.90	220.55
2001	197.36	205.41	209.56	198.11	201.86	196.99	196.53	194.41	174.92	199.09	187.14	188.34	195.44
2002	190.08	194.99	191.78	192.65	193.48	184.76	200.59	198.62	189.66	192.67	190.66	190.01	192.80
2003	194.21	192.26	194.57	190.00	189.13	194.23	197.39	197.18	201.29	208.82	203.42	206.56	197.41
2004	201.03	208.36	219.67	212.63	209.43	211.13	214.32	212.78	214.36	211.53	215.33	218.24	200.68
2005	215.03	214.09	210.62	213.77	216.61	219.48	206.67	216.05	212.28	212.43	217.31	219.01	215.69
2006	212.06	219.10	231.66	222.90	221.65	227.42	220.80	222.95	344.01	216.43	220.84	224.02	231.99
2007	209.77	210.96	221.64	227.43	221.57	221.80	234.18	223.20	220.04	220.56	219.87	228.81	221.65
2008[1]	217.86	219.83	218.30	214.62	213.09	214.41	214.18	200.95	199.99	186.32			209.95

[1] Preliminary.   Source: Bureau of Economic Analysis, U.S. Department of Commerce (BEA)

Corporate Profits After Tax -- Quarterly   In Billions of Dollars

Year	First Quarter	Second Quarter	Third Quarter	Fourth Quarter	Total	Year	First Quarter	Second Quarter	Third Quarter	Fourth Quarter	Total
1997	599.1	619.4	641.5	629.6	622.4	2003	689.5	727.4	770.7	811.8	749.9
1998	562.9	547.6	554.2	548.6	553.3	2004	901.5	920.3	916.2	957.4	923.9
1999	593.2	592.9	582.1	602.5	592.7	2005	1,031.0	1,060.4	956.2	1,089.4	1,034.3
2000	551.8	560.5	551.5	547.2	552.8	2006	1,180.3	1,206.8	1,226.6	1,184.8	1,199.6
2001	556.2	565.2	516.9	614.4	563.2	2007	1,169.3	1,204.0	1,217.3	1,177.6	1,192.1
2002	654.5	675.8	698.5	746.0	693.7	2008[1]	1,190.6	1,126.5	1,121.3		1,146.1

[1] Preliminary.   Source: Bureau of Economic Analysis, U.S. Department of Commerce (BEA)

Change in Manufacturing and Trade Inventories In Billions of Dollars

Year	Jan.	Feb.	Mar.	Apr.	May	June	July	Aug.	Sept.	Oct.	Nov.	Dec.	Average
1999	10.4	36.8	66.7	31.2	44.4	61.6	67.2	42.5	58.0	50.4	121.1	70.9	50.6
2000	69.5	59.5	17.5	38.8	82.8	129.5	8.7	87.4	10.1	77.7	26.4	5.8	63.7
2001	1.7	-40.5	-73.0	-36.6	-38.9	-105.1	-68.2	-34.2	-75.3	-200.6	-139.2	-78.7	-65.2
2002	-0.9	-31.5	-47.8	-20.1	33.6	27.8	78.5	3.5	-106.8	18.5	33.0	-86.0	17.6
2003	-118.4	-60.3	-18.3	0.1	111.8	89.5	24.1	-39.4	78.7	54.4	57.5	45.7	17.6
2004	16.6	108.5	107.0	101.2	88.6	153.5	139.9	373.6	-12.2	54.3	166.0	29.5	72.8
2005	130.5	84.6	60.3	40.0	218.4	-5.7	-66.0	57.9	272.9	81.3	78.8	305.6	54.5
2006	85.9	-49.7	129.5	82.7	169.3	169.3	92.2	93.2	65.9	22.9	28.3	4.2	85.2
2007	37.8	43.6	-17.0	59.5	68.1	55.0	75.6	62.7	87.7	23.8	53.3	96.3	53.4
2008[1]	169.4	78.5	35.6	81.4	66.2	133.3	202.6	34.8	-64.9	-99.6			63.7

[1] Preliminary. *Source: Bureau of Economic Analysis, U.S. Department of Commerce (BEA)*

Productivity: Index of Output per Hour, All Persons, Nonfarm Business -- Quarterly (1992 = 100)

Year	First Quarter	Second Quarter	Third Quarter	Fourth Quarter	Total	Year	First Quarter	Second Quarter	Third Quarter	Fourth Quarter	Total
1997	104.9	106.2	107.1	107.5	106.4	2003	125.2	126.9	130.1	130.0	128.0
1998	108.4	108.7	109.9	110.5	109.4	2004	130.2	131.7	132.2	132.2	131.6
1999	111.5	111.7	112.5	114.4	112.5	2005	133.2	133.4	134.7	134.2	133.9
2000	113.9	115.9	115.7	116.8	115.6	2006	134.8	135.6	135.1	134.9	135.1
2001	116.7	118.3	118.8	120.6	118.6	2007	134.7	136.3	138.7	138.5	137.1
2002	122.7	122.9	124.2	124.1	123.5	2008[1]	139.4	141.0	141.7	141.6	140.9

[1] Preliminary. *Source: Bureau of Economic Analysis, U.S. Department of Commerce (BEA)*

Civilian Unemployment Rate

Year	Jan.	Feb.	Mar.	Apr.	May	June	July	Aug.	Sept.	Oct.	Nov.	Dec.	Average
1999	4.3	4.4	4.2	4.3	4.2	4.3	4.3	4.2	4.2	4.1	4.1	4.1	4.2
2000	4.0	4.1	4.1	3.9	4.1	4.0	4.0	4.1	3.9	3.9	4.0	4.0	4.0
2001	4.2	4.2	4.3	4.5	4.4	4.5	4.5	4.9	4.9	5.4	5.7	5.8	4.8
2002	5.6	5.5	5.7	6.0	5.8	5.9	5.9	5.7	5.6	5.7	6.0	6.0	5.8
2003	5.7	5.8	5.8	6.0	6.1	6.4	6.2	6.1	6.1	6.0	5.9	5.7	6.0
2004	5.6	5.6	5.7	5.6	5.6	5.6	5.5	5.4	5.4	5.5	5.4	5.4	5.5
2005	5.2	5.4	5.1	5.1	5.1	5.0	5.0	4.9	5.1	4.9	5.0	4.9	5.1
2006	4.7	4.8	4.7	4.7	4.6	4.6	4.8	4.7	4.6	4.4	4.5	4.5	4.6
2007	4.6	4.5	4.4	4.5	4.5	4.6	4.7	4.7	4.7	4.8	4.7	5.0	4.6
2008[1]	4.9	4.8	5.1	5.0	5.5	5.6	5.8	6.2	6.2	6.6	6.8	7.2	5.8

[1] Preliminary. *Source: Bureau of Economic Analysis, U.S. Department of Commerce (BEA)*

S&P 500 Index - Logarithmic Scale
(monthly close) through December 2008

Volume of Trading of S&P 500 Stock Index Futures in Chicago   In Thousands of Contracts

Year	Jan.	Feb.	Mar.	Apr.	May	June	July	Aug.	Sept.	Oct.	Nov.	Dec.	Total
1999	1,993.9	2,145.4	3,018.3	1,959.8	2,007.5	2,767.9	1,756.1	2,199.8	3,016.8	2,150.4	1,675.4	2,321.9	27,013
2000	1,910.7	1,916.6	2,956.5	1,651.4	1,684.9	2,225.6	1,078.9	1,358.5	2,148.8	1,681.3	1,636.0	2,211.6	22,461
2001	1,552.0	1,630.8	2,780.9	1,624.2	1,653.0	2,154.4	1,319.7	1,597.5	2,571.2	1,798.3	1,691.7	2,124.2	22,498
2002	1,459.2	1,677.0	2,251.4	1,472.8	1,584.6	2,720.9	2,205.7	1,615.1	2,943.1	1,930.5	1,374.3	2,465.0	23,700
2003	1,442.8	1,343.0	2,900.2	1,256.8	1,415.6	2,782.4	1,222.9	1,079.4	2,411.7	1,118.1	921.3	2,281.5	20,175
2004	944.8	838.6	2,487.0	880.3	937.7	2,135.8	837.4	964.6	2,076.5	866.3	1,105.3	2,101.3	16,176
2005	764.5	873.6	2,330.2	916.2	891.6	2,090.1	618.4	979.1	2,090.2	902.1	880.2	2,041.4	15,377
2006	711.3	772.9	2,198.8	607.5	1,122.0	2,321.6	726.3	890.8	1,883.1	686.3	935.6	1,988.6	14,845
2007	696.3	765.0	2,341.9	614.6	937.9	2,237.8	803.4	1,546.1	1,941.4	854.5	1,130.8	1,967.9	15,838
2008	1,187.3	907.8	2,374.7	761.0	768.2	1,978.9	921.9	729.7	2,491.2	1,588.1	942.0	2,112.2	16,763

Contract value = $250.   *Source: Index and Option Market (IOM), division of the Chicago Mercantile Exchange (CME)*

Average Open Interest of S&P 500 Stock Index Futures in Chicago   In Contracts

Year	Jan.	Feb.	Mar.	Apr.	May	June	July	Aug.	Sept.	Oct.	Nov.	Dec.
1999	399,093	406,516	410,164	381,402	391,035	400,503	372,455	385,809	408,176	394,316	408,751	416,425
2000	369,295	374,365	400,089	379,651	383,677	409,448	380,118	391,867	416,600	413,912	447,245	498,049
2001	488,284	495,621	517,666	498,594	490,148	505,063	485,839	501,281	556,737	529,730	550,201	551,175
2002	495,352	519,023	542,358	513,048	542,839	592,888	594,727	621,558	644,806	607,848	631,224	647,022
2003	596,064	619,738	658,749	622,917	643,030	691,003	611,564	611,578	631,509	582,111	589,392	633,997
2004	612,911	614,843	624,209	595,593	587,717	604,154	586,760	597,581	632,050	636,566	686,531	714,420
2005	678,739	686,413	719,141	681,149	697,818	700,618	656,266	653,430	669,849	642,704	657,097	681,868
2006	655,483	668,113	682,218	653,044	664,790	670,449	625,142	634,579	634,817	609,410	640,481	679,221
2007	634,075	639,584	654,891	634,576	662,438	652,951	602,222	643,716	663,165	595,908	623,469	623,631
2008	566,839	602,738	607,396	560,088	559,320	558,810	551,609	565,810	578,027	627,531	633,531	603,664

Contract value = $250.   *Source: Index and Option Market (IOM), division of the Chicago Mercantile Exchange (CME)*

Volume of Trading of E-mini S&P 500 Index Futures in Chicago   In Thousands of Contracts

Year	Jan.	Feb.	Mar.	Apr.	May	June	July	Aug.	Sept.	Oct.	Nov.	Dec.	Total
1999	576	636	775	602	843	868	887	1,065	1,144	1,237	1,072	964	10,669
2000	1,306	1,388	1,489	1,462	1,676	1,550	1,403	1,439	1,683	2,109	1,843	1,673	19,021
2001	2,226	2,231	3,191	3,067	2,931	2,905	2,925	3,478	3,601	5,255	4,021	3,289	39,119
2002	4,933	5,337	5,609	7,165	7,564	9,772	14,277	11,200	11,765	17,175	11,054	9,892	115,742
2003	13,584	12,631	15,820	13,520	12,846	15,040	14,854	10,860	15,354	14,558	11,002	11,108	161,177
2004	13,087	11,355	18,033	14,993	15,889	12,428	14,361	12,921	12,755	14,636	13,705	13,039	167,203
2005	15,447	12,561	18,478	20,182	16,591	17,371	14,400	17,759	18,786	22,929	16,088	16,503	207,096
2006	18,716	16,095	21,357	18,174	24,750	30,359	21,629	19,107	21,986	22,377	23,616	19,760	257,927
2007	21,632	22,507	37,944	20,399	26,266	39,351	35,295	55,547	37,578	38,649	46,727	33,454	415,348
2008	55,257	40,368	56,108	38,472	36,217	49,724	53,375	36,400	76,696	84,259	56,426	50,587	633,889

Contract value = $50.   *Source: Index and Option Market (IOM), division of the Chicago Mercantile Exchange (CME)*

Average Open Interest of E-mini S&P 500 Index Futures in Chicago   In Thousands of Contracts

Year	Jan.	Feb.	Mar.	Apr.	May	June	July	Aug.	Sept.	Oct.	Nov.	Dec.
1999	16.2	25.0	21.0	44.0	20.8	22.1	17.0	25.6	25.0	25.1	30.0	26.5
2000	17.2	25.3	29.6	28.7	38.3	39.9	33.7	45.6	42.4	49.5	66.1	63.1
2001	55.5	68.5	79.9	91.9	110.8	91.6	97.1	126.2	152.3	134.7	224.8	178.7
2002	86.3	120.1	140.0	156.4	225.6	246.3	291.7	349.0	319.3	312.9	419.0	385.2
2003	265.2	356.6	490.0	567.6	741.8	718.5	399.5	492.5	513.4	460.9	467.7	525.3
2004	510.5	576.4	643.1	545.4	579.9	645.8	603.8	698.0	693.5	708.4	979.9	969.3
2005	827.3	901.7	1,013.6	943.3	1,014.9	986.8	932.6	1,060.8	1,110.1	1,042.2	1,166.4	1,211.3
2006	1,149.2	1,194.6	1,334.1	1,211.3	1,402.5	1,525.3	1,371.2	1,512.3	1,582.4	1,549.5	1,754.4	1,810.9
2007	1,625.6	1,825.1	2,037.4	1,943.7	2,088.7	2,060.5	1,735.6	2,105.4	2,151.5	1,972.4	2,095.4	2,172.5
2008	2,208.2	2,418.8	2,442.6	2,076.5	2,180.8	2,311.5	2,405.0	2,467.2	2,566.1	2,987.6	3,114.1	2,942.0

Contract value = $50.   *Source: Index and Option Market (IOM), division of the Chicago Mercantile Exchange (CME)*

STOCK INDEX FUTURES - U.S.

Volume of Trading of NASDAQ 100 Index Futures in Chicago   In Contracts

Year	Jan.	Feb.	Mar.	Apr.	May	June	July	Aug.	Sept.	Oct.	Nov.	Dec.	Total
1999	111,120	132,436	169,368	181,776	172,840	226,193	164,822	176,429	242,149	209,007	218,672	317,418	2,322,230
2000	349,813	366,408	575,942	503,064	460,085	432,062	296,944	310,549	445,334	490,863	400,412	464,454	5,095,930
2001	422,811	416,445	650,488	498,026	487,334	542,305	369,731	369,845	474,133	516,469	391,042	434,690	5,573,319
2002	380,076	367,561	436,495	378,294	443,579	529,496	454,630	334,242	466,898	367,750	315,925	428,341	4,903,287
2003	360,307	301,454	487,916	301,395	330,640	519,597	350,514	251,058	488,363	322,898	259,960	447,119	4,421,221
2004	271,404	268,590	591,556	321,242	297,320	427,805	286,693	245,050	433,251	286,048	226,853	356,171	4,011,983
2005	254,437	198,956	375,435	217,304	170,882	281,483	125,500	159,789	289,113	200,952	155,141	253,066	2,682,058
2006	186,649	162,841	295,163	113,885	169,399	305,557	132,661	149,906	256,605	136,433	140,407	220,364	2,269,870
2007	122,055	111,962	255,491	73,881	97,857	226,877	94,964	124,717	178,645	112,930	121,891	162,108	1,683,378
2008	137,810	90,886	188,815	72,775	80,472	192,723	103,965	83,158	171,532	125,975	58,023	101,279	1,407,413

Contract value = $100.   *Source: Index and Option Market (IOM), division of the Chicago Mercantile Exchange (CME)*

Average Open Interest of NASDAQ 100 Index Futures in Chicago   In Contracts

Year	Jan.	Feb.	Mar.	Apr.	May	June	July	Aug.	Sept.	Oct.	Nov.	Dec.
1999	10,669	14,766	19,786	21,286	23,028	26,938	21,646	22,765	21,808	19,946	23,429	27,876
2000	27,242	34,555	37,795	36,512	37,578	35,314	29,974	32,922	34,754	35,559	44,022	48,757
2001	46,582	49,495	59,916	56,328	49,337	54,394	50,854	55,234	61,665	51,977	61,196	67,769
2002	49,992	52,883	52,617	51,157	65,219	73,151	60,625	67,760	84,317	72,229	77,451	76,660
2003	71,219	79,905	87,252	71,636	77,717	88,914	80,002	83,940	91,685	75,191	85,651	86,480
2004	73,805	74,892	89,874	81,220	80,905	83,282	69,818	71,711	84,355	74,161	83,675	87,172
2005	72,299	81,327	78,387	56,668	57,116	56,836	49,357	53,270	61,369	60,918	59,754	63,712
2006	61,254	62,994	69,322	60,603	65,224	65,908	54,289	57,585	54,235	53,832	68,347	61,397
2007	47,832	51,655	55,782	50,905	59,586	63,132	63,492	67,870	64,324	50,761	53,292	50,372
2008	42,272	52,260	51,385	31,738	37,017	34,864	28,456	30,588	27,761	27,770	31,473	29,459

Contract value = $100.   *Source: Index and Option Market (IOM), division of the Chicago Mercantile Exchange (CME)*

Volume of Trading of E-mini NASDAQ 100 Index Futures in Chicago   In Thousands of Contracts

Year	Jan.	Feb.	Mar.	Apr.	May	June	July	Aug.	Sept.	Oct.	Nov.	Dec.	Total
1999	----	----	----	----	----	29	62	83	90	105	113	193	675
2000	304	382	604	628	745	762	756	883	1,508	1,589	1,446	1,512	11,118
2001	1,845	1,942	2,603	2,873	2,908	2,969	2,529	2,568	2,387	3,935	3,151	2,595	32,304
2002	3,719	3,649	3,652	4,227	4,625	4,713	5,789	4,225	4,337	6,252	4,812	4,490	54,491
2003	5,200	4,620	5,749	5,132	5,075	6,323	6,369	4,816	7,095	6,601	5,254	5,655	67,889
2004	6,157	5,640	8,011	6,387	6,749	5,646	7,139	6,123	6,476	7,322	5,844	5,675	77,169
2005	7,174	6,149	7,336	7,256	5,735	6,233	4,895	5,171	5,624	6,583	5,288	5,008	72,453
2006	6,628	5,803	7,479	5,459	7,386	8,258	6,741	6,315	7,074	6,769	6,333	5,696	79,940
2007	7,122	6,685	8,700	4,976	7,069	8,426	8,122	10,558	6,856	8,916	11,147	6,733	95,309
2008	11,604	8,072	9,677	6,988	7,042	9,912	10,151	7,607	11,523	12,287	7,300	6,571	108,734

Contract value = $20.   *Source: Index and Option Market (IOM), division of the Chicago Mercantile Exchange (CME)*

Average Open Interest of E-mini NASDAQ 100 Index Futures in Chicago   In Contracts

Year	Jan.	Feb.	Mar.	Apr.	May	June	July	Aug.	Sept.	Oct.	Nov.	Dec.
1999	----	----	----	----	----	894	2,410	4,320	3,867	3,037	5,051	8,685
2000	8,582	9,250	11,117	15,625	23,465	26,095	23,863	31,506	30,956	33,123	58,709	54,420
2001	45,370	65,061	79,962	78,094	90,822	95,236	90,803	131,259	132,349	75,686	115,350	124,023
2002	78,070	94,150	98,159	100,849	153,348	176,394	130,337	171,043	162,133	110,952	154,104	155,987
2003	169,160	227,905	258,023	196,739	240,759	257,390	262,564	316,032	287,936	214,659	279,379	244,333
2004	205,078	251,011	251,486	257,573	304,034	261,067	213,080	256,749	299,794	279,170	374,750	384,492
2005	339,077	419,715	382,805	310,664	331,447	290,759	270,134	325,508	307,007	365,277	382,667	371,388
2006	351,240	361,807	345,533	309,746	381,178	427,387	386,930	421,179	437,975	457,275	498,584	433,456
2007	360,663	354,765	423,270	396,080	463,422	454,010	418,512	429,654	451,180	415,073	439,054	408,021
2008	347,374	410,404	424,513	320,046	377,029	358,774	316,037	333,976	336,525	379,643	359,028	302,534

Contract value = $20.   *Source: Index and Option Market (IOM), division of the Chicago Mercantile Exchange (CME)*

Volume of Trading of S&P 400 Midcap Stock Index Futures in Chicago   In Contracts

Year	Jan.	Feb.	Mar.	Apr.	May	June	July	Aug.	Sept.	Oct.	Nov.	Dec.	Total
1999	18,752	20,938	43,395	27,664	16,574	42,709	17,790	18,188	39,723	18,341	19,974	42,073	326,121
2000	16,918	15,298	45,942	23,892	19,863	42,514	12,140	12,515	42,658	21,701	25,334	59,265	338,040
2001	21,527	19,884	58,286	18,061	19,258	50,331	22,029	23,805	50,706	23,741	19,591	51,641	378,860
2002	22,322	22,814	43,819	23,019	22,484	51,775	30,607	23,075	52,375	25,593	21,262	48,105	387,250
2003	18,827	18,392	44,454	15,841	15,194	40,603	15,153	12,082	43,112	15,253	13,109	50,797	302,817
2004	13,647	10,361	46,214	13,921	13,078	45,940	12,602	13,582	36,701	7,923	9,824	36,971	260,764
2005	6,486	5,736	36,685	5,130	7,235	39,025	4,603	7,699	42,503	5,736	4,988	39,232	205,058
2006	5,668	3,739	34,668	3,671	4,619	31,924	2,656	3,311	23,289	3,718	6,409	29,596	153,268
2007	2,854	3,205	26,948	3,716	3,937	22,210	3,906	4,271	17,518	3,610	10,570	15,395	118,140
2008	5,581	3,286	14,864	2,796	3,124	15,896	4,670	3,369	19,246	6,432	4,397	13,563	97,224

Contract value = $500.   *Source: Index and Option Market (IOM), division of the Chicago Mercantile Exchange (CME)*

Average Open Interest of S&P 400 Midcap Stock Index Futures in Chicago   In Contracts

Year	Jan.	Feb.	Mar.	Apr.	May	June	July	Aug.	Sept.	Oct.	Nov.	Dec.
1999	16,191	16,309	14,573	12,154	12,705	14,422	14,263	13,496	13,182	12,699	13,933	14,902
2000	12,810	13,119	13,965	12,495	13,355	14,040	12,957	13,162	15,026	16,143	16,510	17,479
2001	15,246	15,461	17,235	16,953	15,623	16,606	16,334	16,132	16,718	15,109	15,307	15,337
2002	13,691	14,109	14,954	14,340	16,402	16,611	15,121	16,213	17,006	14,695	15,394	16,432
2003	13,793	13,498	14,530	13,120	13,353	13,986	13,123	13,029	13,726	14,014	15,465	17,446
2004	15,911	15,988	16,554	15,870	15,819	17,148	13,939	13,600	14,213	13,339	14,046	14,755
2005	13,078	13,313	14,861	11,812	11,832	13,811	12,380	12,420	14,477	12,890	12,955	13,822
2006	12,168	11,940	12,409	10,999	10,892	10,447	9,307	9,687	9,194	8,442	9,884	9,794
2007	7,793	8,143	8,267	7,972	9,187	8,425	6,729	6,671	6,951	6,166	8,580	8,839
2008	6,501	7,622	7,512	4,254	5,358	5,700	4,578	5,756	6,847	6,601	6,766	5,761

Contract value = $500.   *Source: Index and Option Market (IOM), division of the Chicago Mercantile Exchange (CME)*

Volume of Trading of Dow Jones Industrials Index Futures in Chicago   In Contracts

Year	Jan.	Feb.	Mar.	Apr.	May	June	July	Aug.	Sept.	Oct.	Nov.	Dec.	Total
1999	284,341	262,932	341,744	365,209	364,417	365,429	279,381	342,753	386,373	378,531	266,183	257,805	3,895,098
2000	322,046	340,377	472,179	321,026	284,005	270,374	215,234	211,612	277,620	319,636	267,051	268,010	3,569,170
2001	275,814	310,088	594,326	411,767	377,620	389,919	320,335	410,927	573,479	520,885	375,793	329,898	4,890,851
2002	409,009	472,893	538,804	467,571	456,210	616,754	811,518	539,507	639,154	699,005	427,235	407,665	6,485,325
2003	452,579	426,198	559,372	428,972	410,967	473,432	368,277	286,508	367,845	218,394	157,726	266,032	4,416,302
2004	224,713	207,423	362,668	203,745	208,229	246,564	183,469	149,931	230,829	169,627	152,412	237,528	2,577,138
2005	149,353	107,824	226,113	157,010	124,999	192,165	96,885	121,793	188,541	133,636	108,737	180,349	1,787,405
2006	119,593	111,738	220,880	106,325	152,340	272,494	108,053	97,964	237,988	121,736	111,993	258,743	1,919,847
2007	97,032	97,537	231,466	76,661	127,981	197,380	101,710	119,985	135,432	95,101	91,014	112,518	1,483,817
2008	105,901	82,432	135,860	71,571	51,097	121,220	122,305	76,031	170,465	99,607	53,397	57,771	1,147,657

Contract value = $10.   *Source: Chicago Board of Trade (CBT)*

Average Open Interest of Dow Jones Industrials Index Futures in Chicago   In Contracts

Year	Jan.	Feb.	Mar.	Apr.	May	June	July	Aug.	Sept.	Oct.	Nov.	Dec.
1999	16,794	19,401	19,807	20,492	25,890	22,198	21,556	25,333	23,977	24,847	22,342	17,299
2000	13,713	16,331	20,443	18,157	19,253	17,394	14,367	15,748	14,840	15,087	19,113	20,966
2001	21,830	23,423	28,340	32,497	33,767	29,357	26,792	33,015	35,451	31,997	30,598	27,018
2002	23,862	35,588	37,582	28,714	32,810	34,482	32,412	32,272	34,665	31,923	34,045	31,892
2003	27,032	30,429	34,371	31,160	34,936	36,352	36,773	43,974	41,747	34,066	37,835	39,727
2004	34,656	44,306	50,172	44,494	45,304	46,641	42,790	42,042	45,940	41,250	43,662	53,469
2005	47,754	48,665	48,423	40,068	41,367	36,909	29,042	30,921	37,232	36,378	37,588	43,819
2006	39,641	39,943	43,595	43,351	45,756	53,833	56,451	58,799	60,497	61,996	63,061	69,927
2007	67,567	72,788	54,933	41,615	48,211	42,631	33,406	37,757	35,894	30,936	35,735	34,375
2008	27,564	32,212	33,736	29,240	31,425	32,987	31,175	34,663	36,423	26,685	27,638	23,708

Contract value = $10.   *Source: Chicago Board of Trade (CBT)*

Stock Index Futures - WorldWide

World stocks – World stock markets in 2008 fell sharply due to the global financial crisis and reversed nearly the entire 2003-07 rally. The MSCI World Index, a benchmark for large companies based in 23 developed countries, plunged by –42.1% in 2008, snapping a 5-year string of gains (2003 +33.8%, 2004 +15.2%, 2005 +10.0%, 2006 +20.7%, 2007 +9.6%).

The MSCI World Index peaked at a record high of 1686.32 in October 2007 and then started to fall as the emerging U.S. housing and mortgage crisis started to spill over into the banking industry and the real economy. The MSCI World Index then plunged when the U.S. housing crisis mushroomed into a full-fledged global crisis in September 2008. The Index fell to a new 13-1/2 year low in March 2009, bringing the overall sell-off from the record high to –59.4%.

World stocks plunged as the global economy slid toward recession. The U.S. officially entered a recession in December 2007 and U.S. GDP plunged by –6.2% in Q4-2008. Europe and Japan were also in recessions by the end of 2008. The World Bank in March 2009 predicted that the global economy would shrink for the first time in post-war history and that the volume of trade would decline by the most in 80 years.

Government officials in the U.S., Europe and Asia took strong action to try to halt the panic by cutting interest rates and announcing fiscal stimulus plans. However, the financial crisis was the worst since the Great Depression and the global economy entered a free-fall. By March 2009, much of the panic about the banking system subsided, but the effects of the crisis were still having a severe impact on the real economy. Unemployment rose sharply in the U.S. and Fed Chairman Ben Bernanke said there was a possibility that the U.S. unemployment rate could rise as high as 10%.

Small-Capitalization Stocks – The MSCI World Small-Cap Index, which tracks companies with market caps between $200 million and $1.5 billion, fell –42.9% in 2008 following the small –0.5% decline in 2007. The Index had previously shown four consecutive years of double-digit gains in 2003-06 (2003 +55.5%, 2004 +22.6%, 2005 +14.2%, 2006 +15.8%). The decline in the MSCI World Small-Cap Index in 2008 of –42.9% was just 0.8 points more than the –42.1% decline in the large-cap MSCI World Index's of –42.1%, illustrating that small caps in 2008 fell by roughly the same amount as large-caps.

World Industry Groups – The MSCI Industry Sectors in 2008 produced the following ranked annual returns: Health Care –22.9%, Consumer Staples –24.9%, Utilities –31.4%, Telecom –35.6%, Energy –39.4%, Consumer Discretionary –42.8%, Industrials –44.2%, Information Technology –44.4%, Materials –51.0%, and Financials –55.6%. The Financials were the hardest-hit sector at –55.6%, adding to the decline of –10.5% seen in 2007. Major U.S. and European banks saw huge losses in 2008 and some needed major bailout operations and partial nationalizations. The sectors that are typically thought of as defensive in fact produced the smallest declines, although there was nowhere to hide during the 2008 stock market debacle since even the defensive sectors of Health Care, Consumer Staples and Utilities showed declines of more than 20%.

Emerging markets – Emerging stock markets were hit hard in 2008 as investors fled riskier markets during the global crisis and as traders lifted yen-carry trades. The MSCI Emerging Markets Free Index, which tracks companies based in 26 emerging countries, plunged by –54.5% in 2008, giving back a substantial portion of the 5-year string of double-digit gains in 2003-07.

G7 – In 2008, all of the seven G7 stock markets saw sharp declines. The ranked returns for the G7 stock markets are as follows: UK FTSE 100 –31.3%, Canadian Toronto Composite –35.0%, U.S. S&P 500 –38.5%, German DAX index –40.4%, Japanese Nikkei 225 –42.1%, French CAC40 –42.7%, and Italian MIB –49.5%.

North America – In North America, Mexico's stock market fell sharply but still did better than the U.S. and Canadian stock markets for a surprising eighth straight year. The Mexican Bolsa index closed 2008 down –24.2%, ending the 5-year string of double-digit gains (2007 +11.7%, 2006 +48.6%, 2005 +37.8%, 2004 +46.9%, 2003 +43.5%). The decline in the Mexican Bolsa index of –24.2% in 2008 was less than the declines seen in the U.S. S&P 500 of –38.5% and the Toronto Composite index of –35.0%.

Latin America – Latin America stock markets all closed lower in 2008 except for Ecuador: Ecuador's Guayaqui Bolsa Index +5.9%, Costa Rica's Stock Market Index –4.6%, Venezuela's Stock Market Index –7.4%, Chile's Stock Market Select Index –22.1%, Jamaica's Stock Exchange Index –25.8%, Columbia's General Index –29.3%, Brazil's Bovespa Index –41.2%, Argentina's Merval Index –49.8%, and Peru's Lima General Index –59.8%.

Europe – European stocks in 2008 closed sharply lower as Europe was hit almost as hard as the U.S. by the global financial crisis. The Dow Jones Stoxx 50 index closed –43.4%, adding to the small –0.4% decline seen in 2007. The index had rallied for four consecutive years in 2003-06 before falling in 2007 and 2008 (+10.4% in 2006, +20.7% in 2005, +4.3% in 2004 and +10.5% in 2003). All five of the big European countries saw double-digit losses in 2008: UK FTSE 100 index –31.3%, Spanish IBEX 35 index –39.4%, German DAX index –40.4%, French CAC 40 index –42.7%, Italian MIB index –49.5%.

Asia – Asian stock markets during 2008 plunged along with the rest of the global stock markets. The MSCI Far East Index in 2008 fell by –32.3% following the small gain of +0.3% seen in 2007. The Asian banking system did not see much direct fall-out from the mortgage security problems that plagued the U.S. and banking systems. However, Asian stocks nevertheless fell sharply due to the plunge in global demand and trade that resulted from the financial crisis. China's Shanghai Composite Index in 2008 plunged by –65.4%, but that followed the extraordinary gains of +96.7% in 2007 and +130.4% in 2006.

The ranked closes for the Asian stock markets in 2008 were as follows: New Zealand's Exchange 50 index –32.8%, Malaysia's Kuala Lumpur Composite index –39.3%, South Korea Composite Index –40.7%, Japan's Nikkei 225 –42.1%, Australia's All-Ordinaries index –43.0%, Taiwan's TAIEX index of –46.0%, Thailand's Stock Exchange index –47.6%, Hong Kong Hang Seng –48.3%, Philippines' Composite index –48.3%, Singapore's Straights Times index –49.4%, Indonesia's Jakarta Composite Index –50.6%, India's Mumbai Sensex 30 index –52.4%, Pakistan's 100 Index –58.3%, China's Shanghai Composite index –65.4%, and Vietnam Stock Index –66.0%.

Year	Jan.	Feb.	Mar.	Apr.	May	June	July	Aug.	Sept.	Oct.	Nov.	Dec.	Average
United States													
2002	339.7	332.7	344.9	323.7	320.8	297.5	274.0	275.4	245.1	266.2	281.4	264.5	297.2
2003	257.2	252.8	255.0	275.6	289.6	292.9	297.7	303.0	299.4	315.8	318.1	334.2	290.9
2004	340.0	344.2	338.5	332.8	336.9	342.9	331.2	331.9	335.0	339.7	352.8	364.3	340.9
2005	355.1	361.8	354.9	347.7	358.2	358.1	371.0	366.8	369.4	362.8	375.6	375.2	363.1
2006	384.8	385.0	389.2	394.0	381.8	381.8	383.8	391.9	401.5	414.2	421.0	426.3	396.3
2007	432.3	422.9	427.1	445.6	460.1	451.9	437.4	443.1	458.9	465.7	445.2	441.4	444.3
2008[1]	414.4	400.0	397.6	416.5	420.9	384.8	381.0	385.6	350.6	291.2	269.4		373.8
Canada													
2002	223.6	223.2	229.5	224.0	223.8	208.9	193.1	193.3	180.7	182.7	192.1	193.3	205.7
2003	192.0	191.6	185.4	192.5	200.5	204.1	212.2	219.5	216.9	227.2	229.7	240.3	209.3
2004	249.1	256.9	251.0	241.0	246.0	249.8	247.2	244.9	253.4	259.3	264.0	270.3	252.7
2005	269.0	282.6	281.0	273.9	280.8	289.5	304.7	311.9	321.9	303.5	316.4	329.5	297.1
2006	349.2	341.7	354.0	356.7	343.3	339.4	345.8	352.9	343.8	360.8	372.8	377.3	353.1
2007	381.0	381.3	384.8	392.2	410.9	406.5	405.4	399.3	412.1	427.5	400.1	404.3	400.5
2008[1]	384.5	397.0	390.2	407.4	430.1	422.9	397.3	402.5	343.5	285.4	271.0		375.6
France													
2002	245.5	245.6	257.9	245.5	235.2	214.5	187.9	185.2	152.8	173.3	183.0	168.6	207.9
2003	161.6	151.5	144.1	162.5	164.6	169.7	176.6	182.2	172.5	185.6	188.4	195.8	171.3
2004	200.2	205.0	199.5	202.2	201.9	205.4	200.7	197.8	200.3	204.0	206.5	210.2	202.8
2005	215.3	221.6	223.8	215.2	226.7	232.7	244.9	242.1	253.1	244.1	251.3	259.4	235.9
2006	272.2	275.1	287.3	285.5	271.3	273.2	275.6	284.2	288.9	294.3	293.1	304.9	283.8
2007	308.6	303.5	310.0	327.9	335.9	333.2	316.4	311.6	314.5	321.8	312.0	308.9	317.0
2008[1]	267.9	263.6	259.0	274.9	275.9	244.0	241.7	246.6	221.9	191.9	179.5		242.4
Germany													
2002	302.0	297.9	319.1	298.1	284.9	259.1	218.8	219.5	163.7	186.4	196.3	171.0	243.1
2003	162.5	150.6	143.3	173.9	176.4	190.4	206.2	206.0	192.6	216.2	221.5	234.4	189.5
2004	240.0	237.6	228.0	235.6	231.9	239.6	230.3	223.8	230.2	234.1	243.9	251.6	235.6
2005	251.6	257.2	257.1	247.4	263.7	271.2	288.9	285.6	298.2	291.4	307.1	319.8	278.3
2006	335.5	342.7	353.0	355.3	336.6	336.0	335.9	346.4	355.0	370.6	373.0	390.0	352.5
2007	401.4	397.0	409.0	438.0	466.1	473.4	448.4	451.6	464.8	474.1	465.3	477.0	447.2
2008[1]	405.1	399.0	386.4	410.8	419.6	379.5	383.1	379.7	344.8	294.9	276.1		370.8
Italy													
2002	223.6	220.8	233.9	227.6	214.5	196.7	182.7	183.2	157.1	170.0	185.9	170.0	197.2
2003	162.6	166.3	157.2	173.3	180.5	181.1	181.6	184.4	181.5	189.0	196.3	195.6	179.1
2004	201.3	203.3	199.4	204.9	200.5	206.5	202.1	199.1	206.4	212.2	218.6	229.6	207.0
2005	234.9	237.8	241.0	230.5	237.0	241.1	251.9	249.5	261.7	242.9	252.5	261.4	245.2
2006	271.8	282.9	286.3	285.5	269.9	271.5	274.1	283.7	287.2	296.4	304.2	310.9	285.4
2007	317.4	310.9	317.2	331.5	329.5	319.9	307.4	304.6	302.4	307.0	291.2	286.7	310.5
2008[1]	252.1	251.6	236.2	251.1	249.8	221.0	213.6	217.1	190.3	158.0	151.0		217.4
Japan													
2002	34.7	36.7	38.2	39.9	40.8	36.8	34.3	33.4	32.6	30.0	32.0	29.8	34.9
2003	28.9	29.0	27.7	27.2	29.2	31.5	33.2	35.9	35.5	35.5	35.0	37.0	32.1
2004	37.4	38.3	40.6	40.8	39.0	41.1	39.3	38.4	37.5	37.4	37.8	39.9	39.0
2005	39.5	40.7	40.5	38.2	39.1	40.2	41.3	43.1	47.1	47.2	51.6	55.9	43.7
2006	57.8	56.2	59.2	58.6	53.7	53.8	53.6	56.0	55.9	56.9	56.5	59.8	56.5
2007	60.3	61.1	60.0	60.4	62.0	62.9	59.8	57.5	58.2	58.1	54.4	53.1	59.0
2008[1]	47.2	47.2	43.5	48.0	49.7	46.8	46.4	45.4	39.1	29.8	29.5		43.0
United Kingdom													
2002	230.6	227.9	236.2	232.1	228.7	209.1	189.4	189.0	166.4	179.1	185.0	174.9	204.0
2003	159.1	162.5	160.3	174.7	181.9	182.1	189.0	190.7	187.3	196.3	198.3	203.9	182.2
2004	202.0	207.2	202.9	206.7	203.4	205.9	202.5	204.5	209.8	212.2	216.6	222.7	208.0
2005	225.5	230.5	227.0	221.4	229.4	236.5	244.3	245.6	253.6	246.1	253.2	263.0	239.7
2006	270.5	273.1	281.6	284.0	269.4	274.1	277.5	277.8	281.8	290.1	288.2	297.6	280.5
2007	296.7	295.4	303.3	310.0	317.7	314.5	303.8	301.2	306.4	319.1	303.1	303.6	306.2
2008[1]	277.1	278.3	270.4	286.4	284.7	263.8	254.0	265.0	229.4	201.7	197.1		255.3

[1] Preliminary.   Not Seasonally Adjusted.   *Source: Economic and Statistics Administration, U.S. Department of Commerce (ESA)*

FT-SE 100 Stock Index (weekly close) as of January 02, 2009

Deutscher Aktienindex (DAX) (weekly close) as of January 02, 2009

Toronto 300 Stock Index (weekly close) as of January 02, 2009

Index Value

CAC-40 Stock Index (weekly close) as of January 02, 2009

Index Value

Hang Seng Stock Index (weekly close) as of January 02, 2009

Index Value

Nikkei 225 Stock Index (weekly close) as of January 02, 2009

Index Value

Sugar

The white crystalline substance called "sugar" is the organic chemical compound sucrose, one of several related compounds all known as sugars. These include glucose, dextrose, fructose, and lactose. All sugars are members of the larger group of compounds called carbohydrates and are characterized by a sweet taste. Sucrose is considered a double sugar because it is composed of one molecule of glucose and one molecule of fructose. While sucrose is common in many plants, it occurs in the highest concentration in sugarcane (Saccharum officinarum) and sugar beets (Beta vulgaris). Sugarcane is about 7 to 18 percent sugar by weight while sugar beets are 8 to 22 percent.

Sugarcane is a member of the grass family and is a perennial. Sugarcane is cultivated in tropical and subtropical regions around the world roughly between the Tropics of Cancer and Capricorn. It grows best in hot, wet climates where there is heavy rainfall followed by a dry season. The largest cane producers are Florida, Louisiana, Texas, and Hawaii. On a commercial basis, sugarcane is not grown from seeds but from cuttings or pieces of the stalk.

Sugar beets, which are produced in temperate or colder climates, are annuals grown from seeds. Sugar beets do best with moderate temperatures and evenly distributed rainfall. The beets are planted in the spring and harvested in the fall. The sugar is contained in the root of the beet, but the sugars from beets and cane are identical. Sugar beet production takes place mostly in Europe, the U.S., China, and Japan. The largest sugar beet producing states are Minnesota, Idaho, North Dakota, and Michigan. Sugar beets are refined to yield white sugar and very little raw sugar is produced.

Sugar beets and sugarcane are produced in over 100 countries around the world. Of all the sugar produced, about 25 percent is processed from sugar beets and the remaining 75% is from sugar cane. The trend has been that production of sugar from cane is increasing relative to that produced from beets. The significance of this in that sugarcane is a perennial plant while the sugar beet is an annual, and due to the longer production cycle, sugarcane production and the sugar processed from that cane, may not be quite as responsive to changes in price.

Sugar futures are traded on the Bolsa de Mercadorias & Futuros (BM&F), Kansai Commodities Exchange (KANEX), the Tokyo Grain Exchange (TGE), the London International Financial Futures and Options Exchange (LIFFE), and the ICE Futures U.S. (ICE) exchange. Options are traded on the BM&F, the TGE, the LIFFE and the ICE.

Raw sugar is traded on the ICE Futures U.S. (ICE) exchange while white sugar is traded on the London International Financial Futures Exchange (LIFFE). The most actively traded contract is the No. 11 (World) sugar contract at the ICE. The No. 11 contract calls for the delivery of 112,000 pounds (50 long tons) of raw cane centrifugal sugar from any of 28 foreign countries of origin and the United States. The ICE also trades the No. 14 sugar contract (Domestic), which calls for the delivery of

raw centrifugal cane sugar in the United States. Futures on white sugar are traded on the London International Financial Futures Exchange and call for the delivery of 50 metric tons of white beet sugar, cane crystal sugar, or refined sugar of any origin from the crop current at the time of delivery.

Prices – World sugar prices on the ICE No.11 sugar nearest-futures chart in early 2008 extended the rally seen in the latter half of 2007 to post a new 2-1/2 year high of 15.07 cents per pound in March 2008. That rally was due to the weak dollar and general commodity strength. Sugar prices fell through June on long liquidation pressure but then regained strength through August. Sugar prices fell moderately as the global financial crisis emerged in September but then regained most of the losses in early 2009. Sugar closed 2008 at 11.81 cents per pound, up by +0.99 cents or +9.1% from 2007. Sugar prices were generally strong during 2008 due to continued firm demand for sugar for ethanol production in Brazil, where about one-half of the sugarcane crop goes to ethanol production. Sugar prices were also supported by the decline in world sugar production in the 2008/09 marketing year by -4.7%, which will likely lead to an annual deficit of at least 5 million metric tons. The drop in world production was caused mainly by a 20% plunge in sugar production in India due to a drought, which could turn India into a net sugar importer for the first time since 2006.

Supply – World production of centrifugal (raw) sugar in the 2008-09 marketing year (Oct 1 to Sep 30) fell -4.7% to 158.781 million metric tons, down from last year's record high. The world's largest sugar producers in 2008-09 were Brazil with 20% of world production, India with 14%, and the European Union with 11%. U.S. centrifugal sugar production in 2008-09 fell -35.32% to 1.300 million metric tons. World ending stocks in 2008-09 fell -9.5% to 38.608 million metric tons. The stocks/consumption ratio fell to 23.8% in 2008-09. U.S. production of cane sugar in 2008-09 rose +3.0% to 3.602 million short tons, but beet sugar production fell 10.9% yr/yr to 4.223 million short tons.

Demand – World domestic consumption of centrifugal (raw) sugar in 2008-09 rose by +3.2% yr/yr to a record high of 162.082 million metric tons. U.S. domestic disappearance (consumption) of sugar in 2008-09 rose by +0.9% yr/yr to an almost three-decade high of 10.960 million short tons. U.S. per capita sugar consumption in 2007-08 (latest data) fell -0.6% to 63.1 pounds per year, which is only about two-thirds of the levels seen in the early 1970s.

Trade – World exports of centrifugal sugar in 2008-09 fell -5.5% yr/yr to 48.169 million metric tons, down from last year's record high. The world's largest sugar exporter was Brazil, where exports in 2008-09 rose 2.5% to 20.250 million metric tons and accounted for 42 of world exports. The next largest exporters are Thailand with 11% of world exports and Australia with 8%. U.S. sugar exports in 2008-09 were unchanged yr/yr at 250,000 short tons, but that is down from the 14-year high of 411,000 seen in 2006-07. U.S. sugar imports in 2007-08 fell -3.1% yr/yr to 2.249 million short tons, down from the 23-year high of 3.443 in 2005-06.

World Production, Supply & Stocks/Consumption Ratio of Sugar   In 1000's of Metric Tons (Raw Value)

Marketing Year	Beginning Stocks	Production	Imports	Total Supply	Exports	Domestic Consumption	Ending Stocks	Stocks As a % of Consumption
1999-00	33,545	136,264	36,753	206,562	41,700	127,328	37,281	29.3
2000-01	37,281	130,867	40,414	208,562	38,393	129,818	40,046	30.8
2001-02	40,046	134,432	39,707	214,185	42,358	134,616	36,568	27.2
2002-03	36,540	148,341	41,627	226,508	47,112	138,589	39,758	28.7
2003-04	39,758	142,421	41,876	224,055	46,637	138,913	37,713	27.1
2004-05	37,633	140,829	44,590	223,052	46,943	140,417	32,850	23.4
2005-06	32,850	144,860	46,062	223,772	49,741	142,295	31,064	21.8
2006-07[1]	32,401	164,526	45,634	242,561	50,245	152,964	39,352	25.7
2007-08[2]	39,352	166,574	44,847	250,773	50,989	157,124	42,660	27.2
2008-09[3]	42,660	158,781	47,418	248,859	48,169	162,082	38,608	23.8

[1] Preliminary.   [2] Estimate.   [3] Forecast.   *Source: Foreign Agricultural Service, U.S. Department of Agriculture (FAS-USDA)*

World Production of Sugar (Centrifugal Sugar-Raw Value)   In Thousands of Metric Tons

Year	Australia	Brazil	China	Cuba	European Union	India	Indo-nesia	Mexico	Pakistan	Thailand	United States	Ukraine	World Total
1999-00	5,448	20,100	7,525	4,060	19,498	20,219	1,690	4,979	2,595	5,721	1,720	8,194	136,294
2000-01	4,162	17,100	6,849	3,500	18,519	20,480	1,800	5,220	2,648	5,107	1,687	7,956	130,764
2001-02	4,662	20,400	8,305	3,700	16,153	20,475	1,725	5,169	3,453	6,397	1,790	7,167	134,398
2002-03	5,461	23,810	11,380	2,250	18,675	20,100	1,755	5,229	3,944	7,286	1,550	7,644	146,512
2003-04	5,178	26,400	10,734	2,550	17,132	15,150	1,730	5,330	4,047	7,010	1,580	7,847	142,470
2004-05	5,388	28,175	9,826	1,300	21,648	14,210	2,050	6,149	2,937	5,187	2,054	7,146	140,901
2005-06	5,297	26,850	9,446	1,300	21,373	21,140	2,100	5,604	2,597	4,835	2,054	6,713	144,943
2006-07[1]	5,212	31,450	12,855	1,150	17,757	30,780	1,900	5,633	3,615	6,720	2,850	7,663	164,526
2007-08[2]	4,939	32,100	15,898	1,450	17,740	28,580	1,950	5,852	4,163	7,820	2,010	7,394	166,574
2008-09[3]	4,900	32,450	15,785	1,350	16,900	22,870	2,060	5,850	3,562	7,900	1,300	6,968	158,781

[1] Preliminary.   [2] Estimate.   [3] Forecast.   *Source: Foreign Agricultural Service, U.S. Department of Agriculture (FAS-USDA)*

World Stocks of Centrifugal Sugar at Beginning of Marketing Year   In Thousands of Metric Tons (Raw Value)

Year	Australia	Brazil	China	Cuba	European Union	India	Indonesia	Iran	Mexico	Philip-pines	Russia	United States	World Total
1999-00	183	1,010	2,548	488	2,870	7,374	908	405	941	454	2,650	1,487	33,546
2000-01	518	710	1,851	438	3,493	10,710	1,330	207	1,063	330	3,000	2,013	37,248
2001-02	634	860	1,004	350	3,420	11,985	1,415	207	1,548	322	3,100	1,978	39,964
2002-03	507	210	869	360	2,717	11,670	1,385	167	1,172	239	2,130	1,386	36,734
2003-04	662	270	2,021	267	3,581	9,340	1,340	267	1,194	277	1,050	1,515	37,605
2004-05	543	1,030	2,323	275	4,699	9,070	1,170	402	1,237	405	440	1,721	38,347
2005-06	343	585	1,757	165	5,339	5,730	1,120	452	1,965	239	580	1,208	34,503
2006-07[1]	291	-285	703	165	5,088	5,625	1,170	937	1,294	253	470	1,540	32,401
2007-08[2]	402	-485	1,401	240	4,005	11,300	1,190	1,092	1,718	262	440	1,632	39,352
2008-09[3]	400	465	3,297	285	4,769	10,480	1,290	712	1,560	547	400	1,533	42,660

[1] Preliminary.   [2] Estimate.   [3] Forecast.   *Source: Foreign Agricultural Service, U.S. Department of Agriculture (FAS-USDA)*

Centrifugal Sugar (Raw Value) Imported into Selected Countries   In Thousands of Metric Tons

Year	Algeria	Canada	China	European Union	Indo-nesia	Iran	Japan	Rep. of Korea	Malaysia	Nigeria	Russia	United States	World Total
1999-00	900	1,207	687	1,786	1,949	960	1,650	1,514	1,256	825	5,170	1,484	36,753
2000-01	975	1,211	1,083	1,839	1,591	1,000	1,486	1,574	1,325	714	5,650	1,443	40,404
2001-02	1,015	1,235	1,375	2,025	1,600	1,010	1,407	1,590	1,385	775	4,850	1,393	39,689
2002-03	1,094	1,329	842	2,150	1,600	955	1,483	1,590	1,406	1,000	4,000	1,569	41,754
2003-04	1,185	1,323	1,235	1,900	1,500	760	1,442	1,682	1,484	1,150	3,670	1,591	44,667
2004-05	1,153	1,230	1,360	2,549	1,450	775	1,328	1,652	1,459	1,150	4,300	1,905	45,033
2005-06	1,380	1,313	1,234	2,630	1,800	1,495	1,350	1,669	1,414	1,200	2,900	3,124	45,880
2006-07[1]	1,310	1,350	1,465	4,338	2,420	1,600	1,350	1,680	1,730	1,240	2,950	1,887	45,634
2007-08[2]	1,300	1,407	900	3,650	2,450	970	1,337	1,510	1,530	1,335	2,850	2,228	44,847
2008-09[3]	1,450	1,440	650	3,994	2,200	995	1,342	1,560	1,540	1,485	3,100	2,264	47,418

[1] Preliminary.   [2] Estimate.   [3] Forecast.   *Source: Foreign Agricultural Service, U.S. Department of Agriculture (FAS-USDA)*

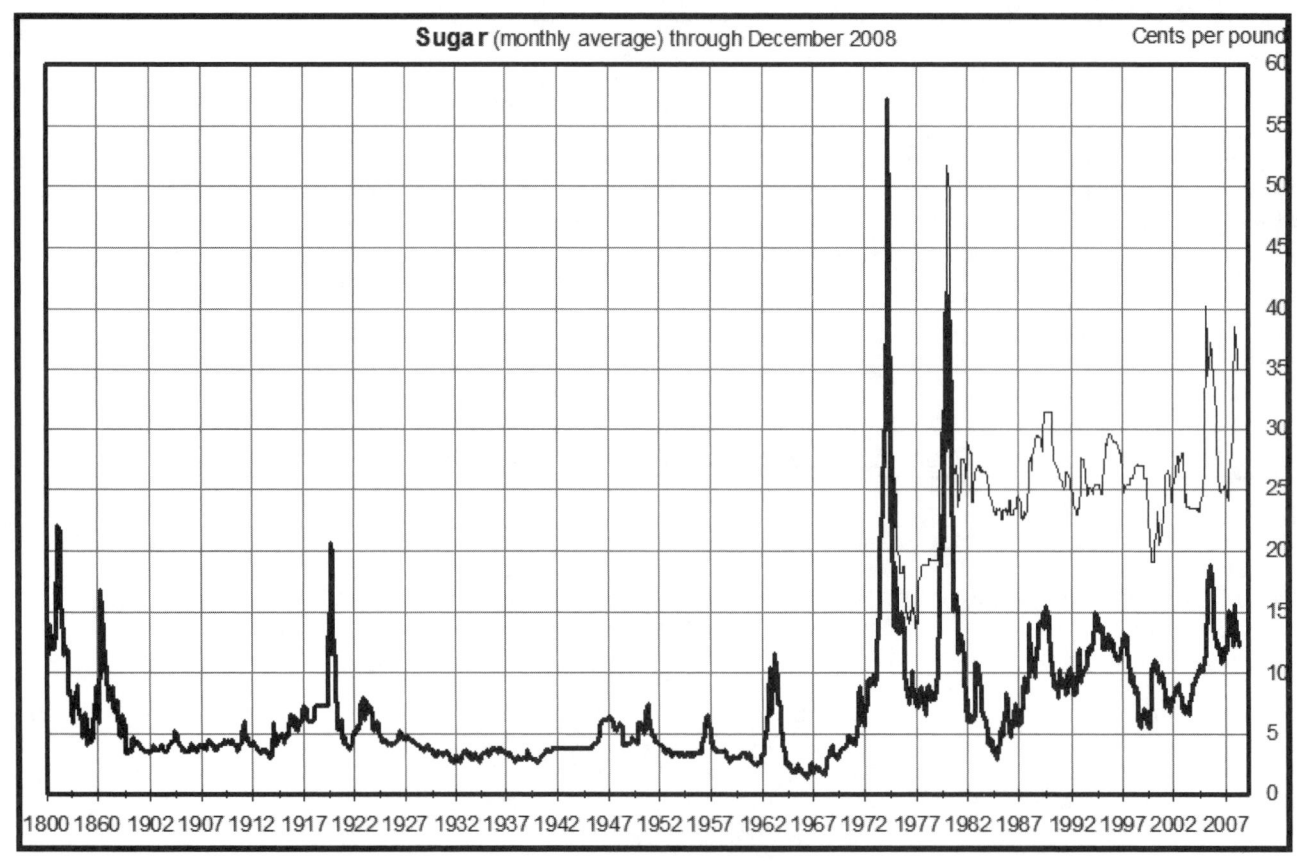

Sugar (monthly average) through December 2008

Centrifugal Sugar (Raw Value) Exported From Selected Countries   In Thousands of Metric Tons

Year	Australia	Brazil	Colombia	Cuba	Dominican Republic	European Union	Guate-mala	India	Mauritius	South Africa	Swazi-land	Thailand	World Total
1999-00	4,123	11,300	959	3,400	185	6,138	1,140	25	426	1,410	284	4,147	41,720
2000-01	3,056	7,700	965	2,932	185	6,607	1,190	1,360	555	1,580	287	3,394	38,260
2001-02	3,594	11,600	1,085	3,070	185	4,793	1,310	1,130	628	1,235	208	4,157	42,332
2002-03	4,114	14,000	1,306	1,798	185	5,600	1,335	1,700	542	1,296	278	5,280	47,471
2003-04	4,157	15,240	1,200	1,942	185	4,900	1,335	250	587	1,025	285	4,860	46,622
2004-05	4,447	18,020	1,231	770	185	6,028	1,569	50	581	1,010	298	3,115	47,141
2005-06	4,208	17,090	988	800	251	8,345	1,241	1,510	548	1,230	320	2,242	49,865
2006-07[1]	3,860	20,850	942	620	225	2,162	1,500	2,680	505	1,267	358	4,705	50,245
2007-08[2]	3,700	19,750	940	950	198	1,386	1,402	4,900	500	1,154	350	4,900	50,989
2008-09[3]	3,900	20,250	940	900	222	1,695	1,590	300	490	1,000	337	5,100	48,169

[1] Preliminary.   [2] Estimate.   [3] Forecast.   *Source: Foreign Agricultural Service, U.S. Department of Agriculture (FAS-USDA)*

Average Wholesale Price of Refined Beet Sugar[2]--Midwest Market   In Cents Per Pound

Year	Jan.	Feb.	Mar.	Apr.	May	June	July	Aug.	Sept.	Oct.	Nov.	Dec.	Average
1999	27.20	27.13	27.00	27.00	27.00	27.00	27.00	27.00	27.00	26.00	26.00	25.20	26.71
2000	23.38	22.25	21.50	21.00	19.75	19.00	19.00	19.00	20.70	21.25	21.00	21.80	20.80
2001	23.13	22.75	22.00	20.50	21.38	21.90	22.50	22.50	24.63	25.75	26.20	26.50	23.31
2002	26.75	26.00	25.95	24.63	24.50	24.00	24.00	25.40	26.25	26.75	27.40	27.88	25.79
2003	27.80	26.50	27.13	27.63	28.00	28.00	27.63	25.50	24.00	24.70	23.94	23.63	26.21
2004	23.70	23.50	23.50	23.50	23.50	23.50	23.50	23.50	23.50	23.50	23.38	23.20	23.48
2005	23.50	23.50	23.25	23.80	24.75	25.88	26.00	26.75	40.10	40.00	40.00	36.90	29.54
2006	34.50	36.50	37.10	36.38	35.00	35.00	35.00	34.50	31.20	28.75	27.19	26.10	33.10
2007	25.50	25.00	24.90	25.00	25.00	25.00	25.38	25.60	25.38	25.00	24.50	24.50	25.06
2008[1]	24.13	26.40	28.00	28.00	29.60	33.25	38.00	38.40	38.50	36.20	35.00	35.00	32.54

[1] Preliminary.   [2] These are f.o.b. basis prices in bulk, not delivered prices.   *Source: Economic Research Service, U.S. Department of Agriculture (ERS-)*

Average Price of World Raw Sugar[1]   In Cents Per Pound

Year	Jan.	Feb.	Mar.	Apr.	May	June	July	Aug.	Sept.	Oct.	Nov.	Dec. Average
1999	8.40	7.05	6.11	5.44	5.83	6.67	6.11	6.39	6.98	6.90	6.54	6.00	6.54
2000	5.64	5.51	5.54	6.48	7.33	8.72	10.18	11.14	10.35	10.96	10.02	10.23	8.51
2001	10.63	10.26	9.64	9.27	9.96	9.80	9.48	8.77	8.60	7.15	7.80	8.02	9.12
2002	7.96	6.81	7.27	7.12	7.33	7.07	8.02	7.86	8.54	8.84	8.87	8.81	7.88
2003	8.56	9.14	8.50	7.92	7.41	6.85	7.18	7.30	6.70	6.74	6.83	6.95	7.51
2004	6.42	7.01	8.23	8.21	8.08	8.41	9.19	8.99	9.10	9.84	9.65	10.19	8.61
2005	10.33	10.51	10.57	10.19	10.23	10.45	10.89	11.09	11.59	12.40	12.86	15.09	11.35
2006	17.27	18.93	18.01	18.21	17.83	16.19	16.61	13.58	12.42	12.09	12.38	12.47	15.50
2007	11.85	11.63	11.44	10.85	10.78	11.05	12.18	11.66	11.61	11.86	11.83	12.47	11.60
2008[2]	13.75	15.16	14.60	13.68	12.23	13.29	14.90	15.58	14.74	12.99	12.87	12.31	13.84

[1] Contract No. 11, f.o.b. stowed Caribbean port, including Brazil, bulk spot price.   [2] Preliminary.   *Source: Economic Research Service, U.S. Department of Agriculture (ERS-USDA)*

Average Price of Raw Sugar in New York (C.I.F., Duty/Free Paid, Contract #12 & #14)   In Cents Per Pound

Year	Jan.	Feb.	Mar.	Apr.	May	June	July	Aug.	Sept.	Oct.	Nov.	Dec. Average
1999	22.41	22.38	22.55	22.57	22.65	22.61	22.61	21.24	20.10	19.50	17.45	17.87	21.16
2000	17.70	17.24	18.46	19.43	19.12	19.31	17.64	18.12	18.97	21.15	21.39	20.56	19.09
2001	20.81	21.18	21.40	21.51	21.19	21.04	20.64	21.10	20.87	20.90	21.19	21.43	21.11
2002	21.03	20.69	19.92	19.73	19.52	19.93	20.86	20.91	21.65	21.94	22.22	22.03	20.87
2003	21.62	21.91	22.14	21.87	21.80	21.62	21.32	21.26	21.34	20.92	20.91	20.37	21.42
2004	20.54	20.57	20.86	20.88	20.69	20.03	20.14	20.10	20.47	20.31	20.40	20.55	20.46
2005	20.57	20.36	20.54	21.21	21.96	21.89	21.94	20.49	21.10	21.71	21.83	21.74	21.28
2006	23.61	24.05	23.10	23.56	23.48	23.32	22.44	21.38	21.27	20.22	19.66	19.59	22.14
2007	20.03	20.59	20.85	20.91	21.27	21.33	22.72	21.80	21.42	20.56	20.25	20.12	20.99
2008[1]	20.24	20.21	20.65	20.54	20.83	21.80	23.76	23.15	23.10	21.46	19.83	20.00	21.30

[1] Preliminary.   *Source: Economic Research Service, U.S. Department of Agriculture (ERS-USDA)*

Supply and Utilization of Sugar (Cane and Beet) in the United States   In Thousands of Short Tons (Raw Value)

	--------------------------- Supply ---------------------------									------------------------------ Utilization ------------------------------					
	------- Production -------			---- Offshore Receipts ----						Net Changes in Invisible Stocks	Refining Loss Adjustment	- Domestic Disappearance -		
Year	Cane	Beet	Total	Foreign	Territories	Total	Beginning Stocks	Total Supply	Total Use	Exports			In Polyhydric Alcohol[4]	Total	Per Capita Pounds
1999-00	4,076	4,974	9,050	1,636	0	1,636	1,639	12,325	10,090	124	-126	0	32	9,993	66.3
2000-01	4,089	4,680	8,769	1,590	0	1,590	2,216	12,575	10,396	141	113	0	33	10,000	65.5
2001-02	3,985	3,915	7,900	1,535	0	1,535	2,180	11,615	10,087	137	-24	0	33	9,785	64.5
2002-03	3,964	4,462	8,426	1,730	0	1,730	1,528	11,684	10,014	142	161	0	24	9,504	63.3
2003-04	3,957	4,692	8,649	1,750	0	1,750	1,670	12,070	10,172	288	23	0	41	9,678	61.0
2004-05	3,265	4,611	7,876	2,100	0	2,100	1,897	11,873	10,542	259	94	0	48	10,019	61.7
2005-06	2,955	4,444	7,399	3,443	0	3,443	1,332	12,174	10,476	203	-67	0	51	10,184	63.2
2006-07[1]	3,438	5,008	8,445	2,080	0	2,080	1,698	12,223	10,424	422	-132	0	53	9,913	62.5
2007-08[2]	3,497	4,740	8,237	2,321	0	2,321	1,799	12,356	10,865	250	0	0	65	10,400	62.1
2008-09[3]	3,602	4,223	7,825	2,249	0	2,249	1,491	11,566	10,960	250	0	0	60	10,500	

[1] Preliminary.   [2] Estimate.   [3] Forecast.   [4] Includes feed use.   *Source: Economic Research Service, U.S. Department of Agriculture (ERS-USDA)*

Sugar Cane for Sugar & Seed and Production of Cane Sugar and Molasses in the United States

								----- Farm Value -----		----- Sugar Production -----				
	Acreage Harvested (1,000 Acres)	Yield of Cane Per Havested Acre Net Tons	--------- Production ---------			Sugar Yield Per Acre (Short Tons)	Farm Price ($ Per Ton)	of Cane Used for Sugar	of Cane Used for Sugar & Seed	--- Raw Value ---		Refined Basis (1,000 Tons)	- Molasses Made -	
Year			for Sugar	for Seed	Total			----- 1,000 Dollars -----		Total (1,000 Tons)	Per Ton of Cane (In Lbs.)		Edible	Total[3]
			---------- 1,000 Tons ----------										-- 1,000 Gallons --	
1999	993.3	35.5	33,577	1,722	35,299	----	25.6	859,175	901,900	----	----	----	----	----
2000	1,023.3	35.0	34,291	1,823	36,114	----	26.1	895,917	941,791	----	----	----	----	----
2001	1,027.8	33.7	32,775	1,812	34,587	----	29.0	951,813	1,003,046	----	----	----	----	----
2002	1,023.2	34.7	33,903	1,650	35,553	----	28.4	961,896	1,007,142	----	----	----	----	----
2003	992.3	34.1	31,942	1,916	33,858	----	29.5	943,646	998,269	----	----	----	----	----
2004	938.2	30.9	27,243	1,770	29,013	----	28.3	771,734	821,118	----	----	----	----	----
2005	921.9	28.9	24,728	1,878	26,606	----	28.4	701,920	754,529	----	----	----	----	----
2006	897.7	32.9	27,962	1,602	29,564	----	30.4	849,157	897,601	----	----	----	----	----
2007[1]	879.6	34.1	28,273	1,696	29,969	----	29.6	837,146	887,000	----	----	----	----	----
2008[2]	869.5	35.3	29,188	1,502	30,690									

[1] Preliminary.   [2] Estimate.   [3] Excludes edible molasses.   *Source: Economic Research Service, U.S. Department of Agriculture (ERS-USDA)*

SUGAR

U.S. Sugar Beets, Beet Sugar, Pulp & Molasses Produced from Sugar Beets and Raw Sugar Spot Prices

Year of Harvest	Acreage Planted (1,000 Acres)	Acreage Harvested (1,000 Acres)	Yield Per Harvested Acre (Sh. Tons)	Production (1,000 Tons)	Sugar Yield Per Acre (Sh. Tons)	Price[3] (Dollars)	Farm Value (1,000 $)	Sugar Production Equivalent Raw Value[4] (1,000 Short Tons)	Sugar Production Refined Basis (1,000 Short Tons)	World[5] Refined #5 (Cents Per Pound)	CSCE #11 World (Cents Per Pound)	CSCE N.Y. Duty Paid (Cents Per Pound)	Wholesale List Price HFCS (42%) Midwest
1999	1,561	1,527	21.9	33,420	----	37.20	1,242,895	----	----	9.10	6.54	21.16	11.71
2000	1,564	1,373	23.7	32,541	----	34.20	1,113,030	----	----	9.97	8.51	19.09	11.32
2001	1,371	1,243	20.7	25,764	----	39.80	1,025,306	----	----	11.29	9.12	21.11	11.90
2002	1,427	1,361	20.4	27,707	----	39.60	1,097,329	----	----	10.35	7.88	20.87	13.05
2003	1,365	1,348	22.7	30,583	----	41.40	1,270,026	----	----	9.74	7.51	21.42	13.24
2004	1,346	1,307	23.0	30,021	----	36.90	1,109,272	----	----	10.87	8.61	20.46	13.20
2005	1,300	1,243	22.2	27,537	----	43.50	1,193,151	----	----	13.19	11.35	21.28	13.58
2006	1,366	1,304	26.1	34,064	----	44.20	1,506,985	----	----	19.01	15.50	22.14	17.03
2007[1]	1,269	1,247	25.6	31,912	----	41.90	1,334,701	----	----	14.00	11.60	20.99	21.22
2008[2]	1,091	1,005	26.7	26,820						15.96	13.84	21.30	24.50

[1] Preliminary. [2] Estimate. [3] Includes support payments, but excludes Gov't. sugar beet payments. [4] Refined sugar multiplied by factor of 1.07.
[5] F.O.B. Europe. *Source: Economic Research Service, U.S. Department of Agriculture (ERS-USDA)*

Sugar Deliveries and Stocks in the United States   In Thousands of Short Tons (Raw Value)

Year	Quota Allocation	Actual Imports	Cane Sugar Refineries Deliveries	Beet Sugar Factories Deliveries	Importers of Direct Consumption Sugar	Mainland Cane Sugar Mills[3]	Total Deliveries	Total Domestic Consumption	Cane Sugar Refineries	Beet Sugar Factories	CCC	Refiners' Raw	Mainland Cane Mills	Total
1999	----	----	5,419	4,536	41	----	9,996	10,167	255	1,499	0	332	1,335	3,421
2000	----	----	5,508	4,433	36	----	9,977	10,091	208	1,554	0	356	1,737	3,855
2001	----	----	5,172	4,680	58	----	9,911	10,075	262	1,500	767	274	1,533	4,337
2002	----	----	5,407	4,291	109	----	9,808	9,994	288	1,472	634	351	1,781	4,525
2003	----	----	5,232	4,219	60	----	9,511	9,713	298	1,300	246	299	1,289	3,432
2004	----	----	4,989	4,668	64	----	9,722	9,901	326	1,817	0	286	1,659	4,088
2005	----	----	5,136	4,710	197	----	10,043	10,212	368	1,753	28	245	1,635	4,029
2006	----	----	5,230	4,195	577	----	10,002	10,162	328	1,429	0	217	1,382	3,357
2007[1]	----	----	5,124	4,707	206	----	10,037	10,265	452	1,792	0	358	1,437	4,039
2008[2]	----	----	5,083	4,867	861	----	10,811	10,995	406	1,806	0	299	1,500	4,012

[1] Preliminary. [2] Estimate. [3] Sugar for direct consumption only. [4] Refined. *Source: Economic Research Service, U.S. Department of Agriculture (ERS-USDA)*

Sugar, Refined--Deliveries to End User in the United States   In Thousands of Short Tons

Year	Bakery & Cereal Products	Beverages	Confectionery[2]	Hotels, Restar. & Institutions	Ice Cream & Dairy Products	Canned, Bottled & Frozen Foods	All Other Food Uses	Retail Grocers[3]	Wholesale Grocers[4]	Non-food Uses	Non-Industrial Uses	Industrial Uses	Total Deliveries
1999	2,312	179	1,361	72	499	346	862	1,263	2,257	71	3,804	5,630	9,434
2000	2,264	168	1,328	71	499	330	817	1,242	2,241	85	3,893	5,491	9,383
2001	2,273	158	1,316	59	484	310	800	1,255	2,250	74	3,927	5,414	9,341
2002	2,075	189	1,223	53	529	297	725	1,322	2,406	99	4,108	5,136	9,244
2003	2,108	214	1,130	52	548	303	632	1,279	2,387	99	4,039	5,034	9,073
2004	2,180	242	1,125	76	603	315	697	1,267	2,398	91	3,956	5,254	9,210
2005	2,297	237	1,131	115	587	336	606	1,262	2,401	92	4,026	5,286	9,312
2006	2,231	228	1,069	88	553	335	535	1,204	2,389	107	3,864	5,057	8,922
2007	2,398	312	1,110	74	609	360	569	1,211	2,412	103	3,877	5,459	9,336
2008[1]	2,312	340	1,108	115	612	427	676	1,212	2,323	97	3,842	5,572	9,414

[1] Preliminary. [2] And related products. [3] Chain stores, supermarkets. [4] Jobbers, sugar dealers.
Source: Economic Research Service, U.S. Department of Agriculture (ERS-USDA)

Deliveries[1] of All Sugar by Primary Distributors in the United States, by Quarters   In Thousands of Short Tons

Year	First Quarter	Second Quarter	Third Quarter	Fourth Quarter	Total	Year	First Quarter	Second Quarter	Third Quarter	Fourth Quarter	Total
1997	2,143	2,401	2,591	2,443	9,578	2003	2,183	2,360	2,464	2,504	9,511
1998	2,233	2,428	2,568	2,458	9,686	2004	2,286	2,368	2,520	2,547	9,722
1999	2,208	2,553	2,655	2,580	9,996	2005	2,335	2,471	2,666	2,571	10,037
2000	2,318	2,484	2,611	2,564	9,977	2006	2,436	2,487	2,690	2,389	10,002
2001	2,370	2,486	2,580	2,474	9,911	2007	2,307	2,535	2,682	2,513	10,037
2002	2,227	2,439	2,645	2,497	9,808	2008[2]	2,513	2,665	2,879	2,754	10,811

[1] Includes for domestic consumption and for export. [2] Preliminary. *Source: Economic Research Service, U.S. Department of Agriculture (ERS-USDA)*

Sugar #11 Futures - ICE Futures U.S.
(weekly close) as of January 02, 2009
Cents per pound

Volume of Trading of World Sugar #11 Futures in New York   In Contracts

Year	Jan.	Feb.	Mar.	Apr.	May	June	July	Aug.	Sept.	Oct.	Nov.	Dec.	Total
1999	683.9	543.5	452.5	688.2	361.9	762.3	346.5	408.3	657.6	344.4	405.5	256.8	5,911
2000	422.5	609.8	501.1	617.6	523.9	717.7	376.8	420.6	622.4	507.6	371.8	242.0	5,934
2001	410.5	545.5	380.6	567.9	427.0	515.6	356.5	419.1	447.3	348.9	414.0	317.4	5,150
2002	568.8	629.5	417.3	693.6	412.2	610.3	529.5	381.0	756.0	402.8	432.1	340.6	6,174
2003	566.0	797.6	443.8	729.5	489.2	719.8	535.9	545.9	760.2	475.3	403.1	674.4	7,141
2004	513.6	1,018.7	1,181.1	993.7	617.3	1,100.6	614.6	679.5	1,248.7	626.5	539.5	632.7	9,767
2005	981.5	1,279.3	957.1	1,258.6	657.6	1,366.8	779.2	1,198.3	1,803.5	915.8	816.6	992.8	13,007
2006	1,444.2	1,601.2	1,092.2	1,467.4	1,147.7	1,459.1	825.0	1,278.6	1,746.7	1,095.7	918.7	1,024.0	15,101
2007	1,322.9	2,189.7	1,659.6	2,023.2	1,819.5	2,679.8	1,559.7	1,326.6	2,175.7	1,565.3	1,452.1	1,489.7	21,264
2008	3,566.7	3,280.8	2,237.7	2,889.5	1,941.8	3,067.4	1,820.2	1,721.4	2,540.9	1,629.9	1,085.5	1,238.1	27,020

Source: IntercontinentalEchange (ICE) formerly New York Board of Trade (NYBOT)

Average Open Interest of World Sugar #11 Futures in New York   In Contracts

Year	Jan.	Feb.	Mar.	Apr.	May	June	July	Aug.	Sept.	Oct.	Nov.	Dec.
1999	165,717	176,465	168,624	188,324	196,864	177,266	142,416	151,621	189,606	161,760	167,549	175,125
2000	191,464	199,031	193,554	187,810	201,756	200,973	172,361	171,808	160,809	154,101	148,035	145,760
2001	157,478	158,192	158,448	167,555	131,640	126,426	112,483	128,181	139,915	146,058	163,358	170,710
2002	184,096	205,138	194,541	187,415	157,738	158,276	149,202	170,667	202,144	207,456	207,598	217,904
2003	244,036	265,758	220,971	192,497	170,867	184,257	180,898	196,857	195,200	185,917	200,605	207,995
2004	246,347	269,863	268,250	275,423	267,362	282,842	300,961	309,436	292,917	322,079	304,462	332,803
2005	375,713	391,006	357,056	352,521	355,922	366,568	404,141	473,757	468,737	464,829	478,097	523,820
2006	526,575	501,074	462,871	474,241	490,201	453,021	457,301	479,420	493,931	447,817	503,364	563,844
2007	632,783	695,426	652,346	686,648	738,708	695,249	674,318	667,523	656,128	681,403	763,910	835,526
2008	1,035,301	1,013,324	973,541	939,615	915,325	885,082	809,433	804,956	774,839	664,164	636,078	644,852

Source: IntercontinentalEchange (ICE) formerly New York Board of Trade (NYBOT)

Sulfur

Sulfur (symbol S) is an odorless, tasteless, light yellow, nonmetallic element. As early as 2000 BC, Egyptians used sulfur compounds to bleach fabric. The Chinese used sulfur as an essential component when they developed gunpowder in the 13th century.

Sulfur is widely found in both its free and combined states. Free sulfur is found mixed with gypsum and pumice stone in volcanic regions. Sulfur dioxide is an air pollutant released from the combustion of fossil fuels. The most important use of sulfur is the production of sulfur compounds. Sulfur is used in skin ointments, matches, dyes, gunpowder, and phosphoric acid.

Supply – World production of all forms of sulfur in 2008 rose +0.9% yr/yr to a new record high production of 69.000 million metric tons. The world's largest producers of sulfur are the U.S with 13.3% of world production, Canada

with 12.8%, China with 12.3%, and Russia with 10.3%. U.S. production of sulfur in 2008 rose by +1.2% yr/yr to 9.200 million metric tons. That was up from the 36-year low of 9.060 in 2006.

Demand – U.S. consumption of all forms of sulfur rose by +7.6% in 2007 to 12.800 million metric tons, well above the 2-decade low of 10.900 million metric tons seen in 2001. U.S. consumption of elemental sulfur fell 2.8% in 2006 (latest data available) to 10.600 million metric tons. U.S. consumption of sulfuric acid fell by -9.6% yr/yr in 2006 to 8.750 million metric tons.

Trade – U.S. exports of recovered sulfur in 2006 (latest data available) fell 7.2% yr/yr to a 14-year low of 635,000 metric tons. U.S. imports of recovered sulfur in 2006 rose by +4.6% yr/yr to a new record high of 2.950 million metric tons.

World Production of Sulfur (All Forms)   In Thousands of Metric Tons

Year	Canada	China	France	Germany	Iraq	Japan	Mexico	Poland	Russia	Saudi Arabia	Spain	United States	World Total
2001	9,444	5,510	1,100	3,421	----	3,743	1,450	1,352	6,130	2,350	668	9,470	61,400
2002	8,925	5,980	1,030	2,499	----	3,191	1,465	1,220	6,500	2,360	685	9,270	62,000
2003	9,028	6,500	906	2,362	----	3,232	1,591	1,240	6,720	2,180	651	9,600	63,500
2004	9,101	7,150	894	2,094	----	3,158	1,825	1,300	6,920	2,249	651	10,100	65,500
2005	8,973	7,710	945	2,185	----	3,256	1,717	1,240	6,950	2,717	651	9,500	65,600
2006	9,047	8,020	945	2,286	----	3,330	1,774	1,240	7,000	2,800	651	9,060	65,700
2007[1]	8,967	8,460	1,306	2,300	----	3,200	1,770	1,324	7,050	3,100	601	9,090	68,400
2008[2]	8,800	8,500	1,300	2,500	----	3,200	1,800	1,300	7,100	3,200	600	9,200	69,000

[1] Preliminary.   [2] Estimate.   *Source: U.S. Geological Survey (USGS)*

Salient Statistics of Sulfur in the United States   In Thousands of Metric Tons (Sulfur Content)

	-- Elemental Sulfur --					By-product Sulfuric Acid[4]	Other Sulf. Compounds	Imports Sulfuric Acid[4]	Exports Sulfuric Acid[4]	Producer Stocks, Dec. 31[5]	Apparent Consumption (All Forms)	Sales Value of Shipments F.O.B. Mine/Plant		
	Native Sulfur[3]	-- Recovered --			Total Elemental Sulfur							Frasch	Recovered	Average
Year	Frasch	Petroleum & Cole	Natural Gas	Total										Total
2001	----	6,480	2,000	8,490	982	----	9,470	1,410	210	232	10,900	----	----	9.99
2002	----	6,750	1,760	8,500	772	----	9,270	1,060	147	181	11,500	----	----	11.82
2003	----	6,970	1,950	8,970	683	----	9,650	908	205	206	11,900	----	----	28.70
2004	----	7,390	1,990	9,380	739	----	10,100	2,400	204	185	12,800	----	----	32.62
2005	----	6,940	1,850	8,790	711	----	9,500	2,680	338	160	12,400	----	----	30.88
2006	----	6,960	1,430	8,390	674	----	9,050	2,430	248	221	12,000	----	----	32.85
2007[1]				8,280	803		9,090	860	100	187	11,900	----	----	36.29
2008[2]				8,400	800		9,200			200	12,800	----	----	100.00

Sulfur Consumption & Foreign Trade of the United States   In Thousands of Metric Tons (Sulfur Content)

	----- Consumption -----			--------- Sulfuric Acid Sold or Used, by End Use[2] ---------					--------- Foreign Trade ---------					
	Native Sulfur (Frasch)	Recovered Sulfur	Total Elemental Form	Pulpmills & Paper Products	Inorganic Chemicals[3]	Synthetic Rubber & Plastic	Phosphatic Fertilizers	Petroleum Refining[4]	Frasch	Exports Recovered	Value $1,000	Frasch	Imports Recovered	Value $1,000
Year														
1999	W	11,700	11,700	10,400	138	174	68	7,770	508	----	685	35,800	----	2,580	51,600
2000	W	11,100	11,100	9,620	136	152	68	7,110	497	----	762	53,700	----	2,330	39,400
2001	W	9,520	9,520	9,530	194	158	68	6,840	591	----	675	48,800	----	1,730	22,100
2002	W	10,400	10,400	8,380	122	27	66	6,660	90	----	687	40,000	----	2,560	26,800
2003	W	10,900	10,900	10,100	225	71	82	6,660	140	----	840	54,400	----	2,870	70,600
2004	W	11,300	11,300	9,290	272	154	70	6,870	248	----	949	63,300	----	2,850	76,800
2005	W	10,900	10,900	9,680	267	312	64	7,000	188	----	684	55,200	----	2,820	70,500
2006[1]	W	10,600	10,600	8,750	246	426	250	6,220	262	----	635	43,800	----	2,950	70,400

[1] Preliminary.   [2] Sulfur equivalent.   [3] Including inorganic pigments, paints & allied products, and other inorganic chemicals & products.
[4] Including other petroleum and coal products.   W = Withheld proprietary data.   NA = Not available.   *Source: U.S. Geological Survey (USGS)*

Sunflowerseed, Meal and Oil

Sunflowers are native to South and North America, but are now grown almost worldwide. Sunflower-seed oil accounts for approximately 14% of the world production of seed oils. Sunflower varieties that are commercially grown contain from 39% to 49% oil in the seed. Sunflower crops produce about 50 bushels of seed per acre on average, which yields approximately 50 gallons of oil.

Sunflower-seed oil accounts for around 80% of the value of the sunflower crop. Refined sunflower-seed oil is edible and used primarily as a salad and cooking oil and in margarine. Crude sunflower-seed oil is used industrially for making soaps, candles, varnishes, and detergents. Sunflower-seed oil contains 93% of the energy of U.S. No. 2 diesel fuel and is being explored as a potential alternate fuel source in diesel engines. Sunflower meal is used in livestock feed and when fed to poultry, increases the yield of eggs. Sunflower seeds are also used for birdfeed and as a snack for humans.

Prices – The average monthly price received by U.S. farmers for sunflower seeds in the first five months of the 2008-09 marketing year (September 2008 through August 2009) was up +2.0% to $23.72 per hundred pounds, which was a new record high.

Supply – World sunflower-seed production in the 2007-08 marketing year (latest data available) fell -5.7% yr/yr to 28.102 million metric tons. The world's largest sunflower-seed producers are the former USSR with 36% of world production, Argentina with 16%, China with 6%, U.S with 5%, and France and India both with a little less than 5%.

U.S. production of sunflower seeds in 2006-07 rose by +34.8% yr/yr to 1.310 million metric tons, which was far below the record production level of 3.309 million metric tons posted in 1979-80. U.S. farmers harvested 2.010 million acres of sunflowers in 2007-08, up +13.5% yr/yr but down from the 7-year high of 2.610 million acres posted in 2005-06. U.S sunflower yield in 2007-08 was up +18.7% to 14.37 hundred pounds per acre, down from the record high of 15.40 hundred pounds per acre in 2005-06.

Demand – Total U.S. disappearance of sunflower seeds in 2007-08 rose +9.4% yr/yr to 1.426 million metric tons, of which 48% went to crushing for oil and meal, 40% went to non-oil and seed use, and 12% went to exports.

Trade – World sunflower-seed exports in 2007-08 fell -37.7% yr/yr to 1.188 million metric tons. The world's largest exporters are the former USSR, which accounted for 35% of world exports in 2005-06 and the U.S., which accounted for 11% of world exports.

World Production of Sunflowerseed   In Thousands of Metric Tons

Crop Year	Argentina	Bulgaria	China	France	Hungary	India	Romania	Africa	Spain	Turkey	States	USSR	Total
1998-99	7,180	524	1,465	1,713	718	944	1,073	1,109	1,097	850	2,392	5,762	27,405
1999-00	5,760	606	1,765	1,868	793	694	1,301	531	579	820	1,969	7,396	26,718
2000-01	2,970	425	1,954	1,833	484	646	721	638	848	630	1,608	7,824	23,099
2001-02	3,730	405	1,478	1,584	632	726	824	929	871	530	1,551	5,468	21,302
2002-03	3,350	645	1,946	1,497	777	1,060	1,003	643	757	830	1,112	7,836	23,985
2003-04	2,990	789	1,743	1,530	992	1,160	1,506	648	763	560	1,209	10,179	26,975
2004-05	3,730	1,030	1,700	1,462	1,186	1,350	1,220	620	785	640	930	8,830	26,414
2005-06	3,840	820	1,830	1,510	1,108	1,490	1,180	520	381	780	1,720	12,132	30,278
2006-07[1]	3,120	1,030	1,850	1,440	1,100	1,450	1,370	300	607	820	997	12,450	29,793
2007-08[2]	4,500	522	1,800	1,308	950	1,400	600	840	703	690	1,310	10,213	28,102

[1] Preliminary.   [2] Forecast.   *Source: Economic Research Service, U.S. Department of Agriculture (ERS-USDA)*

World Imports and Exports of Sunflowerseed   In Thousands of Metric Tons

	---------------------------- Imports ----------------------------					------------------------------------- Exports ------------------------------------						
Crop Year	France	Germany	Netherlands	Spain	Turkey	World Total	Argentina	France	Hungary	Former USSR	United States	Uruguay	World Total
1998-99	395	364	477	576	766	4,015	940	29	152	1,977	291	106	4,080
1999-00	128	124	576	443	486	2,772	265	27	23	1,295	168	28	2,620
2000-01	174	193	413	368	322	2,460	94	11	6	1,865	153	21	2,462
2001-02	43	58	180	172	164	1,202	342	24	14	186	176	130	1,184
2002-03	62	65	148	151	287	1,462	232	3	19	577	123	223	1,586
2003-04	202	60	167	218	630	2,287	45	25	14	1,374	138	127	2,307
2004-05	5	71	24	188	518	1,300	99	20	52	131	117	134	1,186
2005-06	28	63	90	235	391	1,515	45	9	31	664	155	59	1,547
2006-07[1]	49	73	70	233	495	1,943	63	5	42	599	156	13	1,907
2007-08[2]	20	44	33	95	420	1,186	40	4	46	142	150	50	1,188

[1] Preliminary.   [2] Forecast.   *Source: Economic Research Service, U.S. Department of Agriculture (ERS-USDA)*

SUNFLOWERSEED, MEAL AND OIL

Sunflowerseed Statistics in the United States   In Thousands of Metric Tons

Crop Year Beginning Sept. 1	Acres Harvested (1,000)	Harvested Yield Per CWT	Farm Price ($/Metric Ton)	Value of Pro-duction (Million $)	Stocks, Sept. 1	Production	Imports	Total Supply	Crush	Exports	Non-Oil Use & Seed	Total Disap-pearance
2001-02	2,555	13.38	212	326.0	156	1,551	76	1,783	760	235	679	1,674
2002-03	2,167	11.31	267	294.6	109	1,112	98	1,319	319	166	635	1,120
2003-04	2,197	12.13	267	316.2	199	1,209	90	1,498	627	170	538	1,335
2004-05	1,711	11.98	302	272.7	163	930	44	1,137	276	141	630	1,047
2005-06	2,610	15.40	267	487.7	90	1,822	39	1,951	566	178	851	1,595
2006-07	1,770	12.11	320	308.8	356	972	112	1,440	659	182	462	1,303
2007-08[1]	2,012	14.26	478	614.7	137	1,301	87	1,525	683	199	523	1,405
2008-09[2]	2,396	14.29	450	669.3	120	1,553	79	1,752	683	191	627	1,501

[1] Preliminary.   [2] Forecast.   Source: Economic Research Service, U.S. Department of Agriculture (ERS-USDA)

World Production of Sunflowerseed Oil and Meal   In Thousands of Metric Tons

Year	Sunflowerseed Oil — Argen-tina	France	Spain	Turkey	Ex-USSR	World Total	Sunflowerseed Meal — Argen-tina	France	Spain	Turkey	United States	Ex-USSR	World Total
2000-01	1,463	645	503	400	2,383	8,660	1,441	797	585	449	464	2,320	9,962
2001-02	1,308	471	444	299	2,083	7,415	1,268	604	516	336	364	2,104	8,545
2002-03	1,368	487	454	385	2,928	8,653	1,342	599	527	489	173	2,851	9,832
2003-04	1,204	565	459	486	3,394	9,545	1,184	734	534	616	305	3,384	10,974
2004-05	1,507	416	459	451	3,294	9,392	1,509	508	533	572	138	3,432	10,781
2005-06	1,631	400	425	464	4,647	10,987	1,653	494	494	589	299	4,522	12,210
2006-07[1]	1,315	453	429	496	4,993	11,258	1,407	556	499	629	325	4,898	12,634
2007-08[2]	1,692	398	388	417	3,895	9,872	1,709	473	451	549	322	3,944	11,178

[1] Preliminary.   [2] Forecast.   Source: Economic Research Service, U.S. Department of Agriculture (ERS-USDA)

Sunflower Oil Statistics in the United States   In Thousands of Metric Tons

Crop Year Beginning Sept. 1	Supply — Stocks, Oct. 1	Production	Imports	Total Supply	Disappearance — Exports	Domestic Use	Total Disap-pearance	Price $ Per Metric Ton (Crude Mpls.)
2001-02	62	305	16	383	205	168	373	487
2002-03	10	134	28	172	51	109	160	721
2003-04	12	263	12	287	107	162	269	736
2004-05	18	116	34	168	57	101	158	938
2005-06	10	238	26	274	95	154	249	893
2006-07	25	277	71	373	77	269	346	1,242
2007-08[1]	27	287	47	361	77	272	349	1,978
2008-09[2]	12	287	34	333	73	237	310	1,423

[1] Preliminary.   [2] Forecast.   Source: Economic Research Service, U.S. Department of Agriculture (ERS-USDA)

Sunflower Meal Statistics in the United States   In Thousands of Metric Tons

Crop Year Beginning Sept. 1	Supply — Stocks, Oct. 1	Production	Imports	Total Supply	Disappearance — Exports	Domestic Use	Total Disap-pearance	Price USD Per Metric Ton 28% Protein
2001-02	5	358	26	389	26	358	389	97
2002-03	5	153	63	221	3	213	221	101
2003-04	5	301	20	326	12	309	326	125
2004-05	5	133	0	138	3	130	138	91
2005-06	5	272	5	282	6	271	282	88
2006-07	5	316	20	341	13	323	341	114
2007-08[1]	5	328	0	333	17	311	333	183
2008-09[2]	5	327	0	332	9	318	332	176

[1] Preliminary.   [2] Forecast.   Source: Economic Research Service, U.S. Department of Agriculture (ERS-USDA)

Average Price Received by Farmers for Sunflower[2] in the United States   In Dollars Per Hundred Pounds (Cwt.)

Year	Jan.	Feb.	Mar.	Apr.	May	June	July	Aug.	Sept.	Oct.	Nov.	Dec.	Average
2003-04	10.40	11.40	11.50	11.70	12.10	12.80	13.10	13.50	13.70	13.50	13.30	13.60	12.55
2004-05	12.90	12.40	12.80	13.40	13.70	15.00	15.00	15.10	15.40	15.20	15.20	14.40	14.21
2005-06	13.20	12.80	12.20	12.20	11.40	11.20	11.50	11.90	11.80	12.30	12.00	12.40	12.08
2006-07	11.70	12.10	12.50	13.60	13.80	14.90	15.60	15.90	16.60	17.00	18.20	18.40	15.03
2007-08	17.70	17.80	18.30	19.20	19.10	24.20	26.20	25.00	27.50	28.20	28.30	27.70	23.27
2008-09[1]	28.20	25.30	23.60	22.30	19.20								23.72

[1] Preliminary.   [2] KS, MN, ND and SD average.   Source: Economic Research Service, U.S. Department of Agriculture (ERS-USDA)

Tall Oil

Tall oil is a product of the paper and pulping industry. Crude tall oil is the major byproduct of the kraft or sulfate processing of pinewood. Crude tall oil starts as tall oil soap which is separated from recovered black liquor in the kraft pulping process. The tall oil soap is acidified to yield crude tall oil. The resulting tall oil is then fractionated to produce fatty acids, rosin, and pitch. Crude tall oil contains 40-50 percent fatty acids such as oleic and linoleic acids; 5-10 percent sterols, alcohols, and other neutral components. The demand is for the tall oil rosin and fatty acids which are used to produce adhesives, coatings, and ink resins. The products find use in lubricants, soaps, linoleum, flotation and waterproofing agents, paints, varnishes, and drying oils.

Since tall oil and its production are derived from the paper and pulping industry, the amount of tall oil produced is related in part to the pulp industry and in part to the U.S. economy.

Consumption of Tall Oil in Inedible Products in the United States   In Millions of Pounds

Year	Jan.	Feb.	Mar.	Apr.	May	June	July	Aug.	Sept.	Oct.	Nov.	Dec.	Total
2000	91.7	88.1	106.4	97.5	90.9	98.8	91.8	106.6	94.9	93.7	89.4	96.2	1,146
2001	97.7	96.4	104.4	101.6	105.1	100.7	99.9	98.3	102.4	81.4	87.7	74.4	1,150
2002	93.4	132.9	115.0	121.3	109.3	121.6	128.5	130.2	121.5	141.9	115.5	118.6	1,450
2003	136.1	119.9	136.9	126.3	121.7	121.9	119.3	111.6	131.4	124.1	104.9	120.1	1,474
2004	126.8	109.4	136.1	123.7	135.7	160.5	166.9	140.8	125.3	124.6	129.4	110.7	1,590
2005	134.9	115.4	124.5	97.3	144.4	128.3	125.0	127.5	115.6	137.0	120.3	118.2	1,488
2006	120.4	112.1	135.8	120.2	153.2	131.0	140.6	144.3	134.3	129.6	134.8	133.2	1,590
2007	130.9	126.6	117.7	127.0	130.7	128.7	131.2	129.9	128.5	131.1	128.6	123.8	1,535
2008[1]	135.8	131.8	127.4	130.8	144.0	145.9	144.5	151.0	141.2	148.5	127.6	103.7	1,632

[1] Preliminary.   *Source: Bureau of the Census, U.S. Department of Commerce*

Production of Crude Tall Oil in the United States   In Millions of Pounds

Year	Oct.	Nov.	Dec.	Jan.	Feb.	Mar.	Apr.	May	June	July	Aug.	Sept.	Total
2000-01	92.3	91.6	81.4	94.9	83.7	103.7	99.7	99.9	95.1	94.1	105.4	93.0	1,134.8
2001-02	99.1	100.7	86.5	101.8	93.7	105.5	104.2	96.0	88.5	94.7	103.6	91.4	1,165.6
2002-03	102.5	87.3	101.8	108.7	89.8	111.5	108.3	99.6	91.8	109.2	100.8	97.1	1,208.6
2003-04	102.1	87.9	109.0	113.7	96.1	112.1	102.8	106.8	99.2	94.4	108.9	104.1	1,236.9
2004-05	88.1	93.7	99.6	110.0	97.9	109.4	107.3	109.8	101.5	101.0	101.0	98.9	1,218.1
2005-06	95.5	92.1	100.3	103.9	103.4	108.1	110.4	117.6	101.4	104.6	109.7	99.7	1,246.8
2006-07	104.8	103.7	108.5	107.5	105.0	104.5	121.5	125.5	98.1	108.5	122.2	107.9	1,317.7
2007-08	100.0	99.7	107.2	113.6	112.1	115.9	117.2	112.9	103.2	102.8	107.4	105.0	1,297.0
2008-09[1]	107.6	100.7	87.0	90.8									1,158.1

[1] Preliminary.   *Source: Bureau of the Census, U.S. Department of Commerce*

Stocks of Crude Tall Oil in the United States, on First of Month   In Millions of Pounds

Year	Oct.	Nov.	Dec.	Jan.	Feb.	Mar.	Apr.	May	June	July	Aug.	Sept.
2000-01	110.5	102.4	105.4	117.0	118.9	118.2	134.4	139.6	171.7	132.0	160.5	145.4
2001-02	132.7	125.6	142.1	127.9	135.8	155.2	165.6	177.4	190.7	175.4	161.8	155.1
2002-03	160.2	154.1	155.7	160.5	176.0	167.4	156.3	173.4	163.7	180.3	199.3	209.5
2003-04	210.7	207.3	203.0	210.2	209.6	216.3	205.3	207.1	194.1	190.5	196.1	162.2
2004-05	174.1	140.3	124.4	95.0	109.9	108.8	134.0	132.1	130.5	126.3	122.0	121.8
2005-06	107.5	97.3	83.4	81.5	102.8	118.7	82.6	88.3	94.7	93.9	82.0	92.7
2006-07	73.9	61.7	72.1	75.7	97.8	83.4	115.7	132.5	156.1	162.5	164.3	198.4
2007-08	186.8	185.6	168.5	177.0	176.3	162.9	156.3	187.7	182.2	145.1	137.8	138.6
2008-09[1]	135.7	110.8	95.7	110.8	107.5							

[1] Preliminary.   *Source: Bureau of the Census, U.S. Department of Commerce*

Stocks of Refined Tall Oil in the United States, on First of Month   In Millions of Pounds

Year	Oct.	Nov.	Dec.	Jan.	Feb.	Mar.	Apr.	May	June	July	Aug.	Sept.
2000-01	9.6	9.0	9.9	10.2	10.7	12.5	11.8	13.9	12.6	19.5	13.4	21.6
2001-02	22.4	17.2	17.1	19.9	20.7	20.9	21.5	22.7	20.9	18.6	18.4	16.0
2002-03	13.3	16.5	18.7	20.1	20.1	18.6	20.4	19.7	15.8	14.5	13.5	13.9
2003-04	13.1	20.1	19.6	19.9	19.2	13.7	14.3	12.7	16.3	14.2	16.6	17.7
2004-05	14.8	16.6	16.9	17.0	15.2	20.4	16.0	18.2	16.9	17.2	14.5	17.5
2005-06	18.7	28.1	26.9	32.9	28.5	W	6.1	5.3	6.6	4.5	5.9	6.9
2006-07	7.7	7.5	5.3	5.3	5.8	7.3	7.5	7.3	7.9	9.2	6.6	4.2
2007-08	5.9	6.7	5.2	6.4	6.0	7.5	6.8	7.3	6.5	5.4	5.3	8.2
2008-09[1]	6.6	5.0	6.6	5.2	5.3							

[1] Preliminary.   W = Withheld proprietary data.   *Source: Bureau of the Census, U.S. Department of Commerce*

Tallow and Greases

Tallow and grease are derived from processing (rendering) the fat of cattle. Tallow is used to produce both edible and inedible products. Edible tallow products include margarine, cooking oil, and baking products. Inedible tallow products include soap, candles, and lubricants. Production of tallow and greases is directly related to the number of cattle produced. Those countries that are the leading cattle producers are also the largest producers of tallow. The American Fats and Oils Association provides specifications for a variety of different types of tallow and grease, including edible tallow, lard (edible), top white tallow, all beef packer tallow, extra fancy tallow, fancy tallow, bleachable fancy tallow, prime tallow, choice white grease, and yellow grease. The specifications include such characteristics as the melting point, color, density, moisture content, insoluble impurities, and others.

Prices – The monthly average price of tallow (inedible, No. 1 Packers-Prime, delivered Chicago) in 2008 rose +22.8% yr/yr to a record high of 34.18 cents per pound. The wholesale price of inedible tallow in 2008 rose +23.8% yr/yr to a record high of 38.02 cents per pound.

Supply – World production of tallow and greases (edible and inedible) in 2007, the latest available reporting year, rose by +0.9% yr/yr to a record high of 8.617 million metric tons. The world's largest producer of tallow and

greases by far is the U.S. with 45% of world production, followed by Brazil with 7%, Australia with 6%, and Canada with 4%.

U.S. production of edible tallow in 2007 fell –6.6% yr/yr to 1.739 billion pounds, down from the 2002 record high of 1.974. U.S. production of inedible tallow and greases in 2008 fell -1.5% yr/yr to 6.274 billion pounds, which was well below the record high of 7.156 billion pounds posted in 2002.

Demand – U.S. consumption of inedible tallow and greases in 2008 fell 11.6% yr/yr to 2.109 billion pounds, of which virtually all went for animal feed. U.S. consumption of edible tallow in 2007 (latest data available) fell –14.5% yr/yr to 1.354 billion pounds, down from the 2004 record high of 1.565 billion pounds. U.S. per capita consumption of edible tallow in 2007 fell –28.2% to 2.8 pounds per person per year, down from the 2000 and 2004 record high of 4.0 pounds.

Trade – U.S. exports of inedible tallow and grease in 2008 rose +0.1% yr/yr to 361.2 million pounds, and accounted for 5.4% of total U.S. supply. U.S. exports of edible tallow in 2007 (latest data available) rose +41.1% yr/yr to 388 million pounds, and accounted for 21.8% of U.S. supply.

World Production of Tallow and Greases (Edible and Inedible)   In Thousands of Metric Tons

Year	Argentina	Australia	Brazil	Canada	France	Germany	Korea	Nether-lands	New Zealand	Russia	United Kingdom	United States	World Total
1998	146	462	379	256	160	135	19	203	154	202	173	3,679	7,806
1999	160	471	394	285	160	140	18	178	167	186	158	3,979	8,171
2000	161	503	430	293	151	132	17	171	170	178	148	3,948	8,202
2001	142	507	446	296	140	126	15	151	173	171	115	3,503	7,689
2002	147	469	474	305	154	124	14	125	162	178	123	3,826	8,062
2003	154	456	493	289	164	121	15	121	174	183	120	3,707	8,015
2004	178	486	528	343	166	124	15	113	192	181	124	3,714	8,247
2005	184	493	552	348	171	121	15	106	168	176	128	3,797	8,399
2006[1]	181	503	568	357	183	124	16	107	187	180	135	3,808	8,540
2007[2]	194	498	584	359	177	128	16	111	185	185	139	3,839	8,617

[1] Preliminary.   [2] Forecast.   *Source: Foreign Agricultural Service, U.S. Department of Agriculture (FAS-USDA)*

Salient Statistics of Tallow and Greases (Inedible) in the United States   In Millions of Pounds

	Supply				Consumption			Wholesale Prices, Cents Per Lb.	
Year	Production	Stocks, Jan. 1	Total	Exports	Soap	Feed	Total	Edible, (Loose) Chicago	Inedible, Chicago No. 1
1999	7,079	437	7,516	877	229	2,847	3,076	15.1	13.0
2000	7,035	405	7,440	791	146	2,727	2,849	11.7	10.0
2001	6,870	347	7,217	616	107	2,834	2,843	13.7	12.0
2002	7,156	327	7,482	384	W	2,886	2,886	14.8	13.5
2003	6,246	240	6,486	307	W	2,434	2,434	20.3	18.3
2004	6,173	282	6,455	336	W	2,536	2,536	19.8	18.0
2005	6,204	281	6,485	276	W	2,456	2,456	19.0	17.5
2006	6,460	309	6,769	331	W	2,585	2,585	18.6	16.9
2007[1]	6,369	291	6,661	361	W	2,385	2,385	30.7	27.8
2008[2]	6,224	350	6,573	319	W	2,095	2,095	38.0	34.2

[1] Preliminary.   [2] Forecast.   *Source: Foreign Agricultural Service, U.S. Department of Agriculture (FAS-USDA)*

Tallow (monthly average) through December 2008 — Cents per pound

Supply and Disappearance of Edible Tallow in the United States — In Millions of Pounds, Rendered Basis

Year	Stocks, Jan. 1	Production	Total Supply	Domestic Disap-pearance	Exports	Total Disap-pearance	Direct Use	Baking or Frying Fats	Per Capita (Lbs.)
1998	47	1,537	1,586	1,301	246	1,547	868	259	3.1
1999	39	1,729	1,775	1,425	317	1,742	998	262	3.6
2000	33	1,825	1,866	1,581	248	1,829	1,125	283	4.0
2001	37	1,792	1,859	1,455	364	1,819	869	W	3.0
2002	40	1,974	2,023	1,486	511	1,998	974	W	3.4
2003	25	1,966	1,996	1,552	420	1,972	1,108	W	3.8
2004	24	1,818	1,842	1,565	255	1,820	1,163	W	4.0
2005	22	1,813	1,836	1,518	293	1,811	1,116	W	3.8
2006[1]	25	1,861	1,893	1,583	275	1,858	1,160	W	3.9
2007[2]	35	1,739	1,781	1,354	388	1,742	848	W	2.8

[1] Preliminary.   [2] Forecast.   W = Withheld.   *Sources: Economic Research Service, U.S. Department of Agriculture (ERS-USDA); Bureau of the Census, U.S. Department of Commerce*

Average Wholesale Price of Tallow, Inedible, No. 1 Packers (Prime), Delivered, Chicago — In Cents Per Pound

Year	Jan.	Feb.	Mar.	Apr.	May	June	July	Aug.	Sept.	Oct.	Nov.	Dec.	Average
1999	16.30	12.53	11.18	11.38	10.40	11.49	11.50	11.69	14.38	16.37	14.95	13.88	13.00
2000	11.89	10.14	10.67	10.21	11.60	10.74	9.19	9.48	10.07	10.05	9.35	11.23	10.39
2001	12.17	9.46	9.62	10.26	10.19	12.35	15.44	16.83	13.75	11.24	10.60	12.34	12.02
2002	10.00	10.54	12.64	11.06	11.59	15.47	14.80	14.00	14.23	13.98	15.91	18.08	13.53
2003	17.13	15.65	16.60	16.54	16.48	17.30	16.08	15.85	18.70	22.78	23.37	23.08	18.30
2004	23.23	16.72	17.80	21.05	18.01	18.08	19.55	16.92	17.20	14.33	15.61	16.97	17.96
2005	16.20	16.03	18.73	20.95	19.38	18.23	15.11	15.31	17.54	17.40	17.96	16.67	17.46
2006	17.52	17.05	14.98	13.47	14.77	15.27	17.05	17.35	15.59	17.71	20.42	21.46	16.89
2007	22.02	20.78	21.74	25.04	29.16	33.08	32.58	27.67	30.14	31.29	32.87	27.64	27.83
2008[1]	32.19	36.08	40.03	39.66	40.02	45.36	47.55	40.14	36.17	24.39	14.29	14.23	34.18

[1] Preliminary.   *Sources: Economic Research Service, U.S. Department of Agriculture (ERS-USDA)*

Tea

Tea is the common name for a family of mostly woody flowering plants. The tea family contains about 600 species placed in 28 genera and they are distributed throughout the tropical and subtropical areas, with most species occurring in eastern Asia and South America. The tea plant is native to Southeast Asia. There are more than 3,000 varieties of tea, each with its own distinct character, and each is generally named for the area in which it is grown. Tea may have been consumed in China as long ago as 2700 BC and certainly since 1000 BC. In 2737 BC, the Chinese Emperor Shen Nung, according to Chinese mythology, was a scholar and herbalist. While his servant boiled drinking water, a leaf from the wild tea tree he was sitting under dropped into the water and Shen Nung decided to try the brew. Today, half the world's population drinks tea. Tea is the world's most popular beverage next to water.

Tea is a healthful drink and contains antioxidants, fluoride, niacin, folic acid, and as much vitamin C as a lemon. The average 5 oz. cup of brewed tea contains approximately 40 to 60 milligrams of caffeine (compared to 80 to 115 mg in brewed coffee). Decaffeinated tea has been available since the 1980s. Herbal tea contains no true tea leaves but is actually brewed from a collection of herbs and spices.

Tea grows mainly between the tropic of Cancer and the tropic of Capricorn, requiring 40 to 50 inches of rain per year and a temperature ideally between 50 to 86 degrees Fahrenheit. In order to rejuvenate the bush and keep it at a convenient height for the pickers to access, the bushes must be pruned every four to five years. A tea bush can produce tea for 50 to 70 years, but after 50 years, the yield is reduced.

The two key factors in determining different varieties of tea are the production process (sorting, withering, rolling, fermentation, and drying methods) and the growing conditions (geographical region, growing altitude, and soil type). Black tea, often referred to as fully fermented tea, is produced by allowing picked tea leaves to wither and ferment for up to 24 hours. After fermenting, the leaves are fired, which stops oxidation. Green tea, or unfermented tea, is produced by immediately and completely drying the leaves and omitting the oxidization process, thus allowing the tea to remain green in color.

Supply – World production of tea in 2007 (latest available data) rose +5.6% to a record high of 3.871 million metric tons. The world's largest producers of tea in 2007 were China (with 31% of world production), India (25%), Sri Lanka (8%), Kenya (8%), Turkey (5%), and Indonesia (5%).

Trade – U.S. tea imports in 2008 (annualized through November) rose +8.9% to a new record high of 214,038 metric tons. World tea imports in 2006 (latest data available) rose +2.4% to 1.471 million metric tons. The world's largest tea importers were Russia (with 12% of total world imports), the United Kingdom (11%), Pakistan (9%), and the U.S. (7%). World exports of tea in 2006 (latest data available) fell -5.1% to 1.629 million metric tons. The world's largest exporters were Kenya (with 20% of world exports), China (18%), Sri Lanka (13%), India (11%), Indonesia (6%), Vietnam (6%), and Argentina (4%).

World Tea Production, in Major Producing Countries   In Metric Tons

Year	Argentina	Bang-ladesh	China	India	Indo-nesia	Iran	Japan	Kenya	Malawi	Sri Lanka	Turkey	Ex-USSR[2]	World Total
2001	71,117	52,000	721,536	847,000	163,068	51,160	85,000	294,620	36,800	295,090	142,900	25,664	3,073,072
2002	70,457	58,000	765,719	854,000	162,194	63,900	84,000	287,045	39,200	310,000	135,000	26,730	3,192,030
2003	69,866	57,500	788,815	838,000	169,818	63,650	91,900	293,670	41,693	303,230	153,800	26,271	3,228,676
2004	70,389	57,580	855,422	857,000	171,200	40,250	100,700	324,600	50,090	308,090	201,663	22,288	3,401,088
2005	67,871	57,580	953,660	830,750	177,700	59,180	100,000	328,500	38,000	317,200	217,520	24,752	3,550,194
2006	72,129	58,000	1,049,345	892,730	185,000	59,180	91,800	310,580	38,387	310,800	204,600	29,805	3,667,786
2007[1]	72,000	58,500	1,186,500	949,220	192,000	60,000	95,000	315,000	39,000	304,600	191,605	24,941	3,871,339

[1] Preliminary.   [2] Mostly Georgia and Azerbaijan.   *Sources: Foreign Agricultural Service, U.S. Department of Agriculture (FAS-USDA); Food and Agriculture Organization of the United Nations (FAO-UN)*

World Exports of Tea from Producing Countries   In Metric Tons

Year	Argentina	Bang-ladesh	Brazil	China	India	Indonesia	Kenya	Malawi	Papua New Guinea	Sri Lanka	Vietnam	Zim-babwe	Total
2000	49,999	11,000	3,714	230,696	200,868	105,581	217,281	42,400	8,500	287,005	55,600	16,915	1,464,330
2001	58,110	6,400	4,082	252,204	177,603	99,797	207,244	36,587	8,800	293,524	67,900	6,162	1,450,128
2002	57,643	3,964	3,979	254,875	181,617	100,185	288,300	42,596	5,200	290,500	77,000	18,855	1,580,485
2003	59,062	7,348	4,209	262,663	174,246	88,176	293,751	36,924	6,600	297,003	58,600	13,355	1,529,678
2004	67,819	10,635	3,593	282,643	174,728	98,572	284,309	46,200	8,100	298,909	104,000	14,968	1,634,575
2005[1]	68,270	10,297	3,407	288,814	159,121	102,294	347,971	44,600	6,900	307,793	88,000	4,825	1,716,261
2006[2]	72,056	7,450	3,238	288,625	181,326	95,339	325,066	27,503	6,600	204,240	105,000	11,532	1,629,184

[1] Preliminary.   [2] Estimate.   *Source: Food and Agriculture Organization of the United Nations (FAO-UN)*

Imports of Tea in the United States   In Metric Tons

Year	Jan.	Feb.	Mar.	Apr.	May	June	July	Aug.	Sept.	Oct.	Nov.	Dec.	Total
2003	15,051	13,519	15,651	17,810	18,863	15,089	15,290	13,778	11,240	16,417	11,439	13,054	177,201
2004	15,089	14,716	18,355	19,279	18,813	18,782	16,511	14,116	14,530	13,851	14,876	14,698	193,615
2005	16,728	13,977	17,877	20,502	16,696	18,445	15,714	14,146	12,775	14,376	11,276	11,750	184,261
2006	15,660	14,545	17,307	19,003	22,038	20,057	15,690	16,378	14,631	11,807	15,432	13,337	195,885
2007	14,094	12,830	17,312	19,165	19,425	21,156	16,623	15,829	16,136	14,533	15,498	13,964	196,566
2008[1]	15,856	18,000	20,244	21,732	19,547	18,369	17,654	16,458	17,202	16,786	14,354	13,383	209,585

[1] Preliminary.   *Source: Foreign Agricultural Service, U.S. Department of Agriculture (FAS-USDA)*

Tin

Tin (symbol Sn) is a silvery-white, lustrous gray metallic element. Tin is soft, pliable and has a highly crystalline structure. When a tin bar is bent or broken, a crackling sound called a "tin cry" is produced due to the breaking of the tin crystals. People have been using tin for at least 5,500 years. Tin has been found in the tombs of ancient Egyptians. In ancient times, tin and lead were considered different forms of the same metal. Tin was exported to Europe in large quantities from Cornwall, England, during the Roman period, from approximately 2100 BC to 1500 BC. Cornwall was one of the world's leading sources of tin for much of its known history and into the late 1800s.

The principal ore of tin is the mineral cassiterite, which is found in Malaya, Bolivia, Indonesia, Thailand, and Nigeria. About 80% of the world's tin deposits occur in unconsolidated placer deposits in riverbeds and valleys, or on the sea floor, with only about 20% occurring as primary hard-rock lodes. Tin deposits are generally small and are almost always found closely allied to the granite from which it originates. Tin is also recovered as a by-product of mining tungsten, tantalum, and lead. After extraction, tin ore is ground and washed to remove impurities, roasted to oxidize the sulfides of iron and copper, washed a second time, and then reduced by carbon in a reverberatory furnace. Electrolysis may also be used to purify tin.

Pure tin, rarely used by itself, was used as currency in the form of tin blocks and was considered legal tender for taxes in Phuket, Thailand, until 1932. Tin is used in the manufacture of coatings for steel containers used to preserve food and beverages. Tin is also used in solder alloys, electroplating, ceramics, and in plastic. The world's major tin research and development laboratory, ITRI Ltd, is funded by companies that produce and consume tin. The focus of the research efforts have been on possible new uses for tin that would take advantage of tin's relative non-toxicity to replace other metals in various products. Some of the replacements could be lead-free solders, antimony-free flame-retardant chemicals, and lead-free shotgun pellets. No tin is currently mined in the U.S.

Tin futures and options trade on the London Metal Exchange (LME). Tin has traded on the LME since 1877 and the standard tin contract began in 1912. The futures contract calls for the delivery of 5 metric tons of tin ingots of at least 99.85% purity. The contract trades in terms of U.S. dollars per metric ton.

Prices – The average monthly price of tin (straights) in New York in 2008 rose by +24.4% yr/yr to a record high of $11.38 per pound. The 2008 price of $11.38 is more than four times the 3-decade low of $2.83 per pound seen as recently as 2002. The average monthly price of ex-dock tin in New York in 2008 rose by +26.7% yr/yr to $8.60 per pound, and that is also more than four times the 3-decade low of $1.99 per pound posted in 2002.

Supply – World mine production of tin in 2008 rose by +4.1% yr/yr to 333,000 metric tons, which is a new record high. The world's largest mine producers of tin are China with 45% of world production in 2008, Indonesia with 30%, and Peru with 11%. World smelter production of tin rose +6.4% in 2006 (latest data available) to 366,000 metric tons, which is a new record high. The world's largest producers of smelted tin are China with 37% of world production in 2006, Indonesia with 20%, and Malaysia with 9%. The U.S. does not mine tin, and therefore supply consists only of scrap and imports. U.S. tin recovery in 2006 fell –11.2% to 6,810 metric tons, which was a new record low.

Demand – U.S. consumption of tin (pig) in 2007 rose 3.9% to an annualized level of 43,729 metric tons, which is up from the 2006 record low of 42,101 metric tons. The breakdown of U.S. consumption of tin by finished products in 2006 shows that the largest consuming industry of tin is solder (with 40% of consumption), followed by chemicals (24%), tin plate (15%), and bronze and brass (8%).

Trade – The U.S. relied on imports for 80% of its tin consumption in 2008. U.S. imports of unwrought tin metal in 2007 fell 20.1% to 34,600 metric tons, which is an 11-year low. The largest sources of U.S. imports in 2005 were Bolivia (13% of total imports), China (12%), Brazil (8%), and Indonesia (5%). U.S. exports of tin in 2007 rose +16.8% yr/yr to 6,410 metric tons.

World Mine Production of Tin   In Metric Tons (Contained Tin)

Year	Australia	Bolivia	Brazil	China	Indonesia	Malaysia	Nigeria	Peru	Portugal	Russia	Thailand	United Kingdom	World Total
1999	10,011	12,417	13,202	80,100	47,754	7,339	3,300	59,191	2,200	2,500	2,712	----	246,000
2000	9,146	12,464	14,200	99,400	51,629	6,307	2,760	70,901	1,227	2,500	1,930	----	278,000
2001	9,602	12,352	13,016	95,000	61,862	4,972	2,870	38,182	1,174	2,000	1,950	----	246,000
2002	7,017	15,242	12,063	62,000	88,142	4,215	790	38,815	574	1,300	1,130	----	235,000
2003	3,864	16,755	12,217	102,000	71,694	3,359	1,800	40,202	218	2,000	793	----	259,000
2004	1,196	17,569	12,202	118,000	65,772	2,745	1,000	67,675	220	2,500	586	----	301,000
2005	2,819	18,433	11,739	126,000	80,000	2,857	1,500	42,145	228	3,000	129	----	299,000
2006	2,000	18,000	12,000	125,000	90,000	3,000	1,500	38,470	230	3,000	165	----	304,000
2007[1]	2,100	16,000	10,000	135,000	102,000	2,500	----	39,000	100	2,500	100	----	320,000
2008[2]	2,000	16,000	12,000	150,000	100,000	2,000	----	38,000	100	2,000	100	----	333,000

[1] Preliminary.   [2] Estimate.   *Source: U.S. Geological Survey (USGS)*

TIN

World Smelter Production of Primary Tin   In Metric Tons

Year	Australia	Bolivia	Brazil	China	Indo-nesia	Japan	Malaysia	Mexico	Russia	South Africa	Spain	Thailand	World Total
1997	605	16,853	17,525	67,700	52,658	507	34,822	1,188	6,700	----	150	11,986	241,000
1998	655	11,102	14,900	79,300	53,401	500	27,201	1,078	3,000	----	100	15,353	247,000
1999	600	11,166	12,787	90,800	49,105	568	28,913	1,262	4,500	----	50	17,306	267,000
2000	775	9,353	13,825	112,000	46,432	593	26,228	1,204	4,800	----	----	17,076	288,000
2001	1,171	11,292	12,168	105,000	53,470	668	30,417	1,789	4,569	----	----	22,387	289,000
2002	791	10,976	11,675	82,000	67,455	659	30,887	1,748	4,615	----	----	17,548	280,000
2003	597	12,836	10,761	98,000	66,284	662	18,250	1,769	4,100	----	----	15,400	282,000
2004	467	13,627	11,512	115,000	49,872	707	33,914	1,775	4,570	----	----	20,800	308,000
2005	594	13,841	8,986	122,000	65,300	754	36,924	1,700	5,000	----	----	29,400	344,000
2006[1]	600	13,500	9,000	138,000	75,000	853	32,000	1,700	4,980	----	----	28,500	366,000

[1] Preliminary.   *Source: U.S. Geological Survey (USGS)*

United States Foreign Trade of Tin   In Metric Tons

Year	Exports (Metal)	Concentrates[2] (Ore) Total All Ore	Bolivia	Peru	Imports for Consumption — Unwrought Tin Metal Total All Metal	Bolivia	Brazil	China	Indo-nesia	Malaysia	Singa-pore	Thailand	Kingdom
1998	5,020	----	----	----	44,000	5,160	4,710	9,870	7,880	1,870	822	540	790
1999	6,770	----	----	----	47,500	3,850	4,700	13,900	7,930	944	60	20	60
2000	6,640	----	----	----	44,900	6,330	5,860	10,200	5,320	214	20	----	514
2001	4,350	----	----	----	37,500	6,040	5,510	6,360	3,880	674	145	----	118
2002	2,940	----	----	----	42,200	6,150	4,840	7,600	3,340	122	----	----	2
2003	3,690	----	----	----	37,100	5,720	3,000	4,340	3,070	490	----	----	143
2004	3,650	----	----	----	47,600	5,060	4,330	5,310	4,660	6,600	----	500	97
2005	4,330	----	----	----	37,500	5,400	2,150	4,510	5,220	1,530	194	45	67
2006	5,490	----	----	----	43,300	8,160	1,300	4,440	4,600	245	1,090	210	1,370
2007[1]	6,410	----	----	----	34,600	4,340	2,600	4,230	1,680	14	1,730	15	881

[1] Preliminary.   [2] Tin content.   *Source: U.S. Geological Survey (USGS)*

Consumption (Total) of Tin (Pig) in the United States   In Metric Tons

Year	Jan.	Feb.	Mar.	Apr.	May	June	July	Aug.	Sept.	Oct.	Nov.	Dec.	Total
1998	4,410	4,493	4,445	4,508	4,388	4,483	4,273	4,300	4,404	4,402	4,348	4,268	52,720
1999	4,660	4,667	4,790	4,790	4,760	4,700	4,254	4,396	4,340	4,316	4,275	4,227	55,100
2000	4,362	4,466	4,430	4,377	4,466	4,470	4,398	4,476	4,397	4,460	4,244	4,157	47,040
2001	4,252	4,185	4,095	4,141	4,148	4,128	4,055	4,163	4,153	4,197	4,129	3,974	49,620
2002	3,965	3,866	3,868	3,819	4,087	3,887	3,887	3,842	3,835	3,966	3,822	3,811	46,655
2003	3,814	3,808	3,851	3,891	3,701	3,814	3,841	3,850	3,803	3,816	3,764	3,887	45,840
2004	3,851	3,632	3,887	3,837	3,874	4,001	3,844	3,871	3,850	3,870	3,947	3,772	46,236
2005	4,097	3,990	4,027	3,874	3,825	3,918	3,806	3,900	3,824	3,833	3,849	3,699	46,642
2006	3,877	3,694	3,508	3,439	3,447	3,580	3,475	3,420	3,456	3,442	3,407	3,356	42,101
2007[1]	3,381	3,342	3,601	3,365	3,716	3,811	3,585	4,070	3,910	3,734	3,586	3,628	43,729

[1] Preliminary.   *Source: U.S. Geological Survey (USGS)*

Tin Stocks (Pig-Industrial) in the United States, on First of Month   In Metric Tons

Year	Jan.	Feb.	Mar.	Apr.	May	June	July	Aug.	Sept.	Oct.	Nov.	Dec.
1998	6,100	5,570	5,390	5,840	6,170	5,940	5,830	5,580	6,660	6,270	5,880	5,710
1999	5,620	8,120	7,770	7,760	7,760	7,510	7,750	7,560	7,870	7,790	8,390	8,800
2000	8,300	8,330	7,960	7,580	7,810	7,930	8,090	8,240	7,820	8,210	7,200	7,970
2001	8,140	8,330	8,360	8,460	8,270	8,640	8,760	8,760	8,920	9,030	7,630	7,470
2002	7,700	7,320	7,020	6,990	6,870	6,600	6,540	6,590	6,670	7,130	6,880	6,950
2003	7,280	6,980	6,690	6,640	6,390	6,400	6,380	6,420	6,250	6,180	6,190	6,340
2004	6,520	6,010	6,130	6,280	5,850	6,000	5,900	6,290	6,110	6,030	5,900	6,410
2005	6,140	5,260	5,570	5,420	5,770	5,400	5,670	5,830	5,540	5,350	5,330	5,410
2006	5,400	5,380	5,330	5,350	5,400	5,380	5,420	5,400	5,740	5,650	5,650	5,830
2007[1]	5,700	5,970	6,030	6,030	5,860	5,570	5,270	5,270	5,260	5,310	5,920	6,000

[1] Preliminary.   *Source: U.S. Geological Survey (USGS)*

Tin (monthly average) through December 2008 — Cents per pound

Average Price of Ex-Dock Tin in New York[1]   In Cents Per Pound

Year	Jan.	Feb.	Mar.	Apr.	May	June	July	Aug.	Sept.	Oct.	Nov.	Dec.	Average
1999	244.46	251.04	255.13	256.97	269.42	253.64	251.09	251.32	256.38	260.70	278.24	274.51	258.73
2000	283.63	271.70	263.42	259.59	259.70	260.16	257.77	255.92	262.54	254.56	253.64	252.19	261.24
2001	249.32	246.91	243.14	238.33	238.53	231.14	210.17	188.42	179.53	181.38	194.77	195.90	216.46
2002	189.23	183.23	187.65	195.36	201.95	208.01	211.51	188.36	193.79	206.67	205.94	206.63	199.15
2003	212.68	217.98	219.58	217.90	225.40	223.69	225.81	229.58	233.59	248.22	252.93	285.40	232.73
2004	305.34	313.55	357.66	418.57	449.29	438.72	439.24	437.68	438.91	436.80	439.24	414.16	407.43
2005	376.37	393.05	408.41	395.40	394.68	367.81	347.78	347.96	331.01	313.73	300.96	323.43	358.38
2006	338.27	373.87	378.76	420.35	420.53	376.76	400.64	404.26	428.83	461.66	475.57	524.69	417.02
2007	535.46	604.14	648.82	656.53	661.04	659.63	689.99	705.01	700.45	748.39	777.74	756.89	678.67
2008	760.82	800.60	917.15	1,001.99	1,108.30	1,027.62	1,070.50	930.65	850.83	672.97	646.77	532.54	860.06

Source: American Metal Market (AMM)

Average Price of Tin (Straights) in New York   In Cents Per Pound

Year	Jan.	Feb.	Mar.	Apr.	May	June	July	Aug.	Sept.	Oct.	Nov.	Dec.	Average
1999	348.77	356.50	361.11	363.01	372.62	359.05	359.96	357.35	366.06	370.68	392.04	288.77	357.99
2000	400.90	384.13	372.50	368.42	370.13	370.81	366.49	364.65	375.25	363.54	362.94	360.68	371.70
2001	356.37	352.87	348.19	341.59	340.61	329.68	302.57	276.55	263.17	264.88	281.23	279.46	311.43
2002	271.59	263.91	270.54	280.98	288.74	296.02	299.39	269.30	277.60	293.79	292.40	292.95	283.10
2003	304.44	312.32	314.52	312.26	321.92	319.67	322.10	327.16	332.21	350.90	356.46	396.46	330.87
2004	422.33	433.50	485.99	557.29	575.39	570.99	565.68	568.14	572.72	573.79	577.07	550.97	537.82
2005	500.93	519.61	539.30	522.71	522.18	492.64	467.71	466.67	444.80	426.36	411.23	440.30	479.54
2006	464.54	509.45	519.31	574.53	575.57	517.52	548.29	552.06	583.57	623.07	644.19	705.62	568.14
2007	719.05	811.07	873.03	883.74	886.54	884.67	931.50	954.26	949.21	1,012.46	1,049.78	1,025.36	915.06
2008	1,025.05	1,071.97	1,224.20	1,325.79	1,461.85	1,357.22	1,410.60	1,229.27	1,124.02	887.70	841.86	694.41	1,137.83

Source: U.S. Geological Survey (USGS)

TIN

Tin Plate Production & Tin Recovered in the United States   In Metric Tons

| | ------ Tin Content of Tinplate Produced ----- | | | | | | | | | | | | |
| | ------- Tinplate (All Forms) ------- | | | | ---------------------------- Tin Recovered from Scrap by Form of Recovery ------------------------- | | | | | | | | |
Year	Tinplate Waste ----- Gross Weight -----		Tin Content (Met. Ton)	Tin per Tonne of Plate (Kilograms)	Tin Metal	Bronze & Brass	Solder	Type Metal	Babbitt	Anti- monial Lead	Chemical Com- pounds	Misc.[2]	Grand Total
1997	157,000	2,010,000	9,300	4.6	W	12,200	W	W	W	149	W	W	12,300
1998	W	1,700,000	8,900	5.2	NA	NA	NA	NA	NA	NA	NA	NA	NA
1999	W	1,750,000	9,080	5.2	----	----	----	----	----	----	----	----	----
2000	119,000	1,320,000	8,800	6.7	----	----	----	----	----	----	----	----	----
2001	97,800	2,000,000	7,800	3.9	----	----	----	----	----	----	----	----	----
2002	45,900	2,450,000	7,750	3.2	----	----	----	----	----	----	----	----	----
2003	W	2,500,000	7,750	3.1	----	----	----	----	----	----	----	----	----
2004	W	2,550,000	7,700	3.0	----	----	----	----	----	----	----	----	----
2005[1]	W	2,270,000	7,670	3.4	----	----	----	----	----	----	----	----	----
2006[1]	56,400	2,130,000	6,810	3.2									

[1] Preliminary.   [2] Includes foil, terne metal, cable lead, and items indicated by symbol "W".   W = Withheld.   NA = Not available.
Source: U.S. Geological Survey (USGS)

Consumption of Primary and Secondary Tin in the United States   In Metric Tons

Year	Net Import Reliance as a % of Apparent Consumption	Stocks, Jan. 1[2]	---------------------- Net Receipts -----------------------				Available Supply	Stocks, Dec. 31 (Total Available Less Total Processed)	Total Pro- cessed	Consumed in Manu- facturing Products
			Primary	Secondary	Scrap	Total				
1997	85	9,180	39,000	2,360	6,010	47,300	56,500	11,900	44,600	44,400
1998	85	9,280	39,900	2,490	6,240	48,600	57,900	12,000	45,800	45,700
1999	85	9,290	40,500	2,790	6,360	49,700	58,900	11,900	47,000	46,900
2000	86	8,910	41,400	2,990	6,050	50,400	59,300	12,200	47,100	47,000
2001	88	8,830	34,500	2,180	4,770	41,400	50,200	8,220	42,000	41,900
2002	79	8,500	34,200	1,610	4,230	40,100	48,600	8,550	40,000	39,800
2003	89	8,220	32,400	1,380	3,440	37,300	45,500	7,770	37,700	37,400
2004	92	7,680	40,800	4,160	4,350	49,300	57,000	11,800	45,200	44,700
2005	78	8,060	32,500	5,790	3,840	42,200	50,200	9,120	41,000	40,600
2006[1]	79	7,900	46,200	6,150	7,510	59,900	67,800	12,700	55,000	54,500

[1] Preliminary.   [2] Includes tin in transit in the U.S.   NA = Not available.   *Source: U.S. Geological Survey (USGS)*

Consumption of Tin in the United States, by Finished Products   In Metric Tons (Contained Tin)

Year	Tin- plate[2]	Solder	Babbitt	Bronze & Brass	Tinning	Chem- icals[3]	Tin Powder	Bar Tin & Anodes	White Metal	Other	Total	Total Primary	Total Secondary
1997	9,350	15,900	909	3,160	1,210	8,170	W	684	754	3,980	44,400	36,200	8,250
1998	8,900	16,900	1,020	3,610	1,100	8,180	W	704	778	4,260	45,700	37,100	8,620
1999	9,150	18,700	1,610	3,410	905	8,220	W	721	943	3,220	46,900	38,000	8,890
2000	8,800	18,800	1,660	3,360	1,200	8,040	W	714	1,260	3,210	47,000	38,100	8,940
2001	7,800	17,000	770	3,430	1,070	7,590	W	570	1,390	2,230	41,900	34,200	7,630
2002	7,750	13,800	1,310	3,040	679	8,400	W	617	1,320	2,920	39,800	34,000	5,830
2003	7,790	10,600	2,570	2,600	833	8,720	W	852	1,220	2,180	37,400	32,900	4,510
2004	7,700	19,000	728	3,070	798	9,120	W	680	937	2,630	44,700	36,700	7,990
2005	7,250	16,700	554	3,200	790	8,360	W	709	W	3,030	40,600	31,400	9,170
2006[1]	8,220	22,000	637	4,150	868	12,900	W	936	W	4,770	54,500	42,600	11,900

[1] Preliminary.   [2] Includes small quantity of secondary pig tin and tin acquired in chemicals.   [3] Including tin oxide.
W = Withheld proprietary data.   *Source: U.S. Geological Survey (USGS)*

Titanium

Titanium (symbol Ti) is a silver-white, metallic element used primarily to make light, strong alloys. It ranks ninth in abundance among the elements in the crust of the earth but is never found in the pure state. It occurs as an oxide in various minerals. It was first discovered in 1791 by Rev. William Gregor and was first isolated as a basic element in 1910. Titanium was named after the mythological Greek god Titan for its strength.

Titanium is extremely brittle when cold, but is malleable and ductile at a low red heat, and thus easily fabricated. Due to its strength, low weight, and resistance to corrosion, titanium is used in metallic alloys and as a substitute for aluminum. It is used extensively in the aerospace industry, in desalinization plants, construction, medical implants, paints, pigments, and lacquers.

Prices – The price of the mineral ilmenite, a primary source of titanium, in 2008 fell -7.5% to $99 per metric ton. The price of titanium metal sponge traded in the range of $5.87-12.84 per pound in 2006 (latest data available) versus $3.46-12.22 in 2005. The price of titanium dioxide pigments (Anatase) in 2005 (latest data available) traded in the range of $.95-$1.00 per pound versus 90-95 cents per pound in 2004.

Supply – World production of titanium ilmenite concentrates in 2008 fell less than 0.01% yr/yr to 5.650 million metric tons, down from the 2005 record high of 6.090 million metric tons. The world's largest producers of titanium ilmenite concentrates are Australia with 22% of world production in 2008, China (10%), Norway (7%), India (7%), and Vietnam (4%). World production of titanium rutile concentrates in 2008 rose +7.8% yr/yr to 608,000 metric tons, which is a new record high. The world's largest producers are Australia with 51% of world production in 2008 followed by South Africa with 20% and Sierra Leone with 16%.

Demand – U.S. consumption of titanium dioxide pigment in 2008 fell -5.0% yr/yr to 930,000 metric tons, down from 2004's record high of 1.170 million metric tons. U.S. consumption of ilmenite in 2005 (latest data available) fell −12.8% to 1.290 million metric tons, down from 2004's 8-year high of 1.480 million metric tons. U.S. consumption of rutile in 2005 (latest data available) fell 4.7% yr/yr to a 7-year low of 424,000 metric tons.

Trade – U.S. imports of titanium dioxide pigment in 2008 fell by 5.0% yr/yr to 200,000 metric tons, down from the 2005 record high of 341,000 metric tons. U.S. imports of ilmenite in 2005 rose +1.7% yr/yr to 366,000 metric tons.

World Produciton of Titanium Illmenite Concentrates   In Thousands of Metric Tons

Year	Australia[2]	Brazil	China	Egypt	India	Malaysia	Norway	Ukraine	United States	Vietnam	World Total	-- Titaniferous Slag[4] --- Canada	Africa
1999	2,008	96	180	130	378	128	600	537	W	91	4,150	950	1,168
2000	2,173	123	250	125	380	125	750	436	400	174	4,940	910	1,090
2001	2,047	165	300	125	430	130	750	485	500	180	5,130	1,010	1,025
2002	1,956	177	750	125	460	106	750	512	400	170	5,400	900	973
2003	2,063	120	800	125	500	95	840	421	500	310	5,780	873	1,010
2004	1,965	133	840	125	520	61	860	370	500	550	5,940	863	1,020
2005	2,080	127	900	125	550	38	860	375	500	520	6,090	860	1,020
2006	2,367	130	1,000	125	580	35	850	470	500	600	6,700	930	1,230
2007	1,400	127	550		378		377	290	300	254	5,720		
2008[1]	1,250	130	550		378		380	302	200	215	5,640		

[1] Preliminary.   [2] Includes leucoxene.   [3] Approximately 10% of total production is ilmenite. Beginning in 1988, 25% of Norway's ilmenite production was used to produce slag containing 75% TiO2.   NA = Not available.   *Source: U.S. Geological Survey (USGS)*

Salient Statistics of Titanium in the United States   In Metric Tons

Year	--- Titanium Dioxide Pigment --- Production	Imports[3]	Apparent Consumption	------ Ilmenite ------ Imports[3]	Consumption	-- Titanium Slag --- Imports[3]	Consumption	------- Rutile[4] -------- Imports[3]	Consumption	Ores & Concentrates	Scrap	Dioxide & Pigments	Ingots, Billets, Etc.
1999	1,350,000	225,000	1,160,000	1,070,000	1,280,000	678,000	----	344,000	494,000	9,380	8,130	344,000	3,390
2000	1,400,000	218,000	1,150,000	918,000	1,250,000	533,000	----	438,000	537,000	18,900	5,060	423,000	2,980
2001	1,330,000	209,000	1,100,000	1,060,000	1,180,000	594,000	----	325,000	483,000	7,800	7,500	349,000	3,260
2002	1,410,000	231,000	1,110,000	840,000	1,300,000	445,000	----	390,000	487,000	3,810	6,000	485,000	3,460
2003	1,420,000	240,000	1,070,000	804,000	1,300,000	409,000	----	427,000	489,000	10,300	5,320	518,000	3,960
2004	1,540,000	264,000	1,170,000	701,000	1,480,000	457,000	----	360,000	445,000	8,690	9,760	576,000	4,990
2005	1,310,000	341,000	1,130,000	822,000	1,290,000	667,000	----	366,000	424,000	20,900	20,600	486,000	6,350
2006	1,370,000	288,000	1,080,000							32,800	10,800	513,000	7,900
2007[1]	1,440,000	221,000	979,000										
2008[2]	1,500,000	200,000	930,000										

[1] Preliminary.   [2] Estimate.   [3] For consumption.   [4] Natural and synthetic.   W = Withheld.   *Source: U.S. Geological Survey (USGS)*

TITANIUM

World Production of Titanium Rutile Concentrates   In Metric Tons

Year	Australia	Brazil	India	Sierra Leone	South Africa	Sri Lanka	Thailand	Ukraine	World Total
2001	206,000	2,270	19,000	----	134,000	----	----	60,000	421,000
2002	218,000	1,878	18,000	----	138,000	----	----	70,000	446,000
2003	173,000	2,303	18,000	----	108,000	----	----	60,000	361,000
2004	162,000	2,117	19,000	----	110,000	----	----	60,000	353,000
2005	177,000	2,069	19,000	----	115,000	----	----	60,000	373,000
2006	233,000	2,100	19,000	73,802	123,000	----	----	60,000	511,000
2007	297,000	3,000	20,000	79,000	108,000	----	----	57,000	564,000
2008[1]	309,000	3,000	20,000	95,000	121,000	----	----	57,000	608,000

[1] Preliminary.   NA = Not available.   *Source: U.S. Geological Survey (USGS)*

World Production of Titanium Sponge Metal & U.S. Consumption of Titanium Concentrates

| | Production of Titanium (In Metric Tons) — Sponge Metal[2] | | | | | | --- U.S. Consumption of Titanium Concentrates, by Products (In Metric Tons) --- | | | | Rutile (TiO$_2$ Content) | | | |
| | | | | | | | Ilmenite (TiO$_2$ Content) | | | Welding Rod | | | |
Year	China	Japan	Russia	United Kingdom	United States	Total	Pigments	Misc.	Total	Coatings	Pigments	Misc.	Total
1999	----	----	----	----	----	----	1,270,000	13,400	1,280,000	----	469,000	25,800	494,000
2000	----	----	----	----	----	----	1,240,000	13,900	1,250,000	----	513,000	24,100	537,000
2001	----	----	----	----	----	----	1,160,000	15,400	1,180,000	----	455,000	28,500	483,000
2002	----	----	----	----	----	----	1,280,000	16,000	1,300,000	----	464,000	22,900	487,000
2003	----	----	----	----	----	----	1,280,000	16,700	1,300,000	----	466,000	22,500	489,000
2004	----	----	----	----	----	----	1,460,000	19,300	1,480,000	----	418,000	26,700	445,000
2005	----	----	----	----	----	----	1,260,000	34,000	1,390,000	----	394,000	30,000	424,000
2006[1]	----	----	----	----	----	----	NA	NA	142,000	----	----	----	----

[1] Preliminary.   [2] Unconsolidated metal in various forms.   [4] Included in Pigments.   NA = Not available.   W = Withheld.
Source: U.S. Geological Survey (USGS)

Average Prices of Titanium in the United States

Year	Ilmenite FOB Australian Ports[2]	Slag, 85% TiO2 FOB Richards Bay, South Africa	Rutile Large Lots Bulk, FOB U.S. East Coast[3]	Rutile Bagged FOB Australian Ports	Avg. Price of Grade A Titanium Sponge, FOB Shipping Point	Titanium Metal Sponge	Titanium Dioxide Pigments FOB US Plants Anatase	Titanium Dioxide Pigments FOB US Plants Rutile
	Dollars Per Metric Ton					Dollars Per Pound		
2001	$90 - $110	$419.00	$450 - $500	$475 - $565	----	$3.58	$0.92 - $0.94	$1.00 - $1.09
2002	$85 - $100	$445.00	$430 - $470	$400 - $540	----	$3.64	$0.85 - $0.95	$0.85 - $0.95
2003	$80 - $100	$401.00	$415 - $445	$430 - $540	----	$2.72 - $3.95	$0.85 - $0.95	$0.85 - $0.90
2004	$81.00	$347 - $466	$455.00	$550 - $650	----	$3.55 - $6.44	$0.90 - $0.95	$0.90 - $0.95
2005	$80.00	$390 - $555	$470.00	$550 - $650	----	$3.46 - $12.22	$0.95 - $1.00	$0.95 - $1.00
2006	$80.00	$402 - $454	$475.00	$570 - $700	----	$5.87 - $12.84	----	----
2007[1]	$107.00	$418 - $457	$594.00					
2008[2]	$99.00	$404 - $505	$500.00					

[1] Preliminary.   [2] Estimate.   NA = Not available.   *Source: U.S. Geological Survey (USGS)*

Average Price of Titanium[1] in United States   In Dollars Per Pound

Year	Jan.	Feb.	Mar.	Apr.	May	June	July	Aug.	Sept.	Oct.	Nov.	Dec.	Average
2003	3.11	3.11	3.11	3.20	3.24	3.24	3.24	3.24	3.24	3.24	3.24	3.24	3.20
2004	3.24	3.24	3.24	NA	NA	NA	NA	NA	NA	NA	NA	NA	3.24
2005	NA	NA	NA	NA	NA	NA	NA	NA	3.33	3.33	3.33	3.33	3.33
2006	3.33	3.33	3.33	3.33	3.33	3.33	3.33	3.33	3.33	3.33	3.33	3.33	3.33
2007	6.09	9.76	9.76	9.76	NA	NA	NA	NA	NA	NA	NA	NA	8.84
2008	NA	NA	NA	NA	NA	NA	NA	NA	NA	NA	NA	NA	NA

[1] Sponge.   NA = Not available.   *Source: American Metal Market (AMM)*

Average Price of Titanium[1] in United States   In Dollars Per Pound

Year	Jan.	Feb.	Mar.	Apr.	May	June	July	Aug.	Sept.	Oct.	Nov.	Dec.	Average
2003	4.90	4.90	4.90	4.90	4.90	4.90	4.90	4.90	4.90	4.90	4.90	4.90	4.90
2004	4.90	4.90	5.60	5.75	7.61	7.75	7.89	8.50	8.64	9.25	9.25	9.92	7.50
2005	10.60	11.25	11.25	15.44	17.25	20.25	20.25	20.33	22.00	22.00	22.00	22.13	17.90
2006	24.75	24.75	25.53	26.10	27.50	27.58	27.75	27.75	27.75	27.75	27.75	27.75	26.89
2007	27.21	26.50	26.50	25.69	25.32	24.50	24.50	22.15	21.50	20.63	18.90	17.79	23.43
2008	16.62	16.00	15.60	15.50	15.50	15.14	14.95	14.50	14.50	14.50	13.56	13.17	14.96

[1] Ingot, 6Al - 4V.   NA = Not available.   *Source: American Metal Market (AMM)*

Tobacco

Tobacco is a member of the nightshade family. It is commercially grown for its leaves and stems, which are rolled into cigars, shredded for use in cigarettes and pipes, processed for chewing, or ground into snuff. Christopher Columbus introduced tobacco cultivation and use to Spain after observing natives from the Americas smoking loosely rolled tobacco-stuffed tobacco leaves.

Tobacco is cured, or dried, after harvesting and then aged to improve its flavor. The four common methods of curing are: air cured, fire cured, sun cured, and flue cured. Flue curing is the fastest method of curing and requires only about a week compared with up to 10 weeks for other methods. Cured tobacco is tied into small bundles of about 20 leaves and aged one to three years.

Virginia tobacco is by far the most popular type used in pipe tobacco since it is the mildest of all blending tobaccos. Approximately 60% of the U.S. tobacco crop is Virginia-type tobacco. Burley tobacco is the next most popular tobacco. It is air-cured, burns slowly and provides a relatively cool smoke. Other tobacco varieties include Perique, Kentucky, Oriental, and Latakia.

Prices – U.S. tobacco farm prices in 2007 (latest data) rose +1.1% to 168.3 cents per pound from 166.5 cents per pound in 2006. That is, however, far below the record high of 198.4 cents per pound posted in 2004.

Supply – World production of tobacco in 2007 (latest data available) fell by -4.4% yr/yr to 6.326 million metric tons, but still above the 25-year low of 5.976 million metric tons seen in 2003. The world's largest producers of tobacco are China with 38% of world production, followed at a distance by Brazil (with 14% of world production), India (9%), and the U.S. (6%). U.S. production in 2007 rose by +7.1% yr/yr to 353,177 metric tons, where it was down by more than half from the 2-decade high of 810,154 metric tons posted in 1997.

Tobacco in the U.S. is grown primarily in the Mid-Atlantic States and they account for the vast majority of U.S. production. Specifically, the largest tobacco producing states in the U.S. are North Carolina (with 46% of U.S. production in 2006), Kentucky (26%), Tennessee (7%), South Carolina (7%), Virginia (6%), and Georgia (4%).

Flue-cured tobacco (type 11-14) is the most popular tobacco type grown in the U.S. and U.S. production in 2007 rose by +12.5% yr/yr to 503.220 million pounds. The second most popular type is burley tobacco (type 31), which saw U.S. production in 2007 fall -4.8% to 206.805 million pounds.

Total U.S. production of tobacco in 2006 (latest data available) rose +12.7% yr/yr to 727 million pounds, which is less than half of the 2-decade high of 1.787 billion pounds posted in 1997. U.S. farmers have sharply reduced the planting acreage for tobacco. In 2006, harvested tobacco acreage rose by +14.1% yr/yr to 338.950 acres, which is up from the 2005 record low of 297,080 but still far below the 24-year high of 836,230 posted in 1997. Yields have been fairly constant and have averaged about 2,100 pounds per acre for the past 10 years. The farm value of the U.S. tobacco crop in 2007 rose by +8.2% yr/yr to $1.310 billion.

U.S. marketings of flue-cured tobacco (Types 11-14) in the 2006-07 (latest data) marketing year rose by +18.5% yr/yr to 453.8 million pounds. U.S. marketings of burley tobacco (Type 31) in the 2006-07 marketing year rose by +6.9% yr/yr to 217.4 million pounds.

U.S. production of cigarettes in 2006 (latest data) rose by +1.5% to 496.4 billion cigarettes, which was still down sharply from the record high of 754.5 million posted in 1996. U.S. production of cigars rose by +8.2% yr/yr to 3.977 billion in 2006. U.S. production of chewing tobacco in 2006 fell by 3.1% to 38.0 million pounds, which was a record low.

Demand – U.S. per capita consumption of tobacco products in 2006 (latest data) was unchanged at 3.69 pounds per person but there appears to be a shifting from cigarettes to cigars. The 3.69 pounds per capita consumption of tobacco in 2006 is less than half the record high of 9.68 pounds per person that occurred at the beginning of the series in 1970. Per capita cigarette consumption in 2006 fell 1.5% yr/yr to 1,691 cigarettes per person, which was a record low. Per capita consumption of cigars in 2006 rose +1.9% yr/yr to a record high of 47.80 cigars per person. Per capita consumption of loose smoking tobacco in 2006 fell –6.3% yr/yr to 0.15 pounds.

Trade – U.S. tobacco exports in 2004 (latest data available) rose +3.5% yr/yr to 354.0 million pounds, rebounding further from the record low of 325.8 million pounds seen in 2002. Meanwhile, U.S. tobacco imports in 2004 fell –10.9% yr/yr to 561.7 million pounds from the 11-year high of 630.1 million pounds see in 2003. The U.S. exported 111.3 billion cigarettes and 180 million cigars in 2006.

World Production of Leaf Tobacco   In Metric Tons

Year	Brazil	Canada	China	Greece	India	Indo-nesia	Italy	Japan	Pakistan	Turkey	United States	Zim-babwe	World Total
1998	505,353	73,178	2,373,978	137,114	646,000	137,564	132,509	64,000	98,600	250,556	671,250	260,000	6,937,122
1999	629,525	70,215	2,478,295	139,791	736,200	138,000	126,352	64,727	108,800	243,468	586,360	193,183	6,988,557
2000	578,451	53,010	2,563,854	136,593	520,000	146,100	129,937	60,803	107,700	200,280	477,632	227,726	6,697,322
2001	568,505	58,606	2,358,842	142,000	340,000	201,900	130,487	60,600	85,100	144,786	449,760	195,905	6,152,009
2002	670,309	54,550	2,454,105	133,000	550,000	194,500	122,231	58,200	94,500	152,856	398,520	178,408	6,480,287
2003	656,200	46,338	2,262,658	136,000	490,000	200,875	124,985	50,662	88,200	112,158	364,080	102,683	5,975,994
2004	921,281	42,430	2,411,490	133,937	549,900	165,108	117,882	52,659	86,200	133,913	400,060	78,312	6,508,980
2005	889,426	43,000	2,685,743	125,904	549,100	153,470	115,983	47,000	100,500	135,247	290,170	83,230	6,698,999
2006[1]	900,381	43,000	2,746,193	37,252	552,200	177,895	110,000	38,000	112,600	98,137	329,918	44,451	6,615,424
2007[2]	919,393	44,000	2,397,200	18,500	555,000	180,000	100,000	40,000	126,000	98,000	353,177	79,000	6,326,252

[1] Preliminary.   [2] Estimate.   *Source: Food and Agriculture Organization of the United Nations (FAO-UN)*

TOBACCO

Production and Consumption of Tobacco Products in the United States

Year	Cigar-ettes - Billions -	Cigars[3] - Millions -	Plug	Twist	Loose-leaf	Smoking Total Tobacco	Smoking Tobacco	Snuff[4]	Cigar-ettes ----- Number -----	Cigars[3]	Cigar-ettes	Cigars[3]	Smoking Tobacco	Chewing Tobacco	Total Products
1997	722.8	2,324	3.5	1.0	53.7	58.1	11.4	64.3	2,422	37.3	4.10	.61	.11	.60	4.85
1998	679.7	2,751	3.1	1.0	49.2	53.3	11.7	65.5	2,275	37.1	3.60	.61	.12	.53	4.32
1999	611.5	2,938	2.8	0.9	47.2	50.9	14.7	67.0	2,101	38.5	3.50	.63	.13	.51	4.23
2000	594.1	2,825	2.5	0.8	46.0	49.4	13.6	69.5	2,049	38.0	3.40	.62	.13	.48	4.10
2001	562.8	3,741	2.4	0.8	43.9	47.0	12.8	70.9	2,051	41.2	3.50	.68	.15	.47	4.30
2002	532.0	3,819	2.0	0.7	40.2	43.0	15.5	72.7	1,982	41.8	3.40	.68	.16	.43	4.16
2003	499.4	4,017	1.7	0.7	37.9	40.3	17.8	73.8	1,890	44.5	3.20	.73	.16	.40	3.97
2004	493.5	4,407	1.7	0.7	37.0	39.3	16.1	79.3	1,814	47.9	3.10	.79	.15	.37	3.87
2005[1]	489.0	3,674	1.4	0.6	37.2	39.2	17.4	86.7	1,716	46.9	2.90	.77	.16	.36	3.69
2006[2]	496.4	3,977	1.3	0.5	36.1	38.0	16.5	81.8	1,691	47.8	2.90	.78	.15	.37	3.69

[1] Preliminary. [2] Estimate. [3] Large cigars and cigarillos. [4] Includes loose-leaf. [5] Consumption of tax-paid tobacco products. Unstemmed rocessing weight. [6] 18 years and older. NA = Not available. Source: Economic Research Service, U.S. Department of Agriculture (ERS-USDA)

Production of Tobacco in the United States, by States   In Thousands of Pounds

Year	Florida	Georgia	Indiana	Kentucky	Maryland	North Carolina	Ohio	Pennsyl-vania	South Carolina	Tenn-essee	Virginia	Wisconsin	Total
1999	15,312	64,020	11,700	408,492	9,100	448,980	17,052	11,170	78,000	122,601	88,855	2,818	1,292,692
2000	11,475	68,820	7,980	283,065	8,265	406,500	13,200	10,170	81,260	95,958	56,613	2,255	1,052,999
2001	11,700	64,206	9,450	254,653	3,300	386,920	11,956	6,166	78,400	86,893	63,415	3,619	991,223
2002	11,960	53,000	7,800	222,991	1,800	347,920	9,625	6,815	59,475	71,331	64,407	3,817	871,122
2003	11,000	59,400	8,190	225,042	1,595	299,995	8,745	7,880	63,000	65,632	38,818	4,255	802,560
2004	9,800	46,690	8,610	235,003	1,870	350,560	10,976	8,100	63,450	65,381	67,285	3,541	881,875
2005	5,500	27,760	----	174,260	----	278,900	6,732	10,700	39,900	51,670	40,351	----	645,015
2006	2,860	30,090	----	186,780	----	330,580	7,000	16,790	48,300	49,135	47,322	----	727,897
2007	----	39,775	----	197,040	----	383,420	7,175	18,310	46,125	38,636	46,142	----	787,653
2008[1]	----	33,600	----	205,850	----	389,850	6,970	17,630	39,900	52,380	45,970	----	800,527

[1] Preliminary.   Source: Agricultural Statistics Board, U.S. Department of Agriculture (ASB-USDA)

Salient Statistics of Tobacco in the United States

Year	Acres Harvested 1,000 Acres	Yield Per Acre Pounds	Pro-duction Million Pounds	Farm Price cents Lb.	Farm Value Million $	Tobacco (June - July) Exports[2]	Imports[3]	U.S. Exports of — Cigar-ettes	Cigars & Cheroots	All Smoking Tobacco[4]	Stocks — All Tobacco	Fire Cured[6]	Cigar Filler[7]	Mary-land
1997	836.2	2,137	1,787	180.2	3,217	450.1	565.8	217,000	86	487	118.2	2,031	83.3	13.0	15.0
1998	717.6	2,062	1,480	182.8	2,701	461.9	529.6	201,300	93	467	142.5	2,250	84.8	11.4	18.7
1999	647.2	1,997	1,293	182.8	2,356	394.7	480.2	151,400	84	423	151.1	2,301	86.7	11.4	20.6
2000	472.4	2,229	1,053	191.0	2,002	351.4	457.8	148,300	113	397	136.1	2,388	87.8	9.5	16.0
2001	432.3	2,293	991	195.7	1,940	386.7	568.0	133,900	124	411	118.2	1,893	93.8	12.1	13.4
2002	427.3	2,039	871	193.6	1,687	325.8	549.7	127,400	123	338	144.0	1,738	99.5	12.3	9.7
2003	411.2	1,952	803	196.7	1,576	342.1	630.1	121,500	130	343	121.2	1,584	100.5	10.7	8.2
2004	408.1	2,161	882	198.4	1,750	354.0	561.7	118,700	171	361	45.4	1,529	101.5	9.7	7.2
2005	297.1	2,171	645	164.2	1,059			113,300	301			1,455		9.9	5.0
2006[1]	339.0	2,144	727	166.5	1,211			111,317	180			1,167		10.8	0.8

[1] Preliminary. [2] Domestic. [3] For consumption. [4] In bulk. [5] Flue-cured and cigar wrapper, year beginning July 1; for all other types, October 1.
[6] Kentucky-Tennessee types 22-23. [7] Types 41-46.   Source: Economic Research Service, U.S. Department of Agriculture (ERS-USDA)

Tobacco Production in the United States, by Types   In Thousands of Pounds (Farm-Sale Weight)

Year	11-14	21	22	23	31	32	35-36	37	41	41-61	51	54	55	61
1998	812,797	2,340	25,922	11,573	582,336	15,370	9,663	122	9,450	19,744	3,633	3,270	960	2,431
1999	656,752	2,672	24,773	10,630	555,185	14,350	11,640	155	5,920	16,535	4,169	2,252	566	3,628
2000	598,915	2,548	34,167	14,920	362,788	13,395	15,896	165	5,040	10,205	1,070	1,825	430	1,840
2001	579,091	2,202	30,720	12,377	334,066	5,346	13,949	154	4,120	13,318	3,822	3,042	577	1,757
2002	514,385	1,471	23,292	10,145	293,537	4,205	10,570	116	4,410	13,401	4,021	3,151	666	1,153
2003	456,690	839	23,504	10,165	281,698	4,195	11,230	84	5,280	14,155	3,386	3,472	783	1,234
2004	521,535	1,345	24,800	11,006	292,172	5,830	11,798	124	4,140	13,265	3,767	2,744	797	1,915
2005	380,850	----	----	----	203,383	3,000	----	----	2,860	8,621	4,117	----	----	----
2006	447,190	----	----	----	217,255	2,090	----	----	2,600	8,265	4,434	----	----	----
2007[1]	503,220	----	----	----	206,805	2,310	----	----	4,140	11,093	5,195	----	----	----

[1] Preliminary.   Source: Agricultural Statistics Board, U.S. Department of Agriculture (ASB-USDA)

U.S. Exports of Unmanufactured Tobacco   In Millions of Pounds (Declared Weight)

Year	Australia	Belgium-Luxem.	Denmark	France	Germany	Italy	Japan	Nether-lands	Sweden	Switzer-land	Thailand	United Kingdom	Total U.S. Exports
1999	3.2	18.3	14.9	5.6	71.9	15.1	60.3	64.5	3.9	16.1	6.8	9.0	417.5
2000	3.6	23.2	15.7	5.5	86.1	15.8	63.6	19.7	3.5	9.5	7.3	7.3	402.4
2001	3.4	49.7	12.2	11.5	94.8	6.2	51.6	21.6	3.6	14.4	7.7	1.6	410.7
2002	4.5	29.4	13.6	10.3	59.5	8.6	49.6	10.3	1.2	27.3	12.6	6.0	338.2
2003	6.3	61.7	13.5	8.8	55.8	7.6	42.4	9.8	1.6	34.8	3.6	4.8	343.3
2004	3.6	27.4	10.2	16.3	53.5	6.6	34.6	15.8	.6	9.4	8.5	4.0	360.9
2005	2.9	12.7	8.4	10.7	55.3	5.8	21.7	25.4	.7	15.6	3.9	3.2	339.0
2006	4.9	16.8	8.4	7.5	81.2	3.2	3.9	37.0	.7	38.5	3.0	1.1	397.6
2007	3.5	18.0	9.7	13.2	63.1	.7	4.0	24.0	.3	41.7	1.8	.0	411.5
2008[1]	1.1	3.8	6.4	6.4	34.2	.0	.0	39.9	.3	51.8	3.0	.1	326.9

[1] Preliminary.   *Source: Economic Research Service, U.S. Department of Agriculture (ERS-USDA)*

U.S. Salient Statistics for Flue-Cured Tobacco (Types 11-14) in the United States   In Millions of Pounds

Year	Acres Harvested 1,000	Yield Per Acre Pounds	Mar-ketings	Stocks Oct. 1	Total Supply	Exports	Domestic Disap-pearance	Total Disap-pearance	Farm Price cents/Lb.	Placed Under Gov't Loan (Mil. Lb.)	Price Support Level (cents/) Lb.	Loan Stocks Nov. 30	Loan Stocks Uncommitted
1997-98	458.3	2,285	1,014	1,117	2,130	336	541	877	172.0	195.5	162.1	145.3	.0
1998-99	368.8	2,204	815	1,253	2,068	341	492	834	175.5	82.4	162.8	311.5	182.7
1999-00	303.8	2,162	654	2,162	2,816	262	437	699	173.7	136.4	163.2	318.3	144.9
2000-01	250.0	2,396	564	1,189	1,754	238	479	717	179.3	27.4	164.0	256.9	135.9
2001-02	238.1	2,432	544	1,036	1,581	276	389	665	185.7	15.0	166.0	93.2	65.0
2002-03	245.6	2,094	565	916	1,481	220	423	643	182.0	24.8	165.6	17.8	12.8
2003-04	233.4	1,957	508	838	1,345	216	307	522	185.1	59.8	166.3	70.6	68.7
2004-05	228.4	2,283	499	823	1,322	189	338	526	184.5	94.9	169.0	108.2	128.5
2005-06[1]	174.5	2,182	383	796	1,179	258	317	575	147.4	----	----	79.0	----
2006-07[2]	213.1	2,095	454	604	1,058	270	248	518					

[1] Preliminary.   [2] Estimate.   NA = Not available.   *Source: Economic Research Service, U.S. Department of Agriculture (ERS-USDA)*

Salient Statistics for Burley Tobacco (Type 31) in the United States   In Millions of Pounds

Year	Acres Harvested 1,000	Yield Per Acre Pounds	Mar-ketings	Stocks Oct. 1	Total Supply	Exports	Domestic Disap-pearance	Total Disap-pearance	Farm Price cents/Lb.	Gross Sales[3]	Price Support Level cents/Lb.	Loan Stocks Nov. 30	Loan Stocks Uncommitted
1997-98	335.3	1,934	628	751	1,379	168	379	548	188.5	337.9	176.0	105.6	38.5
1998-99	307.1	1,896	590	832	1,422	169	349	520	190.3	431.6	177.8	183.8	142.2
1999-00	303.6	1,829	551	901	1,453	139	273	413	182.9	356.6	178.9	226.6	186.7
2000-01	193.8	1,957	315	1,040	1,355	142	524	666	196.3	169.7	180.5	420.7	336.5
2001-02	167.6	2,033	344	689	1,033	140	245	385	197.3	258.5	182.6	119.3	74.8
2002-03	157.7	1,861	300	648	948	149	221	370	197.4	217.7	183.5	124.2	46.1
2003-04	152.3	1,850	272	578	1,850	174	136	310	197.7	197.3	184.9	91.7	26.5
2004-05	153.2	1,908	280	540	820	228	100	328	199.4	202.3	187.3	115.1	8.5
2005-06[1]	100.2	2,031	203	493	696	208	84	293	156.4	----	----	78.7	----
2006-07[2]	103.6	2,095	217	403	621	190	56	246					

[1] Preliminary.   [2] Estimate.   [3] Before Christmas holidays.   NA = Not available.
Source: Economic Research Service, U.S. Department of Agriculture (ERS-USDA)

Exports of Tobacco from the United States (Quantity and Value)   In Metric Tons

Year	Flue-Cured	Value 1,000 USD	Burley	Value 1,000 USD	Total	Value 1,000 USD	Manu-factured	Value 1,000 USD
1999	86,838	611,054	49,398	404,564	191,975	1,311,643	NA	3,232,862
2000	84,980	606,145	36,649	306,883	179,892	1,204,085	NA	4,012,711
2001	89,930	660,924	42,464	361,567	186,302	1,268,839	NA	2,734,377
2002	73,125	532,713	40,170	334,621	153,427	1,049,709	NA	1,950,188
2003	70,669	519,732	41,876	346,504	155,722	1,038,073	NA	1,843,922
2004	67,183	490,547	58,764	373,001	163,693	1,044,440	NA	1,566,223
2005	62,779	420,532	61,606	412,588	153,762	989,588	NA	1,301,834
2006	88,020	569,431	63,214	409,272	180,368	1,141,374	NA	1,320,283
2007[1]	82,093	541,816	75,905	498,168	186,643	1,207,945	NA	1,122,176
2008[2]	83,564	594,930	43,519	335,499	148,297	1,080,604	NA	761,877

[1] Preliminary.   [2] Forecast.   NA = Not available.   *Source: Foreign Agricultural Service, U.S. Department of Agriculture (FAS-USDA)*

Tung Oil

tung tree are harvested and pressed to yield tung oil. Tung oil is used mostly as an industrial lubricant and drying agent, and is the most powerful drying agent known. It is also used in paints and varnishes, soaps, inks, and electrical insulators. Tung oil is poisonous, containing glycerol esters of unsaturated fats. The oil is also used as a substitute for linseed oil in paints, varnishes, and linoleum, and as a waterproofing agent.

Prices – The price of tung oil in 2007 fell by 2.5% yr/yr to 89.72 cents per pound, down from the 2005 eight-year high of 98.33 cents per pound.

Demand – U.S. consumption of tung oil has fallen

sharply over the past decade. In 2008 (annualized through November) U.S. consumption rose by +1.8% yr/yr to 1.314 million pounds but the 2008 consumption level was only about 7% of 1996's 18-year high of 21.645 million pounds.

Trade – World imports of tung oil in 2007 (latest data available) fell –7.4% yr/yr to 18,329 metric tons. U.S. imports of tung oil in 2007 fell sharply by –40.8% to 1,230 metric tons. The world's largest importers of tung oil are South Korea with 15% of world imports, the Netherlands with 12%, Taiwan with 11%, Japan with 10%, and the U.S. with 7%. The world's largest exporter of tung oil by far is China with 13,313 metric tons of exports in 2007, accounting for 70% of total world exports.

World Tung Oil Trade   In Metric Tons

| | Imports | | | | | | | | Exports | | | | |
Year	Germany	Hong Kong	Japan	Nether-lands	Rep. of Korea	Taiwan	United States	World Total	Argen-tina	China	Hong Kong	Para-guay	World Total
2001	582	36	1,647	1,904	3,390	2,113	4,429	23,544	1,061	17,615	108	1,974	21,991
2002	325	702	1,930	1,793	6,968	5,185	4,166	29,710	916	23,334	589	4,390	30,351
2003	303	306	2,023	1,687	6,396	3,974	4,287	27,419	2,299	19,509	323	2,479	25,951
2004	100	207	1,900	1,778	5,486	3,529	2,975	24,961	1,299	18,850	240	3,626	25,501
2005	43	154	2,067	2,376	3,769	2,938	1,866	22,476	1,035	16,563	171	4,306	23,459
2006[1]	478	104	1,984	2,342	1,828	2,891	2,076	19,783	733	14,668	104	2,876	19,632
2007[2]	1,307	120	1,858	2,119	2,685	2,021	1,230	18,329	956	13,313	100	2,000	19,117

[1] Preliminary.   [2] Estimate.   *Source: The Oil World*

Consumption of Tung Oil in Inedible Products in the United States   In Thousands of Pounds

Year	Jan.	Feb.	Mar.	Apr.	May	June	July	Aug.	Sept.	Oct.	Nov.	Dec.	Total
2002	427	476	583	410	471	454	428	877	695	978	862	886	7,547
2003	685	276	508	317	322	233	270	349	406	269	376	228	4,239
2004	428	400	350	402	264	324	338	310	186	186	101	109	3,398
2005	128	110	144	151	371	127	161	189	92	171	146	110	1,900
2006	174	175	138	103	128	193	198	114	198	134	136	75	1,766
2007	170	81	108	104	176	117	153	83	68	92	75	64	1,291
2008[1]	W	W	141	91	98	W	108	W	W	W	W	W	1,314

[1] Preliminary.   W = Withheld.   *Source: Bureau of the Census, U.S. Department of Commerce*

Stocks of Tung Oil at Factories & Warehouses in the United States, on First of Month   In Thousands of Pounds

Year	Jan.	Feb.	Mar.	Apr.	May	June	July	Aug.	Sept.	Oct.	Nov.	Dec.
2002	W	W	W	W	1,341	1,206	885	516	483	551	560	478
2003	490	W	858	763	722	790	398	W	W	W	W	W
2004	W	W	W	519	229	209	226	137	91	161	121	117
2005	90	128	107	182	130	141	134	122	114	93	116	70
2006	109	99	98	124	81	116	128	85	128	125	76	98
2007	109	135	109	92	66	110	117	153	101	100	36	59
2008[1]	82	87	94	63	29	79	50	78	86	73	W	W

[1] Preliminary.   W = Withheld.   *Source: Bureau of the Census, U.S. Department of Commerce*

Average Price of Tung Oil (Imported, Drums) F.O.B. in New York   In Cents Per Pound

Year	Jan.	Feb.	Mar.	Apr.	May	June	July	Aug.	Sept.	Oct.	Nov.	Dec.	Average
2002	60.50	44.50	44.50	42.00	40.00	40.00	40.00	40.00	40.00	43.75	45.00	45.00	43.77
2003	45.00	45.00	52.80	84.75	85.00	85.00	85.00	85.00	85.00	85.00	85.00	85.00	75.63
2004	85.00	85.00	85.00	85.00	85.00	85.00	85.00	85.00	85.00	85.00	85.00	90.00	85.42
2005	92.50	95.00	97.50	97.50	97.50	97.50	97.50	102.50	105.00	105.00	97.50	95.00	98.33
2006	95.00	95.00	95.00	95.00	95.00	93.75	90.00	90.00	89.00	89.00	89.00	89.00	92.06
2007	85.40	84.33	87.00	85.00	85.00	85.00	85.00	NA	90.00	99.50	100.00	100.71	89.72
2008[1]	107.62	110.79	126.00	130.00	130.00	135.14	139.86	147.62	164.29	175.00	175.00	175.00	143.03

[1] Preliminary.   *Source: Economic Research Service, U.S. Department of Agriculture (ERS-USDA)*

Tungsten

Tungsten (symbol W) is a grayish-white, lustrous, metallic element. The atomic symbol for tungsten is W because of its former name of Wolfram. Tungsten has the highest melting point of any metal at about 3410 degrees Celsius and boils at about 5660 degrees Celsius. In 1781, the Swedish chemist Carl Wilhelm Scheele discovered tungsten.

Tungsten is never found in nature but is instead found in the minerals wolframite, scheelite, huebnertite, and ferberite. Tungsten has excellent corrosion resistance qualities and is resistant to most mineral acids. Tungsten is used as filaments in incandescent lamps, electron and television tubes, alloys of steel, spark plugs, electrical contact points, cutting tools, and in the chemical and tanning industries.

Prices – The average monthly price of tungsten at U.S. ports in 2008 fell by 2.0% yr/yr to $252.50 per short ton, down from the 2006 record high of $265.68 per short ton.

Supply – World concentrate production of tungsten in 2007 (latest data available) fell by -1.3% yr/yr to 89,600 metric tons. That was down from the 2004 record high of 102,000 metric tons. The world's largest producer of tungsten by far is China with 77,000 metric tons of production in 2007, which was 86% of total world production. Russia is the next largest producer at 4.9% with only a miniscule production of only 4,400 metric tons.

Trade – The U.S. in 2008 relied on imports for 61% of its tungsten consumption. U.S. imports for consumption in 2008 fell by –2.1% yr/yr to 3,800 metric tons. U.S. exports in 2008 were negligible at 75 metric tons.

World Concentrate Production of Tungsten   In Metric Tons (Contained Tungsten[3])

Year	Austria	Bolivia	Brazil	Burma	Canada	China	Mongolia	Korea	Portugal	Russia	Rwanda	Thailand	Total
2000	1,600	393	18	74	----	37,000	52	500	743	3,500	108	30	44,000
2001	1,429	532	22	85	----	42,100	63	500	698	5,100	142	50	50,800
2002	1,377	399	24	83	2,295	55,100	35	600	693	5,300	153	31	66,100
2003	1,381	441	30	93	3,636	55,500	40	600	715	5,450	78	208	68,200
2004	1,335	401	262	106	----	60,000	77	600	746	5,500	120	180	69,400
2005	1,350	522	250	100	700	61,000	78	600	815	4,400	120	150	70,100
2006[1]	1,300	870			2,560	79,000		600	780	4,000			90,800
2007[2]	1,300	870			2,600	77,000		600	800	4,400			89,600

[1] Preliminary.   [2] Estimate.   [3] Conversion Factors: WO_3 to W, multiply by 0.7931; 60% WO_3 to W, multiply by 0.4758.
Source: U.S. Geological Survey (USGS)

Salient Statistics of Tungsten in the United States   In Metric Tons (Contained Tungsten)

Year	Net Import Reliance as a % Apparent Consumption	Total Con- sumption	Tool	Stainless & Heat Assisting	Alloy Steel[3]	Super- alloys	Cutting & Wear Resistant Materials	Products Made From Metal Powder	Miscel- laneous	Chemical and Ceramic	Exports	Imports for Con- sumption	Con- sumers	Pro- ducers
2001	59	W	W	389	W	599	5,650	W	----	80	220	2,680	W	W
2002	70	W	W	313	W	426	4,820	W	----	133	94	4,090	W	W
2003	63	W	W	312	W	W	5,210	W	----	129	20	4,690	W	W
2004	73	W	W	259	W	W	6,020	W	----	130	43	2,310	W	W
2005	68	W	W	280	W	W	6,020	W	----	130	52	2,080	W	W
2006	68	W	W	292	W	W	6,590	W	----	118	130	2,290	W	W
2007[1]	68	W	W	W	W	W	W	W	----		109	3,880	W	W
2008[2]	61	W	W	W	W	W	W	W	----		75	3,800	W	W

Columns above: *Net Import Reliance as a % Apparent Consumption*, *Total Consumption*, and the section *-------- Consumption of Tungsten Products by End Uses -------* covers *Steel (Tool, Stainless & Heat Assisting, Alloy Steel[3])*, *Superalloys*, *Cutting & Wear Resistant Materials*, *Products Made From Metal Powder*, *Miscellaneous*, *Chemical and Ceramic*; then *Exports*, *Imports for Consumption*, and *Stocks, Dec. 31 -- Concentrates -- (Consumers, Producers)*.

[1] Preliminary.   [2] Estimate.   [3] Other than tool.   [4] Included with stainless & heat assisting.   W = Withheld.
Source: U.S. Geological Survey (USGS)

Average Price of Tungsten at U.S. Ports (Including Duty)   In Dollars Per Short Ton

Year	Jan.	Feb.	Mar.	Apr.	May	June	July	Aug.	Sept.	Oct.	Nov.	Dec.	Average
2001	83.50	86.00	90.00	93.00	96.15	96.50	93.88	92.88	91.00	89.89	83.84	79.57	87.72
2002	----	70.00	70.00	70.00	70.00	68.13	57.88	59.88	60.25	60.25	60.25	60.25	64.26
2003	60.25	61.55	63.00	63.00	63.00	63.00	63.00	63.00	63.00	63.00	63.00	63.00	62.65
2004	63.00	63.00	66.83	89.77	92.50	92.50	88.95	86.09	87.00	89.86	92.00	93.83	83.78
2005	97.08	109.32	134.13	178.21	272.26	277.61	275.25	237.28	232.50	244.05	255.00	255.00	213.97
2006	255.00	265.66	282.50	275.00	266.36	265.00	265.00	265.00	266.13	267.50	262.00	253.00	265.68
2007	252.50	256.71	261.36	262.50	262.50	262.50	262.50	261.63	252.50	252.50	252.50	252.50	257.68
2008	252.50	252.50	252.50	252.50	252.50	252.50	252.50	252.50	252.50	252.50	252.50	252.50	252.50

U.S. Spot Quotations, 65% WO_3, Basis C.I.F.   *Source: U.S. Geological Survey (USGS)*

Turkeys

During the past three decades, the turkey industry has experienced tremendous growth in the U.S. Turkey production has more than tripled since 1970, with a current value of over $7 billion. Turkey was not a popular dish in Europe until a roast turkey was eaten on June 27, 1570, at the wedding feast of Charles XI of France and Elizabeth of Austria. The King was so impressed with the birds that the turkey subsequently became a popular dish at banquets held by French nobility.

The most popular turkey product continues to be the whole bird, with heavy demand at Thanksgiving and Christmas. The primary breeders maintain and develop the quality stock, concentrating on growth and conformation in males and fecundity in females, as well as characteristics important to general health and welfare. Turkey producers include large companies that produce turkeys all year round, and relatively small companies and farmers who produce turkeys primarily for the seasonal Thanksgiving market.

Prices – The average monthly price received by farmers for turkeys in the U.S. in 2008 rose by +8.7% yr/yr to a record high of 56.5 cents per pound. The monthly average retail price of turkeys (whole frozen) in the U.S. in 2008 rose by +8.7% yr/yr to a record high of 125.0 cents per pound. Turkey prices have more than tripled from the low 40-cent area seen in the early 1970s.

Supply – World production of turkeys in 2008 rose by +3.2% yr/yr to a record high of 5.305 million metric tons. World production of turkeys has grown by more than two and one-half times since 1980 when production was a mere 2.090 million metric tons. The U.S. is the largest producer of turkeys in the world by far with 2.801 million metric tons of production in 2008, which is 53% of world production. The value of U.S. turkey production in the U.S. in 2007 (latest data) was $3.711 billion.

Demand – World consumption of turkeys in 2008 rose by +2.2% to a new record high of 5.129 million metric tons. U.S. turkey consumption of 2.503 million metric tons in 2008 accounted for 49% of world consumption. U.S. per capita consumption of turkeys in 2008 rose +1.7% yr/yr to 17.8 pounds per person per year. U.S. per capital consumption of turkeys has been in the range of 17-18 pounds since 1990, but the USDA is projecting that per capita consumption will drop somewhat.

Production and Consumption of Turkey Meat, by Selected Countries   In Thousands of Metric Tons (RTC)

| | Production | | | | | | | Consumption | | | | | | |
Year	Brazil	Canada	European Union	Mexico	Russia	United States	World Total	Brazil	Canada	European Union	Mexico	Russia	United States	World Total
2000	137	152	2,021	12	7	2,419	4,848	93	137	1,831	146	170	2,223	4,793
2001	165	149	2,100	13	7	2,490	4,938	96	135	1,949	157	171	2,269	4,881
2002	220	147	2,105	13	9	2,557	5,063	130	142	1,932	153	174	2,316	4,959
2003	272	148	2,028	14	12	2,529	5,015	160	137	1,939	170	126	2,301	4,959
2004	315	145	2,032	13	15	2,441	4,974	179	139	1,966	155	112	2,272	4,885
2005	360	155	1,919	14	17	2,464	4,942	199	143	1,888	197	124	2,246	4,865
2006	353	163	1,858	14	19	2,543	4,963	197	144	1,841	200	110	2,295	4,870
2007	458	169	1,790	15	25	2,667	5,140	281	149	1,769	213	100	2,404	5,021
2008[1]	510	172	1,760	15	35	2,801	5,305	300	156	1,750	218	115	2,503	5,129
2009[2]	550	172	1,750	16	40	2,733	5,273	315	158	1,750	223	120	2,457	5,120

[1] Preliminary. [2] Forecast. *Source: Foreign Agricultural Service, U.S. Department of Agriculture (FAS-USDA)*

Salient Statistics of Turkeys in the United States

			Liveweight		Value			Ready-to-Cook Basis			Production		Wholesale Ready-to-Cook	
							Be-		Consumption		Costs			
	Poults Placed[3]	Number Raised[4]	Pro- duced	Price cents	of Pro- duction	Pro- duction	ginning Stocks	Exports	Total	Per Capita	Feed	Total	Pro- duction Costs	3-Region Weighted Avg Price[5]
Year	--- In Thousands ----		Mil Lbs	Per Lb.	Million $	---------- In Millions of Pounds ----------				Lbs. - Liveweight Basis -			
1998	297,798	285,204	7,050.9	38.0	2,683.5	5,215	415	446	4,880	17.7	22.96	36.66	62.12	62.15
1999	297,387	270,494	6,886.4	40.8	2,806.6	5,231	304	378	4,905	17.6	19.00	32.70	57.17	67.81
2000	298,094	269,969	6,942.8	40.7	2,828.5	5,334	254	445	4,903	17.4	19.98	33.68	58.40	68.06
2001	301,721	272,059	7,154.8	39.0	2,796.8	5,489	241	487	5,004	17.5	20.55	34.25	59.11	63.63
2002	296,877	275,477	7,494.9	36.5	2,732.5	5,638	241	439	5,108	17.7	20.85	34.55	59.48	61.09
2003	289,542	274,048	7,487.3	36.1	2,699.7	5,576	333	484	5,074	17.4	22.59	36.29	61.66	60.41
2004	277,717	263,207	7,278.4	42.0	3,054.3	5,454	354	442	5,003	17.0				
2005	293,683	252,053	7,096.0	44.9	3,182.8	5,504	288	570	5,034	16.7				
2006[1]	293,137	262,460	7,463.9	47.9	3,573.7	5,612	206	547	5,065	16.9				
2007[2]	308,402	271,689	7,869.2	47.2	3,710.8	5,880	218	554	5,292	17.5				

[1] Preliminary. [2] Estimate. [3] Poults placed for slaughter by hatcheries. [4] Turkeys place August 1-July 31. [5] Regions include central, eastern and western. Central region receives twice the weight of the other regions in calculating the average.
Source: Economic Research Service, U.S. Department of Agriculture (ERS-USDA)

Turkey-Feed Price Ratio in the United States   In Pounds[2]

Year	Jan.	Feb.	Mar.	Apr.	May	June	July	Aug.	Sept.	Oct.	Nov.	Dec.	Average
1999	6.5	7.1	7.5	7.8	8.2	8.7	9.7	9.5	9.6	10.0	9.9	9.2	8.6
2000	7.6	7.2	7.6	7.9	7.8	8.5	9.5	10.0	10.1	10.0	9.8	8.1	8.7
2001	7.3	7.5	7.7	8.0	8.1	8.3	7.9	7.8	8.3	9.6	9.6	8.1	8.2
2002	7.2	7.2	6.8	6.8	7.3	7.3	6.9	6.3	6.0	6.1	6.5	6.4	6.7
2003	5.7	5.7	5.9	5.9	5.7	5.8	5.9	5.7	6.0	6.3	6.3	5.7	5.9
2004	5.1	4.6	4.5	4.5	4.8	5.2	5.8	7.0	7.9	8.4	8.7	8.2	6.2
2005	6.9	6.9	6.6	6.7	6.9	7.0	7.3	8.0	9.0	9.5	10.0	9.5	7.9
2006	7.0	6.9	6.9	7.3	7.1	7.6	7.7	8.5	9.1	9.6	9.4	5.9	7.8
2007	5.6	5.3	5.5	5.8	5.9	6.1	6.6	6.7	6.6	6.4	6.1	4.9	6.0
2008[1]	4.1	3.6	4.0	4.0	4.3	4.3	4.5	4.7	5.5	5.9	5.6	4.4	4.6

[1] Preliminary.   [2] Pounds of feed equal in value to one pound of turkey, liveweight.   Source: Economic Research Service, U.S. Department of Agriculture (ERS-USDA)

Average Price Received by Farmers for Turkeys in the United States (Liveweight)   In Cents Per Pound

Year	Jan.	Feb.	Mar.	Apr.	May	June	July	Aug.	Sept.	Oct.	Nov.	Dec.	Average
1999	34.8	35.7	37.0	38.7	39.4	41.3	42.0	43.0	44.3	45.3	45.3	42.2	40.8
2000	36.4	35.7	38.2	40.0	40.8	41.8	42.2	43.2	44.8	46.1	47.1	40.5	41.4
2001	36.6	36.3	37.1	37.6	38.2	38.3	38.5	38.7	40.5	44.2	44.5	38.7	39.1
2002	34.1	34.1	32.9	32.9	35.8	37.2	38.6	38.2	37.2	37.2	39.8	38.7	36.4
2003	34.6	34.5	35.1	35.6	34.9	34.9	33.6	32.7	36.2	39.1	41.2	38.2	35.9
2004	34.9	35.0	36.6	38.4	40.1	41.7	43.3	45.1	46.2	48.1	48.7	45.9	42.0
2005	39.3	38.0	38.1	38.8	40.7	42.1	44.6	46.5	50.3	52.5	54.5	53.9	44.9
2006	40.8	39.6	40.3	42.5	43.3	45.4	45.9	48.6	53.3	62.7	66.3	42.7	47.6
2007	40.8	42.4	44.3	46.8	48.3	52.0	55.5	57.2	60.4	61.5	61.6	52.6	52.0
2008[1]	44.8	47.5	52.9	55.1	58.0	60.1	61.1	63.4	66.5	64.6	58.9	44.5	56.5

[1] Preliminary.   Source: Economic Research Service, U.S. Department of Agriculture (ERS-USDA)

Average Wholesale Price of Turkeys[1] (Hens, 8-16 Lbs.) in New York   In Cents Per Pound

Year	Jan.	Feb.	Mar.	Apr.	May	June	July	Aug.	Sept.	Oct.	Nov.	Dec.	Average
1999	57.67	58.84	61.69	63.02	65.55	68.89	71.62	73.57	76.28	79.30	78.99	72.39	68.98
2000	61.58	61.84	65.35	67.38	69.18	70.36	71.55	73.61	76.53	78.74	79.58	70.31	70.50
2001	61.50	61.18	62.38	63.45	65.65	66.00	66.10	66.38	68.81	72.86	73.48	67.71	66.29
2002	60.86	60.03	59.00	59.52	63.52	65.68	66.52	66.56	67.15	67.75	69.79	66.96	64.45
2003	61.04	61.13	61.24	61.43	60.36	60.12	58.18	57.74	61.52	66.08	69.33	66.85	62.09
2004	62.13	61.61	62.62	64.52	66.41	68.95	71.21	73.32	74.69	76.89	78.29	76.05	69.72
2005	67.63	65.34	64.68	65.86	67.69	69.50	72.56	75.98	80.90	82.40	85.75	82.60	73.41
2006	68.29	65.84	67.67	69.75	71.27	72.95	74.95	78.70	84.40	95.83	99.51	74.20	76.95
2007	67.63	69.84	71.66	74.45	76.98	82.12	86.89	89.70	93.12	95.20	94.71	82.47	82.06
2008[2]	73.74	76.40	82.20	85.99	89.19	91.45	92.91	96.85	99.62	97.27	87.44	74.88	87.33

[1] Ready-to-cook.   [2] Preliminary.   Source: Economic Research Service, U.S. Department of Agriculture (ERS-USDA)

Certified Federally Inspected Turkey Slaughter in the U.S. (Ready-to-Cook Weights)   In Millions of Pounds

Year	Jan.	Feb.	Mar.	Apr.	May	June	July	Aug.	Sept.	Oct.	Nov.	Dec.	Total
1999	408.9	361.0	428.8	435.8	438.6	452.4	434.7	464.3	451.3	468.7	487.6	425.4	5,257
2000	396.9	412.4	466.2	413.5	489.2	479.4	422.8	481.6	423.0	494.7	478.2	396.5	5,354
2001	458.3	405.9	458.7	425.1	485.1	460.7	465.1	481.7	409.2	536.2	477.7	413.2	5,477
2002	477.2	442.1	447.8	487.2	496.7	448.0	474.7	475.9	439.4	519.0	488.2	457.9	5,654
2003	473.6	427.1	464.6	471.1	475.8	478.0	483.9	449.3	453.6	522.8	450.3	436.1	5,586
2004	435.5	389.0	466.6	445.2	445.1	462.8	455.4	462.2	451.2	461.5	479.6	434.4	5,389
2005	439.0	396.3	459.4	439.7	456.3	485.8	427.5	483.7	450.6	479.1	478.2	434.4	5,430
2006	443.0	412.4	487.9	430.3	492.8	504.4	453.5	493.6	456.5	535.8	499.7	423.5	5,633
2007	479.0	442.7	478.8	459.6	507.5	495.7	502.0	517.3	456.4	577.8	520.3	457.3	5,894
2008[1]	544.6	504.0	484.5	515.9	517.9	519.7	544.1	503.8	511.5	570.1	507.9	488.2	6,212

[1] Preliminary.   Source: Economic Research Service, U.S. Department of Agriculture (ERS-USDA)

TURKEYS

Per Capita Consumption of Turkeys in the United States   In Pounds

Year	First Quarter	Second Quarter	Third Quarter	Fourth Quarter	Total	Year	First Quarter	Second Quarter	Third Quarter	Fourth Quarter	Total
1998	3.9	3.9	4.2	6.0	18.1	2004	3.6	4.0	4.5	5.0	17.0
1999	3.8	3.8	4.4	5.8	18.0	2005	3.6	3.9	4.2	5.1	16.7
2000	3.7	4.2	4.4	5.5	17.8	2006	3.5	3.9	4.3	5.2	16.9
2001	3.9	3.8	4.3	5.6	17.5	2007	3.8	4.1	4.2	5.5	17.5
2002	3.5	3.9	4.4	5.9	17.7	2008[1]	4.0	4.1	4.3	5.3	17.7
2003	3.6	3.9	4.6	5.3	17.4	2009[2]	4.2	4.2	4.2	5.2	17.8

[1] Preliminary.   [2] Estimate.   Source: Economic Research Service, U.S. Department of Agriculture (ERS-USDA)

Storage Stocks of Turkeys (Frozen) in the United States on First of Month   In Millions of Pounds

Year	Jan.	Feb.	Mar.	Apr.	May	June	July	Aug.	Sept.	Oct.	Nov.	Dec.
1999	304.3	363.8	375.6	374.9	455.4	494.3	556.1	599.0	580.3	596.4	494.5	252.3
2000	254.3	319.4	353.9	391.4	416.9	480.3	506.8	524.0	524.9	528.1	473.9	261.1
2001	241.3	291.4	333.5	355.8	392.6	456.0	506.7	534.2	545.3	542.0	497.9	260.0
2002	240.5	327.1	413.2	457.6	515.2	578.2	644.1	706.2	685.6	672.4	624.9	334.3
2003	333.0	451.9	492.7	549.3	573.5	658.8	718.2	722.5	706.5	647.5	582.7	350.7
2004	354.0	420.5	471.7	504.6	548.8	571.1	597.6	599.6	600.2	527.4	472.3	294.9
2005	288.4	332.9	379.4	414.2	440.1	465.9	506.3	518.9	523.1	477.8	417.6	194.7
2006	206.2	260.5	315.7	377.7	423.7	466.5	507.5	512.2	500.3	464.2	404.2	214.5
2007	218.4	293.4	312.9	346.8	360.2	398.0	448.4	503.5	524.4	504.9	417.0	206.9
2008[1]	260.6	327.6	416.7	428.1	491.3	522.4	562.7	620.7	629.2	621.5	578.0	360.4

[1] Preliminary.   Source: Economic Research Service, U.S. Department of Agriculture (ERS-USDA)

Average Retail Price of Turkeys (Whole frozen) in the United States   In Cents Per Pound

Year	Jan.	Feb.	Mar.	Apr.	May	June	July	Aug.	Sept.	Oct.	Nov.	Dec.	Average
1999	96.9	100.1	98.4	93.6	97.5	100.5	103.1	101.5	101.8	102.5	96.4	97.6	99.2
2000	101.3	102.5	101.5	99.7	102.9	106.5	109.5	104.5	104.4	106.7	98.1	99.4	103.1
2001	108.8	112.5	112.7	109.7	109.4	110.9	111.0	113.5	116.2	114.6	98.0	99.5	109.7
2002	102.2	105.1	106.6	104.0	102.5	107.3	108.0	106.8	106.6	111.7	103.8	98.8	105.3
2003	106.6	105.8	105.5	100.1	106.0	110.6	113.4	116.2	116.7	111.2	100.6	105.4	108.2
2004	108.4	109.4	113.4	108.4	109.0	111.7	112.9	114.2	108.8	112.3	99.6	100.3	109.0
2005	105.8	106.3	106.1	105.8	106.9	108.0	116.5	116.6	112.1	113.7	102.3	106.6	108.9
2006	106.9	119.7	120.9	111.1	108.4	112.8	113.0	110.6	115.1	114.9	97.3	99.1	110.8
2007	110.3	113.6	107.9	108.1	114.6	122.3	122.2	122.9	121.6	124.1	111.3	101.0	115.0
2008[1]	120.7	123.0	115.1	117.0	125.8	123.8	127.0	128.8	132.0	122.2	130.9	133.2	125.0

[1] Preliminary.   Source: Economic Research Service, U.S. Department of Agriculture (ERS-USDA)

Average Retail-to-Consumer Price Spread of Turkeys (Whole) in the United States   In Cents Per Pound

Year	Jan.	Feb.	Mar.	Apr.	May	June	July	Aug.	Sept.	Oct.	Nov.	Dec.	Average
1999	29.9	32.7	28.6	21.3	22.5	22.6	23.2	29.1	18.5	17.6	12.0	19.6	23.1
2000	32.1	33.9	29.1	25.9	27.6	29.5	30.9	23.7	21.1	21.7	13.4	23.1	26.0
2001	39.5	43.3	42.5	39.1	37.7	38.7	38.6	40.5	41.0	35.6	18.7	27.0	36.9
2002	34.2	37.9	40.7	38.3	32.9	35.9	35.9	34.9	35.4	40.2	29.8	24.6	35.1
2003	38.4	37.6	36.8	31.2	38.1	42.9	47.1	50.0	47.2	37.8	25.1	33.2	38.8
2004	39.4	40.4	42.5	35.0	33.5	33.9	33.3	32.5	25.7	26.9	14.0	18.0	31.3
2005	31.3	33.4	33.3	31.5	30.9	29.4	25.6	22.4	24.1	22.9	8.7	16.8	25.9
2006	29.4	44.5	44.8	32.8	28.6	30.8	29.6	22.9	21.5	9.3	-11.3	15.9	24.9
2007	33.7	34.3	27.2	25.2	28.7	30.9	26.5	24.6	19.7	20.0	7.4	9.8	24.0
2008[1]	38.0	37.5	23.7	21.6	27.3	23.4	25.1	23.0	23.4	18.0	33.9	48.8	28.6

[1] Preliminary.   Source: Economic Research Service, U.S. Department of Agriculture (ERS-USDA)

Uranium

Uranium (symbol U) is a chemically reactive, radioactive, steel-gray, metallic element and is the main fuel used in nuclear reactors. Uranium is the heaviest of all the natural elements. Traces of uranium have been found in archeological artifacts dating back to 79 AD. Uranium was discovered in pitchblende by German chemist Martin Heinrich Klaproth in 1789. Klaproth named it uranium after the recently discovered planet Uranus. French physicist Antoine Henri Becquerel discovered the radioactive properties of uranium in 1896 when he produced an image on a photographic plate covered with a light-absorbing substance. Following Becquerel's experiments, investigations of radioactivity led to the discovery of radium and to new concepts of atomic organization.

The principal use for uranium is fuel in nuclear power plants. Demand for uranium concentrates is directly linked to the level of electricity generated by nuclear power plants. Uranium ores are widely distributed throughout the world and are primarily found in Canada, DRC (formerly Zaire), and the U.S.. Uranium is obtained from primary mine production and secondary sources. Two Canadian companies are the primary producers of uranium from deposits in the Athabasca Basin of northern Saskatchewan. Specifically, the companies Cameco accounted for 19% of global mine production in 2000 and Cogema Resources accounted for 15% of world production. Secondary sources of uranium include excess inventories from utilities and other fuel cycle participants, used reactor fuel, and dismantled Russian nuclear weapons.

Prices – The average price of delivered uranium in 2002 (the latest data available) rose by +2.1% yr/yr to $10.36 per pound from $10.15 in 2001. The 2001 price of $10.15 was a record low for the data series that goes back to 1981. The price of delivered uranium in 2002 of $10.36 was roughly one-third of the price of $30 per pound and above seen in the 1980s through 1986 when the price started falling.

Supply – World production of uranium oxide (U308) concentrate in 2003 (the latest data available) rose +7.3% yr/yr to a 13-year high of 56,552 short tons from last 2002's 52,709 short tons. The world's largest uranium producers in 2003 were Canada with 17,050 short tons of production in 2003 (30% of world production), the U.S. with 10,200 short tons of production (18% of world production), and Australia with 9,326 short tons of production (16% of world production). U.S. production in 2003 was the highest since 1983.

U.S. uranium production in 2003 rose +64.4% yr/yr to a 20-year high of 10,200 short tons, up sharply from the record low of 1,315 short tons in 2001. U.S. production had reached a peak of 21,850 short tons in 1980 and production had since fallen steadily to the record low in 2001, which was only 6% of the record level of production.

Trade – U.S. imports of uranium in 2003 (latest data available) rose +0.7% yr/yr to a record high of 53.044 million pounds. The U.S. is being forced to import more uranium as domestic production steadily declines. U.S. exports of uranium fell –14.3% yr/yr to 13.187 million pounds, which was still well above the 7-year low of 8.510 million pounds posted in 1999.

World Production of Uranium Oxide (U₃O₈) Concentrate   In Short Tons (Uranium Content)

Year	Australia	Canada	China	Czech Rep. & Slovakia	France	Gabon	Germany	Namibia	Niger	South Africa	United States	Ex-USSR	World Total
1994	3,050	11,950	----	----	1,700	750	----	2,500	3,800	2,250	1,950	----	41,750
1995	4,900	13,600	----	----	1,250	800	----	2,600	3,750	1,850	3,050	----	43,050
1996	6,450	15,250	----	----	1,200	750	----	3,150	4,300	2,200	3,150	----	46,650
1997	7,150	15,650	----	----	940	600	----	3,770	4,500	1,065	2,900	----	46,550
1998	6,350	14,200	----	----	660	950	----	3,590	4,850	1,250	2,435	----	44,110
1999	7,875	10,680	----	----	450	380	----	3,495	3,790	1,195	2,325	----	39,640
2000	9,830	13,875	655	795	525	----	45	2,430	3,270	1,305	1,890	655	43,475
2001	10,035	16,270	650	595	195	----	----	2,910	3,795	1,135	1,315	1,050	47,395
2002[1]	10,857	17,153	W	0	----	W	W	1,082	W	764	6,206	W	52,709
2003[2]	9,326	17,050	W	W	----	0	0	1,034	0	1,438	10,200	W	56,552

[1] Preliminary.   [2] Estimate.   W = Withheld.   *Source: American Bureau of Metal Statistics, Inc. (ABMS)*

Commercial and U.S. Government Stocks of Uranium, End of Year   In Millions of Pounds U₃O₈ Equivalent

Year	Utility Natural Uranium	Utility Enriched Uranium[1]	Domestic Supplier Natural Uranium	Domestic Supplier Enriched Uranium[1]	Total Commercial Stocks	DOE Owned & USEC Held Natural Uranium	DOE Owned & USEC Held Enriched Uranium[1]
1996	42.2	23.9	13.0	1.0	80.0	83.2	25.3
1997	47.1	18.8	10.3	30.1	106.2	53.2	----
1998	42.1	23.7	35.0	35.7	136.5	24.5	----
1999	44.8	13.5	29.5	39.4	127.1	53.1	----
2000	36.0	18.9	12.6	43.8	111.3	53.1	----
2001	34.4	21.2	9.2	39.0	103.8	53.1	----
2002	31.0	22.4	15.0	32.9	102.1	51.8	----
2003	22.7	23.0	[2]	39.9	85.5	W	W
2004	27.9	29.8	[2]	37.5	95.2	W	W
2005	45.4	19.4	[2]	29.1	93.8	W	W

[1] Includes amount reported as UF₆ at enrichment suppliers.   [2] Included in Enriched beginning 2003.   DOE = Department of Energy
USEC = U.S. Energy Commission   *Source: Energy Information Administration, U.S. Department of Energy (EIA-DOE)*

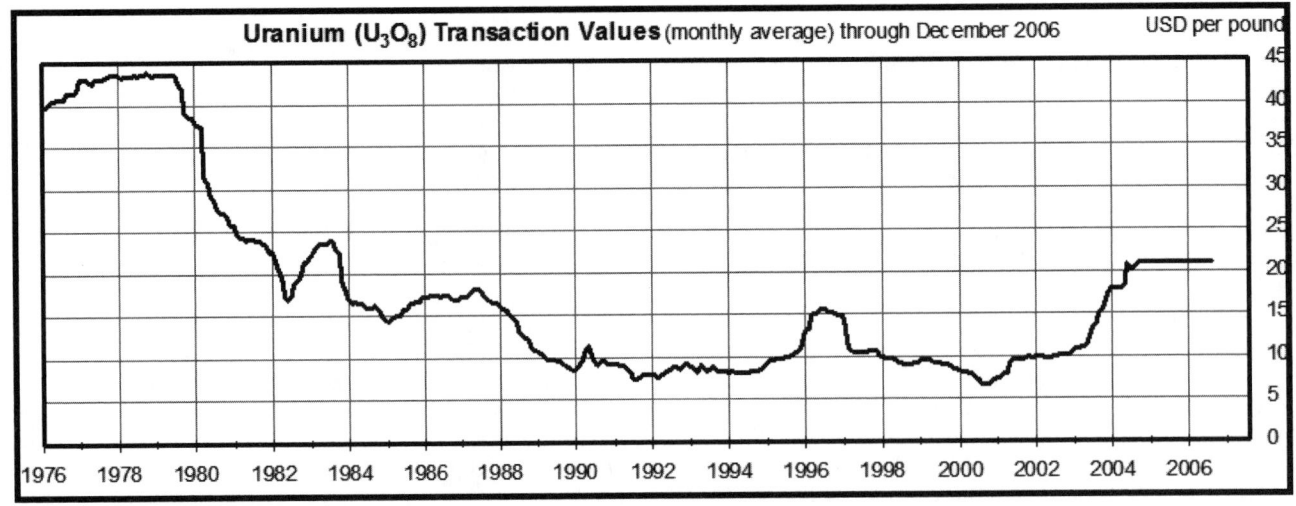

Uranium (U₃O₈) Transaction Values (monthly average) through December 2006   USD per pound

Reported Average Price Settlements for Purchases by U.S. Utilities and Domestic Suppliers   In Dollars Per Pound

Year of Delivery	Contract Price	Market Price[1]	Price & Cost Floor	Total	Contract & Market	Year of Delivery	Contract Price	Market Price[1]	Price & Cost Floor	Total	Contract & Market
	----------------- Averages of Reported Prices -----------------						------------------ Averages of Reported Prices ------------------				
1998	12.53	9.33	13.50	10.31	12.37	2003	----	----	----	10.81	----
1999	12.72	9.52	14.75	11.16	12.57	2004	----	----	----	12.61	----
2000	12.31	9.11	----	11.04	----	2005	----	----	----	14.36	----
2001	11.72	8.04	----	10.15	----	2006	----	----	----	18.61	----
2002	10.73	9.79	----	10.36	----	2007	----	----	----	32.78	----

[1] No floor.   Note: Price excludes uranium delivered under litigation settlements. Price is given in year-of-delivery dollars.   *Source: Energy Information Administration, U.S. Department of Energy (EIA-DOE)*

Uranium Industry Statistics in the United States   In Millions of Pounds U₃O₈

Year	Production Mine	Production Concentrate	Concentrate Shipments	Exploration	Mining	Milling	Processing	Total[1]	Deliveries to U.S. Utilities[2]	Avg Price Delivered Uranium $/lb U₃O₈	Imports	Avg Price Delivered Uranium Imports $/lb U₃O₈	Exports
1998	4.8	4.700	4.900	30	518	160	203	1,120	42.7	12.14	43.7	11.19	15.1
1999	4.5	4.600	5.500	7	310	201	132	848	47.9	11.63	47.6	10.55	8.5
2000	3.1	4.000	3.200	1	157	106	137	627	51.8	11.04	44.9	9.84	13.6
2001	2.6	2.600	2.200	0	81	42	122	423	55.4	10.15	46.7	9.51	11.7
2002	2.4	2.300	3.800	W	W	104	100	426	52.7	10.36	52.7	10.05	15.4
2003	2.2	2.000	1.600	W	W	W	W	321			53.0	10.59	13.2
2004	2.5	2.300	2.300	18	108	W	W	420					
2005	3.0	2.700	2.700	79	149	142	154	648					
2006	4.7	4.100	3.800	188	121	W	W	755					
2007	4.5	4.500	4.000	375	378	107	216	1,231					

[1] From suppliers under domestic purchases.   *Source: Energy Information Administration, U.S. Department of Energy (EIA-DOE)*

Month-End Uranium (U3O8) Transaction Values[1]   In Dollars Per Pound

Year	Jan.	Feb.	Mar.	Apr.	May	June	July	Aug.	Sept.	Oct.	Nov.	Dec.	Average
1997	15.33	15.08	14.85	14.75	14.43	10.95	10.68	10.45	10.55	10.48	10.43	10.53	12.37
1998	10.63	10.63	10.60	10.05	10.00	9.80	9.80	9.73	9.55	9.35	9.25	9.05	9.87
1999	9.03	9.08	9.20	9.20	9.53	9.48	9.48	9.40	9.35	9.23	9.18	9.13	9.27
2000	9.03	8.70	8.55	8.50	8.40	8.18	8.13	7.98	7.88	7.40	7.15	6.80	8.06
2001	6.78	6.83	6.83	7.25	7.38	7.45	7.83	7.95	9.00	9.47	9.44	9.50	7.97
2002	9.58	9.72	9.90	9.76	9.90	9.90	9.88	9.85	9.79	9.85	9.86	9.97	9.83
2003	10.20	10.10	10.10	10.16	10.84	10.90	10.90	11.13	11.47	12.32	13.18	13.98	11.27
2004	14.85	15.47	16.50	17.52	17.75	17.86	17.90	17.90	18.60	20.80	20.20	20.50	17.99
2005	20.55	21.18	21.20	21.20	21.20	21.20	21.20	21.20	21.20	21.20	21.20	21.20	21.14
2006	21.20	21.20	21.20	21.20	21.20	21.20	21.20	21.20	21.20	21.20	21.20	21.20	21.20

[1] Transaction value is a weighed average price of recent natural uranium sales transactions, based on prices paid on transactions closed within the previous three-month period for which delivery is scheduled within one year of the transaction date; at least 10 transactions involving a sum total of at least 2 million pounds of U3O8 equivalent.   *Source: American Metal Market (AMM)*

Vanadium

Vanadium (symbol V) is a silvery-white, soft, ductile, metallic element. Discovered in 1801, but mistaken for chromium, vanadium was rediscovered in 1830 by Swedish chemist Nils Sefstrom, who named the element in honor of the Scandinavian goddess Vanadis.

Never found in the pure state, vanadium is found in about 65 different minerals such as carnotite, roscoelite, vanadinite, and patronite, as well as in phosphate rock, certain iron ores, some crude oils, and meteorites. Vanadium is one of the hardest of all metals. It melts at about 1890 degrees Celsius and boils at about 3380 degrees Celsius.

Vanadium has good structural strength and is used as an alloying agent with iron, steel, and titanium. It is used in aerospace applications, transmission gears, photography, as a reducing agent, and as a drying agent in various paints.

Prices – The price of vanadium in 2008 rose very sharply by +99.3% to $14.75 per pound but still below the record high of $16.28 per pound in 2005.

Supply – Virtually all (99%) of vanadium is produced from ores, concentrates, and slag, with the remainder coming from petroleum residues, ash, and spent catalysts. World production in 2008 from ore, concentrates and slag rose +2.6% to 60,000 metric tons. World production of all vanadium in 2006 (latest data available) 5 fell -0.2% yr/yr to 56,300 metric tons.

The world's largest producer of vanadium from ores, concentrates and slag is South Africa with 23,000 metric tons of production in 2008, which was 38% of world production. The two other major producers are China with 33% of world production and Russia with 27% of world production. Production in Russia and South Africa has been relatively stable in recent years, while China's production grew sharply in the late 1990s. China's production level of 20,000 metric tons in 2008 is a new record high and almost four times the levels seen in the early 1990s.

Trade – U.S. exports of vanadium in 2008 were in the forms of oxides & hydroxides (953 metric tons, +52.2% yr/yr), ferro-vanadium (1,461 metric tons, +72,1%), and pentoxide, anhydride (243 metric tons, -25.7%). U.S. imports of vanadium in 2008 were in the forms of vanadium pentoxide, anhydride (4,100 metric tons, +71.6% yr/yr), ferro-vanadium (3,320 metric tons, +49.6% yr/yr), slag and residues (720 metric tons, -21,7% yr/yr), and oxides & hydroxides (183 metric tons, +335.7% yr/yr).

World Production of Vanadium   In Metric Tons (Contained Vanadium)

Year	Australia	China[3]	Kazak-hstan	Russia	South Africa	Total[4]	Japan[5]	United States[6]	Total	World Total
								From Petroleum Residues Ash, Spent Catalysts		
2003	160	13,200	1,000	5,800	27,172	47,300	560	----	560	47,900
2004	150	16,000	1,000	10,900	23,302	51,400	560	----	560	51,900
2005	100	17,000	1,000	15,100	22,604	55,800	560	----	560	56,400
2006	100	17,500	1,000	15,100	22,000	55,700	560	----	560	56,300
2007[1]		19,000		14,500	24,000	58,500				
2008[2]		20,000		16,000	23,000	60,000				

[1] Preliminary.   [2] Estimate.   [3] In vanadiferous slag product.   [4] Excludes U.S. production.   [5] In vanadium pentoxide product.
[6] In vanadium pentoxide and ferrovanadium products.   Source: U.S. Geological Survey (USGS)

Salient Statistics of Vanadium in the United States   In Metric Tons (Contained Vanadium)

Year	Consumer & Producer Stocks, Dec. 31	Tool Steel	Cast Irons	High Strength, Low Alloy	Stainless & Heat Resisting	Super-alloys	Carbon	Full Alloy	Total	Average $ Per Lb. V₂O₅	Vanadium Pentoxide, Anhydride	Oxides & Hydroxides	Ferro-Vanadium	Ores, Slag, Residues	Vanadium Pentoxide, Anhydride	Oxides & Hydroxides	Ferro-Vanadium
2003	252	143	W	938	70	13	1,030	808	3,240	2.21	185	284	397	3,060	474	74	1,360
2004	336	239	W	1,160	60	17	1,300	1,060	4,050	5.99	240	584	285	2,350	1,040	120	3,020
2005	371	402	W	974	60	36	1,170	1,010	3,910	16.28	254	899	504	1,690	1,370	186	11,900
2006	330	323	W	1,020	61	40	1,210	1,030	4,030	7.86	341	832	389	1,000	1,920	129	2,140
2007[1]	295								4,130	7.40	327	626	154	920	2,390	42	2,220
2008[2]	340								5,190	14.75	243	953	265	720	4,100	183	3,320

[1] Preliminary.   [2] Estimate.   W = Withheld.   Source: U.S. Geological Survey (USGS)

Average Price of Vanadium Pentoxide   In Dollars Per Pound

Year	Jan.	Feb.	Mar.	Apr.	May	June	July	Aug.	Sept.	Oct.	Nov.	Dec.	Average
2003	1.55	1.55	1.55	1.55	1.55	1.55	1.55	1.55	1.55	1.55	1.95	2.10	1.63
2004	2.50	3.43	3.74	5.25	5.25	5.25	5.26	4.64	4.40	5.15	7.00	8.63	5.04
2005	9.65	10.24	13.75	15.00	20.36	26.16	19.96	11.63	11.10	13.74	13.75	11.00	14.70
2006	8.73	9.11	8.78	7.92	8.15	8.08	7.40	7.07	7.85	7.70	7.27	6.70	7.90
2007	6.21	6.34	7.22	8.10	7.98	7.67	7.48	7.36	7.64	7.74	7.67	7.40	7.40
2008	8.03	13.11	15.80	14.60	15.85	17.61	15.65	16.39	15.23	12.83	9.85	8.66	13.63

Source: American Metal Market (AMM)

Vegetables

Vegetables are the edible products of herbaceous plants, which are plants with soft stems. Vegetables are grouped according to the edible part of each plant including leaves (e.g., lettuce), stalks (celery), roots (carrot), tubers (potato), bulbs (onion), fruits (tomato), seeds (pea), and flowers (broccoli). Each of these groups contributes to the human diet in its own way. Fleshy roots are high in energy value and good sources of the vitamin B group, seeds are relatively high in carbohydrates and proteins, while leaves, stalks, and fruits are excellent sources of minerals, vitamins, water, and roughage. Vegetables are an important food for the maintenance of health and prevention of disease. Higher intakes of vegetables have been shown to lower the risks of cancer and coronary heart disease.

Vegetables are best consumed fresh in their raw state in order to derive the maximum benefits from their nutrients. While canned and frozen vegetables are often thought to be inferior to fresh vegetables, they are sometimes nutritionally superior to fresh produce because they are usually processed immediately after harvest when nutrient content is at its peak. When cooking vegetables, aluminum utensils should not be used, because aluminum is a soft metal that is affected by food acids and alkalis. Scientific evidence shows that tiny particles of aluminum from foods cooked in aluminum utensils enter the stomach and can injure the sensitive lining of the stomach.

Prices – The monthly average index of fresh vegetable prices received by growers in the U.S. in 2008 fell by -1.7% to 175.7, down from last year's record level of 178.7.

Demand – The leading vegetable in terms of U.S. per capita consumption in 2007 (latest data available) was the potato with 126.0 pounds of consumption. Runner-up vegetables were tomatoes (90.5 pounds), lettuce (29.5 pounds), sweet corn (26.3 pounds), and onions (21.9 pounds). Total U.S. per capita vegetable consumption in 2007 rose +2.2% at 438.1 pounds. That is about 23% higher than the 356.2 pounds consumed in 1980.

Index of Prices Received by Growers for Commercial Vegetables[2] in the United States   (1990-92=100)

Year	Jan.	Feb.	Mar.	Apr.	May	June	July	Aug.	Sept.	Oct.	Nov.	Dec.	Average
2003	112	113	123	129	138	152	119	138	144	143	180	159	138
2004	127	140	111	127	108	107	100	127	129	155	158	119	126
2005	93	117	165	181	135	138	112	118	127	113	113	152	130
2006	128	115	133	151	156	131	119	152	160	123	119	150	136
2007	177	165	192	181	144	133	126	146	155	196	139	138	158
2008[1]	138	118	134	162	154	153	143	143	174	178	154	155	151

[1] Preliminary.   [2] Includes fresh and processing vegetables.   Not seasonally adjusted.   *Source: National Agricultural Statistics Service, U.S. Department of Agriculture (NASS-USDA)*

Index of Prices Received by Growers for Fresh Vegetables in the United States   (1990-92=100)

Year	Jan.	Feb.	Mar.	Apr.	May	June	July	Aug.	Sept.	Oct.	Nov.	Dec.	Average
2003	147.8	127.5	153.0	167.7	165.0	138.8	133.3	136.6	164.7	156.9	148.4	184.7	152.0
2004	143.8	125.9	140.3	133.1	132.9	101.0	102.8	128.3	141.9	200.0	211.1	143.7	142.1
2005	122.0	152.8	168.5	174.7	144.2	160.0	126.8	132.3	153.3	144.0	163.1	200.8	153.5
2006	207.6	138.8	137.6	174.4	147.9	128.7	134.1	179.5	193.1	167.7	138.3	178.4	160.5
2007	175.3	190.3	222.4	222.5	142.1	145.4	146.0	137.8	162.7	218.3	177.4	204.5	178.7
2008[1]	200.2	158.3	194.1	179.3	170.7	191.7	168.3	146.1	158.7	185.1	200.3	155.9	175.7

[1] Preliminary.   Not seasonally adjusted.   *Source: National Agricultural Statistics Service, U.S. Department of Agriculture (NASS-USDA)*

Producer Price Index of Canned[2] Processed Vegetables in the United States   (1982 = 100)

Year	Jan.	Feb.	Mar.	Apr.	May	June	July	Aug.	Sept.	Oct.	Nov.	Dec.	Average
2003	128.8	129.0	128.9	129.3	129.4	129.3	129.4	129.1	130.0	130.7	131.1	131.3	129.7
2004	131.5	131.7	131.9	131.9	131.7	132.8	133.0	133.3	133.4	134.6	135.4	135.5	133.1
2005	135.7	135.9	136.1	136.3	137.6	137.6	137.7	137.7	137.5	137.7	137.6	138.0	137.1
2006	138.0	136.8	137.1	137.3	138.8	140.2	140.0	140.5	141.4	141.5	142.2	142.2	139.7
2007	142.8	142.9	143.1	143.3	143.5	143.6	143.1	143.1	144.0	143.9	144.2	144.6	143.5
2008[1]	147.8	148.4	149.6	151.2	150.2	151.3	153.3	158.6	162.5	165.0	165.4	167.8	155.9

[1] Preliminary.   [2] Includes canned vegetables and juices, including hominy and mushrooms.   Not seasonally adjusted.   *Source: Bureau of Labor Statistics, U.S. Department of Labor (BLS)*

Producer Price Index of Frozen Processed Vegetables in the United States   (1982 = 100)

Year	Jan.	Feb.	Mar.	Apr.	May	June	July	Aug.	Sept.	Oct.	Nov.	Dec.	Average
2003	133.4	134.1	133.3	134.0	134.1	133.9	134.9	134.2	134.2	135.2	135.1	135.0	134.3
2004	135.1	136.0	135.3	135.3	134.3	134.7	135.4	135.8	136.8	138.1	137.2	137.0	135.9
2005	137.3	137.3	137.4	137.5	137.5	137.4	137.2	136.8	136.6	136.7	136.1	136.4	137.0
2006	137.3	137.7	138.7	138.6	138.8	139.5	139.4	139.3	139.9	142.0	142.7	142.6	139.7
2007	144.0	144.0	144.0	145.2	145.9	146.7	148.2	149.3	149.9	151.5	152.5	153.2	147.9
2008[1]	153.3	153.8	155.6	156.5	156.7	157.1	158.8	161.1	163.9	168.8	171.5	176.6	161.1

[1] Preliminary.   Not seasonally adjusted.   *Source: Bureau of Labor Statistics, U.S. Department of Labor (BLS)*

Per Capita Use of Selected Commercially Produced Fresh and Processing Vegetables and Melons in the United States   In Pounds, farm weight basis

Crop	1999	2000	2001	2002	2003	2004	2005	2006	2007	2008[10]	2009[11]
Asparagus, All	1.2	1.3	1.2	1.2	1.3	1.4	1.4	1.4	1.4	1.4	1.5
Fresh	0.9	1.0	0.9	1.0	1.0	1.1	1.1	1.1	1.2	1.2	1.2
Canning	0.2	0.2	0.2	0.2	0.2	0.2	0.2	0.2	0.1	0.2	0.2
Freezing	0.1	0.1	0.1	0.1	0.1	0.1	0.1	0.1	0.1	0.1	0.1
Snap beans, All	7.6	7.9	7.8	7.2	7.5	7.6	7.6	7.8	7.8	7.3	7.2
Fresh	1.9	2.0	2.2	2.1	2.0	1.9	1.8	2.1	2.2	2.0	2.1
Canning	3.7	4.0	3.8	3.4	3.7	3.7	4.0	3.9	3.5	3.2	3.2
Freezing	2.0	1.8	1.9	1.8	1.9	2.0	1.8	1.9	2.1	2.0	2.0
Broccoli, All [1]	8.3	8.1	7.4	7.5	7.9	8.0	8.1	8.0	8.3	8.6	8.6
Fresh	6.2	5.9	5.4	5.4	5.4	5.3	5.4	5.8	5.6	5.8	5.6
Freezing	2.1	2.3	2.0	2.1	2.6	2.7	2.7	2.3	2.7	2.8	3.0
Cabbage, All	8.8	10.3	10.1	9.5	8.5	9.2	9.0	9.0	9.1	9.2	9.2
Fresh	7.6	8.9	8.8	8.3	7.4	8.1	7.8	7.8	8.0	8.0	8.0
Canning (kraut)	1.2	1.4	1.3	1.2	1.1	1.1	1.2	1.2	1.2	1.2	1.2
Carrots, All [2]	13.1	13.0	13.0	11.6	11.9	11.7	11.8	11.2	10.7	10.7	10.5
Fresh	9.3	9.2	9.4	8.4	8.8	8.7	8.7	8.1	8.1	8.0	7.8
Canning	1.4	1.1	1.4	1.0	1.1	1.0	1.1	1.0	1.1	1.0	0.9
Freezing	2.4	2.7	2.2	2.1	2.0	2.0	2.0	2.1	1.5	1.7	1.8
Cauliflower, All [1]	2.3	2.3	2.0	1.7	1.9	1.9	2.1	2.1	2.1	2.0	2.1
Fresh	1.8	1.7	1.5	1.4	1.6	1.6	1.8	1.7	1.7	1.7	1.7
Freezing	0.5	0.6	0.5	0.3	0.4	0.4	0.4	0.4	0.4	0.3	0.4
Celery	6.5	6.3	6.4	6.3	6.3	6.2	5.9	6.1	6.3	6.4	6.4
Sweet Corn, All [3]	28.3	27.1	27.2	26.2	26.5	26.3	26.7	26.0	26.1	25.0	24.6
Fresh	9.1	9.0	9.2	9.0	9.2	9.0	8.7	8.3	9.2	8.8	8.7
Canning	9.1	9.0	8.7	7.8	8.3	8.2	8.6	8.4	6.9	6.8	6.5
Freezing	10.1	9.0	9.3	9.3	9.0	9.1	9.5	9.3	10.0	9.5	9.4
Cucumbers, All	10.9	11.2	10.0	12.0	10.6	11.3	10.0	9.1	10.2	10.3	9.8
Fresh	6.7	6.4	6.3	6.6	6.2	6.4	6.2	6.1	6.4	6.3	6.3
Pickling	4.2	4.9	3.7	5.4	4.5	4.9	3.8	3.0	3.7	4.0	3.5
Melons	29.0	27.2	28.2	27.3	26.5	24.9	25.0	26.3	25.9	26.5	26.0
Watermelon	15.2	13.8	15.0	14.1	13.6	13.0	13.6	15.1	14.4	15.0	14.8
Cantaloupe	11.4	11.1	11.2	11.1	10.8	9.8	9.6	9.3	9.6	9.8	9.5
Honeydew	2.5	2.3	2.0	2.2	2.2	2.1	1.9	1.9	1.8	1.8	1.8
Lettuce, All	32.5	31.9	31.0	32.2	33.1	33.3	30.6	32.1	30.0	30.0	30.4
Head lettuce	24.9	23.5	23.0	22.6	22.2	21.3	20.9	20.1	18.4	18.3	18.4
Romaine & Leaf	7.6	8.4	8.0	9.6	10.8	12.0	9.7	12.0	11.6	11.7	11.9
Onions, All	20.8	20.4	19.5	20.4	21.4	23.4	22.0	21.7	22.7	22.0	22.6
Fresh	18.5	18.9	18.5	19.3	19.5	21.9	20.9	19.9	21.6	20.7	21.2
Dehydrating	2.3	1.6	1.0	1.1	1.8	1.5	1.1	1.8	1.0	1.3	1.4
Green Peas, All [4]	3.4	3.7	3.3	2.8	3.1	2.8	2.7	2.7	3.0	2.9	3.0
Canning	1.4	1.5	1.4	1.1	1.3	1.2	1.0	1.1	1.1	1.1	1.1
Freezing	2.0	2.1	2.0	1.7	1.8	1.6	1.6	1.6	1.8	1.9	1.9
Peppers, All	11.4	13.3	13.3	14.1	14.0	14.8	15.3	15.8	15.5	15.7	15.8
Bell Peppers, All	6.7	8.2	8.1	8.3	8.4	8.6	9.2	9.5	9.4	9.4	9.4
Chile Peppers, All	4.7	5.2	5.2	5.8	5.6	6.1	6.1	6.4	6.1	6.3	6.5
Tomatoes, All	90.3	89.1	84.8	89.7	89.3	90.6	93.9	84.4	87.9	92.8	92.8
Fresh	19.1	19.0	19.2	20.3	19.4	20.0	20.2	19.8	19.2	20.0	19.4
Canning	71.2	70.1	65.5	69.4	69.9	70.6	73.8	64.6	68.7	72.7	73.4
Other, Fresh [5]	10.5	18.3	17.2	17.8	18.1	19.1	19.9	19.9	19.3	19.7	19.8
Other, Canning [6]	2.5	2.6	2.8	2.4	2.5	2.9	3.1	2.7	2.7	2.8	2.7
Other, Freezing [7]	3.2	3.2	3.2	4.3	3.9	3.8	3.9	3.9	3.9	4.0	4.0
Subtotal, All [8]	290.5	297.1	288.4	294.1	294.3	299.1	298.9	290.2	292.6	297.1	296.8
Fresh	166.1	173.8	172.2	173.7	172.7	176.1	173.0	174.5	174.0	174.5	174.0
Canning	99.6	100.0	93.9	97.7	98.2	100.0	102.9	92.4	95.2	99.1	99.0
Freezing	22.5	21.8	21.2	21.7	21.6	21.6	21.9	21.5	22.5	22.3	22.5
Potatoes, All	136.2	137.9	138.8	132.1	138.4	134.9	125.8	123.5	125.4	120.4	121.0
Fresh	47.7	47.1	46.6	44.3	46.9	45.9	41.4	38.6	39.1	36.9	37.4
Processing	88.5	90.8	92.2	87.8	91.5	89.0	84.4	84.9	86.3	83.5	83.6
Sweet Potatoes	3.7	4.2	4.4	3.8	4.7	4.6	4.5	4.6	5.1	5.1	5.2
Mushrooms	4.1	4.1	3.9	4.1	4.2	4.2	3.9	4.0	3.9	3.9	3.9
Dry Peas & Lentils [9]	0.6	0.8	0.8	0.8	0.6	0.7	0.8	1.2	0.8	0.6	0.8
Dry Edible Beans	7.8	7.6	6.9	6.8	6.7	6.0	6.1	6.4	6.8	6.3	6.5
Total, All Items	442.9	451.7	443.1	441.7	448.8	449.5	440.0	429.9	434.6	433.4	434.2

[1] All production for processing broccoli and cauliflower is for freezing.   [2] Industry allocation suggests that 27 percent of processing carrot production is for canning and 73 percent is for freezing.   [3] On-cob basis.   [4] In-shell basis.   [5] Includes artichokes, brussels sprouts, eggplant, endive/escarole, garlic, radishes, green limas, squash, and spinach. In 2000, okra, pumpkins, kale, collards, turnip greens and mustard greens added.   [6] Includes beets, green limas (1992-2003), spinach, and miscellaneous imports (1990-2001).   [7] Includes green limas, spinach, and miscellaneous freezing vegetables.   [8] Fresh, canning, and freezing data do not sum to the total because onions for dehydrating are included in the total.   [9] Production from new areas in upper midwest added in 1998. A portion of this is likely for feed use.   [10] Preliminary.   [11] Forecast.   NA = Not available.   *Source: Economic Research Service, U.S. Department of Agriculture (ERS-USDA)*

VEGETABLES

Average Price Received by Growers for Broccoli in the United States   In Dollars Per Cwt

Year	Jan.	Feb.	Mar.	Apr.	May	June	July	Aug.	Sept.	Oct.	Nov.	Dec.	Season Average
2001	22.70	32.30	24.70	26.90	25.50	27.00	23.60	27.10	22.90	24.20	22.20	20.00	26.50
2002	55.30	44.40	33.80	24.00	20.80	28.40	27.00	29.60	40.60	24.00	37.10	35.00	31.40
2003	25.20	40.90	28.10	27.10	29.70	24.60	27.00	29.80	49.10	38.90	48.00	40.00	32.70
2004	33.60	28.50	21.60	24.00	27.20	28.70	24.20	29.70	57.00	43.90	44.20	45.40	33.20
2005	22.60	33.30	42.60	39.80	22.40	39.70	22.40	30.50	27.70	22.40	20.90	34.10	28.50
2006	32.50	23.80	27.60	32.40	29.00	51.10	26.20	56.90	39.40	24.60	27.50	53.10	33.70
2007	69.80	25.40	27.60	36.90	26.70	24.80	28.80	38.20	41.80	61.00	38.10	40.70	36.70
2008[1]	47.90	22.90	30.60	52.20	26.70	29.60	26.70	26.60	41.10	57.50	41.20	33.70	36.10

[1]Preliminary.   Source: National Agricultural Statistics Service, U.S. Department of Agriculture (NASS-USDA)

Average Price Received by Growers for Carrots in the United States   In Dollars Per Cwt

Year	Jan.	Feb.	Mar.	Apr.	May	June	July	Aug.	Sept.	Oct.	Nov.	Dec.	Season Average
2001	15.90	16.70	17.30	17.30	17.60	20.10	22.00	19.90	15.70	17.50	18.50	19.50	17.10
2002	19.30	19.70	21.10	21.20	21.30	21.60	20.60	20.10	18.10	17.90	18.70	19.50	19.10
2003	19.30	19.10	18.70	19.40	19.90	20.00	19.90	20.50	19.80	19.10	21.60	24.30	19.00
2004	24.50	24.90	24.60	24.20	24.90	22.50	20.20	18.00	16.70	16.40	17.20	18.00	20.20
2005	20.30	21.00	21.00	21.10	21.20	21.30	21.80	21.40	20.00	21.40	23.10	22.00	20.90
2006	21.40	21.50	21.50	21.50	20.80	21.40	21.50	22.40	19.30	19.80	20.20	19.10	20.60
2007	21.00	28.10	28.30	29.60	32.00	25.90	19.70	17.10	16.10	15.80	15.80	16.20	22.60
2008[1]	16.20	25.90	25.90	25.50	32.00	25.60	25.60	25.50	24.20	23.50	24.60	25.20	24.40

[1]Preliminary.   Source: National Agricultural Statistics Service, U.S. Department of Agriculture (NASS-USDA)

Average Price Received by Growers for Cauliflower in the United States   In Dollars Per Cwt

Year	Jan.	Feb.	Mar.	Apr.	May	June	July	Aug.	Sept.	Oct.	Nov.	Dec.	Season Average
2001	25.70	37.00	23.50	46.50	26.30	37.40	25.60	25.50	24.80	21.70	20.10	20.00	29.20
2002	65.50	30.80	44.10	25.10	26.40	32.70	27.80	24.00	24.70	22.50	37.60	50.00	32.20
2003	24.60	30.70	30.80	20.70	39.50	46.30	27.60	25.30	40.30	25.80	57.00	75.50	35.10
2004	27.30	42.20	24.20	23.50	28.80	46.20	27.60	26.30	31.10	32.20	43.80	54.40	30.80
2005	27.70	38.20	50.60	36.70	29.70	38.10	25.60	31.50	28.50	19.70	25.50	43.90	30.30
2006	33.10	26.40	31.40	32.80	29.00	51.10	26.20	56.90	39.40	24.60	34.80	41.60	32.30
2007	45.70	29.40	51.40	51.60	24.90	30.00	22.30	27.90	27.20	46.20	26.60	52.40	34.30
2008[1]	51.80	30.20	41.70	63.60	24.90	53.90	38.20	43.20	29.50	48.50	36.30	43.90	40.30

[1]Preliminary.   Source: National Agricultural Statistics Service, U.S. Department of Agriculture (NASS-USDA)

Average Price Received by Growers for Celery in the United States   In Dollars Per Cwt

Year	Jan.	Feb.	Mar.	Apr.	May	June	July	Aug.	Sept.	Oct.	Nov.	Dec.	Season Average
2001	14.60	15.00	15.80	19.10	24.00	33.70	13.50	9.33	9.43	8.22	9.01	13.00	14.40
2002	10.10	19.50	23.50	18.60	12.30	9.37	10.80	10.90	11.70	9.98	15.30	9.50	12.80
2003	8.29	11.80	12.60	17.00	11.00	9.34	12.80	11.90	13.30	15.90	23.40	14.50	13.40
2004	20.80	24.40	13.90	15.60	15.00	13.80	12.00	10.00	11.90	15.10	18.10	13.40	14.80
2005	12.90	22.90	28.40	20.80	15.50	9.62	10.00	10.80	12.80	12.20	13.10	10.70	13.90
2006	9.64	10.80	14.90	16.60	12.70	17.80	21.00	23.30	27.70	27.10	22.00	20.20	18.20
2007	33.90	58.90	31.90	18.80	18.30	11.60	11.60	9.64	13.80	13.30	18.60	13.50	20.40
2008[1]	16.20	13.20	13.40	14.00	18.30	30.10	22.40	12.90	12.50	17.20	16.90	20.30	16.90

[1]Preliminary.   Source: National Agricultural Statistics Service, U.S. Department of Agriculture (NASS-USDA)

Average Price Received by Growers for Sweet Corn in the United States   In Dollars Per Cwt

Year	Jan.	Feb.	Mar.	Apr.	May	June	July	Aug.	Sept.	Oct.	Nov.	Dec.	Season Average
2001	32.70	34.00	26.10	18.10	24.60	18.60	19.80	19.20	19.00	23.80	24.80	22.60	19.50
2002	24.80	23.50	26.30	19.40	20.80	18.80	27.90	21.80	22.50	25.80	15.50	18.30	19.20
2003	29.00	24.00	18.90	14.90	16.60	23.20	21.30	20.10	19.70	23.70	30.70	22.60	19.30
2004	30.80	20.70	20.20	17.60	18.10	22.80	21.80	22.90	24.10	33.50	46.70	36.80	20.80
2005	21.30	28.60	26.10	21.50	18.10	22.60	22.20	20.30	24.70	25.50	37.30	21.20	22.10
2006	36.50	35.00	34.00	27.20	15.40	21.60	21.10	22.70	25.90	21.20	20.00	14.40	23.00
2007	27.40	23.60	30.20	25.60	21.40	17.30	22.20	22.80	23.20	21.40	20.60	34.10	22.70
2008[1]	30.80	23.00	28.60	21.00	22.60	19.20	28.10	25.60	24.20	32.70	33.60	22.20	25.90

[1]Preliminary.   Source: National Agricultural Statistics Service, U.S. Department of Agriculture (NASS-USDA)

Average Price Received by Growers for Head Lettuce in the United States   In Dollars Per Cwt

Year	Jan.	Feb.	Mar.	Apr.	May	June	July	Aug.	Sept.	Oct.	Nov.	Dec.	Season Average
1999	10.30	15.50	16.30	20.20	14.00	11.40	12.70	12.00	13.10	13.10	10.70	16.20	13.30
2000	14.60	9.28	14.10	22.80	23.60	13.50	15.00	19.20	29.40	16.20	19.90	12.00	17.30
2001	13.60	22.80	15.10	21.60	18.80	12.10	16.40	26.90	26.20	11.50	10.90	10.00	17.90
2002	26.20	44.10	86.40	14.10	10.20	10.60	11.30	14.60	14.30	13.50	11.90	30.00	21.10
2003	12.10	11.80	9.64	12.50	21.20	32.20	11.90	21.50	23.90	26.30	31.70	21.30	18.10
2004	15.40	19.80	10.40	14.80	10.50	13.30	10.70	17.10	15.20	24.10	14.90	15.70	16.90
2005	11.50	11.70	27.90	30.10	13.90	17.30	11.00	13.50	12.70	12.40	9.81	16.60	15.50
2006	10.50	12.00	19.10	22.40	33.70	11.80	12.20	20.70	16.30	11.80	12.50	22.40	16.90
2007	20.80	15.50	29.70	17.80	13.60	17.80	17.30	23.10	29.20	44.40	17.40	16.00	21.70
2008[1]	17.60	13.30	14.80	21.70	13.60	17.70	17.30	17.20	31.90	32.90	19.50	23.50	20.00

[1] Preliminary.   Source: National Agricultural Statistics Service, U.S. Department of Agriculture (NASS-USDA)

Average Price Received by Growers for Tomatoes in the United States   In Dollars Per Cwt

Year	Jan.	Feb.	Mar.	Apr.	May	June	July	Aug.	Sept.	Oct.	Nov.	Dec.	Season Average
1999	33.50	23.40	22.30	23.70	21.00	29.00	23.10	25.00	26.50	21.30	26.00	28.90	25.80
2000	21.40	21.10	33.00	34.80	23.10	21.80	24.60	33.90	29.50	42.60	47.80	37.60	30.70
2001	43.80	29.10	56.40	19.00	37.80	28.50	27.40	27.60	23.50	28.60	28.50	25.00	30.00
2002	40.50	26.60	38.50	34.30	29.60	33.00	28.50	25.80	23.70	27.60	40.10	38.00	31.60
2003	47.20	31.70	53.30	30.00	23.70	45.70	37.60	41.00	35.70	30.10	30.50	29.10	37.40
2004	34.50	36.30	42.20	44.20	32.20	21.70	23.40	37.80	38.20	67.90	89.00	47.10	37.60
2005	15.40	40.90	40.70	65.10	49.40	40.00	28.00	26.10	46.10	37.30	36.50	96.80	41.80
2006	79.20	46.50	24.80	34.40	23.30	30.90	25.10	27.80	79.80	53.20	28.10	24.80	43.70
2007	35.60	31.20	26.30	52.60	35.60	29.60	26.70	28.60	33.10	41.60	58.70	81.20	34.80
2008[1]	58.20	45.50	66.10	47.40	48.20	58.00	38.60	30.00	26.00	33.80	64.30	37.90	45.40

[1] Preliminary.   Source: National Agricultural Statistics Service, U.S. Department of Agriculture (NASS-USDA)

Frozen Vegetables: January 1 and July 1 Cold Storage Holdings in the United States   In Thousands of Pounds

Crop	2004 July 1	2005 Jan. 1	July 1	2006 Jan. 1	July 1	2007 Jan. 1	July 1	2008 Jan. 1	July 1	2009[1] Jan. 1
Asparagus	14,064	9,280	13,943	9,029	11,929	6,178	9,952	5,409	9,964	7,336
Limas, Fordhook	1,960	8,450	3,502	7,687	2,368	6,543	2,619	7,442	2,209	3,693
Limas, Baby	21,716	48,955	27,360	40,867	21,851	41,849	18,367	40,364	16,213	42,831
Green Beans, Reg. Cut	51,147	151,229	76,655	171,319	24,377	183,610	72,177	183,696	70,854	206,727
Green Beans, Fr. Style	6,596	22,925	8,157	22,341	8,388	27,433	9,303	32,284	12,675	29,548
Broccoli, Spears	50,314	35,882	45,581	35,814	32,699	27,628	23,878	24,078	33,587	36,204
Broccoli, Chopped & Cut	58,843	57,607	62,382	62,561	61,769	46,855	40,715	36,422	49,873	44,562
Brussels sprouts	11,588	23,519	16,028	21,660	10,243	21,650	11,535	21,491	10,392	20,807
Carrots, Diced	49,485	117,745	63,871	128,877	64,540	117,159	53,574	128,121	68,556	152,558
Carrots, Other	75,288	140,440	93,702	150,317	97,528	127,449	51,911	142,063	85,955	155,012
Cauliflower	12,518	37,123	19,916	43,836	18,694	38,196	17,768	36,694	20,334	27,760
Corn, Cut	227,404	502,025	234,965	464,177	188,556	475,671	161,547	461,503	172,494	457,814
Corn, Cob	109,612	242,271	78,525	263,818	71,738	281,694	69,152	256,464	78,251	261,568
Mixed vegetables	56,156	46,892	49,493	55,236	50,856	51,925	43,342	43,868	46,341	47,169
Okra	33,111	33,875	28,097	31,734	26,363	31,507	16,638	23,720	21,505	24,083
Onion Rings	8,426	6,587	6,181	4,757	7,532	7,533	8,136	7,428	5,925	6,634
Onions, Other	28,862	33,278	39,424	43,349	38,192	37,386	26,527	32,010	39,190	29,262
Blackeye Peas	3,004	2,693	1,878	2,348	4,080	4,784	3,136	4,394	2,815	2,687
Green Peas	206,413	230,326	227,162	214,851	222,513	230,351	241,116	232,647	198,133	254,016
Peas and Carrots Mixed	5,674	5,641	5,416	5,227	5,422	4,946	4,654	5,090	4,756	5,304
Spinach	83,287	34,724	87,983	42,464	107,607	52,674	70,443	47,467	80,320	42,561
Squash, Summer/Zucchini	31,326	45,724	39,164	61,518	50,704	64,255	49,275	62,534	46,531	56,888
Southern greens	16,330	17,328	18,905	13,750	17,546	14,826	10,741	12,833	14,231	12,779
Other Vegetables	248,416	363,579	267,205	353,315	238,391	323,249	220,569	373,370	275,882	424,085
Total	1,411,540	2,218,098	1,515,495	2,250,852	1,413,886	2,225,351	1,237,075	2,221,392	1,366,986	2,351,888
Potatoes, French Fries	864,111	838,438	947,971	848,595	877,400	758,254	871,947	820,461	947,666	873,069
Potatoes, Other Frozen	263,341	236,381	242,493	202,504	230,710	196,566	206,261	191,894	242,365	224,694
Potatoes, Total	1,127,452	1,074,819	1,190,464	1,051,099	1,108,110	954,820	1,078,208	1,012,355	1,190,031	1,097,763
Grand Total	2,538,992	3,292,917	2,705,959	3,301,951	2,521,996	3,180,171	2,315,283	3,233,747	2,557,017	3,449,651

Wheat

Wheat is a cereal grass, but before cultivation it was a wild grass. It has been grown in temperate regions and cultivated for food since prehistoric times. Wheat is believed to have originated in southwestern Asia. Archeological research indicates that wheat was grown as a crop in the Nile Valley about 5,000 BC. Wheat is not native to the U.S. and was first grown here in 1602 near the Massachusetts coast. The common types of wheat grown in the U.S. are spring and winter wheat. Wheat planted in the spring for summer or autumn harvest is mostly red wheat. Wheat planted in the fall or winter for spring harvest is mostly white wheat. Winter wheat accounts for nearly three-fourths of total U.S. production. Wheat is used mainly as a human food and supplies about 20% of the food calories for the world's population. The primary use for wheat is flour, but it is also used for brewing and distilling, and for making oil, gluten, straw for livestock bedding, livestock feed, hay or silage, newsprint, and other products.

Wheat futures and options are traded on the Mercado a Termino de Buenos Aires (MAT), Sydney Futures Exchange (SFE), London International Financial Futures and Options Exchange (LIFFE), Marche a Terme International de France (MATIF), Budapest Commodity Exchange (BCE), the Chicago Board of Trade (CBOT), the Kansas City Board of Trade (KCBT), the Minneapolis Grain Exchange (MGE), the Mid America Commodity Exchange (MidAm) and the Winnipeg Commodity Exchange (WCE). The Chicago Board of Trade's wheat futures contract calls for the delivery of soft red wheat (No. 1 and 2), hard red winter wheat (No. 1 and 2), dark northern spring wheat (No. 1 and 2), No.1 northern spring at 3 cents/bushel premium, or No. 2 northern spring at par.

Prices – CBOT wheat prices on the nearest-futures chart in early 2008 extended the rally that began in 2007 and posted a record high of $13.00 per bushel in February 2008. Wheat prices then fell sharply through the rest of 2008. Wheat prices posted a 1-1/2 year low of $4.55 in December, bringing the overall sell-off from the record high to 65%. Wheat prices closed 2008 at $6.1075 per bushel, down -$2.7425 per bushel (–31%) from the 2007 close of $8.85. Wheat prices were pulled higher in 2007 and early 2008 by the rally in corn and soybeans and the competition for planted acreage. Wheat prices also rallied in 2007 and early 2008 based on strong demand and limited supplies with drought in Australia, Canada, and Russia. However, global wheat production rose sharply in 2008/09 by 11.7% to 652.4 million metric tons, thus pushing the global carry-over up 23% to 149.96 million metric tons. The higher wheat production in 2008, combined with the global financial crisis, caused wheat prices to plunge in the latter half of 2008. Global stocks as a percentage of consumption rose to 23.0% in 2008/09, which was a 3-year high and illustrated the more comfortable supplies of world wheat.

Supply – World wheat production in the 2008-09 marketing year rose +11.8% to 682.780 million metric tons, which is a new record high. The world's largest wheat producers were the European Union with 22% of world production in 2008-09, China (17%), India (12%), the U.S. (10%), Russia (9%), and Canada (4%). China's wheat production in 2008-09 rose +3.4% yr/yr to 113.000 million metric tons, but is still well below its record high of 123.289 million metric tons seen in 1997-98. Australia's wheat production rose +45.6% yr/yr to 20.150 million metric tons in 2008-09, but still well below its record high of 26.132 million metric tons in 2003-04. The world land area harvested with wheat in 2008-09 rose +2.6% yr/yr to 224.2 million hectares (1 hectare equals 10,000 square meters or 2.471 acres), remaining above the 210.2 million hectares in 2003-04, which was the smallest wheat harvest area since 1970-71. World wheat yield in 2008-09 rose +8.6% to a new record high of 3.04 metric tons per hectare.

U.S. wheat production in 2008-09 rose +20.9% yr/yr to 2.500 billion bushels, which was still below the record U.S. wheat crop of 2.785 billion bushels seen in 1981-82. The U.S. winter wheat crop in 2008 (latest data available) rose 23.2% yr/yr to 1.868 billion bushels, which was well below the record winter wheat crop of 2.097 billion bushels seen in 1981. U.S. production of durum wheat in 2008 rose +18.4% yr/yr to 84.877 million bushels. U.S. production of other spring wheat in 2008 rose +15.1% yr/yr to 546.744 million bushels. The largest U.S. producing states of winter wheat in 2008 were Kansas with 19% of U.S. production, Oklahoma with 9%, Texas with 5%, Washington with 5%, and Montana with 5%. U.S. farmers planted 63.147 million acres of wheat in 2008, which was up +4.5% yr/yr. U.S. wheat yield in 2008-09 was 44.9 bushels per acre, which was a new record high exceeding the former record yield of 44.2 bushels per acre seen in 2003-04. Ending stocks for U.S. wheat for 2008-09 were at 601.3 million bushels, up +96.6% yr/yr from the 305.8 million bushels in 2007-08.

Demand – World wheat utilization in 2008-09 rose +6.0% yr/yr to a record high of 651.9 million metric tons. U.S. consumption of wheat in 2008-09 rose +20.0% yr/yr to 1.260 billion bushels, which was still below the record high of 1.381 billion bushels seen in 1998-99. The consumption breakdown shows that 75% of U.S. wheat consumption in 2008-09 went for food, 18% for feed and residuals, and 6% for seed.

Trade – World trade in wheat in 2008-09 rose +8.4% yr/yr to a record high of 125.7 million metric tons. U.S. exports of wheat in 2008-09 fell -20.9% yr/yr to 1.000 billion bushes, and remained well below the record of 1.771 billion bushels of exports seen in 1981-82. U.S. imports of wheat in 2008-09 fell -2.3% to 110.0 million bushels, down from the 2006-07 record high of 121.9 million bushels.

World Production of Wheat   In Thousands of Metric Tons

Crop Year	Argen-tina	Australia	Canada	China	European Union	India	Iran	Kazak-hstan	Pakistan	Russia	Turkey	United States	World Total
1999-00	16,400	24,757	26,941	113,880	122,441	70,780	8,500	11,200	17,858	31,000	16,500	62,475	585,817
2000-01	16,230	22,108	26,519	99,640	131,697	76,369	8,088	9,100	21,079	34,450	18,000	60,641	582,899
2001-02	15,500	24,299	20,568	93,873	123,353	69,680	9,459	12,700	19,024	46,900	15,500	53,001	583,078
2002-03	12,300	10,132	16,198	90,290	132,579	71,810	12,450	12,600	18,227	50,550	16,800	43,705	568,708
2003-04	14,500	26,132	23,049	86,490	110,578	65,100	13,440	11,000	19,183	34,100	16,800	63,805	553,899
2004-05	16,000	21,905	24,796	91,952	146,886	72,150	14,568	9,950	19,500	45,400	18,500	58,698	625,700
2005-06	14,500	25,173	25,748	97,445	132,356	68,640	14,308	11,000	21,612	47,700	18,500	57,243	620,044
2006-07[1]	15,200	10,822	25,265	108,466	124,870	69,350	14,500	13,500	21,277	44,900	17,500	49,217	596,101
2007-08[2]	16,300	13,838	20,054	109,298	119,442	75,810	15,000	16,600	23,300	49,400	15,500	55,821	610,991
2008-09[3]	8,400	20,150	28,610	113,000	150,272	78,400	10,000	12,500	21,500	63,700	16,800	68,026	682,780

[1] Preliminary.   [2] Estimate.   [3] Forecast.   *Source: Foreign Agricultural Service, U.S. Department of Agriculture (FAS-USDA)*

World Supply and Demand of Wheat   In Millions of Metric Tons/Hectares

Year	Area Harvested	Yield	Production	World Trade	Utilization Total	Ending Stocks	Stocks as a % of Utilization
1999-00	215.7	2.72	586.7	112.0	580.8	209.5	36.1
2000-01	217.9	2.68	582.9	102.3	583.6	207.3	35.5
2001-02	215.2	2.71	583.1	108.0	587.6	203.2	34.6
2002-03	215.2	2.64	568.7	107.1	603.2	166.8	27.7
2003-04	210.2	2.64	553.9	103.6	580.8	131.9	22.7
2004-05	217.6	2.88	625.7	113.2	605.4	150.8	24.9
2005-06	218.8	2.83	620.0	113.9	617.2	147.5	23.9
2006-07[1]	213.0	2.80	596.1	115.7	619.0	127.0	20.5
2007-08[2]	218.6	2.80	611.0	116.0	615.0	119.6	19.4
2008-09[3]	224.2	3.04	682.8	125.7	651.9	150.0	23.0

[1] Preliminary.   [2] Estimate.   [3] Forecast.   *Source: Foreign Agricultural Service, U.S. Department of Agriculture (FAS-USDA)*

Salient Statistics of Wheat in the United States

Year	Planting Intentions	Winter	Spring	All	Average All Yield Per Acre in Bushels	Value of Production $1,000	Domestic Exports[2]	Imports[3]	Flour	Cereal
		---- Acreage Harvested ----					---- Foreign Trade[5] ----		---- Per Capita[4] ----	
		1,000 Acres					In Millions of Bushels		Consumption In Pounds	
1999-00	62,664	35,436	18,337	53,773	42.7	5,593,989	1,086.5	94.5	144.0	3.8
2000-01	62,549	35,002	18,061	53,063	42.0	5,782,107	1,062.0	89.8	146.0	3.8
2001-02	59,597	31,295	17,338	48,633	40.2	5,440,217	962.3	107.6	141.0	3.8
2002-03	60,318	29,742	16,166	45,824	35.0	5,637,416	850.2	77.4	137.0	3.7
2003-04	62,141	36,753	16,310	53,063	44.2	7,929,039	1,158.3	63.0	137.0	3.7
2004-05	59,674	34,462	15,537	49,999	43.2	7,283,324	1,065.9	70.6	134.0	3.6
2005-06	57,229	33,794	16,325	50,119	42.0	7,171,441	1,002.8	81.4	134.0	3.6
2006-07	57,344	31,117	16,769	46,810	38.7	7,694,734	908.5	121.9	134.0	----
2007-08	60,433	35,952	15,059	51,011	40.5	13,289,326	1,264.1	112.6	----	----
2008-09[1]	63,147	39,614	16,071	55,685	44.9	16,568,211	1,000.0	110.0	----	----

[1] Preliminary.   [2] Includes flour milled from imported wheat.   [3] Total wheat, flour & other products.   [4] Civilian only.   [5] Year beginning June.
Source: Economic Research Service, U.S. Department of Agriculture (ERS-USDA)

Supply and Distribution of Wheat in the United States   In Millions of Bushels

Crop Year Beginning June 1	On Farms	Mills, Elevators[3]	Total Stocks	Production	Imports[4]	Total Supply	Food	Seed	Feed & Residual[5]	Total	Exports[4]	Total Disappearance
	Stocks, June 1		Supply						Domestic Disappearance			
1999-00	277.7	668.2	945.9	2,299.0	94.5	3,336.0	921.0	91.7	279.3	1,299.7	1,086.5	2,386.2
2000-01	226.8	723.0	949.7	2,232.5	89.8	3,267.7	949.6	79.5	300.4	1,329.5	1,062.0	2,391.6
2001-02	197.3	678.9	876.2	1,957.0	107.6	2,931.2	926.4	83.4	182.0	1,191.8	962.3	2,154.1
2002-03	216.8	560.3	777.1	1,605.9	77.4	2,460.4	918.6	84.4	115.7	1,118.7	850.2	1,968.9
2003-04	132.1	359.3	491.4	2,344.8	63.0	2,898.9	911.9	79.7	202.5	1,194.1	1,158.3	2,352.4
2004-05	131.9	414.6	546.4	2,158.2	70.6	2,773.8	909.6	77.6	180.6	1,167.8	1,065.9	2,233.7
2005-06	161.3	378.8	540.1	2,104.7	81.4	2,724.8	917.1	77.1	156.6	1,150.8	1,002.8	2,153.6
2006-07	111.0	460.2	571.2	1,812.0	121.9	2,501.5	937.9	81.9	117.1	1,136.8	908.5	2,045.3
2007-08[1]	73.2	383.0	456.2	2,066.7	112.6	2,619.9	947.3	87.6	15.0	1,049.9	1,264.1	2,314.0
2008-09[2]	25.6	280.2	305.8	2,499.5	110.0	2,915.3	950.0	80.0	230.0	1,260.0	1,000.0	2,260.0

[1] Preliminary.   [2] Estimate.   [3] Also warehouses and all off-farm storage not otherwise designated, including flour mills.   [4] Imports & exports are for wheat, including flour & other products in terms of wheat.   [5] Mostly feed use.
Source: Economic Research Service, U.S. Department of Agriculture (ERS-USDA)

WHEAT

Year	Hard Spring Stocks June 1	Hard Spring Pro-duction	Hard Spring Exports[3]	Durum[2] Stocks June 1	Durum[2] Pro-duction	Durum[2] Exports[3]	Hard Winter Stocks June 1	Hard Winter Pro-duction	Hard Winter Exports[3]	Soft Red Winter Stocks June 1	Soft Red Winter Pro-duction	Soft Red Winter Exports[3]	White Stocks June 1	White Pro-duction	White Exports[3]
1999-00	233	448	230	55	99	44	435	1,051	486	136	454	170	87	247	160
2000-01	218	502	230	50	110	50	458	846	403	133	471	176	91	303	203
2001-02	210	476	216	45	84	50	411	767	349	135	400	199	75	232	147
2002-03	230	351	259	33	80	32	363	620	309	78	321	105	73	233	148
2003-04	145	500	272	28	97	44	188	1,071	512	55	380	140	75	297	192
2004-05	157	525	314	26	90	31	227	856	388	64	380	122	72	306	207
2005-06	159	467	282	38	101	47	193	930	430	88	309	76	63	298	175
2006-07	132	432	250	40	53	35	215	682	281	106	390	146	78	254	197
2007-08	117	449	305	21	72	42	165	956	538	109	352	209	44	221	170
2008-09[1]	68	512	210	8	85	20	138	1,035	460	55	614	190	37	254	120

[1] Preliminary.   [2] Includes "Red Durum."   [3] Includes four made from U.S. wheat & shipments to territories.
Source: Economic Research Service, U.S. Department of Agriculture (ERS-USDA)

Seeded Acreage, Yield and Production of all Wheat in the United States

Year	Seed Acreage - 1,000 Acres Winter	Other Spring	Durum	All	Yield Per Harvested Acre (Bushels) Winter	Other Spring	Durum	All	Production (Million Bushels) Winter	Other Spring	Durum	All
1999	43,281	15,348	4,035	62,664	47.8	34.1	27.8	42.7	1,693.1	503.1	99.3	2,295.6
2000	43,313	15,299	3,937	62,549	44.6	38.4	30.7	42.0	1,561.7	556.6	109.8	2,228.2
2001	41,078	15,609	2,910	59,597	43.5	35.2	30.0	40.2	1,361.5	512.0	83.6	1,957.0
2002	41,766	15,639	2,913	60,318	38.2	29.1	29.5	35.0	1,137.0	388.9	80.0	1,605.9
2003	45,384	13,842	2,915	62,141	46.7	39.5	33.7	44.2	1,716.7	531.4	96.6	2,344.8
2004	43,350	13,763	2,561	59,674	43.5	43.2	38.0	43.2	1,499.4	568.9	89.9	2,158.2
2005	40,433	14,036	2,760	57,229	44.4	37.1	37.2	42.0	1,499.1	504.5	101.1	2,104.7
2006	40,575	14,899	1,870	57,344	41.7	33.2	29.5	38.7	1,298.1	460.5	53.5	1,812.0
2007	45,012	13,297	2,149	60,433	42.2	37.0	33.9	40.5	1,516.0	479.0	71.7	2,066.7
2008[1]	46,281	14,135	2,731	63,147	47.2	40.5	32.8	44.9	1,867.9	546.7	84.9	2,499.5

[1] Preliminary.   Source: Economic Research Service, U.S. Department of Agriculture (ERS-USDA)

Production of Winter Wheat in the United States, by State   In Thousands of Bushels

Year	Colorado	Idaho	Illinois	Kansas	Missouri	Montana	Neb-raska	Ohio	Okla-homa	Oregon	Texas	Wash-ington	Total
1999	103,200	53,960	60,600	432,400	44,160	36,860	81,600	72,100	150,500	29,610	122,400	96,860	1,693,130
2000	68,150	63,900	52,440	347,800	49,400	44,550	59,400	79,920	142,800	45,260	66,000	131,400	1,561,723
2001	66,000	51,830	43,920	328,000	41,040	19,140	59,200	60,300	122,100	28,000	108,800	106,750	1,361,479
2002	36,300	48,510	30,870	270,600	33,440	21,840	50,160	50,220	103,600	29,820	78,300	104,400	1,137,001
2003	77,000	57,600	52,650	480,000	53,070	67,340	83,720	68,000	179,400	47,940	96,600	117,000	1,716,721
2004	45,900	63,000	53,100	314,500	48,360	66,830	61,050	55,180	164,500	47,580	108,500	117,250	1,499,434
2005	52,800	66,430	36,600	380,000	29,160	94,500	68,640	58,930	128,000	47,580	96,000	120,600	1,499,129
2006	39,900	54,670	60,970	291,200	49,140	82,560	61,200	65,280	81,600	38,690	33,600	118,800	1,298,081
2007	94,000	51,830	50,730	283,800	37,840	83,220	84,280	45,990	98,000	40,425	140,600	108,160	1,515,989
2008[1]	57,000	60,000	73,600	356,000	55,680	94,380	73,480	74,120	166,500	44,950	99,000	96,320	1,867,903

[1] Preliminary.   Source: Crop Reporting Board, U.S. Department of Agriculture (CRB-USDA)

Official Winter Wheat Crop Production Reports in the United States   In Thousands of Bushels

Crop Year	May 1	June 1	July 1	August 1	September 1	Current December	Final
1999-00	1,614,799	1,611,559	1,673,222	1,688,582	----	----	1,693,130
2000-01	1,648,805	1,621,966	1,588,376	1,594,321	----	----	1,561,723
2001-02	1,341,381	1,321,126	1,366,192	1,385,048	----	----	1,361,479
2002-03	1,300,726	1,237,671	1,178,320	1,158,710	----	----	1,137,001
2003-04	1,563,314	1,626,376	1,715,912	1,712,150	----	----	1,716,721
2004-05	1,550,395	1,530,742	1,469,735	1,489,408	----	----	1,499,434
2005-06	1,590,862	1,545,971	1,525,302	1,520,848	----	----	1,499,129
2006-07	1,322,831	1,263,766	1,280,005	1,283,134	----	----	1,298,081
2007-08	1,615,613	1,609,679	1,561,907	1,537,262	----	----	1,515,989
2008-09[1]	1,777,532	1,817,364	1,864,245	1,874,857	----	----	1,867,903

[1] Preliminary.   Source: Crop Reporting Board, U.S. Department of Agriculture (CRB-USDA)

Production of All Spring Wheat in the United States, by State   In Thousands of Bushels

	Durum Wheat						Other Spring Wheat							
Year	Arizona	California	Montana	North Dakota	South Dakota	Total	Idaho	Minnesota	Montana	North Dakota	Oregon	South Dakota	Washington	Total
1999	7,275	8,925	9,450	72,000	1,512	99,322	50,560	78,000	108,000	168,000	5,049	59,850	27,280	503,108
2000	8,075	9,700	13,160	78,300	468	109,805	42,750	95,550	77,500	233,600	8,280	60,040	33,480	556,632
2001	7,917	8,505	11,880	54,600	576	83,556	33,320	79,200	65,550	234,600	4,650	64,350	25,830	512,008
2002	8,928	9,000	12,995	48,750	147	79,960	29,900	61,200	75,900	165,200	4,680	24,000	25,370	388,917
2003	11,500	11,500	14,490	58,410	621	96,637	27,060	104,400	60,500	252,800	5,600	56,280	22,345	531,402
2004	9,603	9,000	17,985	52,800	450	89,893	38,710	88,550	88,350	243,950	8,400	71,910	26,250	568,918
2005	7,900	6,555	16,380	68,250	260	101,105	32,400	70,930	81,600	224,400	5,980	67,600	18,700	504,456
2006	7,400	6,435	6,715	31,500	90	53,475	34,310	77,550	63,800	212,350	5,750	42,600	21,250	460,480
2007	7,900	7,125	11,400	43,800	216	71,686	30,600	77,550	55,200	234,000	6,360	52,260	20,562	479,047
2008[1]	14,602	16,275	10,830	42,250	190	84,877	37,440	100,800	59,520	246,400	7,650	68,400	21,210	546,744

[1] Preliminary.   Source: Crop Reporting Board, U.S. Department of Agriculture (CRB-USDA)

Grindings of Wheat by Mills in the United States   In Millions of Bushels -- of 60 Pounds Each

Year	Jan.	Feb.	Mar.	Apr.	May	June	July	Aug.	Sept.	Oct.	Nov.	Dec.	Total
1999-00	-----	234.0	-----	-----	242.2	-----	-----	225.6	-----	-----	226.8	-----	928.7
2000-01	-----	244.7	-----	-----	247.7	-----	-----	223.8	-----	-----	221.3	-----	937.5
2001-02	-----	230.2	-----	-----	238.7	-----	-----	217.0	-----	-----	217.6	-----	903.6
2002-03	-----	230.3	-----	-----	224.4	-----	-----	215.8	-----	-----	217.4	-----	888.0
2003-04	-----	231.8	-----	-----	224.2	-----	-----	214.7	-----	-----	214.5	-----	885.2
2004-05	-----	224.8	-----	-----	222.1	-----	-----	214.9	-----	-----	216.5	-----	878.3
2005-06	-----	229.3	-----	-----	223.4	-----	-----	216.1	-----	-----	217.1	-----	885.9
2006-07	-----	233.3	-----	-----	228.0	-----	-----	222.0	-----	-----	226.1	-----	909.5
2007-08	-----	239.3	-----	-----	236.3	-----	-----	223.5	-----	-----	223.0	-----	922.1
2008-09[1]	-----	234.9	-----	-----	-----	-----	-----	-----	-----	-----	-----	-----	939.6

[1] Preliminary.   Source: Bureau of the Census, U.S. Department of Commerce

Stocks of Wheat in the United States   In Millions of Bushels

	On Farms				Off Farms				Total Stocks			
Year	Mar. 1	June 1	Sept. 1	Dec. 1	Mar. 1	June 1	Sept. 1	Dec. 1	Mar. 1	June 1	Sept. 1	Dec. 1
1999	471.2	277.7	888.1	647.4	979.2	668.2	1,557.0	1,236.3	1,450.4	945.9	2,445.0	1,883.7
2000	424.7	226.8	808.4	623.4	991.8	723.0	1,544.3	1,182.7	1,416.5	949.7	2,352.7	1,806.1
2001	384.8	197.3	696.9	517.9	953.6	678.9	1,459.0	1,105.6	1,338.4	876.2	2,155.8	1,623.5
2002	338.5	216.8	580.2	384.8	871.3	560.3	1,170.8	935.1	1,209.8	777.1	1,751.0	1,319.9
2003	236.3	132.1	687.3	491.9	670.3	359.3	1,351.7	1,028.4	906.6	491.4	2,039.0	1,520.3
2004	257.9	131.9	790.6	531.0	762.7	414.6	1,147.8	899.3	1,020.6	546.4	1,938.4	1,430.3
2005	304.7	161.3	721.4	513.0	679.7	378.8	1,201.9	916.4	984.4	540.1	1,923.3	1,429.4
2006	256.0	111.0	572.0	403.3	716.2	460.2	1,178.5	911.4	972.2	571.2	1,750.5	1,314.7
2007	192.5	73.2	495.0	289.5	664.3	383.0	1,221.9	842.4	856.7	456.2	1,716.9	1,131.9
2008[1]	92.0	25.6	635.7	454.0	617.3	280.2	1,222.4	968.2	709.3	305.8	1,858.1	1,422.2

[1] Preliminary.   Source: National Agricultural Statistics Service, U.S. Department of Agriculture (NASS-USDA)

Wheat Supply and Distribution in Canada, Australia and Argentina   In Millions of Metric Tons

	Canada (Year Beginning Aug. 1)					Australia (Year Beginning Oct. 1)					Argentina (Year Beginning Dec. 1)				
	Supply			Disappearance		Supply			Disappearance		Supply			Disappearance	
Crop Year	Stocks Aug. 1	New Crop	Total Supply	Domestic	Exports[3]	Stocks Oct. 1	New Crop	Total Supply	Domestic	Exports[3]	Stocks Dec. 1	New Crop	Total Supply	Domestic	Exports[3]
1999-00	7.4	26.9	34.4	8.1	19.2	2.8	24.8	27.6	5.2	17.8	.7	16.4	17.1	4.9	11.6
2000-01	7.3	26.5	33.8	7.0	17.3	9.7	22.1	31.8	5.3	15.9	.6	16.2	16.8	5.0	11.3
2001-02	9.7	20.6	30.3	7.7	16.3	5.5	24.3	29.8	5.4	16.4	.6	15.5	16.1	4.9	10.1
2002-03	6.5	16.2	22.7	8.0	9.4	8.0	10.1	18.1	6.1	9.1	1.1	12.3	13.4	5.2	6.8
2003-04	5.7	23.0	28.7	7.2	15.8	3.2	26.1	29.3	5.9	18.0	1.5	14.5	16.0	5.2	9.4
2004-05	6.0	24.8	30.8	8.2	14.9	5.4	21.9	27.3	5.9	14.7	1.4	16.0	17.4	5.0	11.8
2005-06	7.9	25.7	33.6	8.2	16.0	6.8	25.2	32.0	6.4	16.0	.6	14.5	15.1	5.0	9.6
2006-07	9.7	25.3	35.0	9.0	19.4	9.6	10.8	20.4	7.4	8.7	.5	15.2	15.7	4.9	10.5
2007-08[1]	6.8	20.1	26.9	6.3	16.1	4.4	13.8	18.2	6.2	7.5	.3	16.3	16.6	5.1	11.2
2008-09[2]	4.8	28.6	33.4	8.2	19.0	4.7	21.5	26.2	6.5	14.0	.3	8.4	8.7	5.1	3.5

[1] Preliminary.   [2] Forecast.   [3] Including flour.   Source: Foreign Agricultural Service, U.S. Department of Agriculture (FAS-USDA)

WHEAT

Quarterly Supply and Disappearance of Wheat in the United States   In Millions of Bushels

Crop Year Beginning June 1	Beginning Stocks	Production	Imports[3]	Total Supply	Food	Seed	Feed & Residual	Total	Exports[3]	Total Disappearance	Gov't Owned[4]	Privately Owned[5]	Total Stocks
		Supply				Domestic Use				Total Disappearance		Ending Stocks	
1998-99	722.5	2,547.3	103.0	3,372.8	909.7	80.5	542.1	1,380.9	1,042.2	2,426.9	127.9	818.0	945.9
June-Aug.	722.5	2,547.3	24.4	3,294.2	225.7	1.0	424.9	651.6	257.3	908.9	99.8	2,285.5	2,385.3
Sept.-Nov.	2,385.3	----	23.9	2,409.2	240.7	54.9	73.8	221.8	291.8	513.6	126.6	1,769.1	1,895.7
Dec.-Feb.	1,895.7	----	27.7	1,923.4	213.2	1.4	11.6	222.1	246.8	473.0	124.2	1,326.2	1,450.4
Mar.-May	1,450.4	----	27.0	1,477.4	230.1	23.2	31.8	285.4	246.3	531.5	127.9	818.0	945.9
1999-00	945.9	2,299.0	78.8	3,323.7	916.1	88.4	302.4	1,306.9	1,060.6	2,367.5	103.9	340.7	444.6
June-Aug.	945.9	2,299.0	30.6	3,275.5	225.9	6.4	275.2	507.5	323.0	830.5	132.2	2,312.8	2,445.0
Sept.-Nov.	2,445.0	----	19.5	2,464.5	241.1	54.6	-6.6	289.2	289.7	578.9	103.0	1,782.6	1,885.6
Dec.-Feb.	1,885.6	----	19.4	1,905.1	219.2	2.3	30.0	251.4	237.1	488.5	108.7	1,307.8	1,416.5
Mar.-May	1,415.3	----	9.3	914.1	229.9	25.1	3.9	258.8	210.8	469.6	103.9	340.7	444.6
2000-01	949.7	2,228.2	89.8	3,267.7	949.6	79.5	300.4	1,329.5	1,062.0	2,391.6	97.0	779.2	876.2
June-Aug.	949.7	2,228.2	20.4	3,198.3	238.8	1.1	317.9	557.8	287.8	845.6	108.9	2,243.8	2,352.7
Sept.-Nov.	2,352.7	----	25.1	2,377.8	253.0	49.8	-24.5	278.4	293.3	571.6	102.9	1,703.2	1,806.1
Dec.-Feb.	1,806.1	----	21.4	1,827.5	228.2	3.5	11.4	243.1	246.1	489.1	104.4	1,234.0	1,338.4
Mar.-May	1,338.4	----	22.9	1,361.3	229.7	25.2	-4.5	250.3	234.8	485.1	97.0	779.2	876.2
2001-02	876.2	1,947.5	107.6	2,931.2	926.4	83.4	182.0	1,191.8	962.3	2,154.1	99.0	678.1	777.1
June-Aug.	876.2	1,947.5	25.7	2,849.3	233.8	3.5	237.9	475.2	218.3	693.5	97.7	2,058.1	2,155.8
Sept.-Nov.	2,155.8	----	29.0	2,184.9	245.1	51.6	-23.1	273.6	287.8	561.4	96.9	1,526.6	1,623.5
Dec.-Feb.	1,623.5	----	27.6	1,651.0	221.1	2.0	-6.6	216.5	224.7	441.2	96.9	1,112.9	1,209.8
Mar.-May	1,209.8	----	25.2	1,235.0	226.4	26.3	-26.2	226.4	231.5	457.9	99.0	678.1	777.1
2002-03	777.1	1,605.9	77.4	2,460.4	918.6	84.4	115.7	1,118.7	850.2	1,968.9	66.4	425.0	491.4
June-Aug.	777.1	1,605.9	26.7	2,409.6	233.2	2.7	184.5	420.4	240.2	660.7	91.4	1,657.6	1,749.0
Sept.-Nov.	1,749.0	----	23.1	1,772.1	237.8	54.6	-74.7	217.7	234.5	454.2	80.9	1,239.0	1,319.9
Dec.-Feb.	1,319.9	----	12.7	1,332.6	218.9	3.1	14.1	236.1	189.8	425.9	74.1	832.5	906.6
Mar.-May	906.6	----	14.9	921.6	228.4	23.9	-8.2	244.5	185.7	430.2	66.4	425.0	491.4
2003-04	491.4	2,344.8	63.1	2,899.3	911.9	79.6	202.9	1,194.4	1,158.1	2,352.5	60.9	485.5	546.4
June-Aug.	491.4	2,344.8	15.7	2,851.9	230.5	2.1	315.3	547.9	264.9	812.8	60.3	1,978.7	2,039.0
Sept.-Nov.	2,039.0	----	17.8	2,056.7	239.6	53.3	-61.9	231.0	305.4	536.4	60.4	1,459.6	1,520.3
Dec.-Feb.	1,520.3	----	12.9	1,533.2	215.9	2.2	3.1	221.2	291.4	512.6	60.0	960.6	1,020.6
Mar.-May	1,020.6	----	16.7	1,037.3	225.9	22.0	-53.6	194.3	296.4	490.7	60.9	485.5	546.4
2004-05	546.4	2,158.2	70.6	2,775.2	904.6	78.9	188.9	1,172.4	1,062.9	2,235.3	54.0	486.1	540.1
June-Aug.	546.4	2,158.2	17.4	2,722.1	227.5	4.1	265.2	496.8	286.8	783.6	61.9	1,876.5	1,938.4
Sept.-Nov.	1,938.4	----	18.7	1,957.1	235.6	48.2	-57.0	226.8	300.0	526.8	61.7	1,369.0	1,430.3
Dec.-Feb.	1,430.3	----	17.8	1,448.1	216.3	2.4	7.7	226.4	237.4	463.8	55.9	928.5	984.4
Mar.-May	984.4	----	16.7	1,001.1	225.2	24.2	-27.0	222.4	238.7	461.1	54.5	485.6	540.1
2005-06	2,105.0	2,104.7	81.0	4,290.7	914.0	78.0	154.0	1,146.0	1,009.0	2,155.0			571.0
June-Aug.	540.1	2,104.7	19.0	2,663.0	231.0	2.0	263.0	496.0	244.0	740.0	48.3	1,875.0	1,923.0
Sept.-Nov.	1,923.0	----	20.0	1,944.0	238.0	51.0	-61.0	228.0	286.0	514.0	44.1	1,385.4	1,429.0
Dec.-Feb.	1,429.0	----	20.0	1,450.0	219.0	1.0	1.0	221.0	257.0	478.0			972.0
Mar.-May	972.0	----	22.0	995.0	226.0	24.0	-49.0	201.0	222.0	423.0			571.0
2006-07	571.0	1,812.0	121.0	2,504.0	933.0	81.0	126.0	1,140.0	909.0	2,049.0			456.0
June-Aug.	571.0	1,812.0	26.0	2,410.0	233.0	2.0	210.0	445.0	214.0	659.0			1,751.0
Sept.-Nov.	1,751.0	----	29.0	1,780.0	242.0	56.0	-45.0	253.0	212.0	465.0			1,315.0
Dec.-Feb.	1,315.0	----	31.0	1,346.0	224.0	1.0	27.0	252.0	237.0	489.0			857.0
Mar.-May	857.0	----	35.0	892.0	234.0	22.0	-66.0	190.0	246.0	436.0			456.0
2007-08[1]	456.0	2,067.0	112.0	2,635.0	948.0	88.0	30.0	1,066.0	1,263.0	2,329.0			306.0
June-Aug.	456.0	2,067.0	30.0	2,553.0	240.0	1.0	272.0	513.0	323.0	836.0			1,717.0
Sept.-Nov.	1,717.0	----	21.0	1,738.0	245.0	60.0	-120.0	185.0	421.0	606.0			1,132.0
Dec.-Feb.	1,132.0	----	24.0	1,156.0	228.0	2.0	-42.0	188.0	259.0	447.0			709.0
Mar.-May	709.0	----	37.0	746.0	235.0	25.0	-80.0	180.0	260.0	440.0			306.0
2008-09[2]	306.0	2,500.0	110.0	2,915.0	950.0	80.0	230.0	1,260.0	1,000.0	2,260.0			655.0
June-Aug.	306.0	2,500.0	28.0	2,833.0	236.0	1.0	394.0	631.0	344.0	975.0			1,858.0
Sept.-Nov.	1,858.0	----	26.0	1,884.0	250.0	53.0	-132.0	171.0	291.0	462.0			1,422.0

[1] Preliminary.   [2] Forecast.   [3] Imports & exports include flour and other products expressed in wheat equivalent.   [4] Uncommitted, Government only.
[5] Includes total loans.   [6] Includes alcoholic beverages.   *Source: Economic Research Service, U.S. Department of Agriculture (ERS-USDA)*

Wheat Government Loan Program Data in the United States — Loan Rates--Cents Per Bushel

Crop Year Beginning June 1	National Average[3]	Target Rate[4]	Corn Belt (Soft Red Winter)	Central & Southern Plains (Hard Winter)	Northern Plains (Spring & Durum)	Pacific Northwest (White)	Placed Under Loan	% of Production	Acquired by CCC Under Program	Total Stocks May 31	Total CCC Stocks May 31	Outstanding CCC Loans	Outstanding Farmer-Owned Reserve	"Free"
										In Millions of Bushels				
1998-99	258	NA	253	257	258	271	363	14.2	30	946	128	140	0	818
1999-00	258	NA	253	257	258	271	154	6.7	13	950	104	62	0	846
2000-01	258	NA	253	257	258	271	181	8.1	27	876	97	42	0	779
2001-02	258	NA	NA	NA	NA	NA	197	10.1	17	777	99	78	0	678
2002-03	280	386	NA	NA	NA	NA	120	7.5	2	491	66	51	0	425
2003-04	280	386	NA	NA	NA	NA	186	7.9	3	546	61	45	0	485
2004-05	275	392	NA	NA	NA	NA	178	8.3	10	540	54	NA	0	486
2005-06	275	392	NA	NA	NA	NA	170	8.1	1	571	43	NA	0	528
2006-07[1]	275	392	NA	NA	NA	NA	94	5.2	0	456	41	NA	0	437
2007-08[2]	275	392								306	24			

[1] Preliminary.   [2] Estimate.   [3] The national average loan rate at the farm as a percentage of the parity-priced wheat at the beginning of the marketing year.   [4] 1996-97 through 2001-02 marketing year, target prices not applicable.   NA = Not avaliable.
Source: Agricultural Marketing Service, U.S. Department of Agriculture (AMS-USDA)

Exports of Wheat (Only)[2] from the United States — In Thousands of Bushels

Year	June	July	Aug.	Sept.	Oct.	Nov.	Dec.	Jan.	Feb.	Mar.	Apr.	May	Total
1999-00	90,594	110,814	107,168	91,438	96,154	89,211	84,460	71,763	64,198	68,836	73,815	87,789	1,036,240
2000-01	88,581	82,739	104,944	113,785	82,716	86,034	94,705	60,743	85,797	71,502	83,157	68,908	1,023,611
2001-02	59,190	64,911	89,582	86,941	94,598	99,800	81,369	72,114	63,446	78,070	84,211	58,449	932,681
2002-03	63,219	78,013	92,345	73,606	78,866	75,678	69,485	62,769	48,618	65,990	55,764	59,438	823,791
2003-04	54,665	88,042	115,869	125,312	101,168	76,222	79,811	109,607	94,480	96,685	102,588	91,917	1,136,366
2004-05	80,599	97,962	103,222	119,965	92,634	83,947	81,718	77,349	73,131	76,612	81,885	75,575	1,044,599
2005-06	64,553	90,760	83,173	102,761	103,423	77,164	91,531	84,659	71,175	74,420	69,050	72,209	984,878
2006-07	63,115	67,846	78,225	76,431	70,752	60,595	72,226	84,629	75,412	76,512	75,130	85,565	886,438
2007-08	73,088	80,285	153,223	149,168	158,064	116,504	82,343	87,539	84,414	92,251	82,781	79,725	1,239,385
2008-09[1]	77,176	119,492	141,173	117,332	93,462	75,311	54,389						1,162,860

[1] Preliminary.   [2] Grains.   *Source: Economic Research Service, U.S. Department of Agriculture (ERS-USDA)*

United States Wheat and Wheat Flour Imports and Exports — In Thousands of Bushels

Crop Year Beginning June 1	Wheat Suitable for Milling Consump.	Wheat Unfit for Human Consump.	Grain	Flour & Products[2]	Total	P.L. 480	Foreign Donations Sec. 416	Aid[3]	Total concessional	CCC Export Credit	Export Enhancement Program	Total U.S. Wheat
	Imports — Wheat — Wheat Equivalent					Exports — In Thousands of Metric Tons						
2000-01	66,313	----	66,313	23,512	89,824	1,294	1,638	NA	3,109	4,026	0	25,275
2001-02	82,615	----	82,615	24,936	107,551	1,093	875	NA	2,035	4,614	0	25,411
2002-03	49,741	----	49,741	27,633	77,374	1,475	213	NA	2,081	3,633	0	24,295
2003-04	37,156	----	37,156	25,871	63,026	1,211	20	NA	1,628	3,791	0	31,179
2004-05	44,499	----	44,499	26,071	70,570	1,867	12	NA	2,139	2,615	0	26,505
2005-06	54,073	----	54,073	27,281	81,354	969	17	NA	1,191	1,038	0	25,005
2006-07[1]	92,928	----	92,928	28,938	121,866							

[1] Preliminary.   [2] Includes macaroni, semolina & similar products.   [3] Shipment mostly under the Commodity Import Program, financed with foreign aid funds.   NA = Not available.   *Source: Economic Research Service, U.S. Department of Agriculture (ERS-USDA)*

Comparative Average Cash Wheat Prices — In Dollars Per Bushel

Crop Year June to May	Received by U.S. Farmers	No. 2 Soft Red Winter, Chicago	No 1 Hard Red Ordinary Protein, Kansas City	No 2 Soft Red Winter, St. Louis	No 1 Dark Northern Spring 14%	No 1 Hard Amber Durum	No 1 Soft White, Portland, Oregon	No 2 Western White Pacific Northwest	No 2 Soft White, Toledo	Australian Standard White	Canada Vancouver No 1 CWRS 13 1/2%	Argentina F.O.B. B.A.	U.S. Gulf No 2 Hard Winter	Rotterdam C.I.F. U.S. No 2 Hard Winter
			-- Minneapolis --							Export Prices[2] (U.S. $ Per Metric Ton)				
2001-02	2.78	2.69	3.25	2.80	3.61	4.99	3.56	3.67	2.67	157	149	121	125	161
2002-03	3.56	3.40	4.22	3.50	4.47	4.25	3.95	4.58	3.34	185	194	158	160	189
2003-04	3.40	3.66	4.03	3.76	4.39	5.31	3.95	4.24	3.59	182	188	161	156	204
2004-05	3.40	3.01	3.99	3.37	4.66	NQ	3.93	4.04	3.10	177	204	127	151	213
2005-06	3.42	3.13	4.45	3.20	4.98	NQ	3.57	4.35	3.15	191	204	140	168	224
2006-07	4.26	3.98	5.38	4.11	5.41	NQ	4.87	5.48	3.85	227	227	189	204	252
2007-08	6.48	7.71	9.11	7.43	10.81	13.08	9.97	8.68	8.06				340	
2008-09[1]	6.60-7.40	5.39	7.50	5.06	9.04		6.70	7.58	5.36				299	

[1] Preliminary.   [2] Calendar year.   NA = Not available.   *Source: Economic Research Service, U.S. Department of Agriculture (ERS-USDA)*

WHEAT

Wheat (monthly average) through December 2008 — Cents per bushel

Average Price of No. 2 Soft Red Winter (30 Days) Wheat in Chicago   In Dollars Per Bushel

Year	June	July	Aug.	Sept.	Oct.	Nov.	Dec.	Jan.	Feb.	Mar.	Apr.	May	Average
1999-00	2.20	1.94	2.09	2.12	1.98	1.96	2.12	2.34	2.38	2.34	2.30	2.45	2.19
2000-01	2.41	2.14	2.08	2.13	2.36	2.42	2.47	2.57	2.49	2.56	2.52	2.51	2.39
2001-02	2.40	2.56	2.57	2.57	2.68	2.75	2.83	2.96	2.74	2.76	2.75	2.73	2.69
2002-03	2.81	3.19	3.42	3.92	3.89	3.85	3.53	3.32	3.44	3.14	3.08	3.25	3.40
2003-04	3.11	3.23	3.63	3.46	3.42	3.87	3.92	3.90	3.84	3.85	3.92	3.73	3.66
2004-05	3.46	3.26	2.92	2.97	2.82	2.79	2.88	2.93	2.95	3.28	2.92	2.96	3.01
2005-06	3.09	3.22	3.04	2.93	2.99	2.83	2.98	3.11	3.34	3.29	3.21	3.54	3.13
2006-07	3.26	3.43	3.20	3.39	4.40	4.35	4.49	4.19	4.20	4.07	4.25	4.50	3.98
2007-08	5.25	5.52	6.24	7.98	7.89	7.57	8.69	8.55	10.12	10.40	7.72	6.59	7.71
2008-09[1]	7.20	6.87	6.77	5.45	3.76	3.68	4.01						5.39

[1] Preliminary.   *Source: Economic Research Service, U.S. Department of Agriculture (ERS-USDA)*

Average Price Received by Farmers for Wheat in the United States   In Dollars Per Bushel

Year	June	July	Aug.	Sept.	Oct.	Nov.	Dec.	Jan.	Feb.	Mar.	Apr.	May	Average
1999-00	2.50	2.22	2.53	2.58	2.57	2.66	2.52	2.51	2.54	2.59	2.57	2.59	2.53
2000-01	2.50	2.32	2.41	2.44	2.68	2.83	2.87	2.85	2.83	2.87	2.86	2.98	2.70
2001-02	2.74	2.70	2.73	2.85	2.87	2.87	2.88	2.87	2.83	2.87	2.83	2.81	2.82
2002-03	2.92	3.21	3.63	4.21	4.38	4.25	4.06	3.89	3.70	3.55	3.37	3.33	3.71
2003-04	3.08	2.95	3.35	3.39	3.44	3.61	3.68	3.68	3.77	3.83	3.88	3.82	3.54
2004-05	3.55	3.37	3.27	3.36	3.43	3.46	3.40	3.43	3.36	3.42	3.35	3.31	3.39
2005-06	3.23	3.20	3.24	3.36	3.43	3.45	3.53	3.52	3.66	3.79	3.81	4.09	3.53
2006-07	3.98	3.88	3.91	4.06	4.59	4.59	4.52	4.53	4.71	4.75	4.89	4.88	4.44
2007-08	5.03	5.17	5.64	6.76	7.65	7.39	7.71	7.96	9.98	10.60	10.00	8.87	7.73
2008-09[2]	7.62	7.16	7.64	7.43	6.67	6.28	5.97	5.90					6.83

[1] Preliminary.   *Source: Economic Research Service, U.S. Department of Agriculture (ERS-USDA)*

Average Price of No. 1 Hard Red Winter (Ordinary Protein) Wheat in Kansas City — In Dollars Per Bushel

Year	June	July	Aug.	Sept.	Oct.	Nov.	Dec.	Jan.	Feb.	Mar.	Apr.	May	Average
1999-00	2.93	2.68	2.85	2.92	2.80	2.89	2.81	2.90	2.94	2.91	2.84	2.95	2.87
2000-01	3.07	2.97	2.89	3.13	3.41	3.45	3.47	3.54	3.35	3.45	3.41	3.49	3.30
2001-02	3.32	3.20	3.15	3.18	3.28	3.37	3.26	3.29	3.25	3.23	3.24	3.21	3.25
2002-03	3.55	3.92	4.29	5.04	5.10	4.76	4.40	4.06	4.08	3.80	3.79	3.87	4.22
2003-04	3.63	3.34	3.87	3.74	3.79	4.21	4.31	4.32	4.25	4.30	4.35	4.28	4.03
2004-05	4.13	3.97	3.73	4.01	3.95	4.22	4.22	4.14	4.00	4.00	3.76	3.80	3.99
2005-06	3.87	3.83	3.96	4.30	4.57	4.53	4.52	4.46	4.72	4.62	4.86	5.21	4.45
2006-07	5.25	5.27	5.00	5.16	5.62	5.61	5.49	5.29	5.39	5.40	5.52	5.54	5.38
2007-08	6.22	6.28	6.84	8.52	8.89	8.62	9.80	9.97	12.28	12.29	10.29	9.33	9.11
2008-09[1]	9.19	8.68	8.64	7.52	6.17	6.21	6.06						7.50

[1] Preliminary.   Source: Economic Research Service, U.S. Department of Agriculture (ERS-USDA)

Average Price of No. 1 Dark Northern Spring (14% Protein) Wheat in Minneapolis — In Dollars Per Bushel

Year	June	July	Aug.	Sept.	Oct.	Nov.	Dec.	Jan.	Feb.	Mar.	Apr.	May	Average
1999-00	3.73	3.68	3.58	3.55	3.70	3.78	3.64	3.37	3.59	3.65	3.69	3.80	3.65
2000-01	3.78	3.50	3.29	3.17	3.69	3.77	3.52	3.79	3.68	3.63	3.73	3.88	3.62
2001-02	3.81	3.72	3.54	3.52	3.71	3.69	3.59	3.55	3.51	3.51	3.55	3.59	3.61
2002-03	3.64	4.03	4.37	5.24	5.20	4.99	4.47	4.34	4.52	4.36	4.22	4.20	4.47
2003-04	4.12	4.00	4.15	4.03	4.31	4.59	4.43	4.44	4.64	4.63	4.69	4.69	4.39
2004-05	4.56	4.31	4.12	4.68	4.87	5.14	4.93	5.01	4.13	4.79	4.69	4.69	4.66
2005-06	5.03	4.71	4.83	4.80	5.11	5.11	5.28	4.87	4.90	4.83	4.94	5.31	4.98
2006-07	5.59	5.65	4.94	4.86	5.36	5.55	5.44	5.27	5.40	5.55	5.65	5.64	5.41
2007-08	6.19	6.60	6.88	8.20	9.27	9.39	11.06	12.59	19.00	15.60	12.93	12.06	10.81
2008-09[1]	11.46	11.46	9.87	8.51	7.37	6.80	7.78						9.04

[1] Preliminary.   Source: Economic Research Service, U.S. Department of Agriculture (ERS-USDA)

Average Farm Prices of Winter Wheat in the United States — In Dollars Per Bushel

Year	June	July	Aug.	Sept.	Oct.	Nov.	Dec.	Jan.	Feb.	Mar.	Apr.	May	Average
2001-02	2.68	2.67	2.71	2.81	2.82	2.82	2.78	2.81	2.75	2.81	2.75	2.73	2.76
2002-03	2.90	3.19	3.63	4.15	4.32	4.18	3.87	3.66	3.52	3.30	3.19	3.19	3.59
2003-04	2.94	2.89	3.28	3.31	3.37	3.56	3.62	3.66	3.67	3.76	3.79	3.72	3.46
2004-05	3.46	3.31	3.19	3.26	3.34	3.39	3.34	3.28	3.27	3.32	3.27	3.23	3.31
2005-06	3.15	3.15	3.16	3.28	3.34	3.27	3.45	3.45	3.59	3.82	3.74	4.06	3.46
2006-07	3.95	3.82	3.77	4.03	4.63	4.67	4.53	4.53	4.67	4.67	4.87	4.77	4.41
2007-08	5.00	5.13	5.66	6.89	7.55	7.31	7.70	7.75	8.97	10.00	9.61	8.17	7.48
2008-09[1]	7.51	7.10	7.31	6.99	6.05	5.64	5.41	5.29					6.41

[1] Preliminary.   Source: Economic Research Service, U.S. Department of Agriculture (ERS-USDA)

Average Farm Prices of Durum Wheat in the United States — In Dollars Per Bushel

Year	June	July	Aug.	Sept.	Oct.	Nov.	Dec.	Jan.	Feb.	Mar.	Apr.	May	Average
2001-02	3.37	2.74	2.38	3.02	2.91	3.04	3.41	3.44	3.49	3.33	3.33	3.41	3.16
2002-03	3.41	3.44	3.54	4.18	4.43	4.52	4.26	4.23	4.28	4.14	3.93	3.99	4.03
2003-04	3.99	3.85	3.78	3.95	3.89	3.95	3.95	3.96	4.08	4.14	4.19	4.21	4.00
2004-05	4.35	4.09	3.86	3.89	3.87	3.79	3.67	3.64	3.72	3.70	3.63	3.67	3.82
2005-06	3.67	3.72	3.35	3.38	3.39	3.28	3.37	3.29	3.34	3.39	3.41	3.94	3.46
2006-07	3.81	3.83	4.09	4.07	4.55	4.62	4.53	4.71	5.16	5.32	5.46	5.39	4.63
2007-08	5.49	6.69	7.00	8.98	11.70	11.70	11.50	13.10	13.50	15.40	13.80	13.50	11.03
2008-09[1]	8.41	11.80	12.40	11.80	12.00	8.68	8.35	7.86					10.16

[1] Preliminary.   Source: Economic Research Service, U.S. Department of Agriculture (ERS-USDA)

Average Farm Prices of Other Spring Wheat in the United States — In Dollars Per Bushel

Year	June	July	Aug.	Sept.	Oct.	Nov.	Dec.	Jan.	Feb.	Mar.	Apr.	May	Average
2001-02	3.03	2.78	2.84	2.87	2.96	2.91	2.96	2.88	2.86	2.90	2.91	2.91	2.90
2002-03	2.98	3.31	3.66	4.30	4.45	4.26	4.15	4.03	3.82	3.72	3.48	3.55	3.81
2003-04	3.45	3.31	3.42	3.42	3.53	3.68	3.72	3.67	3.84	3.90	3.94	4.01	3.66
2004-05	3.83	3.55	3.38	3.48	3.50	3.57	3.48	3.61	3.49	3.51	3.39	3.37	3.51
2005-06	3.51	3.45	3.43	3.51	3.61	3.71	3.68	3.70	3.83	3.85	3.95	4.18	3.70
2006-07	4.18	4.41	4.11	4.11	4.48	4.48	4.74	4.51	4.73	4.73	4.87	4.98	4.53
2007-08	5.17	5.43	5.53	6.26	6.99	7.00	7.39	8.01	11.10	11.00	10.50	10.70	7.92
2008-09[1]	10.10	9.60	8.22	7.77	7.26	7.12	6.90	6.76					7.97

[1] Preliminary.   Source: Economic Research Service, U.S. Department of Agriculture (ERS-USDA)

WHEAT

Wheat Futures - CME Group (CBT)
(weekly close) as January 02, 2009

Cents per bushel

Volume of Trading of Wheat Futures in Chicago   In Thousands of Contracts

Year	Jan.	Feb.	Mar.	Apr.	May	June	July	Aug.	Sept.	Oct.	Nov.	Dec.	Total
1999	426.5	597.4	710.4	559.2	444.7	674.6	523.5	665.9	536.0	437.7	613.6	380.4	6,570.0
2000	467.1	691.1	522.4	490.7	627.7	759.4	461.1	572.9	388.2	466.3	596.6	364.1	6,407.5
2001	551.8	595.3	536.1	580.0	537.8	720.4	695.3	600.3	385.9	629.5	614.7	354.3	6,801.5
2002	603.0	593.1	501.1	563.1	419.3	689.8	586.4	651.6	682.9	609.4	594.4	378.8	6,872.9
2003	438.0	526.0	411.0	496.8	638.6	661.8	585.1	689.6	536.5	778.9	739.8	465.4	6,967.4
2004	656.9	771.7	783.1	786.2	606.1	786.5	501.7	747.4	520.9	478.7	913.7	402.3	7,955.2
2005	613.0	1,053.6	827.8	937.5	694.7	1,088.0	690.3	1,024.8	660.0	717.4	1,164.5	642.4	10,114.1
2006	889.2	1,421.3	1,059.6	1,300.0	1,511.6	1,617.1	1,067.4	1,659.9	1,365.9	1,938.1	1,613.7	781.2	16,224.9
2007	1,346.2	1,506.0	1,148.0	2,082.5	1,170.5	2,343.7	1,514.4	2,111.3	1,320.3	1,648.4	2,109.7	1,281.8	19,582.7
2008	1,861.3	2,527.7	1,398.7	1,558.6	1,121.6	2,185.7	1,314.2	2,093.6	1,228.1	1,139.0	1,644.5	939.0	19,011.9

Source: Chicago Board of Trade (CBT)

Average Open Interest of Wheat Futures in Chicago   In Contracts

Year	Jan.	Feb.	Mar.	Apr.	May	June	July	Aug.	Sept.	Oct.	Nov.	Dec.
1999	119,096	131,961	118,503	117,905	111,541	117,075	120,365	129,748	128,403	135,884	140,798	124,063
2000	127,419	135,316	123,980	128,462	130,938	133,527	139,194	144,953	141,803	150,592	153,287	134,997
2001	145,802	146,927	137,377	138,876	134,051	151,951	142,399	143,574	136,514	126,772	113,456	104,975
2002	118,192	118,484	112,469	112,870	96,050	98,047	118,041	131,303	129,913	114,544	101,354	82,934
2003	92,679	99,882	95,464	99,500	97,750	96,230	92,484	119,817	110,703	109,449	125,335	120,376
2004	130,101	137,459	141,239	155,383	127,086	135,322	154,623	166,422	154,431	156,290	172,064	182,402
2005	201,297	223,108	218,153	208,149	207,407	223,014	239,219	256,533	276,741	297,319	301,838	298,523
2006	320,974	380,405	389,284	385,698	466,013	491,343	473,749	459,650	455,755	476,906	435,059	426,976
2007	453,140	441,924	405,383	377,162	363,297	401,509	411,971	404,940	379,871	407,669	414,509	423,198
2008	443,193	440,137	400,426	375,845	362,835	359,429	332,360	331,301	294,696	279,041	283,832	250,914

Source: Chicago Board of Trade (CBT)

Commercial Stocks of Domestic Wheat[1] in the United States, on First of Month   In Millions of Bushels

Year	July	Aug.	Sept.	Oct.	Nov.	Dec.	Jan.	Feb.	Mar.	Apr.	May	June
1999-00	248.6	294.9	335.8	354.0	334.6	301.5	277.4	273.7	267.8	266.3	247.6	240.3
2000-01	285.5	310.3	335.3	335.5	306.2	286.6	263.7	251.7	243.2	243.7	224.5	221.0
2001-02	271.0	296.6	318.7	321.9	291.9	251.8	224.5	224.6	217.2	195.6	177.3	176.0
2002-03	193.9	207.7	237.2	241.0	237.7	218.8	195.1	179.7	158.3	133.1	107.2	93.8
2003-04	133.3	171.9	212.0	226.3	220.7	198.1	145.0	126.3	113.1	94.0	89.6	85.4
2004-05	118.3	147.6	174.3	173.5	161.6	137.8	129.8	122.5	113.4	103.8	92.2	88.8
2005-06	127.5	138.6	159.9	163.5	158.5	147.8	137.9	130.9	128.8	122.9	116.7	126.2
2006-07	154.3	172.5	190.3	170.9	166.8	159.5	154.7	146.7	136.3	129.3	116.6	99.2
2007-08	108.6	155.9	173.1	185.7	164.8	151.2	148.3	138.9	123.5	112.3	87.1	78.7
2008-09	98.2	150.4	176.4	214.5	212.9	179.7	167.8	135.9				

[1] Domestic wheat in storage in public and private elevators in 39 markets and wheat afloat in vessels or barges at lake and seaboard ports, the first Saturday of the month.   *Source: Livestock Division, U.S. Department of Agriculture (LD-USDA)*

Stocks of Wheat Flour Held by Mills in the United States   In Thousands of Sacks--100 Pounds

Year	Jan. 1	April 1	July 1	Oct. 1	Year	Jan. 1	April 1	July 1	Oct. 1
1997	6,671	6,040	5,820	6,330	2003	4,265	4,707	4,622	4,554
1998	6,343	6,245	6,210	7,345	2004	4,764	4,666	4,700	4,868
1999	7,544	5,920	5,697	4,265	2005	5,085	4,268	4,637	4,781
2000	5,099	5,217	5,062	5,244	2006	5,211	5,775	5,576	5,587
2001	5,241	5,506	5,178	5,393	2007	5,919	5,884	5,587	6,188
2002	5,377	5,164	4,632	4,184	2008[1]	6,374	6,213	6,168	6,685

[1] Preliminary.   *Source: Bureau of the Census, U.S. Department of Commerce*

Average Producer Price Index of Wheat Flour (Spring[2])   June 1983 = 100

Year	Jan.	Feb.	Mar.	Apr.	May	June	July	Aug.	Sept.	Oct.	Nov.	Dec.	Average
1999	104.8	102.7	105.0	100.5	102.2	102.7	100.7	103.5	101.4	99.8	101.4	96.8	101.8
2000	99.9	99.9	100.2	99.4	100.1	101.7	100.2	100.4	101.2	105.2	103.6	104.4	101.4
2001	104.7	105.1	106.2	105.7	106.9	108.2	107.9	106.8	107.4	110.0	109.5	108.8	107.3
2002	109.6	109.6	110.6	106.5	108.2	108.8	112.6	115.5	120.9	123.0	119.3	116.6	113.4
2003	119.4	121.6	120.2	120.3	122.6	121.6	119.2	122.2	120.4	117.2	121.1	122.4	120.7
2004	123.5	125.1	123.9	124.0	127.6	126.4	125.2	121.0	128.5	127.2	130.2	128.5	125.9
2005	128.5	130.4	130.8	127.6	129.6	130.8	130.3	129.7	130.6	131.4	133.6	131.8	130.4
2006	130.2	134.2	132.8	139.4	142.2	144.2	148.5	141.6	144.2	151.9	151.8	147.5	142.4
2007	144.8	144.6	148.2	153.2	154.3	161.9	167.4	174.0	196.2	209.4	207.1	229.5	174.2
2008[1]	239.6	278.9	293.6	262.8	248.1	246.5	228.5	229.5	214.6	194.9	189.3	179.8	233.8

[1] Preliminary.   [2] Standard patent.   *Source: Bureau of Labor Statistics, U.S. Department of Commerce (BLS) (0212-0301)*

World Wheat Flour Production (Monthly Average)   In Thousands of Metric Tons

Year	Australia	France	Germany	Hungary	India	Japan	Kazakhstan	Rep. of Korea	Mexico	Poland	Russia	Turkey	United Kingdom
1999	154.8	NA	423.6	69.1	196.6	386.5	104.9	152.8	204.8	125.0	899.1	156.6	NA
2000	NA	NA	405.5	73.5	202.5	383.0	120.8	155.9	206.0	125.4	864.0	162.0	374.0
2001	NA	NA	403.1	72.4	197.2	387.2	116.5	142.8	221.1	126.8	866.6	145.2	374.0
2002	NA	NA	415.3	67.6	211.6	389.4	143.4	151.2	218.1	135.2	794.3	139.6	369.0
2003	NA	NA	424.4	70.7	234.1	391.0	137.3	149.3	218.6	143.1	821.3	159.8	365.0
2004	NA	NA	427.3	67.6	239.9	390.1	138.5	157.5	217.6	135.2	799.5	178.4	370.0
2005	NA	NA	415.7	72.3	209.2	384.7	182.2	152.8	219.2	128.6	439.4	191.5	368.0
2006	NA	NA	430.2	62.5	182.5	384.8	189.6	153.8	222.9	143.8	457.7	190.4	366.0
2007[1]	NA	NA	433.8	59.4	181.1	392.7	235.8	146.7	222.9	124.3	455.1	197.8	NA
2008[2]	NA	NA	433.0	56.0	175.1	384.5	206.8	139.5	219.3	109.3	444.6	196.3	NA

[1] Preliminary.   [2] Estimate.   NA = Not available.   *Source: United Nations (UN)*

WHEAT

Production of Wheat Flour in the United States   In Millions of Sacks--100 Pounds Each

Year	July	Aug.	Sept.	Oct.	Nov.	Dec.	Jan.	Feb.	Mar.	Apr.	May	June	Total
1999-00	-----	104.2	-----	-----	108.2	-----	-----	101.1	-----	-----	101.6	-----	415.2
2000-01	-----	108.8	-----	-----	109.7	-----	-----	99.4	-----	-----	97.2	-----	415.1
2001-02	-----	102.1	-----	-----	105.8	-----	-----	96.0	-----	-----	96.3	-----	400.2
2002-03	-----	102.1	-----	-----	100.3	-----	-----	95.9	-----	-----	96.8	-----	395.0
2003-04	-----	103.1	-----	-----	100.5	-----	-----	96.6	-----	-----	96.8	-----	396.9
2004-05	-----	100.9	-----	-----	99.7	-----	-----	95.9	-----	-----	96.2	-----	392.7
2005-06	-----	102.5	-----	-----	100.3	-----	-----	98.1	-----	-----	98.0	-----	398.9
2006-07	-----	104.9	-----	-----	102.5	-----	-----	100.3	-----	-----	102.5	-----	410.1
2007-08	-----	109.0	-----	-----	107.1	-----	-----	101.6	-----	-----	101.9	-----	419.6
2008-09[1]	-----	108.2	-----	-----		-----	-----		-----	-----		-----	432.6

[1] Preliminary.   *Source: Bureau of the Census, U.S. Department of Commerce*

United States Wheat Flour Exports (Grain Equivalent[2])   In Thousands of Bushels

Year	June	July	Aug.	Sept.	Oct.	Nov.	Dec.	Jan.	Feb.	Mar.	Apr.	May	Total
1999-00	4,160	3,638	2,586	6,503	4,576	2,332	3,023	2,924	6,108	2,615	3,193	1,286	42,944
2000-01	3,620	3,805	1,623	3,174	4,165	2,332	2,741	2,236	2,365	2,200	3,868	2,163	34,292
2001-02	1,412	661	1,990	1,005	3,226	2,534	2,479	2,207	3,294	2,301	2,802	2,759	26,670
2002-03	1,474	1,547	753	1,373	2,437	2,854	4,645	1,049	884	1,146	1,083	541	19,786
2003-04	824	1,074	3,444	1,087	765	1,295	1,673	1,789	1,342	1,020	732	1,386	16,431
2004-05	742	1,220	885	770	834	1,005	1,347	955	617	756	722	781	10,634
2005-06	859	686	839	720	840	871	734	572	620	937	1,188	966	9,832
2006-07	720	488	780	610	532	754	756	786	999	941	1,425	2,711	11,502
2007-08	1,467	1,220	1,277	1,135	1,758	2,515	1,960	1,224	1,544	1,328	1,114	1,126	17,668
2008-09[1]	1,417	1,052	1,093	1,053	856	1,055							13,052

[1] Preliminary.   [2] Includes meal, groats and durum.   *Source: Economic Research Service, U.S. Department of Agriculture (ERS-USDA)*

Supply and Distribution of Wheat Flour in the United States

Year	Wheat Ground -- 1,000 Bu. --	Milfeed Production - 1,000 Tons -	Flour Production[3]	Flour & Product Imports[2]	Total Supply	Exports Flour	Exports Products	Domestic Disappearance	Total Population July 1 -- Millions --	Per Capita Disappearance -- Pounds --
						In 1,000 Cwt.				
1998	895,369	7,301	398,914	9,830	408,744	12,574	1,353	394,817	276.2	142.9
1999	917,797	7,040	411,968	9,295	421,263	17,499	1,633	402,131	279.3	144.0
2000	944,868	7,374	421,270	9,666	430,936	16,005	1,693	413,239	282.4	146.3
2001	914,036	7,273	404,521	10,130	414,651	10,507	1,695	402,449	285.4	141.0
2002	889,412	6,893	394,700	11,291	405,991	9,226	2,683	394,082	288.2	136.7
2003	889,188	7,029	396,215	11,145	407,360	5,768	3,953	397,639	291.0	136.7
2004	876,047	6,764	393,925	10,726	404,651	5,152	4,662	394,837	293.6	134.5
2005	884,101	6,826	394,973	11,262	406,235	3,747	4,741	397,748	296.4	134.2
2006	894,527	6,916	403,391	11,740	411,600	3,412	5,867	402,321	299.2	134.5
2007[1]	923,756	7,103	418,836	11,511	429,085	7,158	6,465	415,462	302.1	137.5

[1] Preliminary.   [2] Commercial production of wheat flour, whole wheat, industrial and durum flour and farina reported by Bureau of Census.
Source: Economic Research Service, U.S. Department of Agriculture (ERS-USDA)

Wheat and Flour Price Relationships at Milling Centers in the United States   In Dollars

	At Kansas City					At Minneapolis				
	Cost of Wheat to Produce 100 lb. Flour[1]	Wholesale Price of Bakery Flour 100 lb. Flour[2]	Wholesale Price of By-Products Obtained 100 lb. Flour[3]	Total Products Actual	Total Products Over Cost of Wheat	Cost of Wheat to Produce 100 lb. Flour[1]	Wholesale Price of Bakery Flour 100 lb. Flour[2]	Wholesale Price of By-Products Obtained 100 lb. Flour[3]	Total Products Actual	Total Products Over Cost of Wheat
Year										
2000-01	7.95	9.36	1.06	10.42	2.48	8.24	9.28	.97	10.24	2.01
2001-02	7.64	8.98	1.14	10.11	2.48	8.20	9.11	1.10	10.21	2.01
2002-03	9.66	11.04	1.16	12.20	2.54	9.80	11.03	1.15	12.17	2.38
2003-04	9.43	10.58	1.36	11.95	2.52	9.98	10.67	1.15	11.82	1.84
2004-05	9.33	10.88	.95	11.83	2.50	10.62	11.31	.94	12.25	1.62
2005-06	10.38	11.73	1.03	12.76	2.38	11.35	12.25	.93	13.19	1.84
2006-07	12.41	13.10	1.65	14.76	2.45	12.33	12.75	1.54	14.29	2.11
2007-08	17.87					17.68				
June-Aug.	15.14					14.95				
Sept.-Nov.	20.59					20.41				

[1] Based on 73% extraction rate, cost of 2.28 bushels: At Kansas City, No. 1 hard winter 13% protein; and at Minneapolis, No. 1 dark northern spring, 14% protein.   [2] quoted as mid-month bakers' standard patent at Kansas City and spring standard patent at Minneapolis, bulk basis.   [3] Assumed 50-50 millfeed distribution between bran and shorts or middlings, bulk basis.   *Source: Agricultural Marketing Service, U.S. Department of Agriculture*

Wool

Wool is light, warm, absorbs moisture, and is resistant to fire. Wool is also used for insulation in houses, for carpets and furnishing, and for bedding. Sheep are sheared once a year and produce about 4.3 kg of "greasy" wool per year.

Greasy wool is wool that has not been washed or cleaned. Wool fineness is determined by fiber diameter, which is measured in microns (one millionth of a meter). Fine wool is softer, lightweight, and produces fine clothing. Merino sheep produce the finest wool.

Wool futures and options are traded on the Sydney Futures Exchange (SFE), where there are futures and options contracts on greasy wool, and futures on fine wool and broad wool. All three futures contracts call for the delivery of merino combing wool. Wool yarn futures are traded on the Chubu Commodity Exchange (CCE), the Osaka Mercantile Exchange (OME) and the Tokyo Commodity Exchange (TOCOM).

Prices – Average monthly wool prices at U.S. mills in 2008 (through November) rose by +15.0% yr/yr to a record high of $3.05 per pound. Wool prices in 2008 are almost three times higher than the 3-decade low of $1.09 posted in 2000. The value of U.S. wool production in 2008 was up +7.4% to $32.486 million, more than double the record low of $15.311 million in 2001.

Supply – World production of wool has been falling in the past decade due to the increased use of polyester fabrics. Greasy wool world production in 2007, the latest reporting year for the data series, fell 4.7% yr/yr to a new record low of 2.034 million metric tons. The world's largest producers of greasy wool in 2007 were Australia with 22% of world production, followed by China (19%), and New Zealand (11%).

U.S. wool production of 10,000 metric tons in 2007 accounted for only 0.9% of world production. U.S. production of wool goods fell 15.8% yr/yr in 2008 (9 months annualized) to a record low of 8.0 million yards. That was less that 4% of the record high of 222.5 million yards of wool goods production seen in 1969. The U.S. sheep herd in 2008 fell 4.8% to a new record low of 4.434 million sheep.

Demand – U.S. consumption of apparel wool has dropped sharply, along with production, and it fell 13.5% yr/yr to a record low of 13.333 million pounds in 2006. The breakdown of U.S. mill consumption in 2003, the latest data available, showed that wool usage for carpets was 6.017 million pounds, which was a new record low. Wool usage for apparel production in 2003 was 43.869 million pounds, up +21.8%, up from the 2002 record low of 36.015 million pounds.

Trade – U.S. exports of domestic wool in 2006 (latest data) rose +45.2% yr/yr to 18.000 million pounds. U.S. imports in 2006 rose +17.8% to 7.324 million pounds.

World Production of Wool, Greasy   In Metric Tons

Year	Argentina	Australia	China	Kazakhstan	New Zealand	Pakistan	Rom-ania	Russia	South Africa	United Kingdom	United States	Uruguay	World Total
1998	62,000	689,600	276,759	25,233	265,800	38,500	19,967	47,883	53,045	69,000	22,334	75,503	2,351,701
1999	65,000	687,600	283,152	22,283	252,000	38,700	18,983	40,243	56,032	66,000	21,130	60,293	2,331,342
2000	58,000	671,000	292,502	22,924	257,200	38,900	17,997	39,241	52,671	64,000	21,070	57,218	2,318,945
2001	56,000	657,000	298,254	23,612	236,661	39,200	16,880	39,210	48,649	55,000	19,510	56,744	2,266,377
2002	65,000	587,274	307,588	24,818	228,300	39,430	16,659	41,428	47,502	60,000	18,633	39,376	2,185,911
2003	72,000	551,107	338,058	26,782	229,600	39,700	16,879	44,586	44,156	60,000	17,372	34,922	2,191,770
2004	60,000	509,473	373,902	28,499	217,700	40,000	17,505	47,111	44,156	60,000	17,065	37,271	2,170,613
2005	60,000	519,660	393,172	30,444	215,500	40,000	17,600	48,033	45,000	60,000	16,888	42,009	2,218,612
2006[1]	60,000	438,000	388,777	32,389	224,700	41,020	17,600	49,297	45,000	60,000	17,000	46,709	2,133,404
2007[2]	NA	437,000	395,000	34,172	217,900	41,000	17,700	52,000	45,000	62,000	17,500	50,000	2,034,277

[1] Preliminary.   [2] Estimate.   NA = Not avaliable.   Source: Food and Agriculture Organization of the United Nations (FAO-UN)

Production of Wool Goods[2] in the United States   In Millions of Yards

Year	First Quarter	Second Quarter	Third Quarter	Fourth Quarter	Total	Year	First Quarter	Second Quarter	Third Quarter	Fourth Quarter	Total
1999	25.0	20.9	17.4	14.6	77.9	2004	5.5	5.9	4.2	4.2	19.8
2000	17.9	18.0	13.4	17.4	66.7	2005	4.9	6.9	4.2	4.3	20.3
2001	20.8	12.4	11.0	9.0	53.2	2006	4.1	3.9	2.8	2.8	13.7
2002	7.4	8.6	6.2	5.5	27.7	2007	2.6	2.5	2.2	2.1	9.5
2003	6.5	6.4	5.2	4.9	23.0	2008[1]	2.3	2.1	1.7	1.5	7.5

[1] Preliminary.   [2] Woolen and worsted woven goods, except woven felts.   Source: Bureau of the Census, U.S. Department of Commerce

Consumption of Apparel Wool[2] in the United States   In Millions of Pounds--Clean Basis

Year	First Quarter	Second Quarter	Third Quarter	Fourth Quarter	Total	Year	First Quarter	Second Quarter	Third Quarter	Fourth Quarter	Total
1997	33.1	33.8	30.6	32.8	130.4	2002	11.0	10.5	6.5	W	36.0
1998	29.3	29.6	21.9	17.5	98.4	2003	W	W	W	W	W
1999	17.3	16.8	15.8	13.6	63.5	2004	W	W	W	W	W
2000	17.4	16.1	14.6	13.9	63.0	2005	2.3	5.2	3.9	4.0	15.4
2001	17.0	13.5	11.6	10.9	53.0	2006[1]	3.7	3.8	2.8	3.0	13.3

[1] Preliminary.   [2] Woolen and worsted woven goods, except woven felts.   W = Withheld.   Source: Bureau of the Census, U.S. Department of Commerce

WOOL

Salient Statistics of Wool in the United States

Year	Sheep & Lambs Shorn[4] -1,000's-	Weight per Fleece -In Lbs.-	Shorn Wool Production 1,000 Lbs.	Price per Lb.	Value of Production -$1,000-	Shorn Wool Payment Support -- Cents Per Lb. --	Shorn Payment Rate	Total Wool Production	Raw Wool (Clean Content) Domestic Production	Domestic Wool Exports	Dutiable Imports for Consumption[3] (48's & Finer)	Total New Supply[2]	Duty Free Raw Imports (Not Finer than 46's)	Mill Consumption Apparel	Mill Consumption Carpet
1999	6,158	7.60	46,592	38.0	17,860	----	20.0	46,549	24,575	3,694	21,264	63,955	21,810	63,535	13,950
2000	6,135	7.60	46,446	33.0	15,377	----	40.0	46,446	24,413	6,629	23,902	62,785	21,099	62,041	15,205
2001	5,700	7.60	43,000	36.0	15,311	----	----	43,016	22,712	6,154	15,843	52,128	19,727	52,969	13,310
2002	5,476	7.50	41,322	53.0	21,876	100	18.0	41,078	21,689	8,461	10,526	37,913	14,159	36,015	6,891
2003	5,074	7.50	38,229	73.0	28,126	100	20.0	38,299	20,222	11,067	4,986	29,890	15,749	43,869	6,017
2004	5,073	7.40	37,622	80.0	29,921	100	21.0	37,622	19,864	11,168	6,204	31,355	16,455	NA	NA
2005	5,072	7.30	37,232	71.0	26,272	100	19.0	37,232	19,658	12,422	6,220	25,589	12,156	NA	NA
2006	4,852	7.40	36,019	68.0	24,510	100			19,000	18,000	7,324		9,929	NA	NA
2007[1]	4,657	7.50	34,723	87.0	30,242										

[1] Preliminary. [2] Production minus exports plus imports; stocks not taken into consideration. [3] Apparel wool includes all dutiable wool; carpet wool includes all duty-free wool. [4] Includes sheep shorn at commercial feeding yards.
Source: Economic Research Service, U.S. Department of Agriculture (ERS-USDA)

Shorn Wool Prices   In Dollars Per Pound

Year	US Farm Price Shorn Wool Greasy Basis[1] -- cents/Lb --	Australian Offering Price, Clean[2] Grade 70's type 61	Grade 64's type 63	Grade 62's type 64	Grade 60/62's type 64A	Grade 58's-56's 433-34	Market Indicator[3] Cents/Kg.	Graded Territory Shorn Wool, Clean Basis[4] 62's Staple 3"& up	60's Staple 3"& up	58's Staple 3 1/4"& up	56's Staple 3 1/4"& up	54's Staple 3 1/2"& up
2000	33.0	2.80	1.50	1.69	1.37	1.30	764	1.08	.75	.65	.57	.53
2001	36.0	2.42	1.66	1.69	1.60	1.54	841	1.21	.91	.77	.66	.65
2002	53.0	2.87	2.68	2.70	2.63	2.55	1,051	1.90	1.41	1.40	1.19	1.02
2003	73.0	3.23	3.14	3.16	3.02	2.81	821	2.41	1.73	1.79	1.48	1.24
2004	80.0	3.21	2.75	2.89	2.49	2.33	NA	2.35	1.59	1.74	1.50	1.25
2005	71.0	2.99	2.57	2.65	2.42	2.23	NA	1.86	1.46	1.39	1.41	1.03
2006	68.0	3.17	2.65	2.75	2.47	2.26	NA	1.79	1.45	1.30	1.00	.94
2007	88.0	4.41	3.73	3.90	3.31	2.77	NA	2.65	2.24	1.82	1.32	1.04
2008	NA	4.48	3.57	3.69	3.27	2.79	NA	3.09	2.45	2.25	1.82	1.20

[1] Annual weighted average. [2] F.O.B. Australian Wool Corporation South Carolina warehouse in bond. [3] Index of prices of all wool sold in Australia for the crop year July-June. [4] Wool principally produced in Texas and the Rocky Mountain States.
Source: Economic Research Service, U.S. Department of Agriculture (ERS-USDA)

Average Wool Prices[1] --Australian-- 64's, Type 62, Duty Paid--U.S. Mills   In Cents Per Pound

Year	Jan.	Feb.	Mar.	Apr.	May	June	July	Aug.	Sept.	Oct.	Nov.	Dec.	Average
1999	158	150	157	156	150	149	152	148	139	139	143	137	148
2000	154	146	144	156	156	154	155	151	149	146	140	148	150
2001	160	168	164	158	164	166	167	172	169	159	166	183	166
2002	218	243	250	251	249	259	255	254	268	312	322	328	267
2003	344	346	326	333	296	326	316	308	306	292	285	290	314
2004	304	294	288	281	261	275	277	263	255	255	270	271	275
2005	273	271	268	242	265	266	270	259	252	244	233	236	257
2006	243	256	259	251	258	254	260	260	258	260	308	315	265
2007	352	344	355	367	381	380	378	359	364	393	405	400	373
2008	416	411	407	404	378	376	386	346	317	257	226		357

[1] Raw, clean basis. *Source: Economic Research Service, U.S. Department of Agriculture (ERS-USDA)*

Average Wool Prices --Domestic[1]-- Graded Territory, 64's, Staple 2 3/4 & Up--U.S. Mills   In Cents Per Pound

Year	Jan.	Feb.	Mar.	Apr.	May	June	July	Aug.	Sept.	Oct.	Nov.	Dec.	Average
1999	115	115	115	110	117	122	116	110	105	100	110	95	111
2000	95	95	101	110	125	125	125	120	107	105	105	97	109
2001	95	100	108	129	137	125	127	122	126	130	122	127	121
2002	134	150	170	181	189	200	200	200	198	204	223	233	190
2003	236	260	258	250	223	234	239	243	243	243	232	233	241
2004	233	239	240	240	235	229	233	236	240	236	230	230	235
2005	215	207	200	185	185	185	179	186	195	181	168	140	186
2006	NQ	NQ	162	183	173	171	165	165	165	NQ	212	220	180
2007	186	242	245	279	311	295	285	270	276	NQ	NQ	NQ	265
2008	290	318	319	325	285	295	305	NQ	NQ	NQ	NQ		305

[1] Raw, shorn, clean basis. NQ = No quote. *Source: Economic Research Service, U.S. Department of Agriculture (ERS-USDA)*

Wool (monthly average) through December 2008 — Cents per pound

Wool: Mill Consumption, by Grades in the U.S., Scoured Basis   In Millions of Pounds

| | Apparel Class[1] | | | | | | | | |
| | Woolen System | | | Worsted System | | | | |
Year	60's & Finer	Coarser Than 60's	Total	60's & Finer	Coarser Than 60's	Total	All Total	Carpet Wool[2]
1997	49,038	21,303	70,341	48,153	11,892	60,045	130,386	13,576
1998	31,258	15,079	46,337	42,243	9,793	52,036	98,373	16,331
1999	18,379	10,772	29,151	27,429	6,955	34,384	63,535	13,950
2000	18,503	13,432	31,935	21,732	8,374	30,106	62,041	15,205
2001	16,062	9,849	25,911	NA	NA	27,058	52,969	13,310
2002	9,627	8,482	18,109	NA	NA	17,906	36,015	6,891
2003	6,681	5,309	11,990	NA	NA	31,879	43,869	6,017
2004	NA	NA	NA	NA	NA	NA	NA	NA
2005[3]	NA	NA	NA	NA	NA	NA	NA	NA
2006[4]	NA	NA	NA	NA	NA	NA	NA	NA

[1] Domestic & duty-paid foreign.   [2] Duty-free foreign.   [3] Preliminary.   [4] Estimate.   NA = Not available.   *Source: Economic Research Service, U.S. Department of Agriculture (ERS-USDA)*

United States Imports[2] of Unmanufactured Wool (Clean Yield)   In Millions of Pounds

Year	Jan.	Feb.	Mar.	Apr.	May	June	July	Aug.	Sept.	Oct.	Nov.	Dec.	Total
1999	6.2	3.6	3.9	7.9	3.5	3.0	3.7	3.1	2.6	3.8	2.8	2.5	46.3
2000	4.9	3.8	3.8	4.6	5.1	2.7	3.2	3.7	4.3	3.2	3.5	2.4	45.0
2001	4.9	4.3	4.3	1.5	2.9	2.8	4.0	1.9	2.0	2.8	1.3	1.3	34.1
2002	1.9	1.8	2.6	2.4	2.3	1.5	1.6	1.2	1.9	2.4	2.1	3.1	24.6
2003	2.5	2.8	2.3	2.2	2.1	1.8	1.2	1.1	0.8	1.6	1.1	1.2	20.8
2004	1.3	1.5	2.1	1.8	1.4	2.8	1.6	1.9	2.7	2.4	1.9	1.2	22.7
2005	2.3	1.1	2.0	1.5	1.5	2.0	1.5	1.4	1.0	1.7	1.5	1.0	18.4
2006	1.9	1.0	1.8	1.5	1.3	1.6	0.9	1.5	1.2	1.5	1.6	1.6	17.3
2007	1.3	1.1	1.4	1.4	1.4	1.3	1.1	0.9	0.8	1.0	1.3	1.0	14.3
2008[1]	1.8	0.9	1.4	1.1	1.3	1.1	1.3	0.8	1.2	1.0	0.7	0.7	13.2

[1] Preliminary.   [2] Data are imports for consumption.   *Source: Economic Research Service, U.S. Department of Agriculture (ERS-USDA)*

Zinc

Zinc (symbol Zn) is a bluish-white metallic element that is the 24th most abundant element in the earth's crust. Zinc is never found in its pure state but rather in zinc oxide, zinc silicate, zinc carbonate, zinc sulfide, and in minerals such as zincite, hemimorphite, smithsonite, franklinite, and sphalerite. Zinc is utilized as a protective coating for other metals, such as iron and steel, in a process known as galvanizing. Zinc is used as an alloy with copper to make brass and also as an alloy with aluminum and magnesium. There are, however, a number of substitutes for zinc in chemicals, electronics, and pigments. For example, with aluminum, steel and plastics can substitute for galvanized sheets. Aluminum alloys can also replace brass. Zinc is used as the negative electrode in dry cell (flashlight) batteries and also in the zinc-mercuric-oxide battery cell, which is the round, flat battery typically used in watches, cameras, and other electronic devices. Zinc is also used in medicine as an antiseptic ointment.

Zinc futures and options are traded on the London Metals Exchange (LME). The LME zinc futures contract calls for the delivery of 25 metric tons of at least 99.995% purity zinc ingots (slabs and plates). The contract trades in terms of U.S. dollars per metric ton. Zinc first started trading on the LME in 1915.

Prices – Zinc prices in 2008 fell 43.2% to a monthly average of 88.71 cents per pound, down from the 2006 record high of 158.44 cents per pound.

Supply – World smelter production of zinc in 2008 rose +3.7% to 11.300 million metric tons, which was a new record high. The world's largest producer of zinc is China with 28% of world smelter production, followed by Australia with 13%, and Canada with 6%. U.S. smelter production accounted for only 2.5% of world production in 2006. Australia's production rose rapidly in the 1999-2002 period but the 2006 level of 496,000 metric tons was below the record high of 573,000 metric tons seen in 2002. China's production of 3.1 million metric tons in 2006 was more than five times its production level of 550,000 metric tons seen in 1990. U.S. zinc smelter production in 2006 of 269,000 metric tons was less than half of its production of 796,300 metric tons seen in 1970.

U.S. mine production of recoverable zinc in 2008 rose +11.9% yr/yr to an annualized (through April) level of 832,200 metric tons. U.S. production in 2008 of slab zinc on a primary basis rose by +0.8% yr/yr to 122,000 metric tons, while secondary production fell -4.5% yr/yr to 150,000 metric tons.

Demand – U.S. consumption of slab zinc in 2008 fell by -3.8% yr/yr to a 17-year low of 1,010 million metric tons. U.S. consumption of all classes of zinc fell by -14.5% yr/yr in 2007 to 1.180 million metric tons, which was a new 16-year low. U.S. consumption of slab zinc by fabricators in 2008 (annualized through April) fell by 15.2% yr/yr to 237,600 metric tons, which was a new record low.

The breakdown of consumption by industries for 2006 (latest data) showed that 51% of slab zinc consumption was for galvanizers, 8% for brass products, and the rest for other miscellaneous industries. The consumption breakdown by grades for 2006 showed that 63% was for special high grade, 15% for prime western, 15% for re-melt and other, and14% for high grade. Within that grade breakdown, prime Western consumption has fallen by nearly half in the past 6 years.

Trade – The U.S. in 2009 relied on imports for 73% of its consumption of zinc, up sharply from the 35% average seen in the 1990s. U.S. imports for consumption of slab zinc fell by -18.6 yr/yr to 693,000 metric tons in 2007, while imports of zinc ore fell by -29.2% yr/yr to 271,000 metric tons. The dollar value of U.S. zinc imports in 2007 rose by +11.1% yr/yr to a record high of $3.080 billion. The breakdown of imports in 2007 shows that most zinc is imported as blocks, pigs and slabs (758,000 metric tons); followed by ores (271,000 metric tons); dust, powder and flakes (31,300 metric tons); waste and scrap (21,800 metric tons); dross, ashes and fume (18,600 metric tons); and sheets, plates and other (2,160 metric tons).

Salient Statistics of Zinc in the United States   In Metric Tons

Year	Slab Zinc Production Primary	Secondary	Mine Production Recovered	Imports for Consumption Slab Zinc	Ore (Zinc Content)	Exports Slab Zinc	Ore (Zinc Content)	Consumption Slab Consumed Zinc	as Ore	All Classes³	Net Import Reliance As a % of Apparent Consumption	High-Grade, Price -Cents/Lb.-
1999	241,000	131,000	808,000	1,060,000	74,600	1,880	531,000	1,430,000	----	1,700,000	30	53.48
2000	228,000	143,000	805,000	915,000	52,800	2,770	523,000	1,330,000	----	1,630,000	60	55.61
2001	203,000	108,000	799,000	813,000	84,000	1,180	696,000	1,150,000	----	1,420,000	60	43.96
2002	182,000	113,000	754,000	874,000	122,000	1,160	822,000	1,170,000	----	1,420,000	60	38.64
2003	187,000	150,000	768,000	758,000	164,000	1,680	841,000	1,120,000	----	1,390,000	58	40.63
2004	194,000	156,000	739,000	812,000	231,000	3,300	745,000	1,250,000	----	1,430,000	72	52.47
2005	195,000	156,000	748,000	668,000	156,000	784	786,000	1,080,000	----	1,290,000	67	67.14
2006	113,000	156,000	727,000	851,000	383,000	2,530	825,000	1,150,000	----	1,390,000	78	158.89
2007¹	121,000	157,000	803,000	693,000	271,000	11,000	816,000	1,050,000	----	1,180,000	74	154.40
2008²	122,000	150,000	770,000		44,000		851,000	1,010,000	----		73	89.00

¹ Preliminary.   ² Estimate.   ³ Based on apparent consumption of slab zinc plus zinc content of ores and concentrates and secondary materials used to make zinc dust and chemicals.   *Source: U.S. Geological Survey (USGS)*

World Smelter Production of Zinc[3]   In Thousands of Metric Tons

Year	Australia	Belgium	Canada	China	France	Germany	Italy	Japan	Kazak-hstan	Mexico	Spain	United States	World Total
1999	348.5	232.4	776.9	1,700.0	333.1	333.0	152.8	683.6	249.3	218.9	393.0	371.0	8,550
2000	494.5	251.7	779.9	1,980.0	350.0	327.5	170.3	698.8	262.2	235.1	386.3	371.0	9,020
2001	558.5	259.3	661.2	2,040.0	347.0	358.3	177.8	684.1	277.1	303.8	418.0	311.0	9,320
2002	573.0	260.0	793.4	2,100.0	350.0	378.6	176.0	673.9	286.3	302.1	488.0	362.0	9,840
2003	559.0	244.0	761.2	2,320.0	268.0	388.1	123.0	686.1	279.0	320.4	519.0	351.0	9,980
2004	479.0	263.0	805.4	2,720.0	268.0	382.0	130.0	667.2	316.5	316.9	525.0	350.0	10,500
2005	463.3	257.0	723.0	2,780.0	210.0	334.9	121.0	675.2	356.9	327.2	501.0	351.0	10,400
2006	496.0	219.8	730.0	3,100.0	210.0	300.0	109.0	654.2	300.0	350.0	500.0	269.0	10,600
2007[1]	1,520.0		620.0	2,900.0					390.0	430.0			10,900
2008[2]	1,510.0		660.0	3,200.0					420.0	460.0			11,300

[1] Preliminary.   [2] Estimate.   [3] Secondary metal included.   *Source: U.S. Geological Survey (USGS)*

Consumption (Reported) of Slab Zinc in the United States, by Industries and Grades   In Metric Tons

			----- By Industries -----				----- By Grades -----			
Year	Total	Galvanizers	Brass Products	Zinc-Base Alloy[3]	Zinc Oxide	Other	Special High Grade	High Grade	Remelt and Other	Prime Western
1997	672,000	347,000	76,800	107,000	[4]	141,000	319,000	88,700	57,200	207,000
1998	647,000	320,000	60,300	122,000	[4]	145,000	331,000	72,800	51,700	192,000
1999	614,000	308,000	78,200	105,000	[4]	124,000	317,000	58,400	55,400	184,000
2000	640,000	293,000	82,800	123,000	[4]	NA	332,000	60,600	41,500	206,000
2001	543,000	281,000	74,400	91,200	[4]	NA	294,000	54,000	30,300	165,000
2002	496,000	265,000	86,800	103,000	[4]	NA	294,000	61,400	28,000	113,000
2003	506,000	264,000	87,400	113,000	[4]	NA	310,000	60,000	27,600	109,000
2004	510,000	248,000	96,700	W	[4]	NA	321,000	58,800	33,600	96,200
2005[1]	486,000	238,000	83,900	W	[4]	NA	316,000	62,100	40,300	68,000
2006[2]	504,000	259,000	42,300	W	[4]	203,000	315,000	69,100	73,900	75,400

[1] Preliminary.   [2] Estimated.   [3] Die casters.   [4] Included in other.   W = Withheld.   NA = Not applicable.   *Source: U.S. Geological Survey (USGS)*

United States Foreign Trade of Zinc   In Metric Tons

		----- Imports for Consumption -----						Zinc Ore & Manufactures Exported						
								Blocks, Pigs, Anodes, etc.		Wrought & Alloys				Zinc Ore & Con-centrates
Year	Ores[1]	Blocks, Pigs, Slabs	Sheets, Plates, Other	Waste & Scrap	Dross, Ashes, Fume	Dust, Powder & Flakes	Total Value $1,000	Un-wrought	Un-wrought Alloys	Sheets, Plates & Strips	Angles, Bars, Rods, etc.	Waste & Scrap	Dust (Blue Powder)	
1998	46,300	879,000	16,900	29,200	----	17,600	1,098,690	----	----	----	----	35,000	5,530	552,000
1999	74,600	1,060,000	22,600	26,600	20,000	21,300	1,133,890	----	----	----	----	28,200	5,050	531,000
2000	52,800	915,000	9,380	36,500	15,500	26,700	1,272,750	----	----	----	----	36,100	4,830	523,000
2001	84,000	813,000	7,240	39,300	12,000	26,700	937,110	----	----	----	----	44,000	4,690	696,000
2002	122,000	874,000	1,640	31,200	15,500	30,900	887,785	----	----	----	----	47,700	5,660	822,000
2003	164,000	758,000	1,790	10,300	14,100	27,400	839,705	----	----	----	----	50,200	6,550	841,000
2004	231,000	812,000	2,500	10,800	16,100	24,800	1,142,733	----	----	----	----	53,900	7,640	745,000
2005	156,000	668,000	3,630	9,580	15,800	23,400	1,198,040	----	----	----	----	56,000	9,310	786,000
2006[2]	383,000	895,000	2,050	14,200	31,100	30,100	2,771,580	----	----	----	----	83,800	16,400	825,000
2007[3]	271,000	758,000	2,160	21,800	18,600	31,300	3,079,910	----	----	----	----	102,000	36,600	816,000

[1] Zinc content.   [2] Preliminary.   [3] Estimate.   *Source: U.S. Geological Survey (USGS)*

Mine Production of Recoverable Zinc in the United States   In Thousands of Metric Tons

Year	Jan.	Feb.	Mar.	Apr.	May	June	July	Aug.	Sept.	Oct.	Nov.	Dec.	Total
1999	61.4	57.6	63.0	67.0	61.7	62.8	68.2	72.1	60.8	67.8	61.2	65.9	808.0
2000	64.4	56.6	68.5	64.5	70.2	65.3	68.1	71.4	59.6	62.3	63.5	67.2	814.0
2001	68.4	60.5	62.2	65.2	66.9	66.1	66.7	67.6	60.9	67.1	54.0	55.4	799.0
2002	61.3	60.4	67.8	55.2	63.4	63.8	66.0	67.2	54.4	68.3	61.3	65.5	754.6
2003	65.2	60.2	62.7	54.0	65.2	64.0	64.5	59.6	63.3	58.6	61.0	60.5	738.8
2004	60.4	55.3	57.9	58.5	56.1	59.0	60.8	62.0	61.6	61.6	56.8	56.5	706.5
2005	53.6	56.0	64.1	56.7	53.3	64.6	64.5	68.9	61.8	64.4	51.2	62.3	721.4
2006	58.1	51.4	61.5	54.2	54.3	59.8	64.7	62.3	65.8	66.3	51.5	47.4	697.3
2007	60.3	55.8	63.5	56.6	61.2	64.1	63.1	69.5	61.3	64.6	53.9	69.6	743.5
2008[1]	72.4	67.3	72.1	65.6									832.2

[1] Preliminary.   *Source: U.S. Geological Survey (USGS)*

ZINC

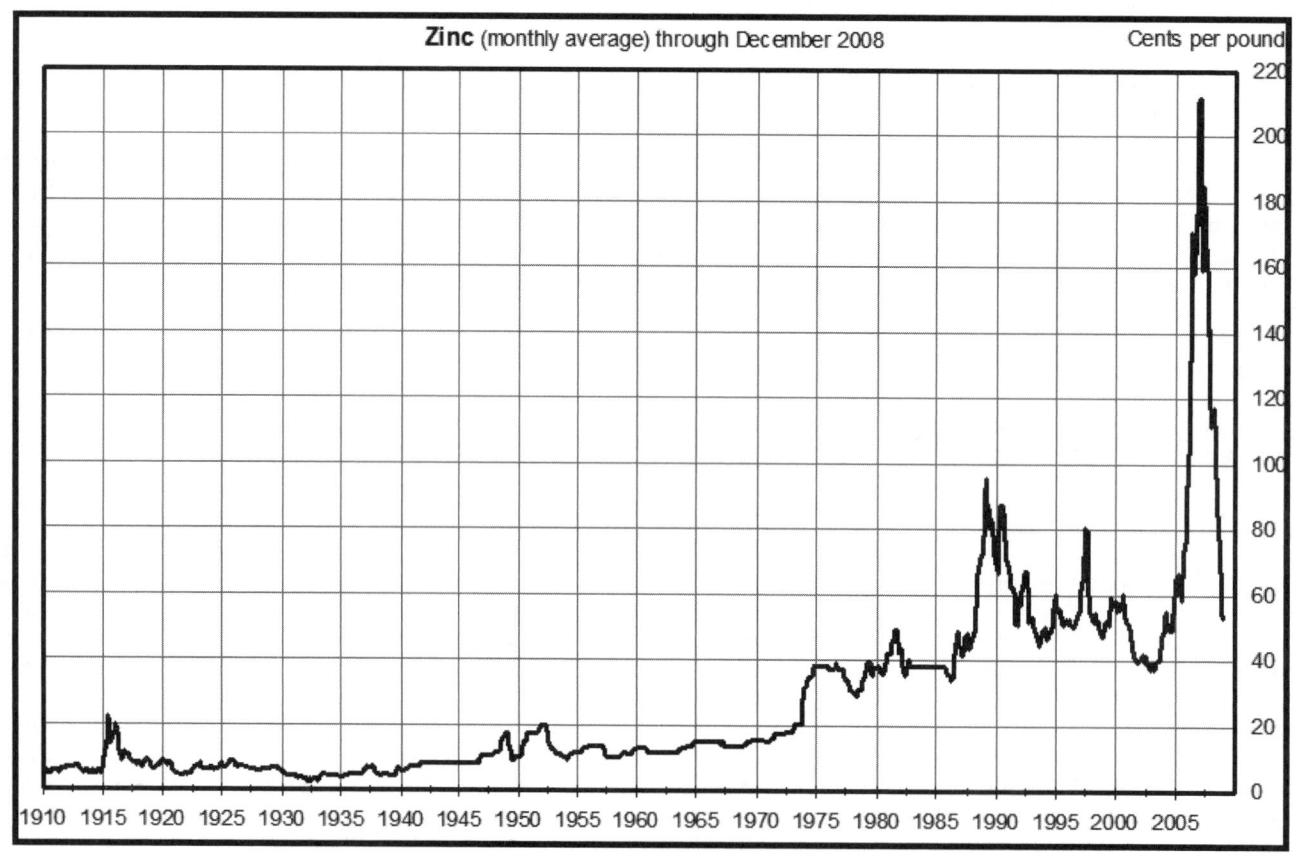

Zinc (monthly average) through December 2008 — Cents per pound

Consumption of Slab Zinc by Fabricators in the United States   In Thousands of Metric Tons

Year	Jan.	Feb.	Mar.	Apr.	May	June	July	Aug.	Sept.	Oct.	Nov.	Dec.	Total
1999	40.5	45.4	43.8	40.3	42.5	47.1	37.8	40.1	42.0	42.8	41.1	39.7	614.0
2000	41.8	44.6	47.7	45.6	44.4	49.1	42.0	43.3	42.6	47.5	43.8	40.2	640.0
2001	45.4	43.5	44.1	42.7	43.6	38.2	30.6	39.2	37.7	35.7	32.1	27.3	543.0
2002	31.2	31.3	30.4	33.1	34.9	34.4	34.3	35.8	36.1	36.1	32.7	33.3	403.6
2003	33.1	33.1	34.4	35.2	34.7	38.2	34.2	35.5	36.8	36.8	35.3	36.4	423.7
2004	35.1	36.2	36.6	36.7	35.9	37.0	33.7	33.6	33.8	34.6	34.3	33.4	420.9
2005	33.6	33.9	34.1	33.5	33.8	34.1	31.3	33.7	34.8	34.7	33.8	34.1	405.4
2006	34.8	34.5	34.8	34.0	33.1	34.2	32.4	33.4	31.4	32.8	32.0	32.4	399.8
2007	33.0	23.1	22.3	23.1	22.7	23.5	22.3	22.7	23.2	23.4	23.4	17.4	280.1
2008[1]	19.7	19.8	21.6	18.1									237.6

[1] Preliminary.   *Source: U.S. Geological Survey (USGS)*

Average Price of Zinc, Prime Western Slab (Delivered U.S. Basis)   In Cents Per Pound

Year	Jan.	Feb.	Mar.	Apr.	May	June	July	Aug.	Sept.	Oct.	Nov.	Dec.	Average
1999	47.29	51.11	51.68	51.07	52.20	50.35	53.73	56.28	59.12	57.07	56.91	58.75	53.84
2000	58.44	54.67	55.60	56.14	57.44	55.67	56.52	58.04	60.53	54.67	53.07	53.00	56.15
2001	51.82	51.29	50.55	48.95	47.54	45.56	43.62	42.53	41.14	39.53	39.99	39.25	45.15
2002	40.98	39.97	42.15	41.66	39.97	39.70	41.01	38.91	39.26	39.08	36.99	38.52	39.64
2003	38.88	38.46	38.48	36.99	37.86	38.57	40.30	39.77	39.84	43.44	44.11	47.60	40.36
2004	49.61	53.31	54.63	51.89	51.88	51.53	49.85	49.31	49.37	53.36	54.61	58.32	52.31
2005	61.10	64.57	66.59	63.55	60.70	61.97	58.26	62.76	67.73	72.10	77.60	87.45	67.03
2006	100.02	106.57	116.10	147.28	170.57	158.11	163.89	164.23	166.56	185.80	210.32	211.82	158.44
2007	183.91	161.21	158.81	171.08	184.68	173.23	169.81	155.93	139.28	140.84	122.63	112.65	156.17
2008	111.49	115.37	117.27	107.07	102.59	89.16	87.44	81.53	81.83	62.25	55.26	53.22	88.71

Source: American Metal Market (AMM)

CRB Yearbook CD

Table of Contents

CRB Yearbooks CD Copyright © Commodity Research Bureau All rights reserved.

QuickSearch is a trademark of dataDisc, Inc.
Segments of this manual reprinted with permission by dataDisc, Inc.

Factual information contained in the CRB Yearbooks CD has been obtained from sources believed to be reliable but are not necessarily inclusive and are not guaranteed in any way and should not be construed as a representation by us.

Chapter 1: Installation

Installing QuickSearch

To run QuickSearch, you will need:
• A computer with a 120 Mhz or faster processor, running any current Windows 2000® XP® Vista® or Macintosh operating system running Parallels or Boot Camp
• At least 32 MB of total RAM installed on your computer; for best performance, we recommend at least 64 MB
• A CD-ROM drive

To Install:
1) Place the disc in the CD-ROM drive. If installation does not start automatically proceed to step 2.
2) Click Start; Select Run
3) Type D:\Autoplay, where D is the letter representing your CD-ROM drive. Press the enter key and follow the instructions.

Chapter 2: Searching and Browsing

Selecting Text to Search

Searches can be conducted across all the text in a *QuickSearch* document (full-text), restricted to a specific field (fielded search), or restricted to a selected table of contents section.

Everywhere in text - searches the full text of the *QuickSearch* document (except for user-defined notes and bookmarks). Choose **Everywhere in text** in the Search dialog box to specify a full-text search.

Fielded Search - searches a specific field and ignores all text outside of that field. To specify a fielded search:

1) Click **Selected field** under **Select where to search**.
2) Select a field from the list of available fields.

Current Table of Contents section - restricts a research only to a Table of Contents (TOC) section.

1) Click the TOC section in the TOC window.
2) Click the Search button on the toolbar OR select Search/Search from the main menu.
3) Click *Current Table of Contents section* under *Select where to search*.

Note: Search results will represent the selected TOC Section and its sublevels.

Types of Searches

Search for Phrase
Type an exact phrase you wish to find, e.g. "Business is the key." Use quotation marks around the search text to distinguish a *phrase search* from a *word search* or choose *Search for phrase* in the **Search/More>>** dialog box. The QuickSearch default setting is a phrase search.

Search for Words
Two types of word searches may be conducted - single words or words in proximity as determined by **Search Operators**. To conduct a word search, choose *Search for word(s)* in the **Search/More>>** dialog box.

1) **Single Word** - Enter any single word, e.g. BUSINESS, to find all occurrences in the document.

2) **Words in Proximity** - Enter any series of words that you wish to find near each other (e.g. BUSINESS INCREASE). Before conducting a *proximity search*, define a search range/proximity in the **Search/ More>>** dialog box. The default setting is 4 words. A typical sentence has 10 words, a typical paragraph has 25 words, and a typical page has 500 words.

Refine Last Search

The **Refine last search** feature can be used to modify your most recent search. (See the Advanced Searching section of this chapter.)

Search Operators

Boolean, wildcard and phrase search operators are available by selecting **MORE>>** in the **Search** dialog box. Double-click on any operator to add it to the Search command line *or* type the operator in the **Type the text to find** box.

To see example of each operator:
- Click the **Search** button and then the **More>>** button.
OR
- Select **Search/Search** from the main menu and **More>>**.
- Click once on the operator you wish to view.

The following operators are available for a word search:

AND (&) - BUSINESS AND INCREASE - Returns all occurrences of BUSINESS and INCREASE in the specified search range that are near each other. "Near" is defined using the Word Proximity setting in the **Search/ More>>** dialog box.

OR (|) - BUSINESS OR INCREASE - Returns all occurrences of the words in the specified search range without regard to proximity.

NOT (~) - BUSINESS NOT INCREASE - Returns all occurrences of the word BUSINESS that are not near the word INCREASE in the specified search range. "Near" is defined using the Word Proximity setting in the **Search/ More>>** dialog box.

Wildcard (*) - Use the asterisk (*) at the end of any part of a word to represent any character or combination of characters. For example, BUSI* may return hits such as *business, businesses, busing*, and *Businowski*. The wildcard operator cannot be used in a phrase search.

Conducting a Search

Basic Searching

1) Click the Search button on the Reader toolbar OR select Search/Search from the main menu.
2) In the **Search** dialog box, select where to search choosing one of the following:
- Everywhere in text
- Selected field*
- Current Table of Contents

*Note: Click a field or a TOC entry before choosing Selected field or Current Table of Contents section.

3) Type the search text (word, words within proximity or phrase) in the *Type the text to find* box or double click on any entry in the **Word Wheel** to select it as search text.
4) Click **Search** in the dialog box. "Hits" will be highlighted in the text and displayed in context in a separate **Hit List** window. The number of hits also will be displayed on the status bar at the bottom of the screen.

Advanced Searching

Search for Words

1) Begin a search by completing steps 1-3 of a Basic Search.
2) Select **More>>** to expand the Search dialog box and change to a *Search for Word(s)* and/or select other **Search Operators** which alter the nature of the search to be conducted. A *Search for Phrase* is conducted unless you select another type of search.
3) Specify the **Word Proximity** in the **Search/ More>>** dialog box, if you are conducting an AND or NOT search. The default proximity is 4 words.
4) Click **Search** in the dialog box. "Hits" will be highlighted in the text and displayed in context in a separate **Hit List** window. The number of hits also will be displayed on the status bar at the bottom of the screen.

Refine Last Search

To refine the last research:
1) Begin a search by completing steps 1-3 of a Basic Search. Click the **More>>** button on the **Search** dialog box to access all search parameters.
2) Click the **Refine last search** box in the lower left corner of the **Search** dialog box.
3) Select the **Boolean** operator to be applied to the refined search (just to the right of the *Refine last search* check box).
4) Preview the format for the refined search in the *Refined Search box* at the bottom of the **Search** dialog box.
5) Type the **[New text to Find]** word(s) in the *Type the text to find box* at the top of the **Search** dialog box.
6) Click **Search**.

Example:

Your first search in the Constitution was for the word "House." If you want to narrow the search results to include only hits of "House" which are not near "senate," you can return to the **Search** dialog box, select **Refine last search**, select the *NOT* operator, specify the word proximity, type "Senate" in the *Type the text* to find box at the top of the **Search** dialog box and click the **Search** button. The **Hit List** will display only hits of "House" which were not located near "Senate" ("near" depends on the proximity that you specified). The final search command would look as follows:

(House) ~ (Senate)

This search could be further refined by selecting **Refine last search** and repeating the steps above.

Example:

If you want to find only occurrences of "House *NOT* Senate" which are near "Representative," return to the Search dialog box, select **Refine last search**, select the *AND* operator, specify the word proximity, type "Representatives" in the Type the text to find box at the top of the **Search** dialog box and click on the **Search** button. The **Hit List** would display only hits of "House" which were near "Representatives" but not located near "Senate" ("near" depends on the proximity that you specified). The final search command would look as follows:

[(House) ~ (Senate)] & (Representatives)

Search Results

Browsing Search Results

Hit List

After conducting a search, each occurrence of the e search text in the document will be displayed in context in a separate **Hit List** window. Double click on any entry in the **Hit List** to move to the corresponding section of text.

Highlighted Hits in the Text

After conducting a search, each occurrence of the search text is highlighted in the text of the document.

1) Click the **First/Previous/Next/Last (Hit)** buttons to move between highlighted hits in the text.
2) The number of the current hit being viewed and the total number of hits are displayed in the Status bar at the bottom of the screen.

Removing the Hit List

1) Click the **Clear** button on the toolbar **OR** select **Search/Clear Search** from the main menu to remove the current **Hit List** window and the highlighting from the hits in the text.
2) Turn off the **Hit List** for future searches by selecting **Edit/Preferences** to open the **Document Preferences** dialog box. Click the **Reader** tab to open **Reader Preferences**. Deselect *Show Hit List?*.

Reader Preferences

Select **Edit/Preferences** from the main menu to open the **Document Preference** dialog box. The box includes three tabs: **Reader**, **Author**, and **Stopper Word List**.

Reader Preferences include:

CD-ROM Drive Letter

Every CD-ROM player is assigned a drive letter. (It is usually the last drive letter after your other drives.)

Default Word Search Proximity

Set the default proximity (the number of words between selected words) to be applied in multiple word (non-phrase) searches.

Show Hit List?

Click **Show Hit List?** to open a **Hit List** automatically after conducting a Search. The Hit List shows "hits" - items found - when you do a search. Browse hits by clicking the **Next/Previous Hit** buttons on the toolbar or selecting **Search/Search** from the main menu. All hits will be highlighted in the text even if a **Hit List** is not activated.

TOC Window Color

Click the **TOC Window Color** button to open a dialog box containing table of Contest background color options. Select from a present color chart, or create a custom color and select it. Click **OK**.
SAVE YOUR DOCUMENT after you select preferences!

Table of Contents Browsing

Hyperlinks

The Table of Contents (TOC) provides a convenient method for accessing any section of the *QuickSearch* document. Each TOC entry is hyper-linked to the corresponding section of text; just click on an entry and *QuickSearch* automatically will move the corresponding section to the text window.

Multiple Levels

QuickSearch TOC's may include up to 32 levels. If there are sublevels in a TOC section, a "+" will appear in front of the TOC entry. To open the next level, click on the "+".

Automatic Tracing

As you move through a *QuickSearch* document (scroll, Next Hit, Previous Hit, etc.) the Table of Contents will "track" your location in the document automatically. A box outline indicates the current TOC section.

Chapter 3: Viewing Images

A *QuickSearch* document may contain *hyperlinked* or *embedded* images. Different methods are used for finding and viewing each type of image

Finding Images

Finding Hyperlinked Images

You can find hyperlinked images in a QuickSearch document by using any of the following options:
- **List** of images
- **Next/Previous Image** buttons or menu selections
- **Search** feature
- **Special formatting**/camera icon

Image List - Open a comprehensive list of hyperlinked images in the document.
1) Click the **Image List** button on the Toolbar **OR** select **Search/Image List** from the main menu.
2) Double click on an image title in the **Image List** to open the image.

Browsing Images - You can browse through images using the **Next/Previous Image** buttons or menu selections.
1) Select **Nest/Previous Image** buttons **OR** Search/ First (Nest, Previous, Last) Image from the main menu.
2) The **Next and Previous Image** buttons or menu selections move the reader sequentially through images in the document.
3) The **First** and **Last Image** menu selections move only to the first or last image in the document.

Searching for Words in Hyperlinked Image Titles - As each hyper-linked image file is added to a *QuickSearch* document, it is given an *Image Title*. The Image Title appears with an optional camera icon at the point you have chosen in the text window. The Image Title is indexed with other text and may be found using a word or phrase search (see Chapter 1 - *Searching & Browsing*).

Look for Special Formatting/Camera Icon – Hyper-linked images can be found by looking for words that have special formatting (the default is double-underlined text). Double click on the specially formatted text to open the image. A camera icon may precede the specially formatted image title. The image can also be opened by clicking on the camera icon.

Finding Embedded Images

Embedded images appear in the text at the point you have chosen. They may be found by:
- Scrolling through text
- Conducting a search for words/phrases that appear near the image.

Scrolling for an Embedded Image

Use the vertical scroll bar to scan text and locate embedded images.

Searching for an Embedded Image*

Search for text that has been placed near an image and marked as hidden.

*Note: **Titles of embedded images will *NOT* appear on an Image List**. The Image List feature is only for hyper-linked images.

Zooming Hyper-linked Images

Marquee Image Zooming*

Marquee Image Zooming allows you to select a portion of a **hyper-linked image** and enlarge it to the size of the image window. *QuickSearch* allows you to zoom to a single pixel.
*Note: Marquee Image Zooming **is available *ONLY* for hyper-linked images**.

1) Click a hyperlinked image title or camera icon to open the image window.
2) Click on and hold the left mouse button and drag a box around the image area you want to enlarge.
3) When the area is defined, release the mouse button. The area selected will fill the Image Window.
4) Steps 2 and 3 may be repeated to continuing zooming.
5) To return the image to its original size, click once on the image with the left mouse button.

Image Panning

Image Panning allows you to use the horizontal/ vertical scroll bars* to move around a **hyperlinked** image that has been enlarged by Marquee zooming.
Click an arrow on the scroll bar **OR** click and drag the horizontal or vertical scroll bar button to move the image across the screen.
*Note: **Scroll bars do not appear on-screen until an image has been zoomed**.

Scale to Gray

Some 1 bit (black & white) hyperlinked images can be sharpened by using the **Scale to Gray** feature. **Scale to Gray** will fill in missing pixels to improve the quality of an image. This feature is particularly useful for viewing scanned document images.

To use Scale to Gray:
1) Open a hyperlinked image
2) Select **View/Scale to Gray** from the main menu
3) **Scale to Gray** will remain active until it is deselected.

Chapter 4: Printing

The **Print** feature will print text and images in the following forms:
- Highlighted lines or blocks of text
- Selected Tables of Contents section(s)
- Search results ("hit" lists)
- Embedded images
- Hyper-linked images
- Zoomed portions of Hyper-linked images

Print Hints

Highlighted text, images and TOC sections will print in order as they are found in the document.

The printed size of Zoomed and Hyper-linked images may vary between portrait and landscape page orientation settings (found via **File/Print Setup**).

You can print *multiple* TOC sections by:
- Using the **Shift** key to select a series of adjacent TOCs.
- Using the **CTRL** key to individually select specific TOCs.
- Using the **Shift** and **CTRL** keys alternately to select specific TOC groupings.

Printing specifications can be set from the Windows Print Manager utility.
Make **Print Setup** modifications *before* you **Print**.

Printing Text or Images

To Print portions of a document:
1) Highlight lines and/or block(s) of text.
2) Click the **Print** button on the toolbar.
OR
Select the **File/Print** from the main menu.
OR
Press **CTRL+P**.

To Print a *Single* TOC section:
1) Click the TOC heading in the **Table of Contents** window.
2) Click the **Print** button on the toolbar.
OR
Select the **File/Print TOC selection(s)** from the main menu.
OR
Click the **right mouse** button and select **Print TOC selection(s)**.
OR
Press **CTRL+P**.
*Note: All the sublevels in the TOC section will be printed.

To Print Multiple TOC sections:
1) Click the first TOC section you want to print from the **Table of Contents** window.
2) Press and hold the **CTRL** key while you click the order TOC sections you want to print. They do not have to be adjacent.
3) When you have finished selecting TOCs, click the **Print** button on the toolbar.
OR
Select **File/Print TOC selection(s)** from the main menu.
OR
Click the **right mouse** button and select **Print TOC selection(s)**.
OR
Press **CTRL+P**.

To Print adjacent TOC sections:
1) Click the *first* TOC section you want to print from the **Table of Contents** window.
2) Press and hold the **Shift** key, and click the last TOC section in the series (all TOC sections between the first and last will be selected automatically).
3) Click the **Print** button on the toolbar.
OR
Select **File/Print TOC selection** from the main menu.
OR
Click the **right mouse** button and select **Print TOC selection(s)**.
OR
Press **CTRL+P**.

*Note: **Multiple TOC Selection functions (highlighting using the** Shift **and/or** CTRL **keys) can be used in combination to select specific TOC groupings**.

To Print Embedded Images:
1) Highlight (double click) the embedded image(s) you want ant to print.
2) Click the **Print** button on the Toolbar.
OR
Select **File/Print** from the main menu.
OR
Press **CTRL+P**.

To Print a Hyperlinked Image:
You can print a **Hyperlinked Image** or a zoomed portion of a Hyperlinked Image.
1) Open the image by double clicking the **Image title** and/or the **camera icon**.
OR
Click the Image List button on the toolbar and double click the Image title from the list.
2) Click the Print button on the Toolbar.
OR
Select File/Print from the main menu.
OR
Press **CTRL+P**.

Print Setup

The Print Setup option allows you to select printer type, page orientation, paper size, paper source, and printer properties (paper, graphics, fonts, device options). Make these selections **before** you print.

To change the Print Setup:
1)   Select **File/Print Setup** from the main menu.
2)   In the **Print Setup** dialog box, click the down arrow in the **Name** pull down menu, select a printer type and enter it in the **Name** window (or click **Network** to access Network printer options).
3)   To select new printer properties select **Properties** and make modifications.
4)   Select **Landscape** or **Portrait**.
5)   Select **OK** to exit.

Page Layout

You can adjust the top, bottom, left, and right margins of a printed page as follows:
1)   Select **File/Page Layout** from the main menu.
2)   In the **Page Parameters** dialog box, set margins (in inches) and click **OK**.

Chapter 5: User Annotations

The reader may customize a *QuickSearch* document by adding "margin" Bookmarks and Notes.

Annotate functions enable the reader to make customized **Bookmarks** in the text and make private, unsearchable comments about a document with **Notes**. The **Bookmark** feature enables the reader to "save his place," while the **Notes** feature allows the reader to "write in the margins" of the text.

Using Bookmarks

To add a Bookmark to a document:
1)   Highlight a portion of text or place the cursor where you would like to add the Bookmark.
2)   Click on the **Bookmark** icon on the Reader toolbar **OR** select **Annotate/Bookmark** from the main menu or select **Insert Bookmark** from the **right mouse** button menu. If text has been highlighted, it is shown in the **Edit Bookmark/Name** text box. If not, enter a name for the bookmark in the text box.
3)   Click **Add** to place the selected text in the **Current Bookmarks** list.
4)   Click **Go to** to scroll text to the point where the bookmark appears.
5)   Click **Close** to close the Bookmark dialog box.

To go to a Bookmark:
1)   Click on the **Bookmark** button on the toolbar **OR** select **Insert Bookmark** from the **right mouse** button menu to open the list of Current Bookmarks.
2)   Highlight the bookmark you want to move to in the text.
3)   Click **Go to**. The selected text will move to the top of the text window.

To edit a Bookmark:
1)   Click on the **Bookmark** icon on the toolbar **OR** select **Annotate/Bookmark** from the main menu **OR** select **Insert Bookmark** from the **right mouse** button menu to open the dialog box containing current bookmarks.
2)   In the **Current Bookmarks** list, click on the bookmark you wish to edit. It will appear in the **Edit Bookmark/Name** window.
3)   Make changes and click **Add**.

To remove a Bookmark:
1)   Click the **Bookmark** icon on the Reader toolbar or select **Insert Bookmark** from the **right mouse** button menu to open the dialog box containing current bookmarks.
2)   In the **Current Bookmarks** list, click on the bookmark you wish to remove. It will appear in the **Edit Bookmark/Name** text box.
3)   Click **Remove**.

Using Notes

To add a Note to a document:
1)   Place the cursor in the text window where you want the note to appear.
2)   Click on the **Notepad** button **OR** select **Annotate/ Notes/Insert** from the main menu **OR** select **Insert Note** from the **right mouse** button menu to open the **Notepad** dialog box.
3)   Type in the note and click **Save**; a Notepad icon appears in the left margin next to the specified line of text.

To View a Note:
1)   Double click the **Notepad** icon in the left margin.
2)   The **Notepad** dialog box displays the note.

To Edit a Note:
1)   Double click the icon of the note you want to edit.
2)   Make changes to text.
3)   Click **Save**.

To Remove a Note:
1)   Place the cursor on the **Notepad** icon and select **Annotate/Note/Delete** from the main menu **OR** select **Delete Note** from the **right mouse** button menu.
2)   A dialog box will ask you to confirm the note deletion.
3)   Click **Yes**. The icon will disappear after scrolling in the document.